# Lecture Notes in Artificial Intelligence     8229

## Subseries of Lecture Notes in Computer Science

### LNAI Series Editors

Randy Goebel
  *University of Alberta, Edmonton, Canada*
Yuzuru Tanaka
  *Hokkaido University, Sapporo, Japan*
Wolfgang Wahlster
  *DFKI and Saarland University, Saarbr*

### LNAI Founding Series Editor

Joerg Siekmann
  *DFKI and Saarland University, Saarbrücken, Germany*

Pengyuan Liu   Qi Su (Eds.)

# Chinese Lexical Semantics

14th Workshop, CLSW 2013
Zhengzhou, China, May 10-12, 2013
Revised Selected Papers

 Springer

Volume Editors

Pengyuan Liu
Beijing Language and Culture University
Applied Language Research Institute
No. 15 Xueyuan Road
Haidian District
Beijing 100083, China
E-mail: liupengyuan@pku.edu.cn

Qi Su
Peking University
School of Foreign Languages
No. 5, Yiheyuan Road
Haidian District
Beijing 100871, China
E-mail: sukia@pku.edu.cn

ISSN 0302-9743                              e-ISSN 1611-3349
ISBN 978-3-642-45184-3                      e-ISBN 978-3-642-45185-0
DOI 10.1007/978-3-642-45185-0
Springer Heidelberg New York Dordrecht London

Library of Congress Control Number: 2013954683

CR Subject Classification (1998): I.2.7, I.2.6, H.3, H.2

LNCS Sublibrary: SL 7 – Artificial Intelligence

© Springer-Verlag Berlin Heidelberg 2013

*Typesetting:* Camera-ready by author, data conversion by Scientific Publishing Services, Chennai, India

Printed on acid-free paper

Springer is part of Springer Science+Business Media (www.springer.com)

# Preface

Chinese Lexical Semantics Workshop (CLSW) 2013 is the fourteenth CLSW conference in the series established in 2000. The previous CLSW were held in different Asia Pacific cities: Hong Kong, Beijing, Taipai, Singapore, Xiamen, Hsin Chu, Yantai, Suzhou, and Wuhan. The scope of the workshop encompassed theoretical linguistics, applied linguistics, computational linguistics, information processing and computational lexicography. Over the past 13 years, CLSW has greatly promoted the academic research and application development of the related fields, and acted as one of the most important meetings in Asia for scholars of Chinese Lexical Semantics.

CLSW 2013 was hosted by Zhengzhou University, China. This year 153 papers were submitted to the workshop. All submissions went through a double-blind review process. Of these, 68 submissions were accepted as regular papers (44.4%) and 4 as short papers (2.6%). They are organized in topical sections covering all major topics of lexical semantics, lexical resources, corpus linguistics, and applications on natural language processing.

On behalf of the Program Committee, we would like to acknowledge Shiwen Yu (Peking University) and Danying Gao (Zhengzhou University), the conference co-chairs, for their tremendous contribution in this event. We are also most grateful to Chu-Ren Huang (Hong Kong Polytechnic University) and the Advisory Committee for their guidance in promoting the workshop. We sincerely appreciate the invited speakers: Gong Cheng (PLA University of Foreign Languages), Chu-Ren Huang (Hong Kong Polytechnic University), Yuming Li (Beijing Language and Culture University), Maosong Sun (Tsinghua University), Haifeng Wang (Baidu Inc.), Houfeng Wang (Peking University), and Hao Yu (Fujitsu Research and Development Center Co. LTD), for their outstanding keynote talks. Also, we would like to thank Chinese Information Processing Society of China (CIPS), National Natural Science Foundation of China (NSFC), Peking University, Henan University, and Zhengzhou University for sponsorship.

Our gratitude goes to all the Program Committee members and reviewers for their efforts to get reviews in on time despite the tight time schedule. We are pleased that the accepted English papers are published by Springer as part of their Lecture Notes in Artificial Intelligence (LNAI) series and that the papers are EI-indexed.

Last but not least, we thank all the authors and attendees for their scientific contribution and participation, which made CLSW 2013 a very successful event.

September 2013

Zhifang Sui
Hong Gao

# Organization

## Conference Chairs

| | |
|---|---|
| Shiwen Yu | Peking University, China |
| Danying Gao | Zhengzhou University, China |

## Advisory Committee

| | |
|---|---|
| Chu-Ren Huang | Hong Kong Polytechnic University, China |
| Donghong Ji | Wuhan University, China |
| Kim Teng Lua | COLIPS, Singapore |
| Mei-chun Liu | Taiwan Chiao Tung University, China |
| Qin Lu | Hong Kong Polytechnic University, China |
| Xinchun Su | Xiamen University, China |
| Shu-Kai Hsieh | Taiwan University, China |
| Shiwen Yu | Peking University, China |
| Chin-Chuan Cheng | National Taiwan Normal University, China/University of Illinois, USA |
| Benjamin Tsou | Hong Kong Institute of Education, China |

## Program Committee

### Chairs

| | |
|---|---|
| Zhifang Sui | Peking University, China |
| Hong Gao | Nanyang Technical University, China |

### Members

| | |
|---|---|
| Xiaojing Bai | Tsinghua University, China |
| Xiaohe Chen | Nanjing Normal University, China |
| Gong Cheng | PLA University of Foreign Language, China |
| Yanbin Diao | Beijing Normal University, China |
| Minghui Dong | Institute for Infocomm Research, Singapore |
| Guohong Fu | Heilongjiang University, China |
| Tingting He | Central China Normal University, China |
| Jiafei Hong | Taiwan Normal University, China |
| Minghu Jiang | Tsinghua University, China |
| Guangjin Jin | Ministry of Education Institute of Applied Linguistics, China |
| Jing-Schmidt Zhuo | University of Oregon, USA |
| Kathleen Ahrens | Hong Kong Baptist University, China |

| | |
|---|---|
| Lingling Mu | Zhengzhou University, China |
| Guiling Niu | Zhengzhou University, China |
| Liming Wang | Zhengzhou University, China |
| Yangdong Ye | Zhengzhou University, China |
| Kunli Zhang | Zhengzhou University, China |
| Dan Zhao | Zhengzhou University, China |
| Zhiyun Zheng | Zhengzhou University, China |
| Qinglei Zhou | Zhengzhou University, China |
| Huibin Zhuang | Henan University, China |

## Publication Committee

### Chair
Pengyuan Liu                    Beijing Language and Culture University,
                                China

### Vice Chair
Xuri Tang                       Huazhong University of Science and
                                Technology, China

### Member
Ying Chen                       China Agricultural University, China

# Table of Contents

## Applications of Natural Language Processing

## Lexical Resources

## Corpus Linguistics

## Other Topics

# A Study on the Interpreting Mechanisms of Puns

Chengfa Lu[1] and Guonian Wang[2]

[1] College of Chinese Language and Literature, Wuhan University, Wuhan, 430072, China
lcfnit@126.com
[2] School of Foreign Languages, China University of Geosciences, Wuhan, 430074, China
13476192792@139.com

**Abstract.** Puns have double meanings. Previous studies on how the two meanings are activated and integrated are far from justifiable or satisfactory. It is suggested in this paper that the Graded Salience Hypothesis (GSH) and Conceptual Blending Theory (CBT) can be combined to solve this question. The GSH assumes that there are two distinct meaning access mechanisms, namely, the lexical access mechanism and contextual access mechanism. The double meanings of a pun are activated through the two mechanisms that run in parallel. However, the integration mechanisms of different types of puns are inconsistent, and it is the differences in the mechanisms that account for the intrinsic reasons why puns are divided into three types.

**Keywords:** puns, interpreting mechanism, Graded Salience Hypothesis, Conceptual Blending Theory.

## 1 Introduction

Different from an ordinary utterance which usually denotes one meaning, a pun has two different meanings. This study attempts to explore how the two meanings are activated and integrated, and the roles that the activation and integration mechanisms play in dividing puns into three types, namely, meaning-unrelated puns, equality puns and primary-secondary puns.

## 2 Previous Studies on the Interpreting Mechanisms of Puns

Previous studies about the interpretation mechanism of puns can be broadly divided into three categories: (1) some interpret puns with the Relevance Theory (RT) [1-4]; (2) others explain them in the combined framework of the Graded Salience Hypothesis (GSH) and RT [5-6]; (3) the rest resort to the Conceptual Blending Theory (CBT) [7-8].

We contend that all the above three explanatory approaches have flaws. First, the relevance theory, lacking in care for puns, is mainly designed for ordinary utterances. The relevance theory stresses that "the principle of relevance does not generally warrant the selection of more than one interpretation for a single ostensive stimulus" [9]. Meanwhile, it is claimed in RT that "The principle of relevance does make it possible

P. Liu and Q. Su (Eds.): CLSW 2013, LNAI 8229, pp. 1–9, 2013.

to use an item-by-item testing strategy in comprehension. It warrants the selection of the first accessible interpretation consistent with the principle, if there is one, and otherwise no interpretation at all." [9]

It is thus evident that the relevance theory mainly focuses on the ordinary utterances with one meaning each. If it is used to explain puns, obstacles emerge. For example, it should be explained why the hearer expends extra mental effort to gain another meaning when he has gotten one. The explanation for this given by Yus is that "humorous effects such as the enjoyment in the resolution of incongruity are worth this extra cognitive effort" [2]. But the question is: how does the hearer know – before he expends extra effort to acquire another meaning – that it will ultimately produce humorous effects?

The second interpreting approach, where the GSH is utilized to explain the activating mechanism and RT to interpret the integration mechanism, produces disorder in that the two theories are intertwined.

The purpose of relevance theory is to lay a unified theoretical basis for cognitive science [9]. This theory attempts to make a consistent interpretation for all verbal communication, establishing itself as an exclusive theory that could by no means be used together with other theories. Additionally, the second explanatory approach requires relevance to account for the meaning salience, resulting in the fact that GSH can not explain the activation mechanism independently, a fact that in turn negates their views.

The drawback in the third approach is that the conceptual blending theory is incapable of explaining the activation mechanism because it only focuses on the integration of semantics. Furthermore, the integration mechanisms of different types of puns differ from one another, as has not been pointed out in previous studies.

We acknowledge that the interpretation process of a pun can be divided into two steps: the activation and integration, which are to be detailed hereinafter with GSH and CBT, respectively.


## 3     The Activation of Two Meanings

Chen believes all puns can be called primary-secondary puns because "the significances of the two meanings of a pun are not of the same size" [10]. However, it is also pointed out that there are another two types of puns: the equality puns  [11] and meaning-unrelated puns [2]. With the help of the Graded Salience Hypothesis (GSH) proposed by Giora [12], we will prove that the activation mechanisms of these three kinds of puns follow the same pattern.

The GSH assumes that there are two distinct mechanisms of semantic comprehension: the bottom-up lexical channel, and the top-down contextual process; and that the two mechanisms run in parallel without interacting with each other. The lexical access mechanism functions in a priority order: the more salient meaning or coded meaning, accessed faster than the less salient one, will first strike our mind due to such factors as conventionality, frequency, familiarity, and typicality. Only when supported by noticeable context can the less salient meaning be activated.

The two meanings of a pun are activated through different mechanisms in parallel. The coded meaning automatically activates itself through the lexical access mechanism, and with the strong support of the context, the less salient meaning can also be activated. The detailed activation process for three different types of puns is depicted below.

### 3.1    The Activation Mechanism of Meaning-Unrelated Puns

The meaning-unrelated puns refer to those puns whose two meanings are not relevant.

(1) A: How many ears does Davy Crockett have?
   B: Two, hasn't he?
   A: No, three. He's got a left ear and a right ear and a wild frontier. (Cited from [2])

(2) *Yi la ke*. (a name of a clothes shop)
   Clothes attract customers.
   The clothes are so delicate that they can absorb customers' attention.

In Case (1), the word "frontier" has two meanings, "pioneering spirit" and "front ear". The former meaning is the coded meaning of the sound activated from the lexical access mechanism, while the latter meaning is the less salient meaning strongly supported by the context. There is no relationship between "pioneering spirit" and "front ear". In Case (2), the two meanings of this pun are "clothes attract customers" and "Iraq." "Iraq" is the coded meaning of the scripts "*Yi la ke*"; "Clothes attract customers" is activated with the assistance of the strong context, i.e., these words appear on the signboard of a clothes shop.

### 3.2    The Activation Mechanism of Equality Puns

The equality puns are those that demonstrate the same significances for their two meanings.

(3) Mr Shen Congwen fell in love with Miss Zhang Zhaohe, but the girl and her father disliked him at first. With the help of Ms Zhang Yunhe, the second-eldest sister of Zhang Zhaohe, Mr Shen was finally accepted by the whole family. Zhang Yunhe telegraphed Mr Shen, with the total text of the telegraph in just one word, "*Yun*"(allowed). (Excerpted from Trendy Old Man and Talented White-haired Woman by Wang Shihua)

(4) *You mianzi mei mianzi, mei mianzi you mianzi, hen pi: bi mianzi.*
   With *mianzi*(face), (you will be sold coal) without *mianzi* (coal dust); without *mianzi*(face), (you will be sold coal) full of *mianzi* (coal dust). (Horizontal third line) Compare *mianzi* (coal dust; face).
   The coal sold to VIPs has no powdered dust, while the coal bought by the poor is mostly dust.

In Case (3), the sound of "*Yun*" has two meanings, "(marriage) allowed" and "(Zhang) Yun (he)" (the matchmaker and telegraph addresser). Case (4) is a traditional Chinese couplet that condemns a coal shop for their discriminated business practices. The coal shopper sells the coal briquette to the seemingly "decent" people who are somehow closely related to him, but sells the coal powder (dust) to the poor or unknown customers. The word "*mianzi*" has two meanings, "face" and "coal powder." There is no relationship between "allowed" and "(Zhang) Yun(he)", nor is there any connection between "face" and "powder." The meanings of "allowed" and "face" are respectively the coded meaning of the two Chinese words. The meanings of "(Zhang) Yun(he)" and "powder" are strongly supported by their contexts. If the name of the telegraph sender did not contain the character "*Yun*", Case (3) could not have been interpreted as a pun. If all the people were sold quality coal briquette, Case (4) would not have made any sense.

### 3.3    The Activation Mechanism of Primary-Secondary Puns

The primary-secondary puns refer to those whose two meanings are of different salience levels, one primary, and the other secondary.

> (5) *Sizhou heidongdongde hai bu rongyi pengbi mei?* (My uncle Mr. Lu Xun)
> Around dark still not easy run into a wall?
> Isn't it very easy to run into a wall in the pitch dark?
> (6) *Dongbian richi xibian yu, diao shi wuqing que youqing.* (Lines from Liu Yuxi's work Zhu Zhi Ci)
> East sunrise west rain, say is no sunshine yet have sunshine.
> Here the rain showers but there the sun shines; some feel it's "*wuqing*" (sunless; merciless) but others believe it's "*youqing*" (sunny; affectionate).

Case (5) has two meanings: 1) it is very easy for one to run into a wall because of the extreme darkness in the room; and 2) it is very easy for a revolutionary to suffer setbacks because of the darkness (harsh environment) in the society. The former meaning is activated through the lexical access mechanism; the latter can only be activated when the listeners are familiarized with the relevant background, that is, Lu Xun was a revolutionary committed to reinventing the society at the time. If the listeners lack such information, the latter meaning will fail to be activated.

In Case (6), the pronunciation of "wuqing" refers to two words: sunless and merciless; the word "youqing" can also be interpreted in two ways: sunny and affectionate (or merciful). The latter meanings of the two terms are the salient meanings, activated through the lexical access mechanism. The former two less-salient meanings are activated through the contextual processes, namely, "rain" and "sun."

In summary, the activation mechanisms of the above-mentioned three types of puns are actually of the same kind. Why, then, do the puns fall into three distinct categories? The reason is that the meaning integration mechanisms for the three types are different.

## 4    The Integration of Two Meanings

The Conceptual Blending Theory (CBT) proposed by Fauconnier provides an approach to analyze the integration mechanism of the two meanings of a pun. CBT claims that there are at least four mental spaces in the conceptual integration network: at least two input spaces (input space 1 & input space 2), a generic space, and a blended space. The structure shared by the input spaces is captured in a generic space, which, in turn, maps onto each of the inputs. The elements of the generic space and relations between the input spaces are selectively projected to the blend, establishing what is called the "emergent structure." Conceptual blending is subsequently achieved through complex mental activities, of which the chief ones are composition, completion and elaboration [13] [14].

- Composition. It includes the blending of two input spaces and thus the generation of new relations between the two.
- Completion. We rarely realize the extent of background knowledge and structure that we unconsciously bring into a blend. Blends recruit great ranges of such background information. Pattern completion is the most basic kind of recruitment. We see some parts of a familiar frame of meaning, and much more of the frame is recruited silently but effectively to the blend.
- Elaboration. We elaborate blends by treating them as simulations and running them imaginatively according to the principles that have been established for the blend. Some of these principles for running the blend will be brought to the blend by completion.

### 4.1   The Integration Mechanism for Meaning-Unrelated Puns

Giora assumes that some meanings are so salient that they resist suppression even when they are not instrumental to the comprehension process and might even divert attention [12]. This phenomenon is very obvious in the puns with two unrelated meanings. In Case (1), the meaning "front ear" is suitable for the current context, while the meaning "frontier" is so salient that it can not be suppressed. The same is true with Case (2).

Therefore, the two activated meanings of meaning-unrelated pun will emerge simultaneously. And yet, they do not share the same abstract structure to generate a generic space. So the two meanings with the same phonetic features can not be integrated, but stand independent of each other.

### 4.2   The Integration Mechanism for Equality Puns

CBT divides integration networks into four kinds: simplex network, mirror network, single-scope network, and double-scope network. Simplex network refers to an especially simple kind of integration network, in which human cultural and biological history has provided an effective frame that applies to certain kinds of elements as values – a frame that is in one input space, with some of those elements in the other. In simplex networks there are no dashes between the organizing frames of the inputs, because the input with the values has no organizing frame that competes with the organizing frame provided by the other input. Accordingly, these networks perform indispensable role compressions. Take Case (3) for example. One input space is the frame of the "telegraph", the other include the two meanings of "*Yun*".

When these two input spaces are composed, the mental space will automatically analyze the prototype of this framework according to the background knowledge: A typical telegraph contains the text body, the addresser and date, etc. And this step is called completion. The next step is to elaborate the prototype: the body of the telegraph is *"Yun"* (allowed), and the addresser is "(Zhang) Yun(he)." The emergent structure of this case is that Ms Zhang Yunhe telegraphed Mr Shen Congwen to tell him "the marriage is allowed." The whole process is shown in Figure 1:

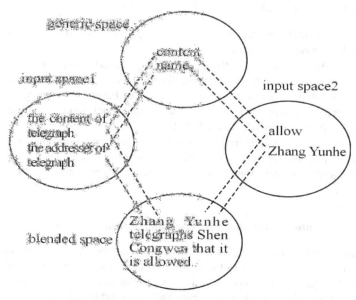

**Fig. 1.** Mapping process of "Yun"

A mirror network is an integration network in which all spaces – inputs, generic, and blend – share the same organizing frame. While spaces in a mirror network share topology at the level of an organizing frame, they may differ at a more specific level. Take Case (4) for example. The organizing frames of the input spaces, generic space and the blended space are the same, that is, the frame of "buying coal" which contains three elements – the buyer, the behavior of buying, and the goods. However, there are differences between the spaces at a more specific level: In input space 1, the buyers are the decent people and the goods are the quality coal briquette; while in input space 2, the buyers are the poor and the goods are the undesirable coal powder. In this level, the two input spaces are opposite to each other. Therefore, the network of Case (4) is a mirror network.

Generally speaking, the networks of equality puns involve only the single network and mirror network. Both of them have the same organizing frame of all the spaces, and the two meanings of the pun are both the essential elements of this framework. As in Case (4), the two meanings of *"mianzi"* are the buyers' social status (having or not having face) and the quality (with or without coal powder) of the goods they bought. Both of them are necessary to understand the framework, so they have the same semantic significance, which is why such puns are called dual-salience or equality puns.

### 4.3    The Integration Mechanism for Primary-Secondary Puns

The networks of primary-secondary puns evolve the single-scope network and double-scope network. A single-scope network has two input spaces with different organizing frames, one of which is projected to organize the blend. Its defining property is that the organizing frame of the blend is an extension of the organizing frame of one of the inputs but not of the other. Take Case (5). The two input spaces are "it is very easy for one to run into a wall because of the extreme darkness in the room" and "it is very easy for a revolutionary to suffer setbacks because of the darkness (harsh environment) in the society."

The organizing frames of the two input spaces are different, but there are also some common abstract structures, i.e., a dark or harsh environment, and an act confronted with difficulties or dangers. The blended space borrows the frame from input space 1 to organize the various elements in the input space 2, thus establishing the emergent structure, as shown in Figure 2.

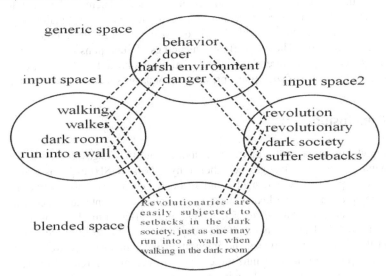

**Fig. 2.** Mapping process of "run into a wall in the dark"

A double-scope network has inputs with different (and often clashing) organizing frames, as well as an organizing frame for the blend that includes parts of each of those frames and that has emergent structure of its own. In such networks, both organizing frames make central contributions to the blend, and their sharp differences offer the possibility of rich clashes. Far from blocking the construction of the network, such clashes offer challenges to the imagination; indeed, the resulting blends can be highly creative.

As in Case (6), the two input spaces are "the weather space" and "the emotional space". And they clash with each other. In weather space, the two opposite kinds of weather coexist at the same time; while in the emotional space, the two opposite emotions are not of the coexistent relationship, but of the relationship between illusion and reality, namely, the lover's feeling of being somewhat merciless to his mate and of being actually passionate. The blended space inherits the coexistent relationship from the weather space, but ignores the fact that the two weather conditions appear in different locations. In stead, the two kinds of weathers are seen as coexisting in the same visual field. The blended space inherits the relationship between illusion and reality from the emotional space, but ignores the fact that being merciless and being affectionate clash with each other. Additionally, the blended space emphasizes the lover's sudden enlightenment of the coexistence of love and non-love, or being merciless and affectionate.

These structures are selective projections, constituting the emergent structure, meaning "The lover, seemingly merciless or ruthless like the changeable, elusive weather, is deeply affectionate for the better half."

Within single-scope network and double-scope network, the organizing frames of the two input spaces are different. Often, one is very vivid and appreciable, such as the "walking space" and "weather space"; while the other is abstract and imperceptible, such as the "revolution space" and "emotion space." Therefore, the listener will have to focus more on the abstract and imperceptible space – the major part of the perception and understanding, with the vivid space becoming the minor part for the listener's interpretation. The two different meanings of such puns respectively belong to the two spaces. The different emphasis or salience attached to the two meanings is justifiable for the name of such puns, primary-secondary puns.

## 5     Conclusions

The interpretation process of a pun can be divided into two stages: semantic activation and semantic integration. The graded salience hypothesis (GSH) explains why the two meanings of a pun can be activated simultaneously. There exist two distinct mechanisms for comprehension, the lexical access mechanism and contextual access mechanism. The two meanings of a pun are activated through different mechanisms in parallel.

The conceptual blending theory (CBT) explicates the integration mechanism of a pun, and the differences between the integration mechanisms may well account for the fact that puns are divided into three types. In meaning-unrelated puns, the two meanings emerge simultaneously with no common structure, and can not be integrated. In equality puns, the two meanings are the essential elements of the organizing frame and they occupy equal status. In primary-secondary puns, the two meanings respectively belong to the two spaces, and the meaning that belongs to the abstract space stands as the focus.

**Acknowledgements.** This study is supported by the Fundamental Research Fund for the Central Universities (No. 2012111010203) and the Fundamental Research Funds for the Central Universities, China University of Geosciences (Wuhan) (CUGW120227).

## References

1. Tanaka, K.: The pun in advertising a pragmatic approach. Lingua 87, 91–102 (1992)
2. Yus, F.: Humor and the search for relevance. Journal of Pragmatics 35, 1295–1331 (2003)
3. Li, L.: The Rhetoric Psychological Mechanism of Puns. Rhetoric Study (2004)

4. Bin, Y.: On Pun in English and Chinese Advertisements —From the Perspective of Relevance Theory. Shandong Foreign Language Teaching Journal, 51–53 (2004)
5. Ai, L., Ai, X.: The Interpretation of Chinese and English Puns: A Cognitive-Pragmatic Approach. Journal of Jiangsu University (Social Science Edition), 75–78 (2010)
6. Lin, Y.: Salience, Relevance and Cognitive Interpretation of English Puns. Foreign Languages and Their Teaching, 19–22 (2009)
7. Lu, Y.: On the Cognitive Interpretation of Advertisement Pun. Journal of Hefei University of Technology, 79–82 (2008)
8. Luo, S.J.: The Cognitive Study on Parody in Advertisements. Foreign Language Research, 52–56 (2010)
9. Sperber, D., Wilson, D.: Relevance: Communication and Cognition. Blackwell, Oxford (2005)
10. Chen, W.: The Origin of Rhetoric. Shanghai Education Press, Shanghai (1997)
11. Gao, W.: The Equality puns. Rhetoric Study 48 (2000)
12. Giora, R.: On our Mind. Oxford University Press, Oxford (2002)
13. Fauconnier, G.: Mappings in Thought and Language. Cambridge University Press, Cambridge (1997)
14. Fauconnier, G., Turner, M.: The Way We Think. Basic Books, New York (2002)

# Semantic-Syntactic Description of Chinese Psycho-verb *Xiang* (想)

Bangjun Xu[1,2], Jingxiang Yin[3], Yi Qin[4], and Qiwang Hu[3]

[1] College of Chinese Language and Literature, Wuhan University, Wuhan 430072
[2] College of Foreign Languages, Central South University of Forestry and Technology, Changsha 410004
veraxu2006@126.com
[3] Naval University of Engineering, Wuhan 430033
13871162120@139.com, huqiwang@sina.com
[4] China University of Geosciences, Wuhan 430074
qinyi18@gmail.com

**Abstract.** This paper summarizes eight parallel semantic senses of the Chinese psycho-verb 想[*Xiang*], i.e. 想象[*xiangxiang*](*imagine*), 关注[*guanzhu*] (*be concerned about*), 想念 [*xiangnian*](*miss*), 回想[*huixiang*](*recall*), 思考 [*sikao*](*ponder*), 认为 [*renwei*](*suppose*), 打算 [*dasuan*](*intend*) and 希望 [*xiwang*](*wish*), with the synonym set of each sense listed. Precise semantic-syntactic analysis and description of the verb are further conducted on the basis of various corpora. A semantic derivation and distribution of the verb's psychological features is also charted.

**Keywords:** Chinese psycho-verb *Xiang* (想), interpretation of sememe, synonyms, semantic-syntactic description, semantic derivation and distribution.

## 1    Introduction

In recent research in syntax and semantics, due attention is paid to psycho-verbs. For the polysemy of the Chinese psycho-verb *Xiang*, studies about it shall contribute considerable efforts in the perspective of lexical semantics in that such psycho-verbs stand as barriers to computer-oriented information processing. The principle of integral descriptions theorized by Moscow Semantic School requires the combination of formal description of lexical meanings and grammatical characteristics in order to integrate the interpretation of the lexical item, its semantic features and syntax rules [1]. This theory emphasizes the importance of combination of semantic interpretation and syntactic description for computer-oriented information processing. Based on this theory, this paper discusses semantic and syntactic characteristics of the psycho-verb *Xiang* while providing assistance to the information processing and language teaching of the verb.

Based on the descriptions of *Xiang* in *The 800 Modern Chinese* Words [*Xiandai Hanyu Babai Ci*] [2], Research on Modern Chinese Primitive Words [*Xiandai Hanyu Shiyi Jiyuanci Yanjiu*] [3], Modern *Chinese Dictionary* [*Xiandan Hanyu Xiangjie*

P. Liu and Q. Su (Eds.): CLSW 2013, LNAI 8229, pp. 10–18, 2013.

*Cidian*] [4], *and* on the analysis of related corpora, eight parallel sememes are summarized as follows: 想象 [*xiangxiang*](*imagine*), 关注 [*guanzhu*](*be concerned about*), 想念[*xiangnian*](*miss*), 回想[*huixiang*](*recall*), 思考[*sikao*](*ponder*), 认为 [*renwei*](*suppose*), 打算[*dasuan*](*intend*) and 希望[*xiwang*](*wish*).

## 2    Interpretations of the Sememes and Their Synsets

It is recorded in *Shuowen Jiezi* (*Xu Shen's Etymological Dictionary*) [5] that "想, 冀 思也" [*Xiang, jisi ye*], which shows that *Xiang* is a kind of psychological and mental activity. Many researches about psycho-activities indicate that psychological processes are categorizable. It is suggested in *General Psychology* [6] that this process can be divided into cognition, emotion and motivation. The polysemy of *Xiang* covers the above three psychological patterns, which are distributed in three spaces, i.e., the space of cognition, emotion and motivation. The division of the three spaces is very significant for the perception of different meanings of the psycho-verb *Xiang* with different syntactic characteristics. Whatever the meaning of this verb is in a certain context, the role of its semantic subject is played by human (or any personalized subject), who possesses psychological capability. The variation of subjective parameter hardly renders any difference in the subtle meanings of the verb. This study, therefore, pays special attention to the objective part of the psychological activity.

### 2.1    *Xiang$_1$*: Imagine

Interpretation of the sememe: the subject of psycho-activity conducts a psycho-action to something (including someone hereinafter) or some situation – which did not exist or happen before the psycho-action took place – so that the image of the thing or situation appears in the brain. *Xiang$_1$* derives from the cognitive space of psycho-activity. Its semantic object is the target of the psycho-action, with examples below:

(1) 我不敢想我的未来。 [*Wo bugan xiang wode weilai.*] (*I can't imagine my future.*)

(2) 你想一下啊，你现在就在阿尔卑斯山上。 [*Ni xiang yixia a, ni xianzai jiu zai A'erbeisishan shang.*] (*Imagine that you're now on the Alps.*)

*Xiang$_1$* has a set of synonyms: 想象[*xiangxiang*](*imagine*), 预见 [*yujian*](*visualize*).

### 2.2    *Xiang$_2$*: Be Concerned about

Interpretation of the sememe: the subject of psycho-activity keeps the image of something or some situation in the brain or memory and concentrates on it. *Xiang$_2$* derives from the cognitive space of psycho-activity. Its semantic object is the target of the psycho-action, with examples like:

(3) 我总想着那件事，太可怕了。 [*Wo zong xiangzhe najian shi, tai kepa le.*] (*I'm always thinking about that terrible encounter.*)

(4) 他们老想着自己腰包。 [*Tamen lao xiangzhe ziji yaobao.*] (*They are usually concerned about their own income.*)

(5) 他只想着自己捞钱，应该下台 。[*Ta zhi xiangzhe ziji laoqian, yinggai xiatai.*]
(*He is only concerned about the money, and should be driven out of his post.*)

*Xiang₂* has a set of synonyms: 想着[*xiangzhe*](*think about*), 记着[*jizhe*](*remember*),
考虑 [*kaolv*](*consider*), 顾虑 [*gulv*](*worry about*), 在意 [*zaiyi*](*care for*), 关心
[*guanxin*](*keep an eye on*), 关注[*guanzhu*](*focus on*).

## 2.3    *Xiang₃*: Miss

Interpretation of the sememe: the subject of psycho-activity keeps the image of something or some situation in the brain or memory, and keeps an emotional relation with
it. *Xiang₃* derives from the space of emotion. Its semantic object is the target of the
psycho-action and emotion, with an example like:

(6) 其实我也很想家 。[*Qishi wo ye hen xiang jia.*] (*Actually, I deeply miss my family.*)

*Xiang₃* has a set of synonyms: 想念[*xiangnian*](*miss*), 思念[*simian*](*long for*), 怀念
[*huainian*](*remember*), 挂念[*guanian*](*have in mind*), 牵挂[*qiangua*](*think of*), 惦念
[*diannian*] (*think about*).

## 2.4    *Xiang₄*: Recall

Interpretation of the sememe: the subject of psycho-activity conducts a psycho-action
to something or some situation – which already existed before the action took place –
so as to bring back the image of the thing or situation to the memory. *Xiang₄* derives
from the space of cognition. Its semantic object is the target of the psycho-action,
with examples like:

(7) 我想起我们曾经的日子 。[*Wo xiangqi women cengjing de rizi.*] (*I recalled our
days of being together.*)

(8) 让我想想他当时说了些什么 。[*Rang wo xiangxiang ta dangshi shuo le xie
shenme.*] (*Let me think/see what he said then.*)

(9) 我好久才想起来过去干的那件蠢事 。[*Wo haojiu cai xiang qilai guoqu gan
de najian chunshi.*] (*It took me much time to recall that stupid mistake I made in the
past.*)

*Xiang₄* has a set of synonyms: 回想[*huixiang*](*look back*), 回忆[*huiyi*](*recollect*).

## 2.5    *Xiang₅*: Ponder

Interpretation of the sememe: the subject conducts a psycho-action to something or an
event so as to obtain the knowledge of the thing or event. *Xiang₅* belongs in the cognitive space of the psycho-activity. Its semantic object is the content or target of the
psycho-action, with examples like:

(10) 我在想怎么处理这个问题 。[*Wo zai xiang zenme chuli zhege wenti.*] (*I am
pondering how to settle the problem.*)

(11) 我在想谁会第一眼看到我的尸体 。 [*Wo zai xiang shui hui diyiyan kandao wode shiti.*] (*I'm thinking about who will first find my corpse.*)

(12) 我在想他俩会不会撞到一起 。[*Wo zai xiang talia hui bu hui zhuang dao yiqi.*] (*I'm considering whether they will run into each other.*)

(13) 我在想那件事情，希望找个对策 。[*Wo zai xiang na jian shiqing, xiwang zhao ge duice.*] (*I'm pondering on that problem carefully in order to find a solution.*)

(14) 让我好好想想 。[*Rang wo haohao xiangxiang.*] (*Let me think about it carefully.*)

(15) 这个问题我想了 3 天。[*Zhege wenti wo xiang le san tian.*] (*This problem took me 3 days to consider.*)

Knowledge is a systematic understanding about some thing or event. On the contrary, image is a kind of direct impression in the brain of the thing or event. "Knowledge has some kind of similarity with reflex of mirror or camera, but they are absolutely different." [7] The image-object of *Xiang$_2$* is a direct impression, which is far from the knowledge-object relation of *Xiang$_5$*. In Example (3), the semantic subject performs a psycho-action on that problem (那件事[*najian shi*]) so as to bring the image of "that problem" to memory. In Example (13), the subject takes up an action with the purpose of obtaining the whole knowledge of "that problem" and the relevant problems. The semantic object of *Xiang$_5$* is expressed by the concrete content of psycho-action (10), the target problem (13) or the way of settling the problem (14). In addition, *Xiang$_5$* is different from *Xiang$_4$*. The utterance "我在想那件事[*Wo zai xiang najian shi.*](*I am thinking about that problem.*)" expresses two meanings, one of which is "recalling how that happened in the way of obtaining the direct expression of the past situation" (as is the case in Example (3)), and the other of which is "thinking about how to settle that problem by means of obtaining the knowledge of it" (as is the case in Example (13)).

*Xiang$_5$* has a set of synonyms: 思考[*sikao*](*ponder*), 考虑[*kaolv*](*consider*), 琢磨 [*zuomo*](*think about*), 思 索 [*sisuo*](*think over*), 思 量 [*siliang*](*calculate*), 推 敲 [*tuiqiao*](*take into account*), 斟 酌 [*zhenzhuo*](*weigh*), 忖 量 [*cunliang*](*rack one's brains*).

## 2.6   *Xiang$_6$*: Suppose

Interpretation of the sememe: the subject applies a psycho-action to something or some event and expresses his/her understanding of the thing or event. It belongs to the cognitive space of the psycho-activity. The semantic object is the subject's judgment about the content of the psycho-action, with an example like:

(16) 我想他应该很快就会回来了 。[*Wo xiang ta yinggai henkuai jiu hui huilai le.*] (*I suppose that he will probably be right back.*)

In some way, *Xiang$_6$* is the consequence of *Xiang$_5$*, has a set of synonyms: 确定 [*kending*](*be sure*), 认为[*renwei*](*believe*), 判断[*panduan*](*gather*), 断定[*duanding*] (*presume*), 推断[*tuiduan*](*assume*), 觉得[*juede*](*infer*).

## 2.7   *Xiang* ₇: **Intend**

Interpretation of the sememe: the subject exerts a psycho-action on some event, which did not happen before the psycho-action took place, and expresses the motivation or planning of fulfilling the event. It belongs to the motivation part of the psycho-activity. The semantic object of the verb is the planning of the subject, with an example like:

(17) 我想明天去看病。[*Wo xiang mingtian qu kanbing.*] (*I plan/intend to see a doctor tomorrow.*)

*Xiang*₇ has a set of synonyms: 打算[*dasuan*](*will do*), 考虑[*kaolv*](*plan to*), 计划 [*jihua*](*intend to*), 准备 [*zhunbei*](*prepare for*), 筹划 [*chouhua*](*arrange*), 拟定 [*niding*] (*work out (a plan)*).

## 2.8   *Xiang*₈: **Wish**

Interpretation of the sememe: the subject imposes a psycho-action to some event, which did not happen before the psycho-action took place, and expresses the desire and emotion of realizing the event. It belongs to the emotional part of the psycho-activity. The semantic object is the desire of the subject, with examples like:

(18) 我很想去，但是……[*Wo hen xiang qu, danshi…*] (*I really want to go, but...*)

(19) 我很想你能像我这么爱你。[*Wo hen xiang ni neng xiang wo zheme ai ni.*] (*I do wish that you could love me like I love you*)

It should be noted that the two sememes 打算 [*dasuan*](*intend to*) and 希望 [*xiwang*](*wish*) devised in this paper are previously regarded as the same meaning in the foresaid Chinese dictionaries. But according to our analysis, they are two different sememes. Professor Zhang Zhiyi mentioned in his report *Sememe Assignment Factors and Extraction of Semantic Features* that every sememe is a function of several variable parameters of morphemes, structural meanings and contextual meanings [8]. It is an assignment collection of several factors of morphemes, structures and contexts. The differentiation of 打算[*dasuan*] (*intend to*) and 希望[*xiwang*](*wish*) into two different sememes is a result of the function with different parameter assignments. Two different *xiang*'s can be extracted in the following examples:

(20) 我想去趟洗手间，你要不要一起？[*Wo xiang qu tang xishoujian.*] (*I'm going to wash my hands, are you with me?*)

(21) 妈妈，我想上厕所。" [*Mama, wo xiang shang cesuo.*] (*Mommy, I want to go to the toilet.*)

From the two cases above we can see that in Example (20), *xiang* is a kind of planning/intention without any emotional factor. While under such internal or external conditions as "the Mom doesn't allow the child to go to the toilet at the time of utterance", the subject of *Xiang* keeps the emotional feeling in some degree on the presumed event, and so 打算[*dasuan*](*intention*) turns into 希望[*xiwang*](*wish*) in (21).

*Xiang*₈ has a set of synonyms:希望[*xiwang*](*wish*), 想要[*xiangyao*](*want*), 期望 [*qiwang*](*hope*).

# 3    Semantic-Syntactic Characteristics of *Xiang*

The enrichment of a verb's meanings is the result of analogy through association and alteration of the contexts for its usage. The systematical description of such linguistic characteristics as syntactic distribution, syntactic transformation and so on, is of great assistance to the description of the description of lexical-semantic systems intrinsic of verbs. "The mapping between the lexical semantic representation of a predicator and the syntactic expression of its arguments is fully predictable. Testing the limits of this hypothesis has proven to be a particularly fruitful way of deepening our understanding of lexical semantic-syntax interface." [9] According to the semantic analysis of *Xiang*, it is suggested that the most important factors for the variation of its meanings are the different language environments (lingual contexts) and the relevant elements of target, content, purpose, and result of the psycho-action. Therefore, it is of great significance to look into the relations between syntactic characteristics and semantic meanings for integral description of the sememes of *Xiang*. This paper will subsequently describe the formal syntactic characteristics of each sememe on the basis of comparison of all the semantic-syntactic relationships. The variation of the subject of *Xiang* does not influence the meaning of the verb. Therefore, only semantic-syntactic characteristics of the semantic object are observed.

## 3.1    Semantic-Syntactic Characteristics of *Xiang*₁

The object of $Xiang_1$ is often presented as NP(1) or S(2) (the parenthesized numbers hereinafter refer back to the corresponding foresaid examples numbered with the same numerals), indicating the image of something or some situation, which didn't exist before the psycho-action, and which may exist thereafter. There might be marks of a future time in the part of NP or S because of the futuristic feature of the object. It can be proved by "future (未来[*weilai*])" in Case (1).

## 3.2    Semantic-Syntactic Characteristics of *Xiang*₂

The object of $Xiang_2$ is often labeled as NP(3)(4) or VP(5), which indicates the image of something or some situation kept in the memory of the subject. The verb can be combined with 着 [*zhe*](*v-ing*) in its syntactic format. Due to the subject's concentration on the image, there will be some words like 总[*zong*](*always*), 老[*lao*](*usually*), 只[*zhi*](*only*) as in Cases (3), (4) and (5) to index the repeatability or uniqueness of concentration.

## 3.3    Semantic-Syntactic Characteristics of *Xiang*₃

The object of $Xiang_3$ is often tagged with NP(6). $Xiang_3$ highlights an emotional feeling from the subject to the target of psycho-action, which bestows the verb with the characteristic of emotion, and which could be proved by the addition of such degree adverbs as 一点[*yidian*](*a little*), 有点[*youdian*](*somewhat*), 一些[*yixie*](*kind of*), 些许[*xiexu*](*a bit*), 非常[*feichang*](*very much*), 很[*hen*](*pretty*), 特别[*tebie*] (*particularly*). When $Xiang_3$ is associated with the degree adverb, it denies the combination of 着 [*zhe*](*v-ing*), as is shown in the following examples:

(22) 他无时无刻不想着自己的祖国。[*Ta wushiwuke bu xiang zhe ziji de zuguo.*] (*He is always missing his motherland.*)

(23) 他很想自己的祖国。[*Ta hen xiang ziji de zuguo.*] (*He misses his motherland very much.*)(\*他很想着自己的祖国。*Ta hen xiang zhe ziji de zuguo. ?He is missing his motherland very much.*)

The object of $Xiang_3$ can hardly express any event, but only the event-related things like 时光[*shiguang*](*time*), 日子[*rizi*](*days*), 岁月[*suiyue*](*years*), 年代[*niandai*] (*decades*) can be predicated. The utterance of "我很想跟他一起旅行的那段日子 [*Wo hen xiang gen ta yiqi lvxing de naduan rizi.*] (*I deeply miss the days of travelling with him.*)" serves as a good case in point for sememe $Xiang_3$, but that of "我很想跟他一起旅行[*Wo hen xiang gen ta yiqi lvxing.*] (*I want to travel with him*)" shifts the verb meaning from $Xiang_3$ (miss) to $Xiang_8$ (wish).

### 3.4 Semantic-Syntactic Characteristics of $Xiang_4$

The object of $Xiang_4$ can be expressed with NP(7)(9) or S(8), which indicates the target of the verb. The kind of S is often introduced by such interrogative pronouns or adverbs as 谁[*shui*](*who*), 什么[*shenme*](*what*), 多少[*duoshao*](*how many/much*), 怎么[*zenme*](*how*), 哪里[*nali*](*where*), 何时[*heshi*](*when*). $Xiang_4$ highlights the process of psycho-action, which is characterized by the overlapping 想想 [*xiangxiang*] in Case (8), and by the combination with lexical forms of time period like 好久[*haojiu*](*much time/for long*) in Case (9). Since the thing or situation indicated in the object existed before the time of verb action, there in the N or S could be the time markers like 曾经[*cengjing*](*once*), 当时[*dangshi*](*then*), 过去[*guoqu*](*in the past*) as shown in Examples (7), (8) and (9).

### 3.5 Semantic-Syntactic Characteristics of $Xiang_5$

The object of $Xiang_5$ is evident primarily in NP(10), S(11) and S(12), which is introduced by such interrogative pronouns or adverbs as[*shui*](*who*), 什么[*shenme*](*what*), 多少[*duoshao*](*how many/much*), 怎么[*zenme*](*how*), 哪里[*nali*](*where*), 何时 [*heshi*](*when*), or constructed partly of V不V [V *bu* V](*V or not V=whether or not V*) pattern. Moreover, the object can be NPs like 事情[*shiqing*](*problem*) or 对策 [*duice*](*solution*) in Case (13), indicating the purpose of the psycho-action. As $Xiang_5$ highlights the process of psycho-activity, it is capable of overlapping the verb as 想想 [*xiangxiang*](*think about*) in Case (14), and of being followed by lexical forms of time period like 3天[*3 days*](*santian*) in Case (15).

### 3.6 Semantic-Syntactic Characteristics of $Xiang_6$

The object of $Xiang_6$ is represented in S(16), which is a kind of cognitive judgment. $Xiang_6$ emphasizes not the process of cognition, but the result of it. Therefore, $Xiang_6$ is not capable of overlapping itself to form 想想. In the S fragment, which means personal judgment, there are usually adverbs of subjective judgment like一定[*yiding*] (*surely*), 肯定[*kending*](*certainly*), 断然[*duanran*](*firmly*), 绝对[*juedui*](*absolutely*) and 或 许 [*huoxu*](*maybe*), 也 许 [*yexu*](*perhaps*), 可 能 [*keneng*](*likely*), 应 该 [*yinggai*] (*supposedly*), 大概[*dagai*](*probably*), 恐怕[*kongpa*](*presumably*).

### 3.7    Semantic-Syntactic Characteristics of *Xiang*₇

The object of *Xiang*₇, which means a plan or intention of the subject, is expressed by VP(17), indicating the content of psycho-action. *Xiang*₇ emphasizes not the process of cognition, but the content. Therefore, *Xiang*₇ cannot be overlapped to form 想想. There can be some markers like 本来[*benlai*](*at first*), 原先[*yuanxian*](*previously*), 最初[*zuichu*](*initially*), 之前[*zhiqian*](*before*) to express the unrealized motivation, as is shown in the following example:

(24) 本来我想做月饼的, 结果成这样了。[*Benlai wo xiang zuo yuebing de, jieguo cheng zheyang le.*] (*At first, I had planned to make some moon-cakes, but they turned out such a mess.*)

### 3.8    Semantic-Syntactic Characteristics of *Xiang*₈

The object of *Xiang*₈, which means a desire of the subject with certain emotion, is denoted in VP(18) and S(19). Due to the emotion of the subject, *Xiang*₈ can be modified by such adverbs of degree as一点[*yidian*](*a little*), 有点[*youdian*](*somewhat*), 一些 [*yixie*](*kind of*), 些许[*xiexu*](*a bit*), 非常[*feichang*](*very much*), 很[*hen*](*pretty*), 特别 [*tebie*] (*particularly*).

To facilitate our understanding, a chart is drafted below (Fig. 1), demonstrating the distribution and relationship of the eight sememes of the verb *Xiang*, which is split into three spaces:

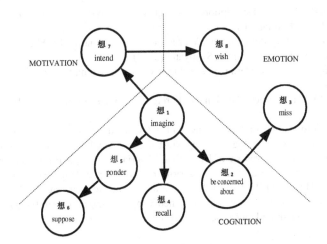

**Fig. 1.** Semantic Distribution of *Xiang* (想)

# 4    Conclusions

On the basis of semantic-syntactic analysis of the psycho-verb *Xiang*, this paper has taken an initiative to suppose its semantic derivation process. As a psychological activity, *Xiang* develops from the prototype sememe into the three spaces of cognition, emotion and motivation by way of context expansion, metonymy and other semantic devices. The original or prototype meaning of *Xiang* is to imagine the prospective thing or situation, and obtain its image. The expansion of the object of the psycho-action extends the prototype meaning to other 2 sememes, namely, 回想 [*huixiang*](*recall with target at a past time as its object*) and 思考[*sikao*](*ponder with concrete content as its object*). Concentration on the image generates the meaning of 关注[*guanzhu*] (be concerned about; with the subject's concentration on the target of psycho-action). Then the sememe 思考[*sikao*](*ponder*) extends to generate  认为 [*renwei*](*suppose*) by means of behavior-result metonymy; the sememe 想象 [*xiangxiang*](*imagine*) extends to produce 打算[*dasuan*](*intend*) through behavior-motivation metonymy. The sememes 打算[*dasuan*](*intend*) and 关注[*guanzhu*](*be concerned about*) stretch to 希望[*xiwang*](wish) and 想念[*xiangnian*](*miss*), respectively, under the contexts of emotion.

This paper has primarily discussed the interaction of the verb's semantic meanings and syntactic patterns; the semantic derivation and distribution of 想 is only just a tentative step. The suggested relationship between the eight sememes of the verb is of reference and assistance to readers who are attempting to gain a more profound comprehension of the verb, and to those who are programming to make information processing smarter and preciser.

# References

1. Apresian, I.D.: Integral Description of Language and Systematic Lexicography. Peking University Press, Beijing (2011)
2. Lv, S.X.: The 800 Modern Chinese Words (The 5th volume of Lv Shuxiang's complete works). Liaoning Education Press, Shenyang (2002)
3. An, H.L.: Research on Modern Chinese Primitive Words. China Social Sciences Press, Beijing (2005)
4. Lin, Z.X.: Modern Chinese Dictionary. Foreign Language Teaching and Research Press, Beijing (2010)
5. Xu, S.: Etymological Dictionary. Zhonghua Book Company, Shanghai (1963)
6. Peng, D.L.: General Psychology. Beijing Normal University Press, Beijing (2001)
7. Ai, S.Q.: Historical Materialism of Dialectical Materialism. People Press, Beijing (1978)
8. Zhang, Z.Y.: http://www.news.ldu.edu.cn/show.php?id=9848,2013-03-20
9. Levin, B.C., Hovav, M.R.: Lexical Semantic and Syntactic Structure. In: Lappin, S. (ed.) The Handbook of Contemorary Semantic Theory, pp. 487–507. Foreign Language Teaching and Research Publishing House, Beijing (2001)

# Chinese Syntactic Analysis Based on Complex Features: A Case Study of the Collocation of 很[*hen*](*very*) and a VP with a Quantitative Complement

Jun Xia

Shenyang Normal University, Shenyang 110034, China
xiajun024@163.com

**Abstract.** Complex features are widely used for lexical description and syntactic analysis in linguistic practice, especially in computational linguistics. The introduction of complex features into Chinese grammar research will benefit both Chinese lexical description and syntactic analysis, consequently Chinese information processing. The paper does a case study of the collocation of 很[*hen*](*very*) and a VP with a quantitative complement, which is a topic of long-term concern in Chinese syntactic analysis, and finds a number of grammatical features with syntactic influence. It provides a reference for Chinese lexical description, Chinese syntactic analysis and the rule-based Chinese information processing.

**Keywords:** complex feature, syntactic analysis, lexical description, 很 [*hen*](*very*), VP with a quantitative complement.

## 1   Introduction

Lexicalism is of great international influence in contemporary linguistic studies, especially in computational linguistic studies. Head-Driven Phrase Structure Grammar (HPSG), Lexical Functional Grammar (LFG) and French word grammar are all lexicalism practices, in which a large amount of syntactic and semantic information is described as complex features of words and the syntactic analysis is mainly done through the unification of complex features; therefore it can be said that complex features and their unification are the main means of lexicalism for syntactic description and analysis.

Early in the 1980s, linguists over the world (mainly computational linguists) began to describe words and analyze sentences with complex features. Today, complex features-based grammars such as HPSG, LFG, word grammar flourish in America, Europe and Japan. Take it for an example, HPSG's description of English, German, Japanese and some other languages has reached a comparatively advanced stage. There is an HPSG international conference every year since 1994, and the coming one, the 20th, will be held in August this year (2013) in Berlin, Germany. In contrast, Chinese linguists, who have done similar works also very early in both theoretical and practical areas, have not moved very far. The complex features-based Chinese studies are mainly related to the translation with foreign languages, so that most features of Chinese words

P. Liu and Q. Su (Eds.): CLSW 2013, LNAI 8229, pp. 19–29, 2013.

found in these researches are based on the comparison of Chinese and foreign languages. To be more exact, only the features of Chinese words that could serve as the counterparts of foreign languages are possible to be found (Feng, 1990). These works have not the solid basis of deep research on Chinese grammar and therefore cannot help answer many questions in Chinese ontological research. For example, what are the syntactically influential features in Chinese? What are the similarities and differences between Chinese syntactic features and that in other languages? How to describe the complex features of each Chinese word? How to analyze each concrete Chinese phrase with complex features? Without satisfactory answers to these questions, it is difficult to promote the complex features analysis in Chinese ontological research. In Chinese ontological research, Zhu(1986) was the first to point out some semantic features with syntactic influence such as verb [+attachment] and verb [+displacement]. Since then, the semantic feature analysis has been used in Chinese ontological research for more than twenty years. But most studies focus only on single feature, rather than complex ones. It can be said that there is a huge gap between the sporadic exploration on semantic features with syntactic influence in Chinese ontological research and the great demand in Chinese computational linguistic research. The former is far from satisfying the latter. The comparatively mature technology and theory about complex features analysis in Chinese information processing and their relatively immature counterpart in Chinese ontological research show the insufficiency of the information exchange between the two academic circles.

In the current situation, we have work to do in two parts: first, to use the comparatively mature technology and theory about complex features analysis into Chinese ontological research, gradually improving Chinese syntactic analysis and lexical description; second, to do a large amount of bottom-up discoveries, namely, to do solid case studies on Chinese phrases one by one so as to accumulate valuable grammatical features. Only with a large number of accurate and effective grammatical features, is it possible to build a great system of Chinese grammatical features and has the complex features analysis its position in Chinese syntactic analysis.

In order to show the advantage of complex features analysis over the traditional analyzing methods, this paper does a case study of syntactic analysis and finds a number of semantic features with syntactic influence in Chinese. It does a little exploring work for both Chinese ontological research and Chinese information processing.

## 2    The Challenges Posed by the Phrase "很[hen](very) + VP with a Quantitative Complement" to Chinese Syntactic Analysis and Lexical Description

In modern Chinese, there is a kind of phrase composed of 很[hen](very) and a VP with a quantitative complement, such as:

[1]  *hen  xia  le         ji     ci    yu*
     很   下   了          几    次    雨
     *Very  drop  le(particle)  several  time  rain*
     (*it has rained for many times*)

[2]  hen   xuanchuan   le              yifan
    很    宣传    了        一番
    very  propaganda  le(particle)   (quantifier)
    (did a lot of propaganda)

[3]  hen   bodong   guo              yizhen
    很    波动    过        一阵
    very   upset    guo(particle)   a while
    (got upset for quite a while)

In all these phrases, 很[hen](very) cannot be collocated solely with the head of VP, so we cannot say 很下[hen xia], 很宣传[hen xuanchuan] or 很波动[hen bodong]. Rather, 很[hen](very) has always semantic relation to the quantitative complements in the VPs. If the quantitative complements in the VPs change, the phrases may not stand legally: [1]

[4]  hen   xia   le              san   ci   yu
  *很   下   了     三   次  雨
    Very   drop   le(particle)      three  time  rain

[5]  hen   xuanchuan   le          si    tian
  *很   宣传   了    四   天
    very  propaganda  le(particle)   four  day

[6]  hen   bodong   guo          yixiaohuier
  *很   波动   过    一小会儿
    very   upset    guo(particle)   a short while

Although 很[hen](very) has semantic relation to the quantitative complements in the VPs, it cannot combine directly with them. Besides, 很[hen](very) has not only relation to the quantitative complement in the VPs, but also relation to other components, such as the verbs. Let's see how the changes of verbs influence the acceptance of the constructions:

[7a]  hen   fei   guo          ji    ci
    很   飞   过    几   次
    very   fly   guo(particle)  several  time
    (have flied for many times)

[7b]  hen   feixing   guo          ji    ci
  *很   飞行   过    几   次
    very   fly   guo(particle)  several  time

[8a]  hen   xuanchuan   le          yifan
    很   宣传   了     一番
    very  propaganda  le(particle)  (quantifier)
    (did a lot of propaganda)

[8b]  hen   huibao   le          yifan
  *很   汇报   了     一番
    very   report   le(particle)   (quantifier)

---

[1] "*" used in front of a phrase shows that it is unacceptable.

[9a]  *hen    pao     guo         yizhen*
      很     跑      过          一阵
      *very   run     guo(particle)   a while*
      *(have run for a long period of time)*
[9b]  *hen   benpao   guo         yizhen*
      *很    奔跑      过          一阵
      *very   run     guo(particle)   a while*

Such a kind of phrases raised challenges to both Chinese syntactic analysis and Chinese lexical description.

Syntactically, they are different from typical head structures whose main syntactic functions are determined by their heads, although VPs are always taken as head structures. We cannot say that 很[*hen*](*very*) has only semantic pointing to the quantitative complements in the VPs, because 很[*hen*](*very*) has also semantic relation to other components of the structures. A single semantic feature does not suffice to describe this phenomenon too, because more than one component affects the legality of the construction. Valency theory, used effectively in composing verb's argument structure, does not work here either. Since Rao(1961) first pointed out such a phenomenon, there are a series of follow-up studies, such as Fan&Rao(1964), Lv(1980), Song(1980), K. Zhan(1981), Lai(1982), Cui(1988), J. Wang (1992 ), Wu(1992), Z. Wang(1993), Peng(1995), Y. Li(1995), Liu(1996), Shao(1997), Meng(1997), Chen(1998), W. Zhan(1998), Chu(1999), Y. Zhang(2004), Lin(2005), Y. Wang(2005), S. Li(2009), B. Zhang(2010). All these studies have deepened more or less the understanding of the phenomenon. However, a thorough syntactic analysis is still absent. It seems that the existing syntactic analysis methods in Chinese ontological research are not sufficient for this task.

Lexically, 很[*hen*](*very*) is a degree adverb in all existing dictionaries. However, such a definition is far from satisfying the explanation of the phrases composed of 很[*hen*](*very*) and a VP with a quantitative complement. We know, in a syntactic unification, each part should have compatible features. So the different changes in the VP that influence the acceptance of the construction may show corresponding grammatical features of 很[*hen*](*very*), which are absolutely more complicated than a simple definition of "degree adverb".

How to meet the challenges? The introduction of complex features would be a good choice. By introducing complex features, we can fully describe the rich features of a word, including not only its part of speech, basic semantics, but also its delicate requirements for its combining objects. With such a method, we can thoroughly describe the syntactic influences of different parts in the phrases composed of 很[*hen*](*very*) and a VP with a quantitative complement.

# 3    The Finding of Features and Their Integration in "很 [*hen*](*very*) + VP with a Quantitative Complement"

## 3.1    The way to Find the Features and the way to Integrate Them

There are two main jobs in analyzing a phrase with complex features. One is to find each single feature, the other is to integrate it.

How to find a single feature? The basic way is replacement, including zero replacement, namely deletion. By observing the syntactic influence of changing different elements at certain syntactic position, or that of the presence and the absence of certain elements, we can draw a feature that does influence the legality of the phrase. In doing this, two principles should be obeyed. First, each feature should be justified; second, each feature should be obtained through certain procedure.

Then how to integrate each single feature? We use systemic method which should abide by four principles. First, features should be compatible; second, there should be as few features as possible; third, similar features should be put together and forming a feature hierarchy; fourth, the set of features should meet the need of syntactic analysis.

## 3.2    Cases of the Features' Finding and Their Integration

To explain every feature in the phrases "很[hen](very) + VP with a quantitative complement" is a task far beyond such a journal paper. So we choose two cases to expatiate.

### Case 1: Some features of the quantitative complement

Through induction many linguists point out that the quantitative complement in the phrases should have the feature [+approximate quantity]. But they cannot explain the illegality of following phrases:

[10] hen    xia    le              yibai         ling    ji     ci     yu
    *很    下    了              一百         零     几     次     雨
        Very drop  le(particle)  one hundred  and    several time   rain

[11] hen    cang   le              ling    dian    ji     dun
    *很    藏    了              零     点     几     吨
        Very store  le(particle)   zero    point   several ton

So we add one more feature [+imaginary quantity] for the quantitative complement, because both 一百零几次[yibai ling ji ci](more than 100 but less than 110 times) and 零点几吨[ling dian ji dun](a few tenths of ton) are not imaginary quantity. The new feature [+imaginary quantity] cannot substitute the feature [+approximate quantity], since we find the following phrases:

[12]  hen    pao    le              shiwanbaqian    li
     *很    跑    了              十万八千        里
        very   run    le(particle)    108,000         Li(500 meter)

[13]  hen    shuo   le              yibaibashi    bian
     *很    说    了              一百八十      遍
        very   say    le(particle)    180           time

In examples [12] and [13], both 十万八千里[shiwanbaqian li](very far) and 一百八十遍[yibaibashi bian](a lot of times) mean imaginary quantity, but they cannot fit in the phrases "很[hen](very) + VP with a quantitative complement", while the feature [+approximate quantity] seems helpful at the situation. So it seems that we should keep both of the features. However, we found more phenomena that cannot be explained by the two features, such as:

[14]  hen   pao    le                    xuduo    tian
      *很    跑    了                    许多     天
      very  run    le(particle)   many     day

[15]  hen   shuo   guo                   ruogan              ci
      *很    去    过                    若干                次
      very  say    guo(particle)  a certain number   time

We then add another new feature [+subjectifiable quantity]. This new feature can not only help explain examples [14] and [15], but also examples [12] and [13]. So now we could integrate the three features [+approximate quantity], [+imaginary quantity], [+subjectifiable quantity]. Only the latter two are necessary, and the former one is redundant.

**Case 2: Some features of the VP**

To explain the contrast between example [7a], [8a], [9a] and example [7b], [8b], [9b], we set a feature [-strong reference]. But why is there such a feature for the verb in the phrases "很[hen](very) + VP with a quantitative complement"? Maybe because 很 [hen](very) in the phrases has always the stress and is the focus of the structure, making other parts of the structure not salient, while the verb with feature [+strong reference] is usually a salient constituent in a structure, making the phrase containing it also salient. Therefore, we set the feature [-salience] for the VP. With such a supposition in the view, we find the feature [+imaginary quantity] of quantitative complement is relevant to the verb's feature [-strong reference]. Because the quantitative constituent with feature [-imaginary quantity] is usually a salient constituent in a structure, the feature [+imaginary quantity] of quantitative complement has the similar function to the verb's feature [-strong reference]. Both of them ensure that the VP containing them has the feature [-salience]. Thus the feature [+imaginary quantity] of quantitative complement, the feature [-strong reference] of the verb and the feature [-salience] of the VP are satisfactorily integrated.

### 3.3    The Complex Features of 很[hen](very) and "很[hen](very) + VP with a Quantitative Complement"

Through a lot of induction and deduction, we get a series of features for the phrases "很[hen](very) + VP with a quantitative complement" and their components. Following is a part of the list.

很 **[hen](very)**: phonetic feature [stress]; semantic features [imaginary quantity], [subjectifiable quantity], [subject inclination of quantity] and [quantitative dimension]; syntactic features [adverb], [modifying a certain kind of syntactic unit].

**quantitative complement**: phonetic feature [stress]; semantic features [imaginary quantity], [subjectifiable quantity], [subject inclination of quantity] and [quantitative dimension].

**VP**: semantic features [imaginary quantity], [subjectifiable quantity], [subject inclination of quantity], [known quantity] and [quantitative dimension]; pragmatic features [salience], [solidarity] and [perfectiveness].

Now we can construct a whole feature structure for the phrases "很[hen](very) + VP with a quantitative complement". Here is an example for the phrase 很跑了几天[hen pao le ji tian](have run for a lot of days).

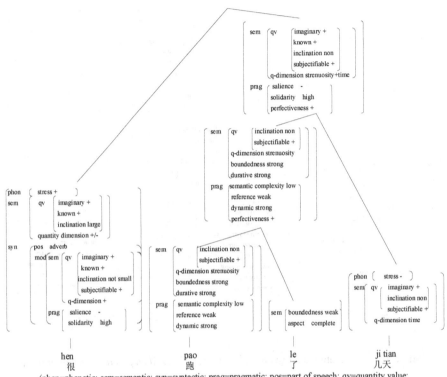

(phon=phonetic; sem=semantic; syn=syntactic; prag=pragmatic; pos=part of speech; qv=quantity value; q-dimension= quantitative dimension)

**Chart 1.** Complex feature analysis for 很跑了几天[hen pao le ji tian](have run for a lot of days)

The complex feature analysis clearly shows the syntactic functions of each component in the phrase. From the chart, we see that the unification is successful and the phrase has two inferential meanings. First, the running was strenuous; second, the running cost very long time.

# 4 Syntactic Analysis Cases of the Phrases "很[hen](very) + VP with a Quantitative Complement"

With the complex features found above, we can do more syntactic analysis now. Here is the analysis of two illegal cases of the phrases "很[hen](very) + VP with a quantitative complement".

**Case 1: syntactic analysis of** 很跑了一百零几天[*hen pao le yibai ling ji tian*]

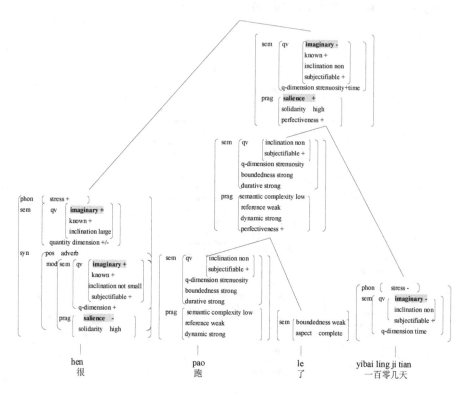

**Chart 2.** Complex feature analysis for 很跑了一百零几天[*hen pao le yibai ling ji tian*]

From chart 2, we see that the semantic feature value [imaginary -] of the quantitative complement determines the semantic feature value [imaginary -] and the pragmatic feature value [salience +] of the VP, which is conflict with the requirement of the complex features of 很[*hen*](*very*), thus the failure of the unification.

**Case 2: Syntactic analysis of** 很奔跑了几天[*hen benpao le ji tian*]
From chart 3(at the next page), we see that the pragmatic feature value [reference strong] of the verb determines the pragmatic feature value [salience +] of the VP, which is conflict with the requirement of the complex features of 很[*hen*](*very*), then the unification fails.

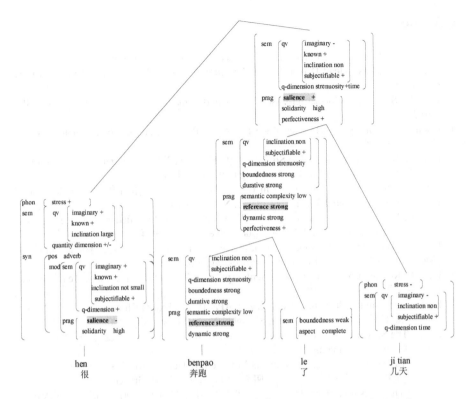

**Chart 3.** Complex feature analysis for很奔跑了几天[*hen benpao le ji tian*]

## 5    Summary

In international linguistic practice, it is very common to use complex features in syntactic analysis and lexical description. The introduction of complex features into Chinese ontological research will absolutely promote the technology of Chinese syntactic analysis and lexical description. Meanwhile, the improvement of Chinese ontological syntactic analysis and lexical description will make itself to offer better service for Chinese information processing. This paper does a case study of the phrases "很[*hen*](*very*) + VP with a quantitative complement", which is a long-standing difficult problem in Chinese syntactic analysis, and finds a number of grammatical features with syntactic influence. We find not only static features but many dynamical features as well. Feng(1990) points out that calculating dynamical features from static features is the key to automatic processing of Chinese, that Chinese syntactic and semantic research work in this area should provide effective rules for this, and that the work needs the thorough cooperation of linguists and computer experts urgently. This work is done with such an attempt. In fact, static features are also not easy to find. Our study here provides a reference for Chinese lexical description, Chinese syntactic analysis and the rule-based Chinese information processing.

# References

1. Bresnan, J.: Lexical-Functional Syntax. Blackwell Publishers Ltd., Oxford (2001)
2. Carl, P., Sag, I.A.: Head-Driven Phrase Structure Grammar. University of Chicago Press, Chicago (1994)
3. Carl, P., Sag, I.A.: Information-Based Syntax and Semantics, vol. 1. Fundamentals, CSLI (1987)
4. Chen, Q.: A Study of "Hen(very) + VP" ("很+VP"考察). Journal of Sichuan Teachers College, No. 3 (1998)
5. Chu, Z., Xiao, Y., Zeng, Q.: The Structures of "Hen(very)" featuring general comparability (通比性的"很"字结构). Chinese Teaching in the World, No. 1 (1999)
6. Cui, S.: The Study of "Hen(very)" in Lu Xun's Works (鲁迅作品中的"很"). Journal of Inner Mongolia National Teacher's College, No. 1 (1988)
7. Fan, J., Rao, C.: A Second Discussion Verb on Phrases Modified by Degree Adverbs (再谈动词结构前加程度修饰). Zhongguo Yuwen, No. 2 (1964)
8. Feng, Z.: The Complex Features in Chinese Sentence Description (汉语句子描述中的复杂特征). Journal of Chinese Information Processing, No. 3 (1990)
9. Lai, H.: Research on the Usage of "Hen(very)" ("很"用法初探). Language Teaching and Linguistic Studies, No. 3 (1982)
10. Li, S.: Study on the Structure "Hen(very) + AP/VP" in Modern Chinese (现代汉语"很'+谓词性成分"研究). Master's Thesis, Shanghai Normal University (2009)
11. Li, Y.: The Structure of "You X" able to Modified by "Hen(very)" (能受"很"修饰的"有X"结构). Journal of Yunmeng, No. 1(1995)
12. Lin, J.: Research on Verbal Constituents Modified by Degree Adverbs in Modern Chinese (现代汉语程度副词修饰动词性成分研究). Master Thesis, Peking University (2005)
13. Liu, S.: The Construction of "Hen(very) VP" in Modern Chinese (现代汉语中的"很VP"格式). Master Thesis, Peking University(1996)
14. Lv, S.: 800 Words in Contemporary Chinese (现代汉语八百词). The Commercial Press, Beijing (1980)
15. Meng, J.: "Hen(very)" that Modifies Verbal Constituents (修饰动词性成分的"很"). Chinese Teaching & Studies, No.3 (1997)
16. Müller, S.: Head-Driven Phrase Structure Grammar: Eine Einführung. Stauffenburg Verlag, Tübingen (2007)
17. Peng, L.: On the Phrases "Hen(very) You(have) NP" (说"很有NP"). Linguistic Researches, No. 2 (1995)
18. Sag, I.A., Wasow, T., Bender, E.: Syntactic Theory: A formal introduction, 2nd ed. CSLI (2003)
19. Shao, J.: On the Principle of Mutually Semantic Selection in Chinese Grammar (论汉语语法的语义双向选择性原则). Journal of Chinese Linguistics, No. 3 (1997)
20. Song, Y.: On the Usage of Degree Adverbs "Zui(most)" and "Hen(very)" (程度副词"最"和"很"的用法). Journal of Hangzhou University, No. 1 (1980)
21. Wang, J.: Verb Phrases Able to be Modified by Degree Adverbs (可受程度副词修饰的动词短语). Journal of PLA University of Foreign Languages, No. 1 (1992)
22. Wang, Y.: The Semantic Study on the Collocation of Indefinite Quantifier and Degree Adverbs in Modern Chinese (现代汉语无定度量词与程度副词同现意义研究). Master Thesis, Shanghai International Studies University(2005)
23. Wang, Z.: On Degree Adverbs "Hen(very)" and "Zui(most)" (程度副词"很"与"最"). Journal of Sichuan Normal University, No. 2 (1993)

24. Wu, S.: On the Modification of "Hen(it very)" on different Phrases (说"很"修饰各种词组). Journal of Jianghan University, No. 5 (1992)
25. Wu, Y.: Introduction to HPSG Theory (HPSG理论简介). Contemporary Linguistics, No. 3 (2003)
26. Zhan, K.: The Sentences with "You" (有字句). Zhongguo Yuwen, No. 1 (1981)
27. Zhan, W.: The Combination of Phrasal Components and the Transmission of Their Functions (语言成分的组合与功能传递). In: International Conference on Modern Chinese Grammar, Peking University (1998)
28. Zhang, B.: The Descriptive Grammar of Modern Chinese (现代汉语描写语法). The Commercial Press, Beijing (2010)
29. Zhang, Y.: Exploration of Adverbs in Modern Chinese (现代汉语副词探索), pp. 66–69. Academia Press (2004)
30. Zheng, D.: The Theory of Word Grammar and Chinese Syntactic Theory (词汇语法理论与汉语句法研究), pp. 1–61. Beijing Language and Culture University Press (1999)
31. Zhu, D.: The Principle of Parallelism in Transformation Analysis (变换分析中的平行性原则). Zhongguo Yuwen, No. 2 (1986)

# A Study on "Chayidian" from the Perspective of Langacker's Cognitive Grammar

Yanli Li

Nanchang Institute of Technology, Nanchang, China
liyanli1110@126.com

**Abstract.** The Chinese adverb "chayidian" (almost) has been a research focus. The previous study mainly discussed the grammatical meaning of "chayidian", the derivation of "chayidian mei P" (D-type, almost not) and how to distinguish the two semantic values of "chayidian mei P" construction. From the perspective of Langacker's cognitive grammar, this paper suggests a new interpretation of these constructions: "chayidian" is a counter-expectation marker word, "chayidian mei P" (D-type) is derived from speaker's profile, and the "expectation rule" constraints the legitimacy of the "chayidian" construction.

**Keywords:** "chayidian" construction, cognitive grammar, expectation.

## 1  Introduction

The usage of the Chinese adverb "chayidian" (almost) is very special. On the one hand, the "chayidian mei P" (almost not P) construction has two possible semantic truth-values, as demonstrated below:

(1) *Ta chayidian mei kao jige.*( B-type)
   He almost not pass examination.
   He almost did not pass (nearly failed) the examination.
(2) *Naniang qiche chayidian mei diaoxia xuanya.* ( D-type)
   The car almost not fall off cliff.
   The car almost fell off the cliff.

The two sentences have the same structure but possess different semantic truth-values: Case (1) means "He passed the exam", while Case (2) means "The car did not fall off the cliff". Mr. Zhu Dexi categorizes these two sentence patterns as B-type and D-type, respectively [1-2].

On the other hand, there exist some factors constraining whether the "chayidian" construction is grammatically legal, as is shown below:

(3) *Zuowei yiming xiaoxuesheng, ta lian daxue shuxue shiti dou chayidian kao jige le.*
   As a pupil, he even college mathematics exam almost pass.
   As a pupil, he almost passed the college mathematics exam.
(4) *Zuowei yiming daxuesheng, ta lian xiaoxue shuxue shiti dou chayidian mei kao jige.*

P. Liu and Q. Su (Eds.): CLSW 2013, LNAI 8229, pp. 30–38, 2013.

As a college student, he even elementary school mathematics exam almost not pass.

As a college student, he almost did not pass (nearly failed) the elementary school mathematics exam.

The two sentences above are acceptable, while the following two are not.

(3)' *Zuowei yiming xiaoxuesheng, ta lian daxue shuxue shiti dou chayidian mei kao jige.

*As a pupil, he even college mathematics exam almost not pass.

*As a pupil, he even almost did not pass (nearly failed) the college mathematics exam.

(4)' *Zuowei yiming daxuesheng, ta lian xiaoxue shuxue shiti dou chayidian kao jige le.

*As a college student, he even elementary school mathematics exam almost pass.

*As a college student, he almost passed the elementary school mathematics exam.

Why does "chayidian mei P" construction have two possible contradictory semantic true-values? How can the hearer accurately identify the appropriate true-value? What are the factors constraining the legality of the "chayidian" construction used in a sentence?

## 2    Previous Studies

The "chayidian" construction has been widely and profoundly studied, mainly with the focus on the following three aspects:

- The grammatical meaning of "chayidian". It is generally believed that "chayidian" is a negative adverb which means that an event was nearly achieved while it did fail to happen, or an event nearly failed to happen while it did happen [3].
- The method of identifying the semantic truth-value of "chayidian mei P" construction, namely, how to distinguish B-type from D-type. By now, the primary method to distinguish the semantic truth-value of this type of construction is based on the "wish" theory put forward by Mr. Zhu Dexi [1-2]. Some scholars claim that there are drawbacks in the wish theory, and put forward modified suggestions. Zhou Yimin assumes that the semantic truth-value should be identified according to the change of speakers' tone and accent [4]. Watanabe Ling [5] and Hou Jinguo [6] hold that the wish theory should be replaced by "intention theory" and "undesirability theory". Mao Jingxiu [7] and Shi Yuzhi [8] suggest that the wish theory overemphasizes the speaker's subjective factors while ignoring the objective factors. They employ positive ingredients and negative ingredients to replace wish and un-wish (undesirability). Dong Weiguang advances a new theory called "tendency theory", holding that the semantics of the true value should be identified from the developmental trend of affairs [9].
- The origin of D-type. Shen Jiaxuan proposed "integration" theory gained Jiang Nansheng's approval [10-11]. Qiu Bin disagreed and claimed that this construction is the result of solidification [12].

Previous researches have greatly deepened our understanding of the "chayidian" construction. However, they also left such questions pending: 1) there are many methods to identify the semantic truth-value of "chayidian mei P" construction, but none is overwhelmingly convincing; 2) they have not clearly explained the reason why the "chayidian mei P" construction is an ambiguous structure; and 3) the differences between the B-type and D-type constructions.

Langacker's Cognitive Grammar (hereinafter referred to as CG) claims that an expression's meaning is not just the conceptual content it evokes; equally important is how that content is construed. This view expands the research range of word meaning. The meaning of word can be more accurately described by analyzing the way a word is construed. For this reason, the usage of a certain word can be consistently interpreted. We believe that the uses of these features are connected to each other. With the help of CG, we will make a unified description of the "chayidian" construction.

# 3     About Cognitive Grammar (CG)

The CG holds that every symbolic structure construes its content in a certain fashion. The relationship between content and construal is just like that between a scene and a particular way of viewing it. CG is generally viewed from four aspects: specificity, focusing, prominence, and perspective [13-15].

## 3.1     Specificity

When we observe things, we can see just the outline if they are far away, and we will see more subtleties if they are closer. The language also possesses such features. In the "Animals-mammals-dog-yellow dog-big yellow dog" series, it become more precise from left to right, as if we gradually narrow the viewing distance, so the resolution is gradually increased. The expression with low resolution is called schema, while that with high resolution is called instantiation, and a schematic characterization is instantiated by any number of more specific ones. The difference between schema and instantiation is relative, e.g. "dog" is the schema of "yellow dog", and is an instantiation of "animal."

## 3.2     Focusing

Focusing refers to the selection of conceptual content for linguistic presentation. Scope is a matter of selection, and sometimes we need to distinguish between an expression's maximal scope and a limited immediate scope. CG emphasizes that there is a conceptual hierarchy. Take "elbow" for example. In conceptualizing an elbow, the conception of an arm other than a body in particular is most directly relevant because a body has major parts including arms, and an elbow is the first and foremost part of an arm. Thus the arm is the immediate scope of elbow, and the body is the maximal scope. This is shown in Figure 1.

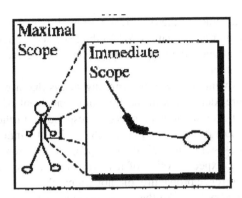

**Fig. 1.** Focusing of "elbow"

### 3.3    Prominence

When attention is directed to a particular object, this object is profiled. An expression can profile either a thing or a relationship. When a relationship is profiled, varying degrees of prominence are conferred on its participants. The most prominent participant, called the trajector (tr), is characterized as the primary focus within the profiled relationship. Often, some other participant is made prominent as a secondary focus, and this is called a landmark (lm).

### 3.4    Perspective

Perspective refers to the viewing arrangement. And the two components of the viewing arrangement are the vantage point and reference point. If we select different vantage points, we will see one thing as "different" scenes, and therefore we will express it differently. For example, when describing an event of a man traveling to a city, the country folks would say "I will go to the city" while the city dwellers would say "I will go back to the city". The reason is that their vantage points are different. And also, if the reference points are different, the expressions are also different. Take, for example, a car moving from point A to point B. If we select point A as the reference point, we will find that the car is farther and farther away from point A; and if point B is set as the reference point, the car is getting increasingly closer to B.

## 4    Grammatical Meaning of "Chiyidian"

Every event has two contradictory states of affair, such as "winning event" having two states of "winning" and "not winning". The sum of the occurrence probabilities of the two states is always an integral 100 percent. Prior to the occurrence of a specific event, we can forecast the result of the event in accordance with the common sense of life experience. For example, if I bought a lottery ticket today, according to common sense, "winning" has a lower probability of occurring, and "not winning" is more likely to happen. I will incline to think that the result of this event is "not winning".

However, the expected values of the occurrence probabilities of the two states are not always the same with their actual values. When the expected values are tremendously different from the actual ones, the adverb "chayidian" will be used. "Chayidian" is a counter-expectation marker.

For example, in this winning event, the winning rule is that it will win if, and only if, the five numbers are identical with the final announcement of winning numbers. This time, the lottery ticket has four numbers corresponding to the announced numbers, with just one number different, and the result is it is not winning.

Although the state of "winning" failed to happen, its occurrence probability is as high as 80%, while the expected value of it is very low, and on the other side, the actual value of the occurrence probability of "not winning" is as low as 20% while the expected value of it is very high. So there is a tremendously quantitative change between the actual and expected values. At this point, the speaker may have a description of "not winning" in two ways:

> (5) a. *Wo chayidian zhongjiang le.* (chayidian P)
> I almost win a lottery.
> I almost won the lottery.
> b. *Wo chayidian mei zhongjiang le.*(D-type)
> I almost not win a lottery.
> I almost won the lottery.

The semantic truth-values of the two sentences above are the same. However the pragmatic meanings of them are different. With the help of CG, they can be interpreted clearly in Figure 2 and 3:

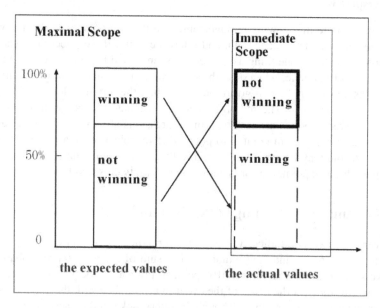

**Fig. 2.** The meaning of (5)a

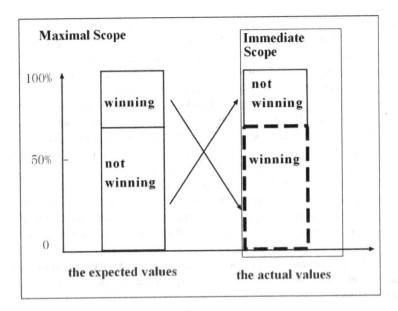

**Fig. 3.** The meaning of (5)b

According to *Modern Chinese 800 Words*, (5)a means that "winning" was nearly achieved while it finally failed, and (5)b means that "not winning" was nearly failed to happen while it did happen [3]. Under the perspective of CG, the interpretation above just describes the immediate scope of this event. The maximal scope of this event is the quantitative change between the actual and expected values.

Because the expectation is that "not winning" will happen, "not winning" naturally becomes the vantage point to observe this event. Standing at this point, the speaker found that "winning" was expected to be at a low occurrence probability (20%), but the actual occurrence probability is as much as 80%, only a little bit away from the reference point of 100%. Meanwhile, as the other state of this event, "not winning" was expected to be at a high occurrence probability (80%), but it had a low actual occurrence probability of 20%, only a little bit away from the reference point of 0.

In Case (5)a, "winning" becomes the trajector (indicated within thick lines), which means that speaker profiled the state of the event that "winning" had a high actual occurrence probability (80%). However, because it was still a little bit away from the reference point (100%), "winning" finally failed to happen (indicated within dashed lines). This sentence is an unmarked negation sentence because it negates a high amount and obtains a slight lower amount. In case (5)b, "not winning" becomes the trajector, which means that speaker profiled the other state of the event that "not winning" had a low actual occurrence probability (20%). However, because it was still a little bit away from the reference point (0), "not winning" failed to disappear and finally happened (indicated inside solid lines). This sentence is a marked negation sentence because it negates a low amount and reaches a slight higher amount.

Let's probe into the B-type with Case (4) as an example. Assume the college student got 61 points in this math exam for kids. It is generally expected that a college student can easily pass the primary school mathematics exam, so the expected value of occurrence probability of "passing the exam" is high and that of "not passing" is low. Actually, he only got 61 points which means the value of "not passing the exam" is very high; if he had lost two more points, he would have failed the exam. Here in this case, "not passing the exam" means that the speaker profiled that the state of "not passing the exam" with a low expected value had a high actual value of its happening probability. Therefore, B-type and "chayidian P" construction share the common point that they profile the same status (side) of the event, and the difference is that: the state profiled by B-type is in a syntactically negative form, while that profiled by "chayidian P" construction is syntactically a positive form.

It should be noted that in the event, quantitative change should not cause qualitative change. Otherwise, the "chayidian" construction will not have survived. Take Case (4) for example. If the college student got 59 points – which means the quantitative change had caused qualitative change – "chayidian" should not have been used because he had already failed the exam.

In summary, the meaning of "chayidian" can mean that an unexpected event nearly happened while it did fail to happen, or an expected event nearly failed to happen while it did happen.

## 5    The Semantic Truth-Values of "Chayidian" Constructions

Heine divided expectation into three kinds, i.e., speaker's expectation, hearer's expectation, and the expectation shared by both the speaker and hearer [15]. In the "chayidian" construction, the expectation mainly refers to the third kind, especially the common sense – norm and normality – that is shared by a certain society.

(6) *Wo chiyidian mei shuaidao.*
    I almost not fall down.
    I almost fell down.
(7) *Qi de wo chayidian mei gei ta yibazhang.*
    Angry I almost give him a slap.
    I was so angry that I nearly slapped him.

"Falling down" is abnormal for normal people, so "not falling down" is a normal state (normality) constituting the semantic truth-value of Case (6). The social norm informs us that "slapping people" is immoral and abnormal, so "not slapping him" stands as the semantic truth-value of Case (7).

Now we are accounting back for Cases (1) to (4). In Case (1), "passing an exam" is generally believed the minimum requirement for those who take the exam, so it is the semantic truth-value other than "not passing the exam". For Case (2), the state of "a car falling off cliff" has low frequency which means falling is abnormal, so "the car not falling off the cliff" is the semantic truth-value. For a pupil, the college mathematics test is too hard to be passed, so "not passing the exam" can be the semantic truth-value and "passing the exam" can not be the semantic truth-value. Case (3) takes "not passing the exam" as its semantic truth-value, so it is legitimately acceptable. While Case (3)' takes "passing the exam" as its semantic truth-value, so it is not unacceptable. Social norm requires that a college student should pass elementary school mathematics exams, so Case (4) survives because its semantic truth-value is "passing the exam", consistent with the social norm. In comparison, Case (4)' fails to survive because its semantic truth-value is "not passing the exam", inconsistent with the social norm.

# 6    Conclusions

The main views of this paper can be summarized as follows:

Firstly, "chayidian" (almost) is a counter-expectation marker word. The expected value and actual value of two possible developments of the same event are in an inverse relationship in terms of their probability of happening, but the quantitative change does not cause a qualitative change.

Secondly, "chayidian mei P (D-type)" (almost not) derives from the speaker's profile. It emphasizes that the occurrence likelihood of the "P" is very low, but not as low as 0; it ultimately does not disappear and is achieved. This sentence pattern is a marked negation. The "almost P" and "almost not P (B-type)" stress that the possibility of its happening is very high, but not as high as 100%; it is eventually unrealized. The latter two are unmarked negative constructions.

Thirdly, the "expectation rule" can distinguish between the semantic true-values of the B-type and D-type that derive from "chayidian mei P" (almost not P). This rule also restricts the legitimacy of the "chayidian P" (almost P) construction in a sentence.

# References

1. Dexi, Z.: A Study on "Cha yi dian". Studies of The Chinese Language (September 1959)
2. Dexi, Z.: The Ambiguity Phenomenon in Chinese Language. Studies of The Chinese Language (February 1980)
3. Nü, S.: Modern Chinese 800 Words. The Commercial Press, Beijing (1980)
4. Zhou, Y.: "Cha dian er mei VP" Sentences in Pekingese. Language Teaching and Linguistic Studies, 24–30 (June 2003)
5. Ling, W.: The Logical Relationship and Semantic Structure of "Chayidian" Sentence. Language Teaching and Linguistic Studies, 81–89 (March 1994)
6. Hou, J.: The Pragmatics of Redundant Negation—A Survey of the Constructions of Chayidian + (Mei) V and Xiaoxin + (Bie) V. Language Teaching and Linguistic Studies, 70–77 (May 2008)
7. Mao, J.: The Opposition Structure in Chinese Language. Language Teaching and Linguistic Studies, 59–71 (February 1985)
8. Shi, Y.: The Differentiation of the Redundant Negation Sentence Including "Chadianr". Chinese Language Learning, 12–16 (April 1993)
9. Dong, W.: The Effect of Linguistic Cognitive Psychology on "Chadianr +DJ" Structure. Language Teaching and Linguistic Studies, 34–40 (March 2001)
10. Shen, J.: Asymmetric and the labeling theory. Jiangxi Education Press, Nanchang (1999)

11. Jiang, L.: Semantic accumulation and constructional integration: An explanation on the asymmetry between affirmation and negation. Studies of The Chinese Language (November 2008)
12. Bin, Q.: On the Routinization of Chadianrmei. The Northern Forum, 67–69 (2007)
13. Langacker, R.W.: Foundations of Cognitive Grammar. Theoretical Prerequisites, vol. 1. Stanford University Press, Stanford (1987)
14. Langacker, R.W.: Foundations of Cognitive Grammar. Descriptive Application, vol. 2. Stanford University Press, Stanford (1991)
15. Langacker, R.W.: Cognitive Grammar, A Basic Introduction, Oxford (2008)
16. Heine, B., Claudi, U., Hünnemeyer, F.: Grammaticalization: A Conceptual Framework. University of Chicago Press, Chicago (1991)

# A Study of Chinese Non-canonical VN Collocations
## From the NLP Perspective

Qiong Wu

College of Chinese Language and Literature, Wuhan University, Wuhan 430072
cindy61361@hotmail.com

**Abstract.** This paper focuses on Chinese non-canonical VN collocations from the NLP perspective. It first makes a classification of the Chinese non-canonical VN collocations, and then talks about their semantic features. This paper argues that, machine recognition of Chinese non-canonical collocations should not only consider the semantic roles of the objects, but also the verbs. Idioms and chunks should be put into the lexicon directly. A flow chart for the machine recognition is offered at the end of this paper.

**Keywords:** semantic features, Chinese non-canonical VN collocations, machine recognition, shallow parsing.

## 1    Introduction

A new language processing strategy - Shallow Parsing, which is also called partial parsing or chunking parsing has appeared in the NLP field recently. Shallow parsing is an analysis of a sentence which identifies the important constituents (noun groups, verbs, verb groups, etc.), but does not specify their internal structure, nor their role in the main sentence. Chinese non-canonical VN collocation is such a constituent, in which the structure is simple, but the semantic relationship is complex. Because of this feature, Chinese non-canonical VN collocation becomes a heated topic in Chinese linguistic research field. Numerous research studies have been carried out on this topic. (Yuan, Y.L.[1], Xie, X.M. & Wang, Y. B.[2], Yang, Y. Z.[3]). However, these studies do not pay much attention on NLP topics such as how to identify the non-canonical objects and how to identify the interpretation by machine translation. With the aim of identifying the semantic roles of the non-canonical objects exactly, this paper talks about the categories of Chinese non-canonical objects and the quality of the verbs. A method is offered in this paper also.

## 2    The Division between Chinese Canonical and Non-canonical Objects

There are diverse kinds of Chinese objects. Previous works focus on the objects' semantic roles and their features. Fan, X. [4]divides the objects into typical and

P. Liu and Q. Su (Eds.): CLSW 2013, LNAI 8229, pp. 39–46, 2013.

untypical categories. Zhang, Y.Q. [5]makes a further analysis on the features of the Prototypical-patient Object. She argues that, the prototypical-patient object has the characteristics of [+patient] and [+change]. Patient means the noun is the object of the verb, and change means the noun can be changed or influenced by the action. Change includes three dimensions:1. The state of the object is changed by the action; 2. The property of the object is changed by the action; and 3. A new product is created by the action. Hence, [±patient] and [±change] can be two prominent features to distinguish non-canonical objects from canonical objects. There is variant of categorizations of Chinese non-canonical objects; and scholars have made categorizations from different perspectives. Meng, C. [6]'s classification is widely covered with circumstance. He divides Chinese objects into 14 categories from the perspective of verb-noun semantic relations. These categories include patient, agent, location, time, instrument, goal and etc. This elaborate classification is authoritative, which can be used in the following analysis. Based on Meng and Zhang's work, Chinese canonical and non-canonical objects can be divided as the following. (see Table 1)

From 1 to 5 in Table 1 are Chinese canonical objects, and from 6 to 14 are Chinese non-canonical objects. With the aim of discussing the latter ones mainly, it's necessary to make a further selection again.

In Table 1, the 14th is *Others*. This kind of object is principally related to Chinese tradition, culture and history. It is not only difficult to get the collocation meaning from the verb and the noun, but also difficult to be reasoned by analogy. For example, 哭鼻子 [*ku bizi*] (*crying*) is a non-canonical VN collocation, and it's hard to say what kind of object 鼻子(nose) is. Besides that, we cannot say 哭嘴 [*ku zui*] (*cry mouth*) or 哭眼睛 [*ku yanjing*] (*cry eyes*) in Chinese, they are ungrammatical collocations. In Chinese, we call such a kind of collocation idioms or chunks. We suggest putting the chunks/idioms into the lexicon.

*Cognate* is another non-canonical collocation in Table 1. A mount of collocations in this kind are Chinese VN separable words, such as 唱歌 [*chang ge*] (*to sing/sing a song*), 走路 [*zou lu*] (*to walk*). From the view of Meng, C., the cognate objects have the characteristics of:

(a) the object does not have new meanings; or
(b) the object have meanings when it co-occur with the verb only.

In sum, we prefer to take the cognates as words than phrases. The cognates should be put into the lexicon as well as the *Others*. Hence, the instrument, manner, time, goal, location, reason and agent objects are the main kinds we will talk in the next section.

**Table 1.** Chinese Canonical and Non-canonical Objects

| Object categories | Patient | Change |
|-------------------|:-------:|:------:|
| 1. Patient objects | + | + |
| 2. Result   objects | + | + |
| 3. Object objects | + | + |
| 4. Causation objects | + | + |
| 5. Equation objects | + | + |
| 6. Instrument objects | − | − |
| 7. Manner objects | − | − |
| 8. Location objects | − | − |
| 9. Time objects | − | − |
| 10. Goal   objects | − | − |
| 11. Reason   objects | − | − |
| 12. Agent   objects | − | − |
| 13. Cognate   objects | − | − |
| 14. Others | − | − |

## 3    Characteristics of Chinese Non-canonical Objects and the Machine Recognition

Selectional restriction is a semantic restriction between words and words in a sentence. NLP pays a lot of attention on semantic selectional restriction, especially on the verb-argument selection. VN collocation is not only a grammatical collocation, but also a semantic collocation. Semantics plays an important role in constructing a correct sentence, as well as syntax.  Some collocations are correct in grammar but not hold in semantics. For example, "*走博士点" [zou boshidian] (*to walk the doctoral program), the verb 走[zou] (to walk) and the noun 博士点 [boshidian] (doctoral program) are grammatically match, but not match in semantics. Hence, semantic research can help us identify non-canonical VN collocation properly.

We made a division between canonical and non-canonical objects in the previous section by commonality. In this section, we will discuss them individually. We try to select the distinctive semantic character of each category, that is, a unique character one category has but the other categories do not have.

In these non-canonical objects, time objects are the easiest to identify. For example, 大干红五月 [dagan hongwuyue] (to work in red May), 做寿 [zuo shou] (to hold a birthday party) and 起五更 [qi wugeng] (to get up at five). The typical feature is [+time]. This feature is not existed in other 6 categories. Hence, to use [±time], we can discriminate time objects from other non-canonical objects.

Among the next six categories of non-canonical objects, the salient one is agent objects. Meng, C. holds the view that agent objects are the executants of an action or an event, which have the character of [+autonomy]. There are some examples such as 吹风 [chui feng] (to blow the wind), 开始新的一年 [kaishi xinde yinian] (to begin a new year) in Chinese. Hence, we can discriminate agent objects from the remaining non-canonical objects by [±autonomy].

Among the rest five categories, the idiosyncratic one is the reason objects. In Chinese, reason objects can be divided into two categories. One is [+animate] category, for example, 哭爹[ku die] (to cry for father), in which the object 爹 [die] (father) has the character of [+animate]. We use reason objects 1 to represent this kind of reason object. Another is [-animate] category, for example, 逃荒 [tao huang] (to escape from a famine), 避雨 [bi yu] (to take shelter from rain). We use reason objects 2 to represent this kind of reason object. The collecting linguistic material shows that, the reason object 2 has another accordant character which is called [+uncontrollable]. 荒 [huang] (famine) in 逃荒，雨 [yu] (rain) in 避雨 and 病 [bing] (sickness) in 养病 [yang bing] (to have a rest because of sickness) all represent the uncontrollable things in an action or an event. Hence, we can use [+animate] and [+uncontrollable] to discriminate reason objects from the rest four non-canonical objects.

The rest non-canonical objects are instrument objects, location objects, manner objects and goal objects. Instrument objects such as 鞭子 [bianzi] (whip) in 抽鞭子 [chou bianzi] (to strap with a whip), 大碗 [dawan] (a big bowl) in 吃大碗 [chi dawan] (to eat with a big bowl), and 毛笔 [maobi] (writing brush) in 写毛笔 [xie maobi] (to write with a writing brush) can be considered as the necessary instrument in an action. They have the common characters of [+shape] and [-abstract]. Location objects have the same characters as instrument objects. For example, 吃饭馆 [chi fanguan] (to eat in an restaurant), 飞北京 [fei Beijing] (fly to Beijing) and etc..饭馆 [fanguan] (restaurant) is a place which prepares and serves food and drinks to people. No matter it is big or small, it always has the character of [+shape]. 北京(Beijing) is a city, though it does not has a shape like restaurants, it do has a shape along the border. There are borders between countries, provinces, cities, towns and etc.. Border lines draw the outlines of districts. For that reason, it is not difficult to understand why people say the shape of China is like a chanticleer, while the shape of Italy is like a high-heel shoe. Chanticleer and high-heel shoe here represent the shape of the country. *Instrument* and *location objects* both have the character of [+shape] but the rest two non-canonical objects do not have. Hence, we can use [±shape] to discriminate *instrument objects* and *location objects* from *manner objects* and *goal objects*.

The next step is to discriminate *instrument objects* from *location objects*. We found that *instrument objects* are moved during an action or an event. Take 抽鞭子 [*chou bianzi*] (*to strap with a whip*) as an example. The whip moved near or far from the object by the action of strap. If a body moves from one position to another, it is said to have a displacement. Strap caused the whip to have a displacement, therefore, the instrument objects have the semantic character of [+displacement]. The location objects do not have a displacement during the action, thus, we can use [+displacement] to discriminate *instrument objects* from *location objects*.

The remaining objects are *manner objects* and *goal objects*. The manner objects are typically used to describe the attribute of things. In 唱C调 [*chang C diao*] (*to sing in the scale of C* ), C调 [*C diao*] (*the scale of C* ) represents the attribute of the song. In 寄特快 [*ji tekuai*] (*to send a mail by express*), 特快 [*tekuai*] (*express*) represents the attribute of the letter (mail) . However, goal objects do not have such a character. Hence, we use [±attribute] to discriminate *manner objects* from *goal objects*.(see fig. 1)

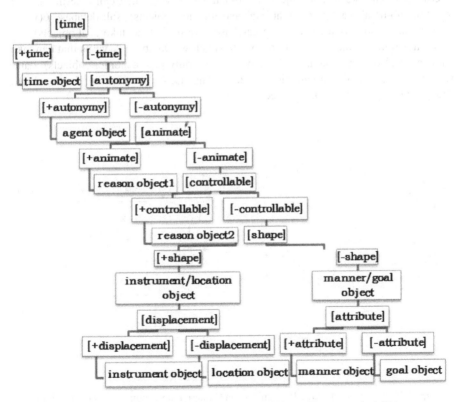

**Fig. 1.** Flow Chart of Machine Recognition on Chinese Non-canonical Object

# 4     Machine Recognition of Non-canonical VN Collocations

In the previous section, we discussed about the semantic features and the machine recognition of non-canonical objects. It is not sufficient to use only the objects' semantic features to achieve machine recognition. We hold the view that the verbs also play a very important role in forming the collocation. In Chinese, 吃馆子 [chi guan-zi], (to eat in the restaurant) and *跑馆子 [*pao guanzi] (to run in the restaurant) have the same structure but the latter one is wrong according to the Chinese grammar. The reason for this is, 吃 [chi] (to eat) and 跑 [pao] (to run) can take different kinds of non-canonical objects. Therefore, it is important to make sure how many kinds of objects a verb can take. Forasmuch, in this section, we focus on both the verb and the objects to offer a machine recognition flowchart of non-canonical VN collocations.

Huang, B. R. [7] is an informative book which focuses on Chinese verbs. It collects 2403 meanings of 1540 Chinese verbs and divides them into 44 grammatical categories. This book also gives details about the different kinds of objects a verb can take which can be the crucial evidence for our research. We build corpus V, in which seven sub-databases are included. These databases are: sub-database 1(verbs that can take time objects), sub-database 2(verbs that can take agent objects), sub-database 3(verbs that can take reason objects), sub-database 4(verbs that can take instrument objects), sub-database 5(verbs that can take location objects), sub-database 6(verbs that can take manner objects) and sub-database 7(verbs that can take goal objects).

We illustrate the machine recognition steps below. Database A(verbs that can take non-canonical objects), database B(verbs that can only take canonical objects), database F(7 categories of non-canonical objects), database C (a combining database) and database D (idioms and chunks). (see Fig.2.)

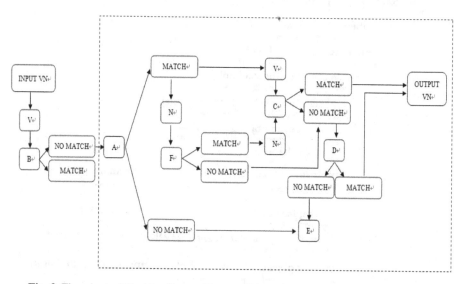

**Fig. 2.** Flowchart of Machine Recognition on Chinese Non-canonical VN collocations

We take 跑北京 [*pao Beijing*] (*to go to Beijing for business*) as an example to illustrate the recognition process. Firstly, the verb 跑 [*pao*] (*to run*) enters into A(verbs that can take non-canonical objects), if it matches, then the object enters into B to check if it matches one of the 7 categories of non-canonical objects. If it matches, then both the noun and the verb enter into C. C not only shows that the verb 跑 [*pao*] (*to run*) can take four kinds of non-canonical objects: location objects, agent objects, manner objects and goal objects, but also shows that the noun Beijing is a location object. The verb and the noun can match in database C. Therefore, this machine recognition finishes successfully, and it gives the output:   pao [V] Beijing [Location Object]. (see Fig.3.)

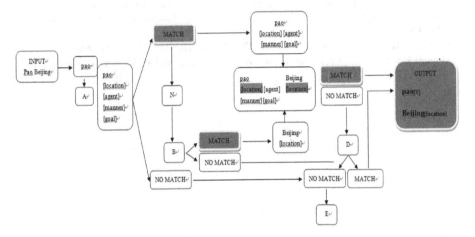

**Fig. 3.** Flowchart of Machine Recognition on *pao Beijing*

## 5    Conclusion

This paper focuses on Chinese non-canonical VN collocations from the NLP perspective. It first discriminates non-canonical objects from canonical objects, and divided the non-canonical objects into seven categories. Then it analyzes the semantic features of each category and offers a flowchart to illustrate the recognition process. This paper argues that machine recognition in Chinese non-canonical objects should not only focus on the objects but also on the verbs. The fourth section gives a description of machine recognition on Chinese non-canonical VN collocations and gives an example in detail at the end of this section. This is a desk study on machine recognition. Further study is needed in the near future. This paper only talks about the recognition process theoretically. Besides that, the materials collected in this research are limited and insufficient. It is better to do future research with the help of large-scale corpus. Finally, this paper talks about Chinese non-canonical objects statically, how to analyze the semantic features dynamically remains a question.

# References

1. Yuan, Y.L.: On the hierarchical relation and semantic features of the thematic roles in Chinese. Chinese Teaching in the World 61, 10–22 (2002)
2. Xie, X.M., Wang, Y.B.: Syntactic Factors of Non-canonical VN Collocations. Linguistic Research 111, 29–33 (2009)
3. Yang, Y.Z.: On the Pragmatic Motivation of Vi. +NP Construction. Chinese Linguistics 17, 58–65 (2007)
4. Fan, X.: An introspection to the Study of Chinese Object. Chinese Language Learning 3, 3–13 (2006)
5. Zhang, Y.Q.: Xiandai Hanyu Shoushi Binyuju Yanjiu. Academia Press, Shanghai (2004)
6. Cheng, J.: The Null Preposition Hypothesis and the applicative construction: A syntactic study of the post-intransitive-verb non-core arguments. Modern Foreign Languages 1, 23–32 (2009)
7. Meng, C.: Hanyu Dongci Yongfa Cidian. The Commercial Press, Beijing (1999)
8. Huang, B.R.: Dongci Fenlei he Yanjiu Wenxianmulu Zonglan. Higher Education Press, Beijing (1998)

# A Talk on "Tongkuai" and "Tongbingkuailezhe"

Wanmei Huang[1], Huali Liu[1], and Xing Chen[2]

[1] College of Arts and Communication, China Three Gorges University,
Yichang Hubei, 443002, China
huangwanmei68@126.com
[2] School of Geography, Beijing Normal University,
Beijing, 100875, China
chenchen19920228@126.com

**Abstract.** "痛快"[Tongkuai] is a common word in modern Chinese, which has three meanings:" 高兴 "[Gaoxing](pleased, very happy, joyful), " 尽兴 "[Jinxing](happily, to one's heart's content ) and " 爽快"[Shuangkuai] (straightforward). The morpheme "Tong" comes from the adverb "Tong", while the adverb "Tong" comes from the grammaticalization of the adjective "Tong". The morpheme "Kuai" derives from the adjective "Kuai". Extended relations occur between the different meanings of the adjective "Kuai", such as "glad" and "fast". This article focuses on the grammaticalization of "Tong" and the extended relations of "Kuai". The lexicalization and grammaticalization of "Tongkuai" are also explained in the paper.

**Keywords:** Modern Chinese, "Tongkuai", Grammaticalization, Lexicalization, Extended meaning.

At present, people are interested in new words so that the related researches are quite popular. Actually, some words in the basic vocabulary of modern Chinese worth more discussion. For instance, the research on finding out the structure type of "痛快"[Tongkuai], the semantic contribution of the morphemes "Tong" and "Kuai" to the compound word "Tongkuai" and the relationships between the popular phrases "痛并快乐着"[Tongbingkuailezhe](pain is happy),"痛而后快"[Tongerhoukuai](painful and then happy) and the commonly used word "痛快"[Tongkuai].

According to Modern Chinese Standardized Dictionary,"痛"[Tong] has three meanings: ① adj. 疼 [Teng](pain) :腰酸背痛 (Back pain); ② adj. 悲伤 [Beishang](sad) : 痛不欲生 (Sad to death ) ; ③ adv. 程度极深[Chengdu jishen](badly, thoroughly, highly, etc.) :痛打,痛改前非等(Beat sb badly, Rectify one's errors thoroughly,etc.) " 快"[Kuai]has seven meanings: ① adj. 高兴 [Gaoxing](glad, happy); ②adj. 速度高, 用时短[Sudu gao, yongshi duan](fast); ③ adj. 锋利 [Fengli](sharp); ④ adj. 敏捷 [Minjie](agile,quick); ⑤ adv. 赶快 [Guankuai](quickly); ⑥adv. 很快[Henkuai](soon); ⑦adj. 直率[Zhishuai](frank)."痛快"[Tongkuai] has three meanings:①adj.高兴[Gaoxing](pleased, very happy) : 心里非常痛快。( he is very happy.） ②adj. 尽情, 尽兴[Jinqing, Jinxing](happily, to one's heart's content) : 他痛快地哭了一场。(He cried happily.) ③adj.爽快, 干脆

P. Liu and Q. Su (Eds.): CLSW 2013, LNAI 8229, pp. 47–55, 2013.
© Springer-Verlag Berlin Heidelberg 2013

*[Shuangkuai, Gancui]( straightforward, frank)* : 他是个痛快人。 *(He is a frank man.)* [1]

Hence, both "Tong" and "Kuai" can be used as adjectives and adverbs, and are therefore multi-category words and polysemes. However, what are the extended relations of the several meanings of the two words? And what are the grammaticalization process and the mechanism of their adjective and adverb usages? The three senses of the dictionary entries of "Tongkuai" are all adjectives with simple functions, which seems that there are no matters of grammaticalization. But as monosyllables, how do "Tong" and "Kuai" become morphemes and finally lexicalized into the disyllabic "Tongkuai"?

# 1    Discussion about "Tong": The Grammaticalization of "Tong"

According to corpora [1], the literature that has the earliest records of "Tong" are *ShanHaiJing* and *ZhouYi*, such as:

(1) 食之已嗌痛，可以已瘑。（周《山海经卷三·北山经》）
*Its meat can cure throat pain and stomach pain. (Zhou.ShanHaiJing)*
(2) 为心病，为耳痛。（周《周易·说卦》）
*This is heart disease and ears pain. (Zhou. ZhouYi)*

According to the two examples above, "嗌痛" *(throat pain）*and"耳痛" *(ears pain)* constitute subject-predicate relationship. That is the earliest usage of "Tong". 《说文解字》*[ShuoWenJieZi](The dictionary wrote at Han dynasty)* tells that"痛,病也。"[2] *("Tong" means sickness.)* So the original meaning of "Tong" is pain which, in this paper, is said as "Tong①". "Tong①" can be extended from "physical pain" to "mental pain" via the mechanism of metaphor, which is recorded as "Tong②". Therefore, "Tong②" is a figurative meaning of "Tong①". The earlier literature that records "Tong②" is *ChuCi*, and the meaning becomes popular after the Eastern Han Dynasty, such as:

(3)痛忠言之逆耳兮，恨申子之沉江。（春秋·屈原《楚辞·七谏》）
*Feel Sad for advice when most needed is least heeded, feel sorry for Shenzi jumping into the Yangtze River. (the Spring and Autumn Period. ChuCi)*
(4)臣痛社稷危也！（东汉·班固《汉书》）
*I feel sad for national crisis. (the Eastern Han Dynasty. HanShu)*
(5) 臣窃痛之。（东汉·班固《汉书》）
*I secretly feel sad. (the Eastern Han Dynasty. HanShu)*

As above, "Tong①" is used as the predicate and there is no object behind it, however, there is always an object after "Tong②". That is the different usage between "Tong①" and "Tong②".

---

[1] Please go to webpages: www.cncorpus.org/ACindex.aspx
*and* ccl.pku.edu.cn/corpus.asp

"Tong" appears in serial verb construction after *the Qin dynasty* and *Han Dynasties*. For example,

(6) 痛以重法绳之。（东汉·班固《汉书》）

*Feel sad for someone to punish him with tough laws. (the Eastern Han Dynasty. HanShu)*

(7)可痛哭者，此病是也。（西汉·刘向《贾谊新书》）

*This is the disease which makes someone feel sad and cry. (the Western Han Dynasty. Jiayi Book)*

According to the researches, "Tong" is usually used together with "哭、惜、恨、悼" *(cry, pity, hate and grieve）* for the reason that this kind of verbs are related to "Tong"and are semantically compatible. When "Tong" is used together with this kind of verbs, "而"*[Er] (so)* can be inserted between them to get the construction "痛而V之" *(Tong so V)*, such as "痛而哭之、痛而悼之" *(feel sad so cry, feel sad so mourn)*. In the Six Dynasties, "Tong" was usually used together with the verbs"搅、拌、揉"*[Jiao, Ban, Rou]（stir, mix, rub, etc）*. For example,

(8) 以匙痛搅令散。（六朝·贾思勰《齐民要术》）

*Stir something energetically with a spoon to make it dispersive. (the Six Dynasties.QiMin YaoShu)*

(9) 以手痛揉。（六朝·贾思勰《齐民要术》）

*Exert oneself to knead with hands . (the Six Dynasties. QiMin YaoShu)*

The examples above put "Tong" into the structural pattern of "以 NP 痛 VP" *(VP emphatically with NP)*. "Tong", just like the prepositional phrase before it, is used as the adverbial of the verb that follows it, so it is the adverb. The adverb "Tong" here is "Tong③". The evolution of "Tong" is finished in *the Six Dynasties*.

In conclusion, "Tong②" is derived from "Tong①" as a result of metaphorical extension in meaning, the process of which is finished in *the pre-Qin period*. From "Tong①" to "Tong②", then to "Tong③", "Tong" finishes its grammaticalization and changes from a verb into an adverb. In the process of grammaticalization, *the Eastern Han Dynasty* is an important transitional stage, and *the Six Dynasties* is a vital period that symbolizes the completion of its grammaticalization.

There are two reasons for the grammaticalization motivation of "Tong". On the one hand, the use of "Tong" together with other verbs provides syntactic conditions for its grammaticalization. On the other hand,"痛,从疒甬聲。"[2](*"Tong" is a phonogram which means sickness. "Yong" represents it pronunciation）* "甬" *[Yong]*, the omitted form of "痛"*[Tong]*, represents both its pronunciation and its meaning. It means "completely" and "thoroughly". Therefore, "Tong" has the meaning "completely" and "thoroughly" since its first coinage, which contributes a lot to its evolution into an adverb that stands for the depth of degree.   In other word, it is laid a semantic basis for it later turned into degree adverbs.

According to the study of the adverb in modern Chinese by *Rongxiang Yang*, "Tong" belongs to modal adverbs[3]. It is considered that the adverb "Tong ③ " is grammaticalized from "Tong②" and "Tong①" so that "Tong③" has the semantic origin of mental "Tong" as well as physical "Tong". No matter what kind of "Tong" it is, the semantic factor of "pain" in it leads to its grammaticalization into a modal adverb. Namely, "Tong③" is a modal adverb in modern Chinese. It is grammaticalized and becomes an adverb that signifies degree in contemporary Chinese.

In fact, both the adjective and the adverb have the same semantic features, such as "status" and "quantity", etc. Therefore, the best part in the grammaticalization chain is the grammaticalization from an adjective to an adverb, namely it is more convenient that the adjective grammaticalize to the adverb. In a word, the sememe of "Tong①" includes [+sensation] [+negative] and [+injury], and the sememe of "Tong②" includes [+mood] [+negative] and [+incident]. If the adjective "Tong" highlights the negative feeling or emotion caused by some reason, the grammaticalized adverb "Tong③" emphasizes the sememe of [+negative] and [act strongly]. One of the two senses belongs to modal depiction, the other expresses the extreme degree. The extreme degree is more ethereal both lexically and semantically than the modal depiction. So "Tong" finishes its grammaticalization process as a modal adverb, and then continues to be grammaticalized to a degree adverb in contemporary Chinese.

In addition, we also consider that in *the Six Dynasties*, the great works of agricultural literature like *QiMinYaoShu*r reserves more spoken langrage at the time, especially the cants in the fields of agricultural production, food storage and process. "Tong" is used together with diverse specific verbs, which is probably the direct cause of its adverb grammaticalization. Or it is speculated that the adverb usage is popular in agriculture and among ordinary people at the beginning, and it enters the basic vocabulary of the modern standard Chinese later. Obviously, spoken language and catchword in every field have made great contributions to language change.

## 2    Discussion about "Kuai": The Extended Meaning of "Kuai"

In *ShuoWenJieZi*, "快，喜也。 从心夬聲。"[2](*"Kuai"means "to be glad". The heart indicates its meaning and "Kuai" represents the pronunciation ) Yucai Duan* explains that the extended meaning of "Kuai" is "fast"[4]. It is clear that the original meaning of "Kuai" is "glad", and the transferred meaning of "Kuai" is "fast". In the literature corpus we have researched, "Kuai" means "happy" and "glad". "Kuai" is an adjective in *pre-Qin period*, and is used causatively sometimes with an object behind it. For example,

(10) 君若来，将待刑以快君志。（春秋《国语·晋语》）

*If the monarch come back, I will be prepared to be punished to pleasure him.(the Spring and Autumn Period. GuoYu)*

(11) 以快楚心。（春秋《左传》）

*Make the monarch of Chu glad. (the Spring and Autumn Period. ZuoZhuan)*

The meaning "fast" of "Kuai" originates from Han Dynasty and is widely used after the Six Dynasties, having the tendency to be adverbialized. For example,

(12) 水有迟快 ……（汉《太平经》）

*The water flows sometimes slowly, sometimes fast. (Han Dynasty.TaiPingJing)*

(13) 使人骑快骡迎至鄴。（六朝《北史》）

*Make sb ride a  fast horse  to meet him in Ye city. (the Six Dynasties. BeiShi)*

(14) 快走踏清秋。（唐·李贺《马诗》）

*Walk fast so as to see the fall beautiful scenery. (Tang Dynasty.Li He. About the horse's Poetry)*

In the above examples, the meaning of "Kuai" is extended from joyful mood to high speed. Why is there this extension? *Zhongshu Qian* thinks that if people are joyful, they will feel time flies[5]. Obviously, this explanation of extended relationship is made from the view of life philosophy. Saying from cognitive psychology or physiological mechanism, happiness is a comfortable mood and feeling, and "畅"[Chang](free) means "no obstacle", like a river which flows smoothly and fast. That's why we say "畅快"[ChangKuai](free and glad). The example of literature is as follows:

(15) 疏河快江。（西汉·刘安《淮南子》）

Dredge the river to make it flow faster. (the Western Han Dynasty. HuaiNanZi)

In this example, "快"[Kuai] (fast) is a causative verb which means "to let the river flows smoothly and fast". Among the literature we have researched, this is a relatively early example that explains "Kuai" as high speed. In this example, "快" [Kuai] (fast) and "疏"[Shu](dredge) are taken as couple examples and there is a causal relationship between them. They also have common semantic features. Dredging results in no obstacle and the no obstacle results in high-speed, which is concerned with mood as well as speed. The common sememe of "glad" and "fast" is [+free]. There is an another viewpoint that the phonetic symbol of "快"[Kuai] is "夬"[Kuai], which means "an open mouth", so the original meaning of "Kuai" is "to open the mouth and speak out the worry frankly and bluntly", and the meanings "comfortable" and "high-speed" derive from this[2]. This view provides us with the evidence for above-mentioned interpretation.

According to *the CCL corpus*, the word"爽快"[Shuangkuai](frank) is used first in *TangWenShiYi* written by the bibliographer *Xinyuan Lu* in *Qing Dynasty*. The example is as follows:

(16) 爽快哀婉，能使诸天欢喜，永於远地流传。（清·陆心源《唐文拾遗》）

*Frankness and pathos make the Gods happy and last forever. (Qing Dynasty.TangWenShiYi)*

"ShuangKuai" appears after "Kuai" is extended to "fast". It means that "*straightforward*, frank" is extended from "fast"directly. Therefore, it can be concluded that the original meaning of "Kuai" has the following relationship with its several transferred meanings:

glad --▶comfortable --▶ unimpeded ⟶ fast ⟶ sharp / frank , agile ↘ quickly

---

2 Please go to this webpage: www.vividict.com/WordInfo.aspx?id=1356

# 3    Discussion about "Tongkuai": The Lexicalization of "Tongkuai"

In the two corpora searched, "Tongkuai" appeared first in *the Six Dynasties*. The adverbialization of "Tong" had already been accomplished then and the use of the word with the meaning "fast" became increasingly popular. In *FaShuYaoLu, the* compiler *Yanyuan Zhang* in *Tang Dynasty* quoted the following sentences from *CaiGuLaiNengShuRenMing* written by *Xin Yang* of *Nan Dynasty*:

(17) 吴人皇象能草，世称沉著痛快。（南朝·羊欣《采古来能书人名》）

*Wu Ren Huang Xiang was good at cursive and people at the time praised his handwriting for its powerfulness and fluency. (Nan Dynasty. CaiGuLaiNengShuRenMing)*

"沉著"*[Chenzhuo]* means "writing vigorously"; 痛快*[Tongkuai]* means "writing straightforwardly and smoothly".沉著痛快*[ChenzhuoTongkuai]* is a terms of calligraphy. Later, it is used to describe the powerfulness and fluency of poems and articles. Afterwards, "Tongkuai" is used alone and turns into a word gradually. For example,

(18) 戴诗壮丽……沉著痛快……（元代·辛文芳《唐才子传》）

*The poems that Dai wrote are magnificent......powerful and fluent. (Yuan Dynasty. TangCaiZiZhuan)*

(19) 因见吕与叔解得此段痛快……（宋·黎靖德《朱子语类》）

*Lv Yushu made an brilliant explanation of the paragraph to make himself glad. (Song Dynasty. ZhuZiYuLei)*

(20)只务自家一时痛快……（宋·黎靖德《朱子语类》）

*Make only himself glad. (Song Dynasty. ZhuZiYuLei )*

"Tongkuai" is more and more frequently used in the literature after *Song Dynasty* and its meaning gets diversified. Its three meanings in modern Chinese already come into being. For example,

(21) 心里一痛快，不觉收了眼泪，……（清·文康《儿女英雄传》）

*He felt very happy and stopped crying. (Qing Dynasty.ErNvYingXiongZhuan)*

(22) 咱们正该心里痛快痛快……（清·文康《儿女英雄传》）

*Now, we should be happy. (Qing Dynasty.ErNvYingXiongZhuan)*

(23) 和尚倒了，就直捷痛快的说和尚倒了……（清·文康《儿女英雄传》）

*Please say monk falls straightforward if it is true. (Qing Dynasty.ErNvYingXiongZhuan)*

(24)索性把台湾的事，谈个痛快罢！（清·曾朴《孽海花》）

*Let's make the thing simple and talk about the Taiwan affairs happily. (Qing Dynasty.NieHaiHua)*

Therefore, it can be claimed that "Tongkuai" is an academic term in the calligraphy circles at first and the public's love of the calligraphic art makes it   break the fields of handwriting, poem and essay. Finally it gets into the common vocabulary from the general vocabulary.

18485 sentences can be found in CCL corpus (ancient Chinese) when "Tong" is used as the searching word and the number before the Six Dynasties is 244. Thus it can be seen that the frequency of the use of "Tong" increased considerably after it changed into an adverb. This is fully consistent with the facts that the frequency of the use of function words is much higher than that of notional words. Further inquiries into the common compound words with "Tong" as the prior morpheme are made in the corpus. The results are as follows:

**Table 1.** Data statistics "Tong+X"

| Example of word | Number of sentence | The literature of first using the word | After the Six Dynasties | Before the Six Dynasties |
|---|---|---|---|---|
| *Tongku* | 1623 | XiHan.*XinShu* | 1620 | 3 |
| *Tongku* | 503 | DongHan.*LunHeng* | 502 | 1 |
| *Tonghen* | 410 | DongHan.*QuanHanWen* | 409 | 1 |
| *Tongxi* | 430 | XiHan.*XinShu* | 425 | 5 |
| *Tongyin* | 524 | the Six Dynasties.*ShiShuoXinYu* | 524 | 0 |
| *Tongdao* | 174 | the Six Dynasties.*QuanLiuSongWen* | 170 | 4 |
| *Tongma* | 134 | the Six Dynasties.*ShiShuoXinYu* | 134 | 0 |
| *Tongji* | 89 | BeiSong.*TaiPingGuangJi* | 89 | 0 |
| *Tongchi* | 44 | BeiSong. *MengXiBiTan* | 44 | 0 |
| *Tonghui* | 20 | Qing.*QiJianShiSanXia* | 20 | 0 |
| *Tongkuai* | 397 | The Six Dynasties.*CaiGuLaiNengShuRenming* | 397 | 0 |

The above table shows that the combination of "Tong+X" appears to be few before *the Six Dynasties*, and it should be a phrase. The frequency of the appearance of "Tong+X" rapidly increases after *the Six Dynasties*. It becomes a regular collocation and is lexicalized finally. In the process of the lexicalization of "Tong+X", the meanings "fast" and "frank" of "Kuai" are obtained. Under the analogy mechanism of grammaticalization, this meaning of "Kuai" occupies the position of "X" and is combined with the adverb "Tong", which results in the word "Tongkuai". At first, the adverb "Tong" and the adjective "Kuai" form a phrase "Tongkuai". Then, with the increasing frequency of its use, the phrase finally becomes a word.

*Rongxiang Yang* holds the view that there are direct grammaticalization and indirect grammaticalization in the notional words' grammaticalizing into adverbs. The so-called direct grammaticalization refers to the direct grammaticalization of a notional word into an adverb and the indirect grammaticalization means that the changing process of the meaning from a notional word into a function word is not reflected on the layer of words, but on the layer of formation morpheme. According to this view, the adverb "Tong③" is grammaticalized directly from the adjective "Tong", which belongs to direct grammaticalization. But the lexicalization of "Tongkuai" belongs to indirect grammaticalization, which means that the formation morpheme "Tong" has already been grammaticalized before the adjective "Tongkuai" becomes a word and the different meanings of the adjective "Kuai" have completed their extension.

According to the literature of foreign language written by *Hopper* and other literature of grammaticalization, *Jiaxuan Shen* induces the nine principles of the theory of grammaticalization, for example, coexistence principle, maintenance principle, frequency principle, gradual changing principle, delay principle and so on[6]. The grammaticalization of "Tong" and the lexicalization of "Tongkuai" reflect those principles well. "Tong" becomes an adverb after grammaticalization, but the usage of it as an adjective still remains. Its two different parts of speech and three meanings coexist in modern Chinese. Meanwhile, after the lexicalization of "Tongkuai", the compound word "Tongkuai" as well as the simple words "Tong" and "Kuai" also exist in modern Chinese.

## 4    Summary: Discussion about "Tongbingkuailezhe"

According to the explanation in the dictionary and the above analyses, the three meanings of the word "Tongkuai" evolve like this: "Tong" in "Tongkuai" is a morpheme that comes from "Tong③", and "Kuai" in "Tongkuai" comes from the meanings such as "glad", "fast" and "frank", etc. Generally speaking, "Tongkuai① "=Tong③+Kuai①("*very happy*"); "Tongkuai②"=Tong③+Kuai①+Kuai②("*very happy and outburst of strong emotions*", "*to one's heart's content*".); "Tongkuai③ "=Tong③+Kuai⑦("*frank and straightforward*"). No matter which meaning it has, "Tongkuai" belongs to modifier-type compound words that "Tong" is the adverbial and "Kuai"is the central word.

Of course, the meaning of a compound word is not equal to a simple addition of the meanings of the morphemes, but the morpheme meaning can directly become a sememe of the semantic meaning of the compound word. Therefore, the explanation of the meaning of a word on the basis of sememe analysis can show the relevance between morpheme meaning and the meaning of the word itself. To understand a compound word easily, the word may be taken apart first to interpret respectively, and then combined to explain the whole.

Finally, "痛 并 快 乐 着 "[*Tongbingkuailezhe*](*pain is happy*)and"痛 而 后 快 "[*Tongerhoukuai*](*painful and then happy*) may belong to de-grammaticalization which is controversial in the Linguistics. Unidirectionality is an important assumption of grammaticalization. It refers to the evolution of the units of a language from vocabulary to grammar by way of grammar continuum chain. In short, the grammaticalization is the evolution from a notional word to a function word, which is a one-way evolution from formal to more formal. De-grammaticalization means that in a certain context a linguistic unit has more automaticity or semantic characteristics at more than one language level (semantically, morphologically, syntactically and so on). The relevant parameters that can judge the de-grammaticalization are re-semantization and de-bonding and so on[7]. After the lexicalization of "Tongkuai", its structure is cohesive and cannot expand. The meaning of it, which is not a simple addition of the two morphemic meanings, is intact and cohesive. The meanings of "Tongbingkuailezhe" and "Tongerhoukuai" are completely different from that of "Tongkuai". "Tong" in "Tongkuai" is "Tong③", and "Tong" in "Tongbingkuailezhe" and "Tongerhoukuai" is "Tong②". The semantic development of "Tong" follows a path opposite to grammaticalization. The adhesiveness and compulsion of the structure "Tongbingkuailezhe" and "Tongerhoukuai" show that they are forceful dismantling and willful extension of the structure of "Tongkuai". Thus, it can be preliminarily concluded that "Tongbingkuailezhe" and "Tongerhoukuai"are the special cases of de-grammaticalization in modern Chinese which was put forward recently in the field of linguistics.

**Acknowledgments.** This work was supported by Hubei province social science fund, Contract No. 2012294.

# References

1. Li, X.: The modern Chinese Standard Dictionary(现代汉语规范词典), vol. 762, pp. 1310–1311. Foreign Language Teaching and Research Press & The Chinese Press, Beijing, China (2004)
2. Xu, S.: Analysis and Interpretation of Chinese Characters(说文解字), vol. 217, p. 154. Zhonghua Press, Beijing (1963)
3. Yang, R.: The study of modern Chinese adverbs(近代汉语副词研究), p. 187. The Commercial Press, Beijing (2007)
4. Duan, Y.: Notes on ShuoWenJieZi(说文解字注), vol. 502, p. 348. Shanghai Ancient Books Publishing House, Shanghai (1988)
5. Yan, C.: Say "Kuai" by Zhongshu Qian(钱钟书说"快"). Nit-Pick on Words 12, 8 (1996)
6. Shen, J.: A Survey of Studies on Grammaticalization("语法化"研究综观). Foreign Language Teaching and Research 4, 17–24 (1994)
7. Yang, K., Wen, X.: Review on De-grammaticalization(《语法化》评介). Foreign Language Teaching and Research 3, 469–473 (2011)

# On *DE*: Its Nature and Features[*]

Huibin Zhuang[1], Wenlei Shi[2], Meihua Wang[3], and Zhenqian Liu[4]

[1] Henan University, Kaifeng, China
[2] Zhejiang University, Hangzhou, China
[3] Inner Mongolia University for Nationalities, Tongliao, China
[4] Shandong University, Jinan, China
{zhuanghuibin,meihua_ehome,levinliu1964}@163.com,
wenleishi@zju.edu.cn

**Abstract.** *DE* in Chinese is special in many aspects. It takes various constituents as its complement, while it itself behaves very much like a clitic. On the basis of the previous works, we carried out an investigation of its syntactic features, such as its derivation and cliticization. The syntactic structure of verb copying constructions in V-*DE* constructions are in fact some adjuncts.

**Keywords:** *DE*, clitic, Pro, forced meaning, Verb copying structure.

## 1    V-*DE* Constraint on Object

V-*DE* constructions in Chinese have challenged many scholars to explore their properties and especially their relationship to other categories. Two types of V-*DE* constructions are most frequently discussed: descriptive and resultative, as shown in (1) and (2) respectively: [1]

(1) 我　跑　得　很　快。
　　 *wo pao de hen kuai.*
　　 I　run *DE*　very　fast
　　 'I run very fast.'
(2) 他　跑　得　很　累。
　　 *ta tiao de hen lei.*
　　 he　jump *DE*　very　tired
　　 'He was very tired from jumping.'

V-*DE* constructions in modern Chinese syntax have a very prominent feature, i.e., if the verb before *DE* requires an NP object semantically, the NP cannot appear after the verb (whether before or after *DE*)[2], as shown below:

---

[*] All correspondence please address to: Zhenqian Liu.

[1] In addition, there is a third kind of "V-*DE*" constructions indicating potential. This kind of "V-*DE*" constructions is not the issue of the current discussion.

[2] It seems that in *gu baihua* (antique vernacular Chinese) and some dialects today, "V-*DE* OC" and "VO *DE* C" can be found. As for "VO *DE* C," according to P. Wei [24], most VOs in them can be analyzed as verbs; and those in dialects are likely from VO *bu* C constructions through analogy.

P. Liu and Q. Su (Eds.): CLSW 2013, LNAI 8229, pp. 56–65, 2013.
© Springer-Verlag Berlin Heidelberg 2013

(3) 他　唱　　得　　我　　不　　想　　写　　信　　了。
　　*ta*　*chang*　*de*　*wo*　*bu*　*xiang*　*xie*　*xin*　*le*.
　　he　sing　*DE*　I　not　want　write　letter　SFP
　　'He sang so loudly (unpleasantly, etc.) that I didn't want to write the letter.'

(4) a. *他　唱　　黄梅戏　　　　得　我　不　想　　写　　信　　了。
　　　*ta*　*chang*　*huangmeixi*　*de*　*wo*　*bu*　*xiang*　*xie*　*xin*　*le*.
　　　he　sing　Huangmei.Opera　*DE*　I　not　want　write　letter　SFP

　　b. *他　唱　　得　黄梅戏　　　　我　不　想　写　　信　　了。
　　　*ta*　*chang*　*de*　*huangmeixi*　*wo*　*bu*　*xiang*　*xie*　*xin*　*le*.
　　　he　sing　*DE*　Huangmei.Opera　I　not　want　write　letter　SFP

　　c. *他　唱　　得　黄梅戏　　　　不　想　　写　　信　　了。
　　　*ta*　*chang*　*de*　*huangmeixi*　*bu*　*xiang*　*xie*　*xin*　*le*
　　　he　sing　*DE*　Huangmei.Opera　not　want　write　letter　SFP

This phenomenon is referred to as V-*DE* Constraint on Object (hereafter abbreviated as VDCO)[3]. Obviously, VDCO has something to do with *DE*.

In the literature, many hypotheses on the nature of *DE* have been put forward. The most influential ones are: (1) *DE* is a special preposition [1]; (2) *DE* is an affix [2-9]; (3) *DE* is an auxiliary [10-14]; (4) *DE* is a complementizer [15]; (5) *DE* is a light verb [16]. Some other scholars argue that *DE*s in different V-*DE* constructions should be treated differently [17-18]. These hypotheses, of course, have captured certain syntactic features of *DE*. None of them, however, could give a sound explanation of VDCO.

Until now, the only view that can better explain this phenomenon is treating *DE* as a (en)clitic [19-22].[4]

What is clitic? According to Spencer, "Clitics are elements which share certain properties of fully fledged words, but which lack the independence usually associated with words. In particular, they can't stand alone and have to be attached to a phonological host" [23]. Judging from its features, *DE* certainly can be treated as a clitic: (1) it cannot stand alone, but crucially depends on the phonological host (appearing only in

---

[3] It is interesting to note that, some scholars may argue that 我*wo* 'I' here is the object of 唱*chang* 'sing' [25-26]. Their evidence is the *ya*-insertion test. They argue that the interjection 呀*ya* can be inserted between a verb and its clausal object, but not between the verb and the postverbal NP object. It is necessary to point out that this test cannot be extended to the resultative V-*DE* construction. For example, I apply it to (i), there is not much contrast produced.

(i) a. 他　唱　　得　我　呀　不　想　　写　　信　　了。
　　　*ta*　*chang*　*de*　*wo*　*ya*,　*bu*　*xiang*　*xie*　*xin*　*le*.
　　　he　sing　*DE*　I　INT　not　want　write　letter　SFP
　　　'He sang so loudly (unpleasantly, etc.), um, that I didn't want to write the letter.'

　　b. 他　唱　　得　呀　我　不　想　　写　　信　　了。
　　　*ta*　*chang*　*de*　*ya*,　*wo*　*bu*　*xiang*　*xie*　*xin*　*le*.
　　　he　sing　*DE*　INT　I　not　want　write　letter　SFP
　　　'He sang so loudly (unpleasantly, etc.), um, that I didn't want to write the letter.'

Very obviously, *wo* 'I/me' cannot be understood as the object of 唱*chang* 'sing'. It must be the subject of the verb/predicate following it, i.e., 不想*bu xiang* 'have no mood'.

[4] J. Huang [27] has actually noticed this possibility. He says "[*DE*] has been historically derived from the verb 得*de* 'obtain'. Phonologically, *DE* is attached to the preceding verb, either as a suffix or a clitic, depending on one's theory...."

the V-*DE* construction); and (2) *DE* cannot be treated as an inflectional affix, because its combination with verbs affects the syntactic structure, while affixes (aspects) do not. This is shown in (5).

(5) a. 张三　　　唱　　　歌。　　　　(SVO)
　　　*Zhangsan　chang　ge.*
　　　Zhangsan　sing　song
　　　'Zhangsan sings a song.'

　　b. 张三　　　唱着/过　　　　　歌。(SVO)
　　　*Zhangsan　chang-ZHE/GUO　ge.*
　　　Zhangsan　sing-*ASP*　　　song
　　　'Zhangsan is singing/has sung a song'

　　c. *张三　　唱　　　得　　歌。　　(SVO)
　　　*Zhangsan　chang　de　ge.*
　　　Zhangsan　sing　*DE*　song

　　d. 张三　　　唱　　　得　　好。(SVC)
　　　*Zhangsan　chang　de　hao*
　　　Zhangsan　sing　*DE*　good
　　　'Zhangsan sings well.'

Obviously, *DE* functions on the syntax level. This is different from affixes which function on the word level.

Assuming this proposal to be on the right lines, VDCO can be explained. According to Ernst [19-20] or J. Tang [21-22], the (en)clitic *DE* is required to be attached to a verb or an adjective preceding it. An overt object NP will impede *DE* to be cliticized to its host; therefore, it is suppressed. Their explanations sound nice, but they are actually redundant. Actually, if *DE* is treated as a (en)clitic, the fact is already explained by the description in Aoun [28] or Jaeggli [29-30]. Aoun suggests clitics are able to absorb both Case and $\theta$-role. This means that the complement NP can get neither a Case nor a $\theta$-role. Of course, it cannot appear in this place. Jaeggli treats clitic as a Case-absorbing element. If so, the complement NP cannot get a $\theta$-role, either. According to the Visibility Condition, an element must be Case-marked in order to be visible for $\theta$-marking. The complement NP is not able to get a Case; of course, it cannot get a $\theta$-role.

## 2    Derivation of *DE*

The proposal that *DE* is a clitic raises the question of how *DE* is derived. The answer can be one of the two assumptions: base-generation (plus movement) or insertion in the derivation. We cannot assume, however, that *DE* is base-generated immediately after V, because, as Chomsky [31] suggests, clitics are nonbranching elements (See also Bošković [32-33]). This means that whether we position *DE* in the complement NP or as the head of a functional category projection, the nonbranching feature will prevent any constituent appearing lower than the position V-*DE* occupies. If *DE* is base-generated in some other places and moves to this position, then it must be generated in a position lower than V-*DE*, because clitics, being different from affixes, cannot be lowered to this place. However, in certain cases, there exists only one word after *DE*, as in (6):

(6)他 生气　 得　 很。
   *ta shengqi de hen.*
   he angry　 *DE* very
   'He was very angry.'

In this case, the possibility of derivation through movement absolutely does not exist: there is no room for *DE* to be base-generated. Accordingly, the only possibility left is that *DE* is inserted. This is also the view held by many scholars on clitics in other languages [34-37].[5] In the present study, *DE* is believed to be inserted when the two constituents join in the mapping process from DS to SS.

Now consider (7), whose derivation is shown in (8) (*DE-I* stands for *DE*-insertion). The tree diagram in (9) demonstrates its structure.[6]

(7) 他 哭　 得　 我 不　 想　　 写　　 信　 了。
   *ta ku de wo bu xiang ∙ xie xin le*
   he cry *DE* I not mood write letter SFP
   'He cried so loudly (unpleasantly, etc.) that I didn't want to write the letter.'

(8) a. Lexicon: *ta, ku, wo, bu, xiang, xie, xin, le...*
      CAUSE (KU (*ta*), ~XIANG (*wo*, XIE (*wo*, *xin*))
   b. DS: *ta ku CAUSE wo bu xiang xiexin le.*
   c. *DE-I* & VDCO: *ta ku DE wo bu xiang xiexin le.*
   d. SS: *ta ku-DE wo bu xiang xie xin le.*
   e. PF: *ta ku de wo bu xiang xie xin le.*

(9)

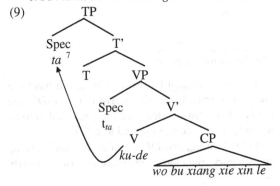

---

[5] Some scholars may argue that since the origins of *DE* in descriptive V-*DE* constructions (*DE*des) and *DE* in resultative V-*DE* constructions (*DE*res) are different (which will be discussed later), they should be studied separately. It is true that in this way, we may "create" a base-generated position for for *DE*res. However, once we get down to the base-generated position of *DE*des, we are still confronted with the above problem. In contrast, a unified account is more proper if we take Economy Principle into account. In the literature, some scholars do treat the two constructions as one (e.g. Junping Li [4](p.560)).

[6] In fact, it is shown in historical documents that the causative *DE*, which came into being very late, is derived through insertion.

[7] In this study, Subject-VP-Hypothesis is adopted, that is to say, subjects of sentences originate in Spec,VP, although in many cases, this movement is not shown unless it is necessary.

(7) is comparatively straightforward, because *ku* 'cry' is a verb that does not require an object. (10), however, is more complex, because the verb in the V-*DE* construction, namely, *ma* 'curse', requires an object. Its derivation is shown in (11) (Q stands for Quantifier) and its structure is shown in (16):

(10) 他　骂　　得　　张三　　　不　想　　写　信　　了。
     *ta*  *ma*  *de*  *Zhangsan*  *bu*  *xiang*  *xie*  *xin*  *le*
     he  curse  DE  Zhangsan  not  want  write  letter  SFP
     'He cursed Zhangsan so much that Zhangsan didn't want to write the letter.'

(11) a. Lexicon: *ta, ma, Lisi, Zhangsan, bu, xiang, xie, xin, le...*
       CAUSE (MA (*ta, Q*), ~XIANG (*Zhangsan*, XIE (*Zhangsan, xin*))
    b. DS: *ta ma Zhangsan/Lisi/ta ziji* CAUSE *Zhangsan bu xiang xie xin le*
    c. DE-I & VDCO: *ta ma* ~~Zhangsan/Lisi/ta ziji~~ DE *Zhangsan bu xiang xie xin le*
    d. SS: *ta ma-DE Zhangsan bu xiang xie xin le*
    e. PF: *ta ma de Zhangsan bu xiang xie xin le*

(12)

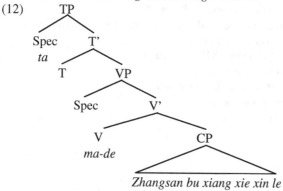

*Zhangsan bu xiang xie xin le*

Because of VDCO, the object of *ma* 'curse' cannot be realized in situ. It has to re-treat. By "retreat," I do not mean that it is eliminated in the derivation of V-*DE* con-struction, but that it is merely "suppressed" or "suspended," i.e., not mapped onto the object position of *ma*. In the present study, it will be represented as a *Pro*[8].

I will call the derivation in (8) and (11) joining, and *DE* a joining marker[9]. The ap-pearance of *DE* can help to join one category to a clause (or, more precisely, a verb).

---

[8] *Pro* here stands for a phonetically empty pronoun. It could be a *PRO*, a *pro*, a zero-topic, or none of them, anticipating more substantial justification later. (Also see J. Huang, A. Li and Y. Li [44].)

[9] It seems that *ge* is another joining marker although its application scope is much narrower. With the help of *ge*, only certain categories (e.g., AP, VP, four-character idioms, and subject-predicate structures) can be joined to a clause (or a verb), as shown below (since *ge* here cannot be treated as a classifier anymore, I will use italic *ge* to gloss it):

(i) a. 问　个　明白　　　b. 说　个　不　停
    *wen*  *ge*  *mingbai*    *shuo*  *ge*  *bu*  *ting*
    ask  *ge*  understand    say  *ge*  not  stop
    'ask what it was all about'  'say sth without stopping'

Of course, *ge* is syntactically different from *DE*, too. It does not behave like a clitic, i.e., the verb preceding *ge* can take its object, as in (ic). Besides, since *ge* is a classifier in nature, nominalization is obligatory before it joins one category to a clause (or a verb). And aspectual marker cannot be present any more afterward. For more discussion, please refer to Y. Zhang [41].

(7) and (10) show that a clause is joined to another clause (or a verb) by *DE*. As a matter of fact, with the help of *DE*, many categories can be joined to a clause (or a verb), as in (13):[10]

(13) a. 他　　跑　　得　　快。
      *ta*　*pao*　*de*　*kuai.*
      he　run　*DE*　fast
      'He runs fast.'

    b. 他　吃惊　　得　　很。
      *ta*　*chijing*　*de*　*hen.*[11]
      he　surprise　*DE*　very
      'She was very surprised.'

    d. 他　骂　得　很　　绝情。
      *ta*　*ma*　*de*　*hen*　*jueqing*
      he　curse　*DE*　very　ruthless
      'He cursed very ruthlessly.'

Their derivation (joining process) can be shown below ((13d) is taken as an instance):

(14) a. Lexicon: *ta, ma, Zhangsan, hen, jueqing….*
    b. DS: *ta ma Zhangsan/ta ziji hen jueqing*
    c. *DE*-I & VDCO: *ta ma ~~Zhangsan/Lisi/ta ziji~~ DE hen jueqing*
    d. SS: *ta ma-DE hen jueqing*
    e. PF: *ta ma de hen jueqing*

(15)

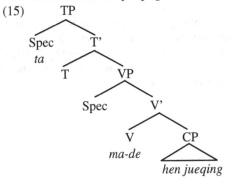

Therefore, *DE* should be viewed as a joining marker that behaves like a clitic. It is inserted in the mapping process from D-structure (DS) to S-structure (SS), when two constituents join. Its function is to join one category $\alpha$ (a word, a phrase or a clause) to another category $\beta$ (a clause or a verb), so as to further describe or interpret the property, action or effect of $\beta$.

---

[10] There is still another situation where a zero-form is joined to a sentence (or a verb). For instance, 看你气得*kan ni qi de* 'look, you are so angry'. Very possibly, this is a result of omission.

[11] To many of us, 很*hen* 'very' in (17b) seems to be an adverb; but according to Nie [43], it should be treated as an adjective.

# 3    Syntactic Structures of V-*DE* Constructions

Compared with (7) and (10), the understanding of (16) is very complex.

(16) 他ᵢ    骂 Pro₁ᵢ/ⱼ 得    Pro₂ᵢ 不    想    写    信    了.
    *taᵢ*    *ma Pro₁ᵢ/ⱼ de*    *Pro₂ᵢ bu*    *xiang*    *xie*    *xin*    *le.*
    he    curse    *Pro DE Pro*    not    want    write    letter    SFP

*Pro₂* in (16) has only one reading, *ta ziji* 'himself'[12], while *Pro₁* has at least three readings, as shown in (17), where verb-copying construction is applied to show the potential objects of the verb *ma* 'curse'.

(17) a.他    骂    人[13]    骂    得    他自己    不    想    写    信    了
    *ta*    *ma*    *ren*    *ma*    *de*    *taziji*    *bu*    *xiang*    *xie*    *xin*    *le*
    he    curse    person    curse    *DE*    himself    not    want    write    letter    SFP
    'He cursed someone so much that he himself didn't want to write the letter.'

  b.他    骂    张三    骂    得    他自己    不    想    写    信    了。
    *ta*    *ma*    *Zhangsan*    *ma*    *de*    *taziji*    *bu*    *xiang*    *xie*    *xin*    *le*
    he    curse    Zhangsan    curse    *DE*    himself    not    want    write    letter    SFP
    'He cursed Zhangsan so much that he himself didn't want to write the letter.'

  c.他    骂    他自己    骂    得    他自己    不    想    写    信    了。
    *ta*    *ma*    *taziji*    *ma*    *de*    *taziji*    *bu*    *xiang*    *xie*    *xin*    *le*
    he    curse    himself    curse    *DE*    himself    not    want    write    letter    SFP
    'He cursed himself so much that he himself didn't want to write the letter.'

A natural question arises then: according to the Binding Theory, *ta ziji*, as an anaphor, must be bound in its governing category (Hereafter referred to as GC), but how is it realized here?

Whether this question can be answered or not depends crucially on how to treat the verb-copying construction. In the literature, there are at least two proposals concerning the syntactic status of the verb-copying construction. The one put forward by L. Cheng [38] treats the duplicated verb as the small (causative) *v*. In this model, the structure of the verb-copying constructions in (17) can be shown as (18):

(18)

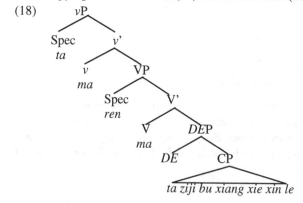

---

[12] For the sake of fluency, I was advised to use 自己*ziji* 'self' instead of 他自己*ta ziji* 'himself'. It is true that here *ziji* is more natural, however, as is well known, the binding condition of *ziji* is very complex and it is hard to precisely show the exact binding relation.

[13] Note that, 人*ren* 'person' here is not specific.

If the structure of the verb-copying constructions is (18), it should be possible for *ta ziji* 'himself' to be bound by the NPs in Spec,VP. This is exactly the situation shown in (19) (Note that it is of VP-shell structure). *Himself* in (19a) is bound by *him*, *herself* in (19b) by *Mary*, *himself* in (19c) by either *John* or *Jim*, and *ta ziji* 'herself' in (19d) by *Mary*. (19e) shows the VP-shell structure of (19d).

(19) a. We showed him a picture of himself.

   b. John gave Mary a picture of herself.

   c. John showed Jim a picture of himself.

   d. 我　让　玛丽　　看　了　　一眼　　她　自己　的　照片。
      wo  rang Mali    kan le    yiyan    ta  ziji   de  zhaopian
      I   let  Mary    see ASP   glimpse  she self   De  photo
      'I let Mary have a glimpse of pictures of herself.'

   e.

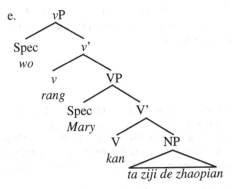

As shown above, *ta ziji* 'himself' in (21a-c) only refers to *ta* 'he' rather than the NPs in Spec,VP. (22). Therefore, it is not an ideal structure, because it cannot prevent the possibility that *ta ziji* 'himself' may be bound by the NPs in Spec,VP. Up to date, only J. Huang's [15] and Gouguet's [39-40] proposals, which treat the verb-copying construction as an adjunct, can prevent this possibility, as shown in (20).

(20)

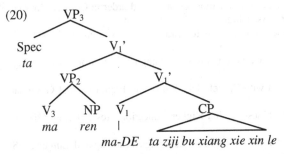

As shown in (20), since the verb-copying construction is an adjunct, the NP in it cannot c-command the anaphor *ta ziji*. That is to say, *ta ziji* in (17a-c) are properly bound by the subjects *ta* 'he'.

# 4    Conclusion

It is one of the most difficult issues for grammarians of Chinese to pin down the nature of *DE*. All the hypotheses put forward before, although have captured certain syntactic features of *DE*, could not give a sound explanation of VDCO. In this paper, *DE* in Chinese is viewed as a clitic inserted in the mapping process from DS to SS. It cliticizes on a verb, and absorbs the Case that the verb assigns to its object (thus forcing them to retreat). This explains the VDCO phenomenon.

**Acknowledgments.** The study is jointly supported by the National Social Science Foundation of China (12BYY049), two projects supported by Social Science Foundation of Shandong Province (under contact 11CWZJ59 and 11BWZJ03 respectively), one project of Humanities and Social Sciences supported by the Education Department of Henan Province (2013-QN-514 ), and one project supported by the Social Science Foundation of Henan University (2012YBRW029).

# References

1. Li, J.: The New Chinese Grammar. Commercial Press, Beijing (1924) (in Chinese)
2. Wang, L.: Modern Chinese Grammar. Commercial Press, Beijing (1943) (in Chinese)
3. Zhu, D.: Lectures on grammatical theory. Commercial Press, Beijing (1982) (in Chinese)
4. Li, J.: On the multiple meanings of V-DE construction. Essays on the Complements in Modern Chinese, pp. 559–571. Beijing Language and Culture University Press, Beijing (1984) (in Chinese)
5. Miao, J.: Chinese Semantic Structure and Forms of Complement. Shanghai Foreign Language Education Press, Shanghai (1990) (in Chinese)
6. Nie, Z.: Several issues on DE. Journal of Liaoning Normal University (Social Science) (3), 52–58 (1992) (in Chinese)
7. Dai, J.X.L.: The head in Wo Pao DE Kuai. Journal of Chinese Linguistics 20, 84–119 (1992a)
8. Dai, J.X.L.: Rethinking case theory for constituency and word order in Chinese. Journal of the Chinese Language Teaching Association 27, 85–110 (1992b)
9. He, Y.: X-bar theory and Chinese Phrase Structure. Linguistics Abroad (2), 36–44 (1995) (in Chinese)
10. Zhang, Z.: The common sense of Chinese Grammar. Shanghai Education Press, Shanghai (1953) (in Chinese)
11. Shi, G.: Problems in Connection with Particle DE. Study and Exploration of Grammar 3, 247–280 (1985) (in Chinese)
12. Huang, B., Liao, X.: Modern Chinese. China Higher Education Press, Beijing (2002) (in Chinese)
13. Fan, X.: On verb copying in "V-DE" sentences. Language Teaching and Linguistic Studies 4, 57–74 (1993) (in Chinese)
14. Li, L.: A Practical Dictionary of Modern Chinese Word Class. Shanxi Education Press, Taiyuan (2000) (in Chinese)
15. Huang, C.-T.J.: Logical Relations in Chinese and the Theory of Grammar. Doctoral dissertation. MIT (1982)
16. Yang, S.: A Minimalist Approach to Mandarin DE. Modern Foreign Languages 1, 51–73 (1998) (in Chinese)

17. Song, Y.: Essays on Modern Chinese Grammar. Tianjin People's Press, Tianjin (1981) (in Chinese)
18. Chen, H.: A new inquiry into the Chinese V-DE complement constructions. Journal of PLA University of Foreign Languages (2), 56–60 (2001) (in Chinese)
19. Ernst, T.: Restructuring and the PSC in Chinese. Ms, Ohio State University (1986)
20. Ernst, T.: Negation in Mandarin Chinese. Natural Language and Linguistic Theory 13, 665–707 (1995)
21. Tang, C.-C.J.: Chinese Phrase Structure and the Extended X'-Theory. Doctoral dissertation, Cornell University (1990)
22. Tang, C.-C.J.: On the distribution of postverbal constituents in Chinese. Bulletin of the Institute of History and Philosophy Academia Sinica 63, 269–300 (1993) (in Chinese)
23. Spencer, A.: Morphological Theory. Blackwell Publisher Ltd., Oxford (1991)
24. Wei, P.: Object Position in Verb-Complement Potential Constructions in Early Mandarin. Language and Linguistics 5, 663–704 (2004) (in Chinese)
25. Li, Y.: Cross-Componential Causativity. Natural Language & Linguistic Theory 17, 445–497 (1999)
26. Huang, C.-T.J., Li, Y.-H., Li, Y.: The Syntax of Chinese. Cambridge University Press, New York (2009)
27. Huang, C.-T.J.: Wo Pao De Kuai and Chinese Phrase Structure. Language 64, 274–311 (1988)
28. Aoun, J.: A Grammar of Anaphora. MIT Press, Cambridge (1985)
29. Jaeggli, O.: Topics in Romance Syntax. Foris, Dordrecht (1982)
30. Jaeggli, O.: Three issues in the Theory of Clitics: Case, Doubled NPs, and Extraction. In: Borer, H. (ed.) The Syntax of Pronominal Clitics, pp. 15–42. Academic Press, Orlando (1986)
31. Chomsky, N.: Bare phrase structure. In: Webelhuth, G. (ed.) Government and Binding Theory and the Minimalist Program, pp. 383–439. Blackwell, Oxford (1995)
32. Bošković, Ž.: On the Nature of the Syntax-Phonology interface: Cliticization and Related Phenomena. Elsevier Science Ltd., Amsterdam (2001)
33. Bošković, Ž.: Clitics as nonbranching elements and the linear correspondence axiom. Linguistic Inquiry 33, 329–340 (2002)
34. Legendre, G.: Morphological and prosodic alignment of bulgarian clitics. In: Dekkers, J., van der Leeuw, F., van de Weijer, J. (eds.) Optimality Theory: Syntax, Phonology, and Acquisition, pp. 423–462. Oxford University Press, Oxford (2000)
35. Embick, D., Noyer, R.: Movement operations after syntax. Linguistic Inquiry 32, 555–595 (2001)
36. Schwarze, C.: On the representation of French and Italian clitics. In: Butt, M., King, T. (eds.) The Proceedings of the LFG 2001 Conference. CSLI Publications, Stanford (2001)
37. Schwarze, C.: On the representation of French and Italian clitics. In: Butt, M., King, T. (eds.) The Proceedings of the LFG 2001 Conference. CSLI Publications, Stanford (2001)
38. Cheng, L.L.-S.: Verb copying in Mandarin Chinese. In: Covert, N., Nunes, J. (eds.) The Copy Theory of Movement, pp. 151–174. John Benjamins Publishers, Amsterdam (2007)
39. Gouguet, J.: Verb copying and the linearization of event structure in Mandarin. Handout for GLOW, Thessaloniki (2004)
40. Gouguet, J.: Adverbials and Mandarin argument structure. In: Bonami, O., Cabredo Hofherr, P. (eds.) Empirical Issues in Syntax and Semantics. Centre national de la recherche scientifique, vol. 6, pp. 155–173. CNRS (2006)
41. Zhang, Y.: From a measure word to an auxiliary word. Contemporary Linguistics 5, 193–205 (2003) (in Chinese)
42. Nie, Z.: On the nature of *hen* in "X de hen" constructions. Zhongguo Yuwen (1), 60–64 (2005) (in Chinese)

# Shǎobuliǎo as Entry in *The Contemporary Chinese Dictionary*: Criteria for Inclusion and Sense Selection

Min Li

Journal Editors' Office, Ludong University, Yantai 264025, China
ytlm85@163.com

**Abstract.** Out of innumerable expressions containing *buliǎo*, *The Contemporary Chinese Dictionary* (*CCD*) includes only 4 as entries, i.e., *shǎobuliǎo*, *duǎnbuliǎo*, *miǎnbuliǎo*, and *dàbuliǎo*. This paper, through a scrutiny of the paradigmatic and syntagmatic variability of *shǎobuliǎo* and a comparison with analogous entries in *CCD*, demonstrates that it is inappropriate for *CCD* to have selected *shǎobuliǎo* in the sense of 'cannot do without' as an entry. Through an analysis of its various usages, the paper proposes that only *shǎobuliǎo* as used before quantity expressions in non-comparative sentences is lexicalized into an independent lexical item and should therefore be included in *CCD* as an entry.

**Keywords:** *The Contemporary Chinese Dictionary*, *shǎobuliǎo*, lexicalization, entry inclusion, sense selection.

## 1 Introduction

*The Contemporary Chinese Dictionary* (*CCD*) includes 4 expressions containing *buliǎo* as entries, i.e., *shǎobuliǎo*, *duǎnbuliǎo*, *miǎnbuliǎo*, and *dàbuliǎo*[1]. Among them, *dàbuliǎo* is lexicalized through the acquisition of new meanings as respectively in *Méi shénme dàbuliǎo de* (It's no big deal) and in *Dàbuliǎo zài páo yítàng* (At worst, I'll go there once more) [1]. It is undoubtedly reasonable for *CCD* to include it as an entry. Out of innumerable *V-buliǎo* expressions, however, why does *CCD* select only *shǎobuliǎo*, *duǎnbuliǎo*, and *miǎnbuliǎo* as entries? Jingti Han, in his account for

---

[1] Because of the strong metalingual nature of this paper, it needs to be noted from the outset that the present text is a translation of the author's Chinese manuscript (by Yujia Jia and Zhengchuan Jia of the School of Foreign Languages at Ludong University). For the sake of space, Chinese constructions discussed or mentioned in the text are not represented in Chinese characters, but are only transcribed in pinyin. Wherever the formal status of a Chinese construction is invariantly above word and its words are always identifiable, spaces between words are assigned. Otherwise, where the formal status of a Chinese construction either alone or within a larger construction, such as *buliǎo* or a non-sentential expression containing *buliǎo*, is not clear or is varying contextually, the whole construction is transcribed holistically without spaces between constituents. If the meaning of a Chinese construction is clear and fixed and must be understood, a rough English translation follows it in brackets. Where meaning is in question or irrelevant, no translation is attempted.

P. Liu and Q. Su (Eds.): CLSW 2013, LNAI 8229, pp. 66–75, 2013.
© Springer-Verlag Berlin Heidelberg 2013

the criteria of entry inclusion in the 5th edition of *CCD*, points out that expressions used in dictionary definitions should be included as separate entries [2]. *Shǎobuliǎo*, *duǎnbuliǎo*, and *miǎnbuliǎo* are all involved in dictionary definitions presumably according to the following logic: The definition of *shǎobudé* necessitates the use of *shǎobuliǎo*, which accordingly becomes an entry word to be defined with *duǎnbuliǎo*, which in turn becomes a headword to be defined with *miǎnbuliǎo*, which is also included as an entry.

A scrutiny of *shǎobuliǎo* in the 6 editions of *CCD*, however, reveals that different editions define it differently. The 1st to 4th editions define it using a synonymous word and exemplifies it in a sentence: '*duǎnbuliǎo* (cannot do without): *Bàn zhège shìr, yīdìng* ～ *nǐ* (In doing this, we cannot do without you).' The 2005 edition defines it in a phrase: '*V. bùnéng quēshǎo* (cannot do without)....' The 2012 edition adds a second definition and an illustrative sentence to the entry: '*V.* ①... ② *miǎnbuliǎo* (be unavoidable): *Gōngzuò shǎng de shì, yǐhòu* ～ *yāo máfan nǐ* (In my future work, I will certainly need your help).'

While the 1st to 4th editions define *shǎobuliǎo* with the synonymous word *duǎnbuliǎo*, which leads to the use of other *V-buliǎo* expressions, the 2005 edition switches to a phrase probably to avoid circular definitions using synonymous words. The 2005 edition seems, however, to have neglected the logic that, since it does not define *shǎobuliǎo* with *duǎnbuliǎo*, it should not have included the latter as an entry and that, if so, it would not have incorporated *miǎnbuliǎo* either. According to its criteria for inclusion, therefore, it should have included only two *buliǎo* expressions, i.e., *dàbuliǎo* and *shǎobuliǎo*.

What we are here concerned with, then, are two questions: Should *shǎobuliǎo* be treated as an entry? Should expressions used in dictionary definitions be included as entries even if they are not lexicalized? In fact, *shǎobuliǎo* is not included as an entry even in such popular CSL learner's dictionaries as *The Commercial Press Learner's Dictionary of Contemporary Chinese* [3] and *A Dictionary of Chinese Usage: 8000 Words* [4]. Evidently, different dictionaries have different criteria for sense selection and there is still no consensus on the inclusion of *shǎobuliǎo* as an entry.

## 2    *Shǎobuliǎo* as Not Lexicalized in the Sense of 'Cannot Do Without'

Although *shǎobuliǎo* is included as an entry in *CCD* in order to define *shǎobudé*, we will not concern ourselves here with whether *shǎobudé* should be selected as an entry or whether it can be appropriately defined with *shǎobuliǎo*. Rather, we are interested in whether *shǎobuliǎo* as a synonym of *shǎobudé* is a lexical item when it means 'cannot do without' and should be included as an entry.

### 2.1    *Shǎobuliǎo* as Isomorphic with Other *V-buliǎo* Expressions

*Shǎobuliǎo*, as used in the definition of *shǎobudé*, is a potential verb-complement construction comprising the verb *shǎo* (lack) and *buliǎo* as its complement.

Although *buliǎo* is not lexicalized into an auxiliary word like *budé*, it has a powerful combining force as an element following certain verbs. Originally, *buliǎo* could only be used after verbs with such semantic features as [+CONSUME], [+CHANGE], or [+MOVE], in which *liǎo*, as a complement to the verbs, had the substantial meaning of 'disappear' as extended from its verb meaning 'end'. As a result of generalization, however, the *V-buliǎo* structure has given rise to abundant verb-complement structures such as *sǐbuliǎo, wàngbuliǎo, shòubuliǎo, yàobuliǎo, dòngbuliǎo, piànbuliǎo, yíngbuliǎo, bànbuliǎo, jiùbuliǎo, zhìbuliǎo, pǎobuliǎo, chéngbuliǎo,* and *hǎobuliǎo,* of which *shǎobuliǎo* is only one. These expressions are essentially the same except for the semantic differences of their verbs. It seems unreasonable, therefore, that *CCD* has selected only *shǎobuliǎo, duǎnbuliǎo,* and *miǎnbuliǎo* as entries from so many isomorphic constructions.

## 2.2   *Shǎobuliǎo* as Paradigmatically Interchangeable with *Quēbuliǎo*

*Shǎo* in *shǎobuliǎo* means 'lack' and is synonymous with the verbs *quē* and *quēshǎo*. In practice, therefore, *quēbuliǎo* or *quēshǎobuliǎo* is often used in contexts where *shǎobuliǎo* may be used, as shown in examples 1-3[2]. There are also various cases where *shǎobuliǎo* and *quēbuliǎo* are used in juxtaposition, as illustrated in examples 4-6.

1. Qǐyè xūyào dǒngshìzhǎng de zhìhuì, dàn gèng <u>quēbuliǎo</u> duōshùrén de cáihuá. (A company needs the wisdom of its top leader, but it depends more on the talent of its staff.)
2. Quánqiú zhìlǐ háowú yíwèn <u>quēbuliǎo</u> dàguó de cānyù. (Global administration certainly involves the role of the big powers.)
3. Zài zhèxie huódòng zhōng jīhū dōu <u>quēshǎobuliǎo</u> jiāzhǎng de shēnyǐng. (Nearly all of these activities witnessed the participation of parents.)
4. Zài nánnǚ guānxi zhōng, yǒu yīzhǒng guānxi, lián dāngshìrén shuāngfāng dōu wúfǎ shuōqīng. Fǎngfú, tā <u>quēbuliǎo</u> tā, tā yě <u>shǎobuliǎo</u> tā. (Among male-female relationships, one relationship is beyond the understanding of even the pair involved. It seems that he cannot do without her just as she cannot part from him.)
5. Qiúduì de chénggōng <u>shǎobuliǎo</u> qiúyuán de nǔlì, gèng <u>quēbuliǎo</u> qiúmí zhízhuó bùbiàn de zhīchí. (The success of the team is indispensible from the efforts of its members, but it relies more on the constant support of its fans.)
6. Zhòngdì <u>quēbuliǎo</u> shuǐ, píngguǒ gèng <u>shǎobuliǎo</u> shuǐ. (Crops rely much on water, but apple trees depend even more on water.)

When a meaning is incorporated into a dictionary, this indicates that the meaning is lexicalized. Lexicalization is the representation of a meaning with a word while non-lexicalization is the expression of a meaning with a non-lexical entity. The fact that *shǎo* and *quē* can be freely substituted by each other proves that *shǎo* in *shǎobuliǎo* is

---

[2] Examples in this paper are mostly cited from PKU-CCL-Corpus or from contemporary news reports accessed via a search at http://www.people.com.cn/. Minor changes, mainly omissions, are sometimes made for the sake of space. Their English versions in the brackets are supplied by the translators of this paper, i.e., Yujia Jia and Zhengchuan Jia.

characterized by paradigmatic variability, i.e., that the combination of *shǎo* and *buliǎo* is temporary rather than fixed. The grammatical status of *shǎobuliǎo* in the sense of 'cannot do without', therefore, should be that of word group or phrase rather than word. As a word group, it should not be included as an entry in *CCD*. Meanwhile, the interchangeability of *shǎo* and *quē* also proves that *shǎobuliǎo* and *quēbuliǎo* share the same usage and should be treated similarly. Unfortunately, however, *CCD* commits an error in meaning selection by including the former and excluding the latter.

### 2.3 *Shǎobuliǎo* as Juxtaposable with Other Verb-Complement Constructions

*Shǎobuliǎo* is also frequently used in juxtaposition with other synonymous verb-complement structures, as illustrated in examples 7-10.

7. Qīnhélì, <u>shǎobuliǎo</u> yīgè zhēn zì, <u>quēbuliǎo</u> yīgè wēn zì, <u>làbuxià</u> yīgè qiān zì. (Affinity cannot be achieved without sincerity, mildness, and modesty.)
8. Yào shíxiàn liángxìng fāzhǎn, <u>líbukāi</u> zhèngcè de zhùlì, <u>shǎobuliǎo</u> hángyè guīfàn hé zìlǜ, gèng <u>quēbuliǎo</u> mínyíng yīyuàn de zìxǐng. (The healthy growth of the private hospitals needs the impetus of favorable policies, the autonomy of the profession, and their own introspection.)
9. Qúnzhòng de láosāohuà, shì lǐngdǎo gànbù shēngcún de yángguāng yǔlù, <u>líbukāi</u>, <u>shǎobuliǎo</u>. (Complaints from the public are the sunshine and water to the leaders' survival, essential and indispensible.)
10. Yào quèbǎo qúnzhòng de xuèhànqián <u>méibuliǎo</u>, <u>shǎobuliǎo</u>! (Ensure that the working people's hard earned money is returned to them, intact.)

*CCD* does not include as entries *quēbuliǎo*, *làbuxià*, *líbukāi*, *líbuliǎo*, and *méibuliǎo*, which are used in juxtaposition with *shǎobuliǎo*, evidently because it does not regard them as words.

## 3 *Shǎobuliǎo* as Not Treated Consistently with Analogous Entries

*CCD* includes *shǎobuliǎo* as an entry only because of its occurrence in one of its definitions, but without considering whether it is a lexical item. This not only spoils the integrity in the inclusion of other analogous entries, but also destroys the consistency in the selection of meanings in similar entry words.

### 3.1 *Shǎobuliǎo* as Included in Imbalance with Analogous Entries

A survey of *CCD* reveals that it includes many three-character potential verb-complement structures, e.g., *láibují/láidejí*, *chībukāi/chīdekāi*, *chībulái/chīdelái*, *huábulái /huádelái*, *shuōbulái/shuōdelái*, *chībuxiāo/chīdexiāo*, *chībuzhù/chīdezhù*, and *kàobuzhù/kàodezhù*. The compilers of a dictionary include a construction as an entry only because they view it as a lexical unit; otherwise, they exclude it only because they do not think it has acquired the status of a word [5]. The incorporation of the above three-character structures into *CCD* as entries implies that its compilers have acknowledged their status as words. Indeed, with the lessening of the mobility of their components and the simultaneous increase in the integrity of their meanings, they have undoubtedly evolved into lexemes. It must be noted, however, *CCD* respects not only the lexical status of its entries, but also their symmetry and balance [6]. That is, it aims to include both the negative and affirmative forms of the verb-complement constructions which coexist symmetrically. Through an examination of *CCD*'s treatment of *shǎobuliǎo* (together with *duǎnbuliǎo* and *quēbuliǎo*), however, we find that the dictionary has neither considered its lexical status nor included its affirmative counterpart as an entry. In fact, although *shǎodeliǎo* as the affirmative form of *shǎobuliǎo* does not appear frequently, it is not infrequently used in rhetorical questions, as shown in examples 11-14.

11. Jiù ná huānwèi zhèháng lái shuō, nǎgè chéngshì <u>shǎodeliǎo</u> ne? (Just think about environmental sanitation work. Which city can do without it?)
12. Yùdào Fāng Wénshān, huàtí nǎnéng <u>shǎodeliǎo</u> Zhōu Jiélún? (With Fang Wenshan, how can we not talk about Zhou Jielun?)
13. Tóngzhìmen xiǎngxiangkàn, ānhǎo jiā, <u>shǎodeliǎo</u> nǚrén ma? <u>Shǎodeliǎo</u> háizi ma? (Think about it, everyone. Can we possess a perfect home without women and children?)
14. Zhè lùshàng huāfèi, nǎyàng <u>shǎodeliǎo</u>! (All the trip expenses must be prepared for.)

This manner of entry inclusion in *CCD* might misleadingly suggest that the negative form of the same structure may have the status of a word while its affirmative form does not. This is, obviously, not consistent with its incorporation of other entries with comparable structures.

## 3.2   *Shǎobuliǎo* as Not Defined Consistently with Analogous *Dàbuliǎo*

Besides *shǎobuliǎo* (together with *duǎnbuliǎo* and *quēbuliǎo*), *CCD* also includes an analogous expression *dàbuliǎo*. As these entries both contain the form *buliǎo*, *CCD* ought to have treated them in the same way, but in fact it fails to treat them consistently. A comparison of the two entries is necessary here.

In the case of *dàbuliǎo*, *CCD* incorporates two of its senses: ①*Adj. liǎobudé* (terrific/extraordinary (mostly used in negative structures)): *Zhège bìng méiyǒu shénme* ～, *chī diǎn yào jiùhuì hǎo de* (This illness is nothing so serious and can be cured with a bit of medicine). ②*Adv. zhìduō yěbuguò* (at most/no more than): *Gǎn bù shàng chē,* ～ *zǒu huíqu jiùshì le* (If we fail to catch the bus, we will at worst have to walk back) [7]. In fact, *dàbuliǎo* has two additional usages besides the two included in *CCD*. Firstly, *dàbuliǎo* is often used to negate the possibility of *dà* (big/large), as in *Tāmen dōushì nóngmíngōng, zhù de fángzi kěndìng* ～ (Since they are all farmer-turned-workers, their houses are certainly not large). Secondly, when it occurs in comparative structures, followed by expressions of quantity, *dàbuliǎo* negates the disparity in terms of the indicated quantity between the entities being compared, as in *Chāoxiǎoxíng cǎisè diànshìjī píngmù bǐ pūkèpái* ～ *duōshǎo* (The screen of an ultra-compact color television set is no larger than a playing card)./*Tā de niánlíng bǐ nǐ* ～ *shí suì* (She is no more than ten years older than you). Neither of these additional senses is included in *CCD*. Why? Because neither has become an inseparable whole with a unique identity; the existence of the affirmative and antonymous counterparts of *dàbuliǎo* (i.e., *dàdeliǎo* and *xiǎobuliǎo*) together with abundant similar constructions can sufficiently guarantee a correct syntactic analysis of it; and, therefore, these two additional senses of *dàbuliǎo* are not lexical units and should not be included in the dictionary. Conversely, the senses of *liǎobudé* (terrific) and *zhìduō yěbùguò* (at most) are the new integral meanings of *dàbuliǎo* generated through lexicalization. They have respectively acquired a holistic property that cannot be reduced to their components and linear relationships. Only these two senses are thus the meanings of *dàbuliǎo* as a lexical item and are accordingly incorporated in *CCD*.

In the case of *shǎobuliǎo*, *CCD* in its 2012 edition presents two of its senses: *V*. ① *bùnéng quēshǎo* (cannot do without); ② *miǎnbuliǎo* (be unavoidable) [7]. Of the two senses, sense ② is the result of semantic extension from sense ①. Evidently, sense ① is not a lexical meaning. The existence of the affirmative and synonymous forms of *shǎobuliǎo* (i.e., *shǎodeliǎo* and *quēbuliǎo*) and numerous analogous constructions, together with its potential structural meaning as is contained in its definition, can sufficiently guarantee a correct syntactic analysis and semantic interpretation of *shǎobuliǎo* in sense ① and thereby reveals that *shǎobuliǎo* in sense ① has not evolved into a lexical item and that sense ① does not possess semantic integrity. *CCD*, however, has included sense ① as a lexical meaning of *shǎobuliǎo*. Apparently, its treatment of *shǎobuliǎo* is not consistent with its handling of *dàbuliǎo*. This is the result of the compilers' application of different criteria or channels for the inclusion of *dàbuliǎo* and *shǎobuliǎo*. Whereas the former is included on the consideration that it has evolved into a lexeme, the latter is incorporated only because it is used in the definition of *shǎobudé* but not on a consideration of whether it is a lexical unit.

## 4    *Shǎobuliǎo* as Lexicalized and Includable in a New Sense

As demonstrated above, *CCD* includes as an entry *shǎobuliǎo* in the sense of 'cannot do without' because it is used in the definition of *shǎobudé*. This is questionable on considering that *shǎobuliǎo* in the sense of *shǎobudé* does not have the status of a word and that the inclusion of *shǎobuliǎo* as used in the sense of 'cannot do without' spoils the balance and consistency of *CCD*'s entry inclusion.

We do not, however, completely object to *CCD*'s inclusion of *shǎobuliǎo* as an entry. Although it is not lexicalized in the sense of 'cannot do without', we think it does have the status of a word when it means 'no fewer/less than' or 'at least'.

### 4.1    *Shǎobuliǎo* as Possessing Manifold Usages

According to one of our surveys, *shǎobuliǎo* possesses five usages [8]. *Shǎobuliǎo* ① means 'cannot do without'. *Shǎobuliǎo* ② means 'be unavoidable'. These first two, as included in the 2012 edition of *CCD*, are the usages of *shǎobuliǎo* as verbs. In fact, *shǎobuliǎo* also possesses three usages as adjectives. *Shǎobuliǎo* ③ denies the possibility of 'few/little', antonymous with *duōbuliǎo*, as illustrated in examples 15-16.

15. Āizhe lājīduī fùjìn de zhùhù, jiāli de wénzi cāngying shǎobuliǎo. (In the houses near rubbish dumps, there are not a few mosquitoes and flies.)
16. Yídàn shèjí dào zànzhù kuǎnxiàng, shǔé kěndìng shǎobuliǎo de. (In the case of any sponsored sum, the amount is surely not small.)

*Shǎobuliǎo* ④ is used in comparative structures, before expressions of quantity, to negate the disparity in terms of the indicated quantity between the entities being compared, as shown in examples 17-18.

17. Bèidòng xīyān shíjì xīrù de yānchén kěnéng bǐ xīyān de rén shǎobuliǎo duōshǎo. (A passive smoker may actually inhale not much less smoke than an active smoker.)
18. Wǒ yě mǎi le hěnduō, bǐ tā shǎobuliǎo jǐjīn. (I bought a lot too, not a few *jin* less than he.)

*Shǎobuliǎo* ⑤ is used in non-comparative constructions, before quantity expressions, to express a quantity of the mentioned entities larger than the indicated quantity, as illustrated in examples 19-20.

19. Zhèxiē dōngxi rúguǒ qù mǎi, zǒng shǎobuliǎo jǐshí yuán, shàng bǎi yuán. (These things, when bought, would cost at least several dozen *yuan* and even a hundred.)
20. Zhèzhǒng qíngkuàng měinián dōu shǎobuliǎo sān sì cì, pèngdào tíngdiàn wǒmen zhǐnéng túhuànnàihé. (There are at least three or four such cases in a year. In the case of a blackout, we can do nothing but sigh.)

In terms of its grammatical function, *shǎobuliǎo* possesses, among the above cases, usages both as verbs and as adjectives. This is predictable as *shǎo* itself may function both as verb and as adjective. Whether it is used as a verb or as an adjective, however, *shǎobuliǎo* can only be included as an entry in the dictionary when it possesses the status of a word. As we have seen earlier, *shǎobuliǎo* ① does not satisfy the criteria for entry inclusion as it is characterized by much mobility among its components, obvious variability in its paradigmatic and syntagmatic relations, and lack of integrity in meaning. In the same way, we have found that *shǎobuliǎo* ②, ③ and ④ do not meet the requirement for inclusion either and that only *shǎobuliǎo* ⑤ satisfies the criteria for inclusion.

### 4.2  *Shǎobuliǎo* as Lexicalized in the Sense of 'No Fewer/Less Than'

The lexicalization of *shǎobuliǎo* ⑤ is mainly reflected in the acquisition of a new meaning by *liǎo*, i.e., 'than', after the weakening of its original meaning, i.e., 'disappear'. As seen above, *liǎo* as a complement in *V-buliǎo* constructions originally means 'disappear'. With the occurrence of the new usage '*shǎobuliǎo* + quantity', the function of *bu* shifts from negating *liǎo* to manipulating the quantity expression behind it, and *liǎo* thereby loses its original meaning and function.[3] Consequently, the identity of *shǎobuliǎo* as a potential verb-complement structure becomes vague and its meaning can no longer be inferred from its component morphemes. Semantic bleaching and reduction, however, are always accompanied by meaning redistribution, which often involves a shift rather than a loss of meaning [9]. As *liǎo* loses its original sense, it also gains a new meaning of comparison ('than') under the synergetic effect of meaning constraint, contextual meaning absorption and pragmatic inference, as can be seen in examples 21-27.

21. Wǒmen wèn, yīge shōumài jìjié néng zhèng duōshǎo qián? Tā xiàoxiào shuō, shǎobuliǎo 1 wàn yuán. (We asked him how much he could earn in a wheat harvest season. He replied with a smile that he could earn at least 10,000 *yuan*.)
22. Nà shíhou zhōnggāodàng hūnyàn jiù 600 duō yuán, xiànzài tóng dàngcì de hūnyàn shǎobuliǎo 1000 *yuán*. (A medium or high grade wedding feast cost only about 600 *yuan* (per table) then, but now a similar feast costs at least 1,000 *yuan*.)
23. Zhè yīlún xiàlái, yīqiè shùnlì, yě shǎobuliǎo 1 gè yuè de shíjiān. (Going through this stage even smoothly will take no less than a month.)
24. Wǎnshàng tā yòu jiānchí fǔzhù xùnliàn, fǔwòchēng, yǎngwòqǐzuò, yǐntǐxiàngshàng, shǎobuliǎo jǐbǎi cì. (In the evenings, he persisted in doing such auxiliary exercises as push-ups, sit-ups and pull-ups for at least several hundred times.)
25. Lú èryé dào shìchǎng chīfàn, jìnqù shǎobuliǎo hǎojǐge zhōngtóu. (Mr. Lu's dinner in the marketplace will at least take several hours.)
26. Qiánduàn shíjiān lái ná yào, měicì dōu shǎobuliǎo yī èrshí yuán, zhècì cái huā le qī yuán. (Formerly, every time the medicine I bought would cost me at least 10 to 20 *yuan*. This time, it cost me only 7 *yuan*.)
27. Yībān láishuō qù gōnggòng chǎngsuǒ jiùcān zǒng shǎobuliǎo sānwǔge péngyou. (Generally a dinner in public places is shared among at least three or more people.)

Firstly, the comparative meaning expressed in '*shǎobuliǎo* ⑤ + quantity' is not the type of explicit comparison conveyed by a comparative structure as in *shǎobuliǎo* ④. Rather, it is a kind of implicit comparison, i.e., one between an implied actual quantity and a stated referential quantity. The sentence in example 21, for instance, contains an implicit comparison between 1 *wàn yuán* (10 thousand *yuan*) as a stated minimum referential quantity and an implied actual quantity which is no less than or probably

---

[3] Evidence for the semantic weakening of *liǎo* may be found in the fact that *liǎo* may sometimes be neglected and dropped out from *A-buliǎo* constructions when they are used in comparative sentences to negate quantity expressions, thereby leading to *A-buduōshǎo/jǐ*... utterances such as: *Zì yě hǎo mófǎng, fǎnzhèng kuàiji de zì bǐ wǒmen xiǎoxuéshēng de zì yě qiángbu duōshǎo.* (The words on the tickets were easy to imitate. Anyway the accountant's handwriting was not much better than that of us pupils.)/*Kàndào bǐ píxiāng gāobu duōshǎo de háizi, lèi de mǎntóu mǎnliǎn dōu shì hàn, wǒ de xīn dōu suì le.* (My heart was broken when I saw my son, not much taller than the suitcase in his hand, was sweating all over under the weight.)/*Wǒ kàn tā bǐ nǐ dàbu jǐsuì.* (It seems that he is not many years older than you.)

more than 10 thousand *yuan*. Apparently, this type of comparative meaning is not an intrinsic quality of *shǎobuliǎo* constructions but is rather a kind of sentential meaning acquired from the context of '*shǎobuliǎo* ⑤ + quantity'.

Secondly, in the context of '*shǎobuliǎo* ⑤ + quantity', what the addresser intends to express is that the actual quantity is at least equal to, or most probably larger than, but never smaller than, the referential quantity stated in the sentence. With the frequent use of the *shǎobuliǎo* construction in this type of comparative meaning, and through contextual meaning absorption and pragmatic inference, this type of comparative meaning is absorbed by *shǎobuliǎo* ⑤ and gradually solidified in it. Thereupon, the meaning of *liǎo* in *shǎobuliǎo* ⑤ shifts from 'disappear' to 'than' and, through semantic reanalysis, *shǎobuliǎo* ⑤ acquires the new comparative meaning, i.e., 'no fewer/less than (a quantity)'.

Thirdly, as '*shǎobuliǎo* ⑤ + quantity' acquires the new comparative meaning, it also obtains a noticeable pragmatic meaning, i.e., that of acknowledging a fairly large quantity as evaluated by the speaker. The acquisition of this meaning of 'subjective large quantity' may be the effect of the meaning of *shǎobuliǎo* as adjective. As can be seen, the basic meaning of *shǎobuliǎo* is 'probably a large quantity' or 'never a small quantity'. When *shǎobuliǎo* ⑤ is used in the context of quantity expressions, the sense of 'large amount' in *shǎobuliǎo* is transferred to the quantity expressions after it under the effect of the 'meaning constraint' mechanism [9] so that the quantity expressed by the *shǎobuliǎo* ⑤ construction pragmatically becomes a subjective large quantity. As Jiaxuan Shen points out, the hearer in a speech event often understands through contextualized inference from the speaker's limited words the implied though not stated meaning of the speaker [10]. If a linguistic construction is often associated with a kind of implied meaning, this implied meaning will be gradually solidified and become intrinsic to the construction, changing or replacing its previous meaning. The acquisition and solidification of the new meaning by *shǎobuliǎo* ⑤ is a typical example of this kind of language development.

The actualization of semantic reanalysis in a construction often leads to a decrease in the syntagmatic and paradigmatic variability of its constituents [11]. This view is now verified by the semantic change and lexicalization of *shǎobuliǎo* ⑤. Manifestly, *shǎo* in *shǎobuliǎo* ⑤ cannot be functionally replaced by its antonym *duō* or by any synonyms. Meanwhile, the affirmative counterpart of *shǎobuliǎo*, i.e. *shǎodeliǎo*, as well as other *V-buliǎo* structures, cannot be used in the context of *shǎobuliǎo* ⑤. This indicates that *shǎobuliǎo* ⑤, through its unique usage, has been lexicalized from a phrasal structure into a lexeme with a unique meaning and unanalyzable form.

# 5     Conclusion

As frequently used constructions in Chinese, *V-buliǎo* expressions need to be carefully scrutinized in the practice of lexicography in order to guarantee a correct selection of senses. Based on a comparison of *shǎobuliǎo* with other *V-buliǎo* constructions and an analysis of its five usages, this paper has demonstrated that, because *shǎobuliǎo* in the sense of 'cannot do without' does not possess the status of a word, its inclusion by *The Contemporary Chinese Dictionary* (*CCD*) as an entry falls short of being appropriate as well as spoils the consistency and balance in the dictionary's sense selection and entry inclusion, and that *shǎobuliǎo* as used before quantity expressions in non-comparative sentences has, under the synergic effect of meaning constraint, contextual meaning absorption and pragmatic inference, acquired a new meaning of comparison and a pragmatic implicature of subjective large quantity and thereby been lexicalized into an independent semantic unit, and should therefore be considered a candidate entry of *CCD*. When *CCD* indeed includes *shǎobuliǎo* in the sense of 'no fewer/less than', the criterion for its inclusion will be consistent with the standard for including other similar three-character entries such as *duǎnbuliǎo*, *miǎnbuliǎo* and such analogous entries as *dàbuliǎo*.

# References

1. Sun, M.: The Lexicalization and Semantic Change of Dabuliao. Ludong University Journal 109, 38–44 (2011)
2. Han, J.: Addition, Deletion, and Balancing: Entry Inclusion in the 5th Edition of The Contemporary Chinese Dictionary. Studies of the Chinese Language 311, 179–186 (2006)
3. Lu, J., Lü, W.: The Commercial Press Learner's Dictionary of Contemporary Chinese. The Commercial Press, Beijing (2007)
4. Liu, L.: A Dictionary of Chinese Usage: 8000 Words. Beijing Language and Culture University Press, Beijing (2000)
5. Zhou, J.: Two-Character Constructions and Dictionary Entry Inclusion. Studies of the Chinese Language 271, 304–309 (1999)
6. Zhou, J.: Problems in New Mandarin Daily News Dictionary. Language Teaching and Linguistic Studies 152, 59–65 (2011)
7. Center for Lexicography, Institute of Linguistics, Chinese Academy of Social Sciences: The Contemporary Chinese Dictionary, 6th edn. The Commercial Press, Beijing (2012)
8. Sun, M., Li, M.: A Study of the Manifold Senses and Uses of Shaoabuliao. Journal of Shandong Youth University of Political Science 159, 123–127 (2012)
9. Chu, Z., Xie, X.: A Number of Issues in the Study of Grammaticalization in Chinese. Chinese Teaching in the World 60, 5–13 (2002)
10. Shen, J.: The Mechanism of the Grammaticalization of Lexical Words: A Review of Grammar via Evolution. Contemporary Linguistics 3, 41–46 (1998)
11. Zhang, X.: The Lexicalization of the Phrase Dao Di into a Temporal Adverb. Language Teaching and Linguistic Studies 151, 95–103 (2011)

# Coercion of Locatives in Mandarin Chinese[*]

Qiang Li

Department of Chinese language and literature, Peking University, Beijing 100871
leeqiang2222@163.com

**Abstract.** The composition of linguistic constituents always involves the consistency of collocation, that is to say, any two constituents in a unit must be the same or similar in meaning, syntax, usage or prosody; If inconsistency appears, one part of the combination will coerce the other to change its own characteristics, or generate a new feature to achieve the goal of combination. This article studies the composition of noun-locative in Chinese and finds that different locatives may coerce nouns to produce appropriate meaning, which mainly manifests in: 1. quantity meaning of noun; 2.meaning of event noun; 3.meaning of nouny verb; 4.meaning of carrier noun's reference; 5.meaning of container noun; 6.shape of noun; 7.meaning of polysemous noun. This article firstly introduces relevant research in generative lexicon, and then describes coercion of locatives and coercion-mechanism in Chinese, finally makes a conclusion and discusses the future work.

**Keywords:** locative, noun, coercion, coercion-mechanism.

Coercion is a common semantic generation mechanism. Pustejovsky (1995) describes the coercion phenomenon in English; Song Zuoyan(2009) illustrates the event coercion in Chinese; Huang Chu-Ren&Kathleen Ahrens (2003) argues that quantifiers in Chinese can also produce coercion. This article studies the composition of noun-locative in Chinese and finds that different locatives may coerce nouns to produce appropriate meaning.[1]

Locatives in Chinese include simple and synthetic ones. "shàng(上'above')、xià (下'below')、qián(前'front')、hòu(后'after')、lǐ(里'in')、wài(外'out')"are simple locatives, which compose synthetic ones with suffix like "biān(边'side')、miàn(面 'surface')". This paper will take "jiān(间'between')、shàng(上'above')、qián(前 'front')、lǐ(里'in')" for example, combining coercion theory in generative lexicon, to

---

[*] This research is sponsored by the national social science fund major projects "Chinese parataxis characteristic research and large knowledge base and corpus construction under the background of international Chinese language education" (Approval No. : 12&ZD175). We hereby express our sincere thanks.

[1] For the composition of noun-locative, some scholars had partially involved, such as Wang Jue(2001), Chu Zexiang (1995, 2008, 2010).This paper aims to describe the semantic selection of locatives and the importance of noun semantic knowledge solution from the perspective of generative lexicon theory. Besides, it will represent coercion mechanism of locative on nouns. Hence, the angle of view in this paper is not completely identical with theirs.

investigate the coercion of locatives on nouns. In this paper, instances are mostly from modern Chinese corpus of Peking University (CCL corpus), while another small part is by collecting other related literature.[2]

# 1    Coercion in Generative Lexicon Theory

William Croft (1991) has pointed that a specific grammatical structure type, including predicate-argument structure type, center word-modifier structure type, verb-adverb structure type, all must satisfy three concepts consistency, that is the unity of conceptual domain, the unity of mental space and the unity of selection. Among them, the unity of selection refers to that predicate and argument must match each other in individuation, quantification number or genericness etc, which is also known as "granularity coercion "(Hobbs1985).The unity of conceptual domain refers to the semantic consistency requirements on verbs and nouns. If inconsistent phenomenon appears, either verb or noun must make a compromise by changing their own semantic type so as to realize mutual matching. For instance:

(1)  Mary enjoyed the book.  (cf. P1991:424)  [3]

Mary wants a beer.  (cf. P1995:110)

The verbs "enjoy" and "want" in the two cases above are supposed to carry objects indicating action and proposition respectively. However, "book" and "beer" refer to things, and do not meet the requirements of semantic type of verb. In this case, type-mismatching appears, which leads to the change of semantic type of object noun into action and proposition.[4] For instance:

(2)  Mary enjoyed reading the book.

Mary wants PRO to drink a beer.[5]

Pustejovsky (1991, 1995) called this phenomenon "type coercion":

TYPE COERCION: a semantic operation that converts an argument to the type which is expected by a function, where it would otherwise result in a type error.

Pustejovsky (1995:113-122) mainly introduced two types of "type coercion". One is subtype coercion, such as "Mary drives a Honda to work". Verb "drive" request the semantics of the object to be vehicle; Honda does not meet semantic requirements directly. According to our encyclopedia knowledge, Honda is a subtype of car, with the semantic dependency relation: Honda<car<vehicle ("<"means subordination). With the semantic relation, Honda can satisfy the semantic selection of verb "drive".

---

[2] Peking University CCL corpus of modern Chinese website:
   http://ccl.pku.edu.cn:8080/ccl_corpus/index.jsp? Dir = xiandai
[3] P1991 means Pustejovsky(1991), the same below.
[4] As to whether semantic type of object noun changes, scholars' views remain to be controversial. Godard&Jayez (1993), Copestake&Briscoe (1992, 1995) and Song Zuoyan(2009) do not agree with "type change". Detailed information can be seen in Song Zuoyan (2009).
[5] PRO is so-called "empty words" in formal syntax, which does not have voice form but has syntactic function, the other three kinds of empty words are NP-trace, pro and variables. For empty words, readers can consult Shi Dingxu(2002:91-97).

In other words, "drive" can coerce "Honda" to produce the interpretation of traffic tools (even if we don't know that Honda is a car brand, we can also infer it must be some kind of traffic tools, and cannot be things for eating or drinking, which suggests that coercion effect of verb "drive" does exists). Another is "true complement coercion", as (1), (2) represents.

Pustejovsky (2006, 2011) further improve and supplement mechanism of argument in the selection and combination, including the distinction in coercion as follows.

> COERCION BY INTRODUCTION: the type a function requires is imposed on the argument type. This is accomplished by wrapping the argument with the type required by the function.
> COERCION BY EXPLOITATION: the type a function requires is imposed on the argument type. This is accomplished by taking a part of the argument's type to satisfy the function.

Next, we take (3) as examples to illustrate these two mechanisms.

(3)  a、 The book fell to the floor.（cf.P2006, the same below）

b、 Mary read a rumor about John.

Verb "fall" in (3a) requires carrying argument which must have physical properties. "Book" contains two kinds of semantic properties: physical•information,[6] and it can provide material properties to meet the requirements of the verb, which is coercion by exploitation. Verb "read" in (3b) requires carrying argument which must have two semantic properties: substance and content. But noun "rumor" is only with content attribute, which can be wrapped by "read", and be imposed upon material properties, which is coercion by introduction.

In short, coercion in generative lexicon theory provides us with an explanation mechanism under syntactic-semantic mismatching cases. Making use of this mechanism, we can restore sentences which are seemingly semantic incompletement or underspecification, and make them clear on semantic transparency. Below we will adopt "coercion" as the main line to study the combination of locatives and nouns in Mandarin Chinese.

## 2    Coercion of Locatives on Nouns in Mandarin Chinese

According to this paper's investigation, coercion of locatives on nouns reflects in seven aspects. Below we will describe them one by one respectively.

### 2.1    Coercion of Locatives on Quantity Meaning of Noun

It mainly manifests in that locatives require nouns to express plural meaning. "jiān(间 'between'), zhījiān(之间'between'), zhōngjiān(中间'between'),zhōng(中'between')" are included. For instance:

---

[6] Such words are called "dot object" in generative lexicon theory, using "•" to connect two dissimilar objects which are different in ontology category. Such as "book", it can be represented as (substance•content).

(4) **a.** yí wèi   jiāoměi   de   nǚtóngchuāng    zhànqǐshēn,   dàdǎn   de   cóng
zhuōzijiān   de   kòngdào zǒuguòlái。
a   beautiful   female classmate   stand up   bravely   from
between   the   tables   gap   come.
'A beautiful female classmate stood up and bravely came from between
the table.'

**b.** tāmen   shuōhuà   zhè   zuǐpízizhījiān   zhāng   de xiāngdāng   de   jiàngé。
they   speak   between   mouths   open   quite   gap
'When they speak, there is a quite large gap between their mouths.'

**c.** wǒ   zhànzài   yǐzizhōngjiān,   xiàngqián   qīng,   xiàozhe。 [7]
I   stand   middle of chairs   forward   tilt   smile
'I stand on the middle of the chair, forward tilting and smiling.'

**d.** tā   shì   liúrìxuéshēngzhōng   dìyīgè   huòdé   lǐxué   bóshì
xuéwèi   de   zhōngguórén。
he   is   among students study in Japan   the first   obtain   science   doctor
degree   Chinese
'He is the first one who obtained science doctor degree among students
studying in Japan.'

Although underscored items in examples 4(a) - (d) above have no quantifiers to be
modified, they must have a plural meaning interpretation, and do not indicate a single
body. We cannot say:

(5) *yìzhāngzhuōzi   jiān   (between a table)
*yìzhāngzuǐpízi   zhījiān   (between a mouth)
*yìbǎyǐzi   zhōngjiān   (middle of a chair)[8]
*yìgèxuéshēng   zhōng   (among a student)

That is to say, looking these nouns alone, they refer either singular or plural meaning, but because of locative's coercion effect, they must be greater than or equal to 2
in number.

---

[7] The anonymous reviewers to this paper points that this sentence seems to have a variety of
understanding. For instance:
(1) jiàoshìlǐyǒu liǎngbǎ yǐzi,  wǒ zhànzài yǐzi zhōngjiān。
(There are two chairs in the classroom, and I stand between them.)
(2) wǒ zhànzài yǐzi zhōngjiān,  érbùshì yǐzi liǎngbiān。
(I stand on the middle of the chair, not on the edge of it.)
There is a subtle difference in the "zhōngjiān(middle)" meaning in above cases. In (1), there
is space between two chairs, "zhōngjiān(middle)" refers to the gap with a space; in (2), we
divide a chair into left, right and center,   and "zhōngjiān(middle)"refers to a particular
location, but not with space.

[8] When "zhōngjiān(middle)" refers to a gap with space, this is a mistake. See note7.

## 2.2     Coercion of Locatives on Meaning of Event Noun

Some nouns in Chinese show the characteristic of strong timeliness, such as "xuě(雪 'snow'),yǔ(雨 'rain'),wǎnfàn(晚饭 'supper')". Such strong timeliness noun often showed double semantic characteristics: eventive and substantive. Some scholars call this kind of noun "event noun"(Han Lei 2004, Wang Shan&Huang Chu - Ren2012); in generative lexicon theory, such words are called dot object or complex type.[9] Event noun shows different semantic roles when combined with locatives. For instance:

(6) **a.**  xuěqián/hòu          (before/after snowing, event)
        xuěshàng/xià/lǐ      (on/below/in the snow, substance)
    **b.**  yǔqián  bèisǎn    (prepare an umbrella before raining, event)
        fēnglǐ yǔlǐ  zǒutiānyá    (walk in wind and rain, substance)
    **c.** shēngmìng  jiùxiàng  fēngqián  de cánzhú.  (life is like the candle before blowing wind, event)
        fēnglǐ yǔlǐ báshè2000km.     (walk 2000km in wind and rain, substance)

Event noun can be expressed as (event • physical object). The above analysis shows when this kind of noun and locatives combine, locatives can decide which semantic facet of nouns is highlighted. In effect, this salience is coercion.

## 2.3     Coercion of Locatives on Meaning of Nouny Verb

There is a special kind of multi-category words in Chinese, which has the nature of verb, such as can be modified by "bù(不'Neg.'), méi(没'Neg.')", can be added with aspect marker "le(了'Asp.'), zhe(着'Asp.'), guò(过'Asp.') ". They also have the nature of noun, such as can be modified by quantifiers. Zhu Dexi (1982:60) called these words "nouny verb". Same as event nouns, locatives can also coerce nouny verb to generate a specific interpretation. For instance:

(7) **a1.** yǎnjiǎngqián,          guófángdàxué       xiàozhǎng     Zhū Dūnfǎ
        shàngjiàng  huìjiànle  lánkèsàdé     jiāngjūn。
        speech before     national defense university   principal    Zhu Dunfa
        admiral     meet     Lank Sade     general
        'Before doing speech, Zhu Dunfa, the principal of national defense universi ty met general Lank Sade.'   (event)
    **a2.** tóngyàng  zài  zhèpiān yǎnjiǎnglǐ,  nín  háikěyǐ kàndào  Qián Zhōngshū
        wénxuépīpíng  de  lìngyímiàn。
        also  in  the  speech,  you  can  see Qian Zhongshu
        literal criticism  another side.
        'Also in the speech, you can see another side of Qian Zhongshu's literal criticism.'(substance)

---

[9] See note6.

**b1.** ānhuīshěng    zài diàochá    <u>fēnxīhòu</u>    rènwéi,   jīnnián quánnián   xià-
liáng          miànjī   3100wànmǔ。
Anhui province    survey    analyze after       think     all this year the summer crops      area       31 million mu.
'After surveying and analyzing, Anhui province thinks that the summer
crops will be an area of 31 million mu all this year.'  (event)

**b2.** nǐ      de    <u>fēnxīlǐ</u>    yǒu   yígè      shífēn      dà de   lòudòng。
you      analysis    has     a       quite      big       mistake
'Your analysis has a quite big mistake.'   (substance)

**c1.** chōngfèn  fābiǎo  yìjiàn,   <u>juédìnghòu</u>   jí  gòngtóng   guànchè zhíxíng。
fully voice     opinion    decide after      together      carry out
'Fully voice opinion, carry out together after deciding.'  (event)

**c2.**  sānzhōngquánhuì  <u>juédìnglǐ</u>,  jiùyǒ  sānchù  shuōdào"gòngtóngfāzhǎn"。
sanzhongquanhui decision in    there   three    involve   "develop together"
'There are three places involving "develop together" in sanzhongquanhui's decision.'  (substance)

This kind of nouny verb can be expressed as (event • abstract object). From the
above examples, we see different locatives coerce nouny verb to generate specific
meaning. Besides, the specific meaning is to rely on dual features of word class of
nouny verb.

### 2.4    Coercion of Locatives on Meaning of Carrier Noun

Some nouns in Chinese do not like event noun, which at the same time contains two
semantic roles of substances and events, but the combination of specific things and
abstract things. Some scholars call such nouns as information noun. or content noun
(Xiang Yuanmao1993, Gu Chuanyu1989). We define them as carrier noun, including
nouns such as book, newspaper, diary, record, form, slogan, etc. These nouns are
composed of concrete material and abstract information, and material is the supporting body of information. For instance, in sentence "jìnxìnshūbùrúwúshū"(尽信书不
如无书 'Blindly believing books is no better than having no books'), the first "shū"
refers to information, while the second "shū" refers to substance; "bàozhǐ"(报纸
'newspaper')can refer to information in "yìbǎnbàozhǐ"(一【版】报纸 'a version of
newspaper'),  while it can also refer to substance in "yìzhāngbàozhǐ"(一【张】报纸
'a piece of newspaper').

When such nouns and locatives combine, specific meaning will be highlighted.
Take "shū(book)" for example:

(8) **a1.** <u>shūshàng</u>    yǒu    zì。
book    on      there    words
'There are words on the book.'    (substance)

**a2.** qīnzì          dào shídì   kǎochá,  héshí  <u>shūshàng</u>   de  jìzǎi。
personally    go    place   inspect    check    book on    record
'Personally go to places to inspect and check the record on the book.'
(content+substance)

**b1.** <u>shūlǐ</u>        jiázhe      yīzhāng      zhàopiàn。
book in      clip      a piece      photo
'A piece of photo clips in the book.'  (substance)

**b2.** <u>shūlǐ</u>        jìzǎizhe      hěnduō      gùshi。
book in      record      many      stories
'Many stories are recorded in the book.'  (content+ substance)

**c1.** <u>shūwài</u>        bāozhe      yīcéng      niúpízhǐ。
book outside      wrap      a piece      kraft peper
'The outside of the book is wrapped with a piece of kraft.' (substance)

**c2.** jiǎngjiǎng    zhèxie      <u>shūwài</u>      de    shìqing。
talk      this      book outside      matter
'Talk about matter outside of the book.'   (content)

**d1.** <u>shūnèi</u>        yǒu      zhàopiàn      chāyè。
book in      there      photo      insert
'There are photo inserts in the book.'  (substance)

**d2.** <u>shūnèi</u>      jīngxuǎnle      yīxiē      zhàopiàn。
book in      select      some      photos
'Some photos are selected in the book.'  (content)

Examples below show that "shū" with locatives "qián(前), xià(下)" only refers to substance. For instance:

(9) **a1.**  <u>shūxià</u>        yāzhe    yīmiàn      xiǎoyuánjìng。
book under    press    a      small  round mirror
'A small round mirror is under the book."   (substance)

**b1.** yīmiàn    jìngzi    fàngzài      <u>shūqián</u>。
a      mirror    lie      book in front of
'A mirror lies in front of the book.'  (substance)

These instances show that, when locatives combine with nouns, they coerce nouns to make appropriate semantic interpretation.


## 2.5    Coercion of Locatives on Meaning of Container Noun

Container nouns have internal space, such as car, chair, etc. At the same time, this kind of noun refers to things which are mostly made up of different parts. For example, the basic structure of "car" is the engine, chassis, body and electrical equipment parts; "chair" consists of legs, back, handrails and cover. When combined with container nouns, locatives will coerce them to produce an interpretation of a certain part. Take " qìchē(car), yǐzi(chair)" for example:

(10) **a.** qìchēshàng / yǐzishàng    (on the car/on the chair)
　　**b.** qìchēlǐ/ yǐzilǐ    (in the car/in the chair)

In group a, locative "shàng" mainly indicates above a certain reference point, and usually refers to exterior contact area.(Liao Qiuzhong1989) In the composition parts of "car/chair", there is "chassis/cover", so "shàng" coerces "car" and "chair" to interpret as meaning of "chassis" and "cover". "lǐ" in group b indicates internal space or range, mainly focuses on the "body", so "car/chair" will be coerced to have internal space object meaning interpretation. "shàng/lǐ" coerces container nouns to have different meaning, which reflects different functions of nouns. Nouns combined with "shàng" have bearing function, others combined with "lǐ" have holding function.

## 2.6  Coercion of Locatives on Shape of Noun' Reference

The entities that nouns refer to always have certain shape, and we often use a noun to refer to these objects with different shape. For example, "xízi"(席子/mat) generally has no shape changes, and it is not a container under the conventional condition. The bearing function of the surface is outstanding. For example:

(11) **a.** miànqián,  pūzhe  xízi,  <u>xízishàng</u>  bǎizhe  shuǐguǒ、gāodiǎn、
guàmiàn、  guàntou、  píngjiǔ  děngděng。
in front  spread mat  on the mat  place  fruit  cookie  noodle
canned food  wine  etc
' In front there put fruits、cookies、noodles、canned food and wine on the mat.'

**b.** dìshàng  yǒu zhāng  cǎoxízi,  <u>xízishàng</u>  tānzhe  yīzhāng  xuānzhǐ。
ground on  there  a  grass mat  mat on  spread  a piece Chinese art paper
'There is a grass mat on the ground, and a piece of Chinese art paper spread out on the mat.'

From the verb "pū/tān(spread)", we can foresee the state of mat is a two-dimensional plane, so can only be combined with locative "shàng".

Combined with "lǐ", which means mat's form has changed from a plane into a container, because mat is soft, can be folded and rolled. In the surface layer of language there will be some specific words that indicate this form change. For instance:

(12) **a.** cóng  juǎnzhe de  <u>xízilǐ</u>  lùchū  yīgēn xiǎobiàn。
from  roll  mat  appear  a  small braid
'A small braid appears from the rolling mat.'

**b.** chēshàng  èrrén  shǒumángjiǎoluàn de jiāng nà xízi kǔnzhā
tuōlāzhe wǎng shāngōu lǐ zǒu。tuōlāzhōng <u>xízilǐ</u> lùchū le yīshuāng
rénjiǎo。
carriage on  two people  hurry  that mat  tie up  pull
toward  ravine  walk  during pulling  mat in  appear  a pair of
feet
'Two people on the carriage hurriedly tied up the mat and pulled it towards the ravine. A pair of feet appeared in the mat during pulling.'

The verb "juǎn(roll)/kǔnzhā(tie up)" act on "xízi", which causes strong form changes. From a plane without space into a container with space, so "xízi" can combine with locative "lǐ".

## 2.7   Coercion of Locatives on Meaning of Polysemous Noun

A noun in Chinese may have different meanings. The combination of these polysemous nouns and locatives is complex. That is to say, locatives will coerce nouns to produce appropriate meaning, such as "dì (地'ground')", which has two meaning: land and farmland. For instance:

(13) **a.** dìshàng /dìxià     (land)
       **b.** dìlǐ/dìqián/dìhòu    (farmland)

"dì" in group a can only be understood as "land", while in group b can only be understood as "farmland". For instance:

(14) **a.** dìlǐ      de      zhuāngjiā     nèngmiáo
         farmland  on     crops        tender plants
         'crops and tender plants on the farmland'
     **b.** 5 mǔ dìqián
         5 mu   farmland  in front
         'in front of 5acres of farmland'
     **c.** dìhòu              zhùzhe      jǐhù       càinóng
         farmland behind    live        a few      vegetable growers
         'a few vegetable growers live behind the farmland'

"dì" with locatives "qián/lǐ/hòu" in above examples is only be understood as the meaning of "farmland". A similar situation is "jī(chicken)", which has meaning of animal or food. In cases below, the meaning of "jī" is different.

(15) **a.**  jīzhōng      (animal)
     **b.**  jīshàng      (food)
     **c.**  jīlǐ         (animal/food)

# 3   Coercion Mechanism of Locatives on Nouns

By investigating we find that different locatives may coerce nouns to produce appropriate meaning, which mainly manifests in: 1. quantity meaning of noun; 2. meaning of event noun; 3. meaning of nouny verb; 4. meaning of carrier noun; 5. meaning of container noun; 6. shape of nouns'reference; 7. meaning of polysemous noun. The combination of locatives and nouns can be summarized as the table below.

| Coercion of locatives on nouns | Coercion Mechanism | Instance |
|---|---|---|
| quantity meaning of noun | coercion by introduction | yǐzijiān(椅子间) |
| meaning of event noun | coercion by exploitation | xuěqián(雪前) xuěshàng(雪上) |
| meaning of nouny verb | coercion by exploitation | yǎnjiǎngqián(演讲前) yǎnjiǎnglǐ(演讲里) |
| meaning of carrier noun | coercion by exploitation | shūqián(书前) shūlǐ(书里) |
| meaning of container noun | coercion by exploitation | yǐzishàng(椅子上) yǐzilǐ(椅子里) |
| shape of noun's reference | coercion by introduction | xízishàng(席子上) xízilǐ(席子里) |
| meaning of polysemous noun | coercion by exploitation | dìshàng(地上) dìlǐ(地里) |

In the table above, "yǐzi" (椅子'chair')and "xízi"(席子'mat') obtain proper interpretation by introduction, namely attributes that locative requires are imposed to them, making them also have such properties, which are not possessed before coercion mechanism works. For example, "jiān"(间'between') imposes concept of number on bare noun "yǐzi", making it possible to express the meaning of number; "lǐ" (里'in') imposes concept of space on "xízi", which originally does not own space, making it possessing space to some extent. Using graphic method in Pustejovsky (2006), it can be expressed as:[10]

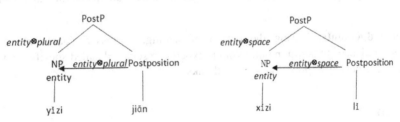

When event noun, nouny verb, carrier noun, container noun and polysemous noun combine with locatives, these nouns obtain proper meaning by exploitation, namely attributes that locative require can be gained from noun. For example, "xuě" (雪'snow') has two meanings: material and event. Combined with "qián", eventive attribute required can be obtained; Combined with "shàng", substantive attribute can be obtained. So, it needs to extract a semantic role of "xuě" to satisfy the requirement of locative. This can be represented as:

---

[10] ⊗ in the figure below is the tensor type constructor, and it introduces a qualia role to a type, making it become a part of this type. For example, beer is natural drink, combined with agentive role "brew", telic role "drink", can be expressed as beer:(liquid$\otimes_A$brew) $\otimes_T$drink.

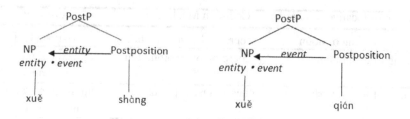

## 4    Conclusions and Future Work

Through describing the combination of nouns and locatives in Mandarin Chinese, we find that locatives can coerce nouns to gain appropriate meaning by introduction and exploitation, concretely manifesting in seven aspects: 1. quantity meaning of noun; 2. meaning of event noun; 3. meaning of nouny verb; 4. meaning of carrier noun; 5. meaning of container noun; 6. shape of noun's reference; 7. meaning of polysemous noun. We think the investigation on the combination of nouns and locatives can richen the essence of coercion, and provide sufficient evidence for the application of coercion.

Of course, this article on studying combination of nouns and locatives is a tentative exploration; more still remain to be further mined. For example, besides seven kinds of coercion mentioned in the paper, whether there exist any other sorts of coercion still needs to study; the combination mechanism remains to be further explained. In addition, from viewpoints of typology, whether other languages, especially China's minority languages have coercion phenomenon is also an interesting and worthy topic.

**Acknowledgements.** During the period of writing, Professor Yuan Yulin gave detailed guidance; In addition, anonymous experts presented detailed specific revision opinion. We hereby express our sincere thanks!

## References

1. Chu, Z.: Latent Form of Noun in Modern Chinese—about Studying Locative after Noun( 现代汉语名词的潜形态—关于名词后添加方位词情况的考察). Research in Ancient Chinese Language (suppl.), 48-53 (1995)
2. Chu, Z., Wang, Y.: The Locations of Spatial Entities and Its Selection for post-Locatives( 空间实体的可居点与后置方位词的选择). Studies in Language and Linguistics 4, 50–62 (2008)
3. Han, L.: An Analysis of Event Nouns in Modern Chinese (现代汉语事件名词分析). Journal of East China Normal University (Philosophy and Social Sciences) 36(5), 106–113 (2004)
4. Hobbs, J.: Granularity. In: Proceedings of the Ninth International Joint Conference on Artificial Intelligence, pp. 432–435 (1985)
5. Chu-Ren, H., Ahrens, K.: Individuals, kinds and events: classifier coercion of nouns. Language Science 25, 353–373 (2003)

6. Qiuzhong, L.: Space Locatives and Reference Point. Studies of the Chinese Language (1), 21–25 (1989)
7. Pustejovsky, J.: The Generative Lexicon. Computational Linguistics 17(4), 409–441 (1991)
8. Pustejovsky, J.: The Generative Lexicon. MIT Press, Cambridge (1995)
9. Pustejovsky, J.: Type Theory and Lexical Decomposition. Journal of Cognitive Science (6), 39–76 (2006)
10. Pustejovsky, J.: Coercion in a general theory of argument selection. Linguistics 49(6), 1401–1431 (2011)
11. Shi, D.: Chomsky's Theory of Syntax—Its Evolution and Latest Development(乔姆斯基的形式句法：历史进程与最新理论). Beijing Language and Culture University Press, Beijing (2002)
12. Song, Z.: Research on event coercion in Mandarin Chinese(现代汉语中的事件强迫现象研究). PhD dissertation of Peking University (2009)
13. Song, Z.: The Latest Developments of Generative Lexicon Theory(生成词库理论的最新进展). Essays on Linguistics 44, 202–221 (2011)
14. Song, Z.: Event Coercion of Mandarin Chinese Temporal Connective hou 'after'. Papers of the 26th Pacific Asia Conference on Language, Information and Computation (PACLIC 26), pp. 644–650
15. Wang, J.: Research on Nouns in Modern Chinese(现代汉语名词研究). East China Normal University Press, Shanghai
16. Wang, S., Huang, C.-R.: Type Construction of Event Nouns in Mandarin Chinese. Papers of the 26th Pacific Asia Conference on Language, Information and Computation (PACLIC 26), pp. 624–633 (2012)
17. William, C.: The role of domains in the interpretation of metaphors and metonymies. In: Geeraerts, D. (ed.) Cognitive Linguistics. Basic Readings, Berlin (1991)
18. Zhu, D.: Grammar Handouts (语法讲义). The Commercial Press, Beijing (1982)

# A Grounding Approach to the Semantic Meaning of the Light Verb *Da*

Fengmei Ren

Foreign Language School, Henan University, Kaifeng 475001
renfengmei@henu.edu.cn

**Abstract.** *Da* has vacant or dull semantic meaning although phonologically it is a verb. Its specific semantic meaning in a certain context is the result of grounding. According to the Grounding Theory of Cognitive Grammar, a bare verb designates a type of process; while a verb in a clause is grounded, and its semantic meaning is an instance of the type of process the bare verb designates. The interpretation of the semantic meaning as an instance of a process type is achieved through the interaction between the speaker and the hearer through which the speaker and the hearer achieve coordinated mental access to the event that the clause designates. On the linguistic level, the speaker anchors the event that the clause designates at a certain position in time and space through the use of grounding elements such as tense and modality, thus singling out the semantic instance of the verb from the instances of its semantic type. Meanwhile, the hearer identifies this semantic instance through these grounding elements, thus achieving coordinated mental access to the same event together with the speaker and making the semantic meaning of the verb specified and grounded.

**Keywords:** light verb *Da*, grounding, interaction, coordinated mental access.

## 1    Introduction

The verb *Da* is frequently and flexibly used in Modern Chinese. It has even been called a "universal verb."  Look at the following corpus:

(1) a.打柴
    *Da* chai
    *Da* firewood
    gather firewood
  c.打饭
    *Da* fan
    *Da* meal
    buy a meal
  e.打灯笼
    *Da* denglong
    *Da* lantern
    hold a lantern

b.打草
    *Da* cao
    *Da* grass
    gather grass
d.打水
    *Da* shui
    *Da* water
    fetch water

P. Liu and Q. Su (Eds.): CLSW 2013, LNAI 8229, pp. 88–96, 2013.

(2)  a.打游击
　　　*Da*  youji
　　　*Da* guerrilla warfare
　　　do things like fighting as a guerrilla
　　c.打基础
　　　*Da*  jichu
　　　*Da* foundation
　　　lay the foundation
　　e.打江山
　　　*Da*  jiangshan
　　　*Da* rivers and mountains
　　　fight for sovereignty over rivers
　　　　　and mountains
　　g.打光棍
　　　*Da* guanggun
　　　*Da*  bachelor
　　　stay single

b.打工
　　*Da* gong
　　*Da* work
　　work
d.打官腔
　　*Da*  guanqiang
　　*Da* bureaucratic jargon
　　talk like a bureaucrat
f.打官司
　　*Da*  guansi
　　*Da*  lawsuit
　　engage in a lawsuit

(3)于是，我 就打了他的手机,
　　Yushi, wo jiu *Da*-le  ta de shouji,
　　So,  I  then  *Da*-le  his cell phone,
　　按照他给我提供的路线，

　　anzhao ta gei wo tigong de luxian,
　　according to he give me offer-de route,

　　找到他住的地下室。

　　zhaodao ta zhu de  dixiashi.
　　find  he  live-de  basement.
　　So I called to his cell phone and found the basement he lived in according to
　　the route he offered to me.
　　五三年打老虎时候儿，那会儿我就在街道办，就做工作。
　　53 nian da laohu shihouer, na  huier wo zai jiedao, jiu zuo gongzuo.
　　53 year Da tiger time, that time I in street bureau, already do work.
　　In 1953 when people were fighting with tigers, I worked at the street bureau.
　　他的篮球打得好 。

　　ta de lanqiu da de hao
　　His basketball play-de well.
　　He plays basketball well.

There are many words in modern Chinese like *Da*, such as "*Nong, Zheng, Gao, Jinxing, Jiayi, Geiyu, Shishi*". Like "do, make, take, have, give" in English, these words are flexible in use yet abstract in meaning, so they are called "light verbs". The concept of "light verb" was first proposed by O. Jespersen in his study of English VNP structure. He discovered that in modern English there is a general tendency to add a verb before a noun that has real semantic meaning and this verb carries the markers of person, tense and aspect, for instance, *have, take, give* in *have* a drink / look / rest; *take* a walk / breath / shower; *give* a sigh / call / smile. The semantic meaning of the light verbs is empty, while the semantic focus is shifted to the subsequent nouns. Jespersen called such verbs "light verbs". (Jespersen, 1949:117) Cattell (1984) also found such linguistic phenomena in English and start using the concept "light verb"; Grimshaw & Mester (1988) observed that in Japanese there are many "light verbs." As an important linguistic phenomenon, the "light verb" phenomenon has aroused the interest of scholars in the academic circle. The study of light verbs is mainly conducted in terms of structuralism. In the mid-1990s, Chomsky (1995) adopted the concept of "light verb" and took light verb as the core of transitive predicates. Meanwhile, he integrated the light verb hypothesis and empty category theory and held that light verbs are semantically empty, they can also be without phonetic forms. Based on their in-depth study of Chinese verbs, Feng Shengli (2002), Zhu Xingfan (2005) and other scholars discovered that there are quite a number of "light verbs" in modern Chinese like the ones listed above. Compared with ordinary verbs, these verbs are relatively empty in meaning, but they do have phonetic forms of verbs. Accordingly, they are called "empty verbs." Based on the characteristics of Chinese verbs, in this paper, we will side with the concept of light verbs by Jespersen, Feng Shengli and other scholars.

As can be seen from the literature collected, existing researches on light verbs are quite rich. Most are based on generative grammar and apply syntactic derivation to explain this phenomenon. Among them the most notable is Larson's (1988) interpretation of light verbs from the perspective of the VP shell. However, generative grammar only focuses on the structure, particularly the syntactic derivation of light verbs without paying adequate attention to their semantic meanings. The research on light verbs from the cognitive perspective is not very abundant. Qiu Wei (2010) found that there is a kind of "delexical structure" in Chinese and English in which the verb head lacks semantic meaning, such as *do a dance, take a breath, give a sigh*; *Jinxing Diaocha (do research), Jiayi Zhengli (put......in order)*. These expressions have one feature in common, that is, the verbs in them have little semantic meaning, while the semantic focus is on the nouns after them. Guided by cognitive linguistics, Qiu Wei held that meanings of light verbs arise through holistic scanning and attraction of semantic prototype. The verbs in the "delexical structure" referred here are light verbs. Cognitive explanation for light verbs has started to focus on the construction of their semantic meaning and it needs to be further deepened. The meaning of a bare light verb is vague and empty, and it is difficult to tell what its specific meaning is. But its semantic meaning is specific and definite in a specific context. In the above example (3), the meanings of *Da* in the underlined phrases are different. *Da* in *Da-le ta-de shouji* means "called (to his cell phone)", *Da* in *Da laohu* means "fighting (with tigers by using sticks and other weapons)", while *Da* in *Ta-de lanqiu da-de hao* means "(he) plays (basketball well)". Triggered by such a semantic abundance of a bare light verb *Da*, we cannot help asking: why does *Da* have so many meanings? What is the cognitive mechanism underlying the specific meaning of *Da* in specific contexts? This paper tries to answer these questions from the perspective of grounding theory in cognitive linguistics. We will first examine the syntactic and semantic features of *Da*.

## 2    The Syntactic and Semantic Features of *Da*

As the syntactic core which carries tense and aspect marker, the light verb *Da* mainly functions as the predicate verb of a clause. *Da* can be used either as an intransitive verb or combine with nouns or noun phrases to form a verb-object construction. It can be followed either by concrete nouns or abstract nouns. In some cases, nouns converted from verbs can be used as its object. The syntactic features of *Da* based on our observation of the corpus are summarized in the table below:

| *Da* as intransitive verb | *Da* as transitive verb | | |
|---|---|---|---|
| | *Da*+ noun | | *Da*+ verbal noun |
| 鸡蛋打了。<br>Jidan da le<br>Egg  da-le<br>The egg is broken. | *Da* + concrete noun | *Da* + abstract noun | 打游击;<br>*Da* youji;<br>*Da*  guerrilla warfare;<br>do things like fighting as a guerrilla |
| | 打老虎;<br>*Da* laohu;<br>*Da* tiger;<br>*beat* the tigers | 打基础;<br>*Da* jichu;<br>*Da* foundation;<br>lay the foundation | |
| 碗打了。<br>Wan da le.<br>Bowl da le.<br>The  bowl  is broken. | 打柴;<br>*Da* chai;<br>*Da* firewood;<br>gather firewood | 打官腔;<br>*Da* guanqiang;<br>*Da* bureaucratic jargon;<br>talk like a bureaucrat | 打招呼<br>*Da* zhaohu;<br>*Da* greeting;<br>greet |
| 瓷器打了。<br>Ciqi da le.<br>Chinaware  da le.<br>The  chinaware is broken. | 打饭;<br>*Da* fan;<br>*Da* meal;<br>buy a meal | 打官司;<br>*Da* guanggun;<br>*Da* lawsuit;<br>engage in a lawsuit | 打躬<br>*Da* gong;<br>*Da* bow;<br>make a bow |

From the semantic point of view, the intransitive verb *Da* means "(fragile things are) broken (when falling down or colliding with other things)". Here the meaning of *Da* is closely related to the meaning of the following nouns which function as patient with the agent invisible. In "Jidan *Da*-le" (The egg is broken), the meaning of *Da* is related to "the egg" which is the patient of *Da*. The agent of *Da* does not appear. The constructional meaning of *Da* is that "due to carelessness, the agent break things which are fragile."

"Jidan da-le"(The egg is broken) refers to the fact that someone breaks the egg because of carelessness. If the agent does appear, the sentence is transformed into "someone da-le jidan". Semantically, this sentence differs from "Jidan da le" in that "someone da-le jidan" implies that "someone broke an egg intentionally" or "someone boiled a poached egg". The same analysis can be applied to the other examples above in the same way.

The use of *Da* as a transitive verb is much more complex. It can be followed by a noun or a verbal noun. They can be either concrete or abstract. *Da* in "da laohu" (fight with tigers) describe the concrete, tangible, visible wrestling scene of fighting with tigers by using sticks and other tools. *Da* in "da chai" (gather firewood) describes a scene in which a peasant in mountainous areas in China climbs up the mountain to gather firewood. Therefore, in the "*Da* + concrete noun" construction, the meaning of *Da* is closely related to the meaning of the concrete nouns after it. The concrete noun as the participant of the process denoted by *Da* activates a specific scene of *Da*.

In the "*Da* + abstract noun" construction, the abstract noun should be understood metaphorically, rather than prototypically. But the abstract noun must have prototypical meaning so as to appear in this construction, although in this configuration its prototypical meaning does not emerge. The prototypical meaning of "*Da* jichu" is "laying foundation for a building" and it metaphorically means "preparing for the future by doing some groundwork. "*Da* jichu" is acceptable while "da bangzhu" (da help; *make help) is not. The reason lies in that "jichu" (foundation) has both prototypical meaning and metaphorical meaning while "bangzhu" (help) in its evolution has become highly abstract.

In the "*Da* + verbal noun" construction, the meaning of *Da* is rather vague, with the semantic focus of the whole phrase being shifted to the subsequent verbal nouns. "*Da* youji" (da guerrilla) means "do things like fighting as a guerrilla" and "da zhaohu" (da greeting) means "greet".

From the above analysis, it can be seen that the light verb *Da* can function as an intransitive verb with the meaning "fragile things falling down or colliding because of careless handling". *Da* as a transitive verb can be followed by concrete nouns and its meaning is closely related to the referential meaning of the following nouns. *Da* as a transitive verb can also be followed by abstract nouns which must have both prototypical and metaphorical meanings with metaphorical meaning salient in the construction. *Da* can be followed by a verbal noun, with the semantic focus of the whole phrase being shifted to the verbal noun which expresses the meaning of the whole structure.

# 3    Grounding Theory

Cognitive linguistics holds that "meaning is conceptualization. (Langacker, 1987: 7). The way human beings conceptualize the world is to abstract and generalize the world with cognitive abilities and then form concepts which are represented in language. The conceptualization of things in the outside world is represented in language by nouns and that of processes is represented by verbs. "A noun profiles (ie. designates) a thing and a verb profiles a process (each in an abstract sense of the term). By itself, however, a simple noun or verb merely specifies a thing or process type, whereas a full nominal or finite clause designates a grounded instance of that type." (Langacker, 2002: 29)

According to grounding theory in cognitive grammar, grounding is one of the basic features of language use. Every sentence is grounded and every language has its own grounding system. (Langacker, 2008: 272) By using certain grounding elements (such as articles, deixis, numerals, quantifiers or tense, modality, etc.), things denoted by nouns and processes denoted by verbs are grounded in time and space, and thereby their meanings becoming more specific and contextual. Grounding is a mental process to locate the things profiled by nouns and processes profiled by verbs in time and space, reality and non-reality, thus making them specified semantically. Therefore, at the cognitive level, to ground a noun or a verb is to put it in a certain context. For instance, a bare noun or verb cannot stand alone in an English sentence, while the verb "work " in the sentence "They work hard" should be considered grounded, with a zero marker to make it coincide with its bare form. Hence it is zero grounding. With grounding elements such as "a" in "a book" being added to a noun, the referential of a noun is identified from a type of things denoted by the noun; while with grounding elements such as –ed in "worked" which denotes the time of the occurrence being added to a verb, the process profiled by the verb is identified. A typical ground includes the speaker (S), the hearer (H), the time and space in which the occurrence takes place, and the interaction of these elements. Grounding functions as a mechanism to enable both the speaker and the hearer to direct their attention at the same thing or process, thus their coordinated mental reference to the same thing or process is achieved . (See Figure 1)

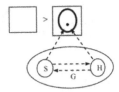

**Fig. 1.** Grounding schema

Grounding is achieved through the cognitive mechanism interaction. The grounding of a verb is a process in which the speaker and the hearer anchor the process profiled by the verb in a specific position in time and space. On the part of the speaker, he (or she) anchors the process in time and space by grounding, i.e., by adding grounding elements to the verb such as tense and modality. Meanwhile, the listener singles out the process by resorting to the grounding elements used by the speaker. Accordingly, the speaker and the hearer's coordinated mental reference to the same process designated by the verb is achieved. The type of process expressed by a bare verb is thus anchored in a specific position in time and space by way of mental interaction (realized through the use of grounding elements) between the speaker and hearer, and the semantic meaning of the verb is thereby specified.

## 4    Grounding of Light Verb *Da*

The Process or event expressed by a clause always occurs at a certain time and space. This is realized by the use of tense and modality in language form. Langacker used a dynamic evolutionary model to model the world we live in, as shown in Figure 2. As the conceptualizer, we tend to understand the world at two levels: reality and non-reality.

Reality includes what happened in history, what is happening now, or what we think happened or is happening.

Reality is depicted in Figure 2 by the cylinder, and C is a conceptualizer (identified as the speaker). The dashed double arrow represents evolutionary momentum, which tends to carry reality along a certain path and precludes it from taking others. Those paths that are not excluded define "potential reality". Reality is often constrained enough that the future course of events can be anticipated with relative accuracy. These predicted events occur in "projected reality", depicted in the figure by the dotted cylinder. For example, the future event reported in *wo xiawu gei ta da dianhua* (I will call him this afternoon) is viewed as an element of projected reality. The speaker's knowledge of his current circumstances allows him to expect reality to evolve in such a way as to include the profiled event in the future. The speaker (the conceptualizer) usually takes his own position along the evolutionary path as a reference to understand the world, and the speaker's position constitutes "present reality", depicted in the figure by the slice of the solid cylindrical section.

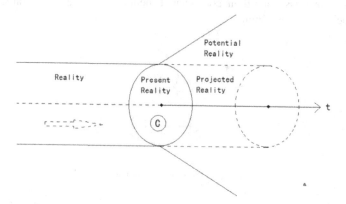

**Fig. 2.** Dynamic evolutionary model, Langacker,1991: 277)

Here we will analyze the grounding of light verb *Da* by integrating the grounding schema and dynamic evolutionary model. As mentioned earlier, through the use of grounding elements, i.e., by adding tense and modal markers to a verb, the conceptualizer (the speaker S) position the designated process in space and time; while the hearer (H), on hearing the grounding elements, singles out the specific process from the type of processes this verb designates. Thus the grounding of the verb is realized through mental interaction between the speaker and the hearer. The mental interaction makes coordinated mental reference to the same event possible and the verb meaning specific and grounded.

According to grounding theory in cognitive grammar, tense and modality are the two major grounding methods. Langacker classified tense in the English language into "present" and "past", while the future tense is viewed as modality. Our emphasis will be on the discovery of how the light verb *Da* is grounded in terms of the past tense. Please look at the following example:

"yushi, wo jiu da-le ta-de shouji, (anzhao ta gei wo tigong de luxian, zhao dao ta zhu de dixiashi)" (So I called him, and found the basement he lived in by following the route he had told me. )

As a conceptualizer, the speaker takes the time and space he is currently in as present reality when he is conceptualizing the occurrence "wo jiu da le ta de shouji" ( I called him), signaled by the letter *e* in Figure 3. By using the past tense marker "le", which functions as a grounding element, the speaker puts the event (e) designated by the clause in a specific position in reality. This position is located before the present reality along the time axis. The hearer identifies the process of *Da* through the grounding element "le". By way of mental interaction, coordination of reference to the same event "I called him" is established as is shown in figure 3. It should be noted that due to the lack of morphological inflections in Chinese, the tense marker of a verb does not always appear. In the sentence "wusan nian da laohu de shihou, na huier wo zai jiedao, jiu zuo gongzuo", *Da* appears in its bare form without any tense marker like "le" or "guo". However the hearer can successfully identify it as a past event. We hold that the tense concept can be expressed in Chinese by other elements except the tense markers (e.g., the time adverbial the year1953, then). We take it as implicit grounding. That is to say, the past tense in Chinese can be realized by tense markers such as "le" and "guo" or by other elements in a clause such as time adverbials "yesterday, last year, once, before, 1953". These elements make the verb's semantic meaning specific and situational, so they can be categorized as grounding elements.

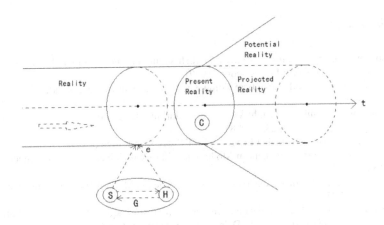

**Fig. 3.** The grounding of *Da* in the past tense

If the event time along the time axis coincides exactly with the time of speaking, the speaker chooses present tense to represent the occurence. In the sentence "ta lanqiu da de hao" (he plays basketball well), by using light verb *Da* in its present tense (zero form, denoted as Ø), the speaker identifies the exact instance of process profiled by *Da* from its other instances. Coordination of reference between the speaker and the hearer is realized through mental interaction. The clause denotes an event that occupies a certain part of the cylinder in the dynamic evolutionary model, rather than being a slice of it. But any slice of it is a full instance coinciding with the speaking time.

In the dynamic evolutionary model, the event described by the clause "ta lanqiu da de hao" (he plays basketball well) (signaled as $e'$) coincides with the slice of current reality in the time axis.

Langacker classified the future process into the category of modality. The future tense not only describes future events, but also reflects the speaker's subjective assessment of the possibility of occurrence and his attitude. Modality as another way of grounding is quite systematic and complex. We will elaborate on this in another paper.

# 5     Conclusion

The concrete meaning of the light verb *Da* in a specific situation arises from the function of grounding and coordination of reference between the speaker and the hearer through mental interaction. Linguistically, by using some grounding elements such as tense markers and modals, the speaker anchors the event designated by *Da* in a specific location in space and time and singles out this process instance among the verb's other instances. The hearer identifies the same event designated by *Da* through the grounding elements used by the speaker. In this way, the speaker and the hearer achieve a coordinated mental reference to the same event that light verb *Da* designates, and thus the semantic meaning of *Da* is specified and grounded.

# References

1. Jespersen, O.: Morphology, Modern English Grammar on Historical Principles, vol. 6. George Allen and Urvin Ltd., London (1949)
2. Cattell, R.: Syntax and Semantics: Composite Predicates in English. Academic Press, Sydney (1984)
3. Grimshaw, J., Armin, M.: Light Verbs and $\theta$-Marking, Linguistic
4. Inquiry, vol. 19, pp. 205–232 (1988)
5. Chomsky, N.: The Minimalist Program. MIT Press, Cambridge (1995)
6. Feng, S.: Light verb movement in Modern and Classical Chinese. Linguistic Science 4(1), 3–16 (2005)
7. Zhu, X.: Light verb of intransitves containing objects. Modern Foreign Languages 28(3), 221–231 (2005)
8. Larson, R.: On the double object construction. Linguistic Inquiry 19, 335–391 (1988)
9. Wei, Q.: Cognitive Approach to Delexical Construction. Foreign Language Education 31, 32–35 (2010)
10. Langacker, R.W.: Foundations of Cognitive Grammar, vol. 1. Stanford University Press, Stanford (1987)
11. Brisard, F.: Grounding: the epistemic footing of deixis and reference. Mouton de Gruyter, Berlin (2002)
12. Langacker, R.W.: Cognitive Grammar: A basic introduction. Oxford University Press, New York (2008)
13. Langacker, R.W.: Foundations of Cognitive Grammar, vol. 2. Stanford University Press, Stanford (1991)

# Affective-Sensitive Operator "*zhenshi*"

Zhifu Liu and Weihua Zhou

College of Art and Communication,China Three Gorges University,Yi Chang, China
zhifuliu1980@163.com, Zwh1154@yahoo.com.cn

**Abstract.** In modern Chinese, "*zhenshi*" is mainly used to elicit the subjective evaluation of the speaker and closely linked to the speaker's affective. It can be seen as an affective-sensitive operator. Based on the corpus of contemporary Chinese fiction, we analyze its syntactic features and lexical semantics in this article, and divide it into two categories: the objective truth and the subjective emphasis.

**Keywords:** zhenshi, affective, sensitive operator, syntactic features, lexical semantics.

## 1    Introduction

In modern Chinese, "*zhenshi*" may be a phrase or a word. According to the differences in the nature of "*zhen*" and "*shi*", "*zhenshi*" at least has the following forms:

a. "*zhenshi1*": "*zhen(true)/adj*" + "*shi(is)/v*";
b. "*zhenshi2*": "*zhen(really)/adv*" + "*shi(is)/v*";
c. "*zhenshi3*": "*zhen(really)/adv*" + "*shi(is) /focus marker*";
d. "*zhenshi4*": *modal adverb*;
e. "*zhenshi5*": *idioms*;

There are several problems concerned with "*zhenshi*". First, "*zhen(true)/adj*" and "*zhen(really) /adv*" are semantically fuzzy, thus a consensus has not been reached on this issue among the academia so far (Hongju Yan, 2010). Second, the meaning of "*zhen(really)/adv*" is not certain. According to *Modern Chinese Dictionary*, it is interpreted as "*dique(really)*" or "*shizai(indeed)*". And the studies of TCFL (Teaching Chinese as a Foreign Language) show that "*dique(really)*" or "*shizai(indeed)*" are not exactly the same (Jinrong Li, 2007; Zeshun Zhang, 2011). Jinrong Li(2007) summarized the meaning of "*dique(really)*" as "affirming the authenticity of the objective situation" and "*shizai(indeed)*" as "subjective confirmation of the high degree traits of things". Third, the studies based on grammaticalization show that "*zhenshi*" has been grammaticalized as a modal adverb in modern Chinese, with its semantic meaning mainly expressed by "*zhen(really)/adv*", its syntactic function similar to "*zhen(really)/adv*", and "*shi(is)*" has been grammaticalized as an intra-word component or suffix (Yisheng Zhang, 2003; Xiufang Dong, 2004). Heyou Zhang (2007) considered that "*shi(is)*" in this case still has a modal function. Hence the complexity of the semantic meaning and function of "*shi(is)*" brings trouble to research.

P. Liu and Q. Su (Eds.): CLSW 2013, LNAI 8229, pp. 97–107, 2013.

As we know, the study of lexicalization and grammaticalization of "*zhenshi*" can reveal the laws of its semantic evolution, but it plays a minor role for Chinese information processing. According to the author of this article, "*zhenshi*" can be treated as an overall structure, and it can be analyzed based on the corpus of contemporary Chinese fiction. The present research receives a total of 3508 cases based on the retrieving of "*zhenshi*" from the corpus of Center for Language and Language Education of Central China Normal University. 570 cases tend to represent objective truth, while 2938 cases tend to represent subjective emphasis. "*Zhenshi*" is mainly used to elicit the subjective evaluation of the speaker and it is closely linked to the speaker's emotion. It can be seen as an affective-sensitive operator. Based on the corpus of contemporary Chinese fiction, we analyzed the syntactic features and lexical semantics in this article, and divided it into two categories: the objective truth and subjective emphasis. For the sake of simplicity, in this article "*zhenshi*" which means objective truth is abbreviated to ZS1 and which means subjective emphasis is abbreviated to ZS2.

## 2    Overall Analysis

From the syntactic point of view, there are two kinds of "*zhenshi*" in corpus: 1) "*zhenshi*" is used alone; 2) "*zhenshi*" is used as a syntactic component in sentence. Semantically it can be divided into two categories: the objective truth and subjective emphasis. Specific statistics is shown in Table1.

**Table 1.** The syntactic and semantic statistics of "*zhenshi*"

| Semantic | Syntactic form | | Frequency | | Affective tendency ratio | |
|---|---|---|---|---|---|---|
| | | | | | positive | negative |
| ZS1 (objective truth) | ZS1 used alone | | 20 | 570 | 0/0% | 0/0% |
| | used as syntactic component in the sentence, X+ZS1+Y | | 550 | | 0/0% | 0/0% |
| ZS2 (subjective emphasis) | ZS2 used alone | | 152 | | 0/0% | 152/100% |
| | used as syntactic component in the sentence | ZS2+idioms or colloquialisms | 1050 | 2938 | 452/43% | 505/48% |
| | | ZS2+adjectives | 331 | | 142/40% | 155/47% |
| | | ZS2+evaluations of varying degrees | 261 | | 113/43% | 148/57% |
| | | ZS2+noun phrases | 697 | | 479/69% | 218/31% |
| | | ZS2+other evaluation components | 447 | | 190/42% | 257/58% |

It can be seen from table 1 that the main function of "*zhenshi*" is to express subjective emphasis, and the subjective "*zhenshi*" which is used alone only expresses negative evaluation. And the evaluation components which are used in the sentences include: idioms or colloquialisms, adjectives, varying degrees evaluations, noun phrases and other evaluation components. All of these evaluation components tend to express negative evaluation.

# 3    ZS1 Expressing Objective Truth

We generalize the syntactic forms of ZS1 in this section. There are 20 cases of ZS1 being used alone to express objective truth. It is mainly used in dialogues or discourses to express the agreement of the truthfulness of a particular situation with an unexpected modal meaning. Specific marks and quantity are shown as below:

a. the modal particle in front of "*zhenshi*": "哦[*o*]", "咦[*yi*]". There are a total of 3 cases, for example.

(1)咦，真是的，怎么没有新牌子的名贵手表呢？

*Goodness, why? Why no famous watches of new bands?*

b. the modal particle behind "*zhenshi*": "呢[*ne*]", "啊[*a*]". There are a total of 3 cases, for example.

(2)真是的呢，论身材，论相貌，你两个都不一样。

*It is true that you two are totally different in both figures and appearances.*

c. "可[*ke*](*emphasis tone*)+*zhenshi*" used alone. There are a total of 3 cases, for example.

(3)你说小王是得理不饶人，可真是。

*Xiao Wang argues a point to death. How excessive he is!*

d. "也[*ye*](*mild tone*)+*zhenshi*" used alone. There are a total of 3 cases, for example.

(4)也真是，苦根拉屎撒尿后哭起来嗯嗯的，起先还觉得他是在笑。

*It's ridiculous, Kugen, finishing bathroom stuff, cries in hum and haw, which sounds like laughing at first.*

e. "还[*hai*](*unexpected tone*)+*zhenshi*" used alone. There are a total of 6 cases, for example.

(5)还真是，中午她没吃饭就走了，老何老于哪还吃得舒坦？

*What a pity, she has gone without lunch, which makes Old He and Old Yu uneasy to swallow a thing.*

f. others. There are a total of 2 cases, for example.

(6)青苗用手一摸，真是，不知啥时候两件衣服都给汗水浸湿。

*Qing Miao touched it with her hand. Indeed, who knows when her clothes got so damp with sweat.*

But "*ke*(*emphasis tone*)+ZS1" and "*ye*(*mild tone*)+ZS1" can also express dissatisfaction, so as a mark, it does not have a distinctive function. It should be noted that, the two meanings of "*zhenshi*" (objective truth/subjective emphasis) are not completely distinct from each other. But an obvious fact is that the context of ZS1 is related to objective events.

There are 550 cases of ZS1 being used as a syntactic component in sentence. The syntactic forms, contexts, frequency and ratios are shown below.

**Table 2.** The analysis of ZS1 as a syntactic component

| Syntactic form | Context | Frequency | Ratio | |
|---|---|---|---|---|
| ZS1…? | doubt | 109 | 20% | 20% |
| 看来/或许[kanlai/huoxu](seem/maybe)+ZS1 | inference/ uncertainty | 43 | 7.8% | 8% |
| ZS1+somebody | unexpected | 19 | 3.5% | |
| 还[hai](unexpected tone)+ZS1 | unexpected | 23 | 4% | 9.6% |
| 倒[dao](unexpected tone)+ZS1 | unexpected | 6 | 1.1% | |
| 竟然[jingran](unexpectedly)+ZS1 | unexpected | 6 | 1.1% | |
| 果真是[guozhenshi](really is)≈ZS1 | unexpected | 24 | 4.4% | 4.4% |
| 要/倘/若[yao/tang/ruo](if)+ZS1 | hypothesis | 24 | 4% | |
| 如果/要是[ruguo/yaoshi](if)+ZS1 | hypothesis | 82 | 14.9% | 22% |
| ZS1…, … | hypothesis | 14 | 2.5% | |
| ZS1+这样[zheyang](like this) | emphasis | 22 | 4% | |
| 才[cai](emphasis tone) + ZS1 | emphasis | 11 | 2% | |
| 我不骗你[wo bu pian ni](I'm not fooling you)+ZS1… | emphasis | 13 | 2.4% | 36% |
| 不是[bushi](not)…, ZS1… | emphasis | 7 | 1.3% | |
| …, 就[jiu](emphasis tone) ZS1… | emphasis | 7 | 1.3% | |
| ZS1…的[de] (modal particle) | emphasis | 16 | 2.9% | |
| A, ZS1 B | emphasis | 8 | 1.4% | |
| 可[ke](emphasis tone)ZS1 | emphasis | 25 | 4.5% | |
| others | emphasis | 90 | 16.4% | |

Obviously, ZS1 always appears in the context of doubt, inference/uncertainty, unexpected, hypothesis and emphasis. ZS1 is a phrase which consists of "zhen(true)/adj" and "shi(is)/v", and the aforementioned five contexts in fact are the conditions of the semantic evolution of "zhenshi".

## 4    ZS2 Which Expressing Subjective Emphasis

ZS2 can be used alone to express discontent. It is generally regarded as an idiom. When it is used in the sentence, evaluation components often follow it. These two cases are analyzed respectively in this section.

## 4.1    ZS2 Used Alone

There are 152 cases of "*zhenshi*" which is used alone and express discontent. The syntactic forms and frequencies are shown below:

**Table 3.** The analysis of ZS2 which is used alone and express discontent

| Syntactic form | Frequency | Example |
|---|---|---|
| ZS2 | 48 | 真是，过个年也不叫人安生！*Jesus Christ, no happiness even in Spring festival.* |
| ZS2+的[de] (*modal particle*) | 40 | 真是的，也不想想自己的身体，要是着了凉还得了！*You fool, think of your health, what if you catch a cold?* |
| ZS2+... | 8 | 睡觉也不安生，真是......*The night is trouble-stuffed. What a shit.* |
| X+可/也[ke/ye](*modal adverb*)+ZS2 | 31 | 贵哥也真是，把老婆带出来干啥呢？*What's wrong with Brother Gui, why he brought his wife here?* |
| X+可/也[ke/ye](*modal adverb*)+ZS2+的[de] (*modal particle*) | 10 | 老爹也真是的，没事净说这些。*Dad, what's wrong? Why would you just say something like this?* |
| X+ZS2+... | 15 | 你这个人真是......钱算得了什么？*Don't be too serious...Money is actually nothing.* |

## 4.2    ZS2+Idioms or Colloquialisms

There are 1050 cases of "*zhenshi*" which are followed with idioms or colloquialisms. The idioms consist of four Chinese characters, a total of 541 cases, accounting for about 52%. The common sayings includes a two-part allegorical saying and metrical verses, sayings consisting of three Chinese characters, and sayings with uncertain count of words. There are a total of 514 cases, accounting for about 48%.

From the syntactic point of view, in this case, "*shi(is)*" is a focus marker, and "*zhenshi*" emphasizes and highlights the evaluation components(the idioms or common sayings ) followed. For example:

(7) 真是无巧不成书，金月波她们来到这儿就发现了毛利这伙儿敌人。

*It was such a coincidence, as soon as their arrival, Jin Yuebo found Mao Li, the enemy Gang.*

Obviously, the idioms and proverbs (including two-part allegorical saying) are the summary of human knowledge and experience, with fixed forms which express the common evaluation or emotion. Therefore, "*zhenshi*" means that the speaker's emotional experience is as the same as people's common emotional experience, that is to say they share a common experience knowledge and form the same evaluation. In the following example, the underlined part shows such consistency. It can be said that "*zhenshi*" means the consistent subjective experience knowledge.

(8)瞅着什么都长气，一天到晚跟她挑不是，真是应了那句话，易同甘苦难共富贵。

*He is always angry and picky to her. <u>Just as the old saying goes</u>: it is easy to share hardships but hard to happiness.*

## 4.3   ZS2+Adjective

There are 331cases of "*zhenshi*" which are followed by adjectives, among which 46 cases are monosyllable adjectives, 218 cases are two-syllable adjectives, and 68 cases are three-syllable adjectives. Generally speaking, '*zhenshi*' in these cases are considered as a modal adverbs, and "*shi(is)*" can be omitted. For example, "*zhenshi haokan(It is really nice-looking)*" can be changed into "*zhen haokan(It is really nice-looking)*", and the meaning remains the same.

I think "*shi(is)*" means "agree with", for example, after removing the word "*shi(is)*" in "*zhenshi(really)*" in cases below, the sentences are still legal. In the example (9), "*zhenshi bucuo. (It's really good.)*" can be changed into "*shi bucuo. (It's good.)*" "*shi bucuo(it's good)*" means the speaker agrees with the evaluation "*bucuo(good)*". The other four examples are the same. Such expression is usually used in the dialogue context.

(9)她有钱，人又漂亮，真是不错。

*She is rich and beautiful. It's really good.*

(10)在知识分子当中工作真是麻烦。

*It is really troublesome to work with the intellectuals.*

(11)做个人真是不容易啊!

*It's so hard to be a man!*

(12) "这个老方真是厉害！"

*What a harsh guy Old Fang is!*

(13)俺爹真是厉害,

*My dad is really amazing.*

It can be said that "*zhen(really)*" is used to further emphasize the agreement "*shi bucuo(it's good)*", so the mood of "*zhenshi+adj*" is stronger than "*zhen+adj*". Even in example (12) (13), I think "*shi(is)*" presupposes that someone has done some evaluation ever before.

(14)"我说王磊可真是没志气。"

*"I think Wang Lei was such a loser"*

(15)"真是不识相啊，这个玉立！"

*"So ungrateful, that Yu Li!"*

## 4.4   ZS2+ Evaluations of Varying Degrees

There are 261 cases of ZS2+ evaluations of varying degrees, including 208 cases of polarity evaluation and 53 cases of non-polar evaluation.

**Table 4.** The analysis of ZS2+ polarity evaluation

| Syntactic form | Frequency | Example |
|---|---|---|
| ZS2+太[*tai*](*too*) X | 81 | 那可真是太棒了。*That was really awesome.* |
| ZS2+X极了[*jile*](*extremely*) | 34 | 那场面真是尴尬极了。*It was really embarrassing to be there.* |
| ZS2+X死了/得要死[*sile/ de yaosi*](*to death*) | 14 | 这个拿刀子的小丫头真是坏死了。*The little bitch with knife in hand is a real bastard.* |
| ZS2+再[*zai*]X也没有[*ye meiyou*](*nothing...as*) | 13 | 能跟你在一起工作真是再好也没有了。*Nothing can be joyful as working with you.* |
| ZS2+X透了/透顶[*toule/ touding*](*extremely*) | 11 | 我真是傻透了。*I was really a champion idiot.* |
| ZS2+够[*gou*](*extremely*) X | 9 | 真是够傻的！*What a simpleton!* |
| ZS2+一点也不[*yi dian ye bu*](*not...at all*) X | 5 | 真是一点也不差。*Not bad at all.* |
| ZS2+好不[*haobu*](*extremely*) X | 5 | 这一下子可真是好不厉害！*Such greatness at a single stroke!* |
| ZS2+说不上来的[*shuo bu shanglai de*](*unspeakably*) X | 4 | 真是说不上来的激动。*(He) was unspeakably excited.* |
| ZS2+X得可以[*de keyi*](*extremely*) | 3 | 真是糊涂得可以。*(He) can never be more stupid.* |
| ZS2+X坏了[*huaile*](*extremely*) | 3 | 可真是吓坏了！*Scared out of my wits!* |
| ZS2+X得不能再[*de buneng zai*](*extremely*)X | 2 | 他们真是愁得不能再愁了。*They cannot be more anxious than that.* |
| ZS2+X尽了[*jinle*](*extremely*) Y | 2 | 他真是丢尽了陈家的脸。*You have made the Chens a real shame.* |
| ZS2+最[*zui*]X不过了[*bu guo le*](*extremely*) | 2 | 他觉得用这两句诗来形容眼前的景象真是最贴切不了。*He was convinced that these two poetic lines are peerless in describing the scenery in front of him.* |
| ZS2+X得不得了[*de bu de liao*](*extremely*) | 2 | 这马真是亮得不得了啦！*That horse is awesomely beautiful.* |
| ZS2+X杀人[*sharen*](*to death*) | 2 | 真是吓杀人哪！*How scaring it is!* |
| ZS2+X得要命[*de yaoming*](*to death*) | 2 | 那些人真是傻得要命。*Those guys are stupid to death.* |
| ZS2+X得紧[*de jin*](*extremely*) | 1 | 真是不通情理得紧呢。*(He) is really not understanding and amenable to reasons.* |
| ZS2+X的不能说[*de bu neng shuo*](*unspeakably*) | 1 | 女人的一辈子，也真是痛苦的不能说。*That woman's whole life was unspeakably sad.* |

**Table 4.** (*continued*)

| | | |
|---|---|---|
| ZS2+大大的[*dada de*](*extremely*) X | 1 | 他才知道这个小孩子真是大大的厉害！ *He finally understands how smart this little child is!* |
| ZS2+一百个[*yi bai ge*](*a hundred percent*) X | 1 | 真是一百个佩服。 *I am a hundred percent convinced.* |
| ZS2+X得出奇[*de chuqi*](*unimaginably*) | 1 | 真是坏得出奇！ *How imaginably evil!* |
| ZS2+X得不行[*de buxing*](*unimaginably*) | 1 | 这会真是馋得不行。 *(He) has never been so greedy than now.* |
| ZS2+X到家了[*daojia le*](*unimaginably*) | 1 | 心想今天真是倒霉到家了。 *What a fucking bad day it is! (He) thinks.* |
| ZS2+贼[*zei*](*unimaginably*) X | 1 | 那老狗日的真是贼精。 *That son of bitch is really crafty.* |
| ZS2+X无比[*wubi*](*extremely*) | 1 | 他真是健美无比。 *He is peerlessly well-built.* |
| ZS2+无比的[*wubi de*](*extremely*) X | 1 | 他们心里真是无比的痛快。 *They were heartily comfortable.* |
| ZS2+X得令人难以想象[*de ling ren nan yi xiangxiang*](*extremely*) | 1 | 真是穷得令人难以想象。 *He was unimaginably poor.* |
| ZS2+出奇地X(chuqi de X/ amazingly) | 1 | 真是出奇地好听。 *That was amazingly pleasing to ears.* |
| ZS2+要多[*yao duo*] X有多[*you duo*] X (*extremely*) | 1 | 真是要多伤心有多伤心。 *(He) was gutted.* |
| ZS2+难以描述的[*nan yi miaoshu de*](*extremely*) X | 1 | 那时真是难以描述的荒凉和艰苦啊！ *The desolation and arduousness there is beyond description.* |

**Table 5.** The analysis of ZS2+non-polar evaluation

| Syntactic form | Frequency | Example |
|---|---|---|
| ZS2+X得很[*de hen*](*very*) | 12 | 那女人可真是丑得很。 *That woman is very ugly.* |
| ZS2+有点[*you dian*](*a little*) X | 8 | 真是有点不幸。 *That was a little bit unlucky.* |
| ZS2+挺[*ting*](*very*) X | 7 | 你们这儿真是挺好看的。 *It is really beautiful here.* |
| ZS2+很[*hen*](*very*) X | 8 | 他看上去真是很帅。 *He looks really handsome.* |
| ZS2+X多了[*duo le*](*more*) | 5 | 同玉儿的爷爷相比，我的爷爷真是可爱多了。 *Compared with Yu'er's Grandpa, my grandpa was for certain cute.* |
| ZS2+大[*da*](*very*) X | 4 | 这个世道真是大变了。 *The society has amazingly changed.* |

**Table 5.** (*continued*)

| ZS2+好[*hao*](*very*) X | 2 | 从她手中拉牵出来的线真是好长好远。*The line stretched out form her hands are really long in distance.* |
|---|---|---|
| ZS2+特别[*tebie*](*very*) X | 1 | 那个人真是特别好。*That guy was really nice.* |
| ZS2+怪[*guai*](*very*) X | 1 | 真是怪可怜的。*What a pity!* |
| ZS2+非常[*feichang*](*very*) X | 1 | 她真是非常幸福。*She was lost in real happiness.* |
| ZS2+蛮[*man*](*very*)X | 1 | 可真是蛮舒服！*That was indeed comfortable.* |
| ZS2+那么[*name*](*very*)X | 1 | 她笑得真是那么快乐和幸福。*She smiles happily and joyfully.* |
| ZS2+不大[*buda*](*a little*)X | 1 | 这个滋味儿真是不大好受。*That feels really unbearable.* |
| ZS2+X不过[*buguo*](*very*) | 1 | 我心里真是气不过。*My anger was nearly uncontrollable.* |

No matter it is polar or non-polar evaluation, in fact, it involves a problem of evaluation criteria. When a speaker wants to make an evaluation, there must be a certain standard of the evaluation. For example, when one says "*That scene is really very embarrassing*", there's always a standard of the embarrassment. Similarly, when one says "*It is really very comfortable!*" there is always a standard of comfort. These standards are mostly the speaker's subjective experience. Therefore, "*zhenshi(really)*" means subjective emphasis, and indicates a psychological process that one's current feeling is similar to his former emotional experience.

## 4.5    ZS2+Noun Phrases

There are 697 cases of "*zhenshi*"+noun phrases. It can be divided into two groups: (1) there is numeral-classifier compound in front of the noun phrase, a total of 338. The numeral-classifiers mainly are 一个[*yige*](*a*), 个[*ge*](*a*), as in example(16)(17); (2) there is no numeral-classifier compound in front of the noun phrase, a total of 359. There are evaluative modifiers in the NP in most cases. Superficially, the sentence "*X zhenshi Y*" is a judgment sentence. In fact, it is an evaluative sentence, which can be seen as an evaluative judgment, and is a subjective judgment. The semantic orientation of "*zhen(really)*" is the evaluative modifier in the NP.

(16)这真是一个俊俏的青年！

*This is a really handsome young man!*

(17)我真是个大笨蛋。

*I am a really big idiot.*

(18)你还真是多面手。

*You really are a generalist.*

(19)你真是老当益壮的老大伯！

*Old uncle, you really have a green old age.*

## 4.6　ZS2+Other Evaluation Components

The other evaluation components behind "*zhenshi*" mainly are the random evaluative components that the speaker expressed according to a specific context. There are 447 cases of this kind. We divide it into two cases: one is the case that "是[*shi*](*is*)" can not be omitted, as in example(20)(21)(22), a total of 276; the other is the case that "是 [*shi*](*is*)" can be omitted, as in example(23)(24), a total of 171.

(20)天呐，真是时代不同了。

*Oh heaven, the world has really changed.*

(21)真是倒他娘的邪霉！

*What a fucking shit!*

(22)真是又爱他，又恨他，又伤心。

*(She) really loves him, but truly hates him either. How sad she is!*

(23)真是受不了你，这是哪门子的歪理啊

*You are totally unbearable, what basis are these false reasoning from.*

(24)你这小子，真是拿你没办法。

*You fool, you are totally out of my reach.*

# 5　Conclusion

In a word, "*zhenshi*" in modern Chinese is mainly used to elicit the subjective evaluation of the speaker and it is closely linked to the speaker's emotion. It can be seen as an affective-sensitive operator. The subjective emphasis function of "*zhenshi*" is based on its function of disclosing objective truth. Objective truth means that the speaker's opinion agrees with the actual situation, while subjective emphasis means that the speaker's current feeling is similar to his former emotional experience.

We made a preliminary statistical analysis of the syntactic and semantic of "*zhenshi*", which will help affective computing for further research. And the formalization method and the specific operating mode of "*zhenshi*" will be researched.

It should be noted that, although "*zhen*(*really*)" can also be used to represent subjective evaluation as in the sentence "*This book is really nice.*" the semantics and functions of "*zhen*" and "*zhenshi*" in some cases are similar, "*zhen*" can be seen as an affective-sensitive operator alone. However, from the above analysis, it can be seen that the evaluative components which are introduced by "*zhenshi*" is more powerful than "*zhen*", so we consider "*zhenshi*" as an affective-sensitive operator in this article.

**Acknowledgments.** This work is supported by a Talent Scientific Research Fund of China Three Gorges University. The author would like to thank the anonymous reviewers for their comments. The remaining errors are ours.

# References

1. Zhang, H.: Semantic Function of "Shi" in Modally Identifying Construction. Journal of Peking University (Philosophy and Social Sciences) 2, 95–101 (2007)
2. Yan, H.: Subjectivity of the Adverb "zhen". Journal of Hunan University of Science & Technology (Social Science Edition) 1, 119–122 (2010)
3. Li, J.: Semantic Patterns and Syntactic Restrictions of "shizai" Sentence. Chinese Teaching in the World 2, 40–53 (2007)
4. Dong, X.: Further Grammaticalization of "shi": From Functional Word to Word-internal Element. Contemporary Linguistics 1, 35–44 (2004)
5. Zhang, Y.: On the Connections Between Diachronic Changes and Synchronic Variations of "adverb+shi" in Chinese. Linguistic Sciences 3, 34–49 (2003)
6. Zhang, Z.: The Semantic Patterns of "shizai" Sentence and How to Teach Them. Chinese Teaching in the World 4, 553–565 (2011)

# On Semantic Category of Speech-Act Verbs in Modern Chinese – With a Case of 请[*qing*](please)

Yuan Tao[1] and Zhanhao Jiang[2,3]

[1] School of Foreign Languages, Shannxi Normal University, Xi'an, China, 710062
taoyuanhuahua@126.com
[2] School of English Studies, Xi'an International Studies University, Xi'an, China, 710128
[3] Post-doctoral Mobile Station, Foreign Language School, Wuhan University, Wuhan Hubei, 430072
jiangzhanhao@xisu.edu.cn

**Abstract.** As one of the speech-act verbs in modern Chinese, *qing* is polysemous, which poses a thorny problem for natural language processing in terms of its sense demarcation and its semantic valence. This article begins with its dictionary definition, and then with the help of such theories as Synset-Allolexeme Theory and Lexical Categorization Theory, categorizes meanings of *qing* as $qing_1$, $qing_2$, $qing_3$, and $qing_4$ on the basis of genuine materials. This article also explores both the semantic senses and semantic valence of each category of *qing*.

**Keywords:** speech-act verbs, semantic categories, semantic valence, machine recognition.

## 1 Introduction

In natural language processing(NLP) and machine translation(ML), sense demarcation of polysemy is a pivotal issue. Meanwhile, it is also a thorny problem because of different collocations and contexts of polysemy. As for NLP, Xiao holds that current researches are too much general in terms of sense delineation and wordnet construction[1]. Therefore, he advances his Synset- Allolexeme Theory which goes: The sense system of given language is based on the primitive word and its allomorphs and therefore such system is a constellation of synomyms. Sememe analysis may reveal the semantic or grammatical relationships between one sense and the remaining senses of given primitive word. Such analysis may meet the needs of specific rather than general semantic delineation in NLP to a great extent. Accordingly, scientific delineation is a prerequisite for automatic tagging and word clustering. Precise and systematic delineation of words must be made before words-clustering is done[1]. According to this theory, our attention should be first directed to the research on lexical semantics in terms of the role lexis plays in lexical system in modern Chinese and then to the systematic study on both semantic categorization and semantic demarcation of primitive words.

Lexical Categorization requires us to target first the research on the position of given word in modern Chinese[2], with *qing* as a case in point in our research. *Qing*, as one of the Imperative Verbs, which are in turn a sub-branch of Speech-act Verbs[3], is a

P. Liu and Q. Su (Eds.): CLSW 2013, LNAI 8229, pp. 108–116, 2013.

primitive word of its kind. In this article, we will first deal with the sentences in which the basic semantic meanings of *qing* are embodied. Such sentences are labeled as Text A. Second, *qing* structures in which fixed semantic meanings are embodied in Chinese lexicon are excluded, for example, 请安[*qing'an*](*courtesy*), 请教[*qingjiao*](*consult*), 请愿[*qingyuan*](*petition*), 请柬[*qingjian*](*invitation card*), 请缨[*qingying*](*request a cord from the emperor (to bind the enemy)*)", 请问[*qingwen*](*excuse me*), which are all labeled as Text B. The remaining sentences in which *qing* is embodied are all labeled as Text C, which are also the items for computer recognition. Text C is complicated for it is the mixture of *qing* itself, its allomorphs and other speech components. Consequently, other morph-syntactic features and semantic parameters must be found to recognize its semantic senses before the computer can recognize its textual function. As a result, in the following section we will focus on its semantic delineation and semantic valence.

## 2    Analyses of Basic Semantic Senses of *Qing*

### 2.1    Sense Demarcation of *Qing*

In the light of Lü's views, basic senses of qing can be categorized as: $qing_1$(meaning request as in Sentence [1]-S[1]), $qing_2$(invite), $qing_3$(entertain or treat) and $qing_4$(as a politeness marker indicating that the addresser hopes that addressee will do something)[4]. In different sentences, semantic category of qing is different due to its different senses. Here are some examples:

S[1] 请你告诉我，我们一定想办法帮忙。 (*Please tell me and we are sure to figure out ways to help.*)

S[2] 由于他的伤势目前还需要进一步治疗，他向足协有关领导请假后很快离开了海南返回深圳。 (*Due to the fact that his wound still needs healing, he reported it to relevant leaders of Soccer Association and asked for leave and soon he left Hainan for Shenzhen.*)

S[3] 刘大娘年老体弱，路况不好，经不住颠簸，建议去县城请医生来治疗。 (*Granny Liu is old and weak and she can't bear the bumpy road and (I) suggest (we) go to the county and invite a doctor.*)

S[4] 1968年，一位四肢瘫痪的美国人请猴子当保姆，每天给他拿这递那，还能让猴子上街区买面包来喂他。 (*In 1968, a paralyzed American engaged a monkey as a baby-sitter and let it go to street to buy bread and feed him.*)

S[5] 陕西凤翔县在元宵节，家家请女儿、女婿吃饭，称为吃十五，并送灯送油，称为添油。 (*In Fengxiang County, Shannxi Province, some families will treat their married daughters and their husband on Lantern Festival and send them some lanterns and oil, which as a custom is called tianyou.*)

S[6] 我对她说 "请坐，尤丽娅•瓦西里耶夫娜! 让我们算算工钱吧。 " (*I said to her: "Uria Vasilievna, be seated, and let us have a discussion on the payment!"*)

In S[1], *qing* means "I made a request of you to tell me what has happened and please tell me…"; in S[2] "…he applied to the Soccer Association for a holiday and asked to leave Hainan for Shenzhen". *Qing* in these two examples is labeled as $qing_1$.

We label *qing* in S[3] and S[4] as $qing_2$ for it can be interpreted as "...suggest that we send for a doctor from county" and "...engage a monkey as a baby-sitter" respectively. While in S[5], we label *qing* as $qing_3$ for it denotes giving somebody a treat, pleasure, service or entertainment. *Qing* in S[6] is marked as $qing_4$ for its meaning has the feature of being imperative, i.e., "Sit down please, Uria Vasilievna!"

## 2.2    Semantic Categories of *Qing* in Different Texts

We label the agent of *qing* in all texts with the parameter X, and the patient, Y.

### *Qing* Denoting X's Request of Y

In Text $Qing_1$, the agent X is in the active position and needs something that Y can provide. Here $qing_1$ is an imperative verb and the sentences in which it is embodied are called "imperative sentences" labeled as $S_{qing1}$. For example, in S[1], X needs Y's help, understanding and support while in S[2], X needs Y's permission and *qing* is the act that X commits to Y, i.e., it is in fact an act of request. In our opinion, $S_{qing1}$ is the first semantic category for the computer to read. Here is one more example:

S[7] 看到你们《读者之友》版经常为普通人说话，帮助普通人，就想请你们为我想想办法。 (*When I read your Reader's Friend Page, I knew you often speak for and help ordinary people and I immediately asked for your help to figure out some ways to help me out.*)

### *Qing* Denoting X's Invitation of Y

In Text $Qing_2$, the agent X performs an active act with his intention and meanwhile X believes that Y may perceive his attention and does as X intends to. Such act is somewhat in an imperative sense. $Qing_2$ as a kind of act, is a predicate, i.e., X extends his invitation to Y on one hand and on the other predicts to what extent Y may perform the act. However, whether Y may accept X's invitation or not is independent of X's intention. Sentences in which $Qing_2$ is contained are tagged as $S_{qing2}$. For example in S[3] and S[4], X sends his invitation to Y to go somewhere or engages Y to do something.

### $Qing_3$ Denoting X's Giving Treat or Service to Y

In Text $Qing_3$, the agent X performs an act on Y, an act denoting X's giving treat or service to Y, such as "treating Y for a meal" or "inviting Y to go to movie". Such act is polite, and beneficial to Y. Although such act is a bit imperative with some causative sense, it is euphemistic, indirect and not against Y's willingness. We mark Text $Qing_3$ as "Treat or Service Sentence" with label as $S_{qing3}$. A good case in point is in S[5].

### $Qing_4$ Denoting X's Hope of Y to do Something

In Text $Qing_4$, X expresses his hope that Y will do something in an indirect way. The events described in the sentences are subjective. The act $Qing_4$ shows X's intention and such sentences can be regarded as "Intention Sentence" and labeled as $S_{qing4}$. A good case in point is S[6] in which *qing* means that "I hope that Uria Vasilievna will have a seat..."

From above-mentioned analyses of *qing* and corresponding materials, we know that the basic senses of *qing* can be categorized as $qing_1$(request), $qing_2$(invite or engage), $qing_3$(entertain or treat) and $qing_4$(as a politeness marker indicating that the addresser hopes that addressee will do something). Among the four categories, implied in and common to them all is the sense of "intention", an active one which demonstrates X's hope or desire of Y to do something.

In addition to the analyses of the basic meanings of *qing*, we have to take into consideration allomorphs of *qing* according to Xiao's Synset-Allolexeme Theory. Such theory holds that the recognition of allomorphs of a verb is one of the problems that computer must handle[1][5]. Therefore, we have to list such allomorphs of *qing* as well as its basic senses in Table 1.

## 3    Semantic Recognition of *Qing* Texts

Xiao holds that human being's speech communication is a process in which speech comprehension and sense recognition moves from syntactic function recognition to sense selection of given lexical items. However, computer recognition takes place with the help of morph-syntactic features as the medium to determine both the meaning and the function of given lexical items[5]. As we mentioned above, when it comes to the sense recognition of *qing*, we should first delimit its texts-Text C, then define *Qing* Text in which the meaning of *qing* is not ambiguous: request( $qing_1$), invite or engage ( $qing_2$), treat or serve( $qing_3$), and its allomorphs( $qing_4$)(see Table 1). Third, we can decide which category each *qing* belongs to. However, before we come to this end, we should dwell on the impact semantic valence of *qing* has on its semantic category.

### 3.1    Semantic Valence of *Qing*1

From what we have analyzed above, we sum up the features of semantic valence of $qing_1$:(1) the agent is a noun, often denoting a person, or an animate or personified organization; (2) the patient is also a noun, denoting a person or an animate or perso-nified organization plus a verbal phrase/another noun+假[*jia*](*holiday*)

**$Qing_1$+Noun(Person or an Animate or Personified Organization)+ a Verbal Phrase**

When Y is a noun(an animate noun), it may be either an individual(person), or other animal or a personified organization such as 你[*ni*](*you*)(singular) in S[1] and 你们 [*nimen*](*you*)(plural) in S[7]. It can also refer to a group of people such as 大家 [*dajia*](*all of you*) in S[8]. After the noun can we place verbal phrase. In the deep structure of this sentence in which *qing* is embodied, action expressed by the verbal phrase is performed by Y as the result of X's request. The agent of this action is in fact Y rather than X. For example, in S[1] the agent of 告诉[*gaosu*](*tell*) is 我[*wo*] (*I*) while in S[7] the agent of 想想办法[*xiangxiangbanfa*](*figure out ways*), 你们 [*ni-men*](*you*)(plural). Verbs after Y suggest semantic features of "help" or "forgiveness".

**Table 1.** Semantic meanings of *qing* and its allomorphs

| Cate-gory | Semantic function | Senses | Intentionality | | Allomorphs* |
|---|---|---|---|---|---|
| | | | Types | Function | |
| $S_{qing1}$ | ask and tell | request | X's hope of Y to do sth. | Statement | 请求、 求、 要求、 恳求、 恳请、央求 |
| $S_{qing2}$ | Imperative | invite and engage | X's invitation of Y to do sth. | Statement | 邀请、邀约、约请、约、敦请、特约 |
| $S_{qing3}$ | Imperative | treat or service | X's giving treat or service to Y | statement | 约请、 约、 敦请、宴请、招待 |
| $S_{qing4}$ | indirect suggestion | suggestion for Y to do sth | X's intention for Y to do sth. | Suggestion | 建议、倡议、提议、 提倡、 首倡、劝、劝告、奉劝、劝说 |

S[8] 赢球让我非常激动，所以今天发言的英文稿还没来得及准备，请大家谅解……(*Winning the match made me excited, so my English speech has not been ready, and I asked for your forgiveness.*)

### *Qing₁*+假(as a Noun)

In this structure, patient Y is 假[*jia*](*holiday*) with abstract meaning. Such structure has the following features in terms of semantic valence:

A. Aspectual markers such as 了[*le*] and 过[*guo*] can be inserted into between请(as a verb) and 假(as the object). Such markers can be used to describe the time when 请假[*qingjia*](*ask for leave*) as an action has happened. i.e., this action took place in the past and 过 is used to show that such action has already happened. Here is one example:

S[9] 本来，女儿已请了假在家照顾他，碰巧那天他又临时替别人顶班。(*The truth is that his daughter has already asked for leave and looked after him at home. He happened to be on duty for others temporarily that day.*)

B. Adverbial phrases denoting time such as 三天[*santian*](*three days*) or 一个月[*yigeyue*](*one month*) can be placed after 请(as a verb) and before 假(as an object).

---

* Sqing1: 请求 [qingqiu], 求 [qiu], 要求 [yaoqiu], 恳求 [kenqiu], 恳请 [kenqing], 央求 [yaoqiu]; Sqing2:邀请[yaoqing],邀约[yaoyue],约请[yueqing], 约[yue], 敦请[dunqing],特约[teyue]; Sqing3:约请[yueqing],约[yue], 敦请[dunqing],宴请[yanqing], 招待 [zhaodai]; Sqing4:建议 [jianyi],倡议[changyi],提议[tiyi], 提倡[tichang],首倡[shouchang],劝[quan], 劝告[quangao], 奉劝[fengquan],劝说[quanshuo]. (English equivalents of those Chinese words are in the corresponding column of "Senses" in the Table.)

Such adverbial phrases are employed to indicate the duration of 请假[*qingjia*](asking for leave), i.e., how long the leave will be. Here is an example:

S[10] 正生已在杭州宗宗宝石有限公司工作，他特地请了三天假，带着贺礼，也带着对哥哥的感激之情赶来。(*Zhensheng has already worked in Zongzong Emerald Co. Ltd. He specially asked for 3-day's leave and with gifts came here to pay a visit to and give his appreciation for his brother.*)

C. 请 as a verb can be reduplicated as in example S[11]:

S[11] 你替他请请假。[4](*You may ask for leave for him.*)

### 3.2    Semantic Valence of *Qing₂*

The features of semantic valence of *qing₂* can be summarized as: (1) the agent is a noun, denoting a person, or an animate or personified thing/organization; (2) the patient is also a noun, denoting a person or an animate or personified thing/organization+ verbal phrase.

### *Qing₂* + Noun Denoting Animate Things

In this structure, X lies in the agent position while Y, the patient position. Their relations can be described as "inviting" and "being invited". However, in the deep structure, whether the event expressed in this structure can take place or not is dependent Y's intention. The agent X doesn't have any control of Y. A good case in point can be found in S[10]. Between *qing₂* and Y can be inserted into aspectual markers such as 了or 过. In addition, directional markers such as 来 [*la*](come near the speaker) or 出 [*chu*](*get away from the speaker*) can also be placed between *qing₂* and Y. Here is an example:

S[12] 张教练为了让孩子们学习进步快，特地请来辽宁体校一名文化教员，及时辅导。(*Coach Zhang specially invited a teacher from Liaoning PE school to come here to teach children literate courses in time.*)

### *Qing₂* + Noun Denoting Animate Things +Verbal Phrase

Such structure features the telescopic form, i.e., Y is both the object of *qing₂* as a verb that precedes Y and the subject of the verb that comes after Y. We may label *qing₂* as $V_1$ and the verb after Y as $V_2$. For example, in S[4], 猴子[*houzi*](*monkey*) is both the object of *qing₂*, "invite" and the subject of 当保姆[*dangbaomu*](*act as a babysitter*). Semantic valence of *qing₂* can also have such features, i.e., to place aspectual markers such as 了 between $V_1$ and Y to indicate time, or to place directional markers such as 来[*lai*](*come near the speaker*) between $V_1$ and Y to indicate direction. When it comes to the meanings, $V_2$ is often used to mean "being engaged in". Here is one more example:

S[13] 许多地方自己谦恭地退让一旁，隆重地请出权威人士来发言。(*In many places, the host himself may retreat behind and formally invites the authority to give a speech.*)

### 3.3    Semantic Valence of *Qing*₃

Similar to *qing*₂ structure, the features of semantic valence of *qing*₃ can be summarized as: (1) the agent is a noun, denoting a person, or an animate or personified thing/organization; (2) the patient is also a noun, denoting a person or an animate or personified thing/organization+verbal phrase. The deep meaning of this structure, i.e., 宴请[*yanqing*](*giving sb. a treat*) or招待[*zhaodai*](*giving sb. a service*) can be made known to the addressee through two ways:

A. In the position of patient, Y can only be some nouns such as 客人[*keren*](*guest*) or 客[*ke*](*guest*). Here is one example:

S[14] 我一个人不愿意喝闷酒，所以想让他陪我，当然是由我请客。 (*I alone don't want to drink myself, so I hope that he may accompany me, of course, it's my treat.*)

B. The deep meaning of *qing*₃ in this structure is dependent on the context in which 请 is embodied as in:

S[15] "谢谢你请我吃饭！ " 他笑了笑，说道 "莫忘了，你也请过我。 " (*Thank you for giving me a meal, smilingly, he said: "don't forget that you have also given me a treat before."*)

In this sentence, the second 请 means *qing*₃ although it is not followed by 吃饭 [*chifan*](*having a meal*). However, the first clause "谢谢你请我吃饭！ " offers us a detailed context, which helps us to delimit the meaning of the second 请 as *qing*₃. In this structure, verbs after Y are often ones denoting pleasure or entertainment.

### 3.4    Semantic Valence of *Qing*₄

Semantic valence of qing₄ is characterized as: (1) the agent X is void in the sentence or is an animate noun denoting a person, or an animate or personified thing/organization; (2) the patient Y takes on such forms as: void, verbal phrases, or a clause. This structure has one more working feature: it can't go with negative words such as 没有 [*meiyou*](*without*) or 不[*bu*](*no or not*).

#### Void/Animate Nouns+ *Qing*₄+Void

This structure epitomizes imperative sentences in Chinese language. *Qing*₄ can be used single with its deep meaning as "this way please!" or "please eat this stuff!", which is shown in S[16]. If a noun precedes *qing*₄, this noun in deep meaning can be interpreted as the patient of *qing*(as a verb). A good case in point is S[17].

S[16] 眼镜先生，彬彬有礼地到她面前，浅浅躬身对她微笑道： "太太，请！ " (*Mister Glasses walked respectfully and politely to her and bowed slightly, smiled and said: "Madam, this way please!"*)

S[17] 狗棍倚在门外，双手捧着烟袋进屋，恭恭敬敬道： "各位老少爷们请！ " (*Gougun leaned against the door, and then holding tobacco pouch in his hands, entered the room and said: "Masters, this way please!"*)

**Void/ Animate Nouns+ *Qing*₄+Verbal Phrase**

This structure is also popular among Chinese imperative sentences. *Qing*, in its deep meaning, suggests euphemism. Without *qing*, the sentence still works, as shown in:

S[18] 今天下午三点召开学生代表会议，请准时出席！（*At 3 this afternoon we have students' representative meeting and please be present on time!*）

**Void+( *Qing*₄)+Clause**

This structure is the same as that in section 3.4.2, i.e., without *qing*, the sentence still works. However, in the clause of this structure, if the subject is void, the clause becomes "void+(*qing*₄)+verbal phrases". Therefore, verb or verbal phrase after *qing*₄ are themselves imperative in meaning, as shown in S[19]:

S[19] 餐厅老板连忙道："不！请你不要误会，事情是这样子的……"（*The canteen boss at once explained: "please don't misunderstand; things turned out to be like this..."*）

In S[19], the patient of *qing* is a clause-你不要误会[*nibuyaowuhui*](*please don't misunderstand*). If we omit *ni*, and the clause turns into(*qing*) *buyaowuhui*; if we go on omitting *qing*, the clause turns into *buyaowuhui*; if we place *ni* in front of *qing*, the structure turns into *nibuyaowuhui* no matter what forms the clause or the structure takes on, their meaning remains the same. In our opinion, structure void+(*qing*₄)+clause is a variation of structure void/animate nouns+ *qing*₄+verbal phrase in section 3.4.2.

# 4    Conclusion

With the help of Synset-Allolexeme Theory and Lexical Categorization Theory, this article explores 请[*qing*](*please*) in Chinese in terms of its semantic meaning and syntactic function on the basis of many genuine materials. Semantically, four semantic categories of *qing* are demarcated while syntactically, the valence of each category of *qing* is analyzed and exemplified. Our analyses will provide some support for machine recognition of *qing* as a polysemy, as well as other words of its kind, which is one of the problems computer must encounter in NLP.

# References

1. Xiao, G.Z.: Structural Description of 打, da, "beat" and Its Synonym Group Construction—A Preliminary Research on Human-Computer Interaction in the Frame of Synset-Allolexeme Theory. Research on Computing Technology and Language. In: Proceedings of 7th International Symposium on Chinese Information Processing. Electrònic Industry Publishing Press, Beijing (2007)
2. Chen, J.S.: Cognitive Lexicography. Fudan University Press, Shanghai (2008)

3. Xiao, S.: Semantic Construction of Speech-act Verb Among Imperative Verbs and Its Synonym Group Construction——A Case Study from the Perspective of Synset-Allolexeme Theory and Lexical Categorization Theory. Chang Jiang Academy 9(4), 168–173 (2010)
4. Lü, S.X.: Eight Hundred Words in Modern Chinese. Liaoning Education Press, Shenyang (2002)
5. Xiao, G.Z.: Factual Exploration of and Theoretic Probe into Chinese Grammar. Hubei People's Publishing Press, Wuhan (2005)
6. Xiao, G.Z., Hu, D.: Semantic Composition and Formal Representation of Synonym set. In: Proceedings of Recent Advance of Asian Language Processing Technologies, Chiang Mai, Thailand, pp. 93–97 (2008)

# A Comparative Study on "Death" Terms in Chinese and Vietnamese

Bich Diep Tu[1] and Guonian N. Wang[2]

[1] College of Chinese Language and Literature, Wuhan University, Wuhan 430072, China
from_green_leaf@yahoo.com
[2] School of Foreign Languages, China University of Geosciences, Wuhan 430074, China
touchbobby@gmail.com

**Abstract.** "Death" is an unavoidable part of life, and sometimes a must topic. For its inauspicious implication, "death" itself is usually euphemized with other terms or phrases in a variety of living languages, including Chinese and Vietnamese. A comparative study is conducted on the various ways of expressing "death" in these two languages. Similarities and differences are revealed in these terms, which serve to unveil the subtle cultural backgrounds in the two nations. The findings are also of assistance to teaching Chinese in Vietnam.

**Keywords:** Chinese, Vietnamese, "death" terms, euphemism, teaching Chinese.

## 1 Introduction

All men are mortal; no one can escape the doomed "birth-illness-aging-death" fate. As Karl Marx has put it, man is the "ensemble of social relations", and his or her physical decease will inevitably impact the relatives and acquaintances around. Death could be a shame or honor; it might also be commonplace or significant. Therefore, there exist various terms for death in most languages, including Chinese and Vietnamese. Chinese, in particular, possesses "death" words and phrases that amount to several tens. For any life, "death" constitutes a big event that relates more or less to the people, nation, society and culture that the deceased has once lived with. The comparative study will attempt to find out – by means of "death" term analysis – the similarities and differences in the two languages and cultures.

## 2 Sememes for Study

In both Chinese and Vietnamese, there under the entry of "die/death" lie quite several senses.

According to *Modern Chinese Dictionary* [1], of the 7 sememes under the entry 死 (die/death/dead), the first goes as follows: [动](生物)失去生命(跟"生、活"相对): ~

P. Liu and Q. Su (Eds.): CLSW 2013, LNAI 8229, pp. 117–125, 2013.

亡、~人 (v. *(of living being) lose one's life (as contrasted to "live"): die a death, someone dies*).

Similarly in *A Vietnamese Dictionary* [2], of the 7 senses under "die/death/dead", the first goes as follows: (Động/tính) Mất khả năng sống, không còn có biểu hiện của sự sống: người ~ để tiếng (v./adj. *lose one's life; showing no sign of life: His name remains even though he is dead*).

Despite the several different sememes of "die/death/dead", it is evident that in both languages the first sense under the entry refers to the fact that a living being loses its life. It is this basic and primitive sense that this paper examines by comparing all possible "death" equivalents or counterparts in the two languages. It suggests that the appropriate choice of terminology for one's death depends on his or her social status, age and religious belief, among many other factors.

## 3    Terms for "Death"

Any man, while alive as a member in the society, is far more than an isolated individual; he belongs to a collectivity and a family; he is placed in a certain social status and expected to have his own religious belief. Therefore, the word "death" is far less than enough to judge one upon his pass-away. An appropriate "death" term for this matter is desired on the basis his social status, age, religious belief, cause of death, funeral tradition, and cultural background.

The inflectional English forms of "death", like "die" and "dead", may correspond equally to their Chinese and Vietnamese counterparts without discrimination, for the reason that the latter two languages are weak in morpheme changes. In other words, the part of speech for "death" terms in Chinese and Vietnamese could be any or all of noun, verb and adjective. Hereinafter, only the most convenient "death" meanings are translated literally into English, without stipulating their original parts of speech in the two Asian tongues.

### 3.1    As per Social Status

Thousands of years have witnessed the feudalist society and history of both China and Vietnam, where social status was seriously and rigidly divided. China, however, had gone through a more tangled and complicated hierarchical development than had Vietnam. Different ways of referring to "death" were adopted subject to the social status and prestige of the deceased. They are generally classified as the following three levels.

**Imperial Rulers.** Emperors or empresses are honored in the Chinese language as 天子 [*tianzi*](*Son of Heaven*), who enjoy the advantage of being addressed differently and vividly from the general public, their subjects. Their death shall be seriously termed as well. The decease of the "God's Son" meant a huge loss to the whole world he or she had been ruling, and would usually impact the general mass as a big bang, a deafening sound from the collapsing mountain. For that reason, they would be reported to have "banged" or "collapsed" (崩 [*beng*](*of mountain or building) collapse*). Besides, other terms that serve the same purpose include 驾崩 [*jiabeng*], 暴崩 [*baobeng*], 崩逝 [*bengshi*], 崩陨 [*bengyun*] and 升霞 [*shengxia*] [3-4].

In Vietnamese, giá băng (directly borrowed from the Chinese 驾崩 [*jiabeng*]) and băng hà (崩霞 [*bengxia*], similar to the Chinese 升霞 [*shengxia*]) are employed for the passing of imperial rulers.

**Officials.** In Chinese, the death of local leuds is termed as 薨 [*hong*] (*demise*), that of prestigious officials as 卒 [*zu*](*obiit*), that of general officials as 逝 [*shi*] (*elapse*), that of officers and scholars as 不禄/不得 [*bulu/bude*](*no salary*), that of marshals and generals as 陨 [*yun*] (*fall*), and that of other noted figures as 困 [*kun*](*sleep*).

While in Vietnamese, the pass-away of officials is euphemized as thất lộc (loss of salary; equivalent to the Chinese 不禄 [*bulu*](*no salary*)) or hoǎng (*demise*, equivalent to the Chinese 薨 [*hong*](*demise*)).

Different terms for "death" are listed in Table 1 on the basis of hierarchical social level of the deceased.

**Table 1.** Hierarchical terms (English equivalents as above) for the deceased

| Hierarchy | Chinese | Vietnamese |
|---|---|---|
| Imperial rulers | 崩[*beng*], 驾崩[*jiabeng*], 暴崩 [*baobeng*], 崩逝[*bengshi*], 崩陨 [*bengyun*], 升霞[*shengxia*] | Giá băng, băng hà |
| Officials | 薨[*hong*], 卒[*zu*], 逝[*shi*], 不禄[*bulu*], 不得[*bude*], 陨[*yun*], 困[*kun*] | thất lộc, hoǎng |

All the terms listed in Table 1 are positive in meaning, paying tribute to the deceased in some way.

As the table indicates, Chinese terms for "death" are larger in number, more delicate in classification and more subtle in meaning than those in the Vietnamese language. It is believed that different cultural backgrounds have played a significant role in these similarities and dissimilarities.

About the hierarchical social status in ancient China, Bao [5] has summarized in her research that people were classified into 10 different social classes in the Zhou Dynasty; Later in the Wei-Jin Periods, the 9-grade system was initiated, with 30 subgrades that distinguished one person from another; There were 29 grades of officials and 45 grades of officers in the Tang Dynasty, with officials in the Song Dynasty ranked on as many as 52 levels. The complicated and various hierarchies, as well as the rigid order imposed to people in that patriarchal clan system, were effective enough to maintain the strict social membership in the "monarch-subject-father-son" bond. One was placed on certain "grade" while living, and was to be addressed accordingly after their death.

Vietnam has long been influenced by the Chinese culture and tradition, but it has adopted and maintained only the parts that fit into its own social and national conditions [6]. Despite the fact that Vietnamese learned from and imitated the patriarchal clan system from China, their hierarchical social system of "grading" people was much more simplified. As a reflection of social background and custom, the Vietnamese language has witnessed "death" terms smaller in number than the Chinese language.

**The General Public.** In both Chinese and Vietnamese, there are the generally known terms for "death" – 死 [*si*](*leave the world*) in Chinese and *chết* in Vietnamese – and other euphemisms like 谢世 [*xieshi*] (*thank the world*) and 逝世 [*shishi*](*leave the world*), etc. Especially in ancient Chinese, there was once the term 迁化 [*qianhua*] (*convert/change oneself in form*) used on very formal occasions.

As everyone exists in certain social group, his or her death will inevitably affect other members in the group physically or spiritually. While talking about or referring to the deceased, some sentiment or feeling will be unconsciously attached to him or her. Generally, people prefer to select some euphemized terms as listed bellow for the "death":

- In Chinese: 去世 [*qushi*](*leave the world*), 永别 [*yongbie*](*farewell*) and 谢世 [*xieshi*](*thank the world*), etc.
- In Vietnamese: (1) mất (*lose*), ngã xuống (*fall down*), vĩnh biệt (*farewell*), all of which are used to refer to the death of those who have sacrificed themselves for the benefits of the general public, those like martyrs, the police and soldiers; (2) về cõi vĩnh hằng (*go to the perpetual world*); (3) khuất núi (*sunset, literally a metaphor*); (4) nhắm mắt xuôi tay (*close the eyes and let go*); and (5) sang bên kia thế giới (*go to another world*).

In some cases, however, the following substitutes for "death" could be scornful or sarcastic:

- In Chinese: 嗝屁 [*gepi*](*breathe one's last*) and 丧命 [*sangming*](*get killed*).
- In Vietnamese: toi (*be over*), ngỏm (*be over*), ngoẻo (*be over*), tiệt (*be lifeless*), bỏ mạng (*get killed*), rồi đời (*end one's life*), and tiêu (*it sucks*).

## 3.2   As per Age

**Die Young.** In Chinese, when one dies before the age of 20, they are usually said to have "died young" (殇[*shang*]). The death of an 8-year-old through 11-year-old is referred to as 下殇 [*xiashang*](*die very young*), that of a 12- to15-year-old as 中殇 [*zhongshang*](*die young*), and that of a 16- to 19-year-old as 上殇 [*shangshang*](*die big*). As for the third sub-category, if a young man or woman is engaged to be married, their death is not called 殇 [*shang*](*die young*). Sometimes 溺 [*ni*](*drowned when young*) or 夭亡 [*yaowang*](*die when small*) is adopted for the death of a young person before adult age. Furthermore, obituary notice for such young deaths often sees the term 疾终 [*jizhong*](*die of illness*) or 云终[*yunzhong*](*end in the cloud*).

In Vietnamese, things are easier. When someone dies at a young age, it is simply chết yểu or chết non (both meaning "death for the young")

**Die Strong.** In China, if one dies in his strong adulthood, they are generally reported to have "passed away", with the Chinese equivalents 逝世 [*shishi*](*pass away from the world*), 去世 [*qushi*](*leave the world*) or 谢世 [*xieshi*](*thank the world*).

In more formal situations such as on the obituary notice, the Vietnamese will use tạ thế (borrowed from the Chinese 谢世[*xieshi*](*thank the world*)), qua đời (*pass away*) or từ trần (*take one's leave*). They could also apply in various other situations for other ages. Another way to address the death of an adult is "hưởng dương + X" (*enjoy a positive life of X, with the real age as "X"*). Furthermore, if one can live a rather long life before his "doomsday", he is believed to have enjoyed his longevity (hưởng thọ).

**Die Old.** The elderly usually enjoy the respect and honor from their offspring and other relatives around in Asian countries. Their death is more remotely and vaguely referred to in China and Vietnam.

• In Chinese: 寿终 [*shouzhong*](*longevity ends*) applies to almost all senior family members. For the death of the No. 1 clan leader, 寿终正寝 [*shouzhong zheng-qin*](*longevity ends and he is sleeping*) or 寿终内寝[*shouzhong neiqin*](*longevity ends and she is sleeping*) will do the trick. The elderly of less prestige are euphemized to have "gone for ever" (长逝[*changshi*]) or "been the past" (作古[*zuogu*]). Children who lose their parents usually regretfully sign that they have "abandoned supporting" (弃养[*qiyang*]).

• In Vietnamese: trăm tuổi (*100 years*), hai năm mươi về chầu trời (*two fifty-years, altogether 100 years;go visit the Heaven*), trút hơi thở cuối cùng (*breathe one's last, usually seen on obituary notice, suffixed by such location of death as in hospital or at home*), and thành người thiên cổ (*become an immortal*).

### 3.3    As per Religion

**Buddhism.** In Chinese, monks or nuns who reach "nirvana" (涅槃[*niepan*] (*a state of being spiritually self-content, relieved and reborn*)) or attain "perfection" (圆寂 [*yuanji*](*a state of being spiritually and morally perfect, with all inner evils or sins removed*) were deemed as the Saints. Later, these two Chinese terms (*translated from the Sanskrit language*) are used to refer to the pass-away of prestigious monks or nuns. Those who practice Lamaism, a Tibetan variation of Buddhism, are crowned with the same honor upon leaving the world. They prefer the term 涅槃 [*niepan*], 坐化 [*zuohua*](*dying in a sitting posture*), 归于极乐 [*guiyu jile*](*returning to the Seventh Heaven*) and 西游 [*xiyou*](*going to the West*).

In Vietnam, viên tịch (equivalent to 圆寂[*yuanji*]) and Niết bàn (equivalent to 涅槃[*niepan*]) are re-borrowings from Chinese, for Vietnam's Buddhism partly initiated from China, and partly from India. Other Vietnamese versions include đi chầu Phật tổ (*go to see Buddha; die*), đi Tây thiên (borrowed from 西游[*xiyou*](*go to the West; die*), về cõi Niết bàn (similar to 涅槃[*niepan*] and 归于极乐[*guiyu jile*](*reach a state of "nirvana"; die*), and trở về cát bụi (*return to dust; die*). It is believed in Buddhism that man derives from dust, and will return to dust.

**Taoism.** Chinese Taoists believe their death is a transformation of "eclosion". In the Taoist religion, several terms are usually used to refer to the death of believers in Taoism: 见阎王 [*jian Yanwang*](*see Pluto, King of the Hell; die*), 登仙 [*dengxian*] (*ascend as Immortal; die*), 驾鹤归西 [*jiahe guixi*](*go to the West on a flying crane; die*) or 含笑九泉 [*hanxiao Jiuquan*](*smile in the Nether World; die*).

Vietnamese borrowed and modified Chinese Taoism, and carried on the term 见阎王 [*jian Yanwang*](*see Pluto*) to mean a Taoist dies. Other similar verb forms are đi buôn muối (*go selling salt; die*) and ngậm cười nơi chín suối (borrowed from 含笑九泉[*hanxiao Jiuquan*](*smile in the Nether World; die*)). In local dialect, "Pluto" (or "Yama") sounds like "muối" (*salt*).

**Christianity.** This is an alien religion that found its believers in both China and Vietnam.

Chinese adopt 归主[*guizhu*](*return to Lord; die*) and 进入天国[*jinru Tianguo*] (*enter the Zion; die*) to mean that a Christian passes away.

The above two terms find their way into the Vietnamese language: về với Chúa (归主[*guizhu*], *return to Lord*) and lên nước Thiên Đàng (进入天国[*jinru Tianguo*], *enter the Zion*). Besides, hiến linh hồn cho Chúa (*sacrifice soul to God*) can also serve the purpose.

**Local Vietnamese Religion.** In local ceremonies, civilians observe days of worshiping their ancestors. On the first and fifteenth days of each lunar month, most households place, in the most solemn spot inside the house, memorial items – a wooden table or cabinet, on which a censer, ancestral portraits and inscribed pillars, traditional rice food, chicken, and fruits (usually a bunch of banana) – to pay respect to their forefathers. In addition, they may also pay tribute to the so-called "Earth God" and other locally-observed "Gods" on those special days. As a reflection and record of this religious practice, several unique terms [7-8] for "death" are listed below:

- về với ông bà ông vải (*meet their forefathers*);
- lên bàn thờ (*go onto the memorial table*);
- lên nóc tủ (*go onto the cabinet*);
- ăn chuối cả nải (*eat a bunch of banana*).

Except the first, the rest three terms are used with an air of satire.

## 3.4    As per Causes of Death

People may perish naturally or accidentally, from illness or of famine, as a martyr or coward.

In positive cases where one dies for a just cause, for the benefits of his country or career, Chinese and Vietnamese words share more similarities than differences. A comparative selection is listed in Table 2:

**Table 2.** Causal terms for the deceased

| Causes | Chinese | Vietnamese |
|--------|---------|------------|
| Positive | 1) 殉[xun](gloriously die for) + reason | 1) tuẫn (gloriously die for) + reason |
| | 殉国 [xunguo](die for one's nation) | tuẫn quốc (same as 殉国) |
| | 殉道 [xundao](die for justice) | tuẫn đạo (same as 殉道) |
| | 殉难 [xunnan](die a martyr) | tuẫn nạn (same as 殉难) |
| | 殉情 [xunqing](die for love) | tuẫn tình (same as 殉情) |
| | 2) 牺牲[xisheng](sacrifice oneself) | 2) hi sinh (same as 牺牲) |
| | 3) 就义[jiuyi](die a martyr bravely) | |
| Negative | 1) 遇难[yunan](die in a murder or accident) | 1) chết (die) + reason |
| | 2) 死于[siyu](die for/of) + reason | chết cháy (burned to death) |
| | 死于车祸 [siyu chehuo](die in a car accident) | chết đói (starved to death) |
| | | chết bệnh (die a patient) |
| | | chết đuối (drowned) |

## 3.5    As per Funeral Tradition

So far, we have discussed different versions for "death". Some are used literally, some orally; some officially, some privately; some chronologically, and some religiously. However, the last stage of one's death, funeral, witnesses different versions as well.

People in China have long observed the "earth-burial" ceremony, and they metaphorize death with 土[tu](dust or earth) or 地[di](ground). The terms 入地[rudi] (enter the ground), 入土[rutu](enter the earth) and 命染黄沙 [mingran huangsha] (relate with yellow sand) are general cases in point. Small hills and highlands are traditionally the favorite places for burial; therefore, 归丘[guiqiu](return to the hill) is another metaphor. Since the departed were placed in wooden coffins, they could also "enter the wood" (入木[rumu]) or "sleep in the wood" (就木[jiumu]).

As a people of farming tradition, deceased Vietnamese are usually buried in the farming field for they have attached their whole life to arable agriculture. Therefore, typical Vietnamese funeral terms for "death" go as follows [9-10]:

- về dưới ruộng (*go back to the field*).
- ngủ với giun (*sleep with the earthworm*).
- chán cơm thèm đất thích nghe kèn (*be fed up with rice but fond of the trumpet*). Ironically referring to those who live a meaningless life (trumpet is one of the musical instruments played at the funeral).
- đắp chiếu (*covered with a matting*). Bamboo matting is used for sitting on or sleeping on, and is also used for covering the dead.
- vào hòm (*in the box/coffin*).
- đi tàu ngầm sáu tấm (*take a six-board submarine*). The coffin made of six pieces of wooden boards that is buried under the field looks like a submarine in the sea.
- xanh cỏ (*change into green grasses*). Green grasses will thrive over the tomb after some time of burial. It refers to "death".
- nhận hoa huệ/hoa cúc (*receive lily/daisy*). These two flowers are common at Vietnamese funerals.

### 3.6    As per Cultural Background

Uniquely different cultural characters in the two nations have also helped create special expression of "death".

In China's Qing Dynasty, all men were required to wear long braids, a hairstyle once exclusively enjoyed by women. When executing male criminals, the persecutors lift their head by the braid before beheading them. "Lifting one's braid" (翘辫子 [*qiaobianzi*]) was thus fabricated to mean one was killed. After the founding of the New China in 1949, the deceased high-profile Communist leaders are usually placed in the graveyard called Beijing Babaoshan (a Mt. name) Revolutionary Cemetery. Another culturally unique term "go up Mt. Babaoshan" has since become a household euphemism for the word "die" [11].

As a socialist country, Vietnam reveres the theorist founders like Marx and Lenin. "Visiting Marx and Lenin" was initiated by former Chairman Ho Chi Minh to refer to the pass-away of a revolutionary or socialist. Meanwhile, there is in this nation's capital Ha Noi a cemetery called "Văn Điển", similar to that in Beijing. Đi Văn Điển (*going to Văn Điển*) is another term for death.

## 4    Conclusions

It is evident from the above discussion that death terms in Chinese – in terms of social hierarchy and age of the deceased – outnumber those in Vietnamese, and are more rigidly used (socially 12 words in Chinese vs. 4 in Vietnamese, and chronologically 11 vs. 8, respectively). China's age-long feudalist social system, as well as the influence of Confucianism (the country's state religion), has deeply shaped the clear-cut social status.

Accordingly, people of different status "monopolize" different euphemistic terms for death. This strongly accounts for the affluent Chinese expressions for pass-away. Similarly, there are uniquely Vietnamese "death" terminologies for its local funeral and burial custom different from that in China.

As is true to both countries, Buddhism and Christianity are incoming religions, which have introduced into Chinese and Vietnamese new "death" words, mostly with similar sounds and like meaning.

Century-long influences from China have also witnessed death word borrowings into Vietnam.

Language is a marker of civilization and reflects social, traditional and religious facts. The death terms detailed in this paper serve as a tentative probe into the two languages. The similarities, as well as differences, are expected to help bridge the understanding of the cultures and social backgrounds in China and Vietnam.

**Acknowledgements.** This study has been partly supported by the National Social Science Foundation Youth Project (12CWW035), and the Fundamental Research Funds for the Central Universities, China University of Geosciences (Wuhan) (CUGW120227). We also appreciate the revision suggestions and comments from several anonymous reviewers.

# References

1. Chao, J.Z., Han, J.T.: Modern Chinese Dictionary, 5th edn. Commercial Press, Beijing (2005)
2. Hoang, P.: A Vietnamese Dictionary. Social Sciences Publishing House, Ha Noi (2002)
3. Pang, Z.X.: On the Types of Euphemism of "Death" in Ancient Chinese and Their Cultural Implications. Journal of Shaoguan University 2, 92–95 (2008)
4. Gu, W.Y.: Expression of Death in Chinese Culture and Their English Versions. Journal of Chongqing Institute of Technology (Social Sciences) 11, 101–107 (2007)
5. Bao, H.L.: Research into the Cultural Factors of Chinese Death Euphemism. Journal of Inner Mongolia University (Humanities and Social Sciences) 6, 77–80 (2000)
6. Tran, Q.V.: Vietnamese Cultural Basics. Vietnam Education Press, Ha Noi (2009)
7. Nguyen, D.T.: Vietnamese Synonyms. Encyclopedia Dictionary Press, Ha Noi (2011)
8. Duong, K.D., Nguyen, Q.H.: The Vietnamese Synonym and Antonym Dictionary. Vietnam National University Press, Ha Noi (2002)
9. Nguyen, N.T.: A Comparative Study of Death Euphemisms in Chinese and Vietnamese, http://cdmd.cnki.com.cn/Article/CDMD-10183-1012359022.htm
10. Li, B., Nong, S.F.C.: A Contrastive Analysis of Chinese and Vietnamese Death Euphemism. Journal of Chongqing University of Arts and Sciences (Social Sciences) 11, 112–115 (2012)
11. Zun, X.H.: A Cultural Probe into Chinese Death Euphemism. Journal of Jiaozuo Teachers College 3, 14–16 (2005)

# Feichang or Tebie – A Study Based on Corpora

Lu Chen and Qi Su

School of Foreign Languages, Peking University
No.5 Yiheyuan Road, Haidian District,
Beijing, 100871, P.R. China
{chenlucrystal,sukia.pku}@gmail.com

**Abstract.** A quantitative study is conducted on two Chinese synonyms *Feichang* and *Tebie* with three corpora: a newspaper corpus, a novel corpus and a spoken corpus. Analyses are conducted on the usage frequency of each word, their distribution on the different registers and the degree of interchangeability. This study provides valid data for the study on the two words.

**Keywords:** Corpus, 非常[*Feichang*], 特别[*Tebie*], Adverb.

## 1    Introduction

Corpus linguistics is an interdisciplinary field that covers subjects as diverse as linguistics, computer science, cognitive linguistics and applied linguistics. Based on real language data, it analyzes a large quantity of linguistic phenomenon from the macro point of view so as to seek the rules behind the language application.

Corpus linguistics has gradually become the mainstream of linguistic study. Nowadays, corpus-based research is having an increasing influence on many areas of language study. Corpus linguistics is not the study of the language itself. It is a corpus-based language research method which includes two aspects: annotation (e.g. part-of-speech tagging) of natural language material and the research on annotated corpus.

There is no doubt that corpus linguistics has a distinguished status in linguistics study. This can be proved by the following two factors: firstly, the profound theoretical basis, such as Firth's view of language, Sinclair's theory and Teubert's philosophy of language and applications of corpus linguistics; secondly, it has various research methods which are not only complementary to each other, but also distinctive enough on themselves, this is also called corpus-driven research and corpus-based study.

Observing the usage variance between synonyms based on the data obtained from corpora is an effective method to discover their using conventions. Chinese synonyms *Feichang* and *Tebie* have a lot of common features, such as their basic semantics and grammatical functions. However, there are many differences in between as well. Therefore, it is misleading to regard them as equal. Based on the argument above, we have conducted a quantitative study on these two Chinese synonyms *Feichang* and *Tebie* by using corpus-based research techniques, and combine the real language data with statistical induction to present the subtle differences in a quantitative form, so that we can distinguish the differences between these two Chinese synonyms.

P. Liu and Q. Su (Eds.): CLSW 2013, LNAI 8229, pp. 126–134, 2013.

## 2     Object for Study

【Entry】非常[*Feichang*]

● Adjective: unusual; special: ～ time; ～meeting.
● Adverb: very; extremely: ～ honor; ～ happy; ～ studious; He is ～ good at speaking.

【Entry】特别[*Tebie*]

● Adjective: distinction; unordinary: ～ style; He has a ～ temper.
● Adverb: particularly: Trains run ～ fast; This program is ～ attractive to the audience.
● Adverb: specifically: After the meeting, the director ～ asked him to stay to discuss the technical problems.
● Adverb: especially: He enjoys traveling, ～ cycling for an outing.

According to the above entries, it is not hard to find that the basic semantic features and grammatical functions of Chinese synonyms *Feichang* and *Tebie* are quite similar: both have two parts of speech, adjective and adverb. Whether those two parts of speech are used equably - in other word, with similar frequencies - will be discussed later.

It is worth mentioning that the fundamental reason of them being treated as synonyms is because both are mostly used as adverb among all of their usages. In this case, one adverb followed by an adjective forms a "～ + adjective" or a "～ + de/ di / de + adjective" structure. This article will only discuss these two cases in detail. Other special cases such as *Feichang* or *Tebie* followed by a verb phrase or some other non-syntactic phenomena will not be covered in this paper.

In addition, we will observe *Feichang* and *Tebie* in different stylistic and discuss their usage distribution on different registers; also, this article attempts to summarize the degree of their interchangeabilities when they are used as synonyms.

## 3     Research Method

### 3.1     Corpora Selection and Construction

The three corpora that we used are:

(1) A newspaper corpus: We adopted the "People's Daily Corpus" which was built by the Institute of Computational Linguistics of Peking University and Fujitsu Research & Development Center. This annotated corpus is based on the "People's Daily" in year 1998, and it works on word segmentation and part-of-speech tagging. Because this corpus covers all the news articles from different pages of the whole year, it eliminates the phraseology biases which are brought by different news stories. The total number of words of this corpus is about 1,945,000.

(2) A novel corpus: We selected 7 novels which have achieved a relatively high click-through rate on the Internet to build this corpus. It includes ancient novels, fantasy novels, children's novels, realistic novels and so on. We tried to eliminate the phraseology differences which are brought by different themes. The total word number of this corpus is about 3,290,000.

(3) A spoken corpus: We adopted the 'Beijing spoken dialect' which was built by the Institute of Languages of Beijing Language and Culture University. It consists of 1.84 million words after being recorded, transcribed, revised and well arranged. The content of this corpus is from recorded conversations. In order to comply with the sociolinguistics sampling principles, the source of this corpus is gathered from interviews which are conducted to nearly 500 people who grew up in Beijing. 210 audio tapes were collected in total. After the revision, 370 people's interviews and 119 audio tapes were classified as valid material and were converted into audio files (wav format) for further processing. As a result, a total number of 1.84 million words were transcribed into texts.

We selected these three corpora because we tried to include as many different stylistic features as possible. The newspaper corpus represents formal written language because of the rigor, formality and openness. The novel corpus includes popular literary works on the Internet hence it possesses obvious, intelligible and entertaining characteristics. Apart from a lot of character dialogues in novels, there are also many formal written languages so the novel corpus is between the written language and the spoken language. In terms of spoken corpus, obviously, it represents the demotic spoken language.

### 3.2    Data Processing

(1) Process corpora: Deleted irrelevant codes on web pages (HTML, XML tags etc.), spaces, dates, carriage returns and other unnecessary characters. Converted web pages into txt files and saved them.

(2) Used the Python program to extract *Feichang* and *Tebie* in each corpus and stored the results for further analysis.

(3) Used ICTCLAS (Institute of Computing Technology, Chinese Lexical Analysis System), developed by the Institute of Computing Technology Chinese Academy of Sciences, to segment and tagged the novel corpus and the spoken corpus that we collected.

Note that in the part-of-speech tagging in ICTCLAS, adjectives, adverbs and distinguishing words are marked as /a, /d and /b respectively. The term 'Distinguishing words' in ICTCLAS is same as the non-adjectives words (that represent attributes or categories) in 'Modern Chinese Dictionary', which means the statistics would not be affected. After the part-of-speech tagging, we could find that the annotation of *Feichang* and *Tebie* is exactly the same as the annotation in "Modern Chinese Dictionary": each word has two usages. This also proves that using ICTCLAS would not affect our final statistical result.

(4) Stored the processed results. This is the last step of preparation.

# 4    Data Results

## 4.1    Information Retrieval

Information was retrieved from each processed file by using the Concordance function of AntConc3.2.4. The result is shown in Table 1.

**Table 1.** Term Frequencies in each Corpus

| | | Total | | Adjective | | Adverb | |
|---|---|---|---|---|---|---|---|
| | | Total Freq | Freq per million words | Total Freq | Freq per million words | Total Freq | Freq per million words |
| Newspaper Corpus | Feichang | 244 | 125 | 8 | 4 | 236 | 121 |
| | Tebie | 630 | 324 | 147 | 76 | 483 | 248 |
| Novel Corpus | Feichang | 557 | 169 | 11 | 3 | 534 | 162 |
| | Tebie | 314 | 96 | 68 | 21 | 246 | 75 |
| Spoken Corpus | Feichang | 247 | 134 | 0 | 0 | 238 | 129 |
| | Tebie | 2391 | 1299 | 140 | 76 | 2251 | 1223 |

## 4.2    Word Structure

As we mentioned before, the most common way of using *Feichang* and *Tebie* is as adverb. In this case, they are followed by an adjective, forming a "~ + adjective" or a "~ + de/ di / de + adjective" structure. We only discuss these two cases in detail, and analyze the results statistically after retrieval.

**Table 2.** Frequencies of Different Usages in each Corpus

| | | Adverb | Adverb of Degree | |
|---|---|---|---|---|
| | | Total Freq | Total Freq | Ratio |
| Newspaper Corpus | Feichang | 236 | 156 | 0.661 |
| | Tebie | 483 | 31 | 0.064 |
| Novel Corpus | Feichang | 534 | 345 | 0.646 |
| | Tebie | 246 | 68 | 0.276 |
| Spoken Corpus | Feichang | 238 | 158 | 0.664 |
| | Tebie | 2251 | 1337 | 0.594 |

**Table 3.** Percent Frequency of each Part-of-Speech for *Feichang* and *Tebie* in Different Corpus

| | | As Adjective | As Adverb | As Adverb of Degree in all Adverbs | As Adverb of Degree |
|---|---|---|---|---|---|
| Newspaper Corpus | Feichang | 0.033 | 0.967 | 0.661 | 0.639 |
| | Tebie | 0.233 | 0.767 | 0.064 | 0.049 |
| Novel Corpus | Feichang | 0.020 | 0.959 | 0.646 | 0.619 |
| | Tebie | 0.217 | 0.783 | 0.276 | 0.217 |
| Spoken Corpus | Feichang | 0 | 0.964 | 0.664 | 0.640 |
| | Tebie | 0.059 | 0.941 | 0.594 | 0.559 |

## 4.3    Statistical Analysis

We used analysis software AntConc3.2.4's Collocates function to retrieve the list of words appearing next to *Feichang* and *Tebie* (R-word) and then sorted them by their occurrence frequencies regardless of their parts of speech. The result is shown in Table 4.

**Table 4.-1.** R-word in Newspaper Corpus

|   | Feichang | Total Freq | Freq per million words | Tebie | Total Freq | Freq per million words |
|---|---|---|---|---|---|---|
| 1 | Important | 26 | 13 | Be | 347 | 178 |
| 2 | attach importance to | 22 | 11 | Administrative Region | 89 | 46 |
| 3 | Happy | 8 | 4 | Want | 18 | 9 |
| 4 | Have | 8 | 4 | conference | 17 | 9 |
| 5 | Satisfy | 7 | 4 | "de" | 9 | 5 |
| 6 | Good | 7 | 4 | Emphasize | 9 | 5 |
| 7 | Necessary | 4 | 2 | At | 8 | 4 |
| 8 | Big | 4 | 2 | attach importance to | 7 | 4 |
| 9 | Like | 4 | 2 | pay attention to | 7 | 4 |
| 10 | Arduous | 3 | 1 | lay stress on | 5 | 3 |
| 11 | "de" | 3 | 1 | "dui" (to/for) | 4 | 2 |
| 12 | Democratic | 3 | 1 | Consultant | 3 | 1 |
| 13 | Broad | 3 | 1 | Important | 3 | 1 |
| 14 | Many | 3 | 1 | Committee | 3 | 1 |
| 15 | grim | 3 | 1 | Many | 3 | 1 |

**Table 4.-2.** R-word in Novel Corpus

|   | Feichang | Total Freq | Freq per million words | Tebie | Total Freq | Freq per million words |
|---|---|---|---|---|---|---|
| 1 | "de" | 154 | 47 | Be | 101 | 31 |
| 2 | Good | 17 | 5 | "de" | 52 | 16 |
| 3 | "zhi" | 14 | 4 | Good | 10 | 3 |
| 4 | Not | 13 | 4 | Like | 10 | 3 |
| 5 | Have | 11 | 3 | Many | 8 | 2 |
| 6 | Reasonable | 8 | 2 | "zhi" | 8 | 2 |
| 7 | Want | 7 | 2 | Have | 6 | 2 |
| 8 | Big | 5 | 2 | Excellent | 3 | 1 |
| 9 | Difficult | 4 | 1 | Not | 3 | 1 |
| 10 | Terrible | 4 | 1 | Still | 2 | 1 |

**Table 4.-2.** (*continued*)

| 11 | Pretty | 4 | 1 | Careful | 2 | 1 |
|---|---|---|---|---|---|---|
| 12 | Satisfy | 4 | 1 | Can | 2 | 1 |
| 13 | Clear | 4 | 1 | Pretty | 2 | 1 |
| 14 | Great | 4 | 1 | Thank | 2 | 1 |
| 15 | fast | 4 | 1 | Little | 2 | 1 |

**Table 4.-3.** R-word in Spoken Corpus

| | Feichang | Total Freq | Freq per million words | Tebie | Total Freq | Freq per million words |
|---|---|---|---|---|---|---|
| 1 | "di" | 24 | 13 | Be | 207 | 112 |
| 2 | Good | 19 | 10 | Many | 164 | 89 |
| 3 | Important | 8 | 4 | Good | 147 | 80 |
| 4 | Joyful | 7 | 4 | "di" | 102 | 55 |
| 5 | Not | 7 | 4 | Big | 70 | 38 |
| 6 | Happy | 6 | 3 | Like | 59 | 32 |
| 7 | Nervous | 5 | 3 | "de" | 50 | 27 |
| 8 | "de" | 5 | 3 | Little | 46 | 25 |
| 9 | Crowded | 5 | 3 | Love | 41 | 22 |
| 10 | Big | 5 | 3 | Not | 41 | 22 |
| 11 | Emphasize | 4 | 2 | Happy | 37 | 20 |
| 12 | Laborious | 4 | 2 | Nervous | 37 | 20 |
| 13 | Like | 4 | 2 | Tall | 33 | 18 |
| 14 | Delighted | 3 | 2 | Have | 30 | 16 |
| 15 | love | 3 | 2 | Crowd | 23 | 13 |

# 5    Analysis and Discussion

## 5.1    Analysis of Adverb Usage

We can learn from Table 2 and Table 3 that *Feichang* is mainly used as adverb and the proportions of this usage in all three corpora are higher than 95%. Among its adverb usages, the adverb of degree ('~ + adjective' or a '~ + de/ di / de + adjective' structure) is the mostly used case and the proportions of this usage are all higher than 60%. The usage of word *Feichang* in three corpora is relatively balanced, which means that the usage of *Feichang* in written language, intermediate language and spoken language is relatively balanced. There are a lot of discussions about using *Feichang* as a distinguishing word, such as [4], [6], and [8] and [12], but their opinions are different to each other and none of them is recognized by authorities yet.

From the obtained data, we can see that this usage is not a common usage, and it often appears in newspaper articles, for example, 非常时期[*FeichangShiqi*](*special period*), 非常阶段[*FeichangJieduan*](*special period*), and TV programs 非常了得 [*FeichangLiaode*](*Very Talented*), and 非常男女[*FeichangNannv*](*Special Boys & Girls*).

Also, *Tebie* is mainly used as adverb, but the proportion is less than that in *Feichang*. The adverb usage proportion of *Tebie* in each corpus varies. The proportions in newspaper corpus and novel corpus are 76.7% and 78.3%, but it reaches 94.1% in spoken corpus. It is worthwhile noting that the proportion of adverb of degree in *Tebie* is also less than that *Feichang*. In newspaper corpus, adverb of degree only accounts for 6.4% and 4.9% of the total usages of adverb and the total grammatical usages. In novel corpus, this usage accounts for 27.6% of the total usages of adverb, and 21.7% of the total grammatical usages. But in spoken corpus, this usage is 59.4% of the total usages of adverb, and 55.9% of the total grammatical usages. Thus, the usage of word *Tebie* in three corpora is not balanced, but adverb is still outstanding. When *Tebie* is used as an adjective, it often appears in newspaper articles in the form of 特别行政区[*TebieXingzhengqu*](*Special Administrative Region*), 特别会议 [*TebieHuiyi*](*special conference*), or "Tebie + 'de' + noun" in oral Chinese. In brief, the usage of *Tebie* is more diverse than *Feichang*. For further information about *Tebie*, please refer to [10], [13].

## 5.2     Analysis of Usage Distribution on the Different Registers

We can also learn from Table 1 and Table 2 that the frequencies of *Feichang* in the three corpora are 125, 169 and 134 per million words. It shows that *Feichang* is used more frequently in semi-formal language and spoken language. This is because it is always in a reduplicated structure, such as 非常非常好[*FeichangFeichangHao*](*very very good*) and 非常非常重要[*FeichangFeichangZhongyao*](*very very important*). That is not suitable for newspaper article's language style. When *Feichang* is used as an adjective, the frequencies are 4, 3 and 0 per million words and when it is used as adverb of degree, the frequencies are 80, 105 and 86 per million words. It is easy to calculate that its frequency in semi-formal language is 1.31 times of in written language and 1.22 times of in spoken language.

The frequencies of *Tebie* in the three corpora are 324, 96 and 1299 per million words. It shows that *Tebie* is used mostly in spoken language, and its frequency is 4 times of in written language, and 13.53 times of in semi-formal language. When *Tebie* is used as an adjective, the frequencies are 76, 21 and 76 per million words and when it is used as adverb of degree, the frequencies are 248, 75 and 1223 per million words. It is easy to find that its frequency in spoken language is 4.93 times of in written language and 16.31 times of in semi-formal language.

From the above statistics we can see that people prefer using *Tebie* in newspaper corpus, but they would use *Feichang* instead for adverb of degree. In novel corpus, *Feichang* is more used than *Tebie*, while in spoken corpus, the preferences are opposite. It means that *Feichang* possesses stronger stylistic feature of written language. While *Tebie* is a colloquial word, since people usually and largely use it in oral communication to emphasize.

### 5.3    Analysis of the Degree of the Interchangeability

We can learn from Table 4 that among the top 10 common collocations in newspaper corpus, there are 6 adjectives collocating with *Feichang*, but there is no adjective collocating with *Tebie*. The first adjective collocating with it is the 13th word, 重要 [*Zhongyao*](*important*), whose frequency is only 1.5 per million words. It is much lower than 13 (per million words) in *Feichang*.

Obviously, the interchangeability of *Feichang* and *Tebie* in newspaper corpus, i.e. in written language is relatively low. Especially when they are used as adverb of degree collocating with an adjective, people prefer *Feichang* rather than *Tebie*.

In novel corpus, there are 9 adjectives collocating with *Feichang*, and 6 with *Tebie*. And there are 2 adjectives collocating with both *Feichang* and *Tebie*, they are 好 [*Hao*](*good*) and 漂亮[*Piaoliang*](*pretty*) which is 15.38%. Their collocation probabilities in *Feichang* and *Tebie* are very close to each other. It indicates that *Feichang* and *Tebie* are interchangeable in a small area in novel corpus, i.e. in semi-formal language; people use 非 常 好 [*FeichangHao*](*very good*), 非 常 漂 亮 [*FeichangPiaoliang*](*very pretty*), and 特别好[*TebieHao*](*very good*), 特别漂亮 [*TebiePiaoliang*](*very pretty*) at a similar frequency.

It is interesting that we found that the collocation probability of structure "*Feichang* +'bu (not)'+ ∼" is much higher than structure "*Tebie* +'bu (not)'+ ∼". We may draw a conclusion that people prefer using *Feichang* in collocations to express negative tone in novels.

In spoken corpus, there are 9 adjectives collocating with *Feichang*, and 7 with *Tebie*. Also, there are 4 adjectives collocating with both *Feichang* and *Tebie*. They are 好[*Hao*](*good*), 大[*Da*](*big*), 高兴[*Gaoxing*](*happy*) and 紧张[*Jinzhang*](*nervous*) which account for 33.33%. It is obvious that the frequencies of 特 别 好 [*TebieHao*](*very good*), 特别大[*TebieDa*](*very big*), 特别高兴[*TebieGaoxing*](*very happy*) and 特别紧张[*TebieJinzhang*](*very nervous*) are much higher than 非常好 [*FeichangHao*](*very good*), 非 常 大 [*FeichangDa*](*very big*), 非常高兴 [*FeichangGaoxing*](*very happy*) and 非常紧张[*FeichangJinzhang*](*very nervous*).

Therefore, there is interchangeability between *Feichang* and *Tebie* to some extent in spoken corpus, but the difference is that people prefer *Tebie* rather than *Feichang*.

In conclusion, although Chinese synonyms *Feichang* and *Tebie* have many common features in their basic semantics and grammatical functions, there are still some differences in use that people should pay attention to. For example, the degree of the interchangeability from high to low is spoken language, semi-formal language and written language. It is also one aspect that shows the different features of these three language styles: the rigor and formality of written language against the popularity and arbitrariness of spoken language. Besides, regarding to certain words and their collocations, people do have strong preferences.

In addition, from [13], there is an opinion that believes *Tebie* has the meaning of 非 常 [*Feichang*](*very*). It also means 特 地 [*Tedi*](*particularly*) and 着 重 [*Zhuozhong*](*especially*). Hence, in terms of the tone of voice, the severity of *Tebie* is slightly higher than *Feichang* However, if *Feichang* is used repeatedly, the severity would increase, which lays more emphasis on the unusualness of the parts it describes. In that situation, the severity is similar to *Tebie*. In other words, *Tebie* equals to "Feichang Feichang". In Han Rongzhu's summary of the usage for degree of adverbs, he believes *Feichang* expresses high extent and *Tebie* expresses extreme extent. These researches can also help us to understand the subtle differences between *Feichang* and *Tebie* from different aspects so that we can use them more precisely.

## 6    Conclusion

From the process and statistical research on the three corpora, *Feichang* and *Tebie* are both mostly used as adverb, particularly used to denote degree. *Feichang* is rarely used as adjective and *Tebie*'s non-adverb usage is a bit higher. In terms of registers, *Feichang* is more likely to be used in written language while *Tebie* is more in spoken language. From the interchangeability point of view, they can be replaced by each other to some extent, such as in spoken language. We have also noticed that in some other context, these two words cannot be changed by the other, such as in newspaper articles.

This paper's analysis explains that *Feichang* and *Tebie* are only partially identical. Their meanings and voice of tones are a little different and the usage and collocations are also different in varies registers. Therefore, we need to fully use corpus linguistics method to analyze different corpora to understand and use synonyms correctly.

## References

1. Huang, C., Zhao, H.: Chinese Word Segmentation: A Decade Review. Journal of Chinese Information Processing 5(21) (2007)
2. Zhu, H., Zeng, Z.: Analysis on "Tebie" and "Youqi". Modern Chinese 2 (2010)
3. Pu, H., Guo, S.: On the Characteristics, Range and Classification of Adverbs of Degree. Journal of Shanxi University (Philosophy and Social Sciences) 2 (2003)
4. Gong, J.: Complex "Feichang". Modern Chinese 4 (2008)
5. Pang, K.: Analysis on distinguishing words. Journal of Shangqiu Teachers College 6(19) (2003)
6. Deng, L.: Study on "Feichang+N". Journal of Sichuan College of Education 19(7) (2003)
7. Wei, N.: The Methodology and Related Notions of Corpus Linguistics. Foreign Languages Research 5 (2009)
8. Yu, Q.: The "Feichang" Phrase - A Linguistic Phenomenon Calling for Special Attention and Study. Applied Linguistics 1 (2000)
9. Han, R.: The Degree Adverbs in Modern Chinese. Chinese Language Learning 2 (2002)
10. Zhang, S., Liu, H.: Word class position of distinguishing words in modern Chinese. Journal of Huaibei Coal Industry Teachers' College (Philosophy and Social Sciences) 10(29) (2008)
11. Ding, X.: The development and research of corpus linguistics. Contemporary Linguistics 1 (1998)
12. Zhang, Y.: The modern trend of Chinese rhetoric learning in the perspective of an unacquainted collocation "Feichang X". Rhetoric Learning 2 (2008)
13. Huang, Y.: A Comprehensive Analysis of "Very" and "Special". Journal of China Three Gorges University (Humanities & Social Sciences) 6(31) (2009)

# Inchoative State of Emotions

Shan Wang[1,2] and Chu-Ren Huang[1]

[1] Dept. of Chinese and Bilingual Studies, The Hong Kong Polytechnic University,
Hung Hom, Kowloon, Hong Kong
[2] Division of Linguistics and Multilingual Studies, Nanyang Technological University,
HSS-03-31, 14 Nanyang Drive, Singapore 637332
shan.wang@connect.polyu.hk, churen.huang@polyu.edu.hk

**Abstract.** This paper provided two linguistic evidences to identify the inchoation of emotions: 開始 *kāishǐ* 'begin' and (不)起來 *(bù)qǐlái* 'literally (not) stand up, meaning (not) begin to'. It collected and annotated the data in Sinica Corpus and Gigaword Corpus based on some guidelines. Compared to Chang et al. (2000), our results indicate that though in total Type A emotions (such as 高興 *gāoxìng* 'happy') outnumber Type B emotions (such as 快樂 *kuàilè* 'joyful') in expressing inchoation (Chang et al. 2000); depression and sadness of Type B has a higher tendency of being inchoative. This research not only deepens the understanding to emotion, but also helps question-answering tasks in natural language processing.

**Keywords:** inchoative state, emotion, corpus.

## 1 Introduction

Various emotions are common human feelings. Tremendous amount of work has been conducted to emotions in the fields of computational linguistics, linguistics, neurosciences, etc.. However, very few studies have concerned about the inchoation of emotions. This paper answers these questions: (a) Emotions usually last in human mind for some time. Is there any linguistic evidence that indicates the inchoation of emotions? (b) How to collect and annotate suitable data? (c) Do different types of emotions differ in expressing inchoation?

By answering these questions, this research not only deepens the understanding to emotion, but also helps question-answering tasks in natural language processing.

## 2 Ways to Identify the Inchoation of Emotions

Chang et al. (2000) noticed that verbs of emotion can represent either a homogeneous state or an inchoative state. They used 了 *le* 'perfective aspect' to differentiate the two states. In (1), 高興 *gāoxìng* 'happy' is a homogenous state, while in (2) it is an inchoative state. The results are shown in Table 1.

P. Liu and Q. Su (Eds.): CLSW 2013, LNAI 8229, pp. 135–142, 2013.

(1) 他 的 朋友 非常 高興。(Sinica)
Tāde péngyǒu fēicháng gāoxìng.
his    friend    very       happy
'His friends are very happy.'

(2) 這時 我 又 高興 了 起來 。(Sinica)
Zhèshí      wǒ   yòu   gāoxìng
At this time   I     again   glad
le          qǐlái.
Perfective aspect begin to
'At this time I was glad again.'

**Table 1.** Verbs of Emotional Association with the Sentential Final Particle 了 le 'perfective aspect'

| Subtypes | Type A | | | Type B | | | Typ e A / Typ e B |
|---|---|---|---|---|---|---|---|
| | Words | | Freque ncy | Words | | Freque ncy | |
| happiness | 高興 | gāoxìng | 'happy' | 20 | 快樂 | kuàilè | 'cheerful' | 10 | 2.0 |
| depression | 難過 | nánguò | 'grieved' | 9 | 痛苦 | tòngkǔ | 'painful' | 0 | 0 |
| sadness | 傷心 | shāngxīn | 'sad' | 2 | 悲傷 | bēishāng | 'sorrowful' | 1 | 2.0 |
| regret | 後悔 | hòuhuǐ | 'regret' | 7 | 遺憾 | yíhàn | 'regretful' | 0 | 0 |
| angry | 生氣 | shēngqì | 'angry' | 14 | 憤怒 | fènnù | 'wrathful' | 0 | 0 |
| fear | 害怕 | hàipà | 'be afraid' | 5 | 恐懼 | kǒngjù | 'fear' | 2 | 2.5 |
| worry | 擔心 | dānxīn | 'worry' | 6 | 煩惱 | fánnǎo | 'trouble' | 3 | 2.0 |

Aspectualizers can be used to test the stage of an event (Freed 1979, Brinton 1988, Smith 1991, 1994). 開始kāishǐ 'begin', 起來qǐlái 'literally stand up, meaning begin to ', 中斷zhōngduàn 'interrupt', 停止tíngzhǐ 'stop', 結束jiéshù 'end', and 完成 wánchéng 'complete' are common aspectualizers in Mandarin Chinese (Wang 2012, Wang & Huang 2013). Out of them, 開始kāishǐ 'begin' and 起來qǐlái 'literally stand up, meaning begin to; meaning begin to' can illustrate the inchoation of an event (Chang 1994, Huang & Chang 1996). For example, 跑起來pǎo qǐlái 'begin running' means the start up of the running event. This paper applies the aspectualizers開始 kāishǐ 'begin' and (不) 起來 (bù)qǐlái 'literally (not) stand up, meaning (not) begin to' to test the initiation of emotions. 0 is an instance of using 開始kāishǐ 'begin' to represent inchoation and 0 is an example of using 起來qǐlái 'literally stand up, meaning begin to' to represent it.

(3) 不少 球迷 開始 傷心 。(gigaword)
Bùshǎo     qiúmí      kāishǐ   shāngxīn.
Not a few   ball fan   begin   sad
'Not a few ball fans began feeling sad.'

(4) 談到 狗 ， 阿杜 忍不住 難過 起來。(gigaword)
Tándào        gǒu, Ā-dù   rěnbuzhù
speaking of   dog   A-do   could not help but

nánguò  qǐlái.
sad          begin to
'Speaking of dogs, A-do could not help but sad.'

# 3    Annotation Guidelines

The data collected in this paper are taken from two corpora: Academia Sinica Balanced Corpus of Modern Chinese (Sinica Corpus)[1] and Chinese Gigaword Corpus (2nd edition)[2]. The former is a Mandarin Chinese corpus containing 10 million words. The texts in the corpus are collected from different sources, such as philosophy, science, arts, etc. The later contains a total of 1.1 billion characters from Taiwan's Central News Agency China's Xinhua News agency and Singapore's Zaobao.  Both corpora are segmented and tagged with Part-of-Speech.

Chang et al. (2000) classified emotion verbs into seven subtypes, namely happiness, depression, sadness, regret, angry, fear, and worry. They identified a total of 33 verbs, each with a frequency of over 40 in Sinica Corpus as listed in Table 2.

**Table 2.** Verbs of Emotion with a Frequency of over 40 in Sinica Corpus

|            | 快樂   | kuàilè    | 'cheerful'  |
|------------|--------|-----------|-------------|
|            | 高興   | gāoxìng   | 'happy'     |
|            | 愉快   | yúkuài    | 'pleasant'  |
|            | 樂     | lè        | 'joy'       |
| happiness  | 喜悅   | xǐyuè     | 'joyous'    |
|            | 開心   | kāixīn    | 'joyful'    |
|            | 歡樂   | huānlè    | 'gay'       |
|            | 歡喜   | huānxǐ    | 'joy'       |
|            | 快活   | kuàihuo   | 'merry'     |
|            | 痛快   | tòngkuài  | 'delighted' |
|            | 痛苦   | tòngkǔ    | 'painful'   |
|            | 難過   | nánguò    | 'grieved'   |
| depression | 沉重   | chénzhòng | 'heavy'     |
|            | 沮喪   | jǔsàng    | 'depressed' |
|            | 痛心   | tòngxīn   | 'distressed'|

---

[1] http://www.sinica.edu.tw/SinicaCorpus/
[2] http://www.ldc.upenn.edu/Catalog/CatalogEntry.jsp?
catalogId=LDC2005T14

**Table 2.** (*continued*)

| | | | |
|---|---|---|---|
| sadness | 傷心 | *shāngxīn* | 'sad' |
| | 悲傷 | *bēishāng* | 'sorrowful' |
| regret | 遺憾 | *yíhàn* | 'regretful' |
| | 後悔 | *hòuhuǐ* | 'repent ' |
| anger | 生氣 | *shēngqì* | 'angry' |
| | 氣 | *qì* | 'angry' |
| | 憤怒 | *fènnù* | 'wrathful' |
| | 氣憤 | *qìfèn* | 'indignant' |
| fear | 怕 | *pà* | 'fear' |
| | 害怕 | *hàipà* | 'be afraid' |
| | 恐懼 | *kǒngjù* | 'fear' |
| | 畏懼 | *wèijù* | 'awe' |
| worry | 擔心 | *dānxīn* | 'worry' |
| | 煩惱 | *fánnǎo* | 'trouble' |
| | 擔憂 | *dānyōu* | 'be anxious' |
| | 煩 | *fán* | 'bother' |
| | 憂心 | *yōuxīn* | 'sorrow' |
| | 苦惱 | *kǔnǎo* | 'distressed' |

We used the emotion words in Chang et al. (2000) as keywords and collected all data in two structures: (i) 開始*kāishǐ* 'begin' +emotion word, with window size as 5 tokens, and (ii) emotion word +(不)起來*(bù)qǐlái* 'literally (not) stand up, meaning (not) begin to', with window size as 1 token. These data are not ready to use, so we made the following annotation guidelines. The annotated data are free for sharing.

(I) Disambiguate emotional words with multiple meanings. For example, 生氣 *shēngqì* 'angry' is a homonym. Chinese WordNet divides it into 生氣1 *shēngqì* 'angry' 1 and 生氣2 *shēngqì* 'angry' 2 as shown in Table 3 and Table 4.

Only 生氣1 *shēngqì* 'angry' 1 has emotional meaning, while 生氣2 *shēngqì* 'angry' 2 does not. When we automatically collect the 生氣*shēngqì* 'angry' sentences from Sinica Corpus, both 生氣*shēngqì* 'angry' are included. As both Sinica Corpus and Gigaword Corpus are not tagged with word senses, we must manually exclude 生氣2 *shēngqì* 'angry' 2 from our study.

(II) Make clear the modifying relation between 開始 *kāishǐ* 'begin' and the emotions.

**Table 3.** Senses of 生氣1 *shēngqì* 'angry' [1]

生氣1　ㄕㄥ　ㄑㄧˋ　　　*shēngqì* 'angry'

| 詞義 01：不及物動詞，VH | |
|---|---|
| 領域 | |
| 釋義 | 形容因不符合自己的心意而產生不愉快的情緒。 |
| 語義關係 | 同義詞「氣(0700)」、「生 1(1510)」 |
| 英文對譯 | fume, 01225225V, |
| 例句 | 改到成績不好的同學，錯！錯！錯！三十分，就令我很<生氣>。 |
| | 他從來不惹母親<生氣>，有好吃的食物總讓母親先吃，對母親非常孝順。 |
| | 總覺自己好像被社會欺瞞了些什麼，這種隱約的感覺令她不由<生氣>起來。 |

**Table 4.** Senses of 生氣2 *shēngqì* 'angry' [2]

生氣2　ㄕㄥ　ㄑㄧˋ　　　*shēngqì* 'angry'

| 詞義 01：名詞，Na | |
|---|---|
| 領域 | |
| 釋義 | 普通名詞。生物體所具有的生命力。 |
| 語義關係 | 同義詞「生意 2(0120)」 |
| 英文對譯 | energy, 10119788N, , vitality |
| 例句 | 心中的抑鬱難以形容，生命多采，失去她，彷彿一切都沒有了<生氣>！ |
| | 在我的認識中，她是個完全坦率而<生氣>盎然的靈魂，這些特質倒隱掩了她嬌小的身型。 |
| | 歐威尼已從水源地用塑膠管引水到部落，並在空地開墾，種植小白菜、油菜等，綠油油的顏色，增添不少<生氣>。 |

(5) 在 羅布 林卡 工作 了 43年 的 扎西 對 羅布 林卡 開始 維修 感到 很 高興。(gigaword)

Zài luóbùlínkǎ　　gōngzuò le
at　Norbulingka work　　perfective aspect
43 nián de　zhāxi　duì　　　luóbùlínkǎ
43 year DE　Tashi　towards　Norbulingka
kāishǐ wéixiū gǎndào hěn　gāoxìng.
begin repair feel　　very　happy

'Tashi who worked at Norbulingka for 43 years is very pleased that Norbulingka started repairing. '

In (5), 開始*kāishǐ* 'begin' modifies the common verb 維修*wéixiū* 'repair' rather than the emotion高興*gāoxìng* 'pleased', so it is not the case we want.

(III) When an emotional word is in an adverbial position, it is not modified by 開始 *kāishǐ* 'begin'.

(6) 比賽 雙方 的 教練員 就 開始 愉快 地 接受 了 記者 的 採訪 。 (gigaword)

Bǐsài    shuāngfāng de    jiàoliànyuán jiù
game    both sides    DE   coach              at once
kāishǐ yúkuàide    jiēshòu le
begin   pleasantly accept   perfective marker
jìzhě        de        cǎifǎng.
reporter  DE    inverview

'The coaches of both sides begin pleasantly to accept the reporter's interview.'

In (6), the emotion word 愉快*yúkuài* 'pleasantly' acts like an adverb that modifies 接受*jiēshòu* 'accept'. Thus 開始*kāishǐ* 'begin' does modify 愉快*yúkuài* 'pleasantly' but 接受*jiēshòu* 'accept'. Such cases are not acceptable in this study.

(IV) When an emotion has an epistemic marker ahead, this paper treats 開始*kāishǐ* 'begin' as modifying the emotion.

(7) 在 那 之後 ， 我 就 上場 打球 ， 而 當 我 發現 自己 必須 多一點 士氣 時 ， 開始 感到 愉快 。 (gigaword)

Zàinàzhīhòu, wǒ jiù            shàngchǎng
after that          I     at once    enter the field
dǎqiú,        ér    dāng wǒ fāxiàn zìjǐ          bìxū
play ball   but when I    find    myself   must
duō  yīdiǎn shìqì      shí,        kāishǐ gǎndào
more a little morale    when, begin    feel
yúkuài.
pleasant

'After that, I at once entered the field to play ball; and when I found myself must have a little more morale, I began to feel pleasant.'

In (7), 感到*gǎndào* 'feel' is an epistemic word, which is highly connected to the experiencer of the emotion 愉快*yúkuài* 'pleasant'. For such a case, we treat 開始 *kāishǐ* 'begin' as referring to the emotion 愉快*yúkuài* 'pleasant'.

# 4    Inchoation of Emotions

Chang et al. (2000) further divide the words in Table 2 into Type A and Type B based on five criteria: (a) the distribution of its grammatical functions; (b) its selectional restrictions when it functions as an adjunct; (c) its occurrence in imperative and evaluative constructions; (d) its verbal aspect or aktionsart; (e) its transitivity. The subtypes and words in the two types are as follows.

Type A : (a) happiness: 高興 gāoxìng 'happy', 開心 kāixīn 'joyful', 痛快 tòngkuài 'delighted'; (b) depression: 難過 nánguò 'grieved', 痛心 tòngxīn 'distressed'; (c) sadness: 傷心 shāngxīn 'sad'; (d) regret: 後悔 hòuhuǐ 'regret'; (e) anger: 生氣 shēngqì 'angry'; (f) fear: 害怕 hàipà 'be afraid' ; (g) worry: 擔心 dānxīn 'worry', 擔憂 dānyōu 'be anxious about', 憂心 yōuxīn 'sorrow'.

Type B: (a) happiness: 快樂 kuàilè 'cheerful', 愉快 yúkuài 'pleasant', 喜悅 xǐyuè 'joyous', 歡樂 huānlè 'gay', 歡喜 huānxǐ 'joy', 快活 kuàihuo 'merry'; (b) depression: 痛苦 tòngkǔ 'painful', 沉重 chénzhòng 'heavy', 沮喪 jǔsàng 'depressed'; (c) sadness: 悲傷 bēishāng 'sorrowful'; (d)regret: 遺憾 yíhàn 'regretful'; (e) anger: 憤怒 fènnù 'wrathful', 氣憤 qìfèn 'indignant'; (f) fear: 恐懼 kǒngjù 'fear', 畏懼 wèijù 'awe'; (g) worry: 煩惱 fánnǎo 'trouble', 苦惱 kǔnǎo 'distressed'.

Chang et al. (2000) find that Type A words are predominately inchoative, while Type B words are rarely like this. Our data as a whole supports this conclusion as shown in Table 5. In total, there are 856 cases of Type A that express inchoative states, compared to only 148 cases of Type B.

**Table 5.** Inchoative State of Emotion in both Sinica Corpus and Gigaword Corpus

| Subtypes | Type A | | | Type B | | |
|---|---|---|---|---|---|---|
| | Words | | Frequency | Words | | Frequency |
| happiness | 高興 gāoxìng | 'happy' | 101 | 快樂 kuàilè | 'cheerful' | 49 |
| | 開心 kāixīn | 'joyful' | 16 | 愉快 yúkuài | 'pleasant' | 6 |
| | 痛快 tòngkuài | 'delighted ' | 0 | 喜悅 xǐyuè | 'joyous' | 7 |
| | | | | 歡樂 huānlè | 'gay' | 2 |
| | | | | 歡喜 huānxǐ | 'joy' | 5 |
| | | | | 快活 kuàihuo | 'merry' | 3 |
| depression | 難過 nánguò | 'grieved' | 10 | 痛苦 tòngkǔ | 'painful' | 2 |
| | 痛心 tòngxīn | 'distressed' | 0 | 沉重 chénzhòng | 'heavy' | 28 |
| | | | | 沮喪 jǔsàng | 'depressed' | 4 |
| sadness | 傷心 shāngxīn | 'sad' | 1 | 悲傷 bēishāng | 'sorrowful' | 6 |
| regret | 後悔 hòuhuǐ | 'regret' | 28 | 遺憾 yíhàn | 'regretful' | 0 |
| anger | 生氣 shēngqì | 'angry' | 13 | 憤怒 fènnù | 'wrathful' | 3 |
| | | | | 氣憤 qìfèn | 'indignant' | 0 |
| fear | 害怕 hàipà | 'be afraid' | 56 | 恐懼 kǒngjù | 'fear' | 7 |
| | | | | 畏懼 wèijù | 'awe' | 3 |
| worry | 擔心 dānxīn | 'worry' | 530 | 煩惱 fánnǎo | 'trouble' | 21 |
| | 擔憂 dānyōu | 'be anxious about' | 65 | 苦惱 kǔnǎo | 'distressed' | 2 |
| | 憂心 yōuxīn | 'sorrow' | 36 | | | |
| TOTAL | | | 856 | | | 148 |

However, when we added the total Number of each subtype, we noticed some differences in representing inchoative states as shown in Table 6. When expressing depression, Type A is only 29% of Type B. Similarly, the sadness group of Type A is only 17% of Type B. Moreover, the worry group of Type A contributes a huge portion of the properties of Type A. The results indicate that Type B is more likely to have an inchoative state than Type A when it is a depressive or sad emotion. This is due to the reason that such kind of negative emotions may easy be spotted.

**Table 6.** Total No. of Type A and Type B Emotions in both Sinica Corpus and Gigaword Corpus

| Subtype | Type A No. | Type B No. | Type A / Type B |
|---|---|---|---|
| happiness | 117 | 72 | 1.63 |
| depression | 10 | 34 | 0.29 |
| sadness | 1 | 6 | 0.17 |
| Regret | 28 | 0 | 0 |
| Anger | 13 | 3 | 4.33 |
| Fear | 56 | 10 | 5.60 |
| Worry | 631 | 23 | 27.43 |
| TOTAL | 856 | 147 | 5.82 |

## 5    Conclusions

This paper first proposed two aspectualizers 開始 *kāishǐ* 'begin' and (不)起來 *(bù) qǐlái* 'literally (not) stand up, *meaning* begin to' to identify the inchoation of emotions, which is complementary to the 了 *le* 'perfective aspect' test in Chang et al. (2000). Then it introduced four guidelines for corpus data annotation. With a large data set from both Sinica Corpus and Gigaword Corpus, it re-examined the inchoative state of emotions. It found that though in total Type A emotions outnumber Type B in expressing inchoation, depression and sadness of Type B have a higher tendency of being inchoative.

**Acknowledgments.** This work is supported by a General Research Fund (GRF) sponsored by the Research Grants Council, Hong Kong (Project No. 543810) and the studentship of The Hong Kong Polytechnic University.

## References

Brinton, L.J.: The Development of English Aspectual Systems: Aspectualizers and Post-verbal Particles. Cambridge University Press, Cambridge (1988)

Chang, L.-L., Chen, K.-J., Huang, C.-R.: Alternation Across Semantic Fields: A Study on Mandarin Verbs of Emotion. Computational Linguistics and Chinese Language Processing 5(1), 61–80 (2000)

Chang, S.-M.: V-qi-lai Constructions in Mandarin Chinese: A Study of Their Semantics and Syntax (現代漢語「起來」的語意及句法研究). National Tsing Hua University, Hsinchu (1994)

Freed, A.F.: The Semantics of English Aspectual Complementation. Springer (1979)

Huang, C.-R., Chang, S.-M.: Metaphor, Metaphorical Extension, and. Grammaticalization: A Study of Mandarin Chinese -qilai. In: Goldberg, A.E. (ed.) Conceptual Structure, Discourse, and Language, pp. 201–216. Cambridge University Press, Cambridge (1996)

Smith, C.S.: The Parameter of Aspect. Kluwer Academic Publishers, Boston (1991)

Smith, C.S.: Aspectual Viewpoint and Situation Type in Mandarian Chinese. Journal of East Asian Linguistics 3(2), 107–146 (1994)

Wang, S.: Semantics of Event Nouns. The Hong Kong Polytechnic University, Hong Kong (2012)

Wang, S., Huang, C.-R.: Aspectualizers and Their Selected Nouns. In: Paper presented at The 21st Annual Conference of the International Association of Chinese Linguistics (IACL-21), National Taiwan Normal University, Taiwan (2013)

# Research on the Description of Tibetan Information Domain Frame Semantic Structure[*]

Rdo Rje Sgrol Ma[**]

Northwest University for Nationalities
No.1, Minde Road, Chengguan District, Lanzhou, China
Djzm868@sina.com

**Abstract.** This paper analyzed the frame and the frame semantics based on cases. And it also used the frame as the basic unit for describing Tibetan lexical semantics to build the frame hierarchical structural system in Tibetan information domain, and to describe every sub-property semantic of sub-frame in this system as well. The describtion included definitions of sub-framework, core frame, noncore frame, word element and so on. The description laid the theoretical foundation for achieving further research on series of semantic understanding for Tibetan phrases, sentences, and sections.

**Keywords:** Tibetan, Information, Frame Semantics, Description.

## 1  Information Domain

The term"Information" first appeared in "The Book of Changes"," The middle sun biases west, the full moon goes wane, the world becomes full or empty, the information goes by time. " The phrase means " the noon arrives, the sun is going to the west; the moon will begin to be smaller after it is full; between heaven and earth everything is abundance or weakness, all these information goes by time." So in China since ancient time it concluded that in changes of objective world related with the occurrence, the growth, and the result of itself to their ups and downs, meeting and parting, rise and decline, moving and stationary, gain and loss etc. These phenomena were called information. [1] Recently the "information" gradually becomes a kind of fixed news genre, therefore information is named news. And actually the information is the main part of the news, to report the dissemination of current events. Thus information domain semantic frame describes the situation of the event message exchange with someone or something in the frame. The information is a kind of carrier concerning

---

[*] This paper was supported by Northwest University for Nationalities' Special Funds Project of Central Universities Foundation, the project number is zyz2011102, and National Natural Science Foundation, the project number is 61262053.

[**] Brief introduction of author: Rdo Rje Sgrol Ma (1970-), woman, Qinghai Guide, Associate Professor, Master; the research aspect: Tibetan Frame Semantics, Tibetan Information Process.

P. Liu and Q. Su (Eds.): CLSW 2013, LNAI 8229, pp. 143–152, 2013.

how the people get messages. The messages are contained in the news, and people get the news in order to gain the message. In Tibetan, the information is "mi dang bya dngos kyi gnas tshul sbel ba dang phar tshur bskur bai gtam mam aphrin no"[མི་དང་བྱ་དངོས་ཀྱི་གནས་ཚུལ་སྦེལ་བ་དང་ཕར་ཚུར་བསྐུར་བའི་གཏམ་མམ་འཕྲིན་ནོ།།](For the release of the current situation of People and things and People exchanges between language and letters, etc ) [2]. The sentences containing these words using in Tibetan news mediums such as "agod pa, sbel pa, gtong pa, bsgrgs pa" [འགོད་པ། སྦེལ་པ། གཏོང་པ། བསྒྲགས་པ།](Publish ,issue ,Broadcast, Broadcast) and so on have made a description of exchanging information scene for an event. For example, by reporting a verb "agod pa"[འགོད་པ།]( Report ) it activates this kind of scene—— the information holder of an official or individual (insiders) via TV, newspaper, webs or other forms to report what they knew to share with other side who (groups or individual called informed party) have right to hear. The insiders disseminate the situation of the event information to informed party. At this moment, insiders lost the content of the information or message; the informed party received this information. In this scene it usually included someone who knew the information, someone who need the information, as well as the information implied the content of the information itself. In short, in this scene it needs these participants —— insiders, informed parties, and exchanging message. These scenes could be activated by the word "agod pa" [འགོད་པ།]( Report ) under the   contextual circumstances of news mediums.

## 2    The Frame and Semantic Frame

The "frame" in this paper is not the framework composed by the beams and columns for withstanding the vertical and horizontal loads in civil engineering, but a linguistic term. The term "frame" is first used by anthropologist Bateson in anthropology.[3] But the concept of frame theory was first proposed by American computer scientist Minsky, who thought our knowledge as a form of information structure stored in the memory, it is the frame.[4] The so-called frame is "presenting of a typical scene information structure "and this is frame theory. According to Minsky's frame theory, we can imagine the frame is like a piece of cloth with full of tied nets, every junction in the net supposed to have its own "obligations", which presents some typical feature of its corresponding situation. [5] In the twentieth century after 70s, Charles Fillmore first used Minsky's conception of frame in the field of cognitive science, [6] and after this definition was devised for several times, Fillmore (1992s) thought the frame was the cognitive structure of the word when encoding its definition. From cognitive linguistics, the frame is any kind of conceptual system, to understand any of concepts in this system must know the whole system in advance, referencing any concept will be related to   other concepts in this system. [7] In semantic theory, the frame is about a thing of unchanging class or the structure of encoding the surround knowledge, and specifies the function of each part. [8] All these definitions above, we know that when we recognize Tibetan word "bsgrks pa" [བསྒྲགས་པ།](Announce), besides the elements like "sgrog pa po" [སྒྲོག་པ་པོ།] (Announced the party)( political parties or state organs, individual ) "nyan pa po" [ ཉན་པ་པོ ](Listeners), and "sgrog byi bya ba" [ སྒྲོག་བྱིའི་བྱ་བ ](Theme), we should  know its conceptual structure in advance,  namely the knowledge of semantics frame. The semantics frame provided  the meaning of the word "bsgrags pa"[ བསྒྲགས་པ ](Announce) in Tibetan daily life, and the background and motivation of using it in Tibetan discourse. Bump points of these information foreground and  background  consisted  of  the  frame  of  word  "bsgrags pa"[ བསྒྲགས་པ ](Announce).  Taking word "sgrog pa"[ སྒྲོག་པ ](preach) as an exmple, verb "sgrog pa"[ སྒྲོག་པ ](preach) is focused on  the action between "sgrog pa po[ སྒྲོག་པ་པོ ]" and "sgrog byi bya ba"[ སྒྲོག་བྱིའི་བྱ་བ ](Theme); and "nyan pa po"[ ཉན་པ་པོ ](Listeners) provided  the background information in semantic understanding and described the concept "sgrog pa"[ སྒྲོག་པ ](preach).

The semantic frame is not the meaning of word itself. Although there is similar, close, and related meaning of word its own, it still has distinction between them. In Tibetan "agod pa"[ འགོད་པ ](Publish), "spel gtong"[ སྤེལ་གཏོང ](Broadcast), these words means report, as verbs the lexical meanings is about the information of people or things tells to groups", and "report" has different meaning in different frames. For example "He wrote a report". The semantic frame of "report" in that sentence means "entity (cognitive object)" and reported paper, this shows how the word playing the roles in the frame and meaning of frame elements.[9]

Please consider the sample sentence below:

Example 1: yus hruau sa agul gyi gnod atshe thebs pi yul dngos la song bi gsar agod pas rang kyi mthong thos skor gleng ba.

[ ཡུལ་ཤུལ་ས་འགུལ་གྱི་གནོད་འཚེ་ཐེབས་པའི་ཡུལ་དངོས་ལ་སོང་བའི་གསར་འགོད་པས་རང་ཉིད་ཀྱི་མཐོང་ཐོས་སྐོར་གླེང་བ། ]

(The Reporter who witnessed the Yushu earthquake talks about what he saw and heard.)

The viewpoint of this sentence is "gsar agod pa"[ གསར་འགོད་པ ](Reporter). For the whole sentence, the content of the report is "gsar agod pas rang nyid kyi mthong thos skor gleng ba".[ གསར་འགོད་པས་རང་ཉིད་ཀྱི་མཐོང་ཐོས་སྐོར་ གླེང་བ ]( The Reporter report the thing what he saw and heard.)The preposition "sa"[ ས ](Industry preposition) indicated "gsar agod pa"[ གསར་འགོད་པ ](Reporter) who implemented an action or behavior is talking "gleng ba[ གླེང་བ ]"(Talk). The content of the talking is "mthong thos"[ མཐོང་ཐོས ](One's sees and hears). "yus hruau"[ ཡུལ་ཤུལ ](Yushu) is the place where he saw and heard the information. "sa agul gyi gnod atshe thebs pa"[ ས་འགུལ་གྱི་གནོད་འཚེ་ཐེབས་པ ](Earthquake victims) is the scene being seen and the reason . We could collect those sporadic knowledge, and gather them through the main string——viewpoint, and can form "gleng ba"[ གླེང་བ ](Talk) for convex pointed information domain and semantic sub-frame "gleng ba"[ གླེང་བ ](Talk) in the class of "News report". We are going represent the convex with a graphical as convex and concave points, dashed box (a) represented convex points, and dashed box (b) represented concave points in the example 1, so the whole discourse elements of foreground and background are formed (in picture 1).

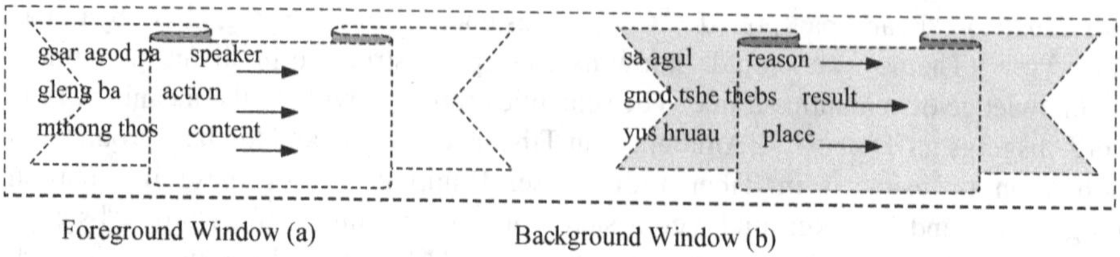


**Fig. 1.** consisted example 1's factors of foreground and background

In terms of example 1, core frame elements of semantic sub-frame "gleng ba"[གླེང་བ།](Talk) is the foreground part which included talker and content of talking. Non-core-frame elements is the back-scene or background part which included contents, means, methods, places, spaces, cause, and goals and so on. The definition of sub-frame, frame core elements and non core elements, and word elements etcetera are consisted of a frame semantic. Therefore, different semantic frame has its own different frame semantic structure; a specific lexical unit with specific sense and relevant frame element are combined "frame semantic structure".

# 3 Description of Tibetan Information Domain Frame Semantic Structure

## 3.1 Tibetan Information Domain Frame Layer Structural System

It is necessary to build a frame category hierarchy system in order to analyze or research Tibetan frame semantics classification and structure easily in some fields. Tibetan information domain falls into four hierarchies. They are information frame domain, information frame sub-domain, information frame class, and information sub-frame. For information frame sub-domain, it devides into news report and message exchange according to information reported form and information disseminated form (in picture 2).

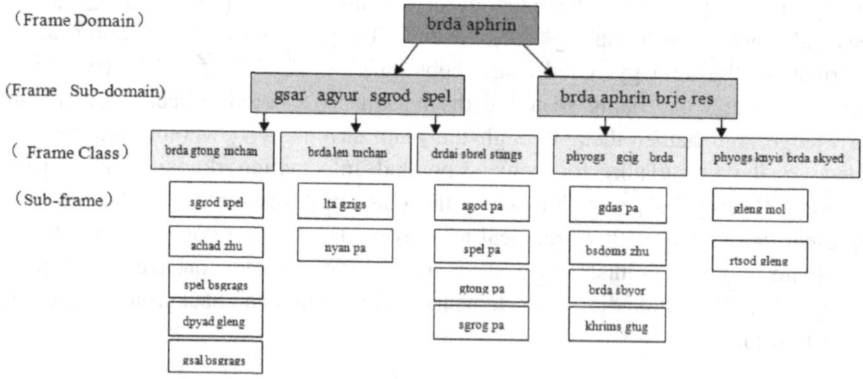


**Fig. 2.** The Information Domain Frame Hierarchical Structural Picture

Among the four hierarchical systems of information domain above, if between domain frame and classified frame, classified frame and subclass frame, sub-frame and sub-domain, sub-frame and sub-frame, it gets two-digit 01-99 to present frame domain, classified frame, subclass frame, and sub-frame valued range, in the hierarchical system word "agod ba"[འགོད་པ](Publish) presented as code 01010301. These following numbers showed word "agod ba"[འགོད་པ](Publish), the name of a sub-frame. Among those numbers: the first 01 means first domain, such as "brda aphrin"[བརྡ་འཕྲིན](Message) in the picture 2 above; the second 01 shows first sub-frame that presented second layer in hierarchical system, such as "gsar akyur sgrog sbel"[གསར་འགྱུར་སྒྲོག་སྦེལ](News report); the third 03 presented the third layer sub-frame in hierarchical system, such as "brdi sbrel stangs"[བརྡའི་སྦྲེལ་སྟངས](Links manner); the fourth 01 presented the first word "agod ba"[འགོད་པ](Publish) in the last layer of sub-frame, it can be used to indicte the frame codes to distinguish the members of sub-frame, such as frame domain, classified frame, and subclass frame. The frame codes present relationship of the frame layers and layers in some sub-frames, as well.

## 3.2    Description of Tibetan Information Domain Sub-frame Property

Description of Tibetan information domain sub-frame property actually is how to use formal presentation to present the semantic property of sub-frame. Thereby we would use every name of sub-frame as the start point to observe this frame name to analyze the usage of Tibetan words in Tibetan linguistic environment; and it also can be research approach of Tibetan interpretation to dig the contained sporadic semantic knowledge and to combine those semantic knowledge together to form a conceptual structure. Therefore, three aspects s going to be mainly described the description of Tibetan information domain sub-frame property below.

### 3.2.1    The Description of Tibetan Information Domain Sub-frame

For sub-frame "sgrog sbel"[སྒྲོག་སྦེལ](Report) in Tibetan information domain, it can be presented by frame code (frame classified hierarchical level number), sub-frame definition, and the description of this frame usage in Tibetan daily life. Look at the description of sub-frame "sgrog sbel"[སྒྲོག་སྦེལ](Report).

Frame code: 01010101
Name of sub-frame: sgrog sbel[སྒྲོག་སྦེལ](Report)
Frame definition: tsgags par dang rgyang sgrog brnyin aphrin sogs brgyud de aphrin    gsar    phyir    sgrog    cing    sbel    bar    fya    bai
[ཚགས་པར་དང་རྒྱང་སྒྲོག་བརྙན་འཕྲིན་སོགས་བརྒྱུད་དེ་འཕྲིན་གསར་ཕྱིར་སྒྲོག་ཅིང་སྦེལ་བར་བྱ་བའོ]
English definition: to tell the crowds about the news through newspapers, magazines, broadcasts, and TVs or other ways, i.e.reported news.

### 3.2.2    The Description of Tibetan Core Information Domain and Non Core Frame

To understand the semantic frame "sgrog sbel"[སྒྲོག་སྦེལ](Report), first the definition of "sgrog sbel"[སྒྲོག་སྦེལ](Report) must be clear , and then from the frame definition of "sgrog sbel"[སྒྲོག་སྦེལ](Report) we could firstly recognize that verb "tell" activating a series of questions from the explanation of the definition "to tell the crowds about the news". For examples, "who told ", "told what", " told whom" and so on.  A series of knowledge points understanding that frame semantic can be gained from these questions, such as "sgrog pa po"[ སྒྲོག་པ་པོ ](Reporter), "sgrog byi bya ba"[ སྒྲོག་བྱེ་བྱ་བ ](Report theme), "nyan pa po"[ ཉན་པ་པོ ](Listener), and "sgrog stangs"[སྒྲོག་སྟངས](Way of reporting). Secondly, the way of "sgrog"[སྒྲོག](Report) are newspapers, magazines, broadcasts, TVs, network etc. They introduce media to report the news or events, in other words what kind of genre the news are used. In that case, the genre and the medium are another important knowledge point we need while understanding the frame semantics. Thirdly, above every knowledge point at process of cognitive understanding of the whole frame definition, some are playing main roles, but some are not; some exist, but some do not; some are necessary, but some are not. Those knowledge points which are necessary factors while understanding the frame semantics are called core frame. Those knowledge points which are less necessary or secondary factors while understanding the frame semantics are named noncore frame. All of the knowledge points will be linked together in the cognitive processes to form the whole frame semantics of sub-frame. Next the frame definition "sgrog sbel"[ སྒྲོག་སྤེལ ](Report) will act as starting point to determine elements of core or noncore frame, and to make semantic descriptions.

**Table 1.** The description of core frame and non core frame property

| Sub-frame | | sgrog spel |
|---|---|---|
| **Frame Interpretation** | | tshags par dang rgyang sgrog brnyan aphrin sogs brgyud de aphrin gsar  phyir sgrog cing spel bar byaao |
| core | brda sgrog mkhan | **reported side** | brda dang gnas tshul phyi la bshad mkhan dper na. a khu ston pas rgyal bor khyi skad sgrod tu bcug. |
| frame | brda spel mkhan | | brda dang gnas tshul sogs phyir khyab ajug pa  nub byang slob chen gyis slob raai glu ba mchog bcu adems sgrug gi agran sdur |
| elements | | | gnas ts hul dra bar bkod. |
| | sgrod byi bya ba | content | aphrin brdaam gnas tshul |
| | aphrin sbyor | medium | aphrin brdaam gnas tshul rnams sgrog byed kyi lag cha ste . tshags par brnyan aphrin rgayng sgrog  agrem brda la sogs na |
| | sgrog yul | object | aphrin brdaam gnas tshul sogs sgrog pai yul aphrin gsar bsgrags nas mi yongs la shes su ajug. |
| non | sgrog stangs | mode | aphrin brdaam gnas tshul sogs phyir sgrog par byed pai rnam paam byed thabs |
| core | Brdai kha phyogs | aspect | skad dang brda la sogs pa sprod par byed paai kha phyogs. dper na. tshogs aduai dgongs don phyi la bsgrags. |
| frame | | | |
| elements | brgyud rim | approach | go rim du ma adus paai don. dper na. zas mi lag brgyud nas song na je n     yung yin. gtam mi kha brgyud nas bshad na je mang yin |
| | dus tshod | time | aphrin brdaam gnas tshul khyab sgrog byed paai dus. |
| | rgyu rkyen | reason | bya baam dngos po gang rung zhig    dper na. sman bcos byas pas nad sel. skyed paai rgyu rkyen |
| | abras bu | result | rgyu rkyen sna tshogs kyi dbang gis bskyed paai abras bur go. |

Sgrog sbel[ སྒྲོག་སྦེལ་ |](frame definition): tsgags par dang rgyang sgrog brnyin aphrin sogs brgyud de aphrin gsar phyir sgrog cing sbel bar fya bai

[ ཚགས་པར་དང་རྒྱང་སྒྲོག་བརྙན་འཕྲིན་སོགས་བརྒྱུད་དེ་འཕྲིན་གསར་ཕྱིར་སྒྲོག་ཅིང་སྦེལ་བར་བྱ་བའི།] [10] ( We use through newspapers, radio, television and other media to spread the news) From definition "sgrog cing sbel"[ སྒྲོག་ཅིང་སྦེལ་བ ](Transmission) elicited "sgrog mkhan"[ སྒྲོག་མཁན ](Communicators), "sbel mkhan"[ སྦེལ་མཁན ], "sgrog byi ba"[ སྒྲོག་བྱེད་བྱ་བ ](Communication), "sgrog stang"[ སྒྲོག་སྟངས ](Mode of transmission), "brdi kha phyogs"[ བརྡི་ཁ་ཕྱོགས](Direction), "aphrin sbyor"[ འཕྲིན་སྦྱོར ](Media) and so on. From verb "brgyud"[བརྒྱུད ](Through)" the medium of news report was educed, such as "tshags par"[ ཚགས་པར ](News paper), "rgyang sgrog"[ རྒྱང་སྒྲོག ](Broadcast), "bryan aphrin"[བརྙན་འཕྲིན ](Television). And "aphrin gsar"[འཕྲིན་གསར](News) is a form of the news report. Then, core frame and noncore frame of the frame "sgrog sbel"[ སྒྲོག་སྦེལ་ |](Report ) is below. (In table 1).

### 3.2.3   The Description of Tibetan Information Domain Lexical Units

In the frame system, each frame includs its own corresponding lexical units, which has the same background of frame semantics. The lexical unit is a combination of a word and a sense, which means ithas a specific meaning. For example, the report frame "sgrog sbel"[ སྒྲོག་སྦེལ་ |](Report) involves the following lexical units "sgrog sbel"[ སྒྲོག་སྦེལ་ |](Report), "sgrog pa"[ སྒྲོག་པ |](preach), "bsgrag pa"[ བསྒྲག་པ ], "bkod pa"[ བཀོད་པ ], "sbel pa"[ སྦེལ་པ ](issue), "gtong ba"[ གཏོང་བ ](Broadcast), "bsgrags pa"[ བསྒྲགས་པ ](Announce), "bshad pa"[ བཤད་པ ](Say), "khrom bsgrags"[ ཁྲོམ་བསྒྲགས ](Announcement), "gsal bsgrags"[ གསལ་བསྒྲགས ](Explanation), "bkod"[བཀོད](announce), "bshad na[ བཤད་ན ] etc. We look at some examples as follow,

Example 1: One piece of Tibetan news of Qinghai People's Radio and Television in January 2013.

si ri yvai aphrin gtong <sub>&lt;sgrog mkhan&gt;</sub> gis <sub>&lt;gyed sgra&gt;</sub> bsgrags <sub>&lt;bya tshig&gt;</sub> ai <sub>&lt;abrel sgra&gt;</sub> gnas tshul <sub>&lt;bya ba&gt;</sub> ltar na <sub>&lt;sbyor tshig&gt;</sub>. tshes bcu bzhiai nyin <sub>&lt;dus tshod&gt;</sub> si ri yvai srid gzhung dmag dpung dang ngo rgol phyogs gi drag chos pa <sub>&lt;akrug rtshod byed mkhan&gt;</sub> sa <sub>&lt;byed sgra&gt;</sub> si ri yvai rgyal sa tva mva hri kiai lho nub nye adabs kyi muau aa tva mus yva grong rdal <sub>&lt;sa gnas&gt;</sub> nas <sub>&lt;gnas gzhi&gt;</sub> akhrug rtshod byas <sub>&lt;rgyu rkyen&gt;</sub> te <sub>&lt;lhag bcas kyi phrad&gt;</sub>. mi bcu gsum rkyen lam du shor <sub>&lt;mjug abras&gt;</sub>.

སི་རི་ཡུའི་འཕྲིན་གཏོང་ཁང་ གིས་མ་བསྒྲགས་པ་ ཨེ་རྒྱུ་ འབྲེལ་སྒྲ་ གནས་ཚུལ་ ཆགས་ ལྟར་ན་ སྦྱོར་ ཚིག་ཚེས་བཅུ་བཞིའི་

ཉིན་ དུས་ཚོད་སི་རི་ཡུའི་སྲིད་གཞུང་དམག་དཔུང་དང་དང་ངོ་རྒོལ་ཕྱོགས་ཀྱི་དྲག་ཆོས་པ་ སསི་རི་ཡུའི་རྒྱལ་ས་ཏྭ་མྭ་ཧི་ཀིའི་ ལྷོ་ནུབ་ཉེ་འདབས་ཀྱི་མུའུ་ཨཱ་ཏྭ་མུས་ཡྭ་གྲོང་རྡལ་ནས་ གནས་གཞིའཁྲུག་རྩོད་བྱས་ ཏེ།ལྷག་བཅས་ མི་བཅུ་གསུམ་ རྐྱེན་ལམ་དུ་ཤོར།མཇུག་འབྲས།

Example 2: An English report.

According to the Syrian News Agency's <sub>&lt;reported side&gt;</sub> report <sub>&lt;word element&gt;</sub>, Syrian government army and armed opposition <sub>&lt;the two side of fighters &gt;&lt;the time&gt;</sub> in Syrian capital city Damacus at southwest suburbs of Jose Adami Town <sub>&lt;fighting place &gt;</sub> fought <sub>&lt;event /reason&gt;</sub> to cause 13 people died <sub>&lt; the result &gt;</sub> on 14<sup>th</sup>.

Through examples above, we can realize the verb lexicag mkhan" རྟོག་ཨསན། > (reported side), "dus tshod" དུས་ཚོད > (the time), "sa gnas" ས་གནས > (the place), "rgyul unit "sgrags pa" < བསྒྲགས་པ > as objective word (it s a word that can activate a frame in a certain sentence.) in this sentence. The frame elements for activating a frame are "bya ba" བྱ་བ > (the event), "sgro rkyen" སྒྲོ་རྐྱེན ?(the reason), "mjug abras" འཇུག་འབྲས> (the result) etc. These frame elements activate the whole frame.

### 3.2.4    The Features of Tibetan Information Domain Sub-frame Semantics

The word elements appeared in the report "sgrog sbel"[ སྒྲོག་སྦེལ ](Report) are sub-frame. lexical units in Tibetan information domain. Mainly the verb elements take place in report class, such as "sgrod pa"[ སྒྲོད་པ ](preach), "bsgrag pa"[ བསྒྲག་པ](preach), "sbel    pa"[  སྦེལ་པ  ](issue),    "gtong    ba"[   གཏོང་བ   ](Broadcast),    "bsgrags pa"[ བསྒྲགས་པ ](Announce) and so on. All these verbs show that the reported side has information. Through report behavior it lead the information holder side would make changes about right to know the truth and the range; the information shift from holder side to unknown side, the action is independent, the direction of the action is outgoing. The process of the implementation of the action is first to report and then to learn the situation. Thereby, the information domain lexical units can activate a group of the semantic features, which could be described as: [+ independent events] and [+shifting from right to know the truth into passenger side].

## 4    Knowledge Representation of Tibetan Information Domain Frame Semantics

There are four hierarchical systems in Tibetan information domain frame. They are one frame domain, two frame sub domains, five frame classes and seventeen frame forms. The frame reflects a scene of discourse. Each frame has a related inferior hierarchical frame. Therefore, in other words the scene is bigger or smaller, and it also has classified hierarchies; the frame also has classified hierarchies as well. Semantic frame is a multi-hierarchical system, which could be divided into frame domain, frame sun domain, frame class, sub-frame etc. Different hierarchy between frame and frame or same hierarchy between frame and frame are related, but different with each other. They consisted of an organic frame hierarchical network system, which is called frame network for short. If we use frame network to present Tibetan information frame semantics the specific expressed as follows:

```
Frame classes :: =<frame1>|<frame2>|<frame3>……
    Frames   :: =< ZWGNY(concept smantics oriinal frame  )><ZWCHY ( word meaning
              frame)>
    ZWGNY:: =[ZSBT (representation body groove)] & <YYJS (semantic role
              groove)>
        ZSBT:: =string(the elements in the smallest indivisible concept
              collections)
      YYJS:: =string(the elements in the semantic relationships)
      string:: =word sequences (meta-language symbols)
    ZWCHY:: =<CHY(word groove)> &[<CSY(word meaning groove)>]&[CL(word cases
              groove)]& <CX(POS groove)>
    CHY:: =string(word prototype)
    CSY:: =string(word definition and meaning)
    CL:: =sting(example of lexical items, for helping to eliminate the
         ambiguities)
    CX:: =N (noun)|V (verb)|A (adjective)|D (adverb)|P (preposition)|R
    (pronoun)|
```

According to the above, " | " presents "or", "&" presents "and", " [ ]" presents "options", "< >" presents "required", "( )" presents "explanation". This kind of frame network can be easily transformed into object-oriented representation, which provided technical support to the achievement of Tibetan semantic hierarchical understanding.

# 5    Conclusion

In the processing of Tibetan natural language, for those Tibetan words, phrases, sentences and chapters which are based on the understanding of the semantic content and researching on translation are impossible to stand away from the supporting of technology of foundation engineering as Lexical Semantic Knowledge Base. But as a matter of fact, the attribute description of frame semantic is a description of Tibetan Lexical semantic information or for a semantic knowledge. Although, using a framework form to express lexical semantic information could reflect more on the primary and secondary relations within the framework of elements and the Framework Knowledge incidence relations and structural hierarchy, we still have an inadequacy in this description method. And it is the spot which need to be strengthened and improved in the future work.

# References

[1] Huan, L.H.: Information Source. Happy to Learn Chinese: Primary Version (6), 15 (2009)
[2] Gros, T.K.B. (ed.): Chinese-Tibetan-English Dictionary of New Daily Vocabulary, p. 566. Sichuan People's Publishing House, Chengdu (2009)
[3] Tannen, D.: Framing in Discourse. Oxford University Press, New York (1993)
[4] Weilin, M.: The Frame Theory and Meaning Construal. Foreign Language Teaching 10, 18–21 (2007)
[5] He, Y.J.: Research on Translation Under Frame Semantics. Chinese Russian Teaching 27(3), 54–57 (2008)

[6] Ungerer, F., Schmid, H.J.: An Introduction to Cognitive Linguistics. Beijing Foreign Language Teaching and Research Press, Beijing (2001)

[7] Yin, L.F. (ed.): Cognitive Linguistics Generality, p. 119. Beijing University Publishing House, Beijing (2008)

[8] Man, Z.S.: The Relations Between the Semantic Frames and the Fields. Foreign Language Teaching (10), 1–3 (2001)

[9] Yan, H.X., Wei, L., Ru, L.: Description Systems of the Chinese Frame Net Database and Software Tools. Journal of Chinese Information 21(5), 27 (2007)

[10] Gros, T.K.B. (ed.): Chinese-Tibetan-English Dictionary of New Daily Vocabulary, p. 27. Sichuan People's Publishing House, Chengdu (2009)

# Research on the Semantic Features of Dimensional Adjective *gao* 'high/tall' and *di/ai* 'low/short' in Chinese

Ying Wu

School of Foreign Studies, Hunan University of Science and Technology,
Xiangtan 411201, China
wuyingywu@foxmail.com

**Abstract.** In this paper, firstly, we mainly discuss the use of dimensional adjectives *gao* 'high/tall' and *di/ai* 'low/short'. Secondly, we analyze the inherent semantic features of *gao* 'high/tall' and of nouns combined with *gao* 'high/tall'. Finally, we study the differences between *di* 'low' and *ai* 'short'. *Gao* 'high/tall' can both have a dimensional use, and have a positional use. *Di* 'low' only has a positional sense, and *ai* 'short' only has a dimensional sense.

**Keywords:** *gao* 'high/tall', *di/ai* 'low/short', semantic features.

## 1    Introduction

There are no related researches on the spatial sense of *gao* 'high/tall' and *di/ai* 'low/short' in Chinese, except the work of Yongjun Ren. However, his research does not cover the semantic essence of *gao* 'high' and *di/ai*, 'low/short'.[1] Though there are many studies of dimensional adjectives corresponding to the concept of *height* in many different languages, such as English, German, Italy, and Swedish, we can't adopt their study method and research findings to deal with Chinese dimensional adjectives, because the denotation and the usage of *gao* 'high' as an dimensional adjective in Chinese are different from those of its counterparts denoting *gao* 'high' in other language. Therefore, in this article, we will give a thorough and detailed account of the sense of the Chinese dimensional adjective *gao* 'high/tall' and *di/ai* 'low/short' by evidence from the corpus.[1]

The dimensional adjectives *gao* 'high/tall' and *di/ai* 'low/short' are commonly used to describe the upward, vertical dimension of an object. *gao* 'high/tall' can both have a dimensional sense, as is the case of *gao lou* 'tall building', and have a positional sense, as is the case of *yun hen gao* 'high clouds'. *Di* 'low' only has a positional sense, as in *di kong* 'low sky', and *ai* 'short' only has a dimensional sense, as in *ai shan* 'short hill'. The dimensional sense is consistent with the positional sense in essence, since both senses indicate the vertical distance from the reference plane to a point of an object. The only difference between them is that the dimensional sense glosses as inherent 'vertical

---

[1] The corpus data in this paper are from the Part of Novels in Contemporary Chinese Corpus at Peking University (online).

P. Liu and Q. Su (Eds.): CLSW 2013, LNAI 8229, pp. 153–162, 2013.

dimension' measured from the underside (or a reference plane) to the top of an object, but the positional sense glosses as 'vertical extension' over a certain reference point, which is usually the ground.

The use of *gao* 'high' is symmetrical with that of *di/ai* 'low/short'. The objects which can be described by *gao* 'high' also can be described as *di/ai* 'low/short', such as, *gao/ai shan* 'tall/short mountain', *gao/di kong* 'high/low sky'. Therefore, in this article, we will take *gao* 'high/tall' as an example to investigate the semantic features of *gao* 'high/tall' and *di/ai* 'low/short'. As for the semantic similarities and differences of *di* 'low' and *ai* 'short', we will further discuss in detail.

The spatial dimensional features referred to by the dimensional adjectives can be presented out depending on the features of objects denoted by nouns which the adjectives can modify. Ungerer and Schmid claim that the semantic features of adjectives are interwined with the semantic features of nouns which they are used to modify.[2] Therefore, in this article, we will discuss the semantic features of *gao* 'high/tall', then move on to show what nouns the adjective rather combines with, and discuss qualities of these objects that the nouns refer to.

## 2     Inherent Semantic Features of *Gao* 'High/Tall'

There are many related researches of dimensional adjectives corresponding to the nouns height in many different languages. Bierwisch(1967) deals with German *hoch* 'high' and *niedrig* 'low'. He states that *hoch* 'high' and *niedrig* 'low' should be comprehended in terms of one-dimensionality and verticality.[3] Clark(1973) and Lyons(1977) are of opinion that English *high-low*, *tall-short* have ground level as their reference plane. Furthermore, the adjectives involve a vertical direction.[4][5] Lang(1989) encompasses German adjectives *hoch-niedrig* 'high/tall-low' and believes that the relevant scale for them is expressed as Vert that should be considered a semantic prime.[6] Vogel(2004) studied the Swedish adjective *hog* 'high' and *lag* 'low'. He claims that *hog* 'high' and *lag* 'low' refer to vertical dimension, which is considered being measured from a reference plane to the top of the object.[7] Through the researches on Chinese *gao* 'high/tall', We consider that Chinese *gao* 'high/tall' describe the vertical extension, which extends or reach far up. Furthermore, the adjective relates to an upward direction. In this section, we will introduce arguments for the vertical orientation of *gao* 'high/tall', where related research on highness has merely assumed a verticality, without discussing the issue any further, then move on to the direction, and then go on to treat the extensibility of the vertical dimension.

### 2.1     Verticality

The adjective *gao* 'high/tall' is associated with the vertical axis, and the vertical dimension referred to by *gao* 'high/tall' is more salient than other dimensions of an object. Verticality can be considered the primary feature of *gao* 'high/tall'. The vertical orientation of *gao* 'high/tall' in Chinese can be separated into three types, that is, inherent verticality, canonical verticality and temporary verticality. We would like to elaborate further on this quality and shed more light upon this issue.

## Inherent Verticality

Among objects described as *gao* 'high/tall', some objects keep fixed, permanent vertical orientation, such as *gao ta* 'tall tower', *gao shu* 'tall tree', *gao lou* 'tall building' and *gao shan* 'tall mountain'. Such objects have inherent tops, bottoms, or fixed foundations. We define this fixed, permanent vertical orientation as 'inherent verticality'. The objects with this quality can not move and keep the vertical orientation inherently relative to the ground level. The distribution in the corpus is the following: in 428 out of 640 instances, *gao* 'high/tall' combines with a noun which corresponds to an object having an inherent vertical orientation. Among these objects with inherent verticality, what is the most in number can be listed as the three large category of objects, that is, the category of *shan* 'mountain', the category of *shu* 'tree' and the class of *fang wu* 'building'.

## Canonical Verticality

Some objects, which have vertical orientation that is common or customary if it is to serve a certain purpose is assumed to have a canonical verticality. Of course, their orientation can be changed in the special situation. One example is a cup, which has to stand upright to keep the water inside, but sometimes can be placed horizontally when it is cleaned and dried. We call this ordinary and customary vertical orientation as 'canonical verticality'. Such objects can move here and there. 'Movable objects' not only refer to objects which can move depending on their own force, such as, people and animal, but also refer to objects moved depending on the external force, such as desk, wardrobe and bookstore. Of the 640 instances in the corpus, *gao* 'high/tall' describes an object having an canonical verticality in 204 cases.

These objects with inherent or canonical verticality carries its verticality no matter how it is turned or held and they are still described as *gao* 'high/tall'. As Clark(1973) has pointed out , a tall person lying on the bench is still tall, not long, since we do consider human beings as upright objects.[4] Even a person's shadow, though it typically falls on a horizontal surface, can be described as tall, since it reflects a human body with canonical verticality, such as in (1).

(1) Na shi hou, xi tian luo jin can xia, ta zhan zai huang gou po shang, *gao gao de shen ying* tou she zai dan hui se de tian mu shang.

'At that time, when the sky in the west lost all residual sunset clouds, he stood on the waste valleys slope, and tall figure projected on the light-grey sky.'

Usually, a person's shadow is discerned as *chang* 'long', since its canonical orientation is horizontal. One such use is shown in example

(2) Qing chen de yang guang ying zhao zai ta de shen shang, zai di shang tou xia *chang chang de shen ying*.

'The sunlight on early morning shined upon her body and threw long figure on the ground.'

A person's shadow with canonical horizontal orientation can be referred to by *gao* 'high/tall' further provides an argument for the important role of customary practice of the vertical dimension in the cognition of people.

**Temporary Verticality**

Some objects, which have not the vertical height by itself, receive the vertical height temporarily by the way that they are placed vertically. Objects like this is assumed to have temporary verticality. In the corpus, there are only 18 instances of combination of *gao* 'high/tall' and nouns denoting objects with temporary vertical orientation. In(3), one example is shown:

(3) Zhou Jin zai chu fang ba guo wan piao pen nong de ding dang xiang, yi huir, duan zhe yi wan *gao gao de mian tiao* lai, zuo zai wo dui mian xi xi liu liu di chi.

'In the kitchen, Zhou Jin get boiler, bowl, gourd ladle, basin to chink, in a short while, she held a bowl of noodles in high position, sitting my opposite to eat.'

In example(3) *mian tiao* 'noodles' is lacking an actual vertical height, whereas, they gain the vertical orientation temporarily through one person's action, such as pile, fold.

## 2.2    Direction

Objects, to which height is assigned, are directed upwards. Objects must have the upward direction in order to qualify for description as *gao* 'high/tall'. As Lang(1989) point out, the dimension of high starts at the foot point and goes upwards.[6] We believe that the upward direction of the objects combined with the adjective *gao* 'high/tall' relates to the fixed bottom of an object. The bottom of an object support the whole weight of it to overcome the gravity to make it exist, so the direction of object is opposite to the direction of gravity, that is, its direction is upward which is coincident with that of *gao* 'high/tall'. Therefore, *gao* 'high/tall' tend to combine with objects with the fixed bottom. If these objects are measured, they can be performed from the point of support to the top. Objects, which are attached to the upper end of some other objects to prevent it from falling on the ground, directed downwards, are not referred by *gao* 'high/tall', though they have the vertical orientation. Objects such as curtains, pigtail, hair, wicker and rattan hanging from other objects are not discerned as *gao* 'high/tall' but as *chang* 'long'. There are some objects that have no supported point, such as pictures and couplets stuck on the wall, are not referred by *gao* 'high/tall', because they are considered directing downwards. Take *yu shui guan* 'rain pipe' as another example, rain pipe closed to the wall of the building, which have the vertical orientation, is not described as *gao* 'high/tall', but *chang* 'long', because the direction of rain pipe depends on its function of transporting the rain downwards from the top of the building and so it has downward direction. These facts provide an argument for the implicit direction of *gao* 'high/tall'.

## 2.3    Extensibility

Objects described as *gao* 'high/tall' extends far up from the reference point and the distance it extends is not in the scope which people can see, that is to say, people can not see the top of the tall objects, such as high build, especially, the skyscraper, whose top disappears in the sky. Objects referred by adjectives *shen* 'deep' also have same quality with *gao* 'high/tall', such as *shen jing* 'deep well', *shen hai* 'deep sea', *shen dong* 'deep cave', whose bottom disappear downwards in the ground and can not be seen. Assembly, the left and right ends of objects described as *chang* "long", can be out of sight, such as *chang chang de he liu* 'long river', *chang chang de ma lu* 'long road'. Unlike *gao* 'high/tall', the distance between left ends and right ends of objects referred by *kuan* 'wide' must be in sight, that is to say, the whole dimension must be seen, such as, *kuan jie dao* 'wide street', *kuan ma lu* 'wide road'. In (4), a instance is shown to illustrate this quality of gao 'high/tall'.

(4) zai xiao wu de jiao luo nar, *gao gao de yan chong wang gao kong shen qu*, zhan qu le zhe ge xiao fang jian de si fen zhi yi.

'In the corner of the cottage, tall chimney stretches out to the sky, and occupies the a quarter of this small room.'

# 3    Semantic Features of Nouns Combined with *Gao* 'High/Tall'

Through examining the nouns which combined with *gao* 'high/tall' in corpus, we find out that the main features of objects denoted by noun are as follows: fixed shape, gestalt structure, maximal vertical dimension, function of vertical dimension highlighted.

## 3.1    Fixed Shape

Usually, objects described as *gao* 'high/tall' need to be has fixed shape, and these objects are usually composed of the rigid material, such as building, trees, table. However, objects without fixed shape are made of soft material, such as rope, cane, hair, clothing, curtains, can't be described as *gao* 'high/tall'. Some objects with fixed shape is formed by stacking many soft objects, such as bun, ricks, breast, and another objects with fixed shape is formed by taking the hard material as a support point and the soft material as composed element, such as nose, cheekbone, tent and so on. In addition to a few objects, such as flame, spray, the objects corresponding to nouns combined with *gao* 'high/tall' in the corpus all have fixed shape. This is because in order to maintain the vertical dimension, objects must have fixed shape, whether they are hard or soft objects. Although some objects are made of soft materials, they are made to have the fixed shape in some way and keep the vertical dimension, so they can be described as *gao* 'high/tall'. The example (5) show how the adjective *gao* 'high/tall' describes an object made of soft materials.

(5) Gou wu guang chang shang shu li zhe liang ge *gao gao de chong qi zhu*, shang mian gua zhe liang lie ju da zi fu.

'Two column which is filled with gas set up on the shopping square, adorned with two large scroll on which are written characters.

In example(5), if the column is not full of gas, it is soft and has not a fixed shape, but, once it is filled with gas, it has a fixed shape and has the vertical dimension, so the noun denoted by objects can be described as *gao* 'high/tall'.

In the corpus, only in a few instance, *gao* 'high/tall' combine with a noun which corresponds to an object not having a fixed shape, but having temporary shape in order to maintain the vertical dimension, such as *gao gao de hai lang* 'high waves of the sea', *gao gao de huo yan* 'high flame'.

### 3.2    Gestalt Structure

Dirven&Taylor(1988) claim that tall entities are seen as whole structures, physically discontinuous with the background against which they are viewed. [8] In brief, gao 'high/tall' profiles an entity in its entirety, as a Gestalt. That is to say, *gao* 'high/tall' combines with nouns referring to objects profiled against their background and are not integral part of a larger structure. We can speak of *gao gao de shu jia* 'tall bookcase', because a bookcase can be viewed against the background of the wall in front of which it is standing. But we can not say of *gao men* 'tall door', even though the vertical dimension and shape of the door may be identical to those of the bookcase. The reason is that a door is an integral part of the wall; it is physically continuous with the wall, and cannot be viewed against a distinct background. Resemble to this, we can not speak of a man with a *gao e tou* 'tall forehead', or a chair with *gao tui* 'tall legs'. In my corpus, the background of some tall objects can be present in the sentence, in (6), one instance is shown.

(6)na shi tian ye shang zhan xian le luan qi ba zao de fan rong, yi xie qing zhuan dui qi de xiao *gao lu zhi shen yu da pian de shui dao yang miao zhi zhong.*

'At that time, the prosperity in a mess are shown on the field, some small tall furnace formed by piling up some black brick involved in large of rice seedlings.'

In example (6), the background of *gao lu* 'tall furnace' is rice seedlings.

### 3.3    Maximal Vertical Dimension

Goy(2002) and Vogel(2004) states that high either refers to objects whose maximal dimension is vertical, or to objects whose vertical dimension is as big as a human being or bigger.[9][7] In my corpus, the adjective *gao* 'high/tall' is combined with nouns that clearly refer to objects with their maximal dimension along the vertical axis in a majority of the cases, such as *gao shu* 'tall tree', *gao gan* 'tall pole', *gao ta* 'tall tower', *gao cao* 'tall grass', *gao ge zi* 'tall stature', *gao cao dui* 'tall mow', *gao mao zi* 'tall cap' and so on.

There is another group where it is uncertain whether the dimension, referred to by *gao* 'high/tall', is the maximal dimension. Such uses refer to mountains, buildings, rock, cliff, and so on. Though the vertical dimension of these objects is not maximal, at least, they are taller than a human being or other objects around them.

### 3.4    Functionally Salient Vertical Dimension

In my corpus, there are also a few examples where *gao* 'high/tall' clearly refers to a non-maximal dimension of the objects, but a vertical and minimal extension, such as wall, threshold, fence and pillow. We also find out that we can speak of *gao qiang* 'tall wall', *gao gao de zha lan* 'tall fence', but can not say of *gao li ba* 'tall hedges' which has the same shape with that of fence and wall. The reason is because the vertical dimension of objects combined with *gao* 'high/tall' is functionally important.

Walls and fences can be used to prevent sth. from coming in or out. threshold can be used to keep some dirty out of door. A pillow can be used to promote sleeping. The function of these objects come true through their vertical dimension which is the focus paid a close attention to by people, but the length and width on horizontal orientation don't make function for people, so they are not noticed and filtered in the process of perceiving. Conversely, the vertical dimension of these objects has very important function for people, so it has prominent saliency in the process of perceiving, which determinate to the combination of *gao* 'high/tall' and these objects. However, the function of the fence is used to divide area which is not related to its vertical dimension, but its horizontal dimension, so it is only described as *chang* 'long', but *gao* 'high/tall'.

Most of the time, when we say that " an object X is too high", it usually means "this object X is too high to......". For instance, As for a child who wants to climb over the wall, even if the wall is very short (is shorter than a human being), he also will say "the wall is too high", which is because he can not climb over the wall, and at this time, the wall play a role for child. But for an adult, it cannot be said that "the wall is too high", because the wall doesn't play its role for him. Example (7) show how the objects play a role for people.

(7)ta jia de yuan zi li zhong zhe ling ren ji dong de pu tao, wo he guo qing ceng jing you guo yi ge zhou mi de ji hua, jiang yuan nei de pu tao zai mou ge shen ye xi jie yi kong, ke shi ta jia de *wei qiang tai gao le.*

'The excited grapes are planted in her yard, Guo Qing and I had a thorough plan that we will rob all grapes in a deep night. But the wall in her yard is too high.'

## 4    Differences between *Di* 'Low' and *Ai* 'Short'

In Chinese, the difference between *di* 'low' and *ai* 'short' is very clear. *di* 'low' usually has a positional use, but *ai* 'short' usually has a dimensional use. There are many instance concerning the use of *di* 'low' and *ai* 'short', some example are as follows:

The positional use: *tian kong di* ' the sky is low', *yun cai di* 'the clouds are very low', *chuang hu di* 'a window is low', *tian hua ban di* 'a celling is very low'

The dimensional use: *ai shu* 'a short tree', *ai deng* 'a short bench', *ai qiang* 'a short wall', *ai wu* 'a short house', *ai zhuo* 'a short table'

Generally, *di* 'low' are not interchangeable for *ai* 'short', for example, we can speak of *shen cai ai de nan ren* 'a man with a short figure' but can not speak of *shen cai di de nan ren* 'a man with a low figure'. we can say of *tian kong di* 'the sky is low', but can't say of *tian kong ai* 'the sky is short'. But as above mentioned, the positional sense is inherently consistent with the dimensional sense. And both refers to vertical distance from the reference point to a point of an object. The actual amount of vertical distance referring to by *di* 'low' is the same with that of *ai* 'short', for instance, when an object with one meter is located on the ground, we say that the object itself is 1 meter high and it is zero high in position; When the object goes up 1 meter above the ground, we say the object is 1 meter high in position, so the number value of their vertical distance is the same. Because of the same meaning between *di* 'low' and *ai* 'short', the two words can be used to as a morpheme constitute a word *di ai* 'very short' with a semantic focus on the morpheme *ai* 'short'. So if we don't emphasize the positional height or the dimensional height, but only pay attention to the actual number value of the vertical distance, *di* 'low' can be interchangeable for *ai* 'short'. In my corpus, the same objects can be described both by *di* 'low' and by *ai* 'short'. Such instances are given in (8)-(11).

(8) zhong nian nan ren qing wo men jin le fang man gu lao jia ju de li wu, *wu ding hen ai*, shang mian you yi ge ge lou.

'The middle-aged man invited us to come into the inner room filled with old furniture. The roof is very low on which there is a loft.'

(9) ren zi xing de lu xi *wu ding hen di*, gei yang tie lu zi de yan hui xun de you hei.

'The herringbone roof made of reed mat is very low, which was smoked very dark by smoke from the tinplate furnace.'

(10) na zuo nong jia *xiao wu* hai zai, que xian de po bai han chen, you *di* you xiao, xiang ge zhu wo.

'The big farm house was still there, but appeared dilapidated and unsightly, low and small, like a pighome.'

(11) tie dao bei, yi pian shu lin, lin wai ji jian *ai wu*, xiang zi suan ji zhe, zhe da gai jiu shi bai fang zi le.

'A few low houses stood beside the forest which lies to the north of a railway, Xiang Zi considered that this is probably the White House.'

Usually, *wu ding* 'a roof' should be described by *di* 'low' in its positional sense, but *wu ding* 'a roof' in (8) is called by *ai* 'short' in its dimensional sense; *fang wu* 'a house' should be referred to by *ai* 'short' in its dimensional sense, but it in (10) is called by *di* 'low' in its positional sense. There another such instances, *di fang yan* 'low eaves'—*ai fang yan* 'short eaves', *di ling* 'low collar'—*ai ling* 'short collar', *di cao cha zi* 'low grass stubble'—*ai cao cha zi* 'short grass stubble'.

Another fact is that objects with a functional top can be both described as *ai* 'short' and as *di* 'low', because the boundary of the dimensional height and the positional height of objects with a functional top is very obscure and their height can both be interpreted as a dimensional height and as a positional height, such as *chuang* 'bed' and *tai zi* 'platform' which can be both said of *di chuang* 'low bed', *di tai* 'low platform' and said of *ai chuan* 'short bed', *ai tai* 'short platform'.

(12) yi zhang *ai chuang*, shang mian pu you yi zhang lu xi, lu xi shang you gai you yi zhang chang chang de ruan ruan de xiang pu ye zi bian cheng de dian zi.

'There is a low bed on which a reed mat is spread, which carries a long soft mat weaved by cattail leaves.'

(13) yao shi you ren bu de yi cang zai zhe jian wu li, ta bi ding cang zai zhe kuai bu man de hou mian, yin wei *chuang tai di*, yi gui you bu gou hou.

'If someone is obliged to hide in this house, he will undoubtedly hide in the back of the cloth, because the bed is too low and the chest is not thick enough.'

*Chuang mian* 'the surface of a bed' and *zhuo mian* 'the surface of a table' is the part with the main function which is used often by people and is the focus of concern, so the distance from the surface of bed and table to the ground not only can be understood as the inherent dimensional height of the bed and table, but also can be understood as the positional height.

## 5    Conclusion

We have studied the semantic features of *gao* 'high/tall' and *di/ai* 'low/short' in detail on the basis of the previous researches, and have gained some understandings about the semantics of *gao* 'high/tall' and *di/ai* 'low/short'. These studies not only make us understand the senses and the semantic features of *gao* 'high/tall' and *di/ai* 'low/short' deeply and correctly, but also can supply with the theoretical basis for the dictionary compilation and the foreign Chinese teaching.

This article has only studied the spatial senses of *gao* 'high/tall' and *di/ai* 'low/short'. Many metaphorical senses of *gao* 'high' and *di*'low' have derived from its spatial senses. Which metaphorical senses *gao* 'high' and *di* 'low' have? What is the relationship between the spatial senses and the metaphorical senses, as well as, between the metaphorical senses? What is the mechanism of their evolution? As for these questions, we will do more researches in further.

**Acknowledgments.** Financial Support from Project Supported by Humanities and Social Sciences Youth Research Fund of Education Department(12YJC740113), Philosophy and Social Sciences Research Fund of Hunan Province(Xiang Zhe She Ling[2011], NO: 12).

## References

1. Ren, Y.-J.: Study on The Semantics of the Spatial Dimensional Words in Modern Chinese. Master Degree Thesis in Yanbian University, 9-13 (2000)
2. Ungerer, F., Schmid, H.-J.: An Introduction to Cognitive Linguistics. Longman, London (1996)
3. Bierwisch, M.: Some Semantic Universals of German Adjectival. Foundations of Language 3, 1–36 (1967)
4. Clark, H.: Space, time, semantics, and the child. In: Terry, M. (ed.) Cognitive Development and the Acquisition of Language, pp. 27–63. Academic Press, New York (1973)
5. Lyons, J.: Semantics, pp. 702–710. Cambridge University Press, Cambridge (1977)

6. Lang, E.: The semantics of dimensionsal designation of spatial objects. In: Manfred, B., Edward, L. (eds.) Dimensional Adjectives: Grammatical Structure and Conceptual Interpretation, pp. 263–417. Springer, Berlin (1989)
7. Vogel, A.: Swedish Dimensional Adjectives, Doctor's Degree Thesis in Stockholm University. Almqvist & Wiksell International, Stockholm, 170–202 (2004)
8. Dirven, R., Taylor, J.: The conceptualization of vertical space in English: the case of tall. In: Rudzka-Ostyn, B. (ed.) Topic in Cognitive Linguistics, Philadelphia, pp. 379–402 (1988)
9. Goy, A.: Grounding meaning in visual knowledge. In: Coventry, K.R., Olivier, P. (eds.) Spatial Language. Cognitive and Computation Perspectives, pp. 121–145. Kluwer Academic, Dordrecht (2002)

# Cognitive Semantic Analysis on 口[kǒu](*mouth*) and 嘴[zuǐ](*mouth*)

Lijuan Li[1] and Zhifu Liu[2]

[1] School of Chinese Language and Literature,
Central China Normal University, WuHan, China
`lilij10@163.com`
[2] College of Art and Communication, China Three Gorges University, Yi Chang, China
`zhifuliu1980@163.com`

**Abstract.** 口[kǒu](*mouth*) and 嘴[zuǐ](*mouth*) form a pair of synonyms in Chinese. This article aims to find out the differences between them through the cognitive semantic analysis on the words composed of 口[kǒu](*mouth*) and 嘴[zuǐ](*mouth*). Investigation shows that the word-formation ability of 口[kǒu](*mouth*) is stronger than that of 嘴[zuǐ](*mouth*), and the semantic extensions of 口[kǒu](*mouth*) and 嘴[zuǐ](*mouth*) are limited by their original meaning, which reflects different cognitive interpretations.

**Keywords:** 口[kǒu](*mouth*), 嘴[zuǐ](*mouth*), Cognitive semantics, Differences.

## 1    Introduction

Fuyi Xing had interesting examples about 口[kǒu](*mouth*) and 嘴[zuǐ](*mouth*) (Xiande Zhao, 2007), such as:

a) 昨天我亲口跟他说过这件事。
*I had told him this matter personally yesterday.*
b) ？昨天我亲嘴跟他说过这件事。
*? I had kissed and told him this matter yesterday.*

Both of the semantic of 口[kǒu](*mouth*) and 嘴[zuǐ](*mouth*) can refer to a part of the vocal organ, why is example b) unacceptable? The possible answer is that 亲嘴[qīnzuǐ] means "kiss" specifically. But another question arises, namely we use 亲嘴[qīnzuǐ] but not 亲口[qīnkǒu] to express the meaning of "kiss". It involves the cognitive semantic differences between 口[kǒu](*mouth*) and 嘴[zuǐ](*mouth*) and their different word-formation abilities. Many scholars had studied the semantic differences of them. Xiyao Shi (1994) and Wei Zhang (2005) analyzed the semantic differences of 口[kǒu](*mouth*) and 嘴[zuǐ](*mouth*). Chuanfeng Lü(2006) discussed the semantic evolution of 嘴[zuǐ](*mouth*) and the diachronic substitution between 口[kǒu](*mouth*) and 嘴[zuǐ](*mouth*). The agreed of the differences between them can be summarized as follows:

P. Liu and Q. Su (Eds.): CLSW 2013, LNAI 8229, pp. 163–172, 2013.
© Springer-Verlag Berlin Heidelberg 2013

a) As a part of body organ, 口 [*kǒu*](*mouth*) particularly means the inner cavity part of the mouth, 嘴[*zuǐ*](*mouth*) can mean the part around the mouth.

b) 嘴[*zuǐ*](*mouth*) can also mean the cheek.

c) The words composed of 口[*kǒu*](*mouth*) are often used in written language and ancient materials, and emerged earlier.

d) The words composed of 嘴[*zuǐ*] (*mouth*) are often used in oral language, and emerged later.

e) 嘴[*zuǐ*](*mouth*) is always used to express negative meaning.

f) 嘴[*zuǐ*](*mouth*) has a great advantage when used alone, while the compound words composed of 口[*kǒu*](*mouth*) are still used in abundance.

As a word, there is a process of gradually replacing between 口 [*kǒu*](*mouth*) and 嘴[*zuǐ*](*mouth*), but the differences of the original meanings and the cognitive semantics are the main reason for the differences at the synchronic level. In this article, based on *Modern Chinese Standardized Dictionary*, *Contemporary Chinese Dictionary* and the words retrieved from www.cncopus.org, we try to find out the differences between 口[*kǒu*](*mouth*) and 嘴[*zuǐ*](*mouth*) through the cognitive semantic analysis.

## 2     The Further Explanations of the Dictionary Entries

In this section, we will categorize the entries of 口[*kǒu*](*mouth*) and 嘴[*zuǐ*](*mouth*) listed in *Modern Chinese Standardized Dictionary* and *Contemporary Chinese Dictionary*, and make further explanations with the relevant words retrieved from www.cncopus.org.

### 2.1     Entries of 口[*kǒu*](*mouth*)

(1) n. eating organ of human beings and animals; the part of vocal organ.

This meaning can be further divided into: a) refers to eating and vocal organ, such as 口疮[*kǒuchuāng*](*aphtha*), 口臭[*kǒuchòu*](*bad breath*), 口罩[*kǒuzhào*](*gauze mask*), etc; b) only refers to vocal organ, such as 口哨[*kǒushào*](*whistle*), 口技[*kǒujì*](*oral stunts*), etc; c) mainly refers to organs of speaking, such as 随口 [*suíkǒu*](*speak thoughtlessly*), 顺口 [*shùnkǒu*](*read smoothly*), 脱口 [*tuōkǒu*](*blurt out*), 改口 [*gǎikǒu*](*correct oneself*), 有口无心 [*yǒukǒuwúxīn*](*be sharp-tongued but not malicious*), 信口胡言 [*xìnkǒuhúyán*](*just a nonsense*), 百口莫辩 [*bǎikǒumòbiàn*](*inexcusable*), 众口一辞[*zhòngkǒuyìcí*](*unanimously a speech*), etc; d) only refers to eating organ, such as 口服 [*kǒufú*](*take orally*), 病从口入 [*bìngcóngkǒurù*](*disease enters by the mouth*), etc.

(2) n. a person's feeling and preference of the taste of food.

It should be noted that it further refers to the taste of food, such as 口感 [*kǒugǎn*](*mouthfeel*), 口淡[*kǒudàn*](*tastelessness*), 可口[*kěkǒu*](*good to eat*), etc.

(3) n. utterance

The examples in *Modern Chinese Standardized Dictionary* are 口才 [*kǒucái*](*eloquence*), 口气 [*kǒuqì*](*tone*), 口音 [*kǒuyīn*](*voice*). Further semantic analysis shows that these three words are related to verbal expressions and do not mean utterance. According to the specific examples, the meanings related to utterance can be further divided into the following four categories: a) related to utterance, such as 口碑 [kǒubēi](public praise), 口彩 [kǒucǎi](blessing words), 口舌 [kǒushé](words), 口实[kǒushí](handle), 借口[jièkǒu](excuse), etc. b) related to speaking, such as 口快 [kǒukuài](too eager to talk), 口气 [kǒuqì](tone), etc. c) verbal, oral, such as 口传[kǒuchuán](spread from mouth to mouth), 口供[kǒugòng](verbal confession), 口令[kǒuling](command), 口试[kǒushì](oral test), 口授[kǒushòu](oral instruction), etc. d) verbally, orally, such as 口称 [kǒuchēng](orally claim), 口是心非 [kǒushìxīnfēi](affirm with one's lips but deny in one's heart), 口服心服 [kǒufúxīnfú](not mere professed obedience but submission with a good grace), etc.

(4) n. people in a family

It should be noted that it can also refer to animals, for example, 牲口 [shēngkou](draught animals).

(5) n. the part of a container which interlinks with the outside world.

It should be noted that the original meaning of 胃口 [wèikǒu](appetite) is also the part of the stomach which interlinks with the outside world.

(6) n. generally refers to the part of an object which interlinks with the outside world.

It should be further noted that in the words such as 袖口 [xiùkǒu](cuff of a sleeve) and 领口 [lǐngkǒu](neckband), the sleeve and collar are all considered as container. In the words 心口 [xīnkǒu](pericardium) and 胸口 [xiōngkǒu](chest), the chest is considered as a container, it is gestalt cognition. The meaning of 虎口 [hǔkǒu](part of the hand between the thumb and the index finger) is also based on gestalt cognition. 口 [kǒu](mouth) in the words 缺口 [quēkǒu](insufficiency), 突破口 [tūpòkǒu](sally port) and 茬口 [chákǒu](opportunity) are abstract.

(7) n. passageway

This meaning can be further divided into: a) the passageway of buildings. For example, 门口 [ménkǒu](doorway). b) the passageway of natural objects. For example, 河口 [hékǒu](river mouth).

(8) n. particularly refers to the gateway in the Great Wall.

(9) n. particularly refers to port.

(10) n. professional emphasis; industry

(11) n. broken place (on the surface of human body or object), the shape of the broken place is always linear or circular.

(12) n. the edge of knife, scissors and other sharp weapons.

It should be further noted that the meaning of 风口[fēngkǒu](a place where there is a draught) is a metaphor.

(13) n. the age of the horse and the mule. (Their age can be judged from the number of tooth and the degree of tooth abrasion.)

(14) quantifier. a) used for human beings or certain animals. b) used for some artifacts with edges. c) used for actions or things related to mouth.

It should be noted that, 接口 [jiēkǒu](interface) refers to the interconnected part of two different systems or two parts with different characteristics of a system and it is usually divided into hardware interface and software interface. 端口 [duānkǒu](port ) particularly refers to the interface of computer which was used to connected to the peripheral device. Therefore, 口 [*kǒu*](*mouth*) in these two words means interconnected part. 插口[*chākǒu*](*socket*) refers to a socket into which something can be inserted. 口[*kǒu*](*mouth*) in this word means a hole, and it isn't a part of a container which interlinks with the outside world.

## 2.2    Entries of 嘴[*zuǐ*](*mouth*)

(1) n. the mouth through which an animal or human beings may take food into the body; a part of the vocal organ.

It should be noted that the meanings can be further divided into: a) eating and vocal organs, such as 咧嘴 [*liězuǐ*](*grin*), 尖嘴 [*jiānzuǐ*](*sharp-tongued*), 嘴角 [*zuǐjiǎo*](*corners of the mouth*), etc. b) vocal organ, such as 笨嘴[*bènzuǐ*](*inarticulate*), 七嘴八舌[*qīzuǐbāshé*](*with seven mouths and eight tongues, all talking at once*), etc.
(2) n. something which looks like a mouth.

It should be further noted that it can also be used to refer to geographic names, such as 肖公嘴 [*Xiaogongzui*], 陆家嘴 [*Lujiazui*], 邹家嘴 [*Zoujiazui*], 石塘嘴 [*Shitangzui*], etc.
(3) n. food.
(4) n. uterance.

It should be noted that the meanings can be further divided into: a) speaking, such as 嘴笨[*zuǐbèn*](*inarticulate*), 嘴刁[*zuǐdiāo*](*sharp-tongued*), etc. b) something spoken, such as 接嘴[*jiēzuǐ*](*respond*), 插嘴[*chāzuǐ*](*interrupt*), 回嘴[*huízuǐ*](*retort*), etc.

# 3    The Cognitive Analysis of Words Which Consist of口 [*kǒu*](*mouth*)

## 3.1    The Metaphors of 口[*kǒu*](*mouth*)

### 3.1.1    Shape Metaphor

Generally, a mouth has two kinds of shapes, round or linear. So broken place (on the surface of human body or object) is the extended meaning of 口[*kǒu*](*mouth*), such as 伤口[*shāngkǒu*](*wound*), 创口[*chuāngkǒu*](*wound*), etc. Because of the feature of being not connected, the meaning is further extended to "interspace", such as 缺口 [*quēkǒu*](*insufficiency*), 茬口[*chákǒu*](*choice*), etc. The mouth is an opening space of the body, based on which it can be extended to refer to a place like a hole, such as 插口 [*chākǒu*](*socket*). The meaning of 口[*kǒu*](*mouth*) in the words such as 心口 [*xīnkǒu*](*precordium*), 胸口 [*xiōngkǒu*](*chest*), and 虎口 [*hǔkǒu*](*part of the hand between the thumb and the index finger*) is based on the cognition of gestalt. The semantic evolution path can be summarized as follow:

the pace like a hole      the edge of knife, scissors and other sharp weapons

↑                ↑

abstract opening space ← 口 [kǒu] (mouth)→broken place→abstract interspace

↓

gestalt opening space

### 3.1.2  Function Metaphor

The main function of the mouth is eating. We consider the body as a container, and the mouth is the passageway of the body to the outside world. By metaphor, mouth's function as a passageway can be projected to other objects, so it can refer to the part of the object which interlinks with the outside world. A typical example is 瓶口 [píngkǒu](bottleneck). The follows are the other meanings which are evolved from the function of mouth based on metaphor. a) Generally refers to the part of an object which interlinks with the outside world, such as 舱口[cāngkǒu](hatch), 井口[jǐngkǒu](the mouth of a well), 袖口[xiùkǒu](cuff of a sleeve), etc. b) passageway of buildings and natural objects, such as 门口[ménkǒu](doorway), 河口[hékǒu](river mouth), etc. c) particularly refers to the gateway in the Great Wall. d) particularly refers to port. e) profession, industry. Different professions, industries are just like different channels where people can develop, such as 对口[duìkǒu]( fit in with one's vocational training or speciality). The semantic evolution path can be summarized as follow:

port

↑

eating organ→the parts of the objects...→passageway of buildings and natural objects

↓                ↓

profession; industry    gateway in the Great Wall

### 3.2   The Metonymy of  口 [kǒu](eating organ)

Using metonymic mechanism, 口 [kǒu](mouth) is extended to refer to a person's feeling and preference of the taste of food, such as 口淡[kǒudàn](tastelessness), 口轻 [kǒuqīng](not salty), 口重[kǒuzhòng](salty), etc. Another further extended meaning is the taste of food, such as 可口[kěkǒu](tasty), 爽口[shuǎngkǒu](tasty and refreshing), etc. As we all know, people who want to live must eat. Therefore, 口 [kǒu](mouth) is transferred to refer to human beings, such as 人口 [rénkǒu](population), 两口 [liǎngkǒu](couple), 糊口[húkǒu ](make a living to feed the family). The semantic evolution path can be summarized as follow:

human beings←口[kǒu](eating organ)→a person's feeling and preference of the taste of food→the taste of food

### 3.3    The Metonymy of 口[kǒu](vocal organ)

As a vocal organ, the main function of 口[kǒu](mouth) is speaking. The meanings of 口[kǒu](mouth) based on metonymic mechanism are listed below. a) utterance, b) speaking, c) verbal, oral, d) verbally, orally. The semantic evolution path can be summarized as follow:

utterance

↑

speaking←口[kǒu] (vocal organ)→verbal→verbally

# 4    The Cognitive Analysis of Words Which Consist of 嘴 [zuǐ](mouth)

### 4.1    The Metaphor of 嘴[zuǐ](human organ)

According to *GuangYun*, the original meaning of 嘴[zuǐ](mouth) is the same with beak. The most distinctive feature of a beak is pointed. Chuanfeng Lü(2006) listed the recessive semantic features of 嘴[zuǐ](mouth): [+sharp], [+hard], [+outstanding]. It is based on the above understanding of 嘴[zuǐ](mouth) that people draw an analogy between嘴[zuǐ](mouth) and other things, such as 烟嘴[yānzuǐ](cigarette holder), 山嘴 [shānzuǐ](spur), 壶嘴[húzuǐ](spout). Some geographic names also have such kind of metaphor. The semantic evolution path can be summarized as follow:

嘴[zuǐ] (the mouth of animal)→the part of an object that looks like a beak

### 4.2    The Metonymy of 嘴[zuǐ](eating organ)

Using metonymic mechanism, 嘴 [zuǐ](mouth) is extended to refer to food. For example, 零嘴[língzuǐ](snack). The semantic evolution path can be summarized as "嘴[zuǐ] (eating organ)→food".

### 4.3    The Metonymy of 嘴[zuǐ](vocal organ)

As a vocal organ, the main function of 嘴[zuǐ](mouth) is speaking. The meanings of 嘴 [zuǐ](mouth)based on metonymic mechanism are listed below. a)speaking, b)utterance. The semantic evolution path can be summarized as "utterance←(vocal organ)嘴 (zuǐ)→speaking".

Based on the above analysis, we summarize the cognitive meanings of 口 [kǒu](mouth) and 嘴[zuǐ](mouth) as follows.

**Table 1.** The comparison of the cognitive meanings of 口[*kǒu*](*mouth*) and 嘴[*zuǐ*](*mouth*)

|  | Cognitive feature | 口[*kǒu*](*mouth*) | 嘴[zuǐ](mouth) |
|---|---|---|---|
| human organ | shape metaphor | broken place | the part of an object that looks like a beak |
|  |  | gestalt opening space |  |
|  |  | the place like a hole |  |
|  |  | abstract interspace |  |
|  |  | abstract opening space |  |
|  |  | the edge of knife, scissors and other sharp weapons |  |
|  | function metaphor | the part of an object which interlinks with the outside world |  |
|  |  | passageway of buildings and natural objects |  |
|  |  | port/ gateway in the Great Wall |  |
|  |  | profession, industry |  |
| eating organ | function metonymy | human beings | food |
|  |  | a person's feeling and preference of the taste of food |  |
|  |  | the taste of food |  |
| vocal organ | function metonymy | speaking | speaking |
|  |  | utterance | utterance |
|  |  | verbal |  |
|  |  | verbally |  |

As it can be seen, a) as a human organ, both 口[*kǒu*](*mouth*) and 嘴[*zuǐ*](*mouth*) have metaphors based on their shape, but there is no further semantic extension of嘴 [*zuǐ*](*mouth*). At the same time, 嘴[*zuǐ*](*mouth*) does not have the metaphor which is based on the channel function of 口[*kǒu*](*mouth*). b) as a eating organ, 嘴[*zuǐ*](*mouth*) has only one extended meaning, but 口[*kǒu*](*mouth*) has three. c) as a vocal organ, the difference of extended meaning between 口[*kǒu*](*mouth*) and 嘴[*zuǐ*](*mouth*) is that口 [*kǒu*](*mouth*) can transfer to mean "verbal" and "verbally".

# 5    Statistical Analysis of Word-Formation of 口[kǒu](mouth) and 嘴[zuǐ](mouth)

Based on the above analysis, we count the frequency of the words consisted of口 [kǒu](mouth) and 嘴[zuǐ](mouth) which were retrieved from www.cncopus.org.The total of the words consisted of口 [kǒu](mouth) is 602, and the total of the words consisted of嘴[zuǐ](mouth) is 129. Table2 lists the words of top 10.

**Table 2.** Statistical analysis of word-formation of 嘴[zuǐ](mouth)

| Order number | Word | Occurrence number | Frequency ‰ |
|---|---|---|---|
| 1 | 嘴[zuǐ](mouth) | 955 | 0.0999 |
| 2 | 嘴里[zuǐlǐ](in the mouth) | 466 | 0.0488 |
| 3 | 嘴唇[zuǐchún](lip) | 342 | 0.0358 |
| 4 | 嘴巴[zuǐbā](mouth) | 302 | 0.0316 |
| 5 | 嘴角[zuǐjiǎo](corners of the mouth) | 119 | 0.0125 |
| 6 | 嘴上[zuǐshǎng](mouth) | 84 | 0.0088 |
| 7 | 插嘴[chāzuǐ](interrupt) | 75 | 0.0078 |
| 8 | 嘴边[zuǐbiān](lips) | 70 | 0.0073 |
| 9 | 张嘴[zhāngzuǐ](open one's mouth) | 49 | 0.0051 |
| 10 | 大嘴[dàzuǐ](big mouth) | 42 | 0.0044 |
| 11 | 七嘴八舌[qīzuǐbāshé](gabble) | 41 | 0.0043 |
| 12 | 吵嘴[chǎozuǐ](quarrel) | 40 | 0.0042 |

From the frequency point of view, the frequency of 嘴[zuǐ](mouth) and the words consisted of嘴[zuǐ](mouth) is much lower than that of口[kǒu](mouth) and the words consisted of口[kǒu](mouth). The reason probably is that the corpus is about written language.

Among the above listed words, the original meaning of 嘴[zuǐ](mouth) appears much more frequent, and extended meaning less. Only in such words as 插嘴 [chāzuǐ](interrupt) and吵嘴[chǎozuǐ](quarrel), the meaning of嘴[zuǐ](mouth) is extended meaning, while others are original meaning. In the words such as 一口 [yīkǒu](a mouthful) and 开口[kāikǒu](open one's mouth), the meaning of 口 [kǒu](mouth) is original meaning. In the phrase 一口气[yīkǒuqì](one breath), 口 [kǒu](mouth) is a measure word, and the others use extended meaning. We can draw a conclusion that although both 口[kǒu](mouth) and 嘴[zuǐ](mouth) mean the eating organ and vocal organ of human beings and animals in modern Chinese, 嘴 [zuǐ](mouth) is mainly used as original meaning, but口[kǒu](mouth) is mainly used as extended meaning.

**Table 3.** Statistical analysis of word-formation of 口[kǒu](mouth)

| Order number | Word | Occurrence number | Frequency ‰ |
|---|---|---|---|
| 1 | 口[kǒu](mouth) | 2045 | 0.214 |
| 2 | 人口[rénkǒu](population) | 1545 | 0.1617 |
| 3 | 出口[chūkǒu](exit) | 686 | 0.0718 |
| 4 | 门口[ménkǒu](doorway) | 619 | 0.0648 |
| 5 | 进口[jìnkǒu](entrance) | 435 | 0.0455 |
| 6 | 一口[yīkǒu](a mouthful) | 400 | 0.0419 |
| 7 | 一口气[yīkǒu qì](one breath) | 354 | 0.037 |
| 8 | 开口[kāikǒu](open one's mouth) | 346 | 0.0362 |
| 9 | 口号[kǒuhào](slogan) | 340 | 0.0356 |
| 10 | 口气[kǒuqì](tone) | 308 | 0.0322 |
| 11 | 口袋[kǒudài](pocket) | 288 | 0.0301 |
| 12 | 窗口[chuāngkǒu](window) | 213 | 0.0223 |

## 6    Synonym Discrimination

From the semantic evolution point of view, as an eating and vocal organ, both 口 [kǒu](mouth) and 嘴[zuǐ](mouth) can be used for human beings and animals. 口 [kǒu](mouth) is used for human beings first, then animals. 嘴[zuǐ](mouth) is used for animals first, then human beings. So the semantic extension of them is limited by their original meaning.   The main features of the mouth of human beings include: when the mouth is open, it is round, and when the mouth is closed, it is just like a line. The most significant feature of the beak is outstanding. The metaphorical meaning of 口 [kǒu](mouth) and 嘴[zuǐ](mouth) can not be separated from these features. Although 口[kǒu](mouth) and 嘴[zuǐ](mouth) have some semantic extensions in common, such as "speaking" and "utterance", the word-formation ability of them is opposite, for example:

a)嘴尖[zuǐjiān](sharp-tongued)/*口尖[kǒujiān]
b)嘴软[zuǐruǎn](hesitate to criticize)/*口软[kǒuruǎn]
c)嘴硬[zuǐyìng](stubborn and reluctant to admit mistakes or defeats )/*口硬[kǒuyìng]
d)铁嘴[tiězuǐ](be skilled in debate)/*铁口[tiěkǒu]

It can be seen that, the opposition of the word-formation ability of 口[kǒu](mouth) and 嘴[zuǐ](mouth) shows that the extended meaning was limited by the semantic features of the original meaning, but it is not universal, for example:

a) 吵嘴[*chǎozuǐ*](*quarrel*)/*吵口[*chǎokǒu*]
b) 多嘴[*duōzuǐ*](*gossipy*)/ ?多口[*duōkǒu*]
c) 嘴刁[*zuǐdiāo*](*sharp-tongued*)/ ?口刁[*kǒudiāo*]
d) 嘴乖[*zuǐguāi*](*clever and pleasant when speaking to elders*)/ ?口乖[*kǒuguāi*]

## 7    Conclusion

In a word, the word-formation ability of 口[*kǒu*](*mouth*) is stronger than that of嘴 [*zuǐ*](*mouth*), and the semantic extensions of口[*kǒu*](*mouth*) and嘴[*zuǐ*](*mouth*) are limited by their original meanings, which reflects different cognitive interpretation of Chinese people. Based on the analysis above, we are able to account for the difference of 亲嘴[*qīnzuǐ*](*kiss*) and 亲口[*qīnkǒu*](*personally*) mentioned at the beginning of the article. On the one hand, it is associated with the feature of 嘴[*zuǐ*](*mouth*),such as [outstanding], so we say亲嘴[*qīnzuǐ*](*kiss*); on the other hand, from the frequency point of view, in most cases, the meaning of口 [*kǒu*](*mouth*) is the extended meaning when it was used to form a word, but the meaning of 嘴[*zuǐ*](*mouth*) is the original meaning.

**Acknowledgments.** This work is supported by a Talent Scientific Research Fund of China Three Gorges University. The author would like to thank the anonymous reviewers for their comments. The remaining errors are ours.

## References

1. Lü, C.: The Evolvement of the Acceptation of the Common Used Word "Zui" and Its Diachronic Subrogation with "Kou". Studies in Language and Linguistics 1, 107–109 (2006)
2. Zhao, X.: The Charm of Oral Expression of Professor Xing Fuyi. Chinese Teaching & Studies 3, 58 (2007)
3. Li, X.: Modern Chinese Standardized Dictionary. Foreign Language Teaching and Research Press (2004)
4. Shi, X.: The Semantic and Pragmatic Analysis of "Kou" and "Zui". Chinese Language Learning 1, 11–14 (1994)
5. Zhao, Y.: An Introduction to Cognitive Linguistics, pp. 119–122. Shanghai Foreign Language Education Press (2001)
6. Xiong, Z.: Cognitive Foundations of the Classifier "Kou" and its Syntactic Behaviors. Journal of Chaohu College 2, 96–100 (2003)
7. Zhang, W.: Analysis of "Kou" and "Zui". Language Teaching and Linguistic Studies 2, 77–80 (2005)

# The Acquisition of Chinese Ergative Verbs and the Verification of Relevant Rules in Semantic Role Labeling

Mengxiang Wang[1,2], Yang Liu[1,2], Houfeng Wang[1,2], and Longkai Zhang[1,2]

[1] Institute of Computational Linguistics, Peking University, Beijing 100871, China
[2] Key Laboratory of Computational Linguistics (Ministry of Education),
Peking University, Beijing 100871, China
{wmx1984,liuyang,wanghf}@pku.edu.cn, zhlongk@qq.com

**Abstract.** Ergative verb is a small class of Chinese verbs. Compared with other general verbs, it has different syntactic, semantic features. According to the grammatical viewpoint and the requirement of Chinese information processing, the thesis generalizes those verbs that can enter into "NP$_1$+V+NP$_2$" and "NP$_2$+V" as ergative verbs, those verbs with causative features synchronously called typical ergative verbs, the others called atypical verbs. Based on this assumption, combining with the tagged corpus in Chinese Prop-Bank, we find ergative verbs have their own semantic role labeling features which the general verbs don't have, which will be useful to improve the accuracy of Semantic Role Labeling.

**Keywords:** Chinese information processing, Chinese ergative verbs, Semantic role labeling.

## 1 Introduction

First of all, we can see a special language phenomenon:

*(1)Steve Jobs changed the world.*
*(2)The world changed*

The "change" in those sentences can either have two arguments or one, that is to say it can be used as transitive verb or intransitive verb. When it is used as transitive verb, it is causative; we can rewrite this sentence as "Steve Jobs make the world changed". It makes no difference whether the "world" is the Object in transitive clauses or the subject intransitive clauses. Its semantic role should always be "Object". Take the difference of the argument against syntactic arrangement into consideration, the linguists name the "change" in sentence (1) as "causative verb" while "ergative verb" in sentence (2). However, dictionaries list the "change" as one word, so we conclude those words that can takes two arguments or one only could be used as ergative verb and accusative verb at the same time, as ergative verb also can be called unaccusative verb as someone said.

P. Liu and Q. Su (Eds.): CLSW 2013, LNAI 8229, pp. 173–180, 2013.

Ergative verb have been a focus of Sino-foreign grammatical studies all the time. The Ergative Theory was originated from the western long time ago and went back to the "Ergative structure" (it refers to a kind of passive construction) that is suggested by Tesniere in 1959. Previously there are deep studies about Ergative structure. Both the Unaccusative Hypothesis by Perlmutter (1978) and Burzio Generalization by Burzio (1986) have a very detail testing and research about ergative structure. However, some people from the Chinese academia keep reserved opinions, such as Lv Shu Xiang (1987). Despite this, most people are positive about this. Such as Huang Zheng De (1990), Li Lin Ding (1990), Xu Lie Jiong, Shen Yang (1998), Xu Jie(1999), Zeng Li Ying (2006) and so on .All of them have studied ergative verb and ergative phenomenon from grammatical and semantic viewpoint. It's worth pointing out that some of the theory have not been applied and used enough when processing the Chinese information about ergative verb. Therefore, in this thesis, combining with the requirement of Chinese information processing, we would like to give a new definition of ergative verb to make full use of the general rule of labeling and to improve the accuracy of Semantic Role Labeling.

# 2      How to Justify and Extract Ergative Verbs

The ergative verb is regarded as a small class of verbs while its definition is still remained controversial. According to the general grammatical viewpoint and the requirement of Chinese information processing, we will re-justify and extract the ergative verbs.

## 2.1      The Definition and Measurement of Ergative Verbs

The western linguists generalize those verbs that can enter "$NP_1$+V+$NP_2$" and "$NP_2$+V" into ergative verbs. Whereas as Chinese does not have obvious formal features as its paratactic and topic language, there are too many verbs that can transformed from"$NP_1$+V+$NP_2$" to "$NP_2$+V", therefore it has always been the bone of contention among grammatical scholars. As Gu Yang (1996) and Yang Su Ying's viewpoint (1999), some people hold the opinion that it does not tally with reality to limit ergative verb as intransitive verb only, the measurement of ergative verb should be "Vi+NP "and "NP+Vi", which means those arguments that can change the location in one sentence takes behind the transitive verb is ergative verbs. Some people like Tan Jing Chun (1997) thought that ergative verbs are causative verbs which are wrong as well. Because some words like "die" does not have causative meaning and people often misunderstood it as ergative verb, such sentence as "Wang Mian die father/ Wang Mian's father die".

From the opinion above, one thing is sure that an ergative verb can have argument precede or after it.

Formally, it can transform between "$NP_1$+V+$NP_2$" and "$NP_2$+V", which is a necessary requirement of ergative verbs. Any words that can not be transformed by this pattern are absolutely not ergative verbs. Word like "awaken" can not be followed by an argument, so it can not be an ergative verb. The problem is, in the Chinese academic circles: Combining the special feature of Chinese, though some verbs can be transformed between "NP$_1$+V+NP$_2$" and "NP$_2$+V", it can not become an ergative verb. For example , if we define the verb "wash" as an ergative verb since it can be transformed from sentence "I washed the clothes "to "clothes was washed", while in the sentence "I washed one piece of clothes" ,"one piece of clothes" can not be put ahead ,does that mean "wash" is not an ergative verb ? As another example, Li Lin Ding (1990) thought "walk" is ergative verb because "walk" is an motional verb, you can say "he walked by an mountain "A mountain been walked by", while Zeng Li Ying (2006) do not think so. Because she believes that ergative verbs should have causative meaning in some way semantically. The reason why there is disagreement when give ergative verb a definition is how to measure it correctly. The problem above is from the covering of theory, in this thesis; the issue is to handle the Chinese information processing on the purpose of processing people's language better by extract the feature of ergative verb. Therefore it is necessary for us to give ergative verbs a new definition.

Although there is no final definition in the circle of Chinese academic, but they have come to a conclusion that is, "the basic requirement or a must requirement for ergative verbs is transform the sentences between two arguments sentence to one argument sentence". Though the most controversial issue is those verbs that can transform between "NP$_1$+V+NP$_2$ and "NP$_2$+V" but can not be regarded as ergative verbs at the same time, most of these verbs which can enter this format are different as common verbs. For example, there are two verbs "wash" and "beat". The "wash" may be is not a typical ergative verb but can enter the format"NP$_1$+V+NP$_2$ and "NP$_2$+V", we can say "we wash clothes" or "Clothes washed". But to "beat", which is regarded as an general action verb, we can hardly say "Man beat".

Therefore, as to Chinese information processing, when we define a class of verbs, we should not only pay attention to the difference but also have a deep thinking about the covering of its feature. For example, if we pick up decades of the recognized ergative verb strictly from 20,000 verbs, it has no meaning though those were approved by grammatical scholars. According to this kind of situation, we can just define the ergative verb by the basic way in the circle of grammatical, and then classify them into typical and atypical ergative verbs; thereafter we can classify them again according to their features and actual demand, in this way we can enlarge the covering of ergative verb.

On these grounds, it concludes: Generally, the verbs can either followed by two arguments or one only, besides if it can transform from two arguments to one argument sentence, we can conclude them as ergative verbs. If these verbs also have the feature of causative or spontaneous meaning, they can be named as typical ergative verbs. Otherwise they will be atypical ergative verbs. Such as the word: "turn off", when we are transforming it from two argument sentence to one .we can say, "He turned off the light" or "the light has been turned off", it has the feature of causative or spontaneous meaning, so we can say that "turn off" is a typical ergative verb. Another example "walk", it can transform between two arguments to one argument sentence, but it does not have the feature of causative or spontaneous meaning, so it is an atypical ergative verb.

If formally identify them, we can refer to the measurement that Zeng Li Ying pointed out:

**I.** Transform between "$NP_1+V+NP_2$" and "$NP_2+V$"

这　件　事　感 动　了　小李。

zhe jian shi    gan dong le xiao li

*This thing moved        Mr. Li*

小　李　　感动　了。

*xiao li    gan dong    le*

*Mr. Li was moved*

**II.** In imperative clause "让(rang)+NP+V" ( "make +NP+V")

这　件　事　让　小　李 感　动　了。

*zhe jian shi    rang    xiao li    gan dong le*

*This    thing    make Mr. Li    moved*

**III.** The Verb can modify itself. "$NP_2$+自己（zi ji）+V" ( "$NP_2$+oneself +V")

灯　　自己　熄灭 了

*Deng    zi ji    xi mie le*

*The light itself died out.*

The different conclusion we have with Zeng is that we believe those verbs that qualify standard I can be named as ergative verb, if it suits to II and III also, then it will be typical ergative verb, otherwise atypical ergative verb.


## 2.2    Extraction of Typical Ergative Verb

In Chinese, where there is context, there is hope that arguments are precede or behind a verb. This makes it hard for some of us to measure ergative verb. As Wang Huihui (2002) defined the feature of the verb "consume", since it does exist such sentence as "we consumed a lot of things" "Things consumed", and he thought "consume" is an ergative verb. However, in fact consume in "$NP_2$+V"structure hardly been used .So when we know the requirement of ergative verb, It is key to extract them. We can not just define it by our rhythm whether it can be transformed or not, but also some the practice of corpus.

It is simple to explain why Verb-object ergative verb can not be ergative verb, generally, ergative verb can follow object, yet there is object in Verb-object sentence, so it is hard to have another.

As for the relation between "V + C (complement)" and ergative verb, Shen Yang (2012) pointed: each ergative verb have the "V + C" Verb's features grammatically and semantically. What is more, "V + C" is the basic form of ergative structure.

This point may be too absolute, but explains the relation between "V + C" and erga-tive verb. One thing is positive, it is very easy for those verbs that reflects "V + C" to become ergative verbs .because "V + C" itself is causative such as "煮 糊 [zhuhu]overcooked" is for sure "something being overcooked". Typical ergative verbs is causative as "减弱[jianruo]weaken" and "加强[jiaqiang]strengthen" are "V + C" structure. In this way, we find new measurement to extract ergative verbs. We can pay much more attention to "V + C" other than "V + O" .However, some of the verbs like "express/match" in "V + C" structure is not ergative verbs, thus we still need to refer to the above measurement to select .We once select 531 ergative verbs out of 678 verbs from "V + C" in CCD（Chinese Concept Dictionary） . One thing need to be pointed out is:  it is not necessary to take ergative verbs into "V + C" verbs .According to what the viewpoint in the circle of grammar, the "V + C" structure is countless, and not all verbs in "V + C" are ergative verbs. I would love to refer to the CDD that invented by Language department In Beijing University. It contains prac-tical corpus and many "V + C" that can define ergative verbs included. Once the dic-tionary expanded "V + C", we must exam it again, both sentence and verbs should qualify the measurement I.

Combing the measurement Modern Chinese corpus in CCL and measurements above, we found there are 173 typical ergative verbs in Modern Chinese verb Dictionary.

## 3    The Rule of Semantic Role Labeling That Related to the Argument of Ergative Verb

The noun that followed verb is the argument of verb; it is the same as Semantic Role. Here I would like to discuss the Semantic Role labeling of ergative verbs, which is role labeling of argument "NP$_1$"and"NP$_2$". It is sure that ergative verbs can also use with other Semantic Cases, however, these Cases can be cite by specific Case-mark and most of them is Peripheral Cases, so we will not have further discussion about it. For example, "Steve Jobs changed the world with technology" we focus on the Se-mantic Role of "Steve Jobs" and "the world", "technology" here was introducing by "with", its Semantic Role is "Instrumental", the noun that followed the ergative verb "change" is not a must argument , so it is out of the range of this study .

When ergative verb follows with NP$_1$ and NP$_2$, in accordance with the rule of se-mantic role, the Agent should be put on the location of the subject, the Patient should be on the object's location. Such as in the *Modern Chinese verb Dictionary* the NP$_1$ precedes the ergative verb is labeled as the Agent and the word after NP$_2$ is labeled as the Patient .For example "The state-owned enterprise changed the quitting time", *Modern Chinese verb Dictionary* labeled the noun precedes verb as "Agent" and the noun after as "Patient". However, after study the Modern Chinese verb Dictionary the non-labeling Semantic Components related to typical ergative verb have the Semantic role as "Experiencer" and "Theme" except for "Agent" and "Patient".

In this thesis, we believe that the labeled "Experiencer" and "Theme" should be concluded into "Agent" and "Patient". There are two situations that "Experiencer" labeled, one is related to Relative verb (eg. "是[shi](is)", 叫[jiao](named)), we not usually consider this kind of relation verb, the other situation is one who non-spontaneous do something. These sentences do not have an object sometimes. As "The windmills turn up slowly" was labeled as "Experiencer", some have an object and the object was labeled as "Theme" .Such as "My wife lost her handbag" the two arguments were labeled as "Experiencer" and "Theme". The ergative verb with semantic role as "Experiencer" usually is "NP+V" structure, but also can enter into "NP$_1$+V+NP$_2$". In the dictionary, the sentence like "the temperature reduced" should follow an Experiencer, so can we label the "temperature" in the sentence that "He lowered the temperature" as "Experiencer"? Definitely not, because "lower" was controlled by him and the temperature it selves can not change itself. Besides, I have found that the "Agent" and "Patient" do not appear at the same time, so do the "Experiencer" and "Theme". According to Fillmore's theory of "One-instance-per-clause principle", if two cases show at the same time in one sentence, then we must distinguish them. We can merge them when they are two kinds of semantic cases; therefore, it is reasonable to conclude "Experiencer" and "Theme" into "Agent" and "Patient".

For this reason, even though there is some little mistake about semantic role labeling in the structure of "NP1+V+NP2" or "NP2+V", even "NP1" or "NP2" does not have the feature of "Experiencer", yet we can still regard them as "Agent" and "Patient", Because the "NP1+V+NP2" offen can be regarded as a causative form, we can understand this as the actor make the "object" become one state. The actor may not do anything but the "object" changes, so it is "Experiencer".

When the ergative verb follows one argument, on the basis of Chinese grammar features, the argument precedes the verb, and the semantic role should be "Agent". Whereas if ergative verb follows one argument, then the argument precedes the verb is "Patient". Because the features of the ergative verb decides that any "NP2+V" form can changed into "NP1+V+NP2", the relation between NP2 and the verbs never change. NP1 is the causer, the ergative verb happens for the reason of the causer, and the causer can be omitted. NP2 can be regarded as the cause; it is the Experiencer thing affected. For instance, "Attention is distracted" He distracted his attention", no matter how we change it, the relations between "attentions" and "distract" is the same, so does their semantic role while it is obvious that it can not be the doer, because "attention" can not happen Spontaneous but man does.

Therefore, The front- and rear labeling is different between ergative verbs and general verbs the way it labels semantic role, especially when the syntactic positions is flexible. We can think of it this way, any ergative verbs that follow two arguments, the argument behind is the Patient, the ergative verb follow only one argument and the argument precedes the verb is tend to be the Patient.

# 4     Experimental Verification

Generally speaking, the argument preceding the general verb is more likely to be the Agent, but to ergative verb, it is different.

According to methods above, there are 173 typical ergative verbs among the more than 2000 verbs in the *"Modern Chinese verb Dictionary"*. Then, we combine the Chinese Propbank data resources for testing. In Propbank, the initiator of the general action (Agent usually) labeled A0, the content or object which relate to the general action (Patient usually) labeled A1.We can see the instances of Chinese semantic role in the Propbank database:

**Table 1.**

| 1: 冷 战 结 束 以后 *leng zhan jie shu    yi hou.* (after the end of Cold War) | Segmentation | Etymology | Verb | Role |
|---|---|---|---|---|
| | *leng zhan* | NN | — | (*A1*) |
| | *jie shu* | VV | *jie shu* | — |
| | *yi hou* | LC | — | — |
| 2: "糖 脉 康" 颗粒 不 仅 降 低 血 糖 *"tang mai kang" ke li    bu jin jiang di    xue tang* *("tang mai kang" not only reduce blood glucose)* | " | PU | — | ( |
| | *tang mai kang* | NN | — | (*A0-B*) |
| | " | PU | — | — |
| | *ke li* | NN | — | (*A0-I*) |
| | *bu jin* | CC | — | — |
| | *jiang di* | VV | *jiang di* | — |
| | *xue tang* | NN | — | (*A1*) |

Firstly, in order to increase the credibility of the data and make the data cover a wider range, we extract 2 different typical range ergative verbs for 2 times. One is strictly according to the *"Modern Chinese verb Dictionary"*, the other one is conclude the 479 verbs which are dynamic complement structure in the CCD. Then, we brought Chinese Propbank 4559 unergative verbs as detection object again for comparing, which is to find the differences between ergative verbs and unergative verbs(or general verbs) ,especially in the Agent and Patient's use. The results shown in table2:

**Table 2.**

| VERB  SEMANTIC ROLE  PROPOTION  % DISTRIBUTION | unergative verb (*Chinese Propbank*) 4559 | ergative verb (*Modern Chinese verb Dictionary*) 173 | ergative verb (*CCD*) 652 |
|---|---|---|---|
| No A1& No A0 | 22.1 | 10.6 | 10.7 |
| A1& No A0 | **32.7** | **54.4** | **51.5** |
| No A1& A0 | 11.2 | 4.0 | 5.0 |
| A1&A0 | 34.0 | 30.9 | 32.8 |
| One argument with A0 precedes | **64.8** | **19.9** | **22.3** |
| One argument with A1 precedes | **35.2** | **80.1** | **77.7** |
| One argument with A0 follows | 5.2 | 1.0 | 0.9 |
| One argument with A1 follows | 94.8 | 99.0 | 99.1 |
| Two arguments with A0 precedes | 93.7 | 97.1 | 97.5 |
| Two arguments with A0 follows | 95.5 | 98.1 | 96.7 |

The data on the second line shows, compared with any action verbs, the "Patient" is more important than the "Agent" in the argument that follows the ergative verb. Because the ergative verb A1 appears more often than un-ergative verb .Most of all, referring to the date on the fifth and sixth line, we found when ergative verb follows one argument, the argument precedes the verb is more likely to be the Patient while the argument precedes the un-ergative verb (general verb) is tend to be the Agent.

Besides, combining the data on other lines, we can come to a conclusion that in the structure $NP_1+V+NP_2$, Most of the $NP_2$ plays an role as Patient, while $NP_1$ as the Agent. When in NP+V structure, then mostly NP is the Patient. The above data basically validated the semantic role labeling rule under the condition of one argument.

# 5    Other Discussion

Even though we have found that tendency of ergative verb with preceded argument and the argument followed on the process of semantic role labeling, However, from the data above we can know that even with one argument in the sentence, there is 20% of the argument before ergative verb is the Agent .Therefore, When the argument is the Agent ? How to improve the accuracy of semantic role labeling? Further discussion need to be made in the future.

**Acknowledgments.** This research was partly supported by China Postdoctoral Science Foundation (No.2013M530456), National High Technology Research and Development Program of China (863 Program) (No.2012AA011101) and National Social Science Foundation of China. (No. 12&ZD227).

# References

1. Aho, A.V., Ullman, J.D.: The Theory of Parsing, Translation and Compiling, vol. 1. Prentice-Hall, Englewood Cliffs (1972)
2. Perlmutter, D.M.: Impersonal passives and unaccusative hypothesis. Berkeley Linguistic Society 4, 157–189 (1978)
3. Burzio, L.: Italian syntax: A government-binding approach. Reidel, Dordrecht (1986)
4. Yung, G.: Characteristics of generative grammar and verb in the lexicon. Contemporary Linguistics (3), 1–16 (1996)
5. Huang, C.-T.: Two kinds of transitive verbs and two kinds of intransitive verb in Chinese. In: The 2nd Symposium on International Chinese Language Teaching. World Chinese Press, Taipei (1990)
6. Lv, S.: "sheng" and "bai". Studies of The Chinese Language 1, 1–5 (1987)
7. Li, L.: Verbs in Modern Chinese. China Social Sciences Press, Beijing (2000)
8. Lin, X., Wang, L., Sun, D.: Modern Chinese verb Dictionary. Beijing Language and Culture University Press, Beijing (1994)
9. Yang, S., Sybesma, R.: On the Nature of Unaccusatives and Unaccusative Structures. Chinese Teaching in the World 26(3), 306–321 (2012)
10. Tan, J.: Causative Verbs and Relevant Sentences Patterns, Grammar Research and Exploration, vol. (8). The Commercial Press, Beijing (1997)

# Internal Semantic Structure and Conceptual Hierarchy of Antonymous Compounds in Modern Chinese

Jinzhu Zhang

The PLA University of Foreign Languages, Kunshan 215300, China
95339041@qq.com

**Abstract.** As a closed word class with higher prominence, antonymous compounds are unique and self-contained in the modern Chinese vocabulary system. The internal semantic structure of antonymous compounds is unpredictable from the meaning of their components and surface grammatical structure, which presents three different conceptual hierarchies.

**Keywords:** Antonymous Compounds, Typical Quantification Reference, Conceptual Integration, Conceptual Hierarchy.

## 1    Introduction

Antonymous compounds are a kind of coordinate compounds composed of two opposite or relative monosyllabic morphemes, such as 上下 [*shangxia*] (*up and bottom*), 长短[*changduan*] (*long and short*), 涨落[*zhangluo*] (*rise and fall*), 大小[*daxiao*] (*big and small*), and 来往[*laiwang*] (*come and go*), etc. As a a closed word class with higher prominence, antonymous compounds are of irregular coordinate meaning and are unique and self-contained in the entire modern Chinese vocabulary system. The fact that their surface syntactic structure is inconsistent with the internal semantic structure has not yet attracted enough attention. For example:

> Example 1.
> (a)这里有大小岛屿五千多个。
> [*Zhe li you   da xiao dao yu wu qian duo ge.*]
> *There are more than five thousand islands.*
> (b)一个人的艺术生命的长短，决定于他的综合修养。
> [*Yi ge ren de yi shu sheng ming de chang duan, jue ding yu ta de zong he xiu yang.*]
> *The length of the artistic life of a person is decided by his comprehensive accomplishment.*
> (c)由于海水的涨落以及风引起的海水的运动，海岸线会经常移动。
> [*You yu hai shui de zhang luo yi ji feng yin qi de hai shui de yun dong, hai an xian hui jing chang yi dong.*]
> *Due to the fluctuation of sea and movement caused by wind, the coastline often moves.*

P. Liu and Q. Su (Eds.): CLSW 2013, LNAI 8229, pp. 181–190, 2013.

In Example 1a, 大小[*daxiao*] (*size*) is not equal to 大[*da*](*big*)+小[*xiao*](*small*). Instead, it indicates not only "big" and "small" size but all metrics related to an area; in Example 1b, 长短[*changduan*] (*length*) means the attribute of the length of one's life. That is to say 长短[*changduan*](*length*) is not equal to 长[*chang*](*long*)+短[*duan*](*short*); in Example 1c, 涨落[*zhangluo*](*fluctuation*) means the fluctuation of actions and does not have the timeliness of verb 涨[*zhang*](*rise*)and 落[*luo*](*fall*), i.e. 涨落[*zhangluo*](*fluctuation*) is not equal to 涨[*zhang*](*rise*)+落[*luo*](*fall*).

In view of the above findings, this article collects 232 antonymous compounds from the Modern Chinese Dictionary. Based on the statistical results, the syntactic property of word-formation components is mainly distributed in nominal, verbal and adjectival category.

According to the statistical data, we can see that there are 88 of V+V (verb+verb) compounds, accounting for 37.93%; 79 of N+N (noun+noun), accounting for 34.05%; and 61 of the A+A (adjective+adjective), accounting for 26.29%.

From the cognitive point of view, categorization is one of the most basic cognitive activities. It refers to the similarity in differences in reality and is able to classify different things into category, thus forming the process and ability of the concept. Antonymous compounds express its entire category or related category through two typical word-formation components, which means that the antonymous coordinate morphological structure also has the function of categorization. Category represents a high generalization schema of THING, and can be defined as a region of a cognitive category. Region refers to a set of the interconnected entities. In this case, the entities does not necessarily mean the discrete specific objects and can refer to any perceived and related things, such as "objects, relationships, feelings", etc.

Prototype nouns outline a region that is bounded, which means a set of entities involved in a particular dimension is bounded, as shown in Fig.1a; Verbs outline a region representing a process, with each verb being a point in process, as in Fig.1b; adjectives represent the atemporal relations, as in Fig.1c.

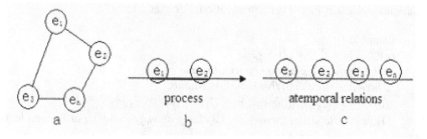

**Fig. 1.** Conceptual schema of word class category [1]

From the perspective of lexical semantics, antonymous compounds refer to the entire category or superordinate category, with the semantic feature of [+universal quantification]. Dexi Zhu [2] pointed out that universal quantification means "without exception in one set or scope", which is defined at the syntactic level[3-5].

We discuss the universal quantification mainly on the static vocabulary level. Among the compounds, universal quantification presents different types.

## 2　Internal Semantic Structure of Antonymous Compounds

Based on the analyses of 232 antonymous compounds, the universal quantification is not only restricted by the components, its own semantic and syntactic properties, but related to the degree of conceptual integration of antonymous compounds. According to their syntactic property, we roughly divide compounds into three categories: N+N, A+A, V+V. We'll discuss the relations among components, conceptual hierarchy and universal quantification according to the three categories.

### 2.1　The Universal Quantification of N+N

N+N Compounds consist of nominal morphemes, such as 左右[*zuoyou*] (*left and right*), 内外[*neiwai*] (*inside and outside*), 前后[*qianhou*] (*front and back*), 上下 [*shangxia*] (*up and down*), 表里[*biaoli*] (*surface and inside*), 始末[*shimo*] (*beginning and end*), 早晚[*zaowan*] (*morning and night*).

Nominal morphemes generally belong to the complementary oppositeness, as in Fig.2[6-7].

**Fig. 2.** Complementary oppositeness of N+N

The entire category is made up of two entities or members, which coordinately refer to the universal quantification of the entire category. For example, 前后[*qianhou*] (*front and back*) refers to the entire space category; 始终[*shizhong*] (*beginning and end*) refers to the whole process from the beginning to the end. All N+N compounds have the semantic feature of universal quantification, which is realized by two typical components. Word-formation components and antonymous compounds are at the same conceptual level. We call this type holistic universal quantification, as diagrammed and exemplified in Fig.3 with the bold line.

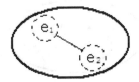

**Fig. 3.** Holistic universal quantification schema of N+N antonymous compounds

## 2.2    The Universal Quantification of A+A

A+A Compounds consist of adjectival morphemes, such as 大小[*daxiao*] (*big and small*), 高低[*gaodi*] (*high and low*), 长短[*changduan*] (*long and short*), 深浅 [*shenqian*] (*deep and shallow*), 冷暖[*lengnuan*] (*cold and warm*), 老少[*laoshao*] (*old and young*), ect.

Adjectival morphemes generally belong to the polar oppositeness, which has intermediate state in between, as shown in Fig.4[6-7].

**Fig. 4.** Polar oppositeness of A+A

Internal semantic structure of A+A is more complicated and can be divided into three types:

### 2.2.1    The Holistic Universal Quantification
Example 2.

(a)城中的 170 多条河道纵横交错，把陆地分割成 110 多个大小岛屿。

[*Cheng zhong de 170 duo tiao he dao zong heng jiao cuo, ba lu di fen ge cheng 110 duo ge da xiao dao yu.*]

*The city is criss-crossed with more than 170 canals, which divide the land into more than 110 islands.*

(b)从铁门栏看进去，房子还未上好窗子，一些长短的木块尚在院心。

[*Cong tie men lan kan jin qu, fang zi hai wei shang hao chuang zi, yi xie chang duan de mu kuai shang zai yuan xin.*]

*Seen through the steel fence, the window has not yet been installed; some sticks are still in the yard.*

In Example 2a and 2b, the semantic extension of antonymous compounds 大小 [*daxiao*] (*big and small*), 长短[*changduan*] (*long and short*) are more than the simple addition of "大[*da*] (*big*)+NP" and "小[*xiao*] (*small*)+NP", "长[*chang*] (*long*)+NP" and "短[*duan*] (*short*)+NP". It indicates not only "big and small" or "long and short" size, but all metrics related to area property and length property. Thus, A+A also has the universal quantification, which is same as N+N, belonging to the holistic universal quantification. Word-formation components and antonymous compounds are also at the same conceptual level, as shown in Fig.5.

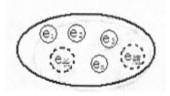

**Fig. 5.** Holistic universal quantification schema of A+A antonymous compounds

Here, the integrity of category is highlighted with the bold line. However, the entities or members are with dotted line.

### 2.2.2    The Arbitrary Universal Quantification
Example 3.

(a)国家无论大小，一律平等。

[*Guo jia wu lun da xia, yi lv ping deng.*]

*Countries, in any size, are equal.*

(b)电视剧无论长短，必须符合艺术创作规律。

[*Dian shi ju wu lun chang duan, bi xu fu he yi shu chuang zuo gui lv.*]

*TV series, in any length, must conform to the artistic creation rules.*

In Example 3, "countries" or "TV series", in any attribute value, must conform to the condition expressed by the predicate without exception.

Such A+A compounds refer to all entities or members of the entire category and also have the universal quantification. This type focuses on the individual category instead of the entire category, highlighting the entire category by highlighting several entities or members. We call this arbitrary universal quantification. In arbitrary universal quantification, components and compounds are still at the same conceptual level. This type is illustrated in Fig.6 where solid lines represent all entities or members, the dotted line represents the entirety.

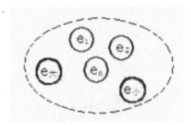

**Fig. 6.** Arbitrary universal quantification schema of A+A antonymous compounds

The two types of universal quantification, the holistic and the arbitrary, actually reflect two types of human cognitive models: one is Synoptic Mode, a kind of static internal view, in which human points of view are still within a space; the other is Sequential Mode, a kind of dynamic external view, human points of view are in multiple space transformation[8]. The holistic universal quantification corresponds to the Synoptic Mode, and the arbitrary to the Sequential Mode. According to image schema (image scheme), the holistic universal quantification corresponds to the whole scheme, highlighting the entirety and ignoring the details and the relations between entirety and parts; while the latter corresponds to the set scheme [9].

### 2.2.3    The Governing Universal Quantification
The governing universal quantification refers to superordinate attribute category or related category. Superordinate category can govern or cover all entities or members of a subordinate category or set. Accordingly, this type also has universal

quantification. When it comes to the levels of categorization, the word-formation components are in the basic or subordinate level category and the A+A antonymous compounds are in the superordinate level category, which can also correspond to the set scheme. Set scheme is also hierarchical as smaller units constitute a larger one step by step, presenting the shape of a pyramid.

Example 4.

(a)绒毛的长短标志着棉花的优劣。

[*Rong mao de chang duan biao zhi zhe mian hua de you lie.*]

*The length of the villi marks the cotton quality.*

(b)小马要过河，不知道水的深浅。

[*Xiao ma yao guo he, bu zhi dao shui de shen qian.*]

*The pony wants to across the river, but doesn't know the depth of the water.*

(c)这些桥大小不一，千姿百态、风格迥异。

[*Zhe xie qiao da xiao bu yi, qian zi bai tai, feng ge jiong yi.*]

*The size of these bridges is different, and they are in various styles.*

In Example 4, the A+A antonymous compounds 长短[changduan] (length), 深浅 [shenqian] (depth), 大小[daxiao] (size) respectively refer to   their own superordinate attribute categories. The governing universal quantification is illustrated in Fig.7.

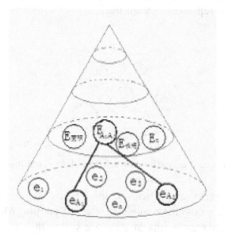

**Fig. 7.** Governing universal quantification schema of A+A antonymous compounds

In addition, there are some A+A antonymous compounds, such as 老少[*laoshao*] (*old and young*), 老小[*laoxiao*] (*old and young*), 虚实[*xushi*] (*virtual and real*), 异同[*yitong*] (*different and same*), etc, which are different from others in that they experience two times of conceptual integration rather than only one time. For instance, 老少[*laoshao*] (*old and young*), the internal semantics refers to all people of different ages. The process of conceptual integration is that: firstly two morphemes referring to the attribute value are adjectival, and then through the conceptual metonymy, they are transferred as the superordinate attribute category 老人 [*laoren*] (*the old*) and 年轻人[*nianqingren*] (*the young*), as shown in Fig.8a; secondly, through the holistic universal quantification, the two typical nominal morphemes 老[lao] (*the old*) and 少 [*shao*] (*the young*) refer to all the people of different ages, as shown in Fig.8b. We can see that the components and the antonymous compounds are in the different categories and also belong to the governing universal quantification schematized in Fig.8.

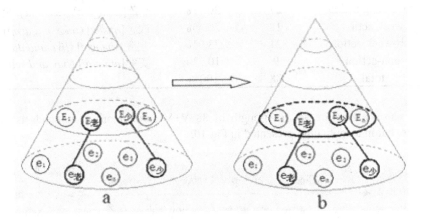

**Fig. 8.** Governing universal quantification schema of A+A antonymous compounds

## 2.3   The Universal Quantification of V+V

The V+V antonymous compounds consist of verbal morphemes and belong to directional or complementary oppositeness, as shown in Fig.9.

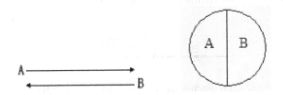

**Fig. 9.** Directional and complementary oppositeness of V+V

We found that the internal semantic structure of the V+V antonymous compounds is related with the strength of the word-formation components action. The action strength of the word-formation components is restrained by the typical features of its verb timeliness. The stronger the verb timeliness is, the stronger the action is, and vice versa. The advantaged syntactic function of verb timeliness can act as predicate verb, and can take the marks of tense and aspect in Chinese 着[zhe], 了[le], 过[guo][2].

Based on the action strength of the word-formation components, we divide V+V into five groups, as shown in Table 1.

**Table 1.** The distribution of the strength of the V+V antonymous compounds action.

| strength of action | number | percentage | example |
|---|---|---|---|
| strong action | 13 | 14.8% | 出没[chumo] (appear and disappear) |
| sub-strong action | 27 | 30.7% | 涨落[zhangluo] (rise and fall) |
| weak action | 18 | 20.4% | 取舍[qushe] (take and drop) |
| sub-weak action | 21 | 23.9% | 生死[shengsi] (live and die) |
| non-action | 9 | 10.2% | 买卖[maimai] (buy and sell) |
| total | 88 | 100% | |

We can see that the action strength of 88 V+V antonymous compounds is not discrete, but in a continuum presented in Fig.10.

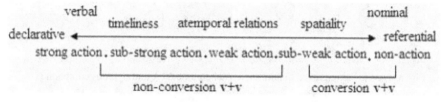

**Fig. 10.** Continuum of the strength of V+V action

From the Fig.10, we find that antonymous compounds with V+V of strong action, sub-strong action, weak action and part of sub-weak action are consistent with their conceptual level, referring to the whole process from the event $V_1$ to the event $V_2$, with a holistic universal quantification, as shown in Fig.11.

**Fig. 11.** Holistic universal quantification schema of V+V antonymous compounds

However, some of sub-weak action V+V lose the ability of being a predicate verb and cannot take the marks of tense, aspect:

*兴亡[xingwang] (thrive and perish)着[zhe]/了[le]/过[guo]

*兴衰[xingshuai] (rise and fall) 着[zhe]/了[le]/过[guo]

*存亡[cunwang] (exist and perish) 着[zhe]/了[le]/过[guo]

*得失[deshi] (get and lose) 着[zhe]/了[le]/过[guo]

The syntactic function of sub-weak action V+V compounds is to be the subject, object and attributive in the sentence, e.g.,

Example 5.

(a)农业国家的兴衰往往依赖于上天的恩威。——subject

[*Nong ye guo jia de xing shuai wang wang yi lai yu shang tian de en gui.*]

*The rise and fall of agricultural country always depends on god's will.*

(b)周恩来现在所做的事情关系着国家的生死存亡。——object

[*Zhou Enlai xian zai suo zuo de shi qing guan xi zhe guo jia de sheng si cun wang.*]

*What Zhou Enlai does now influences the survival of our country.*

(c)朝鲜又处于危急存亡的关头。——attributive

[*Chao xian you chu yu wei ji cun wang de guan tou.*]

*North Korea is under a critical situation.*

From the three examples above, we can conclude that the compounds have already lost the typical feature "timeliness of components", and its internal semantics refers to the nominalization of whole event. The conceptual category of compounds is detached from the category of components, which means the compounds and components are not in the same category. This type of V+V compounds embedded within a whole event process refers to the related category, which is inconsistent with the definition of the governing universal quantification schematized in Fig.12.

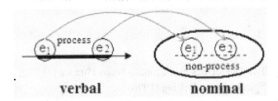

**verbal**                **nominal**

**Fig. 12.** the governing universal quantification schema of V+V antonymous compounds

**Table 2.** The distribution of three type universal quantification in antonymous compounds

| Antonymous compounds | | Universal Quantification | | |
| --- | --- | --- | --- | --- |
| | | the holistic | the arbitrary | The governing |
| N+N | | + | | |
| A+A | | + | + | + |
| V+V | strong action | + | | |
| | sub-strong action | + | | |
| | weak action | + | | |
| | sub-weak action | + | + | + |
| | non-action | | | + |

Non-action V+V compounds transfer their components' semantics into related categories, showing no obvious universal quantification.

Based on the preceding analysis, we can conclude that most antonymous compounds have universal quantification. However, the universal quantification presents in three different types. The holistic and the arbitrary universal quantification are at the same conceptual level, with low degree of conceptual integration, while the governing universal quantification crosses the different conceptual categories with higher degree of conceptual integration, and is hard to separate the compounds' semantics from those of their components, which in turn causes some difficulties during acquisition.

## 3    Conclusion

The specialty of antonymous compounds is that they have regular coordinate grammatical structure, but its semantics cannot be derived from the surface grammatical structure as simply as "1+1=2". With no doubt, the internal semantic structure is so complex and most antonymous compounds have the typical semantic feature [+universal quantification], which presents in three different types. The generation of universal quantification is not accidental, but associated with Antonymous Coordinate Morphological Construction, which is different from the general syntactic word-formation and reflects that Chinese, to some extent, different from English—a language of hypotaxis [10], shows the characteristics of parataxis.

## References

1. Zhang, M.: Cognitive Linguistics and Chinese Noun Phrases (认知语言学与汉语名词短语). China Social Science Press, Beijing (1998)
2. Zhu, D.X.: Lectures on Grammar(语法讲义). The Commercial Press, Beijing (1982)
3. Lu, J.M.: The Quantification Subject Sentence and Others(周遍性主语句及其他). J. Zhongguo Yuwen (1986)
4. Shi, Y.Z.H.: The Grammatical Forms and Motivation(语法的形式和理据). Jiangxi Education Press, Nanchang (2001)
5. Dong, Z.C.: Research on Universal Quantification Expressions in Chinese(汉语全称量限表达研究). PhD Thesis at Nankai University(2010)
6. Shen, J.X.: Asymmetrical Phenomena and Markedness in Chinese Grammar(不对称和标记论). Jiangxi Education Press, Nanchang (1999)
7. Jiang, S.Y.: The Summary Research on the Modern Chinese(近代汉语研究概要). Peking University Press, Beijing (2005)
8. Talmy, L.: Typology and Process in Concept Structuring. Toward a Cognitive Semantics, vol. 2. MIT Press, Cambridge (2000)
9. Yuan, Y.L.: Container Metaphor, Set Metaphor and Relative Grammatical Phenomenon(容器隐喻、套件隐喻及相关的语法现象). J. Zhongguo Yuwen (2004)
10. Deng, Y.H.: The Type Research on Coordinate Phrases in Chinese and English(英汉联合短语的类型研究). J. Foreign Language Education (2005)

# Markedness of Opposite

Jing Ding and Chu-Ren Huang

CBS The Hong Kong Polytechnic University
amanda.ding@connect.polyu.hk,
churenhuang@gmail.com

**Abstract.** In the studies of opposite pairings, the saying that some opposite pairs have one member as unmarked and the other marked "covers a number of disparate and independent phenomena" (Lyons 1977: 305). A lot of work has been done on selecting criteria for determining the unmarked/marked members (e.g., Lehrer 1985). This paper reviews the three most used criteria (morphological mark, semantic meaning and context-frequency) in previous studies and examines the theoretical criteria with natural language facts, especially with examples of Chinese. The aim is to discuss whether such criteria are capable in practical using.

## 1 Introduction

The concept of **markedness** has been used in many linguistic researches. Started from the phonological field of distinguishing words with different features, then it is synchronically introduced into the areas such as morphology, syntax, pragmatics, cognitive linguistics, language acquisition, and of course lexical semantics. However, a close look at the using of marked/markedness may find the term is overused in some many cases that the sense itself has been developed into many different meanings. And for the causes to the markedness/unmarkedness within one pair, Haspelmath (2006: 25) mentions some possible candidates like structural asymmetries, phonetic difficulty and pragmatic inferences.

Among the various related terms and categories, however, this paper only deal with the markedness that can appear in the opposite pairings, which mainly from the aspects of morphology, semantics and frequency in contexts. Other aspects, although very interesting and sometimes also closely related, such as phonology or psychology, have to be saved for our later paper, due to the limitation of time and writing.

## 2 Markedness and Its Criteria

The best summarized and also the most cited list of markedness criteria is that of Lehrer (1985). The eight criteria she presents cover most (if not all) of the standards people use to determine markedness, and three of which are mentioned most frequently as the main practical approaches.

P. Liu and Q. Su (Eds.): CLSW 2013, LNAI 8229, pp. 191–195, 2013.

## 2.1   Morphological Markedness and Opposite

This standard claims that the word member which takes a morphological mark is considered as the marked one. Languages like English usually add prefixes to produce the derivational morphemes. Many of them are negative prefixes such as *un-, a-, in-, dis-, non-*. Such prefixes are very common in English vocabulary. Lehrer (2002) reports that *un-* and *in-* are the most productive prefix of negation and both of them can generate contradictories and contraries antonyms. Examples of contradictories are like *mortal: immortal* and *true: untrue*; while ones of contraries like *happy: unhappy* and *wise: unwise*. And, some prefixes, such as *non-*, are also able to create opposites which are complementaries, for example, *grammatical: nongrammatical*. According to Zimmer (cf. Lehrer 2002) "most of the non- derivatives listed in Webster's International Dictionaries have neutral stems, with a few negative ones" (2002: 504).

However, in most of the case, for the words which have lexical and morphological antonyms, Lehrer notes, "the morphological antonym will have more general meaning than the lexical antonym" (2002: 504). For example, *happy: unhappy/sad, unhappy* negates the meaning of being happy while not indicate what kind of emotion is being hold by the subjective; on contrast, sad definitely points out the emotional status, not angry or depress, but the one of showing sorrow.

The negative morphology is widespread in many languages. In Chinese, we have the negative prefixes such as *bu4-("not"), mei3-("not"), fei1-("not"), fan3-("against"), wei4-("not yet")* and so on. But in Chinese, the situation is a little bit more complex than that of English. Since Chinese words are combined by characters, the suffixes usually also take one character position, and that will make the derived one more likely to be treated as a compound or even a phrase, which is considered to be less likely to combine an opposite pair with the stem word. For example, *hao3 ("good"): bu4 hao3 ("not good")/ huai4 ("bad")*. The word *bu4 hao3 ("not good")* negates the semantic meaning of *hao3 ("good")* in a wider scale than only asserting *huai4 ("bad")*; but my intuition, if I am right with most of the native Chinese speakers, would probably prefer to take *huai4 ("bad"): bu4 hao3 ("not good")*, as one opposite pairing, since it is more balance in both phonology and morphology. Only very few Chinese words take the derivational morphemes within the new characters. The most common example is *wai1 ("not straight, not upright")*. The upper radical of it is *bu4 ("not")* and the bottom radical is *zheng4 ("upright")* and the whole meaning of *wai1* is almost the same as *bu4 zheng4*[1]. But this kind of morphology is very rare in Chinese. Hence, for the most cases in Chinese, the stem word and the derived one with a negative suffix would probably not be considered as constructing an opposite pair in morphological aspect.

## 2.2   Semantic Markedness and Opposite

From the semantic aspect of distinguishing marked and unmarked members, it is important to decide which one has a neutralized reading. Usually, the one which can be used in a how-question or a related nominalization of measurement is considered to be the unmarked member.

---

[1] The pronunciation of *bu4 zheng4* is actually *bu2 zheng4*, due to the phonetic restriction of Chinese compounds.

For the neutralized *how*-questions, it is normal to accept the saying like:

*How long is it?*

rather than:

*How short is it?*

The first sentence is always considered as a natural way to ask for the length of something, without any supposition for its length. So the answer to the first question is free from the limitation of length range--- it can be thousands and millions of miles, like for the distance from earth to the sun, but also can be only a few millimeters, like for the height of a cell.

In contrast, when using the sentence of "How short is it", the speaker is actually having the supposition that the object he or she refers to is supposed to be short, or shorter than expected length. So if a basketball player falls to pass the height selection, then others might ask: "How short is he?" Even in this case, the player is probably higher than the majority of population.

Hence, the marked questioned, could be both *How short is he?* or *How tall is he?*, "carry with the presupposition that the object in question has already been placed towards one end of the scale rather than the other"(Lyons 1968: 467), while, "the unmarked member is less likely to be 'biased' or 'committed'" in "asymmetrical entailments" (1985: 400; 2002: 500).

Secondly, Nominalization of measurement is also used as a common criterion. It is natural to use one of the pair as Quantity Measure Adjective (Lehrer 1985: 400). To the question of "How long is it", we usually answer: "It is 5 feet long." But not: "It is 5 feet short." Unless in: "It is 5 feet shorter than you want." It is the same situation for ratios: utterances like "A is twice / half as long as B" are preferred than "A is twice / half as short as B" in most of the discourses.

Another Another kind of neutral nominal is seen in the name of property. We may already notice that the word "length", which derives from the word "long", is now used as the name for property of both *long* and *short*. The above question of "How long is it" can also be uttered as "What is the length of it", but not "what is the shortness of it". Similarly, is "shortness", rather than "length", is selected to ask for the property of something, there is likely to be the supposition that the object is in the scale of being short, or shorter than expectation. According to Lyons (1968), the fact of the neutralization is that people may feel one of the opposite pair is 'positive' while the other 'negative'. So for the *long: short* pair, *long* is treated as a more-than-normal size, and *short* as less-than-normal size. In general, people prefer to neutralize the 'more than' one as the 'unmarked' antonym.

Haspelmath notes on the markedness "as specification for a semantic distinction: in English opposition *dog/bitch*, *dog* is the unmarked member because it can refer to male dogs or to dogs in general" (2006: 26). Hence, "the difference between marked and unmarked is not that between A and non-A, but between A and indifference between A and non-A" (2006: 29) A widely mentioned example in English is that of *married: unmarried*, with a prefix *un-* the later word is seen to have a marked meaning of the persons who are not married, implying the fact that married status is more normal. Or, in Haspelmath's words: "the marked member is semantically more specific than the unmarked member." (2006: 29) It is the same as Lehrer's earlier assumption: "the unmarked member denotes more a quantity" (1985: 400; 2002: 499).

Additionally, positive and negative are also used as replacing labels for the unmarked and marked words. Lehrer thinks "the unmarked member is evaluatively positive; the marked is negative" (Lehrer, 1985: 400). The crucial weakness of such standard is that positive/negative is no less ambiguous than mark/unmark. Take positive as the preferred one by people while negative the reverse one. For pairs such as *good: bad*, it is of course easy to say that *good* is positive and *bad* is negative. But in some other pragmatic involved examples the situations would be more complicate. In the case of traffic light, *green* is positive to pedestrian while negative to drivers, and, *red* is negative to pedestrian while positive to drivers.

## 2.3    Markedness and Frequency

Due to the unbalanced using of pair members, it is not hard to guess that they may share different distributions in everyday language. The unmarked one of course enjoys higher appearance, compared with the other marked one, since the later mainly uttered when a certain property, like being short, is emphasized.

Some early dated researches already notice that the unmarked member of an opposite pair can be more frequent than the marked one (for example, Greenberg 1966; Zwicky 1978). Waugh (1982) explains it as the unmarked one can appear in more contexts. Similarly, Lehrer (1985) also notes, due to a wider range of contexts and its neutralized meaning in some contexts, the unmarked ones should be more frequent.

However, Haspelmath (2006) presents his suspicion on such saying. According to Leech et al. (2001), the unmarked gradable antonym members are one to five times more frequent than the marked pairing members, which, to Haspelmath, cannot be satisfactorily reasoned with wider range of contexts such as neutralized questions or statements. He offers another possibility that of the shorter expression of one pairing should be easier for using. He supposes such hypothesis would be supported by many studies in the field of phonology. Meanwhile, as to the fields like morphology or syntax, Haspelmath also admits, it seems lack of evidence (2006: 46).

## 3    Conclusion

These criteria offered by previous studies try to provide a practical standard for defining the marked/unmarked of certain word in a pairing. However, sometimes we may also find crash within these criteria. Let's take *impartial: partial* for example. In this pair, *impartial* is the one with a morphological mark but with a wider and neutral meaning in reading. On the other hand, *partial*, which stems from the root word *part*, has an abnormal understanding and denotes less of the quantity, according to Lehrer's (1985, 2002) criteria. That is to say, the negated word does not carry a semantic negative but positive meaning. The first and second rules do not agree on the same conclusion in this case. Similar crashes can also be found easily with other pairings, for instance, *unbiased: biased, unprejudiced: prejudiced* and most ironically, *unmarked: marked*.

However, it is not enough, to conclude that the trying to have a determined and universal standard for marked fails in the end. Rather, it is better to admit that the concept of being marked is still too abstract and more work need to be done on determining the criteria. In that sense, I am strongly agree with Haspelmath: not to have a general but unambiguous term as marked or unmarked but to be replaced with more clear-defined and straightforward terms such as "frequency of use, phonetic difficulty, and generalized conversational implicatures", which specifically indicate the individual "substantive factors" behind the asymmetrical phenomena with opposite pairings (2006: 27, 63).

# References

1. Haspelmath, M.: Againstmarkedness (and what to replace it with). Journal of Linguistics 42, 25–70 (2006)
2. Lyons, J.: Introduction to Theoretical Linguistics. Cambridge University Press, Cambridge (1968)
3. Lyons, J.: Semantics, vol. 1. Cambridge University Press, Cambridge (1977)
4. Alan, C.D.: Lexical Semantics. Cambridge University Press, Cambridge (1986)
5. Lehrer, A.: Markedness and antonymy. Linguistics 21, 397–429 (1985)
6. Lehrer, A.: Paradigmatic relations of exclusion and opposition I: gradable antonymy and complementarity. In: Cruse, D.A., Huandsnurcher, F., Job, M., Lutzeier, P.R. (eds.) Handbook of Lexicology, pp. 498–508. de Gruyter, Berlin (2002)
7. Lehrer, A., Lehrer, K.: Antonymy. Linguistics and Philosophy 5, 483–501 (1982)
8. Greenberg, J.: Language universals, with special reference to feature hierarchies. Janua-Linguarum, Series Minor 59. Mouton, The Hague (1966)
9. Zwicky, A.: On markedness in morphology. Die Sprache 24, 129–143 (1978)
10. Waugh, L.R.: Marked and unmarked: a choice between unequals. Semiotica 38, 299–318 (1982)
11. Leech, G., Rayson, P., Wilson, A.: Word frequencies in written and spokenEnglish based on the British National Corpus. Longman, Harlow (2001)

# On the Lexical Differences between South and North as Revealed by Diachronic Substitutions of Commonly Used Body-Part Terms

Wen-Hui Chou

Department of Chinese Literature of Tunghai University Taichung, Taiwan 40348
chouwhq@yahoo.com.tw

**Abstract.** This paper is concerning about the Middle Ancient Chinese lexical researches: It is an important task to discover the linguistic differences between the South and the North during the Southern and Northern Dynasties period. Prior discussions have always concentrated on phonological aspects, while lexical studies are nearly entirely absent. In this paper, we propose a systematic methodology to unearth lexical differences. By investigating diachronic substitutions of the commonly used body-part terms, we try to prove that the northerners tended to use the ancient word while the southerners adopted the new word yan in formal writing. This will partly confirms Yan Zhitui's(顏之推) point: "southerners often use vernacular words while northerners use archaisms." In the future, more studies of this kind will reveal the overall lexical differences between South and North, and will help us to understand the "Yan Zhitui Puzzle".

**Keywords:** the Middle Ancient Chinese, the Lexical Differences between South and North, the Diachronic Substitutions of Commonly Used Terms.

## 1    Introduction

*Yanshi Jiaxun - Yincipian*: "The south has gentle waters and lands, with sounds that are clear and focused, but their words are flippant and superficial, as the people use more vulgar vocabulary. The north has deep waters and powerful mountains, the people have low and serious tones, with slowness and mistakes, but they are plain and direct, more frequently use vocabulary from the ancient times". Based on this, Mr.Lu Guoyao proposed the term "Yan Zhitui's Puzzle." This puzzle points to the north-south distinctions in medieval phonology and vocabulary. However, these were only a few words that did not specifically describe the differences concretely, resulting in confusion among scholars. Since the 1960s, many scholars have discussed the north-south differences in phonology[1], but there have not been breakthroughs in terms of vocabulary. Thus, when Mr.Lu discussed phonology, he used "Half Solution of Yan

---

[1] As early as scholars began enthusiastically discussing the nature of *Qieyun* in 1961, they already discussed north-south differences in phonology, as Wang (1961), Tsou (1961), He (1961), Huang (1962), Chou (1963), etc.

P. Liu and Q. Su (Eds.): CLSW 2013, LNAI 8229, pp. 196–207, 2013.

Zhitui's Puzzle and its Half Solution" as the title, stating that phonology could be analyzed using Tong-Tai dialect, but it does not address vocabulary. The difficulty in interpreting vocabulary is that there is no obvious system; however, even though there are many vocabulary, there are still commonalities to be found. This study seeks to propose a method to systematically research differences in vocabularies, using the diachronic substitutions of commonly used terms under the unique framework of middle ancient vocabulary to explain the phenomenon of vulgarities in the south and ancient words in the north, in order to unveil the mysteries of the "Yan Zhitui's Puzzle."

The attempt to solve the "Yan Zhitui's Puzzle" first requires understanding of the features of middle ancient vocabulary. During this period, in terms of vocabulary development, there was development of disyllablization, with rich and diverse disyllabic structures. Politics and rivers separated the north and south during the Northern and Southern Dynasties, forming two sets of standard words. The two sets of standard words had distinct vocabularies after separate development.[2] The north-south difference was not only in terms, but also in disyllabic structure. Disyllablization and lexical difference between south and north must be compared at the same time in order to gain a comprehensive overview of the evolution of middle ancient vocabulary. Regardless of north or south, mixing the disyllabic structures would not be able to find the internal evolutionary rules of disyllablization. If the disyllabization is not emphasized, then research on similarities and differences in the north and south would require expenditure of energy without being able to gain systematic evidence. For instance, searches for lexical difference between south and north tend to sift through the literature records as if panning for gold, which takes a lot of time without leading to a lot of research gains. This shows that when researching middle ancient vocabulary, "disyllablization" and "north-south difference" are two topics that must be studied together or else their significance would both be lost.

Other than these two main points, there is another key that needs to be overcome to solve the puzzle. The so-called differences and similarities between the north and south actually are "more similar than different." In most cases, there were no major differences in the north-south vocabularies and expressions. In searching for the "small differences" between north and south, the research subject is very important, otherwise one would be lost in the sea of words. This study believes that language systems tend to move with the times; when this changing system was divided into two in the Northern and Southern Dynasties, Jinling and Yexia were affected by different factors. With the passage of time, it was impossible for the two languages to remain the same. Thus, if we seek to find lexical difference between south and north, we should begin with the changes in vocabulary, and one way to begin is with the diachronic substitutions of commonly used terms. In a dynamic evolution process of the diachronic substitutions of commonly used terms, when the standard words of Luoyang were separated by the politics and rivers, the two sets of standard words were formed for Jinling and Yexia, the substitutions of original terms would certainly have developed differently. Compared to uncommonly used terms with no

---

[2] Chou (2012a) discussed and explained the rich middle ancient disyallbic combinations and the general similarities and specific differences between the north and south.

substitution changes, commonly used terms with higher term frequencies would be even more likely to demonstrate north-south differences. Therefore, using the diachronic substitutions of commonly used terms as the beginning in researching north-south differences would likely be especially fruitful.

At the current time, research on substitution of commonly used terms in history has already been substantial in research on middle ancient vocabulary. Quantitative research is a common method, but at the beginning of substitution development, there were few examples, which tend to not be effective evidence. This problem is the difficulty in researching ancient Chinese terms and vocabularies. Unlike good word sense of modern Chinese linguistic studies as a foundation, researchers often need to rely on written evidence. They rely on quantitative comparisons excessively, and low term frequency would result in inadequate evidence. If it is possible to place research on the diachronic substitutions of commonly used terms in a systematic framework, even though there are few pieces of individual proof, when the same changes are occurring in different structures, there would be sufficient evidentiary power to construct a set of rules. Middle ancient Chinese provides for such an environment. As previously stated, there were many forms of middle ancient disyllabic structure, although there were not many individual examples for a set of diachronic substitutions of commonly used terms, they could be prevalent among different types of disyllabic structures, then such substitution could be proven. Then, input the factors of north-south difference, the different speeds in the diachronic substitutions of commonly used terms could be used to clearly see the lexical difference between south and north.

In the history of the Chinese language, middle ancient Chinese was in a key transitional point. Studying the differences in the two sets of standard words based in Jinling and Yexia helps us to understand the divergent development in the Northern and Southern Dynasties, as well as to explore the flux and competition between these two sets of standard words during the Sui and Tang dynasties; this is an important issue in the history of the Chinese language.

## 2    Research on Commonly Used Terms

Research of commonly used terms began with a reflection on traditional scholium. Unlike traditional scholium's emphasis on investigation of difficult terms, a new beginning in lexicological research was taking note of the usage and evolution of common terms in daily life. With the development of lexicology, research of commonly used terms has gradually received more attention. This study differs from investigation of difficult terms; other than identifying the meaning of terms, it also focuses on defining commonly used terms, the evolution of commonly used terms, and the substitution of commonly used terms. Wang Wei-hui (1999: 1-10), Bai Yun (2012: 1-10) described the history of research on commonly used terms: since the 1920s and 1930s, a group of scholars led by Li Ching-hsu began exploring commonly used terms, then in the 1940s and 1950s Wang Li began "new scholium" studies, describing in *Manuscript of Chinese History* the evolutionary traces of multiple sets of commonly used terms; then Chiang Shao-yu pointed out the importance of research on commonly used terms on lexical systems. Research on commonly used terms has gradually received more attention from scholars. Other than articles, there were specialized chapters or monographs such as Li Tzong-jiang's *Evolution of Common Words in Chinese*, Hsu Shi-yi's "Chapter 8 Exploration of Language Source and Evolution of Vocabularies" in *Research on the Vocabularies of Ancient and Vernacular Vocabularies*, and Wang Wei-hui's *Evolution of Common Words in East Han-Sui*. After 2000, this became a trend, with many articles3, as well as multiple published doctoral dissertations, as Lai Ji-chuan's "Comparative Study on Lun Yu and Common Words in the Annotates of Han and Wei", Rui Tung-li's "Original Meanings of the Single-syllable Common Words in Ancient Chinese", Gao Hai-yang's "Social Classification of Common Words in Beijing Dialects", Chang Ching-ching's "Evolution of Several Common Words in Contemporary Chinese", Yang, Shi-tie's "Study of Common Words in Early Qin Chinese", Yu Fei's "Research into the Common Words of Two Han Dynasties", and the recently published Bai Yun's *Common Synchronic and Diachronic Verbs in Chinese*.

For research on commonly used middle ancient terms, Wang Wei-hui's *Evolution of Common Words in East Han-Sui* was an important milestone. The book researched the substitutions of 41 sets of middle ancient commonly used term such as nouns, verbs, and adjectives over time, investigating large amounts of corpus, using sample sentences and statistical data to combine qualitative and quantitative studies, describing the rhythm of common term evolutions and reasons for substitutions of new and old terms. The advantage of this book was that it emphasized the characteristics of corpus, separating oral and written terms. More importantly, it noticed the importance of middle ancient disyllabic structure, emphasizing the differences between old and new term combinations and relationships. However, in terms of middle ancient vocabulary research, one flaw is that it did not consider the lexical difference between south and north. The following will discuss "mu/yan (eye)" in the researcher's study, in turn accentuate that the research on commonly used middle ancient terms must consider lexical difference between south and north.

"Mu" and "yan" is a set of commonly used terms that have been substituted over time, and have been mentioned by previous scholars. At earliest, "mu" was found in oracle bone writing, while "yan" was first found in extant literature in the Warring States period, which originally referred to eyeballs, and later gradually replaced "mu". Wang Wei-hui summarized the views of previous scholars, listing various supplementary references, to state that at first "yan" referred to "eyeballs" as stated by Wang Li. However, it did not replace "mu" in the Tang Dynasty, but as stated by Fang (1987), it was frequently used as "mu" in literature in the Han Wei and Six Dynasties. Wang Wei-hui also compared Buddhist sutras and Chinese literature, deriving the conclusion that "the replacement of [mu] by [yan] in oral speech would not have been later than the end of Han Dynasty" (Wang, 2000:29). Based on the fact that "yan"

---

[3] For instance, Wang Dong researched "Ou/jiao (corner)"; Lu Chuanfeng researched "he/in (drink)" and "zui/kou (mouth)"; Ding Chongming researched names for male spouses; Ye Guichen, Wang Yuewen, and Li Mingdi researched "shu/fu/kun/bang (to tie)"; Zheng Yanhua researched common terms "ya/chuang (window); Long Dan researched "ya/chi (teeth)"; and Xu Zhilin researched "quan/gou (dog)".

frequently appeared in Chinese texts, and its powerful ability to form other compounds, fifty or sixty terms such as "zuo yan (left eye)," "shuang yan (both eyes), and "mei yan (eyebrows and eyes)," and many of which were not interchangeable with "mu," Wang believed that "by the end of the Six Dynasties, in literary language [yan] had also gradually replaced [mu], but after this [mu] remained a part of the literary vocabulary system, coexisting with [yan] in the long term." (Wang, 2000:31)

Wang did raise real examples, but did not consider the differences in terms of "yan" and "mu," so there may have been overgeneralization. In comparing Buddhist sutras to Chinese texts, Buddhist sutras did indeed use "yan" more than "mu." However, in Chinese texts, the uses of "mu" was several times greater than "yan" during the Northern and Southern Dynasties, and had not been replaced by "yan." Considering the regional differences between texts containing "mu" and "yan," other than differences in oral speech and written text, there were clear north-south differences. Chou (2012b) researched this issue, finding that in northern texts, combinations with "yan" only appeared in Buddhist sutras or oral data, many of which were in neologisms; non-verbal tests were still primarily "mu," which conforms to Yan Zhitui's so-called "many ancient terms in their speech." On the other hand, in southern Chinese texts, disyllabic structure already showed the replacement of "mu" by "yan," which can be seen as an annotation for "many of the words are vulgar." Compared to Wang, this could better analyze the north-south differences, as well as the substitution of "mu" and "yan."

## 3    Differences and Similarities in Substitution of Commonly Used Terms for Body Parts in the North and South

Seen from the appearance of terms, other than the Buddhist sutra data, there was a greater ratio of ancient language being used in northern literature; there was greater usage of new terms in the south compared to in the north, which could be said that the north has more vocabulary from the ancient times and the south has more vulgar terms. However, in-depth observation of disyllabic structure could be better used to analyze the lexical difference between south and north.

In terms of parallel structure, two terms for body parts could be listed in parallel, the significance of disyllabic structure includes the simple addition of two body part terms such as  Case 1 "mianmu" referring to "face and eyes," there were also extended meanings such as in Case 2 "yanmian (social face)."

(1) 其　病中　　熱脹，　　面目　　浮腫。（《黃帝內經》）
　　 qi  bingzhong  rezhang　  *mianmu*  fuzhong. (Huangdi Neijing)
　 The   illness   fever bloating   face and eyes   bloated
　'In illness, there was fever bloating, with face and eyes bloated.'

(2) 吾　亦　何　面目　見　於　至尊？（《魏書•京兆王傳》）
　　 wu  yi  he  *mianmu*  jian　 yu  zhizun  (Weishu, Jingzhaowangchuan)
　　 I   also  what   social face  see   in   emperor
　'With what social face could I see the emperor? '

Thus, discussing substitution not only involves ancient words or new terms, but also whether there were changes in the compound terms. On the whole, there have been examples of using ancient words in the north and south, and other than simple addition, the meanings of compounds could also be brand new. The usage of new terms (such as using "yan" to substitute "mu" in mianyan) generally appears in southern texts, and the term meanings were always simple addition (as in Case3). This is an in-depth way of seeing "vulgar terms in the south."

(3) 其　根頭　似　蛇　　面眼。（《異苑》）

   *qi*  *gentou*  *si*  *she*  **mianyan** *(Yiyuan)*
   its  head  like  snake  face and eyes.
   'Its  head looked like the face and eyes of a snake. '

Since parallel structure involved placing two terms for body parts, if these two both have substitutions, the disyllabic combination shows which was substituted first. In terms of the substitutions of "shou/tou" and "mu/yan," the substitution of the former was before that of the latter. Thus, in the Northern and Southern Dynasties, we can discover that northern and southern texts both had "shoumu" formed by two ancient terms; southern texts included two new terms "touyan." However, when new was mixed with the old, then there was only "toumu" (Case 4)[4] and no "shouyan" or "yanshou," because the substitution of "shou" -- "tou" was earlier than that of "mu" -- "yan". When "tou" replaced "shou," "mu" may not have been substituted for "yan" yet, thus, there could be the combination of "toumu," then if "shou" was not substituted for "tou," it was because the substitution time was even earlier, so "mu" also had not been substituted, and naturally there would be no "shou" and "mu" combination. Similar conditions were also seen in the combination restrictions of "shou/tou" and "zu/jiao," because the substitution of "zu/jiao" was also later, so similarly there was no combination of "shou/jiao."

(4) 有　頭目　口喙，　無　手足，　而　動搖。（《宋書．五行志》）

   *you*  **toumu**  *kouhui,*  *wu*  *shouzu,*  *er*  *dongyao (Songshu, Wuxingzhi)*
   have  head and eyes  mouth,  no  hands and feet, .conj  move.
   'it had head and eyes and mouth, no hands and feet, and it moved on its own. '

Observation of different groups of terms being substituted more clearly shows the process of substitution. In terms of the group with earlier substitution, "tou/shou" used the combination of the ancient term "shou," other than few meanings of simple additions, there were many compound extended meanings such as "mianshou" to refer to young males (Case 5) to the inner palace governed by women (Cases 6-7), "shouling" refers to leaders (Case 8), "shouzu" refers to from head to feet (Case 9), "shouwei" refers to an amount of time (Cases 10--11) and space (Case 12) that can be calculated from beginning to end. These examples appeared in northern and southern texts; using the new term "tou" generally added up two terms simplistically, such as

---

[4] The reason that there was no combination of "mutou" was because the sequence of tones, "mu" is the entering tone, and tends to be in a later position, thus there was no combination of "mutou."

"touyan" (Case 13), "toumian (head and face)" (Case 14), "toujing (head and neck)" (Case 15), "touxiang (head and nape of neck)" (Case 16), "toujiao (head and feet)" (Case 17). There were few cases of extended meanings such as "touling (leader)" (Case 18). These cases mostly appeared in southern texts. In the north, other than Buddhist sutra information, they could also be found in more verbal texts in the north, such as "toujiao" (Case 19).

(5) 又 納 面首 生口 , 不 以 送 臺 , 免 官。( 《宋書 . 臧質 傳》 )

*you na **mianshou** shengkou, bu yi song tai, mian kuan. (Songshu, Zang Zhi Zhuan)*

also  accept young men servants,     no  use  send authorities  no official position.

'(He) also accepted young men and servants rather than sending them to authorities; this resulted in him being relieved of his position. '

(6) 為 主 置 面首 左右 三十 人。( 《魏書 . 劉子業傳》 )

*wei zhu zhi **mianshou** zuoyou sanshi ren. (Weishu, Liu Zi Chuan)*

for  princess. Arranged  young men  nearby  thirty  men.

'Arranged thirty handsome young men  for the princess. '

(7)帝 乃 為 主 置 面首 左右 三十 人。( 《宋書 . 前廢帝本 紀》 )

*di nai wei zhu zhii **mianshou** zuoyou sanshi ren. (Songshu, Qian-feidi Benji)*

Emperor  thus for  princess. arranged  young men  nearby  thirty  men.

'Thus the Emperor arranged thirty handsome young men for the princess. '

(8) 津 隨 賊 中 首領 ( 《魏書 . 楊津傳》 )

*jin sui zei zhong **shouling** (Weishu, Yang Jin Chuan)*

Jin  follow  thieves. among  the leader

'Jin followed the leader among thieves.'

(9) 通 以 大 袈裟 覆 衾 蒙 首足。( 南朝梁 《陶弘景集》 )

*tong yi da jiasha fu qin meng **shouzu** (Nanchaoliang Tao Hongjing Ji)*

General  use  big  Taoist priest cloak  cover  bedquilt cover head to feet.

'Used a large Taoist priest cloak to cover the head to feet. '

(10) 首尾 十 載 , 遂 忝 三州 七郡。( 《宋書 . 劉敬宣傳》 )

***shouwei** shi zai, sui tian sanzhou qijun. (Songshu, Liu Jingxuan Chuan)*

the time has been ten years, hence be three prefectures seven districts.

'The time has been ten years, and I have been an official in three prefectures and seven districts. '

(11) 惠蔚　首尾　　五　　載，無　所　　厝　意。(《魏書．崔光傳》)

*Huiwei* **showei** *wu zai, wu suo cuo yi.    (Weishu, Cui Guang Chuan)*

Huiwei from beginning to end   five years no        pay   attention

'Huiwei did not pay much attention   in the five years from beginning to end. '

(12) 自　項城　　至　長安，連　旗　千里，首尾　不　絕。(南朝宋《世說新語》)

*zi xiangcheng zhi zhangan, lian qi qianli,* **shouwei** *bu jue. (Nanchao-song Shishuo Xinyu)*

from     xiangcheng   to   zhangan,    continued flag   thousand miles continued no break

' The flags continued for a thousand miles from Xiangcheng to Changan without any break '

(13) 奉　月　初　告，承　極　不　平復，頭眼　半體　疢　恒　惡。(《王獻之集》)

*Feng yue chu gao, cheng ji bu pingfu,* **tuoyan** *banti chen heng e. (Wang Xianzhi Ji)*

As month beginning notice, from very not well the head and the eyes half side of the body illness still bad

'The notice from beginning of the month said that the body was still not being well, the head and the eyes and half side of the body were still in discomfort. '

(14) 賊　斫　綜　頭面，凡　四　創，綜　　當時　悶絕。(《宋書．潘縱傳》)

*zei zhuo zong* **toumian,** *fan si chuang, zong dangshi menjue. (Songshu, Pan Zong Chuan)*

bandits   cut     Zong head and face, all four   wounds   Zong   then     fainted

'The bandit cut Pan Zong's head and face, cutting four wounds, then Pan Zong fainted.'

(15) 見　一　竹竿　雉　頭頸　　　盡　　就，身　猶　未　變 (《異苑》)

*jian yi zhugan zhi* **tuojing** *jin jiu, shen you wei bian (Yiyuan)*

see one   bamboo pheasant  the head and neck    all  be , body still not   change

'(He) saw that a bamboo pole had turned into the form of a pheasant, the head and neck had changed, only the body was still the same. '

(16) 苦　頭項　　　　腰　　痛 (《王氏脈經》)

*ku* **tuoxiang** *yao* tong *(Wangshi Mojing)*

troubled   the head and the neck   waist     pain

'Troubled by pain in the head and the neck and waist '

(17) 得 一 物, 大 如 水牛, 青色 　 無 頭腳 （南朝宋《異苑》）

*de yi wu, da ru shuiniu, qingse wu **toujiao** (Nanchaosong, Yiyuan)*

get one thing size as buffalo ,green 　 no 　 head and feet

'Obtained something the size of a water buffalo, the color is green, with no head and feet. Sometimes it moved on its own. '

(18) 衣 被 　 故敝, 　 必 　 責 　 頭領。 （《宋書. 后妃傳》）

(Songshu, Houfeizhuan)

*yi bei 　 gubi, 　 bi 　 ze 　 **touling** (Songshu HoufeiChuan)*

clothes blankets worn-out must punish team leader

'If the clothes and blankets are worn-out, the team leader must be punished. '

(19) 小者 去 　 頭腳。 （北魏 《齊民要術》）

*xiaozhe qu **toujiao**. (Beiwei Qimin Yaoshu)*

small 　 remove the head and feet

'If small, remove the head and feet. '

Compared to "shou" -- "tou," the group of later substitution, "mu" -- "yan" had different expressions. Disyllabic structures using the ancient term "mu" were generally simple meaning additions, "bimu (nose and eyes)", "toumu (head and eyes)", "koumu (mouth and eyes)", "shoumu (hands and eyes)", "mushou (eyes and hands)", "shenmu (body and eyes)", there were fewer combinations with extended meanings, such as "mianmu (social face" (Cases 2), "meimu (fabrications)" (Case 20), "ermu (informants/attention)" (Case 21--22), which also appeared in northern and southern texts. As for the combinations that used the new term "yan," these tended to be simple additive meanings, such as "yanbi (eyes and nose)," "kouyan (mouth and eyes)", "mianyan (face and eyes)", "meiyan (eyebrows and eyes)", "yaner (eyes and ears)", "yanzu (eyes and feet)". Other than Buddhist sutras, these tended to be found in southern texts.

(20) 鼠輩 欲 輕 相 　 間構, 曲 生 　 　 眉目 。 （北齊 武成帝〈宣敕定州〉）

*shubei yu qing xiang jiangou, qu sheng **meimu**. (Beiqi Wuchengdi Xuanchi Dingzhou)*

bad people want casual each other frame casual creat fabrications

'These bad people wanted to frame him, so they created fabrications, and they should be killed according to the law. '

(21) 布 耳目 　 以為 　 視聽 。 （《宋書•劉穆之傳》）

*bu ermu 　 yiwei 　 **shiting**. (Songshu, Liu Muzhi Zhuan)*

arrange informants for what he saw and heard

'(Muzhi ) made informants tell him what they saw and heard so he knew the whole. '

(22)於是　　內為　　朋黨,　　防蔽　　耳目。(《魏書·皇后列傳》)

*yushi  neiwei    pengdang,  fangbi*  **ermu**.  *(Weishu, Huanghou Liechuan)*

therefore    gather    followers,    cover up    attention

'(The empress) gathered her followers to cover up the public attention.'

As for the mix of new and old, such as "toumu" and "touzu", are also seen frequently in southern texts, with no extended meanings.

Comparisons in the previous statement show that southern literature had more new terms. In the process of vocabulary substitution, simple addition of disyllabic structure was more easily substituted, thus these combinations appeared in many early terms at the start of substitution. If substitution had gone on for some time, then the simple additive compounds of ancient terms gradually disappeared, with only combinations with extended meanings left, such as the expression of "shou". The new term "tou" also gradually appeared in northern texts with more verbal characteristics; in the south combinations relating to "tou" began to have extended usages. At the beginning of substitution, such as the substitution of "yan" for "mu," and the simple additive compounds relating to "mu" had not all been replaced, while the new term "tou" tended to all be simple additive compounds in the south, while the new terms were rare in northern texts.

# 4    Conclusion

Observing the evolution of the diachronic substitutions of commonly used terms in the framework of middle ancient disyllablization clearly shows that the competition between old and new terms is not simplistic. Single syllable terms metabolized with the changes in time, new terms (such as "tou" and "yan") replaced old terms, completing substitution. However, the situation for disyllabic structure is relatively complex, it was difficult for old terms to be replaced from their tight disyllabic structures, especially the disyllabic compounds with extended meanings stayed as they were; but the looser disyllabic structures changed with the times, and were ultimately replaced by new terms. In-depth analysis of lexical difference between south and north could show the differences in substitutions speeds – faster in the south and slower in the north. Different types of diachronic substitutions of commonly used terms all show that the substituted new terms generally appeared in the south, which proves Yan Zhitui's statement that the south has more vulgar language while the north has more ancient language; the thousand-year mystery could be unraveled. This study not only analyzes the similarities and differences in north-south vocabularies, but can also analyze different substitution principles for single-syllabic terms and disyllabic structure in commonly used terms; this is a study with significant meaning.

# References

1. Wang, L.: Manuscript of Chinese History. Chung Hwa Book Company, Beijing (1980) (reprint)
2. Wang, F.Y.: Discussion on Anthology. Cultural Education Press, Changchun (1993)
3. Bai, Y.: Common Synchronic and Diachronic Verbs in Chinese. China Social Sciences Publishing House, Beijing (2012)
4. Wang, W.H.: Evolution of Common Words in East Han-Sui. Nanjing University Press, Nanjing (2000)
5. Li, T.J.: Evolution of Common Words in Chinese. Chinese Dictionary Publishing House (1999)
6. Chou, J.H.: Vocabularies in the Ghost Fictions of Wei, Jin, Northern and Southern Dynasties. Ba Shu Books, Chengdu (2006)
7. Chou, C.M.: The Characteristics of Qie Yun and its Phonetic Basis, Wen Xue Ji. Chung Hwa Book Company, Beijing (1963)
8. Chou, W.H.A.: Observation of the Characteristics of Chinese and Ancient Chinese Vocabularies. Wan-Juan Book Company, Taipei City (2012)
9. Gao, M.: Research into the Vocabularies in Chinese Ancient History Books. Tianjin Ancient Books Publishing House, Tianjin (2008)
10. Hsu, S.Y.: Research on the Vocabularies of Ancient and Vernacular Vocabularies. Shanghai Education Press, Shanghai (2000)
11. Chen, S.L.: A Comparative Study on the Language in Wei, Jin, Northern and Southern Texts and Buddhist Sutra. Chung Hwa Book Company, Beijing (2008)
12. Huang, J.G.: Investigation of the Classification of Word Meaning in Ancient Culture. Shanghai Education Press, Shanghai (1995)
13. Huang, J.G.: Distinction between Synonyms in Ancient Chinese and Mandarin Chinese. Shanghai Guji Publishing House, Shanghai (2002)
14. Guan, S.H.: Introduction to the Vocabularies in Ancient Chinese. Student Book, Taipei City (2006)
15. Fang, Y.H.: Does using "Yan" as "Mu" start in Tang Dynasty? Literature Study (3) (1987)
16. Wang, T.: A Diachronic Investigation of the Substitution of "Yu/Jiao". Journal of Yanan University, Social Science Edition (4) (2005)
17. Wang, T., Luo, M.Y.: Northern and Southern Dialects in the Northern and Southern Dynasties. Journal of Central South University of Technology, Social Science Edition (4) (2006)
18. Wang, T.: A Comparative Study on the Differences between Northern and Southern Word Usage in Northern and Southern Dynasties. Journal of Chang Jiang (3) (2008)
19. Wang, H.: The Naming and Characteristics of Qie Yun. Studies of the Chinese Language (4) (1961)
20. He, J.Y.: The Characteristics of the Phonetic System of Qie Yun – A discussion with Wang Hsian and Tsou Rong-fen. Studies of the Chinese Language (9) (1961)
21. Lyu, C.F.: A Diachronic Investigation of the Substitution of "He" and "Yin". Journal of Language and Literature Studies (9) (2005)
22. Lyu, C.F.: The Evolution of the Word Meaning of "Zui" and a Diachronic Investigation of the Substitution with "Kou". Language Study (1) (2006)
23. Li, L.: A Glimpse into the Northern and Southern Differences Among the Common Words Used in Northern and Southern Dynasties. Journal of Zhanjiang Normal College (4) (2011)

24. Chou, W.H.B.: The Similarities and Differences between the Common Languages in North and South – From the substitution of "yan" and "mu". Bulletin of Chinese Linguistics 6(1) (2012)

25. Tsou, R.F.: The Characteristics of Qie Yun and its Position in the Phonetic History of Chinesel. Studies of the Chinese Language (4) (1961)

26. Hsu, C.L.: A Diachronic Investigation of the Substitution of "Quan" and "Gou". Journal of Guangdong Education Institute (6) (2007)

27. Huang, B.C.: The Fundamental Problems of the Phonetic System of Qie Yun - A discussion with Wang Hsian and Tsou Rong-fen. Studies of the Chinese Language (2) (1962)

28. Yeh, G.C., Wang, Y.W., Li, M.C.: A Diachronic Investigation of the Substitution of "Shu", "Fu", "Kun" and "Bang". Journal of Hunan University of Science & Technology (6) (2007)

29. Cheng, Y.P.: A Diachronic Investigation of the Substitution of "You" and "Chuang". Journal of Hainan Radio (2) (2007)

30. Lu, G.Y.: "Yan Zhitui's Puzzle" and its Half Solution (1). Studies of the Chinese Language (6) (2002)

31. Lu, G.Y.: "Yan Zhitui's Puzzle" and its Half Solution (2). Studies of the Chinese Language (2) (2003)

32. Lu, G.Y.: A Collection of Lu Guo-yao's Papers on Linguistics. Jiangsu Education Publishing House, Nanjing (2003)

33. Long, D.: The Semantic Field of "Yachi" in Wei-Jin and its Evaluation Over Time. Language Study (4) (2007)

34. Lai, J.C.: Comparative Study on Lun Yu and Common Words in the Annotates of Han and Wei, Doctoral thesis, Sichuan University (2004)

35. Rui, T.L.: Original Meanings of the Single-syllable Common Words in Ancient Chinese, Doctoral thesis, Zhejiang University (2004)

36. Li, L.: Vocabularies in Wei Books, Nanjing: Doctoral thesis, Nanjing Normal University (2006)

37. Gao, H.Y.: Social Classification of Common Words in Beijing Dialects, Doctoral thesis, Beijing Language and Culture University (2006)

38. Chang, C.C.: Evolution of Several Common Words in Contemporary Chinese, Doctoral thesis, Soochow University (2007)

39. Yang, S.T.: Study of Common Words in Early Qin Chinese, Doctoral thesis, Anhui University (2007)

40. Yu, F.: Research into the Common Words of Two Han Dynasties, Doctoral thesis, Jilin University (2008)

# Semantic Derivation of the Lexical Item *Shen* in Mandarin Based on Conceptual Metaphor

Xiangyun Qiu

Department of Taiwan Institute of Literature,
National Changhua University of Education, Taiwan
chuss@cc.ncue.edu.tw

**Abstract.** The Mandarin word '*Shen*' (body)has determined its semantic derivation through conceptual metaphor and metonymy, further resulting in the phenomenon of polysemy. This research discusses how metaphors have influenced the semantic derivation of Mandarin term '*Shen*' used in Taiwan, analyze the term's various semantic derivatives, through ontological metaphor, container metaphor, spatial metaphor, metaphor in Buddhist realm, and metonymies of 'the part for the whole', 'the whole for the part' , 'the physical for the abstract', and finally generate a semantic relationship schema.

**Keywords:** Mandarin; *shen*; metaphor; metonymy; polysemy.

## 1    Introduction

Human beings start to understand the world from their own body and then further from exploring outside world. As a subject, human beings use their own experience as a prototype of conceptual cognition, and they base on their own body they are most familiar with as a reference to future construction of a new concept through metaphors. The '*Shen*(body)' can be said as the 'source concept' of understanding the world by human beings[1].

Physical metaphor is the mapping of people's own sensory experiences to external objects. The interaction between *Shen* and outside world has affected the formation of human cognition [2]. Gestalt theory, with body experience as the original source, can help us to construct the physical existence of the self and external world and then the concept of space and time, etc, body experience turns our concepts into a variety of image schema, thus body metaphor can be said to be the 'primary interface' [3].

Metaphors are one of the foundational ways of extending lexical meanings, and the principle governing polysemous relations is the metaphorical mapping of image schema [3].The phenomenon of polysemy is the result of continuous development of people's cognition abilities.

P. Liu and Q. Su (Eds.): CLSW 2013, LNAI 8229, pp. 208–219, 2013.

It is very common that the Mandarin term *Shen* exhibits extended meanings motivated by metaphors. All parts of the body from head to feet contribute to the source domain of cognitive metaphors and their semantic derivatives are developed through conceptual metaphors and metonymy. The metaphors in view of overall concept of *Shen* are rare seen. Ou Hsiu-Hui [4] discussed its development of polysemy from concrete to abstract meanings from the perspective of metaphors.Among which, metonymy and metaphor play a key role in extended meanings and cognition. How the commonly used words associated with Taiwan Mandarin term *Shen* present their extended meanings through metaphors? Can we construct a clearer system of its semantic derivative relationship schema? This article is to analyze its metaphor and metonymy types to understand the formation of the concept of ethnic awareness and then will be helpful for us to correctly grasp the word's meanings and for future language teaching job.

## 2    The Metaphorical Representations of Taiwan Chinese *Shen*

The so-called "conceptual metaphor" is to map the originally known experience to the unknown target domain, so as to achieve the purpose of re-understanding of the characteristics of target domain [5]."Cognitive metaphor" can be divided into two categories, "metaphor" and "metonymy"; among which,"metaphor" is the mapping process of different domains based on their similarities.

"*Shen*, the general term of the body, or specifically refers to the body" [6]. In addition, *Shen* in the ancient Oracle looks like 𠂤 ,and 𫝀 , which all portrait the silhouette of a standing person with a big belly. However, in most of the modern Chinese *Shen* words do not have the original meaning, instead they are extended meanings. MOE's Dictionary of Commonly Used Characters contains 610 entries of commonly used phrases composed of *Shen*[6], where the rich semantic expressions explainits phenomenon of polysemy. Conceptual metaphor is one of the key mechanisms of extending meanings. Base on Lakoff and Johnson( 1980 )[7], we will look at the metaphoric representation of Taiwan Chinese *Shen* derivatives.

### 2.1   Ontological Metaphor

As Lakoff and Johnson [7] state, ontological metaphor is composed of two categories: entity/substance metaphor and container metaphor. The former uses concrete objects to understand a bstract concepts. The mapping of other concrete domains of the Mandarin term *Shen* is represented as below:

**1. *Shen* Is an Object or the Appearance of an Object:** *Shen* originally refers to the human body, which is then projected onto other appearances of external objects. As it is mapped to animal domain, there are phrases such as *Shi Shen* (the body of lion), *Yu Shen* (the body of fish); *Shu Shen* (tree trunk) in plant domain; *He Shen*(river bed), *Qiao Shen*(bridge deck), *Che Shen*(automobile body), *Ji Shen* (aircraft body), *Wu Shen*(housestructure), *Qiang Shen*(frame), *Qin Shen* (body of instrument), *Dao Shen*(blade) are in other object domains, where the human body is mapped to other entities, referring to their appearances or main parts. Those examples as mentioned above all map the human body to other external wholeness of objects, representing semantic derivatives formed by personification metaphor.

The appearances of objects can apply the metaphor of the human 'body,' similarly, the human body can be the metaphor of other objects. For example, *Fei Shen*(fly) sees the human being as a flying object, *Zhi Shen*(be exposed to) and *Xian Shen*(be caught up) as objects within a container, and *Yu Huo Fen Shen*(horny) as combustible substances. Other words such as *Liang Shen* (tailor), *Qu Shen* (lean), *Tuo Shen* (rely on) and *Qian Shen* (retreat) all derive from the metaphors of countable, bendable, reliable and livable items and are the mapping of ontological metaphor to different domains.

**2. *Shen* Is a Container:** *Ren Shen* (the human body) is characterized with an accommodation, so 'the body' can be the metaphor of a container; for instance, *Man Shen* (all over the body), *Li Shen* (make one's home) implicitlysee the body as containers which can be refilled, and filled where as such metaphor is rarely seen.

**3. *Shen* Is the Abstract Realm of Buddhist Doctrine:** Metaphor is the mapping of concrete domain to abstract domain. As Buddhist doctrine is so abstract and deep that the superior Buddhist realm is almost beyond description, the Buddhist Sutras in Mandarin often used *Shen* as the metaphor of various abstract states in Buddhism. For instance, *Jin Shen*(golden body) and *Bu Huai Zhi Shen* (unrotton body) refer to eternal spiritual soul while Buddhist terms such as *Bao Shen*(Sambhogakaya), *Se Shen*(rupa-kaya),*Hua Shen* (three Buddha bodies showing for enlightenment of living beings), *Fa Shen* (the unmanifested body of the law) describe the lofty realm of the invisible and abstract by the tangible 'body' metaphor.

Heine [8] observed that when parts of the body are used to describe the items in the domain of inanimate objects, their shapes, functions, and relative positionsplay animportant role in aligning the human body with ontological metaphor. Here you can see a variety of representations of ontological metaphor of Mandarin Chinese *Shen* either based on physical similarity (eg. *Chuan Shen*), functional similarity (eg.*Man Shen*) or spatial similarity (eg.*Li Shen*). The "similarity" metaphor may be related to the likeness in shape or appearance, or the spiritual resemblance in quality or state; from physical to spiritual likeness, *Shen* can be the metaphor of abstract Buddhist realm.

## 2.2    Orientational Metaphor

Human beings live in the space where they move their body and perceive the changes in the space, thus forming the orientational metaphor. Lakoff and Jackendoff [7] pointed out that the metaphorical spatial orientation is not arbitrary, instead it is based on our physical and cultural experience. People use their body as a reference point to construct a series of orientational metaphors. Chinese *Shen's* orientational and spatial metaphor is then further mapped to abstract temporal domain. The representations follow as below:

**1. *Shen* Is Where the Space Is:** Heine [8] says that orientational markers are mainly sourced from body part words. Many body part words in Chinese occur the phenomenon of spatial concepts due to their extended meanings. For instance, *Tou* (head), *Mian*(face), *Shou*(hands), *Jiao* (feet) originally refer to the head of human beings, but turn out to form *Qian Tou*(front), *Hou Mian*(back), *Gao Shou*(master), *Shan Jiao*(foothills)through metaphor and analogy, expressing the spatial concept. The human 'body' exists in the space and *Shen* is the basis of cognition, thus forming the orientational metaphorical words such as *Shen Shang* (on the body), *Shang Shen*(upper body), *Xia Shen* (lower body), *Qi Shen*(get up), *Shen Bian*(around), *Bao Zai Wo Shen Shang* (count onme), *Re Huo Shang Shen*(get into trouble), *Tong Shen*(throughthe whole body), *Zhou Shen* (all over the body), *Shen Wai*(apart from the body), and *Ren Wu Zai Shen*(duty call). Among them is the special death metaphor with *Guo Shen* (pass away), which is a special case of orientational metaphor in Taiwan Chinese.

**2. *Shen* Is the Basis of Time:** Metaphor causes the phenomenon of semantic transfer, and the metaphorical body part words can be projected onto the domain of concrete items, container domain, space domain,but also onto the time domain[9] . Many temporal expressions are realized by orientational metaphors as the body movement in the space is similar to the change of time, translating many time metaphors into spatial metaphors. The concept of time in Mandarin mostly derives from spatial concept; for instance, *Qian Shen*(past life) refers to the past, *Shen Hou*(after death) to the future, *Yi Zhuan Shen*(at a glance) to very soon, *Sui Shen*(carry on one's person) to any time, *Zhong Shen Wei Fu*(father forever), *Zhong Shen Da Shi*(getting married)to a life time.   These are the semantic samples extending from space domain to time domain.

It is worth noting that *Qian Shen* and *Shen Qian* refer to the past while *Shen hou* refers to after death, where temporal metaphors as *Qian*(front) and *Hou*(back) may come up with different perceptions due to the metaphorical reference points, including these two metaphorical systems, *Ji Shen Zai Dong* (moving ego) and *Shi Jian Zai Dong* (moving time) [10]. In the concept of time as *Shi Jian Zai Dong*, *Qian* is the time course experienced, and *Hou* is regarded as that not yet experienced. For instance, *Qian/Hou Tian* (the day before/after), *Qian/Hou Bian Chang* (the first/second half), *Qian/Hou Shi* (previous/future lives), *Jin Hou* (in the future), *Yi hou* (later), *Qian Yin Hou Guo* (cause and effect), *QianRenZaiShu, Hou Ren Cheng Liang* (One generation plants the trees, another gets the shade.), etc. The following figure shows the metaphorical model of 'moving time' metaphor[11] [12]:

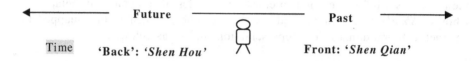

**Fig. 1.** Metaphoricalmodel of time of orientation-'moving time'metaphor

Regardless of time and place, people take *Ji Shen* (one's own body) as starting point to understand the external objects from near to farther place, from themselves to other people and entities, from concrete to abstract objects. As the 'body' is one of the visible entities, it can form other 'ontological' or 'container' metaphors. Moreover, due to people living in the space, 'spatial' or 'orientational' metaphors are constructed and extended to time metaphors. The whole world seems to have become a cognitive world based on the human perception of their body. People usually use their own sensory experience to understand the world.

The above is the metaphorical representation of Chinese *Shen*. The original meaning of *Shen* is the human body, but with the similarity to its shape, position, function and appearance, six types of semantic metaphors derived from *Shen* such as 'substance metaphor,' 'appearance metaphor,' 'container metaphor,' 'abstract Buddhist realm metaphor,' 'space metaphor' and 'time basis metaphor' have been presented. Overall, 'metaphorical' derivatives are structural and systematic.

## 3     The Metonymies of the Taiwan Chinese *Shen*

Metonymy is the replacement between objects of the same domain based on proximity. Depending on different categorization methods, there are many kinds of metonymy, but it can be mainly divided into three kinds: the part for the whole, the whole for the part, the part for the part [13]. The following is those examplesof metonymy:

## 3.1    The Part Stands for the Whole

**1. *Shen* stands for Human Beings or the Human Body:** The body originally refers to the torso of the human body, but it can be mapped to other abstract concepts such as the person's identity, characteristics and status based on the correlation. Those words include *Yi Shen*(alone), *Dan Shen*(single), *Du Shen*(single), *Gu Shen*(alone),*Zhi Shen*(alone), *Shen Ying*(figure), *Sheng Xing*(physique), *Xi Shen* (body wash), *Sui Shen*(portable), *Qi Shi Shen*(begging body), *Huang Pao Jia Shen*(acclaim emperor), *Sheng Zai Fu Zhong*(being in happiness), in which those *Shen* sappy the metonymy of the person itself.

**2. *Shen* stands for Existence of Individuals:** The existence of the body represents that of individuals. Further, the human shape has become the metonymy of human individuals, highlighting the existence of individuals. Such worlds are *Qi Shen*(habitat), *Rong Shen*(shelter), *An Sheng*(shelter), *Tong Shen* (through the whole body), *Ting Shen*(step forward), *Xian Shen* (caught up), *Cha Shen* (get involved), *Cang Shen*(hide), *Ying Shen* (shadow body), *Ying Shen* (stealth), *Yin Shen* (invisible), *Zheng Shen* (self identify), *Ba Shen* (get out), *Xian Shen* (show up), *Hun Shen* (full of), *Fen Shen* (the double), *Ti Shen* (the double), *Shan Shen*(dodge), *Wei Shen* (committment), *Dong Shen*(leave), *Ting Shen* (come forward), *Shen Chu* (living), *Shen Xian* (caught), *Ce Shen Qi Jian* (get involved), *Xian Chu Yuan Shen* (show true colors), *Quan Shen Er Tue* (get out), *Zhi Shen Shi Wai* (stay out), etc.

**3. *Shen* stands for Oneself:** Among the existence of enormous individuals, people realizethat the most important thing is their "self" existence; as "*Shen Zai Gu Wo Za*" (The body exist, before I am), the self extends its meaning to "self, onself" which has long been used before. For instance, in Texts of Taoism, "*Wu Suo Yi You Da Huan, Wei Wu You Shen*"(What makes me liable to great calamity is my having the body.)   Also in Xue Er of the Analects of Confucius, "*Wu Ri San Xing Wu Shen*" (I examine myself three times a day.) Both *Shen*s represent 'oneself.'   Further, those words in Chinese such as *Zi Shen* (itself), *Ben Shen* (in itself), *Lao Shen* (an elderly woman referring to herself), *Qie Shen*(Women referring to themselves in ancient time), *Qin Shen* (in person), *Qie Shen* (vital), *Shen Jiao* (teaching by example), *Gan Tong Shen Shou* (empathy), *Yi Shen Zuo Ze* (lead by example), and *Yin Huo Shao Shen* (draw the fire upon oneself), either in view of referring to oneself or to others, are all examples of metonymy by using *Shen* to represent "oneself."

**4. *Shen* stands for Life:** As "*Shen Zai Gu Wo Zai*" (The body exist, before I am,), so '*Shen*' has become the metonymy of "human life." Such words include *Shang Shen* (harmful), *Fang Shen* (self-defense), *Hu Sheng* (defense), *She Shen* (sacrifice), *Jian Shen* (donate body), *Xun Shen*(perish), *Zang Shen* (bury body), *Shen Wang* (dead), *Shen Gu*(death), *Yang Shen* (self-cultivation), *Quan Shen Zhi Ji* (a plan to save one's life), *Ren Shen Bao Xian* (life insurance), *Yi Shen Bao Guo* (give one's body for the nation), *You Guo Wang Shen* (die for one's country), *Sha Shen Cheng Ren*(die for a just cause), *Fen Shen Sui Gu*(die the cruelest death), *Fen Bu Gu Shen* (selfless), *Ming Zhe Bao Shen* (wise to play it safe), *Yun Shen Sui Shou* (sacrifice one's life), *Qing Shen Zhong Yi* (die for justice), *Yu Hai Quan Shen* (play safe), *Qing Shen Ying Jiu*(in a effort to rescue), and *Xun Yi Wang Shen* (die for justice).

**5. *Shen* stands for Physique:** *Shen Zi Gu* (the body) refers to human physique, so *Shen* can be the metonymy of human physique such as *Shen Zi Ruo* (weak), *Shen Zi Gu* (the body), *Jian Shen* (fitness), *Shen Qiang Ti Zhuang* (strong and healthy), *Shen Xin Ju Pi* (physically and mentally fatigue), and *Lao Shen Jiao Si* (exhausted and worried).

**6. *Shen* stands for Abilities:** *Shen* is used to refer to a certain ability of the body. Some parts of *Shen* (the body) and *Shou* (hands) turn out to be the metonymy of various abilities of one's hands, feet, the body and eyes. This belongs to the metonymy of the part for the whole, which occurs only with *Shen Shou Bu Fan* (extraordinary skill), *Hun Shen Jie Shu* (play all one's cards), etc.

## 3.2    The Whole Stands for the Part

**1. *Shen* stands for Parts of the Body:** Such words use the general term *Shen* to represent other unspecified parts of the body. For instance, *Xia Shen* (lower part of the body) refers to genitals, and *Shen Zhang* (physically challenged) means the person who is disabled from some of his physical part of his body. These words are euphemism that implicitly presents some clear parts of the body by the general term *Shen*. Other examples include *Shu Shen* (bind oneself), *Yao Shen* (waist), *Zhe Shen* (shelter), *Bi Shen* (shelter), *Quan Shen Shi Bing* (seriously ill), and *Shu Shen Jiu Bu* (surrender).

**2. *Shen* stands for Objects on the Body:** For instance,*Ci Qing* (Tattoo) means the tattoo on the body somewhere; *Suo Shen* (frisk) means to search the hidden items on someone' body; *Yi Shen Guang Xian* (dress classy) refers to the outfit one is wearing. Those words use the metonymy of *Shen* to represent those items that are located on the body.

**3. *Shen* stands for the Baby Inside the Body:** As previously mentioned that in the ancient Oracle and bronze inscriptions, the *Shen* itself depits the shape of the person with a big belly standing side ways, some draw out the symbols for the baby in pregnant belly,referring to the shape of big belly, namely the pregnant women.  In the Book of Poetry, Da Ya, Da Ming: *Da Ren You Shen, Sheng ci Wen Wang* (Da-ren became pregnant, and gave birth to our king Wen.) Taiwanese and Hakka still use '*You Shen*' to describe pregnant women, which is the metonymyof new life in the belly; '*Sun Shen*' refers to abortion, and others as *Dai Shen* Zi, *Huai Shen Zi, Zhong Shen Zi* and *Shuang Shen Zi,* all means 'pregnant,' which are deliberately obfuscated euphemism using the metonymy of the whole for the part.

## 3.3    The Part Stands for the Part (the Concrete Replacing the Abstract)

**1. *Shen* sands for Efforts:** As *Shen* refers to the person's external appearance and *Xin* (heart) means the person's inner thoughts, generally these two words are used as the oppositions.  However, *Shen* sometimes can be the metonymy of the body and the person's efforts(*Xin Li*), so those examples such as *Tou Shen* (indulged),*Xian Shen* (devotion) and *Zhi Shen* (endeavor) are all metonymies using *Shen* to represent "effort."

**2. *Shen* stands for Social Status:** *Shen* represents the existence of individuals and also the existence of *Wo* (I).Living in the society, every *Shen*(person) will naturally obtain different feedback, so *Shen* can be the metonymy of people's values and status in the society. Such examples as *Shen Shi* (life experience), *Shen Jia*(family background), *Shen Jia*(one's values), *Shen Fen* (identity), *Chu Shen* (origin), *Ji Shen* (rise in society), *Yin Shen* (unrotten corpse), *Shen Wei* (as a), *Fang Xia Shen Duan* (dropping one's pride), *Shen Xian Ming Yang* (become famous), *Shen Bu Yu Shi* (lack of good oppurtunity), *Li Shen Chu Shie* (conduct oneself in society), *Gong Cheng Shen Tui* (mission accomplished), *Shen Jian Shu Zhi* (wear different hats), *Shen Ju Yao Zhi*(occupy an important position) are all metonymies using *Shen* to represent people's social status.

**3. *Shen* stands for Virtue or Chastity:** Since *Shen* is the metonymy of representing inner thoughts with external part, maintaining theirself spiritual perfection is called *Xiu Shen* (self-cultivation), which uses *Shen* as the metonymy of people's inherent virtues. Chinese people are greatly affected by Confucian culture, which emphasizes on moral character, so there are many examples using "body" to represent "virtues" in ancient and modern texts. Others such as *Bu Zhan Shen* (not get involved), *Du Shan Qi Shen* (the perfection of individual morality), *Jie Shen Zi Hao* (keep your nose clean), *Ren Shen Gong Ji*(Name calling), *Shu Shen Zi Xiu* (constrain themselves with morality and self-cultivation), *Chi Shen Yan Jin* (exercise proper restaints), *Ren Wu Ren Shen* (Rich land makes a house luxurious, virtue makes a person shine), *ZhuoShen Bu Zhu* (out of control, especially morally), *RuShenBai Ming* (disgrace themselves and lose reputation), *ShenBai Ming Lie* (Totally discredited) are the metonymies of moral value judgments.

**4.** *Shen* **stands for Liberty:** *Shen* refers to the independent existence of individuals, once *Shen* cannot represent oneself, which means one loses personal liberty. This way *Shen* turns out to be the metonymy of *Ren Shen Zi You* (personal liberty.) Such metonymies include *Mai Shen* (sell oneself), *Shu Shen*(ransom), *Dian Shen Mai Ming* (sacrifice one's life) and *Shen Bu You Ji* (invulnerable) .

**5.** *Shen* **stands for a State or a Scenario:** Some words with *Shen* have their original meanings, but as they gradually expand their semantic usage, the state that *Shen* exists has become the metonymy of state and scenarios of other events.Therefore, *Zhan Shen* implies getting involved in one's state and *Tuo Shen* means getting away from a certain scenarios, which are metonymies of replacing a certain state by parts of the body. Other metonymies of scenarios are *Fan Shen* (restart life), *Bian Shen* (turn into), *Nuan Shen* (warm up), *Re Shen* (warm up), *Yao Shen Yi Bian*(suddenly), *Chou Shen Shi Wai*(get away one's work), *Ca Shen Er Guo* (passing by), etc.

**6.** *Shen* **stands for Manners or Attitude:** The action events of *Shen*(the body)can be the metonymy of the attitude of those who launch the events. These words with the body representing attitude are very common. For instance, *Tou Da* (big head) and *Xian Hong* (blush) refer to headache and shame; *Deng Yan* (stare at) and *Duo Jiao* (stomp) means angry. Among those words with *Shen*, *Qian Shen* (bow), means respectful; *Ping Shen* (you may rise) originally refers to the standing posture after the worship on bended kneesand is used by the ancient emperor to indicate the ministers forgoing the formality. All the examples use body's actions with *Shen* to express the emotional attitude of those who initiate. Nevertheless, some scholars think that the attitude is expressed by the entire verb phrases or words, not just by *Shen* itself.

**7.** *Shen* **stands for a Quantifier:** In conceptual metaphor, people see abstract things as concrete ones so that they can be referred, classified, categorized, and quantified. There are many examples of metonymy in Chinese using words with *Shen* to represent a quantifier. For instance, *Yi Tou Niu* (a cow), *Yi Yan Kan Chuan* (see through), *Yi Mian Dao* (one-sided), *Yi Bi Zi Hui* (a rebuff), *San Jiao Mao* (one's skill is not good enough), *Yi Shou Hao Cai*(good cook), and *Yi Du Zi Qi* (very angry). Other Chinese words with *Shen* as a quantifier include *Yi Shen Shang* (serious injuries), *Yi Shen Han* (sweating all over), *Yi Shen Shi Dan* (full of courage), and *Yi Shen Wu Yi* (very talented). These are temporary quantifiers where you can only say *Yi* (one), not *Er* (two) *Shen Shang*, *San* (three)*Shen Shang* or other phrases. However, *Shen* later has officially become the quantifier of categorization and calculation as *Yi Shen Shan* (one shirt) and *Er Shen Shan* (two shirts) in Taiwan Hakka and *San Shen* (three Buddha statues) and *Pu Sa Wu Bai Shen* (five hundred Buddha statues).

The above are the metonymies of Chinese word '*Shen*." Metonymy has a referential function. You can see the specific case that *You Shen* in Chinese remains the usage of ancient language; *Po Shen* and *Chi Shen* are metonymies of people's virtues and behaviors, representing abstract domain with concrete domain; *Shen* is not only seen as a temporary quantifier, it is used as officially quantifiers for calculating clothes or Buddha statues. *Shen* provides metonymies of entities,which shows various functions of the conceptual metaphor such as alternative, reference, categorization andquantification.

## 4    Conclusion

As previously mentioned, besides the original meaning of *Shen* (the body), there are six categories of metaphors such as substance, appearance, container, abstract Buddhist realm, spatial and time metaphor. For the metonymy of *Shen*, the first one is the part replacing the whole, extending meanings from *Shen* to human or human body, individual existence, oneself, one's life, efforts, and abilities. The second is the whole replacing the part, deriving from *Shen* the metonymies of body parts, objects on the body and the baby inside the body. The third is the part replacing the part, where *Shen* extends its meaning into eight categories: efforts, social status, chastity, virtues and conduct, personal liberty, state and scenarios and manners and attitude. To conclude, *Shen*, in addition to its original meaning, the semantic derivatives through metaphor and metonymy are as many as 24 kinds, creating a diversity of semanticderivatives. We can see that the polysemy of *Shen* is not developed separately, instead it is motivated by metaphor and metonymy, building a derivative relationship from concrete to abstract. Among them, we can see more examples of metonymies than metaphors. The following shows how those derivatives formed:

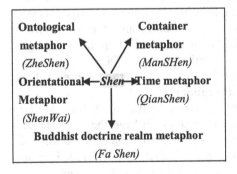
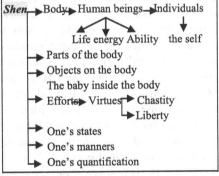

**Fig. 3.** The derivative diagram of metaphors

**Fig. 4.** The derivative diagram of metonymy

The following figure shows metaphorical derivatives from Chinese Shen (the body) seen before:

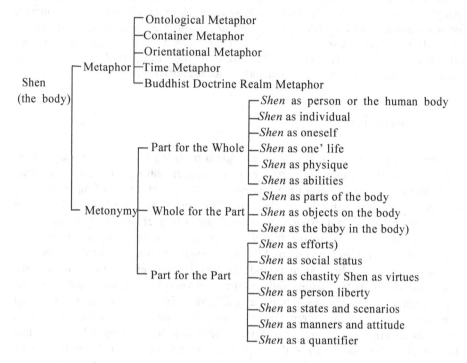

**Fig. 2.** The metaphorical relationship diagram of the Shen words

We can see from the above that cognitive metaphor and metonymy has impact on the semantic expansion where the former mostly applies radiation model and latter uses concatenation model. The metaphors highlight the similarity between two objects using the "analogy strategy", while metonymies focus on partial characteristics of a whole object using the "focus strategy" to quickly highlight the message with the intended meaning. Furthermore, in Taiwan Mandarin there are several metaphorical words rarely seen in modern Chinese such as *Guo Shen* (passed away) and *You Shen* (pregnant).

Conceptual metaphor is to gradually map concrete entities to abstract domain and the simple to the complex. With the central meaning of *Shen*(the body), layers of extended meanings through the metaphor and metonymy models are formed, where each kind of semantic derivatives is not separately discovered, instead, somewhat is correlated between them. The key to understanding the central and other meanings is to learn about the cognitive models of metaphor and metonymy [14]. The complex phenomenon of polysemy can be clearly analyzed through metaphor and metonymy to construct a meaning chain within a range of words [15]. Furthermore the overall understanding of semantic system feature sand semantic development can help us master Chinese semantic core content, proving that the body metaphor is indeed the primary interface for human beings to understand the world. Cognitive metaphor also provides us cognitive theories to understand the systematicity of polysemy and to precisely obtain the core meanings. This way we can easily track the context of semantic derivative system.

# References

1. Rong, H.B.: Semantic Research of Body Language, PHD thesis of Institite of Linguistic Studies, Shanghai International Studies University (2009)
2. Huang, S.F.: Embodied Cognition, Language and Cognition. In: Su, L.I.-W., Biq, Y.-O. (eds.), p. 341. National Taiwan University Press, Taipei (2009)
3. Cao, F., Tsai, L., Liu, H.: Body and metaphor: the first interface of language and cognition. The Crane Bookstores, Taipei (2001)
4. Ou, H.-H.: From metaphor looks at the word meaning gradation cognition of equivocal character-Take "the body" the character as an example. Da-Yeh Journal of General Education 1 (1998)
5. Shu, D.-F.: Metaphor and Metonymy: Similarities and Differences. Journal of Foreign Languages, General Serial No.151(3), 26–34 (2004)
6. Ministry of Education (2011), The Revised Mandarin Chinese dictionary: http://dict.revised.moe.edu.tw/
7. Lakoff, G., Johnson, M.: Metaphors we live by. U.S.A. University of Chicago Press, Chicago (1980)
8. Heine, B.: Cognitive Foundations of Grammar. Oxford University Press, NewYork (1997)
9. Zhao, X.: Cognitive Research of Body Language Semantic transfer. PHD thesis of School of Foreign Language and Literature, Fudan University (2010)
10. Zhou, R.: Psychological realityBased on Cognitive Metaphor–Experimental Evidence on Temoral and Spatial Metaphoric Representation. Foreign Language Teaching and Research 2, 88–93 (2001)
11. Fan, J.-H.: Metaphorical Use of Spatial Concepts "Front/Back". Journal of Beijing University of Aeronautics and Astronautics (Social Sciences Edition) 19(1), 66–69 (2006) (in Chinese)
12. Lai, L.-Y.: Love Metaphor of Pop music lyrics in Taiwanese (1980-2010), master's thesis of Graduate Institute of Taiwanese Literature, National Changhua Normal University of Education, p. 140 (2011)
13. Shie, J.-S.: Cognitive Linguistic Account of Conventional Metonymies in Contemporary Mandarin Chinese in Taiwan. Journal of Humanities and Social Sciences 4(1), 55–67 (2008)
14. Ling, Z.: A Cognitive Research of Polysemy. Journal of Wenzhou Vocational and Technical College 7(1), 60 (2007)
15. Huo, C.: Cognitive Interpretation of Polysemy –noun examples in parts of the body, master's thesis of Foreign Languages and Cultures, Nanjing Normal University (2011)

# On Acronyms in Chinese: A Prosodic Perspective

Jianfei Luo

Beijing Language and Culture University, Beijing, China
nch1980s@gmail.com

**Abstract.** Acronym is one way to create new words on the basis of existing expressions, but it is required to meet the codes of a language and its natural rhythm. In Chinese, disyllable is the best unit in the prosodic model. In order to form disyllables, some information is even dropped out. The creation of monosyllabic and trisyllablic acronyms is limited. Monosyllables can appear only in disyllabic feet; while trisyllables only appear on the condition that the disyllabic words cannot meet ideographic requirement. Trisyllabic words have disyllabliz- ing tendency. Few acronyms with four or five syllables can be found due to the fact that they go against the principle of economy.

**Keywords:** acronym, natural foot, prosodic, prosodic word.

## 1   Introduction

Acronym, formed on the basis of the Economy Principle, is a kind of convenient and practical way to simplify expressions. It meets the needs of daily communication. Acronyms are generally derived from complex words or fixed phrases.

In the literature, Chinese acronyms are studied from many aspects. Tian Zong & Xiao Jiugen(2006) have studied its forming methods or mechanism and Zhang Zhiguo & Yang Ling (2003) its causes. Its features, principles and some other aspects are also discussed in some theses or dissertations. Generally speaking, when scholars carry out research on acronyms, they focus mainly on their classification, causes, features, and the relationship between the original words and acronyms. Moreover, According to some scholars, statistics shows that more than 70% of the acronyms are disyllables. Our question is: is the number of syllables related with the formation of acronym? If the answer is yes, how does the number of syllable affect the formation of the acronyms?

## 2   Basic Models of Acronym Formation

We propose that the following assumptions: Chinese acronyms need to go through two processing programs from the original type (words or expressions) to the output. The first one is to extract the key words. In this program, the most important elements are the meaning, information and the focus of Chinese original words. When getting down to the processing or integration, we may have more than one option. Here, the

P. Liu and Q. Su (Eds.): CLSW 2013, LNAI 8229, pp. 220–228, 2013.

restriction of prosodic words and natural foot must be taken into consideration. Applicable acronyms cannot be obtained without these two steps. A chart is provided below to show the process:

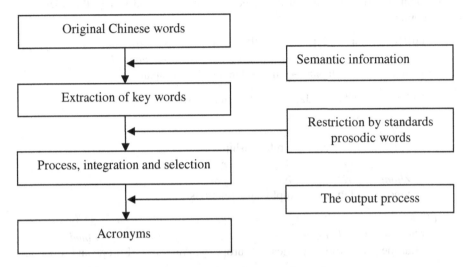

**Fig. 1.** Basic models of acronym formation

## 3      Relationship between Acronyms and Prosodic Words

### 3.1     A Monosyllable Cannot Stand Alone

In the standard prosodic word system, the monosyllable cannot make a foot. For example (f refers to foot, while σ refers to syllable):

This conclusion is drawn in accordance with the requirement of Chinese natural foot. In a word whose meaning are not from the inside characters, like 德谟克拉西[*de mo ke la xi*] (democracy) or a word consisting of duplicated serial like 55555, a monosyllable cannot stand alone, i.e., [...*/σ/...]. The reason is that in Chinese a monosyllable cannot form an independent foot. The natural foot denies the independence of monosyllables.

According to the theory we mentioned above, though in Chinese certain category can be briefed as monosyllable, their existence must be constrained by the requirement of prosodic words and natural foot. A monosyllabic acronym cannot stand by itself, but appear together with another monosyllable. When examined specifically, we can find that most Chinese monosyllabic acronyms are nouns indicating certain places. For example, "日"[*Ri*] (Japan) is a short form for "日本"[*Riben*] (Japan), "中"[*Zhong*] (China) is short for "中国" [*Zhongguo*] (China), so we have phrases like "

中日友好"[*Zhongri youhao*] (friendship between China and Japan), "中日邦交" [Zhongri bangjiao] (Sino Japan diplomatic relations).

**3.1.1** Combine two acronyms of the same kind and then add some other elements. For example:

(1)中国    +  日本 →    中   +  日  →  中  日
*Zhongguo* + *Riben* → *zhong* +  *ri*  → *zhong ri*
China    +  Japan → China+ Japan → Sino Japan

(2)中日[*Zhongri*] (Sino Japan) + other elements:

a.  中      日      关系
*Zhong*   *ri*      *guanxi*
Sino     Japan     relationship

b.  中      日      邦      交
*Zhong*   *ri*      *bang*    *jiao*
Sino     Japan     diplomatic relations

(3) 欧洲   +   北  美   →   欧  +  美   →   欧美
*Ouzhou* + *Bei mei*   →   *Ou* + *Mei*  →   *Oumei*
Europe  + North America → Europe  + America →Europe and America

(4)欧美[*Oumei*] (Europe and America) + other elements:

a.  欧    美      电影
*Ou*   *mei*    *dianying*
European and American movies

b.  欧    美      服装
*Ou*   *mei*    *fuzhuang*
European and American clothes

**3.1.2** An acronym and a monosyllabic element make a disyllabic word, such as"赴韩 "[*fuhan*] (go to South Korea), "访美"[*fangmei*] (visit US), "亲日"[*qinri*] (Pro-Japanese Diplomacy). This kind of combination has two restrictions:

First of all, they often appear on the written texts and seldom appear in oral Chinese. For example:

(5)访   美      赴  美       *去  美
*fang  mei*    *fu  mei*      *qu  mei*
visit US       go to US       go to US

Secondly, most words collocating with this kind of acronym are "Disyllabe-templated Mono-Word". Namely, these monosyllables should embed in disyllables models. For example:

(6)访  美   *访   美国   *访   学  者   *访   著  名  学  者
*fang mei*  *fang Meiguo*  *fang  xuezhe*   *fang  zhuming  xuezhe*
visit US    visit US      visit  scholar      famous visiting scholar

| (7)赴 | 日 | *赴 | 日 | 本 | *赴 | 宴 | 会 | *赴 | 学 | 术 | 会 | 议 |
|---|---|---|---|---|---|---|---|---|---|---|---|---|
| *fu* | *ri* | *\*fu* | *Riben* | | *\*fu* | *yanhui* | | *\*fu* | *xueshu* | *huiyi* | | |
| go to Japan | | go to Japan | | | go to party | | | go to academic meeting | | | | |

From the above examples we can see, although certain category is briefed as a monosyllable, its number is limited. The reason is that in Chinese, a monosyllable cannot form a foot itself. A standard prosodic word is made of two syllables. In order to meet this requirement, a monosyllabic component can only stand side by side with another monosyllabic element, forming a foot.

## 3.2    Disyllables as the Best Mode

A foot consists of at least two constituents (Foot Binarity Principal). Since a monosyllable in Chinese cannot form a foot ($\sigma \neq f$), a disyllable becomes the only choice, and in the theory of Prosodic Morphology, it is considered to be the Foot Binarity Principal.

For Chinese acronyms, disyllable is the most common form. No matter how many syllables or feet are there in the original Chinese words, people always trend to select two symbolized syllables for short. We will analyze the formation of disyllable acronym from combination of different feet later.

3.2.1 For those words which originally consist of three syllables, i.e., 2+1 or 1+2, there are four ways to form acronyms:

(8) 2+1 → 1+1

| 机关 | 枪 | → | 机 | 枪 |
|---|---|---|---|---|
| *jiguan* | *qiang* | | *ji* | *qiang* |
| machine gun | | | machine | gun |

(9) 2+1 → 2+0

| 后勤 | 部 | → | 后勤 |
|---|---|---|---|
| *houqin* | *bu* | | *houqin* |
| logistics | department | | logistics department |

(10) 1+2 → 1+1

| 副 | 高 | 级 | → | 副 | 高 |
|---|---|---|---|---|---|
| *fu* | *gao* | *ji* | | *fu* | *gao* |
| associate | senior | | | associate senior | |

(11) 1+2 → 0+2

| 毛 | 白杨 | → | 白杨 |
|---|---|---|---|
| *mao* | *bai yang* | | *bai yang* |
| white poplar | | | white poplar |

3.2.2 For those words which originally consist of four syllables, i.e., 2+2, the deriving ways are as follows:

(1) V+V: 惩教 [*chengjiao*] (punishment and education)—惩罚教育 [*chengfa jiaoyu*] (punishment and education)

(2) N+N: 档级 [*dangji*] (level)—档次和级别 [*dangci    jibie*] (level)

(3). V+N: 倒币 [*daobi*] (resell the currency as profit)—倒卖货币 [*daomai huobi*] (resell the currency as profit)

(4) Modified structure: 杜诗 [*dushi*] (Dufu's poetry)—杜甫的诗 [*Dufu de shi*] (Dufu's poetry)

3.2.3 For those words which originally consist of five syllables, i.e., of three or more than three feet. The way is as follows:

(1). Select one character from every foot with overall significance to compose the acronym. Such as [[鞍山]钢铁公司] [*Anshan gangtie gongsi*] (Anshan Iron and Steel Company)—鞍钢[*An gang*] (Anshan Iron and Steel Company), [[彩色照片]打印][*caise zhaopian dayin*] (print chromo photograph)—彩印[*caiyin*] (print chromo photograph).

This type is in accordance with the rule of natural foot and semantic information. It is the most common way to form disyllabic words. More specifically, we select the most informational key words, which best represent the rhythms and information, to form acronyms.

(2). Abandon a foot (or super foot) and select one syllable from each of the rest feet to make a disyllable acronym. For example, [[香港]壁球总会] [*Xianggang biqiu zonghui*] (Hong Kong Squash)—壁总[*bi zong*] (Hong Kong Squash), [[乙型肝炎][表面抗原]] [*yixing ganyan biaomian kangyuan*] (hepatitis B surface antigen)—表抗 [*biao kang*] (hepatitis B surface antigen).

This method is not in complete accordance with the basic principle of "information equivalence", so the composition of a completed foot or a super foot generally carries the overall semantic information with it. Once these compositions are completely abandoned, some semantic information will also be lost. As a result, it will be ambiguous or unclear. Take 壁总[*bi zong*] (Hong Kong Squash) as an example, if this news is broadcast in Hong Kong, people there naturally know that it refers to 香港壁球总会[*Xianggang biqiu zonghui*] (Hong Kong Squash). However, if there are 台湾壁球总会[*Taiwan biqiu zonghui*] (Taiwan Squash), 北京壁球总会[*Beijing biqiu zonghui*] (Beijing Squash), we cannot abandon the foot completely; instead, we use the information of the first foot to make it clear. Then we may have some new acronyms, such as 港壁总[*Gang bi zong*] (Hong Kong Squash), 台壁总[*Tai bi zong*] (Taiwan Squash) and 京壁总[*Jing bi zong*] (Beijing Squash).

In general, disyllabic acronyms have advantages in number, productivity and formation methods. Being the main way to form acronyms Chinese, they take a large proportion of all the Chinese acronyms. Of course, their forming method is generally in accordance with attributes of "information equivalence". Those that are not of complete information equivalence can be used only in a certain situation or by adding certain parts which have strong presuppositions so as to avoid ambiguity.

### 3.3 Conditions in Deriving Trisyllabic Words and Their Transitions to Disyllabic Words

In the study of natural foot, disyllabic words are generally considered as the best natural modes. Although a trisyllabic word forms a super foot, it is weaker in the stability and rhythms than a disyllabic word. Generally speaking, under the same conditions of grammar, semantics and pragmatics, disyllabic words are preferred. This is also true of Chinese acronyms. Specifically speaking, there are three points we should pay attention to. First, the number of trisyllabic acronyms is much less than that of disyllabic acronyms. Second, the productivity of trisyllabic acronyms is weaker than disyllabic ones. What is more, some trisyllabic acronyms have the tendency to become disyllabic, and after the transformation, most disyllabic acronyms are used more often than the original trisyllabic ones.

#### 3.3.1 Formation Method of Trisyllabic Acronym

(1) The existence of disyllabic acronym needs more semantic information. For example:

(12)调研[*diaoyan*] (research)—调研员[*diaoyan yuan*] (researcher)

(13)防洪[*fanghong*] (flood control)—防洪墙[*fanghong qiang*] (anti-flood wall)

(14)夜大[*yeda*] (night university)—夜大生[*yeda sheng*] (night university student)

(15)劳保[*laobao*] (labor insurance)—劳保鞋[*laobao xie*] (safety shoes)

(16)测绘[*cehui*] (mapping)—测绘局[*cehui ju*] (mapping agency)

(17)扫盲[*saomang*] (eliminate illiteracy)—扫盲班[*saomang ban*] (literacy class)

(2) For some original three-foot words, we cannot abandon a certain foot and select only two syllables from the rest feet. Since it will not stand for the whole meaning of the words or it will make ambiguity. For example, 清查住房办公室[*qingcha zhufang bangongshi*] (inventory housing office)—查房办[*chafang ban*] (inventory housing office).

If in this example we keep only 查[*cha*] (check), and left the object, a listener or reader will not know what it refers to. However, if we call it 房办[*fangban*] (housing office), people will misunderstand it as 房屋办公室[*fangwu bangong shi*] (housing office or other offices relative to the house). In this case, the acronym will lose the meaning of 清查 [*qingcha*] (check), which means to check. Thus, generally one symbolized character of each foot must be taken to form a trisyllabic acronym.

#### 3.3.2 Relation between Trisyllabic Acronym and Natural Foot

In the formation of trisyllabic acronyms, we can find two kinds of internal modes if we consider the relationship between acronym and natural foot.

(1) The technical model is consistent with natural foot, such as 清查住房办公室[*qingcha zhufang bangongshi*] (inventory housing office)—查房办[*chafang ban*] (inventory housing office). That is to say, we select one key character/syllable from each foot to symbolize the information of the whole foot to form

an acronym. Just like the examples above, we select the element in a [2+1] way, which is consistent with the natural foot.

(2) The technical model is not in accordance with the natural foot, such as 城运会[*chengyun hui*] (city sports meeting), 初职班[*chuzhi ban*] (the primary professional class), 二商局[*ershang ju*] (the second commercial bureau).

The acronym 城运会[*chengyun hui*] (city sports meeting) is formed with the character 城[*cheng*] (city) from the foot 城市[*chengshi*] (city) and characters 运[*yun*] (sports) and 会[*hui*] (meeting) from the trisyllabic super foot 运动会[*yundonghui*] (sports meeting). The mode of this acronym is [1+2], namely 城 + 运会 [*cheng+yunhui*] (city sports meeting), however, if we follow people's intuition or Chinese natural foot, we should read like [2+1], 城运+会[*chengyun+hui*] (city sports meeting). More examples:

**Table 1.** The mismatch between three-syllable acronym and natural foot

| Original words | Syncopated by the structure | Syncopated by natural foot |
|---|---|---|
| 初级职业班<br>*chuji zhiye ban*<br>The primary professional class | 初 + 职班<br>*chu + zhiban*<br>The primary professional class | 初职 + 班<br>*chuzhi + ban*<br>The primary professional class |
| 第二商业局<br>*dier shangye ju*<br>the second commercial bureau | 二 +商局<br>*er + shangju*<br>the second commercial bureau | 二商 + 局<br>*ershang + ju*<br>the second commercial bureau |
| 传授技艺的讲习所<br>*chuanshou jiyi de jiangxisuo*<br>technical skills institute | 传 +习所<br>*chuan + xisuo*<br>technical skills institute | 传习 +所<br>*chuanxi + suo*<br>technical skills institute |
| 船舶运输研究所<br>*chuanbo yunshu yanjiusuo*<br>transportation research institute | 船 + 研所<br>*chuan + yansuo*<br>transportation research institute | 船研 + 所<br>*chuanyan + suo*<br>transportation research institute |

The chart above can be summarized as: there are two different situations in the internal structure in trisyllabic acronyms. The first kind is the elements of acronym consistent with the natural foot, and the other one is the elements of acronym in conflict with the natural foot. However, no matter in which mode it is, our reading sense is eventually realized by the natural foot.

### 3.3.3  Relations between Trisyllabic Acronym and Disyllabic Acronym

Some acronyms can be realized either as disyllables or trisyllables. More often than not, disyllabic acronyms play important roles, for example, some examples are given below:

(18) 上  影  厂   上  影
*Shang* *ying* *chang*  *Shang* *ying*
Shanghai film studio  Shanghai film studio

(19) 社  科  联   社  联
*she* *ke* *lian*  *she* *lian*
social science association social science association

(20) 微  型  机   微  机
*weixing* *ji*  *wei* *ji*
microcomputer  microcomputer

(21) 工  体 场   工  体
*gong* *ti* *chang*  *gong* *ti*
Worker Stadium  Worker Stadium

Besides, in Spoken Chinese, the ambiguity of some disyllabic acronyms can be eliminated under certain situations. Take 山东师范大学[*Shandong shifan daxue*] (Shandong Normal University) as an example, we can call it either as 山师大[*Shan shida*] (Shandong Normal University) or 师大[*shida*] (Normal University) for short. When using these two acronyms in Jinan (the capital city of Shandong Province where Shandong Normal University is located), people can easily understand them. But people outside of Jinan may get confused with 师大[*shida*] (Shandong Normal University), because there are some other normal universities except Shandong Normal University in Jinan. This also happens to 港壁[*gangbi*] (Hong Kong Squash) and 港壁总[*Gang bizong*] (Hong Kong Squash). Thus, standard disyllabic acronyms can be used as long as we can avoid the ambiguity.

### 3.4 Tetrasyllabic Acronym and Disyllabic Acronyms

There are mainly two ways to form a tetrasyllabic acronym. Firstly, two apposite disyllabic acronyms form a tetrasyllabic acronym. Such as 反腐倡廉[*fanfu changlian*] (combat corruption and unhold integrity), 反骄破满[*fanjiao poman*] (combat arrogance and complacency), 反帝反殖[*fandi fanzhi*] (combat imperialism and colonialism). The rhythm modes of these words are very similar to some Chinese idioms. Besides, we can also form a tetrasyllabic acronym by selecting two syllables from the original super-syllable words plus an existing word. Such as, 反帝同盟[*fandi tongmeng*] (anti-imperialist Union), 反猎人士[*fanlie renshi*] (anti-hunting people), 非洲民盟[*Feizhou minmeng*] (Africa Union).

The first foot mode is actually the combination of two standard prosodic words which is a "standard compound prosodic word". It accords with the standard mode of rhythm and has its special rhythm property; it can also be taken apart and used by itself, while the second kind of foot mode can be selectively abbreviated again. For example, 非洲民盟[*Feizhou minmeng*] (Africa Union)→ 非盟[*fei meng*] (Africa Union). It can become the standard disyllabic foot.

# 4 Summary

We can make a conclusion from the analysis above.

(1) The formation of Chinese acronym is creation and process of the existing Chinese words. It should meet the codes of language and natural rhythm.

(2) In Chinese language, disyllable is the best unit in prosodic model. Therefore when people create acronyms, they prefer disyllables regardless of the number of foot, even with some information missed.

(3) The natural mode of Chinese trisyllabic noun phrases is [2+1] mode. So when we create the acronym, we prefer the mode of [2+1].

(4) The mode of tetrasyllabic acronym is [2+2], which is very similar to composite prosodic words. Acronyms with more than five syllables are called super composite prosodic words.

**Acknowledgements.** This research is sponsored by Beijing Language and Culture University graduate innovation project (13ycx018). Thank Cen Ling from Central China Normal University for helping the translation.

# References

1. Chao, Y.R.: A Grammar of Spoken Chinese. University of California Press, Berkeley (1968)
2. Chomsky, N.: Knowledge of language: its nature, origin and use. Praeger, New York (1986)
3. Duanmu, S.: A Formal Study of Syllable, Tone, Stress and Domain in Chinese Languages. Doctoral Dissertation, MIT (1990)
4. Feng, S.: Interactions Between Morphology, Syntax and Prosody in Chinese (Revised Edition). Peking University Press, Beijing (2009) (in Chinese)
5. Feng, S.: Studies on Chinese Prosodic Grammar. Peking University Press, Beijing (2005) (in Chinese)
6. Feng, S.: The Prosodic Syntax of Chinese. Shanghai Education Press, Shanghai (2000) (in Chinese)
7. Hayes, B.: A Metrical Theory of Stress Rules. Doctoral Dissertation, MIT (1980)
8. Li, W.: Study of Way of Formation and Standarization of abbreviation in contemporary Russian and Chinese. Dissertation for the Master Degree. Harbin Institute of Technology, Harbin (2006) (in Chinese)
9. Liberman, M., Prince, A.: On stress and linguistic rhythm. Linguistic Inquiry 8 (1997)
10. Tian, Z., Xiao, J.: Form Pattern of Chinese Abbreviation and Its Mechanism. Journal of Jiangxi Normal University (Social Sciences) 39(6), 36–41 (2006) (in Chinese)
11. Zhang, Y.: A Study of Chinese Lexical Abbreviations from the Perspective of Optimality Theory, Dissertation for the Master Degree, Xiangtan University, Hunan (2008)
12. Zhang, Z., Yang, L.: Analysis of the Causes of Abbreviation. Shandong Foreign Language Teaching Journal 93(2), 22–24 (2003) (in Chinese)

# Regularity and Idiomaticity in Chinese Separable Verbs

Lulu Wang[1,2] and Stefan Müller[3,*]

[1] Dept. of Chinese Lang. & Lit., Peking University, 100871 Beijing, China
[2] School of Lang. & Lit. Communication University of China,
100024 Beijing, China
hettylulu@gmail.com
[3] Dept. of Philosophy and Humanities, Free University of Berlin, 14195 Berlin, Germany
Stefan.Mueller@fu-berlin.de

**Abstract.** This paper deals with the lexical representation of Chinese Separable Verbs (thereafter SVs) within the framework of Head-Driven Phrase Structure Grammar (HPSG). We argue that SVs are syntactically flexible, but semantically decomposable or non-decomposable expressions, which are similar to the idiomatic expressions in English. For decomposable SVs, we specify the verbal parts of SVs selecting the nominal parts via the LID feature proposed by Sag (2007a). For decomposable SVs, we introduce a special lexical entry of the head verb to specify the idiomatic meaning with the co-occurring nominal part. For non-decomposable SVs, the syntactic structure is represented as a head-complement-phrase consisting of the head verb and the complement with an empty SLASH value. The meaning of idiomatic SVs is represented at the head.

**Keywords:** Separable Verb, Semantic Constraint, Cooccurrence Restriction, HPSG.

## 1 Introduction

This paper deals with idiomatic expressions like lǐfà in (1a). These elements have word-like properties and are traditionally called compounds (Smith, 1999). As (1b) shows these idiomatic expressions can appear discontinuously and hence are called separable verbs/words/idioms (Li, 2001), phrasal verbs, or compound verbs. This terminology reflects the two-fold nature of such expressions, that is, as a word or a phrase.

(1)   a.  jīntiān kěyǐ qù **lǐfà**    le.
          today can to haircut Mood
          'It is OK to have a haircut today.' (from 'wéichéng')

      b.  gūyé     gāng **lǐ** le    **fà** huílái.
          son-in-law just cut PERF hair back
          'Just having had a haircut, the son-in-law was back.' (from 'wéichéng')

---

\* Stefan Müller was involved in discussing the phenomena discussed here and the analysis suggested in this paper, he read earlier versions of the paper several times and contributed crucial insights, therefore I decided to list him as a coauthor. However, the responsibility of mistakes is mine.

P. Liu and Q. Su (Eds.): CLSW 2013, LNAI 8229, pp. 229–240, 2013.
© Springer-Verlag Berlin Heidelberg 2013

Apart from their adjacent realization, separable verbs interact in various ways with the rest of the grammar: their parts can be separated by adjuncts and they interact with control, passive, and topicalization. However, the meaning of the SVs is the same whether they are realized as continuous items (words) or discontinuously in syntactic constructions.

This paper offers a lexical account of Chinese SVs in HPSG. To start with, we give a general presentation of the flexibility and frozenness of SVs. Then we go through the literature on SVs and idiomatic expressions in HPSG in Section 3. In Section 4, we will analyze the syntactic and semantic representations of SVs. A short conclusion is given in the end.

## 2  Phenomenon

### 2.1  Basic Facts

In mandarin Chinese, separable verbs (thereafter SVs) denote to the expressions that behave either as words in (1a) or as phrases in (1b).[1]

(2)   a.  zhōngruì yě  hěn  **yōumò**.
          name      also very humorous
          'Zhongrui is humorous too.' (from 'sòng shìqióng zì shù')

      b.  shīfù,  nǐn yòu  **yōu**  le   yī  **mò**.
          master, you again conceal PERF one silent
          'Master, you have made a joke again.'(from 'shīfù yuèláiyuè yōumò')

In the examples in (1) and (2), the word 'lǐfà' is an intransitive verb and the word 'yōu-mò' is an adjective. The verbal parts are separated by the past particle and they behave like a verb-object phrase. The semantic contribution of the discontinuous realization is the same as the one with continuous realization. It should be noted that the meaning of separable verbs is not necessarily composed of the meanings of their parts. For instance, 'fà' is a bound morpheme that appears in nouns like 'tóufà' (hair) or 'máofà' (fur). In the case of 'lǐfà', 'fà' means 'tóufà'. If the meaning were compositional, the meaning of the following example should be the same with (1b). However, the meaning is not the same, since the verb has multiple meanings as 'tidy up' or 'groom'.

(3)   lǐ     le    tóufà
      tidy/cut PERF hair
      'tidy the hair or cut the hair'

In the separable verb construction, we only have a specialized meaning 'cut hair'.

### 2.2  Syntactic Flexibility

Many constituents can be inserted in between the verbal and nominal morphemes of the SVs, including aspect particles (4a–c), numerals (4b), classifiers (4b–c), adjectives (4c), and others.

---

[1] Most examples are selected from the Mandarin Corpus of Peking University.
   http://ccl.pku.edu.cn:8080/ccl_corpus/index.jsp?dir=xiandai

(4)  a.  tā  gāng lǐ-le      fà.
         he just  cut-PERF hair
         'He just had a haircut.'

     b.  wǒ zuò-le      yī  gè  mèng.
         I    make-PERF one CL dream
         'I dreamt.'

     c.  wǒ xǐ-le        gè  tòngkuài zǎo.
         I   wash-PERF CL cool       bath
         'I have taken a nice shower/bath.'

The nominal morpheme can be raised to the post-*ba* NP position (5a) or the subject position (5b).

(5)  a.  wǒ zuótiān   bǎ  zǎo xǐ-le.
         I    yesterday BA bath wash-PERF
         'I have taken the bath yesterday.'

     b.  zǎo wǒ zuótiān    xǐ-le.
         bath I   yesterday wash-PERF
         'As for the bath, I have taken one yesterday.'

It also allows for verb reduplication (6).

(6)  nǐ  bǎ  nà  tiáo yú  huí-huí-guō.
     you BA that CL  fish back-back-pan
     'You should cook that fish again.'

However, not all SVs can be used in topic and verb reduplicated sentences.

(7)  a.  fà  lǐ  le     méiyǒu?
         hair cut PERF not
         'Have you had your hair cut?' from ('yǔfǎ jiǎngyì')

     b.  *mò  yōu  le      méiyǒu
          silent conceal PERF not

     c.  tā  lǐfà     lǐ-chū    le   míngqì.
         he haircut haircut-out PERF fame
         'He became famous due to giving others a haircut.'

     d.  *tā yōumò      yōu-chū  le   míngqì.
          he make-a-joke conceal-out PERF fame

The separability of SVs is related to the individual verbal and nominal parts. In SVs, some morphemes that form part of the compound contribute their individual meanings to the compound (e.g. *bāo* (peel) and *pí* (skin)), but others do not (e.g. *zǎo*[2]). We observe that these differences are related to the boundness of the individual morphemes, and therefore we classify SVs into four subtypes in the following table:

---

[2] *zǎo* does not have a meaning alone, it only denotes the meaning of 'taking a shower/bath' when combined with the verb *xǐ*.

**Table 1.** The Compositional Patterns of SVs

|  | V-free | V-bound |
|---|---|---|
| N-free | A: *lĭfà (have a haircut)* | B: *zuòmèng (make a dream)* |
| N-bound | C: *xĭzăo (take a bath)* | D: *yōumò (make a joke/humorous)* |

For type A, the meaning of the expression can be derived from the parts, which is similar to decompositional idioms discussed by Nunberg, Sag, and Wasow (1994). But the difference is that the meanings of SVs are the combination of the literal meanings of the parts, rather than the idiomatic meanings as in idioms like *spill the beans* = divulge the information. Type B is similar to the light verb construction in German and Persian (Müller, 2002; 2010), since the nominal morpheme behaves like the predicative noun. Here, *zuò* (make) is semantically vacuous and *mèng* (dream) contributes the 'dream' relation. The whole compound means 'dreaming'. While in C, the meaning of the verb is specified by the nominal morpheme. For example, the literal meaning of *xĭ* is 'wash'. It only refers to 'taking a shower/bath' when combining with *zăo*. Type D is similar to non-decomposable idioms in that the meaning of the whole compound cannot be derived from the meanings of the parts compositionally.

### 2.3    Semantic Idiomaticity

Nunberg, Sag and Wasow (1994) develop an account for decomposable and non-de-composable idioms. In particular, idioms like 'spill the beans' are semantically decom-posable, since the idiom can be constructed as 'divulge the secrets'; in contrast, idioms like 'kick the bucket' are non-decomposable, as the idiom is interpreted as a whole. The idea of decomposability captures the internal regular structure of the idioms. But van der Linden (1989) and Abeillé (1995) favor an analytical account, rather than the de-composable or compositional idea. Because 'beans' only denotes 'secrets' with the verb 'spill', rather than any other verb. We agree with the emphasis on the whole meaning of the idioms. That is also true with the phrasal SVs.

For a phrasal SV, its meaning is the same with that of the continuous version. As in (1), the verbal phrase means 'having a haircut', which is the same with that of the word 'lĭfà'. But this is not to deny that some phrasal SVs are analytical. For example, the verbal part 'lĭ' can be modified by the aspect particle and verbal classifier and the nominal part 'fà' can also be modified by the nominal classifier. These facts show that 'lĭ' and 'fà' function similarly to the verbs and the nouns in a verb-object relation. However, the meaning of 'lĭ' in the phrasal case is restricted to the meaning of 'cut' in a 'haircut' relation, rather than other verbal meanings in the dictionary, such as 'groom' in (8), 'notice of', or 'manage'. The nominal part 'fà' means 'hair'. Similar to the case with the 'beans' in 'spill the beans', which only denotes 'secrets' with the verb 'spill', the verbal part 'lĭ' only means 'haircut' with the nominal part 'fà'.

(8)  tā yòu shuā le    yīxià   yá,   **lĭ**   le    yīxià    tóufà.
     he again brush PERF one-time teeth, groom PERF one-time hair
     'He brushed his teeth and groomed his hair again.' (from 'tíhú ànjuàn')

Admittedly, not all SVs are semantically analytical. A frequently raised example is 'yōumò', in which neither the verbal part nor the nominal part has a meaning related to the phrasal meaning of 'making a joke'. The following sentence can not be simply interpreted compositionally. The parts of the compound is meaningless. The meaning of the phrase can only be captured when the two parts are interpreted as a whole.

(9) shīfù, nín yòu **yōu**    le    yī **mò**.
master, you again conceal PERF one silent
'Master, you have made a joke again.'(from 'shīfù yuèláiyuè yōumò')

The above evidence shows that no matter what the parts mean, only the whole complex meaning counts. Such phrasal SVs represent the complex idiomatic meanings with internal syntactic structures. In short, the semantic composition of SVs are either decomposable (for literal use) and non-decomposable (for idiomaticity). In addition, the semantic idiomaticity is related to the syntactic flexibility.

To summarize, separable verbs in Chinese include both the phrasal usage and word usage. The degree of the syntactic flexibility of SVs is related to the flexibility of their verbal and nominal parts. In along with the syntactic flexibility, the semantic constraints could be classified as decomposable and non-decomposable.

# 3    Previous Studies

Previous studies pay much attention on defining the boundaries of SVs, that is, are they words or phrases? As the expression could be separated, some linguists (lǚ 1979) claim a phrasal view. But some others (Lin 1953) consider them as words, or compound words, since the semantic meaning is unchanged and the expansion is limited. Still, most linguists (first suggest by Lu 1957) prefer an analysis of capturing the two-fold nature and denote them as 'separable words'.

Similar to the issue above, it is also difficult to tell the segmentation unit in word identification, since it is unclear to treat them as words or phrases. It is also assumed that there is a gray area between the boundary of word and the phrase. In order to distinguish the borderline, Smith (1995) designs a system to predict the separability of the discontinuous words and to get the lexicalization score based on the constituents between the verbal and nominal parts that are stored in the database. In automatic processing, Fu (1999) suggest a character-based method to recognize them. She define a character with basic syntactic and semantic information. A word is defined in derivation rules. Similar to this idea, Li (2001) provides a more complete analysis in the framework of HPSG, which is CPSG in his thesis. He claims that this issue is a long-standing problem at the interface of Chinese morphology and syntax. He also encode the syntactic and semantic information in the lexicon.

Hence, we believe that the continuous or discontinuous usage of the SVs is related to the internal parts and the usage as a word or a phrase should be treated separately. Concerning their syntactic flexibility and semantic idiomaticity, SVs are similar to idiomatic expressions in English and many other languages. We will have a quick overview of the studies on English, German, and French idioms, and an important paper to Chinese separable verbs as well.

## 3.1    Idioms in HPSG

Previous proposals on idioms in HPSG mainly focus on two issues: lexicon selection and semantic specification. For lexicon selection, most work suggests a feature to identify the co-occurrence constituents as in Erbach (1992), Erbach and Krenn (1994), Sag and Wasow (1999), Sailer (2003), Soehn (2004), Sag (2007, 2012), and Ritcher and Sailer (2009), only Riehemann (1997), Riehemann and Bender (1999) make use of the semantic underspecification to denote the co-occurring constraints. Soehn and Sailer (2003) point out that the disadvantage of Riehemann's analysis is that not all idiom parts have a literal lexical counterpart. Instead, they propose a COLL feature and they claim that the overall utterance must be identical with the sign in COLL lists of all the lexical signs of this utterance.

Concerning the identification of the lexicon, Erbach (1992) introduces a feature LEXEME below CONTENT INDEX. Soehn and Sailer (2003) point out that if it is below INDEX, it only confines to the nouns and excludes other constituents. Thus, they modify the INDEX feature to separate LEXEME from the traditional INDEX features. This is not true with works in MRS where verbs do have an INDEX, which is also a KEY feature. Moreover, Soehn (2003, 2004), Richer and Sailer (2009) propose a new feature of 'LISTEME'. This feature identifies a particular word or phrase. As they put the LISTEME below HEAD, it is available for selection and the LISTEME value of a projection is the same as the one of the head (Soehn, 2004). Another feature of FORM (Pollard and Sag 1994, Sag and Wasow 1999) is similar to PHON in LFG, which is also under the HEAD. Sag (2007) introduces LID[3] in Sign-based Construction Grammar, which not only identifies the co-occurrence strings, but also specifies the idiomatic meaning. Richter and Sailer (2009) argue that this approach can not deal with locative modifiers, since they are not on the ARG-ST list. Richter and Sailer (2004) use another system for combinatorial semantics in HPSG, namely Lexical Resource Grammar (LRS).In LRS, the sign is not considered a single content object, it is rather conceived of as a list of subexpressions of the final logical form. This kind of semantic representation is called discontinuous.

In light of these works, we find out that two issues are the most important: (1) It is necessary to put a lexicon identifier in the syntax. To follow a general version, we choose 'LID' to identify the co-occurrence morphemes under HEAD feature.(2) Although the approach of semantic underspecification is not sufficient to constraint the co-occurrence relation, it is approval that idioms have idiomatic meanings in contrast to their literal meanings. I agree with Riehemann (1997) and Sag (2007), there is necessity to specify the idiomatic relations from literal relations.

## 3.2    Li 2001

Li (2001) proposes three types of V-X idioms based on their different degrees of 'separability' between V and X.

---

[3] Sag (2010): "LEXICAL-IDENTIFIER (LID) is used to individuate lexical items semantically; the value of LID is a frame that canonically specifies the (fine-grained) meaning of a lexeme. As for *pull the strings*, the noun *strings* will default to its literal interpretation except when its LID value is resolved to the idiomatic relation *i_strings_rel* by the lexical entry for the idiomatic verb *pull*."

- V-N1: freely separable, e.g. *xǐzǎo* (wash-bath: *take a bath*);
- V-N2: less separable, e.g. *shāngxīn* (hurt-hart: *sad* or *heart-broken*);
- V-A/V: least separable, e.g. *kànjiàn* (look-see: *have seen*).

To take V-N1 idioms as an example, Li suggests that they are similar to the ordinary transitive VPs, but the semantics of the idiom should be given directly in the lexicon, and the V and N must co-occur.

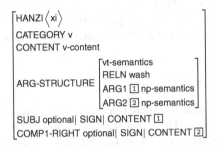

**Fig. 1.** xǐ(*wash*)-NP

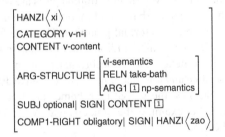

**Fig. 2.** xǐ-zǎo(*take a bath*)

In the above grammars, Li (2001) distinguishes the literal and idiomatic meaning of the verb *xǐ*. This distinction is also related to the syntactic and semantic differences. As in figure 1, the verb is a transitive verb. But the verb in figure 2 is only used in *xǐzǎo*. Further, Li (2001) proposes a lexical rule to capture the semantic link between the following two entries.

We agree with the distinction of the literal and idiomatic meanings of the verbal parts. But the lexical rule in Figure 3 is not necessary, since the parts of the SVs can form either a word or a phrase.

## 4 Analysis

In this section, we will propose the analysis in two aspects: the syntactic co-occurrence and the semantic constraints of SVs. Before our analysis, we first distinguish the SVs into two subtypes: word SVs and phrasal SVs, based on their continuous and discontinuous nature. To capture the isomorphism relation between the usage as a word and

$$\begin{bmatrix} \text{HANZI} \left\langle \boxed{1} \right\rangle \\ \text{CATEGORY } \boxed{1} \text{ v-n-ii} \\ \text{COMP1-RIGHT obligatory| SIGN| HANZI} \left\langle \boxed{2} \right\rangle \end{bmatrix} \rightarrow \begin{bmatrix} \text{HANZI} \left\langle \boxed{1},\boxed{2} \right\rangle \\ \text{CATEGORY } \boxed{1} \text{ v} \\ \text{COMP1-RIGHT null} \end{bmatrix}$$

**Fig. 3.** The V_N_ii Rule

a phrase, we define the word SVs as the phrasal SVs without any grammatical objects in between. Thus, in our grammar, the word and phrasal forms of SVs are both realized as phrasal entries. To note that, this analysis is only accounted for the decomposable SVs. That is because there is no connection between the word and phrasal usages of the non-decomposable SVs.

### 4.1  Syntactic Co-occurrence

Following Li (2001), we agree that there is a co-occurrence relation between the verbal and nominal parts of the phrasal SVs. The question is whether they are mutual selection or single selection. Some linguists (Soehn 2003/2004, Richer and Sailer, 2009) have proposed a mutual selection analysis of English and German idioms with the feature of LISTME. However, SVs are different from the tradition idioms, in that they are only idiomaticity in the construction. The verbal and nominal parts are actually constituents of many other words or phrases. The verbal parts function like the transitive verbs, which are represented as bi_val_verb in the formal grammar. Thus, we follow the analysis of Sag (2007) and Müller (2010) on English idioms and Persian complex predicates. We also use the feature of LID to denote the co-occurrence relation.

In detail, the decomposable and non-decomposable SVs have different selection constraints. For decomposable SVs, the verbal morphemes are free, but they require the fixed nominal morphemes. For example, the syntactic features of *lǐfà* (cut-hair) is shown in the following lexical entry:

$$\begin{bmatrix} \textit{word} \\ \text{SYNSEM|LOC|CAT} \begin{bmatrix} \text{HEAD } \textit{verb} \\ \text{SUBCAT} \left\langle \text{NP, NP} \begin{bmatrix} \text{HEAD} & \textit{noun} \\ \text{LID} & \textit{fà} \end{bmatrix} \right\rangle \end{bmatrix} \end{bmatrix}$$

**Fig. 4.** The lexical entry of 'lǐ' in 'lǐ-fà' (*cut-hair*)

For non-decomposable SVs, the syntactic flexibility is less free than that of the decomposable SVs, since they do not allow for topicalization as the example (7) shows. So we treat them as the head-complement-structure phrase with the empty SLASH value to block the extraction, that is, the SLASH value of the argument is specified as the empty list and hence the extraction of this element is blocked since it is incompatible with the specification of the trace or any other way of introducing a non-local dependency.

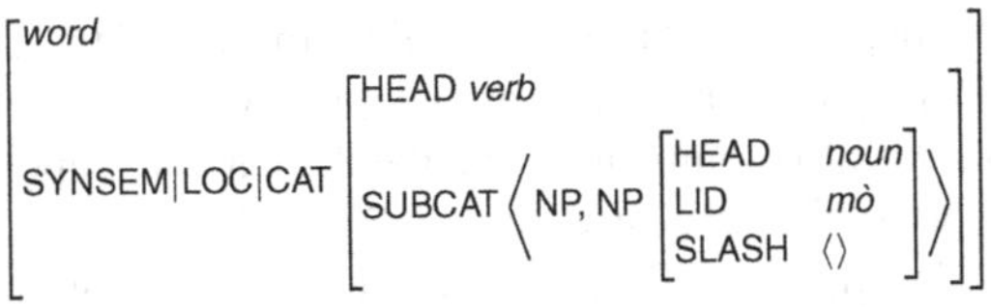

$$
\begin{bmatrix}
\textit{word} \\
\text{SYNSEM|LOC|CAT}
\begin{bmatrix}
\text{HEAD } \textit{verb} \\
\text{SUBCAT } \left\langle \text{NP, NP}
\begin{bmatrix}
\text{HEAD} & \textit{noun} \\
\text{LID} & \textit{mò} \\
\text{SLASH} & \langle\rangle
\end{bmatrix}
\right\rangle
\end{bmatrix}
\end{bmatrix}
$$

**Fig. 5.** The lexical entry of 'yōu' in 'yōu-le-yī-mò' (*make a joke*)

## 4.2 Semantic Constraints

Recalling the discussions in section 2.3, the semantic meanings of SVs are either analytical in decomposable ones or non-analytical in non-decomposable ones. In the case of a decomposable SV, the verbal part specifies a fixed meaning with the co-occurring nominal part, which is similar to the decomposable idioms in English. In light of the analysis in Sag (2007), we also introduce a special lexical entry for the verbal part of the SV, that selects a fixed nominal part and specifies an idiomatic relation. For instance, the literal meanings of *lǐ* include 'to tidy up', 'to cut', or 'to notice'.[4] It means '(*hair*)*cut*' only when it selects *fà* (hair) as the object. Followings are the lexical items of *lǐ* in *lǐ-tóufà* (figure 6) and *lǐ-fà* (figure 7).[5]

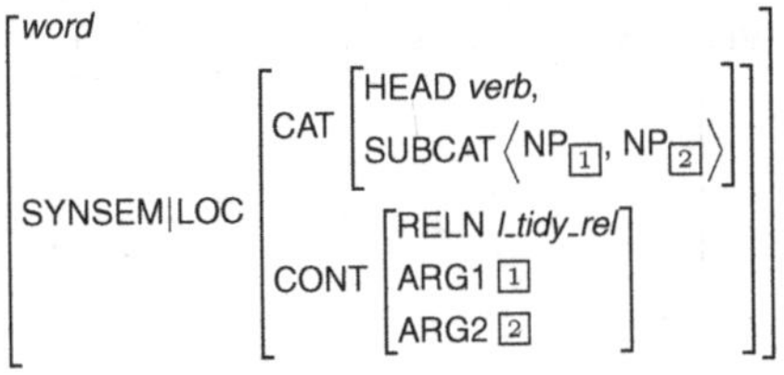

$$
\begin{bmatrix}
\textit{word} \\
\text{SYNSEM|LOC}
\begin{bmatrix}
\text{CAT}
\begin{bmatrix}
\text{HEAD } \textit{verb,} \\
\text{SUBCAT } \langle \text{NP}_{\boxed{1}}, \text{NP}_{\boxed{2}} \rangle
\end{bmatrix} \\
\text{CONT}
\begin{bmatrix}
\text{RELN } \textit{l\_tidy\_rel} \\
\text{ARG1 } \boxed{1} \\
\text{ARG2 } \boxed{2}
\end{bmatrix}
\end{bmatrix}
\end{bmatrix}
$$

**Fig. 6.** The lexical entry of *lǐ*(tidy)

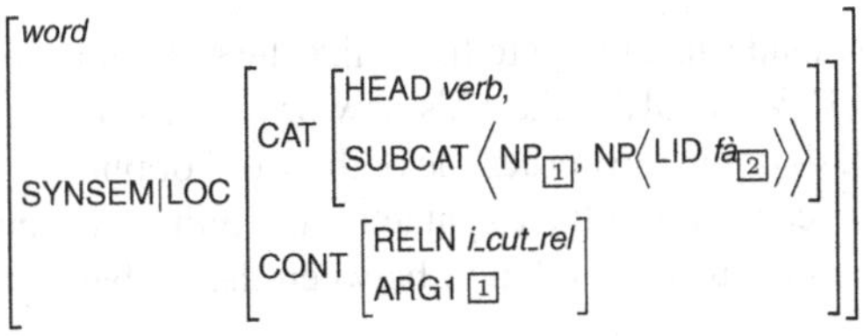

$$
\begin{bmatrix}
\textit{word} \\
\text{SYNSEM|LOC}
\begin{bmatrix}
\text{CAT}
\begin{bmatrix}
\text{HEAD } \textit{verb,} \\
\text{SUBCAT } \langle \text{NP}_{\boxed{1}}, \text{NP}\langle \text{LID } \textit{fà}_{\boxed{2}} \rangle \rangle
\end{bmatrix} \\
\text{CONT}
\begin{bmatrix}
\text{RELN } \textit{i\_cut\_rel} \\
\text{ARG1 } \boxed{1}
\end{bmatrix}
\end{bmatrix}
\end{bmatrix}
$$

**Fig. 7.** The lexical entry of *lǐ* (cut)

For non-decomposable SVs, the semantics is represented at the HEAD, and the nominal parts do not contribute semantically. Following Erbach (1992), we denote them as

---

[4] lǐ₁ (*tidy*) - tóufà (*hair*) / wénjiàn (*files*); lǐ₂ (*cut*) - fà (*hair*); lǐ₃ (*notice*) - rén (*people*) / tā (*him*)
[5] *l* is short for *literal*, and *i* is short for *idiomatic*.

*e_rel.* Then the semantics of the phrase is identical to that of the HEAD via the Semantic Inheritance Principle[6]. Since the nominal parts do not contribute anything, the semantics of the phrase is also compatible with the Semantic Compositional Principle[7]. With these semantic principles, the Head Feature Principle[8] and the Head-Complement Rule[9], the structural description (SD) of the lexical entry in figure (5) is defined as in figure (8).

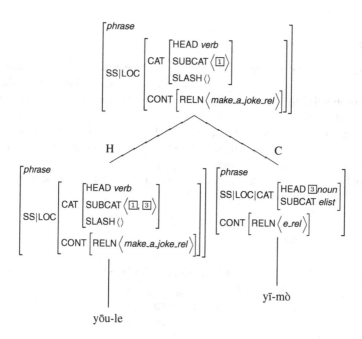

**Fig. 8.** The lexical SDs of 'yōu-le-yī-mò'(*make a joke*)

## 5    Summary

In this paper, we have made an attempt to formalize the separable verbs (SVs) in HPSG. The new ideas are: (1) We analyze the SVs as words or as phrases separately, which avoids the problem of defining the borderline of the word or phrase. (2) We classify SVs into four basic types according to their syntactic flexibility and semantic idiomaticity. (3) To illustrate the co-occurrence relation between the verbal and nominal parts, we

---

[6] The CONTENT value of a phrase is token-identical to that of the head daughter. (Pollard and Sag, 1994)

[7] In any well-formed phrase structure, the mother's RESTR value is the sum of the RESTR values of the daughters. (Sag and Wasow, 1999) In this SD, the RESTR is represented as RELN.

[8] The HEAD value of any headed phrase is structure-shared with the HEAD value of the head daughter. (Pollard and Sag, 1994)

[9] See Müller (2007:54).

make use of the feature LID following Sag (2007) and Müller (2010). (4) The semantics of the decomposable SVs is analytical, the HEAD specifies the idiomatic meaning with the co-occurring nominal complement. For non-decomposable SVs, the semantics of the expression is inherited from the HEAD daughter, and the complement contributes nothing.

**Acknowledgments.** We would like to thank the anonymous reviewers of CLSW 2013 for comments on the earlier version of this paper. Special thanks go to Yulin Yuan, Janna Lipenkova, Felix Bildhauer and Philippa Cook for their insightful criticisms. This paper is supported by China Scholarship Council and National Social Science Foundation of China (12&ZD175).

# References

1. Sag, I.A.: Remarks on locality. In: Müller, S. (ed.) Proceedings of the 14th International Conference on Head-Driven Phrase Structure Grammar, pp. 394–414. CSLI Publications, Stanford (2007)
2. Smith, S.: Discontinuous compounds in mandarin chinese: A lexicalization algorithm. Master's thesis, University of Manchester (1999)
3. Li, W.: The morpho-syntactic interface in a Chinese phrase structure grammar. PhD thesis, Simon Fraser University, Canada (2001)
4. Nunberg, G., Sag, I.A., Wasow, T.: Idioms. Language 70(3), 491–538 (1994)
5. Müller, S.: Complex predicates: Verbal complexes, resultative constructions, and particle verbs in german. In: Studies in Constraint-Based Lexicalism, Stanford, vol. 13 (2002)
6. Müller, S.: Persian complex predicates and the limits of inheritance-based analyses. Journal of Linguistics 46(2) (2010)
7. van der Linden, E.J.: Idioms and flexible categorial grammar. In: Everaert, M., van der Linden, E.J. (eds.) Proceedings of the First Tilburg Workshop on Idioms, Tilburg, pp. 127–143 (1989)
8. Abeillé, A.: The flexibility of French idioms: A representaion with Lexical Tree Adjoining Grammar. In: Everaert, M., van der Linden, E.J., Schenk, A., Schreuder, R. (eds.) Idioms: Structural and Psychological Perspectives, pp. 15–42. Lawerence Erlbaum Associates (1995)
9. Lü, S.X.: Issues on Chinese Grammar (Hanyu Yufa Fenxi Wenti). The Commercial Press (1979)
10. Lin, H.D.: Issues on continuous verbs. Studies of The Chinese Language 10 (1953)
11. Lu, Z.W.: Chinese Lexion (Hanyu De Gouci Fa). The Science Press (1957)
12. Fu, A.P.: Chinese sentence tokenization in a chinese english mt system. Journal of Chinese Information Processing 5 (1999)
13. Erbach, G.: Head-driven lexical representation of idioms in hpsg. In: Proceedings of the Interantional Conference on Idioms, Tilburg (1992)
14. Krenn, B., Erbach, G.: Idioms and support verb constructions. In: Nerbonne, J., Netter, K., Pollard, C.J. (eds.) German in Head-Driven Phrase Structure Grammar. CSLI Lecture Notes, vol. (46), pp. 365–396 (1994)
15. Sag, I.A., Wasow, T.: Syntactic Theories: a formal introduction. CSLI Publications (1999)
16. Sailer, M.: Combinatorial Semantics and Idiomatic Expressions in Head-Driven Phrase Structure Grammar. PhD thesis, Universität Tübingen (2003)
17. Soehn, J.P.: License to coll. In: Müller, S. (ed.) Proceedings of the 11th International Conference on Head-Driven Phrase Structure Grammar, pp. 261–273. CSLI Publications (2004)

18. Sag, I.A.: 2. In: Sign-Based Construction Grammar: An informal synopsis. CSLI Publications (2012)
19. Richter, F., Sailer, M.: Phraseological clauses in constructional hpsg. In: Müller, S. (ed.) Proceedings of the HPSG 2009 Conference. CSLI Publications (2009)
20. Riehemann, S.Z.: Idiomatic constructions in hpsg. Presented at the Cornell HPSG Workshop (1997)
21. Riehemann, S.Z., Bender, E.: Absolute constructions: On the distribution of predicative idioms. In: Bird, S., Carnie, A., Haugen, J., Norquest, P. (eds.) WCCFL 18 Proceedings, pp. 476–489. Cascadilla Press (1999)
22. Soehn, J.P., Sailer, M.: At first blush on tenterhooks. about selectional restrictions imposed by nonheads. In: Jäger, G., Monachesi, P., Penn, G., Wintner, S. (eds.) Proceedings of Formal Grammar, pp. 149–161 (2003)
23. Pollard, C., Sag, I.A.: Head-driven phrase structure grammar. In: Studies in Contemporary Linguistics, vol. 68, Chicago (1994)
24. Müller, S.: Head-driven Phrase Structure Grammar: Eine Einfürung, 1st edn. Stauffenburg Einfürung, vol. 17. Stauffenburg Verlag, Tübingen (2007)

# The Reason for the Popularity of *"hold zhu"*[*]

Zheng Kan and Dekuan Xu[**]

School of Chinese, Ludong University, Yantai 264025
419643530@qq.com, xudekuan@tom.com

**Abstract.** The paper explores the newly coined expression "hold zhu" in Chinese in terms of its origin, semantics and the reasons for its popularity, and forecasts its development in the future and its influence on Chinese language with a conclusion that a right attitude should be held for the new expressions like these in order that the vocabulary of Chinese language will be enriched and developed in a healthy way.

**Keywords:** *"hold zhu"*, meaning, popularity, development.

On 9, August, 2011, in one Taiwan TV program called "University", a girl named Xie Yilin shocked the audience with her exaggerated style and bizarre behavior. She said:

"就算走错party，整个场面我也要hold住。"
*jiusuan zoucuo party, zhengge changmian wo yeyao hold zhu*
"Even if I went to the wrong party, I should hold the whole situation."

After being uploaded to "Youku", the viewers of that video quickly exceeded one million in 11 days. The expression "hold zhu" became popular rapidly and was widely used by people. On 27, December, 2012, we searched the relevant entries about "hold zhu" on Baidu and Google, and found 432 million on Baidu and 44.8 million on Google, showing the wide popularity of this expression. Why is this expression so popular? We will make a thorough inquiry about it in the following parts.

## 1    The Origin of *"hold zhu"*

Some people think that the expression "hold zhu" is of a long history spreading from Guangdong and Hong Kong, it's a word of English-Chinese mixture. Since the "hold zhu" became popular, many netizens from the dialect regions of China all said that "hold zhu" was already in existence. There is "吼住"(*houzhu, which means to catch*)in Jianghan Plain of Hubei Province, and "候住"(*houzhu, which means to wait*) used by people from Nanning City of Guangxi Autonomous Region. Still some people believe that "hold zhu" firstly appeared in Stephen Chow's film "Out of the Dark". And then

---

[*] Project fund: Key social science popularization and application project of Shandong Province "On language hot spots – linguistics behind hot words and expressions" (12-KPZZ-07).
[**] Corresponding author.

P. Liu and Q. Su (Eds.): CLSW 2013, LNAI 8229, pp. 241–247, 2013.

some people regard it emerges from Xie Yilin and quickly became popular. Different people have different opinions about the origin of "hold zhu", but I personally prefer the first argument. There should be particular historical and cultural reasons and the accumulation in the in use for the prevalence of each word, as when Xie Yilin said "hold zhu", the expression is not baseless creations of its own. There is certainly such using situation in her life circle or dialects, and this expression quickly became popular with her exaggerated performances.

## 2　The Meaning of "hold zhu"

In the Webster's Advanced Learner's Dictionary, the meaning for "hold" is "to bear or carry oneself". The third term for the entry "zhu" in the sixth edition of Modern Chinese Dictionary is to be used as verb complement. "Hold" is a verb, and "zhu" is its complement, so the combination of "hold" and "zhu" is consistent with the Chinese structure "verb + complement". It is possible to restore "hold zhu" into the structure of Chinese words. "Hold" has such meanings as "grip; reserve; detain; contain; approve; remain unchanged; effective". Then can the combination of "hold" and "zhu" also keep the original meaning of "hold" or some new meanings emerge in the process of spreading ? Here are a few examples:

- 男人hold 住了自己的爱情。

  *nanren hold zhu le ziji de aiqing*

  "The man has grasped his love"

- 2012年，世界人口将达70亿，地球你hold住吗？

  *2012 nian, shijie renkou jiang da 70 yi, diqiu ni holdzhu ma*

  "The population on earth will be 70 million in 2012. Can the earth bear it?"

- 面对零食，我得hold住。

  *miandui lingshi, wo dei hold zhu*

  "In the face of snack, I must control myself."

- 朋友，你hold得住网络吗？

  *pengyou, ni hold de zhu wangluo ma*

  "Dear Friend, can you keep yourself away from the Internet?"

- ·今天的表演hold住了全场的观众。

  *jintian de biaoyan holdzhu le quanchang de guanzhong*

  "The show today attracted all the audience"

- 800米长跑，别人都累得倒下了，我却hold住了。

  *800 mi changpao, beiren dou leide daoxia le, wo que holdzhu le*

  "I succeeded in the 800 meters long-distance race, although all other people are exhausted."

- 开发商还能hold住房价吗？

  *kaifashang haineng holdzhu fangjia ma*

  "Can the estate agent keep the high price of commercial residential building?"

- ·谢娜的开场太搞笑了，hold不住了。

  *Xie Na de kaichang tai gaoxiao le, hold buzhu le.*

  The opening of Xie Na is very funny, I can't keep myself from laughing.

- ·亲们，狂风暴雨般的考试要hold住啊！

  *qin men, kuangfeng baoyu ban de kaoshi yao houzhu a*

  Dear friends, you must not fail in the stormy exam!

In the sentence above, each expresses one aspect of the meanings of "hold zhu". The meanings include "grasp, bear, control, keep oneself away from, attract, succeed, keep" etc. On the basis of different sentences and different context, "hold zhu" can express different meanings, most of which are positive.

There are nineteen senses in the Oxford Advanced Learner's English-Chinese Dictionary. They are: (1)to carry sth (2)to put your hand on part of your body (3)to remain strong and safe or in position (4)used to tell sb to stop doing sth or not to do sth (5)to consider that sth is true (6)to have sth you have gained or achieved (7)to have a particular job or position (8)to support the weight of sb/sth (9)to have enough space for sth/sb (10)to defend sth against attack (11)to keep sb and not allow them to leave (12)to have a meeting (13)to have a belief or an opinion about sb/sth (14)to wait until you can speak to the person you have telephoned (15)to remain the same (16)to keep sb's attention or interest (17)to own or have sth (18)to keep sth so that it can be used later (19) to remain strong and safe or in position.

We can see the positive and neutral senses are absorbed in Modern Chinese. The (4)(5)(11)(17) senses are not found in "hold zhu" in Chinese. At the same time, new senses such as "reserved and explicit" and "to cheer sb. on " are added.

The structure of "hold zhu" is "English morpheme + Chinese morpheme". In Chinese, its English pronunciation and writing are retained and the meaning in Chinese is also mostly equal to that in English. In the Chinese-western mixed words, Chinese morpheme is to express a category or description, like "*xiu*(show)", in 时装秀 (*shizhuang xiu*, fashion show), 脱口秀 (*tuokou xiu*, talk show) and 表演秀 (biaoyan xiu, show display). The Chinese morpheme "zhu" doesn't express a category or description. The morpheme is a complement for a verb indicating a result. For the pronunciation, no similar sound to be used to replace the morpheme. In all the written articles, the original English writing is also kept.

# 3    The Reasons of "hold zhu"

## 3.1    The Economy Principle of Language

The American linguist George Kingsley Zipf put forward "a principle of least effort". The word "hold " has nineteen meanings in English. In different context, the word can express different meaning. We don't need different word in different context. In word formation, this word is an English-Chinese mixture. They are simple, concise and vivid. "hold zhu" have the expressive force and covering power. So they fit the economy principle. The word is productive. It can be used as a transitive verb to be followed by "爱情(aiqing, love), 网络(wangluo, internet) and房价(fangjia, price of commercial residential building)", and can be used as an adjective with an adverb coming before it as in "十分hold住 (shifen hold zhu, to hold to a much high degree )". It also has affirmative form and negative form hold不住 (hold bu zhu, cannot hold) hold 得住 (hold de zhu, can hold) . The various parts of speech of "hold zhu" and the extension of its meaning lead to generalization of its meaning and range of its use amplifies.

Nowadays, in field of vocabulary, disyllables predominate. The pronunciation of "hold zhu" also fit the economy principle. The pronunciation of "hold" is [həuld], the combination produces the speech sound change: [d] is not pronounced. "hold zhu" is pronounced as [hou tsu]. The pronunciation is a special phenomenon of elision. This process turns the three-syllable pronunciation into a bisyllable pronunciation. It complies with the tide that disyllables predominate. "Hold zhu", the expression has the sound beauty of rhythm and tempo: its sounds powerful and cordial. All the above characteritics of the expression are in line with the economy principle.

## 3.2    Meeting the Demand of the Development of the Theory of Linguistic Adaptation

As Verschueren points out in the book Understanding Pragmatics, the use of language is the process of language choice based on the language internal and external reasons. The reasons why human beings can select languages while using them is that languages have variability, negotiability and adaptability. When people are communicating, they choose relevant context adaptation consciously and unconsciously. Contexts include communicative context (language users, the social, psychological world and physical world) and linguistic context. In the show "University", Xie Yilin spoke English from the beginning to the end so as to comply with the local atmosphere and situation of communicating in Hong Kong and Macao. That's why "hold zhu" came from and being spread broadly. This expression is meant to comply with the situation of communicating namely to adjust to the audience's mental, social and physical world. "hold zhu" has been an expression that is widely used in a fastest way and also is the most popular in the Internet. If there exists a similar context, users could think of "hold zhu" and use it.

### 3.3    The Factors of the Development of Society

The function of language is communication. Communication is to meet the need of the development of society. As society develops constantly and new things spring up, people need to know and denote the new things and satisfy the need of communication. Different components of the language system differ greatly in terms of their connections with the social development. Vocabulary, which is most sensitive to the social development and changes most quickly, has the most direct connection with the social development. With the fast social development, the expression of communication is marked with emotions. Over the past 20 years, frequent exchanges between China and the West have brought in a great number of new vocabulary into the Chinese vocabulary system. "hold zhu" is concise whereas has great expressive power and is attractive and amusing. It keeps the pace with the times and expresses people's feelings as a whole.

### 3.4    Promoting the Development of the Mass Media

The open and free network media creates conditions for prevalence of "hold zhu". As a newly emerging medium, Internet offers a free and open communication platform for the spread of many new words. Meanwhile, the expression "hold zhu" has been widely used in TV, newspaper, magazines and so forth. The masses can come across and be familiar with the expression in a variety of channels so as to further use it. At the same time, among the increasingly competitive era, all the media, for the sake of interest maximization, are scrambling to disclose the controversial or hot figures and events to draw public    attention. Generally speaking, the headlines titled with "hold zhu" are more likely to arouse people's curiosity. Since all media favor the expression extremely, the frequency of "hold zhu" among masses has increased.

### 3.5    Being in Line with the Masses' Social Cultural Psychology

Nowadays, most netizens are much younger, and they prefer characteristic innovation for they don't want to be stereotype. While the vogue and novel "hold zhu" has catered to masses' intention to be original and changeable, the expression definitely demonstrates their personalities. "hold zhu", vivid, visual and witty, creates the relaxed and pleasant atmosphere for people. In the competitive society, pressure floods everywhere, while the witty "hold zhu" can calm down people's restless mood. Masses prefer to use new, vivid and lively words to ease the ambience and to enrich vocabulary.

The widely-used phrase also reflects the masses' language cognition psychology of "following suit": people is apt to keep close pace with fashion, no matter what is in style.

That is, the masses are taking the initiative to imitate the communication mode of people with a better financial condition and a higher rank. The survey suggested that the users of "hold zhu" are relatively young , and that they generally like surfing the Internet, who have the common characters that their literacy level is much higher as well as the English level. Generally, the literacy of their chat fellows is in line with that of their own. Consequently, when "hold zhu" becomes popular, the originally frequently-used term can cause the use frequency much higher. With the trend that the netizens are younger and younger, the masses, particularly the teenagers, have played a significant role in the wide spread of the term. Being in adolescence, young people's desire to show their personality is much stronger. What's more, with her exaggerated and twisted performance and her Chinese-English mixed language, Xie Yilin has successfully attracted the audience, which catered the psychology of worship of foreign things and favor of novel matters to make the term popular. At last, "hold zhu" can help to deliver the meaning of "being persistent and being easy and confident to face the reality", which has the positive significance among the masses.

## 4    The Development and Future of "hold zhu"

The result of language contact at the Sino-western culture collision created the new Chinese expression "hold zhu" by absorbing some elements from English. The popularity of "hold zhu" shows the needs for human communication and enriches human's language life. "Hold zhu" belongs to expressions containing foreign letters. With the trend of global communicating, there will be more and richer such expressions in Chinese. However, as society develops, the expressions like "hold zhu" may disappear someday for they cannot stand the test of time and communication needs. With the development of society, there exists another possibility that this kind of words will be accepted by society and become part of general vocabulary. Although "hold zhu" conforms to the principle of economy because it can express more than one meanings, it's hard for the people who speak English less to understand it and it's necessary to give an additional illustration and explanation, so in this sense, it conflicts with the principle of economy to some degree.

## 5    Conclusion

Whether "hold zhu" will be used for a long period of time in the future needs the test of time and the mass. Such newly-coined expressions enrich human language life, bring vigor to the language and make the language more expressive. Language has its own development rule closely connected with the development of society. We should have a right attitude toward the new expressions like "hold zhu". To enrich Chinese vocabulary and make it develop in a healthy way, it's necessary to guide the use of these expressions through a rational and standardized way, neither rejecting them totally nor and using them in every situation without limit.

# References

1. Ye, F., Xu, T.: Essentials of linguistics. Peking University Press, Beijing (2007)
2. Lü, Z., Jia, D.: On New expression "hold zhu", Modern Chinese (2012)
3. Chen, C.: The eastern-western mixed expression "hold zhu". Jiannan Literature (2012)
4. Hong, J.: On "hold zhu". Learning Chinese (2012)
5. Zhou, Y., Yang, Y.: The popular expression "hold zhu". Overseas English (2012)
6. Hu, L., Guo, X.: "Hold zhu"–the network expression. Bi Jie College Journal (2012)
7. Verschueren, J.: Understanding Pragmatic. Edward Arnold Publishers Ltd., London (1999)
8. Xu, D.: On Foreign morpheme. In: Language Teaching and Research in the Information and Network Era. Qunyan Press, Beijing (2005)

# The Semantic Functions of Prepositions and Postpositions in Chinese Spatial Circumpositions -- A Perspective from Language Typology

Lei Cai[1,2]

[1] College of Chinese Language and Literature, Wuhan University, Hubei, P.R.C.
[2] Faculty of Foreign Studies, Hubei University, Hubei, P.R.C.
celena@hubu.edu.cn

**Abstract.** Circumposition is an important syntactic structure in Chinese grammar with unique typological value. By studying the structural and semantic typological features of prepositions and postpositions in circumpostions, we can better the theoretical framework of Chinese adpositional system. The present study analyses the semantics of a typical spatial circumposition – "zai-shang/li/zhong" (在…上/里/中), and the findings suggest that prepositions and postposition bear different semantic functions by setting restrictions on the law of adposition omission. Two general rules serve as the semantic motivations for adposition omission: the mandatory rule of syntactic semantics and the rule of spatial semantic self-sufficiency.

**Keywords:** typological features, preposition, postposition, spatial circumposition, semantic functions, adposition omission.

## 1 Introduction

The terminology of circumposition was first put forward by Greenberg (1995), the founder of the modern word order typology and then was introduced by Liu Danqing (2002) to the framework of Chinese adposition studies. According to Liu, it is "a kind of adposition combining a preposition preceding NP and a postposition following NP "(2002:316), such as "zai...shang" (在…上), "gen...si de" (跟…似的), etc. Some circumpositions are usually used to describe and mark spatial relations, so they are called spatial circumpositions, and "zai...shang/li/zhong" (在…上/里/中) is one typical example.

However, circumposition has been the Cinderella of Chinese language study for far too long. The traditional approach to Chinese adpositions mainly centres around the discussions on prepositions. Few studies incorporated postpositions into the theoretical framework of adposition studies, and postpositions are often categorized into different word classes or even find no place in any word class at all. According to Liu (2004), adposition is the superordinate of preposition and postposition, and only when postposition is incorporated into the Chinese adpositional system, can it be possible to establish a perfect theoretical framework of Chinese adposition studies.

P. Liu and Q. Su (Eds.): CLSW 2013, LNAI 8229, pp. 248–257, 2013.
© Springer-Verlag Berlin Heidelberg 2013

Besides, circumpositions have received little attention. By searching the journal articles on CKNI (National Knowledge Infrastructure), we found only 4 articles themed with "circumposition", and 30 articles with "circumposition" as a key word. What's more, there are even fewer researches on the semantic functions of prepositions and postpositions in circumpositional structures from the perspective of typology. Thus, it is necessary to conduct the study in this regard since it can not only help us better understand the typological properties of Chinese adpositions, but also offer us a special perspective to the interface study of the adpositional semantics and syntax.

## 2 The Semantic Functions of Prepositions and Postpositions in Spatial Circumpositions

Prepositions and postpositions in spatial circumpositions differ a lot in terms of the size of the syntactic domains that they govern, the degree of semantic abstraction, thematic roles, and semantic functions. Then what distinguishes them in semantic functions? Will these distinctions have some influence on the law of omission of adpositions? The mysteries will be unveiled in this section.

### 2.1 The Degree of Semantic Abstraction of Prepositions and Postpositions

Hopper and Traugott (1993) categorized adpositions into two groups according to their degree of semantic abstraction: primary adpositions with greater degree of semantic abstraction, and secondary adposition with less degree. In preposition-dominant languages, the preposition that precedes the other is more semantically abstract. For example, in the English prepositional structure "from inside the room", "from" is more semantically abstract as a marker for the source; while "inside" is more concrete in semantics as a marker for denoting specific locations. In the languages with circumpositions, prepositions differ from postpositions in the degree of semantic abstraction. In general, the more abstract the adposition is, the larger syntactic domain it governs, and the vice versa (Liu, 2002). Based on the degree of semantic abstraction, Liu classifies Chinese adpositions into three categories: 1) primary adpositions: relators, such as "lai" (来), "er" (而), "yi" (以), the postpositions which mainly function as the relators between prepositional phrases and VP; 2) secondary adpositions: basic relational adpositions, such as "zai" (在), "cong" (从), "dao" (到), the prepositions to mark basic thematic relations; 3) tertiary adpositions: concrete relational adpositions, such as "shang" (上), "li" (里), "qian"(前), "hou" (后), which covers most of the postpositions.

Based on Liu's classification of adpositions, we can define the preposition "zai" in the typical spatial circumposition "zai…shang/li/zhong" (在…上/里/中) as a secondary adposition which marks basic relations, and the postposition "shang/li/zhong" (上/里/中) in the structure as tertiary adposition, which marks concrete relations. Compared to "shang/li/zhong" (上/里/中), "zai" (在) is more semantically abstract and governs a larger syntactic domain.

## 2.2 The Differences in Semantic Functions between the Preposition and Postposition

According to Zlatev (2007), space is not a self-contained "semantic field", but an important part of the background for conceptualization and meaning, and the most common way of defining spatial semantics is in terms of a class of expressions for spatial meaning, such as spatial prepositions. As far as Chinese is concerned, the typical expressions of spatial semantics are spatial circumpositions, e.g. "zai...shang" (在...上), "zai...li" (在...里).

Moreover, due to the property as function words, the adpositions, especially the prepositions, have inherent syntactic semantics. As Rapaport (2002) stated, each item in a syntactic structure (pattern) bears a syntactic semantics, a kind of meaning derived from its role determined by its relationships to other items in the complete system of expressions. In this sense, prepositions and postpositions in spatial circumpositions bear both spatial semantics and syntactic semantics. They both function on the semantics and syntax of the whole sentence, which may lead to either semantic coherence or semantic redundancy. Besides, they may also raise some mandatory demand on the syntactic structure and the omission of some constituents.

"zai...shang/li/zhong" (在......上/里/中)is a typical spatial circumpositional structure which depicts static spatial relations. In this structure, "zai" (在) is the preposition with no specific spatial semantics but only a mark for static locational relationship without inflection. "shang/li/zhong" (上/里/中) is the postposition to mark specific spatial relationship and location, which is grammaticalized from content words. By comparing the preposition "zai" (在) and postposition "shang/li/zhong" (上/里/中), we can find that postpositions play the major role in expressing spatial meanings, and they are used to depict the specific dimension of spatial domain or relative locations of objects. For example[1],

(1) 我 与小五 在 床上 躺了 一会儿。
Wǒ yǔ xiǎowǔ zài chuángshang tǎng le yíhuìer.
        in bed lied
Xiao Wu and I lied in bed for a while.

(2) 我 晚上 睡 在 桥洞 里。
Wǒ wǎnshang shuì zài qiáodòng li。
            slept in arch of bridge
I slept under the bridge in the nights.

(3) 有 时候 我 被 吊 在 空 中 好几个小时。
Yǒushihòu wǒ bèi diào zài kōng zhōng hǎo jǐgè xiǎoshí.
                hang in air
Sometimes I had to remain hanging in midair for several hours.

---

[1] All the examples are quoted or adapted from the sentences in CCL corpus.

In the examples above, the postpositions "shang" (上), "li" (里) and "zhong" (中) undertake the job of marking spatial relations to specify the location of the target people or object and to denote the spatial properties of the landmark or place. For example, "chuang" (床) in (1) is regarded as a 2-dimensional space with the properties of a surface, which requires the use of postposition "shang" (上) to express the "support" semantics and "surface" semantics. The landmark "qiaodong" (桥洞) in (2) is viewed as a 3-dimensional space with the property of "containment", which requires the use of postposition "li" (里) to express the meaning of "containment". The noun "kong" (空) in (3) is relatively special which is usually treated as an abstract infinite 3-dimensional space, so the postposition "zhong" (中) can mark the location of "I" when "hanging in midair" as a point somewhere above viewers but still within their vision.

In contrast to the postpositions, the spatial meaning of the preposition "zai" (在) is weakened to an abstract marker of spatial location, whose major function in terms of spatial semantics is to foreground the location. Nonetheless, "zai" (在) keeps its syntactic semantic function as a relator. Since "zai" (在) has its origin of being a verb, it still remains some properties of a verb. For instance, "zai" (在) links the two NP constituents – "xiaowu"(a person's name) and "chuang" (床) in (1), and it remains the existential meaning of the verb "zai" (在). In (2) and (3), "zai" (在) works as a relator of VP and NP to achieve semantic coherence, such as its function of linking the verb "tang" (躺) and the noun "qiaodong" (桥洞) in (2), and "diao" (桥) and "kong" (空) in (3). Compared to its spatial semantic function, the syntactic semantic function of "zai" (在) seems much more important.

## 3    The Semantic Motivation for the Omission of Adpositions

The omission of adpositions is one of the important typological features of Chinese adpositions, and it has aroused the attention of some scholars.

### 3.1    The Semantic Motivation for the Omission of Prepositions

Zhang Yisheng (2000) discussed some general rules of adposition omission from the angle of semantics, collocations, syntactic positions and phonetics. He proposed that all the prepositions that precede prepositional phrases with locatives can be omitted. However, Chu Zexiang (2010) challenged this proposal by counting the occurrence frequency of "zai" (在) preceding locatives in corpus. His research findings show that "the frequency of occurrence and omission of "zai" (在) preceding locatives is about half and half···Zhang's idea needs revisiting"(2010:130). Chu conducted an in-depth research on the law of omission of "zai" (在) and generalized the rules governing the omission of "zai" (在) according to its omission frequency in different syntactic positions as follows: attributive > initial modifier > preceding VP > following VP.

Many factors may affect the omission of prepositions, which involves semantics, syntax, pragmatics and phonetics, but among which the most important one is semantic motivation. Basically speaking, there are two general rules in effect: *the mandatory rules of syntactic semantics* and *the rule of spatial semantic self-sufficiency*.

**The Influences of the Mandatory Rule of Syntactic Semantics on Preposition Omission.** Since the preposition "zai" (在) only functions as a marker of spatial location, it has a weak role in expressing spatial meanings. Therefore, its major role in the sentence is to function as a relator. When the circumposition "zai···shang/li/zhong" (在···上/里/中) precedes or follows VP, the vacancy between VP and NP, or that between the NPs governed by adpositions needs to be filled by a relator. In this case, "zai" (在) cannot be omitted. For example,

(4) 我　靠　　在　　　　一棵　大树　　上。
　　Wo　kao　zai　　　yike　dashu　shang.
　　　　lean　against　　a big tree
　　I leaned against a big tree.

(5) 他　在　　报纸　　　　上　看到了一条惊人的消息。
　　Tā　zài　bàozhǐ　　shàng　kàndàole yītiáo jīngrén de xiāoxī.
　　he　in　newspaper
　　He came across a piece of surprising news in newspaper.

As we can see in the examples above, "zai" (在) has its position either between VP and NP or between two NPs as a relator as required by the mandatory rule of its syntactic semantics. "Zai" (在) in (4) links the verb "kao" (靠) and NP "yi ke dashu" (一棵大树), and in example (5), the co-occurrence of two NPs that "zai" (在) governs – "ta" (他) and "baozhi" (报纸), requires the occurrence of "zai" (在) as an adhesive. Once "zai" (在) is omitted, the whole sentence will become unintelligible and unacceptable.

When "zai" (在) works as a relator between two NP constituents, it also has the function of eliminating ambiguity for it can help distinguish the semantic domains of different NP constituents (Liu, 2002). Let's have a look at example (6) a, where "zai" (在) is situated between two NPs – "women gao pingmianhua de" (我们搞平面画的) and "waiguoren" (外国人), If "zai" (在) is omitted, the semantic domains of 2 NPs will be mixed up since the NP preceding "zai" (在) appears to be the attributive of the NP following "zai" (在), and then the semantics of the reorganized structure will be "the foreigners like us who engage in 2-dimentional art". Thus, the use of "zai" (在) in this case can effectively be free of structural ambiguity.

(6) a. 我们　　搞　平面画的　　　在 外国人　　眼中　　　　都不吃香。
　　Wǒmén　gǎo　píngmiànhuàde　zài　wàiguórén　yǎnzhōng　dōu bù chīxiāng.
　　we　　　　　　　　　　　in foreigners' eyes

People like us who engage in 2-dimensional art are not popular with foreigners.

However, suppose the circumposition is moved to the beginning of the sentence, the vacancies between the constituents that require the occurrence of preposition may disappear, and "zai" (在) in this case can be omitted. Compare the following examples:

(6) b. (在)　外国人　　眼中，　我们　　搞　平面画的，　　都不吃香。
　　zài　wàiguórén yǎnzhōng, Wǒmén gǎo píngmiànhuàde, dōu bù chīxiāng.

(7) a. 林彪　在　东北　　战场　　　上　较　充分地　　　显示出他的
　　　Línbiāo zài  dōngběi  zhànchǎng shàng jiào chōngfèn de xiǎnshìchū tāde
　　　　　On  Dongbei  battlefield
　　　指挥才能。
　　　zhǐhuī cáinéng.

(7) b. (在)　东北　　　　战场　　　上，林彪较充分地显示出他的指挥才能。
　　　Zài  dōngběi  zhànchǎng shàng, Línbiāo jiào chōngfènde xiǎnshìchū tā de
　　　zhǐhuī cáinéng.
　　　Lin Biao fully displayed his talents in military leadership on the battlefield in
　　　Dongbei.

(8) a. 叶子　在　　微风　　中　　轻轻晃动。
　　　Yèzi  zài  weīfēng  zhōng  qīngqing huàngdòng.
　　　　　leaves in  breeze

(8) b. (在) 微风　　中，叶子轻轻晃动。
　　　Zài weīfēng zhōng, yèzi qīngqing huàngdòng.
　　Leaves swayed gently in breeze.

If we move the circumposition in (7) a to the beginning of the sentence, the positions of the 2 NPs governed by "zai" (在) get changed as well. Then the NP "women gao pingmianhua de" (我们搞平面画的) is no longer governed by "zai" (在), so the potential structural ambiguity disappears. As a result, the mandatory rule of syntactic semantics of "zai" (在) can be applied nowhere. It is also true in the case of (8) b and (9) b, where there is no need for a relator between NP and VP when the circumposition is moved to the initial position. Here "zai" (在) plays the function only as a marker of spatial location with no restrictions on syntactic structure. Then when the mandatory rule of syntactic semantics fails, what may have a decisive role in the omission of "zai" (在)? Now the rule of spatial semantic self-sufficiency gets into the act.

**The Influences of the Rule of Spatial Semantic Self-sufficiency on Preposition Omission.** As conforms with the economy principle of language, there is usually no need to use the syntactic mark of the same category when the intrinsic semantics of a word is self-sufficient for the purpose of avoiding semantic redundancy. Hence, when the syntactic semantic functions of prepositions have no restrictions on the sentence structure, and the "NP + postposition" structure is semantically self-sufficient in expressing spatial meanings, "zai" (在) can be omitted. In example (6) (7) (8) b, when the circumposition is moved to the beginning of the sentence, "zai" (在) only functions as a marker of spatial semantics since the major role of describing the spatial locations is played by postpositions like "zhong" (中) and "shang" (上). Here, the combination of word of place and postposition can sufficiently express the spatial meaning which leaves the role of "zai" (在) unimportant, so "zai" (在) in this sense can be omitted. In addition, the initial position of the circumposition serves to highlight the spatial semantics of the structure as the focus. In this case, the use of "zai" (在) as a marker of spatial semantics will lead to semantic redundancy, which partly explains the omission of "zai" (在).

Besides its omission in the initial position of the sentence, will the omission of "zai" ( 在 ) in other positions also be influenced by the rule of spatial semantic self-sufficiency? Let's review the following examples:

(2) b. 我　晚上　　　睡　桥洞里。
　　　 Wǒ　wǎnshang　shuì　qiáodòngli.

In (2) b, when "zai" (在) is omitted, the sentence is still semantically and syntactically legal. Though it appears that the mandatory rule of syntactic semantics works in (2) a since "zai" (在) links the verb "shui" (睡) and the NP "qiaodong" (桥洞), in fact whether "zai" (在) occurs or not doesn't affect the validity of the sentence. In the sentence, the VP and NP can form a verb-object relation, which does not necessarily requires a relator. In other words, what is in effect for the omission of "zai" (在) in this case is not the syntactic requirement but the semantic requirement. The NP "qiaodong" (桥洞) which bears an intrinsic spatial meaning integrated with the postposition "li" (里) constitutes a sufficient spatial meaning, which not only specifies the spatial location of the agent but also the spatial properties of "qiaodong" (桥洞). Consequently, whether or not "zai" (在) occurs doesn't affect its spatial semantic self-sufficiency.

When the circumposition appears as an attributive, the preposition "zai" (在) is often omitted. For instance,

(9) a. 他 在　狱中　　所写材料
　　　 Tā zài yùzhōng　suǒxiěcáiliào

　　　 in  prison　written materials

(9) b. 他　狱中　　所写材料
　　　 Tā yùzhōng　suǒxiěcáiliào

　　　 the materials he wrote in prison

(10) a. 这些　　在　树林中　　　　睡觉的人
　　　　 zhèxiē　zài　shùlínzhōng　shuìjiào de rén

　　　　 those　 in　woods　　　sleeping

(10) b. 这些　树林中　　睡觉的人
　　　　 zhèxiē shùlínzhōng　shuìjiào de rén

　　　　 those men sleeping in woods

As shown in (9) b and (10) b, when "zai" (在) is omitted, the "word of place + postposition" structure in each sentence as the attributive still fulfills its function of specifying the location or the spatial properties of the modified objects. As a result, the spatial semantic self-sufficiency remains satisfied, which justifies the omission of "zai" (在).

## 3.2    The Semantic Motivation for the Omission of Postpositions

Not only prepositions, but also postpositions can be omitted. Try to compare the following four pairs of circumpositions:

(12) a. 在 家 里            b. 在 家 (里)
       zài  jiā  li            zài  jiā
       at    home            at    home

(13) a. 在 桌上            b. 在 桌 (上) *
       zài  zhuō shang            zài  zhuō
       on desk            on desk

(14) a. 在 梦中            b. 在 梦 (中) *
       zài  mèng zhong            zài  mèng
       in dream            in dream

(15) a. 在 武汉 里 *            b. 在 武汉
       zài Wǔhàn li            zài  Wǔhàn
       in  Wuhan            in  Wuhan

By comparing the examples above, we can see an interesting phenomenon. When the postposition "li" (里) in (12) is omitted, the circumposition is still semantically valid. However, in (13) b and (14) b, the circumpositions sound unacceptable when the postpositions "shang" (上) and "zhong" (中) are omitted. The case is different in (15) a where the circumposition becomes unacceptable when the postposition "li" (里) appears. So what rule underlines the postposition omission? Basically speaking, the omission of postpositions also has much to do with the rule of spatial semantic self-sufficiency. If the NP in the circumposition can satisfy the demand for spatial semantic self-sufficiency, the postposition can be omitted.

The postposition "li" (里) in (12) can be omitted because the NP "jia" (家) is a typical word of place, which can be semantically self-sufficient even in the absence of postposition. But "zhuo" (桌) in (13) and "meng" (梦) (14) are common nouns whose locative meaning can only be formed by combining with postpositions to mark the specific spatial relations and locations. Therefore, when postpositions are omitted, the NPs themselves can not express spatial meanings, and the structure will become unintelligible as a result. Then why "Wuhan" (武汉) in (15) as a typical word of location can not occur with "li" (里)? It is closely linked to the spatial property of "Wuhan" (武汉). It is a word of absolute location, that is to say, its location does not vary with the change of observers' (or speakers') perspective or reference points. What's more, this kind of words usually refers to a large 3-dimensional space with boundaries, whose spatial meaning overlaps that of "li" (里). Hence, the co-occurrence of NP and the postposition will lead to semantic redundancy, and the postposition omission in this case is the demand of economy principle of language.

### 3.3    The Semantic Motivation for the Omission and Co-occurrence of Prepositions and Postpositions

There is another phenomenon worthy of note in terms of the omission of adpositions in circumpositions, i.e. the preposition and postposition in the same circumposition may both occur or be omitted at the same time, or occur alone in the absence of the other. For instance,

(16) a.    家 有   贤妻,  外 有   良友

　　　　　jià yǒu   xiánqī, wài yǒu   liángyǒu

(16) b.    家里 有   贤妻,  外面   有   良友

　　　　　jiāli yǒu   xiánqī, wàimian yǒu liángyǒu

(16) c.    在   家有   贤妻,  在 外 有   良友

　　　　　zài jiā yǒu xiánqī, zài wài yǒu liángyǒu

(16) d.    在 家里 有 贤妻,   在 外面   有 良友

　　　　　zài jiāli   yǒu xiánqī, zài wàimiàn yǒu liángyǒu

　　　　　At home there's a good wife, outside home there're good friends

From (16) a to d, the preposition and postposition occur in the following patterns: both omitted; preposition omitted while postposition occurs; postposition omitted while preposition occurs; co-occur. What is interesting is all the four structures are acceptable. It can also be explained by the rule of spatial semantic self-sufficiency. Both "jia" (家) (home) and "wai" (外) (outside) are typical words of location, so they themselves alone can meet the demand of spatial semantic self-sufficiency. So whether the preposition and postposition occur or not doesn't affect the intelligibility and validity of the structure. But if we have a close look at the four structures, we can find the degree of acceptability of (16) d is weaker than the other three. This is mainly because the co-occurrence of the preposition and postposition brings about semantic redundancy, which goes against the economy principle of language. However, a speaker may use this kind of structure on purpose out of pragmatic reasons, then the word of place in the structure will become the foreground and focus of the topic as a result.

## 4    Conclusions

Circumposition is an important syntactic structure in Chinese grammar with the unique typological value. By studying the structural and semantic typological features of prepositions and postpositions in circumpostions, we can perfect the theoretical framework of Chinese adpositional system. The analysis of the semantics of the typical spatial circumposition – "zai...shang/li/zhong" (在...上/里/中) reveals that the preposition and postposition bear different semantic functions, which set restrictions on the law of adposition omission respectively. As the findings indicate, the preposition "zai" (在) has two major semantic functions: the spatial semantic function to mark or foreground spatial relations and locations; and the syntactic semantic function as a relator to link different constituents. While the major semantic function of postpositions is to mark specific spatial locations and properties. Two general rules serve as the semantic motivations for adposition omission: the mandatory rule of syntactic semantics and the rule of spatial semantic self-sufficiency. Though these two rules may not cover all the motivations underlying adposition omission, they can offer reasonable explanations to most common cases, which may bring some enlightments to Chinese adposition studies by portraying the typological features of Chinese adpositions.

# References

1. Chu, Z.X.: The Study on Chinese Spatial Phrases (汉语空间短语研究). Beijing University Press, Beijing (2010)
2. Greenberg, J.H.: Circumfixes and Typological Change. In: Elizabeth, C.T., Re-becca, L., Susan, S. (eds.) Papers from the Fourth International Conference on Historical Linguistics, pp. 233–241. John Benjamins, Amsterdam (1980)
3. Liu, D.Q.: Circumpositions in Chinese (汉语中的框式介词). Contemporary Linguistics 4, 241–253 (2002)
4. Liu, D.Q.: Word Order Typology and Adposition Theories (语序类型学与介词理论). The Commercial Press, Beijing (2004)
5. Hopper, P.J., Traugott, E.C.: Grammaticalization. Cambridge University Press, Cambridge (1993)
6. Rapaport, W.J.: Holism, Conceptual-Role Semantics, and Syntactic Semantics. Minds and Machines 12, 3–59 (2002)
7. Zhang, Y.S.: The Function Words in Modern Chinese. East China Normal University Press, Shanghai (2000)
8. Zlatev, J.: Spatial Semantics. In: Dirk, G., Hubert, C. (eds.) The Oxford Handbook of Cognitive Linguistics, pp. 318–350. Oxford University Press Inc., New York (2007)

# On the Meaning Representation of Fuzzy Words

Xiaoju Cui, Mianzhu Yi, and Wuying Liu

Foreign Languages University of Luoyang, Henan Prov., 471003, China
cxj841018@sohu.com, mianzhuyi@gmail.com, wyliu@nudt.edu.cn

**Abstract.** The basic characteristic of fuzzy language is the meaning uncertainty and fuzziness of the language units, such as words and sentences, and how to represent such fuzzy meaning formally is a problem that is worth studying. This paper attempts to analyze and explore the formal meaning representation of Chinese fuzzy words.

**Keywords:** fuzzy language, fuzzy words, meaning representation.

## 1 Introduction

### 1.1 Motivation and Research Object

The fuzzy language reflects the ambiguity of human thinking and understanding, which is objective and inevitable. Marx once said: A thing is itself and changing continuously, which has a contradiction of invariability and variability [1]. Therefore, all materials in the world are in the unceasing and absolute movement, while stillness is a certain period of development and is relatively temporary. So, people mostly take the continuous movement as a background when they distinguish the properties of things and use a limited discrete model to characterize a continuous process of infinite development [2]. This will inevitably lead to ambiguity in people's understanding of the properties of things, which has reflection in fuzzy language, such as fuzzy words and sentences. This paper mainly discusses the fuzzy words in Chinese.

Currently, semantic problem is the bottleneck of language information processing. The fundamental precondition of solving this problem is a symbolic and formal representation of the meaning of various elements in language systems. So that the computer can more accurately understand and process natural languages. The fundamental property of the fuzzy language is the semantic ambiguity. This paper attempts to explore a formal meaning representation of fuzzy words.

### 1.2 Outline

The next section discusses in detail the representation method of fuzzy word meaning. In section 3 the specific process of the fuzzy word meaning representation is explored. Finally, section 4 gives a summary of this study and an outlook on the further work.

P. Liu and Q. Su (Eds.): CLSW 2013, LNAI 8229, pp. 258–265, 2013.

# 2    Meaning Representation Method of Fuzzy Words

Choosing the representation method of fuzzy word meaning, we mainly consider three aspects, which are explained respectively in the subsections of this section as follows.

## 2.1    Language Meaning Representation and Ontology

To a certain extent, the language meaning representation is an expression of language ontology. Ontology is an explicit specification of conceptualization [3]. Conceptualization refers to systems and models formed by the relationship between concepts. Therefore, simply speaking, ontology is a standardized description of the relationship between concepts. The ontology can be classified as universal ontology, domain ontology, language ontology and task ontology. Language ontology is an expression of the relationship between concepts through language resources. WordNet, a famous language ontology, developed by Princeton University, uses synonym sets (synsets) to express concepts, where the relationship between synsets express the relationship between concepts [4].

Langacker (1987, 1999, 2000) suggested that the meaning is conceptualization [5]. Each language symbol carries some meanings, in other words, the language has a semantic level. In view of this, we can express the relationship between concepts through semantic representations, namely, semantic ontology. Although the problem of semantic ontology construction is also a hard one, we would like to express a point of view: since the meaning representation of language can be seen as a form of semantic ontology, we can learn from ontology knowledge representation methods in order to formally represent the language meanings.

## 2.2    Characteristics and Structure of Frames

There are many representation methods of ontology knowledge, such as predicate logic, rules, semantic networks, and frames. Compared with other representation methods, the frames representation method has advantages of strong adaptability, clear structure, and flexible reasoning [6].

Frames were proposed by Marvin Minsky (1975) based on the psychological model formed in people's understanding of situations and stories [7]. A frame is an artificial intelligence data structure used to divide knowledge into substructure by representing "stereotyped situations". Frames are connected together to form a complete idea. In frames representation, a frame, the unit of knowledge, is made up of slots, facets and values. Each frame represents a concept. Slots represent the intrinsic and extrinsic attributes of a concept, namely, relationships between this concept and any other concepts. Facets represent the type of the allowable fillers of slots. Usually value and sem are two frequently used facets, where the filler of the former is the actual numerical value of the corresponding slot, and the filler of the latter is the selectional restriction on the filler of the slot. It can be said that the frames in framework representation are actually encapsulated structures of multiple pairs of attribute-value.

## 2.3    The Relationship between Word Meanings and Concepts

A word in the language is the expression of a concept or some concepts. Sergei Nirenburg and Victor Raskin (2004) suggested that the language meanings are directly connected not to the outside world (denotation, or extension relations), but to the concept [8]. In one of his papers Lezin said that each sememe of a word can be correspondent to a certain concept-class in the OWL ontology, and the indication of a word sememe in the conceptual taxonomic hierarchy is an important component of the word meaning interpretation [9]. According to the view of the cognitive linguistics, the language meaning is not the direct mapping from the objective world to the language system, on the contrary, when the information of the objective world reflects to the human brain, it should be processed and controlled by the cognitive mechanism of human brain to form certain concepts, and while these concepts are expressed by the particular language symbols, the language meanings are established [10]. So it can be said that the word meanings are closely related to the concepts and the later is the main source of the former.

The semantic difference of words which describe the same concept usually exhibits in different values of one or several attribute-slots. For instance, the expression of the concept "HUMAN" includes a group of words listed as follows:

"儿童" [ertong] (*children*)
"少年" [shaonian] (*juvenile*)
"青年人" [qingnianren] (*younger*)
"中年人" [zhongnianren] (*middle-aged*)
"老年人" [laonianren] (*old folks*)

Obviously, the semantic difference between above words is different age attribute values of the human concept.

Based on the three aspects discussed in the above subsections, we believe that frames are a suitable choice to represent the meaning of words, of course, including fuzzy words. In the following section we will explore the specific process of the fuzzy word meaning representation by frames.

# 3    Meaning Representation Process of Fuzzy Words

Before representing the fuzzy word meanings, it should have a deep understanding of the fuzzy words and their semantic features. In the view of this, this section begins with an analysis of the fuzzy word characteristics.

## 3.1    Fuzzy Words and Their Semantic Features

Fuzzy language reflects people's fuzzy understanding of the state of things. From a distribution point of view, fuzzy words in the language are mainly concentrated in the attribute adjectives to express attributes, such as <"较热"[jiaore](*hotter*), "热" [re](*hot*), "冷"[leng](*cold*), "较冷"[jiaoleng](*colder*) >, <"较大"[jiaoda](*larger*),

"大"[da](*large*), "小"[xiao](*small*), "较小"[jiaoxiao](*smaller*) >, <"较好"[jiaohao] (*better*), "好" [hao](*good*), "坏" [huai](*bad*), "较坏"[jiaohuai] (*worse*) >.

Fuzzy words have a certain semantic ambiguity, but this ambiguity reflects the interval continuity of attribute values, which does not affect the correct understanding and using of these words. So, fuzzy words also have some semantic clarity, which mainly manifested in two aspects:

(1) Each fuzzy word is a description of a certain attribute-concept, such as <"较热" [jiaore](*hotter*), "热"[re](*hot*), "冷"[leng](*cold*), "较冷"[jiaoleng](*colder*) > is a description of the attribute-concept "TEMPERATURE", and <"较大"[jiaoda] (*larger*), "大"[da](*large*), "小"[xiao](*small*), "较小"[jiaoxiao](*smaller*) > is a description of the attribute-concept "SIZE".

(2) Fuzzy words, which describe the same attribute-concept, have some hierarchical properties. For instance, the fuzzy words <"较热"[jiaore](*hotter*), "热" [re] (*hot*), "冷"[leng](*cold*), "较冷"[jiaoleng](*colder*) > are hierarchical to describe high and low temperature value (TV), TV("较热"[jiaore](*hotter*)) > TV("热" [re](*hot*)) > TV("冷"[leng](*cold*)) > TV("较冷"[jiaoleng](*colder*)).

It can be said that people are based on no other than the above two clear semantic features of fuzzy words to understand and use them correctly. Understanding-based intelligent language information processing simulates human cognitive powers and operations to language concepts. So the meaning representation of fuzzy words only need to make their clear semantic features symbolic and formal. As to the formalization of the first clear semantic feature, it is only needed to introduce the slot-value pair that indicates the attribute-concepts, which are described by the fuzzy words. However, it is difficult and complicated to formalize the second clear semantic feature. For this reason it will give a deep analysis of the hierarchical properties of fuzzy words in the following subsection.

## 3.2    Hierarchical Properties of Fuzzy Words

Through certain analysis and research, we find that each attribute-concept that the fuzzy adjectives describe has a continuous gradient interval, and people tend to use limited discrete model to express the continuous gradient interval approximately, which will generate the fuzzy words. For example, the temperature concept has a continuous gradient temperature value, and all the adjectives which express that concept such as "较热"[jiaore] (*hotter*), "热" [re](*hot*), "冷" [leng] (*cold*), "较冷" [jiaoleng] (*colder*), and others form a discrete sequence that people use to describe the continuous temperature attribute approximately.

By the analysis of several discrete sequences of fuzzy words, we found that the formation of these discrete sequences has certain regularity. Let's take the discrete sequence of fuzzy words that is correspondent to the concept "TEMPERATURE" for example. Among these words there are five adjectives which have relatively independent meanings: "极冷"[jileng](*impossibly cold*), "冷"[leng](*cold*), "温暖" [wennuan](*warm*), "热"[re](*hot*), "极热"[jire](*incredibly hot*). From these five words " 冷"[leng](*cold*) and "热"[re](*hot*) are two basic ideal cognitive prototypes that people formed in the cognitive domain[1] "temperature" based on idealized cognitive model[2], while "极冷"[jileng](*impossibly cold*) and "极热"[jire](*incredibly hot*) are the two maximum that go beyond the basic cognitive prototypes mentioned above respectively in the interval of temperature variation, and "温暖"[wennuan](*warm*) implies the opposite unity of "冷"[leng](*cold*) and "热"[re](*hot*). The five words divide the continuous interval of temperature variation into four subintervals and all the other words which express the concept "TEMPERATURE" lies in the four intervals. This can be shown in the following figure:

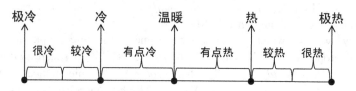

**Fig. 1.** Distributive regularity of the discrete sequence of fuzzy words that is correspondent to the concept "TEMPERATURE"

As shown in Fig.1, "很冷"[henleng] (*very cold*), "非常冷"[feichangleng] (*very cold*) denote the section that approaches "极冷"[jileng](*impossibly cold*) in the interval between "极冷"[jileng](*impossibly cold*) and "冷"[leng](*cold*), while "较冷" [jiaoleng] (*colder*) denotes the section that approaches "冷"[leng](*cold*); "有点冷" [youdianleng](*a little cold*) denotes the interval between "冷"[leng](*cold*) and "温暖" [wennuan](*warm*), while "有点热"[youdianre] (*a little hot*) denotes the interval between "温暖"[wennuan](*warm*) and "热"[re](hot). It is easy to find that this distributive regularity of the discrete sequence which is correspondent to the continuous temperature concept is also effective to discrete sequences representing other concepts.

### 3.3     Distributed Model of Fuzzy Words

Based on the analysis in the above subsection, we try to do the formal modeling as follows: A and B, respectively, represent two opposing cognitive prototypes about an attribute-concept. A represents the positive cognition prototype, such as "热" [re](*hot*), "高"[gao](*high*), and "好"[hao](*good*), etc. B represents the negative cognitive prototype, such as "冷"[leng](*cold*), "低"[di](*low*), and "坏"[huai](*bad*), etc. C represents the opposite unity of A and B. Max(A) and Max(B) represent the two maximum that go beyond A and B respectively in the interval of corresponding attribute variation, such as "极冷" [jileng](*impossibly cold*), "极热" [jire](*incredibly*

---

[1] The term "Cognitive Domain" was proposed by R.W. Langacker. He defined it as the context for the characterization of a semantic unit [11].

[2] The term "Idealized Cognitive Model" was proposed by G.P. Lakoff. He defined it as the unified rational routine conceptualization formed in people's understanding of things [11].

*hot*), "极热"[jihao](*wonderful*), "极坏"[jihuai](*worst*), etc. We use [0, 1] to represent the continuous gradient interval of an attribute, and lets Max(B)=0, B=0.25, C=0.5, A=0.75, and Max(A)=1. The abstract mathematical distributed model of fuzzy words is shown below.

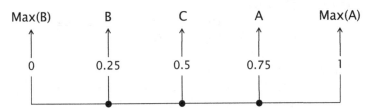

**Fig. 2.** The abstract mathematical distributed model of fuzzy words

By this model it can numeric-formally represent meanings of the fuzzy words that people use to approximately express the continuous gradient interval of an attribute. Still taking the discrete sequence of fuzzy words representing the temperature concept for instance, let x as any word in this sequence and $TV_R(x)$ corresponds to the relative temperature value denoted by x. According to the model in Fig. 2, we can represent the hierarchical properties of the words in the temperature sequence as the machine-readable numeric features shown as follows:

```
TVR("极热"[jire](incredibly hot))=1
TVR("极冷"[jileng](impossibly cold))=0
TVR("温暖"[wennuan](warm))=0.5
TVR("热"[re](hot))=0.75
TVR("冷"[leng](cold))=0.25
0.9(the rounded (0.75+1)/2 to one decimal digit)<TVR("非常
热"[feichangre](very hot))<1
0.75<TVR("较热"[jiaore](hotter))<0.9
0.5<TVR("有点热"[youdianre](a little hot))<0.75
0.25<TVR("有点冷"[youdianleng](a little cold))<0.5
0.1(the rounded (0+0.25)/2 to one decimal digit)<TVR("较冷
"[jiaoleng](colder))<0.25
0<TVR("非常冷"[feichangleng](very cold))<0.1
```

### 3.4    Fuzzy Word Meaning Representation with Frames

In view of the above exploration and analysis, we add to a frame that will be used to represent a fuzzy adjective meaning two attribute slots:

Domain: the filler of the domain slot should be the attribute-concept expressed by the fuzzy adjective

`Range`: the filler of the range slot should be the relative value denoted by the adjective.

Following are some demonstrative fuzzy adjectives whose meanings have been represented with the above defined frames:

```
高[gao](high)
        domain    value    height-attribute
        range     value    0.75

较高[jiaogao](higher)
        domain    value    height-attribute
        range     sem      >0.75&<0.9

低[di](low)
        domain    value    height-attribute
        range     value    0.25

较低[jiaodi](lower)
        domain    value    height-attribute
        range     sem      >0.1&<0.25
```

As shown in the instances above, we represent the fuzzy adjectives meanings in the form understood by computer. Comparing the domain attribute, computer knows that these four words all describe the height concept (height-attribute). Comparing the range attribute, computer knows that different words from these four imply different comparable height values (HV), that is HV("较高"[jiaogao](*higher*)) > HV ("高"[gao](*high*)) > HV("低"[di](*low*)) > HV("较低"[jiaodi](*lower*)).

## 4    Conclusion

Formal representation of language meanings is a problem of the understanding-based intelligent language information processing nowadays. The fundamental property of the fuzzy language is the semantic ambiguity. This paper attempts to explore a representation method of Chinese fuzzy words. There are also many fuzzy sentences in Chinese. In the further researches, we will work on the representation method of Chinese fuzzy sentences.

## References

1. Li, Q.: Fuzzy Semantics Introduction. Social Sciences Documentation Publishing House, Beijing (2007)
2. Li, X.: Ambiguity: the Mystery of Human Knowledge. People's Publishing House, Beijing (1985)

3. Gruber, T.: Ontolingua: a Translation Approach to Portable Ontology Specification. Knowledge Acquisition 5(2), 199–220 (1993)
4. Miller, G.A., Beckwith, R., Fellbaum, C., Gross, D., Miller, K.: Introduction to WordNet: an On-line Lexical Database. International Journal of Lexicography 3(4), 235–244 (1990)
5. Shu, D.: Cognitive Semantics. Shanghai Foreign Language Education Press, Shanghai (2008)
6. Ma, S., Zhu, X.: Artificial intelligence. Tsinghua University Press, Beijing (2004)
7. Minsky, M.: A Framework for Representing Knowledge. In: Winston, P.H. (ed.) The Psychology of Computer Vision. McGraw-Hill (1975)
8. Nirenburg, S., Raskin, V.: Ontological Semantics. The MIT Press, Cambridge (2004)
9. Lezin, G.V.: Ontological Semantics of the Text: Formatting of Interpretation in the Semantic Dictionary,
   http://rcdl.ru/doc/2009/141_147_Section04-2.pdf
10. Li, K.: Formal Semantics in Linguistics. Journal of Graduate School of Chinese Academy of Social Sciences 15(2), 112–117 (2009)
11. Zhang, Y.: Cognitive Expressions of Concepts — Comparisons among Frame, Cognitive Domain and Idealized Cognitive Model. Journal of Mudanjiang College of Education 10(3), 39–40 (2009)

# Internal Structure Types and Semantic Relation Types of Chinese Complex Cardinal Numerals

Ping Liu

College of Foreign Languages
South-Central University for Nationalities
Wuhan, Hubei, PRC 430074
liuping354@hotmail.com

**Abstract.** Chinese complex numerals have two types of structures: atom-base structure and round-remainder structure. This paper studies on the structural and semantic relationship between them. We hold that the former is either parallel to or consisted by the latter. Together with atoms and bases, they form the structure hierarchy of Chinese numeral system. The semantic relationship between constituents in atom-base structures is multiplication whose expression is word order, and that in round-remainder structures is addition and it can be expressed as word order or words. While the Chinese example Greenberg (1978) gives is wrong, order does function as a morpheme indicating semantic relationship and there are nine pairs of such Chinese cardinal numerals.

## 1   Introduction

The reference grammar of Dutch, the *Algemene Nederlandse Spraakkunst* (Haeseryn, Romyn, Geerts, de Rooij & van den Toorn 1997), studies the formation of numerals under the theme of word classes and word formation, Hurford's studies of numerals (Hurford 1975, Hurford 1987, Hurford 2003, Hurford 2007) study them as syntactic constructs, especially in Hurford (2007: 777), whereas Booij (2010) considers Dutch numerals as a mixed bag of derived words, compounds, and syntactic idioms, which form a complex network of constructional schemas of varying degrees of abstractness.

Existing studies about Chinese cardinal numerals take them as word and word structures (Zhu 1958), simple words and compound words (Zhang 1982, Xiao and Li 1997, Zhao 1999), or simple words and phrases (Hu 1984). This paper considers numerals under the heading of three forms: word, compound word and phrase, and the last two together as complex numeral. Listed in Table 1 are typical examples of each form.

About the structural composition of numerals, Zhu(1958) puts forward that there are three basic concepts:系数词 (xi shu ci, atom word, coefficient word), 位数词 (wei shu ci, base word) and 系位结构 (xi wei jiegou, atom-base structure), to which Xiao & Li(1997) adds 整零构造 (zheng ling gouzao, round-remainder structure). They have named the structural system of Chinese cardinal numerals and the two types of Chinese complex numerals: atom-base structure and round-remainder

P. Liu and Q. Su (Eds.): CLSW 2013, LNAI 8229, pp. 266–274, 2013.

Table 1. Forms of Chinese cardinal numerals

| value | Chinese cardinal numeral | pronunciation | numeral form |
|-------|--------------------------|---------------|--------------|
| 3 | 三 | san | Word |
| 30 | 三十 | sanshi | compound word |
| 33 | 三十三 | sanshi san | compound word |
| 33 | 三十又三 | sanshi you[1] san | Phrase |
| 3003 | 三千零三 | sanqian ling[2] san | Phrase |

structure. However, there are so far no systemic study on differences and relations between the two types of structures, or on their internal semantic relationships. This paper introduces, analyzes and compares the two structures. It also explores the semantic relationships between their constituents and corresponding formal expression of these relationships. Furthermore, it studies on order as a morpheme indicating semantic relationship. It holds that though Greenberg (1978)'s related Chinese example is wrong, order does indicate semantic relationship in Chinese cardinal numerals and there are nine pairs of such numerals.

This paper consists of six sections. Section 1 is an introduction. Section 2 introduces the connotations of atom-base structure and round-remainder structure, as well as their significances. In section 3 the relationship between the two structures is introduced, the continuous hierarchy of Chinese definite numeral system they constructed together with atoms and bases is also described. Section 4 focuses on the semantic relationships between constituents in Chinese complex numerals and their formal expressions. Section 5 focuses on order as a morpheme indicating semantic relationship. Section 6 is a conclusion. It concludes the paper and inquires about research prospects.

## 2    Atom-Base Structure and Round-Remainder Structure

Dexi Zhu's *Numerals and Numeral Phrases* (1958) is the first systematic Chinese study on Chinese numerals and numeral phrases, also the first on the subject from a structural point of view. In the article and *Lectures on Grammar* (1982), he puts forward the concept of *atom-base structure* — a term for structures composed by atoms and bases — and the concepts of *atom-base combination* and *complex atom-base structure*,[3] which can be summarized as Figure 1.

---

[1] "有(you)" means "again" here.

[2] "零(ling)" usually means "zero", but it refers to both "zero" and "remainder" here. See part 4 for detailed explanation.

[3] This article will use the latter term.

$$
\text{numeral phrase} \left\{ \begin{array}{l} \text{atom-base structure} \\ \text{combination of atoms and bases}^{4} \\ \text{complex atom-base structure} \end{array} \right.
$$

**Fig. 1.** Relation net of Chinese numeral phrases (Zhu 1958)

On this basis, Xiao and Li (1997) first puts forward the concept of *round-remainder structure*: the kind of complex numerals composed by two or more atom-base structures, atom-base structure and atom, or 十 (10) and atom. For example: 四万三千五百 *(si wan san qian wu bai, 43500)*, 二十二 *(er shi er, 22)*, 十一 *(yi, 11)*, and so on.

After comparing these two structural systems, the following questions will appear: isn't round-remainder structure a combination of *combinations of atom-base structures* and *complex atom-base structure*?[5] What are the distinctive differences between the two? Do they belong to the same level?

The raise of round-remainder structure has the following values: First, it reflects the understanding of the overall structural features of a class of complex numerals, while Zhu (1958, 1982) simply parallels three types of structures. Second, it reflects the ordering characteristics of the overall numerical value of a class of complex numerals: from left to right, from round to fractional, from large to small, while Zhu (1958, 1982) simply concludes the structural characteristics. This is proved by the features Xiao and Li (1997) has summarized about round-remainder structures: combination of individual values in terms of meaning, ordering from round to fractional in terms of syntactic position.

However, though Xiao and Li (1997) has the above positive significances, it has just done a simple description of the relationship between the two structures: "From the angle of structural relationship and semantic features, Chinese definite numerals system is one composed by atom-base structures and round-remainder structures." We can see that they think there is only a simple parallel relationship between the two structures.

It is not the case, though. A hierarchical relationship at structural and semantic level can be found by further comparing their structural features and semantic content.

---

[4] Dexi Zhu's *Lectures on Grammar* holds that combinations of atom-base structures fall into the following two categories: 1) Atoms act as the end of a combination, indicating units; 2) 十一 *(shi yi, 11)*, 十二 *(shi er, 12)*,...... 十九 *(shi jiu, 19)* , where 十 *(shi, 10)* acts as base, and its atom is an omitted 一 *(yi, 1)*.

[5] Because Xiao G.Z. & Li Y.Z. (1997) also pointed out that: a round-remainder structure can act as the *atom* of a complex atom-base structure. For example, the atoms of 五千四百二十万 *(wu qian si bai er shi wan, 54.2 million)* and 四千三百八十一亿 *(si qian san bai ba shi yi yi, 438.1 billion)* are respectively 五千四百二十 *(wu qian si bai er shi, 5420)* and 四千三百八十一 *(si qian san bai ba shi yi, 4381)* .

## 3    Relations between Atom-Base Structure and Round-Remainder Structure

Structurally, atom-base structure is either parallel to or consisted by round-remainder structure. They form a continuous hierarchy of Chinese definite numeral system together with atoms and bases.

First of all, they are parallel. Atom-base structures like 二十 *(er shi, 20)*, 三十 *(san shi, 30)* and round-remainder structures like 四万零五 *(si wan ling wu, 40005)*, 三万五 *(wan wan wu, 35000)* are all members of Chinese numeral system. As numerals, they have no difference from atoms like 二 *(er, 2)*, 三 *(san, 3)*, 四 *(si, 4)* or bases like 十 *(shi, 10)*, 百 *(bai, 100)* and 千 *(qian, 1000)*.

Second, a round-remainder structure may consist of several atom-base structures. Round-remainder structures reflect the ordering features of different numerical values, that is to say, "the positional arrangement of constituents from round to fraction" (Xiao and Li, 1997), while the consisted structures are still atom-base structures. For example, in the round-remainder structure 三百五十 *(san bai wu shi, 350)*, 三百 *(san bai, 300)* is a round number, 五十 *(wu shi, 50)* is relatively fractional, therefore, this numeral's structure is round-remainder, but as consisted structures, both 三百 and 五十 are atom-base structures.

In this sense, a complex numeral with only one atom-base structure and no other constituents can be called *a round structure without fractional elements*, for its end is open. For example, 三百 *(san bai, 300)*. It may be followed by a tens digit and a unit digit, or only one of them. Even the lowest-valued atom-base structure, tens digit, can be followed by fractional numeral. For example, 二十 *(er shi, 20)* can be followed by an atom like 二 *(er, 2)*.

Finally, they compose a continuous hierarchy of Chinese cardinal numeral system together with atoms and bases.

Both atom-base structure and round-remainder structure can be structural types of modern Chinese complex numerals, but the two types of structures are not at the same level, because as mentioned above, round-remainder structure may consist of several atom-base structures. At the same time, atom-base structure consists of atoms and bases. Therefore, the hierarchy of Chinese cardinal numeral system can be illustrated as Figure 2.

In this hierarchy, every level can be used alone to form a numeral, the lower level can also be a component of the higher level. For example, 三 *(san, 3)*, 十 *(shi, 10)*, 三十 *(san shi, 30)*, 三百 *(san bai, 300)*, 三百三十 *(san bai san shi, 330)* are all independent numerals, while the atom 三 and the base 十 are constituents of the atom-base structure 三十, just as the atom-base structures 三十 and 三百 are both constituents of the round-remainder structure 三百三十.

Thus, there are both differences and connections between the two types of structures. They form a unity of oppositeness in Chinese numeral system. They are not simply two paralleled structures, but rather two consecutive levels in the hierarchy of Chinese cardinal numerals. The former is parallel to and also contained in the latter—parallel in function, contained in structure. Their relationship is similar to that between words and phrases in the grammatical unit hierarchy of language system.

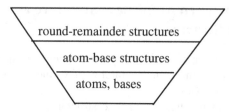

**Fig. 2.** Structural hierarchy of Chinese cardinal numeral system

# 4 Semantic Relationships between Constituents in Chinese Complex Numerals and Their Formal Realizations

The semantic relationship between constituents of atom-base structures "is multiplication"(Zhu, 1958). In round-remainder structure, the numerical semantic relationship between two or several atom-base structures, atom-base structure and atom, or 十 *(shi, 10)* and atom, is addition.

It is worth noting that because a round-remainder structure consists of atom-base structures, the relationship between the atoms and bases in these atom-base structures is still multiplication. In other words, the semantic relationship between the constituents in atom-base structures is only multiplication, while in round-remainder structures there are two types of relationship: addition and multiplication. For example:

(1) 十六 *(shi liu, 16) = 1 × 10 +6* (round-remainder structure, addition and multiplication)
(2) 三百一十 *(san bai yi shi, 310) = 3 × 100 +1 × 10* (round-remainder structure, addition and multiplication)
(3) 五千〇二十五 *(wu qian ling er shi wu, 5025) = 5 × 1000 +2 × 10 +5* (round-remainder structure, addition and multiplication)
(4) 四万零五 *(si wan ling wu, 40005)= 4 × 10000 +5* (round-remainder structure, addition and multiplication)

Considering these together with atoms and bases, the numbers of semantic relationship types of these structures also form a hierarchy: 0 -> 1 -> 2.

In round-remainder structure, the order of the numerical computation is first multiplication then addition, for example, 三百四十五 *(san bai si shi wu, 345) = 3 × 100 +4 × 10 +5*. This shows that the atom-base structure is more basic, which further reflects round-remainder structures may consist of atom-base structures.

In modern Chinese, constituents of Chinese complex numerals mainly have two types of semantic relationships: addition and multiplication. The only special case we observed so far is 半百 *(ban bai, half hundred)*. 半 *(ban, Half)* is not an atom, but a fraction with the meaning of *1/2*. Literally, the numeral means *1/2 × 100*. The numerical semantic relationship between the constituents is multiplication, but the overall numerical value is *100 divided by 2*. Should it be concluded that the semantic relationship in this complex numeral is division? It is not the case, but that the semantic relationship between its internal constituents is still multiplication. The reason is that it is about the type of semantic relationship between constituents, not the relationship between the value it expresses and the individual constituents in it.

In terms of relationship between structure and meaning, atom-base structure reflects that the order of constituents in multiplication is from atom to base, while round-remainder structure reflects that the order of constituents in addition is from the round part to the remainder part.

What are the formal expressions of semantic relationships in atom-base structure and round-remainder structure (that is, multiplication and addition)? Xiao and Li (1997) holds that the formal realization for addition in round-remainder structure can be 零 *(ling, zero, remainder)*, 又 *(you, again)*, 有 *(you, have)*. There is no related research on other formal expressions.

I hold the view that in Chinese numerals, there are one kind of formal expression for multiplication and two for addition.

The formal expression of multiplication in Chinese numerals is order, that is, the order of *atom in the front, base in the back.* [6]For example, in 三十 *(san shi, 30)*, the semantic relationship between the two constituents 三 *(san, 3)* and 十 *(shi, 10)* is multiplication, i.e., *3 × 10*. While in 十三 *(shi san, 13)*, the relationship is addition: *10 +3*. This is because the base 十 *(shi, 10)* goes in the front and the atom 三 *(san, 3)* follows, being opposite to the order of *atom-base* which indicates multiplication.

The semantic relationship *addition* has two types of formal expressions.

One is order, i.e., *base in the front, atom in the back*, like the above-mentioned 十三 *(shi san, 13)*, the semantic relationship is addition.[7] If it is 三十 *(san shi, 30)*, the relationship is multiplication.

The other one is overt words, e.g., 又 *(you, again)*, 有 *(you, have)*, 零 *(ling, zero, remainder)*, 单 *(dan, odd)*, 丹 *(dan, the same as* 单*)*, and so on. These words not only indicate the value distribution of *round + remainder* in round-remainder structures, but also mark the semantic relationship of *addition*. For example,

(5) 三千零五十 (san qian ling wu shi, 3050)

(6) 壬戌年春节住院有感（时年八十有三也）

ren xu nian chun jie zhu yuan you gan (shi nian ba shi you san ye)

Reflections on Being Hospitalized in Renxu Chinese New Year (At the Age of Eighty Three)

(Zi Yaohua, *Chinese Finance* (中国金融 (zhong guo jin rong), 19, 43-47, (1982))

In these overt words, 零*(ling, zero, remainder)* is rather special, because it can be an overt word connecting round word and remainder, also a word expressing the absence of atoms on specific digit positions, in which case, 零 can not be in the initial or the final position, nor be doubled. That is to say, in a Chinese numeral, regardless of the number of absent atoms in a series, there can be only one 零 to replace the absent ones. For example, 1001 should be 一千零一*(yi qian ling yi)*, not 一千零零一 *(yi qian ling ling yi)*. This usage of 零 is not an expression of semantic relationship, but an expression of the numerical meaning. Only when used as a sign to connect

---

[6] See part 5 for detailed explanation.

[7] The same as note 4.

round part and the remainder, can it be a formal expression of addition. The former can not be omitted, while the latter can, which is because when the latter is omitted, there is still word order to express the addition relationship between the round part and the remainder.

All the above can be summarized as in Table 2.

**Table 2.** Structure types, semantic relationships and their formal expressions

| structure type | semantic relationship | formal expression |
|---|---|---|
| atom-base | multiplication | order of *atom in the front, base in the back* |
| round-remainder | multiplication | |
| | addition | 1. order of *base in the front, atom in the back*<br>2. overt words like 又、有、零、单、丹, etc. |

# 5    Word Order as a Morpheme Indicating Semantic Relationship in Chinese Numerals

Concerning word order as an overt morpheme indicating semantic relationship in numerals, Greenberg (1978) has done some related research. It argues that in certain numerical expressions in languages, the arithmetical operations themselves are represented by overt morphemes including word order. That is to say, these morphemes have to express different arithmetical operation. For example, the *and* in *one thousand and fifty* which indicates addition, is such a morpheme.

However, the Chinese example it gives is questionable. It says: "In MANDARIN 32 is expressed as 3, 10, 2 in which the order is significant. For example, 2, 10, 3 would represent 23." (Greenberg 1978: 264) Surely enough, 三十二 (san shi er) is 32, 二十三 (er shi san) is 23, numerical values are different in the two cardinal numerals. Nevertheless, it does not mean that the arithmetical operations in them are different. The arithmetical operation between 三 and 十 in 三十二 is multiplication, so is the one between 二 and 十 in 二十三. The arithmetical operation between 三十 and 二 in 三十二 is addition, so is the one between 二十 and 三 in 二十三. Therefore, the arithmetical operations are not different in the two numerals.

In numerals, *semantic relationship* is what Greenberg calls *Arithmetical operation*. Then, the following question becomes natural: Does order of constituents indicate different semantic relationship in Chinese cardinal numerals? The answer is YES. It exists only in nine pairs of numerals: 一十(10)-十一(11), 二十(20)-十二(12)...九十 (90)-十九(19). Their value, semantic relationship and structure are as listed in Table 2.

Based on related discussion in part 4 and part 5, in these Chinese numerals, the order of *atom in the front, base in the back* indicates multiplication, while the order of *base in the front, atom in the back* indicates addition.

**Table 3.** Order indicating different semantic relationship

| Chinese numerals | Value | Semantic relationship | Structure | Chinese numerals | Value | Semantic relationship | Structure |
|---|---|---|---|---|---|---|---|
| 十一 | 11 | 10+1 | base-atom | 一十 | ·10 | 1×10 | atom – base |
| 十二 | 12 | 10+2 | base-atom | 二十 | 20 | 2×10 | atom – base |
| 十三 | 13 | 10+3 | base-atom | 三十 | 30 | 3×10 | atom – base |
| 十四 | 14 | 10+4 | base-atom | 四十 | 40 | 4×10 | atom – base |
| 十五 | 15 | 10+5 | base-atom | 五十 | 50 | 5×10 | atom – base |
| 十六 | 16 | 10+6 | base-atom | 六十 | 60 | 6×10 | atom – base |
| 十七 | 17 | 10+7 | base-atom | 七十 | 70 | 7×10 | atom – base |
| 十八 | 18 | 10+8 | base-atom | 八十 | 80 | 8×10 | atom – base |
| 十九 | 19 | 10+9 | base-atom | 九十 | 90 | 9×10 | atom – base |

# 6    Conclusion

In summary, the semantic relationships between constituents in Chinese complex numerals have only two types: addition whose formal expression is the order of *base-atom* or overt words like "零、又、有、单、丹" etc. and multiplication whose formal expression is the order of *atom-base*. While the Chinese example Greenberg (1978) gives is wrong, order does function as a morpheme indicating semantic relationship and there are nine pairs of such Chinese cardinal numerals. At the same time, Chinese cardinal numeral system has a clear hierarchy: atoms, bases --> atom-base structure --> round-remainder structure.

Do other types of semantic relationships exist in other languages? Are there other forms of expressions for different semantic relationships? Is the ordering for addition and multiplication in other languages the same as that in Chinese? Do other types of structures like *base-atom structure* and *fraction-round structure* exist? Do cardinal numeral systems of other languages have clear hierarchies like that of Chinese? These questions provide room for further study.

**Acknowledgements.** This article is sponsored by Major Projects of Chinese National Social Science Foundation (11&ZD189), the National Natural Science Foundation of China (61173095) and the Social Science Research Fund of Central South University for Nationalities (YSY10008).

# References

1. Booij, G.: Constructions and Lexical Units: An Analysis of Dutch Numerals. In: Olsen, S. (ed.) New Impulses in Word-Formation. Linguistische Berichte Sonderheft, vol. 17, pp. 1–14. Helmut Buske Verlag, Hamburg (2010)

2. Greenberg, J.H.: Generalizations About Numeral Systems. In: Greenberg, J.H. (ed.) Universals of Human Language. Word Structure, vol. 3, pp. 249–295. Stanford University Press, Stanford (1978)
3. Haeseryn, W., Romyn, K., Geerts, G., de Rooij, J., van den Toorn, M.: Algemene Neerlandse spraakkunst. Martinus Nijhoff/Wolters Plantyn, Groningen/Deurne (1997)
4. Hu, F.: Numerals and Quantifiers 数词和量词. Shanghai Education Press, Shanghai (1984)
5. Hurford, J.R.: A Performed Practice Explains a Linguistic Universal: Counting Gives the Packing Strategy. Lingua 117, 773–783 (2007)
6. Hurford, J.R.: Language and Number: The Emergence of a Cognitive System. Basil Blackwell, Oxford (1987)
7. Hurford, J.R.: The Interaction Between Numerals and Nouns. In: Plank, F. (ed.) Noun Phrase Structure in the Languages of Europe, pp. 561–620. Mouton de Gruyter, Berlin (2003)
8. Hurford, J.R.: The Linguistic Theory of Numerals. Cambridge University Press, Cambridge (1975)
9. Xiao, G., Li, Y.: System, Characteristics and Historical Evolution of Chinese Definite Numerals 汉语确数词的系统构成、使用特点和历史演进. Journal of Wuhan Institute of Education 16, 34–44 (1997)
10. Zhang, Z.: Collected Works of Zhang Zhigong 张志公文集. Chinese Grammar, vol. 1. Guangdong Education Press, Guangzhou (1991)
11. Zhao, S.: Collected Works on Comparison Between Chinese and English Grammar 汉英对比语法论集. Shanghai Foreign Languages Education Press, Shanghai (1999)
12. Zhu, D.: Lectures on Grammar语法讲义. The Commercial Press, Beijing (1982)
13. Zhu, D.: Numerals and Numeral Phrases数词和数词结构. Zhongguo Yuwen 70, 185–187 (1958)

# Comparison and Analysis between Chinese and African Languages in the Usage of Negative Words

Shan Xiao

International Education College, China University of Geosciences, 430074
wdxshan@gmail.com

**Abstract.** The teaching of Chinese negative words is a very important component in teaching Chinese as a foreign language. In the research of Linguistic Typology, the contrastive investigations between Chinese Language and African Languages are very few. Malagasy Language is one representative of African Languages System. In this paper, we mainly focus on the negative words of the Chinese Language and the Malagasy Language by comparison and do the quantitative research on the base of empirical research in order to find out the types of translated errors. Therefore, the comparison and the analysis of the two languages can help to find out the deep causes of those errors. This is the key to the success in the teaching of vocabulary.

**Keywords:** Africa, Malagasy Language, Chinese Language, Negative Words, Analysis of Errors.

## 1 Introduction

The development of Sino-African relations can be traced back to the 15th century. After the founding of New China, with the establishment of the friendly partnership between China and Africa governments, all aspects of interaction of two different worlds have been developed significantly. Under the new situation of China-Africa cooperation, how to shorten and stride over the cultural differences and build up closer relationship is facing severe challenges now.

Language is the carrier and the foundation of culture. Study on the differences between Chinese and African Languages can better promote the cultural exchanges of two regions. On the other hand, it can also help African Chinese learners to grasp Chinese language rules faster and better. 'Due to the interference of the mother tongue, students who have different mother tongues make different errors on learning Chinese. ' [4]

From the collected research materials until now, there is very little research on Chinese Language Teaching specifically for the African countries. One of the main reasons is the diversity of African Languages. 'In the records of anthropologists and the research of Jacques Leclere, Africa has 6-7 language families in the World 16 language families.'[3] The other main reason is the African Language System experienced the borrowing of a large number of foreign words and colonial forces in the development of languages. Historical and practical reasons both cause to the

P. Liu and Q. Su (Eds.): CLSW 2013, LNAI 8229, pp. 275–287, 2013.

studies of African Languages are quite difficult so far, let alone the comparative analyses between Chinese and African Languages. Madagascar is the largest island country in Africa. 98% of the island's residents use Malagasy Language which is one of representative languages in African Language Families. This paper introduces the negative words comparison and analysis between Chinese Language (CL) and Malagasy Language (ML), combined with the dynamic corpus research to explore the negative error types and reasons which the primary Madagascar students are most likely to make while learning this kind of words.

## 2    Features and Usage Comparisons of Negative Words between CL and ML

The basic sentence order of ML is 'Predicate-Object-Subject'. This is also one of the characteristics of ML. [9] Such as Affirmative Sentence:

(1) Mamaky            boky            aho.
读[du](read)      书[shu](book)      我[wo] (I)
This is 'I read the book.'
(2) Mpianatra                              izy.
是学生[shi xue sheng](is a student)    她[ta](She)
This is 'She is a student.'

Usually there is only one negative form that is using negative word 'tsy (no/not)' in the beginning of the sentence to negate the predicate part in ML. Its form is 'tsy+verb/adjective'. The meaning and function are equal to Chinese negative word '不[bu](no/not)'. Such as 'tsy+mamaky(not read)' 'tsy+mora(not cheap)' and etc. Meanwhile, other constituent parts and word order of the sentence will not be changed. For example:

(3) Tsy              mamaky        boky          aho.
不[bu](no/not)    读[du](read)    书[shu](book)    我[wo],(I)
This is 'I do not read book.'
(4) 这件衣服不便宜。
Tsy              mora          ity      akanjo      ity.
不[bu](no/not) 便宜[pianyi](cheap) 这[zhe](this)衣服[yifu](dress)这[zhe] (this)[1]
This is 'This dress is not cheap.'

### 2.1    Comparison of Predicate Verb Negation

Negative word '不[bu](no/not) ' in CL can not only negate the subjective intention of speaker, but also negate a past or future action or activity with the predicate verb form not be changed. For example:

---

[1] Here two 'ity' combined together mean 'this' in ML.

(5)昨天我去叫他，可是他不去。

[*zuo tian wo qu jiao ta , ke shi ta bu qu*]

*Yesterday I called him, but he did not go.*

(6)明天你去找他，他也不去。

[*ming tian ni qu zhao ta , ta ye bu qu*]

*Tomorrow you go to find him, he would not go either.*

However, negative word 'tsy' in ML does not quite correspond to Chinese negative word '不[*bu*](*no/not*) ' . Although it was put in front of the predicate verb as same as 'bu', the predicate verb should capitalize the first letter for different tenses. The predicate verb negation for past tense is 'tsy+N-verb' while the future tense is 'tsy+H-verb'. Examples are as shown in Table 1.

**Table 1.** Subjective Intention Negation between CL & ML

|      | Predicate Verb | Past Tense | Future Tense |
|------|----------------|------------|--------------|
| CL   | qu (go)        | bu + qu    | bu + qu      |
| ML   | mandeha (go)   | tsy+ Nandeha | tsy + Handeha |

If you want to express the objective negation which used to illustrate the action or state did not appear until the speaker speaks, we choose another negative word '没/没有[*mei/mei you*] (*no/not*)' instead of 'bu' in CL but not distinguish between tenses. For example:

(7)昨天他没来上课。

[*zuo tian ta mei lai shang ke.*]

*He did not go to school yesterday.*

(8)到现在他都没有来。

[*dao xian zai ta dou mei you lai.*]

*He did not come until now.*

But in ML, they still use the negative word 'tsy' for objective negation. When the past action or state does not appear, the predicate verb negation is 'tsy+T-verb'. When the current action or state does not occur, the predicate verb negation is 'tsy+verb'. Examples are as shown in Table 2.

**Table 2.** Objective Negation between CL & ML

|      | Predicate Verb | Past Action/State | Current Action/State |
|------|----------------|-------------------|----------------------|
| CL   | lai (come )    | mei/mei you +lai  | mei/mei you+ lai     |
| ML   | Tonga(come)    | tsy +Tonga        | tsy+tonga            |

In addition, the negation of verb complements and helping verbs such as '能/会'[*neng/ hui*](*can/would*)] will be different according to the subjective intention of speaker or objective condition limitation with tenses as well in CL. For example:

(9)昨天她生病了，所以没能去学校。

    [*zuo tian ta sheng bin le, suo yi mei neng qu xue xiao*]

    *She was sick yesterday, so she could not go to school.*

(10)现在我去不了学校。

    [*xian zai wo qu bu liao xue xiao*]

    *I can not go to school now.*

(11)明天我不会去你家的。

    [*ming tian wo bu hui qu ni jia de*]

    *I will not go to your house tomorrow.*

But in ML, although they negate the verb complements and helping verbs base on tenses, they do not distinguish from the subjective intention or objective condition. They still use 'tsy' to negate. Therefore, their negation can assume three forms: 'tsy+afaka+N-verb' (Past Tense), 'tsy+afaka+Verb' (Present Tense), 'tsy+afaka+H-verb' (Future Tense) .Examples are as shown in Table 3.

**Table 3.** Negation of Verb Complements and Helping Verbs between CL&ML

|  | Verb Complements/ Helping verbs | Past Tense | Present Tense | Future Tense |
|---|---|---|---|---|
| CL | neng +qu (can go) | mei +neng qu | bu+nengqu | bu+hui+qu |
| ML | afaka+ mandeha (can go) | tsy+afaka Nandeha | tsy+afaka Mandeha | tsy+afaka Handeha |

## 2.2    Comparison of Predicate Adjective Negation

On predicate adjective negation, when we want to negate the property or state of things, we use different negative words to express the differentia between subjective evaluation and objective judgment. For example:

(12)这双鞋不贵。

    [*zhe shuang xie bu gui*]

    *These shoes are not expensive.*

(13)那村口的树叶还没黄呢。

    [*na cun kou de shu ye hai mei huang ne*]

    *Those leaves in the village have not turn to yellow yet.*

In example 12, people have a subjective evaluation on the price of shoes which is 'not expensive', we use 'bu' to negate. But in example 13, whether the leaves 'yellow' or not is an objective fact which can not be changed with people's will. We use 'mei/meiyou' to negate.

However, the predicate adjectives negation does not distinguish between subjective and objective in ML. They keep on using 'tsy' to negate. So the example 12 and 13 in ML are translated in Malagasy language as followed.

(12a) Tsy     lafo     ity     kiraro     ity.
   [*not expensive     these     shoes     these*]
   *These shoes are not expensive.*

(13a) Ary     mbola     tsy     mavo ihany ny felan'ry hazo eo am-pidiran'tanàna    ry.
   [*Interjection still not yet yellow till    one leave that tree village         that*[2]]
   *Those leaves in the village have not turn to yellow yet.*

Furthermore, predicate adjective negation does not be affected whatever the tenses. For example:

(14) Mbola tsy     voky aho,     dia     efa          lasa     izy. (Past Tense)
   [*still    no/not    full      I ,     then    already    leave    she*]
   *I was not even full, but she had already left.*

(15) Hakelina sakafo ity, tsy    mahavoky    ahy.(Present Tense/General Statement)
   [*a    little      food     this  no/not   will full      I*]
   *I can not be full for such a little food.*

(16) Zara raha nitondra sakafo kely    ianao, tsy    mahavoky    ianao.(Future Tense)
   [*only/just   bring/take    food such little you ,no/not    will full    you*]
   *You only take such a little food, you will not be full.*

In short, the predicate negation forms in ML as above are shown by the same negative word 'tsy'. But for the predicate verbs, the first letter will be changed due to different tenses, while the predicate adjectives are unaffected by the tenses.

# 3    Analyses of Errors on Chinese Negative Words

Analysis of errors can be divided into 8 steps: Corpus Collection, Errors Identification ,Errors Correction, Error Types Selection, Formal Description, Rules Interpretation, Reasons Exploration and Teaching Suggestion.[8]This shows that if we want to know the errors which Madagascar students made when they study the Chinese negative words , it is necessary to start from the corpus collection and investigation.

## 3.1    Objects of Investigation

The objects of investigation of this research are three classes of Madagascar students. They are all   zero-based Chinese learners in China University of Geosciences(CUG) of 2011.Class 1 has 22 students who learned Chinese for about 10 months from September 2011 to June 2012.We called Advanced Level(A– Level). Class 2 has 17 students who learned Chinese for about 9 months from October 2011 to June 2012.We called Intermediate Level (I– Level). Class 3 has 16 students who learned Chinese for about 5 months from February 2012 to June 2012.We called Elementary Level (E– Level). The totals of people are 55.

## 3.2    Types of Corpus

The corpuses for this investigation are all based on single sentences[3] by filling the blanks with proper Chinese negative words. The purpose is to investigate how the

---

[2] Here two 'ry' combined together mean 'that' in ML.

[3] The single sentences here also include the simple 'Question-Answer' sentence such as 'Did you eat? Not yet.'

zero-based Chinese learners use and what kinds of error types they made after studying the Chinese negative words 'bu' and 'mei /mei you' for different levels.

## 3.3    Research Methods

We can do different statistics and analysis on the same corpus for various study purposes, and come to a series of related research conclusions by comparing the data scientifically. According to our purpose, we adopt questionnaire survey, static and synchronic research methods and statistical analysis in this paper.

## 3.4    Statistical Process and Result Analysis

We have designed 11 types of negative sentences according to the different structures and usages of 'bu' and 'mei/mei you' for student to fill in by the given words or cues. In order to avoid the accuracy of conclusions because of the limitation of questionnaire and also for language comparison research in the future, we put 'bu' negative single sentences and 'mei/mei you' single sentences together to investigate. All together are 40 sentences[4]. The questionnaires were fully taken back availably at last, and we arranged all the data and generalized the result as shown in Table 4.

**Table 4.** Error Types and Rate of Negative Structure of Madagascar Students

| Content Investigation | | Correct Rate | | | Average Correct Rate | Error Rate Rank |
|---|---|---|---|---|---|---|
| Negative Words | Types of Negative Structures | A – Level | I – Level | E – Level | | |
| bu | (1) bu +太[tai] (too much/very)+verb | 98.7 | 88.3 | 62.7 | 83.2 | 8 |
| | (2) bu+太[tai] (too much/very)+adj. | 99.5 | 97.7 | 92.4 | 96.5 | 11 |
| | (3)verb+bu +verb complements | 70.7 | 61.4 | 35.7 | 55.9 | 1 |
| | (4)bu+太[tai](too much/ very)+helping verb+verb | 75.6 | 82.0 | 87.1 | 81.6 | 7 |
| | (5)single 'bu' | 90.4 | 90.3 | 89.7 | 90.1 | 9 |
| | (6)comparative sentence with 'bu' | 83.2 | 77.3 | 45.6 | 68.7 | 4 |
| mei /meiyou | (7)mei/mei you+verb | 77.9 | 70.0 | 30.6 | 59.5 | 2 |
| | (8)mei/mei you+adj. | 81.4 | 76.4 | 61.5 | 73.1 | 6 |
| | (9)mei+helping verb+verb | 71.2 | 70.6 | 69.0 | 70.3 | 5 |
| | (10)single 'mei/mei you' | 93.4 | 92.8 | 88.7 | 91.6 | 10 |
| | (11)comparative sentence with 'mei/mei you' | 83.9 | 79.5 | 40.7 | 68.0 | 3 |

---

[4] See the Appendix.

From Table 4, we may find out some problems: First one is that we may see the highest correct average correct rate is 98.7% while the lowest is only 30.6%.Why there is a big gap between them for different types of negative structures? The second one is that Number 3 and Number 2 are both negative structures of 'bu' which always taught in primary stage. But why they have such a big different error rate between them? The third one is the comparative sentence structures with 'bu' and 'mei/mei you' which are always learned in advanced stage .It is relatively difficult for Chinese learners to understand the meaning of comparison and grape the usage of these kinds of structures well. So the error rates are both correspondingly higher. However, also is predicate verb negation, why the error rate of Number 7 is so much higher than Number 1? And if the confusion of Chinese negative word of 'bu' and 'mei/ mei you' is the fundamental cause of this error, but why in contrast the correct rate of single 'bu' or 'mei/ mei you' structure is such high?

### 3.5    Summary and Analysis of Error Types

With these questions we re-sort and summarize all the error sentences in the questionnaires once again and come to the conclusion that there are three main types of errors which Madagascar students easily to err.

**Confusion between Verb Complements Negation and Helping Verbs Negation.**
This type of error usually presents that the verb complements negation is replaced by helping verbs negation and the error rate is very high. For examples:

(17)*We could not find the car to go to school.*

　　False: 我们不能找车去学校。

　　[*wo men bu neng zhao che qu xue xiao.*]

　　True: 我们找不到车去学校。

　　[*wo men zhao bu dao che qu xue xiao.*]

(18) *He could not fall asleep because he was sick.*

　　False: 他生病了，不能睡觉。

　　[*ta sheng bing le , bu neng shui jiao.*]

　　True: 他生病了，睡不着觉。

　　[*ta sheng bing le , shui bu zhao jiao*]

(19)*You can not learn the Chinese well if you don't work hard.*

　　False: 如果你不努力的话，就不能学汉语好。

　　[*ru guo ni bu nu li de hua ,jiu bu neng xue han yu hao.*]

　　True: 如果你不努力的话，就学不好汉语。

　　[*ru guo ni bu nu li de hua,  jiu xue bu hao han yu.*]

(20)*The plane would not fly because of the bad weather.*

　　False: 因为天气不好，所以飞机不会飞。

　　[*yin wei tian qi bu hao, suo yi fei ji bu hui fei.*]

　　True: 因为天气不好，所以飞机飞不了。

　　[*yin wei tian qi bu hao, suo yi fei ji fei bu liao.*]

(21)*Today is not the weekend, so I can not go home.*

    False: 今天不是周末，所以我不会回去家。

    [*jin tian bu shi zhou mo , suo yi wo bu hui hui qu jia.*]

    True: 今天不是周末，所以我回不了家。

    [*jin tian bu shi zhou mo , suo yi wo hui bu liao jia.*]

All the above false examples substitute 'verb+bu+verb complements (such as: 到 [*dao*],着[*zhe*],了[*le*])' structure for 'bu+helping verbs+verb' structure which are semantic confusions. While teaching, the CL teacher for foreigners tend to interpret the 'bu+能/会[*neng/ hui*](*can/would*)' as 'the speaker does not have the ability to do something subjectively or the action can not happen due to the objective reasons'. That plays a great impact in understanding the meaning of sentence for foreigners including the Madagascar students. However, when we negate the verb complements such as '找到[*zhao dao*](*find out*)' '学到[*xue hao*](*study well*)' in CL, we just put negative word 'bu' after the verb and before the complement. That is why Madagascar students use 'bu+helping verbs+verb' to represent all the situations when the action can not be accomplished. Also as mentioned in Chapter 2.1, ML does not distinguish the subjective intention from objective condition, so they use the same 'tsy+afaka(*can*)+Verb' structure to express the verb complements negation. In addition, the tense is another main factor to affect the negative word choice in ML. In example 20, Madagascar students think 'the plane will not fly' because of the bad weather. And in example 21, they think 'I will not go home 'because today is not the weekend. They were all expressed as future tense and reflected directly into CL learning. And only the helping verb '会[*hui*](*would*)' contains a future tense meaning in CL, so that is the reason why they choose 'bu hui' instead of 'bu neng' or 'verb+bu+verb complements' in this case. The cognition between Malagasy and Chinese are totally different.

**Misuse of the Negative Words 'bu' and 'mei/ mei you'.**
Negative words 'bu' and 'mei/ mei you' can be used both before the predicate to mean 'no' or 'not'. And as mentioned in Chapter 2.1, there is only one negative word 'sty' in ML. So the Madagascar students often misuse these two negative words or use 'bu' instead of 'mei/ mei you' simply and one-sidedly in the early learning days. But 'mei/ mei you' has its own requirements of tense and aspect, especially for the negation of occurred actions or states in the past. For examples:

(22)*I can not test well in this exam because I was not prepared.*

    False: 这次考试我不准备，所以不能考好了。

    [*zhe ci kao shi wo bu zhun bei, suo yi bu neng kao hao le.*]

    True: 这次考试我没准备，所以考不好了。

    [*zhe ci kao shi wo mei zhun bei , suo yi kao bu hao le.*]

There are two kinds of negations in example 22. One is the misuse of the negative words 'bu' and 'mei/ mei you'. Because the action 'prepare' was happened before the speaker talked, so we should use 'mei/mei you' instead of 'bu' to negate. Another one is the confusion between verb complements negation and helping verbs negation that is 'bu neng kao hao' should be instead of 'kao bu hao' to mean the 'can not test well'.

(23) *I feel he was not unhappy at all.*

    False: 我觉得他一点也不不开心。

    [*wo jue de ta yi dian ye bu bu kai xin.*]

    True: 我觉得他一点也没有不开心。

    [*wo jue de ta yi dian ye mei you bu kai xin.*]

In this example, 'not unhappy' is the state of 'he' which had already occurred. So we should also use 'mei/mei you' to negate rather than 'bu'. There are a lot of these errors existed mainly because of the characteristics of negative word in ML.

Nevertheless, we discovered that there is no problem for Madagascar students to use the single 'bu' or 'mei/ mei you' structure. Examples are as follows.

(24)A: 你没有吃饭吗？

    [ni mei you chi fan ma?]

    *Haven't you had your dinner yet?*

    B: 没有。

    [*mei you.*]

    *Not yet.*

(25)A: 你不回家吗？

    [*ni bu hui jia ma?*]

    *You do not go home?*

    B: 不，（我不回家）。

    [*bu, wo bu hui jia.*]

    *No, I will not go home.*

The reason is that ML does not use 'tsy' but another negative word 'Tsia' to answer the question. 'Tsia' is only used in this situation and also does not distinguish between 'bu' and 'mei/ mei you' as the function of 'tsy'.So students generally can easily to choose the correct Chinese negative words to answer based on the same negative words shown in questions. But it does no mean that the students really know the nuances of meaning and usage between single 'bu' and 'mei/mei you' structures.

**Misunderstanding of Comparative Sentence with Negative Words.**
The Chinese comparative sentence structures with negative words are often learned in advanced stage for foreign students. Meanwhile, the characteristics of negative word in ML also influence the learning of comparative sentence with 'bu' or 'mei/ mei you'. Examples are as follows.

(26)*He is not taller than me.*

    False: 他不我高。[ta bu wo gao.]

    True: 他不如我高。[ta bu ru wo gao.]

This example is the misusage of 'mei/mei you', 'bu' and '不如[*bu ru*](*not...than*)'. 'mei/mei you' and 'bu ru' have the comparative function but 'bu' does not have.

(27)*The CDs which he has is less than mine.*

    False: 他有的光盘比我的没那么多。

    [*ta you de guang pan bi wo de mei na me duo.*]

    True: 他有的光盘没我的那么多。

    [*ta you de guang pan mei wo de na me duo.*]

The error in this example is that the negative object '我的[*wo de*] (*mine*)' is not in the scope of negation.

(28)*The life in China is not as good as in Japan.*

　　　False: 中国的生活没有日本的那么好。

　　　[*zhong guo de sheng huo mei you ri ben de na me hao.*]

　　　True: 中国的生活没有/不如日本那么好。

　　　[*zhong guo de sheng huo mei you/ bu ru ri ben na me hao.*]

This example belongs to the phenomenon that 'macro-objective item' is omitted by 'de-structure'. [6]It is often seen in oral Chinese but is somewhat difficult to be accepted in grammar.

Furthermore, tense auxiliary word redundancy and misusage in negative sentences are also seen in our questionnaires such as:

(29)*He did not return to his country, but live in Beijing instead.*

　　　False: 他没有回国了，而是就住在北京。

　　　[*ta mei you hui guo le , er shi jiu zhu zai bei jing.*]

　　　True：他没有回国，而是就住在北京。

　　　[*ta mei you hui guo, er shi jiu zhu zai bei jing.*]

(30)*She did not look old.*

　　　False: 她看上去一点也不老了。

　　　[*ta kan shang qu yi dian ye bu lao le.*]

　　　True：她看上去一点也不老。

　　　[*ta kan shang qu yi dian ye bu lao.*]

In example 29, the negative word 'mei/mei you' can not be used with '了[*le*]' (*past tense marker*) together. Example 30 is the tense auxiliary word 'le' redundancy.

## 4　　Conclusions

This paper introduces the semantic and usage comparison between Chinese negative words and Madagascar's negative words. According to the questionnaires, we find out the main error phenomenon and types which Madagascar students easily made in learning the Chinese negative words. Positive and negative transfer of mother tongue affect them a lot, especially the non-one-to-one correspondence between negative words 'bu', 'mei/mei you' and 'tsy'. And because the negative words changed in different context by tenses or aspects, plus the cognitive differences between Chinese and Malagasy is also another direct factor to decide the accuracy of negative expression.

Therefore, textbook selection, content arrangement, teaching strategies, no matter what it is, should be based on the characteristics of Madagascar student step by step. The first step is to tell them how to distinguish the difference between 'bu' and 'mei/mei you', and the second step is to import the Chinese cognitive viewpoint and the distinguishable approach on subjective evaluation and objective judgment in particular. The third step is not only to reinforce the exercises concentrate on the priorities and difficulties which have the high error rate, but also to guide the students to correct the errors which they made with more positive and relaxed attitude as well.

# References

1. Li, T.G.: The Usage of 'Bu' and 'Meiyou' and Time Restriction("不"、"没有"的用法及其所受的时间限制). J. Chinese Language Learning 2, 1–7 (2003)
2. Lv, S.X.: Eight Hundred Words of Modern Chinese Language(现代汉语八百词). The Commercial Press, Beijing (2001)
3. Mesmin, T., Athanase, B., Louise, A.N.: African Languages and Cultural Identity. In: Museum in International, p. 42. Yilin Press, Beijing (2008)
4. Wang, J.Q.: Research On Language System of Chinese Learner(汉语作为第二语言的学习者语言系统研究). The Commercial Press, Beijing (2006)
5. Xiao, X.Q.: Chinese Interlinguage and Grammar Study(汉语中介语语法问题). The Commercial Press, Beijing (2008)
6. Yuan, Y.L.: An analysis of the interlinguage errors with respect to méiyǒu(试析中介语中跟"没有"相关的偏误). J. Chinese Teaching in the World 2, 56–70 (2005)
7. Yao, X.B.: Interlanguage And Teaching Chinese as a Foreign Language(中介语与对外汉语教学). Academia Press, Shanghai (2009)
8. Zhou, X.B.: Steps in the Grammar Error Analysis in LCFL(非母语者汉语语法偏误研究程序). J. Journal of Yunnan Normal University (Teaching And Research on Chinese as a Foreign Language) 1, 1–9 (2009)
9. Zhi, F.S.: A Kaleidoscopic View of the World's Languages(世界语言博览). Shanghai Foreign Language Education Press, Shanghai (2008)

# Appendix: Single Sentences in Questionnaire

1.这衣服_____(干净)。 *This cloth is _____. (clean)*

2.汉语学习_____(难)。 *Chinese Learning is _____. (difficult)*

3.在这个地方她_____(很有名)。 *She is _____ (very famous) in this place.*

4.这天气___, 正好(…冷…热)。 *The weather is just right, _____ (...cold...hot).*

5.睡懒觉是一种_____的习惯（好）。 *Get up late is _____ habit. (good)*

6.我对这个地方_____(熟悉)。 *I am _____ this place.(familiar with )*

7.我们_____去学校(找车)。 *We _____ to go to school. (can find car)*

8.我觉得他一点也_____(开心)。 *I feel he is _____. (happy)*

9.今天不是周末，所以我_____ （能回家）。
   *Today is not the weekend, so I _____. (can go home)*

10.这次考试我_____ （准备），所以_____(考好)。
   *I_____in this exam because I _____. (can test well , prepare)*

11.我今天早上_____ （能） 去上课，去医院看病了。
   *I _____ to school, I went to see the doctor this morning. (can go)*

12.因为大卫的眼睛_____(能看)东西，所以他的听力非常好。
   *Because David's eyes _____ anything, so his listening is very good. (can see)*

13.春节的时候人太多了，所以他_____(能买到)火车票。
   *There were so many people in spring festival so he _____ the ticket. (can buy)*

14.因为天气不好，所以飞机_____ (飞)。

*The plane _____ because of the bad weather.(would fly)*

15.她做了很多菜，吃了三天也_____(能吃完)。

*She made lots of dishes that_____ for 3 days.(can finish)*

16.她看上去一点也_____(老)。 *She _____.( look old)*

17.这么点荣我_____(吃饱)。 *I _____ for such a little food. (can be full)*

18.这事情要保密，_____告诉别人(能)。

*This thing is a secret, you_____ other people. (can tell)*

19.今天下雨，所以我们_____(能出去)踢球。

*Today is raining day, so we_____ and play football. (can go out)*

20.看样子他是_____了(会来)。 *It seems that he_____. (will come)*

21.如果我说实话，你_____(会)骂我吧？

*You_____ (would scold) me if I tell you the truth?*

22.他_____ (回国)，而是就住在北京。

*He_____, but live in beijing instead. (return to his country)*

23.他生病了，_____(睡觉)。 *He_____, because he was sick.(can fall sleep)*

24.如果你不努力的话，就_____(学好汉语)。

*You _____ if you do not work hard.(can study well)*

25.没有钱的话，你什么也_____(买)。

*You_____ anything if you do not have money.(can buy)*

26.我逛了一天的街，但是什么也_____(买)。

*I went to shopping for a whole day, but I _____ anything. (buy)*

27.她说她_____ (是坐飞机来)。*She said she_____. (come by plane)*

28.妈妈身体不好，我每天都提醒她_____(忘)了吃药。

*Mom's health is not good, so I remind her _____ to eat medicine. (forget)*

29. A:你没有吃饭吗？ B ：_____。 (否定回答)

*A: Haven't you had your dinner yet? B: _____. (Negative answer)*

30. A:你不回家吗？ B:_____，我_____回家。(否定回答)

*A: You do not go home? B: _____, I _____ go home. (Negative answer)*

31. A:我不去了。你呢？B:_____,我要去。(否定回答)

*A: I can not go there. How about you? B:_____ , I will go. (Negative answer)*

32. A:他是不是离开了？B:_____,他去厕所了。(否定回答)

*A: Is he gone or not?B: _____, he went to the bathroom.(Negative answer)*

33. A: 一整天我都没有看到他，你看到了吗？B:_____，我没看到。(否定回答)

*A: I haven't seen him for a whole day. Did you see him?*

 *B: _____. (Negative answer)*

34.他_____我高。 (他矮我高) *He is_____ than me. (I am higher.)*

35.他家的光盘_____多。 (他少我多)

*The CDs which he has is _____ as mine. (I have more CDs.)*

36.中国的生活_____那么好。（日本生活更好）

*The life in China is _____ than in Japan. (Life in Japan is better.)*

37.英语_____汉语那么难。（汉语更难）

*English is_____ as Chinese.(Chinese is much more difficult.)*

38.武汉的楼_____上海那么高。（上海楼更高）

*The buildings in Wuhan are _____ as in Shanghai. (Buildings in Shanghai are higher.)*

39.我的汉语水平_____别人差。（我的汉语也和别人一样好）

*My Chinese is_____ than others. (My Chinese is also good compared to others.)*

40.他不经常运动，所以身体_____我好。（我身体更好）

*He does not often do the sports, so his health is_____ than mine. (My health is better.)*

# The Chinese Word-Form Transformation Related to the Development of Visual Behavior Categories

Xiaofang Ouyang

School of Chinese Linguistics & Literature/Center for Study of Language & Information, Wuhan University, Luojia Mountain, 430072, Wuhan, P.R. China
bbrirao@126.com

**Abstract.** The cognitive development of visual behavior categories has been proceeding from the simple to the complex and from the concrete to the abstract. Reflected on the language level, it has caused the word form transformations of visual verbs in Chinese. The transformation includes the creation of compound characters and compound words. In Old Chinese, producing new compound characters based on 目 [*mu*](*eye*) is the best way to reflect the complication of visual behavior categories. The rich visual characters and their explanations in *Shuo Wen Jie Zi* show that the ancient ancestors' cognitive maturity of visual behavior categories is high. The main way to record the development of visual behavior categories is generating new compound words. Through studying the internal structures, semantic relationships between morphemes and significant features of 153 compound verbs related 看 [*kan*](*look*), we found that the word-formation abilities of those core morphemes are unequal because they have different stylistic features. And the compound verbs sharing one visual morpheme have the same significant features which could be used to distinguish the synonyms in the visual verb group.

**Keywords:** Visual behavior Categories, word form transformation, compound characters, compound words, cognition.

## 1 Background

According to the cognitive science, objects are grouped into different categories by human beings in their process of recognizing the world. Basic-level categories are cognized the earliest since they are perceptually and conceptually the most salient. With those basic-level categories as the base and reference, people cognize all the other things in the world. That results in the generation of the subordinate, superordinate and other complicated and abstract categories. All the categories are organized orderly in a hierarchical structure. Cognition is the foundation of language, and language is the window of cognition. The cognitive development of categories determines the formation and evolution of the corresponding words. Conversely, the rich linguistic facts are the best clues about categorization and the development of human cognition.

P. Liu and Q. Su (Eds.): CLSW 2013, LNAI 8229, pp. 288–296, 2013.
© Springer-Verlag Berlin Heidelberg 2013

The visual behavior expressed by the verb 看[kan](look) is the basic way for human beings to get information from the objective world. Because of its importance for human survival, the visual behavior is cognized first. The basic-level visual category developed longitudinally to the super-ordinate ones, such as 感官[ganguan](sense), and the sub-ordinate ones, such as 仰视[yangshi](look up to),瞟[piao](look sidelong at), 窥视[kuishi](look through a tiny hole or gap). It also developed laterally to some complicated or abstract categories, such as 看望[kanwang](visit), 观赏[guanshang](view and admire), 看待[kandai](treat or regard). After constructing the paradigmatic semantic network related to 看[kan](look) and analyzing all the 209 verbs in the network, we found rich linguistic representations matched with the cognitive development of visual behavior categories from the simple to the complex and from the concrete to the abstract. Word form transformation, word meaning extension, changes of syntactic functions and shifts of pragmatic functions are included. [1-2]

This paper studies the word form transformation that reflects the development of visual behavior categories. With the development of human cognition, many new categories are generated constantly. The existing words can be used to represent those categories. But if the existing words cannot meet that need, new forms will be produced based on the old materials. That is called word form transformation in this paper. Because the Chinese characters are ideograph and the relationship between Chinese characters and words is very complicated, the word form transformation here includes the creation of compound characters and compound words.

## 2    Producing New Compound Characters to Represent the Development of Visual Behavior Categories

In Modern Chinese, many compound characters with 目[mu](eye) as their idea component are used to represent the complex visual behavior categories, such as 盯[ding] (stare at), 瞪[deng](glare at), 瞟[piao](look sidelong at), 睃[suo](look askance at), 瞥[pie](shoot a glance at). So are some compound characters in which the 目 [mu](eye) is hidden, like 望 ( 朢 [1] )[wang](look far into the distance), 观 ( 觀)[guan](watch), 窥(窺)[kui](peep), etc. In addition, the 目[mu](eye) can be directly used to express the visual behavior, especially in Ancient Chinese. For example, 项羽 目之，问为谁[Xiang Yu mu zhi, wen wei shui](Xiang Yu looked at him and asked who he was).[2]

The cognitive science research shows that people always cognize their own bodies first, the surroundings second and then the other abstract things. And the human body is the basic reference point of cognition. We can believe that 目[mu] could be the initial language form of visual behavior category. Later, 视[shi](look) became the core of visual behavior words and then 看[kan](look) took the role of 视[shi]. But 目 is always

---

[1] 朢 is the traditional form of 望. The 臣 in it looks like an upright eye in the oracle bone inscription.
[2] This sentence is quoted from *Han Shu*.

the basic element. It is the most creative idea component of visual characters. In Old Chinese, monosyllables played a dominant role in the lexicon system. That is to say, One Chinese character is just a word. And at that time, the system of Chinese characters was still in the development stage. So generating new compound characters based on 目 [*mu*](*eye*) became the best way to reflect the complication of visual behavior categories. There are at least 57 visual characters with 目 as their idea component and 视[*shi*] (*look*) as their explanation word in *Shuo Wen Jie Zi* and more than half of them are not used now. For example, 瞠[*tang*](*look with glassy eyes*), 膴[*wu*](*look slightly*), 睘 [*qiong*](*look in horror*), 眽[*mo*](*look greedily*), 睒[*shan*](*look quickly*), 瞀[*mao*](*lower eyes and look cautiously*), etc. The explanations of those characters in *Shuo Wen Jie Zi* show that ancient ancestors' cognitive maturity of visual behavior categories is high. They distinguished different visual behaviors from multiple angles, including the movement and status of eyes, the agent of visual behavior, the attitude or emotion when looking, the purpose of visual behavior and so on.

All of those monosyllables formed a relatively complete lexicon system of visual behavior. A visual word group with 视[*shi*] (*look*) as the core can be constructed. And the word group may be more complete than the one with 看[*kan*](*look*) as the core in Modern Chinese, since many concepts are expressed by phrases now. There are also some monosyllables are still in use. But their meanings have changed more or less. 看 is the typical example. The original meaning of 看[*kan*] is looking in the distance with a hand shading eyes. Now it becomes a basic-level category word with rich sense items. A few visual characters only exist as bound morphemes in Modern Chinese, such as 视[*shi*](*look*), 观[*guan*](*observe or watch*) and 瞻[*zhan*](*look forward or up*). Most visual compound characters die out. We attribute that to three reasons:

(1) The Chinese character system and lexicon system need to be simplified and reduced. So many monosyllables close or related in meaning made the character and vocabulary system too large and complicated. It was harder to write, memorize and recognize all the characters and words. People also found it relatively more difficult to choose the proper words. That went against language principle of simplicity. Simplification and reduction should be done.

(2) The phonetic system restricts the formation and development of the word system. The number of syllables in each language is limited, while the semantic information is infinite. That will lead to the phenomena of homonym. With the simplification of the phonetic system of Old Chinese, a large number of homonyms were produced. The conflict between syllables and meanings were sharpened. A good solution is the reduction of the monosyllables and the disyllabification of vocabulary.

(3) The abstract thinking ability of human being is further enhanced. With the development of society, the content of people's life had changed a lot and human cognitive ability had been improved fast. The angle of people to observe, analyze and generalize things and phenomena changed from seeking differences on common ground to seeking common points while reserving differences. Correspondingly, the main way to reflect difference between categories in language level shifted from producing new monosyllables or compound characters to generating disyllabic compound words with old materials.

The emergence and disappearance of visual monosyllables are just a small part of the evolution of Chinese lexicon system. But the producing and existing of those visual compound characters are the evidence of the development of visual behavior categories. Besides, some common visual words in Modern Chinese such as 盯 [ding](stare at), 瞪[deng](glare at) are not found in *Shuo Wen Jie Zi*. That shows some new compound characters were produced to express visual behavior categories after the Eastern-Han Dynasty, while deriving from dialects cannot be ruled out either.

## 3    Generating New Compound Words to Represent the Development of Visual Behavior Categories

From above, the way of generating new monosyllables to reflect the development of visual behavior categories were restricted. Generating disyllabic compound words became the main way. We made an exhaustive research on visual verbs in Modern Chinese and found 153 disyllabic words in all 209 verbs.[3] But the shift in the way is not an overnight process. Almost every compound word experienced a process of lexicalization in which materials like sentences or phrases develop into or recruited to form lexical items. So did the visual compound words. Usually they were made up temporarily with two monosyllables first, and were solidified and take shape gradually because of frequent co-occurrence. The meanings of those two monosyllables were further integrated into a new word meaning. That process embodied the proximity principle of human cognitive psychology. If two words always appear in a particular linear order, people will consider them as entirety and pay less attention to the internal structure between two components and the meanings of each one. The grammar distance between the two words will be shortened and even disappear. A new disyllabic word comes into being finally.

In the process of generating disyllabic words, which monosyllables had been used to make new collocations was very critical. From the angle of word formation, it is about morpheme choosing. After analyzing the 153 visual disyllabic verbs, we get 9 morpheme combination types[4] as following:

(1) Visual verb morpheme[5] + Visual verb morpheme: 21 words[6,] such as 瞅 见[choujian]( see by a glance), 顾盼[gupan](look around);

(2) Visual verb morpheme + Visual-like verb morpheme[7]: 7 words, such as 观察[guancha](observe), 视察[shicha](inspect);

---

[3] All the visual verbs are selected from the Contemporary Chinese Dictionary (2005).[3]

[4] The internal order of two morphemes is ignored here. For example, "Visual verb morpheme+ Visual-like verb morpheme" includes two cases, visual verb morpheme being in front and back.

[5] Visual verb morpheme refers to the morpheme which has the meaning of visual behavior. For example, 看[kan],视[shi],瞧[qiao],瞅[chou],见[jian],观[guan],览[lan],瞥[pie],望[wang], 瞻[zhan],眺[tiao],瞭[liao],瞰[kan],窥[kui].

[6] There are 21 visual disyllabic verbs fitting into this combination type. The same below.

(3) Visual verb morpheme + Non-visual morpheme: 87 words, such as 看管 [kanguan](guard), 俯视[fushu](look down);

(4) Visual-like verb morpheme + Visual-like verb morpheme: 3 words, such as 阅读[yuedu](read), 察验[chayan](examine);

(5) Visual-like verb morpheme + Non-visual morpheme: 16 words, such as 拜读 [baidu](have the honor to read), 诊察 [zhencha](examine (a patient));

(6) Visual-like verb morpheme + Eye noun morpheme[8]: 1 word, 目验 [muyan](verify with one's own eyes);

(7) Non-visual morpheme + Eye noun morpheme: 12 words, such as 目送 [musong](watch sb go), 放眼[fangyan](take a broad view);

(8) Non-visual morpheme + Non-visual morpheme: 5 words, such as 打量 [daliang](look sb up and down), 检查[jiancha](check up);

(9) Syllable + Visual verb morpheme: 1 word, 睥睨[pini](look askance at)[9].

Through studying the internal structures and semantic relationships between morphemes, we found that the compound verbs with two visual morphemes can be divided into two kinds:

(1) Two morphemes are at the same level. They explain each other, complete each other and restrict each other in order to express the meaning more clearly and specifically. For example, 看望[kanwang] is made up of two polysemantic morphemes, 看[kan] and 望[wang]. Both of 看 and 望 have the meaning of "visit" while each of them has many other meanings. Through combining them together, only the meaning of "visit" can be activated. Accordingly, 看望[kanwang] will be understood clearly as "visit" only. In addition, using two synonymous visual morphemes together can depict the action state vividly, since some visual behaviors contain repeated visual actions of the agent. For example, 顾盼[gupan](look around) with 顾[gu](look back or look) and 盼 [pan](look) together shows us a vivid scene that a person is looking right and left, forward and back.

(2) Two morphemes are in the relation of superordinate and hyponym. Usually the morpheme behind is the superordinate concept, such as 窥视[kuishi]. 窥[kui] means "look through a tiny hole or gap" and 视[shi] means "look". 视[shi] is the superordinate morpheme of 窥[kui] and indicates the semantic category of 窥[kui]. But now we feel that the sememe "look" of 窥[kui] is weakening under the influence of 视[shi]. 窥[kui] and 视[shi] are turning to the modifier

---

[7] Some verb morphemes like 察[cha], 读[du], 阅[yue], 验[yan], 赏[shang], often occur with visual morphemes and their meanings are directly related to visual behavior. We call them visual-like verb morphemes.

[8] Eye noun morpheme refers to the noun morpheme which means "eye". For example, 目[mu], 眸[mou], 眼[yan] and 睛[jing].

[9] 睥睨[pini] is a binding word. But now 睨[ni] can stand alone as a word. So we consider it a morpheme here.

component and the modified. 窥视[*kuishi*] is more like a modifier-head compound verb and the meaning is similar to the monosyllable 窥[*kui*]. The compound verbs with only one visual morpheme occupy the highest proportion. There are much more compound verbs with visual morpheme behind (X + visual morpheme) than those with visual morpheme in the front (visual morpheme + Y). The X usually describes the visual behaviors from different angles, such as method, state, reason or goal. For example, 凝视[*ningshi*](*gaze fixedly*), 扫视[*saoshi*](*glance around*), 鸟瞰[*niaokan*](*take a bird's-eye view*), 赏阅[*shangyue*](*read and appreciate*), 诊察[*zhencha*](*examine (a patient)*). The Y complements the visual behaviors with corresponding result or effect. For example, 视察 [*shicha*](*inspect*), 看顾 [*kangu*](*look after*), 观赏 [*guanshang*](*view and admire*).

Synchronic phenomena in language reflect the diachronic evolution. Through studying the visual compound verbs in Modern Chinese, we can know the diachronic development of visual vocabulary and explore their origins.

1.  The imbalance of word-formation abilities of the core morphemes shows that most visual compound verbs are generated in written style because the morphemes have different stylistic features.

视[*shi*] is the most productive visual morpheme, far ahead of others. There are 43 disyllabic verbs with 视[*shi*] as their core morpheme. 看[*kan*] is much less productive although the verb 看[*kan*] is the most common visual word in Modern Chinese. There are 21 compound verbs containing the morpheme 看[*kan*]. 望[*kan*], 16 verbs, and 观[*guan*], 14 verbs, come in order after it.

视[*shi*] is the core defining word of visual behavior verbs in *Shuo Wen Jie Zi*. It shows that 视[*shi*] is the most common visual verb at that time, just like 看[*kan*] in Modern Chinese. Research shows that 看 had displaced 视[*shi*] in spoken Chinese as the most widely used visual verb at the end of Han Dynasty and the beginning of the Three-kingdom Period and taken the place of 视[*shi*] in written Chinese after Jin Dynasty.[4] That is to say, 看[*kan*] has been the core visual word for about 1500 years. Why is the word-formation ability of the morpheme 看[*kan*] relatively poor? Comparing the compound words containing 看[*kan*] with the ones containing 视[*shi*], we found that the latter have obvious features of written style. Usually they don't appear in oral communication, while 看[*kan*] and the phrases with 看[*kan*] as the head are used a lot. For example, we say 生气地看[*shengqi de kan*](*look angrily at*) instead of 怒视[*nushi*](*look angrily at*) in oral communication. Some vivid visual verbs, such as 盯[*ding*], 瞟[*piao*], 瞄[*miao*] are used frequently. Even non-visual phrases are often used to describe the visual behavior, such as 给了…一个白眼 [*geile…yige baiyan*](*give…a dirty look*). Other visual verbs containing 观[*guan*], 望 [*wang*], 览[*lan*], 眺[*tiao*], 瞰[*kan*] also have the written style color. It shows that most visual compound verbs were generated in written Chinese and are usually used in literary language. It is less likely to combine this kind of words in spoken Chinese.

The visual verbs with strong oral color, such as 瞧[*qiao*] and 瞅[*chou*], have seldom formed compound words.

From the above, we can see that the word-formation ability of visual morphemes is related to their own stylistic features and the style of the context. The lexicon system of dialects can also provide evidence for that conclusion. Dialects exist in spoken form. Though the modern Chinese dialects have been influenced deeply by Mandarin, the basic words almost remain unchanged. In the author's dialect[10], there are only 3 visual verbs which are all monosyllables and there is not any visual compound verb.

2.    The compound verbs sharing in one visual morpheme have the same significant features which could be used to distinguish the synonyms in the visual verb group.

The main visual morphemes are 视[*shi*], 看[*kan*], 望[*wang*] and 观[*guan*]. The semantic difference between 望[*wang*] and others is relatively obvious. 望[*wang*] means "look far into the distance" and the corresponding extended meaning is "expect or hope". The compound words with the morpheme 望 inherit the semantic feature and also follow the path of meaning extension. For example, 眺望[*tiaowang*](*look into the distance from a high place*), 展望[*zhanwang*](*look into the distance*) and 瞻望[*zhanwang*](*look far ahead*) can collocate with 未来[*weilai*](*the future*). Compared with 观看[*guankan*](*watch*), 观望[*guanwang*](*look on from the sidelines*) has a distinct sense of distance. Comparing 细看[*xikan*](*look carefully*) with 谛视[*dishi*](*look carefully*), 偷看[*toukan*](*look stealthily*) with 窥视[*kuishi*](*look stealthily*[11]), we can find the stylistic difference between 看 and 视.

The differences between 视[*shi*] and 观[*guan*] are amplified through their respective compound word groups. 视 [*shi*] is always combined with the morphemes expressing method and the visual activity get modified from different angles. For example, 正视[*zhengshi*](*look squarely at*), 注视[*zhushi*](*look attentively at*), 仰视 [*yangshi*](*look up*), 怒视[*nushi*](*look angrily at*) and etc. All the visual activities expressed by those verbs emphasize focusing the sight on one point. Differing from 视 [*shi*], 观 [*guan*] usually focuses on the overall grasp. For example, 观察 [*guancha*](*observe*) and 观摩[*guanmo*](*view and emulate*). So 观 [*guan*] is more easily related with appreciation. Thus, 赏[*shang*](*admire*) can be combined with 观 [*guan*] to form 观赏[*guanshang*](*view and admire*) but not 视赏[*shishang*]. Correspondingly, 观[*guan*] can be used as a noun morpheme which means "view or sight", such as 奇观[*qiguan*](*marvelous sight*), 蔚为大观[*weiwei daguan*](*present a splendid sight*). Extended to psychological domain, 观[*guan*] also means "outlook, concept, notion, idea", such as "乐观[*leguan*](*optimism*), 悲观[*beiguan*](*pessimism*), 人生观[*renshengguan*](*outlook on life*), 世界观[*shijieguan*](*world outlook*)". All of

---

[10] The author's hometown is Pingjiang located at the junction of Hunan, Hubei and Jiangxi. Pingjiang diatect is a branch of Gan dialect.

[11] The original meaning of 窥[*kui*] is "look through a tiny hole or gap". "Look stealthily" is the extended meaning.

those show the overall grasp of 观[*guan*]. The mental verbs containing 视[*shi*], such as 重视[*zhongshi*](*attach importance to*), 蔑视[*mieshi*](*despise or show contempt for*) and 歧视[*qishi*](*discriminate*), imply that some attitude is highly targeted. That proved the point-focus of 视[*shi*]. We can say that if the synonym discrimination is done based on the comparison between word groups, the nuances can be discovered more easily.

In addition, we feel the visual word group is in disequilibrium. Many visual compound verbs don't have their oppositions in semantic meaning. There are several visual or mental verbs related to negative emotions, such as 怒视[*nushi*](*look angrily at*), 敌视[*dishi*](*be hostile to*) and 仇视[*choushi*](*look upon with hatred*). But there is no one related to positive emotions. Besides, several verbs have been produced to express the same one visual behavior from different angles, while some visual activities have only one or don't have lexical representation. For example, 斜视[*xieshi*], 瞟 [*piao*], 睃[*suo*], 乜斜[*miexie*], 睨[*ni*] and 睥睨[*pini*] are all used to express "look askance", and only 平视[*pingshi*] means "look at the front horizontally", while no word are produced to express "look with rolling eyes". Facts show that the lexical system is the representation of categorization, but the words don't reflect all the cognitive concepts. Only the concepts human paid attention to can be represented by words. If some concepts which were important in a certain period and got their lexical representations lose their positions, the corresponding words will die out. For example, 牻[*mang*](*black and white cow*), 牭[*si*](*four-year-old cow*), 犍[*jiu*](*the cow of great strength*) and 牰[*you*](*the cow of black eye socket*) were once common in the farming period and have disappeared now. So observing and studying the development and evolution of visual verbs at the language level is an effective way to know the cognitive process of visual behavior categories.

# 4    Conclusion

Language is the window of cognition. There are two ways of word form transformation to reflect the cognitive development of visual behavior categories. Producing new compound characters based on 目[*mu*](*eye*) is more common in Old Chinese. The rich visual characters and their explanations in *Shuo Wen Jie Zi* show that the ancient ancestors' cognitive maturity of visual behavior categories is high. A relatively complete lexicon system of visual behavior was formed at that time. But with the development of human cognition and the evolution of language system, a great change happened to the visual lexicon system. Generating new compound words with old visual morphemes became the main way to record the development of visual categories.

After an exhaustive research on the 153 visual disyllabic verbs, we get 9 combination structures and two kinds of semantic relationships between morphemes. The word-formation abilities of visual morphemes are different. 视[*shi*] is the most productive, far ahead of others. 看[*kan*], 望[*wang*] and 观[*guan*] come in order after it. The imbalance of word-formation abilities of the core morphemes shows that most visual compound verbs are generated in written style because the morphemes have different stylistic features. The compound verbs sharing in one visual morpheme have the same significant features which could be used to distinguish the synonyms in the visual verb group. In addition, the visual words don't match all the cognitive concepts so strictly. Many visual compound verbs don't have their oppositions in concept. Several verbs have been produced to express the same visual behavior from different angles, while some visual activities have only one or don't have lexical representation. More attention should be paid to the diachronic and synchronic lexical systems at the language level, and then we may discover the secrets of human cognition.

**Acknowledgments.** This research is supported by the Major Projects of National Social Science Foundation of China (11&ZD189) and the Post-70s Scholars Academic Development Program of Wuhan University: Interdisciplinary Research Team of Applied Linguistics.

# References

1. Ouyang, X.F.: The Cognitive Study of the Paradigmatic Semantic Network Related to Kan, Doctoral Dissertation of Wuhan University (2009)
2. Ouyang, X.F.: The Research on Sequential Meaning Extension: A Case Study on the Polysemy of 看(kan). In: Ji, D., Xiao, G. (eds.) CLSW 2012. LNCS, vol. 7717, pp. 438–447. Springer, Heidelberg (2013)
3. Chinese Academy of Social Sciences Research Institutes of Language Department of Dictionary: Contemporary Chinese Dictionary, 5th edn. Commercial Press, Beijing (2005)
4. Wang, W.H.: The Research of the Evolution of Chinese Common Words from Eastern Han to Sui Dynasty. Nanjing University Press, Nanjing (2000)

# Qualia Modification in Mandarin Neologism:
# A Case Study on Prefix "Wéi 微"

Lingchen Chou and Shukai Hsieh

Graduate Institute of Linguistics
National Taiwan University
qazwert78@gmail.com
shukaihsieh@ntu.edu.tw

**Abstract.** Language change is a ubiquitous and inevitable phenomenon in daily usages, represented by both novel interpretations and usages of old words, as well as through the development of entirely new words called neologisms. This study aims to give a theoretical account of the prefix微[*wéi*] in Mandarin, which recently has extended its meanings by combing with modified nouns in varied contexts, for instance, 微電影[*wéi-diànyǐng*] (*short film*), 微環島[*wéi-huándǎo*] (*riding bicycle to travel the northern coastline of Taiwan*), 微開車[*wéi-kāichē*] (*riding motorcycle*) and so on. To analyze this phenomenon through the lens of lexical semantics, we follow the *Generative Lexicon Theory* to explore the selective binding of *wéi* +noun modification in terms of qualia structure. The result shows that *wéi* has a high preference for selection of the FORMAL role but excludes TELIC. Possible explanations are given for the underlying reasons for psychological preferences in perceiving FORMAL components of objects, such as shape and color, rather than the specification of function or purpose.

**Keywords:** neologism, qualia structure, the Generative Lexicon.

## 1 Introduction

Language is flexible and changes easily and frequently. With people's daily usage, new words and meanings have emerged spontaneously. In this study, we will take a look at *wéi*, which can function as verb, adjective, and adverb. Among these usages, three core senses with high frequency and familiarity can be identified in the Chinese Wordnet[1]and the on-line Chinese dictionary of the Ministry of Education[2]: (1) Small amount of something (*wéi-bó* 'slight'); (2) small size, micro- (*xì-wéi* 'tiny'); and (3) low degree (*wéi-hóng* 'reddish').

---

[1] http://lope.linguistics.ntu.edu.tw/cwn
[2] http://dict.revised.moe.edu.tw

P. Liu and Q. Su (Eds.): CLSW 2013, LNAI 8229, pp. 297–305, 2013.
© Springer-Verlag Berlin Heidelberg 2013

However, recently a new usage of *wéi* has emerged. It has become more common to combine *wéi* with many modified nouns to form novel meanings, such as 微電影 [*wéi-diànyǐng*] (*short film*), 微賴床[*wéi-làichuáng*] (*to sleep one to two hours late*), and 微漫畫 [*wéi-mànhuà*] (four-page comics). These new words are traditionally called 'neologisms', "a word or phrase created for a new (unknown before) object or expressing a new notion." (Akhmanova, 1996)

Previous studies on neologisms primarily took a historical or social perspective, specifying the motivations or origins of new words. These studies focused on issues such as Taiwanese loanwords forming neologies in Mandarin Chinese (Hsieh, 2005), ways in which properties of systemization of lexical determine the relationship between neologisms and general words (Deng, 2005), and comparisons of lexical differences in spoken neologisms between Taiwan and mainland China (Wang, 2007).

Rather than focusing on history or origins to understand how neologisms emerge, this study instead aims to focus on the underlying mechanism of lexical semantic composition in neologism. The study explored whether there were particular factors or characteristics of certain nouns that made them more likely to be combined with *wéi* to form a neologism. To conduct this analysis, the study used the model of selective binding and qualia modification from Generative Lexicon Theory (Pustejovsky, 1995), to explore semantic analysis of nouns combined with *wéi*, as well as the classification of these nouns.

# 2     Qualia Structure in the Generative Lexicon Theory

Before reporting on the analysis, the paper will briefly review the theoretical context and purpose of using this approach.

## 2.1     Overview

In order to account for rich and multiple meanings of a lexical item, the sense-enumeration approach seems not appropriate; although it gives an exhaustive account of meanings, the lists that are generated are often cumbersome and hard to analyze. On the other hand, the *Generative Lexicon Theory* (*GL Theory*, henceforth) provides a simpler and clearer way to shed light on both lexical semantic information and the generative nature of creativity in language. Qualia structure, as one of four levels of lexical knowledge representation proposed by the *GL Theory,* contains four basic roles: (1) CONSTITUTIVE: the relation between an object and its constituents or proper parts, e.g. material, parts and component elements; (2) FORMAL: that which distinguishes the object within a large domain, e.g. shape, orientation, and color; (3) TELIC: purpose and function of the object; (4) AGENTIVE: factors involved in the origin or "bringing about" of an object, e.g. creator, artifact, natural kind and causal chain. (Pustejovsky, 1995)

As argued by Pustejovsky, the qualia structure provides us the structural conceptual template, over which semantic compositional computation may apply to the denotation of a lexical item. For example, in the case of polysemy with adjectival modification, the semantic generative device, called selective binding, takes the adjective as a function and applies it to a quale within the noun which it modifies. That is, it selects the quale of the noun that is in composition within the resulting interpretation. The following examples illustrate these two issues:

(1)  a. a well-built house
     b. a two-story house
     c. a vacation house
     d. a brick house

It is apparent that *a well-built house* represents the "making" of that house is good, which relates to the AGENTIVE role of *house; a two-story house* indicates the "shape" of that house is two-floor, which relates to the FORMAL role; "vacation" and "brick" actually point out the "purpose" of that house is living for vacation and the "material" of it is brick, which connects to the TELIC and CONSTITUTIVE role. Based on this view, it shows that the noun *house* actually contains four qualia, and one of them will be selected while being modified by different adjectives.

Johnston and Busa (1996) took this perspective and proposed *Qualia Modification* observing the relational structure between modifiers and heads in compounds. For example, in concepts like *bread knife* and *wine glass,* the modifying nouns represent the function or purpose of head nouns, which can be categorized as TELIC Qualia Modifications. Other examples such as *bullet hole* and *lemon juice* indicate AGENTIVE Qualia Modifications, *glass door* and *silicon breast* demonstrates CONSTITUTIVE Qualia Modifications.

## 2.2  Studies on Qualia Modification in Mandarin Chinese

Since this study focuses on Mandarin Chinese, three studies related to both qualia modification and Mandarin Chinese will be reviewed in this section.

Wang and Huang (2010) pointed out adjectival modifications to Mandarin nouns, especially in two cases: "*cháng+* noun" and "adjective+ *túshuguǎ*". The results showed the adjective *cháng* can modify different types of nouns such as (1) *cháng+* natural type nouns *(cháng-fǎ* 'long hair'); (2) *cháng+* artifactual type nouns *(cháng-tímù* 'long title'). Additionally, when different adjectives modify a particular noun, some of them can select multiple facets of the noun whereas others might only pick up one facet. For example, in the phrase *hǎo de túshū-guǎn* 'good library', the adjective *hǎo* can specify a library which is well-built (AGENTIVE role), large (FORMAL role) or filled with lots of collections (CONSTITUTIVE role); while others like *dà túshū-guǎn* 'large library' and *gǔ-laǒ de túshū-guǎn* 'old library', adjectives *dà* and *gǔ-laǒ* can only modify one quale of the noun.

Lee et al. (2010) proposed a more detailed cross language survey of qualia modification in noun-noun compounds, exploring these combinations in Chinese, German, and Japanese (among other languages). In examples in Mandarin such as *fàn-wǎn* 'rice bowl' and *yóu-jǐng* 'oil well', some former nouns clarify the function and purpose of latter ones (TELIC qualia modification), and other nouns serve as AGENTIVE qualia modification *(jǐng-shuǐ* 'water from a well'), CONSTITUTIVE qualia modification *(bolí-mén* 'glass door'), or FORMAL qualia modification *(wèi-ái* 'stomach cancer').

On the other hand, Wang and Huang (2011) specifically investigated the 'modifier-head' type in compound event nouns, discovering that the modifier actually acts as a qualia role of the head. For example, *táotài-sài* 'elimination game' shows that the TELIC role of the modifier *táotài* provides the core meaning of the compound. This also indicates that contrasting to the Righthand Head Rule (Williams 1981), the modifier is in fact sometimes able to supply more semantic information than its head.

# 3    Methods

Current balanced corpora of Mandarin Chinese in Taiwan such as Academic Sinica Balanced Corpus of Modern Chinese was released a relatively long time ago (1990), which makes it difficult to extract neologisms based on its data. Nevertheless, the World Wide Web (WWW) provides both conventional and novel usages of language, serving as an appropriate approach to investigate diachronic change. ". . . Although the web is young and old documents are often removed, there are first examples in which language change is documented." (Volk, 2002). Because of the dearth of information regarding the current emergence of the new usage of *wéi* in existing corpora, Internet searches, especially using the Google search engine, became the main source of data for this study. Furthermore, online social networks provide a communicating platform and used by every generation, but most especially the youth where created usages and interpretations of language often come from (Boyd, 2007).

Using these two sources, our data can be categorized into two corpora: web pages retrieved from the Google search engine, including blogs[3], news articles[4], and general web pages[5]; and the web version of PTT[6] (an on-line discussion board usually used by college students in Taiwan). To avoid incorrect interpretations caused by language specific and cultural differences, the data are only restricted to the domains of web pages and discussion boards in Taiwan. Proper names such as 微電子[*wéi-diànzǐ*] (*microelectronics*), 微博[*wēi-bó*], 微奈米[*wēi-nàimǐ*] (micronano) and so on are also excluded.

---

[3]  http://www.google.com.tw/#q=%22%E5%BE%AE%22&hl=zh-
     TW&site=webhp&tbm=blg&source=lnms&sa=X&ei=NoZVUaKQH8rikgXPuYH
     YBQ&ved=0CA0Q_AUoAw&bav=on.2,or.&fp=d7df41498d07ba25&biw=1920
     &bih=989

[4]  http://www.google.com.tw/#q=%22%E5%BE%AE%22&hl=zh-
     TW&site=webhp&tbm=nws&source=lnms&sa=X&ei=qINVUcXtBoXYkAW5toH
     YDw&ved=0CAsQ_AUoAQ&bav=on.2,or.&fp=94f36680bb864f01&biw=1920
     &bih=989

[5]  http://www.google.com.tw/#q=%22%E5%BE%AE%22&hl=zh-
     TW&site=webhp&source=lnms&sa=X&ei=eIZVUcC4IIfwkgXHz4HoDg&ved=
     0CAYQ_AUoAA&bav=on.2,or.&fp=94f36680bb864f01&biw=1920&bih=989

[6] http://www.google.com.tw/search?as_q=&as_epq=%22%E5%BE%AE%22&as
     _oq=&as_eq=&as_nlo=&as_nhi=&lr=lang_zh-
     TW&cr=&as_qdr=all&as_sitesearch=ptt.cc&as_occt=any&safe=images
     &as_filetype=&as_rights=

Our research rationale was to classify the qualia role selected by the prefix *wéi* in Mandarin neologism, and see whether there is a tendency of *wéi* to be used more frequently in particular forms of qualia modification. As for the analyzing approach, the GL Theory will be the primary theoretical apparatus.

## 4    Results and Discussion

Overall there were 75 example sentences, retrieved between 2009 and 2012.[7] In order to precisely understand novel interpretations of *wéi*+ noun phrase, we first read over the whole context, and after thorough confirmation of the meaning, the selected qualia role of each noun phrase was then analyzed. The following is part of the collected data:

**Table 1.** Data of prefix wéi in neologism

| SENTENCE | QUALIA |
|---|---|
| 台中微設計早午餐咖啡館<br>[*wéi-shèjì*] (*wéi-design*) | FORMAL |
| 腳踏車，微環島<br>[*wéi-huándǎo*]<br>(*wéi-travel around an island*) | CONSTITUTIVE |
| 微鼓勵<br>[*wéi-gǔlì*] (*wéi-encourage*) | FORMAL |
| 精緻無比的微雪景<br>[*wéi- xuějǐng*] (*wéi-snow*) | AGENTIVE |
| 這就是- 微神奇寶貝<br>[*wéi- shénqí bǎobèi*] (*wéi-Pokemon*) | AGENTIVE |
| 台中99元豬肉微火鍋<br>[*wéi- huǒguō*] (*wéi-hotpot*) | FORMAL |

Considering 75 sentences, the selected qualia role of noun phrases belonging to CONSTITUTIVE had 3 sentences, while FORMAL had 62, TELIC had 0, and AGENTIVE had 10. This finding seems quite reasonable, since the FORMAL role pertains to characteristics that can be perceived by our senses (such as size, color, etc.) and that serve to distinguish one object from another. It therefore makes sense that a main source for new lexical items and meanings would be people talking about what they perceive. The TELIC role, on the other hand, refers to purposes or functions of an object, which would make it harder to modify, and thus a less preferred

---

[7]    However, by using the Baidu search engine, we have discovered that the usage of 微電影 [*wéi-diànyǐng*]( *wéi-movie*)is as prevalent as in China, whereas others are not apparent. One article has specifically pointed out the new notion of *wéi* (http://money.163.com/12/0607/02/83C4B3KD00253B0H.html), showing 微酒店[*wéi-jiǔdiàn*]( *wéi-hotel*),微設計[*wéi-shèjì*]( *wéi-design*), and so on.

selection for qualia modification. In addition to comparing the preferences underlying the selective binding of the prefix *wéi* in the various role categories, it is also interesting to look inside each group and have more detailed discussion.

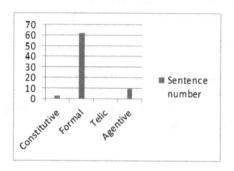

**Fig. 1.** Sentence number of each qualia structure

The first group is the CONSTITUTIVE role, and the examples are presented as follow:

(1) 腳踏車，微環島
 jiǎo-tà-chē, wéi-huán-dǎo
 foot step car, small around island
 'Riding bicycle to travel the northern coastline of Taiwan'

(2) 寫高雄一年輕城市的微歷史
  xiě-gāo-xióng – nián-qīng-chéng-shì de wéi-lì-shǐ
  write high powerful — year light city market POSS small undergo history
  'To write about the local history of the young city Kaohsiung'

In sentence (1), the reason why the author used *wéi-huándǎo* was mentioned directly in his blog; he suggested that since people usually view *huándǎo* as riding their bicycles around the whole coastline of Taiwan, his one-day trip of riding his bicycle around only the northern coastline can be called *wéi-huándǎo*. As the northern coastline is part of the whole of Taiwan, it is obvious that the prefix *wéi* has selected the CONSTITUTIVE role of *huándǎo* as to form a new interpretation. Sentence (2) provides the same view point: *wéi-lìshǐ* refers to only the local part of the whole history of Kaohsiung city, which indicates the same selective binding between *wéi* and the following noun phrase.

The second group is the FORMAL role, containing most sentences among all four qualia. 微電影[*wéi-diànyǐng*] (*short film*) is a salient instance and currently popular usage of the prefix *wéi*. Some people might take its literal English translation *micro cinema* as the meaning, but in fact *micro cinema* is a term first coined in 1994, indicating the usage of home basements as movie exhibition places (MacDonald 2008). It also has some other characteristics such as low-budget film making, tendency of being shot on video camera or 16mm camera, actors are usually unknown by public and so on. Some properties seem to overlap those of *wéi-diànyǐng,* but the most salient feature of what people use in Mandarin is the shorter length of the movie, which only lasts approximately ten minutes. Based on this understanding, the analysis of its qualia role should be FORMAL rather than AGENTIVE. Other examples include 微及格 [*wéi-jígé*] (*almost pass the test*), 微漫畫 [*wéi-mànhuà*] (*four-page comics*), 微推理 [*wéi-tuīlǐ*] (*a detective story not about murder or serious crimes but daily trivial matters*) and so on.

The last group will be those sentences grouped in the AGENTIVE role, related to the source or origin of an object. Phrase such as 微李安 [*wéi-lǐān*] refers to the famous international director *lǐān,* indicating that someone has the interest of filming and holds a dream of becoming a well-known director. Another example is 微開車 [*wéi-kāichē*] (*wéi-driving*). One might guess it may be related to properties of vehicles or the style of driving cars due to the implication of *kāichē* 'driving a car', but actually and surprisingly it means 'riding a motorcycle'. 微獵殺 [*wéi-lièshā*] (*wéi-hunting*) is a similar instance describing the scene of a cat bites off a mouse's head and tears it apart. The reason why the author uses *wéi* might be our stereotype of *lièshā* 'hunting' — the predator chasing other animals and ferociously killing them. Compared to lions or leopards, cats are relatively tame and their hunting should not be as cruel as that of their larger predatory cousins. These following noun phrases that either refers to the proper name or implies the change of source is included under the AGENTIVE role.

Based on the analysis above, there are three interesting points we can make if we take a closer look. First, by adding *wéi,* one can make the relatively inferior events sound better, hiding the truth under the surface. Phrases like *wéi-kāichē, wéi-jígé,* and 微整形[*wéi-zhěngxíng*] (taking plastic surgery on partial or small parts of body) are the all similar examples which can either place the phrase's implication under AGENTIVE role, or else reduce the degree or narrow the scope (FORMAL role) in order to make the literal meanings sound better or higher-class.

Second, apparently the prefix *wéi* tends to select the FORMAL role of the modified nouns in forming a novel interpretation much more frequently, and, at least in this data set, never selects the TELIC role. One possible explanation is elements in FORMAL are actually what people can have direct access to, such as the appearance, weight or color of objects, causing people to use these kinds of characteristics to form new words. Another possible reason is related to the nature or original meaning of the word. As Pustejovsky (2000) proposed the qualia selection properties, adjectives such as *useful* and *effective* can pick the TELIC qualia of the following noun to modify since they are words which actually specify the condition of objects being used, which also indicates the purpose or function of those objects. However, three highly familiar meanings of *wéi:* (1) Small amount of something; (2) small size, micro-; and (3) low degree, seem to have nothing to do with describing how objects are used, placing a much larger emphasis on their formal appearance while excluding the function or purpose of those concepts, and therefore excluding as well the possibility of selecting TELIC role when generating the neologism.

Third, since the tendency to generate *wéi* in new language based on noun combinations in the FORMAL role, it is possible to predict that if one day we encounter a newly-created word such as 微教授 [*wéi-jiàoshòu*] *(wéi-professor),* we will be easily able to take its qualia structure and try to guess its novel implication. A more interesting question might how long this trend might last—will *wéi* continue to be a productive prefix generating new word combinations, or will this trend of using *wéi* soon die out?

## 5    Conclusion

As shown in this paper, the emergence of the new usage of *wéi* combines various kinds of modified nouns to form novel meanings. Among 75 examples collected from the Internet using the Google search engine and the PTT bulletin board, the study found that neologisms using *wéi* have high tendency to be selected based on the FORMAL qualia role of the following noun, with somewhat lower preferences for selection based on the CONSTITUTIVE and AGENTIVE qualia roles, and apparently full exclusion of the TELIC qualia role. The cause of this phenomenon may be people's general daily access to ready perception of the FORMAL qualia role of objects such as shape, magnitude and color. As for the TELIC role, given the complication of readily identifying the purpose and function of novel objects and concepts, we assume that since there appears to be no direct specifying relationship between *wéi* and other nouns in its current primary usages, it is possible that no such new forming will be generated in the future. In addition to its implications for discussing how the use of *wéi* might grow and change in the future, we also think this study shows great promise for thinking about the qualities of qualia modification in both Mandarin and other languages. We believe this study raises interesting questions about the interplay of language use and cognition in the processing of language, and think it can be of use in understanding the generative and creative qualities of language in many other contexts.

## References

1. Lee, C., Chang, C., Hsu, W., Hsieh, S.: Qualia Modification inNoun-Noun Compounds: A Cross-Language Survey. In: Proceedings of the 22nd Conference on Computational Linguistics and Speech Processing (ROCLING 2010), pp. 379–390. National Chi Nan University, Taiwan (2010)
2. Hsieh, C.: Taiwanese Loanwords in Mandarin Chinese: Language Interaction in Taiwan. Taiwan Papers, Taiwan (2005)
3. Boyd, D.: Why Youth (Heart) Social Network Sites: The Role of Networked Publics in Teenage Social Life. In: Buckingham, D., The John, D., Catherine, T. (eds.) MacArthur Foundation Series on Digital Media and Learning: Youth, Identity and Digital Media, pp. 119–142. The MIT Press, London (2007)
4. Pustejovsky, J.: The Generative Lexicon. The MIT Press, London (1996)
5. Pustejovsky, J.: Events and the Semantics of Opposition. In: Tenny, C., Pustejovsky, J. (eds.) Events as Grammatical Objects. Cambridge University Press (2000)

6. Volk, M.: Using the Web as Corpus for Linguistic Research. In: Pajusalu, R., Hennoste, T. (eds.) Catcher of the meaning. A Festschrift for Professor HaldurÕim, University of Tartu, Tartu (2002)
7. Johnston, M., Busa, F.: Qualia Structure and the Compositional Interpretation of Compounds. In: Proceedings of the ACL SIGLEX Workshop on Breadth and Depth of Semantic Lexicaons, pp. 77–88. Santa Cruz, California (1996)
8. Akhmanova, O.S.: Dictionary of Linguistic Terms. Sovietencyclopedia, Moscow (1966)
9. MacDonald, S.: Canyon Cinema: The Life andTimes of an Independent Film Distributor. Universityof California Press (2008)
10. Wang, S., Huang, C.: Adjectival Modification to Nouns in Mandarin Chinese: Case Studies on "cháng+ noun" and "adjective+ túshūguǎn". In: Proceedings of Pacific Asia Conference on Language, Information and Computation, Tohoku University, Sendai, Japan (2010)
11. Wang, S., Huang, C.: Compound Event Nouns of the 'Modifier-head' Type in Mandarin Chinese. In: Proceedings of the 54th Pacific Asia Conference on Language, Information, and Computation. Nanyang Technological University, Taiwan (2011)
12. Deng, T.: On the General Lexical Properties of English Neologism. Shandong Foreign Language Teaching Journal (2005)

# A Concise Review of the Answers to Fundamental Issues of Lexical Semantics

Shengjian Ni[1] and Donghong Ji[2]

[1] College of Chinese Language and Literature, Wuhan University, Wuhan, China
hijackon@163.com
[2] Computer School, Wuhan University, Wuhan, China
Donghong_ji2000@yahoo.com.cn

**Abstract.** There is relationship of inheritance and development between different schools of lexical semantics, which have their own emphases on dissimilar language phenomena and try to solve distinct problems of lexical semantics. The understanding of this relationship helps make explicit the drawbacks of existent study and future tendency, which is conducive to the development of natural language processing.

**Keywords:** lexical semantics (LS), LS schools, fundamental problems, natural language processing (NLP).

## 1    Introduction –Fundamental Problems of LS

LS flourishes with related subjects such as NLP, etc. LS acts as the base for many applications, such as second language acquisition and learning, dictionary compiling, and computational linguistics[1].

According to the requirements of related subjects, Paradis points out that there are five questions (or issues) that are of central importance to any theory of lexical semantics that makes claims to be a coherent framework within which lexical meanings can be described and explained. These five questions are:

1. What is the nature of meaning in language?
2. What is the relation between words and their meanings?
3. How are meanings of words learned and stored?
4. How are meanings of words communicated and understood by language users?
5. How and why do meanings of words change? [1]

Of these questions, questions (1) and (2) are more basic than the others. Paradis points out that:

> The answers to these five questions make up the fundamental theoretical assumptions and commitments which underlie different theories of lexical semantics, and they form the basis for their various methodological priorities and explanations for word meanings in language. [1]

P. Liu and Q. Su (Eds.): CLSW 2013, LNAI 8229, pp. 306–317, 2013.

In the following section, a concise review is offered about how different schools of LS have tried to answer these questions, which is expected to be helpful in making clear what have been done about these five issues and what should be done in the future, especially for application studies, such as NLP, etc.

## 2 Answers of Different LS Schools to the Five Issues of LS

According to time and relationship of inheritance between different LS Schools, Geeraerts[2] divides LS into five schools: historical-philological semantics, structuralist semantics, generativist semantics, and Neo-structuralist semantics, cognitive semantics. These schools places distinct importance on and offers diverse answers to the five issues, as is to be discussed separately in this section.

### 2.1 Nature of Meaning in Language

In historical-philological semantics, meaning is a psychological type of entity and a kind of thought; and meaning changes result from psychological processes [2]. Structuralist semantics emasculates psychology from historical-philological semantics and thought that the nature of meaning lies in the relationship between language units and the main clue of all of its theories focuses on the description of relations. Generativist semantics renews the mental reality of historical-philological semantics[2], adopting a meaning viewpoint of mentalism. Neo-structuralist semantics, while inheriting main viewpoints and methods of structuralist semantics, considers the psychological adequacy of meaning.

None of the above explanations about the nature of meaning are satisfactory. Cognitive semantics, which inherits and develops the cognitive and psychological orientation of historical-philological semantics, provides the most rich and systematic explanation about the nature of meaning.

Cognitive semantics, a subfield of cognitive linguistics, shares these two slogans:

(1) Meanings are based on the bodily experience ;
(2) Meanings are in the head.

This kind of semantic view explains the nature and source of meaning, implying that meaning is embodied and creative[3], and categories and concepts are formed based on human's experience of the outside and inner worlds, and finally words are created to express these categories or concepts. While experiencing the world to form concepts, the following processes are undergone: perception, presentation, categorization and conceptualization, etc. Conceptualization is the last and key stage of the formation of concepts. Meaning, based on perception, presentation, and categorization, is the result of conceptualization[4][5]. In cognitive linguistics, presentation is expressed with image schemata.

Wang Yin points out that conceptualization involves many cognitive styles and cognitive structures. These cognitive styles include embodiment, categorization, metonymy, metaphor, and construal, activation, relevance, conceptual blending, etc., and cognitive structures includes all kinds of image schemata[3].Cognitive styles and cognitive structures exist side by side and promote each other. Cognitive structures come from cognitive styles and once formed, they act as the base for cognitive styles, which means that meaning is established on world knowledge and there is no clearcut boundary between language knowledge and world knowledge[6].

According to cognitive semantics, word meaning is not the mirror image of the outside world; and the formation and understanding of word meaning involves all the cognitive styles touched upon in the process of conceptualization; and the presentation of word meaning can not do without image schemata; and the generative mechanism trying to explain polysemy can not avoid metonymy, metaphor and construal, concept blending, etc.[7].

Cognitive subjects, with different natural or cultural backgrounds, may own different cognitive styles which may lead to diverse conceptualizations and meanings for the same entity or event. Wang Yin proves with many examples that during the process of categorization and conceptualization, people may understand the same entity or event from different angles, paying attention to different characteristics or parts of it and lexicalize it[3]. And thus the same entity or event might be endowed with different meanings in different languages or cultures.

The understanding of the nature of meaning determines the ways of how to represent the meaning of a word and the meaning generation mechanism based on the representation, which in turn influences the understanding of word meaning(s) in contexts. The question of the nature of meaning is the most basic and it is the starting point of rational explanation and correct understanding of word meaning(s), which is crucial to many applications such as word sense disambiguity (WSD) in NLP because the understanding of the nature of meaning determines the principle, methods, and even the effect of WSD.

Main contents of this section is shown in table 1.

**Table 1.** Studies or views about the nature of meaning

| LS schools | Studies or views. |
|---|---|
| historical-philological semantics | Psychological entity, a kind of thought. |
| Structuralist semantics | Relations between language units. |
| Generativist semantics | Psychological entity (a mentalism view of meaning). |
| Neo-structuralist semantics | Extended relations between language units and psychological entity. |
| Cognitive semantics | Meanings are based on the bodily experience; meanings are in the head. |

## 2.2    Relations between Words and Their Meanings

Three LS schools have comparatively rich studies on this issue, of which structuralist semantics and Neo-structuralist semantics focuses on syntagmatic and paradigmatic relations between words, while cognitive semantics emphasizes senses of the same word (form).

Structuralist semantics has three theoretical clues: lexical field theory, componential analysis, and relational semantics. Structuralist semantics observes that the nature of meaning lies in relations between language units and all its main theoretical clues are description of relations.

Structuralist semantics offers such word relations as synonymy, hyponymy, antonymy, and partonymy (meronymy), homonymy, polysemy, etc. Relational semantics of structuralist semantics emphasizes description of synchronic semantic relations, observing that meaning is expression network with all kinds of semantic relations. It can be said that componential analysis is the method of lexical fields and word relations are the content of lexical fields. A clear understanding of word relations is conducive to discovering the distinctive features of a lexical field, which is the base for determining word semantic features.

Some branches of Neo-structuralist semantics, including WordNet project, Mel'čuk's lexical function theory (1982), and distributional corpus analysis, develop relational semantics.

WordNet offers such word relations such as *troponymy* and *entailment*. Troponymy is dedicated to expressing special way(s) of doing an action. E.g. to *sleepwalk, stride, shuffle, stroll, slouch,* etc. are particular ways of walking and these verbs are troponyms of *walk*. *Entailment* refer in particular to certain relations between verbs, e.g. *to snore* entails *to sleep.*

Word relations mentioned above are restricted to limited metalinguistic paradigmatic relations. In Mel'čuk's Meaning-Text Theory, more relations between words and expressions are discerned and expressed with lexical functions. As a result, paradigmatic relations are expanded greatly and syntagmatic relations are also expressed richly. Lexical functions convey both semantic and grammatical relations. For detail, we can refer to Mel'čuk[8]. Lexical functions are universal, usable in all languages.

Lexical functions provide abundant, multidimensional structures for lexical description. From the perspective of practice, an Explanatory Combinatorial Dictionary (ECD)(the main contents of which are lexical functions) constructs more information sources than WordNet do for a word form and has aroused strong interest in lexicographers and computational linguists. However, because it is very time-consuming to construct an ECD, the quantity of vocabulary of existing ECDs and number of languages which has established an ECD are much less, which restricts the application of ECD.

Syntagmatic relations expressed by lexical functions are not deep or complete enough because of lexical functions' lack of extensive distributional basis, which can be remedied by distributional corpus analysis. Distributional corpus analysis, because of its continuous renovation and dynamicity, has been the absolute dominant method in NLP.

The main developments of distributional methods of LS came from the application of distributional thought in large-scale corpus, which leads to the appearance of distributional corpus analysis. According to Geeraerts, distributional corpus analysis takes a radical usage-based rather than system-based approach: it considers the analysis of actual linguistic behaviour to be the ultimate methodological foundation of linguistics[2].

Distributional corpus analysis disambiguates word senses according to collocation and it digresses from the mainstream of structuralist semantics as collocation is in essence contextual. Combined with statistical methods, distributional corpus analysis overcomes many weaknesses of rule-based methods, such as:1) so far, no suitable system of semantic primitives has been demarcated or established ; 2) there has been no way of differentiating linguistic knowledge from extralinguistic knowledge.

The biggest disadvantage of distributional corpus analysis is that its theoretical backgrounds are not always clear and extralinguistic knowledge is usually not considered by it.

Cognitive semantics remedies these disadvantages of distributional corpus analysis, offering many related methods to explain word sense relations and these methods include the prototype theory, metaphor and metonymy, idealized cognitive models, image schemata, etc. While explaining word sense relations, image schemata are the bases, metaphor and metonymy are the cognitive mechanisms concerned, and prototype effect and polysemy are the phenomena or results to be explained.

Cognitive semantics observes that cognitive models are in the form of image schemata but not propositions, and operations of metaphor and metonymy are based on image schemata[9][10]. In virtue of the operations of metonymy and metaphor based on image schemata , more categories and concepts, especially abstract ones, are formed, which in turn result in more image schemata, and during this process human being develops their abstract thinking and inferring ability, complex concepts are formed from simple ones, and all kinds of conceptual structures are also produced. Thus we have prototypical models of categorical structures and the phenomenon of polysemy.

Thus, image schemata, metaphor and metonymy, prototype effect, polysemy are in fact unified and they form a series with immanent logical relations :

Image schemata > metonymy and metaphor > prototype effect≥polysemy

' > ' stands for 'appear or exist prior to' which means that the appearance or existence of the former is a prerequisite for the latter to appear and the former can be used to explain the latter. E.g. image schemata, metonymy and metaphor, prototype effect can be used to explain polysemy, while image schemata can be used to explain the mechanism of metonymy and metaphor. No wonder, Lakoff points out that *idealized cognitive models* (equivalent to *image schemata* in this paper) are the source of categorical structures and prototype effect [11].

Production of prototype effect involves both metonymy and metaphor, with metonymy being the more fundamental mechanism, as metaphor is often based on metonymy. There are two kinds of prototype effect:

(1) The structure represented by a sense with certain denotation embodies prototype effect. E.g. when the word *fruit* is understood as 'something which grows on a tree or bush and which contains seeds or a stone covered by a substance that you can eat', its denotation unanimously includes *apple, cherry, pear*,etc. However, such things as *cucumber, tomato, bitter gourd* may or may not be included as *fruit* according to such factors as culture, regions and eating habits. In this situation, different degrees of prototypicality of these members of *fruit* embody prototype effect.

(2) Structure formed by the senses of the same word (form) can also embodies prototype effect. E.g. the original sense of the word *fruit* is 'something which grows on a tree or

bush and which contains seeds or a stone covered by a substance that you can eat' and this sense is expanded to mean 'result', 'achievement', 'production' , etc., which have only different degrees of meaning overlap with the original meaning of *fruit*.

In short, good solution of the question of the relations between words and their senses is one of the keys to reasonable explanation of language phenomena, understanding language, and constructing language resources. Frequently-used resources in NLP such as linguistic ontologies, WordNet, FrameNet, etc. all have rich studies about relations between words and their meanings, however, there is still deficiency which is remedied by lexical functions of Meaning-Text Theory to a great degree. Applied fully, lexical functions can not only express more relations between words and their meanings but also substitute a lot of work previously done by syntactic transformation to save much time and labor, which is meaningful for many NLP applications as textual entailment recognition.

Main studies or views of different LS schools about relations between words and their meanings are summarized and shown in table 2 below.

**Table 2.** Relations between words and their meanings

| LS schools | Studies or views |
|---|---|
| historical-philol-ogical semantics | Relations between word meanings: semasiological change--chain change of word meaning. |
| Structuralist semantics | Lexical field theory, componential analysis and relational semantics (limited number of meta-linguistic paradigmatic relations. |
| Generativist semantics | Katz semantics: inheritance of semantic feature. |
| Neo-structuralist semantics | Related contents of structuralist semantics are expanded, e.g. lexical functions:paradigmatic relations are expanded greatly and syntagmatic relations are also conveyed sufficiently. |
| Cognitive semantics | Explanatory adequacy: relations between words and their senses are produced through all kinds of cognitive styles--image schemata are the basis, metonymy and metaphor are mechanism, and prototype effect and polysemy the results. |

## 2.3    Acquisition and Storage of Word Meanings

Though historical-philological semantics adopts methods of cognition, psychology and explanation while studying meanings, its emphasis is placed on explaining the psychological factors involved in understanding meanings in contexts. Though it points out that word meanings are stored in mental structures, it offers no concrete studies.

Structuralist semantics treats language as an isolated, automatic system and basically does not discuss the acquisition or storage of word meanings. However, from the study of structuralist semantics it can be inferred that relations between words (and even language units) can be seen as means of storing word meanings.

Adopting the related viewpoints of historical-philological semantics, generativist semantics offers concrete mental structures for storing the meanings of words.

Neo-structuralist semantics, inheriting many viewpoints and some methods of structuralist semantics, studies meaning in an extensive cognitive context and offers many ways for storing word meanings. E.g. Jackendoff's Conceptual Semantics, Bierwisch's Two-Level Semantics, and Pustejovsky's Generative Lexicon all touch upon word meaning storage because of their formalized representations of word meanings.

Conceptual Semantics considers the combination of linguistic and extra-linguistic knowledge and offers methods to distinguish the two kinds of knowledge. Conceptual Semantics observes that: (1) there is no need to express all the information about the usage of language in word presentation and part of the task (e.g. visual memory, perceptual knowledge, etc.) can be expressed by other cognitive models; (2) formalized representation of word meanings do not need to include all the information related to explaining the conceptual ability of language users; (3) information of word meanings should be put in the level of 'conceptual structure' in which linguistic and extra-linguistic knowledge (e.g. perceptual knowledge and motor schemata, etc.) can interact with each other and word meaning no longer owns a privileged position[12].

Conceptual structure constructs an interface between linguistic and extra-linguistic knowledge, and the interface's function can be embodied by an entry as follows:

$$
\begin{bmatrix}
drink \\
\\
V \\
- <NP_i> \\
[\text{event CAUSE ([thing]}_i, [\text{eventGO([thing LIQUID]}_j, [\text{path} \\
\text{TO ([place IN ([thing MOUTH OF ([thing]}_i)])])])])]
\end{bmatrix}
$$

**Fig. 1.** The conceptual structure of the word *drink*[13]

Conceptual Semantics' differentiation between linguistic and extra-linguistic knowledge is static, ignoring the dynamic interaction between the two kinds of knowledge in concrete contexts. Two-Level Semantics tries to deal with this kind of interaction. Like Conceptual Semantics, Two-Level Semantics also adopts a modular view of cognition, observing that:

> Cognitive behaviour is determined by the interaction of systems and subsystems that operate as largely autonomous modules of the mind. In particular, polysemy in natural language may be adequately described by distinguishing between two levels of knowledge representation: semantic form and conceptual structure[2].

According to Geeraerts, 'Semantic form' and 'Conceptual structure' express linguistic and extra-linguistic knowledge respectively[2]. A semantic form expresses only one sense of a word (form), however, the interaction between a semantic form and a conceptual structure in certain contexts can produce a series of explanations, which means that Two-Level Semantics emphasizes dynamic relations between words and meaning changes. E.g., $\lambda x[\text{PURPOSE}[x \, w]]$ is a abstract logical expression and words with the semantic feature PURPOSE can substitute x to get a comparatively concrete expression. If the word *university* is understood as 'a institution providing advanced study and teaching', it has the semantic feature PURPOSE and can substitute x to get this expression:

λx [PURPOSE[x w] & advanced study and teaching [w]]

This can be understood as: there is an x (*university*) which owns a semantic feature PURPOSE that exists in a (mental) space (marked as 'w') independent of language as the schema 'advanced study and teaching'-a kind of conceptual structure. The two levels of knowledge is related to each other in the space w. If we want to express another semantic feature 'the place or buildings where a university lies' of the word *university*, this expression can be used: λx [building [x] & purpose [x w]].

According to Geeraerts, the most elaborate formalized componential model in contemporary semantics is the Generative Lexicon defined by Pustejovsky (1995a)[2], which uses word sense presentation structure as in F.g. 2 to store word meanings and grammatical information.

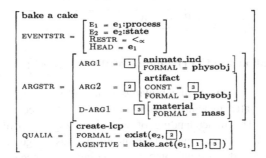

**Fig. 2.** Semantic representation of verb phrase '*bake a cake*' [14]

All image schemata, including idealized cognitive models, frames and scripts, from cognitive semantics are word meaning storage means. Frames are the most fundamental and can be integrated with other image schemata in application studies. LS shools prior to cognitive semantics lack studies in the origin of meanings, which is remedied by cognitive semantics based on Embodied Philosophy. It is pointed out that:

> Embodied Philosophy observes that the combination of body experience and mental ability produces concepts and meanings; language comes from practice and is closely related to conceptual structures and cognitive styles; and linguistic forms and concepts are interdependent and there is large quantity of instances of iconicity[3].

Wang Yin explains in detail the origin of words and their meanings from two aspects:

(1) Lexical construction (including origin of lexicon, embodied categorization, conceptualization, lexicalization, and embodied metaphor, embodied metal lexicon, spatialized compound words and affixes);

(2) the embodiment of lexical categories (including the division of parts of speech, conversion of parts of speech, and gender, number and case of nouns, time, aspect and voice of verbs)[3].

Embodied Philosophy describes the formation of language and meaning from the level of all human languages. To an individual human being, embodiment and mentality are both essential factors in acquiring a language. The study of Littlemore[15] offers good evidence for the importance of embodiment in language and meaning formation. Main contents of this section is summarized in table 3.

**Table 3.** Studies or views about acquisition and storage of word meaning

| LS schools | Studies or views. |
|---|---|
| historical-philological semantics | Meanings are the results of mental processes (acquisition) and represented with mental structures (storage). |
| Structuralist semantics | Word meanings are stored in language system, especially in word relations. |
| Generativist semantics | Recovers and develops historical-philological semantics, offering concrete mental structures to represent word meanings. |
| Neo-structuralist semantics | Formalized conceptual structures from Jackendoff's Conceptual Semantics, Bierwisch's Two-Level Semantics, and Pustejovsky's Generative Lexicon (meaning storage). |
| Cognitive semantics | Embodied Philosophy. |

## 2.4    Communication and Understanding of Word Meanings

This issue is closely related to the previous issue. Word meaning storage means represent abstract, static meanings, while ostensive utterances express concrete, dynamic meanings. The understanding of word meanings involves many factors: ostensive utterances, word meaning storage means such as image schemata triggered by these utterances, and the current contexts (including time, space, relations between communicators,etc.), all kinds of cognitive ability and styles, and so on.

**Table 4.** Studies or views about communication and understanding of word meanings

| LS schools | Studies or views |
|---|---|
| historical-philological semantics | Explaining meaning changes in contexts: differentiation between'usual meaning'and 'occasional meaning'--the basis of meaning changes is to regulate 'usual meaning'into'occasional meaning'. |
| Structuralist semantics | Semanteme (from lexical field theory and componential analysis), word relations and distribution. |
| Generativist semantics | Projection rules based on a tree diagram way of word meaning representation. |
| Neo-structuralist semantics | Conceptual semantics : conceptual structure (static). Two-Level Semantics : interaction between two levels of knowledge representation--*semantic form* and *conceptual structure* of autonomous modules of the mind. The Generative Lexicon : semantic generation mechanisms based word representation. |
| Cognitive semantics | Image schemata and semantic generation mechanisms based on them (including metonymy, metaphor, and conceptual blending theory, etc.) |

Studies about communication and understanding of word meanings comes mainly from two LS schools--Neo-structuralist semantics and cognitive semantics. The Generative Lexicon of Neo-structuralist semantics not only offers elaborate word meaning representation mechanisms but also semantic generation mechanisms based on the presentation mechanisms.

Two of the core tasks of cognitive semantics are word meaning representation mechanisms and corresponding semantic generation mechanisms. Idealized cognitive models, frames and scripts are all word meaning representation mechanisms; and metonymy, and metaphor are the semantic generation mechanisms based on these image schemata. The answers of different LS to the issues discussed in this section is shown in table 4 in a nutshell.

## 2.5    Ways and Reasons for Word Meaning Changes

Historical-philological semantics thinks that meaning changes are the results of mental processes; and the change mechanisms which can be established through studying historical classification of words, correspond to human's mode of thinking; and metonymy and metaphor are considered not only as linguistic notions but also as human's cognitive ability[2].

Historical-philological semantics's fundamental method is to explain meaning changes in contexts and it develops a kind of pragmatic, usage-based meaning change theory based on the differentiation between 'usual meaning' and 'occasional meaning':

> The basis of meaning changes is to regulate 'usual meaning' into 'occasional meaning'; meaning changes are important objects of study, the focal point of which is *semasiological change* (the phenomenon of adding new senses to an existing word) but not onomasiological change (the phenomenon of expressing a new sense with a coined word) .

*Semasiological change* is first divided into connotational change and denotational changes. Denotational change is further divided into analogical change and non-analogical change. Analogical change is the process of copying the polysemy of another word, which may takes place in one language or between different languages. Non-analogical change involves four mechanisms: specialization ('narrowing' of meaning), generalization ('expansion', 'extension', or 'broadening' of meaning), metonymy, and metaphor. Denotational change alters only attributes (usually concomitant meanings, such as social meanings or emotional meanings) of a word[2]. Structuralist semantics are not interested in meaning changes, especially diachronic meaning changes. Generativist semantics is interested in only synchronic meaning changes. Neither generativist semantics nor Neo-structuralist semantics is interested in diachronic meaning changes.

Cognitive semantics pay attentions both to diachronic and synchronic meaning changes and its methods for explaining prototype effect and polysemy can in fact be used to explain meaning changes. There is large quantity of this kind of studies, such as Wang Yin[3]. The main contents of this section is shown in table 5.

**Table 5.** Studies or views about the ways and reasons for word meaning changes

| LS schools | Studies or views |
| --- | --- |
| historical-philological semantics | semasiological changes; meaning changes are also the results of mental process and change mechanisms correspond to human's mode of thinking. |
| Generativist semantics | Tries to use tree diagrams to analyze words and *projection rules* are used to finish analysis of synchronic meaning changes. |
| Neo-structuralist semantics | Carries out exploration into synchronic meaning changes in virtue of word representations, e.g., the Generative Lexicon offers systematic semantic generation mechanisms based on word sense representations. |
| Cognitive semantics | Is interested in both diachronic and synchronic meaning changes and offers the most elaborate ways for explaining (polysemy) and meaning changes. |

# 3    Conclusion

When different LS schools try to answer those fundamental questions of LS, they have different emphases and advantages; and there are both conflicts and complementarity between their viewpoints and methods. All studies of these fundamental questions boil down to this issue: how to represent/store word meanings with suitable forms and how to disambiguate word senses and explain polysemy based on these representations. This is one of the core problems both for daily linguistic understanding and linguistic applications (e.g. NLP). To get more satisfactory solution to this issue,  the following thing should be helpful: using cognitive semantics as the foundation, different schools of LS should learn from each other and at the same time refer to the research methods and results of related subjects such as NLP, cognitive science, and psychological linguistic, artificial intelligence, etc., which will certainly bring about breakthrough for explaining, understanding and generating word meanings and which has special significance for breaking through bottlenecks in NLP.

# References

[1] Paradis, C.: Lexical Semantics. In: Chapelle, C. (ed.) The Encyclopedia of Applied Linguistics, Wiley-Blackwell, Oxford, UK (to appear, 2013)
[2] Geeraerts, D.: Theories of Lexical Semantics, pp. 10–30. Oxford University Press, New York (2010)
[3] Yin, W.: Explorations of Cognitive Linguistics. Chongqing Publishing House, Chongqing (2005)
[4] Ungerer, F., Schmid, H.J.: An Introduction to Cognitive Linguistics. p. iv. Foreign Language Teaching and Research Press, Beijing (2001):
[5] Langacker, R.W.: Ten Lectures on Cognitive Grammar. In: Yuan, G., Fuyin, L. (eds.) p. v. Foreign Language Teaching and Research Press (2007)
[6] Langacker, R.W.: Cognitive Grammar: A Basic Introduction. Oxford University Press, New York (2008)

[7] Fauconnier, G., Turner, M.: The way we think: Conceptual blending and the mind's hidden complexities. Basic Books (AZ) (2008)

[8] Mel'čuk, I.: Lexical Functions: A Tool for the Description of Lexical Relations in a Lexicon. In: Wanner, L. (ed.) Lexical Functions in Lexicography and Natural Language Processing. J. Benjamins, Amsterdam (1996)

[9] Lakoff, G., Johnsen: Metaphors we live by, p. 68. The University of Chicago Press, London (2003)

[10] Dingfang, S.: The Basic Principle, Study Objectives and Methods of Cognitive Semantics. Shandong Foreign Language Teaching Journal 5, 3–11 (2005)

[11] Lakoff, G.W.: Fire, and Dangerous Things: What Categories Reveal about the Mind. The University of Chicago Press, Chicago (1987)

[12] Jackendoff, R.: Conceptual Semantics and Cognitive Linguistics. Cognitive Linguistics 7, 93–129 (1996)

[13] Jackendoff, R.: Semantic Structures Cambridge, p. 93. MIT Press, MA (1990)

[14] Pustejovsky, J.: The Generative Lexicon, pp. 105–140. Massachusetts Institute of Technology, Massachusetts (1996)

[15] Littlemore, J.: Applying Cognitive Linguistics to Second Language Learning and Teaching. Palgrave Macmillan, London (2009)

# A Semantic Study of the Adverb *Jiu* in Mandarin Chinese

Lei Zhang and Peppina Po-lun Lee

Department of Chinese, Translation and Linguistics, City University of Hong Kong
leizhang@my.cityu.edu.hk,
ctpllee@cityu.edu.hk

**Abstract.** This paper investigates the semantics of the adverb *jiu* in Mandarin Chinese. In the spirit of Paris [6], we claim that the nuclear meaning of *jiu* is to build up a relation between two units; more precisely, between the asserted value and its alternatives, between the actual value and the reference value, between the asserted value and the relevant open sentence, and/or between two successive events. Based on this, we argue that according to its semantics the adverb *jiu* can be classified into three: focus adverb *jiu*, sufficiency operator *jiu* and *jiu* with the 'close to' meaning. Focus adverb *jiu* can be further divided into exclusive adverb *jiu*, scalar adverb *jiu* and *jiu* indicating emphatic assertion according to its semantic properties. When *jiu* takes the 'close to' meaning, it either acts as a temporal adverb or implies two events happened/will happen in quick succession.

**Keywords:** focus adverb, exclusive adverb, scalar adverb, sufficiency operator, emphatic assertion.

## 1    Introduction

In Mandarin Chinese the adverb *jiu* has diverse usages. Various studies have been conducted to define the semantics of *jiu*, which still remains to be controversial, with many issues yet to be resolved. Based on previous analyses, in this paper, we will propose an alternative analysis. Along the line of Paris [6], we put forward that the nuclear meaning of *jiu* is to establish a relation between two units, which to be more specific, a relation between the asserted value and its alternatives, between the asserted value and the reference value, between the asserted value and the relevant open sentence, and/or between two events that occur one after another. Based on this, in accordance with its semantic functions *jiu* is classified into three: focus particle *jiu*, sufficiency operator *jiu* and the adverb *jiu* which expresses the 'close to' meaning.

The rest of this paper is organized as follows: Section 2 makes a brief introduction on the previous analyses of the semantics of the adverb *jiu*. In Sections 3 through 5 we provide an alternative account of the semantics of the adverb *jiu*, in which Section 3 deals with the focus adverb *jiu*, Section 4 discusses sufficiency operator *jiu,* and Section 5 focuses on the case that *jiu* takes the 'close to' meaning. Section 6 concludes this paper.

P. Liu and Q. Su (Eds.): CLSW 2013, LNAI 8229, pp. 318–327, 2013.
© Springer-Verlag Berlin Heidelberg 2013

## 2    Literature Review

The semantics of the adverb *jiu* is an issue of great debate. Previous studies like [1-2] among others have provided unified accounts for various usages of *jiu*. Lu [8] suggests that the basic meaning of *jiu* is to restrict scope, and *jiu* usually takes the mood of stressing 'small quantity'. Biq [1-2] points out that as a focusing adverb *jiu* marks a simple focus(ing). Paris [6] puts forward that the discourse function of *jiu* allows it to establish a relation between two units that need not be explicit linguistic expressions. Lai [4-5] argues that *jiu* is a scalar particle, which presupposes a change of state of the truth value of a proposition and the point at which this change occurs is located 'farther down' than what is expected on the relevant scale. Similar to Lai's account, Chen [7] considers that *jiu* indicates 'the fact is deviated from expected', which to be more specific, implies 'earlier or less than expected'.

However, no consensus has been reached on the core meaning of *jiu*. Moreover, the unified accounts provided by previous analyses, i.e. treating *jiu* as a simple focus marker, a scalar particle or an adverb of denying expectation, are inadequate to account for all the phenomena of *jiu*.

## 3    Focus Adverb *Jiu*

In this chapter, we will focus our discussion on the cases where *jiu* serves as a focus adverb, which builds up both a relation between the asserted value and its alternatives, and a relation between the asserted value and the relevant open sentence.

Generally speaking, in terms of its semantic properties, focus adverb *jiu* can be further divided into three: scalar adverb *jiu*, *jiu* indicating emphatic assertion and exclusive adverb *jiu*. In what follows, we will discuss them one by one.

### 3.1    Scalar Adverb *Jiu*

As a scalar adverb, *jiu* induces a scale and evaluates the asserted value denoted by its interacting focus phrase as the relative minimal/lowest value on the relevant scale. In such a case, *jiu* establishes the following relations between two units: on the one hand, the asserted value makes the relevant open sentence true; on the other hand, the asserted value together with the alternatives introduced is ordered on a scale and in contrast to the alternatives it is evaluated as the relative lowest value. See (1).

(1) a. 张三　　下星期一　就　去 北京。
Zhangsan <u>xia xingqiyi</u> *jiu* qu Beijing.
Zhangsan next Monday JIU go Beijing
'Zhangsan will go to Beijing as early as next Monday.'

b. 三　个　人　就 能　搬动　那 张　桌子。
<u>San ge ren</u> *jiu* neng bandong na zhang zhuozi.
three CL person JIU can move that CL table
'As few as three people can move that table.'

It is argued that in the case that *jiu* acts as a scalar particle, the semantic contribution of *jiu* to the sentence in which it occurs is considered to be as follows: a sentence with *jiu* presupposes the corresponding sentence without *jiu*; and a sentence with *jiu* entails either (a) none of the alternatives can satisfy the relevant open sentence, or (b) the alternatives introduced can fulfill the open sentence in question. To be more specific, when the associated element of *jiu* can be evaluated as the 'threshold value', a sentence with *jiu* entails that the alternatives can satisfy the open sentence; otherwise, it entails no alternatives can make the open sentence true. In other words, *jiu* has quantificational force. See also (1).

Sentence (1a) presupposes 'Zhangsan will go to Beijing next Monday'. For (1a), the alternatives introduced by the asserted value *xia xingqiyi* 'next Monday' are ordered according to time. *Jiu* evaluates the asserted value as 'early' and excludes the possibility that the alternatives located in the higher position such as 'next Tuesday', 'next Wednesday', 'two weeks later' can satisfy the open sentence 'Zhangsan will go to Beijing in t'. Thus (1a) entails 'Zhangsan will not go to Beijing at the alternative time values'. (1b) presupposes 'three people can move that table'. In this sentence the asserted value *san ge ren* 'three people' is evaluated as the threshold value and (1b) entails that the alternatives in the higher position like 'four people' can make 'x can move that table' true.

In what follows, we will discuss which usages of *jiu* can be subsumed under the scalar adverb *jiu*. Here the classification of *jiu*'s usages made by Lü et al [9] is used for reference.

First, *jiu* associates with a temporal or durational expression and indicates that the event or change of state considered will happen 'earlier' or has happened 'a long time ago' in contrast to the expected or stipulated value. Consider (3).

(3) 晚饭　　一会儿　　就　好。
  Wanfan　yihui'er　*jiu* hao.
  supper a-while JIU ready
  'Supper will be ready as early as in a little while.'

Second, the associated element of *jiu* introduces a set of alternatives which are ordered on a quantity-related scale, *jiu* evaluates the quantity denoted by the asserted value as 'small'. This is illustrated in (4).

(4)五百　　　块　就　够　了。
  Wubai　　kuai *jiu* gou　le.
  five-hundred CL JIU enough SFP
  '(As few as) five hundred dollars is enough.'

Third, the alternatives introduced can be ranked in some other ways. See below.

(5) 中学生　　　　　就 能 答对 这 个 问题。(Scale of education degree)
  Zhongxuesheng　　*jiu* neng dadui zhe ge　wenti.
  middle-school-student *JIU* can answer-right this CL question
  'Even middle school student can give the right answer to this question.'

(6) [中型]_F　　　货车 就 够 用 了。(Scale of size)
  [Zhongxing] _F huoche *jiu* gou　yong　le.
  medium　　　truck　JIU enough use SFP
  'As small as a [medium] _F truck is enough.'

### 3.2  *Jiu* Indicating Emphatic Assertion

In this case *jiu* is to emphatically assert that its interacting element has the property denoted by the relevant part of the sentence or determines the actuation of the relevant event, as shown in (7) and (8). Moreover, usually *jiu* is not related to a scale. In such a case, *jiu* establishes the following relations: (a) the asserted value satisfies the relevant open sentence; and (b) the asserted value introduces a set of alternatives. Compared with the alternatives, the asserted value is the most salient one from a certain aspect, i.e. the asserted value is uppermost in the addresser's mind.

(7) a.`[张三]　就 会　说 英语。
　　　`[Zhangsan] *jiu* hui shuo Yingyu.
　　　Zhangsan　JIU can speak English
　　　'Zhangsan can speak English.'

　b. 你 要 的 书，`[我　手头] 就 有。
　　Ni　yao de shu, `[wo shoutou] *jiu* you.
　　you want DE book　I　hand　JIU have
　　'The book you want, I have it at hand.'

(8) a. 你 在 `[图书馆]　就 能 打印。
　　Ni zai `[tushuguan] *jiu* neng dayin.
　　you in　library　JIU can　print
　　'You can print in the library.'

　b. 我　　`[明天] 就 有 时间。
　　Wo `[mingtian] *jiu* you shijian.
　　I　tomorrow JIU have time
　　'I have time tomorrow.'

In (7a) *Zhangsan* is the emphatic part of the sentence, and *jiu* emphasizes that the individual *Zhangsan* has the property of 'being able to speak English'. Unlike sentences with the exclusive adverb *jiu*, the possibility of the alternatives introduced being able to speak English would not be excluded in such a case. In (7b) the subject *wo shoutou* 'at hand of mine' is the emphatic part which is associated with *jiu*; and *jiu* emphasizes that *wo shoutou* would make the proposition 'x has this book' true. For (8a), *tushuguan* 'library' as a member of the set of possible places is highlighted, which makes 'you can print in x' true. For (8b), emphasis is on the temporal adverb *mingtian* 'tomorrow' and *jiu* emphasizes that *mingtian* fulfills 'I have time at t'.

In this case, the meaning conveyed by *jiu* needs to be distinguished from both exclusive adverbs which excludes the possibility that the alternatives introduced satisfies the relevant open sentence and additive adverbs which indicate there are some other alternatives fulfill the relevant open sentence. *Jiu* associates with the alternatives and implies that there exists some alternative(s) but not all alternatives that can make the relevant open sentence true. Put in another way, one may say that *jiu* holds existential but negated universal quantificational force under such a case. As for which alternatives can fulfill the relevant open sentence and which cannot, *jiu* imposes no restriction on it. Consider below.

(9) 都　谁　会　说　英语？

    *Dou* shui hui shuo Yingyu?

    DOU who can speak English

    'Who can speak English?'

(10) a. 张三　　和 李四会 说　英语。

       Zhangsan he Lisi hui shuo Yingyu.

       Zhangsan and Lisi can speak English

       'Zhangsan and Lisi can speak English.'

   b. 只有　　张三　　会　说 英语。

       Zhiyou　 Zhangsan hui　shuo Yingyu.

       ZHIYOU Zhangsan can speak English

       'Only Zhangsan can speak English.'

   c. 我们　都　会 说 英语。

       Women *dou* hui shuo Yingyu.

       we　DOU can speak English

       'We all can speak English.'

(11) `[张三　　和李四] 就 会 说 英语。

    `[Zhangsan he Lisi] *jiu* hui shuo Yingyu.

    Zhangsan and Lisi JIU can speak English

    'Zhangsan and Lisi can speak English.'

For easy demonstration, suppose there are six people in the domain of discourse. The three sentences in (10) can be used to answer the question in (9). (10a) is the list reading, namely all the qualified people are listed. In (10b) the exclusive adverb *zhiyou* quantifies over *Zhangsan*, in (10c) the universal quantifier *dou* quantifies over *women* 'we', and thus the exhaustive readings are gotten in these two sentences. However, neither (7a) nor (11) can be used to reply to (9), which shows that quantificational force does exist in *jiu* under such a case.

### 3.3 Exclusive Adverb *Jiu*

In the case of being an exclusive adverb, the semantic relations built up by *jiu* are as follows: (a) the asserted value makes the open sentence in question true; and (b) the asserted value introduces a set of alternatives which cannot satisfy the relevant open sentence. Here *jiu* can pass the two tests of exclusive particles.[1] *Jiu* quantifies over the alternative set and excludes these alternatives as possible values for the relevant open sentence. Hence it passes the quantification test. A sentence with *jiu* entails the

---

[1] König [3] assumes a focus particle to have the following three properties: (a) a sentence with a focus particle entails the relevant sentence without this particle; (b) a focus particle quantifies over the alternative set; and (c) a focus particle may include or exclude the alternatives as the possible values for the relevant open sentence. Furthermore, based on property (c), focus particles may be divided into two subgroups: exclusive adverbs and inclusive adverbs. Moreover, both of them can be tested by the two tests: quantification test and entailment test. Note that, roughly speaking, adverbs belong to particles.

corresponding sentence without *jiu* and thus *jiu* passes the entailment test. Consider (12) and (13).[2]

(12) `[就] 张三　会　说　法语。
　　 `[*Jiu*] Zhangsan hui shuo Fayu.
　　 JIU Zhangsan can speak French
　　 'Only Zhangsan can speak French.'

(13) 我　`[就]　知道 你 会 来。
　　 Wo `[*jiu*] zhidao ni hui lai.
　　 I　JIU　know you will come
　　 'I did know that you would come.'

In (12) the asserted value *Zhangsan* introduces a set of individuals, and *jiu* excludes people in the set other than *Zhangsan* as possible values for the open sentence 'x can speak French'. In (13) the proposition *wo zhidao ni hui lai* 'I knew you would come' introduces an alternative proposition *wo bu zhidao ni hui lai* 'I did not know you would come', which is excluded, as it fails to satisfy the requirement of the discourse.

Sentences (12) and (13) entail the corresponding sentences (14) and (15) respectively.

(14) 张三　会　说　法语。
　　 Zhangsan hui　shuo　Fayu
　　 Zhangsan can speak French
　　 'Zhangsan can speak French.'

(15) 我　知道　你 会 来。
　　 Wo zhidao ni　hui　lai.
　　 I　know you will come
　　 'I knew that you would come.'

It is therefore observed that the exclusive adverb *jiu* contributes to the meaning of the sentence in two ways: (a) A sentence with *jiu* presupposes the corresponding sentence without *jiu*; and (b) a sentence with *jiu* entails that none of the alternatives can fulfill the relevant open sentence. See (16).

(16) `[就] 他 读　过　这 本　书。
　　 `[*Jiu*] <u>ta</u> du　guo zhe ben shu.
　　 JIU he read ASP this CL book
　　 'Only he has read this book.'

Sentence (16) presupposes that he has read this book and entails that no other alternatives introduced by *ta* 'him' would make the proposition 'x has read this book' true.

To conclude, when *jiu* serves as an exclusive adverb, two usages are involved.

One is the emphatic usage, in which *jiu* interacts with either the predicate to its right or the whole sentence exclusive of *jiu* itself.[3] See also (13), in which *jiu* is used to confirm the event, which is denoted by the relevant sentence and has been introduced in the previous discourse.

---

[2] In this case *jiu* is usually phonologically stressed, although it is not the focus.

[3] Note the case that the associated element occurs to the left of *jiu* is excluded because in such a case *jiu* is used to express emphatic assertion, which does not have the property of exclusiveness.

The other is the limiting use of *jiu*. In this case *jiu* usually indicates 'no other(s)' or implies the asserted value is located lower than the excluded alternatives on the relevant scale. Its semantics is equivalent to the adverb *zhi* 'only'. In general, the limiting *jiu* requires its associated element to occur in its c-command domain.

(17) 张三     `[就] 会 [听] F 英语。
    Zhangsan `[*jiu*] hui [ting] F Yingyu
    Zhangsan   JIU can listen-to English
    'Zhangsan only can [listen to] F English.'

(18) 张三     `[就] 买 了 [三] F 本 书。
    Zhangsan `[*jiu*] mai le [san] F ben shu.
    Zhangsan   JIU buy ASP three   CL book
    'Zhangsan only bought [three] F books.'

It is argued that the exclusive adverb *jiu* has either a scalar use or a non-scalar use, which is determined by two factors, i.e. the usages of *jiu* and the context.

In the emphatic case, *jiu* indicates that in contrast to the alternatives, only the associated element of *jiu* can satisfy the discourse. The alternatives introduced are generally the negation of the asserted value. It is difficult to say that the asserted value and its alternatives are ordered on a scale. As a result, in this case *jiu* has the tendency to take a non-scalar use.

In the limiting case, whether *jiu* has a scalar use or not is highly determined by the context. Consider (12) and (18) again. For (12), when there is a relevant expectation or stipulation on the number of individuals who can speak French, *jiu* has a scalar use, which indicates that the asserted value does not reach the expectation or stipulation; and when there does not exist any relevant expectation/stipulation, *jiu* has a non-scalar use, which signals 'Zhangsan but no one else can speak French'. In (18) *jiu* tends to have a scalar use due to the following reason: the focus phrase *san ben shu* 'three books' will introduce a set of alternatives which only differ in the position of focus. Here the excluded alternatives are ordered according to the quantity of books.

## 4     Sufficiency Operator *Jiu*

In the case that *jiu* functions as a sufficiency operator, it associates with an element to its left, i.e. the subordinate clause, and indicates that the antecedent is sufficient to make the consequent true. The core meaning of the adverb *jiu* manifests as follows: (a) the antecedent, namely the asserted value, makes the consequent true; and (b) the asserted value introduces an alternative set. Similar to the case of emphatic assertion, in this case the relation between the asserted value and its alternatives is loose. It is difficult to judge which alternative(s) is/are qualified and which are not, because *jiu* focuses on the sufficient relation between the antecedent and the consequent. Here *jiu* is usually treated as a marker of sufficient condition by previous studies like [1-2], [4-6] and so forth. This is demonstrated in (19).

(19) a. 如果　你去，我　就　不　去　了。
　　　　Ruguo ni qu,　wo *jiu* bu　qu　le.
　　　　if　　you go　I JIU NEG go SFP
　　　　'If you go, I will not go.'

　　b. 你　请　我，我　就　去。
　　　　Ni qing　wo, wo *jiu*　qu.
　　　　you invite　I　I　JIU go
　　　　'If you invite me, I will go.'

In (19a) the antecedent clause *ta qu* 'he goes' can make the consequent clause *wo bu qu le* 'I will not go' true. In (19b) the antecedent clause *ta qing wo* 'he invites me' can satisfy the consequent clause *wo qu* 'I will go'.

In fact, the types of subordinate clauses that can interact with *jiu* are not restricted to conditional clauses, and can be purposive clauses, reason clauses and the like, as shown in (20)[4].

(20) a. 因为　　临时　　有　事，　就　在　长沙　　逗留了　两　天。
　　　　Yinwei　linshi　you shi,　*jiu*　zai Changsha douliu le　liang tian.
　　　　because temporary have things JIU　in Changsha　stay ASP two CL
　　　　'Because of the temporary emergency, (we) stayed in Changsha for two days.'

　　b. 为了　赶　时间，　　就　少　休息　一会儿。
　　　　Weile gan shijian,　　*jiu* shao　xiuxi yihui'er.
　　　　for catch-up-with time JIU few　rest　a-while
　　　　'In order to save time (let's) take less rest.'

# 5　*Jiu* with the 'Close to' Meaning

In the case that *jiu* holds the 'close to/near' meaning, two cases are involved: one is that, *jiu* indicates 'immediate future', to be more specific, *jiu* implies that the actual time value is close to and higher than the reference time value on the relevant temporal scale, which can be treated as a temporal adverb, as seen in (21); and the other is that, generally *jiu* signals that two events happened/will happen in quick succession, more precisely, *jiu* implies that two events are close in time and this relation can be demonstrated on an indirect temporal scale. For easy illustration it is called successive *jiu*, as shown in (22).

(21) 我　就　走。
　　　Wo *jiu* zou.
　　　I　JIU　go
　　　'I will go immediately.'

---

[4] The two examples in (13) are cited from [9].

(22) a. 我 说　完 就 走。
　　　Wo shuo wan *jiu* zou.
　　　I　say finish JIU go
　　　'I will go immediately after I have said it.'
　　b. 我　说　完　就　走　了。
　　　Wo shuo wan *jiu* zou le.
　　　I　say finish JIU go ASP
　　　'I went immediately after I had said it.'

For (21), *jiu* indicates that the event *wo zou* 'I go' will happen within a short time span with regard to the speech time, *jiu* acts as a temporal adverb. In (22a) and (22b), successive *jiu* signals that the two events will happen/happened in quick succession.

## 6    Concluding Remarks

This paper has explored the core meaning of the adverb *jiu* and discussed its semantic functions. It is claimed that the various usages of *jiu* can be derived from the basic meaning of *jiu* as establishing a relation between two units. As a focus adverb, *jiu* not only establish a relation between the asserted value and the relevant open sentence but also a relation between the asserted value and its alternatives. According to its semantic properties, focus adverb *jiu* can be further divided into three: exclusive adverb *jiu*, scalar adverb *jiu* and adverb *jiu* indicating emphatic assertion. As the name implies, exclusive adverb *jiu* has the property of exclusiveness and it interacts with an element to its right or the whole sentence exclusive of *jiu* itself. In the limiting case, exclusive *jiu* has either a scalar use or a non-scalar use which is highly determined by the context; whereas in the emphatic case it tends to take a non-scalar use. Scalar adverb *jiu* associates with an element to its left and induces a scale. Moreover, it evaluates the asserted value as a lower value. In the case of expressing emphatic assertion, *jiu* interacts with an element to its left and emphatically asserts that its associated element has the relevant property or determines the actuation of the event in question. Sufficiency operator *jiu* indicates that the antecedent is sufficient to satisfy the consequent. *Jiu* with the 'close to' meaning signals that the asserted value is close to the reference value on the relevant (indirect) temporal-related scale.

**Acknowledgments.** Part of the results reported in this paper is supported by the RGC General Research Fund (GRF) CityU 146311 from the Hong Kong SAR government. The authors thus acknowledge the generous support of the relevant party. Sincere thanks also go to the anonymous reviewers for their invaluable comments. As usual, the authors alone are responsible for all potential errors that may exist in the paper.

## References

1. Biq, Y.O.: The Semantics and Pragmatics of *Cai* and *Jiu* in Mandarin Chinese. PhD dissertation.Cornell University (1984)
2. Biq, Y.O.: From Focus in Proposition to Focus in Speech Situation: *Cai* and *Jiu* in Mandarin Chinese. Journal of Chinese Linguistics 16, 72–108 (1988)

3. König, E.: The Meaning of Focus Particles—a Comparative Perspective. Routledge, London (1991)
4. Lai, H.L.: Rejected Expectations: The Scalar Particles *Cai* and *Jiu* in Mandarin Chinese. PhD Dissertation. The University of Texas at Austin (1995)
5. Lai, H.L.: Rejected Expectations: The Scalar Particles *Cai* and *Jiu* in Mandarin Chinese. Linguistics 37(4), 625–661 (1999)
6. Bai, M.L. (Paris): Xiandai Hanyu *Cai* he *Jiu* de Yuyi Fenxi. ZhongguoYuwen 5, 390–398 (1987)
7. Chen, L.M.: On *Jiu* and *Cai*. Contemporary Linguistics 1, 16–34 (2005)
8. Lu, B.F.: Fuci *Jiu* de Yixiang Fenhe Wenti. Chinese Language Learning 1, 31–34 (1984)
9. Lü, S.X., et al. (eds.): Modern Chinese 800 Words. The Commercial Press (1980)

# Homonomous Extension of Semantic Meaning

Ping Chen

School of Humanity and Teacher Education, Wuyi University, Wuyishan, Fujian 354300
shnchp_158@163.com

**Abstract.** During the semantic evolution of words, there exists the phenomenon of several words changing their meanings in the same or reverse directions by following the same law, which is that these words contain the same, similar or opposite nucleus-sememes. Research on the phenomenon of this kind of semantic evolution is conducive to the correct analysis of the extension of a word's meaning and the exploration of the systematicness and regularity in the semantic evolution process.

**Keywords:** homonomous extension of semantic meaning, nucleus-sememe, systematicness.

## 1    About the Homonomous Extension of Semantic Meaning

The meaning of a word is in the process of a progressive evolution. A word can develop many meanings; Different meanings are not fragmented but associated with each other. Therefore, vocabulary research requires further study of the law of word's semantic revolution. Over past decades, Chinese scholars have studied the law of semantic meaning extension from multiple perspectives. They have summed up a series of methods and patterns concerning semantic evolution, among which lateral linkage during the process of semantic evolution has also attracted scholars' great attention.

[1]Jialu Xu puts forward the idea of "synchronous extension", deeming that the extending of a word's meaning often brings along similar changes for interrelated words, i.e. "synchronous extension". He also expounded the following six aspects: the definition and the category of the synchronous extension; synchronous extension's impact upon the development of language; the role of synchronization extension and linguistic analysis; previous attentions to synchronous extension; the basis of synchronous extension. Then [2]Xiaoshen Wang discuses four types of synchronous extensions in medieval Chinese vocabulary: the synchronous extensions of synonyms, antonyms, antisense combination and synchronous extension in an intricate fashion. [3]Lansheng Jiang proposes the statement of "parallel extension", referring to two or above synonyms (including homoionym) or antonyms (including words with opposite meanings) influencing each other, extending in the similar direction on the basis of their original meanings and then producing the same or opposite extended meanings. "The parallel extension" is essentially equivalent to [1]Jialu Xu's "synchronous extension". [3]Lansheng Jiang holds that "the synchronous extension" can easily be mistaken as extension at the same time which is not exactly consistent with the case that

P. Liu and Q. Su (Eds.): CLSW 2013, LNAI 8229, pp. 328–341, 2013.

parallel semantic extension comes in sequence. [4]Weiguang Dong presents the idea of "lateral linkage". He thinks lateral linkage can be expressed in two ways: according to the consistency that lies in the development and tendency of meanings inside the extension set, the establishment of a set can be seen as an gradually progressive process. Then if the first established extension sequence exerts an influence on the subsequent sequence, this kind of influence is the impact of "lateral linkage". What Dong emphasizes is the latter, and he points out that a semantic extension set may be affected by two types of forces: vertical driving force and parallel lateral convergent force that develop from inside. [5]Bo Zhang puts forward the idea of corresponding extension. He thinks that although the perspective of research and literature referred of Shaoyu Jiang's idea of "meaning produced by relative causes", Zongda Lu and Ning Wang's idea of "extension series of overlapped 'line' and 'segment'", Jialu Xu's "synchronous extension" and so on are quite different, but they've all revealed an important phenomenon during the process of semantic extension, namely inside the meaning system, the movement of a word's meaning tends to affect the corresponding change of one or more other correlative words' meaning. In many cases the semantic extension of related words, in other words, is not irrelevant and going independent, but a correlated, consistent and orderly covariation. [5]Bo Zhang defines this situation as "the corresponding extension". [6]Li Feng advocates the idea of homonomous extension of semantic meaning. He considers this as the phenomenon of meaning change that comes with many words' changing by following the same extension law.

Although all of the above arguments have different names, but the essence is the same, which explains the phenomenon that there exists the same extension set in different words. And they also hold roughly the same view that the reason of this phenomenon is that under the influence and drive of a particular extension set, there follows other extension sets. As cited above, the idea of "synchronous extension" used the word "drive", "parallel extension" used "influencing each other" and "comes in sequence", "lateral linkage" used "parallel lateral convergent force" and "corresponding extension" used "affect".

We believe that the view of "drive" and "influence" is questionable. Word meaning is extended along the direction guided by the original meaning's features. It can clearly be seen that extensions have rules to follow. So in the same language environment, the laws will work, resulting in the same series of extended meanings. That is to say the reason why there exists the same extension series is that common law is in action, rather than one influences or drives the existence of the other. Zongda Lu and Ning Wang had also expounded on the relationship of meanings between word and word. They points out according to the relationship of meanings, word and word can be either relative or overlapping i.e. two words has different extension series, but they have different numbers of the same or similar meanings. [7]Zhengjian Luo also points out that the synchronous extension reveals the internal law of language: the extended meanings of homoionyms and synonyms are similar or the same as well. [6]Li Feng advocates the idea of homonomous extension of semantic meaning. He considers this as the phenomenon of meaning change that comes with many words' changing by following the same extension law. This argument demonstrates more clearly the phenomenon that the extended meanings of words that are meaning identical, similar or opposite tend to be the same, similar or opposite as well. But [6]Li Feng does not completely put aside the argument of "influence, drive". He also believes that "the evolvement of the meaning ...... is interactional and mutually driven".

As to the phenomenon of different words extending their meanings along the same path, this paper will name it as "homonomous extension of semantic meaning" which is first proposed by Li Feng, and use the analytical approach concerning nucleus-sememes to explore the inherent law during the process of semantic evolution process.

# 2     Homonomous Extension in the Same Direction

In the process of homonomous extension, there are a few words which extend into the same or related meanings along the same direction. We call this phenomenon as "homonomous extension in the same direction". For example:

## 2.1     轻 [qīng] (light), 薄 [báo] (slight)

轻 and 薄 both has the extended meaning of "make light of" or "slight".

轻 [qīng] (light), 《说文解字》 Shuo Wen Jie Zi: 轻,轻车也。(轻[qīng] refers to a lightweight car). Its original meaning is a simple and flexible car. Its extended meaning is "make light of", as is shown in the sentence: 我尝闻少仲尼之闻，而轻伯夷之义者(《庄子》)(I have also heard of the saying that Confucius knows very little and Bo Yi's noble virtue should **be made light of**.in Zhuangzi.)

薄 [báo], 《说文解字》 Shuo Wen Jie Zi: 薄，林薄也。(薄 [báo] refers to staggered clusters of grass and woods or dense mulberry leaves eaten by silkworm.). Originally mean to be grass. 《淮南子·俶真》 Huai Nan Zi•Chu Zhen: 鸟飞千仞之上，兽走丛薄之中。(Birds fly high in the sky, the beasts run in **dense clusters of grass and woods**.)You Gao made such notes: 聚木曰丛，深草曰薄。(Trees gathered together are called woods, grass gathered called **dense clusters**.) Its extended meaning is "slight", as is shown in the sentence: Mencius said: '于不可已而已者，无所不已。于所厚者薄，无所不薄也。(If you give up things that should not be given up, then there is nothing wrong to give up; if you slight those who should have been treated kindly and generously, then there is nothing wrong to **slight** anybody.) in 《孟子·尽心上》 Mencius • Jin Xin Shang.

## 2.2     譬[pì] (draw an analogy)、喻[yù] (inform)、详[xiáng](scrutinize)、审 [shěn] (exhaustive)

譬, 喻, 详, 审 all have the extended meaning of "understand" or "be clear about".

譬[pì], 《说文解字》 Shuo Wen Jie Zi: 譬，谕也。(譬[pì] means to tell.)It originally means to draw an analogy, as is shown in the sentence:取譬不远，昊天不忒。(Let me **draw an analogy** without going too far. Heaven's punishment would be surely right.) It extends to the meaning of "understand" or "be clear about", as is shown in 《后汉书》*Houhanshu*: 唯匈奴未赔圣德, 威侮二垂, 陵虐中国。(*Only huns still don't **understand** the kindness of the emperor, pose a threat to the western and northern borders and bully wantonly the central plains.*)

喻[*yù*], 《说文解字》*Shuo Wen Jie Zi*: 谕, 告也。(喻[*yù*]*means to inform, belonging to the category of articulating in meaning.*) 《广韵•遇韵》*Guangyun• Yuyun*'s comment is: 喻, 同谕。(喻[*yù*] is essentially equivalent to谕[*yù*].) 《广雅• 释诂三》*Guangya • Shigusan*: 喻, 告也。(喻[*yù*] means to inform.) The original meaning of 喻[*yù*] is to inform and enlighten, as is shown in 《礼记·学记》*Liji • Xueji*: 和易以思, 可谓善喻矣。(*Only when students can feel happy and comfortable, as well as be diligent in thinking can a teacher be thought as good at **enlightening** others.*) The extended meaning of 喻[*yù*] is to understand or be clear about something, as is expounded in 《论语·里仁》*The Analects • Benevolence* : 子曰：君子喻于义，小 人喻于利。(*Confucius said : What is **understood** by the man of honor is righteousness, that of the man of disgrace is only benefit.*)

详[*xiáng*], 《说文解字》*Shuo Wen Jie Zi*: 详, 审议也。(详*[xiáng] means to examine and discuss.*) [8]Shunhui Zhang said: "Perhaps 'examine and discuss' means to censor what one says." The original meaning of 详[*xiáng*] is to scrutinize and try, as is seen in 《书·蔡仲之命》 *Shu • The Order on Cai Zhong*: 详乃视听, 罔以侧言改厥 度。(*To **scrutinize** is to see and listen, don't listen to gossips and change state statutes.*) Its extended meaning to "understand" or "be clear about" something, as is seen in Qian Tao's 《五柳先生传》*Biography of Mr. Wuliu*: 先生不知何许人也， 亦不详其姓字。(*Nobody knows where he comes from and no one **is clear about** his name.* )

审[*shěn*], 《说文解字》*Shuo Wen Jie Zi*: 宷, 悉也。知宷谛也。(宷*[shěn] is equivalent to* 悉*[xi], meaning to be detailed and know all the related information.*) 《 说文解字》*Shuo Wen Jie Zi*: 悉, 详尽也。(defines "悉*[xi] as to be in detail.*") The original meaning of 审[*shěn*] is to be exhaustive and thorough, as is seen in 《礼记· 中庸》*Liji • Zhongyong*: 博学之, 审问之，慎思之，明辨之，笃行之。(*One should learn extensively, question **thoroughly**, think carefully, distinguish clearly and practice earnestly.*) Its extended meaning is to understand and be clear about something, as is seen in 《公孙龙子·白马》*Gong Sun Long Zi • White Horse*: 故黄、 黑马一也，而可以应有马，而不可以应有白马，是白马之非马，审矣。(*Then, with the same yellow or black horse, you can say there is a "horse", but you can't say there is a "white horse". Therefore a "white horse" is different from a "horse". This is a very **clear** sense to see.*)

## 2.3  疾[*jí*] (*hate*), 忌[*jì*] (*abhor*)

疾[*jí*] and 忌[*jì*] both have the extended meaning of "be jealous of".

疾[*jí*] has the meaning of "hate" and "detest", as is seen in 《书·君陈》*Shu • Junchen*: 尔无忿疾于顽，无求备于一夫。(*You should not angrily **detest** he who is obstinate. Don't expect to ask one person to be perfect.*) It extends the meaning of "be jealous of", as is seen in 《商君书·修权》*Shang Jun Shu • Xiu Quan*: 公私之分别，则小人不疾 贤，而不肖者不妒功。*Only when the distinction between between public and private* *interests is clear will a man of narrow horizons not **be jealous of** a man of talent, nor will people with no accomplishments envy those who have made great achievements.*)

忌[*jì*]，《说文解字》*Shuo Wen Jie Zi*: 忌，憎恶也。(忌*[jì]* means "abhor".) Its original meaning is "detest" or "resent", as is implied in 《诗·大雅·瞻卬》*Shijing • Daya • Zhanyang*: 舍尔介狄，维予胥忌。(*The king has discarded all foresights. He hates me for no other reason than **resenting** my faithfulness and uprightness.*) 《毛传》*Mao Zhuan* : 忌，怨也。(忌*[jì]* refers to "resent".) Its extended meaning is "envy", as is implied in 《抱朴子·汉过》*Baopuzi • Hanguo*: 忌有功而危之，疾清白而排之。(*Because of **jealousy**, he may do harm to meritorious people; for envying men of noble morality, he may squeeze them out.*)

### 2.4    明[**míng**] (wise), 暗[**àn**](not bright)

明[*míng*] and 暗[*àn*] has the extended meaning of "wise" and "fatuous" respectively.

The original meaning of 明[*míng*] is the sun and moon's light, as is expounded in 《易·系辞下》*Yijing • Xicixia*: 日往则月来，月往则日来，日月相推，而明生焉。(*When the sun sets, the moon rises; When the moon fades, the sun appears. The alternation of the sun and the moon produces **light**.*) It can be extended as "wise" or "sage", as is seen in 《论语·颜渊》*The Analects*: 浸润之谮，肤受之愬，不行焉，可谓明也已矣。(*If secretly sow vituperation that seeps in like water and direct slander that hurts like keenly-felt pain won't work with you, then you can be called **wise**.*)

暗[*àn*]，《说文解字》*Shuo Wen Jie Zi*: 暗，日无光也。(暗*[àn] means the sun losing its light.*) 暗[*àn*] originally means "insufficient light" and "not bright", as is seen in 《韩非子·解老》*Hanfeizi • Jie Lao*: 以为暗乎，其光昭昭；以为明乎，其物冥冥。(*You think the road very dark, in fact it was shining; you think the road is very bright, actually it is somber.*) It is extended as "fatuous" or "incapable". 《荀子·天论》*Xunzi • Tian Lun*: 上暗而政险，则是虽无一至者，无益也。(*The king being **fatuous** and the government tyrannic, even if none of these phenomena exists, there is no benefit.*)

## 3    Homonomous Extension in the Opposite Direction

There is another kind of phenomenon in the process of semantic evolution: a few words extend their meanings in the direction that is opposite to one another. We call it as "homonomous extension in opposite directions". For example:

### 3.1    憾[**hàn**] (resentment), 恨[**hèn**] (regret)

憾[*hàn*]'s original meaning is "resentment", as is seen in 《国语·齐语》*Guoyu • Qiyu*: 山泽各致其时，则民不苟；陵阜、陵、墐、井、田、畴均，则民不憾。(*Open and close particular areas of mountains or rivers in appropriate time, then the civilians would not cut wood and hunt slinkingly; allocate farmland fairly, then the farmers will* *not harbour **resentment**.*) It is extended as "regret", as is implied in 《左传》*Zuozhuan*: 美哉，犹有憾。(*Good but there are still **regrets**.*)

恨[*hèn*] originally refers to "regret" or "repentance", as is seen in 《史记》*ShihChi*: 梁惠王曰：寡人恨不用公叔座之言也。(*King Lianghui said: I **regret** that I didn't follow Gong Sunzuo's advice.*) It is extended as "resent". 《荀子》*Xunzi*: 处官久者 士妒之，禄厚者民怨之，位尊者君恨之。(*Officials may envy those who have been of high rank for a long period of time; ordinary people may bear a grudge against those who are of high salary; the king may **resent** those who are of very honorable status.*)

憾[*hàn*] and恨[*hèn*] extend their meanings in the opposite direction. 憾[*hàn*] extends from the meaning of "resentment" into that of "regret". 恨[*hèn*] extends from the meaning of "regret" into that of "resentment".

### 3.2　怨[yuàn] (resent), 非[fēi] (violate)

怨[*yuàn*], 《说文解字》*Shuo Wen Jie Zi*: 怨，恚也。(怨[*yuàn*] *is literally equal to* 恚 [*huì*] *(malevolence).*) Its original meaning is "resent". 《史记》*Shih Chi*: 武安由此大 怨灌夫、魏其。(*Since then, An Wu **resented** Guanfu and Qi Wei.*) It is extended as "go against". 《管子》*Guanzi*: 夫名实之相怨久矣。(*The fame has **gone far against** the fact.*)

非[*fēi*], 《说文解字》*Shuo Wen Jie Zi*: 非，违也。(非[*fēi*] *refers to "violate".*) Its original meaning is "violate". 《诗经》*Shijing*: 无非无仪。(*Don't **violate** the views of the elders and your husband; don't do improper things.*) Its extended meaning is "resent". 《国语》*Guoyu*: 今既无事矣，而非和，于是加宠，将何治为？(*Now the nation is in peace, but you **resent** Mr. He. If the king has a higher opinion of you, how you will govern the country?*)

怨[*yuàn*] and非[*fēi*] extend their meanings in the opposite direction. 怨[*yuàn*] extends from the meaning of "resent" into that of "violate". 非[*fēi*] extends from the meaning of "violate" into that of "resent".

### 3.3　望[wàng] (look into the distance), 希[xī] (hope)

望[*wàng*], 《说文解字》*Shuo Wen Jie Zi*: 望，出亡在外，望其还也。(望[*wàng*] *means gazing at the distance, hoping people to come back.*) 望[*wàng*] originally means "look into the distance", as is implied in《诗·卫风·河广》*Shijing • Weifeng • Heguang*: 谁谓宋远，跂予望之。(*Who says our Song kingdom is far away from here? I can see it by standing on my tiptoes and **looking into the distance**.*) It is extended to the meaning of "hope." 《孟子·梁惠王上》*Mengzi • King Lianghui I*: 王如知此，则无 望民之多于邻国也。(*If you, my Majesty, understand this, you won't **hope** your country's population larger than that of your neighboring countries.*)

希[*xī*] means "hope".《南齐书》*Nanqishu*: 沥肠纾愤，仰希神照，辩明枉直。(*To vent out of accumulated resentment in the heart, **hope** Gods to give enlightenment and identify the merits.*) It is extended to the meaning of "see" or "look", as is seen in 《管 子》*Guanzi*: 上惠其道，下敦其业，上下相希，若望参表，则邪者可知也。(*Keep* *submissive and obedient to the emperor, take your responsibilities seriously, **observe** these two parts like watching the benchmark, then the evil man can be found out.*)

望[*wàng*] and希[*xī*] extend their meanings in the opposite direction. 望[*wàng*] extends from the meaning of "look" into that of "hope". 希[*xī*] extends from the meaning of "hope" into that of "look".

# 4     The Law of Homonomous Extension

Different words share similar process and results of semantic evolution. "This is definitely not coincidental. There are a great amount of situations like this in Chinese." The academic world have many interpretations of this kind of phenomenon, including above mentioned Jialu Xu's "synchronous extension", LanSheng Jiang's "parallel extension", Weiguang Dong's "lateral linkage" and Bo Zhang's "corresponding extension" etc.. But, why different words have the same extension process? Whether there are laws to follow? We discussed from the perspective of the core meaning.

[9]Lianrong Zhang(1995), the first person to research word's core meaning, points out that among all the meanings of a word, there is one meaning (note: sememe) at the core of the entire meaning structure and all the other meanings is associated with it. He also points out that the research of the development of a word's meaning should depend on the understanding of the nucleus-sememe, including the determination of each word's meaning in each period and the study on the emergence and development of each meaning. [10]Yunlu Wang(2008) argues that the nucleus-sememe is the soul of a word's meaning. Originated from the original meaning, the core meaning winds through the core part of all meanings and the evolution and development of the word's meaning. The research of nucleus-sememe can clearly explain the emergence of most of the word's meanings and the connection between them.

Both scholars regard the research of nucleus-sememe as of great significance to the research of the development and evolution of the word's meaning. Likewise, the analysis of the word's nucleus-sememe can reveal well the law during the process of homonomous extension.

## 4.1     轻 [*qīng*] (*light*), 薄 [*báo*] (*slight*)

The main meanings of 轻[*qīng*]are: ①lightweight car. ②An object's weight is quite small. ③ cheap, inexpensive. ④low status. ⑤dexterous, portable. ⑥readily, easily. ⑦reduce, weaken. ⑧make light of, contempt.

The original meaning of 轻[*qīng*] is a small flexible car. Its nucleus-sememe 小 [*xiǎo*] (*little*) appears throughout the various meanings of 轻[*qīng*]. That is to say every extended meaning of 轻[*qīng*] is derived from the nucleus-sememe 小[*xiǎo*] (*little*), so is the extended meaning "make light of, belittle". It is thus clear that the nucleus-sememe 小[*xiǎo*] (*little*) is the law of 轻[*qīng*]'s semantic extension.

The main meanings of 薄 [*báo*] are: ①staggered clusters of grass and woods. ② small thickness. ③slight. ④bland. ⑤phony, mean. ⑥alleviate, diminish. ⑦despise, disdain.

The original meaning of 薄 [*báo*] is brushwood. Brushwood is comparatively lower than the jungle. Therefore, 薄 [*báo*] has the characteristic of being short and low. Hence "being short and low" is the nucleus-sememe of薄 [*báo*].   The extended meaning "despise" means looking down upon those with lower ability. So, the nucleus-sememe "being short and low" is the law of 薄 [*báo*]'s semantic extension.

Through the analyses above we can see that the nucleus-sememe 小[*xiǎo*] (*little*) is the law of 轻[*qīng*]'s semantic extension and the nucleus-sememe "being short and low" is the law of 薄 [*báo*]'s semantic extension. They have the same (similar) nucleus-sememe, which is the determinant that both 轻[*qīng*] and 薄 [*báo*] have the extended meaning of "make light of" or "belittle" and which is the law of homonomous extension as well.

**4.2**   **恶[è] (offence), 难[nán] (difficult), 憎[zēng] (detest), 畏[wèi] (weird), 骇 [hài] (abnormal), 惊 [jīng] (abnormal), 怪 [guài] ( strange), 震 [zhèn] (extraordinary)**

| Word | Original Meaning | Nucleus-sememe | Extended Meaning |
|---|---|---|---|
| 恶[è] | offence, bad words and deeds caused by negligence etc. | bad | be afraid of |
| 难[nán] | difficult, not easy, issues being tough to deal with | tough | be fearful of |
| 憎[zēng] | detest, being hostile to nasty persons or things | nasty persons or things | dread |
| 畏[wèi] | with an ugly and weird image | ugly and weird | fear |
| 骇[hài] | horse running madly for reacting to abnormal stimuli | abnormal circumstance | scared |
| 惊[jīng] | horse running wildly for reacting to abnormal stimuli | abnormal stimuli | frightened |
| 怪[guài] | bizarre, unusual, strange things | strange | dread |
| 震[zhèn] | fast thunder | extraordinary situation | frightened |

恶[è], 难[nán], 憎[zēng], 畏[wèi], 骇[hài], 惊[jīng], 怪[guài] and 震[zhèn] all have the similar extended meanings of "fear", "dread" and all that, belonging to homonomous extension. Their shared law of extension consists in the same (similar) nucleus-sememe "tough, abnormal."

## 4.3   乐[yuè] (pleasan), 嘉[jiā] (beautiful), 好[hǎo] (good looking ),喜[xǐ] (joy), 善[shàn] (fine)

| Word | Original Meaning | Nucleus-sememe | Extended Meaning |
|---|---|---|---|
| 乐[yuè] | musical instruments that give pleasant sound | pleasant | be keen on |
| 嘉[jiā] | people or things that are good or beautiful | beautiful | like |
| 好[hǎo] | woman being good looking | good looking | love |
| 喜[xǐ] | joy, pleasure | wonderful things | enjoy |
| 善[shàn] | fine characters of people or things. | fine | fancy |

乐[yuè], 嘉[jiā], 好[hǎo], 喜[xǐ], 善[shàn] all have the similar extended meanings of "love", "fancy" and all that. This is because they share the same law of extension, i.e. the same (similar) nucleus-sememe "pleasant, fine."

## 4.4   待[dài] (wait), 容[róng] (hold)

待[dài],《说文解字》Shuo Wen Jie Zi: 待，竢也。(待[dài] refers to wait.) Its original meaning is "wait", that is, allow someone/something to arrive or do things after a period of time. Its nucleus-sememe is "allow". When the object allowed is "other people's faults or different points of view", then待[dài] is extended as "tolerate".《国语·晋语八》Guoyu • Jinyu 8: 以其五贤陵人，而以不仁行之，其谁能待之？(If he uses his five advantages to oppress others, instead of pursuing righteousness, who would **tolerate** him? )

容[róng],《说文解字》Shuo Wen Jie Zi: 容，盛也。(容[róng] means "contain".) Its original meaning is "hold", i.e., to accommodate a certain number of people or issues within a fixed space or scope. Its nucleus-sememe is "hold". When the object held is "someone/something to arrive or be done after a period of time", then "hold" is abstracted into "allow". Therefore, the extended meaning of "wait" emerges.《宣和遗事》Xuan He Yi Shi: 至军门，军吏止帝于小室，曰："元帅尙未起，可俟于此。" 容移时，有小黄头奴至，曰："元帅请国主。"(To the barrack's door, an officer led the emperor into a small room and said: "Marshal has not get up, you wait here". After a moment's **waiting**, a servant came and said, "Marshal invites you to come.")

待[dài] and 容[róng] have similar nucleus-sememes "allow" and "hold". But they extend in the opposite direction: 待[dài] extends from "wait" to "tolerate". 容[róng] extends from "hold" to "wait". This is homonomous Extension in the opposite direction, sharing the same law of extension with the same (similar) nucleus-sememes.

## 4.5    好[hǎo] (good looking) ，恶[è] (offence)

The original meaning of 好[hǎo] is "woman being good looking". Its nucleus-sememe is "good looking (better than general)". The characteristic of its nucleus-sememe can be abstracted as "very" or "so". So 好[hǎo] is extended as an adverb of degree to enhance the extent, as is seen in 《西地锦》 *Xi Jin Di*, written by Xiaoyou Shi of Song dynasty: 风儿又起，雨儿又煞，好愁人天色。(*The wind blows, the rain stopped. The weather makes me feel so sad.*)

The original meaning of 恶[è] is offence, i.e. bad words or deeds caused by negligence. Its nucleus-sememe is "bad (more than general)". The characteristic of its nucleus-sememe can be abstracted as "very" or "quite". So 恶[è] is extended as an adverb of degree to enhance the extent, as is seen in 《淮南子·墬形训》 *Huai Nan Zi • Di Xing Xun*: 其人大面短颐，美须恶肥。(*That person has a big face, short cheeks, long beard and a very fat body.*)

好[hǎo] and 恶[è] are a pair of antonym, but their nucleus-sememes have the same characteristics: "more than general". Therefore, both of them are extended to the adverb of degree which enhance the extent.

## 4.6    软[ruǎn] (soft), 强[qiáng] (hard bow)

软[ruǎn] means being soft. The nucleus-sememe is "insufficient resistance of stress".

Its main extended meanings are:

① soft, mild. 《端午日赐衣》 *Clothes Bestowed on Dragon-boat Festival,* a poem written by Fu Du of Tang dynasty: 细葛含风软，香罗叠雪轻。(*It is made from the finest silk cloth, being as soft as the gentle breeze. It is so fragrant and as light as a stack of snow.*)

② feeble. 《夜宴曲》 *Song of the Banquet*, a poem written by Jianwu Shi of Tang dynasty: 被郎嗔罚琉璃盏，酒入四肢红玉软。(*Blamed by the man, she was punished to drink another cup of wine. After drinking, her arms and legs became very feeble.*)

③ Not strong, timid. 《西厢记诸宫调》卷一 *Xi Xiang Ji Zhu Gong Diao Volume I*, written by Jieyuan Dong of Jin dynasty: 早见女孩儿家心肠软，誠得颤着一团。(*Knowing that the girls are timid, he purposely frighten them into a circle.*)

④ Make someone change his mind. 《西游记》第十九回 *Journey to the West Chapter19*: 你莫诡诈欺心软我，欲为脱身之计。(*Don't you expect to cheat me, fool me and make me change my mind in order to escape.*)

⑤ Inferior. Laoshe's 《四世同堂》六三 *Four Generations Under One Roof • Chapter 63*: 压轴是招弟的《红鸾禧》，大轴是名角会串《大溪皇庄》只有《红鸾禧》软一点。(*Zhaodi's Hong Luan Xi is the penultimate one. The finale is Da Xi Huang Zhuang which is played by famous Chinese opera actors. The former is slightly inferior to the latter.*)

⑥ Slightly less, less than. Juyi Bai's 《题朗之槐亭诗》 *Ti Lang Zhi Huai Ting Shi*: 春风可惜无多日，家酝唯残软半瓶。(*It's a pity that the spring is coming to an end. The wine made at home is less than half a bottle.*)

The original meaning of强[*qiáng*] is a hard bow. Its nucleus-sememe is "sufficient resistance of stress". The main meanings hence extended are:

① Violent; tyrannical. 《老子》 *Lao Tse*: 心使气曰强。 (When the heart is filled with anger, it becomes **violent**.)

② Strong and healthy. 《荀子·劝学》 *Xunzi • Quanxue*: 蟥无爪牙之利，筋骨之强 。 (*Earthworm has neither sharp teeth and paws nor **strong** muscles and bones.*)

③ Determined, staunch. 《书·皋陶谟》 *Shu • Gaotaomo*: 强而义。 (*Be **determined** and righteous.*)

④ Make sb become strong. 《礼记·学记》 *Liji • Xueji*: 故君子之教喻也，道而弗 牵，强而弗抑，开而弗达。 (*Therefore the man of honor will teach by knowing how to enlighten students. He will make them understand reasons by instruction rather than force, **make them become stronger** rather than restrain their development and give them inspiration rather than reveal everything.*)

⑤ Good, superior. 景强偏感高僧上，地胜能令远思开。 (*Good sceneries make you feel **superior** than others; brilliant ground will broaden your mind.*)

⑥ Slightly more, surplus. 《木兰诗》 *Poems of Mulan*: 策勋十二转，赏赐百千 强。 (*Mulan was recorded a great number of feats and rewarded **numerous** properties.*)

软[*ruǎn*] and强[*qiáng*] are a pair of antonyms. Their nucleus-sememes (respectively "insufficient resistance of stress" and "sufficient resistance of stress")are also on the contrary. Based on the nucleus-sememes which are on contrary to each other, they are extended as roughly opposite meanings. Opposite nucleus-sememes are then the law of homonomous extension.

In conclusion, homonomous extension means a group of words with the same, similar or opposite nucleus-sememes carry on their semantic evolution along the same or opposite directions according to the characters of the shared nucleus-sememes. These identical, similar or opposite nucleus-sememes are the laws.

# 5    The Research Value of Homonomous Extension

## 5.1    Conducive to the Correct Analysis of Semantic Extension

The introduction of sememe analysis research makes the research of semantic extension more detailed. It is helpful to better understand the implied reasons why extension happens. But sememe analysis [11] "is more subjective. The definition of sememes and the analysis of meaning structure do inevitably have subjective components." To ensure the objectivity of the extension analysis to the largest extent, we put it in the whole extension system to get summarizations. While taking full advantage of homonomous extension is also beneficial to the correct understanding of the evolution of word's meaning and helps to avoid the subjectivity of sememe analysis. Homonomous extension is a kind of lateral parallelism, that is to say one meaning tends to be in different extension series. The analysis of a word's one particular sememe may be subjective, but if other extension series also have this kind of phenomenon, then you can decide to a great extent the correctness of the analysis. For instance:

怜[*lián*], 《说文解字》 *Shuo Wen Jie Zi*: 怜，哀也。(怜*[lián] refers to sympathy.*) It originally means to "be pitiful and sympathetic". 《尔雅·释诂下》 *Erya • Shigu II*: 怜，爱也。(怜*[lián] means cherish.*) "Sympathy" and "cherish" these two meanings of怜[*lián*] appears to two irrelevant kinds of feelings. Is there a connection of extension between them? What is the reason if there is? It is hard to give a definite answer just from the meanings of 怜[*lián*]. Let's look at another meaning system.

愍[*mǐn*], 《说文解字》 *Shuo Wen Jie Zi*: 愍，痛也。(愍*[mǐn] means grief.*) Its original meaning is to grieve. 《广韵·轸韵》*Guangyun • Zhenyun*: 愍，怜也。(愍*[mǐn]* is equal to sympathy.) 《广雅·释诂一》*Guangya • Shigu I*: 愍，爱也。(愍*[mǐn]* refers to love.) In the meaning system of 愍[*mǐn*], there are also meanings like "pitiful" and "love". Thus we can roughly determine that there are extended relations between these meanings, while the implied reasons between them can be summed up in combination with two other meaning systems.

惜[*xī*], 《说文解字》 *Shuo Wen Jie Zi*: 惜，痛也。(惜*[[xī] means pity.* ) 《广雅·释诂一》 *Guangya • Shigu I*: 惜，爱也。(惜*[[xī] refers to cherish.* )

痛[*tòng*], 《说文解字》 *Shuo Wen Jie Zi*: 痛，病也。(痛*[tòng]* means pain or disease.) *Grand Chinese Dictionary*: 痛，怜爱。(痛*[tòng]refers to love tenderly.*)

怜[*lián*], 愍[*mǐn*], 惜[[*xī*] and 痛[*tòng*] all can be extended as "love". They have in their original meanings a common sememe "injury", which is the reason why they all have the extended meaning "love". Then why does each semantic composition of "love" have such a sememe "injury"? We can learn from the specific context.

愍[*mǐn*], 《敦煌变文集》 *Dunhuang Bianwenji*: 鸭儿水上学浮沈，任性略无顾恋心；可惜愍鸡肠寸断，岂知他是负恩禽。(*Baby ducks carelessly learn swimming in the river and have no sense of gratitude; poor **hen** endures hardships and does know they are so ungrateful children*) Lihong Jiang interprets: "愍鸡[*mǐn*][*jī*]means the hen that **fosters** the ducks. 愍[*mǐn*] refers to foster."

惜[*xī*], 《韩非子·难二》 *Hanfeizi*: 夫惜草茅者耗禾穗，惠盗贼者伤良民。(***Cherish** thatch will damage crops. Tolerate thieves would harm innocent civilians.*)

怜[*lián*], 《遗悲怀三首》 *Yi Bei Huai Sanhou* by Zhen Yuan of Tang dynasty: 谢公最小偏怜女，嫁与黔娄百事乖。(*Mr. Xie **adored** his niece the most and nothing went well since she married Qian Lou.*)

痛[*tòng*], the first act of Shen Hong's *Slumdog Tragedy*: 姑妈痛我，舍不得让我去学徒弟。*Aunt **loves** me very much and she won't let me go to school.*)

In these cases, 愍[*mǐn*] and惜[*xī*] means "take care of". 怜[*lián*] and 痛[*tòng*] means love dearly. They all have the meaning of "protect from harm", that is to say "love" is an emotion orientation and one of its behavioral expressions is to protect the loved one from any harm.

These four words' process of extending the meaning "love" can be analyzed in sememes like:

| 愍[mǐn]: | ① Grief, sorrow. | People or objects + get hurt or damaged + in a bad mood, sorrowful |
|---|---|---|
| | ② Care, foster. | Care + foster + protect from harm |
| 惜[xī]: | ① Pitiful, sorry. | Things + broken, lost + heartbroken, regret |
| | ② Love, cherish. | Take care of + protect from damage |
| 怜[lián]: | ① Sympathy, pity | Other people + get hurt + sympathy + care |
| | ② Love dearly | Concern and care for + protect from harm |
| 痛[tòng]: | ① Pain or disease. | Body + get hurt + feel painful |
| | ② Hurt. | Things + get hurt |

## 5.2　Conducive to Explore the Systematicness and Regularity of Semantic Evolution

The evolution and extension of the meaning are not a single, isolated process. Both of them have the systematicness, of which an important embodiment is "homonomous extension". From the above analyses and academic researches, we can see that the systematicness exists in many situations:

计[jì], 揆[kuí], 度[duó], 量[liáng], 卜[bǔ], 测[cè], 料[liào], 谓[wèi], 云[yún], 想[xiǎng], 猜[cāi] and 意[yì] all extend from the nucleus-sememe "judge" to the meaning of "guess". 恶[è] , 难[nán], 憎[zēng], 畏[wèi], 骇[hài], 惊[jīng], 怪[guài], 震[zhèn] all extend from the nucleus-sememe "abnormal situation" to the meaning of "fear". 乐 [yuè], 嘉 [jiā], 好 [hǎo], 喜 [xǐ], 善 [shàn]all extend from the nucleus-sememe "wonderful things or people" to the meaning of "love". 愍[mǐn], 惜[xǐ], 怜[lián], 痛[tòng] have the common nucleus-sememe "hurt". The meaning "love" then is extended.

苦[kǔ], 痛[tòng], 恶[è] and 怪[guài] share the common feature of "being unusual". 苦 [kǔ] and 痛 [tòng] are feeling psychologically or physiologically unusual, i.e. uncomfortable feeling; 恶[è] and 怪[guài]refers to unusual things, namely things that are inferior or weird. According to the common nucleus-sememe "unusual", they all extend to the meaning "very".

善[shàn], 喜[xǐ], 好[hǎo] can all be extended as "easy", but not extended directly by the original meaning. All the original meanings of these three words have the nucleus-sememe "wonderful", hence extended as "be emotionally fond of 'wonderful' things" and "tend to behaviorally 'love' them". "Love" is the "tendency" in behavior. While "easy" means things "tend to" make a particular change which leads to "easy". The extension process is as follows :

善[shàn], 喜[xǐ], 好[hǎo]　(wonderful)　love, be fond of　(tendency)　easy

As a result, the analysis of a specific semantic evolution needs to look for as many words of the same nucleus-sememe as possible (mainly synonyms and near-synonyms) in order to form homonomous extension series. The exploration of homonomous extension not only can realize the mutual verification of each series' extension process, but also ensure the objectivity of the analysis of meaning extension and make the seemingly complex Chinese meaning extension more systematic, conducive to the systematic study of the sematic evolution of Chinese words.

# References

1. Xu, J.: About the Synchronous Extension. J. Chinese Language (1), 50–57 (1987); (许嘉璐《论同步引申》.中国语文1987年第1期. 50-57)

2. Wang, X.: A Tentative Study on the Synchronous Extension of Medieval Chinese Vocabulary. Journal of Nankai (4), 66–70 (1998); (王小莘《试论中古汉语词汇的同步引申现象》.南开学报.1998年,第4期. 66-70)

3. Jiang, L.: Parallel Extension of Interrelated Words, A Modern Chinese Sourcebook, pp. 309–320. The Commercial Press, M. Beijing (2000) (江蓝生《相关词语的类同引申》.见《近代汉语探源》.北京：商务印书馆.2000:309-320.)

4. Dong, W.: Lateral Linkage of a Semantic Extension Set. J. Language Studies (2), 79–87(1991) (董为光《词义引申组系的"横向联系"》.语言研究.1991年,第2期. 79-87)

5. Zhang, B.: Corresponding Differentiation of Words and Cognate Meaning-Differentiated Words Series. J. Ancient Chinese Studies (4), 23–30 (1995) (张博《词的相应分化与义分同族词系列》.古汉语研究.1995年,第4期. 23-30)

6. Feng, L.: Homonomous Extension of Semantic Meaning and Interpretations in Chinese Dictionary. J. Dictionary Studies (2), 8–13 (1986) (冯利《"同律引申"与语文词典的释义》.辞书研究.1986年,第2期. 8-13)

7. Luo, Z.: Introduction of Chinese Word Meaning Extension, pp. 106. Nanjing University Press, M. Nanjing (1996) (罗正坚《汉语词义引申导论》.南京：南京大学出版社.1996年, 106)

8. Zhang, S.: Interpretations of Shuo Wen Jie Zi. M. Zhengzhou: Zhongzhou Painting and Calligraphy Organization, 5(22) (1983) (张舜徽《说文解字约注》卷五.郑州:中州书画社,1983年. 22. )

9. Zhang, L.: About the Nucleus-semem of Words. J. Chinese Language Studies (3) 31–36 (1995) (张联荣《谈词的核心义》.语文研究.1995年第3期. 31-36)

10. Wang, Y.: Study on the Nucleus-sememes of Chinese Words - Also on the Systematic Methods of Methods of Dictionary's Compilation of Word Meaning. X. Tang, H. Huang.: Study on Language and Cognition, pp.135-136. Social Science Academic Press, M. Beijing (2008) (王云路师《论汉语词汇的核心义——兼谈词典编纂的义项统系方法》.唐孝威、黄华新主编《语言与认知研究 》（第2辑）.北京市：社会科学文献出版社.2008年. 135-136)

11. Zhang, Z., Zhang, Q.: Lexical Semantics, vol. 33. The Commercial Press, Beijing (2005); (张志毅、张庆云《词汇语义学》.北京:商务印书馆 年 33 (2005)

# The Design and Completion
# of Jiangsu Tourism Q&A System

Li Zhang

School of Chinese Language and Literature, Nanjing Normal University,
122# Ninghai Road, Nanjing, 210097
zl_yuyi@163.com

**Abstract.** Bridging the gap between the user's query and the tourism information has been a major challenge for Q&A systems. State-of-the-art approaches
address this issue implicitly from an information extraction view. The effectiveness of these Q&A systems is highly dependent on the availability of names
of tourism sites. Without the name of tourism sites in users' questions will
cause mistakes. Moreover these Q&A systems can not deal with real question
sentences but only some query words. In this paper we try to solve the above
problems by analyzing user's query sentences and then construct databases of
Q&A and tourism information. We explore strategies to return precise and appropriate answers. Now Jiangsu Tourism Q&A has launched an online service
and it will be applied to other areas more widely in the future. Experiments
show that the Jiangsu Tourism Q&A is feasible and effective.

**Keywords:** Q&A, Tourism, Query classification.

# 1    Instruction

The natural language understanding technique in Q&A systems is not well developed.
But there has been many practical systems in specific domains. Over the past few
years, tourism question answering (TQA) portals like Yunnan Tourism Question Answer Model have attracted great attention in China (Yu et.al, 2007). This Q&A system fosters interactive creation of content by allowing users to search some tourism
information. However, it demands that questions must include the names of tourism
sites and it returns a full list of tourism information instead of more related sentences.
Thus, the answers generally include much more information than need.

We want to develop a Q&A system to deal with tourism information in Jiangsu
province in China. It is called the Jiangsu Tourism Q&A (JSQA) System. JSQA aims
to provide online Q&A service smarter which requires real questions and generates
precise and appropriate answers. So there are two major challenges in our tourism
Q&A system that is how to deal with real questions and how to return appropriate
answers.

We address the above problems by constructing two databases Q&A database
(QADB) and tourism sites database (TSDB). The former can deal with real question

P. Liu and Q. Su (Eds.): CLSW 2013, LNAI 8229, pp. 342–349, 2013.
© Springer-Verlag Berlin Heidelberg 2013

sentences and return natural answers. The latter can store a large number of tourism information in Jiangsu. They are stored in MySQL and use PHP to design the system. Now Jiangsu Tourism Q&A has bridged the gap between users' queries and tourism information; and it has launched an online service.

In the following, we will describe the structure of our system. Section 2 is concerned with the construction of QADB and TSDB in MySQL. Section 3 details the operating mechanism of JSQA about integration of two databases. Finally, we conclude in Section 4.

## 2    Construction of Databases

### 2.1    Q&A Database

Our approach of handling exact answers is to establish two databases that store all kinds of question-answer pairs and much tourism information. One is Q&A database (QADB) which satisfies the answer pattern for the question.

We have designed a list of 30 questions of tourism to investigate what people often do in asking about tourism information and then consulted 600 informants. We record all kinds of questions and answers from questionnaires and collect a 200 question-answer pairs database based on tourism. We also collected some question-answer pairs from tourism web sites. With analyzing questions, we found that the questions people often used in tourism Q&A dialogs can be classified from four respects shown in Table 1. The division of four kinds of question-answer pairs is the basic tragedy in our Q&A system.

**Table 1.** Four Query Types

| ID | Example | Explanation |
|----|---------|-------------|
| 1 | 我想去中山陵看看。(*I want to go to Dr. Sun Yat-sen's Mausoleum.*) | Only names of tourism sites contained like Dr. Sun Yat-sen's Mausoleum |
| 2 | 南京的公园有哪些？(*Some parks in Nanjing.*) | Only tourism attributes contained like Nanjing and park |
| 3 | 中山陵在哪个城市？(*What city is the Dr. Sun Yat-sen's Mausoleum at?*) | Both names and attributes contained |
| 4 | 你好！(*Hello!*) | Neither names and attributes contained |

Using the answer patterns and questions that derived from questionnaires and webs, we automatically label chunks as meaning being same or different. The total number of chunks used in formulating QADB is 150. There are 50 different themes about 279 different keywords in Table 2 and 50 different answers in Table 3. The rest are question-answer details in Table 4.

Those three tables in the QADB are keyword table, answering model table and matching table. Every table has some fields. As in keyword table are PKID, PKEY and MATCH meaning sequence numbers of keywords, keywords that are synonymous in each row and match values respectively. In answering model table, PRID means sequence numbers of answers and PRE is the abbreviation of specific answers. The last field PID means main sequence numbers in matching table.

**Table 2.** Keyword Table

| PKID | PKEY | | MATCH |
|---|---|---|---|
| 1 | 你好 | Hello | 0 |
| 2 | 哪里/地方/地点/城市/哪儿 | City | 0 |
| 3 | 星级/级别/等级 | Star Level | 0 |
| 4 | 票价/收费/门票/价格/花费 | Ticket Price | 0 |
| 5 | 类型/特色/特点/好玩/属于 | Style | 0 |

**Table 3.** Matching Table

| PID | PKID | PRID |
|---|---|---|
| 1 | 1. Hello | 1. Hello! |
| 2 | 2. City | 2. The city is: |
| 3 | 3. Star Level | 3. The star level is: |
| 4 | 4. Ticket Price | 4. The ticket price is: |
| 5 | 5. Style | 5. The style is: |

**Table 4.** Answering Model Table

| PRID | PRE | |
|---|---|---|
| 1 | 你好！ | Hello! |
| 2 | 景点所在地是： | The city is: |
| 3 | 景点的星级是： | The star level is: |
| 4 | 景点票价是： | The ticket price is: |
| 5 | 景点的类型是： | The style is: |

For each question we develop a set of synonymous keywords by judging all questions in questionnaires. Because the grammatical structure of Chinese is different from that of English, the approach of handling Chinese queries is to match them with keywords stored each row in Table 2, instead of identifying query types that give a fairly clear indication of the type of answer like who and what. So we name a theme each row like city, star level and style etc. For example, considering the following questions: "中山陵在哪个城市 (*What city is the Dr. Sun Yat-sen's Mausoleum at?*)". The keyword "城市 (*City*)" recorded in row 2 in Table 2 is clear about the expected answer like city. We call the word "城市 (*City*)" a theme of keywords. This is simple non-structured knowledge that goes as far as identifying Nanjing as a city, park as a style and Dr. Sun Yat-sen's Mausoleum as a name. If there is one keyword in users' question, the theme of keywords will tell us directly that one theme is being looked for.

Once the theme of keywords has been found, it is possible to decide what the answer (or answer model) should be in Table 3. Aimed at this purpose Table 4 is used as a medium from question to answer.

## 2.2    Tourism Sites Database

The other database in JSQA is tourism sites database (TSDB) which satisfies user's demand of tourism information. In tourism domain, Jiangsu tourism information is necessary for system to output exact answers.

The work for pre-construction: we have collected much information about 500 tourism sites in Jiangsu province from books, webs and questionnaires.

The main table used in formulating TSDB is Table 5. There are ten fields in it like ID, name, city, and star level, ticket price, style, bus, hotel, phone number, address etc. The first six fields are common in users' queries that JSQA mainly handles in practice in Table 5. These six fields are marked up with a special symbol to divide names from attributes which is easy for JSQA to recognize.

**Table 5.** Tourism Information Table

| ID | Name | City | Star Level | Ticket Price | Style |
|----|------|------|-----------|--------------|-------|
| 1 | 中山陵<br>Dr. Sun Yat-sen's Mausoleum | 南京<br>Nanjing | 4A | 免费<br>Free | 陵墓<br>Mausoleum |
| 2 | 夫子庙秦淮河风光带<br>The Confucian Temple | 南京<br>Nanjing | 4A | 免费<br>Free | 寺庙<br>Temple |
| 3 | 玄武湖公园<br>Xuanwu Lake | 南京<br>Nanjing | 4A | 免费<br>Free | 公园<br>Park |

Experiments have proved that names of tourism sites inputted are sometimes different from those recorded in Table 5. For example, users always input "秦淮河 (*Qinhuai River*)" or "夫子庙 (*the Confucian Temple*)" instead of "夫子庙秦淮河风光带 (*Landscape along the Qinhuai River and the Confucian Temple*)" recorded. Besides, many names consist of tourism attributes such as "山 (*Mountain*)", "寺 (*Temple*)" and "湖 (*Lake*)". It is hard to decide whether combining tourism attributes with names or not. If extra words are not accepted in tables, the presence of tourism attributes may cause the answer to be judged inexact. For instance, JSQA may return nothing if only word "玄武 (*Xuanwu*)" instead of "玄武湖 (*Xuanwu Lake*)" is inputted when a user want to know something about Xuanwu Lake. In order to avoid confusion, approaches of solving the problem are that tourism information must be recorded exactly in Table 5 first and different representations of the same tourism site like "玄武湖 (*Xuanwu Lake*)" and "玄武 (*Xuanwu*)" can be recorded in the same field to increase possibility of success.

Another table in TSDB is a temporary table which is cache space that record specific tourism ID after users' queries and tourism information are matched.

# 3        Operating Mechanism of JSQA

Figure1 shows the structure of the data flow and the modules involved, outlining the approach to analyze user's queries and then return answers in JSQA.

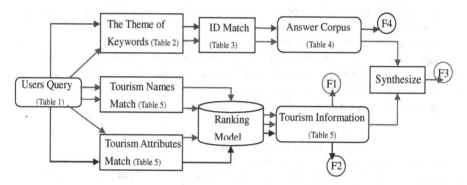

**Fig. 1.** The structure of the data flow and the modules involved

## 3.1        KIA Principle

The group of the theme of keywords, ID-match and answer pairs is called KIA which is a key process to handle users' queries in Figure 1and uses tables in QADB.

Now we introduce KIA as below: First the user's query is matched with keywords. And the theme of keywords tells us one theme being looked for by maximum match value in Table 2. Then PKID of that theme is recorded. Second, we can get the PRID corresponded with the PKID in Table 3. At last, JSQA returns the answer whose ID is that PRID in Table 4. For example, given the question "这个景点在哪个城市？ (*What city is this tourism site at?*)", the theme of keywords is "城市 (*City*)" which is clear about the expected answer like city after matching with PKID. PKID is 2 when the theme of keywords is city in Table 2 and the module of ID-match tells us its PRID is also 2 in Table 3. At last JSQA returns "景点所在地是: (*The city is :*)" in answer pairs. So we know ID-match is used as medium in KIA mechanism from the theme of keywords to answer pairs.

## 3.2        Tourism Matching and Ranking

On the basis of Yunnan Tourism Question Answer Model, the decision that matches only names of tourism sites with users' queries caused our system to output a lot of inexact answers. Next we will describe some experiments where we change the decision to tourism matching and ranking called M2 in Figure 1.

M2 must use tables stored in TSDB. There are 500 candidate tourism sites containing much information about tourism attributes. First the user query is matched with not only names of tourism sites but also tourism attributes. Second match value is added to plus one when information is matched between tourism sites and the user query. Once they have a match value, some candidate tourism sites are extracted from Table 5 to temporary table; they are sorted by match value assigned a rank in reverse order and placed as first answers outside the table. The first tourism site is the best answer which will be returned.

### 3.3 Query Type

Once the focus of the query has been found, it is possible to decide what the query type should be. After analyzing 18000 queries, we find names of tourism sites and tourism attributes are core focuses that capture the differences among four kinds of user queries in Table 1. So, users' queries can be classified by whether there are names and attributes in. The focus of the query is called query type. Different query types determine what modules use to get exact answers in Figure 1.

For example, given the query "我想去看看苏州的园林 (*I want to go to gardens in Suzhou.*)", the focus "苏州 (*Suzhou*)" and "园林 (*Garden*)" are all tourism attributes and no name is in. So its query type is NO.2. With this query type, JSQA will start appropriate modules F2 shown in Figure 1.

Classifying the user query before analyzing helps alleviate problems related to matching with keywords and tourism information on Q&A described above.

### 3.4 Integration

This is contrast to the usual QA paradigm that the user query is used to search two databases QADB and TSDB of answers. In this case the query is used to match with the theme of keywords and tourism information that are associated with answers. However, this involves addressing the word mismatch problem between the user query and answers before adding tourism information which is the major challenge for tourism Q&A.

JSQA has four functions. They are F1~F4 shown in Figure1 that start different modules to handle the user query according to query types. On the basis of Jiangsu tourism, which function being started in system is determined by the focus in users' queries. To summarize, the focus formula is [±names of tourism sites] [± tourism natures]. So F1~F4 will be started by those query types in Table1 respectively.

First, F1 is used to return all information about one certain tourism site if only its name contained in the user query. And F1 starts modules of names matching and ranking. Second, F2 is used to return all information about some certain tourism sites if different tourism attributes contained which starts modules of attributes matching and ranking. Third, F3 is used to return some certain information about one tourism site if both in. F3 is the most complex function which starts all modules to get last answer in Figure 1. And only a single answer was returned for each query. F4 is used to return other replies if neither in.

For example, given the query "中山陵在哪个城市？ (*What city is the Dr. Sun Yat-sen's Mausoleum at?*)", its query type is NO.3 in Table 3 because both the name "中山陵 (*Dr. Sun Yat-sen's Mausoleum*)" and the attribute "城市 (*City*)" contained. Then F3 will start. Processes in F3 are two steps. Step1: the theme of keywords 城市

(*City*) in the query tells JSQA that the theme city is being looking for. After ID-match, answer pairs can return the answer model "景点所在地是：(*The city is :)*". Stpe2: the word "城市 (*City*)" is not only a theme of keywords but also a tourism attribute. So both tourism name and attribute matching are started to filter tourism information which satisfies "中山陵 (*Dr. Sun Yat-sen's Mausoleum*)" and "城市 (*City*)". Sorted by match value assigned a rank in reverse order, the first answers "南京 (*Nanjing*)" can be placed outside. At last, the answer model and the answer are synthesized. The exact answer "景点所在地是：南京 (*The city is: Nanjing.*)" can be returned.

## 4     Conclusion

In this paper, we introduced the design and implementation of JSQA. To solve problems associated with query classification and tourism information described above, Q&A database (QADB) and tourism sites database (TSDB) perform well in our system. The former can deal with real question sentences and return natural answers. The latter can store a large number of tourism information in Jiangsu. On the basis of two databases, JSQA can return four kinds of precise and appropriate answers in a more related sentence by using approaches of analyzing the theme of keywords and four query types.

JSQA has launched an online service and will be applied to other areas like education. Although our system is still a single-round Q&A system, experiments show that the JSQA is feasible and effective. At last, we have the hope to assume that there is scope for its improvement to be a multi-round Q&A system through modifying algorithm, designing a better matching mechanism and adding tourism information and question-answer pairs.

**Acknowledgement.** This paper is supported in part by National Social Science Fund of China under contract 10CYY021, China PostDoc Fund under contract 2012M510178, Jiangsu PostDoc Fund under contract 1101065C, A Project Funded by the Priority Academic Program Development of Jiangsu Higher Education Institutions.

## References

1. Feng, Z.W.: Man-machine Interaction and Linguistic Research. 人机对话与语言研究. Language Planning, China (1987)
2. Dong, S.H.: Progress and Challenge of Human-Computer Interaction. 人机交互的进展及面临的挑战. Journal of Computer-Aided Design & Computer Graphics (1), 16 (2004)
3. Chen, H., Han, J.Q., Deng, H.Q., Li, X.M.: Research and Implementation of Specific Domain Based Human Computer Dialogue. 面向特定领域人机对话模型研究与实现. College of Information Science and Technology. Peking University, Beijing (2004)

4. Zhang, G., Liu, T., Zheng, S.F., Che, W.X., Qin, B., Li, S.: Research on Open-domain Chinese Question-Answering System. 开放域中文问答系统的研究与实现, Collection of Information Retrieval Laboratory, Harbin Institute of Technology, China, vol. 1 (2003)
5. Richard, J.C., Stefan, M.R.: A Simple Question Answering System. In: Proceedings of the Ninth Text Retrieval Conference (TREC-9), London, UK (2000)
6. Abraham, I., Salim, R.: IBM's Statistical Question Answering System. In: Proceedings of the Ninth Text Retrieval Conference (TREC-9), New York, USA (2000)
7. Tatsunori, M., Shimpei, K., Madoka, I.: Answering Contextual Questions Based on the Cohesion with Knowledge. International Journal of Computer Processing of Oriental Languages (20), 115–135 (2007)
8. Xia, T., Fan, X.Z., Liu, L.: ALICE Mechanism Analysis and Application Study. ALICE机理分析与应用研究, vol. 23. Computer Applications, China (2003)
9. Yu, Z.T., Deng, J.H., Han, L., Mao, C.L., Zheng, Z.Y., Guo, J.Y.: A FAQ Ques-tion Answering System Based on Restricted Domain. 受限域FAQ中文问答系统研究. Journal of Computer Research and Development (44), 388–393 (2007)
10. Xu, Z.C., Hu, X.P., Li, Y.M., Huang, M.F.: A Man-Machine Interaction Soft-ware-Robot for E-Commerce Order. 电子商务订单拟人化实时处理的人机对话软件机器人研究. Journal of Harbin Institute of Technology 38 (2006)
11. Luke, W., Laura, T.: PHP and MySQL Web Development, 4th revised edn. Addison-Wesley Educational Publishers Inc. (2008)
12. Nie, Q.P.: PHP+MySQL Dynamic Web Development and Whole Instance. PHP+MySQL动态网站开发与全程实例. Tsinghua University Press, China (2009)
13. Amit, S.: Entity based Q&A retrieval. In: Proceedings of the 2012 Joint Conference on Empirical Methods in Natural Language Processing and Computational Natural Language Learning, PA, USA, pp. 1266–1277. Association for Computational Linguistics (2012)

# The Extracting Method of Chinese-Naxi Translation Template Based on Improved Dependency Tree-To-String

Lei Li[1,2], Zhengtao Yu[1,2,*], Cunli Mao[1,2], and Jianyi Guo[1,2]

[1] School of Information Engineering and Automation, Kunming University of Science and Technology, 650500 Yunnan, China
[2] Key Laboratory of Intelligent Information Processing, Kunming University of Science and Technology, 650500 Yunnan, China
ztyu@hotmail.com

**Abstract.** Be aimed at the problem that the loss of aligned information which caused by the different syntactic structure between Chinese and Naxi language, we put forward a method of template extraction based on improved dependency tree-to-string which could improve the effect of translation template. First of all, the method analyzes the dependency-tree of source language and the string of target language, according to the relationship of alignment, maps the dependency-tree of source language to the string of target language. Then, according to the dependency relationship of the words in the source language, we get aligned words and the unaligned words in the source language, at the same time, merge and extend the unaligned words to the aligned words. Finally, we could extract the translation template by the recursive method. In addition, we do some comparative experiments about the improved and the former method. The experimental results show that the improved method has better effect; the Accuracy is increased by 5.14%. In the process of translation, the method can effectively solve the loss of the unaligned words.

**Keywords:** Chinese- Naxi, Translation template, Improved dependency tree to string, Merge operation.

## 1    Introduction

The language of Naxi is a unique language in Lijiang of China, which belongs to the Dongba hieroglyphs. In the syntactical aspects, the order of the words in the sentence and the verb collocation are the main means to constitute the syntax. Because the language of Naxi is a typical "Verb-final" language [1], and has a great difference with Chinese in the grammatical structure, there are still many problems to be solved in the bilingual translation. At present, syntax-based statistical machine translation is the mainstream method in SMT. For example; the statistical machine translation model based on string-to-tree which is proposed by Japan's Yamada [2] inosculates the message of target language, and gets the result that the generated target language

---

* Corresponding author.

P. Liu and Q. Su (Eds.): CLSW 2013, LNAI 8229, pp. 350–358, 2013.
© Springer-Verlag Berlin Heidelberg 2013

is more consistent with the rules of grammar. Liu [3] proposed the statistical machine translation model based on tree-to-string. The model uses the structural information of source language in phrase tree, and combines the method of tree-to-string to complete the translation. Liu Yang et al. [4] proposed the statistical machine translation model based on tree-to-tree. It uses the information of source languages and target languages in parse tree into machine translation adequately, and gets good results. Liu Qun et al. [5] proposed the method of statistical machine translation based on dependency tree-to-string. First, the method analyzes the dependency structure of the source language, and then uses the relationship of alignment which is analyzed before to map the dependency-tree to the target language for extracting the translation template. Because the method puts the dependency relationship into the process of translation and the syntactical analysis is simple relatively, the method has been widely used.

There are great structural differences between Chinese and Naxi language, and there are many unaligned words in the bilingual translation. Such as Figure 1.

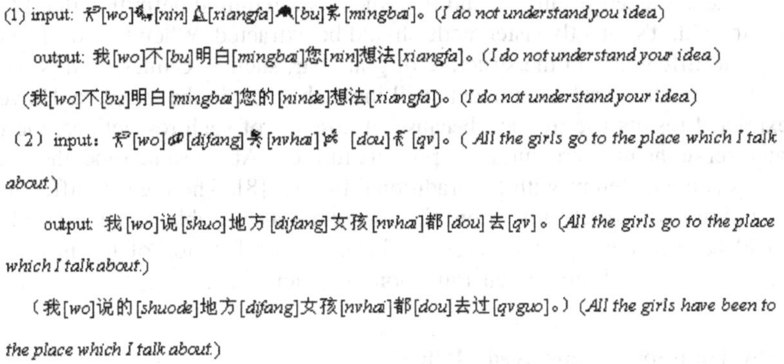

(1) input: 我[wo]你[nin] 你[xiangfa] 不[bu]意 [mingba]。 (I do not understand you idea)

output: 我[wo]不[bu]明白[mingba]您[nin]想法[xiangfa]。 (I do not understand your idea)

(我[wo]不[bu]明白[mingba]您的[ninde]想法[xiangfa])。 (I do not understand your idea)

（2）input: 我[wo]地方[difang]女孩[nvha] 都 [dou]去 [qv]。 ( All the girls go to the place which I talk about)

output: 我 [wo]说 [shuo]地方 [difang]女孩 [nvha]都 [dou] 去[qv] 。 (All the girls go to the place which I talk about)

（我[wo]说的 [shuode]地方 [difang]女孩[nvha]都 [dou]去过 [qvguo]。） (All the girls have been to the place which I talk about)

**Fig. 1.** The example of translation

In the above example, some words don't appear in Naxi language. This causes these words missing in the process of translation, and leads to the result that the Chinese sentences can't be properly understood. If we use the method of statistical machine translation based on the dependency tree-to-string, it'll lead to the problem of the unaligned words missing in the results. The main reason is the template doesn't pay attention to the translation of unaligned words. In this paper, we put forward an extracting method of Chinese-Naxi translation template based on improved dependency tree-to-string. In the process of template extraction, it merges and extends the unaligned words into the translation template, and solves the problem caused by unaligned words in the statistical machine translation.

## 2     The Improved Method of Translation Template Extraction

### 2.1     The Definition of the Improved Translation Template

Because the extracting results are from Chinese dependency-tree and corresponding fragments of Naxi string, the template is defined as a triplet (CDT, NS, A).

Among them, "CDT" is the fragment of Chinese dependency-tree, "NS" is the corresponding string of Naxi language, and "A" is aligned relationship between "CDT" and "NS". For the element of "A" in the triplet, the section of <D, S> must be consisting with the aligned matrix of the entire sentence [6]. That is:

$$\forall (i, j) \in M, i \in D \leftrightarrow j \in S \tag{1}$$

In fact, it is required the both side of translation section should be corresponding. Otherwise, translation template will not be generated for the words. But the improved method does not need all of the words correspond to each other. It is because that the method could get the aligned words and associated unaligned words according to the context of dependency-tree in the source language. As the unaligned words appeared, the method will uses the merged operation to integrate the unaligned words with the associated aligned words, and generate a translation template.

For the element of "CDT" in the triplet, we use tree-let to take place of sub-tree. Because if the extracted result is a sub-tree, there is a required definition that [7] if a node is extracted, it's directly sister' node should be extracted. When the two languages have great differences in the structure of grammar, such as Chinese and Naxi language, some non-structural components will inevitably lost in the template. However, if the extracted results use tree-let, because of absence of such restrictions, the template can reserve the non-structural components furthest. At the same time, the tree-let of CDT has some different with the traditional tree-let [8]. The biggest difference is that the traditional tree-let only allow the root node as variable, but the tree-let of CDT could have a number of different variables in the location of the non-central node. This is good for ability of generalization in the template.

## 2.2    The Thinking of Improved Method

As the translation templates have been defined, we analyze the dependency-tree of the source language, and get the aligned words and the associated unaligned words due to the context of the words in the dependency-tree. Then, it combines the unaligned nodes to the associated aligned nodes in a "CDT" according to the dependency of the two words. Finally, using the method of post-order to travel the dependency-tree of source language, and extract the "CDT" in the dependency-tree of source language and its corresponding "NS" as a whole part to conserve in the template. For the parent nodes in the dependency-tree of source language, we not only extract the template corresponding to it, but also make its child nodes represented by non-terminal. At last, merge the non-terminal into it as the extracted result.

## 2.3    Marked the Attributes

After the "CDT" and the "NS" being extracted, it also need to mark the attributes of each node in the tree-let of the "CDT", each node contains three attributes: a central word, central word tags and partial order of the node relative to its parent node. Among them, the attribute of central word and central word tags are similar with the traditional method [9] based on dependency tree-to-string. The difference is the partial order is defined in the tree-let. Because of the language of Naxi is a typical

"Verb-final" language, partial order is aim at finding the correct relative positions in the matching process. For example, if a node relate to its parent node is at the second position in the left sub-tree from right to left, it's partial order in the original dependency-tree is -2. Now, if we extract a tree-let from its parent node and the tree-let only contains one node on the left, the partial order of the node is -1, instead of -2.

After traveling the whole tree and marking on the "CDT", all translation templates can be stored as a translation template set. Extracted translation template is shown in Figure 2.

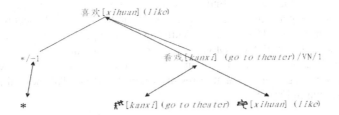

**Fig. 2.** The translation template after Generalization

## 3      The Algorithm of Extraction

Before the extraction of translation template, bilingual training corpus must do syntactical analysis in Chinese side to get the aligned relationship. Then, algorithm gets the corresponding target string of Naxi according to the aligned relationship. Finally, algorithm uses the improved translation template to extract. The dependency-tree which is got by aligned relationship is shown in Figure 3.

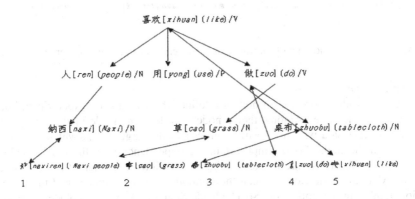

**Fig. 3.** The Dependency tree is used in the algorithm for extraction

The entire algorithm of extraction consists of two steps: First step, algorithm of extraction gets the aligned words and associated unaligned words in the target language based on the context of the source language, and merges the associated un-aligned words into the aligned words, then marks each node's related attributes. Second step, extractor will extract translation template on each node recursively according to the attributes which marked in the first step.

## 3.1    Merged Operation and Node Annotation

### Merged Operation

The merged operation analyzes the Chinese dependency-tree, and gets the dependencies between aligned words and unaligned words due to the dependencies of the words in the Chinese dependency-tree. Then, it scans the dependency-tree of Chinese from the bottom to the top. If it finds the unaligned node, it will merge the unaligned node in Chinese dependency-tree into the aligned nodes as a whole according to the achieved dependencies. Then continue with the above operation, until all unaligned nodes are merged completely. Obviously, using such operations could extract and preserve the different syntactical structure between the Chinese and the Naxi, and use this information to get more suitable results when decoding. The new aligned relationship is shown in Figure 4.

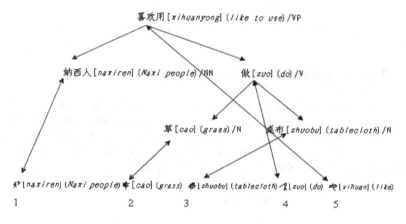

**Fig. 4.** The aligned relationship of each node in the dependency tree after the merge operation

### Node Annotation

In Chinese dependency-tree, each node all defines three attributes: Node-Span, Sub-tree Span, and Include. Among them, node's Node-Span is defined as a closed interval; it is consisted with the position number of the target string which is corresponding with the node. For example, if in the dependency-tree, the corresponding target words node of "A" are located at 1, 3, 4 positions in the target string. Node-Span of "A" is the collection between the minimum position number and the largest position number in this collection. So The Node-Span of "A" is [1, 4].Node's Sub-tree Span is defined as the closed interval formed by the node's Node-Span and its direct child node's Node-Span. For example, if in the above example that node "A" is a direct child node of node "B", and Node-Span of node "B" is [2, 3].Then the Sub-tree Span of node "B" is [1, 4].

In addition to these two attributes, the algorithm also introduces a third attribute: Include. This at-tribute is an indicator with the value of {0, 1}.It can be getting based on the node's Node-Span and Sub-tree Span. The leaf nodes do not have a child node, so its Node-Span and Sub-tree Span are the same. If a node's Node-Span and Sub-tree Span are exactly identical, the node is a leaf node. Its value is set to "1", and otherwise the value is "0". The purpose to introduce this attribute is to find the leaf node, because only the leaf nodes may be extracted independently. For the aligned relationship of the nodes in Figure 3, all nodes' value of attributes is shown in Table 1.

**Table 1.** The three attributes of all nodes

| 节点[jiedian](node) | Node Span | Subtree Span | Include |
|---|---|---|---|
| 纳西人[naxiren](Naxi people)/NN | [1, 1] | [1, 1] | 0 |
| 喜欢用[xihuanyong](like to use)/VP | [5, 5] | [1, 4] | 1 |
| 草[cao](grass)/N | [2, 2] | [2, 2] | 0 |
| 做[zuo](do)/N | [4, 4] | [2, 3] | 1 |
| 桌布[zhuobu](tablecloth)/N | [3, 3] | [3, 3] | 0 |

## 3.2    Translation Template Extraction

After marking the attributes of each node, algorithm of extraction runs recursively. If the value of the node's Include is "0", the algorithm will extract the template directly, then generalize the node and generate translation templates with its parent node. If the value is "1", algorithm will generate all the possible translation templates whose root node is the above node. The method is to merge the translation template of the child nodes and the combination of the child nodes. The details of this algorithm is given below, the translation templates according to the algorithm are shown in Table 2.

```
/ * Description of the algorithm
  * Input: the nodes of dependency-tree which marked va-
    riety of attributes
  * Output: extracted translation templates
  * "n" is some node, "T" is the number of nodes-1,"R"
    and "L" are two empty stacks /
    for i=0 to T do
      if n.include!=1 then
      Mark the position of its parent node, and ex-
      tract the template to join the "R" and "L"
      else if  n.include==1 then
      Take the elements whose parent node location is
      "i" in the stack "L" with n.value to generate
      translation template then join in "R"
      L(1) = "*"
          L(1).value and n.value generate translation
          templates then join in "R"
      end if
    end for
Output R
```

**Table 2.** The final translation template. (* represents a variable after generalization)

| Treelet | String |
|---|---|
| (纳西人[naxiren] (Naxi people)/NN/0) | 木*[naxiren] (Naxi people) |
| (桌布[zhuobu] (tablecloth)/N/0) | 毳[zhuobu] (tablecloth) |
| (做[zuo] (do)/V/0) | 乚[zuo] (do) |
| (做[zuo] (do)/V/0 (桌布[zhuobu] (tablecloth)/N/1)) | 毳[zhuobu] (tablecloth) 乚[zuo] (do) |
| (做[zuo] (do)/V/0 (*/1)) | •乚[zuo] (do) |
| (草[cao] (grass)/N/0) | 丰[cao] (grass) |
| (喜欢用[xihuanyong] (like to use)/VP/0 (*/-1)) | 乞[xihuan] (like) |
| (喜欢用[xihuanyong] (like to use)/VP/0 (*/-1)) (草[cao] (grass)/N/0) | 丰[cao] (grass) • 乞[xihuan] (like) |
| (喜欢用[xihuanyong] (like to use)/VP/0 (*₁/-1) (*₂/1)) | • • 乞[xihuan] (like) |

# 4 Experiments and Analysis

## 4.1 The Preparation of Experimental Data

Due to the research of Naxi language translation is in the initial stages, few corpuses can be used in the Naxi language. So we organize, collect and develop the corpuses of Chinese-Naxi by ourselves (Training corpus, The development set, The test set).The Naxi language is from the dictionary of Chinese-Naxi and Nine-year compulsory education in elementary school, junior high school textbook (Naxi language).In order to improve the accuracy of the translation, we select 15,987 pairs of sentences from the training corpus as the development set which is written based on the thesaurus recently. The test set uses pre-collected 7,327 pairs of sentences and the average length of these sentences are 11.7 words. Specific situation is shown in Table 3.

**Table 3.** The condition of all Corpus

| | The number of Sentence/pairs of sentence | The number of the words in Naxi | The number of the words in Chinese |
|---|---|---|---|
| The parallel corpus | 35k | 548k | 822k |
| The training corpus | 24k | 295k | 547k |
| The development set | 16k | 146k | 235k |
| The test set | 7k | 70k | 109k |

## 4.2   Experiments and Results

### The Selection of Experimental Tools

In order to test the effect of improved template ex-traction model, we design comparative experiments in the direction of Chinese to Naxi. Experimental system is used the "Silk Road" (Version 1.0) as the prototype [10]. Dependency syntactical parser uses the "ctbparser" [11].

We use the training corpus to train the translation template. At first, use "ctbparser" to analyze the Chinese sentence in the bilingual corpus. Then, get a XML file which has been segmented and aligned. Finally, we use the traditional template extraction method and the improved template ex-traction method to extract the template from the XML file. After extraction, it will derive the experimental results to test from development set and the test set, and use the BLEU-3 and the Accuracy as an evaluative index for evaluation.

### The Analysis of Experimental Results

We analyze the experimental results. 17,260 (not repeated) translation templates are extracted by using the improved method. Among them, 2340 could match with the test set. The experimental results are shown in Table 4.The experimental results given in the table show that in the case using the same language model and decoder, the value of BLEU-3 is increased by 1.74%, and the value of Accuracy is increased by 5.31% using the improved translation template extraction model in the development set. The experiments in the test set, the value of BLEU-3 is increased by 1.66%, and the value of Accuracy is increased by 4.98%.The experiment results show that using the improved method to extract the template can improve the performance of SMT.

**Table 4.** The results of these experiments

| The Method of Extraction | Development set (15187) | | Test set (7327) | |
|---|---|---|---|---|
| | BLEU-3 | Accuracy | BLEU-3 | Accuracy |
| Traditional Method | 21.25% | 63.76% | 22.46% | 67.39% |
| Improved Method | 22.99% | 68.98% | 24.12% | 72.37% |

## 5    Conclusions and Future Work

Due to the loss of aligned information which is caused by different structure between Chinese and Naxi, we put forward an extracting method of Chinese-Naxi translation template based on improved dependency tree-to-string. The experimental results show that for languages with the different grammatical structure, the improved method has greatly improved than the former method in the value of BLEU-3 and Accuracy. In the future, we will expand the scale of corpus, and apply the method of dependency tree-to-dependency tree and tree-to-forest to the Chinese-Naxi statistical ma-chine translation in order to improve the performance of system.

**Acknowledgments.** This work was supported by National Natural Science Foundation of China, Contract No. 61163022.

# References

1. Yang, J.: The milepost of Naxi pictographs-"dictionary of Naxi pictographs". Journal of Chinese Books and Culture 2(1), 31–33 (1997)
2. Yamada, K., Knight, K.: A Decoder for Syntax-Based Statistical MT. In: Proceedings of the ACL, pp. 295–302 (2007)
3. Liu, Z., Wang, H., Wu, H.: Example based machine translation based on TSC and statistical generation. In: Proceedings the Tenth Machine Translation Summit, pp. 25–32 (2005)
4. Liu, Y., Lv, Y., Liu, Q., Xiong, H.: The method of translation template extraction Based on the model of tree to tree. Journal of Chinese Information Processing 20(5), 29–39 (2006)
5. Liu, Q., Xiong, D., Lin, S.: A survey of Syntax-based in the Statistical Machine Translation. Journal of Chinese Information Processing 22(2), 28–39 (2008)
6. Xiao, T., Li, T., Chen, R., Zhu, J., Wang, H.: The method of realignment for statistical machine translation. Journal of Chinese Information Processing 24(1), 110–117 (2010)
7. Dang, Z., Zhou, Q.: The automatic conversion of Phrase trees to dependency trees. Journal of Chinese Information Processing 19(3), 21–27 (2005)
8. Quirk, H., Menezes, A., Cherry, C.: Dependency Tree-let Translation: Syntactically Informed Phrasal SMT. In: Proceedings of ACL, pp. 115–124 (2005)
9. Huang, Y., Lv, Y., Liu, Y., Liu, Q.: The algorithm of align the template based on dependency trees to string translation model. Journal of Chinese Information Processing 17(3), 37–45 (2007)
10. Stolcke. Silk Road- A Language Modeling Toolkit. In: Proceedings of International Conference on Spoken Language Processing, pp. 901–904 (2006)
11. Cao, H., Zhao, T., Li, S.: Based on head-driven model Chinese tree bank (CTB) syntax analysis. Journal of Communications of High Technology 17(1), 15–20 (2007)

# A Customized Lexicalized Reordering Model for Machine Translation between Chinese and English

Fei Su[1], Jin Huang[2], and Kaile Su[1]

[1] Department of Computer Science
Peking University
{feisu,kaile}@pku.edu.cn
[2] Youdao Inc.
Beijing, China
huangjin@rd.netease.com

**Abstract.** Lexicalized reordering model is adopted in state-of-the-art phrase-based machine translation systems to help formulate a better word reordering of translation results. The most widely-used MSD (Monotone, Swap, Discontinuous) reordering model is designed generically and has been used in every language pair without customization. However, in the scenarios of translation between Chinese and English, the word reordering distance tends to be long due to the syntax difference between English and Chinese, in which case MSD model is likely to deliver unappropriate results.

Based on intensive investigation on large English-Chinese bilingual corpus, we redesign the orientation set of the reordering model and propose a new lexicalized reordering model MLR (Monotone, LeftDiscontinuous, RightDiscontinuous), which is tailored for C2E and E2C MT. MLR can handel long-distance word reordering well. The superiority of MLR is verified in our empirical studies and has already been applied to Youdao online translation system (http://fanyi.youdao.com)[1].

**Keywords:** Machine translation, Phrase-base model, Lexicalized reordering model.

## 1 Introduction

Despite an enormous progress in the field of machine translation (MT) in recent years, the word reordering problem remains intractable, for it is the syntax difference that leads to the word reordering between two languages in translation, while the related syntax analysis is far from perfect till now.

---

[1] The work was done during the internship of the first author at NetEase Youdao.

P. Liu and Q. Su (Eds.): CLSW 2013, LNAI 8229, pp. 359–367, 2013.
© Springer-Verlag Berlin Heidelberg 2013

## 1.1   The MSD Lexicalized Reordering Model

To tackle the word reordering problem without deep syntax analysis, [1] has introduced MSD lexicalized reordering model, which becomes one of the major components in current phrase-based MT.

In this model, the relative position of a phrase pair according to the previous one is classified into three orientations: Monotone, Swap and Discontinuous (Figure 1).

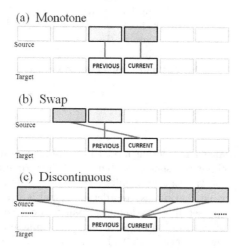

**Fig. 1.** MSD Model

For example in Figure 2, the prepositional phrase (PP) "on Monday" in the first sentence pair is classified as Discontinuous, "in Washington" in the second sentence is classified as Swap, "went to" in the first sentence is classified as Monotone.

**Fig. 2.** Word reordering in E2C translation

The reordering tendency of a phrase pair is measured by conditional probability. In the training corpus, for each extracted phrase pair $(e, f)$, we count its total occurrence $\#(e, f)$; and $\#(o, e, f)$, its occurrence for a certain orientation $o \in Ori$, where

$$Ori = \{Monotone, Swap, Discontinuous\} \tag{1}$$

The orientation conditional probability for a phrase $(e, f)$ is as follows:

$$P(o|e, f) = \frac{\#(o, e, f)}{\#(e, f)} = \frac{\#(o, e, f)}{\sum_{o' \in Ori} \#(o', e, f)} \tag{2}$$

The log conditional probability is used as a feature in the translation step to help determine the position of each phrase pair. For instance, the phrase pair with target side "on monday" has the biggest probability in the orientation "Discontinuous", thus suggesting that this phrase should not be placed right after the previous one.

## 1.2  Word Reordering between Chinese and English

Comparing to the translation between English and other European languages, the word reordering distance tends to be longer in translation between English and Chinese. This attributes to their syntax difference in prepositional phrases (PP), for most of the reordering in C2E or E2C MT are related to PP.

A PP is usually put after its attached host in English. However, there is an opposite syntax of PP in Chinese. We can see from Figure 2, no matter the PP is attached to a noun phrase (as in the first pair) or a verb phrase (as in the second pair) in English, it is located in front of its host in both two Chinese sentences.

Today, when we acquire the C2E or E2C translation results yielded by a state-of-the-art MT like Google Translation, a plenty of reordering mistakes can still be found.

## 1.3  Lexicalized Model Should Be Customized

Statistics from our Chinese-English corpus (a bilingual corpus of about 2M sentences) shows that, of all three reordering orientations in MSD, Discontinuous takes the largest proportion 49.3%, while Swap only takes 3.2%. This unbalance is not found when translating English into other European languages. It can be explained by syntax difference on PP. A PP in English has to be reordered across two or more phrases to the front of its attached host in Chinese, in which case the orientation is classified as Discontinues. Unfortunately, the overwhelming Discontinuous brings out the following two problems:

**Less Informative**: comparing to Monotone and Swap, Discontinuous contains less information about the reordering direction for it is direction-neutral (see Figure 1). The huge amount of Discontinuous renders lexical reordering features less efficient.

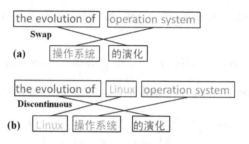

**Fig. 3.** MSD classification is unstable

Based on intensive investigation on our 2M English-Chinese bilingual corpus, we find a more appropriate way to divide the reordering relationship in E2C (C2E) MT. In the next section, we propose a new lexicalized reordering model customized for translation between English and Chinese.

## 2    A Customized Lexicalized Reordering Model for C2E and E2C MT

### 2.1    A New Lexicalized Model: MLR

Based on the characteristics of word reordering between Chinese and English, we propose a lexicalized model MLR, which applies the following orientations:

$Ori = \{Monotone, LeftDiscontinuous, RightDiscontinuous\}$

In MLR, The original Discontinuous in MSD is divided into LeftDiscontinuous and RightDiscontinuous, while Swap is merged into RightDiscontinuous (4).

Comparing to MSD, MLR has the following advantages:

First of all, LeftDiscontinuous and RightDiscontinuous keep more information on reordering direction. For example, In E2C MT, PPs such as "on monday" tend to be reordered to the **left** of its host. This tendency can be clearly observed in MLR, but not in MSD (see Table 1, the data is based on the 2M Chinese-English corpus).

**Table 1.** $P(o|e, f)$ on MLR and MSD with $e =$ "on monday"

| MLR | Mono | L-Dis | R-Dis |
|-----|------|-------|-------|
|     | 0.289 | **0.612** | 0.099 |
| MSD | Mono | Swap | Disc |
|     | 0.289 | 0.187 | **0.524** |

Secondly, MLR behaves more consistently comparing to MSD. To illustrate this, we go back to two similar cases in Figure 3, which are classified differently as Swap and Discontinuous in MSD. Now they are all classified as RightDiscontinuous. Hence the fact that a PP in English tends to be reordered to the left of its attached host in Chinese can be easily observed in MLR.

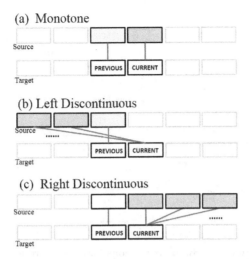

**Fig. 4.** MLR Model

In addition, in MLR three reordering types are more evenly distributed in E2C training corpus. we made a statistics on the proportion of reordering relationships when translating about 2M English news sentences into Chinese, the results are shown in Figure 5.

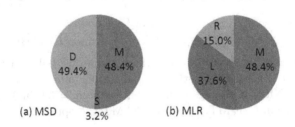

**Fig. 5.** Orientation distribution in the training corpus

## 2.2   Define Orientation: Word Alignments or Phrase Alignments

Orientation probability $P(o|e, f)$ is calculated in phrase extraction step. The orientation can be defined based on word alignments, or phrase alignments (Figure 6).

Previous works usually define orientations based on word alignments (Figure 6 (a) ), which also results in the problem of excess Discontinuous. For example in Figure 6 (b), the two occasions will be classified separately as Monotone and Swap in phrase-based definition, but both of them will be recognized as Discontinuous in word based-based definition, in which case the information of reordering direction is lost.

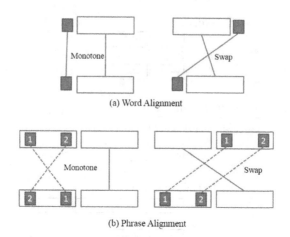

(a) Word Alignment

(b) Phrase Alignment

**Fig. 6.** Define Monotone and Swap orientations based on word alignments and phrase alignments

In the MLR model, we define the orientation based on phrase alignments.

### 2.3   Smoothing for MLR

Most of the extracted phrases have very limited occurrences in the corpus (in our experiments, nearly half of the phrases occur only once), which leads to over-fitting. To avoid this, a simple add-N smoothing is applied to $P(o|e, f)$:

$$P(o|e, f) = \frac{\#(o, e, f) + smooth}{\sum_{o' \in Ori} \#(o', e, f) + smooth * |Ori|} \tag{3}$$

In Moses, *smooth* is set to 0.5 by default, while we believed that its value should be adjusted according to the specific corpus and language pairs. In our experiments on NIST data set, we find that $smooth = 3.0$ in MLR yields the best performance in C2E MT, while in E2C MT the optimal value is still 0.5.

## 3   Experiments and Evaluation

The MT system in our experiments is based on Moses [2]. Word alignments are generated by GIZA++ [3]. Feature parameters are tuned by Z-MERT [4].

We extract about 2M English-Chinese sentence pairs from several large bilingual websites (mostly news, such as China Daily news and Xinhua news). There are about 61M English words and 60M Chinese words. Of all these sentence pairs, we sample 1000 as our development set to tune parameters, the rest of them are used as training set. The experiments are based on two MT directions: E2C and C2E. BLEU [5] and NIST [6] are used as the evaluation standards. Translation results are evaluated on NIST05 and NIST06 data sets.

Besides the basic MSD lexicalized model, other reordering models have been proposed.

**MSLR**: It is a reordering model with four orientations: Monotone, Swap, Left-Discontinuous, RightDiscontinuous. It is first proposed by [7]. Comparing to MLR, it splits RightDiscontinuous into two parts, which again causes the problem of inconsistency mentioned in section 1.3.

**Hierarchical Phrase Reordering Model**: It is proposed by [8], and is proved promising in later experiments. The model is still based on MSD. It expands the definition of Swap to make the three orientations more evenly distributed. In our experiments, We find that in many cases, Swap in hierarchical model is equivalent to LeftDiscontinuous in MLR. Comparing to MLR, hierarchical reordering model is more sophisticated.

Under the same parameter settings, the above two models are also compared with MLR.

The C2E and E2C results are listed in Table 2 and Table 3. It seems that MSLR is not a good choice in either direction. Hierarchical model has desirable records in C2E direction but not in E2C. Comparing to the baseline MSD, the adoption of MLR yields 0.5% BLEU gain on average in both direction.

Comparing the results of MLR to that of basic MSD, we notice an interesting phenomenon: except for improving the word order, MLR also improves the word selection of the translation result to make it more readable. There are two possible reasons: 1. A better reordering feature can help segment the source sentence in the right way, for a reasonable segmentation such as PP often has a higher reordering feature score; 2. After the reordering of a translation is improved, the language model feature plays a better role to improve the word selection. The further reason of this phenomenon is still under investigation.

In summary, we believe that MLR is a better option for reordering model in both C2E and E2C MT. This has also been proved in our user log evaluation sets besides NIST data sets.

**Table 2.** C2E MT evaluation

| Model | NIST 05 | | NIST 06 | |
|---|---|---|---|---|
| | BLEU | NIST | BLEU | NIST |
| MSD | 0.3152 | 8.7658 | 0.3024 | 8.5761 |
| MSLR | 0.3179 | 8.8359 | 0.3057 | 8.6238 |
| Hierachy | **0.3215** | **8.8513** | 0.3076 | 8.6273 |
| MLR | 0.3208 | 8.8501 | **0.3083** | **8.6344** |

**Table 3.** E2C MT evaluation

| Model | NIST 05 | | NIST 06 | |
|---|---|---|---|---|
| | BLEU | NIST | BLEU | NIST |
| MSD | 0.3407 | 8.9178 | 0.3438 | 8.9264 |
| MSLR | 0.3405 | 8.9154 | 0.3442 | 8.9267 |
| Hierachy | 0.3421 | 8.9536 | 0.3471 | 9.0775 |
| MLR | **0.3450** | **8.9727** | **0.3490** | **9.0864** |

## 4    Related Work

The basic lexicalized reordering model is proposed by [1], which is equivalent to MSD. It is also adopted by [9] and [7]. Later, orientation with four types *MonotoneAdjacent, MonotoneGap, ReverseAdjacent* and *ReverseGap* is proposed in [7] and [10]. It is equivalent to MSLR. In [11], reordering problem is treated as a binary classification task with the output {*straight, inverted*}.

Most of the previous works define the orientation based on word alignments, except for [8], which is based on phrase alignments. Notice that MLR is also based on phrase alignments.

Our work in this paper is mainly based on phrase-based translation model. The hierarchical phrase-based model [12] treat the word reordering problem in a completely different way, thus is beyond the scope of our discussion here.

## 5    Conclusions

In this paper we focus on improving the word reordering in machine translation between Chinese and English. After observing that the original MSD reordering model yields unbalanced orientation results (too much Discontinuous), we propose MLR, a lexical reordering model customized for C2E and E2C MT. We compare it with other popular reordering models in our experiments and has proved its superiority. Our work has already been put into practice in Youdao Translation (http://fanyi.youdao.com).

In the future, we intend to test the feasibility of MLR lexicalized model on other language pairs, and explore other reasonable ways to divide the reordering relationship.

**Acknowledgements.** The authors would like to thank Junjie Yao for his kindly help in formulating the paper, and thank Xin Chen and Qifeng Sun in Youdao inc, for their constructive instructions. This work is supported by 973 Program (2010CB328103).

## References

1. Tillmann, C.: A unigram orientation model for statistical machine translation. In: Proceedings of HLT-NAACL 2004: Short Papers. Association for Computational Linguistics, pp. 101–104 (2004)
2. Koehn, P., Hoang, H., Birch, A., Callison-Burch, C., Federico, M., Bertoldi, N., Cowan, B., Shen, W., Moran, C., Zens, R., et al.: Moses: Open source toolkit for statistical machine translation. In: Proceedings of the 45th Annual Meeting of the ACL on Interactive Poster and Demonstration Sessions. Association for Computational Linguistics, pp. 177–180 (2007)
3. Och, F., Ney, H.: Improved statistical alignment models. In: Proceedings of the 38th Annual Meeting on Association for Computational Linguistics. Association for Computational Linguistics, pp. 440–447 (2000)

4. Zaidan, O.: Z-mert: A fully configurable open source tool for minimum error rate training of machine translation systems. The Prague Bulletin of Mathematical Linguistics 91(-1), 79–88 (2009)
5. Papineni, K., Roukos, S., Ward, T., Zhu, W.: Bleu: a method for automatic evaluation of machine translation. In: Proceedings of the 40th Annual Meeting on Association for Computational Linguistics. Association for Computational Linguistics, pp. 311–318 (2002)
6. Doddington, G.: Automatic evaluation of machine translation quality using n-gram co-occurrence statistics. In: Proceedings of the Second International Conference on Human Language Technology Research, pp. 138–145. Morgan Kaufmann Publishers Inc. (2002)
7. Ohashi, K., Yamamoto, K., Saito, K., Nagata, M.: Nut-ntt statistical machine translation system for iwslt 2005. In: Proceedings of International Workshop on Spoken Language Translation, pp. 128–133 (2005)
8. Galley, M., Manning, C.: A simple and effective hierarchical phrase reordering model. In: Proceedings of the Conference on Empirical Methods in Natural Language Processing. Association for Computational Linguistics, pp. 848–856 (2008)
9. Koehn, P., Axelrod, A., Mayne, A., Callison-Burch, C., Osborne, M., Talbot, D.: Edinburgh system description for the 2005 iwslt speech translation evaluation. In: International Workshop on Spoken Language Translation (2005)
10. Nagata, M., Saito, K., Yamamoto, K., Ohashi, K.: A clustered global phrase reordering model for statistical machine translation. In: Proceedings of the 21st International Conference on Computational Linguistics and the 44th Annual Meeting of the Association for Computational Linguistics. Association for Computational Linguistics, pp. 713–720 (2006)
11. Xiong, D., Liu, Q., Lin, S.: Maximum entropy based phrase reordering model for statistical machine translation. In: Proceedings of the 21st International Conference on Computational Linguistics and the 44th Annual Meeting of the Association for Computational Linguistics. Association for Computational Linguistics, pp. 521–528 (2006)
12. Chiang, D.: Hierarchical phrase-based translation. Computational Linguistics 33(2), 201–228 (2007)

# Incorporating Hierarchical Dirichlet Process into Tag Topic Model

Ming Zhang[1], Tingting He[1,*], Fang Li[2], and Li Peng[1]

[1] School of Computer, Central China Normal University, WuHan, China
{mingzhang0309,theloveyboy}@gmail.com, tthe@ccnu.edu.cn
[2] Engineering & Research Center for Information Technology on Central China Normal University, Wuhan, China
Fang__lf@163.com

**Abstract.** The Latent Dirichlet Allocation (LDA) is a parametric approach and the number of topics must be predefined. So it is natural to try to capture uncertainty regarding the number of topics. This paper proposes a Tag Hierarchical Dirichlet Process (THDP) that automatically infers the number of topics while also leveraging the tag information associated with each document. In this model, we assume that an author is clear in his mind that the content will contains which aspects and for each aspect he will choose a tag to describe it, and then we consider problems involving groups of tag, where each tag within a group is a draw from a mixture model and it is desirable to share topic between groups. In this setting it is natural to consider Hierarchical Dirichlet Process, Where the well-known clustering property of the Dirichlet process provides a nonparametric prior for the number of topic within each tag. Experimental results on corpora demonstrate superior performance over the THDP model.

**Keywords:** Hierarchical Dirichlet Process, Topic Model, Tag.

## 1    Introduction

With the rapid development of web 2.0, the internet has brought a large amount of resources, such as blogs, twitter, and encyclopedia. These resources contain a wealth of information, which can be applied to a variety of fields in information processing to improve the service quality, but it is too deficiency to use tradition human professional to dispose the information when the large volume of information emerge people like tidewater. In natural language processing (NLP), computer programs face several tasks that require human-level intelligence, or the programs should be endowed with the ability of language understanding. One core of the issue is how to automatically obtain knowledge from the web and effectively use them to help our life.

In recent years, blog has become more and more popular. As of 16 February 2011 (2011-02-16), there were over 156 million public blogs in existence. On October 13, 2012, there were around 77 million Tumblr[1] and 56.6 million WordPress[2] blogs

---

* Corresponding author.

P. Liu and Q. Su (Eds.): CLSW 2013, LNAI 8229, pp. 368–377, 2013.
© Springer-Verlag Berlin Heidelberg 2013

in existence worldwide. Blog is a service that allows people to publish messages to share with others what have happened. People not only note down their personal life, but also exchange their opinions towards a broad range of topics. For example, they may express their feelings on politicians or global events. Based on this content, a great deal of interest and meaningful word has been done, such as opinion summarization, sentiment analysis.

A blog is a discussion or informational site published on the World Wide Web and consisting of discrete entries typically displayed in reverse chronological order. It can be seen as knowledge based on wide coverage and good scalability.

Tagging has recently emerged as a popular way to organize user generated content for Web 2.0 applications, such as blogs and bookmarks. In blogs, users can assign one or more tags for each blog. Usually, these tags can reflect the concerned subjects of the contents. Tags can be seen as labeled meta-information about the content, and they are beneficial for knowledge mining from blogs.

In this paper, we extend the Tag topic model (TTM)[3] by crystallized HDP[4] as prior distribution. We assume that an author is clear in his mind that the content will contains which aspects before he writes a blog and for each aspect he will choose a tag to describe it. The THDP represents each document with a mixture of tags, each tag can be viewed as a multinomial distribution over topics and each topic is associated with a multinomial distribution over words. Then we use the clustering property of the Dirichlet process to infer the number of topics. After estimating the parameters of the model, we get the tag-topic and topic-word distributions, then the tags are regarded as concepts, and the top words arranged to the top topics under the tags are selected as the contexts.

The remainder of this paper is organized as follows: Section 2 reviews the related works. Section 3 describes the related models. Section 4 presents the THDP model and introduces the parameter estimation process. Section 5 shows the experimental results synthetic documents and blog corpus. At last, we conclude the paper in Section 6.

## 2    Related Works

Recently, the methods of Nonparametric Bayesian process are widely used. Most existing work on HDP are focused on video surveillance[5], image understanding[6,7] and image annotation[8]. Cowans[9] apply HDP model on information retrieval. Xu[10] proposed HDP-HTM that combines HDP with a Hierarchical Transition Matrix study evolutionary clustering. Yee crystallized HDP as prior distribution of LDA to infer the topic number. Williamson[11] presented the focused topic model for learning sparse topic mixture patterns; this model integrates desirable features from both the HDP and the Indian buffet process (IBP). Chan[12] improve the focused topic model by leveraging contextual information about the author(s) and document venue.

This paper proposes a Tag Hierarchical Dirichlet Process (THDP) that automatically infers the number of topics while also leveraging the tag information associate with each document.

# 3    Overview of Related Models

## 3.1    Tag Topic Model(TTM)

The TTM was proposed by Li in 2011. This model extends LDA by adding a tag layer, the generative process with TTM is as follows.

 For each of the D documents d, choose $\psi_d \sim$ Dirichlet($\eta$)
 For each of the L tags t, choose $\theta_l \sim$ Dirichlet($\alpha$)
 For each of the K topics k, choose $\varphi_k \sim$ Dirichlet($\beta$)
 For each of the $N_d$ words $w_i$ in document d
  - choose a tag   $t_i \sim$ Multinomial($\Psi_d$)
  - choose a topic $z_i \sim$ Multinomial($\theta_t$)
  - choose a word $w_i \sim$ Multinomial($\varphi_z$)

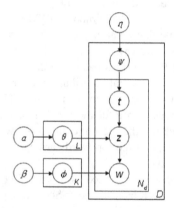

**Fig. 1.** The Tag topic model

The TTM has superior performance on the semantic knowledge acquisition from the corpora, but it must define the topic number and the time complexity of the model is too difficult to detect a best fit value for the corpora.

## 3.2    HDP

We have a nonparametric Bayes model of LDA by using the HDP, called HDP-LDA, The generation process of HDP-LDA is

$$G_0 \mid \gamma, \; H \sim DP(\gamma, H)$$
$$G_j \mid \alpha_0, G_0 \sim DP(\alpha_0, G_0)$$
$$\theta_{ji} \mid G_j \sim G_j$$
$$x_{ji} \mid \theta_{ji} \sim F(\theta_{ji})$$

The hyper parameters of the HDP consist of the baseline probability measure H, and the concentration parameters $\gamma$ and $\alpha_0$. The baseline H provides the prior distribution for the factors $\theta_{ji}$. The distribution $G_0$ varies around the prior H, with the amount of variability governed by $\gamma$. The actual distribution $G_j$ over the factors in the jth group

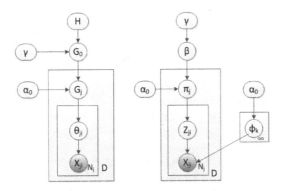

**Fig. 2.** Directed graphical representations of HDP

deviates from $G_0$, with the amount of variability governed by $\alpha_0$. If we expect the variability in different groups to be different, we can use a separate concentration parameter $\alpha_j$ for each group j.

Using a stick-breaking process (SBP), $G_0$ and $G_j$ are represented as sun of point masses given by

$$G_0 = \sum_{k=1}^{\infty} \pi_k \delta_{\psi_k}, G_j = \sum_{k=1}^{\infty} \theta_{j,k} \delta_{\psi_k}, \tag{1}$$

$$\theta_j \sim DP(\alpha_0, \pi), \psi_k \sim Dir(\beta), \tag{2}$$

$$\pi_k = \tilde{\pi}_k \prod_{l=1}^{k-1} (1 - \tilde{\pi}_l), \tilde{\pi}_k \sim Beta(1, \gamma_0) \tag{3}$$

The construction of $\pi$ in Eq.(3) is called the stick-breaking construction and is denoted by $\pi \sim SBP(\gamma_0)$.

## 4     THDP

### 4.1     Model Description

HDP is one of the most popular nonparametric Bayesian approach. The basic idea is that Dirichlet process has a good clustering characteristic and we do not predefine the amount of the category. So the model will become more intelligent.

The THDP topic model draws upon the strengths of the two models (TTM, HDP); using the topic-based representation to model both the content of documents and the tag. As in the THDP model, a group of tags, $T_d$, indicate the mainly purpose of the

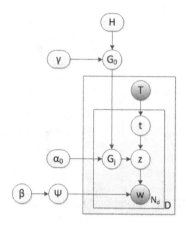

**Fig. 3.** The THDP model

blog. For each word in the document a Tag is chosen uniformly at random. Then, as in the topic model, a topic is chosen from a distribution over topics specific to that tag, and the word is generated form the chosen topic.

We can describe the generative process as follows:

$G_0 \sim DP(\gamma, H)$
For each of the document d, chosen a tag t
For each of the tag t in document d, chosen
  $-G_j \sim DP(\alpha_0, G_0)$
For each of the $N_d$ words $w_i$ in document d
  - chose a topic $z_i \sim G_j$
  - chose a $w_i \sim$ Multinomial $(\psi)$;

Given an underlying measure H on multinomial probability vectors, we select a random measure $G_0$ which provides a countable infinite collection of multinomial probability vectors; these can be viewed as the set of all topics that can be used in a given corpus. For the lth tag in the jth document in the corpus we sample $G_j$ using $G_0$ as a base measure; this selects specific subsets of topics to be used in tag l in document j. From $G_j$ we then generate a document by repeatedly (1) choose a tag with the equal probability from the tag sets associate with the document and (2) sampling specific multinomial probability vectors $z_{ji}$ from $G_j$ and sampling words $w_{ji}$ with probabilities $z_{ji}$. The overlap among the random measures $G_j$ implement the sharing of topics among documents.

## 4.2    Parameter Estimation Process

The published inference algorithms relevant to the HDP belong to Gibbs sampling and variational methods (including collapsed ones). In this paper, we focus on a Gibbs sampling method that empirically proved effective while staying close to the parametric case.

Due to the space limit, we only show the sampling formula, the more inference and equation can be seen[13]; each $(t_i, z_i)$ pair is drawn for word $w_i$ conditioned on all other variables:

$$P(t_i = l, z_i = k \mid \cdot) \propto \frac{n_{l,k}^{-d,i} + \alpha_0 \pi_k}{n_l^{-d,i} + \alpha_0} \cdot \frac{n_{k,w}^{-d,i} + \beta_v}{n_{k,\cdot}^{-d,i} + \beta_0} \tag{4}$$

Where $t_i = l$ and $z_i = k$ represent the assignments of the ith word in the document to tag l and topic k. $n_{l,k}^{-d,i}$ is the number of times that tag l is assigned to topic k, except the current instance, $n_{k,w}^{-d,i}$ is the number of times that word w is assigned to topic k except the current instance.

We need to use the Chinese restaurant process procedure for sampling $\alpha_0$ and $\pi$, where a document, word, and topic represent respectively a restaurant, a customer, and a dish served at a table. The number of tables serving topic k in tag l, i.e., $m_{d,k}$, is sampled using the Stirling numbers of the first kind denoted by $str(\cdot)$:

$$p(m_{l,k} = m \mid n_{l,k}, \alpha_0, \pi_k) = str(n_{d,k}, m)(\alpha_0 \pi_k)^m \frac{\Gamma(\alpha_0 \pi_k)}{\alpha_0 \pi_k + n_{l,k}} \tag{5}$$

The conditional posterior for the mixing proportions $\pi$ is also given as a stick-breaking construction as follows.

$$\tilde{\pi}_k \sim Beta(1 + m_{.,k}, \gamma_0 + \sum_{l=k+1}^{T} m_{.,l}), \tilde{\pi}_T = 1 \tag{6}$$

$$\pi_1 = \tilde{\pi}_1, \pi_k = \tilde{\pi}_k \prod_{l=1}^{k-1} (1 - \tilde{\pi}_l) \tag{7}$$

## 5    Experiment and Result

### 5.1    Dataset and Pre-processing

The dataset used in the experiment is from the blog corpus during October 2011 and December 2012, which is constructed by National Language Resources Monitoring and Research Center, Network Media Branch. After filtering out blog texts with no tags or containing less than 100 words and some preprocessing such as remove stop words and extremely common words, filter out the non-nominal words and retain only the nouns or nominal phrases. The dataset containing the tags and context of N = 927 blog, with W = 10438 words in the vocabulary and T = 558 tags.

### 5.2    Experiment Results

We use both the perplexity and topic numbers for performance evaluations. The perplexity is a standard measure for estimating the generalization performance of probabilistic model, and it is monotonically decreasing in the likelihood of the test data. Lower perplexity score indicates better generalization performance. Fig.4 shows the perplexities with three different numbers of topics for the TTM and THDP, the result shows that the THDP performs better than the TTM. Fig.5 shows the model we proposed infers the number of topics, we initialize the number of topics number to 0, while the number of iterations increases, the topics number also increase, but when the iteration is beyond 600, the topics number will be stable. For the dataset we used in this experiment, the topics number is 114.

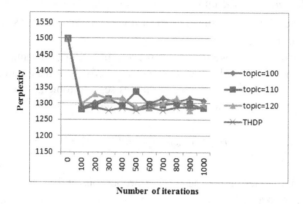

**Fig. 4.** The perplexities for different topic numbers of TTM and THDP

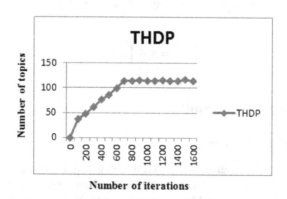

**Fig. 5.** The topic number for different iteration of THDP

## 5.3    Examples of Tag and Topic Distribution

There is no quantitative measure for distributions of topic model, so we evaluate them by observing the top tags assigned to each tag and the top words assigned to the corresponding topics. Fig.6 displays some examples learned by the THDP model.

Each topic is illustrated with the top 10 words and the top 5 tags for the corresponding topics.

As show in the Fig.6, each topic is shown with the 10 words and 5 tags that have the highest probability condition on that topic. In topic 16, the tag "黄岩岛(Huangyan Island)", "中国(China)", "菲律宾(the Philippines)", "南海(South China Sea)" and "军事(military)" are the five top tags and the probabilities are 0.2045,0.0847,0.0754,0.0492,0.0324. This means when an author writes a blog associate with Huangyan Island he will be choose the topic 16 first.

In topic 82, we can see the 5 top tags are similar to the topic 16, but the probabilities are not the same. Compare topic 16 with topic 82, we know exactly what is the difference between topic 16 and topic 82, the topic 16 is regard to the territorial sovereignty between China and the Philippines and the topic 82 is concerning something about the Philippines.

At last, we use the PMI-IR[14] to calculate the co-occur probability between two words in the search engine. The formula used in the experiment is as follows:

$$PMI - IR(tag, word) = \log_2 \frac{Hits(tag \& word)}{Hits(word)} \tag{8}$$

Hits(tag & word) is the number of times that the tag and the word co-occurs. Hits(word) is the number of times that the word occurs.

In the experiment, we calculated the PMI-IR between the tag and the top 20 words that assigned to the related topics of this tag. Tab. 1 shows the results of PMI-IR between the tag "股票(stock)" and the top words assigned to topic 31. From the table, we can find that the PMI-IR can demonstrate superior performance over the THDP model.

Table 1. PMI-IR between the tag "股票(stock)" and top words

| word | PMI-IR | word | PMI-IR |
|---|---|---|---|
| 期货(future) | 0.7595 | 机构(institution) | 0.1214 |
| 股海(unit sea) | 0.6509 | 因素(factor) | 0.0854 |
| 利空(bad news) | 0.5398 | 政策(policy) | 0.0813 |
| 股市(stock market) | 0.5080 | 会议(meeting) | 0.0794 |
| 市值(market value) | 0.5038 | 区间(interval) | 0.0670 |
| 货币(monetary) | 0.4894 | 经济(economic) | 0.0621 |
| 利好(good news) | 0.4145 | 节点(node) | 0.0469 |
| 收益(return) | 0.3276 | 行情(conjuncture) | 0.0440 |
| 强势(dominance) | 0.2289 | 中央(central) | 0.0324 |
| 周期(cycle) | 0.1531 | 市场(market) | 0.0056 |

**Topic 11**

| WORD | PROB. |
|---|---|
| 经济(economic) | 0.0739 |
| 欧洲(europe) | 0.0695 |
| 国家(country) | 0.0529 |
| 危机(crisis) | 0.0466 |
| 债务(debt) | 0.0422 |
| 市场(market) | 0.0345 |
| 财政(financial) | 0.0288 |
| 问题(problem) | 0.0279 |
| 德国(germany) | 0.0275 |
| 希腊(greece) | 0.0263 |

| TAG | PROB. |
|---|---|
| 欧债危机(European debt crisis) | 0.1021 |
| 德国国债(German Bund) | 0.0926 |
| 债务危机(debt crisis ) | 0.0714 |
| 欧元(Euro) | 0.0546 |
| 德国(germany) | 0.0365 |

**Topic 31**

| WORD | PROB. |
|---|---|
| 期货(future) | 0.1885 |
| 股海(unit sea) | 0.0998 |
| 利空(bad news) | 0.0757 |
| 股市(stock market) | 0.0684 |
| 市值(market value) | 0.0554 |
| 货币(monetary) | 0.0388 |
| 利好(good news) | 0.0323 |
| 收益(return) | 0.0295 |
| 强势(dominance) | 0.0258 |
| 周期(cycle) | 0.0249 |

| TAG | PROB. |
|---|---|
| 股票(stock) | 0.0745 |
| 股市(stock market ) | 0.0658 |
| 大盘(the big board) | 0.0249 |
| 财经版(business sections) | 0.0217 |
| 欧洲(Europe) | 0.0104 |

**Topic 16**

| WORD | PROB. |
|---|---|
| 中国(China) | 0.1012 |
| 菲律宾(the Philippines) | 0.0868 |
| 黄岩岛(Huangyan Island) | 0.0752 |
| 南海(South China Sea) | 0.0395 |
| 主权(sovereignty) | 0.0305 |
| 领土(territories) | 0.0277 |
| 军舰(warship) | 0.0260 |
| 渔船(fisher) | 0.0257 |
| 海域(sea area) | 0.0254 |
| 菲方(Philippine side ) | 0.0223 |

| TAG | PROB. |
|---|---|
| 黄岩岛(Huangyan Island) | 0.2045 |
| 中国(China) | 0.0847 |
| 菲律宾(the Philippines) | 0.0754 |
| 南海(South China Sea) | 0.0492 |
| 军事military | 0.0324 |

**Topic 82**

| WORD | PROB. |
|---|---|
| 菲律宾(the Philippines) | 0.1250 |
| 基诺(Jino) | 0.0759 |
| 发言人(addressor) | 0.0670 |
| 三世(triple world) | 0.0580 |
| 总统(president) | 0.0536 |
| 船只(ships) | 0.0491 |
| 渔民(fisherman) | 0.0446 |
| 帕纳塔格(Panatag) | 0.0402 |
| 潟湖(lagoon) | 0.0357 |
| 发布会(Conference) | 0.0223 |

| TAG | PROB. |
|---|---|
| 菲律宾(the Philippines) | 0.1024 |
| 总统(president) | 0.0547 |
| 国家(country) | 0.0438 |
| 中国(China) | 0.0217 |
| 黄岩岛(Huangyan Island) | 0.0168 |

**Fig. 6.** An illustration of 4 topics from 114–topic solution for the dataset, Each topic is shown with the 10 words and 5 tags that have the highest probability conditioned on that topic

## 6    Conclusion

In this paper, we propose a THDP model. The model uses the HDP as the prior distribution of TTM, which infer the topic number of dataset automatically and links the tags to the topics of the document and capture the semantic of a tag in the form of topic distribution. Example results on the dataset are used to demonstrate the consistent and promising performance of the proposed THDP, the computational expense of the proposed model is comparable to that of related topic model.

**Acknowledgement.** This work was supported by the NSF of China (No.90920005, No.61003192), the Major Project of State Language Commission in the Twelfth Five-year Plan Period (No.ZDI125-1), the Project in the National Science &Technology Pillar Program in the Twelfth Five-year Plan Period (No.2012BAK24B01), the Program of Introducing Talents of Discipline to Universities (No.B07042), the NSF of Hubei Province (No.2011CDA034) and the self-determined research Funds of CCNU from the colleges' basic research and operation of MOE (No.CCNU10A02009 and No.CCNU10C01005 ).

# References

1. About Tumblr.com (accessed October 13, 2012)
2. WordPress.com Stats (accessed October 13, 2012)
3. Tingting, H., Fang, L.: Semantic KnowledgeAcquisition from Blogs with Tag-Topic Model. China Communications 9(3), 38–48 (2012)
4. The, Y.W., Jordan, M., Beal, M., Blei, D.M.: Hierarchical Dirichlet processes. Journal of the American Statistical Association 101(476), 1566–1581 (2006)
5. Wang, X., Tieu, K., Gee-Wah, N., Grimson, W.E.L.: Trajectoryanalysis and semantic region modeling using a nonparametric Bayesian model. In: Proceedings of the IEEE Conference on Computer Vision and Pattern Recognition, pp. 1–8. IEEE, Anchorage (2008)
6. Sudderth, E.B., Torralba, A., Freeman, W.T., Willsky, A.S.: Describing visual scenes using transformed objects and parts. International Journal of Computer Vision 77(1-3), 291–330 (2008)
7. Sudderth, E.B.: Graphical Models for Visual Object Recognition and Tracking [Ph. D. dissertation]. Department of Electrical Engineering and Computer Science, Massachusetts Institute of Technology, USA (2006)
8. Yakhnenko, O., Honavar, V.: Multimodal hierarchical Dirichlet process model for predicting image annotation andimageobject label correspondence. In: Proceedings of the SIAM International Conference on Data Mining, pp. 281–294. SIAM, Sparks (2009)
9. Cowans, P.J.: Information retrieval using hierarchical Dirichlet processes. In: Proceedings of the 27th Annual International ACM SIGIR Conference on Research and Development in Information Retrieval, pp. 564–565. ACM, New York (2004)
10. Xu, T.B., Zhang, Z.F., Yu, P.S., Long, B.: Evolutionary clusteringby hierarchical Dirichlet process with hidden Markov state. In: Proceedings of the 8th IEEE International Conferenceon Data Mining, pp. 658–667. IEEE, Pisa (2008)
11. Williamson, S., Wang, C., Heller, K.A., Blei, D.M.: The IBP compound Dirichlet process and itsapplication to focused topic modeling. In: ICML (2010)
12. Chan, X., Zhou., M., Carin, L.: The contextual Focused Topic Model. In: KDD, pp. 96–104 (2012)
13. Issei, S., Kenichi, K., Hiroshi, N.: Practical Collapsed Variational Bayes Inference for Hierarchical Dirichlet Process. In: KDD, pp. 105–113 (2012)
14. Turney, P.D.: Mining the Web for Synonyms: PMI- IR versus LSA on TOEFL. In: Flach, P.A., De Raedt, L. (eds.) ECML 2001. LNCS (LNAI), vol. 2167, pp. 491–502. Springer, Heidelberg (2001)
15. Heinrich, G.: "Infinite LDA"– Implementing the HDP with minimum code complexity (2011)
16. Deng, H., Han, J., Zhao, B., Yu, Y., Lin, C.: Probabilistic topic models with biased propagation onheterogeneous information networks. In: KDD (2011)
17. Blei, D.M., Ng, A.Y., Jordan, M.I.: Latent Dirichlet Allocation. Journal of Machine Learning Research 3(4-5), 993–1022 (2003)
18. Heinrich, G.: Parameter estimation for text analysis (2005)
19. Steyvers, M., Griffiths, T.: Probabilistic topic models. Handbook of latent semantic analysis 427(7), 424–440 (2007)
20. Ranganathan, A.: The Dirichlet Process Mixture (DPM) Model (2004)

# Naxi-Chinese Bilingual Word Alignment Method Based on Entity Constraint

Xiuzhen Yang[1,2], Zhengtao Yu[1,2,*], Jianyi Guo[1,2], Xiao Pan[1,2], and Cunli Mao[1,2]

[1] School of Information Engineering and Automation, Kunming University of Science and Technology, 650500 Yunnan, China
[2] Key Laboratory of Intelligent Information Processing, Kunming University of Science and Technology, 650500 Yunnan, China
ztyu@hotmail.com

**Abstract.** This paper proposes Naxi-Chinese bilingual word alignment method based on entity constraint for the characteristic that entity and entity is alignment in bilingual alignment. First, we mark the corpus of Naxi word segmentation and entity label, using Conditional Random Fields constructs the model of Naxi word segmentation and entity recognition to achieve Naxi word segmentation and entity recognition. Then, using entity alignment constraint relation of Naxi-Chinese sentence uses the specific marker to mark out bilingual entity of Naxi-Chinese sentence. Finally, we introduce features, such as fertility probabilities and distortion probabilities et al, and achieve the Naxi-Chinese bilingual alignment model by GIZA++. Naxi-Chinese bilingual word alignment experimental result shows the method proposed by this paper has better effect compared to only use IBM Models.

**Keywords:** Conditional random fields, Entity alignment constraint, Fertility probabilities, Distortion probabilities.

## 1 Introduction

Naxi language is the character that is created and used by the Naxi people of Lijiang. It is the unique pictograph that is still in use in the world. Naxi language information processing platform and the construction of bilingual word aligned corpus about machine translation are very important. So far, in the Naxi information platform construction, we make 4186 Naxi characters and map their Unicode. Constructing 3900 Naxi-Chinese-English three language dictionary; Achieving Naxi phonetic, Chinese, English input method; Achieving Web embedding fronts technology of Naxi pictographs[1][2]; Constructing a small-scale Naxi-Chinese parallel corpus[3][4]; However, there are a little job to be done in Naxi-Chinese bilingual word automatic alignment. Carrying out Naxi-Chinese bilingual word alignment method is the basis of constructing large-scale Naxi word aligned corpus.

---

[*] Corresponding author.

P. Liu and Q. Su (Eds.): CLSW 2013, LNAI 8229, pp. 378–386, 2013.

Bilingual word alignment as intermediate implicit process is proposed by Brown et al[5]. It uses expectation maximization to estimate the probability of word alignment. Word alignment tool GIZA++[6] based on IBM Models are develop by Franz Och et al. GIZA++ has achieved bilingual word automatic alignment of Chinese-English, English-French, English-Khmer. Because IBM Models are based on models of one-to-many, and there are certain language features, for instance, entity is important element or feature of bilingual sentence. The exiting entities have corresponding relationship, these characteristics have certain impact on word alignment. This paper researches that entity constraint relation has impact on Naxi-Chinese bilingual word alignment, then, proposing Naxi-Chinese bilingual word alignment method based on entity constraint.

## 2 Naxi-Chinese Word Alignment Method Idea Based on the Entity Constraints

The idea of Naxi-Chinese word alignment method mainly uses that there are alignment relationship among entities in bilingual alignment process. The existing entity recognition method can effectively recognize entity of bilingual sentence. We mark out bilingual entity alignment relationship, and using these relationships increase by the accuracy of bilingual word alignment. Its realization process is: first, using Conditional Random Fields[7]segments word for Naxi sentence, then, recognizing the entities of Naxi and Chinese, then, the corresponding entities are replaced by the same mark. Finally, we align to the replaced sentence to get the alignment result.

## 3 Naxi-Chinese Bilingual Word Alignment Method Based on Entity Constraint

### 3.1 Naxi Word Segmentation

As with Chinese word segmentation, there also exits the problem of Naxi word segmentation in Naxi language. We choose Naxi characters of Naxi sentence as feature, then, marking word segmentation corpus. Using Conditional Random Fields constructs Naxi segmentation model.

### 3.1.1 Definition of Feature Templates

In the paper, according to Naxi language characteristic and the feature what conditional random fields[8] use the last $n$ characters and the next $m$ characters for contextual information of the current character. In this paper, the next two characters of the current character, the next two characters of the current character and architectural features among them are used. The feature templates what we use is as following:

(1) $C_n$  (n=-2,-1,0,1,2)

(2) $C_n \ C_{n+1}$  (n=-2,-1,0,1,2)

(3) $P_u \ (C_0)$

Among them, $C$ denotes Naxi character. $C_0$ denotes the current character. n denotes the position of relative to the current character. For instance, in sequence "ᚠᚠ[naxi](Naxi)ᚠ[ren](people)ᚠ[nvhai](girl)ᚠ[xihuan](like)", if the current character is "ᚠᚠ[naxi](Naxi)", $C_{-1}$ denotes "ᚠ[ren](people)". $P_u$ ($C_0$) denotes current character is punctuation or not. Feature templates (1) and (3) are all the features of single sequence element. Feature template is combination features of element sequence.

### 3.1.2 Naxi Sentence Word Segmentation Model Based on Conditional Random Fields

Firstly, Naxi sentence is divided into single character. Then, the single character is marked. The marked information is divided into two groups, one group as training corpus, other group as testing corpus. The paper takes $X = x_1, x_2, \ldots, x_N$ as Naxi character sequence in corpus, $Y = y_1, y_2, \ldots, y_N$ as forecasting Naxi word sequence, so we can build the following model: $X$ has known, conditional probability of $Y$ can be calculated by the following formula:

$$P_\wedge(Y \mid X) = \frac{1}{Z_X} \exp\left(\sum_{j=1}^{N}\sum_{i} \lambda_i f_i\left(y_{j-1}, y_j, X, j\right)\right) \tag{1}$$

Among the, $Z_x = \sum_{y \in Y} \exp\left(\sum_{j=1}^{N}\sum_{i} \lambda_i f_i\left(y_{j-1}, y_j, X, j\right)\right)$ denotes normalizing factor, $f_i\left(y_{j-1}, y_j, X, j\right)$ denotes feature function, $\lambda_i$ denotes feature function corresponding weight.

The defined feature template is integrated into model by feature function, such as: when $x_{j-1}$ denotes word "ᚠᚠ[naxi](Naxi)", $x_j$ denotes word "ᚠ[ren](people)", $y_{j-1}$ corresponding mark denotes word's beginning, $y_j$ corresponding mark denotes $y_{j-1}$ corresponding mark denotes word's end, the feature function equal to 1. So the defined $C_n$ $C_{n+1}$ is integrated into model. Weight of feature function $\lambda_i$ can pass model training to get corresponding valuation. Generally, we use maximum likelihood estimation, its likelihood function can be calculated by the following formula:

$$L_\wedge = \sum_{i=1}^{M} \log\left(P_\wedge\left(Y_i \mid X_i\right)\right) - \sum_k \frac{\lambda_k^2}{2\sigma_k^2} \tag{2}$$

The right of equality's sign, the second item denotes Gaussian priori value, among them, $\sigma^2$ denotes Prior variance. We use Limited Memory BFGS(L-BFGS)[9] to resolve optimal value of likelihood function. Weight $\lambda_i$ is trained out, so Conditional Random Fields model can be built.

Testing corpus is input this model, the most probable marked sequence can pass Viterbi arithmetic to obtain, formula is as follows:

$$Y^* = \arg\max_{Y} P(Y \mid X) \tag{3}$$

In output's results, the marked word combination in corresponding $Y^*$ is the final Naxi segmentation result.

### 3.1.3 The Result of Naxi Word Segmentation

We collect 8000 pairs training the Naxi corpus and achieve manual word segmentation for Naxi sentence and entity label to get training corpus. Using Conditional Random Fields gets Naxi word segmentation and entity recognition model, the result of Naxi sentence word segmentation is shown in figure 1:

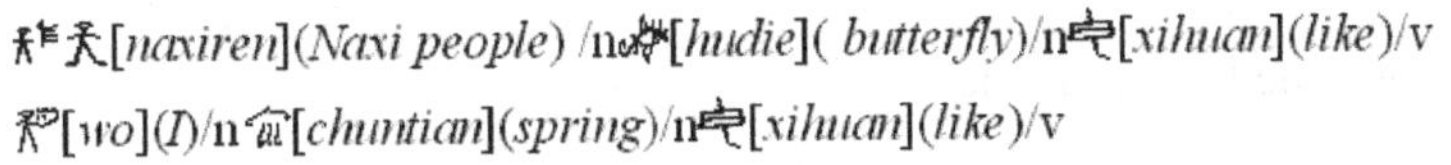

꫞ꪻ[*naxiren*](*Naxi people*) /n꫞[*hudie*]( *butterfly*)/n꫞[*xihuan*](*like*)/v

꫞[*wo*](*I*)/n꫞[*chuntian*](*spring*)/n꫞[*xihuan*](*like*)/v

**Fig. 1.** The result of Naxi word segmentation

### 3.2 Naxi - Chinese Word Alignment Method Based on IBM Models

Currently, IBM Models[10] are seen as basic models or contrast models by the researchers in the word alignment domain. There are 5 IBM Models in Naxi-Chinese bilingual word alignment method and it is more advance from the previous model that means IBM Model2 is overcome the problem/lack point in IBM Model 1...et al. IBM Model 5 is the most advance among other 4 models.

(1) IBM Model 1

Word sequence of Naxi source language sentence is defined as $s_1^l = s_1 s_2, ..., s_l$, word sequence of Chinese source language sentence is defined as $t_1^m = t_1 t_2, ..., t_m$. If $s_l$ and $t_m$ are alignment each other, we introduce Naxi-Chinese bilingual word alignment relation $\alpha_m$. This model has the most simple form, the translation probability of IBM Model 1 is defined as:

$$P(t \mid s) = \frac{\varepsilon}{(l+1)^m} \sum_{a_1} ... \sum_{a_m=0}^{l} \prod_{j=1}^{m} tr(t_j \mid s_{a_j}) \tag{4}$$

$\varepsilon$ is a normalization constant. $l$ denotes the length of input sentence. $m$ denotes the length of input sentence. $tr(t_j \mid s_{a_j})$ denotes the translation probability of word pair $(t_j, s_{a_j})$, among given constraints, each source language word $s$ must meet the following formula:

$$\sum_{t} tr(t \mid s) = 1 \tag{5}$$

IBM Model 1 can use EM algorithm circular iterative algorithm, it considers all the possible alignment in the training process. In addition this model has the only local maximum value, and the starting point of the iterative and calculation process has nothing to do.

(2) IBM Model 2

Compared with IBM Model 1 introduces set of alignment probabilities, namely:

$$a(a_j | j,m,l) = P(a_j | a_1^{j-1}, t_1^{j-1}, m, l) \tag{6}$$

It needs to meet limited condition:

$$\sum_{i=0}^{l} a(a_j | j,m,l) = 1 \tag{7}$$

Hence the basic form of model is:

$$P(t|s) = \varepsilon \sum_{a_1=0}^{l} \cdots \sum_{a_m=0}^{l} \prod_{j=1}^{m} tr(t_j | s_{a_j}) a(a_j | j,m,l) \tag{8}$$

IBM Model 2 can also use EM algorithm circular iterative algorithm to get the estimated value of the model parameters.

(3) IBM Model 3

Compared with IBM Model 2 introduces fertility probabilities, namely:

$$n(\phi | s_i) = P(\phi | \phi_1^{i-1}, s) \tag{9}$$

$\phi$ denotes the number that word $s_i$ produces target language word. It reflects possibility of one word corresponding to multiple words. Hence we can get form of IBM Model 3:

$$P(t|s) = \sum_{a_1=0}^{l} \cdots \sum_{a_m=0}^{l} P(t,a|s)$$

$$= \sum_{a_1=0}^{l} \cdots \sum_{a_m=0}^{l} \binom{m-\phi_0}{\phi_0} P_0^{m-\phi_0} P_1^{\phi_0} \prod_{i=1}^{l} \phi_i! n(\phi_i | s_i) \prod_{j=1}^{m} tr(t_j | s_{a_j}) d(j | a_j, m, l) \tag{10}$$

$d(j|a_j,m,l)$ denotes distortion probabilities, it reflects difference of alignment position. $P_0$ denotes the probability of word not empty. $P_1$ denotes the probability of word corresponding to empty.

In general, the initial value that IBM Model 3 uses can be random, but in order to get better result uses the parameter that IBM Model 2 iterates finally as input of IBM Model 2.

Compared with IBM Model 3, IBM Model 4 introduces the concept of parts of speech, and the calculation of distortion probabilities is further perfected. Meanwhile it considers different fertility probabilities' words. It has impact on the translation result of word pair. Compared with IBM Model 4, IBM Model 5 revises the influence of empty word alignment.

Because mathematical logic of IBM Model is relatively rigid, and it considers comprehensively for the possibility of word alignment, in most cases using IBM Models can get a better word alignment result.

### 3.3    Naxi-Chinese Bilingual Word Alignment Method Based on Entity Constraint

Through we analyze for the Naxi-Chinese bilingual word alignment result, we find there is alignment relationship among entities in the bilingual, entity only aligns to entity, there is not alignment relationship between the entity and the non-entity. We introduce the entity alignment constraint for this characteristic, designing bilingual word alignment process is shown in figure 2:

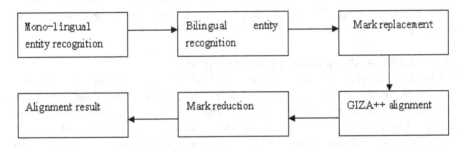

**Fig. 2.** Word alignment realization process based on entity constraint

Word alignment realization process based on entity constraint is shown in figure 2: first, recognizing the entities of Naxi and Chinese, then, the corresponding entities are replaced by the same mark, then, we align to the replaced sentence to get the alignment result. Finally, the mark in bilingual sentence is reverted to the original entity to get the final result.

### 3.3.1    Mono-lingual Entity Recognition and Mark Replacement

(1)   Mono-lingual entity recognition

The entities that we recognize can be divided into three kinds of words: entity class (including person name, geography name), time class (including time, date) and numeric class (including quantity, ordinals)[11]. According to the need, we set up four kinds of entities: person name, geography name, numeral, temporal word. Specifically, we complete entity recognition like this:

Naxi language end: firstly, we use Conditional Random Fields to segment and mark part of speech for Chinese sentence, then we use Conditional Random Fields to recognize entity for the sentence.

Chinese end: firstly, we use ICTCLAS to segment and mark part of speech for Chinese sentence. Because ICTCLAS contains the model of entity recognition, we can use the model to mark entity for sentence.

(2)   Bilingual entity recognition

The paper mainly recognizes entity for person name, geography name, numeral, temporal word. Because the entity has certain rules, the entity of source language is translated into the entity of target language with the aid of Naxi-Chinese dictionary.

(3) Mark replacement

Naxi-Chinese corresponding entities are replaced by RM, DM、SC 和 SJC. RM stands for person name. DM stands for geography name. SC stands for numeral. SJC stands for temporal word. For instance, "𖿢 [chuntian](spring)" is translated into "春天[chuntian](spring)" in Chinese, so, "𖿢 [chuntian](spring)" is replaced by SJC. Like this, "春天[chuntian](spring)"'is also replaced by SJC.

Different entities are replaced by different marks in the same sentence. Such as, "𖿢 [chuntian](spring)"and " 𖿢 [qiutian](autumn)"'are recognized and they are all numeral, so, they are replaced by SC1, SC2 in Naxi end. Like this, "春天 [chuntian](spring)"and '秋天[qiutian](autumn)" are replaced by the same mark in Chinese end.

### 3.3.2    GIZA++ Alignment and Mark Reduction

The marked bilingual sentence is aligned by GIZA++. In the paper, the mark that restrains bilingual end has been aligned. For instance, 'RM1' of Naxi end only aligns with 'RM1' of Chinese end. 'RM2' of Naxi end only aligns with 'RM2' of Chinese end. We do not permit 'RM1' of Naxi end aligns with 'RM2' of Chinese end.

On the basis of bilingual word alignment, we scan original bilingual sentence and let the mark revert to the corresponding entity.   The result is the final alignment result.

## 4    The Experiment and Result Analysis

In order to verify Naxi-Chinese bilingual word alignment method based on entity constraint we extract 200 sentences as evaluation data from 8000 sentences. Then, 200 evaluation data is aligned artificially. Finally, 8000 Naxi-Chinese corpus including 200 evaluation data are aligned by Naxi-Chinese bilingual alignment method that the paper proposes. In the paper, we choose alignment method that only uses IBM Models to compare with this method. Precision, recall, F-measure and AER are seen as standard that evaluates the quality of word alignment. $A$ denotes the set of waiting for evaluating alignment results. Among them the results of artificial alignment are marked two categories. $S$ denotes deterministic alignment set. $P$ denotes nondeterministic alignment set. The formula is as the following:

$$precision = \frac{|A \cap P|}{|A|} \tag{11}$$

$$recall = \frac{|A \cap S|}{S} \tag{12}$$

$$F - Measure = \frac{2 \times precision \times recall}{precision + recall} \times 100\% \tag{13}$$

$$AER = 1 - \frac{|A \cap S| + |A \cap P|}{|A| + |S|} \tag{14}$$

The results are as following (Table 1).

Table 1. The Comparison Experiment of Naxi-Chinese bilingual word alignment method

| Type | Precision (%) | Recall (%) | F-Measure (%) | AER (%) |
|---|---|---|---|---|
| IBM Models | 79.25 | 81.32 | 80.27 | 20.12 |
| IBM Models and Entity Recognition | 85.13 | 87.32 | 86.21 | 15.48 |

The experimental results show: compared with using IBM Models, using IBM Models and entity recognition make precision, recall and F-Measure be increased. AER is decreased. So, Naxi-Chinese word alignment method that this paper proposes is more effective.

## 5    Conclusion

This paper proposes Naxi-Chinese bilingual word alignment method based on entity constraint for the characteristic that entity and entity is alignment in bilingual alignment. First, using Conditional Random Fields segments word for Naxi sentence, then, we get through restraining bilingual entity to improve the effect of word alignment.

**Acknowledgements.** This work was supported by National Natural Science Foundation of China, Contract No. 61163022.

## References

1. Guo, H., Che, W., et al.: Web Embedding Fonts Technology of Naxi Pictographs. Computer Engineering 17(31), 203–207 (2005)
2. Guo, H.: The Design and Development of Outlines Font of Naxi Hieroglyphic and the Embedding Fonts Technology of Naxi Hieroglyphic. Kunming, Kunming University of Science and Technology (2005)
3. Zhao, F., Yu, Z., Xian, Y., et al.: Naxi-Chinese Bilingual Corpus and Building a Bilingual Corpus Alignment. Journal of Guangxi Normal Uniwersity: Natural Science Edition 27(01), 20–24 (2009)
4. Zhao, F.: Naxi-Chinese Bilingual Translation Method Research. Kunming, Kunming University of Science and Technology (2010)
5. Brown, P.F., Mercer, R.L., et al.: The Mathematics of Statistical Machine Translation: Parameter Estimation. Computational Linguistics 19(2), 263–311 (1993)
6. Och, F.J., Ney, H.: A Systematic Comparison of Various Statistical Alignment Models. Computational Linguistics 29(1), 19–51 (2003)

7. Tang, J., Hong, M., Li, J., et al.: Tree-structured Conditional Random Fields for Semantic annotation. In: 5th International Semantic Web Conference, Athens, USA, pp. 640–653 (2006)
8. Zhao, H., Huang, C., Li, M.: An Improved Chinese Word Segmentation System with Conditional Random Field. In: Fifth Sighan Workingshop on Chinese Language Processing (SIGHAN-5), pp. 162–165 (2006)
9. Zheng, W.-N., Bo, P.-B., Liu, Y., Wang, W.-P.: Fast B-spline curve fitting by L-BFGS. Computer Aided Geometric Design 29(7), 448–462 (2012)
10. Nagao, M.: A Framework of a Mechanical Translation between Japanese and English by Analogy Principle. In: Artificial and Human Intelligence, pp. 173–180. North-Holland, Amsterdam (1984)
11. Zhao, J.: A Survey on Named Entity Recognition, Disambiguation and Cross-Lingual Coreference Resolution. Journal of Chinese Information Processing 23(2), 3–17 (2009)

# Real Scene Oriented Chinese Text Automatic Proofreading Technology[*]

Jian Jiao and Yangsen Zhang

Institute of Intelligent Information Processing, Beijing Information Science & Technology
University, Beijing 100192
zys@bistu.edu.cn

**Abstract.** Traditional Chinese text automatic proofreading technology is mainly focused on one or more pre-set error types, the proofreading performance in a real scene needs to be improved. This paper proposes a real scene oriented Chinese text proofreading system model for Chinese text automatic proofreading. Real scene oriented Chinese text automatic proofreading strategy is provided after analyzing performance requirements of automatic proofreading system for the real scene. The model is expected to provide new thoughts for future development of proofreading for Chinese text.

**Keywords:** automatic proofreading for Chinese text, real scene oriented, N-Gram model, Combination of rules and statistics.

## 1 Introduction

Modern text editing system has greatly improved the speed of publications. At the same time, it brings forward challenge to text proofreading. Traditional manual proofreading is not only slow and expensive but also heavily dependent on the proofreader's experience and energy. Besides, obvious errors may be neglected due to the omission of the proofreader. There are growing demands for Chinese automatic text proofing in various areas including news, promotions, literature and history.

Chinese scholars began to explore the Chinese text automatic proofreading technology since 1990s, and a series of proofreading models and methods were proposed which laid the foundation for practical application of Chinese text automatic proofreading. Professor Yangsen Zhang proposed an automatic error-detection model [1, 6] for Chinese text proofreading by the combination of rule-based and statistical methods, which led to positive results. According to the emergence regularity of a single character after word segmentation in Chinese text, Professor Zhang proposed the concept of "non-multi-words errors" with a set of rules for error-detection. And then,

---

[*] This paper is funded by the Natural Science Foundation of China (NSFC, Grant No.61070119), the Project of Construction of Innovative Teams and Teacher Career Development for Universities and Colleges Under Beijing Municipality (Grant No. IDHT20130519) and the Beijing Municipal Education Commission Special Fund (Grant No. PXM2012-014224-000020).

P. Liu and Q. Su (Eds.): CLSW 2013, LNAI 8229, pp. 387–395, 2013.

a text automatic error-detection model was established. Combined with which the binary and ternary statistical model of word and the binary and ternary statistical model of part of speech, text automatic error-detecting model and implementation algorithm are established. Professor Zhensheng Luo proposed a method combining pattern matching and sentence component analysis for the realization of syntax error checking [2, 5]. The method detects various kinds of syntax errors by two-step scanning. The first-step scans the collocation errors based on pattern matching method and the second-step scans component related errors exploiting a predicate head driven sentence components analyzing method. The combination of these two methods results in a good experimental performance.

At present, the study of Chinese text automatic proofreading focus on syntax and semantic levels. Chinese syntax and semantics are not only more complex than English, but also is not clear in the definition of Chinese word and does not have the temporal variation as well as English vocabulary. All of this led to the difficulties of the syntax analysis. Researches abroad are not fully applicable [7-10]. Although domestic scholars have done a lot of fruitful work, there is still a long way to go with the real practical of Chinese text proofreading. Lexical studies based on statistical laws have been widely used because of its significant effect on the proofreading. Therefore, lexical level proofreading is in the core status while the syntactic and semantic level proofreading is in the auxiliary status in real scene Chinese text proofreading field.

## 2    Performance Requirements of Automatic Proofreading System for the Real Scene

Compared with practical systems applied to real scenes, academic proofreading systems mainly focus on factors such as recall rate, etc. while ignoring temporal and spatial consumptions. Thus, user experience of these systems needs to be improved. Therefore, we come up with the performance requirements applied to the real scene of Chinese text automatic proofreading system. Specific indicators are as follows:

- Accuracy rate is more important than recall rate

Accurate rate is defined as:

$$p = \frac{The\ number\ of\ correctly\ identified\ errors}{The\ total\ number\ of\ errors\ identified\ by\ system} \times 100\% \tag{1}$$

Recall rate is defined as:

$$r = \frac{The\ number\ of\ correctly\ identified\ errors}{The\ total\ number\ of\ errors\ in\ the\ test\ text} \times 100\% \tag{2}$$

From the definition above we can see that improving recall rate will lead to a decline in accuracy rate and with the increasing of accurate rate, recall rate will decline. In the real scene, from a psychological perspective, users are more patient of neglected errors than that the correct vocabulary was marked wrong. Therefore, the design of our system focuses on accuracy rate. An algorithm is designed to calculate the confidence level of the determination that a word is erroneous, and only the words with a confidence level above a certain threshold will be marked as error.

- Space requirements is more important than time requirements

The existed Chinese text automatic proofreading systems do not apply to the real scene because they have high time and space complexity. In order to improve the display effects, scholars tend to adopt the approach of space for time which may reduce the time of proofreading but lead to great memory demand at the same time. Due to the rapid development of computer hardware technology, the storage issue has been greatly improved. But for most ordinary users too great storage occupation is still unbearable. By contrast, on the premise of smooth operation, users can perform other actions to mitigate the negative effects brought by the time consumption. Based on this, during algorithm design process, we adopt the approach of time for space to optimize the date storage and query solutions in order to reduce the storage space. This strategy has important realistic meaning on large amount of text automatic proofreading.

- Regional locating exceed point locating

Another major difficulty in Chinese text automatic proofreading is error locating. There are two main solutions for the problem. One is called precise locating and another is called full-word locating. For example, when proofreading the wrong word "精忠抱国[jingzhongbaoguo]", the single Chinese word "抱[bao](hug)" will be marked in the precise locating while in the full-word locating all the four single Chinese words will be marked. There is a great difference of the complexity in error locating using different strategies. For error-detection based on word continuation relations, precise locating is easier than full-word locating. However, when comes to error-detection that based on syntax analysis, it is quite the reverse. We will use the error-detection based on word continuation relations for the purpose of quickly locating the errors. In order to make it easier to locate errors and improve the locating accuracy, we believed that region locating is more important than the point locating which means that the mark scope covers error word but not limited in the error word. This is equivalent to weaken the full-word locating strategy. The method not only greatly reduces the difficulty of error locating but also meets our request on automatic proofreading system.

## 3    Real Scene-Oriented Chinese Text Automatic Proofreading Strategy

At present, the theory and practice of text proofreading are immature. It is commonly agreed that automatic error-detection and error-correction should be carried out on lexical, syntax and semantics levels respectively [3, 4]. Since lexical level proofreading theory and practice are relatively mature than the other two levels and have more satisfactory performance, we will take lexical proofreading as the core of our system while syntactic and semantic levels proofreading as complement. Overall proofreading strategy of the system is as follows:

- Conducted error-detection and error-correction by several rounds of scanning
- Achieved lexical errors locating by using the relationship of single word continuation and lexical continuation
- Achieved syntactic and semantic errors locating by using the syntax and semantic rules
- Applied compress mapping on lexical knowledge base and word knowledge base to reduce the memory usage
- The flow of the system is as follows:
- First, filter the wrong words in the first round of text scanning using the common error words knowledge base. Common error knowledge base is organized at the form: "error word + space + right word". When the error word was detected, recording its position in the text and replacing it with the right one. Then we get the intermediate text one.
- Second, accomplished word segmentation and name entity identification with the help of segmentation system and specialized dictionary which included common slang knowledge base, idioms and poems knowledge base. Then we get the intermediate text two.
- Third, scan intermediate text two. Record the start position and length of the character sequence. Determine the location of error words and obtain the to-be-annotate error words knowledge base with the help of word continuation relations. Texts without lexical error were collected to form the intermediate text three.
- Fourth, scan the intermediate text three. Exploited the syntax and semantic rules and the collocation knowledge base to determine the error position.
- Finally, calculate the confidence value of the possible error word. If the confidence value of the word is higher than the certain threshold, the word would be determined as error word.

There are two major problems in the lexical proofreading system: the construction of knowledge base and fast search strategy of the dictionary. A practical method was presented to construct the knowledge base and take advantage of it to improve the query speed. The realization will be described in detail in part four. We will still use accurate rate, recall rate and F-score which have been widely used to evaluate the performance of the system. The F-score was defined as follows:

$$\text{F-Score} = \frac{2 \times p \times r}{p + r} \times 100\%, \text{ p is accurate rate and r is recall rate} \qquad (3)$$

## 4    The Realization of Real Scene-Oriented Automatic Proofreading System

### 4.1    The Construction of the Knowledge Base

The knowledge base used by the system include the common error word knowledge base, idioms knowledge base, slang knowledge base (including the three-character scripture, One Thousand Character Primer, the collection of 300 song poems), Chinese place name knowledge base, single word knowledge base, word co-occurrence knowledge base, grammar rules knowledge base and semantic collocation knowledge base. All the knowledge bases are obtained by counting People's Daily corpus which contains 25 million Chinese characters in 2000. We use N-Gram model to get the word co-occurrence knowledge base. An n-gram model predicts $X_i$ based on $X_{i-(n-1)}...X_{i-1}$. In probability terms, this is $P(X_i \mid X_{i-(n-1)}...X_{i-1})$. We get the common wrong word knowledge base in the way of combining rules and statistics. The concrete realization of the program as follows:

- Count error words in large amounts of texts that include input errors and habitual errors.
- Count the frequency of words, idioms and slangs in large amount of texts and sorting them.
- Select K-words with highest occurrence frequency, replace common error words to form error-word set.
- Make rules, build the error word knowledge base, according the rules the error word that caused by the bad input will be put into the knowledge base.

The core thought of automatic proofreading based on statistics is to create co-occurrence and collocation knowledge base by counting the word collocation in a large amount of texts. Therefore, the storage and usage of knowledge base became a key bottleneck of system performance. We proposed a knowledge base compression-mapping program to reduce the memory usage when loading knowledge base. The main idea is as follows:

- The knowledge base was divided into existential knowledge base (idioms, slangs, poems, place names, etc.) and associated knowledge base (common error word knowledge base, the word co-occurrence knowledge base, collocation knowledge base, etc.).
- Huffman-encoding Chinese characters according to their occurrence frequency, the existential knowledge base was converted into Huffman-encoded character form.
- The form of associative knowledge base: "word + space + word" or "word + space + word + statistics information (word frequency, mutual information)". A Hash function was used to map the lexical items in the dictionary to a closed interval. And at the same time to ensure that only if the lexical items are in the dictionary the mapping result would belongs to the interval. That is:

$$\forall x \in \Omega, \text{Hash}(x) \in R, \forall y \notin \Omega, \text{Hash}(y) \notin R \qquad (4)$$

Through the compression and mapping process to the knowledge base, the runtime storage of the system has been decreased. But also, in part, more process time would be consumed.

## 4.2    Proofreading on Lexical Level

Lexical Proofreading is the core of proofreading system. It utilized technology such as bidirectional maximum matching, word continuation relationship etc. Proofreading on lexical level is divided into three main steps. The first step is to filter the error word. Replace the error word in the text with the right one by using the common error word knowledge base and record the error word position at the same time. We classify the errors in the text to three types: missed words, repeated words and misspelled words. After analyzing 305 common errors in the sample, we found that misspelled words error in all errors accounted for 64.9% while missing words error accounted for 17.7%. Thus, most of the errors will be recognized in the first step of filtering error words. The common error word knowledge base plays a decisive role in the process. After error word replacement we got the intermediate text. The most kind of errors are missing words or repeated words. We use the word continuation relations knowledge base to check the continuous force of Chinese single words. This aims to find out whether there are errors in step two. Our research shows that when the threshold of co-occurrence frequency is set at 1 to 2, the system will get the best effect. The word segmentation was carried out by using the ICTCLAS. In the final step, we achieved error locating using bidirectional pinyin knowledge base and the Five-stroke Method.

### 4.3 Proofreading on Syntax and Semantics Level

Syntax analysis aimed to determine whether there is a syntax error by checking the grammatical components collocation of the sentence. It is mainly reflected in collocations, punctuation and the relationship of organization or people. The proofreading based on collocation of words and punctuation depends on the rules. One of the rules is as follows:

**Rule 1**: if nouns exist at the right side of the measure word collocates with noun, select the most nearest noun as the collocation word. If there are several nouns adjacent to each other, select the far most one as the collocation word.

The proofreading based on relationship of organization or people is mainly depends on looking up the knowledge base which we have constructed before. The existing syntax analysis technology is immature and semantic knowledge is multifarious lead to a high cost on syntax and semantic proofreading in the real scene. At the same time, as most audiences who use the automatic are well educated, it is hard to see errors like "我吃了一块石头 (I ate a stone)". It is not reasonable to focus on such case in real scene oriented proofreading system.

### 4.4 The Confidence Value Computation

After several rounds of proofreading process, we get a set of candidate error words. We will calculate the confidence value for each word and mark the word as error word if its confidence value is higher than the threshold. As we know from above, the candidate set contains two types of error. One can be found by common error word filtering. This kind of error will be marked directly. And another kind of error is found by calculating the word co-occurrence frequency. We adopt the following strategy to locate the error word:

- Filtering out the word with higher occurrence frequency according to the Chinese single word knowledge base.

- Calculate the edit distance between the word in the candidate set and the word in the lexical knowledge base, and record the minimum distance.
- Filtering out the word sequences that their edit distance lower than 1 and remark the others as the error words.

The Leveshtein Distance algorithm can be used to calculate the words edit distance because the length of word is short. Filtering out potentially correct words by calculating confidence level will cause drop in recall rate, however, this will largely avoid the phenomena that correct words are marked error. This is consistent with our performance requirements of the automatic proofreading system.

## 5  Analysis of the Experimental Results

149 common error sentences were selected to testify the proposed system. The results compared with Microsoft Word and the latest free Black Horse automatic proofreading system as follows:

**Table 1.** Comparison of our system and others

|  | Accurate rate | Recall rate | F-Score |
|---|---|---|---|
| Our System | 88. 46% | 78. 63% | 83. 26% |
| MS Word | 87. 10 | 69. 83% | 77. 51% |
| Black horse2004 | 90. 03% | 72. 45% | 80. 28% |

The system is showed in Fig.1:

县里的按装队早就到了，谁知发生了这一意外情况，只能推迟开工。
陈科长的棋艺在厂里首屈一指，但碰到这样一位高人，只能甘败下风。
年轻意味着责任，意味着希望，意味着未来，怎么能遇到一点挫折就自抱自弃呢？
文坛浮躁成风。他曾写过一篇长文，对此作了尖锐的针贬。
眼看大雁南飞，秋风一阵紧似一阵，寒夜还是没有影儿，团部几位领导急得一愁莫展。
随着警报响起，空气顿时紧张起来，卫兵穿流不息地在院子里进进出出。
机构重碟，人浮于事，效率低下，已是普遍现象。你说不改革行吗？
一走进渡假村的大门只见两棵挺拔的白杨迎风站立，仿佛在夹道欢迎来宾似的。
造这堵围墙，是考虑小区的安全，谁知事与愿违，却防碍了救护车的通行。
远远望去，门上贴着一符对联，喜气洋洋。
迎面是一座花园，花园后高楼耸立，不时轨穿梭而过。真是天翻地复的变化啊！
原定五年完成临摹任务，但自经历这场变故，他已失去了一股作气的心劲。
没有笨鸟先飞的自觉，没有竖定决心，还谈什么攀登科学的险峰？
自小生长在山区，黝黑的脸庞，宽阔的肩背，透露出内心的粗匡。
食不裹腹，衣不蔽体目已成为历史，今天，人们对饮食的要求，已提高到一个崭新的阶段。
这块表虽说款式陈旧，但走时还挺准的，你就凑和用吧。
正是春节前夕，侯车室里人头攒动，人声鼎沸，几乎找不立足的地方。
接到信后，真是迫不急待，连夜赶到县城，坐等第一班车。

**Fig. 1.** Screen shot of the system

Experiment result shows that the accuracy rate and recall rate of our system on proofreading single Chinese word error are higher than Microsoft Word. And because our system can also find syntax errors and semantic errors, it is significantly better than the black horse proofreading system. However, the accuracy rate of our system is lower than the black horse proofreading system because of the lack of high quality corpus. In order to minimize the storage space we did not use the word co-occurrence model, which resulted in errors like "我们用户党中央的正确决定" (The word "用户" in this sentence is wrong and the right one should be "拥护" which has the same pronunciation with "用户") cannot be detected. And the similar rationale applies to the black horse proofreading system.

## 6    Conclusion

In this paper, a suitable model for the real scene oriented Chinese text automatic proofreading system is introduced, and the performance indicators and specific implementation strategy of the system are identified. It gives a new solution to reduce system space utilization and improve user interaction experience. However, a feasible strategy to reduce system time cost is not proposed. Besides, due to the fact that the error-correction strategy depends on error-detection strategy and that there are several kinds of error-detection strategies in our system, the error-correction strategy is not introduced in this paper. Through long-term design, improvement and refinement of automatic text proofreading systems, we have the following experiences:

- The performance of statistics-based automatic proofreading system relies on the construction of corpus. Compared with domain-independent proofreading system, domain-dependent systems are more practical since they have far better performance and lower cost. Therefore, we believe that the design and construction of automatic proofreading system could take a domain-dependent training and proofreading pattern.
- The granularity of proofreading strategy based on rules is too big which results in an unsatisfactory effect. Strategy combining statistics and rules give full play to the comprehensiveness of the statistical methods and the definiteness of rules. Proofreading strategy based mainly on statistics and supplemented by rules has a higher practical value.
- The word co-occurrence frequency strategy has the lowest cost among all proofreading schemes based on word continuation relation. Also, it has few obvious disadvantages compared with other strategies such as strategy using mutual information.
- Encoding method determines the memory usage of the system. The compression algorithm designed to various knowledge bases is essential to the practical of automatic proofreading system.

## References

1. Zhang, Y., Cao, Y., Yu, S.: A Hybrid Model ofCombining Rule-based and Statistics-based Approaches for Automatic Detecting Errors in Chinese Text. Journal of Chinese Information Processing 20(4) (2005); (张仰森,曹元大,俞士汶. 基于规则与统计相结合的中文文本自动查错模型与算法. 中文信息学报

2. Luo, W., Luo, Z., Gong, X.: Study of Techniques of Automatic Proofreading for Chinese Texts. Journal of Computer Research and Development 41(1) (2004); (骆卫华,罗振声,宫小瑾. 中文文本自动校对技术的研究. 计算机研究与发展

3. Wu, Y., Jin, P., Guo, T.: Coarse-Grained Word Sense Disambiguation Using Features Described in the Lexicon. Journal of Chinese Information Processing 21(2) (2007); (吴云芳,金澎,郭涛. 基于词典属性特征的粗粒度词义消歧. 中文信息学报

4. Chen, X., Xu, P., Zhang, Y.: Automatic proofreading techniques for texts digitization. Application Research of Computers 25(5) (2008); (陈翔,徐平先,张玉志. 面向文本数字化的自动纠错方法. 计算机应用研究

5. Luo, W., Luo, Z., Gong, X.: Study of Semantic Errors Checking in Automatic Proofreading for Chinese Text. Computer Engineering and Applications 39(12) (2003); (骆卫华,罗振声,宫小瑾. 中文文本自动校对的语义级查错研究. 计算机工程与应用

6. Zhang, Y., Ding, B.: Automatic Errors Detecting of Chinese Texts Based on the B-i neighborship. Journal of Chinese Information Processing 2(18) (2001); (张仰森,丁冰清. 基于二元接续关系检查的字词级自动查错方法. 中文信息学报

7. Baker, C.F., Fillmore, C.J., Lowe, J.B.: The Berkeley FrameNet Project. In: COlING-ACI 1998, pp. 86–90 (1998)

8. Johnson, C.R., Fillmore, C.J.: The FrameNetTagset for Frame-Semantic and Syntactic Coding of Predicate-Argument Structure. In: Proc. of the 1st Meeting of the North American Chapter of the Association for Computational Linguistics (ANLP-NAACI 2000), pp. 56–62 (2000)

9. Dolan, W., Vanderwende, L., Richardson, S.D.: Automatically Deriving Structured Knowledge Bases from On-Line Dictionaries. In: Proc. of the Pacific Association for Computational Linguistics (1993)

10. Richardson, S.D., Dolan, W.B., van der Wende, L.: MindNet: Acquiring and Structuring Semantic Information from Text. In: COLING-ACI 1998, pp. 1098–102 (1998)

# Chinese Text Feature Dimension Reduction Based on Semantics[*]

Zhenlei Du, Yangsen Zhang, Ruijuan Zheng, and Lin Jiang

Institute of Intelligence Information Processing,
Beijing Information Science and Technology University, Beijing 100192, China
dzl1215@126.com

**Abstract.** Feature dimension reduction is an important step in text categorization, but traditional feature dimension reduction method ignores semantic information of features. In order to solve this problem, this paper, with the semantic dictionary, proposes a new feature dimensionality reduction processing method. The word-semantic knowledge base is constructed on the basis of HowNet and The Semantic Knowledge-base of Contemporary Chinese. By using the knowledge base and the feature extraction method, text feature is mapped to semantic feature and the dimensional reduction of feature space is realized. Naïve Bayes method is introduced to verify the categorization performance. The experimental results indicate that the proposed approach has a good performance of high dimension reduction and categorization.

**Keywords:** Feature Dimension Reduction, Semantics, Knowledge Base, Text Categorization.

## 1 Introduction

The rapid development of Internet technology brings human beings into the era of big data, in which information is abundant and updates constantly. Especially, with the emergence of various mobile terminals and social networking in recent years, mass text messages constantly emerge and spread every day. These messages bring large amount of information to the user, make it difficult to find, filter and manage information. Therefore, finding needed information quickly and accurately and filtering out irrelevant data has gained focus from both industry and academic community. Meanwhile, the research of text categorization technology has received continuous attention. Text categorization is the process in which a given text, by its characteristics (content or attributes), was associated with one or more categories under the predefined classification system [1].

[*] This paper is funded by the Natural Science Foundation of China (NSFC, Grant No.61070119), the Project of Construction of Innovative Teams and Teacher Career Development for Universities and Colleges Under Beijing Municipality (Grant No. IDHT20130519) and the Beijing Municipal Education Commission Special Fund (Grant No. PXM2012-014224-000020).

P. Liu and Q. Su (Eds.): CLSW 2013, LNAI 8229, pp. 396–405, 2013.

The process of text categorization as a whole can be divided into two phases of training and categorization. The training phase is to construct categorization model through the connection between text data set and categorizations, and make preparations for the categorization stage. The categorization stage is the process of labeling unknown text category according to the training result, including five steps of text preprocessing, text representation, feature dimension reduction, training of the classifier and performance evaluation. Currently the mainstream of text representation is using vector space model (VSM) for representation of text features. That is, constructing text-entry matrix by calculating frequency of entries appeared in the text. However, since the vector's attributes may involve all Chinese words [2], the matrix dimension is very large, which makes text categorization very complicated. The method to solve this problem is dimension reduction of text feature matrix at first.

## 2    Survey of Commonly Used Feature Dimension Reduction Methods

In text categorization, the high dimensional issue of feature space is one of the main obstacles [3]. Commonly used dimension reduction methods include feature selection and feature extraction. Feature selection generally refers to, by a certain criterion, choosing related features from numerous raw features that can best reflecting the statistical characteristics of model categories, i.e. finding best feature to describe the text subset, or feature set reduction in essence [4]. Commonly used feature selection methods include: document frequency (DF), mutual information (MI), information gain (IG), statistics (CHI), expected cross entropy (ECE), weighted evidence for text (WET), etc. [5~7].

Basically the idea is to first rate each feature word independently by using some evaluation function, and then collect feature words with higher score as text feature subset. These methods select feature set that representing text by feature frequency or correlation statistics information between features and categories, and noise in feature space can be effectively removed. However, they are not satisfactory in solving the problem of data sparseness, as they ignore the synonymous and redundant relation between words.

Feature extraction is a mapping or transforming from the original measurement space to feature space, namely, by means of constructing a feature scoring function, the value of feature space data from the measured space can be retrieved, and then features with highest value can be extracted to form a feature set. At present major feature extraction methods are principal component analysis (PCA), latent semantic indexing (LSI), non-negative matrix factorization (NMF), etc. [8]. Feature extraction is to form a new set of features by changing the nature of the original feature space, in which combination features often only have mathematical sense.

Part of speech of the Chinese language are more flexible, dimension reduction methods that have better performance in English may not be applicable to the Chinese. Therefore, this paper focused on the study seeking efficient feature extraction method, reducing the dimension of feature space and improving the efficiency and accuracy of the text representation. Based on the characteristics of Chinese text, we extract feature words using chi-square statistics and semantic feature knowledge base constructed on the HowNet and The Semantic Knowledge-base of Contemporary Chinese (SKCC), eliminate redundant features, and achieve the dimension reduction based on semantic features. In theory, it can fundamentally improve the categorization accuracy, in view of the semantic relation within the whole text, between sentences and between phrases.

# 3    Construction of Word-Semantic Knowledge Base

At present, major semantic resources of Chinese text are SKCC and HowNet, etc. SKCC describes semantic class of every word, while words of the same semantic category will have relatively strong semantic similarity. For example, nouns "car" and "bicycle" both belong to the class of vehicle, thus the semantic difference between them is smaller than that between "car" and "rice" (belonging to the class of foods). The tree-structured semantic class system has a detailed description for the semantics of the words in the semantic tree with different words belonging to different leaf nodes.

Using sememe to describe semantic information of words, HowNet greatly reduces the complexity of Chinese words. As a unique feature of HowNet, it has more than 2,000 carefully selected "semantic primitives" that can't be further segmented, including 10 categories of sememes: events, the entities, attribute values and so on [9]. Eight complex relations exist between sememes, including hyponymy, synonymy, antonymy, etc. composing a complex net structure. Hyponymy is most important among all relations. Sememe relations can be simplified into a tree structure, i.e. each category of sememes form a tree structure, and each tree node is a sememe.

Semantic class has standard tree structure and sememes can also be approximated to, with similar structure. Both sememe and semantic class can express the semantic difference between two words clearly and accurately, providing effective way for scientific quantification of word semantics and scientific computation of semantic research. Through a comprehensive study of knowledge in the HowNet and SKCC, this paper extracts semantic knowledge to verbs, nouns and adjectives.

## 3.1    Structure Design of Word-Semantic Knowledge Base

In the HowNet, the sememe description of a single word is not fixed. After investigating the situation of sememe representation of word semantics, this paper maps the semantics of verbs and adjectives to their main sememes, and those of nouns are mapped to main sememes and five auxiliary sememes, namely, PartPosition, Whole, Domain, Host, Modifier. As for SKCC, since semantic information is relatively weak, all such semantic information is mapped to semantic class attributes. Finally, all the properties of the two dictionaries are combined to form a new word-semantic mapping. Statistically, more than 80,000 "word-semantic" mappings are extracted. After further manual correction, we remove some basic words (with themselves as sememes in HowNet), and delete semantic items for words with interpretations too general in SKCC (as opposed to sememes in HowNet) while retaining their sememes. Storage structure is shown in Table 1.

Table 1. Storage structure of "Word-Semantic Mapping" knowledge base

| POS | Main sememe | PartPosi-tion | Whole | Do-main | Host | Modi-fier | Semantic |
|---|---|---|---|---|---|---|---|
| Noun | | | | | | | |
| Verb | - | - | - | - | - | | |
| Adjec-tive | - | - | - | - | - | | |

Note: "-" indicates this does not exist.

### 3.2    Algorithm Design of Word-Semantic Knowledge Base

**Algorithm 1.**Construction algorithm of word-semantic knowledge base

**Step1:** Load HowNet and SKCC, then read the HowNet information and store into haHownet, read semantic dictionary information in the SKCC and store into haSemantic;

**Step2:** Circularly scan haHownet, retrieve current word and its part of speech, store into CurWord and CurPos, respectively;

**Step3:** If CurPos is a verb or an adjective, choose its main sememe as partial semantic mapping, while taken advantage of CurWord to obtain corresponding semantic class information from haSemantic, the above two are encapsulated as current word's full semantic mapping;

**Step4:** If CurPos is a noun, choose its main sememe and the five secondary sememe mentioned in the last section as partial semantic mapping of the current word; while taken advantage of CurWord to obtain corresponding semantic class information from haSemantic, the encapsulation of the above two as current word's full semantic mapping;

**Step5:** When traversal of haHownet is done, store the word-semantic mapping information of all words in a text according to the format of table 1;

**Step6:** End.

## 4    Feature Dimension Reduction Based on the Semantics

### 4.1    Word-Semantic Mapping

By observation, we found that there are a large number of words that have same semantics in the training samples. For example: words "Audi", "Audi car", "car", "front", "rear", etc. may appear multiple times in a document. Previously established word-semantics knowledge base is utilized to reconstruct character vectors with corresponding word-semantic mappings, thus the original document is mapped from basic concepts level to semantic level. By replacing basic level word statistical information with semantic information as the feature item in feature vector space, not only the document information or category information can be mapped into several feature properties to achieve feature dimension reduction but also the meaning of this document and its category information can be highlighted.

For each document $D_i$ in document set, the feature vector constituted by keywords can be expressed as,

$$D = D_i(d(t_1, w_{i1}), d(t_2, w_{i2}), \ldots, d(t_t, w_{it})) \tag{1}$$

Where $t_j (j = 1, 2, \ldots, t)$ is feature items, $w_{ij}(i = 1, 2, \ldots, n)$ is the weight of feature item $t_j$ in the i-th document.

In word-semantic mapping for key word $t_j$ in document $D_i$, the semantics information should be obtained firstly for words having double meanings of sememe definitions and word semantics. If the semantic information does not exist, then sememe information should be obtained. As the HowNet and SKCC currently include limited entries and some keywords are not included in the HowNet, we have kept the original form for these keywords. The compactness of inner category information is strengthened by semantic replacement, and the distinguishability between categories is more obvious, making categorization more accurate.

## 4.2    Weight Evaluation Based on Semantics

TF-IDF is commonly used among methods of feature weight evaluation. The TF-IDF value of entry $t_i$ in a document could be defined by the following formula,

$$TF\text{-}IDF_i = TF_i \times \log(\frac{N}{n_i}) \tag{2}$$

Among the formula $TF_i$ is frequency of entries appearing in the document; $N$ is the total number of all training documents; $n_i$ is the number of documents that contain entry $t_i$. In practical applications, taken into account the influence of text length to the weights, normalization should be done to the weight formula and weights should be normalized to the interval of [0, 1].

$$TF\text{-}IDF_i = \frac{TF_i \times \log\dfrac{N}{n_i}}{\sqrt{\sum(TF_i \times \log\dfrac{N}{n_i})^2}} \tag{3}$$

TF-IDF takes the ratio of the number of times that feature word $t_i$ appearing in document D to the number of documents containing $t_i$ as the weight of word $t_i$. Term frequency (TF) is used to calculate the ability of the term describing the document, inverse document frequency (IDF) is used to calculate the ability of the word distinguishing documents. TF-IDF considers the smaller the probability of a word appearing in the text, the greater the capability it distinguishes different categories. The inverse document frequency (IDF) is an adjustment to the weights of TF, aiming to highlight important words and suppress secondary words. The semantic and keyword vector space weight evaluation formed after semantic mapping is divided into two parts: the keywords section are evaluated using equation (2), and $d(s_s, w_{is})$ section are evaluated using the following semantic weight calculation method,

$$d(t_s, w_{is}) = d(t_s, w_{is}) p(t) \qquad (4)$$

Where $p(t)$ is the probability of entry $t_s$ corresponding to each semantic interpretation.

New semantic feature vector space consisting of semantic items and keyword items is generated by the feature vector space of formula (1),

$$D = D_i(d(s_1, w_{i1}), d(s_2, w_{i2}), ..., d(s_s, w_{is}), d(t_1, w_{i1}), d(t_1, w_{i2}), ..., d(t_1, w_{it})) \qquad (5)$$

Where $t_j (1 < j < t)$ is reserved keyword items; $s_i (1 < i < s)$ is semantic items, while $d(s_s, w_{is})$ is the weight of semantic item $s_i$ in text $D_i$. The changes of semantic and keyword vector space dimension formed after semantic mapping are shown in Figure 1.

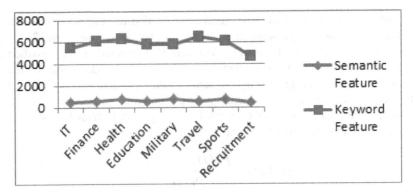

**Fig. 1.** Changes of keyword vector to semantic vector

## 4.3    Semantic-Based Feature Extraction

According to the distribution of feature items in the document, the significance of feature in the feature space is calculated and features of high value are retained. Y.Yang [10] compared feature extraction methods for text categorization, and it showed that $\chi^2$ statistics method selects fewer features while ensuring categorization results.

$\chi^2$ statistics method measures the degree of correlation between feature item t and document class c, and assumes a first order degrees of freedom distribution exists between t and c. The higher the statistical value of some feature to some class, the bigger correlation with it, and more categorical information carried with it. Let N be the total number of documents in the training corpus, c is a specific category, t represents a feature, A is the number of documents that belong to category c and contain feature t, B is the number of documents that does not belong to category c but contain feature t, C is the number of documents that belong to the category c but do not contain feature t, D is the number of documents that neither belong to c nor contain feature t. $\chi^2$ value of t for c could be calculated by the following formula,

$$\chi^2(t,c) = \frac{N \times (AD - CB)^2}{(A+C)(B+D)(A+B)(C+D)} \tag{6}$$

Features fall below a specific threshold should be removed from the original feature space, and those above the threshold should be reserved as document representation.

Chi-square value of the items could be calculated with the results after semantic replaced using $\chi^2$ statistical. The feature items could be sorted according to $\chi^2$ statistical value; feature words meeting the threshold constraint could be retained; and redundant features could be eliminated and rebuild to form a new feature space.

## 4.4    Text Categorization Based on the Semantic Features

In this paper, a Naive Bayesian (NB) based classification method is used. Assuming that $D(w_1, w_2, ..., w_n)$ represents the document vector to be classified, and $w_i(i = 1,2, ..., n)$ represents features of document D. Documents to be classified are firstly processed through word-semantic mapping to constitute semantic feature space, and are then processed through semantic feature extraction to form a new semantic feature space, dimension reduction is then achieved.

Assuming there exists a set of categories $C(c_1, c_2, ..., c_n)$. With Bayes' theorem, the categorization model could be abstracted as,

$$P(c_i \mid D) = \frac{P(D \mid c_i)P(c_i)}{P(D)} \tag{7}$$

Because $P(D)$ can be regarded as a constant for all classes, equation (7) can be simplified as,

$$P(c_i \mid D) = P(D \mid c_i)P(c_i) \tag{8}$$

Meanwhile, since all the properties of the categorization model are assumed to be mutually independent in NB. $P(c_i)$ is a constant, and the following derivation can be obtained from equation (8),

$$P(c_i \mid D) = P(D \mid c_i)P(c_i) = P(w_1, w_2, ... w_n \mid c_i)P(c_i) = \pi_{i=1}^{n} P(w_i \mid c_i) \tag{9}$$

Taking maximum of equation (9), i.e., if there are

$$P(c_k \mid D) = Max\{P(c_1 \mid D), P(c_2 \mid D), ..., P(c_n \mid D)\} \tag{10}$$

Then the maximum class is selected as the category of the document for a given document D.

## 5     Experimental Results

Text experiment data used in this paper comes from the classified corpus of Chinese news text provided by *Sogou* open experimental platform. We have collected 16,888 texts after removal of duplicate documents, English documents and damaged documents. Then texts are divided into eight categories, as finance, IT, health, sports, travel, education, military and recruitment. Each document is about 100 to 5,000 words in length. We extract more than 14,000 articles from pre-processed texts as training corpus, and extract more than 3,300 articles from the Internet as test corpus to conduct the Naive Bayesian categorization experiments.

To evaluate the result of categorization, we use the general method of performance evaluation: the Recall rate, the Precision rate and $F_1$ value. For some specific category:

$$\mathrm{Re}\,call = \frac{\#of\ correct\ positive\ predictions}{\#of\ positive\ examples} \tag{11}$$

$$\mathrm{Pr}\,ecision = \frac{\#of\ correct\ positive\ predictions}{\#of\ positive\ predictions} \tag{12}$$

$$F_1 = \frac{2 \times \mathrm{Re}\,call \times \mathrm{Pr}\,ecision}{\mathrm{Re}\,call + \mathrm{Pr}\,ecision} \tag{13}$$

In order to validate the semantic replacement's influence on categorization results, we have collected and analyzed experiment data before and after the semantic replacement. Categorization experiment results are shown in table 2 and table 3:

**Table 2.** Experimental result before semantic mapping

| Category | Precision | Recall | $F_1$ |
|---|---|---|---|
| Military | 0.9397 | 0.8416 | 0.8879 |
| Finance | 0.5512 | 0.7874 | 0.6485 |
| IT | 0.6850 | 0.7527 | 0.7173 |
| Health | 0.8911 | 0.8824 | 0.8867 |
| Sports | 0.6533 | 0.9891 | 0.7868 |
| Travel | 0.8300 | 0.8157 | 0.8228 |
| Education | 0.8357 | 0.5262 | 0.6459 |
| Recruitment | 0.7185 | 0.6929 | 0.7055 |

**Table 3.** Experimental result after semantic mapping

| Category | Precision | Recall | F1 |
|---|---|---|---|
| Military | 0.9534 | 0.8564 | 0.9023 |
| Finance | 0.5465 | 0.8246 | 0.6573 |
| IT | 0.6825 | 0.9613 | 0.7983 |
| Health | 0.8738 | 0.9193 | 0.8960 |
| Sports | 0.7120 | 0.9921 | 0.8290 |
| Travel | 0.8231 | 0. 8093 | 0.8161 |
| Education | 0.8476 | 0.6335 | 0.7251 |
| Recruitment | 0.7407 | 0.6329 | 0.6826 |

Experimental results show that the recall rate, accuracy and $F_1$ value of text categorization have been somewhat improved by using the semantic features based dimension reduction method proposed in this paper. Figure 2 shows the improvements of $F_1$ value, especially in categories of IT, sports and education. Other categories also show slightly enhancements and thus somewhat proved the feasibility of the proposed method in this paper. Due to the introduction of category information of the training document collection into semantic feature space, while keeping the feature words of training document as far as possible, through the joint modeling of keyword information and categories, and the consideration of semantic correlation between keyword and category information, the categorization precision of some individual classes gains improvement to a certain extent. However, for texts of travel and recruitment categories, due to over-generalization of semantic features of keywords, distinctions among categories are reduced, making the categorization results decreased.

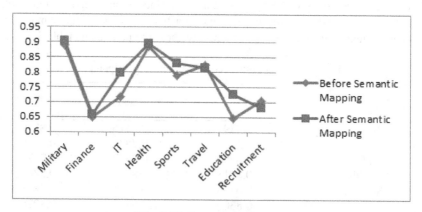

**Fig. 2.** F1 Comparison diagram

# 6    Conclusion

Dimension reduction is the bottleneck to the efficiency of text categorization. Semantic knowledge based text categorization is the focus of current research. This paper proposed a semantics-based feature dimension reduction method. Word-semantic knowledge base is extracted from HowNet and SKCC, and is used to map text to semantic feature space. $\chi^2$ statistical method is used to extract features from semantic feature space, and text feature dimension reduction on semantic level is thus achieved. Experimental results show that this dimension reduction method is feasible to some extent. Simple semantic dimensionality reduction reduces the distinguishing degree of words in the category information. From the perspective of semantic knowledge, there are a variety of collocations between words in the document. Word collocations are not only restricted by the semantic composition features, but also affected by the thinking habits and cultural customs. Therefore, they cannot be completely replaced by decontextualized words and semantics. Semantic collocations can effectively express the relationship among most words. Building semantic knowledge base on semantic level has significance importance in future research. We will further investigate the method of building semantic collocation, and the method of reducing feature dimensions to improve the efficiency of text categorization.

# References

1. Zong, C.: Statistical Natural Language Processing, pp. 340–353. Tsinghua University Press, Beijing (2008)
2. Dai, L., Huang, H.: A Comparative Study on Feature Selection in Chinese Text Categorization. Journal of Chinese Information Processing 18(1), 26–32 (2004)
3. Lewis, D.D.: Feature Selection and Feature Extraction for Text Categorization. In: Proceedings of the Workshop on Speech and Natural Language, pp. 23–26 (1992)
4. Liu, H., Wang, Y.: Mixed Method of Reducing Feature in Text Classification. Computer Engineering 35(2), 194–196 (2009)
5. Chen, J.: Research of Feature Selection Method for Chinese Text Classification. Northwest Normal University, Gansu (2012)
6. Zhang, B.: Analysis and Research on Feature Selection Algorithm for Text Classification. University of Science and Technology of China, Anhui (2010)
7. Wu, J., Kang, Y.: A Study on Feature Dimension Reduction in Text Categorization. Natural Science Journal of HaiNan University 25(1), 62–66 (2001)
8. Gao, M., Wang, Z.: Comparing Dimension Reduction Methods of Text Feature Matrix. Computer Engineering and Applications 30, 157–159 (2006)
9. Dong, Z., Dong, Q.: Theoretical Findings of HowNet. Journal of Chinese Information Processing 4(21), 3–9 (2007)
10. Yang, Y.: A Comparative Study on Feature Selection in Text Categorization. In: Proceeding of the Fourteenth International Conference on Machine Learning, pp. 412–423 (1997)

# Semantic Automatic Error-Detecting for Chinese Text Based on Semantic Dependency Relationship[*]

Jiayuan Li, Yangsen Zhang, Jinjin Zhu, and Zewei Zhang

Institute of Intelligence Information Processing,
Beijing Information Science and Technology University, Beijing 100192, China
ljyuan0616@126.com

**Abstract.** Automatic error-detecting for Chinese text is one of the important issues in the field of Chinese Information Processing. The current study of text error-detecting focuses on words-level and syntactic-level, but semantic error-detecting has not got enough attention. For this reason, we studied semantic collocations of sentences, and built up a words dependency knowledge base; at meanwhile, combined with the description of concept of words in HowNet, we proposed a semantic error-detecting strategy for Chinese text. Experimental results show that this method has a better performance in semantic error-detecting.

**Keywords:** Automatic proofreading for Chinese text, semantic error-detecting, semantic collocation, dependency grammar.

## 1 Introduction

Automatic error-detecting of text is one of the main applications of natural language processing. As early as the 1960s, researchers abroad initiate the research of automatic error-detecting of the English text. Up to this date, automatic error-detecting technology for English text is relatively mature, and there are a number of practical commercial systems, such as Microsoft Office Word. In the early 1990s, domestic researchers began to build Chinese text automatic proofreading system. The current study of Chinese text automatic proofreading methods has made great achievements and has been put into practical application, such as Black Horse Collation System, KINGSOFT WPS2000 etc. Errors appeared in Chinese text could be divided into three types: word-level errors, syntax-level errors and semantic-level errors[1], in which, the proportion of word-level errors is larger than syntax-level and semantic-level. At present, there are abundant studies on word-level error-detecting. For example, the model and algorithm based on the combination of rules and statistics proposed by literature [2] have achieved good effects. In contrast, research on syntax

[*] This paper is funded by the Natural Science Foundation of China(NSFC, Grant No.61070119), the Project of Construction of Innovative Teams and Teacher Career Development for Universities and Colleges Under Beijing Municipality(Grant No. IDHT20130519) and the Beijing Municipal Education Commission Special Fund (Grant No. PXM2012-014224-000020).

P. Liu and Q. Su (Eds.): CLSW 2013, LNAI 8229, pp. 406–415, 2013.

and semantic error-detecting is still not enough and proofreading results are not so good as word-level error-detecting. To improve the accuracy and recall rate of text automatic error-detecting, syntax-level and semantic-level approaches are the main concern of current research.

This paper proposes a novel semantic error-detecting strategy for Chinese text which focuses on semantic collocations among notional words in sentences. Firstly, dependency syntax parser is used to extract collocations of notional words. Meanwhile, a words dependency collocation knowledge base is built with the help of concepts of HowNet vocabularies. Then, we can find out semantic collocation errors in test text, using semantic collocation information in the knowledge base. The overall effect of the text error-detecting has been improved.

## 2　Errors in Chinese Text

A word or phrase is considered wrong because it is not suitable for its context, that is, the word or phrase has an improper collocation with other words[3]. In accordance with the errors encountered in Chinese text, errors can be divided into word-level, syntax-level and semantic-level.

(1) Word-level errors: these errors are mainly caused by misspelled words, repeated words, missed words or translocated words, etc. They can be subdivided into two kinds: one is caused by a string which cannot be found in knowledge base, while the other is caused by a string can be found in the dictionary, but usage of that word in the sentence is improper. For example:

example 1: 接到信后，他迫不急（及）待的连夜赶到县城。(*After receiving the letter, he rushed at once to the town that very night.*) (error of the first type)

example 2: 在未来的日子里，水将比珍珠还珍惜（珍贵）。(*In the future, water is more precious than pearls.*) (error of the second type)

(2) Syntax-level errors: these errors are defined as syntax exceptions destroying the whole structure of the sentence, and the syntax exceptions are caused by missed words, repeated words or useless words. For example:

example 3: 通过此次学雷锋活动，给同学们上了具有深刻意义的一课。(*The activities of learning from Lei Feng has a profound significance to students.*) (The elements of sentence is redundant or incomplete)

(3) Semantic-level errors: Some errors are neither word-level error nor syntax-level error, but some semantic collocation errors between sentence elements. For example:

example 4: 她穿了一双粉色的手套，非常可爱。(She wore a pair of pink gloves, very cute.) (collocation error between "穿[chuan] (*wear*)" and "手套[shoutao] (*glove*)") example 5: 我们带着太阳（太阳镜）好不好？(We take the sun ok?) (collocation error between "带着[daizhe] (*take*)" and "太阳[taiyang] (*sun*)" )

# 3    Semantic-Level Error-Detection Technology and Its Implementation

A domain independent text error proofreading system is consisted of error detection and error correction components of lexical, syntactic and semantic, and semantic error-detecting is only part of the system. After word and syntax error-detecting, semantic collocation of sentence elements still needs further examination, this is, semantic-level error-detecting[3]. Semantic-level error-detecting here doesn't check the reasonableness of the whole semantic frame of a sentence, but the semantic collocation of sentence elements, so there is no need to build up semantic framework of the whole sentence. In this paper, semantic dependency collocations based error-detecting method is proposed: Before error-detecting, large-scale corpus is processed to obtain dependency relations of sentence elements and dependency treebank is built. Then a word dependency collocation knowledge base is constructed with the dependency treebank as knowledge source. After that, on the basis of the constructed word dependency collocation knowledge base and the "HowNet"[4], we construct a semantic dependency collocation knowledge base. During error-checking, the sentence that needs to be proofread is firstly analyzed to get its sentence elements and word dependency collocations. Then, combined with HowNet, we translate the word dependency collocations into semantic dependency collocations. Finally, according to the semantic collocation information in the semantic dependency knowledge base, error-detecting system would determine whether the word collocations are semantically correct.

## 3.1    Building Up Dependency Treebank and Extracting Collocations

### 3.1.1    The Theory of Dependency Grammar
In the 1970s, Robinson put forward four axioms about dependency relation, which laid a foundation for dependency grammar, the four axioms are [5]:

(1) Only one member in a sentence is independent;
(2) The other members are directly dependent on a particular member;
(3) Any member cannot dependent on two or more than two members;
(4) If member A is directly dependent on member B, and member C is between A and B, then member C directly depends on B or a member between A and B.

In the 1990s, Chinese scholars initiated the research that applied the analytical method of dependency grammar to Chinese corpus linguistics. And combined with the practice of Chinese grammar, they proposed the fifth axiom of dependency grammar[6,7]:

The members on both sides of the central member are unrelated.

Connexion is one of the core concepts of dependency grammar. Words dependency relation, which is binary relation of word pairs, is established by connexion. One word of the word pair credited as head, the other one credited as dependent. Dependency relations reflect a semantic collocation relation between the head word and the dependent word. The collocation relation displayed a phenomenon that head word dominates the dependent word, and at the meantime, the dependent word is controlled by the head word. The dominant relationship reflects the dependency collocation information of words.

### 3.1.2 Building Up Dependency Treebank and Extracting Words Collocations

Before semantic error-detecting, words dependency collocations and dependency information of sentence elements must be found. First of all, by using syntactic parser implemented by Harbin Institute of Technology, corpus that mainly comes from the *People's Daily* is parsed. The accuracy of HIT syntactic parser can be as high as 86%. Based on the above work, we constructed a large-scale dependency treebank, with the treebank corpus totaling about 31 million words and its annotation information including the parts of speech, dependency types, etc. For example, "这位饱经风霜的老人将出现在体育场。(*The weather-beaten old man will appear in the stadium.*)", this sentence's parsing result is shown in figure 1:

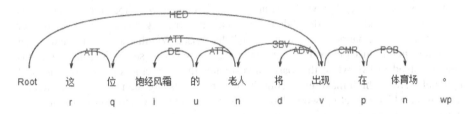

**Fig. 1.** The parsing result of "这位饱经风霜的老人将出现在体育场。"

Dependency parse result can be represented as "$A_i \leftarrow A_j$", where $A_i$ and $A_j$ are the two words in the dependency relations, and the symbol "$\leftarrow$" indicates the relation type, the arrow points to head word $A_j$. The $A_i$ is the dominant word, $A_j$ is dominated by $A_i$, and directly dependent on $A_i$.

The corpus we performed syntactic parse mainly comes from *People's Daily*. Dependency treebank describes the dependency collocations contained in sentences in detail. By parsing the corpus with dependency parser, a large-scale dependency treebank is constructed. The dependency treebank is stored in the form of XML, the format is shown in figure 2:

For example: "二〇〇〇年到来的钟声，就要鸣响在我们这个星球的寥廓上空。(*The bell of the arrival of 2000 will ringing in the boundless sky.*)"

```
<sent id="0" cont="二〇〇〇年到来的钟声，就要鸣响在我们这个星球的寥廓上空。">
  <word id="0" cont="二〇〇〇年" pos="nt" parent="1" relate="ADV" />
  <word id="1" cont="到来" pos="v" parent="2" relate="DE" />
  <word id="2" cont="的" pos="u" parent="3" relate="ATT" />
  <word id="3" cont="钟声" pos="n" parent="6" relate="SBV" />
  <word id="4" cont="，" pos="wp" parent="-2" relate="PUN" />
  <word id="5" cont="就要" pos="d" parent="6" relate="ADV" />
  <word id="6" cont="鸣响" pos="v" parent="12" relate="SBV" />
  <word id="7" cont="在" pos="p" parent="11" relate="DE" />
  <word id="8" cont="我们" pos="r" parent="7" relate="POB" />
  <word id="9" cont="这个" pos="r" parent="10" relate="ATT" />
  <word id="10" cont="星球" pos="n" parent="7" relate="POB" />
  <word id="11" cont="的" pos="u" parent="12" relate="ATT" />
  <word id="12" cont="寥廓" pos="a" parent="13" relate="ATT" />
  <word id="13" cont="上空" pos="nl" parent="-1" relate="HED" />
  <word id="14" cont="。" pos="wp" parent="-2" relate="PUN" />
</sent>
```

**Fig. 2.** The storage format of "二〇〇〇年到来的钟声，就要鸣响在我们这个星球的寥廓上空"

In this sentence, parent node of each word is shown behind corresponding words. For example, the word "二〇〇〇年[erlinglinglingnian] (*the year 2000*)", its "parent= 1", the word with "id =1" is "到来[daolai] (*arrival*)", therefore, dependency relation exists between "二〇〇〇年" and "到来".

With the treebank as knowledge source, word dependency collocations in sentences are discovered, and a word dependency collocation knowledge base is built for further construction of semantic collocation knowledge base. Whether the combinations of verbs and nouns in Chinese text are correct with respect to semantic collocation has been resolved in [8], while this paper investigates the correctness of combinations of notional words, which make great contributions to expressing the meaning of sentence. Therefore, when extracting word dependency collocations, we add notional words dependency collocations into words dependency collocation knowledge base. Notional words include nouns, verbs, adjectives, adverbs, numerals, quantifiers and pronoun, etc. The storage format of word dependency knowledge base is shown in table 1:

**Table 1.** Format of word dependency knowledge base

| ID | pre-collocate | post-collocate | frequency |
|---|---|---|---|
| ... | ... | ... | ... |

## 3.2 Building Semantic Dependency Collocation Knowledge Base Based on HowNet

Dependency grammar points out syntactic collocations of each word in sentence, and the meaning of a sentence is based on the collocation relations. Besides, dependency grammar can obtain the collocation information about the long-distance words, which has nothing to do with the physical location of the sentence elements. Therefore, we use the dependency parser and HowNet semantic information to find out possible semantic collocations in Chinese text, and then, we combined the semantic collocations with related algorithm to implement semantic error-detecting, such as the following two sentences:

example 1：学校开展了学雷锋的活动。(*School has started the activities of learning from Feng Lei.*)

example 2：学校开展了学雷锋。(*School has started learning from Feng Lei.*)

Dependency trees of the above sentences can be obtained through dependency parse. From the dependency tree of example 1, we can get all the word dependency collocations, but here, only the dependency collocations of national words are taken into account. Dependency collocations of the word "开展[kaizhang] (*start*)" in example 1 are:

（学校[xuexiao] (*school*)←开展）（开展→活动[huodong] (*activity*)）
dependency collocations of the word "开展" in example 2 are:
（学校←开展）（开展→学[xue] (*learn*)）

HowNet gives definition and tagged part-of-speech for each word in HowNet. According to HowNet, actually, the first feature (also is the main feature) of each word is the field the word belongs to. Usually, main feature can be used to describe the meaning of words, but for some fields of large category, it need to narrow the field by additional features.

According to the definitions of HowNet vocabularies, it can be found that the main feature (also is main sememe) of a word can be used to describe the meaning of the word. Many words contain more than one part-of-speech. For different parts-of-speech, the corresponding main sememes are also different. Therefore, according to the correspondence between word in HowNet and its part-of-speech in a sentence, we can get corresponding main sememe and sememe collocation with respect to its word dependency collocation. The sememe collocations of the word "开展" in above two example sentences show as follows:

（场所[changsuo] (*place*)←成长[chengzhang] (*grow up*)）
（成长→事情[shiqing] (*thing*)）
（场所←成长）（成长→模仿[mofang] (*imitate*)）

Based on the above insights, combining the definition of the HowNet vocabulary with dependency grammar theory, a semantic dependency collocation knowledge base can be built. According to sememe of HowNet, we translated the word dependency collocations into sememe dependency collocations, as a result, semantic information of collocation knowledge base has been enriched[9]. The following semantic automatic error-detecting algorithm is carried out on this basis.

This system built up a sememe collocation knowledge base by calculating the frequency and mutual information(MI) of all sememe collocations. Frequency and mutual information reflect the rationality of semantic co-occurrence from two aspects, thus, they can be seen as parameters when assess whether a semantic collocation is reasonable. For example the sememe collocations extracted from example 1 and example 2, according to sememes collocation rules, we predicate the collocation "成长→模仿" is unreasonable collocation. Thus, the error-detecting system can find out the semantic errors in the test text. The storage format of semantic dependency collocation knowledge base is shown in table 2.

**Table 2.** The storage format of semantic dependency collocation knowledge base

| ID | pre-sememe | post-sememe | frequency | MI |
|----|-----------|-------------|-----------|-----|
| ... | ... | ... | ... | ... |

### 3.3    The Algorithm of Semantic Automatic Error-Detecting

On the basis of semantic collocation knowledge base, we can realize semantic automatic error-detecting better. It's important to note that this proofreading system just check whether the collocation of two semantics is reasonable, instead of the whole semantic framework of sentence. The algorithm of semantic error-detecting is described as follows:

**Algorithm 1.** The algorithm of semantic error-detecting

Step1. Read the semantic dependency collocation knowledge base and HowNet information, and save them to hash table respectively;

Step2. Using dependency parser to analyze proofreading text sentence by sentence, generate dependency trees for all sentences, and save the trees to the file named test.xml;

Step3. Read file named test.xml sentence by sentence, combine with HowNet, translate notional word collocations extracted from all sentences into semantic dependency collocations and formatted as "sem1+sem2";

Step4. Look for semantic dependency collocation "sem1+sem2" in semantic dependency collocation knowledge base, according to frequency and mutual information of the collocation assess whether the semantic collocation is correct. Set frequency for feq, mutual information for MI, if feq=0, conclude that the collocation is error, than set error coefficients E=1, and turn to step5; if feq<3 and MI<2, concluded that the collocation may be wrong, than set E=0.5; Otherwise, set E=0 and turn to step6;

Step5. Call the error indication module to display errors and explain;

Step6. End.

# 4    Experimental Results and Analysis

In order to evaluate the automatic error-detecting system objectively, error-detecting system adopts the following performance indexes to measure system performance:

The accurate rate is defined as:

$$p = \frac{\text{The number of correctly identified errors}}{\text{The total number of errors identified by system}} \times 100\% \qquad (1)$$

The recall rate is defined as:

$$r = \frac{\text{The number of correctly identified errors}}{\text{The total number of errors in the test text}} \times 100\% \qquad (2)$$

The F-score was defined as:

$$F - \text{Score} = \frac{2 \times p \times r}{p+r} \times 100\% \qquad (3)$$

This experiment adopt People's Daily Corpus as training corpus when constructing dependency treebank, and 290 real texts for evaluation texts. The full evaluation texts are 6781 words, including 221 errors, in which there are 58 semantic errors. Because semantic error-detecting module is a part of proofreading system, it cannot be run separately. Therefore, there are experiments for comparison test. The first is: word error-detecting combined with syntax error-detecting to proofread; the second is: combining all three level (word-level, syntax-level, and semantic-level) to proofread. The experimental results are shown in table 3:

**Table 3.** Experimental results of two methods

| experimental method | precision | recall rate | F-Score |
| --- | --- | --- | --- |
| The first | 67.59% | 83.44% | 74.68% |
| The second | 69.66% | 84.16% | 76.23% |

From the experimental results, it can be seen that the precision, recall rate and F-score have been improved due to the incorporation of semantic error-detecting module. And better performance has been achieved on the combination of word and semantic error-detecting. However, the improvement is not significant. The main reason is that the proportion of semantic collocation errors is relatively small in all errors. In this experiment, semantic collocation errors accounted for 26%. Besides, some legal collocations were reported as illegal by the semantic error-detecting module. The main reasons are:

(1) Training corpus is not enough. *People's Daily* is the official newspaper of Central Committee of the Chinese Communist Part[10], it's mainly associated with news stories, and its filed coverage is not comprehensive enough, therefore, leading to data

sparseness. For this reason, the semantic dependency collocation knowledge base is incomplete, leading to many legal semantic collocations cannot be found in semantic dependency knowledge base, and eventually, some legal collocations were reported as illegal.

(2) When assessing whether a collocation is correct, the thresholds of frequency and mutual information of the collocation may influence the result.

(3) There are some wrong parse results when analyzing sentences by dependency parser, thus, this wrong corresponding collocations may lead to misjudgment.

(4) The semantic of new word and its solution are not taken into account, which is the reason for misjudgment.

## 5     Conclusion

This paper proposes a semantic automatic error-detecting strategy based on semantic dependency collocation knowledge base and HowNet. A semantic collocation knowledge base is constructed using dependency grammar. Semantic error-detecting experiment is carried out with satisfactory results. The experimental results show that automatic error-detecting in semantic-level is feasible and contributes to text proofreading. However, there're more work to be done in future work, such as improving construction method of knowledge base to expand its scale; proposing a solution for semantic collocation of new words, and making a further improvement for system's performance.

## References

1. Watterson, C., Jurosher, J.R., Bensema, W.D.: Experimental Confirmation of an HF Channel Model. IEEE Transactions on Communication Technology 18(6), 792–803 (1970)
2. Zhang, Y., Cao, Y., Yu, S.: A Hybrid Model of Combining Rule-based and Statistics-based Approaches for Automatic Detecting Errors in Chinese Text. Journal of Chinese Information Processing 20(4), 1–7 (2005); (张仰森, 曹大元, 俞士汶. 基于规则与统计相结合的中文文本自动查错模型与算法. 中文信息学报
3. Luo, W., Luo, Z., Gong, X.: Study of Semantic Errors Checking in Automatic Proofreading for Chinese Text. Computer Engineering and Applications 39(12), 116–117 (2003); (骆卫华,罗振声,宫小瑾.中文文本自动校对的语义级查错研究. 计算机工程与应用
4. Dong, Z., Dong, Q.: HowNet Knowledge Database [OL] (2000), http://www.keenage.com
5. Tesniere, L.: Element de Syntaxe Structural. Klincksieck, Paris (1959)
6. Zhou, M., Huang, C.: Approach to the Chinese Dependency Formalism For the Tagging of Corpus. Journal of Chinese Information Processing 8(3), 22–24 (1994); (周明,黄昌宁. 面向语料库标注的汉语依存体系的探讨. 中文信息学报

7. Liu, W., Wang, M., Zhong, Y.: On Study of Hierarchy Structure of Dependency Relations in Chinese. Journal of Chinese Information Processing 10(2), 32–45 (1996); (刘伟权,王明会,钟义信.建立现代汉语依存关系的层次体系. 中文信息学报

8. Guo, C., Zhang, Y.: Study of Semantic Automatic Error-detecting for Chinese Text Based on Sememe Matching of HowNet. Computer Engineering and Design 31(17), 3924–3928 (2010); (郭 充. 张仲森.基于《知网》义原搭配的中文文本语义级自动查错研究. 计算机工程与设计

9. Chen, J., Luo, Z.: An Approach to Word Sense Disambiguation Based on Collocation. Microcomputer Information 24(3), 187–188 (2008); (陈佳,罗振声. 一种基于语义搭配的汉语词义消歧方法. 微计算机信息

10. Baidu, http://baike.baidu.com/view/38274.htm

# Studies on a Hybrid Way of Rules and Statistics for Chinese Conjunction Usages Recognition

Lijuan Zhou[1,2] and Hongying Zan[1]

[1] Zhengzhou University, Zhengzhou, China
lz683@uowmail.edu.au, iehyzan@zzu.edu.cn
[2] University of Wollongong, Wollongong, Australia
lz683@uowmail.edu.au

**Abstract.** Conjunction is a kind of functional words. Different conjunctions may contain different usages. The same conjunction may have different usages in different contexts. Studies on conjunction usage recognition are helpful for automatic understanding of modern Chinese texts. This paper adopts a hybrid way of rules and statistics to identify conjunction usages. Experiment results show that the methods combining rules and statistics are helpful for automatic recognition of conjunction usages. Among them, F measure of the participle and part-of-speech tagging corpus of the April , May, June 2000 People' s Daily achieves 91.42%, 90.88%, 90.92% respectively in open test.

**Keywords:** Conjunction, Rule, Statistics, Usage Recognition.

## 1 Introduction

Conjunction is mainly used to connect words, phrases, small clauses or sentences, indicating the relationship between words, phrases, clauses or sentences. Although the number of conjunctions is not very large, their functions and usages are complex and diverse. They have strong personality, a wide range of usages and high appearance frequency [1]. So conjunction plays an important role in modern Chinese grammar.

Conjunction usages refer to the places where conjunction with some meanings can be used. The same conjunction may indicate different meanings in different contexts and have different usages, such as the following sentences including conjunction "此外(moreover)" from [2]:

(1)小余会说北京话和上海话，此外也懂点儿广州话(Xiao Yu can speak Beijing language and Shanghai language. Moreover, he also knows a little Guangzhou language.)

(2)他一生就写过这两部书，此外没有别的著作了(He wrote only the two books in his life. Moreover, he didn't write other books.)

The conjunction "此外(moreover)" stands for "there is something except this" in the first clause while the conjunction "此外(moreover)" stands for "there is nothing except this" in the second. The conjunction "此外(moreover)" refers to different meanings in the two clauses. So their usages are different. The words are positive

P. Liu and Q. Su (Eds.): CLSW 2013, LNAI 8229, pp. 416–424, 2013.

after the conjunction "此外(moreover)" in the first sentence, while the words are positive after the conjunction "此外(moreover)" in the second sentence.

Semantic information could be understood preferably after all different usages are surveyed. At present, conjunction usage dictionary contains 315 conjunctions and 696 usages [3], [4]. Therefore, recognizing usages manually is time-consuming and labor-consuming in the large-scale corpus. To determine the use of conjunctions by people cost not only time but also labor. Automatic recognition is a method that the machine recognizes usages automatically. Its research is helpful for the analysis of modern Chinese chapters. The results that machine automatically recognizes in the above sentences are shown as follows. They are ID of usage in angle brackets [5].

(1)小余/nr　会/v　说/v　北京话/nz　和/c　上海/ns　话/n　，/w　此外 /c<c_ci3wai4_1>　也/d　懂/v　点儿/q　广州/ns　话/n (Xiao Yu can speak Beijing language and Shanghai language. Moreover, he also knows a little Guangzhou language.)

(2)他/r　一生/n　就/d　写/v　过/u　这/r　两/m　部/n　书/n　，/w　此外 /c<c_ci3wai4_2>　没有/v　别的/r　著作/v　了/y(He wrote only the two books in his life. Moreover, he didn't write other books.)

## 2 Related Work

Yu et al. [6] initially put forward the thoughts of building the "Trinity" knowledge base of modern Chinese functional words and defined functional words as adverb, preposition, conjunction, auxiliary, modality and position words. Zan et al. [7] constructed modern Chinese functional words knowledge base which contains usage dictionary, usage rule base and usage corpora of functional words. Liu et al. [8] discussed automatic recognition of adverb usages based on rules preliminarily. Zhang [9] studied automatic recognition of common Chinese adverb usages based on statistics. These studies mainly aim at constructing knowledge base of functional words or automatic recognition of adverb usages. However, studies on conjunction usages which are applied to machines are limited, such as recognition of conjunction usages.

Author [3], [4] preliminarily studied automatic recognition of modern Chinese conjunction usage is based on rules on the basis of studies of other function words and realized automatic recognition of a small number of conjunctions usages based on statistics. The statistical recognition and rule recognition are performed separately here. Rule-based method is simple and easy to understand. But it cannot be obtained automatically through machine learning and is difficult to adjust according to actual data. So rule-based method is incomplete and it is difficult to distinguish, write and optimize, such as the following sentences including conjunction "可是(however)" from Zhang [10]:

(1)佃农家的生活自然是很苦的，可是由于母亲的能干，也勉强过得下去(The life of tenant farmer is very hard. However, he can support it because of the effort of mother.)

(2)青春啊，永远是美好的，可是真正的青春，只属于永远力争上游的人，永远忘我劳动的人，永远谦虚的人(Youth is always nice. However, true youth belongs to people with aim high, ecstasy labor and modest.)

The conjunction "可是(however)" all stands for the relationship of transition in the two sentences. The meaning of the words are different before and after the conjunction "可是(however)" in the first sentence and they are opposite. The words after the conjunction "可是(however)" are supplements of front words in the second sentence. The two usages can be understood by readers, but it is difficult to depict with the same or different meanings through rules.

Empirical method based on the statistics obtains language knowledge from training data automatically or semi-automatically, sets up effectively statistical language model and optimize according to the actual situation of training data constantly. But single usage or usages with sparse distribution could not be recognized by statistical method. There are 156 single usages in 696 usages [3], [4]. Therefore statistical method may have a large negative influence on the recognition results in this situation.

This paper aims to adopt the combinational methods of rule and statistics to recognize conjunction usages and use their upsides as possible to improve the effects of automatic recognition of conjunction usages according to their advantages and disadvantages.

## 3    Automatic Recognition of Conjunction Usage by Combining Rules and Statistics

### 3.1    Combinational Methods

This paper adopts five different combinational methods to recognize conjunction usage. Method RSc is mainly an improvement of rule-based method. The original rule-based method is that if a rule of a conjunction could be matched successfully by sequence, the recognition process will end. Now all rules of a conjunction would be matched. If there are more than one match results, statistical recognition module would be called. If statistical recognition results are in the rule results, statistical recognition results are the final result. If the two results are inconsistent with each other, find the existing usage distribution rate according to the file "C_D_Pr_Ps.txt" to select the usage with the highest rate as the final result. The file "C_D_Pr_Ps.txt" records usage distribution rate, rule precision and statistical precision of every usage of every conjunction. Fig. 1 is the flow chart of recognizing the usage of a conjunction in method RSc. Among them, the file "C_D_Pr_Ps.txt" records example date as follow:

```
$所以
@<c_suo3yi3_1a>#0.474#0.995#0.9648
@<c_suo3yi3_1b>#0.486#1#0.9522
@<c_suo3yi3_1c>#0.04#0.857#0.9286
```

"<c_suo3yi3_1a>", "<c_suo3yi3_1b>"and "<c_suo3yi3_1c>" are the three usages of conjunction "所以(so)". The date that is separated by "#" after each usage is respectively usage distribution rate, rule precision and statistical precision from left to right.

Method RSr, RSs, RScrs are improvement of method RSc. Method RSr is that finding usage rule precision replacing finding usage distribution rate of method RSc. Method RSs is that finding usage statistical precision replacing finding usage distribution rate of method RSc and choosing the high accuracy as the final result. High usage distribution rate does not mean high recognition precision. High recognition precision does not mean high usage distribution rate. Therefore, using only one factor as a criterion is not sufficient. Method RScrs takes into account usage distribution rate and recognition precision. If results are rule recognition results, usage distribution rate will be multiplied rule recognition precision, while if results are statistical recognition results, usage distribution rate will be multiplied statistical recognition precision. Finally, the usage with bigger product date is the final result.

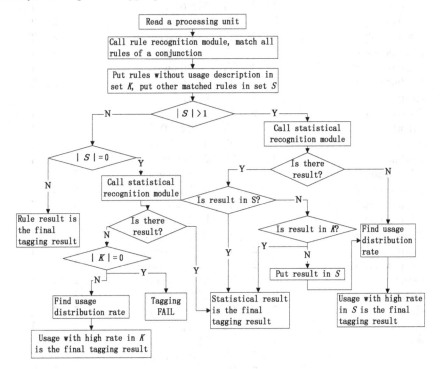

**Fig. 1.** Flow chart of method RSc based on rules and statistics

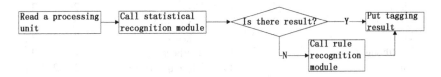

**Fig. 2.** Flow chart of method SR based on rules and statistics

Method SR disposes conjunctions of multiple usages and single usages separately. Statistical recognition module will be called for conjunctions of multiple usages. Rule recognition module will be called for conjunctions with no recognition results. If a rule can be matched successfully, recognition result will be outputted. Conjunctions with no recognition results contain three types as following: conjunction with single usage, such as "与(and), 以便(in order), 而是(but)" etc., conjunction with sparse usage distribution, such as "倘若(if), 不然(otherwise)" etc., and conjunction that total number of appearing is less than 6 times, such as "如若(if), 甚或(even)", etc.. Flow chart is shown in Fig. 2.

**Table 1.** Context window size and feature template of conjunctions which are corresponding with model

| word | L | R | T | word | L | R | T |
|---|---|---|---|---|---|---|---|
| 并(and) | 2 | 7 | $T_3$ | 那(then) | 2 | 9 | $T_3$ |
| 并且(and) | 2 | 2 | $T_3$ | 那么(then) | 2 | 4 | $T_3$ |
| 不但(not only) | 2 | 5 | $T_2$ | 那末(then) | 2 | 2 | $T_3$ |
| 不光(not only) | 2 | 2 | $T_3$ | 乃至(and even) | 2 | 2 | $T_2$ |
| 不仅(not only) | 2 | 2 | $T_3$ | 且(moreover) | 2 | 5 | $T_3$ |
| 不论(no matter) | 2 | 2 | $T_3$ | 然而(however) | 2 | 3 | $T_3$ |
| 不如(not so as) | 2 | 2 | $T_3$ | 任(let) | 2 | 2 | $T_3$ |
| 诚然(indeed) | 2 | 2 | $T_2$ | 如(if) | 2 | 2 | $T_3$ |
| 除非(only if) | 2 | 9 | $T_3$ | 如果(if) | 2 | 2 | $T_3$ |
| 但(but) | 9 | 4 | $T_3$ | 如果说(if) | 2 | 2 | $T_3$ |
| 但是(but) | 5 | 6 | $T_2$ | 若(if) | 2 | 2 | $T_3$ |
| 而(while) | 2 | 3 | $T_1$ | 甚至(even) | 2 | 3 | $T_1$ |
| 而且(but also) | 2 | 2 | $T_3$ | 虽(although) | 2 | 2 | $T_3$ |
| 尔后(thereafter) | 2 | 2 | $T_3$ | 虽然(although) | 2 | 2 | $T_3$ |
| 反之(conversely) | 2 | 2 | $T_3$ | 所以(so) | 2 | 2 | $T_3$ |
| 非但(not only) | 2 | 5 | $T_3$ | 同时(meanwhile) | 6 | 7 | $T_3$ |
| 否则(otherwise) | 3 | 2 | $T_3$ | 无论(no matter) | 2 | 3 | $T_1$ |
| 固然(no doubt) | 2 | 2 | $T_2$ | 无奈(however) | 2 | 3 | $T_3$ |
| 何况(much less) | 2 | 2 | $T_3$ | 要不(otherwise) | 2 | 3 | $T_3$ |
| 和(and) | 6 | 5 | $T_3$ | 要不是(but for) | 2 | 2 | $T_3$ |
| 还是(still) | 9 | 7 | $T_3$ | 要么(or) | 2 | 3 | $T_3$ |
| 或(or) | 2 | 2 | $T_3$ | 要是(suppose) | 2 | 2 | $T_3$ |
| 或是(or) | 2 | 2 | $T_3$ | 一方面(on the one hand) | 2 | 2 | $T_3$ |
| 或者(or) | 2 | 2 | $T_3$ | 以(in order to) | 2 | 2 | $T_3$ |
| 及(and) | 4 | 2 | $T_3$ | 以及(as well as ) | 2 | 2 | $T_3$ |
| 即便(even if) | 2 | 2 | $T_3$ | 以至(up to) | 3 | 5 | $T_3$ |
| 即使(even if) | 2 | 2 | $T_2$ | 以至于(so that) | 2 | 2 | $T_3$ |
| 既(since) | 2 | 2 | $T_1$ | 抑或(or) | 2 | 5 | $T_1$ |
| 既然(since) | 2 | 3 | $T_3$ | 因(because) | 2 | 2 | $T_3$ |
| 假如(if) | 2 | 2 | $T_3$ | 因此(so) | 2 | 2 | $T_3$ |
| 尽管(although) | 2 | 2 | $T_3$ | 因为(because) | 5 | 3 | $T_3$ |
| 可(but) | 2 | 2 | $T_3$ | 与其(rather than) | 2 | 2 | $T_1$ |
| 可见(as you see) | 2 | 3 | $T_3$ | 只是(just) | 2 | 2 | $T_3$ |
| 可是(however) | 2 | 2 | $T_3$ | 只要(so long as) | 2 | 2 | $T_3$ |
| 况且(moreover) | 2 | 2 | $T_3$ | 只有(only if) | 8 | 2 | $T_3$ |
| 另一方面(on the other hand) | 2 | 2 | $T_2$ | 总之(in conclusion) | 2 | 2 | $T_3$ |
| 哪怕(even) | 3 | 9 | $T_3$ | | | | |

### 3.2    Statistical Recognition Module

Conjunction usage recognition problem can be seen as a sequence marking problem that identify usage of conjunction sequence. Conditional Random Field (CRF) can use words, part of speech and other multi-level resources. Therefore, this paper adopts CRF model to recognize conjunction usage.

CRF model [11] is a discriminate model proposed by Lafferty in 2001. CRF is an undirected graph model which calculates conditional probability of output node under the condition of giving input node. It inspects conditional probability of tagging sequence corresponding to input sequence. Its training target is to maximize conditional probability. In recent years, CRF has been confirmed that this model can perform very well in Natural Language Processing, such as Chinese word segmentation [12], Chinese Named Entity Recognition [13], Chinese Word Sense Disambiguation [14].

The paper adopts CRF++ 0.53[1] toolkit for conjunction usage recognition. Corpus needs to be transformed into feature files identified by the toolkit firstly. Feature files contain multiple blocks. A block can form a Chinese sentence and there is an empty line in two blocks. Each block contains multiple tokens and each token must be written in a line. A token contains many columns and every column is separated by spaces or tabs. The definition of the token can be chosen according to specific tasks, such as words, parts of speech, etc. In the experiment, words and parts of speech of the context of conjunction is the basis of recognizing conjunction usage. The paper selects different range of words and parts of speech according to the size of the context window.

In order to get better statistical recognition effects, statistical recognition module adopts the best model pre-trained of every conjunction to realize open test. So the focus of statistical recognition module is how to find the best model. This paper chooses the participle and POS tagging corpus of three months of People's Daily (2000.1-2000.3) and adopts four folds cross-validations. Content window size is from 2 to 10 and feature template is the above three. The model corresponding to the highest recognition precision is the best model. Table 1 shows the left window size (L), the right window size (R) and feature template (T) model corresponding to the best model of 73 conjunctions with multiple usages.

### 3.3    Rule Recognition Module

Rule recognition module adopts the method of the author's article [3], [4] and uses six features: F, M, L, R, N, E according to conjunction usage rules. F stands for head of the sentence which contains target conjunction, M stands for before target conjunction but not contiguous, L stands for before target conjunction and contiguous, R stands for behind target conjunction and contiguous, N stands for behind target conjunction but not contiguous, E stands for the end of the sentence that contains target conjunction. Rule recognition module devises six verifiers according to six features. If one rule can be matched successfully according to priority sequence, recognition program will end. If all the rules cannot be matched, recognition result is "FAIL". The specific recognition processes are:

---

[1] http://crfpp.sourceforge.net/

(1) Initialize tagging corpus and usage rule base. Split corpus into paragraphs for conjunctions that connect sentences or paragraphs according to line break. Split corpus into sentences for conjunctions that connect words, phrases or small clauses according to full stop, question mark, exclamation mark or line break. The processing units that contain sentences and paragraphs are read into memory with dynamic array. Usage rules are read into memory with hash table.

(2) Read the processing unit which needs to be tagged, find all conjunctions which need to be tagged and corresponding rules and dispose the processing unit to get corresponding dictionary and the original sentence, as well as the location of functional words which need tagging in dictionary and the original sentence.

(3) Search the rules of functional words which need to be tagged, read their usage rules in sequence. Then determine the kind of verifier to analyze and match usage rules and to determine the tagging result. At last, output the processing unit and read the next processing unit when all the conjunctions of the current processing unit are tagged. The tagging program is over when there is no a processing unit which needs tagging.

## 4    Experiments and Results Analysis

The experimental corpus is the participle and POS tagging corpus of three months of People's Daily (2000.4-2000.6). Evaluation criteria are precision (P), recall (R) and F measure (F) of all conjunctions in every month. The paper adopts open test of the above five combinational methods to recognize conjunction usage and compares with single rules method (R) and statistical method (S). The statistical method also adopts the best model in Table 1 for open test. The results are shown in Table 2. Among them, C# stands for the total number of conjunctions tagged manually in every month.

As can be seen from the table, whether it is P, R or F, the results of method SR are the highest, about 91%, while the results of method R are the lowest, about 84%. They also explain that rules summarized manually are one-sided. Although precision of method S is close to that of method RS, recall rate of method S is the lowest in the seven methods. This is mainly because of the conjunctions with single usage, sparse usage distribution. Method SR uses the advantages of rule and statistics, so its results are the best. The results of method RScrs are higher than those of methods RSc, RSr and RSs. They verify that usage distribution rate, rule precision and statistical precision have an impact on the recognition results. The results of method RSr are higher than those of methods RSc, SR and they show that influence of rule is large when one factor is taken into account. The results of method RSc, RSr, RSs and RScrs are lower than that of method SR since results of RSc, RSr, RSs and RScrs mainly depend on the rule recognition results and result of method SR largely depends on statistical results. So it is reasonable from theory that SR results are higher than those of RSc, RSr, RSs and RScrs. In addition, the results of five combinational methods are higher than that of a single method such as method R or S from F measure. It implies that the method of combining rule and statistics is feasible for conjunction usage recognition.

**Table 2.** Conjunctions usages recognition results with different methods

| corpus | method | C# | P(%) | R(%) | F(%) |
|--------|--------|-----|------|------|------|
| | R | | 84.63 | 84.36 | 84.50 |
| | S | | 90.31 | 79.49 | 84.56 |
| | RSc | | 87.21 | 87.18 | 87.19 |
| 2000.4 | RSr | 31209 | 87.36 | 87.34 | 87.35 |
| | RSs | | 86.98 | 86.96 | 86.97 |
| | RScrs | | 87.36 | 87.34 | 87.35 |
| | SR | | 91.43 | 91.41 | 91.42 |
| | R | | 83.29 | 83.03 | 83.16 |
| | S | | 89.70 | 79.07 | 84.05 |
| | RSc | | 85.99 | 85.98 | 85.98 |
| 2000.5 | RSr | 27611 | 86.15 | 86.15 | 86.15 |
| | RSs | | 85.86 | 85.86 | 85.86 |
| | RScrs | | 86.21 | 86.20 | 86.20 |
| | SR | | 90.88 | 90.88 | 90.88 |
| | R | | 85.76 | 85.54 | 85.65 |
| | S | | 89.80 | 79.77 | 84.49 |
| | RSc | | 87.33 | 87.33 | 87.33 |
| 2000.6 | RSr | 31807 | 87.50 | 87.49 | 87.49 |
| | RSs | | 87.21 | 87.21 | 87.21 |
| | RScrs | | 87.61 | 87.61 | 87.61 |
| | SR | | 90.93 | 90.92 | 90.92 |

## 5    Conclusions

This paper takes advantage of the upsides of rules and the statistics and initially proposes five methods combining rules and statistics to recognize conjunction usages. Experimental results show that combinational methods are effective and improve precision and recall of automatic recognition of conjunction usage. Then it will promote the studies on automatic recognition of other modern Chinese functional words and advance other research related to Chinese information processing in the field of natural language processing.

In the future, the present author will focus on the case studies to discuss whether the five combinational methods are applicable for all conjunctions and expect to improve automatic recognition of conjunction usage so that it can be applied to automatic recognition of conjunction structure phrases and new polar words. Moreover, combinational methods are applied to studies on the automatic recognition of other modern Chinese functional words to promote automatic understanding of modern Chinese text content.

**Acknowledgements.** This work is supported by the National Natural Science Foundation of China (No. 60970083, 61272221), the National High Tech Research Plan of China (863 Plan) (No. 2012AA011101), the Open Project Program of National Laboratory of Pattern Recognition, Institute of Automation, Chinese Academy of Sciences and the key project of Science and technology research of  Henan department of education (12B520055).

# References

1. Zhou, G.: Conjunctions and Relevant Problems. Education Press, Hefei (2002)
2. Lv, S.X.: Modern Chinese Eight Hundred words. Commercial Press, Beijing (2007)
3. Zan, H.Y., Zhou, L.J., Zhang, K.L.: Studies on the Automatic Recognition of Modern Chinese Conjunction Usages. In: Huang, D.-S., Gan, Y., Bevilacqua, V., Figueroa, J.C. (eds.) ICIC 2011. LNCS, vol. 6838, pp. 472–479. Springer, Heidelberg (2011)
4. Zhou, L.J., Zhang, K.L., Yuan, Y.C.: The Studies on Automatic Recognition of Rule-based Modern Chinese Conjunction's Usages. In: Proceedings of the Fifth National Youth Conference on Computational Linguistics, Wuhan, pp. 96–102 (2010)
5. Zan, H.Y., Zhang, K.L., Chai, Y.M., Yu, S.W.: Formal Description of Modern Chinese Adverb Usages. In: Proceedings of the 8th Chinese Lexical Semantics Workshop, Hongkong (2007)
6. Yu, S.W., Zhu, X.F., Liu, Y.: Knowledge-base of Generalized Functional Words of Contemporary Chinese. Journal of Chinese Language and Computing 13(1), 89–98 (2003)
7. Zan, H.Y., Zhang, K.L., Chai, Y.M., Yu, S.W.: Studies on the Functional Word Knowledge Base of Contemporary Chinese. Journal of Chinese Information Processing 21(5), 107–111 (2007)
8. Liu, R., Zan, H.Y., Zhang, K.L.: The Automatic Recognition Research on Contemporary Chinese Language. Computer Science 8(A), 172–174 (2008)
9. Zhang, J.H.: Studies on Automatic Recognition of Common Chinese Adverb's Usages Based on Statistics. Ph.D. thesis, Zhengzhou University (2010)
10. Zhang, B.: Modern Chinese Functional Words Dictionary. Commercial Press, Beijing (2006)
11. Lafferty, J., McCallum, A., Pereira, F.: Conditional Random Fields: Probabilistic Models for Segmenting and Labeling Sequence Data. In: Proceedings of the 18th ICML 2001, Williams College, Montreal, pp. 282–289 (2001)
12. Zhao, H., Huang, C., Li, M.: An Improved Chinese Word Segmentation System with Conditional Random Field. In: Proceedings of the Fifth SIGHAN Workshop on Chinese Language Processing (SIGHAN-5), Sydney, pp. 162–165 (2006)
13. Zhou, J.S., Dai, X.N., Yi, C.Y., Chen, J.J.: Automatic Recognition of Chinese Organization Name Based on Cascaded Conditional Random Fields. Chinese Journal of Electronics 34(5), 804–809 (2006)
14. Ding, D.X., Qu, W.G., Xu, T., Dong, Y.: Research of Disambiguating Combinational Ambiguity in Chinese Word Segmentation Based on CRF. Journal of Nanjing Normal University 8(4), 73–76 (2008)

# Minimum Error Rate Training
# for Bilingual News Alignment

Can Wang, Yang Liu, and Maosong Sun

Department of Computer Science and Technology
State Key Lab on Intelligent Technology and Systems
National Lab for Information Science and Technology
Tsinghua University, Beijing 100084, China
acanthu@gmail.com,
{liuyang2011,sms}@tsinghua.edu.cn

**Abstract.** News articles in different languages on the same event are invaluable for analyzing standpoints and viewpoints in different countries. The major challenge to identify such closely related bilingual news articles is how to take full advantage of various information sources such as length, translation equivalence and publishing date. Accordingly, we propose a discriminative model for bilingual news alignment, which is capable of incorporating arbitrary information sources as features. Chinese word segmentation, Part-of-speech tagging and Named Entity Recognition technologies are used to calculate the semantic similarities between words or text as feature values. The feature weights are optimized using the minimum error rate training algorithm to directly correlate training objective to evaluation metric. Experiments on Chinese-English data show that our method significantly outperforms two strong baseline systems by 12.7% and 2.5%, respectively.

**Keywords:** Bilingual News Alignment, Minimum Error Rate Training, Discriminative Model.

## 1 Introduction

A hot event usually leads to many news articles written in different languages from multiple sources, which often exhibit diverse standpoints and viewpoints. While identifying, analyzing, and summarizing such diversity from multilingual news articles is of great value, how to find multilingual news articles on the same event turns out to be the first obstacle. Therefore, there is an urgent need for multilingual news alignment: given news articles in different languages, find out the correspondence.

As a special case of multilingual news alignment, bilingual news alignment has attracted attention from a number of authors. Yang et al. (1997) propose to use cross-lingual information retrieval techniques to identify the correspondence between multilingual texts. Steinberger et al. (2002) calculate the semantic similarity of news in different languages using a multilingual thesaurus. Vu et al. (2009) present a feature-based method to include useful information sources. However, these efforts suffer from two major drawbacks:

P. Liu and Q. Su (Eds.): CLSW 2013, LNAI 8229, pp. 425–435, 2013.

* The alignment model is not discriminatively trained. Information sources usually have different contributions to predicting alignment. It is important to recognize such differences to take full advantage of information sources.

* The optimization objective is not directly related to evaluation metrics. Most previous methods are heuristic or generative. Even for discriminative methods, the optimization objectives are usually maximum likelihood or maximum a posteri, which are not directly related to evaluation metrics. Therefore, maximizing likelihood, posterior or heuristic does not necessarily result in the maximum in terms of evaluation metric.

To alleviate these problems, we propose a linear model for bilingual news alignment. The model is capable of incorporating arbitrary information sources as features to predict the alignment of bilingual news articles. Each feature is associated with a weight to represent the degree of importance. We use the minimum error rate training (MERT) algorithm (Och, 2003) to optimize feature weights with respect to evaluation metrics directly. Experiments on Chinese-English data show that our method significantly outperforms two strong baseline systems by 12.7% and 2.5%, respectively.

## 2     Related Work

The core task of bilingual news alignment is how to evaluate the similarity between two news articles written in different languages. And the difficulty is how to overcome the semantic ambiguities and language barriers.

Similarity between monolingual documents is usually measured by metrics such as cosine similarity, Jaccard coefficient or Pearson correlation coefficient (Huang et al., 2008). But these lexical similarity methods cannot always identify the semantic similarity of texts like "I own a dog" and "I have an animal" (Mihalcea et al., 2006). Then researchers try to utilize corpus or knowledge like WordNet to design semantic metrics for any two words and then calculate the semantic similarity between texts.

Similarity between bilingual documents is more difficult. Yang et al. (1997) use cross-lingual information retrieval techniques such as example-based term translation method, generalized vector space model (GVSM), latent se-mantic indexing (LSI) method to identify the correspondence between bilingual texts. Leek et al. (1999) use machine translation tools to help cross-language topic tracking. Steinberger et al. (2002) represent European document contents using descriptor terms of a multilingual thesaurus EUROVOC and measure the semantic similarity based on the distance between the two documents' representations. Vu et al. (2009) use Discrete Fourier Transform (DFT) score of a word's frequency chain to measure time distribution similarity as a feature to evaluate the bilingual news similarity.

Because of the differences in data sets, the performances of cross-language information retrieval or bilingual document alignment are different, but they are always poor, and worse on Chinese-English test. Vu et al. (2009) achieve a precision of 31.5% in English-Chinese corpora, and 63.4% in English-Malay corpora on Top-1 retrieval test.

Previous methods, whether monolingual or bilingual, all try to represent documents into a unified semantic space, and then calculate the similarity. But they are either not for the news alignment or cannot make full use of the news articles' characteristics. We propose a linear model, and incorporate useful information sources as features such as bilingual vector space model cosine similarity, text graph similarity, named entity similarity, news publishing date interval. We use the minimum error rate training (MERT) algorithm to optimize feature weights with respect to evaluation metrics directly, and achieve a precision of 58.63%, which significantly out-performs two strong baseline systems.

The rest of this paper is organized as follows. In section 3, we give a formal description of our model and training method. Section 4 describes the features and the score functions we use. In Section 5, we evaluate our model in Chinese-English news alignment task. Section 6 points to a conclusion.

# 3  Approach

## 3.1  The Model

Compared with generative models, discriminative models can extend conveniently and integrate various features into them. This paper gives a discriminative framework for bilingual news alignment based on the linear modeling approach. Within this framework, we can de-sign various feature functions according to the bilingual news knowledge. Each feature function is associated with a feature weight. Given a Chinese news article, for every English news article candidate, we can calculate the linear combination of features as an overall score. The alignment result is the one with the highest overall score. A linear model not only allows for easy integration of new features, but also admits optimizing feature weights directly with respect to evaluation metrics.

For bilingual news alignment, we propose a linear model:

$$score(e,c) = \sum_{m=1}^{M} \lambda_m h_m(e,c) \tag{1}$$

$e$ and $c$ represent an English news article and a Chinese news article respectively. $h_m(e,c)$ is a feature function with weight $\lambda_m$. For a news pair $<e,c>$, the linear combination of all features gives its overall score $score(e,c)$.

## 3.2  Training

Minimum error rate training (MERT) (Och, 2003) is an algorithm for optimizing parameters (i.e., feature weights) in statistic machine translation. MERT doesn't optimize parameters through maximum likelihood estimation, it tries to find parameters that result in the best F-measure or best value of other metrics directly. MERT optimizes only one parameter each time and keep all other parameters fixed. This process runs iteratively over M parameters until the overall loss on the training corpus does not decrease. Similarly, in the task of bilingual news alignment, we can use MERT algorithm to optimize the weight of each feature function with respect to the final precision of the alignments directly.

Let $S$ be the size of the Chinese news set needed to find their alignments. For each Chinese news $c_s$ to align to, there are $K$ English news candidates $Cands_s=\{e_{s,1}, e_{s,1},...,e_{s,K}\}$ to align from. Parameters $\lambda_1^M=\{\lambda_1,\lambda_2,...,\lambda_M\}$ are the weights of features $h_1^M=\{h_1,h_2,...,h_M\}$. $e_{s,right}$ represents the right alignment of $c_s$ tagged by human in the candidates. We use precision as the evaluation metric of bilingual news alignment, so our goal is to find a set of feature weights that maximize the precision on the training corpus:

$$\hat{\lambda}_1^M = \arg\max_{\lambda_1^M}\left\{\sum_{s=1}^{S}\delta(\hat{e}(c_s;\lambda_1^M),e_{s,right})\right\} \qquad (2)$$

$$\hat{e}(c_s;\lambda_1^M)=\arg\max_{e\in Cands_s}\left\{\sum_{m=1}^{M}\lambda_m h_m(e,c_s)\right\} \qquad (3)$$

After given initial values and ranges of the parameters, in each iteration, MERT optimizes parameters from the first dimension to the last. For instance, when adjusting the $i$-th dimension parameter $\lambda_i$, MERT keeps the other parameters fixed. So the overall score of the alignment between $e_{s,k}$ and $c_s$ is:

$$score(e_{s,k},c_s)=\sum_{m=1,m\neq i}^{M}\lambda_m h_m(e_{s,k},c_s)+\lambda_i h_i(e_{s,k},c_s) \qquad (4)$$

$$= a_{s,k}+b_{s,k}\lambda_i$$

where $a_{s,k}=\sum_{m=1,m\neq i}^{M}\lambda_m h_m(e_{s,k},c_s)$, $b_{s,k}=h_i(e_{s,k},c_s)$.

It's a linear function with parameter $\lambda_i$ corresponding a line. So the set of candidates in $Cands_s$ defines a set of lines. The decision rule in Equation (3) states that $\hat{e}(c_s;\lambda_1^M)$ is the line with the highest model score for a given $\lambda_i$. The selection of $\lambda_i$ for each news pair ultimately determines the precision at $\lambda_i$.

As the precision can only change if we move to a $\lambda_i$ where the highest line is different than before, Och (2003) suggests only evaluating the precision at values in between the intersections that line the top surface of the cluster of lines. Figure 1 shows four candidate alignments in dimension $\lambda_i$. The upper envelope is highlighted in bold, it's constituted by the topmost line segments. The upper envelope indicates the best candidate alignments the model predicts with various values of $\lambda_i$. We just need to find the critical intersections where the topmost line changes one by one in the direction of $\lambda_i$ growing, rather than all possible K2 intersections be-tween the K lines. We can find the closest inter-section on current topmost line to current critical inter-section as a new critical intersection and then update the new current topmost line and new current critical intersection to find the next critical intersection. In the interval (leftbound, $\lambda_{ia}$], $e_{s,2}$ has the highest score. Similarly, the best candidate are $e_{s,3}$ for ($\lambda_{ia}$,

$\lambda_{ib}$], $e_{s,4}$ for ($\lambda_{ib}$, $\lambda_{ic}$], $e_{s,1}$ for ($\lambda_{ic}$, *rightbound*]. The optimal can be found by collecting all topmost lines related intersections on the training corpus and choosing one $\lambda_i$ that results in the maximal precision value.

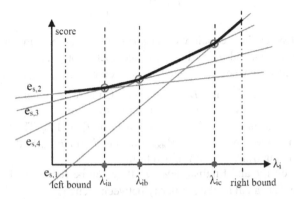

**Fig. 1.** An example of MERT algorithm

## 4    Bilingual News Alignment Features

The most significant advantage of discriminative model is to define useful features that capture various characteristics of bilingual news alignment. We can include various metrics such as bilingual vector space model as features directly. In our model, the feature set is composed of linguistic-dependent features and linguistic-independent features. We extract linguistic-dependent features such as bilingual vector space model (BVSM) cosine similarity, bilingual text graph similarity, bilingual named entity similarity, and linguistic-independent features such as news publishing date interval, content length difference. Title of news is an important characteristic too. We also use length difference, bilingual cosine similarity, and bilingual named entity similarity between news titles as features in our model. Because titles are always short, building text graphs of titles is insignificant, we don't use bilingual text graph similarity between titles as a feature in our model.

When calculating the feature values, a bilingual dictionary is used. It can be obtained after word alignment process in machine translation by a statistical machine translation toolkit GI-ZA++, which implements IBM models and HMM model for word alignment. This dictionary can give the translation probability of any two words in different languages.

### 4.1    Linguistic-Dependent Features

**Bilingual Vector Space Model Cosine Similarity**
VSM is a popular model for measuring similarity between monolingual documents with *tfidf* weights. Let $D=\{d_1, d_1,..., d_{|D|}\}$ be a set of documents and $T=\{t_1, t_2,..., t_u\}$

the set of distinct terms occurring in $D$. For term $t$ in document $d$, its *tfidf* weight is defined as:

$$tfidf(d,t) = tf(d,t) \times \log\left(\frac{|D|}{df(t)}\right) \qquad (5)$$

Here $tf(d,t)$ denotes the frequency of term $t$ in $d$, $df(t)$ is the number of documents in which term $t$ appears, and $|D|$ is the size of the document set.

Then document $d$ can be represented by a vector $\vec{t_d} = (tfidf(t_1), ..., tfidf(t_u))^T$. For bilingual documents, let $D_C$ and $D_E$ denote the Chinese document set and English document set respectively. Their distinct term sets are $T_C = \{t_{c1}, t_{c2},..., t_{cm}\}$ and $T_E = \{t_{e1}, t_{e2},..., t_{en}\}$, $m$ and $n$ are the term numbers in $T_C$ and $T_E$. The bilingual dictionary can be represented by a matrix $P_{m \times n}$, element $P_{ij}$ in $P_{m \times n}$ is the probability of Chinese term $t_{ci}$ being translated to English term $t_{ej}$.

For Chinese news $d_c$ and English news $d_e$, they can be represented by vectors $\vec{t_{d_c}}$ and $\vec{t_{d_e}}$, then we can calculate the similarity between them as:

$$SIM(d_c, d_e) = \frac{(P^T \vec{t_{d_c}}) \cdot \vec{t_{d_e}}}{|P^T \vec{t_{d_c}}| \times |\vec{t_{d_e}}|} \qquad (6)$$

**Bilingual Text Graph Similarity**

Keywords can imply the topic of a text, so we assume that the similarity between bilingual news can be measured through calculating the similarity of their keywords. Rada et al. (2004) propose an innovative unsupervised graph-based model for keyword extraction. In bilingual news alignment, we build a text graph for each news article at first. Before the text graph is created, preprocessing like word segmentation on Chinese texts, stemming on English texts and Part-of-speech tagging on both sides. After moving stopwords, we choose words tagged with noun, verb and adjective as terms to build text graphs, each distinct term generates a vertex. If two terms co-occur in a fixed-size window (i.e., 3) in the origin news article text, an undirected line will be generated between the two vertexes that represent the two terms. After we run Google's PageRank (Brin and Page, 1998) on the graph, we get the weight of each vertex. The vertexes are ranked by their weights, and we extract terms whose corresponding vertexes rank in top 25% as keywords. Finally, we calculate the translation probability of the two key-word sets to evaluate the similarity between Chinese news dc and English news de as:

$$p(d_c, d_e) = \frac{\sum_{i=1}^{I} w_{c_i} \sum_{j=1}^{J} p(e_j | c_i)}{\sum_{i=1}^{I} w_{c_i}} + \frac{\sum_{j=1}^{J} w_{e_j} \sum_{i=1}^{I} p(c_i | e_j)}{\sum_{j=1}^{J} w_{e_j}} \qquad (7)$$

where $\{c_1, c_2,..., c_I\}$ and $\{e_1, e_2,..., e_J\}$ are the sets of keywords in Chinese news $d_c$ and English news $d_e$ respectively. $p(e_j | c_i)$ and $p(c_i | e_j)$ are the probabilities of translating $c_i$ to $e_j$ and $e_j$ to $c_i$, which given by the bilingual dictionary. $w_{c_i}$ and $w_{e_j}$ are weights of vertexes representing $c_i$ and $e_j$ in the two text graphs respectively.

**Bilingual Named Entities Similarity**
Named entity mainly refers to the terms of person names, place names or organization names. Friburger et al. (2002) and Montalvo et al. (2007) point out the effect of named entity recognition in improving monolingual and bilingual document clustering respectively. So we extract named entities through named entities recognition tools released by Stanford University, and then calculate the similarity between the two named entity sets as a feature according to Equation (7).

### 4.2    Linguistic-Independent Features

In bilingual news alignment, some features are linguistic-independent, but they often imply the alignment of two bilingual news. We integrate two linguistic-independent features in our model. One is news publishing date interval, the other is the ratio of the difference to the sum of the two news texts' lengths. A short interval and a small length difference ratio may imply the two news are possibly aligned to each other.

## 5    Experiments

### 5.1    Experimental Setup

The experiments were conducted on a Chinese-English corpora. The data are from two websites of two news publications: Xinhua News[1] (Chinese) and The New York Times[2] (English). The news are published in October 2011, and the topics contain Japan nuclear leak, Thailand floods, Mexican drug, Yemen unrest and so on. We choose 203 Chinese news and 215 English news which can represent the hot topics in the month. Table 1 shows the statistics of our refer-ence data for bilingual news alignment. For each Chinese news, we tagged one or n most similar English news from the 215 English news candidates. Table 2 shows the alignments in-formation between the bilingual news.

**Table 1.** Statistics on evaluation data

|  | news number | words | terms | size | average length |
|---|---|---|---|---|---|
| Chinese news | 203 | 122249 | 10091 | 761KB | 602 |
| English news | 215 | 190550 | 16484 | 1331KB | 886 |

---

[1]  http://www.xinhuanet.com
[2]  http://www.nytimes.com

**Table 2.** Alignments information of the data, n denotes the number of English news tagged aligned with one given Chinese news

| n | 1 | 2 | 3 | 4 | 5 | 6 | 8 | 9 | 12 | total |
|---|---|---|---|---|---|---|---|---|----|-------|
| These Chinese news number | 152 | 17 | 15 | 3 | 1 | 6 | 2 | 3 | 4 | 203 |

We use precision of the right alignments to evaluate our model:

$$precision = \frac{the\ number\ of\ right\ alignments}{the\ number\ of\ Chinese\ news\ in\ test\ data} \qquad (8)$$

We use 4-fold cross-validation to train and test our model, and calculate the average precision as final precision of our model.

## 5.2   Baseline

**Baseline 1: Bilingual Vector Space Model (BVSM)**
We calculate the BVSM cosine similarity score be-tween the bilingual news according to Equation (6) in section 4 and choose the candidate with the high-est score as the aligning result.

**Baseline 2: Machine Translation Based Method**
We translate Chinese news into English by Bing's translation API[3]. Then we use vector space model and calculate the monolingual cosine similarity score. We choose the candidate with the highest score as the aligning result.

## 5.3   Results

The experiments use 4-fold cross-validation to get the average precision of our model. We also recorded the time each method cost. Table 3 shows the results.

It is worth noting that our approach results in a better precision than the two base-lines and is much more efficient than the machine translation based method. The time cost in our approach is mainly spent on processes of part-of-speech tagging and named entity recognition. While machine translation based method spent more than 95% time on translation. Machine translation consumes a lot of resources and time, so MT-based method cannot meet the needs of bilingual news alignment.

**Table 3.** Performance of the methods

| Method | Precision | Cost   Time (s) |
|--------|-----------|-----------------|
| Baseline1 | 45.84% | 4 |
| Baseline2 | 56.18% | 168 |
| Our Method | 58.63% | 13 |

---

[3] http://www.microsoft.com/en-us/translator/developers.aspx

We also evaluated the contributions of each feature. We excluded one feature and trained the model again. The more new model declined, the more important this feature is. Table 4 shows the contribution of each feature.

**Table 4.** Contribution of each feature

| Features the Model Use | Precision | Decline |
|---|---|---|
| ALL | 58.63% | 0.00% |
| ALL-LEN | 57.62% | -1.01% |
| ALL-NE | 55.17% | -3.46% |
| ALL-GRAPH | 52.25% | -6.38% |
| ALL-BVSM | 51.24% | -7.39% |
| ALL-DATE | 51.73% | -6.90% |
| ALL-TitleFeatures | 54.19% | -4.44% |

In Table 4, ALL denotes all of the features, and LEN for length difference feature, NE for named entity feature, GRAPTH for text graph feature, BVSM for bilingual vector space model feature, DATE for news publishing date interval feature, TitltFeatures for the features related   to news titles. From Table 4 we can find that the most im-portant features in our model are bilingual vec-tor space model cosine similarity, news publish-ing date interval and text graph similarity. The length difference feature is not obvious. The title features are also important in the bilingual news alignment model. Named entity recognition can also help the task of bilingual news alignment. An example of the weights of parameters opti-mized by MERT algorithm is shown in Table 5.

**Table 5.** An example of the weights of parameters opti-mized by MERT algorithm

| Feature | Publish Date Interval | Content Length Difference | Content BVSM Cosine Similarity | Text Graph Similarity |
|---|---|---|---|---|
| Weight | -0.060 | -0.067 | 3.504 | 2.737 |
| Feature | Content Named Entities Similarity | Title Length Difference | Title BVSM cosine similarity | Title Named Entities Similarity |
| Weight | 0.049 | -0.072 | 2.208 | 0.772 |

## 6    Conclusion

In this paper, we proposed a bilingual news alignment model based discriminative frame-work. We designed various features according to the characteristics of the news such as bilingual vector space model cosine similarity, bilingual text graph similarity, bilingual named entity similarity, news publishing date interval and the difference between the news lengths. Technologies such as Part-of-speech tagging and Named Entity Recognition are used to calculate the semantic similarities between words or text as feature values. We used mini-mum error rate training algorithm to optimize the feature weights. Experiments on Chinese-English news data show that our model outperforms bilingual vector space model and ma-chine translation based method, especially more efficient than the latter.

In bilingual news alignment, our model relies on the bilingual dictionary. While many Out-of-Vocabulary (OOV) words often appear in news, which usually result in a bad precision. In future work, we will try to improve our model by using knowledge of Wikipedia and WordNet to solve OOV problem and evaluate semantic similarity between words more precisely.

**Acknowledgements.** This research is supported by the 863 Program under the grant No.2012AA011102 and No. 2011AA 01A207 and by the Singapore National Research Foundation under its International Research Centre @ Singapore Funding Initiative and administered by the IDM Programme Office.

# References

1. Friburger, N., Maurel, D., Giacometti, A.: Textual similarity based on proper names. In: Proceedings of the Workshop Mathematical/Formal Methods in Information Retrieval (MFIR 2002) at the 25th ACM SIGIR Conference, pp. 155–167 (2002)
2. Huang, A.: Similarity Measures for Text Document Clustering. In: Proceedings of New Zealand Computer Science Research Student Conference (NZCSRSC), pp. 49–56 (2008)
3. Jagarlamudi, J., Daume III, H., Udupa, R.: From Bilingual Dictionaries to Interlingual Document Representations. In: Proceedings of the 49th Annual Meeting of the Association for Computational Linguistics (ACL): Shortpapers, pp. 147–152 (2011)
4. Liu, Y., Liu, Q., Lin, S.: Discriminative Word Alignment by Linear Modeling. Computational Linguistics 36(3), 303–339 (2010)
5. Mihalcea, R., Corley, C., Strapparava, C.: Corpus-based and Knowledge-based Measures of Text Semantic Similarity. Proceedings of American Association for Artificial Intelligence (AAAI) 6, 775–780 (2006)
6. Mihalcea, R., Tarau, P.: TextRank: Bringing Order into Texts. In: Proceedings of the Conference on Empirical Methods in Natural Language Processing (EMNLP), vol. 4(4) (2004)
7. Montalvo, S., Martínez, R., Casillas, A., Fresno, V.: Bilingual News Clustering Using Named Entities and Fuzzy Similarity. In: Matoušek, V., Mautner, P. (eds.) TSD 2007. LNCS (LNAI), vol. 4629, pp. 107–114. Springer, Heidelberg (2007)
8. Och, F.J.: Minimum error rate training in statistical machine translation. In: Proceedings of the 41st Annual Meeting on Association for Computational Linguistics (ACL), pp. 160–167 (2003)
9. Pouliquen, B., Steinberger, R., Ignat, C., Kasper, E., Temnikova, I.: Multilingual and cross-lingual news topic tracking. In: COLING 2004 Proceedings of the 20th International Conference on Computational Linguistics Article No. 959 (2004)

10. Pouliquen, B., Steinberger, R., Deguernel, O.: Story tracking: linking similar news over time and across languages. In: Proceedings of the Workshop on Multisource Multilingual Information Extraction and Summarization, pp. 49–56 (2008)
11. Steinberger, R., Pouliquen, B., Hagman, J.: Cross-lingual Document Similarity Calculation Using the Multilingual Thesaurus EUROVOC. In: Gelbukh, A. (ed.) CICLing 2002. LNCS, vol. 2276, pp. 415–424. Springer, Heidelberg (2002)
12. Vu, T., Aw, A.T., Zhang, M.: Feature-based Method for Document Alignment in Comparable News Corpora. In: Proceedings of the 12th Conference of the European Chapter of the ACL, pp. 843–851 (2009)
13. Yang, Y., Carbonell, J.G., Brown, R.D., Frederking, R.E.: Translingual Information Retrieval: Learning from Bilingual Corpora. Artificial Intelligence Journal Special Issue: Best of IJCAI 1997, 1–20 (1998)

# Hedge Detection with Latent Features

Qi Su[1], Huanqing Lou[1], and Pengyuan Liu[2]

[1] Peking University, Beijing 100871, China
[2] Beijing Language and Culture University, Beijing, 100083, China
{sukia,louhuanqing,liupengyuan}@pku.edu.cn

**Abstract.** In the current internet environment, the issue of information credibility is crucial given that anyone can put up information on the Web freely. Hence, it is urge and necessary to develop computational approaches to distinguish reliable information from the unreliable, inaccurate one. In the year 2010, CoNLL proposed a new shared task of hedge detection, aiming to push uncertainty detection for natural language processing applications. Among the pro-posed approaches, sequence labeling models exhibit promising performance. However, only shallow features (e.g. word, lemma, POS tags, etc.) were explored in the existing research. In this paper, we aim to exploit the advantage of topical features in sequence labeling based hedge detection. The experimental results illustrate the effectiveness of the high-level features.

## 1 Introduction

Nowadays people are increasingly relying on the Web to seek information. However, the quality of online information is potentially inaccurate given that some content can be generated by anyone freely. Under the circumstance, in the year 2010, the Conference on Computational Natural Language Learning (CoNLL) proposed a shared task to develop uncertainty detection in natural language sentences. In the task, hedges, the linguistic devices to show uncertainty, were annotated in two types of corpora. Automatic systems need to identify sentences which contain hedges and display hesitation or uncertainty. A further task of speculative scopes detection was proposed as well.

The problem of hedge detection can be treated as a sequence labeling task in the sense that it distinguishes linguistic expressions inside the scope of hedges from the outside ones. Accordingly, some sequence labeling model (e.g. conditional random fields and svm-hmm) have been widely adopted and have generated competitive prediction for hedge detection (Tang et al., 2010). However, only shallow features (e.g. lemma, part-of-speech tags, etc) were examined in the existing research.

In this paper, we aim to explore the feasibility and effectiveness of high-level features for sequence labeling based hedge detection. Recently, some work has been performed on the non-linear dependence in conditional random fields (CRFs) and latent features of data to improve the performance of a CRF model (Maaten et al., 2011). Generally speaking, high-level features usually show some advantages over shallow features (Nallapati et al., 2010). Using high-level features (e.g. topic models) for document representation has been an area of considerable interest in machine learning (Wei and Croft, 2006). It projects words to a lower dimensional latent space

P. Liu and Q. Su (Eds.): CLSW 2013, LNAI 8229, pp. 436–441, 2013.

thus improves generalizability to unseen items, and helps disambiguate some ambiguous items. Furthermore, it can capture the underlying information from both labeled and unlabeled data in providing a semi-supervised manner for sequence labeling.

## 2    Related Work

The study of hedge as a linguistic term goes back at least to Lakoff (1972). In Lakoff (1972)'s definition, hedges are "words whose job is to make things fuzzier or less fuzzy". Accordingly, the function of Lakoff's hedge is actually two-fold: to weaken or intensify the speaker's commitment to a proposition. The term was then widely discussed and narrowed down by some linguists only to keep it as a detensifier. It includes a wide range of expressions cutting across parts of speech (Hyland, 1998), e.g. auxiliaries (*may, might*), hedging verbs (*suggest, question*), adjectives (*probable, possible*), adverbs (*likely*), conjunctions (*or, and, either...or*), nouns (*speculation*), etc. While some of these hedge cues, especially the epistemic verbs such as *may, might*, are general words to be applied across domains, many are unique to a particular domain (Clausen, 2010). The complication of hedge detection is thus in the sense that the same word types occasionally have different, non-hedging uses.

The detection of uncertainty within the society of natural language processing has received considerable attention recently (Farkas et al., 2010). The task can be treated as a binary classification problem. Light et al. (2004) utilized a SVM classifier with bag-of-word features to identify speculative sentences in MEDLINE abstracts. As a comparative research, they also compiled a hand-crafted list of hedge cues. The presence of a hedge cue, i.e. a token or multi-word expression indicating that the speakers cannot back up their opinions or statements with facts, is considered to be a high precision feature of uncertainty. Medlock and Briscoe (2008) conducted a weak supervised Bayesian learner to derive the probability of a token being a hedge cue, and further classified speculative and non-speculative sentences according to the identified features. Kilicoglu and Bergler (2008) proposed to incorporate syntactic information to refine the potential hedge cues. In Medlock (2008)'s research, they compared different shallow features and showed that the information of part-of-speech tags and stemming can only marginally improve the accuracy of a bag-of-word representation. However, using bigrams brought a statistically significant improvement. Szarvas (2008) extended the methodology of Medlock, and discussed the effect of n-gram features and a semi-supervised feature selection solution. Ganter and Strube (2009) proposed a method to automatically detect the sentences containing uncertainty based on Wikipedia weasel tags and syntactic patterns.

## 3    Sequence Labeling with High-Level Features

In this section, we describe how we model hedge detection as a sequence labeling task, and focus on the generation of high-level features using Latent Dirichlet Allocation.

### 3.1     Sequence Labeling

Given an observation sequence $x=(x_1, x_2, \ldots, x_n)$, the goal of sequence labeling is to assign each unit in $x$ a sequential label $y=(y_1, y_2, \ldots, y_n)$. Within the setting, there has emerged many models, e.g. Hidden Markov models (HMM), conditional random fields (CRF), Max-margin Markov networks (M3N), SVM-struct, etc.

As a discriminative learning model, CRF is recognized as one of the mainstream methods in labeling sequential data. More specifically, it is an undirected graphical model which defines a single log-linear distribution function over label sequences Y given the observation sequence X, as illustrated in Figure 1.

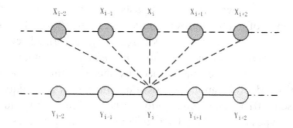

**Fig. 1.** Graphical Structures of CRF

The model calculates the conditional probabilities of the various possible labels of an output token and chooses the one with maximum probability (Lafferty et al., 2001) as:

$$P(y \mid x) = \frac{1}{Z_x} \exp(\sum_{t=1}^{N} (\psi(x, y, t) + \phi(x, y, t)))$$

where

$$\phi(x, y, t) = \sum_{y} w_y^T f_y(x, y, t)$$

is the potential function defined on the vertex at the $t^{th}$ position, which measures the compatibility between the local observations around the $t^{th}$ position and the output label.

$$\psi(x, y, t) = \sum_{y, y'} u_{y, y'} f_y(x, y, t)$$

is the potential function defined on an edge connecting two labels. $Z_x$ is a normalization constant for each x as

$$Z_x = \sum_{y} \exp(w_y^T \phi(x, y))$$

Although powerful for sequence labeling, CRF does not fit for the modeling of complex/nonlinear relationship between input features and output labels (Peng et al, 2009). Another limitation of a CRF model is that it is not easy to incorporate the unlabeled data. For achieving good performance accuracy, a lot of training data is needed for the CRF. Hence, conceptually, it will be helpful to incorporate nonlinear and complex relationship into the CRF model. A hybrid framework which combines generative model and discriminative model can utilize best features of both approaches.

### 3.2    Latent Dirichlet Allocation

As a generative graphical model, Latent Dirichlet allocation (LDA), introduced by Blei et al (2003), resembles the probabilistic Latent Semantic Indexing model (pLSI) in the basic generative process. In LDA, however, the topic mixture is drawn from a conjugate Dirichlet prior thus to produce semantically consistent predictions. The likelihood for a document with word vector $w$ can then be yielded by:

$$P(w) = \int_\theta (\prod_{n=1}^{N} \sum_{z_n=1}^{k} p(w_n \mid z_n; \beta) p(z_n \mid \theta)) p(\theta; \alpha) d_\theta$$

The likelihood of the whole data collection is calculated by multifying the likelihood of all the documents:

$$P(W) = \prod_{m=1}^{M} P(w_m)$$

The model of LDA is used to model the underlying topic structures of texts. Incorporating CRF with LDA generated topic features is a straight-forward extension of CRF (Nallapati et al., 2010). In this paper, we perform LDA training and inference by Gibbs sampling, then train the CRF model by adding topic IDs as additional external features. As an unsupervised model, LDA allows us to train and infer on an unlabeled dataset, thus relax the restriction of the labeled dataset used for CRF training.

## 4    Corpus and Features

We collect a set of manually annotated biological scientific articles to be our training corpus. In the corpus, hedge cues are identified manually and tagged with the <ccue> tags. If there is at least one token or multi-word expression recognized as a hedge cue, the whole sentence will be identified as "uncertain". On top of the labeled data, we also utilize the additional unlabeled data for the training of LDA, thus to capture the underlying information from both the labeled and unlabeled data.

For the acquirement of effective sequence learning processes, we explore three different levels of feature set.

**Level 1:** token; whether the token is a potential hedge cue (occurring in the pre-extracted hedge cue list) or part of a hedge cue; its context within the scope of [-2, 2]

**Level 2:** lemma; part-of-speech tag; whether the token belongs to a chunk; whether it is a named entity

For the two levels of features, basically, we adopt the feature templates used in Tang et al. (2010). The level 2 features are acquired using GENIA tagger[1] for both corpora.

---

[1] http://www-tsujii.is.s.u-tokyo.ac.jp/GENIA/tagger

In level 3, topical features generated by the LDA model are added to the previous feature set.

**Level 3**: topic ID (inferred by the LDA model)

## 5    Experiments

As a baseline, we use a naïve matching of hedge cues, in which a single word (token) or multi-word expression will be identified as a hedge cue if it occurs in a pre-extracted list of hedge cues. The list was generated from the training corpus. Table 1 shows the experimental results using all the settings on the test set.

**Table 1.** Experimental Result on the Test Corpus of Biological Articles

|             | Precision | Recall | F-score |
|-------------|-----------|--------|---------|
| Single word | 44.16%    | 96.58% | 60.60%  |
| Multiword   | 43.99%    | 96.84% | 60.50%  |
| CRF         | 91.24%    | 76.46% | 83.20%  |
| +GENIA      | 86.88%    | 86.48% | 85.77%(+2.57) |
| +LDA        | 86.81%    | 86.82% | 86.31%(+0.54) |

As shown in the table, a significant improvement can be found between the baselines and all the other experimental settings. Comparing with the naïve matching of single-word hedge cues, the model based on multi-word cues shows slightly better recall but drops in precision, thus achieving a very similar F-score. The performance of sequence labeling outperforms both naïve methods significantly. Even the CRF with Level 1 features provides substantial improvement over the methods of naïve matching. With the introduction of the features generated by GENIA tagger, e.g. part-of-speech tags, named entity tags and chunks, the performance of CRF get improvement of up to 2.57 percentage points.

The topics generated by LDA are effective, since the feature further improved the F-score by around 0.54%. However, the improvement is not significant comparing to the result based on GENIA tagging. The reason is probably that the basic unit we dealt with is a short segment (sentence). Although we have introduced unlabeled data trying to discover the hidden topics and reduce the sparseness, the size of the external dataset is not large enough. Yet as what we have observed from the experiments, the introduction of more external data has the potential to obtain a richer set of hidden topics, thus to improve the expected performance.

## 6    Conclusion

This paper focuses on the task of hedge detection. We discussed the high-level/ latent features for hedge detection in the context of a sequence labeling model. It can be concluded from the experimental results that the prediction generated from high-level features outperforms both the baselines and the basic CRF methods. Our work suggests a potential research direction of incorporating topical information for hedge detection.

# References

1. Blei, D., Ng, A., Jordan, M.: Latent dirichlet allocation. Journal of Machine Learning Research, 993–1022 (2003)
2. Farkas, R., et al.: The CoNLL 2010 Shared Task: Learning to Detect Hedges and their Scope in Natural Language Text. In: Proceedings of the Fourteenth Conference on Computational Natural Language Learning (CoNLL 2010): Shared Task, Uppsala, Sweden, pp. 1–12 (2010)
3. Ganter, V., Strube, M.: Finding Hedges by Chasing Weasels: Hedge Detection Using Wikipedia Tags and Shallow Linguistic Features. In: Proceedings of the ACL-IJCNLP 2009 Conference Short Papers, pp. 173–176 (2009)
4. Hyland, K.: Hedging in scientific research articles. John Benjamins B.V., Amsterdam (1998)
5. Lafferty, J., et al.: Conditional random fields: Probabilistic models for segmenting and labeling sequence data. In: Proceedings of ICML 2001, pp. 282–289 (2001)
6. Lakoff, G.: Linguistics and natural logic. In: The Semantics of Natural Language, pp. 545–665. Reidel, Dordrecht (1972)
7. Light, M., Qiu, X., Srinivasan, P.: The Language of Bioscience: Facts, Speculations, and Statements in Between. In: Proceedings of the HLT-NAACL 2004 Workshop: Biolink 2004, Linking Biological Literature, Ontologies and Databases (2004)
8. Medlock, B., Briscoe, T.: Weakly Supervised Learning for Hedge Classification in Scientific Literature. In: Proceedings of the ACL (2007)
9. Nallapati, R., Surdeanu, M., Manning, C.: Blind Domain Transfer for Named Entity Recognition using Generative Latent Topic Models. In: Proceedings of the NIPS 2010 Workshop on Transfer Learning Via Rich Generative Models (2010)
10. Peng, J., Bo, L., Xu, J.: Conditional Neural Fields. In: Advances in Neural Information Processing Systems, NIPS (2009)
11. Szarvas, G.: Hedge Classification in Biomedical Texts with a Weakly Supervised Selection of Keywords. In: Proceedings of ACL 2008: HLT, pp. 281–289 (2008)
12. Wei, X., Croft, W.: LDA-Based Document Models for Ad-hoc Retrieval. In: Proceedings of SIGIR 2006 (2006)

# Research on Weighted Complex Network Based Keywords Extraction

Zhi Zhou[1], Xiaojun Zou[1], Xueqiang Lv[2], and Junfeng Hu[1],[*]

[1] Key Laboratory of Computational Linguistics, Ministry of Education,
Peking University, Beijing, 100871, P.R. China
{zhizhou,zouxj,hujf}@pku.edu.cn
[2] Beijing Key Laboratory of Internet Culture and Digital Dissemination Research,
Beijing Information Science and Technology University, Beijing, 100101, P.R. China
lxq@bistu.edu.cn

**Abstract.** Based on the complex network theory, this paper constructs a weighted lexical network to extract keywords from the text automatically. The current related researches mainly focus on the measures of nodes' contribution to the whole network, while this paper lays emphasis on the construction of lexical network. By introducing linguistic knowledge, we center on reasonable selection of nodes, proper description of relationships between words, enhancement of node attributes, and etc. Experiments indicate that the lexical network constructed by our approach achieves preferable effect on accuracy, recall and F-value—when selecting the top three results, the three indices increase by 6.67%, 3.96% and 4.97% on average than the classic TF-IDF method respectively.

**Keywords:** Chinese Information Processing, Keywords Extraction, Complex Network, Phrase Combination.

## 1 Introduction

As a means of text indexing, keywords are a set of words or phrases representing the theme of a given text and widely applied in the fields of information retrieval, text classification, knowledge mining, and etc. For example, keywords are used in search engines to index documents and in topic identification systems to indicate topic category.

Since author-assigned keywords are absent in many real texts and it is time-consuming and laborious to assign manually, automatic keywords extraction is therefore a research field worthy of investigation. Numerous methods have been developed to address this issue in recent decades. Luhn adopted term frequency (TF) to characterize the importance of terms [1]. However, this criterion is too simple and fails to extract keywords with low frequency. Salton and Buckley improved this method by introducing the inverse document frequency (IDF), which is known as the classic TF-IDF algorithm [2]. Turney further treated

---

[*] To whom all correspondence should be addressed.

P. Liu and Q. Su (Eds.): CLSW 2013, LNAI 8229, pp. 442–452, 2013.
© Springer-Verlag Berlin Heidelberg 2013

keywords extraction as a supervised learning task, where all phrases in the text are potential candidates and keywords are recognized by using a decision tree based strategy [3]. Frank proposed a naive Bayesian learning scheme to extract keywords, which is also a supervised learning strategy [4]. Li et al. explored a maximum entropy principle to extract keywords automatically for Chinese texts [5].

The idea of viewing keywords extraction from a network perspective has received great attentions in recent years. Network based approach exhibits several advantages over the other methods mentioned above in nature. Firstly, networks prove adept in problem representation, as there are seldom objects and the relationships among them in a problem domain that fail to be described as nodes and edges in networks. Secondly, the problems can be solved by taking into account global information computed from the entire network, rather than relying only on local information [6]. Specific to the problem of keywords extraction, the network based approach has the following advantages: The relationships between words are described as edges which keeps more context information; The dependence on the background corpus is weakened and keywords can be extracted from a single text utilizing its own information; Moreover, unlike supervised learning methods, it does not need training corpus, which avoids the data sparse problem caused by the deficiency of training corpus. Therefore, many researches on network based keywords extraction have been performed. Network based keywords extraction of English or Chinese texts was studied by Matsuo [7], Zhu [8], Ma [9], and et al. respectively. The network based keywords extraction generally contains two steps: The first step is to represent the text as a network, in which each node corresponds to a word and each edge corresponds to the potentially useful relationship between words; The second step is to design a node contribution measure which quantifies the importance of each node in the network and words are ranked according to this measure, and finally the ones on top are selected as the keywords of the text. The researches mentioned above are mainly focused on the designation of new measures to depict node importance (namely, optimizing the second step): Matsuo et al. proposed the difference of extended path length with and without node $v$ (denoted as $CB_v$) to evaluate its importance, Zhu et al. explored the average path length increment (denoted as $\Delta L_v$) to determine the importance of the node $v$, Ma et al. improved this method by combining $\Delta L_v$ and clustering coefficient increment ($\Delta C_v$).

Yet little attention has been devoted to the construction of lexical network (namely, optimizing the first step) so far. The reasonable representation of texts directly affects the accuracy of keywords extraction, over-simplified or over-detailed description of lexical relationships will reduce the performance of keywords extraction—the former leads to information deficiency while the latter results in introduction of noise. This paper attempts to represent texts as lexical networks more accurately by introducing linguistic knowledge, namely, reasonable selection of words from texts as lexical nodes from a linguistic perspective, proper description of relationships between words, enhancement of node attributes, and etc. The rest of this paper is organized as follows. In Section

2, the construction of lexical network is elaborated, including the selection of lexical nodes, the representation of relationships between words, the reflection of the node differences; Section 3 describes the concrete steps of our proposed algorithm for keywords extraction; Section 4 presents some experimental results and analysis, including keywords extraction from a single document as well as comparison with other related algorithms; The final section concludes this paper and discusses some possible future works.

## 2    Network Construction

The keywords consists mainly of phrases and partly of words with rich but definite meanings. Compared to words, phrases are seen as a better feature of text representation due to their stable structures and integrate meanings [10], for example, the meaning of the phrase *natural language processing* is clearer than that of any separated word—*natural, language* or *processing*. We selected 100 Chinese scientific papers from *Journal of Chinese Information Processing* to conduct a statistical analysis. In these papers, there are 410 author-assigned keywords in total, of which 329 are phrases (accounting for 80.2%) and only 19.8% are words. Since the Chinese word segmenter usually splits sentences into words rather than phrases. Thus the Chinese phrase structure rules [11] summarized by Zhan are applied to combine words to phrases in this paper. Considering that both phrases and words are candidates of keywords, this paper only combines words co-occurring in high frequency into phrases (rather than all co-occurring words). The combination strategy is defined as

$$
Compound(w_i, w_j) = \begin{cases} Cat(w_i, w_j), & \begin{aligned} &\text{if Neighbor}(w_i, w_j) > \theta \\ &\text{and } (w_i, w_j) \text{ meets the} \\ &\text{combination rules,} \end{aligned} \\ \varPhi, & \text{otherwise.} \end{cases} \tag{1}
$$

where $Cat(w_i, w_j)$ and $\varPhi$ denote the combination operation and no operation for the neighboring word pair $(w_i, w_j)$ respectively, $Neighbor(w_i, w_j)$ denotes the co-occurrence times of the pair $(w_i, w_j)$, the threshold $\theta$ is determined partly by the length of the text, i.e., the longer the text is, the greater $\theta$ is.

Theoretically, each word in the text has a possibility to be keywords. However, through the statistical analysis of the collected papers mentioned above, the words with part-of-speech (POS) tag of noun or verb have more chance to be keywords, whereas the words with POS tag of pronoun, preposition or adverb seldom appear as keywords. Table 1 summarizes the POS distribution of the author-assigned keywords collected from the 100 papers mentioned above. It can be seen that noun and verb predominate in the author-assigned keywords, accounting for 59.0% and 34.4% respectively. Note that the unknown words are mainly long terms, English phrases, English abbreviations and etc. tokenized and marked by the segmenter and POS tagger. In this paper, the words selected

**Table 1.** The part-of-speech distribution of the author-assigned keywords collected from the selected 100 papers

| POS | Nouns | Verbs | Unknown Words | Adjectives | Others |
|---|---|---|---|---|---|
| # of keywords | 242 | 141 | 24 | 2 | 1 |
| Proportion | 59.0% | 34.4% | 5.9% | 0.5% | 0.2% |

as nodes in the network construction are restricted to nouns, verbs and unknown words.

The noise in lexical network can also be reduced by word frequency. When an author elucidates a certain topic, keywords are usually frequently referred to. Words with extremely low frequency (for instance, appear only once) have a relatively small possibility to be keywords. Most of the low-frequency words are more of noise than keyword candidates, affecting the judgment of other important lexical nodes. Table 2 presents the frequency distribution of the author-assigned keywords in the 100 papers mentioned above. Among them, keywords with frequency 3 or above are up to 336 while keywords with frequency less than 3 amount to 74. To reduce noise in lexical network construction, words with low-frequency in the text are removed and a percentage is set as the removal-threshold to adapt to different text length.

**Table 2.** The frequency distribution of the author-assigned keywords collected from the selected 100 papers

| Frequency | 0 | 1 | 2 | 3 | 4 | 5-10 | 11-20 | Above 20 |
|---|---|---|---|---|---|---|---|---|
| # of keywords | 42 | 19 | 13 | 21 | 16 | 68 | 70 | 161 |
| Proportion | 10.2% | 4.6% | 3.2% | 5.1% | 3.9% | 16.6% | 17.1% | 39.3% |

The edges between the nodes in the network represent the lexical co-occurrence relationships between words. This co-occurrence is determined by the size of the *associated span* [12], which is defined as the maximum textual distance within which the two words associate with each other semantically in a sentence. If the associated span is set too small, some long-range associations between words will be lost; On the other hand, if the value is set too large, a lot of redundant information will be embodied. Cancho et al. pointed out that when the associated span is 2, the lexical network of English text displays the small-world features [13]. Liu et al. demonstrated that the associated span of the Chinese text is also 2 and provided linguistic explanations [14]. This paper therefore selects associated span as 2 to count the co-occurrence of words. In addition, we assume that the co-occurrence interrupted by any punctuation is invalid.

On the choice of the weight of edges, Matsuo, Zhu, and et al. constructed a *binary lexical network* to extract keywords, i.e., the relationship between two words is simply defined as with or without associations. This paper adopts *weighted lexical network*, a network with more descriptive power, of which the weight of a edge represents the association strength of the two nodes (words) it connected. A straightforward approach is to take the co-occurrence frequency of the word pair as its edge weight in the network, for instance, the weighted network constructed by Lin et al. [15]. However, this weight design method is rough and may lead to poor results in some case. Considering the following situation, high co-occurrence of word pair $(w_1, w_2)$ might not indicate that $w_1$ and $w_2$ are closely associated, if $w_1$ (or $w_2$) appears frequently in the text. Hence, to depict the relationship of the pair $(w_1, w_2)$ more accurately, we should consider not only their co-occurrence frequency, but also the frequency of both $w_1$ and $w_2$. *Jaccard coefficient* is such a measure, which is defined as

$$ J(w_i, w_j) = \frac{d(i, j)}{d(i) + d(j) - d(i, j)} , \tag{2} $$

where $d(i, j)$ is the co-occurrence frequency of the word pair $(w_i, w_j)$, $d(i)$ $(d(j))$ is the number of sentences containing the word $w_i$ $(w_j)$. The larger the Jaccard coefficient is, the closer the association of $w_i$ and $w_j$ is. Jaccard coefficient is more suitable than the co-occurrence to reflect the association or relationship of two words.

In network theory, the attributes of the node reflect the characteristics of the node itself. On the modeling of nodes, networks constructed by most current researches do not differentiate the nodes, and the differences among them are only reflected by edges indirectly, which is not reasonable from the linguistic point of view. In fact, words represented by nodes are different—Intuitively, just considering the words themselves rather than the relationships among them, the chance of some words to be keywords is higher than others. This differences of words (nodes), for instance, word length, IDF and so on, can be represented as node attributes. Generally, the longer the word is and the larger the IDF is, the higher the possibility of the word being keywords is. In addition to word length and IDF values, other linguistic knowledge or domain knowledge' can also be introduced by other means to enrich the node attributes.

## 3    Algorithm

After the construction of lexical network that represents the text, keywords can be extracted through some measures that quantify the importance of nodes in the network. The more important a node is, the greater the possibility of the word (which corresponds to the node in the network) being keywords is. Taking the measure *closeness centrality* as an example, which is defined as

$$ C_c(w_i) = \frac{1}{\sum_{j=1}^{n} dist(w_i, w_j)} , \tag{3} $$

where $n$ denotes the total number of nodes, $dist(w_i, w_j)$ denotes the distance from node $w_i$ to $w_j$ which presents the cost of the node $w_i$ to $w_j$ and can be derived from the shortest path algorithm. As Jaccard coefficient represents edge weight of the adjacent two nodes (i.e., the larger the Jaccard coefficient is, the closer the two nodes are), a transformation of *edge weight* to *edge cost* is required to apply the shortest path algorithm. For simplicity, we define the edge cost function as

$$cost(w_i, w_j) = \frac{1}{J(w_i, w_j)} \ . \tag{4}$$

The *closeness centrality* is a measure that reflects how close a node is to all other nodes in the network. Further more, we define a compound measure that takes node attributes (i.e., words length $strlen(w_i)$ and $IDF(w_i)$) into account when computing the score associated with a node in the network,

$$C_{im}(w_i) = (1 + \beta \times IDF(w_i))(1 + \alpha \times strlen(w_i))C_c(w_i) \ , \tag{5}$$

where $\alpha$ and $\beta$ are adjustable parameters (in the experiments, we took the empirical values $\alpha = 0.071$, $\beta = 0.002$). In fact, $(1 + \alpha \times strlen(w_i))C_c(w_i)$ reflects the importance of $w_i$ weighted by its length $strlen(w_i)$ in the single text (or lexical network), $(1 + \beta \times IDF(w_i))$ reflects its specificity in the entire text set (which can be viewed as a global network).

As an example, we take closeness centrality to measure the importance of lexical nodes, and the keywords extraction steps can be designed as follows,

1. Process the word segmentation for the input text and count the adjacent frequency $Neighbor(w_i, w_j)$ for each word pair $(w_i, w_j)$;
2. Combine words to phrases in terms of Equation (1) (the input to this step is $Neighbor(w_i, w_j)$ and text length);
3. Select nodes in terms of part-of-speech, i.e., remove pronouns, prepositions, adverbs and etc., and retain nouns, verbs and unknown words;
4. Count the frequency for each word $w_i$, and remove words with low-frequency in the text (the threshold is text-length related);
5. Count the co-occurrence in terms of the pre-set association span, i.e., 2;
6. Compute the Jaccard coefficient $J(w_i, w_j)$ for each pair $(w_i, w_j)$ in terms of Equation (2) and construct the lexical network of the text;
7. Remove all small *connected components* in the network except for the largest one;
8. Compute the edge cost $cost(w_i, w_j)$ for each connected node pair $(w_i, w_j)$ in terms of Equation (4);
9. Compute the closeness centrality $C_c(w_i)$ for each node $w_i$;
10. Compute the compound importance measure $C_{im}(w_i)$ for each node $w_i$ in terms of Equation (5);
11. Rank the nodes (words) in terms of their compound importance and choose the top $K$ words as keywords of the input text.

## 4   Experimental Results

In order to evaluate the performance of the network constructed in this paper, we randomly selected a scientific paper, extracted keywords using our designed algorithm and compared with the author-assigned keywords. The paper selected

**Table 3.** The author-assigned keywords of the paper "Study on the Smart-Input Method of Chagatai Letters and Transcription Signatures for Digitalized Chagatai Digitalizing System" (in Chinese) in *Journal of Chinese Information Processing*, 2007(6)

| NO. | The Author-Assigned Keywords |
|:---:|:---:|
| 1 | 计算机应用/computer application |
| 2 | 中文信息处理/Chinese information processing |
| 3 | 古维吾尔文(察合台文)/ancient Uyghur(Chagatai language) |
| 4 | 数字化整理/digitalization |
| 5 | 智能输入法/smart IME |
| 6 | 撰写符号/transcription signatures |
| 7 | UNICODE |

for testing was "Study on the Smart-Input Method of Chagatai Letters and Transcription Signatures for Digitalized Chagatai Digitalizing System" (in Chinese) published in *Journal of Chinese Information Processing*, 2007(6). The keywords assigned by the authors are shown in Table 3.

Among the keywords, "计算机应用"(*computer application*) and "中文信息处理"(*Chinese information processing*) were not considered in our experiments, as they are disciplines generic keywords and never appear in the original paper. We adopted the Chinese Lexical Analysis System (ICTCLAS) [16] to segment the raw text and tag each word with a part of speech in all the experiments of this section.

**Table 4.** The top 10 extracted keywords when our algorithm is applied

| Rank | Keywords | Rank | Keywords |
|:---:|:---:|:---:|:---:|
| 1 | 察合台文/Chagatai language | 6 | 方案/scheme |
| 2 | 转写符号/transcription signatures | 7 | 输入/input |
| 3 | 智能输入法/smart IME | 8 | 使用/use |
| 4 | 维吾尔文/Uyghur | 9 | 字母/letter |
| 5 | 智能输入/smart input | 10 | 拼写/spelling |

As is shown in Table 4 that words combination strategy used in our algorithm combined words to phrases effectively. Among the top five phrases, some are exactly the same as the author-assigned keywords (i.e., the first and the third) while the others slightly differ from the author-assigned keywords. Although "维吾尔文"(*Uyghur*) and "古维吾尔文"(*ancient Uyghur*), "转写符号" (*transcription signatures*) and "撰写符号" (*transcription signatures*) are different literally in Chinese, the former of each pair (extracted by our algorithm) closely resembles the latter (assigned by the authors) in meanings and can be adopted as keywords of the text. This experimental result shows that the lexical network built in this paper can be applied to extract keywords of Chinese texts effectively.

To further validate the advantages of the network constructed in this paper, we compared it with some other related algorithms. In comparison with other network-based approaches, our algorithm adopted the same node importance measure as that proposed in other methods respectively and the difference was only in network construction. The test set adopted was the 100 Chinese papers obtained from *Journal of Chinese Information Processing* mentioned above and the author-assigned keywords were taken as the answers to calculate accuracy, recall and F-value.

Zhu et al. built a binary lexical network by selecting the top 25% of high-frequency words as network nodes. When two words were in the same sentence, an edge between the corresponding nodes was added to construct the network. They also designed an average path length increment $\Delta L_v$ as the node importance measure. When adopting the same measure $\Delta L_v$, the comparison results with the approach designed by Zhu et al. are shown in Table 5.

**Table 5.** The comparison results with the approach designed by Zhu et al.

| TOP N | | 3 | 4 | 5 | 10 | 15 |
|---|---|---|---|---|---|---|
| Average Accurate(%) | Zhu's Approach | 15.00 | 13.75 | 12.80 | 9.20 | 7.53 |
| | Our Approach | **26.33** | **24.50** | **22.60** | **15.40** | **11.60** |
| Average Recall(%) | Zhu's Approach | 9.00 | 10.91 | 12.72 | 17.99 | 21.93 |
| | Our Approach | **15.68** | **19.43** | **22.55** | **30.79** | **34.53** |
| Average F-Value(%) | Zhu's Approach | 11.25 | 12.17 | 12.76 | 12.17 | 11.21 |
| | Our Approach | **19.66** | **21.67** | **22.57** | **20.53** | **17.37** |

This experimental result shows that, with the same measure $\Delta L_v$, our method achieves better effect on accuracy, recall and F-value than the approach designed by Zhu et al. This indicates that, compared with binary network, the weighted network describes the relationships between the words more accurately, which improves the performance of keywords extraction.

Lin et al. built a simple weighted network, taking the co-occurrence frequency of the words as the edge weight, and combined weighted centrality and boundary-node based betweenness as the node importance measure. When adopting the same measure, the comparison results between the approach designed by Lin et al. and our approach are shown in Table 6.

As is shown in the Table 6, with the same measure, our method achieves better effect on accuracy, recall and F-value than the approach designed by Lin et al., especially when comparing the top three extracted keywords. The reason is that the lexical network we designed utilizes linguistic knowledge to keep more text information while filtering out much of the noise, and thus is more effective.

We also compared our approach with TF-IDF method, and closeness centrality is selected as the measure of our approach. The experimental results are shown in Table 7. It can be seen from Table 7 that the accuracy, recall and F-value of our method are better than those of the TF-IDF method, because the network keeps the association information between words and we also introduced linguistic

**Table 6.** The comparison results between the approach designed by Lin et al. and our approach

| TOP N | | 3 | 4 | 5 | 10 | 15 |
|---|---|---|---|---|---|---|
| Average Accurate(%) | Lin's Approach | 24.33 | 22.50 | 21.60 | 15.90 | 12.20 |
| | Our Approach | **27.67** | **24.25** | **23.20** | **17.30** | **12.87** |
| Average Recall(%) | Lin's Approach | 14.15 | 17.54 | 21.01 | 31.23 | 35.76 |
| | Our Approach | **16.17** | **18.99** | **22.93** | **33.94** | **38.04** |
| Average F-Value(%) | Lin's Approach | 17.89 | 19.71 | 21.30 | 21.07 | 18.19 |
| | Our Approach | **20.41** | **21.30** | **23.06** | **22.92** | **19.23** |

knowledge into it, while the TF-IDF method only utilizes word frequency in the text and inverse document frequency in the background corpus.

**Table 7.** The result compared with TF-IDF approach

| TOP N | | 3 | 4 | 5 | 10 | 15 |
|---|---|---|---|---|---|---|
| Average Accurate(%) | TF-IDF Approach | 24.00 | 23.00 | 21.40 | 15.50 | 12.00 |
| | Our Approach | **30.67** | **26.50** | **24.60** | **17.00** | **12.33** |
| Average Recall(%) | TF-IDF Approach | 14.03 | 18.03 | 20.88 | 30.47 | 35.26 |
| | Our Approach | **17.99** | **20.65** | **24.12** | **33.52** | **36.40** |
| Average F-Value(%) | TF-IDF Approach | 17.71 | 20.21 | 21.14 | 20.55 | 17.91 |
| | Our Approach | **22.68** | **23.21** | **24.36** | **22.56** | **18.42** |

Further, as to the network designed in this paper, different node importance measures may achieve different performances in keywords extraction. Comparing the experimental results from Table 5 to Table 7, it can be seen that closeness centrality is relatively preferable.

Numerically, all of the three indices, i.e., the average accuracy, recall and F-value, are relatively low in the experimental results above, whatever method is adopted. One reason is that these methods can only extract words appeared in the text. The recall and F-value will significantly reduced if the author-assigned keywords do not appear in the text (Note that these keywords account for 10.2% according to Table 2). Another important reason is that the exact match is used in the evaluation above, which means an extracted keyword is judged as right if and only if it is exactly the same as one of author-assigned keywords. However, limited by the phrase combination strategy, no combination, partial combination or over-combination of the phrases splited by the segmenter is likely to happen, and any of them may lead to the extracted keywords mismatching with the author-assigned keywords. If this mismatch happens, the extracted keyword is judged as wrong, though it is close to the author-assigned keyword in semantic. Taking the paper "Study on the Smart-Input Method of Chagatai Letters and Transcription Signatures for Digitalized Chagatai Digitalizing System" mentioned above as an example, the author-assigned keyword "古维吾尔文" (*ancient Uyghur*) only appears once in the text, whereas the phrase "维吾尔文" (*Uyghur*) appears 12 times. Although splited by the segmenter, "维吾尔" (*Uyghur*) and "文" (*language*) were combined successfully into "维吾尔文" (*Uyghur*) when the combination strategy was applied, and this combined phrase was extracted as a keyword. However, it was judged as wrong only because it is not literally the same as "古维吾尔文" (*ancient Uyghur*).

## 5  Conclusions and Future Work

This paper constructs a lexical network to extract keywords based on the characteristics of network as well as linguistic knowledge. Rather than designing a node importance measure, this research focuses on the construction of lexical network, including reasonable selection of nodes, proper description of relationships between words, enhancement of node attributes, and etc. In the experiments, our approach was compared with three competitive baseline approach, namely, binary network, simple weighted network and TF-IDF approach. Experiments indicate that the lexical network constructed by our approach achieves preferable effect on accuracy, recall and F-value—when selecting the top three results, the three indices increase by 6.67%, 3.96% and 4.97% on average than the classic TF-IDF method respectively.

For the future work, improvements can be made in the following aspects. Firstly, not only the reflection of words to the text theme, but also the semantic relationships between the candidates (i.e., inclusion or similarity) should be considered in keywords extraction to reduce the information redundancy among the extracted keywords. Secondly, more linguistic knowledge (the syntax dependency tree, for instance) can be explored to construct direct weighted networks; Thirdly, a more reasonable evaluation method should be designed to evaluate effectiveness of the keywords extraction, for example, the combination of exact match and similar match.

**Acknowledgments.** This work is partially supported by the Chiang Ching-kuo Foundation for International Scholarly Exchange under the project "Building a Diachronic Language Knowledge-Base" (RG013-D-09) and the Opening Project of Beijing Key Laboratory of Internet Culture and Digital Dissemination Research (ICDD201102).

## References

1. Luhn, H.P.: A Statistical Approach to Mechanized Encoding and Searching of Literary Information. IBM Journal of Research and Development 1(4), 309–317 (1957)
2. Salton, G., Buckley, C.: Term-weighting Approaches in Automatic Text Retrieval. Information Processing and Management 24(5), 513–523 (1988)
3. Turney, P.D.: Learning to Extract Keyphrases from Text. National Research Council, Canada, NRC Technical Report ERB-1057 (1999)

4. Frank, E., Paynter, G.W., Witten, I.H.: Domain-specific Keyphrase Extraction. In: Proceedings of the 16th International Joint Conference on Artificial Intelligence, Stockholm, Sweden, pp. 668–673. Morgan Kaufmann (1999)

5. Li, S.J., Wang, H.F., Yu, S.W., Xin, C.S.: Research on Maximum Entropy Model for Keyword Indexing. Chinese Journal of Computers 27(9), 1192–1197 (2004) (in Chinese)

6. Mihalcea, R., Tarau, P.: TextRank: Bringing Order into Texts. In: Proceedings of the Conference on Empirical Methods in Natural Language Processing (EMNLP 2004), pp. 404–411 (2004)

7. Matsuo, Y., Ohsawa, Y., Ishizuka, M.: KeyWorld: Extracting Keywords from A Document as A Small World. In: Jantke, K.P., Shinohara, A. (eds.) DS 2001. LNCS (LNAI), vol. 2226, pp. 271–281. Springer, Heidelberg (2001)

8. Zhu, M., Cai, Z., Cai, Q.: Automatic Keywords Extraction of Chinese Document Using Small World. In: Proceedings of the International Conference on Natural Language Processing and Knowledge Engineering, pp. 438–443 (2003)

9. Ma, L., Jiao, L., Bai, L., Zhou, Y., Dong, L.: Research on a Compound Keywords Detection Method Based on Small World Model. Journal of Chinese Information Processing 3(23), 121–128 (2009) (in Chinese)

10. Liu, H.: The Theoretical and Experimental Justifications of Phrase Advantage in Chinese Information Processing. Applied Linguistics (4), 129–135 (2007) (in Chinese)

11. Zhan, W.D.: A Study of Constructing Rules of Phrases in Contemporary Chinese for Chinese Information Processing. Doctoral Thesis. Peking University (1999) (in Chinese)

12. Zhao, P., Cai, Q.S., Wang, Q.Y., Geng, H.T.: An Automatic Keyword Extraction of Chinese Document Algorithm Based on Complex Network Features. Pattern Recognition and Artificial Intelligence 20(6), 827–831 (2007) (in Chinese)

13. Cancho, R.F.I., Sole, R.V.: The Small World of Human Language. Proceedings of the Royal Society of London, Series B, Biological Sciences 268(1482), 2261–2265 (2001)

14. Liu, Z.Y., Sun, M.S.: Chinese Word Co-occurrence Network: Its Small World Effect and Scale-free Property. Journal of Chinese Information Processing 21(6), 52–58 (2007) (in Chinese)

15. Lin, Y.X., Liang, Y.H., Han, Y., Zhang, Y.G., Yao, J.M.: Keyphrase Extraction of Chinese Documents Based on Weighted Complex Network. Microelectronics & Computer 26(10), 65–73 (2009) (in Chinese)

16. Zhang, H., Liu, Q., Cheng, X., Zhang, H., Yu, H.: Chinese Lexical Analysis Using Hierarchical Hidden Markov Model. In: Proceedings of the Second SIGHAN Workshop, pp. 63–70 (2003)

# Automatically Predicting the Polarity of Chinese Adjectives:
# Not, a Bit and a Search Engine

Ge Xu[1,2,3], Churen Huang[1], and Houfeng Wang[2]

[1] Faculty of Humanities, The Hong Kong Polytechnic University, Hong Kong
[2] Institute of Computational Linguistics, Peking University, Beijing, 100871
[3] Department of Computer Science, MinJiang University, Fuzhou, 350108

**Abstract.** The SO-PMI-IR method proposed by [1] is a simple and effective method for predicting the polarity of words, but it suffers from three limitations: 1) polar paradigm words are selected by intuition; 2) few search engines nowadays officially support the NEAR operator; 3) the NEAR operator considers the co-occurrence within 10 words, which incurs some noises.

In this paper, for predicting the polarity of Chinese adjectives automatically, we follow the framework of the SO-PMI-IR method in [1]. However, by using only two polarity indicators, 不 [bu](*not*) and 有点 [youdian](*a bit*), we overcome all the limitations listed above.

To evaluate our method, a test set is constructed from two Chinese human-annotated polarity lexicons. We compare our method with Turney's in details and test our method on different settings. For Chinese adjectives, the performance of our method is satisfying. Furthermore, we perform noise analysis, and the relationship between the magnitude of SO-PMI-IR and accuracy is also analyzed. The results show that our method is more reliable than Turney's method in predicting the polarity of Chinese adjectives.

**Keywords:** sentiment analysis, polarity, Chinese adjective.

## 1 Introduction

The polarity (semantic orientation) of a word represents an evaluative characterization of a word's deviation from the norm for its semantic group, for example, "beautiful" is positively oriented, as opposed to "ugly" [2].

Predicting the polarity of words or building polarity lexicons automatically is a key task in sentiment analysis, which supports many other related works. Many research works have been carried out to address this problem, and some sentiment lexicons have been built [3–6].

In this paper, we propose a method for predicting the polarity of Chinese adjectives. Although our method follows the framework of [1, 7], we do not select polar paradigm words by intuition, but adopt only two polarity indicators which are strongly linguistics-based. Furthermore, our method does not require the NEAR operator as [1, 7], thus is not limited on specific search engines.

P. Liu and Q. Su (Eds.): CLSW 2013, LNAI 8229, pp. 453–465, 2013.

In our method, the two polarity indicators are 不[*bu*](*not*) and 有点[*youdian*](*a bit*). The only basic operator required for search engines is the "exact phrase" operator, to make sure that search engines return the hit number of the exact phrase. This operator is supported by various mainstream search engines and usually is double quotation marks(""). In our method, SO-PMI-IR(*word*) is

$$log_2[\frac{hits("不\text{word}")hits("有点")}{hits("有点\text{word}")hits("不")}].$$

Two examples are investigated in Table 1.

**Table 1.** Two examples using our method

| 美丽[*meili*](*beautiful*) | 丑陋[*choulou*](*ugly*) |
|---|---|
| hits("不")= 7,440,000,000 | hits("不")= 7,440,000,000 |
| hits("不美丽")=2,260,000 | hits("不丑陋")= 416,000 |
| hits("有点")=509,000,000 | hits("有点")=509,000,000 |
| hits("有点美丽")=113,000 | hits("有点丑陋")= 184,000 |
| SO-PMI-IR=0.4524 >0 | SO-PMI-IR=-2.6927 <0 |
| positive | negative |

The result is correct because 美丽[*meili*] is the Chinese adjective for "beautiful", and 丑陋[*choulou*] is for "ugly". At first sight, this method seems extremely simple. However, after detailed analyzing and verifying in our paper, we will show that our method is both strongly linguistics-based and of high performance.

## 2    Related Work

As a pilot work, [8] try to predict the polarity of adjectives in an unlabeled corpus. They think the polarity of conjoining adjectives is subject to linguistic constraints, and use a clustering algorithm to divide all adjectives into two clusters. A notable characteristic of the work in [8] is that the authors use no polar seed, but identify the dominant cluster as positive based on semantic markedness in linguistics. This is to say, the approach uses special prior knowledge compared with those approaches using polar seed words.

In [1], the polarity of a given phrase is calculated by comparing its similarity to a positive paradigm word (excellent) with its similarity to a negative paradigm word (poor) through a search engine. Although we can see a search engine as a large-scale unlabeled corpus, Turney's method does not extract the relation between words from the corpus to build a graph, which is adopted in [8] and many other graph-based approaches. Our work is most similar to Turney's method, the difference between our method and Turney's method will be discussed in section 3.2.

[9] describe and evaluate a new method of automatic seed word selection for unsupervised sentiment classification of product reviews in Chinese. The authors find that in Chinese it is more common to say "not good" than "bad", and use this observation to identify suitable positive seeds for the given corpus. The way that the authors identify

positive seeds is related to our method in this paper; however they use it to construct only an initial set of positive seeds and do not explain the construction from a linguistic perspective.

In [10], the authors propose a simple approach to generate a high-coverage polarity lexicon of both individual words and multi-word expressions, using only a Roget-like thesaurus and a handful of affixes. The authors point out that based on marking theory, overtly marked words, such as "dishonest", "unhappy", tend to have negative polarity, whereas their unmarked counterparts, "honest" and "happy", tend to have positive polarity. Thus they use 11 antonym-generating affix patterns to generate overtly marked words and their unmarked counterparts, which are then used as the set of seed words. Similar to [9], this work uses the negative affixes (positive indicators) to construct only an initial set of seeds. In contrast, in our method, we use both positive indicator (not) and negative indicator (a bit), and do not adopt any thesaurus.

[11] propose a knowledge-based method to automatically determine the polarity of DSAAs (dynamic sentiment ambiguous adjectives) in Chinese such as "large", "small", "high" and "low". One feature of their method is to use "a bit" to construct patterns for polarity identification, because the authors assume that "a bit" commonly modifies cases with negative polarity. Compared with [11], our work covers all Chinese adjectives, and furthermore, we use "not" which provides another type of asymmetry in polarity.

The related work above can be summed as follows. The two polarity indicators (not and a bit) for our method are mentioned in some of the above works, however, they only use one of the two indicators in rule-based patterns or to extract a set of polar words, and never use the two indicators simultaneously. Furthermore, no deep analysis from a linguistic perspective is provided. By using the two Chinese polarity indicators and the framework of [1] , we can make a binary classification on the polarity of any Chinese adjective. The remarkable application of linguistic knowledge (semantic markedness) in [8] motivates us to search for more reliable linguistic clues (instead of selecting seeds) in the task of predicting the polarity of Chinese adjectives.

## 3   Our Method

### 3.1   Linguistics-Based Polarity Asymmetry

**The Pollyanna Principle.** Pollyanna is a character in the book *Pollyanna* written by Eleanor H. Porter (1913), who is a young girl fervently holding a naively optimistic and grateful outlook on life.

In [12], the authors propose the Pollyanna Hypothesis which states that people will prefer to look on the bright side rather than the gloomy side of life, thus resembling the optimistic heroine in the novel *Pollyanna*. Interpreting it in a communicative framework as the Pollyanna Principle means postulating that participants in a conversation will prefer pleasant topics of conversation to unpleasant ones [13].

The Pollyanna Principle can be used to explain the asymmetry in polarity, and such asymmetry offers us polarity indicators (not and a bit) for identifying polar words. We can see that "not" is much more related with positive words and "a bit" is much more related with negative words, and such asymmetry is cross-cultural and spotted in different languages.

**Positive Indicator: Not.** In the milestone work of [12], the authors propose that negative affixes are applied significantly more often to E+ (evaluatively positive words) members of pairs to make the E- opposite than to the E- (evaluatively negative words) members to make the E+ opposite. This is to say, the formations from E- to E+ by negative affixes such as *broken-unbroken, violent-nonviolent* are rare compared with the formations from E+ to E- such as *happy-unhappy, moral-immoral*.

The authors propose that this is because E+ words have prior appearance in a language historically as well as in development of language in individuals, and negative affixes must be applied to *already existent* meaningful forms (E+ words are dominant). Therefore, negative affixes are used to attach positive words much more than to negative ones. Note that the work of [12] is based on cross-cultural and developmental data, which shows the possibility that our method is transferred to languages other than Chinese.

We can also understand the asymmetry from the perspective of pragmatics. As pointed out by [14], negation is often experienced as an unpleasant sort of construction, speakers may employ various sorts of indirection to soften the ill effects of a negative utterance; contrariwise, hearers may systematically strengthen the interpretation of negation to compensate for such euphemism.

Suppose that **p** and **q** are a pair of opposite assertions, and **p** is positive, **q** is negative. Commonly, listeners will systematically infer **not-p** to the strong opposite assertion **q**, and ignore the logical possibility of something being neither **p** nor **q** [14].

In this paper, we only concentrate on the negation of adjectives. When a positive adjective is negated, the meaning becomes the opposite of the adjective. However, when a negative adjective is negated, the meaning is normally not the opposite of the adjective, but only the cancellation of the negative polarity, see Table 2:

Let's explain the asymmetry in negation of polarity using a pair of opposite sentences and show why "not" is much more related with positive words than negative ones.

Suppose that a speaker wants to express "He is a stupid person". According to the Pollyanna Principle, the speaker tends to use some indirect and implicit expressions that are weaker than "stupid". Thus the speaker uses "not smart" instead of "stupid", because "not smart" is weaker than "stupid". The listener of this sentence normally knows that the sentence has been weaken by using the Pollyanna Principle, thus he will automatically understand the "not smart" to be "stupid", instead of a middle evaluation between "smart" and "stupid", thus recovering the original intention of the speaker.

In contrast, when the speaker wants to express "He is a smart person", we can say it directly, without the need of euphemism, and we will not replace "smart" with "not stupid". In such cases, "not stupid" becomes an infrequent or unnecessary expression.

Therefore, **"not"** can be considered as an indicator for positive polarity. This is to say, **the more possible a polar adjective is modified by "not", the more possible the word carries positive polarity.**

**Table 2.** Examples of negation

| Sentences | Negation of sentences |
|---|---|
| He is happy. | He is not happy. (=He is sad.) |
| He is a smart person. | He is a not smart person. (=He is a stupid person.) |
| It is interesting. | It is not interesting. (= It is boring.) |
| He like her. | He doesn't like her. (=He hates her.) |
| He is sad. | He is not sad. (≠He is happy.) |
| He is a stupid person. | He is not a stupid person. (≠He is a smart person.) |
| It is boring. | It is not boring. (≠It is interesting.) |
| He hates her. | He doesn't hate her. (≠He like her.) |

**Negative Indicator: A Bit.** It has been noticed in linguistics that the use of the minimizers like "a bit", "a little" are restricted to bad situations [15, 16, 13, 17, 18].

[15] claims that in a sentence with "a little/a bit/somewhat", there is an implication of "more than expected", so that the use of these expressions is restricted to unfavorable contexts, which is also observed in [16, 17]. When a minimizer like "a little/a bit/somewhat" is used to modify a positive word, generally it is infelicitous. See Table 3 for some examples, asterisks (*) in the table mean infelicitous.

**Table 3.** Examples of "a bit"

| |
|---|
| The paint is a bit dirty. His shirt is somewhat short. He is somewhat stupid. |
| *The paint was a bit clean. *He is a bit smart. *She is a bit beautiful. |

Similar to the positive indicator (not), the asymmetry on polarity when using "a bit" is also cross-cultural and observed in many languages. For example, [18] argues that Dutch has comparable general restrictions for "a bit", and also this phenomenon is observed in Japanese [19], Hebrew and Chinese [20].

The asymmetry on polarity when using "a bit" can also be explained from the perspective of pragmatics.

When faced with bad situations, speakers tend to understate the degree to which things are bad. Thus the 'minimizing' degree adverbs such as "somewhat/a little/a bit" are specialized towards negatively evaluated terms [13]. When a word with negative polarity is modified by the quantifier meaning "a bit", its negative value is actually diminished, and brought closer to the mid point of the evaluative scale [20]. Therefore, according to the Pollyanna Principle, minimizers like "somewhat/a little/a bit" can occur only in a context where the speaker's utterance is construed negatively. In contrast, the positively evaluated terms are actually immune to such reduction [20], thus "a bit" is less frequently used to modify a positive word. If a situation is good, then it is normally unacceptable to use "a bit" to modify the positively evaluated terms because there is no need to mitigate a good situation, which is inconsistent with the Pollyanna Principle.

To sum up, when expressing negative meanings, we often need to soften the expression by euphemism, thus we use "a bit" to reduce the strength of the negative situation, make the situation look like better. In contrast, when expressing positive meanings, we seldom modify them using "a bit".

Therefore, **"a bit"** can be considered as an indicator for negative polarity. This is to say, **the more possible a polar adjective is modified by "a bit", the more possible the word carries negative polarity.**

### 3.2   Implementation of Our Method

Given a search engine and the two Chinese polarity indicators (not and a bit), we can now make a binary classification on the polarity of all Chinese adjective.

Since our method follows the work in [1, 7], we at first introduce briefly their work.

In [1, 7], the polarity of a given phrase is calculated by comparing its similarity to positive paradigm word(s) with its similarity to negative paradigm word(s), and the authors define SO-PMI-IR(*word*) as:

$$log_2\left[\frac{hits(word\ NEAR\ PPW)hits(NPW)}{hits(word\ NEAR\ NPW)hits(PPW)}\right]$$

, where PPW is the positive paradigm word(s) and NPW is the negative paradigm word(s); $hits(query)$ is the number of hits returned from a search engine after submitting the $query$, and NEAR is an operator supported by the search engine to offer co-occurrence within a window of 10 words. If the SO-PMI-IR value is positive, the word has positive polarity, otherwise negative polarity.

To avoid division by zero, 0.01 is added to the hits. Polar paradigm words are selected by intuition.

In our method, SO-PMI-IR(*word*) is

$$log_2\left[\frac{hits("不word")hits("有点")}{hits("有点word")hits("\ 不")}\right].$$

The query "不word" is formed by adding 不 (not) immediately before the word with no spaces in between. The double quotation marks ("") of "不word" are the "exact phrase" operator used to make sure that search engines return the hits number of the exact phrase. The query "有点" is formed in the same way.

Our method is different from Turney's in the following three aspects:

1. Instead of polar paradigm words, we use only two polarity indicators: 不[*bu*](*not*) and 有点[*youdian*](*a bit*), which are strongly linguistics-based.
2. Instead of the NEAR operator, queries in our method only need the "exact phrase" operator (normally, double quotation marks), which is widely supported by search engines and simpler than the NEAR operator.
3. Furthermore, the NEAR operator considers the co-occurrence within 10 words, which incur some noises. In our method, there are no such noises from co-occurrence. We will explain this further in section 5.1.

Our method is especially suitable for Chinese adjectives because 有点 (a bit) can be used to modify almost all Chinese adjectives as 不 (not) can. According to [21], almost all Chinese adjectives can be prefixed by 很[*hen*](*very*), thus Chinese adjectives can be seen as gradable adjectives. Theoretically, 有点 (a bit) as a degree adverb can precede almost all Chinese adjectives, thus it is reasonable to construct a query for any search engine by adding 有点 (a bit) before an adjective.

## 4    Experimental Setting

### 4.1    Test Set

Our method requires no training data, so we only need to construct the test set.

For our test set, two Chinese sentiment lexicons are used: Hownet sentiment lexicon[1] and NTUSD (NTU Sentiment Dictionary)[2]. Both Hownet sentiment lexicon and NTUSD contain positive and negative terms. Hownet is a Chinese ontology dictionary, and HowNet sentiment lexicon is built for public use based on Hownet. NTUSD was automatically generated by enlarging an initial manually created seed vocabulary by consulting a Chinese synonym dictionary and the Academia Sinica Bilingual Ontological WordNet [22].

We use the ICTCLAS package[3] to perform word segmentation and POS tagging on the two lexicons according to PKU code [23]. Then we use the intersection of the two sets of adjectives from the two lexicons as our test set[4]. The test set contains 720 Chinese adjectives, in which 339 adjectives are positive and 381 adjectives are negative.

To use the intersection of two lexicons is to guarantee that the test set is high-quality in polarity tagging. We also conducted experiments on full test set of both dictionaries (Hownet sentiment lexicon and NTUSD), similar results are observed. So, in our paper, we only consider the intersection of two dictionaries (720 Chinese adjectives) as the test set.

## 5    Experimental Results

### 5.1    Comparison with Turney's Method

**Accuracy.** In this experiment, we compare three results in Table 4:

---

[1] http://www.keenage.com/download/sentiment.rar
[2] http://nlg18.csie.ntu.edu.tw
[3] http://www.ictclas.org
[4] If an adjective is segmented by ICTCLAS, it is removed from the test set.

1. **Turney(2)** means using the method in [7] with the two polar paradigm words: 出色[*chuse*](*excellent*), 糟糕[*zaogao*](*poor*);
2. **Turney(20)** means using the method in [7] with the 20 polar paradigm words as in [24];
3. **Ours** means our method in section 3.2.

The AltaVista search engine used in [7] does not support NEAR operator any more, so we adopt an online Chinese corpus[5] which supports all sorts of query operators such as the NEAR and the "exact phrase" operators. Such a choice can also be seen as an advantage of our method over Turney's method for predicting the polarity of Chinese adjectives, because it is not easy to find search engines which both contain large-scale Chinese corpora and support the NEAR operator.

The adjectives in test set are sorted in the descending order of the absolute value of their SO-PMI-IR and the top ranked words (the words with highest confidence) are then classified. For example, the third column in Table 4 shows the accuracy when the top 75% are classified and the bottom 25% (with lowest confidence) are ignored.

Table 4. Comparison with Turney's method: Accuracy

| Percent of full set | 100% | 75% | 50% | 25% |
|---|---|---|---|---|
| Size of test set | 720 | 540 | 360 | 180 |
| Acc@Turney(2) | 0.6847 | 0.5926 | 0.6528 | 0.8333 |
| Acc@Turney(20) | 0.8222 | 0.8648 | 0.9333 | 0.9000 |
| Acc@Ours | 0.8042 | 0.8685 | 0.8806 | 0.9667 |

In Table 4, our method is much better than **Turney(2)** and is comparable with **Turney(20)** which uses 20 carefully selected polar paradigm words. The large accuracy difference between **Turney(2)** and **Turney(20)** shows the influence of selecting polar paradigm words on performance. According to [7], polar paradigm words are selected by intuition and are based on opposing pairs (good/bad, nice/nasty, excellent/poor, etc.). The selecting of polar paradigms is subjective and can be influenced by the knowledge of researchers, and even the genre of the corpus. However, in our method, only two polarity indicators are used, which are strongly linguistics-based and immune to intuition.

**Noise Analysis.** Although **Turney(20)** has similar performance with our method, its accuracy (see the *Acc@Turney(20)* row in Table 4) does not increase smoothly as we decrease the percentage of the test set that is classified, which shows that the magnitude of SO-PMI-IR in Turney's method is no longer a good indicator of the confidence in the classification of a word. Such a phenomenon is also spotted in [7] when the corpus is small. We will analyze it in more detailed way as follows.

To reduce the influence of data sparseness, we remove the adjectives that have zero hit in both polarities. For **Turney(20)**, 692 adjectives have at least one nonzero hit number from either the query constructed using positive paradigm words or using negative

---

[5] http://ccl.pku.edu.cn/, 477 million Chinese characters.

paradigm words. For our method, the number is 654. The number of the shared adjectives is 631. We use the 631 adjectives as the new test set. Table 5 shows the relationship between the size of test set and accuracy. Also, The adjectives in test set are sorted in the descending order of the absolute value of their SO-PMI-IR; when size of test set is 10%, only the top 10% words (the words with highest confidence) are then classified.

**Table 5.** Comparison with Turney's method: Noise analysis

| Percent of full set | Size of test set | Acc@ Turney(20) | Acc@ Ours |
|---|---|---|---|
| 100% | 631 | 0.8368 | 0.8225 |
| 90% | 567 | 0.8660 | 0.8624 |
| 80% | 504 | 0.8929 | 0.8948 |
| 70% | 441 | 0.9048 | 0.9070 |
| 60% | 378 | 0.9233 | 0.9180 |
| 50% | 315 | 0.9333 | 0.9397 |
| 40% | 252 | 0.9206 | 0.9524 |
| 30% | 189 | 0.9101 | 0.9524 |
| 20% | 126 | 0.8889 | 0.9603 |
| 10% | 63 | 0.9524 | 0.9683 |

In Table 5, the third and fourth columns are two accuracy lists for **Turney(20)** and our method respectively. From top to bottom, the accuracy list of our method increase monotonously, but the the accuracy list of **Turney(20)** fluctuates sharply.

The trend difference of the two accuracy lists can be explained by the difference of how two methods choose co-occurrence contexts. Our method only considers the word before the target adjective as the context, which reduces the noise incurred from long-distance co-occurrence. In contrast, Turney's method uses the NEAR operator, which allows the co-occurrence within a window of 10 words. For Turney's method, "He is rich but stupid", "Good and Evil", "The camera is not cheap and ugly" are all noises because a positive word co-occurs with a negative word within a window of 10 words. However, our method is naturally immune to these noises, because the context in our method is minimized. Each of the two polarity indicator is added before the target adjective to construct a query, thus there is no noise caused by long-distance co-occurrence.

Therefore, as for our method, the magnitude of SO-PMI-IR is always a good indicator of the confidence in the classification of a word. We would further investigate the relationship between the magnitude of SO-PMI-IR and accuracy in section 5.3.

## 5.2   Comparison on Different Search Engines and on Different Corpus Sizes

We test our method on different search engines: Baidu[6], Jike[7], Sougou[8], YahooCn[9], and AltaVista[10]. The results are satisfying and stable, see Table 6.

---

[6] http://www.baidu.com
[7] http://www.Jike.com
[8] http://www.sougou.com
[9] http://www.yahoo.cn
[10] http://www.altavista.com

**Table 6.** Comparison on different search engines

| Percent of full set | 100% | 75% | 50% | 25% |
|---|---|---|---|---|
| Size of test set | 720 | 540 | 360 | 180 |
| Acc@Baidu | 0.8694 | 0.9407 | 0.9639 | 0.9833 |
| Acc@Jike | 0.8639 | 0.9333 | 0.9528 | 0.9667 |
| Acc@Sougou | 0.8222 | 0.8889 | 0.9361 | 0.9611 |
| Acc@YahooCn | 0.8417 | 0.9185 | 0.9583 | 0.9944 |
| Acc@AltaVista | 0.8375 | 0.8926 | 0.9194 | 0.9556 |

We also test our method on different corpus sizes, see Table 7.

Although Baidu is the largest Chinese search engine in the world, its hit number returned has a maximum (100,000,000), thus it is hard to obtain the accurate hit number in some cases (especially for frequent words). Here, we adopt Jike as the default search engine because it can return accurate hit numbers and has a large-scale Chinese corpus.

We reduce the corpus by adding "site:SiteName" to every query submitted to Jike, which restricts the search results to the Web pages in the Internet domain "SiteName". Three SiteNames are used; they are "sina.com.cn" (160 million pages), "163.com" (42 million pages) and "tianya.cn" (10 million pages). Together with the corpus of Jike without site restriction (13 billion pages), we have four corpora of different sizes. The comparison is given in Table 7.

**Table 7.** Comparison on different corpus size in the Jike search engine

| Percent of full set | 100% | 75% | 50% | 25% |
|---|---|---|---|---|
| Size of test set | 720 | 540 | 360 | 180 |
| Acc@ 13 billion pages | 0.8639 | 0.9333 | 0.9528 | 0.9667 |
| Acc@ 160 million pages | 0.8778 | 0.9352 | 0.9611 | 0.9778 |
| Acc@ 42 million pages | 0.8653 | 0.9167 | 0.9472 | 0.9556 |
| Acc@ 10 million pages | 0.8625 | 0.9204 | 0.9528 | 0.9833 |

From Table 7, we can see that the corpus size does not affect accuracy significantly when using our method. In [7], the authors report accuracy on General Inquirer (GI) lexicon[11] and use different experimental settings, so we can not compare Tunery's method with ours directly. However, when they change the corpus from 350 million web pages (at least one hundred billion words) to 7 million web pages (at least two billion words), we see significant drop in accuracy.

### 5.3 The Relationship between the Magnitude of SO-PMI-IR and Accuracy

For our method, after the analysis in section 5.1, the absolute value of SO-PMI-IR can be seen as a good indicator for classification accuracy. In this section, we will explore

[11] http://www.wjh.harvard.edu/~inquirer/

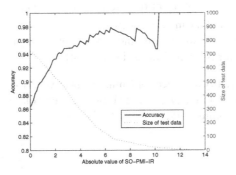

**Fig. 1.** The relationship between SO-PMI-IR and accuracy

how confident we can be on the polarity classification by our method when obtaining the SO-PMI-IR of a Chinese adjective.

Figure 1 is based on the experiment on the Jike search engine (see the *Acc@Jike* row in Table 6), when the absolute value of SO-PMI-IR becomes larger, the size of test set decided by the absolute value becomes smaller. If the absolute value of SO-PMI-IR is larger than one, we have at least 90% confidence that the test set is correctly classified. If the absolute value of SO-PMI-IR is larger than two, we have almost 94% confidence that the test set is correctly classified; at the same time, the size of test set is around 500, which is 70% of the full test set.

In Figure 1, the accuracy curve initially increases monotonously when the absolute value of SO-PMI-IR increases. When the absolute value of SO-PMI-IR is larger than six, the accuracy curve fluctuates because the size of test set becomes very small, and is very sensitive to wrong classification. However, the accuracy is still over 94%.

The trend in Figure 1 is also spotted in other settings (different search engines, different test set etc.) for our methods. Compared with the method in [7], the absolute value of SO-PMI-IR in our method is a good indicator for the accuracy of polarity classification in both the large-scale corpora (see Figure 1) and the small-scale corpus (see Table 5), thus we can control the quality of the polarity classification by the absolute value of SO-PMI-IR.

## 6 Conclusion and Future Work

In this paper, we propose a method to predict the polarity of Chinese adjectives. The merits of our method are summarized as follows:

1. Our method is simple, and the accuracy of predicting the polarity of Chinese adjectives is satisfying.
2. Different from [7], our method does not depend on specific search engines which support the NEAR operator.
3. Our method only considers the word before the target adjective as context, which reduces the noise incurred by using the NEAR operator in [7]. Therefore, in our

method, the magnitude of SO-PMI-IR is always a good indicator of the confidence in the classification of a Chinese adjective.

4. Our method only uses two polarity indicators (not and a bit), and avoids selecting polar paradigm words by intuition as in [1, 7, 24].

Our method is currently designed for Chinese adjectives. However, we also note that the method is applicable to many Chinese verbs and even polar nouns. We will address such problems in our future work.

# References

1. Turney, P.: Thumbs up or thumbs down? Semantic orientation applied to unsupervised classification of reviews. In: Proceedings of the Association for Computational Linguistics (ACL), pp. 417–424 (2002)
2. Hatzivassiloglou, V., Wiebe, J.: Effects of adjective orientation and gradability on sentence subjectivity. In: Proceedings of the International Conference on Computational Linguistics, COLING (2000)
3. Stone, P.J.: The General Inquirer: A Computer Approach to Content Analysis. The MIT Press (1966)
4. Esuli, A., Sebastiani, F.: Sentiwordnet: A publicly available lexical resource for opinion mining. In: Proceedings of LREC, pp. 417–422 (2006)
5. Strapparava, C., Valitutti, A.: Wordnet-affect: an affective extension of wordnet. In. In: Proceedings of the 4th International Conference on Language Resources and Evaluation, Lisbon (2004)
6. Wilson, T., Wiebe, J., Hoffmann, P.: Recognizing contextual polarity in phrase-level sentiment analysis. In: Proceedings of the Human Language Technology Conference and the Conference on Empirical Methods in Natural Language Processing (HLT/EMNLP), pp. 347–354 (2005)
7. Turney, P.D., Littman, M.L.: Measuring praise and criticism: Inference of semantic orientation from association. ACM Transactions on Information Systems (TOIS) 21(4), 315–346 (2003)
8. Hatzivassiloglou, V., McKeown, K.: Predicting the semantic orientation of adjectives. In: Proceedings of the Joint ACL/EACL Conference, pp. 174–181 (1997)
9. Zagibalov, T., Carroll, J.: Automatic seed word selection for unsupervised sentiment classification of chinese text. In: COLING 2008 (2008)
10. Mohammad, S., Dorr, B., Dunne, C.: Generating high-coverage semantic orientation lexicons from overtly marked words and a thesaurus. In: Proceedings of the Conference on Empirical Methods in Natural Language Processing (EMNLP 2009), Singapore (2009)
11. Wu, Y., Wen, M.: Disambiguating dynamic sentiment ambiguous adjectives. In: Proceedings of COLING 2010 (2010)
12. Boucher, J., Osgood, C.E.: The pollyanna hypothesis. Journal of Verbal Learning and Verbal Behaviour 8, 1–8 (1969)
13. Leech, G.: Principles of pragmatics. Longman, London (1983)
14. Israel, M.: The pragmatics of polarity. In: Horn, L., Ward, G. (eds.) The Handbook of Pragmatics, pp. 701–723. Blackwell, Oxford (2004)
15. Bolinger, D.: Degree Words. Mouton, Paris (1972)
16. Ernst, T.: Towards an integrated theory of adverb position in English. Indiana University, Bloomington (1984)

17. Quirk, R., Greenbaum, S., Leech, G., Svartvik, J.: A comprehensive grammar of the English language. Longman, London (1985)
18. Klein, H.: Adverbs of degree in Dutch and related languages. John Benjamins Publishing Company, Amsterdam (1998)
19. Sawada, O.: The meanings of positive polarity minimizers in japanese: a unified approach. In: The Proceedings of SALT 20 (2010)
20. Yariv-Laor, L., Sovran, T.: The structure of linguistic asymmetry: Evidence from hebrew and chinese. Poznań Studies in Contemporary Linguistics 34, 199–213 (1998)
21. Zhu, D.: Lecture Notes on Chinese Grammar. The Commercial Press (1982) (in Chinese)
22. Ku, L., Chen, H.: Mining opinions from the web: Beyond relevance retrieval. Journal of the American Society for Information Science and Technology 58(12), 1838–1850 (2007)
23. Yu, S., Duan, H., Swen, B., Chang, B.: Specification for corpus processing at peking university: Word segmentation, pos tagging and phonetic notation. Journal of Chinese Language and Computing 13 (2003) (in Chinese)
24. Yuen, R., Chan, T., Lai, T., Kwong, O., T'sou, B.: Morpheme-based derivation of bipolar semantic orientation of chinese words. In: Proceedings of COLING 2004 (2004)

# Research on Micro-blog Sentiment Analysis

Xinpo Lou, Yumei Chai, Hongying Zan, Ruicong Xu, Yingjie Han, and Kunli Zhang

School of Information Engineering, Zhengzhou University, Zhengzhou, China
pdslouxinpo@163.com,
{ieymchai,iehyzan,ieyjhan,ieklzhang}@zzu.edu.cn

**Abstract.** Micro-Blog is a kind of important media on the Internet, which conveys the users' point of view in simple and convenient ways. The research related to micro-blog has got extensive attention from the academic and industrial areas. This paper aims to study on the analysis of Chinese micro-blog emotion, proposing a template-based algorithm for the automatic discovery of micro-blog emotional neologisms. It uses a combination method of dictionaries and rules on Chinese micro-blog sentiment analysis.

**Keywords:** Sentiment Analysis, Polar Word, Parsing, Micro-Blog.

## 1 Introduction

Micro-blog, short for micro-blog, is a social medium platform allowing its users to share, disseminate and retrieve information. Through WEB, WAP and web-client components, users can form their private networking groups. Within the 140-character limit, consumers can update and share messages with others instantly. Meanwhile the large scale micro-blog text brings natural language processing new opportunities and challenges. Among the masses of twitter messages, the emotional ones are in the majority, which contain very precious opinion resources. Comments on products are very valuable for both sellers and buyers; and the ones on hot issues of society, are also very important for governments to learn what netizens think about the specific events.

Sentiment analysis, also known as opinion mining, aims at analyzing the subjective and appraisive text of subjectivity, mining opinions and comments, for the purpose of presenting them to readers in an intuitive way. The messages containing personal feelings in twitter are rather rich, and sentiment analysis on them has already aroused attention of numerous scholars both at home and abroad. There have already existed many micro-blog sentiment analysis systems intended for information written in English, such as TweetFeel, Twendz and Tweeter Sentiment.

In sentiment analysis, two kinds of technologies have been adopted .One method is based on machine learning, which mainly regards sentiment word and theme relational feature as classification feature, marks training sets and testing sets and conducts, sentiment analysis with it. Naïve Bayes[1,2], Support vector machine[2,3], and Maximum Entropy[4] are the common classification methods. The methods above require manually annotated corpus, which are laborious, and inconsistency. Pang et al[7]

P. Liu and Q. Su (Eds.): CLSW 2013, LNAI 8229, pp. 466–479, 2013.

firstly applied this method to chapter-level sentiment analysis tasks, and pointed out that it has a distinct advantage in sentiment analysis, compared to unsupervised learning. Xie et al[8] put forward Multiple strategies for Chinese micro-blog sentiment analysis method, based on hierarchical structure. Another method combines emotion dictionary with regulations. Turney et al[6] suggest that through the emotional words and the templates, the sentiment analysis can go on with comments on cellphones, banks, movies, and tour destinations. Go A et al[9] prefer to classify micro-blog on the Twitter by making use of distance-supervision. And Park A et al[10] propose a suggestion of collecting and marking the English micro-blog text automatically to analyze the emotion and mining comments. The method of combining emotional words with rules, with high accuracy, is simple and can be achieved easily, but it can not recognize new sentiment words online.

This paper mainly discusses Chinese micro-blog's sentiment analysis. Micro-blog corpus includes numerous Internet words traditional sentiment dictionaries lack. Thus a basic sentiment-word dictionary is constructed by scanning micro-blog artificially. Meanwhile, some templates are summed up according to the features of Chinese micro-blog. Through these templates, new internet words can be found out automatically and based on the features of Chinese micro-blog, some rules can be drawn. This paper realizes opinion sentence identification and sentiment analysis, combining the network sentiment dictionary with rules. It has a good performance in the NLP&&CC2012 Assessment organized by China Computer Federation (CCF).

## 2    The New Discovery of Micro-blog Sentiment Words

With the help of scanning micro-blog corpus manually, the basic Internet sentiment word dictionary is constructed. Network information's quite real-time, so a tremendous amount of information pours in every day, including some new-born network vocabulary. Based on the new words extracted manually, we summarize some templates, according to where these words appear frequently, and recognize the new words automatically by means of templates. The corpus referred to includes data of Sina micro-blog, as well as sample data from Tencent micro-blog offered by CFF, and all the themes are connected with social news. There are 13500 messages in the corpus.

### 2.1    Template's Extraction

Go on with the syntactic analysis of the LTP[5] developed by Harbin Institute of Technology Computing and Information Retrieval Centre.

　　Eg. 我们对这个员工的所作所为感到遗憾。(*We feel sorry for what the worker has done.*)

Result after syntactic analysis as Figure 1:

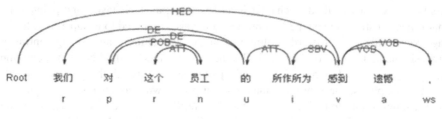

**Fig. 1.**

**Template Extraction algorithm description:**
**Input** : Micro-blog Text Sets D after word segmentation
**Output:** Template Set M
1    M = φ
2  **for** each text d ∈D **do**
3      **for**  i =1..L **do**   //L is the count of the words in d
4          **if**  $W_i$ is sentiment word then    //$W_i$ is the sentiment word
5              $M_i$← $W_i$ part-of-speech and the dependence relationship
6              $Count_i$←$Count_i$ + 1
7          **end if**
8      **end for**
9  **end for**
10   calculate frequency($M_i$)
11  **return**   frequency($M_i$) template(>threshold)

Seven templates are chosen manually, in order to extract network sentiment words. For example, in VOB, if the object is an adjective, then it is chosen as an alternative sentiment word. As the example, 感到[*gandao*](*feel*)_遗憾[*yihan*](*regret*) (VOB) have an interdependent relationship, we regard "遗憾"[*yihan*](*regret*) as the spare sentiment word.

According to the interdependent relationship, we select templates which have the highest probability of interdependent relationship. Frequency($M_i$) represents the template's assessment, and it is defined as follows:

$$frequency(M_i) = \frac{the\ number\ of\ emotional\ words\ from\ M_i}{the\ number\ of\ words\ from\ M_i}$$

The threshold value in this paper is 0.5, the extraction template is shown in Table 1.For each template $T_r$, there is a sentence set $C_r$.

## 2.2    Finding the Candidate Emotional Words

### 2.2.1    Selecting the Candidate Emotional Words
The sentiment terms can be found by following the steps: split the Chinese micro-blog into single sentences following punctuation clause(which are ended with'。', '!','? '), and that's to say each sentence is an independent row. Then do words

segmentation, tagging, and syntactic analysis. At last, place the processed results into an array. Travel the array from beginning to end, select emotional words according to templates, and put these words into the pending list.

The algorithm for the discovery of sentiment words:

**Input:** Template sets M, Micro-blog text sets D

**Output:** Candidate sentiment word lists CPList, template extraction sentence sets SentList

```
1   CPList  =  φ
2   for each text d ∈D do
3       for each sentence s in text d do
4           preprocess for s
5           for each template m ∈M do
6               if s satisfy m then
7                   CPList← CPList ∪ { Sentiment words extracted from s in accordance with the template 8
                        m }
9                   SentList← SentList ∪ {s}
10              end if
11          do for
12      end for
13  end for
14  return CPList
```

**Table 1.** Candidate sentiment word discovery template

| Template | Description | Examples |
|---|---|---|
| DA（Degree adverb + Adjective) | Extract the adjective following after adverb of degree. | 惠普和戴尔必须扼制新联想，只不过他们显得过于急躁。(*HP and Dell must hold back New Lenovo, but they just seem too impatient.*) 她非常漂亮。(*She is very pretty.*) |
| VOB（Verb-object) | If the objective is adjective, then set this adjective as the candidate sentiment words. In structure VOB，if the subject is a noun，containing structure DE，then extract the word before "的" as the candidate sentiment words. | 当然,新联想也不容盲目乐观。(*Of course, New Lenovo allows no blind optimism.*) 她是一个热心肠的人。(*She is very warm-hearted.*) |
| ADV (Adverbial) | ① In structure ADV，if there is "地/u", then extract the word before "地/u"as the candidate sentiment words. ② In structure ADV, if there is no "地/u", then select the adjective in the structure as the candidate sentiment words。 | 讽刺地说(*ironically speaking*) 尽管一系列冲突事件对戴尔在中国的品牌形象造成了极其恶劣的影响。(*Even though a series of conflicts caused very bad effects on Dell's brand image in China.*) |

**Table 1.** (*continued*)

| DEI（Dei） | In template DEI, extract the words after "得"as the candidate sentiment word. | 讲得好(*good point*)<br>比如最喜欢做比较和攻击性广告也做得最成功的宝洁。(*For example, P&G, whose favorite is making comparative and aggressive ads and who is also the most successful.*) |
|---|---|---|
| SBV（Subject-verb） | In structure SBV, if the predicate is an adjective, then set this adjective as the candidate sentiment word. | 成就显著(*remarkable achievements*)<br>戴尔的直销模式在一定意义上突破了销售网络不足的缺陷。(*In a way, the direct sales model of Dell makes up for the lack of selling network.*) |
| VV（Verb-verb） | Set the verb as the candidate sentiment word. | 戴尔表示会尊重竞争对手。(*Dell pledged to respect their rivals.*)<br>一方必将赢得最终的胜利。(*One party will certainly win the final victory.*) |
| COO（Coordinate） | In structure of coordination with comma, if there is one word in the seed lists, others are also sentiment words. | 苹果手机和平板电脑漂亮、大方、实用。(*Iphones and ipads are beautiful, powerful and practical.*)<br>只要跨过国际化的障碍，成功、胜利、机遇就属于中国企业。(*Success, victory and opportunity will belong to Chinese enterprises as long as they cross the barrier of internationalization.*) |

## 2.3  The Candidate Emotional Word Set Denoising

In recent years, many statistical computer learning models have been widely used in natural language processing, including: Hidden Markov Model, Support Vector Machine, Maximum Entropy, Maximum Entropy Markov Model and Conditional Random Fields. In this paper, we adopt the conditional random field statistical model to denoise the candidate emotional word set. This method can make the best of the context as well as add some external features.

The experiment chooses $C_r$ corresponding to $T_r$ as the training corpus. Testing corpus comes from sentences based upon templates. Statistical methods regard speech and part-of-speech as features. We can compare the results of window training experiment with different features in order to detect the size of the best feature window of every sentiment term.

## 2.4  The Polarity Identification of Emotional Words

The emotional words' polarity identification requires the conjunction list, the impact factor list and the basic Network sentiment word list. Words we mainly used are coordinating conjunctions and adversative conjunctions. The conjunctive list (see Table 2) is mainly used for the polarity identification of emotional words, and if it is a conjunction, the sentiment terms around them have the same polarity. If it is an adversative conjunction, the situation is opposite. In an article, some words don't have own sentiment, but affect greatly the polarity identification, and to a certain degree, they can strengthen, weaken and deny the part-of speech, such as some degree adverbs, negative adverbs and so on, which are called impact factors. The tags "a, b, c, d, n" in the impact factor list(see Table 3) respectively represent "strengthen positively

,weaken positively, weaken negatively and deny", and a represents the sentiment term. For example, "那些政策让罪恶和腐败无处遁形"(*These policies make sins and corruption have no place to hide.*),and this sentence contains coordinating conjunctions '和'[*he*](*and*) and the word '罪恶'[*zuie*](*sins*) has a negative direction. The word '腐败'[*fubai*](*corruption*) is detected through regulations in table 1, and then we can get the preliminary judgment that the word '腐败' is negative. Check whether there are impact factors around the word '腐败', if it does exist, we should change its polarity according to the tagging of the impact factor.

The judgment of emotional words' polarity can be done as the following steps: scan the whole candidate sentiment word list, and delete the terms that are not 'n, v, d, a, c, i, l' from the array. Thus, select terms which are more likely to be emotional words according to polarity identification. Then put the positive ones and negative ones respectively into their corresponding forms after finishing the emotional words polarity identification according to the conjunction structure and the basic emotional word list.

**Table 2.** Conjunction Examples

| Conjunction | Examples |
|---|---|
| 与[yu](and) | 联想作为跨国企业的成熟与理智、冲劲和开拓(*As an international enterprise, Lenovo's maturity, reasonability, pushfulness and pioneering spirit.*) |
| 和[he](and) | 保持了理智和谨慎(*keep reasonable and cautious.*) |
| 但是[danshi](but) | 这台笔记本外观很漂亮，但是散热很糟糕。(*This lap-top is very good-looking, but its thermal dissipation is terrible.*) |
| 然而[raner](however) | 她外面很美，然而，内心却很丑陋。(*She has good appearance and ugly heart.*) |

**Table 3.** IF(Impact Factor)Examples

| IF | Examples |
|---|---|
| A/n 透顶/z a/n | 糟糕透顶[*zaogaotouding*](*awful*) |
| A/n 轻微/a b/n | 危害轻微[*weihaiqingwei*](*slight harmness*) |
| A/n 不大/d c/n | 风险不大[*fengxianbuda*](*small risks*) |
| 很/d 难/a A/n d/n | 很难实现[*hennanshixian*](*hard to achieve*) |
| 不/d A/n n/n | 不稳定[*buwending*](*unstable*) |

**Algorithm for the judgment of sentiment words' polarity:**

**Input:** Candidate sentiment word lists CPList, Conjunction word lists CList, Weibo text sets D
**Output:** Positive sentiment word list PList, Negative sentiment word list NList
1   **for** each text d ∈D **do**
2     Extract sentences containing conjunctions to make the data sets M
3   **end for**
4   **repeat**
5   **for** each candidate sentiment word w ∈CPList **do**
6       **for** each data m ∈M **do**
7         judge the part-of-speech of w is not n、v、d、a、c、i、l，otherwise delete it
8         find sentences with w，judge the polarity based on the conjunction structure
9         **if** w fulfils the rules of negative factor，**then** negate the polarity
10      **end for**
11 **if** w is positive   **then** w is in PList
12 **else** w is in NList
13 **end for**
14 **until**   W =φ

# 3     Analysis of Micro-blog Sentiment Tendency

The process of sentiment analysis is divided into two parts: First, determine whether each sentence in Micro-blog is subjective or not; Second, estimate the sentiment tendency of perspective sentences: positive, negative, or neutral.

## 3.1   Opinion Sentences' Recognition

In the micro-blog, sentences with emotion words or symbols can express obvious feelings better, so we call them opinion sentences. As for opinion sentence recognition, without the corpus training, sentiment words play an important role in analyzing the emotion's polarity. It identify whether a sentence is an opinion sentence with the help of a sentiment word is an available method, and considering that the traditional sentiment dictionary doesn't perform well on micro-blog, we create a basic Network sentiment word dictionary in this paper, enriching the vocabulary automatically via the algorithm in Section 2. In traditional sentiment analysis, emotion words are classified into positive and negative words, and the corresponding dictionary has been created. For example,'善良'[*shanliang*](*kind-hearted*) is a positive word, while'丑陋'[*choulou*](*ugly*) is a negative word. Some regulations have been added to the dictionary, such as "改进了+名词"[*gaijinle + mingci*](*improved + noun*),"提高了+名词" [*tigaole + mingci*](*improved + noun*)，"优化了+名词" [*youhuale + mingci*]( *optimized + noun*) and so on. The nouns at the back are the evaluation objects. For example ,in the micro-blog,"新的苹果手机，改进了摄像头，改进了电池，改进了触控，还从3G变成了4G，比以前更nb。"(*The new iphones have improved on camera, battery and touch device and upgraded from 3G to 4G, which are even more freaking awesome than ever*.) It satisfies the rule "改进了+名词", and its evaluation objects are " 摄 像 头 [*shexiangtou*](*camera*) 、 电 池 [*dianchi*](*battery*) 、 触 控 [*chukong*](*touch*)".

There are emoticons together with characters in the micro-blog. Take Sina for an example, its micro-blog provides some default emotions, and emotions' manifestation in the text is "/" followed by the text, like"/哈哈"[*haha*](*Aha*). One message can contain several emoticons, and here positive and negative emotions' classification is also based on them.

### 3.2      The Orientation Recognition of Opinion Sentences

Analyzing the orientation of sentiment words in sentences is a common practice of judging whether the micro-blog's sentiment orientation is positive, negative or neutral. If there is a single sentiment word in the micro-blog, and it's the word that decides the orientation of the post; if there are several sentiment words, then calculate the total number of positive words and negative words respectively, and that the number is equal indicates that it's positive, and if not, it depends on whose total is larger.

After analysis, we find that the negative adverb often leads to the polarity reversal of sentiment fragments. Therefore, the system creates a negative factor table including 64 negative adverbs to solve the problem. Separate analysis for the two more complicated negative questions is given as follows:

1)   Double negation: We stipulate that it can be called double negation only if there are two negatives in the same fragment(with the border of , ？ ！) and there isn't any sentiment word between two negatives.

2)   The location of negative words: in this system, the sentiment word's location has been designated in the negative factor table. For example, in"不必/d An/n" An represents the location of sentiment words, and the sentiment word is after the negative word.

**Micro-blog tendency judgment algorithm based on sentiment word dictionary and rules:**

**Input** : Micro-blog sets T = {$t_1$,$t_2$,$t_3$,……,$t_n$},Sentiment word dictionary Dict, Emotion symbol sets Emotions ;

**Output:** Sentiment tendency set List from Micro-blog sets T

```
1   k=0
2   List = φ
2   for each Micro-blog set t∈T do
3       k=k+1
4       score = 0
4       for Micro-blog emotion icon e in tk do
5           if(e ∈ Emotions)    then score = score + δ (e);
6       end for
7       for i = 1…L do      //L is the word counts in tk
8           if(wi ∈ Dict)    then
```

**if**($w_i$ satisfies the rule of negative factor)    **then**    score = score - f($w_i$)
else score = score + f($w_i$)
9       **end for**
10      **if**(score > 0)    **then** List[k]='POS'
11      **else if**(score == 0) **then** List[k]='OTHER'
12      **else** List[k]='NEG'
13 **end for**
14 **return** List
**Attention** :

$$\delta(e) = \begin{cases} 1 & e \in Positive\,Emotion \\ -1 & e \in Negative\,Emotion \end{cases} \qquad f(w) = \begin{cases} 1 & w \in Positive\,Dict \\ -1 & w \in Negative\,Dict \end{cases}$$

# 4    Results and Analysis of the Experiment

## 4.1    Experimental Set-Ups

The data used in this paper come from test corpus of NLP&CC2012 micro-blog sentiment analysis held by China Computer Association, which includes about 3400 posts, and 20 themes have been given, covering living, education, politics and so on, and tagged with each corresponding result artificially (see Table 4).Use the unified format to save the micro-blog, and a post's storage and definition are as follows:

<weibo id="4">
<sentence id="1">小心我们中国人民解放军发两颗核导弹给你们尝尝。 (*Beware that we PLA send you two nuclear missiles.*)</sentence>
<sentence id="2">最后我也会说是"不小心"误发的。(*Eventually, we would also say that launch is a careless mistake.*)</sentence>
<sentence id="3"> 看你丫的嚣不嚣张！(*Dare you to be arrogant.*)</sentence>
<hashtag id="1">菲军舰恶意撞击 (*Philippine warships's malicious clash.*)</hashtag>
</weibo>

In the example, <weibo id="4">indicates the identifier number of Micro-blog is 4 , <sentence id="1">the sentence number is 1, <hashtag >indicates the topic of Micro-blog.

This experiment uses Precision,    Recall rate and F-measure to estimate the results. The following computational formula is :

$$Precision = \frac{\#system\_correct}{\#system\_proposed}$$

$$Recall = \frac{\#system\_correct}{\#gold}$$

$$F - measure = \frac{2 \times \Pr ecision \times \mathrm{Re}\, call}{\Pr ecision + \mathrm{Re}\, call}$$

#gold is the counts of manually annotated results, #system_correct is the matched results between system and manual work, #system_proposed is the count of the system results。

**Table 4.** Micro-blog manually annotated results

| Files | Positive sentences | Negative sentences | Neutral sentences | Total sentences | Neutral percentage |
|---|---|---|---|---|---|
| Life | 85 | 424 | 263 | 772 | 34.07% |
| Education | 239 | 335 | 292 | 866 | 33.72% |
| Politics | 53 | 492 | 326 | 871 | 37.43% |
| Events | 64 | 515 | 328 | 907 | 36.16% |
| Total | 441 | 1766 | 1209 | 3416 | 35.39% |

## 4.2    Select Emotional Words in Micro-blog

The basic emotional word list is selected by scanning the corpus manually, including 436 words that have positive connotations and 2254 words that have negative connotations. According to the basic emotional word list and syntax analysis, we got the template results (see Table 5).

**Table 5.** Template Extraction Results

| Template | DA | VOB | ADV | DEI | SBV | VV | COO |
|---|---|---|---|---|---|---|---|
| Precision | 0.5796 | 0.5110 | 0.5306 | 0.5357 | 0.5745 | 0.5127 | 0.8788 |

Extract the sentiment words with the templates, the results are in Table 6 after denoising using statistical methods:

Eventually, we got 2198 emotional words selected from the corpus to be analyzed on their polarity.

We need to preprocess the corpus, and choose all the sentences with conjunction. The following is an example of sentences which contain conjunction '和'[*he*](*and*) :

**Table 6.** Sentiment word Extraction results

| Template | Word counts | Precision |
|----------|-------------|-----------|
| DA | 384 | 0.6710 |
| VOB | 694 | 0.6572 |
| ADV | 601 | 0.6247 |
| DEI | 168 | 0.5258 |
| SBV | 394 | 0.6851 |
| VV | 123 | 0.5983 |
| COO | 57 | 0.8889 |

The data format for coordinating conjunction '和' with an context window data of 5:

0  1  2  3  4  5  6  7  8  9  10  11  12  13  14  15  16  17  18  19  20 21
政策 n 让 v 所有 v 的 u  罪恶 n 和  p 腐败 a  都 d  无处  d  遁  Vg 形 Ng

The process of judging the emotion polarity is just like a snowballing, obtained by multiple iterations, and that's to say expansion terms and basic emotional words merge, getting a larger scale emotional word list, and then restart the emotional words polarity identification, to get a new expansion vocabulary. Repeat it several times until it won't increase any more. For more details (see Table 7)

**Table 7.** Sentiment word variation

| Frequency | Positive words | Negative words |
|-----------|----------------|----------------|
| Initial | 436 | 2254 |
| Iteration once | 552 | 3458 |
| Iteration twice | 598 | 3965 |
| Iteration ten times | 612 | 4104 |
| Final(after 17 times) | 648 | 4240 |

The results for the judgment of undetermined sentiment words' polarity are shown in Table 8:

**Table 8.** Results for Polarity Judgement of Sentiment words

| Part of speech | Precision |
|---|---|
| Positive emotional words | 0.665 |
| Negative emotional words | 0.652 |
| Total | 0.653 |

From the chart above, we can see the accuracy of the results is not so high. After analysis, we find two main reasons. Firstly, the accuracy of the syntax analysis can affect the results; secondly, data selected by templates may contain some noise. The emotional word find algorithm based on templates, to a certain extent, enables emotional resources' automatic construction, and decreases time-consumption and energy-consumption if we select emotional words by scanning the corpus manually. The emotional words dictionary used here is a micro-blog emotional word list which is formed by removing noise words artificially in the results of the emotional words find algorithm that is based on templates.

### 4.3    Recognition of Opinion Sentences

The recognition of opinion sentences is described as follows: for each sentence in every micro-blog, judge whether the sentence is an opinion sentence or not. The definition doesn't include sentences written to express one's feelings or will. The natural language processing lab of Zhengzhou University (ZZUNLP) took part in NLP&&CC2012, with the result of ZZUNLP. The average result covers each term's average result of 53 results submitted by 34 enterprises who have been evaluated (see Table 9).

**Table 9.** Perspective sentence recognition results

| Evaluation results | Precision | Recall | F measure |
|---|---|---|---|
| ZZUNLP | 0.765 | 0.647 | 0.701 |
| Average results | 0.727 | 0.615 | 0.647 |

### 4.4    Sentiment Polarity Analysis

Sentiment orientation analysis can be described as follows: judge the sentiment orientation of each opinion sentence in micro-blog. Data set contains each sentence of every micro-blog and the orientation analysis should be based on recognition of opinion sentences. The sentiment orientation covers POS, NEG and OTHER (see Table10). Xie lixing et al, using the statistical model, put forward multi-strategy methods based on the hierarchy structure according to the hierarchy (see Table 11).

**Table 10.** Sentiment orientation analysis results

| Evaluation results | Precision | Recall | F measure |
|---|---|---|---|
| ZZUNLP | 0.902 | 0.584 | 0.709 |
| Average results | 0.745 | 0.455 | 0.552 |

**Table 11.** Comparison result

| Method | Precision |
|---|---|
| Dictionary and rule-based method | 0.690 |
| Hierarchy structure strategy-based method | 0.672 |

Through the comparison between Table 9 and Table 10, we can get the conclusion that both of them have a high accuracy, but a low recall rate. The main reasons are as follows: As for opinion sentences recognition and sentiment orientation analysis, we mainly use the dictionary, which has its limitations; besides, there are also some sentiment sentences without emotional words in micro-blog affecting the experimental results. From the comparison analysis of Table 11, the method based on combining the dictionary with regulations is better than that based on statistics, which indicates that the former method used in the paper does have some effect on Chinese micro-blog sentiment analysis.

## 5    Conclusion

In recent years, as a new kind of medium, micro-blog has become increasingly important. The sentiment analysis research about micro-blog has just begun, so further corresponding research needs to be done to verify the method of this paper. More attention should be paid include collecting sentiment corpus and tagging in the micro-blog text. This paper adopts the method of combining sentiment words dictionary with regulations, and makes some achievements, but there is still much to improve. For further study, we'll create the network dictionary, taking connections between micro-blog users and those between messages into consideration, to increase the accuracy rate.

**Acknowledgements.** This work is supported by a grant from the Natural Science Foundation of China (No.60970083, No.61272221), 863 projects of National High Technology Research and Development (No.2012AA011101), the Science and Technology Research Project of the Education Department of Henan Province (No.13B520381, NO.12B520055), and the Open Projects Program of National Laboratory of Pattern Recognition.

# References

1. Riloff, E., Wiebe, J., Wilson, T.: Learning Subjective Nouns Using Extraction Pattern Boostrapping. In: CoNLL 2003, pp. 25–32 (2003)
2. Lin, W.H., Wilson, T., Wiebe, J., Hauptmann, A.: Which Side are You on? Identifying Perspectives at the Document and Sentence Level. In: CoNLL 2006, pp. 109–116 (2006)
3. Riloff, E., Patwardhan, S., Wiebe, J.: Feature subsumption for opinion analysis. In: EMNLP 2006 (2006)
4. Pang, B., Lee, L.L.: A sentiment Education: Sentiment Analysis Using Subjectivity Summarization based on Minimum Cuts. In: ACL 2004, Spain, pp. 271–278 (2004)
5. Che, W., Li, Z., Liu, T.: LTP: A Chinese Language Technology Platform. In: Proceedings of the Coling 2010: Demonstrations, Beijing, China, pp. 13–16 (August 2010)
6. Turney, P.: Thumbs up or thumbs down semantic Orientate-on Applied to Unsupervised Classification of reviews. In: ACL 2002, pp. 417–424 (2002)
7. Pang, B., Lee, L., Vaithyanathan, S.: Thumbs up? Sentiment classification using machine learning techniques. In: ACL 2002, pp. 79–86 (2002)
8. Xie, L., Zhou, M., Sun, M.: Hierarchical structure based Hybrid Approach to Sentiment Analysis of Chinese Micro Blog and Its Feature Extraction. Journal of Chinese Information Processing 26(1), 73–82 (2012)
9. Go, A., Bhayani, R., Lei, H.: Twitter sentiment Classification Using Distant Supervision (2009)
10. Pak, A., Paroubek, P.: Twitter as a Corpus for Sentiment Analysis and Opinion Mining. In: Proc. of Language Resources and Evaluation Conference. [s. n.], Lisbon (2010)
11. Lafferty, J., Mccallum, A., Pereira, F.: Conditional Random Fields: Probabilistic Models for Segmenting and Labeling Sequence Data. In: Proceedings of the 18th ICML 2001, pp. 282–289 (2001)

# Named Entity Recognition
# Based on Bilingual Co-training

Yegang Li[1,2,3], Heyan Huang[1,2,*], Xingjian Zhao[1,2], and Shumin Shi[1,2]

[1] School of Computer Science and Technology, Beijing Institute of Technology, Beijing, China
{lyg8256,hhy63,wisedo,bjssm}@bit.edu.cn
[2] Beijing Engineering Applications Research Center of High Volume Language Information
Processing and Cloud Computing (Beijing Institute of Technology), Beijing, China
[3] Department of Computer Science and Technology,
Shandong University of Technology, Zibo, Shandong, China
lyg8256@bit.edu.cn

**Abstract.** Named entity recognition (NER) is a very important task in natural language processing (NLP). In this paper we present a semi-supervised approach to extract bilingual named entity, starting from a bilingual corpus where the named entities are extracted independently for each language. Then a bilingual co-training algorithm is used to improve the named entity annotation quality, and iterative process is applied to extract named entity pairs with higher bilingual conformity ratio. This leads to a significant improvement of the monolingual named entity annotation quality for both languages. Experimental result shows that the annotation quality of Chinese NE is improved from 87.17 to 88.28, and improved 80.37 to 81.76 of English NE in F-measure.

**Keywords:** named entity recognition, bilingual co-training, natural language processing.

## 1 Introduction

NER is a frequently needed technology in natural language processing applications. State-of-the-art supervised statistical models for NER typically require large amount of labeled data and linguistic expertise to be sufficiently accurate, which makes it difficult to build high-quality models for so many languages.

Recently, there have been some works which offered hope for creating NER analyzers in many languages, using parallel English-foreign language data, a high-quality NER tagger for English, and projected annotations for the foreign language[1]. Parallel data has also been used to improve existing monolingual taggers or other analyzers in both languages[2].

Both Chinese and English have their own special features that can be employed for entity extraction. Chinese does not have white space for tokenization or capitalization, features which, for English, can help identify name boundaries and distinguish names

---

* Corresponding author.

P. Liu and Q. Su (Eds.): CLSW 2013, LNAI 8229, pp. 480–489, 2013.

from nominal. Using bilingual co-training allows us to capture such indicative information to improve Chinese name tagging. For example,

1. Results from Chinese name tagger : <PER>金庸新[*jinyongxin*]( *Jin Yong-xin*)</PER >小说[*xiaoshuo*](*novel*).
2. Results from English name tagger: the new novels of <PER>Jin Yong</PER>
3. Name tagging after using bilingual co-training: < PER >金庸[*jinyong*]( *Jin Yong*)</PER >新小说[*xinxiaoshuo*]( *new novels*)

"金庸新" and "金庸" in Chinese can be a PER name, while its English translation "Jin Yong" indicates that "金庸" is more likely to be a PER name than "金庸新".

On the other hand, Chinese has some useful language-specific properties for entity extraction. For example, standard Chinese family names are generally single characters drawn from a fixed set of 437 family names, and almost all first names include one or two characters. The suffix words (if there are any) of ORG and GPE names belong to relatively distinguishable fixed lists. For example,

1. Results from English name tagger : The captain of a ferry boat who works on ⟨PER⟩　Lake Constance　⟨/PER⟩ ...
2. Results from Chinese name tagger: 在 ⟨ LOC ⟩ 康斯坦茨湖 [kangsitancihu]( Lake Constance) ⟨/LOC⟩ 工作的一艘渡船的船长...
3. Name tagging after using bilingual co-training: The captain of a ferry boat who works on ⟨LOC⟩　Lake Constance　⟨/LOC⟩ …

"Lake" in English can be the suffix word of either a PER or LOC name, while its Chinese translation "康斯坦茨湖" indicates that "Lake Constance" is more likely to be a LOC name.

To solve the problems, a semi-supervised learning framework with the help of parallel corpus is proposed in this paper. We propose a semi-supervised approach using a bilingual co-training model to carry out English and Chinese NER. To ease error propagations from the projected annotations, we correct the projected annotations with a maximum entropy model. The maximum entropy model addresses the Named Entity alignment of a bilingual corpus, which builds an alignment between each source NE and its translation NE in the target language. A Named Entity alignment, however, is not easy to obtain. It requires both Named Entity Recognition and alignment to be handled correctly. NEs may not be well recognized, or only parts of them may be recognized during NER. When aligning bilingual NEs in different languages, we need to handle many-to-many alignments. Although this makes the task more difficult, it greatly reduces the chance of errors introduced by previous steps and therefore produces much better performance on our task.

The rest of this paper is organized as follows: In section 2, we discuss related work on NE recognition and alignment. In section 3, we discuss bilingual co-training algorithm. Section 4 gives the overall framework of NE alignment with our maximum entropy model. Feature functions are also explained in this section. We show experimental results and compare them with baseline systems in Section 5. Section 6 concludes the paper and discusses future work.

## 2    Related Work

NER, including proper names, temporal and numerical expressions, has been widely addressed by symbolic, statistical as well as hybrid approaches. Its major part in information extraction (IE) and other NLP applications has been stated and encouraged by several editions of evaluation campaigns such as MUC[3], the CoNLL-2003 NER shared task[4] or ACE[5], where NER systems show near-human performances for the English language. Our model builds upon prior work on co-training and cross-lingual projection for named entities. Other interesting work on aligning named entities in two languages is reported in [1-2],[6-9].

Our bilingual co-training approach is related to bilingual labeling models presented in previous work. Still, there are some disadvantages for previous work based on parallel corpora. First, current NE alignment methods are not accurate enough, and many noises could be introduced during the word alignment stage. Second, *manual annotation* is usually obtained from a few limited domains, leading to a bad affect on statistical supervised learning methods. Following of previous work we focus on the task of bilingual NE recognition. In contrast, our bilingual co-training model does not require large amount of labeled data, since we conduct our experiments with the co-training algorithm.

## 3    Bilingual Co-training

Starting with a set of labeled data, co-training algorithms attempt to increase the amount of annotated data using large amounts of unlabeled data. The process may continue for several iterations. In natural language processing, co-training was generally found to bring improvement over the cases when no additional unlabeled data are used. One important aspect of co-training consists in the relation between the views used in learning. Blum and Mitchell[10] states conditional independence of the views as a required criterion for co-training. Abney[11] shows that the independence assumption can be relaxed, and co-training is still effective under a weaker independence assumption.

In this work, we apply co-training by regarding the parallel Chinese-English sentences as weaker independent views for NE identity. Instances are selected by bilingual conformity ratio on a set of unlabeled instances, and the instances most confidently labeled are added to the labeled data. This procedure preserves the distribution of labels in the labeled data as instances are labeled and added. The bilingual conformity ratio can be defined as follows:

$$conformity\_ratio = \frac{1}{n}\sum_{U}\frac{1}{K}\sum_{k=1}^{K} conformity(ws_i, wt_j)_k$$

$$conformity(ws_i, wt_j)_k = \begin{cases} 1 & T(ws_i) = T(wt_j) \\ 0 & T(ws_i) \neq T(wt_j) \end{cases}. \tag{1}$$

Where $(ws_i, wt_j)_k$ represents k($1 \le k \le K$) pair word in the parallel sentence, and $T(ws_i), T(wt_j)$ represent the annotations of NE. The bilingual co-training algorithm is discussed as follows.

---

1. Given:

   (a) A set Ls of source labeled examples

   (b) A set Lt of target labeled examples

   (c) A set Us of source unlabeled examples

   (d) A set Ut of target unlabeled examples

---

4. Classifiers

   (e) Use Ls to train the classifiers Classifier(s)

   (f) Use Lt to train the classifiers Classifier(t)

5. Loop for m iterations

   (g) Create a pairs pool $\overline{U}s$ and $\overline{U}t$, with examples from Us and Ut, create $\overline{U}s$ and $\overline{U}t$ by labeled the examples in $\overline{U}s$ and $\overline{U}t$ with Classifier(s) and Classifier(t),calculate $conformity\_ratio(\overline{U}s, \overline{U}t)$ ,

   $max \leftarrow conformity\_ratio(\overline{U}s, \overline{U}t)$, create $\tilde{L}t^* \leftarrow null$ , $\tilde{L}s^* \leftarrow null$

   (h) Loop for 10 iterations

   (i) Create $(\hat{L}s, \hat{L}t)$ with k pairs sentences extracted from $(\overline{U}s, \overline{U}t)$ , projected annotations from $\hat{L}s$ to $\hat{L}t$ ,create $\tilde{L}t$ by corrected the projected annotations with $\hat{L}t$

   (ii) $classifier(t) \leftarrow classfier(Lt \cup \tilde{L}t)$ , train Classifier(t), label $\overline{U}t$ with Classifier(t), update $conformity\_ratio(\overline{U}s, \overline{U}t)$ , if $conformity\_ratio(\overline{U}s, \overline{U}t) > max,$ then $max \leftarrow conformity\_ratio(\overline{U}s, \overline{U}t)$ , $\tilde{L}t^* \leftarrow \tilde{L}t$

   (iii) $Lt \leftarrow Lt \cup \tilde{L}t^*$ , train classifier(t) with Lt: $classifier(t) \leftarrow classfier(Lt)$

---

(i)  Loop for 10 iterations

    (i)  Create $(\hat{L}s, \hat{L}t)$ with k pairs of sentences extracted from $(\overline{U}s, \overline{U}t)$, projected annotations from $\hat{L}t$ to $\hat{L}s$, create $\tilde{L}s$ by corrected the projected annotations with $\tilde{L}s$.

    (ii)  $classifier(s) \leftarrow classfier(Ls \cup \tilde{L}s)$ , train Classifier(s), labeled $\overline{U}s$ with Classifier(s), update $conformity\_ratio(\overline{U}s, \overline{U}t)$ , if $conformity\_ratio(\overline{U}s, \overline{U}t) > \max$,             then $\max \leftarrow conformity\_ratio(\overline{U}s, \overline{U}t), \tilde{L}s^* \leftarrow \tilde{L}s$.

    (iii)  $Ls \leftarrow Ls \cup \tilde{L}s^*$ , $classifier(s) \leftarrow classfier(Ls)$.

---

# 4    Corrective NE Projection Annotation

To ease error propagations from the projected annotations, we corrected the projected annotations with a Corrective model.

## 4.1    Projection NE Candidate

For each word in the source language NE, we find all the possible projection word in target language through the word alignment [12]. Next, we have all the projection words as the "seed" data. With an open-ended window for each seed, all the possible sequences located within the window are considered as possible candidates for NE projection. Their lengths range from 1 to the empirically determined length of the window. During the best candidate projection NE selection, the NE alignment model discussed as follows is applied to search the best projection NE.

## 4.2    NE Alignment Model

There are several valuable features that can be used for NE alignment. Considering the advantages of the maximum entropy model [13] to integrate different kinds of features, we use this framework to handle our problem. Suppose the English NE $Ne_c^d$, and the Chinese NE $Nc_a^b$. Suppose also that we have M feature functions $f_m(a_k, Nc_a^b, N\tilde{e}_c^d), m = 1, 2, \cdots, M$ . For each feature function, we have a model parameter $\lambda_m, m = 1, 2, \cdots, M$ . The alignment probability can be defined as follows [14]:

$$P(a_k \mid Nc_a^b, N\tilde{e}_c^d) = \frac{\exp\left(\sum_{m=1}^{M} \lambda_m f_m\left(a_k, Nc_a^b, N\tilde{e}_c^d\right)\right)}{\sum_A \exp\left(\sum_{m=1}^{M} \lambda_m f_m\left(a_k, Nc_a^b, N\tilde{e}_c^d\right)\right)} \qquad (2)$$

In our approach, we adopt 3 features: translation feature, the source NE and target NE's co-occurrence feature, and length of NE pair feature. Next, we discuss these three features in detail.

**Translation Feature**

The translation feature here is used to represent how close an NE pair is based on translation probabilities. Given a parallel corpus aligned at the sentence level, we can achieve the translation probability between English chunk and Chinese chunk with IBM Model [15].

$$P(F \mid E) = \frac{1}{(n+1)^m} \prod_{j=1}^{m} \sum_{i=1}^{n} t(f_j \mid e_i) \qquad (3)$$

Suppose the candidate English NE, $E = e_1, e_2, \cdots, e_m$ consists of m English words and the candidate Chinese NE, $C = c_1, c_2, \cdots, c_n$ is composed of n Chinese characters. The translation probability of the NE pair is computed as follows,

$$P(Nc \mid Ne) = \frac{1}{(n+1)^m} \prod_{j=1}^{m} \sum_{i=1}^{n} t(c_j \mid e_i) \qquad 1 \le j \le n, 1 \le i \le m \qquad (4)$$

We defined translation feature as follows,

$$f_m\left(a_k, Nc_a^b, N\tilde{e}_c^d\right) = \log(P(Nc_a^b \mid N\tilde{e}_c^d)) + \log(P(N\tilde{e}_c^d \mid Nc_a^b)) \qquad (5)$$

The scores between the candidate Chinese NEs and the English NEs are calculated via this formula as the value of translation feature.

**Co-occurrence Feature**

If a source NE and a target NE co-occur very often, there exists a big possibility that they align to each other. This probability is a good indication for determining bilingual NE alignment. The co-occurrence feature can be defined as follows,

$$f_m\left(a_k, Nc_a^b, N\tilde{e}_c^d\right) = \frac{count(Nc_a^b, N\tilde{e}_c^d)}{count(Nc_a^b, *)} + \frac{count(Nc_a^b, N\tilde{e}_c^d)}{count(*, N\tilde{e}_c^d)} \qquad (6)$$

Where $count(Nc_a^b, N\tilde{e}_c^d)$ is the number of times $Nc_a^b$ and $N\tilde{e}_c^d$ appear together. $(Nc_a^b, *)$ is the number of times that $Nc_a^b$ appears.$(*, N\tilde{e}_c^d)$ is the number of times that $N\tilde{e}_c^d$ appears.

**Length Feature**

When translating NE across languages, we notice that the difference of their length is also a good indication for determining their relation. The length feature [16] can be defined as follows,

$$f_m\left(a_k, Nc_a^b, N\tilde{e}_c^d\right) \approx f_m\left(a_k, \left|Nc_a^b\right|, \left|N\tilde{e}_c^d\right|\right) = \frac{\left|Nc_a^b\right| - \delta\left|N\tilde{e}_c^d\right|}{\sqrt{\left(\left|Nc_a^b\right| + 1\right)^{\sigma^2}}}$$

$$\delta = \frac{1}{n}\sum_{i=1}^{n}\left(\frac{count(Ne_i)}{count(Nc_i)}\right), \sigma^2 = \frac{1}{n}\sum_{j=1}^{n}\left(\frac{count(Ne_j)}{count(Nc_j)} - \frac{1}{n}\sum_{i=1}^{n}\left(\frac{count(Ne_i)}{count(Nc_i)}\right)^2\right) \quad (7)$$

Where $count(Ne_i)$ is the character number of $Ne_i$ and $count(Nc_j)$ is the character number of $Nc_j$.

## 5     Experimental Results

### 5.1     Experimental Setup

We perform experiments to investigate the performance of the above framework. We take the NiuTrans[17] bilingual training data consists of 100K Chinese-English sentence pairs as our unlabeled corpus. The training and test data sets consist of the Penn Xinhua News corpus sections 1–206 and section 206-305, respectively. They are annotated with 3 types of NE such as person name (PER), location name (LOC) and organization name (ORG).

To achieve the most probable aligned Chinese NE, we use the published package YASMET[1] to conduct parameter training and re-ranking of all the NE candidates. YASMET requires supervised learning for the training of the maximum entropy model. We acquire a large annotated training set from NiuTrans corpus.

This paper maintains a pool of 1000 unlabeled instances by random selection. The classifier proposes labels for the instances in this pool. We choose 100 instances for each classifier with high confidence while preserving the class distribution observed in the initial labeled data, and add them to the labeled data.

---

[1] http://www.isi.edu/~och/YASMET.html

The automatically generated annotation was then evaluated by calculating precision and recall with respect to this gold standard. Precision is defined as

$$P = \frac{\#of \quad correct \quad annotated \quad NEs}{\#of \quad all \quad annotated \quad NEs}$$

Recall is defined as :  $R = \dfrac{\#of \quad correct \quad annotated \quad NEs}{\#of \quad all \quad correct \quad NEs}$

The F-score, a combined measure of NE annotation's precision and recall, is defined as:  $F = \dfrac{2PR}{P+R}$

### 5.2    Baseline System

We formulate the named entity recognition task as the classification of each word with context to one of the classes that represent region information and named entity's semantic class. MALLET[2] includes tools for sequence tagging for applications such as named-entity extraction from text. Algorithms include Hidden Markov Models, Maximum Entropy Markov Models, and Conditional Random Fields (CRF).

We employ a CRF method in Chinese language as Chinese NER baseline system, and employ MALLET in English language as English NER baseline system. The Chinese and English baseline NE tagging performance on different entity types is shown in Table 1 as follows.

**Table 1.** Baseline F-Measure (%) of NE Tagging

| NE Type | Chinese NE(F-value) | English NE(F-value) |
| --- | --- | --- |
| PER | 89.59 | 81.22 |
| LOC | 88.48 | 80.43 |
| ORG | 84.54 | 79.69 |
| ALL | 87.17 | 80.37 |

### 5.3    Bilingual Co-training Results

Based on the testing strategies discussed in Section 3, we perform all the experiments and get the performance for bilingual co-training. NE tagging performance on different entity types are shown in Table 2 as follows.

---

[2] http://mallet.cs.umass.edu/index.php

**Table 2.** Bilingual co-training F-Measure (%) of NE Tagging

| NE Type | Chinese NE(F-value) | English NE(F-value) |
|---------|---------------------|---------------------|
| PER | 90.86 | 82.31 |
| LOC | 89.53 | 82.01 |
| ORG | 85.71 | 80.42 |
| ALL | 88.28 | 81.76 |

We restrict the bilingual co-training model to use only features similar to the ones used by the baseline model. We obtain performance much better than that of the baseline model. In this set of experiments, we compare our bilingual co-training method with a named entity recognition system based on CRF method. As shown in table 2, NE improves F-measure over the supervised baseline. For Chinese, it achieves 88.28% in F-measure of all type of NE, which outperforms the supervised baseline by 1.11%. For English, it achieves 81.76% in F-measure of all type of NE, which outperforms the supervised baseline by 1.39%.

The projected data is not completely clean and brings some errors into the final results. But it avoids the acquisition of large annotated training set and the performance is still much better than traditional recognition models.

## 6    Conclusions

Traditional word alignment approaches cannot come up with satisfactory results for NE alignment. Consider that bilingual text can provide valuable additional information for named entity tagging, we propose a novel approach using a bilingual co-training model for NE recognition. The following part proved the assumption that more unlabeled data is used, the better performance is got. This is because additional cross-domain data makes the classification of NE tags more accurate in cross-domain.

While our approach has only been tested on Chinese and English so far, we can expect that it is applicable to other language pairs. The approach is independent of the baseline tagging/extraction system, and so can be used to improve systems with varied learning schemes.

Due to the inconsistency of NE translation, some projected NE is not correct. We may need some manually-generated rules to fix this. This problem will be investigated in the future.

**Acknowledgements.** This work was supported by project of the National Natural Science Foundation of China (No. 61132009, 61201352, 61202244), and the National Basic Research Program of China (973 Program) (2013CB329300, 2013CB329606), and MSRA UR Project (95116953).

# References

1. Das, D., Petrov, S.: Unsupervised part-of-speech tagging with bilingual graph-based projections. In: Proceedings of the 49th Annual Meeting of the Association for Computational Linguistics: Human Language Technologies, Portland, Oregon, USA, pp. 600–609 (June 2011)
2. Burkett, D., Petrov, S., Blitzer, J., Klein, D.: Learning better monolingual models with unannotated bilingual text. In: Proceedings of the Fourteenth Conference on Computational Natural Language Learning, Uppsala, Sweden, pp. 46–54 (July 2010)
3. Marsh, E., Perzanowski, D.: Muc-7 evaluation of ie technology. In: Overview of Proceedings of the Seventh Message Understanding Conference (MUC-7), vol. 20 (1998)
4. Tjong Kim Sang, E.F., De Meulder, F.: Introduction to the conll-2003 shared task: Language independent named entity recognition. In: Proceedings of CoNLL, Edmonton, Canada, pp. 142–147 (2003)
5. Doddington, G., Mitchell, A., Przybocki, M., Ramshaw, L., Strassel, S., Weischedel, R.: The automatic content extraction program-tasks, data, and evaluation. In: Proceedings of LREC, vol. 4, pp. 837–840 (2004)
6. Huang, F., Vogel, S., Waibel, A.: Automatic Extraction of Named Entity Translingual Equivalence Based on Multi-Feature Cost Minimization. In: ACL 2003 Workshop on Multilingual and Mixed-language Named Entity Recognition, Sapporo, Japan, pp. 9–16 (2003)
7. Moore, R.C.: Learning Translations of Named-Entity Phrases from Parallel Corpora. In: EACL 2003, Budapest, Hungary, pp. 259–266 (2003)
8. Donghui, F., Yajuan, L., Ming, Z.: A new approach for English-Chinese named entity alignment. In: Proceedings of the Conference on Empirical Methods in Natural Language Processing EMNLP, pp. 372–379 (2004)
9. Sungchul, K., Kristina, T., Hwanjo, Y.: Multilingual Named Entity Recognition using Parallel Data and Metadata from Wikipedia. In: Proceedings of the 50th Annual Meeting of the Association for Computational Linguistics, Jeju, Republic of Korea, July 8-14, pp. 694–702 (2012)
10. Blum, A., Mitchell, T.: Combining labeled and unlabeled data with co-training. In: Proceedings of the 11th Annual Conference on Computational Learning Theory (COLT 1998), Wisconsin, MI, pp. 92–100 (1998)
11. Abney, S.P.: Bootstrapping. In: Proceedings of the 40th Annual Meeting of the Association for Computational Linguistics, Philadelphia, PA, pp. 360–367 (2002)
12. Och, F.J., Ney, H.: A Systematic Comparison of Various Statistical Alignment Models. Computational Linguistics 29(1), 19–51 (2003)
13. Berger Adam, L., Della Pietra Stephen, A., Della Pietra Vincent, J.: A maximum entropy approach to natural language processing. Computational Linguistics 22(1), 39–72 (1996)
14. Och, F.J., Ney, H.: Discriminative training and maximum entropy models for statistical machine translation. In: Proceedings of the 40th Annual Meeting on Association for Computational Linguistics, pp. 295–302. Association for Computational Linguistics (July 2002)
15. Brown, P.F., Della Pietra Stephen, A., Della Pietra Vincent, J., et al.: The mathematics of statistical machine translation: Parameter estimation. Computational Linguistics 19(2), 263–311 (1993)
16. Church, K.W.: Char align: A program for aligning bilingual texts at the character level. In: The 31st Annual Meeting of the Association for Computational Linguistics, Columbus, Ohio, pp. 1–8 (1993)
17. Tong, X., Jingbo, Z., Hao, Z., et al.: NiuTrans: An Open Source Toolkit for Phrase-based and Syntax-based Machine Translation. In: Proceedings of the 50th Annual Meeting of the Association for Computational Linguistics System Demonstrations, Jeju, Korea, pp. 19–24 (July 2012)

# Phrase Filtering for Content Words
# in Hierarchical Phrase-Based Model

Xing Wang[1], Jun Xie[2], Linfeng Song[2], Yajuan Lv [2], and Jianmin Yao[1]

[1] School of Computer Science &Technology, Soochow University, Suzhou, China
{20114227047,jyao}@suda.edu.cn
[2] Key Laboratory of Intelligent Information Processing, Institute of Computing Technology,
Chinese Academy of Sciences, Beijing, China
{xiejun,songlinfeng,lvyajuan}@ict.ac.cn

**Abstract.** When hierarchical phrase-based statistical machine translation systems are used for language translation, sometimes the translations' content words were lost: source-side content words  is empty when translated into target texts during decoding. Although the translations' BLEU score is very high, it is difficult to understand the translations because of the loss of the content words. In this paper, we propose a basic and efficient method for phrase filtering, with which the phrase' content words translation are checked to decide whether to use the phrase in decoding or not. The experimental results show that the proposed method alleviates the problem of the loss content words' and improves the BLEU scores.

**Keywords:** hierarchical phrase-based model, content words, phrase filtering.

## 1    Introduction

The Hierarchical phrase-based model (Chiang,2005)was proposed by David Chiang in 2005. The model is a synchronous context-free grammar translation model that learns context-free grammars from a bilingual word-aligned corpus. Learned grammar phrases are used during decoding. Compared to the phrase-based model(Koehn et al.,2003), the hierarchical phrase-based model using hierarchical phrases can capture the reordering between the phrases, the model has superior performance. Compared to syntax-based translation models(Liu et al.,2006; Xie et al.,2011), hierarchical phrase-based model learns context-free grammars from a bitext without any syntactic information. Therefore hierarchical phrase-based model becomes one of the most active models in study .

Hierarchical phrase-based model extracts huge numbers of synchronous context-free grammar phrases from a bilingual word-aligned corpus. However the model is prone to learn noisy phrases due to noise in the training corpus or wrong word alignment. Specifically, since some content words have no counterpart in translation, the model extracts noisy phrases omitting content words. Using phrases that omitting contents words leads to syntax and semantic errors in translation. Here are some samples that using some noisy phrases in our Baseline experiments:

P. Liu and Q. Su (Eds.): CLSW 2013, LNAI 8229, pp. 490–498, 2013.
© Springer-Verlag Berlin Heidelberg 2013

Example1: 房间的灯不亮  —>  the light does not work    noisy phrase: *房间 的 X —> the X*

Example2: 您是在这儿用餐还是带走?  —>  here or to go ?  noisy phrase: *您 是 在 X —>X*

The translation is fluent in example 1, but it uses a noisy phrase (房间 的 X -> the X). The noisy phrase leads to the lack of the content word "房间", and the translation remains ambiguous because of the use of noisy phrase. The translation in example 2 using the noisy phrases leads to the semantic error. The reason why the above phenomenon occurs is the use of noisy phrases during decoding. The alignment mistakes cause the model inevitably to extract the noisy phrases. Therefore, it is necessary to detect the phrases' content words translation. Filtering noisy phrases can reduce the model's phrases table and accelerate the decoding speed to improve the quality of the translation.

The remainder of the paper is organized as follows: Section 2 describes the proposed method of phrases filtering; Section 3 introduces the experimental setup; The experimental results and the discussions are presented in Section 4; Section 5 concludes the paper and suggests directions for future work.

## 2    Phrase Filtering

We can find using the noisy phrases causes the deterioration in the quality of the translation output through above examples. Alignment mistakes cause source side's content words have no counterpart in the target side, resulting in extracting noisy phrases. Using the noisy phrases during decoding, the translation's content words lost. However, BLEU metric, the most popular gain function for automated MT evaluation, treats all characters equally, so BLEU score can't describe the content words omitting in the translation.

Therefore it is necessary to filter noisy phrases. For each phrase, we recognize phrase's content words in source side, then check source side's content words have its counterpart or not. Filtering the phrases that source side's content words have no counterpart to avoid omitting content words during decoding.

### 2.1    Content Words Recognition

Before check source side's content words have counterpart or not, we need to recognize the content words in phrase's source side.

The ideal approach is tagging sentences in training corpus before word alignment step. then do word alignment with part-of-speech information. But this processing method is flawed: for example, the word "计划" in different contexts will be marked as the verb "计划/ v" or the noun "计划/ n". Word alignment toolkit GIZA++ treat "计划/ v " and "计划/ n " as different words. Tagging the sentences means that we expand word alignment space, we will face a serious problem of data sparse. In this paper, Using above method with 260k sentence pairs of training corpus degrade the quality of translation.

Therefore, the reorganization of content words should consider both the data sparse problem and part-of-speech tagging accuracy. This paper proposes a compromise method shown in Figure 1:

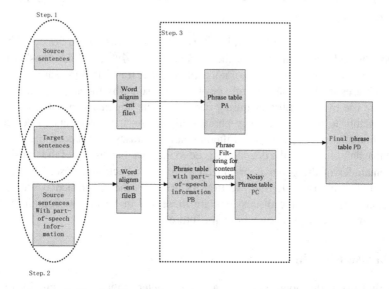

**Fig. 1.** The flowchart of content word recognition for phrase filtering

Step .1: Align words between source side and target side. Then we can obtain bilingual alignment information and bilingual word alignment file A.

Step 2: Tag the source sentence. Using source side with part-of-speech information, target side and the bilingual alignment information in Step.1 to generate bilingual word alignment file B.

Step.3: Bilingual word alignment file A can be used to generate a common phrase table PA. Bilingual word alignment file B can be used to generate a phrase table PB with source side's part-of-speech information. Filtering phrase table PB through checking source side's content words have counterpart or no, then the noisy phrase table PC can be obtained. The phrases in the noisy phrase table PC will be removed from the common phrase table PA. The remainder of the common phrase table PA is the final phrase table PD used during decoding.

## 2.2    Phrase Filtering

Alignment mistakes may appear in word align step. The alignment mistakes cause the model extract the noisy phrases, some noisy phrases' content words in source side have no counterpart in its target side, while a correct phrase's content words in source side should have the counterpart in the target side.

Definition 1: For a phrase X -> $<\gamma, \alpha>$, if any content word in source side $\gamma$ have no counterpart in the target side, we called it pseudo source side content words empty phrase.

Definition 2: If a phrase X -> <γ, α>, if any content word in target side α have no counterpart in the source side, we called it pseudo target side content words empty phrase.

Pseudo source side content words empty phrase and pseudo-target side content words empty phrase are called by a joint name pseudo content words empty phrase.

Why we call it pseudo content words empty phrase ? we can think about the situation: the content words' counterpart is appear at the other side in fact, but it has no alignment to its counterpart due to alignment mistakes. We will use a synonym expansion method to alleviate this problem in another section below.

Filtering the phrase by checking its' content words in source side have counterpart or not. pseudo content words empty phrases are filtered directly, the model won't use these phrases during decoding. For example, the phrase（那样$_1$ 的 东西 。$_2$ $\longrightarrow$ like$_1$ that$_1$ .$_2$）(the subscripts indicate word alignments), its source side words "的" "and "东西"have no counterpart in its target side. So this phrase is a pseudo content words empty phrase, it will be filtered out directly in the phrase filtering strep.

## 2.3 Hierarchical Phrase Filtering

Simply checking the phrase is pseudo content words empty phrase or not will filter a large number of qualified phrases, For example, the phrase（做$_1$ 了$_1$ 很 傻$_2$ 的 事 。$_3$ $\longrightarrow$ acted$_1$ like a$_4$ fool$_4$ .$_3$）(source words "做""了"align to the target word"acted"). The phrase will be filtered because the source content word "事" has no counterpart in its target side. There are a lot of idiomatic expression that source side's content words can not find its counterpart in the word alignment step, then lots of qualified phrases are treated as content words empty phrases mistakenly, they will not appear during decoding.

According to the introduction of hierarchical phrase-based model, its phrases divided into the initial phrases and hierarchical phrases. The initial phrases mainly deal with the translation of the string. And the hierarchical phrases process sentence's structure, it is responsible for the sentence overall tone sequence. The above idiomatic expression misjudgment pseudo content words empty phrase generally does not involve the reordering of sentence, so we can only check hierarchical phrases in this step.

## 2.4 Synonym Expansion

In the above phrase filtering step, we only check phrases' content words in source side have counterpart or not. In this way, the phrase（负$_1$ 的 力量 。$_2$ $\longrightarrow$ positive$_1$ force .$_2$）,we filter the phrase because the source content word "力量" has no counterpart in its target side. It isn't a noisy rule in fact. We consider the use of alignment vocabulary translation probability to help filtering phrases, to make up for mistakenly filtered phrase.

Lexicalization probability is the probability of the word the A translated to the target language word B in a bilingual corpus. Now we consider the word"力量"translation probability in the bilingual corpus in descending order of translation probability:

Pr(power | 力量) = 0.292
Pr(emphasized | 力量) = 0.138
Pr(strength | 力量) = 0.123
Pr(capability | 力量) = 0.076
Pr(of | 力量) = 0.046
............

We use two pruning strategy to select the word A's basic translation in a bilingual corpus: First, the histogram pruning strategy. Set pruning value α, choose the top maximum probability α translation as lexicalized words translation. For example, let α = 5, basic translations of the word "力量" are {power, emphasized, strength, capability, of}. Second, the threshold pruning strategy. Lexicalization probability is greater than the pruning threshold β translation can be used as the basic translation of words. For example, let β = 0.1, the basic translations of the word "力量" are {power, emphasized, strength}.

As we know, concepts are represented by Wordnet (Miller 1995, Fellbaum 1998a) synonym sets and are expanded by following the typed links included in Wordnet. so we can use basic translation the WordNet synonym expansion. The word "power", the basic translation of the word "力量" , find its synonyms through WordNet. We can obtain the word "force" and other words, therefore the phrase （负 $_1$ 的 力量 。$_2$ —> positive$_1$ force $_{.2}$) is recalled. In this way we can make up for alignment mistakes, and recall the mistakenly filtered phrases.

Definition 3: If a phrase X -> <γ, α, ~>, if any content word in source side γ have no counterpart in the target side and the phrase can't be recalled through Wordnet Synonym expansion, called source side content words empty phrase.

Definition 3: If a phrase X -> <γ, α, ~>, if any content word in target side γ have no counterpart in the source side and the phrase can't be recalled through Wordnet Synonym expansion, called target side content words empty phrase.

Source side content words empty phrase and target side content words empty phrase are called by a joint name content words empty phrase.

## 3    Experimental Setup

We carried out MT experiments for oral translation from Chinese to English. The training data includes IWSLT10 test set and the indoor bilingual corpus that we obtained from the Web, consists of about 260k parallel pairs. The tuning set is IWSLT03 test set. The test set includes IWSLT07 test set and IWSLT08 test set. We uses Giza++ alignments (Och and Ney, 2000) symmetrized with the grow-diag-final-and heuristic. Chinese word segmentation and Chinese part-of-speech tagging were done by our indoor tool named PBCLAS. we used SRI Language Modeling Toolkit (Stolcke, 2002) to train a 5-gram model with modified Kneser-Ney smoothing on the 6,000k English sentences.

The experiment using the minimum error rate training (Och, 2003) for optimizing the feature weights. Our evaluation metric is IBM BLEU(Papineni et al.,2002),which performs case-insensitive matching of n-grams up to n = 4.

This paper set six systems to verify the function of filter phrase filtering, initial phrase filtration, filter hierarchical phrase, synonym expansion. They are divided into two groups: nouns group and nouns and pronouns group. Describe as follows:

Baseline: Using the common phrase table without any processing during decoding.
Filter-all: Using phrase table that all phrase checked during decoding.
Filter-nonX: Using phrase table that only initial phrase checked during decoding.
Filter-X: Using phrase table that only hierarchical phrase checked during decoding.
Filter-nonX + WordNet: Using phrase table that only initial phrase checked and recalled the mistakenly filtered through Wordnet synonym expansion during decoding.

Filter-X + WordNet: Using phrase table that only hierarchical phrase checked and recalled the mistakenly filtered through Wordnet synonym expansion during decoding.

## 4    Experimental Results and Discussions

The Baseline system use the phrase table without any processing during decoding. the phrase table consists of 7,885,749 phrases. Some phrases' source content words have no counterpart in the target side, Result in table 2 example : some system's output omit some content words. According to our statistics, 8 percent of all sentences in IWSLT07 test set and 6.4 percent of all sentences in IWSLT08 test set have the same problem in our Baseline's output. Therefore it is necessary to filter the phrase table.

Experiment divided into two groups: the first group is phrases' source nouns and pronouns recognize and check, and the second group is phrases' source nouns recognize and check.

**Table 1.** Experimental results on test set

| | | nouns and pronouns group | | | nouns group | | |
|---|---|---|---|---|---|---|---|
| | | IWSLT07 | IWSLT08 | | IWSLT07 | IWSLT08 | |
| | | BLEU(%) | BLEU(%) | number of filtered phrases | BLEU(%) | BLEU(%) | number of filtered phrases |
| **Baseline** | | 48.42 | 54.34 | | 48.42 | 54.34 | |
| **Filter-all** | | 48.68 | 54.05 | 333,613 | 49.82 | 53.08 | 143,114 |
| **Filter-nonX** | | 48.49 | 54.33 | 192,455 | 48.66 | 54.38 | 87,947 |
| **Filter-X** | | 48.73 | 53.67 | 141,158 | **49.55** | **55.16** | 55,167 |
| **Filter-nonX +** | α=5 | 48.64 | 54.33 | 155,882 | 48.68 | 53.79 | 58,297 |
| **WordNet** | β=0.1 | 48.49 | 54.33 | 178,514 | 48.66 | 54.38 | 68,195 |
| **Filter-X +** | α=5 | 48.83 | 53.99 | 124,046 | 49.55 | 55.16 | 51,340 |
| **WordNet** | β=0.1 | 48.73 | 53.67 | 132,057 | 49.55 | 55.16 | 52,473 |

In the first experiment group, compared to the Baseline, the system Filter-X's result shows that the filtering of initial phrases have an effect on the translation. From the example 1 in Table 2 we can see ,during decoding ,the translation's semantics is more accurate avoid using the noisy phrase. But the system Filter-nonX's BLEU score decrease in IWSLT08 test set. The reason is that some omitted content words expression are reasonable in the set references, such as Example 2 in Table 3.the phrase（X 什么 东西 —> what X）that used in the Baseline System is reasonable. System Filter-nonX+WordNet and systems the Filter-X+WordNet's BLEU score improve a little contrast to corresponding system Filter-nonX and system Filter-X, but they recall a number of mistakenly filtered phrases. the translation output changes not much because the recalled phrases' length is long and they are hardly used during decoding.

**Table 2.** Part of the quality improved obviously translation

| example1 | original text | 房间 的 灯 不 亮 。 |
| | Baseline's output | the light does not work . |
| | New output | the light in the room is not working . |
| example2 | original text | 原文：今天 有 好多 旅客 。 |
| | Baseline's output | there are lots of passengers . |
| | New output | there are so many passengers today . |

**Table 3.** Part of the quality improved not obviously translation

| example1 | original text | 请问 这 是 什么 东西 ？ |
| | Baseline's output | what is this ? |
| | New output | what is this item ? |
| example2 | original text | 请 给 我 炒 鸡蛋 。 |
| | Baseline's output | scrambled eggs , please . |
| | New output | i 'd like scrambled eggs . |

In the second experiment group. compared to the Baseline sytstem, System Filter-nonX's BLEU scores improve   significant in two test sets: IWSLT07 test set, increased by 1.03 percent (0.4955 vs .4842) ,and IWSLT08 test set , increased by 0.82 percent (0.5516 vs 0.5434). Compared to the first experiment group, these systems are also greatly improved. This group retains part of idiomatic expression phrases. From the example3 in Figure 3, and the phrase（请 给 我 X —> X   please）is filtered in the first experiment group, but it retain in the second experiment group. It is the same to the phrase（请 您 告诉 我 X —> please tell me the X）. System Filter-nonX+WordNet and system Filter-X+WordNet successfully recall a number of mistakenly filtered phrases but improve BLEU score a little. Overall, compared to the Baseline, other systems' BLEU score improves; it proved that our method is effective.

The system Filter-X's BLEU score improves more than the system Filter-nonX's BLEU score. Because system Filter-nonX filter more idiomatic expression phrases, removing these phrases deteriorate the translation quality. System Filter-nonX+WordNet and system Filter-X+WordNet 's results show that recalling the mistakenly filtered phrased though Wordnet can help system perform better.

## 5    Concludes the Paper and Future Work

This paper presents a phrase filtering method to filter phrase that source-side content words   is empty when translated into target texts for hierarchical phrase-based model, which can accelerate the decoding speed as well as improve translation quality. Experimental results on IWSLT test sets show that the method can improve the BLEU score as well as solve content words omit problem in translation.

Future work will be focusing on the following two aspects. First, for the initial phrase processing. We learn to recognize the idiomatic expression to filter the initial phrase more effective, and we can adding more information to recognize the idiomatic expression phrases. Second, We can try to build the phrase filtering model, and use the soft constraints for the noisy phrases to improve the experimental performance.

**Acknowledgement.** The authors were supported by High-Technology R&D Program (863) Project No 2011AA01A207, National Natural Science Foundation of China (No. 61003152, 61272259, 61272260, 90920004), the Special fund project of the Ministry of Education Doctoral Program (No. 20103201110021), the Natural Science Foundation of Jiangsu Province (No. BK2011282), the Major Project of College Natural Science Foundation of Jiangsu Province (No. 11KJA520003) and the Natural Science Foundation of Jiangsu Province, Suzhou City (No. SYG201030 , SH201212).

## References

1. Chiang, D.: A hierarchical phrase-based model for statistical machine translation. In: Proceedings of the 43rd Annual Meeting on Association for Computational Linguistics, pp. 263–270. Association for Computational Linguistics (2005)
2. Koehn, P., Och, F.J., Marcu, D.: Statistical phrase-based translation. In: Proceedings of the 2003 Conference of the North American Chapter of the Association for Computational Linguistics on Human Language Technology, pp. 48–54 (2003)
3. Liu, Y., Liu, Q., Lin, S.: Tree-to-string alignment template for statistical machine translation. In: Proceedings of the 21st International Conference on Computational Linguistics and the 44th Annual Meeting of the Association for Computational Linguistics, pp. 609–616 (2006)
4. Xie, J., Mi, H., Liu, Q.: A novel dependency-to-string model for statistical machine translation. In: Proceedings of the Conference on Empirical Methods in Natural Language Processing, pp. 216–226 (2011)

5. Och, F.J., Ney, H.: Improved Statistical Alignment Models. In: Proceedings of the 38th Annual Meeting on Association for Computational Linguistics. Association for Computational Linguistics (2000)

6. Stolcke, A.: SRILM-an extensible language modeling toolkit. In: Proceedings of the 7th International Conference on Spoken Language Processing 2002, pp. 901–905 (2002)

7. Och, F.J.: Minimum error rate training in statistical machine translation. In: Proceedings of 41st Annual Meeting on Association for Computational Linguistics, pp. 160–167. Association for Computational Linguistics

8. Papineni, K., Roukos, S., Ward, T., et al.: Bleu: a Method for Automatic Evaluation of Machine Translation. In: Proceedings of the 40th Annual Meeting on Association for Computational Linguistics, pp. 311–318. Association for Computational Linguistics (2002)

9. Miller, G.A.: WordNet: A Lexical Database for English. Communications of the ACM 38(11), 39–41 (1995)

10. Fellbaum, C. (ed.): WordNet: An Electronic Lexical Database. MIT Press, Cambridge (1998)

# Complex Query Expansion Based on Weighted Shortest Path Length in Key Term Concurrence Network

Hua Yang[1, 2], Mingyao Zhang[3], Donghong Ji[4,*], and Guozheng Xiao[2]

[1,2] School of Mathematics and Computer Science,
Guizhou Normal University, Guiyang, 550001, China
yanghuastory@foxmail.com
[2] College of Chinese Language and Literature, Wuhan University, Wuhan, 430072, China
gzxiao@foxmail.com
[3] School of Foreign Languages and Literature, Wuhan University, Wuhan, 430072, China
myzhang@whu.edu.cn
[4] School of Computer, Wuhan University, Wuhan, 430072, China
dhji@whu.edu.cn

**Abstract.** We build a key term concurrence network based on a large-scale document set. On the basis of the concept of the shortest path length in the large-scale key-term complex network, we propose a novel method of query expansion for complex query, which is a kind of short text. We accomplish information retrieval task for complex query expressed in natural language to testify the performance of the query expansion method. Experimental results show that our novel method turned out effective, but need to acquire good initial analysis for original complex user query.

**Keywords:** information retrieval, query expansion, complex query, complex network, semantic relevance.

## 1    Introduction

Performance of Information Retrieval (IR) can be improved by query expansion (QE) [1, 2]. According to the source of the expanded term, the methods can be categorized as three [3] :   1) Methods based on global corpus, simply referred as Global Analysis. These methods compute co-occurrence frequency, point-wise information, etc., on the basis of the whole corpus to obtain expanded terms [4-8] . 2) Methods based on small part of the corpus, simply referred as Local Analysis. These methods are based on the two-stage retrieval process and the assumption that the top k documents retrieved in first stage are related. The expanded terms are obtained from the k documents; 3) Methods based on manual semantic dictionaries. These methods obtain expanded terms from the manual-annotated resources which contain semantic relations among terms, e.g., semantic dictionaries, such as wordnet [9-11].

---

* Corresponding author.

P. Liu and Q. Su (Eds.): CLSW 2013, LNAI 8229, pp. 499–507, 2013.

In this paper, a method is proposed which is different from the above-mentioned three categories of methods. The new method obtains expanded terms for original user query by employing the concept of shortest path length in graphic science and the new method is used to expand complex query described in natural language. The key step is to obtain terms that are highly related to the complex query. This work is factually to evaluate semantic relatedness between a term and a short text, i.e., the above-mentioned complex query. For the convenience of understanding, the remaining part of this paper is organized as follows. Section 2 presents our method. Section 3 presents the experimental results and analysis. Section 4 compares our method with traditional methods. Section 5 points out what the future work is for query expansion based on our work.

## 2    Query Expansion Based on Shortest Path Length in Complex Network

The main idea of using the concept of shortest path length to expand query is as follows: Firstly, to   construct large-scale key term co-occurrence network (KTCN); Secondly, to use the lengths of the shortest path to evaluate the semantic relatedness between two terms and then obtain expanded term, and weigh them before inputting the expanded query to the retrieval system.

```
Input: large-scale document set corpus
Output•Key term network KTCN

 1) KTCN=empty graph ∅ .
 2) for each document D in corpus
        acquire D's key terms list LD
          for each paragraph P in D
            for every pair of terms (K1,K2) that K1, K2∈ LD
               if K1 and K2 co-occurs in P
                  if edge (K1, K2) does not exist in KTCN
                        create a new edge (K1,K2), and weight
                        this edge 1;
                  else
                     increase weight (K1, K2) by 1;
 3) MaxEdgeWeight=maximum of all edge weight in KTCN;
 4) for each edge e in KTCN
            e's new weight=MaxEdgeWeight-e's original weight
    +1;   //Note 1
```

**Fig. 1.** The process of constructing KTCN

## 2.1 Network Construction

The construction process of KTCN is shown in Fig. 1. L, the list of key terms of the corpus is also acquired. After the operation of Note 1 in Fig. 1, the smaller the value of an edge weight, the more times the two terms corresponding to the two nodes of the edge in KTCN co-occurred in the Corpus.

## 2.2 Initial Analysis for Complex Query

Current research of Chinese QE technique focuses mainly on expanding single term, which assumes that the user query is a short term and expresses complete concept meaning. However, user query may be a complex query, i.e., a query expressed in natural language, such as "列举全球变暖的危害 (lie ju quan qiu bian nuan de wei hai, *List the damages resulting from global warming*)". Little QE work focuses on complex query and the prevalent approaches go like this: segment the original Chinese query Q into the vector Qa composed of multiple terms and expand each term in Qa respectively. These approaches ignore some valuable information, such as term combination and term concurrence in the complex query. Take the query "列举全球变暖的危害(lie ju quan qiu bian nuan de wei hai, *List the damages resulting from global warming*)" for example, this query can be segmented as {列举 (lie ju, *list*) , 全球 (quan qiu, *global*) , 变暖 (bian nuan, *warming*) , 危害 (wei hai, *damage*)}. Intuitively , "全球变暖(quan qiu bian nuan, *global warming*)" expressed the users' intention better than "全球(quan qiu, *global*)" and "危害(wei hai, *damage*)"; moreover, the combined term "全球变暖(quan qiu bian nuan, *global warming*) " has turned into a semantic unit with more special connotation than the single term "全球 (quan qiu, global) ''" or "'变暖(bian nuan, *warming*) ''". We initially weight the terms in the list as the ratio of length of each term to the length of original complex query. For example, for the query "列举全球变暖的危害(lie ju quan qiu bian nuan de wei hai, *List the damages resulting from global warming*)", the resultant vector of initial analysis is Qa={<变暖(bian nuan, *warming*), 0.166667>, <气候(qi hou, *climate*), 0.166667>, <气候变暖(qi hou bian nuan, *climate warming*), 0.333333>, <全球 (quan qiu, *global*) , 0.166667>, <全球气候(quan qiu qi hou, *global climate*), 0.333333>, <全球气候变暖(quan qiu qi hou bian nuan, *global climate warming*), 0.5>, <危害(wei hai, *damage*), 0.166667>}.

## 2.3 Setting of Expansion Length

Shortest path length between two nodes in KTCN is used to define the semantic relatedness between the two corresponding terms: it is assumed that the smaller the numerical value of the shortest path length between two nodes in KTCN, the higher semantic relatedness for the two corresponding terms. For example, for an initially-analyzed complex query Qa = {<变暖(bian nuan, *warming*), 0.166667>, <气候(qi hou, *climate*), 0.166667>, <气候变暖(qi hou bian nuan, *climate warming*),

0.333333>, <全球(quan qiu, *global*) , 0.166667>, <全球气候(quan qiu qi hou, *global climate*), 0.333333>, <全球气候变暖(quan qiu qi hou bian nuan, *global climate warming*), 0.5>, <危害(wei hai, *damage*), 0.166667>}, we call each term in Qa as expanding source, notated as Ts. For each Ts in Qa, we obtain the expanded term vector including ExtNum initially expanded terms. ExtNum is the notation of expansion length. It is worth mentioning that it is difficult to compute shortest path in very large-scale network. For the details of computing, see another of our paper to be published.

### 2.4    Weighting Strategy for Expanded Term

The elements in initially-expanded vector for each source term, i.e., Ts, are sorted ascending according to the relatedness value to the source term. The strategy for weighting each expanded term is shown in Fig. 2.

### 2.5    Retrieval Process

#### 2.5.1    Inverse Indexing
The supporting project of this paper is to explore how to evaluate the semantic relatedness between terms within complex network composed of terms. The purpose of this paper is to verify the validity of corresponding methods based on complex network. Therefore, the inversion indexing does not adopt unigram or bigram as item to be indexed, but use key term as the unit to be indexed instead. The indexing process is as follows: if T is a key term of document T, create indexing item for this pair of key term and document, with the form of {T, {D, F}}, where F is the occurrence frequency of T in D as key term.

#### 2.5.2    Retrieval of Related Document
The result of retrieval, i.e. the document set retrieved for complex user query, is sorted non-descending according to the document score that is also the relatedness value between query and document. The strategy for score each document is shown in Fig. 3. In the strategy, if an expanded term is expanded by more than one source term, its weight is accumulated. This accumulation is a noteworthy but implicit operation happened actually in the retrieval process because it differentiates our method from the methods concentrating on query expansion methods which assume that user query is a single term instead of complex query.

## 3    Experimental result

### 3.1    Corpus and Evaluating Parameters

IR4QA (Information Retrieval for Question Answering) task in NTCIR-7 [12-14]is used to test the performance of our methods. KTCN is constructed on Chinese corpus for IR4QA have node number of 713218 and edge number of 19042384, which establish a large-scale network. Average Precision (AP), Q-measure (Q) [15]   and nDCG[16]   are used to test the performance of system for IR4QA task.

```
Input: Initially analyzed query Qa, with the element form of <term,
initialWeight>; expanding length ExtNum; factor alpha which is used
to treat the terms expanded from long source term and short source
term differently; factor beta is used to assure the importance of
term in original query.
Output: expanded vector with the element form of <term, final-
Weight>.
1) QAE=empty;
2) for each Es in Qa{
       source term InitTerm=Es.term;
        InitWeight=Es.InitialWeight;
       Set InitTerm as the starting node, obtain ExtNum terms which
has the shortest path lengths to the starting node, store the Ex-
tNum terms in a tempory vector Vtemp, and sort the terms nondes-
cending according to its shortest path length to the source term;
       L=Vtemp.length;
       for(i=1;i<=L;i++){
               W=Vterm[i]•
               tmpScore=(L-i+1)/L;
               search E with E.term=W in QAE;
               if(faild)
                   adding new element <W,alpha×InitWeight+ tmpScore> into
                       QAE;
               else   update the E<W,WT> in QAE as
                       <W,WT+alpha×InitWeight+ tmpScore>;
       }
  }
3) tempMaxWeight=maximum of weight for terms in QAE
   for each element EQAE(W,WT) in QAE
     TotalInitWeight=sum of weights of elements in QA;
     for each EQA(W,WT) in QA
         if (EQAE.W == EQa.W)
             EQAE.WT=•TotalInitWeight/ EQA.WT•×tempMaxWeight×beta;
```

**Fig. 2.** Strategy for weighting expanded terms

## 3.2    Experimental Result and Analysis

After numerous trial tests, it is verified that the best result is obtained when al-pha≈200 and beta≈15. Table 1 lists the results when alpha=200 and beta=15. It can be seen that the best result is obtained when expanding length ExtNum is set as about 25. The performance may be better than that listed in table 1, but to what extent the performance can be good can not be verified since our result is not used to participate in the process of pooling. The detailed reason for that is described in Ref. [14] .

```
Input: Vector V1 of terms after expanding, with the element
 form of <term, finalWeight>; Inversion Indexing File InvIdx
 with the form describe in section 2.5
Output: resultant vector after retrieval, with the element
 form of <Document, Score>
1) for each document D in the corpus{
        new a temporary element EVd;
        EVd.Document=D;
        EVD.Score=0;
        Add EVD to Vd;
    }
2) for each EQAE=•T•WT•in V1{
        for each EVd=(D•SD) in Vd{
            search item •EQAE.T•EVd.D• in InvIdx;
            if(success)
                read the triple•EQAE.T•EVd.D•F• from InvIdx
                // Note: F is the frequency that EQAE.T oc-
                curs in EVd.D as key term
            EVd.SD = EVd.SD+ EQAE.WT ;
        }
    }
3) Sort elements in Vd non-descending by score;
```

**Fig. 3.** Scoring strategy for retrieved document

For the best result obtained, we investigated the distribution of AP score, as shown in Fig. 4. It can be seen in Fig. 4  that the performance of our retrieval system is extremely unstable. The standard deviation reached 0.2231 with the average of only 0.4135. For the 97 topics evaluated in NTCIR-7 IR4QA task, the number of topics with AP higher than 0.675 reached 18, of which the number of topics whose AP score between 0.775 and 0.8 reached 9. On the other hand, 22 topics are scored lower than 0.2, of which 8 topics are scored close to 0. We investigated the reason for the extreme instability. It is found that the topics of low score are always badly analyzed at the first step---initial analysis for original query. For example, for the topic ACLIA1-CS-T42, i.e., "谁是本拉登? (shui shi ben la deng? Who is Bin Laden?)", the initial analyzing result is empty, which leads to the score of 0 for this topic. For the topic of ACLIA1-CS-T74,  i.e., "列举中俄之间发生的事情 (lie ju zhong e zhi jian fa sheng de shi qing, list the events happened between China and Russia. )", the initial analyzing result is {(俄之间(e zhi jian, between Russia and), 0.25), (发生(fa sheng, occur), 0.166667), (发生的事情(fa sheng de shi qing, event occurred), 0.416667), (事情(shi qing, event),0.166667),  (之间(zhi jian, between),   0.166667) }, where "俄之间(e zhi jian, between Russia and)" is a Chinese character string carrying no meaning in Chinese, and "发生(fa sheng, occur)", "发生的事情(fa sheng de shi qing, event occurred)", "事情(shi qing, something)", "之间(zhi jian, between)" mean "happen", "event happened", "event", "between" in English. It is clear that each term is in the initially-analyzed query is of little relevance to the intention of original user query, which leads to the extremely low score of 0.007 for this topic. These phenomena lead to the conclusion that the bottleneck of our retrieval system is the stage of initial analysis of original query instead of stage of query expansion. This brings both good and bad messages. The bad one is that the performance of our retrieval system depends heavily on the performance of initial query analysis, which is still a difficulty in NLP technique. The good message is that the performance of strategy for finding the most semantically-related term for a given term and the strategy for weighting expanded term perform well, which conforms to the purpose of the supporting project of this paper, which is to evaluate the semantic relatedness between terms by using relative theory in the   researching field of complex network.

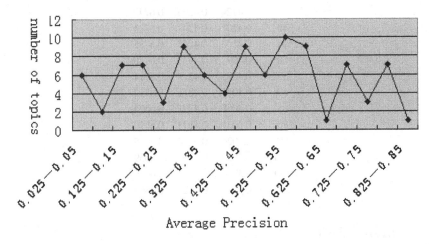

**Fig. 4.** Distribution of number of topics for AP score

## 4    Comparison with the Traditional Methods

Compared with the traditional methods referred in Section 1, the method employed in this paper (called KTCN-QE) is novel. KTCN-QE does not depend on manual resources, which is expensive. KTCN-QE can avoid the sensitivity of Local Analysis while requiring only one-stage retrieval process. KTCN-QE employed the global information of the whole corpus as Global Analysis does. However, unlike Global Analysis, KTCN-QE does not need to compute relatedness between every pair of terms, which means better real-time performance. KTCN-QE can adapt it to the situation that the generation, disappearance, and modification of documents in the corpus, which is the real situation of the web. This feature originated from the operation when the change of the documents happens. The operations only include adding edge, increasing weight, decreasing weight, delete edge, and so on. For the same reason, when KTCN-QE is used for retrieving information in massive documents, e.g., the documents on the web, the edge weight of the network can be more precise and will express the semantic relatedness strength more precisely and make better performance for query expansion.

**Table 1.** Result with different expanding length

| ExtNum | AP | Q | nDCG |
|---|---|---|---|
| 1 | 0.3577 | 0.3728 | 0.6135 |
| 5 | 0.3969 | 0.4106 | 0.6527 |
| 10 | 0.4024 | 0.4162 | 0.6586 |
| 15 | 0.3879 | 0.4021 | 0.6442 |
| 20 | 0.4039 | 0.4181 | 0.6602 |
| 25 | 0.4135 | 0.4276 | 0.6745 |
| 30 | 0.4131 | 0.4269 | 0.6743 |
| 35 | 0.4124 | 0.4263 | 0.6742 |
| 40 | 0.4101 | 0.4241 | 0.6721 |
| 45 | 0.4103 | 0.4243 | 0.6735 |
| 50 | 0.4093 | 0.4233 | 0.6720 |
| 55 | 0.4082 | 0.4223 | 0.6714 |
| 60 | 0.4075 | 0.4218 | 0.6712 |
| 65 | 0.4060 | 0.4201 | 0.6694 |
| 80 | 0.4031 | 0.4173 | 0.6670 |
| 90 | 0.4026 | 0.4164 | 0.6665 |
| 100 | 0.4021 | 0.4160 | 0.6659 |
| 150 | 0.3954 | 0.4094 | 0.6606 |
| 200 | 0.3878 | 0.4021 | 0.6566 |

## 5   Future Work

The purpose of this paper is not just to expand query but also to use query expansion to verify the validness of our method for evaluating relatedness between a term and a short text. As far as query expansion is concerned, the work listed below is worth being carried out. As mentioned above, the bottleneck lies in the initial analysis of original query. Therefore, using unigram and bigram as items to be inversion-indexed is one method to solve that problem. Another way to overcome the bottleneck is to investigate the connectivity of terms of the original user query in the network to lower the initial weight of the term in original query, which is less relative to the semantic meaning of the query.

**Acknowledgements.** This paper is supported by Natural Science Foundation Project (61070243), Major Project of Invitation for Bid of National Social Science Foundation (11&ZD189), Guizhou High-level Talent Research Project (TZJF-2010-048), Guizhou Normal University PhD Start-up Research Project (11904-05032110011), and Governor Special Fund Grant of Guizhou Province for Prominent Science and Technology Talents (identification serial number "黔省专合字(2012)155号").

# References

1. Van, R.C.: A new theoretical framework for information retrieval. In: Proceedings of 1986 ACM Conference on Research and Development in Information Retrieval, pp. 194–200. ACM, New York (1986)
2. Baeza-Yates, R., Ribeiro-Neto, B.: Modern information retrieval. Addison-Wesley, Harlow (1999)
3. Ding, G.D., Bai, S., Wang, B.: Local Co-occurrence Based Query Expansion for Information Retrieval. Journal of Chinese Information Processing 20(003), 84–91 (2006) (丁国栋, 白硕, 王斌. 一种基于局部共现的查询扩展方法. 中文信息学报 20(003), 84–91 (2006))
4. Van, R.C.: A theoretical basis for the use of co-occurrence data in information retrieval. Journal of Documentation 33(2), 106–119 (1977)
5. Crouch, C.J., Yang, B.: Experiments in automatic statistical thesaurus construction. In: Proc. of the AGM2SIGIR Conference on Research and Development in Information Retrieval, pp. 77–88. ACM, New York (1992)
6. Chen, H., Yim, T., Fye, D., et al.: Automatic thesaurus generation for an electronic community system. Journal of the American Society for Information Science 46(3) (1995)
7. Sch, H., Pedersen, J.O.: A cooccurrence-based thesaurus and two applications to information retrieval. Information Processing and Management 33(3), 307–318 (1997)
8. Lin, D., Zhao, S., Qin, L., et al.: Identifying synonyms among distributionally similar words, pp. 1492–1493. Lawrence Erlbaum Associates Ltd. (2003)
9. Miller, G.A., Beckwith, R., Fellbaum, C., et al.: Introduction to wordnet: An on-line lexical database*. International Journal of Lexicography 3(4), 235–244 (1990)
10. Richardson, R., Smeaton, A.F.: Using WordNet in a knowledge-based approach to information retrieval (1995)
11. Smeaton, A.F., Berrut, C.: Thresholding postings lists, query expansion by word-word distances and POS tagging of Spanish text (1996)
12. Mitamura, T., Nyberg, E., Shima, H., et al.: Overview of the NTCIR-7 ACLIA Tasks: Advanced Cross-Lingual Information Access. In: Proceedings of the Seventh NTCIR Workshop Meeting, Tokyo Japan (2008)
13. Tetsuya Sakai, E.: Overview of the NTCIR-7 ACLIA IR4QA Subtask (2008)
14. Sakai, T., Kando, N., Lin, C., et al.: Overview of the NTCIR-7 ACLIA IR4QA Task. In: Proceedings of the Seventh NTCIR Workshop Meeting, Tokyo, Japan (2008)
15. Sakai, T.: Evaluating information retrieval metrics based on bootstrap hypothesis tests. IPSJ Digital Courier 3, 625–642 (2007)
16. Kek, J.K., Cumulated, J.: gain-based evaluation of IR techniques. ACM Transactions on Information Systems (TOIS) 20(4), 422–446 (2002)

# Design and Implementation of Chinese Spam Review Detection System

Xiujuan Xu[1], Tianqi Han[1], Zhenlong Xu[2], Yu Wang[1], and Yu Liu[1,*]

[1] School of Software, Dalian University of Technology, DaLian, China, 116620
{xjxu,yuliu}@dlut.edu.cn, simon.hon.90@gmail.com,
karenwangyu2004@163.com
[2] School of Management, Dalian University of Technology, DaLian, China, 116620
white_bird@yeah.net

**Abstract.** This paper designs and implements a Chinese spam review detection system based on rules. The main rules include the following three types: (1) Calculating the similarity between two comments, i.e., if the similarity is larger than a specified threshold, the two comments are viewed as review spam; (2) Calculating the correlation degree between comments and the product, i.e., if the degree is smaller than a specified threshold, the comment is viewed as review spam. (3) Detecting whether stuffing exists in the keyword, meta field or keywords of the web page. If they exist, the comments are viewed as review spam. In addition, we proposed a Naive Bayes Classifier in the review detection system. We selected 500 comments randomly and signed the comments true or false manually. Then 400 comments were selected to train and the other 100 comments were used to test. Finally, precision of the algorithm was attained. Experimental results show that the operation effect of our system is satisfactory.

**Keywords:** Review Spam, Information Processing, Vector Space Model, Naive Bayes Classifier.

## 1 Introduction

Most e-commerce websites allow users to comment on the products they purchase, so customers can express views, such as love, praise, criticism, disgust on these products. Customers always browse the products comments before shopping. Therefore, if customers could not learn more about the commodity information, the review of the product on shopping sites will have direct or indirect influence on customer purchase behavior. According to a survey, investigated by the China Internet Network Information Center (CNNIC) based on an e-commerce websites comment on customers' purchasing behavior, 43.3% of people will focus on product reviews of other customers before buying products [1]. Some users will publish some spam reviews to the commodity, deliberately touted or vilify some certain commodities, these spam reviews to

---

* Corresponding author.

P. Liu and Q. Su (Eds.): CLSW 2013, LNAI 8229, pp. 508–518, 2013.

a certain extent affected the comment information reference value, confuse the public, and mislead customers. Our spam reviews detection system is designed to solve the above problems, so as to find and remove the false comments from the text, stay true review, improve the precision and accuracy of sentiment analysis, and to provide reliable reference data for the user.

In recent years, it is one of the hotspots about spam reviews of English in text mining. In 2010, Ee-Peng Lim et al. [2] studied the problem of English spam reviews, and found several characteristics of the spam reviews. First, the spam reviews targeted on specific commodity. Secondly, spam review had a deviation from most people's comments. Estimating spam degree of each evaluator using the scoring method, he then selected a high suspicious set to do further analysis experiment. That same year, G. Wu et al. [3] discussed how to identify suspicious evaluation from the twist angle; they found that the overall evaluation of the level may distort a target evaluation by dishonest people. Evaluation of Nitin Jindal et al. [4] was committed to find unusual comments from the suspicious reviewers' comments. In 2011, Fangtao Li et al. [5] proposed the use of semi-supervised learning algorithm Co-Training to identify fake reviews, respectively analysis of spam reviews recognition problem from review and reviewer. In 2012, Wang et al. [6] proposed using the network method of social evaluation to detect online spam reviews. There are less domestic study on spam review, analysis of [7][8] most related work focuses on the comment spam.

## 2    Design of Spam Reviews System

In our paper, we analyze, design and realize an online review spam detection system according to several common types of reviews spam. Firstly we designed the rules of online review spam detection system based on sufficient analysis of the B2C e-commerce website product reviews. Then we used our algorithm to analyze the reviews based the rules so as to obtain the accuracy of this rules. Finally we analyzed 500 reviews with the Bayesian method.

### 2.1    Overall Process

In order to identify some common type review spam, the general work flow is shown in figure 1. The system is divided into 5 modules: reviews preprocessing, Chinese word dividing, keywords extracting, review comment analyzing and other parameters analyzing. Whereby, effective ICTCLAS [9] Chinese word segmentation system is used for the module of Chinese word dividing as the Chinese word segmentation module of this system.

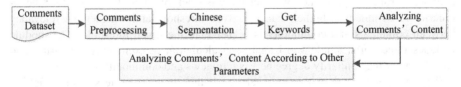

**Fig. 1.** Overall Flow

## 2.2   Reviews Preprocessing

In the preprocessing step, the main work is to carry on the preliminary screening for comments. In e-commerce sites, the situation always exists that a user buys the same products several times. Thus the problem arises that the user writes many comments on the same commodity. Analyzing these comments written by the same user, we can find that most content has very high similarity and the scoring almost the same. If these comments can't be processed, it will lead to two problems in the later process:

1) When it comes to calculate the average value of a characteristic calculation of all the comments, the user's comments weight will be higher than other users' as the user has published several similar comments, which is unfair for others and resulting in the statistical error.
2) According to these rules, the comments which have high similarity will be regarded as spam. In this way, even if the user's comments are not actually reviews spam, due to the presence of some high similar comments, it will also be judged as review spam, resulting in the errors of judgment.

These problems can be avoided by pretreatment. So in the preprocessing stage, this paper scans the review data and only saves the latest comment by the same user.

## 2.3   Keywords Extraction

In the online review spam detection system, the main work of the keywords extraction is extracting related words of the commodity information. It can be divided into 3 categories:

1) Object representing a feature of the products: quality, price, cost performance, color etc. ;
2) Object related to the purchase and delivery of products: delivery speed, service, packaging etc. ;
3) Polarity words, including positive words and negative evaluation.

In order to extract the keywords accurately, this paper uses the TF-IDF algorithm to compute each word's TF-IDF weight based on Chinese segmentation results. It ranks all the extracted words according to the weight from high to low, and selects the top 100 words as keywords.

## 2.4   Analyzing Review Comment

In the analyzing review comment module, this system mainly analyzes the review comments from 3 aspects, i.e., whether there is stack of single word, whether the similarity of comment is higher than the given threshold and whether the relevancy between comments and commodity is higher than the given threshold. The module includes three parts: single word analysis, calculation of comments similarity, and calculation of the similarity degree between reviews and commodity.

The analysis of single word is to analyze whether there are useless element field or keyword stuffing of page content in the comments. For example, the comment, "very

very very good", will be considered as review spam, and it can be detected in this analysis process.

The calculation of similarity between comments is to use the vector space model to calculate the similarity between comments. We can get the proper threshold by our experiment, and define the comment as review spam if similarity exceeds the threshold. For example, while calculating the similarity between "Apple mobile phone is really good" and "Apple's quality is good, well done", we use the calculation first level annotation to the former comment, then we get the result as "apple /n mobile phone /n is really /a good /a". As to the latter one, we get the result as "Apple's quality is good, well done". Upon the retention of nouns, verbs, adverbs, adjectives, the former comment can be expressed as a vector; the latter comment can be expressed as a vector. This two comments similarity can be expressed as a formula (1).

$$\text{Sim}(D_1, D_2) = \frac{\sum_{k=1}^{8} w_{1,k} \times w_{2,k}}{\sqrt{(\sum_{k=1}^{8} w_{1,k}^2)(\sum_{k=1}^{8} w_{2,k}^2)}} \tag{1}$$

Then we selected the appropriate threshold to determine whether the two comments should be classified as false.

Computing reviews and commodity related degree, the TF-IDF algorithm is first used [10] to calculate each word TF-IDF weights, and then to choose the low weight as keywords. This is mainly based on the following considerations: due to the use of the TF-IDF algorithm, calculated weights on more words tend to appear more times in a single comment in a few pieces of comments, so the choice of higher weights words as keywords is not suitable for product reviews of short text. Therefore, the lower weights words are chosen as keywords so that more people use them as keywords. Once keys words are extracted, correlation and calculation of comments would be done respectively and those correlations below the given threshold are regarded as spam review.

## 2.5     Analysis According to Other Parameters

In addition to the analysis above, we also analyze reviews from other angles. Review authenticity judgment is not limited to the judgment of review contents and other parameters are considered in the system. Information beyond review contents is analyzed in this module. We first analyze the buying time and reviewing time and then analyze the user level.

A comment usually involves several parameters: (1) buy time; (2) review time; (3) number of reply; (4) content of reply; (5) user level; (6) user grade. According to the actual situation (1), (2), (5) and (6) of these four parameters can be used for analysis.

Reviewers post false comment due to the following three reasons: (1) a reviewer posts multiple reviews in a same user name; (2) a reviewer posts multiple reviews in different user names; (3) different reviewers post multiple reviews. Case (1) has excluded in the pretreatment process. For the case (2) and (3), according to the concept of the group review spam proposed in the literature [2], buy time and review time of multiple reviews were likely to happen in a shorter time interval. Therefore, the accuracy rate could be higher by defining a time window and adjust the size of the time window to detect review time of false reviews posted by group review spam. Moreover, due to unified review on a product with similar content and same score, reviewers in the same spam review group often have same user level and same score to the same product, which are two additional bases in identity of the user.

Chinese:

English:

> *Fast, good, happy.*
> *Advantage: Fast, good, happy.*
> *Disadvantage: No shortcoming has ever been found.*
> *Experience: Fast, good, happy.*
> *The comment is useful or no useful for me?*
> *1 Kenshin_1225 re:*
> *2999, is true or false?*
> *2 mu19831130 re:*
> *Unhappy' 'I was cheated by so-call Laoliu special selling''''*
> *3Yao_XX re:*
> *Why is the iPhone put to panic buying with 4999 price?*
> *4 Chinese:*瑞兔 *[Pinyin:RuiTu] (English:GoodRabbit) re:*
> *They know we are looking forward to buy iPhone, so they put it on first webpage, but 4999 price, hehe.*
> *'Untimed' Very creative!*
> *5 caca9905 re:*
> *If I could not find iPhone with 2999 price today, I would not come back to 360.com website again in my life.*
> *6 LiiSa re:*
> *False...4999 price on the first webpage*
> *7 Chinese:*楽楽风尘 *[Pinyin:LeLeFengChen] (English: HappyWindDust) re:*
> *Everyone should go to ask "JingDongLiuDongQiang", what's going on with 2999 price, occurred or not?*
> *It is very obvious, JingDong is cheated us!*

**Fig. 2.** Reply of a user comment

In addition, after much investigation, most customers did not have the habits to review or reply after reading other people's product reviews. For example, 4452 product reviews used in this paper, only 479 product reviews get reply from other users, of which 269 product reviews only have one reply and little relevance with product information. Therefore, the number of reply and reply contents to the review is not universal, which is not suitable for analysis. For example, Figure 2 is a typical crawling product reviews.

## 3 Naïve Bayes Classifier

Process of bias classification mainly contains preprocessing stage, training stage and classification stage as shown in figure 3. In the collection of all the products review, we randomly selected 500 reviews. Then, 400 comments were selected from the 500 comments to make a training set and the other 100 comments for testing set.

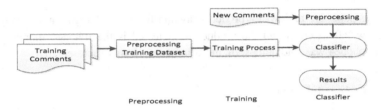

**Fig. 3.** Naïve Bayes Classifier Processing

Firstly, to preprocess 400 comments in the training set, we need set a property for each comment to manual annotation of the 400 comments, for example, 1 for true, 0 for false. In this way, the training set is divided into 2 categories, denoted as $C = \{C_0, C_1\}$, where $C_0$ represents spam review collection, $C_1$ represents the no-spam review set. Prior probability of each $C_i$ is $P(C_i)$, $i=0,1$. For the new review $d$, which belongs to the $C_i$ class conditional probability is $P(d|C_i)$. According to Bias theorem, the posterior probability of $C_i$ is $P(C_i|d)$, as shown in equation (2).

$$P(C_i \mid d) = \frac{P(d \mid C_i)P(C_i)}{P(d)} \tag{2}$$

P (d) could be ignored, for all $C_i$ classes are constants, and then the equation (2) is simplified into equation (3).

$$P(C_i \mid d) \propto P(d \mid C_i)P(C_i) \tag{3}$$

In order to avoid the $P(C_i)$ equal to 0, the Laplace smoothing algorithm was adopted, as shown in equation 4.

$$P(C_i) = \frac{1 + |D_{c_i}|}{|C| + |D_c|} \tag{4}$$

Among them, |C| is the number of classes in training set, |C|=2; $|D_{C_i}|$ is the number of documents in the training set belonging to the class of Ci; $|D_C|$ is the total number of document in training set , and $|D_C|$=500.  Using equation 4 we calculated $P(w_j|C_i)$, it represents the classifier prediction probability word $w_j$ happened in the documentation of the class $C_i$.

$$P(w_j \mid C_i) = \frac{1+TF(w_j,C_i)}{|V|+\sum_{k=1}^{|V|}TF(w_k,C_i)} \tag{5}$$

In equation 5, |V| represents the total number of words feature list, TF($w_j$, $C_i$) represents the frequency of the word $w_j$ expressed in all document of $C_i$   class.

# 4    Experimental Results

Data in this paper are reviews on product crawling from 京东[Jingdong] (360buy.com) (http://www.360buy.com) and the product we selected is the iPhone4 mobile phone. Since the iphone4 was sold quite well, the comments are very representative.

## 4.1    Experimental Data

Experimental data included a total of 4452 user reviews. Each review consists of the following information: user name, user location, buy time, review time, the number of reply, number of comments, general impression, advantages, shortcomings, and the use of experience, star rating, and degree of membership. Online comments section as shown in figure 2.

## 4.2    Experimental Results

First, all review are read and preprocessed, with 183 reviews filtering out made by the same user and   4269 comments left. After the preprocessing of review, average user score is 4.81 points. When adding user dictionary, the system added 15 users. After the Chinese word segmentation, extraction of the system   total to 3757 words, including 1530 nouns, 1483 verbs, 450 adjectives and adverbs 294.

After the keyword extraction, the system entered the review content analysis. For the data in Anhui Province as an example, our system discovers 35 spam reviews in this area. After the single word detection, no comments were detected as problem comment. While detecting high similarity in comments for each user, 7 comments were found with problems. Figure 4 shows that review No.844 and No.853.exhibit that these two reviews' overall impression, advantages and use the experience are exactly the same. Furthermore, the "deficiency" description in reviews is the default content in 360buy.com. As this review has no value to other potential customers, they could be considered as spam reviews.

Chinese:

| 序号 | ID | 地点 | 购买时间 | 评论时间 | 总体印象 | 优点 | 不足 | 使用心得 | 星星评分 | 会员等级 |
|------|----|------|----------|----------|----------|------|------|----------|----------|----------|
| 844 | 曝盖球 | 安徽 | 2011-05-21 | 2011-7-13 8:15:53 | 还不错挺好的 | 还不错挺好的 | 暂时还没发现缺点哦！ | 还不错挺好的 | 5 | 62 |
| 853 | darkdanceing | 安徽 | 2011-07-11 | 2011-7-12 18:00:20 | 帮别人买的，不知道啊 | 帮别人买的，不知道啊 | 暂时还没发现缺点哦！ | 帮别人买的，不知道啊 | 5 | 62 |

English:

| Order | ID | Province | Buying Time | Comments Time | Overall Impress | Advantage | Disadvantage | Experience | Star | Rating |
|-------|----|----------|-------------|---------------|-----------------|-----------|--------------|------------|------|--------|
| 844 | PanGaiQiu | Anhui | 2011-05-21 | 2011-7-13 8:15:53 | Not bad, good | Not bad, good | No shortcoming have ever been found | Not bad, good | 5 | 62 |
| 853 | darkdancing | Anhui | 2011-07-11 | 2011-7-12 18:00:20 | Buy it for others, I don't know | Buy it for others, I don't know | No shortcoming have ever been found | Buy it for others, I don't know | 5 | 62 |

**Fig. 4.** Review Contents

After deleting the spam reviews, average points are 4.78 for the rest of reviews, slightly lower compared with the previous 4.81, indicating that part of the spam reviews give scores higher than the average score of the products, thereby raising the overall score of products. Table 1 shows identify of the user grade distribution for the spam reviews in our system. As can be seen from the table, the middle level user created spam reviews most.

Figure 5 shows a group of typical review spam found, and our figure shows only part of them. These reviews have the following features:

1) Content of the comments is same. The four columns (overall impression, advantages, shortcomings, experience) of the review are the same content.
2) Comments and commodity are not of high degree of correlation. The comment could use to describe variety of commodities, so it is more likely to be a spam review.
3) Locations of users are the same place
4) The purchase date is the same day
5) Users make the comment in a very short time region. By the statistics, there are total 81 items of this review spam. The comment time is from 2011-07-09 15:09:35 to 2011-07-09 16:04:36. Lots of same comments are made by the limited time, even not to one hour. So it would be more possible to comment a spam review.
6) The user names are all consisted of 10 Arabic numerals with high similarity. The user level and user score are also the same.

Based on the above analysis, it has high possibility that these comments are review spams.

**Table 1.** The degree distrubution of spam reviewers

| Degree | Number of Customers |
|--------|---------------------|
| 50 | 40 |
| 56 | 37 |
| 60 | 60 |
| 61 | 172 |
| 62 | 495 |
| 63 | 173 |
| 88 | 55 |

Chinese:

| 序号 | ID | 地点 | 购买时间 | 评论时间 | 回复数目 | 总体印象 | 优点 | 不足 | 使用心得 | 星级 | 会员 |
|---|---|---|---|---|---|---|---|---|---|---|---|
| 959 | 6395798245 | 北京 | 2011-06-02 | 2011-7-9 16:12:38 | (共0条回复) | 质量好有发票 | 有发票价格也合理 | 暂时还没发现缺点哦! | 有发票价格也合理 | 5 | 62 |
| 960 | 9183025567 | 北京 | 2011-06-02 | 2011-7-9 16:12:01 | (共0条回复) | 质量好有发票 | 有发票价格也合理 | 暂时还没发现缺点哦! | 有发票价格也合理 | 5 | 62 |
| 961 | 8767958975 | 北京 | 2011-06-02 | 2011-7-9 16:11:35 | (共0条回复) | 质量好有发票 | 有发票价格也合理 | 暂时还没发现缺点哦! | 有发票价格也合理 | 5 | 62 |
| 962 | 8675139105 | 北京 | 2011-06-02 | 2011-7-9 16:11:27 | (共0条回复) | 质量好有发票 | 有发票价格也合理 | 暂时还没发现缺点哦! | 有发票价格也合理 | 5 | 62 |
| 963 | 8945714122 | 北京 | 2011-06-02 | 2011-7-9 16:11:21 | (共0条回复) | 质量好有发票 | 有发票价格也合理 | 暂时还没发现缺点哦! | 有发票价格也合理 | 5 | 62 |
| 964 | 7024462211 | 北京 | 2011-06-02 | 2011-7-9 16:10:11 | (共0条回复) | 质量好有发票 | 有发票价格也合理 | 暂时还没发现缺点哦! | 有发票价格也合理 | 5 | 62 |
| 965 | 5018770523 | 北京 | 2011-06-02 | 2011-7-9 16:09:56 | (共0条回复) | 质量好有发票 | 有发票价格也合理 | 暂时还没发现缺点哦! | 有发票价格也合理 | 5 | 62 |
| 966 | 6315142022 | 北京 | 2011-06-02 | 2011-7-9 16:09:41 | (共0条回复) | 质量好有发票 | 有发票价格也合理 | 暂时还没发现缺点哦! | 有发票价格也合理 | 5 | 62 |
| 967 | 8774434477 | 北京 | 2011-06-02 | 2011-7-9 16:09:35 | (共0条回复) | 质量好有发票 | 有发票价格也合理 | 暂时还没发现缺点哦! | 有发票价格也合理 | 5 | 62 |
| 968 | 5286972346 | 北京 | 2011-06-02 | 2011-7-9 16:09:22 | (共0条回复) | 质量好有发票 | 有发票价格也合理 | 暂时还没发现缺点哦! | 有发票价格也合理 | 5 | 62 |
| 969 | 1071646012 | 北京 | 2011-06-02 | 2011-7-9 16:09:14 | (共0条回复) | 质量好有发票 | 有发票价格也合理 | 暂时还没发现缺点哦! | 有发票价格也合理 | 5 | 62 |
| 970 | 1354784853 | 北京 | 2011-06-02 | 2011-7-9 16:09:00 | (共0条回复) | 质量好有发票 | 有发票价格也合理 | 暂时还没发现缺点哦! | 有发票价格也合理 | 5 | 62 |
| 971 | 1405157179 | 北京 | 2011-06-02 | 2011-7-9 16:08:55 | (共0条回复) | 质量好有发票 | 有发票价格也合理 | 暂时还没发现缺点哦! | 有发票价格也合理 | 5 | 62 |
| 972 | 1041923238 | 北京 | 2011-06-02 | 2011-7-9 16:08:53 | (共0条回复) | 质量好有发票 | 有发票价格也合理 | 暂时还没发现缺点哦! | 有发票价格也合理 | 5 | 62 |
| 973 | 3911542495 | 北京 | 2011-06-02 | 2011-7-9 16:08:26 | (共0条回复) | 质量好有发票 | 有发票价格也合理 | 暂时还没发现缺点哦! | 有发票价格也合理 | 5 | 62 |
| 974 | 6124088612 | 北京 | 2011-06-02 | 2011-7-9 16:08:17 | (共0条回复) | 质量好有发票 | 有发票价格也合理 | 暂时还没发现缺点哦! | 有发票价格也合理 | 5 | 62 |
| 975 | 6834080409 | 北京 | 2011-06-02 | 2011-7-9 16:08:04 | (共0条回复) | 质量好有发票 | 有发票价格也合理 | 暂时还没发现缺点哦! | 有发票价格也合理 | 5 | 62 |
| 976 | 2807909902 | 北京 | 2011-06-02 | 2011-7-9 16:07:57 | (共0条回复) | 质量好有发票 | 有发票价格也合理 | 暂时还没发现缺点哦! | 有发票价格也合理 | 5 | 62 |
| 977 | 3747437739 | 北京 | 2011-06-02 | 2011-7-9 16:07:55 | (共0条回复) | 质量好有发票 | 有发票价格也合理 | 暂时还没发现缺点哦! | 有发票价格也合理 | 5 | 62 |
| 978 | 9610581854 | 北京 | 2011-06-02 | 2011-7-9 16:07:48 | (共0条回复) | 质量好有发票 | 有发票价格也合理 | 暂时还没发现缺点哦! | 有发票价格也合理 | 5 | 62 |
| 979 | 8885801018 | 北京 | 2011-06-02 | 2011-7-9 16:07:21 | (共0条回复) | 质量好有发票 | 有发票价格也合理 | 暂时还没发现缺点哦! | 有发票价格也合理 | 5 | 62 |
| 980 | 5858056818 | 北京 | 2011-06-02 | 2011-7-9 16:07:20 | (共0条回复) | 质量好有发票 | 有发票价格也合理 | 暂时还没发现缺点哦! | 有发票价格也合理 | 5 | 62 |
| 981 | 7640032335 | 北京 | 2011-06-02 | 2011-7-9 16:07:02 | (共0条回复) | 质量好有发票 | 有发票价格也合理 | 暂时还没发现缺点哦! | 有发票价格也合理 | 5 | 62 |
| 982 | 5133453506 | 北京 | 2011-06-02 | 2011-7-9 16:07:01 | (共0条回复) | 质量好有发票 | 有发票价格也合理 | 暂时还没发现缺点哦! | 有发票价格也合理 | 5 | 62 |
| 983 | 9623550729 | 北京 | 2011-06-02 | 2011-7-9 16:06:26 | (共0条回复) | 质量好有发票 | 有发票价格也合理 | 暂时还没发现缺点哦! | 有发票价格也合理 | 5 | 62 |
| 985 | 5871695855 | 北京 | 2011-06-02 | 2011-7-9 16:04:20 | (共0条回复) | 质量好有发票 | 有发票价格也合理 | 暂时还没发现缺点哦! | 有发票价格也合理 | 5 | 62 |
| 986 | 5127992214 | 北京 | 2011-06-02 | 2011-7-9 16:04:11 | (共0条回复) | 质量好有发票 | 有发票价格也合理 | 暂时还没发现缺点哦! | 有发票价格也合理 | 5 | 62 |
| 988 | 3787282131 | 北京 | 2011-06-02 | 2011-7-9 16:03:56 | (共0条回复) | 质量好有发票 | 有发票价格也合理 | 暂时还没发现缺点哦! | 有发票价格也合理 | 5 | 62 |
| 989 | 3444375881 | 北京 | 2011-06-02 | 2011-7-9 16:03:53 | (共0条回复) | 质量好有发票 | 有发票价格也合理 | 暂时还没发现缺点哦! | 有发票价格也合理 | 5 | 62 |
| 992 | 4870333686 | 北京 | 2011-06-02 | 2011-7-9 16:01:46 | (共0条回复) | 质量好有发票 | 有发票价格也合理 | 暂时还没发现缺点哦! | 有发票价格也合理 | 5 | 62 |
| 1004 | 5407651563 | 北京 | 2011-06-02 | 2011-7-9 16:00:19 | (共0条回复) | 质量好有发票 | 有发票价格也合理 | 暂时还没发现缺点哦! | 有发票价格也合理 | 5 | 62 |

English:

| Order | ID | Province | Buying Time | Comments Time | Number of Reply | Overall Impress | Advantage | Disadvantage | Experience | Star | Rating |
|---|---|---|---|---|---|---|---|---|---|---|---|
| 959 | 6395798245 | Beijing | 2011-06-02 | 2011-7-9 16:12:38 | 0 | Good Quality with a receipt | The price is reasonable with a receipt | No shortcoming have ever been found | Good Quality with a receipt | 5 | 62 |
| ... | ... | Beijing | 2011-06-02 | 2011-7-9 16:... | 0 | Good Quality with a receipt | The price is reasonable with a receipt | No shortcoming have ever been found | Good Quality with a receipt | 5 | 62 |
| 983 | 9623550729 | Beijing | 2011-06-02 | 2011-7-9 16:06:26 | 0 | Good Quality with a receipt | The price is reasonable with a receipt | No shortcoming have ever been found | Good Quality with a receipt | 5 | 62 |
| 985 | 5871695855 | Beijing | 2011-06-02 | 2011-7-9 16:04:20 | 0 | Good Quality with a receipt | The price is reasonable with a receipt | No shortcoming have ever been found | Good Quality with a receipt | 5 | 62 |
| 986 | 5127992214 | Beijing | 2011-06-02 | 2011-7-9 16:04:11 | 0 | Good Quality with a receipt | The price is reasonable with a receipt | No shortcoming have ever been found | Good Quality with a receipt | 5 | 62 |
| 988 | 3787282131 | Beijing | 2011-06-02 | 2011-7-9 16:03:56 | 0 | Good Quality with a receipt | The price is reasonable with a receipt | No shortcoming have ever been found | Good Quality with a receipt | 5 | 62 |
| 989 | 3444375881 | Beijing | 2011-06-02 | 2011-7-9 16:03:53 | 0 | Good Quality with a receipt | The price is reasonable with a receipt | No shortcoming have ever been found | Good Quality with a receipt | 5 | 62 |
| 992 | 4870333686 | Beijing | 2011-06-02 | 2011-7-9 16:01:46 | 0 | Good Quality with a receipt | The price is reasonable with a receipt | No shortcoming have ever been found | Good Quality with a receipt | 5 | 62 |
| 1004 | 5407651563 | Beijing | 2011-06-02 | 2011-7-9 16:00:19 | 0 | Good Quality with a receipt | The price is reasonable with a receipt | No shortcoming have ever been found | Good Quality with a receipt | 5 | 62 |

**Fig. 5.** Typical Spam Reviews

Chinese:

| 3091 | QQ519397501 | 北京 | 2011-04-26 | 2011-5-12 17:23:17 | (共0条回复) | .......... | .......... | .......... | .......... | 3 | 93 |
|---|---|---|---|---|---|---|---|---|---|---|---|

English:

| 3091 | QQ519397501 | Beijing | 2011-04-26 | 2011-5-12 17:23:17 | 0 | ..... | ..... | ..... | ..... | 5 | 62 |
|---|---|---|---|---|---|---|---|---|---|---|---|

**Fig. 6.** Another type of spam reviews

Figure 6 shows another type of comments that would be judged as a spam review. There are no meaningful words in the comment. This kind of comment is of no reference value, so the system judged it as a spam review.

In addition, there are 145 comments, which is of low relation with the commodity. Table 2 shows the accuracy of Bayesian algorithm in the situation with different selected training sets and threshold. From the present experimental results, the accuracy can be up to 70%. Table 5.2 shows that the experiment results are quite different when choosing different training set and threshold. This is because commodity comment is a type of short text. The frequency of the words is different in real reviews and spam reviews with different training set, and also have a big difference in other process of comments test. So there are some big differences in the result.

**Table 2.** Results of Naive Bayes Classifer

| Comment number in the training dataset | Comment number in the test dataset | Threshold | Accuracy |
|---|---|---|---|
| 100,101,...,499 | 0,1,...,99 | 0 | 53% |
| 0,1,...,399 | 400,401,...,499 | 0 | 36% |
| 0,2,...,498,499 | 1,6,11,...,496 | 0 | 47% |
| 0,1,...498,499 | 2,7,12,...,497 | 0 | 42% |
| 0,1,...497,499 | 3,8,13,...,498 | 0 | 51% |
| 0,1,...497,498 | 4,9,14,...,499 | 0 | 57% |
| 1,2,...,498,499 | 0,5,10,...,495 | 0 | 53% |
| 0,2,...,498,499 | 1,6,11,...,496 | -0.01 | 66% |
| 0,1,...,498,499 | 2,7,12,...,497 | -0.01 | 54% |
| 0,1,...,497,499 | 3,8,13,...,498 | -0.01 | 57% |
| 0,1,...,497,498 | 4,9,14,...,499 | -0.01 | 70% |
| 1,2,...,498,499 | 0,5,10,...,495 | -0.01 | 70% |

# 5    Conclusions

This paper designs and implements the key process of Chinese spam reviews detection system, including vector space model, TF-IDF algorithm and Bayesian algorithm. A detailed description of the design and ideas of every rule was described. And our system test some comments to carried out subsequently. Content of commodity comment are short text, and vector space model is used. It is based on the rules system, the existing framework. It is representative for the existing review spam and the spam reviews detection of single commodity.

As the algorithms in our paper are based on rules, and the regulations are limited, our system exist some problems. For example, in the choice of keywords without processing stop-word, it might have a certain extent effect on the result. Because the system does not further process the Chinese word segmentation results, the similarity of words is not considered, which might ignore some of review spam. We would further do our research this problem in the future.

**Acknowledgments.** This work was under Grand by the Natural Science Foundation of China (No. 61003176, 61202441, 71101014, 71211140349), the Talent Science Research Start-up Foundation of Dalian University of Technology (No.1600-852018).

# References

1. China Internet Network Information Center. 2009 annual report of China online shopping market, 38–42 (2009)
2. Lim, E.-P., Nguyen, V.-A., Jindal, N., Liu, B., Lauw, H.W.: Detecting product review spammers using rating behaviors. In: Proceeding CIKM 2010 Proceedings of the 19th ACM International Conference on Information and Knowledge Management, pp. 939–948 (2010)
3. Wu, G., Greene, D., Smyth, B., Cunningham, P.: Distortion as a validation criterion in the identification of suspicious reviews. Technical Report UCD-CSI-2010-04, University College Dublin (2010)
4. Jindal, N., Liu, B., Lim, E.: Finding Unusual Review Patterns Using Unexpected Rules. In: CIKM 2010: 19th ACM International Conference on Information and Knowledge Management, Toronto, Ontario (2010)
5. Li, F., Liu, N., Jin, H., Zhao, K., Yang, Q., Zhu, X.: Incorporate Reviewer and Product Information for Review Rating Prediction. In: Proceedings of the Twenty-Second International Joint Conference on Artificial Intelligence, IJCAI 2011 (2011)
6. Wang, G., Xie, S., Liu, B., Yu, P.S.: Identify Online Store Review Spammers via Social Review Graph. Journal of ACM Transactions on Intelligent Systems and Technology (TIST) 3(4) (September 2012)
7. Xia, H., Liu, J.: Credibility Analysis of Comments of Virtual Community Based on Text Similarity Computing. Journal of Modern Information 31(9), 33–37 (2011)
8. Yang, F., Li, J.: Survey on research of opinion spam in user-generated-content. Application Research of Computers 28(10), 3601–3605 (2011)
9. ICTCLAS, http://ictclas.org/
10. Shi, C., Xu, C., Yang, X.: Study of TFIDF algorithm. Journal of Computer Application 29(6), 167–180 (2009)

# Usage-Based Automatic Recognition of Grammar Errors of Conjunctions in Teaching Chinese as a Second Language

Yingjie Han[1], Aiying Lin[2], Yonggang Wu[1], and Hongying Zan[1]

[1] College of Information Engineering, Zhengzhou University,
Zhengzhou, Henan 450001, China
{ieyjhan,iehyzan}@zzu.edu.cn, wygchina@sina.com
[2] College of Science, Agricultural University of Henan, Zhengzhou, Henan 450002, China
linay_2000@163.com

**Abstract.** Foreign students learning Chinese grammar make errors for many reasons, among which the inappropriate use of functional words maintains a great proportion. Methods for the automatic recognition of the errors are limited. We start with the conjunctions in Chinese functional words knowledge base, analyze and summarize the appropriate usage and problematic usage of conjunctions, and propose a usage-based method to detect the grammar errors which are caused by inappropriate use of conjunctions. The results based on HSK prove that the method is simple and effective. It will be of great help in teaching Chinese as a second language.

**Keywords:** Usage, Rule, Grammar Error, Automatic Recognition.

## 1 Introduction

Grammar errors are often made by foreigners who study Chinese, the reasons for which include positive transition and negative transition of their mother language. Many scholars focus on grammar errors in teaching Chinese as a second language. Human-oriented solutions have been studied a lot, but automatic solutions are few.

Li et al. [1-3] point out that about half of grammar errors can be related to inappropriate use of functional words. Functional words are specific parts in modern Chinese which are used frequently with flexible usage but have no meaning. They are a hard part for foreigners to learn. The triune contemporary functional knowledge base (CFKB) has been built, which includes usage base, rule base, and corpus of functional words [4-6]. It provides the basis for automatic recognition of usage of functional words and automatic comprehension of semantics. The deep-going application of CFKB has been conducted. Han et al. [7] discussed the automatic recognition of part-of-speech and segmentation errors based on the automatic annotation of auxiliary words. In this paper, the author conducted usage-based automatic recognition of grammar errors based on usage rule base of conjunctions. Conjunctions are chosen as the research object for the reason that they have relational words such as conjunctions and adverbs which can be beneficial to automatic recognition of overrepresentation and omission of conjunctions.

P. Liu and Q. Su (Eds.): CLSW 2013, LNAI 8229, pp. 519–528, 2013.

## 2     Related Works

Li [1] compared the functional words which have similar meaning, and show their difference in order to use them more appropriately. Li [2] compared 30 grammar items, provided the examples, and then proposed a targeting teaching strategy. Jin [3] compared the synonym, investigated their usage rules, and found the condition of their usage on syntax. Lu [8] classified grammar errors as the following four classes such as addition, overrepresentation, omission and disorder. Wang [9] discussed the practicability of automatic recognition of grammar errors and pointed out that some grammar errors can be automatically recognized by computers.

## 3     Usage-Based Automatic Recognition of Grammar Errors of Conjunctions

HSK dynamic composition corpus [10] is the answer sheet of foreigners who attended the modern Chinese proficiency examination. The errors they made are classified into characters, words, sentences, sectors, chapters and punctuation. They are annotated and corrected by manual works. The specific remarks are shown in Zhang [11]. According to 322 conjunctions in CFKB, there are 6423 sentences which contain grammar errors extracted from HSK. Some of the conjunctions have other parts of speech at the same time. For example, 和[he](and) can be a conjunction, or a preposition. After screening inspection, there are 2952 sentences which contain grammar errors of conjunctions left. Table 1 shows the top ten conjunctions where grammar errors most probably occur.

**Table 1.** The type and distribution of grammar errors of Conjunctions in HSK (top 10)

| word in Chinese | word | Total Errors (piece) | Addition (piece) | Overrepresentation (piece) | Omis-sion(piece) |
|---|---|---|---|---|---|
| 而[er] | but | 634 | 251 | 289 | 94 |
| 和[he] | and | 403 | 92 | 115 | 196 |
| 而且[erqie] | but also | 305 | 29 | 261 | 15 |
| 以[yi] | according to | 239 | 49 | 126 | 64 |
| 因为 [yinwei] | because | 233 | 48 | 85 | 100 |
| 与[yu] | and | 125 | 23 | 40 | 62 |
| 如果[ruguo] | if | 114 | 37 | 36 | 41 |
| 因[yin] | due to | 121 | 20 | 18 | 83 |
| 但[dan] | but | 100 | 45 | 14 | 41 |
| 所以[suoyi] | so | 96 | 37 | 19 | 40 |

Taking the corpus of the People Daily of Jan.1998 and Jan.2000 to Jun.2000 into consideration, the top 20 frequently used conjunctions and their occurrence frequency are shown in Table 2. '-' denotes that the Chinese word has no corresponding word in English.

**Table 2.** Frequently-used conjunctions and their occurrence frequency (top 20)

| word in Chinese | word | Frequency (per month) | word in Chinese | word | Frequency (per month) |
|---|---|---|---|---|---|
| 和[he] | and | 12818 | 如果[ruguo] | if | 402 |
| 而[er] | but | 1682 | 而且[erqie] | but also | 376 |
| 并[bing] | and | 1560 | 既[ji] | as | 369 |
| 与[yu] | and | 1374 | 则[ze] | - | 354 |
| 但[dan] | but | 1344 | 因此[yinci] | so | 342 |
| 及[ji] | and | 760 | 以[yi] | according to | 300 |
| 或[huo] | or | 682 | 但是[danshi] | but | 278 |
| 以及[yiji] | and | 537 | 因为[yinwei] | because | 269 |
| 同时[tongshi] | meanwhile | 460 | 虽然[suiran] | although | 210 |
| 不仅[bujin] | not only | 412 | 只有[zhiyou] | only | 200 |

Table 1 shows conjunctions that foreigners often make mistakes on. Table 2 shows the most frequently used conjunctions. With the two tables taken into consideration, 而 [er](*but*), 而且 [erqie](*but also*), 和 [he](*and*), 如果 [ruguo](*if*), 因为 [yinwei](*because*) and 与[yu](*and*) are chosen to be intensively studied.

Usage-based automatic recognition on grammar errors of conjunctions in teaching Chinese as a second language follows the steps bellow.

Step1. Process HSK composition corpus, following automatically tagging, words part-of-speech and segmentation according to Yu [12], and the errors are corrected to eliminate their influence on automatic recognition on grammar errors.

Step2. Manually annotate and proof usage of conjunctions of processed HSK corpus according to usage rule bases, then human-proofed corpus can be acquired.

Step3. Automatically annotate usage of conjunctions of processed HSK corpus according to usage rule base by computer. After annotating, automatic annotated corpus can be acquired.

Step4. Compare the automatic annotated corpus and human-proofed corpus, the precision and the recall of automatic recognition can be achieved.

Step5. Analyze and evaluate the results, fraction of coverage and mutual exclusion rate of rules are taken into consideration. Rules are refined and extended. The order of rules is adjusted to enhance the ability of automatic recognition on grammar errors of conjunctions.

Step6. Repeat step 3, 4 and 5, the best results of automatic recognition of grammar errors are chosen.

The precision can be computed as formula (1): F denotes the amount of sentences recognized by the usage rules. F+ denotes the amount of the sentences which are recognized correctly.

$$\mathrm{Pr}\,ecision = \frac{F^+}{F} \tag{1}$$

The recall can be computed as formula (2): S denotes the amount of sentences in which grammar errors exist. F+ denotes the amount of the sentences which are recognized correctly.

$$\mathrm{Re}\,call = \frac{F^+}{S} \tag{2}$$

### 3.1 Appropriate Usage-Based Automatic Recognition on Grammar Errors of conjunctions

The rules of conjunction usage in CFKB list formalize description of appropriate usage of every conjunction, which are regular expressions. For example, the rules of appropriate usage of 和[*he*](*and*) are shown as bellow.

$和
@<c_he2_1a>→M ^M→、 #{、 }
@<c_he2_1c>→B~B ^B→<v_d>|<a_d>
@<c_he2_1b>→(、 |与|同|及|以及)B~B(、 |与|同|及|以及) ^B→n|r
@<c_he2_1b>→M|N ^M→~*(、 |与|同|及|以及) ^N→(、 |与|同|及|以及)*~
@<c_he2_2>→A~不A ^A→a|v
@<c_he2_2>→M ^M→不论|不管|无论

These rules provide a useful way to automatically recognize the grammar errors on conjunction 和[*he*](*and*). If the usage of 和[*he*](*and*) in a sentence can't be recognized by the appropriate usage rules, it means a grammar error occurred. According to this, for the six conjunctions which are chosen, the precision and the recall of automatic recognition on grammar errors are shown in Table 3.

**Table 3.** Results of appropriate usage-based automatic recognition of grammar errors of conjunctions

| word in Chinese | word | Addition | | Overrepresentation | | Omission | |
|---|---|---|---|---|---|---|---|
| | | Precision (%) | Recall (%) | Precision (%) | Recall (%) | Precision (%) | Recall (%) |
| 而[er] | but | 0 | 0 | 100 | 0.99 | - | - |
| 而且 [erqie] | but also | 83.33 | 16.13 | 100 | 20.29 | - | - |
| 和[he] | and | 100 | 25.00 | 100 | 17.86 | - | - |
| 如果 [ruguo] | if | 0 | 0 | 0 | 0 | - | - |
| 因为 [yinwei] | because | 100 | 17.02 | 100 | 12.20 | - | - |
| 与[yu] | and | 0 | 0 | 0 | 0 | - | - |

The results show that grammar errors can be recognized automatically by appropriate usage of conjunctions to some extent and the precision is high, such as 而且[erqie](*but also*), 和[he](*and*) and 因为[yinwei](*because*). This informs that the appropriate usage rules have strong ability on recognition of grammar errors. If the conjunction in the sentence can't be recognized by the appropriate usage rules, then there are grammar errors about the conjunction in the sentence. With this method, we can examine the grammar errors of functional words. But we can also see from Table 3 that not only the precision of 而[er](*but*), 如果[ruguo](*if*), and 与[yu](*and*) but also the recall of all the conjunctions is very low. The reason is that appropriate usage rules lay much emphasis on appropriate usage of conjunctions but not on the problematic forms. For omission, it can't be automatically recognized by the appropriate usage rules of conjunctions which presented by '-'. The reason is that in order to recognize the grammar errors of conjunctions, the conjunctions must exist in the sentence.

### 3.2 Problematic Usage-Based Automatic Recognition of Grammar Errors of conjunctions

The capacity of appropriate usage is limited, for they are used for recognizing appropriate usage but not for recognizing problematic usage of conjunctions. In order to improve the capacity of recognition, we summarize and extract inappropriate usage rules of typical grammar errors of conjunctions according to reference [1-3, 8, 10] to extend rule base. For example, the rules of problematic usage of 和[he](*and*) are shown as bellow.

$和

(1) @<c_he2_e>→F ^F→~
(2) @<c_he2_e>→E ^E→~
(3) @<c_he2_e>→LR ^L→v ^R→{d}v
(4) @<c_he2_e>→L|R ^L→p|d|a|c|, |、|。|？|！ ^R→, |。|、|？|！
(5) @<c_he2_e>→M ^M→《*!()》)
(6) @<c_he2_e>→MLR ^M→(n|r)*v*(n|r) ^L→(n|r) ^R→(n|r)*v*n

Rule (1) indicates that 和[he](and) is used at the head of the sentence. Rule (2) indicates that 和[he](and) is used at the end of the sentence. Rule (3) indicates that 和[a](and) is used to connect verb. Rule (4) indicates that either 和[he](and) is used next to a preposition, a adverb, a adjective, a conjunction, ' , ', ' 、 ', ' 。 ', ' ? ', ' ! ' or ' , ', ' 、 ', ' 。 ', ' ? ', ' ! ' is used next to 和[he](and). Rule (5) indicates that 和[he](and) is used in embrace or in title. Rule (6) indicates that 和[he](and) is used to connect simple sentence.

**Table 4.** Results of problematic form usage-based automatic recognition of grammar errors of conjunctions

| word in Chinese | word | Addition | | Overrepresentation | | Omission | |
|---|---|---|---|---|---|---|---|
| | | Precision (%) | Recall (%) | Precision (%) | Recall (%) | Precision (%) | Recall (%) |
| 而[er] | but | 100 | 6.72 | 100 | 22.44 | - | - |
| 而且 [erqie] | but also | 90.00 | 29.03 | 96.00 | 34.78 | 77.78 | 46.67 |
| 和[he] | and | 91.67 | 60.44 | 98.31 | 56.86 | - | - |
| 如果 [ruguo] | if | 100 | 13.89 | 100 | 7.14 | 43.10 | 63.97 |
| 因为 [yinwei] | because | 83.33 | 31.91 | 100 | 20.00 | 44.44 | 8.00 |
| 与[yu] | and | 94.12 | 69.57 | 100 | 45.45 | - | - |

### 3.2.1 Problematic Usage-Based Automatic Recognition on Addition

Addition refers to the situation in which in some grammar forms, an ingredient must be used, but when grammar forms are changed, the ingredient is forbidden to use. Foreigners who just began to learn Chinese didn't understand the condition of the change [8]. Some examples in HSK are shown as bellow.

(1) 你们两位自己小心{CD 和[he](and)}照顾吧。
   *You two have to take care of {CD and} yourselves.*
(2) 换言之，父母要先放下对新潮流的主观{CD 与[yu](and)}成见，先进入孩子的世界去感受他们所发經驗的。

*In other words, parents should put down the subjective {CD and} prejudice, and go into children's world and feel them.*

{CD} indicates addition, followed by additional words. The precision and the recall of addition are shown in Table 4.

From Table 4 we can draw out that after extending the rule base and adding rules of problematic usage of conjunctions, the precision and the recall are improved to a great extent. Sentence (1) and (2) are the correctly recognized ones. 和[*he*](*and*) can be used to connect nouns and pronouns, and indicates the coordinative relation. The problematic usage of和[*he*](*and*) in sentence (1) can be detected by using rule (3) @<c_he2_e>→LR ^L→v ^R→{d}v. Similarly, 与[*yu*](*and*) can be used to connect nouns and pronouns, and indicates the coordinative relation. The problematic usage of 与[*yu*](*and*) in sentence (2) can be detected by the rule @<c_yu3_e>→LR ^L→a ^R→n. But to other words such as 如果[*ruguo*](*if*) and 而[*er*](*but*), the results are not so good. These words have very flexible usage, and have no difference between appropriate usage and problematic usage. Moreover, it is hard to formulate its problematic usage. Sentence (3) and (4) are the examples which can't be recognized correctly. 而[*er*](*but*) can be used to connect a verb, its usage in sentence (3) is right, so the addition can't be recognized only by usage. 如果[*ruguo*](*if*) can be used with or without related words, so the addition in sentence (4) can't be recognized.

(3) 她也常常和我谈话，{CD 而[*er*](*but*)}告诉我为什么爸爸生气了。

*She often talk to me, {CD but} telling me why my dad was angry.*

(4) 父母不放心{CD 如果[*ruguo*](*if*)}我一个人去留学。

*My parents worry about that {CD if} I study abroad by myself.*

### 3.2.2   Problematic Usage-Based Automatic Recognition on Overrepresentation

Overrepresentation is caused by choosing the inappropriate one from the two or more description [8]. Examples of HSK composition base are shown as bellow:

(5) 我也希望有关的人员来{CC 和[*he*](*and*)}我公司工作，工钱一定是很好的

*I hope someone will work for {CC and} my company, the job is well-paid.*

(6) 他用他的做法提醒我努力学习、并且{CC 而且[*erqie*](*but also*)}使我丰富地了解社会。

*He reminded me of hard studying by his own behavior, and {CC but also} made me understanding the society.*

{CC} denotes overrepresentation, followed by the overrepresented words. The correct word which manually added is before '{ }'.

Table 4 shows that the precision and the recall are improved to some extent after extending the rule base of conjunctions. Sentence (5) and (6) are the examples that can be recognized correctly. But the results of some words such as 如果[*ruguo*](*if*) and 因为[*yinwei*](*because*) are not so good. Sentence (7) and (8) are the examples which can't be recognized correctly. They are all about errors at semantic level, and can't be recognized by usage rules.

(7) 有些是通过{CC 因为[*yinwei*](*because*)}亲戚朋友介绍，有些却是偶然相遇才認識的。

*Some of them are introduced by {CC because} their relatives, but others are casually encountered.*

(8) 因为{CC 如果[*ruguo*](*if*)}我在这儿刚刚得了胃病，所以不能随便吃东西。

*Because {CC if} I have got stomach trouble here, I should not eat food casually.*

### 3.2.3    Problematic Usage-Based Automatic Recognition on Omission

Omission refers to errors in which words or ingredients are missed in sentence [8]. Examples of HSK composition base are shown as bellow:

(9) 抽烟不仅是对自己的身体有不好的影响，{CQ 而且[*erqie*](*but also*)}会伤害别人的健康。

*Smoking is a bad habit, it will not only do harm to our own body {CQ but also} hurt others' health.*

(10) 面对挫折时，{CQ 如果[*ruguo*](*if*)}我没有想到好机会，只想自己的苦境，那么现在的我到底怎样生活呢。

*I haven't thought out a good idea to face the frustration. {CQ if} I only care for my own suffering, and how can I lead a life now.*

{CQ} denote omission, followed by the missing word.

From Table 4 we can see that 而[*er*](*but*) ,和[*he*](*and*) and 与[*yu*](*and*) have no related words. The omission of them can't be recognized, and the results are shown in '-'. Those words which can be associated with other words, such as 而且[*erqie*](*but also*), 如果[*ruguo*](*if*)  and 因为[*yinwei*](*because*) can be recognized by rules of their related words. Sentence (9) and (10) are examples which can be recognized correctly. But sometimes 而且 [*erqie*](*but also*), 如果 [*ruguo*](*if*) and 因为 [*yinwei*](*because*) can be used alone without connecting with any related words, so it is hard to detect the missing words. Sentence (11) and (12) are examples which can't be recognized correctly.

(11) 虽然我们现代人的生活很紧张[BQ, ]但{CQ 如果[*ruguo*](*if*)}我们尽量试试谈话，这个代沟的问题能解决。

*Although modern life is stressful [BQ,] but {CQ if} we try to talk to each other, the problem of generation gap can be solved.*

(12) 这次我到北京大学学习，正是{CQ 因为[*yinwei*](*because*)}她的坚定支持。

*This time can I come to study in Peking university is {CQ because} of her support.*

## 4    Conclusions

Usage rules of conjunctions can be a simple, practicable and effective way on automatic recognition of grammar errors of conjunctions. It doesn't need training samples or much cost. But it is hard to detect the error types. For example when the rules of 和[*he*](*and*) are used to detect a single error type, its precision is 98.31% at most, and the recall is 60.44% at most. But when they are used to detect different error types, the micro average precision is 50.44% and the micro average recall is 32.39%. The reason is that it is hard to write the rules for the recognition of distinct error types. It needs to be pointed out is that some factors in the corpus can also influence the results.

(1) Some of the sentences in which conjunction grammar errors occurred include many other error types are hard for automatic recognition. Sentence (13) is an example.

(2) Some of the grammar errors not only appear at the grammar level, but also at the semantic level. It is hard for the usage-based method to detect semantic errors; sentence (14) is an example.

(13) 凡事都要有计划，经过一番的冷静思考后再{CC才}去实行，从小她就强调这点；[BC, ]如果遇到什么{CC任何}困难，要随机应变地{CC的}去处理，找出事情的失败[F败]{CQ原因}再{CC而}加以纠正；[BC, ]最重要{CQ的}还要不灰心去做{CJs}，直到成功为止。

*It needs a plan with which everything goes well, it should be carried out after {CC until} calm thought, and that's what she emphasized all the time; [BC,] if you are faced with any difficulty, be flexible, when the {CQ reason} of failure is found out, then {CC but} correct it; [BC,] the most important {CQ thing} is to do it insistently {CJs}, and wait for success.*

(14) 随着生活水平的不断提高，贫者对{CC 和[he](and)}富者的反感越来越深，盗案也越来越多！

*With the improvement of living standards, the poorer have increasingly hate on {CC and} the richer. The thefts happen frequently.*

At last, one error type mentioned by Lu [8] is disorder, which means the order of some ingredients in the sentence is wrong. By now, it can't be recognized automatically only by using usage rules of functional words. We need other knowledge base to support the recognition.

## 5    Future Works

The usage of functional words can be helpful to natural language understanding, machine learning, parsing, and information retrieval etc. The next steps are to

(1) Mine the application of CFKB in teaching Chinese as a second language and promote its quality and value.
(2) Move on to automatic recognition of other type of error and improve its indexes.
(3) Automatically provide error types, causes, correcting advice and revision suggestion based on recognition results.
(4) Find users for CFKB, combine the theory and practice, and extend the application field of CFKB.

**Acknowledgements.** This work is supported by a grant from the Natural Science Foundation of China (No.60970083, No.61272221), 863 projects of National High Technology Research and Development (No.2012AA011101), the Science and

Technology Research Project of the Education Department of Henan Province (No.13B520381, NO.12B520055), and the Open Projects Program of National Laboratory of Pattern Recognition.

# References

1. Li, X.Q.: Teaching materials of Modern Chinese functional words. Peking University Press, Beijing (2005) (in Chinese)
2. Li, D.Z.: The analysis of errors in foreigners learning Chinese. Beijing language and culture. University Press, Beijing (2007) (in Chinese)
3. Jin, L.X.: The analysis of functional words in teaching Chinese as a secondary language. Peking University Press, Beijing (2006) (in Chinese)
4. Zan, H.Y., Zhang, K.L., Chai, Y.M., Yu, S.W.: Studies on the Functional Word Knowledge Base of Modern Chinese. Journal of Chinese Information Processing 21(5), 107–111 (2007) (in Chinese)
5. Zan, H.Y., Zhang, K.L., Zhu, X.F., Yu, S.W.: Research on the Chinese Function Word Usage Knowledge Base. International Journal on Asian Language Processing 21(4), 185–198 (2011)
6. Zan, H.Y., Zhou, L.J., Zhang, K.L.: Studies on the Automatic Recognition of Modern Chinese Conjunction Usages. In: Huang, D.-S., Gan, Y., Bevilacqua, V., Figueroa, J.C. (eds.) ICIC 2011. LNCS, vol. 6838, pp. 472–479. Springer, Heidelberg (2011)
7. Han, Y.J., Zhang, K.L., Zan, H.Y., Chai, Y.M.: The Automatic Discovery on Auxiliary Word Usage-Based Part-of-Speech and Segmentation Errors for Chinese Language. Application research of computers 28(4), 1318–1321 (2011) (in Chinese)
8. Lu, J.J.: The analysis of grammar errors in foreigners learning Chinese. Language Teaching and Linguistic Studies (1), 49–64 (1994) (in Chinese)
9. Wang, J.: Feasibility Analysis of Computer Aided Chinese Grammar Error Identification. Applied linguistics (1), 135–142 (2011) (in Chinese)
10. HSK dynamic composition corpus base (in Chinese), http://202.112.195.192:8060/hsk/index.asp
11. Zhang, B.L.: The annotation instruction of HSK dynamic composition corpus base (in Chinese), http://202.112.195.192/hsk/help2.asp
12. Yu, S.W., Duan, H.M., Zhu, X.F., et al.: The processing standard on part of speech, Segmentation and spelling of corpus of Beijing University. Journal of Chinese and Computing 13(2), 121–158 (2003) (in Chinese)

# Comparison and Optimization of Microblogging Segmentation Methods

Huanqing Lou[1], Qi Su[2], and Jinsong Huang[1]

[1] Key Laboratory of Computational Linguistics,
Ministry of Education Institute of Computational Linguistics,
School of Electronics Engineering and Computer Science, Peking University, Beijing, China
[2] School of Foreign Languages, Peking University, Beijing, China
{lhq,sukia,hjs}@pku.edu.cn

**Abstract.** Nowadays microblog has become a big source of information, and an important spreading channel as well. Owing to its unique characteristics, it is not effective to do valuable segmentation with exist-ing tools. By comparing the results of four mainstream segmentation tools on microblog corpus, this article analyzes that how segmentation tools with differ-ent characteristics influenced the seg-mentation results, and furthermore summed up the weakness of existing segmentation tools. Finally, the author proposed a "microword" centered seg-mentation method based on CRFs, which offers a new method of resolving segmentation problem in microblog.

**Keywords:** Chinese word segmentation, microblog, segmentation algorithm, microword.

## 1    Introduction

From Directory Portal Site to Full-Text Search Engine, and now to SNS, the presenta-tion form of information on the net keeps changing constantly. Microblogging, as a new access to network socializing, is now sweeping the world. Only during the first half of 2011, the number of Chinese microblog users experienced a rapid increase from 63,310,000 to 195,000,000, an increase of up to 208.9%. By the end of June 2012, this number has reached 274 million, which means more than half of all Chi-nese Internet users are microblogging[1]. Constantly updated and widely spread, micro-blog is now playing an increasingly important role in information production and dissemination. In addition, the semi-real-name system makes the content more valua-ble. On the other hand, the length-limited rule, user groups, and writing style has spawned a lot of cyber words and self-making words, such as the recently more popu-lar "航母Style", "十动然拒" and so on. Challenges, therefore, have been brought in improving both the accuracy and the efficiency of the new terms identification. Organized by the Institute of Computational Linguistics, Peking University, CIPS-SIGHAN-2012 Chinese Word Segmentation Evaluation has focused on the

---

[1] Data from CNNIC issued "The 28th China Internet network development report".

P. Liu and Q. Su (Eds.): CLSW 2013, LNAI 8229, pp. 529–537, 2013.

investigation of adaptation capabilities of traditional segmentation algorithms for Microblogging text. Academically or practically speaking, the study of microblogging segmentation is now necessary and urgent.

Traditional Chinese word segmentation algorithms can be broadly classified into two categories. One is lexicon based method. The idea is "segmentation". This method includes maximum-matching segmentation and statistical segmentation [1] (Huang and Zhao, 2007). The other is character tagging method [2] (Xue, 2003). The idea is "word-building". By transfer the segmentation problems into sequence labeling problems, it then uses machine learning algorithms to solve them. Nowadays, some segmentation system in plain text has already reached an F value of 97% [3] (Che, 2010), but the performance on microblogging corpus is not satisfying. As microblogging corpus has characteristics such as colloquial and semi-structure, existing dictionaries and training libraries are difficult to meet the requirements to make fine results. So the use of semi-supervised machine learning methods [4] (Sun and Xu, 2011) has become a good choice, which also brings us effective results. Moreover, there exists a number of micro-Bo semi-structured text (such as @, #, URL and emoticon symbols, etc.).If we could make good use of them, not only can we reduce interference, but also identify the emotional coloring of corpus [5] (Yuan and Purver, 2012).

## 2    Microblog and Microword

Microblog is a compound word consisting of "micro" and "blog". It is a broadcast social net-work platform for sharing short messages through poster-follower mechanism. "Micro" means the content is short, and "blog" shows its social attributes. Content-length limit is the fundamental difference between microblog and traditional blog. Most microblog sites limit the content-length to 140 characters. It's difficult for users to publish well-organized content in such a short paragraph, therefore microblog content is usually a sentence with one or two keywords. On the other hand, people microblog anytime and anywhere. They usually post with-out a second check, so a large part of microblog corpus has a strong colloquial feature: words are chosen arbitrarily, and a lot of cyber words as well as made-up words come out. The other feature of microblog corpus is semi-structure. In order to achieve social interaction purpose, microblog site defined some specific symbols. For example, "@username" is used to push the article to target user as through notification, and "#topic#" is used to add this microblog post to a topic forum consisting of other posts with the same symbol. Although these elements are not linguistic units in conventional sense, they serve as a whole to express a specific meaning. It is widely acknowledged that semantic units in microblog play a very important role, and its concept shall expand from the narrow definition in linguistics to a microblog-specific term, "microword."

In this article, the microword is defined as a sequence of characters in a microblog which can express specific meaning as a whole, such as the username (including author, users mentioned in content, etc.), topic, and hot words and so on. They became non-linguistic words because of some rules set in microblog, but also bear specific semantics, so we can treat them as broader lexes.

# 3    Comparison of Microblog Segmentation Results from Existing Tools

Chinese word segmentation has always been a fundamental subject in Chinese information processing, and there are many related re-searches. Segmentation algorithms mentioned in the citation have already achieved fine results in experiments. However, in practice the segmentation with single algorithm is not ideal, therefore most of the existing segmentation tools take good advantage of complementarity of these algorithms, coupled with optimization of details, so as to achieve a more satisfactory result.

Segmentation tools varied. Some are heavy-weight, powerful dedicated segmentation libraries, and the others are lightweight segmentation components relying on other projects. This article selects four widely-used and constant-updated segmentation tools, namely ICTCLAS segmentation system[2], IKAnalyzer[3], Pangu segmentation system[4] and SCWS segmentation system[5], and uses them on "NLPIR microblog corpus"[6]. The following table shows their features

**Table 1.** Segmentation Tools and Their Features

| Tools | Features |
|-------|----------|
| ICTCLAS | Using a Hierarchical Hidden Markov Model and N-shortest path algorithm, and unifying all aspects of Chinese lexical analysis into one complete theoretical framework. |
| IKAnalyzer | Using a unique "forward iteration most granular segmentation algorithm", supporting simple ambiguity handling and combining output of quantifiers in multi-processor mode. |
| Pangu | Lightweight segmentation tool, using a combination of dictionary-based and statistics-based segmentation algorithms, having multivariate segmentation features and good recognition of unknown words. |
| SCWS | A machinery Chinese word segmentation engine based on word frequency dictionary, meeting the basic rules of word recognition according to the pre-acquisition of word frequency dictionary, supplemented by certain proper nouns (e.g., names, places, numbers, years, etc.). |

---

[2] Project home: http://www.ictclas.org
[3] Project home: http://code.google.com/p/ik-analyzer/
[4] Project home: http://pangusegment.codeplex.com/
[5] Project home: http://www.xunsearch.com/scws/
[6] By Dr. ZHANG Huaping from Beijing Institute of Technology, including 230 thousand microblog corpus consist of content, author, time, etc.

According to the diction, this article divides microblog corpus into three categories: colloquial, literary and semi-structured. Colloquial corpuses are close to the spoken language with more casual words. Literary corpuses are short articles (such as news, proverbs, etc.). Semi-structured corpuses use some microblog-reserved characters to express certain structured meaning. The table below shows some examples of these categories:

**Table 2.** Categories of Microblog Corpus

| Categories | Examples |
|---|---|
| colloquial | 工资未涨，房租先行。这下给我涨了30%。我了个去啊。明年交房以后，就是卖血也得装好住进去，再也不受这份气了 |
| literary | 央行数据显示，2009年全国使用非现金支付工具办理支付业务约214.3亿笔，金额716万亿元，同比分别增长16.9%和13.1%。其中，银行卡业务197亿笔 |
| semi-structured | #暗黑3#暴雪大神延续跳票的传统@我爱大菠萝 |

We select 100 microblog posts from the "NLPIR microblog corpus library"(50 colloquial, 20 literary, 30 semi-structured) and manually segment them into a test set, then we use the latest version of the tools mentioned above to carry out segmentation on the test set and com-pare the results:

**Table 3.** Segmentation Tools Performance on Test Set

| Tools | ICTCLAS | IKAnalyzer | Pangu | SCWS |
|---|---|---|---|---|
| $P_{col}$ | 0.7375 | 0.8663 | 0.8026 | 0.8427 |
| $R_{col}$ | 0.7261 | 0.8322 | 0.781 | 0.8354 |
| $F_{col}$ | 0.7318 | 0.8489 | 0.7917 | 0.839 |
| $P_{lit}$ | 0.8854 | 0.8021 | 0.9136 | 0.932 |
| $R_{lit}$ | 0.8641 | 0.7881 | 0.9023 | 0.9282 |
| $F_{lit}$ | 0.8746 | 0.795 | 0.9079 | 0.9301 |
| $P_{ss}$ | 0.5021 | 0.6366 | 0.5712 | 0.6123 |
| $R_{ss}$ | 0.4874 | 0.6233 | 0.5641 | 0.602 |
| $F_{ss}$ | 0.4946 | 0.6299 | 0.5676 | 0.6071 |

We can see each tool has an adept area. The difference of their performances on each type is very significant. Overall, the literary type, which is most similar to traditional blog content, obtains the best segmentation re-sults. The semi-structured type's recognition rate is rela-tively low, since no pretreatment is performed to the corpus. In terms of individual tool, SCWS has the best overall performance, and then IKAnalyzer follows. The other two tools do well on literary corpus, but not so satisfactory on the other two types corpus with more microblog characteristics.

In order to show an intuitive result, the authors list the segmentation results of different tools and identify the difference in bold to make it obvious (IKAnalyzer ignores all punctuation symbols):

**Table 4.** Segmentation Results on Colloquial Corpus

| Tools | Results |
|---|---|
| ICTCLAS | 工资/未/**涨**/，/房租/先行/。/这/**下**/给/我/涨/了/30%/。/我/了/个/去/**啊**/。/明年/交/**房**/以后/，/**就**/是/卖/血/也/得/装/好/住/进去/，/再/也/不/受/这/**份**/气/了 |
| IKAnalyzer | 工资/**未涨**/房租/先行/**这下**/**给我**/**涨了**/**30**/我/了/个/去/**啊**/明年/**交房**/以后/**就是**/**卖**/**血**/也/**得**/**装好**/住/**进去**/**再也**/**不受**/**这份**/**气了** |
| Pangu | 工资/未/**涨**/，/房租/先行/。/这/**下**/给/我/涨/了/30/**%**/。/我/了/个去啊/。/明年/交/**房**/以后/，/**就是**/卖血也/**得**/装/**好**/住/进/去/，/**再也**/不受/这份气/了 |
| SCWS | 工资/未涨/，/房租/先行/。/**这下**/给/我/**涨了**/30/%/。/**我了**/个/去/**啊**/。/明年/交/**房**/以后/，/**就是**/**卖**/**血**/也/**得**/装好/住/进去/，/**再也**/不受/这份/气了 |

**Table 5.** Segmentation Results on Literary Corpus

| Tools | Results |
|---|---|
| ICTCLAS | 央行/数据/显示/，/2009年/全国/使用/**非现金**/支付/工具/办理/支付/业务/约/214.3亿/笔/，/金额/716/万/亿/元/，/同比/分别/增长/16.9%/和/13.1%/。/其中/，/**银行**/**卡业务**/197亿/笔 |
| IKAnalyzer | 央行/数据/显示/2009年/全国/使用/**非**/**现金支付**/工具/办理/支付/业务/约/214.3**亿笔**/金额/716/万/亿元/同比/分别/增长/16.9/和/13.1/其中/**银行卡**/业务/197亿笔 |
| Pangu | 央行/数据/显示/，/2009/年/全国/使用/**非**/**现金**/支付/工具/办理/支付/业务/约/214.3/**亿笔**/，/金额/716/万亿/元/，/同比/分别/增长/16.9/%/和/13.1/%/。/其中/，/**银行卡**/业务/197/亿/笔 |
| SCWS | 央行/数据/显示/，/2009/年/全国/使用/**非现金**/支付/工具/办理/支付/业务/约/214.3/亿/笔/，/金额/716/万/**亿元**/，/同比/分别/增长/16.9/%/和/13.1/%/。/其中/，/**银行卡**/业务/197/亿/笔 |

Colloquial corpus chooses words in a casual style, starting with two four-character phrases, antithesis neatly. Followed is more typical spoken language, and the author uses the "给我" to enhance the tone, which the existing segmentation tools cannot recognize it as an in-dependent word. As for the next phrase, "我了个去", there is no lexical rule at all. As we can see, IKAnalyzer has a smaller segmentation particle size, which meets the needs of colloquial text segmentation best. For the reorganization of the network made-up words, each tool has its own result, but no one is correct.

Literary corpus are similar to the ordinary web page text. There are a number of terms and quantifiers, and the segmentation tools vary on them with no harm. But phrases like "银行卡", "非现金" are key information of the context, and wrong segmentation on them can cause a great loss. In scope of this post, SCWS performs best, Pangu secondly, and the other two have relatively big mistakes.

**Table 6.** Segmentation Result on Semi-Structured Corpus

| Tools | Results |
|---|---|
| ICTCLAS | #/暗黑/3/#/暴/雪/大/神/延续/跳/票/的/传统/@/我爱/大/菠萝 |
| IKAnalyzer | 暗黑/3#/暴雪/大神/延续/跳票/的/传统/我/爱/大菠萝 |
| Pangu | #/暗黑/3/#/暴雪/大神/延续/跳票/的/传统/@/我/爱/大/菠萝 |
| SCWS | #/暗/黑/3/#/暴/雪/大神/延续/跳票/的/传统/@/我爱/大/菠萝 |

Structured text in microblog is a double-edged sword. It can be used to guide the identification of unknown words, and even get more precise disambiguation. However, if we just do the segmentation directly to the corpus as to plain text, we won't be able to find the word "暗黑3", furthermore we get a wrong result "菠萝"[7]. In actual test set, microblog usernames can be bizarre, the topics are of various length, and many double slash symbols are left by forwarding. All these can make semi-structured corpus without pretreatment seem messy, leading to unsatisfactory segmentation result.

As for the comparison test, tools using frequency-first intelligent granularity method perform better on microblog corpus. But overall, due to the features of microblog corpus, tools used in this test didn't reach a satisfactory result. Also we found that in order to achieve the desired results, segmentation tools must reduce in-dependence on dictionaries, while enhance ambiguity resolution and the ability to identify new words. On the other hand, for semi-structured microblog corpus, we should take full advantage of the information brought by the structuration and process them separately in the final result. To achieve this goal, we cannot simply treat microblog corpus as plain text, nor can we treat every single microblog post in isolation. This leads us to abandon the traditional corpus-centered processing mode, and use another micro-word-centered mode, which takes full advantage of user information and topic information.

---

[7] "暗黑3" is the Chinese abbreviation for Diablo III, a computer game developed by Blizzard company, and "大菠萝" is a nick-name for "暗黑3" which means "big pineapple".

# 4 Comparison of Microblog Segmentation Results from Existing Tools

The method we proposed is an intelligent microblog segmentation algorithm considering the context and author's language habits. There are two main steps: first is performing preprocessing on microblog corpus to get microwords, and second is doing segmentation using the CRF model.

The main objective of preprocessing is to establish a microword-centered feature corpus. First, we need to maintain a microword dictionary, identifying the author, topic, user name with predetermined rules and adding them to the dictionary. For each microword we maintain a small corpus set. If some microword appears in a post, the post will be added to the corpus set corresponding with the microword, and this corpus set is the feature corpus set of the microword. The purpose of this step is to make factors which have a natural clustering feature (such as author, topic) the center of consideration, and make the features more centralized. For example posts of the same author can be considered as sharing the same style of word using, and posts under the same topic should be more relevant. Preprocessing can identify the microword directly, so as to reduce the burden of the new word recognition. More importantly, it prepares feature libraries for CRF algorithm.

CRF (conditional random field) is a machine learning model mainly used for text labeling in NLP field. If we use it to label the location in-formation of each word, the result we get is segmentation for the sentence. Unlike algorithms based on dictionary, the idea of the CRF is word-grouping rather than word-cutting. This method not only considers the frequency in-formation, but also considers the context, which leads to good learning ability. It has a better effect in ambiguity resolution and new words recognition. Compared to algorithms such as HMM, MEMM which are also based on probability, CRF algorithm has neither output independence assumption nor local restriction of normalization on nodes. Therefore it can get the global optimal value, which is very suitable for handling microblog corpus.

We use CRF++ toolkit[8] to perform segmentation test. The training and test platform is Intel ® Core ™ 2450 dual-core i5 - four threads, 2.5 GHz. During the training process, we use a model file trained from the People's Daily tagging set, and then choose 10 relevant posts for each microword as the feature corpus. Finally we make them into one model file. The training uses 6 segmentation tags: S (single words), B (beginning), E (ending), and M/M1/M2 (middle). Segmentation result is shown in the following table:

**Table 7.** Effect of CRF Segmentation Algorithm

| Corpus Type | P | R | F |
|---|---|---|---|
| colloquial | 0.8901 | 0.8723 | 0.8811 |
| literary | 0.9155 | 0.9142 | 0.9148 |
| semi-structured | 0.9112 | 0.9051 | 0.9081 |

---

[8] Project home: https://code.google.com/p/crfpp/

Result shows that the CRF-based algorithm has an obvious improvement on microblog segmen-tation. Because of the preprocessing on mi-crowords, this algorithm is superior to the other existing tools on the semi-structured corpus. On colloquial corpus, this algorithm is slightly bet-ter than CSWS, but the advantage is small, which might because the scale of characteristic corpus compared with conventional corpus is too small and the training effect is not obvious. As to Literary corpus, this algorithm uses an older conventional corpus which is not so com-pleted and updated as the CSWS's 2010 dic-tionary, so the segmentation result is a bit infe-rior. To be intuitive, we also give the segmenta-tion results:

**Table 8.** Segmentation Result of CRF Based Algorithm

| Categories | Results |
|---|---|
| colloquial | 工资/未/涨/，/房租/先/行/。/这下/给我/涨了/30/%/。/我了个去/啊/。/明年/交/房/以后/，/就是/卖血/也/得/装好/住进/去/，/再/也/不/受/这份/气/了 |
| Literary | 央行/数据/显示/，/2009/年/全国/使用/非/现金/支付/工具/办理/支付/业务/约/214.3/亿/笔/，/金额/716/万/亿/元/，/同比/分别/增长/16.9/%/和/13.1/%/。/其中/，/银行/卡/业务/197/亿/笔 |
| semi-structured | #/暗黑 3/#/暴雪/大神/延续/跳票/的/传统/@/我爱大菠萝 |

We can see the segmentation result of this colloquial example is fairly average, but mi-croword "我了个去" is correctly recognized. The overall effect for literary example is good, though some new words will be mistakenly broken up. As to the semi-structured example, because of the preprocessing, topics and user names can be recognized properly. The algo-rithm is trained on topic #暗黑3# related cor-pus, so the word "暴雪" can be recognized.

From all above, we can see that the CRF-based algorithm has achieved similar result with exist-ing segmentation tools on colloquial and literary corpus, and shows distinguishing advantages on semi-structured corpus by giving a big im-provement on P, R, F values. We believe that if there are enough microblog tagging corpus for training, the CRF-based algorithm shall gain a greater improvement.

# 5    Conclusion

After classification, filtering, labeling on mi-croblog corpus, and comparing the results of various segmentation tools, we get the following conclusions.

First, we classify microblog content according to the writing style. Then we filter 100 posts out from thousands and label them. Our goal is to make the segmentation results more comparable under the premise that the accuracy of segmen-tation can approximately reflect the real situa-tion, and then find the advantages and disad-vantages of different segmentation tools as well as the deficiency of existing segmentation tools on microblog corpus. These works can give ide-as to improve segmentation methods.

Second, microwords are relevant to each other. For example the content of two topics "暗黑2" and "暗黑3" are more likely to be relevant, so their feature corpus can learn from each other to build a larger, higher-level feature corpus.

Third, the labeled corpus and formation rules used in training are not enough, which may cause that the features of each microword are not properly reflected. Next thing to do is pro-moting the microblog corpus labeling work.

The treasure of microblog is giant, and segmen-tation is a powerful tool to dig it. We will do further study on the microblog segmentation methods, including deeper excavation of the relationship between microwords and establish-ing multi-level feature libraries. We will opti-mize the CRF-based segmentation algorithm, and on this basis, explore the selection and connection method for microwords. At the same time we would try our best to promote the microblog corpus labeling work, providing more resources for the study of microword.

# References

1. Huang, C., Zhao, H.: Chinese Word Segmentation: A Decade Review. Journal of Chinese Information Processing 21(3), 8–20 (2007)
2. Xue, N.: Chinese Word Segmentation as Character Tagging. International Journal of Computational Linguistics and Chinese Language Processing 8(1), 29–48 (2003)
3. Che, W., Li, Z., Liu, T.: LTP: A Chinese Language Technology Platform. In: Proceedings of the COLING 2010, pp. 13–16 (2010)
4. Sun, W., Xu, J.: Enhancing Chinese word segmentation using unlabeled data. In: Proceedings of the Conference on Empirical Methods in Natural Language Processing 2011, pp. 970–979 (2011)
5. Yuan, Z., Purver, M.: Predicting Emotion Labels for Chinese Microblog Texts. In: CEUR Workshop Proceedings, Vol. 917(4), pp. 40–47 (2012)

# The Category Structure in Wikipedia: To Analyze and Know How It Grows

Qishun Wang[*], Xiaohua Wang, Zhiqun Chen, and Rongbo Wang

Institute of Cognitive and Intelligent Computing, Hangzhou Dianzi University,
Hangzhou 310018, China
qishun.wang@gmail.com, wxhhie@sohu.com,
{5792523,12498354}@qq.com

**Abstract.** Wikipedia is a famous encyclopedia and is applied to a lot of famous fields for many years, such as natural language processing. The category structure is used and analyzed in this paper. We take the important topological properties into account, such as the connectivity distribution. What's the most important of all is to analyze the growth of the structure from 2004 to 2012 in detail. In order to tell about the growth, the basic properties and the small-worldness is brought in. Some different edge attachment models based on the properties of nodes are tested in order to study how the properties of nodes influence the creation of edges. We are very interested in the phenomenon that the data in 2011 and 2012 is so strange and study the reason closely. Our results offer useful insights for the structure and the growth of the category structure.

**Keywords:** Wikipedia, complex network, category structure, growth.

## 1    Introduction

### 1.1    Wikipedia

Wikipedia is a collaboratively edited, multilingual, free Internet encyclopedia supported by the non-profit Wikipedia Foundation. Many people devote their knowledge to the Wikipedia in their own languages. There are editions of Wikipedia in 285 languages so far, such as English, Chinese and Japanese. It has become the largest and most popular encyclopedia in the world. Its corpus can be applied to many fields, such as natural language processing, information retrieval, information extraction, ontology building and so on [1].

### 1.2    Category Structure

Wikipedia provides many useful structures, such as the structure of categories, pages and images. They are useful in the area of data mining, a lot of useful knowledge can be mined and results can be used in related fields to improve the performance. In this

---

[*] Corresponding author.

P. Liu and Q. Su (Eds.): CLSW 2013, LNAI 8229, pp. 538–545, 2013.
© Springer-Verlag Berlin Heidelberg 2013

paper we mainly use the structure of categories to analyze the topology and the growth of the structure.

Wikipedia seeks to create a summary of all human knowledge in the form of an on-line encyclopedia, with each topic of knowledge covered encyclopedically in one article, so in order to represent information and knowledge hierarchy, the category structure is set up. When authors write new articles, they are encouraged to assign some useful categories to their articles, in order to organize and sort articles easily, both articles and categories can belong to more than one category [1]. For example, the article Teacher falls in the category Educators, and the category Educators also belongs to the following twenty-four: Schoolteachers, Academics, Lecturers, Deaf educators and so on. The categories also can assign themselves to other more general categories, for instance, Language teacher training belongs to Teacher training, which in turn belongs to Teaching. The structure is a graph in which multiple organization schemes coexist, not a simple tree-structured taxonomy.

We download a complete snapshot of Chinese Wikipedia dated August 2012 from the official website. It contains many meaningful structures, such as category structure and page structure, and the former is applied in our paper. Each record in this dataset has a property which tells us when it was created or modified, offering a chance to study how the network grows and evolves over time. To build the network which represents organization of this knowledge, we traverse all the links and filter the links only when its type is category. The structure is transformed and then used to build a complex network, which its node is a category and its edge is the relation between the categories. The resulting network consists of $N \approx 2.5*10^5$ nodes and $E \approx 5.3*10^6$ edges, the vast majority (99.6%) of these nodes belonging to a single connected cluster [giant component (GC)].

## 1.3    The Dataset

We consider the category and its link structure of a complete snapshot of Chinese Wikipedia dated August 2012, consisting of $N \approx 2.5 * 10^5$ entries and $E \approx 5.3 * 10^6$ links. Each record in this dataset has a property which tells us when it is created, offering a chance to study how the network grows over time. To process our dataset first of all we traverse all the links and filter the links only when its type is category. Then we transform the original structure to the structure which will be used in our experiment. Finally the structure is used to build a complex network, which its node is a category and its edge is the relation between the categories. After above steps we deserve a complex network to use in the following research.

## 2    Topological Features

In this section, some topological properties are analyzed in order to show the relation between the categories, such as the connectivity distribution [2].

The first and essential statistical character of large-scale, complex networks is the connectivity distribution $P(k)$, which indicates the probability that a randomly selected node has k connections. It represents the importance or the connectivity of the reality networks, that is, the influence of the node in the network.

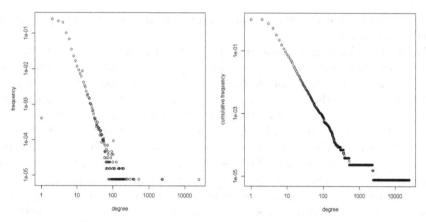

**Fig. 1.** Connectivity distribution of the category structure

Fig. 1 shows the connectivity distribution and the cumulative connectivity distribution of the network, which is the fraction of nodes with degree greater than or equal to k. Some networks, notably the category structure, the Internet, the world wide web, and some social networks are found to have degree distributions that approximately follow a power law: $P(k) \sim k^{-\alpha}$, where $\alpha$ is a constant, in the category network the $\alpha$ is equals with 2.987, with a fat tail. From Fig. 1 we can see that this network is inhomogeneous: the majority of the nodes have less than three links but a few nodes have a large number of links, guaranteeing that the system is fully connected. So according to the fact we can make the conclusion that the category network is a small-world and scale-free network.

# 3    Growth of the Structure

## 3.1    Basic Properties

Wikipedia was founded in 2001, but the input page lacked of the Chinese input function until 2004. So we can hold the view that the Chinese Wikipedia is really developed from 2004, not from 2001.

In Table 1 the data show the growing trend of the category structure between 2004 and 2012. The growing trend of the network's properties is very obvious. The number of nodes and the number of edges grows approximately linearly over time, with the number of edges growing at a faster pace, so the average node degree increases year by year. On average, the network gains about 15977 new nodes and about 33125 new edges per year.

**Table 1.** Properties of the network from 2004 to 2012: number of nodes N, number of edges E, ratio of the growth rate of edges and nodes <k>, average path length <l>, average clustering coefficient <C>

| Year | N | E | <k> | <l> | <C> |
|------|------|------|------|------|------|
| 2004 | 109 | 69 | 0 | 1.115 | 0 |
| 2005 | 6862 | 7405 | 1.086 | 2.249 | 0.006 |
| 2006 | 13614 | 19545 | 1.798 | 4.242 | 0.008 |
| 2007 | 20782 | 29498 | 1.389 | 3.994 | 0.016 |
| 2008 | 33652 | 50273 | 1.614 | 5.520 | 0.029 |
| 2009 | 48025 | 71486 | 1.476 | 5.742 | 0.037 |
| 2010 | 74067 | 120790 | 1.893 | 7.690 | 0.033 |
| 2011 | 101253 | 178972 | 2.140 | 16.955 | 0.036 |
| 2012 | 127925 | 265075 | 3.228 | 14.097 | 0.122 |

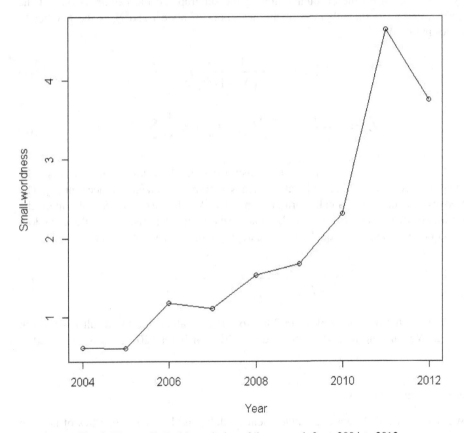

**Fig. 2.** The small-worldness index of the network from 2004 to 2012

## 3.2    Small-Worldness Index

Many evidences point out that this network has the small-world effect. For instance, the connectivity distribution can be fit with a power law distribution; the average clustering coefficient is high which indicates that nodes tend to create tightly knit groups characterized by a relatively high density of ties; the average path length is low which states that the relationship between any nodes is close.

But these conclusions can't quantify how much small-world the network is. So the measure which is named the small-worldness is proposed in order to be able to categorize the networks into the two broad classes of small-world and not small-world [3-4].

The characteristic path length is defined as the mean of geodesic length over all pairs of nodes [5], it is considered as the global efficiency ($E_{global}$) of the network, where N is the number of nodes in the network. The local efficiency ($E_{local}$) of the network can be obtained by averaging $E_i$ over nodes, in which $E_i$ is the local efficiency that is based on the efficiency among the subgraph of the neighbors ($G_i$) of the node i, and $G_i$ is the subgraph of the neighbors of node i and $N_i$ is the number of nodes in $G_i$ [6].

$$E_{global} = \frac{1}{N(N-1)} \sum_{i,j} l_{ij} \tag{1}$$

$$E_i = \frac{1}{N_i(N_i-1)} \sum_{j,k \in G_i} l_{jk}, \quad E_{local} = \frac{1}{N} \sum_i E_i \tag{2}$$

A special index was proposed to measure the small-worldness in networks. The measure based on global and local efficiency measures is taken into account [7]. The S shows the degree of small-worldness in networks, the larger the S is the more the small-world the network is. The Barabasi-Albert model is used to build a random network, and its scale is equal with the category structure's scale in each year.

$$S = \frac{E_{local}}{E_{local-random}} \times \frac{E_{global}}{E_{global-random}} \tag{3}$$

After all the S in network from 2004 to 2012 is calculated, the result is drawn in Fig. 2. We can find that S is increased year by year before 2012, but is decreased in 2012.

## 3.3    Edge Creation

We mainly test different edge attachment models based on the properties of node in order to study how the creation of individual edges is influenced by the properties of the nodes [8].

When authors start to write a new article, what they first to do is to find the references which are most cited by other articles. This phenomenon also exists in the network, the nodes which have more links point out that they are famous in the network and always referenced by other nodes. So according to these facts we can suppose that the probability of creating a new link with a node is related to the number of its existing connections. The probability is also related to the node's age. Because when new category joins the structure, they might choose the category which had lived longer to connect normally.

The method [9] is used and results are showed in Fig. 3. We can see in Fig. 3 that P(Degree) $\propto$ Degree$^{0.755}$, denoting how nodes with higher degrees are more likely to attract new edges than nodes which have fewer connections. A strange phenomenon can be observed in Fig. 3 that there is a spike at age 0, which represents that at first the number of created edges quickly goes down and then grows again. This denotes that older nodes benefit from receiving incoming links. The overall effect suggests that there is an abnormal spike of links created when a node joins the network followed by lower levels of edge creation: older nodes tend then to establish further links [9].

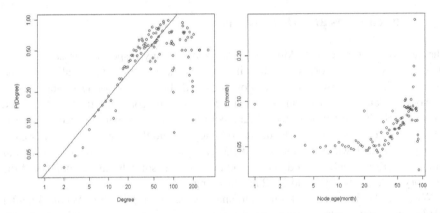

**Fig. 3.** Probability of creating a new link as a function of node degree (left panel), and probability of creating a new link as a function of the node's age (from October, 2004) (right panel)

### 3.4 What Happened in 2011 and 2012

From the data in Table 1 and Fig. 2 we are able to observe a suspicious phenomenon. The average path length in 2011 is twice larger than in 2010, but it decreases in 2012. The average clustering coefficient is almost equal with the coefficient in 2011, but in 2012 it is triple as large as in 2011. The small-worldness index in 2011 is twice larger than in 2010, but becomes smaller in 2012.

Let us analyze the reason why this phenomenon occurred. Wikipedia was described as "an effort to create and distribute a free encyclopedia of the highest possible quality to every single person on the planet in their own language." Some volunteers wrote a lot of articles in low quality, tampered the articles malicious and added error contents to the articles. As a result, the credibility of the Wikipedia was declined, which led to the result that the average path length and the small-worldness index of the network became larger abnormally. So some related rules were enabled to increase the editing quality of the article and the related contents in pages, it resulted in the fact that the authors couldn't create new entries and modify old entities easily. It is among the reasons for the trend that "unprecedented numbers of the millions of online volunteers who write, edit and police [Wikipedia] are quitting year by year", which was reported by the Wall Street Journal [10-11].

After the rules were enabled, the actions of adding new entries and modifying old entries became more rigorous, some experts modified or deleted the wrong or malicious contents in order to make the category structure more rigorous which increased the credibility of the Wikipedia. We can observe the data in Table 1 and Fig. 2, in 2012 the average path length and small-worldness index becomes smaller, the average clustering coefficient becomes larger, it shows that the category structure in 2012 became more rigorous. So we can believe that in 2013 more volunteers will attend the project to make the Wikipedia more reliable in order to serve the public better.

## 4    Conclusions and Discussions

The category structure in Wikipedia is analyzed in many respects. The connectivity distribution of the network shows that it is a network which has the small-world and scale-free features. After the basic properties and the small-worldness index of the network are analyzed, we can understand how the category structure evolutes and grows clearly. The creation of the relation between categories is influenced by properties of the categories, such as the degree of category and the length of time after category was created which is also called the category's age. As a novel view of our paper, we offer a sophisticated understanding to the reason why the arguments of the category structure in 2011 and 2012 are so strange.

What we should do in the future is to analyze the future growth of Wikipedia after 2013. According to the research results we can give some useful opinions to the development of Wikipedia in the future. So this work is meaningful.

**Acknowledgements.** This study was partly supported by National Natural Science Foundation of China 61202281.

## References

1. Medelyan, O., Milne, D.: Mining Meaning From Wikipedia. International Journal of Human-Computer Studies 67, 716–754 (2009)
2. Newman, M.E.J.: The Structure and Function of Complex Networks. Siam Review 45, 167–256 (2003)
3. Humphries, M.D., Gurney, K.: Network 'small-worldness': a Quantitative Method for Determining Canonical Network Equivalence. PLoS One 3(4), e0002051 (2008)

4. Humphries, M.D., Gurney, K., Prescott, T.J.: The Brainstem Reticular Formation is a Small-world, Not Scale-free, Network. Proceedings of the Royal Society B: Biological Sciences 273(1585), 503–511 (2006)
5. Boccaletti, S., Latora, V., Moreno, Y., Chavez, M., Hwang, D.U.: Complex Networks: Structure and Dynamics. Physics Reports 424(4), 175–308 (2006)
6. Latora, V., Marchiori, M.: Efficient Behavior of Small-world Networks. Physical Review Letters 87(19), 198701 (2001)
7. Jalili, M.: Error and Attack Tolerance of Small-worldness in Complex Networks. Journal of Informetrics 5(3), 422–430 (2011)
8. Barabási, A.L., Albert, R.: Emergence of Scaling in Random Networks. Science 286(5439), 509–512 (1999)
9. Allamanis, M., Scellato, S., Mascolo, C.: Evolution of a Location-based Online Social Network: Analysis and Models. In: 12th ACM Int'l Conference on Internet Measurement. ACM, Boston (2012)
10. Angwin, J., Fowler, G.A.: Volunteers Log Off as Wikipedia Ages. Wall Street Journal 23 (2009)
11. Rawlinson, K.: Wikipedia Seeks Women to Balance its 'Geeky' Editors. The Independent (2011)

# On Constructing a Chinese Task-Oriental Subjectivity Lexicon

Xiaoying Xu[1], Jianhua Tao[2], and Ya Li[2]

[1] School of Chinese Language & Literature, Beijing Normal University, 100875, Beijing, China
xuxiaoying2000@bnu.edu.cn
[2] NLPR, Institute of Automation, Chinese Academy of Sciences, 100190, Beijing, China
{jhtao,yli}@nlpr.ia.ac.cn

**Abstract.** Affective language computing has drawn considerable interest in natural language processing area, multiple domains have been developed in this area. Constructing an emotion corpus plays a fundamental role in affective language processing. Large amounts of recent works have tackled this issue and several emotion lexicons had been established, however, the task of the lexicon had not been examined clearly and little attention had been paid to clarify the role of the emotion word applied in different tasks. In this paper, three basic issues on establishing a Task-oriental subjectivity lexicon for multiple application domains, i.e., the principle of collecting and annotating the emotion terms in different tasks, the models of the emotion theory and the composition of isolated and contextual-based terms are discussed in-depth. Finally, the method for building this lexicon is also examined.

## 1    Introduction

Affective information is important for human language technology and there is now considerable interest in affective language processing (Xie Lixing, Zhou Ming, Sun Maosong, 2012; Long Jiang, Mo Yu, Ming Zhou et. al., 2011). Human's emotion is sophisticated, as concerning as affective computing in general, Picard (1997) notes that phenomena vary in duration, ranging from short-lived feelings, through emotions, to moods, and ultimately to long-lived, slowly-changing personality characteristics.

Affective language processing relates to multiple domains and multiple tasks. The automatic detection and synthesis of emotion can be applied in text, speech, facial and body gesture, and the tasks of emotion computing include lots of domains, e.g., opinion mining and market analysis, affective computing, or natural language interfaces such as dialogue system, e-learning environments or educational/edutainment games et. al..

For realizing the tasks in different domains, Machine-learning Methods and Language-modeling Methods are two major approaches. Within the Language-modeling Methods, constructing an subjectivity corpus plays an important and fundamental role.

P. Liu and Q. Su (Eds.): CLSW 2013, LNAI 8229, pp. 546–554, 2013.

Large amounts of recent works have tackled this issue and several emotion corpus had been established (Esuli and Sebastiani, 2006; Xiaoying Xu et al, 2009; Xiaoying Xu et al, 2012). However, most of the corpus can be categorized into two types, the domain-in-general corpus and the domain-specific corpus. In these two kinds of corpus, the task of the lexicon had not been examined clearly, which will necessarily result in the confusion on issues of the composition and annotation of entries. Moreover, due that most of the corpuses are established by automatic and semi-automatic methods, little attention will be paid to clarify the role of the emotion word applied in different tasks.

In this paper, we discuss three basic issues on establishing a task-oriental subjectivity lexicon for multiple application domains. The principle of collecting and annotating the emotion terms in different tasks will be discussed in-depth, the models of emotion theory and the composition of isolated and contextual-based terms are explored. Finally, the method for building this lexicon is also examined.

This paper is organized as follows: Section 1 is the introduction of the paper. Section 2 is a brief review of previous related work.   Section 3 discusses three basic issues on constructing a Task-oriental subjectivity lexicon. Section 4 presents the methods used in our corpus. Section 5 discusses the conclusion and future research.

## 2     Previous Research

Large amounts of recent works have pay attention to the issue of term's emotion annotation. Most of the previous works (Esuli and Sebastiani, 2006; Hatzivassiloglou and McKeown, 1997; Kim and Hovy, 2004; Takamura et al., 2005; Kaji and Kitsuregawa , 2007; Xiaoying Xu et al, 2012) established their lexicons automatically or semi-automatically based on some available resource. Few of the previous works (Wiebe and Mihalcea, 2006; Cerini et al., 2007; Karo Moilanen and Stephen Pulman, 2008; Xiaoying Xu et al, 2009) established their lexicons manually. Most of the works focus on the emotion information of the isolated words, while a few of the works (Xiaoying Xu et al, 2012) have tackled with the contextual-based orientation of the words and expressions.

Regarding the Chinese corpus established by automatic and semi-automatic method (Zhu Yanlan, Min Jin ,Zhou Yaqian, Huang Xuanjing, Wu Lide, 2006; Xiaojun Wang, 2008), the available resources used in these researches, including the Hownet's desired/undesired annotation, the Contemporary Chinese Language Orientation Usage Dictionary's commendatory/derogatory annotation , and the synonyms, semantic similarity and semantic correlation in Hownet and some synonym dictionaries, are not designed for the affective computing and thus are not suitable for being utilized directly (Xiaoying Xu et. al., 2009). For the corpus established manually, little of them examine the task of the corpus and pay attention to the function of the terms when applied in different processing systems (Xiaoying Xu & et. al., 2009; Ying Chen, Sophia Y. M. Lee and Chu-Ren Huang, 2009).

# 3    The Basic Issues in Constructing an Task-Oriental Emotion Lexicon

Three basic issues, including the task-oriental principle, the models of the emotion theory and the composition of isolated and contextual-based terms in constructing a Task-oriental emotion corpus will be discussed in this section.

## 3.1    Task-Oriental Corpus: From Attitude to Feeling and Personality

According to the introduction and the review of the previous research in section 1 &2, we can see that the emotion corpus can be used in lots of domains in natural language processing    fields, e. g., opinion mining and market analysis, or natural language interfaces such as dialogue system, e-learning environments or education-al/edutainment   games et. al.

Different domain has different tasks, the composition and the analyzing prospective of emotional terms differ accordingly in different domain. The typical difference of three main affective computing domains is illustrated as follows.

**Opinion Mining Field: Attitude-Dominant.**
Within opinion mining field, three subtasks can be identified, determining document subjectivity, (Pang and Lee, 2004; Yu and Hatzivassiloglou, 2003), determining document polarity (Pang and Lee, 2004; Turney, 2002) and determining the strength of document orientation (Wilson et al., 2004). In this area, a coarse-grained affective computing (Shanahan et al., 2006), which is attitude assessment, has become the most salient trend. Meanwhile, the coarse-grained polarity-driven approach is often criticized as too general to satisfy some applications, and the fine-grained affective information which detect emotion expressions also have drawn more and more attentions recently. At the same time, some work now considers longer-term affective states. For example, Mishne (2005) aims to classify the primary mood of weblog postings.

Generally, This field focus on the human's attitude, the polarity of "thumb up/thumb down" matters (Turney, 2002).The fine-grained feelings also must be categorized into attitude system, for example, "愤怒 anger" and "喜悦 happy" means "strongly negative" while "strongly positive", but the feeling of "激动 excited"can represent "strongly negative" and "strongly positive" respectively in different context. In Xiaoying Xu (2009), we discussed in detail on how to establish and annotate this kind of corpus and manually categorized 116533 entries of Chinese Hownet terms.

**Speech Synthesis and Speech Recognization: Feeling and Personality.**
Within speech synthesis & speech recognition systems, it's important to satisfy the need for natural human-like and expressive emotional speech for natural human-computer interact purpose. In this task, the emotional state, i. e. the feeling of the utterance and the personality of the speaker are valuable. Accordingly, in this field, both the spontaneous feeling and the stable personality must be analyzed. For example, "经得住（考验）  withstand (the test)" means "positive" and "thumb up" in

opinion mining task, but it means "neutral" feeling and "calm" personality in the Speech Synthesis & Speech Recognition task.

**Dialogue System----Attitude, Feelings and Personality.**
Within dialogue system, both opinion and the expressiveness are valuable. For the content understanding, opinion must be taken into account; for the natural and expressive interact, feeling and personality are important. So all the three dimensions, e.g., the attitude, feeling and personality must be analyzed in this task. Dialogue System has been shown to benefit from the detection of attitude and feelings already.

### 3.2    Emotion Theory: Typical and Discrete Categories vs. the Circumplex Model

There are two basic theories in the study of emotion: those which identify different emotions as discrete categories, which exist without reference to each other, and those in which different emotions are represented as points in emotional space, a space which is defines along two or three general dimensions (e.g., arousal, valence, approach-avoid ) (Sophie  K.   Scott, Disa Sauter, Carolyn McGettigan, 2009). A dominant approach in the former class of theories is the theory of basic emotions, there is a subset of emotions that are recognized across different cultures (i.e., are universal), that can be processed in a rapid and automatic way, and that are implemented in different neural systems (Ekman et al., 1969; Ekman, 1992a, b). In contrast, a dominant dimensional account of emotions is the circumplex model (Russell, 1980, 1997). In this model, emotions are points in emotional space along the dimensions of arousal and valence. Russeel's Arousal and Valence Model (AVM) is as follows:

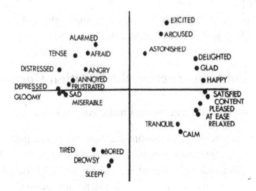

**Fig. 1.** Russeel's Arousal and Valence Model

In affective language processing area, the discrete category model has been broadly used. Recently, several research began to use the circumplex model in their work (Jia Jia et. al., 2011; Yi-Hsuan, Y., L. Yu-Ching, S. Ya-Fan, and H.H.Chen, 2008; Yi-Hsuan, and H.H.Chen, 2011).

In our lexicon, we annotate the terms into three separate AVMs, i.e., the attitude AVM, feeling AVM and personality AVM. Three AVMs consist of different term entries, while the same term will have different annotation in different AVM.

### 3.3    Isolated Word vs. Contextual-Based Term

Human expresses their emotion in several hierarchies of their language as well as the body and facial gestures. Emotional word/phrase, degree word, negative word, conjunction, rhetoric, punctuation and other linguistic expressions and even the world acknowledge can impact the affective meaning of the sentence.

Though most of the corpus mentioned above only focus on the orientation and emotion information of isolated emotion word, the degree word, negative word, conjunction have been applied to parse the subjectivity of the sentence (Xie Lixing, Zhou Ming, Sun Maosong, 2012). Considering that human expresses their emotion in several hierarchies of their language, we propose to add the rhetoric expressions, subjective phrase and sentence patterns, as well as the Chinese buzzwords into our corpus.

In Xiaoying Xu et al (2012), we paid attention to vehicle (the source concept part of the metaphor) orientation of the term, which can not only significantly increased the entry of the term orientation lexicon, but also add the indispensable contextual-based orientation to the lexicon.

The subjective phrase and sentence pattern have been discussed in lots of Chinese linguistic researches (Zheng Juanman, 2010; Chang Yuzhong, 1993), the phrases and patterns, discussed in the previous articles and resources, such as "真是的，整一个……" will be collected in our corpus.

The Chinese Buzzwords, such as "我可以说脏话吗（May I speak obscene words）" "你妈喊你回家（ Your mother calls you go back home）" are used high frequently to express affective information in the web, and mostly, they consist of no emotion word. They will also be labeled in our corpus.

## 4    The Method of Constructing the Emotion Corpus

### 4.1    Previous Automatic and Semi-automatic Annotation

The studies applying the methods of automatic and semi-automatic annotation have two subcategories:    Lexicograph-based Methods and Corpus-based Methods.

Lexicograph-based Methods rely on the lexical semantic knowledge and glosses in existing lexicographic resources alongside known non-neutral seed words. The resources applied commonly are WordNet synsets (Esuli and Sebastiani, 2006; Zhu Yanlan, Min Jin, Zhou Yaqian, Huang Xuanjing, Wu Lide, 2006), WordNet-Affect (Strapparava and Valitutti, 2004) , commendatory and derogatory dictionaries (Li Juan, Zhang Quan, Jia Ning, 2009) and synonym dictionaries(Li Juan, Zhang Quan, Jia Ning, 2009).

Corpus-based Methods (Hatzivassiloglou and McKeown, 1997; Kaji and Kitsuregawa, 2007) extend their lexicon based on varied context information and semantics connection indicated in the large-scale corpus. Wang Zhimin, Zhu Xuefeng, Yu Shi-wen(2006) applied Corpus-based Methods to described and formulized the word emotional trends in their Grammatical Knowledge-base of Contemporary Chinese, they tagged the word emotions by the approach of using both qualitative and quantitative methodology based on the statistics result in People's Daily tagging corpus.

## 4.2    Previous Human Annotation Studies

Comparing with the automatic and semi-automatic annotation studies, human annotation studies are conducted much less in quantity. Wiebe and Mihalcea (2006) marked up WordNet senses as subjective, objective or both with good agreement. Cerini et al. (2007) established the Micro-WNOp corpus which is a list of about 1000 WordNet synsets annotated by for polarity. Karo Moilanen and Stephen Pulman (2008) built a core sentiment lexicon contains 41109 entries tagged with positive (+), neutral (N), or negative (-) prior polarities. They furthermore maintain an auxiliary lexicon of 314967 known neutral words such as names of people, organizations, and geographical locations.    Fangzhong Su and Katja Markert(2008) investigated the reliability of manual subjectivity labeling of word senses and marked up subjectivity/attitude (subjective, objective, and both) of word senses as well as polarity/connotation (positive, negative and no polarity).

## 4.3    Annotating the Corpus According to Different Duties

In this paper, we propose to use different method to annotate the emotion corpus according to different tasks.

For annotating the isolated words which have stable meanings, we suggest the manual annotating method discussed in Xu Xiaoying et. al. (2009). In Xu Xiaoying et. al.(2009), we established an opinion-mining orientation corpus,    which is a domain-specific emotion corpus, our annotators are required to tag the sentences' polarity and the key polarity words in obtaining the sentences' polarity    for a large amount of real subjective text before annotating our lexicon. We also discussed the relations between word subjectivity/polarity and other criterions popularly used in the ready-made sources and established a very clear annotation guideline. Thirdly, our work divided the lexicon into three types, i.e. objective, positive and negative for avoiding the bias and confusion in tagging. Finally, we verify the reliability of our lexicon both in the agreement between the annotators and in sentence polarity judging system. The experimental results showed significant high agreement and a very promising result considering the simple recognition method and verifying our approach's high reliability.

For the contextual-based terms, such as the emotions categories of the vehicle of the metaphor, we propose the automatic tagging method used in Xu Xiaoying et. al. (2012). In Xu Xiaoying et. al. (2012), we established a metaphor parsing scheme based on the vehicle annotation corpus. According to mapping relation between the vehicle and the words with semantic orientation which are co-appeared in simile sentences collected from large-scale corpus, we automatically label the vehicle orientation. Then, we parse the metaphor polarity based on the vehicle orientation corpus and extend the metaphor parsing to opinion mining. The results demonstrated the effectiveness of our approach and verified our approach's high reliability.

# 5     Conclusion and Future Work

In this paper, we discuss the framework and the method for establishing a task-oriental subjectivity lexicon. The detailed procedures and the consistency evaluation of annotation as well as the reliability of this lexicon will be demonstrated in future work.

**Acknowledgements.** The work was supported by the National Science Foundation of China (No. 60873160, 90820303, 61233009, 61273288, 61203258), 863 Programs (No. 2009AA01Z320), and the Singapore National Research Foundation under its International Research Centre @ Singapore Funding Initiative and administered by the IDM (CSIDM) Programme Office.

# References

1. Esuli, A., Sebastiani, F.: Determining Term Subjectivity and Term Orientation for Opinion Mining. In: Proceedings of EACL 2006, 11th Conference of the European Chapter of the Association for Computational Linguistics, Trento, IT (2006)
2. Pang, B., Lee, L.: A Sentimental Education: Sentiment Analysis Using Subjectivity Summarization Based on Minimum Cuts. In: Proceedings of ACL 2004, 42nd Meeting of the Association for Computational Linguistics, Barcelona, ES, pp. 271–278 (2004)
3. Strapparava, C., Valitutti, A.: Wordnet-affect: an Affective Extension of Wordnet. In: Proceedings of the 4th International Conference on Language Resources and Evaluation, Lisbon (2004)
4. Cerini, S., Compagnoni, V., Demontis, A., Formentelli, M., Gandini, C.: Micro-WNOp: A Gold Standard for the Evaluation of Automatically Compiled Lexical Resources for Opinion Mining. In: Language Resources and Linguistic Theory: Typology, Second Language Acquisition, English Linguistics (2007)
5. Chang, Y.: Functional Dictionary of Idioms in Vernacular Language. Beijing Language and Culture University Press (1993)
6. Ekman, P., Sorenson, E.R., Friesen, W.V.: Pan-cultural Elements in Facial Displays of Emotion. Science 164, 86–88 (1969)
7. Ekman, P.: Are There Basic Emotions? Psychology Review 99, 550–553 (1992a)
8. Ekman, P.: An Argument for Basic Emotions. Cognitive Emotion 6, 169–200 (1992b)
9. Esuli, A., Sebastiani, F.: SentiWordNet: A publicly Available Lexical Resource for Opinion Mining. In: Proceedings of the Fifth International Conference on Language Resources and Evaluation (LREC 2006), Genoa, Italy (May 2006)
10. Su, F., Markert, K.: Eliciting Subjectivity and Polarity Judgments on Word Senses. In: Proceedings of the 22nd International Conference on Computational Linguistics (Coling 2008), Manchester (2008)
11. Hatzivassiloglou, V., McKeown, K.: Predicting the Semantic Orientation of Adjectives. In: Proceedings of ACL 1997 (1997)

12. Shanahan, J.G., Qu, Y., Wiebe, J.: Computing Attitude and Affect in Text: Theory and Applications. Springer (2006)
13. Martin, J.: Computational Model of Metaphor Interpretation. Academic Press (1990)
14. Jia, J., Zhang, S., Meng, F., Wang, Y., Cai, L.: Emotional Audio-visual Speech Synthesis Based on Pad. IEEE Transactions on Audio, Speech, and language Processing 19(3), 570–582 (2011)
15. Kaji, Kitsuregawa, M.: Building Lexicon for Sentiment Analysis from Massive Collection of HTML Documents. In: Proceedings of EMNLP-CONLL (2007)
16. Moilanen, K., Pulman, S.: The Good, the Bad, and the Unknown: Morphosyllabic Sentiment Tagging of UnseenWords. In: Proceedings of ACL 2008: HLT, Short Papers (Companion Volume), Columbus, Ohio, USA, pp. 109–112 (2008)
17. Kim, S.-M., Hovy, E.: Determining the Sentiment of Opinions. In: Proceedings of COLING (2004)
18. Li, J., Zhang, Q., Jia, N.: Semantic Orientation Identification for Chinese Opinion Terms. Computer Engineering and Applications 45(2), 131–133 (2009)
19. Long, J., Mo, Y., Ming, Z., et al.: Target Dependent Twitter Sentiment Classification. ACL (2011)
20. Gilad, M.: Experiments with Mood Classification in Blog Posts. In: Proceedings of ACM SIGIR 2005 Workshop on Stylistic Analysis of Text for Information Access (2005)
21. Picard, R.: Affective Computing. The MIT Press, MA (1997)
22. Russell, J.A.: A Circumplex Model of Affect. Journal of Personality and Social Psychology 39(6), 1161 (1980)
23. Scott, S.K., Sauter, D., McGettigan, C.: Brain Mechanisms for Processing Perceived Emotional Vocalizations in Humans. In: Brudzynski, S.M. (ed.) Handbook of Mammalian Vocalization. Academic Press, UK (2009)
24. Strapparava, C., Valitutti, A.: WordNet-Affect: an Affective Extension of Word-Net. In: Proceedings of LREC 2004 (2004)
25. Takamura, H., Inui, T., Okumura, M.: Extracting Semantic Orientations of Words using Spin Model. In: Proceedings of ACL 2005 (2005)
26. Turney: Thumbs up or Thumbs down? Semantic Orientation Applied to Unsupervised Classification of Reviews. In: Proceedings of ACL (2002)
27. Stoyanov, V., Cardie, C.: Toward Opinion Summarization: Linking the Sources. In: Proceedings of the Workshop on Sentiment and Subjectivity in Text, Sydney, pp. 9–14. Association for Computational Linguistics (July 2006)
28. Wang, Z., Zhu, X., Yu, S.: Research on Word Emotional Evaluation Based on The Grammatical Knowledge-base of Contemporary Chinese. Computational Linguistics and Chinese Language Processing 2(4) (2005)
29. Wiebe, J., Micalcea, R.: Word Sense and Subjectivity. In: Proceedings of ACL 2006, Wilson et al. (2006)
30. Xu, X., Li, Y., Tao, J., Li, X.: Automatic Parsing of the Metaphor Polarity for Opinion Mining. In: Proceedings of Oriental Cocosda, Macau (2012)
31. Xu, X., Li, Y., Hu, L., Tao, J.: Categorizing Terms' Subjectivity and Polarity Manually for Opinion Mining in Chinese. In: Proceedings of ACII, Amsterdam (2009)
32. Xie, L., Zhou, M., Sun, M.: Hierarchical Structure Based Hybrid Approach to Sentiment Analysis of Chinese Micro Blog and Its Feature Extraction. Journal of Chinese Information Processing 26(1) (2012)
33. Yi-Hsuan, Y., Chen, H.H.: Prediction of the Distribution of Perceived Emotions Using Discrete Samples. IEEE Transactions Audio, Speech, and language Processing 19(7), 2184–2196 (2011)

34. Yi-Hsuan, Y., Yu-Ching, L., Ya-Fan, S., Chen, H.H.: A Regression Approach to Music Emotion Recognition. IEEE Transactions Audio, Speech, and language Processing 16(2), 448–457 (2008)
35. Chen, Y., Lee, S.Y.M., Huang, C.-R.: A Cognitive-based Annotation System for Emotion Computing. In: Proceedings of the Third Linguistic Annotation Workshop, ACL-IJCNLP 2009, August 6-7, pp. 1–9. Suntec, Singapore (2009)
36. Yu, H., Hatzivassiloglou, V.: Towards Answering Opinion Questions: Separating facts from Opinions and Identifying the Polarity of Opinion Sentences. In: Proceedings of EMNLP 2003 (2003)
37. Zheng, J.: On the Construction of Derogatory Idioms in Modern Chinese. The PHD Dissertation of Jinan University (2010)
38. Zhu, Y., Min, J., Zhou, Y., Huang, X., Wu, L.: Semantic Orientation Computing Based on HowNet. Journal of Chinese Information Processing 12(11) (2006)

# Concepts Extension from HNC to Lexical Semantic Web through Constructing Synsets

Li Feng[1] and Qian Xu[2]

[1] College of International Exchange, Shenzhen University, Shenzhen 518060
lily_von@126.com
[2] Foregin Language Department, Shenzhen University, Shenzhen 518060
abbyxu1990@163.com

**Abstract.** HNC designs a theoretical framework for machine to understand the meaning of natural language and offers different ways to represent abstract as well as concrete concepts. However, it doesn't mention some concrete concepts closely related to people's daily life and fails to reveal the connotations of them. This paper based on the "Synset-Lexeme Anamorphosis" Method tries to realize a word cluster centered with concept nodes by constructing synonym sets and tries to reveal detailed semantic connotations of words. It aims to reach an effective docking between HNC and lexical semantic web to make the current Semantic Web more complete and perfect.

**Keywords:** HNC Concepts Representation, "Synset-Lexeme Anamorphosis" Method, Construction of Synset, Word-meaning Description.

## 1   Introduction

HNC (Hierarchical Network of Concepts) theory proposed by Huang Zengyang constructs a theoretical framework of natural language representation and understanding through concept association network. Three kinds of semantic webs are designed to cluster abstract concepts: primitive concepts web, basic concepts web and logical concepts web (Huang, 1999). Nevertheless, these concept webs do not extend to the words and their connotations of concrete concepts, even at the lowest level of HNC.

A complete concept network should not merely conclude abstract concepts, but should extend itself to concrete concepts of concrete words, reveal and process all the connotations of semantic (word) meaning. Words are the carrier of concepts, and word meaning is the content of concepts. Therefore, the study of concepts is supposed to focus on word meaning. But so far, revealing the connotations of word meaning is still a difficult problem, which "has not been solved by HNC, as well as other schools" (Xiao Guozheng, 2011). Under this circumstance, Xiao Guozheng puts forward the "Synset-Lexeme Anamorphosis" Method in order to construct the synonym sets of concrete concepts with the purpose of clustering concrete concepts and revealing the connotation and semantic features of each concrete concept. It is supposed to reach a refined representation system of word meaning in the Semantic Web, and to realize an

P. Liu and Q. Su (Eds.): CLSW 2013, LNAI 8229, pp. 555–563, 2013.

extension from HNC association network to lexical semantic web and make a connection between the two.

## 2    Concepts Representation System in HNC

The partial association network at word level represents itself as a concept representation system in HNC. It divides concepts into two kinds----abstract ones and concrete ones, and lays its emphasis on the former.

### 2.1    The Representation of Abstract Concepts

In HNC Theory, five primitives {v, g, u, z, r} (refer to dynamic, stative, attribute, value, and effect respectively) are used to describe external features of abstract concepts; meanwhile, network level symbols are used to express their connotations (Huang, 1997). For example, the concept nodes of the word "思维活动[*siweihuodong*] (*conceptual work*)" are described in HNC like the following:

Line 8思维活动[*siweihuodong*] (*conceptual work*)

80 思考[*sikao*] (*to think*) vg，思维[*siwei*] (*thought*) g，想法[*xiangfa*] (*idea*) r

800 概念[*gainian*] (*concept*) r，观点[*guandian]* (*point of view*) z

"思考[*sikao*] (*to think*)，思维[*siwei*] (*thought*)，想法[*xiangfa*] (*idea*)，概念[*gainian*] (*concept*)，观点[*guandian]* (*point of view*)"are all the abstract concepts of the word "思维活动[*siweihuodong*] ( *conceptual work*)". The letters stand for the external features of this word: "vg" means that the concept "思考" possesses dynamic and stative features at the same time; those concepts with no "v" all have the stative feature. The difference among "思维[*siwei*] (*thought*)"，"思考[*sikao*] (*to think*)"，"想法[*xiangfa*] (*idea*)" and "概念[*gainian*] (*concept*)"，"观点[*guandian]* (*point of view*)" is that "思考[*sikao*] (*to think*)" and "思维[*siwei*] (*thought*)" are the beginning of "思维活动[*siweihuodong*] (*conceptual work*)"，and "概念[*gainian*] (*concept*)"，"想法[*xiangfa*] (*idea*)"，"观点[*guandian]* (*point of view*)" are the result. In the result, "z" is the value of "r" (Xiao et al., 2011).

Numbers in HNC are the network level symbols. They are used to express the connotations of concepts. The number "8" indicates that the words followed are all the concepts of "思维活动[*siweihuodong*] (*conceptual work*)" at the "8" line in the concepts network. Those concepts started with the same number belong to the same level. Line "80" is the sublayer of line "8", and line "800" is the sublayer of line "80".

It is certain that the method of representing the abstract concepts in HNC is relatively comprehensive. It combines internal features and external features of words. To some extent, it successfully clusters the abstract concepts of one word and describes them hierarchically. But this method just shows the positions of these concepts, instead of their semantic connotations and differences in meaning.

## 2.2    The Representation of Concrete Concepts

Because of the complexity of concrete concepts, it is difficult to normalize their representation. Therefore, HNC adopts a method of subordinating the concrete concepts to primitive concepts and basic concepts of abstract ones, rather than explain them in detail. For example,

夫妻[*fuqi*] (*couple*)          p411

交通工具[*jiaotonggongju*] (*vehicle*)     pw22b

现代探测设备[*xiandaitanceshebei*] ( *modern detection equipment*) w9219

"p, pw and w9" are the symbols used to describe  different categories of concrete concepts in HNC (p: human w: objects pw: common artifacts w9: modern products).

To represent the concrete concept "夫妻[*fuqi*] (*couple*)", the category "p" for "human" needs to be subordinated to primitive concept node 411 of line 4, indicating "marrying"; for "交通工具[*jiaotonggongju*] (*vehicle*)", the category "pw" for "common artifacts" needs to be subordinated to primitive concept node 22b, indicating "self-transferring objects", etc.

Although subordinating representation method is rough and approximate, it has a great significance in establishing a connection between abstract concepts and concrete concepts. Moreover, this method represents the connection with symbols, which is beneficial for computing semantic distance (Huang, 1997). Nevertheless, some common concrete concepts and their hyponymy concepts in daily communication are not mentioned or labeled in HNC.

Consequently, to make the network more complete, both abstract and concrete concepts need to be extended to more hypogenous levels to build a connection with words and their connotations of concrete concepts.

It seems impossible to describe the meanings of words one by one. But if the synonyms of one concept are clustered, then group description is an effective method to finish this huge project. "Synset-Lexeme Anamorphosis" method is the one to achieve this goal.

## 3    "Synset-Lexeme Anamorphosis" Method

"Synset-Lexeme Anamorphosis" Method put forward by Xiao (2007) is a new method to construct synonym sets. The purpose of the method is to construct a refined word-meaning structure that can reveal the differences and connections of concrete concepts, and build the meaning representation system shared by human and computer.

The Method believes that concepts are limitless, but they can be represented by limited lexemes in any language. Lexemes can be divided into basic lexemes and un-basic lexemes. The semantic system in one language is a synset system that consists of basic lexemes and their variants. If the letter $\sum$ stands for chunk system, S stands for multiword chunks, $V_0$ for basic lexemes and $V_1$, $V_2$, $V_3...V_n$ for variants, their relations should be like this:

$$\Sigma = \{S_1, \ S_2, \ S_3 \ldots \ldots S_n\} \quad ; \quad S = \{V_0, \ V_1, \ V_2, \ V_3 \ldots \ldots V_n\}$$

**Key Terms in "Synset-Lexeme Anamorphosis" Method**

According to Xiao, lexeme refers to "an individual unit as well as a set of individuals combined by one basic word meaning with particular phonetic forms or graphic forms" (Xiao Guozheng, 2007). That means the term lexeme has two meanings. One meaning is that one lexeme is one word itself; the other one is that lexeme is a set of words and their variants. Its properties of individuality and clustering enable the synset to connect with the concept nodes in HNC. These nodes are represented in the form of individual lexeme (e.g. 夫妻[*fuqi*] (*couple*)), while synset is a cluster of lexemes (e.g. synset夫妻 [*fuqi*] (*couple*)). No matter for individual lexeme or a synset lexeme, they describe the same concept.

The lexeme anamorphoses refer to the variants of lexeme in practical use (Gao Mingkai, 1962). They are synonyms with same concepts and references but have different word forms in synset construction. What people use in practical are the lexeme anamorphorses or variant lexemes.

Basic lexeme is the representative lexeme of a synset. It is the standard of finding and validating anamorphoses. Therefore, in the synset construction, general words in the standard modern Chinese should be chosen as basic lexemes rather than dialect or unfamiliar words. The synonymy set is typically represented by basic lexemes and collects variant lexemes as its members. For example, in the synset {夫妻[*fuqi*] (*coople*), 夫妇[*fufu*](*husband and wife*), 伉俪[*kangli*] (*couple*), 伴侣[*banlv*] (*companion*), 两口子[*liangkouzi*] (*couple*), 两公婆 [*lianggongpo*] (*couple*),……}, "夫妻 [*fuqi*] (*couple*)" is the basic lexeme and the rest members are the variant lexemes of it.

After the validation of basic lexeme, the connotations of all the variant lexemes in the synset can be described in the form of "basic lexeme + distinctive features", which greatly simplifies word-meaning description.

The word-meaning description means that the description of the semantic compositions of words. Word meaning and concept meaning are not exactly equivalent. The former concludes two parts: basic meaning and extra meaning (Zhang Zhiyi & Zhang Qingyun, 2005); the latter equals to the basic meaning to some degree (Xiao et al., 2011). Thus, the description of semantic composition concludes the two parts too. The basic meaning is the synset's concept meaning, owning the property of generality; the extra meaning relates to the distinctive features, which can distinguish one word from others. The respective description of basic meaning and extra meaning clearly presents similarities and differences of synonyms.

# 4    Constructing Synsets with Different Positional and Semantic Relations

The foundation of constructing synsets is that the word set has the same concept meaning. According to the positional and semantic relations of concepts (Wang

Dechun, 1997), we can construct different synsets with different relations. If a concept concludes another concept, they have a relation of hyponymy. And then we can construct a "superordinate synset" and a "hyponymy synset". When two concepts are apposed, a "compeer synset" can be constructed. When the hyponymy concepts include more refined concrete concepts, they can be collected into a subset of the hyponymy synset, or hyponymy sub-synset in short form.

## 4.1    Superordinate Synset

This paper exemplifies "夫妻[*fuqi*] (*couple*)" to describe the construction of synset. The word "夫妻[*fuqi*] (*couple*)" is a node at the lowest level in HNC system. Actually it includes two hyponymy concepts: "丈夫[*zhangfu*] (*husband*)" and "妻子[*qizi*] (*wife*)". Hence "夫妻 [*fuqi*] (*couple*)" is relatively a superordinate concept. In speech communication, this concept is usually expressed by other words. These words with same concept, reference and different word forms can be put into one synset together with "夫妻[*fuqi*] (*couple*)".

According to Wikipedia, "夫妻 [*fuqi*] (*couple*)" refers to the legal marriage relationship of men and women after a ceremony.[1] Based on its definition, the semantic composition of "夫妻[*fuqi*] (*couple*)" can be described as: 夫妻[*fuqi*] (*couple*) [ + male and female + legal marriage relationship]. Its synonyms are "夫妇[*fufu*] (*husband and wife*)", "伉俪[*kangli*] (*couple*)", "伴侣[*banlv*] (*companion*)", "两口子[*liangkouzi*] (*couple*)", "两公婆[*lianggongpo*] (*couple*)", "老两口[*laoliangkou*] (*old couple*)", "小两口[*xiaoliangkou*] (*young couple*)" etc. Because "夫妻[*fuqi*] (*couple*)" is a standard word in modern Chinese and can be used in both oral and written Chinese, it is chosen as the basic lexeme in constructing its synset. The different word forms varied by place, age and language style in this set are all the anamorphoses of the word "夫妻[*fuqi*] (*couple*)". To describe them in the form of "basic lexeme + distinctive features" is like the following:

夫妻[*fuqi*] (*couple*) =[+male and female+ legal marriage relationship]

Lexeme anamorphoses and their semantic compositions are:

夫妇[*fufu*] (*husband and wife*)=[coople+ husband's name can be added + written form]

伉俪[*kangli*] (*couple*)=[ coople + husband's name can be added + successful + matched+ written form+ commendatory]

伴侣[*banlv*] (*companion*)=[ coople+ husband or wife + written form]

两口子[*liangkouzi*] (*couple*)=[coople+ northern dialect+ oral]

两公婆[*lianggongpo*] (*couple*)=[coople+ southern dialect+ oral]

老两口[*laoliangkou*] (*old couple*)=[ coople+ northern dialect+ oral+ old]

小两口[*xiaoliangkou*] (*young couple*)=[ coople+ northern dialect+ oral+ young]

The description way "basic lexeme +distinctive features" is not only concise and clear, but is easy to find the differences among these word.

---

[1] http://zh.wikipedia.org

## 4.2  Hyponymy Synset

A hyponymy synset can be constructed when a concept contains hyponymy anamorphoses. For example, the aforementioned "夫妻[*fuqi*] (*couple*)" includes two hyponymy concepts "丈夫[*zhangfu*] (*husband*)" and "妻子[*qizi*] (*wife*)".

The wife"妻子[*qizi*] (*wife*)", also refers to "老婆[laopo] (wife)", in ancient time was called "娘子 [*niangzi*] (*lady*)", "夫人[*furen*] (*madam*)". Those are all the appellations of the female side in marriage. The semantic compositions of "妻子 [*qizi*] (*wife*)" and " 丈夫[*zhangfu*] (*husband*)" are described as the following:

妻子[*qizi*] (*wife*) [+men and women+ marital+ to female+ appellation]

Its hyponymy lexeme anamorphoses and their semantic compositions are (Feng Li, 2013):

堂客[*tangke*] (*wife*) =[wife + south-central dialect]

媳妇[*xifu*] (*wife*) =[wife + northern dialect]

孩子他妈[haizitama] (children's mom) =[wife+ northern dialect + face-to-face addressing]

内人[*neiren*] (*my wife*) =[wife +self-abasing terms]

老婆（子[*laopo (zi)*] (*old biddy*) =[wife +informal]

爱人[*airen*] (*lover*) =[wife+ northern dialect+ respectful appellation + endearing appellation)]

夫人 [*furen*] (*madam*) =[wife + respectful appellation]

太太④[*taitai*] (*Mrs.*)=[wife +husband's surname] （④means that the word "太太 [*taitai*] (*Mrs.*)" is the fourth sense in the fifth edition of Modern Chinese Dictionary ）

The synset description of "丈夫[*zhangfu*] (*husband*)" will not be mentioned here for lack of space.

## 4.3  Compeer Synset

A compeer synset is composed by two or more apposed synsets. It is automatically generated after the apposed synsets are constructed. For example, the synsets of "丈夫 [*zhangfu*] (*husbands*)" and "妻子[*qizi*] (*wives*)" are constructed as the hyponymy synsets of "夫妻[*fuqi*] (*coople*)".

In addition, the two apposed concepts"丈夫[*zhangfu*] (*husband*)" and "妻子[*qizi*] (*wife*)" have special variants of same appellation, that is, they have the same appellation variants like "配偶[*peiou*] (*spouse*)，爱人[*airen*] (*lover*)，那口子[*nakouzi*] (*partner*)，老伴 [*laoban*] (*husband or wife*)，……". Their semantic compositions can be described as the following:

配偶[*peiou*] (*spouse*)=[husband or wife +often in formal document +written form]

爱人[*airen*] (*lover*)①=[husband or wife+ oral +respectful]

那口子[*nakouzi*] (*partner*)=[husband or wife +northern dialect)+ oral +casual]

老伴[*laoban*] (*husband or wife*)=[husband or wife + old + oral]

Those are the compeer synset of both "丈夫[*zhangfu*] (*husband*)" and "妻子[*qizi*] (*wife*)".

## 4.4 Hyponymy Sub-synset

Through the diachronic study on the concept "妻子[*qizi*] (*wife*)", its hyponymy concepts can be divided into subclasses, which compose the hyponymy sub-synset.

In the time of polygamy, "妻子[*qizi*] (*wife*)" also had the appellations of "原配（元配）[*yuanpei*] (*first wife*)", "正室①[*zhengshi*] (*legal wife*)", "二房[*erfang*] (*second wife*)" and "小老婆[*xiaolaopo*] (*concubine*)" etc. They all refer to the female spouse in a legal marriage of polygamy (excluding "妾Φ[*qie*] (*concubine*)", "姨太[*yitai*] (*concubine*)" and "陪房[*peifang*] (*maids that accompanied the bride to her husband's house*)", which were not protected by law). The descriptions of semantic compositions of hyponymy sub-synset are:

原配/元配[*yuanpei*] (*first wife*)=[wife + the first one + former appellation]

大老婆[*dalaopo*] (*first wife*)=[wife + vulgar appellation of "原配" + former appellation]

正室①[*zhengshi*] (*legal wife*)=[wife +legally married + same status with "原配" + former appellation+ written form]

"正室①[*zhengshi*] (*legal wife*)" could be the first wife or the remarried one, having the same status as the official wife.

二房[*erfang*] (*second wife*)=[wife + the second + lower status + former appellation+ written form]

小老婆[*xiaolaopo*] (*concubine*)=[wife + after the second one +lower status +former appellation + oral]

Here ① refers to the first sense of the word in the fifth edition of Modern Chinese Dictionary (2005).

All the words aforementioned appeared in the old times, and they can be called former appellation variants.

Another kind of spouse titles is about the remarried wives after the death of the first one, like "继室[*jishi*] (*remarried wife after the first one's death*)", also called "继配[*jipei*] (*remarried wife after the first one's death*)"and "填房[*tianfang*] (*remarried wife after the first one's death*)". They are all legal wives. Differently, "填房[*tianfang*] (*remarried wife after the first one's death*)" is mostly a young widow or an older girl.[2] Their semantic compositions are:

继室/继配[*jishi*]/ [*jipei*] (*remarried wife after the first one's death*) =[ wife + remarried + same status with "原配" + former appellation]

填房[*tianfang*] (*remarried wife after the first one's death*)=[ wife + remarried widow/ older girl/ wife's sister) + same status with "原配" +former appellation]

Those constructions of synsets not only cluster the scattering synonyms but also describe each concept's connotation in detail, clearly revealing the similarities and differences among the synonyms and presenting their positional and semantic relations (as in Figure1).

---

[2] http://baike.baidu.com/view/243895.htm

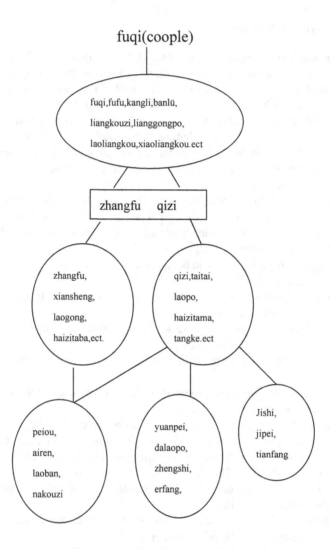

**Fig. 1.** Synset Relations of the Concept

# 5    Conclusion

The "Synset-Lexeme Anamorphosis" method originating from HNC Theory is the succession, development and extension of HNC. It helps to construct the synonym sets with refined semantic structures. The word meaning description system constructed with this method is able to reveal the differences and connections of concrete concepts, and this system is complementary to the concepts representation system in HNC.

**Acknowledgement.** This research is supported by the second-phase expansion items of "985 Project" of Wuhan University----"The Interdisciplinary Platform of Linguistic Science and Technology and Modern Society Construction" and "The Theoretical Exploration and Technological Realization of Chinese Semantic Web Based on Concept Features". Item number: 985yk006.

## References

1. Feng, L.: The Connotations of Lexical Primitives and Their Functions in Constructing Synsets (《词义基元的内涵及其在同义词群建构中的作用》). Hubei Society and Science (《湖北社会科学》) (3), 113–116 (2013)
2. Gao, M.: On Lexemes in Language System (《论语言系统中的词位》). Journal of Peking University (《北京大学学报》) (1) (1962)
3. Huang, Z.: HNC (Hierarchical Network of Concepts) Theory— New Thought for Studying on How Computers Understand Language (《HNC（概念层次网络）理论——计算机理解语言研究的新思路》). Tsinghua University Press, Beijing (1999)
4. Huang, Z.: The Essentials of HNC Theory (《HNC理论概要》). Journal of Chinese Information Processing (《中文信息学报》) 11(4) (1997)
5. Modern Chinese Dictionary, 5th ed. (《现代汉语词典(第5版)》). The Commercial Press, Beijing (2005)
6. Wang, D.: Introduction to Linguistics (《语言学概论》). Shanghai Foreign Language Education Press, Shanghai (1997)
7. Xiao, G.: The Description of the Lexical Meaning Structure of the Verb "da" and the Construction of its Synset——A Study on "Synset-Lexeme Anamorphosis" Shared by Human and Computer (《动词"打"本义的结构描写及其同义词群建构——一种人机共享的"词群-词位变体"研究初探》). Assembly Documents on the 7th Chinese Information Processing Conference (《第七届中文信息处理国际会议论文集》). Electronic Industry Press, Beijing (2007)
8. Xiao, G., et al.: The Mapping from Space of Concept Primitives to Space of Word Meaning Primitives (《从概念基元空间到语义基元空间的映射——HNC联想脉络与词汇语义结构表述研究》). Journal of East China Normal University (《华东师范大学学报》). Philosophy and Social Sciences (1) (2011)
9. Zhang, Z., Zhang, Q.: Lexical Semantics (《词汇语义学》). The Commercial Press, Beijing (2005)

# Construction and Application of the Knowledge Base of Chinese Multi-word Expressions

Lei Wang[1,3], Shujing Li[1], Weiguang Qu[2], and Shiwen Yu[3]

[1] School of Foreign Languages, Peking University Beijing 100871
[2] School of Computer Science, Nanjing Normal University Nanjing 210000
[3] Institute of Computational Linguistics, Peking University Beijing 100871
{wangleics,lishujing}@pku.edu.cn, wgqu@njnu.edu.cn,
yusw@pku.edu.cn

**Abstract.** In a language, Multi-word Expressions (MWEs, also called "idiomatic expressions" or "set phrases") are very common in everyday usage. Most linguists hold that MWEs be an inclusive concept that should consist of not only lexical units such as idioms, idiomatic expressions, *xiehouyu*[1], proper nouns, but also non-lexical units such as proverbs, maxims and adages. Even those that are statistically idiosyncratic are to be listed in MWEs. In NLP tasks like word segmentation and semantic role labeling remain a bottle-neck problem. Therefore, to construct a knowledge base for MWEs with relatively complete entries and tagged attributes will be an effective solution for the above-mentioned problem. This paper introduces relevant information about the construction and application of an MWE knowledge base by the Institute of Computational Linguistics at Peking University(ICL/PKU), in which the author expects to provide due help to research in this regard.

**Keywords:** Chinese multi-word expressions, knowledge base, construction and application.

## 1 Introduction

As a language evolves and develops, some combinations of words with good prevalence and high frequency of usage will become fixed and thus multi-word expressions will come into being. Generally speaking, MWEs are universal in all kinds of languages around the world. For instance, a typical MWE structure—idiom—exists in every language. (Baldwin 2003) defines an MWE as such: 1. decomposable into multiple simplex words; 2. Lexically, syntactically, semantically, pragmatically and/or statistically idiosyncratic. The first indicates that MWEs in form should be decomposed into several individual words while the second shows an MWE should be of sense semantically, syntactically, lexically or statistically. Thus, MWEs generally possess decomposability structurally but their meanings cannot be deduced from individual constituents, i.e. words.

---

[1] 歇后语, An idiomatic two-part double pun. Part one is akin to a riddle, while part two is usually a double pun based on part one and reveals the metaphorical meaning of part one.

P. Liu and Q. Su (Eds.): CLSW 2013, LNAI 8229, pp. 564–571, 2013.
© Springer-Verlag Berlin Heidelberg 2013

Since an MWE can serve as a word, a phrase or a sentence syntactically, its composition usually cannot be changed when syntactic analysis is conducted. This is mainly due to the fact that the rules of their composition are inherited historically from speakers' habits of expression rather than grammatically from reasonable analysis. Therefore, MWEs usually are regarded as the most difficult part of the formalization of a language and cannot be identified and analyzed by grammatical rules available. From a semantic perspective, for each constituent of an MWE does not reflect its meaning as a whole, the semantic role labeling for its constituents poses a great challenge to an NLP task. Moreover, for its huge number few lexicons can include MWEs completely.

## 2    The Definition and Classification of MWEs for Chinese Information Processing

With respect to Chinese information processing, techniques relating to word processing have become the basis of many other tasks—Chinese character input, word segmentation, speech recognition and synthesis, full-text information retrieval, text classification and machine translation. In most cases, word processing provides a platform for other NLP tasks. However, there is the problem of defining segmentation units for MWEs that extend to different categories no matter what techniques -- based on rules or on statistics -- will be applied. Therefore, to construct a knowledge base for MWEs with relatively complete entries and tagged attributes will be an effective solution for the above-mentioned problems.

Before the concept of MWE was introduced into Chinese language, structures as such are generally called "熟语shuyu (idiomatic expressions)" or "习语xiyu(habitual expressions)". The *Dictionary of Modern Chinese*(Lv & Ding 1996) defines *shuyu* as: a fixed expression that can only be used as a whole and not be analyzed by grammar rules and whose constituents cannot be changed, such as "慢条斯理, 无精打采, 不尴不尬, 一来二去, 乱七八槽, 八九不离十. etc.". In his book about English idiomatic expressions, (Fiedler 2007) defines them as: a multi-word language unit that is mainly used by habit with relatively fixed syntactic-semantic structure. It tends to be used as a whole to promote its effect of expression. Thus, it is known to us that by definition it is essential for MWEs to be "fixed" no matter in Chinese or English and based on that there still exist a large number of disputes on how to define idiomatic expressions accurately, be it from a semantic, grammatical or pragmatic perspective.

On balance, there are some characteristics about *shuyus* that linguists have reached the following consensus. (Hu 1998) believes that in the lexicon of a language some words are often used together instead of being used individually to express certain ideas more effectively. These combinations of words are defined as *shuyu*, which should includes idioms, idiomatic expressions, *xiehouyus*, proverbs, adages, etc. Expressions as such cannot be changed in constitution.

The difference lies in that some researcher (Wu 1986) believes that a *shuyu* shall only consist of those whose grammatical functions are only limited to words. Namely although *shuyus* appear longer in formal structure and richer in semantic content and are often in the form of phrases, they are equal to words in terms of usage, composition and popularity and are close to words syntactically. They shall include idioms, proverbs, *xiehouyus* and idiomatic expressions. However, some researcher(Zhou 1994) holds that an MWE cannot function just as words but also as independent sentences in which adages and maxims shall also be included and need to be analyzed syntactically.

Since MWEs are present in authentic text in a large number, it is quite unavoidable to tag them appropriately in order for them to be processed by computer. Currently, corpora play an even more significant role in NLP tasks and a lot more work need to be done when building a large-scale corpus. Our principle of marking up MWEs shall not only demonstrate their linguistic features but also the availability for natural language processing, in which the latter should be laid more emphasis. However, there are many problems when conducting word segmentation for MWEs in texts. Some MWEs like idioms or idiomatic expressions, if being segmented and tagged by their constituents, will bring about more difficulties for understanding. For instance, the idiom "鸡飞狗跳(ji fei gou tiao, chickens fly and dogs jump)" means "a chaos" metaphorically in Chinese. But after we segment it with ICTCLAS(Zhang et al 2003)[2], the result is as the following:

$$鸡/n \quad 飞/v \quad 狗/n \quad 跳/v$$

It is noticeable that each constituent is segmented and tagged with its POS, which renders it rather difficult to understand its real meaning. Whereas the proverb "只要功夫深，铁杵磨成针。(zhi yao gong fu shen, tie chu mo cheng zhen, If you work at it hard enough, you can grind an iron rod into a needle.)" will be segmented and tagged as:

$$只要/c \quad 功夫/n \quad 深/a \quad ，/w$$
$$铁杵/n \quad 磨/v \quad 成/v \quad 针/n \quad 。/w$$

Its true meaning can hardly be related to its literal meaning if we look at it character by character.

For the above knowledge, aiming at Chinese information processing we classify the MWEs into two categories: those processed as words and those processed as sentences. Each of the two categories can also be subdivided into several categories as Fig. 1 shows.

Due to the fact that the MWEs treated as words such as idioms, *xiyus* and proper nouns will be processed as words in a sentence, we tag them as "word" in the MWE knowledge base for the purpose of NLP tasks in order to stress their indivisibility. Different from other researchers, we have not classified abbreviations into an individual category but regard them as variants of proper nouns. This is mainly because abbreviations are often used when people feel some proper nouns are rather lengthy and expect to use them in a concise and convenient way. In a sense abbreviations will be thought as words only when the proper noun it represents forms a correct mapping with it. In practice abbreviations should be treated as a word that cannot be further segmented when conducting POS tagging, which makes it fairly close to idioms and *xiyus* with respect to grammatical attributes. Thus it is appropriate to mark them as the variants of proper nouns.

---

[2] www.ictclas.org

In addition, we have not classified terms as an individual category for the following reasons: 1) Terms are of relativity. A word/phrase that is considered as a term in one discipline may not be considered as a term in another. 2) Terms possess the same features as proper nouns both formally and grammatically. Therefore, they should be treated as the same category in language information processing. Given the fact that we need keep accordance with our corpus in terms of tagging, we still adopt the ICL/PKU tagging system for proper names—to tag a proper noun both internally and externally. For instance, "北京大学" should be tagged as "[北京/ns 大学/n]nt".

The criterion for distinguishing idioms and *xiyus* is whether they are metaphorical, i.e. whether we can get their meanings from looking at them literally. We classify those that cannot be understood literally into idioms whereas those whose meanings can be seen easily from their compositions are classified into *xiyus*. For instance, "画蛇添足(hua she tian zu, to draw a snake and add feet to it)" is an idiom whereas "名副其实(ming fu qi shi, be true to the name)" is a *xiyu*. Another issue is the number of characters that an idiom or *xiyu* should have. We define that if an idiom or a *xiyu* can function as a sentence they will not be classified into either of the categories.

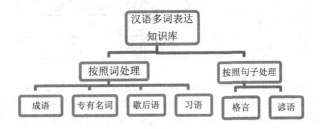

**Fig. 1.** Categories of MWE knowledge base

Now the numbers of each categories in the MWE knowledge base constructed by ICL/PKU are shown in Table 1:

**Table 1.** The numbers of each MWE category

| 序号 | 多词表达类别 | 条目数 |
|------|------------|--------|
| 1 | 成语 | 8377 |
| 2 | 习语 | 29742 |
| 3 | 专有名词[3] | 1402 |
| 4 | 歇后语 | 14309 |
| 5 | 格言 | 326 |
| 6 | 谚语 | 571 |

---

[3] Here refers to the Term Knowledge Base of Computational Linguistics built by ICL/PKU.

# 3     The Tagging Methods of the MWE Knowledge Base at ICL/PKU

At present, the two knowledge bases that have fairly complete information are the idiom knowledge base and the *xiyu* knowledge base, which are constructed through the 973 National Basic Research Program of China (No. 2004CB318102)(Wang et al 2012). Beside the fields that are listed in *Grammatical Information Knowledge Base for Modern Chinese*(Yu et al 1998) about idioms and *xiyus*, the properties of each entry in the above-mentioned two knowledge bases can be classified into four categories: lexical, semantic, syntactic and pragmatic, each of which also includes several fields in its container -- the SQL database. Table 2 shows the details about the fields.

**Table 2.** Property categories of CIKB

| 类别 | 属性字段 |
|------|----------|
| 词汇 | 条目,拼音, 全拼音,变体,释义,来源 |
| 语义 | 近义,反义,直译,意译,英语近似 |
| 语法 | 构成,句法功能 |
| 语用 | 频率,情感色彩,等级 |

There are three fields of translation as we can see in Table 2. In spite of the fact that a literal translation of an idiom will not reflect its metaphorical meaning generally, it will still be of value to those who expect to get familiar with the constituent characters and may want to connect its literal meaning with its metaphorical meaning, especially for those learners of Chinese as a foreign language. "变体Bianti" refers to a variant form of the idiom that was caused by random misuse, literary malapropism, etc. For instance, "山盟海誓(shan meng hai shi)" can also be written as "海誓山盟". The field "Frequency" is an integer that shows the frequency of the idiom in 55-year (1947-2002) People's Daily Corpus. In the field of "Emotion", we define the emotion types as "appreciative (A)", "derogatory (D)" and "neutral (N)".

Those MWEs that need to be processed as sentences such as proverbs, adages and maxims usually function as sentences in texts. In general, the author expects to express some specific intention when using the MWEs as such—the moral behind the MWE. Actually in text processing, if we try to understand the MWE literally, i.e. by the characters or words that constitute it, mistakes will often be made. Thus we believe that the best replacement will be the moral that a proverb, adage or maxim has. For instance, when the proverb "宁做蚂蚁腿，不学麻雀嘴。(ning yao ma yi tui, bu xue ma que zui. An ant's legs are much better than a sparrow's beak.)" is introduced, the author wants to express the meaning "实干要比空谈重要(shi gan yao bi kong tan zhong yao. Actions speak louder than words.)". So there is a field "寓意(*yuyi*, moral)" added to the MWE knowledge base that holds "conciseness" as its most important principle, i.e. to use the simplest language to describe its meaning. For instance, the meaning of the above-mentioned proverb "实干要比空谈重要" is more concise and direct than the lengthy one "我们宁要像蚂蚁一样实干也不要像麻雀一样光靠嘴来说。(wo men ning yao xiang ma yi yi yang shi gan ye bu yao xiang ma que yi yang guang kao zui lai shuo. We prefer those who work hard like ants to those who chatter like sparrows.)".

The fields of the MWEs in the knowledge base that need to be processed as sentences such as proverbs, adages and maxims include: pinyin, *bianti*, English translation(optional), tenor, vehicle, moral, etc. For their low frequency of appearance in the People's Daily Corpus, we have not counted their frequency. Because this type of MWEs often has metaphorical meanings, we set up "tenor" and "vehicle" fields for future research with this respect.

# 4    Research on Metaphor Based on MWE knowledge Base

In everyday use, many MWEs have metaphors. A metaphor is used on two objects that seem unrelated but have internal relationships by analogies to create a rhetoric that is able to transfer the meaning from one object to the other in order to promote the effect of expression. (Richards 1986) points out in his book *The Philosophy of Rhetoric*: A metaphor should have two parts: One is the tenor (also called "the source") that is the object to be described and the other is the vehicle (also called "the target") that is the object to be transferred onto meaning. For instance, Shakespeare's well-known quote "All the world's a stage, and all the men and women merely players: They have their exits and their entrances." compares the "world" to the "stage" for the purpose of describing the abstract concept "world" by a simple object "stage". Here the "world" is the tenor while the "stage" is the vehicle. "Men" and "women" are tenors of the second level and "exits and entrances" are the common descriptive predicates used to describe "men" and "women". The last sentence shows the same attributes both the tenor and the vehicle have.

Research on MWEs that have metaphors is helpful to natural language processing, lexicography, teaching Chinese as a second language, theories and practice of translation, etc. The previous research on MWEs mainly focuses on bigram combination of words, while when recognizing and processing MWEs that have more than two words, the experiments usually produce dissatisfactory results. Our research expends the measurement criterion of MWEs and includes those whose number of words is more than two with an attempt to provide more quantitative methods and basis for computing.

Based on the MWE knowledge base, we can also conduct statistical research on metaphors in MWEs, from which we will obtain linguistic knowledge about statistical facts and data. In Table 3 nouns with high frequency of appearance of idioms, *xiyus*, proverbs and *xiehouyus* in the MWE knowledge base are counted and we hope by doing that we will know more about what nouns play significant roles in various MWEs.

**Table 3.** Nouns in various MWEs

| 成语 | | 习语 | | 谚语 | | 歇后语 | |
|---|---|---|---|---|---|---|---|
| 名词 | 频率 | 名词 | 频率 | 名词 | 频率 | 名词 | 频率 |
| 风 | 260 | 心 | 526 | 人 | 112 | 人 | 496 |
| 虎 | 248 | 风 | 487 | 雨 | 37 | 儿 | 185 |
| 龙 | 234 | 人 | 481 | 水 | 24 | 头 | 181 |
| 凤 | 220 | 天 | 474 | 天 | 20 | 狗 | 175 |
| 金 | 188 | 龙 | 358 | 路 | 18 | 瞎子 | 171 |
| 马 | 186 | 日 | 352 | 山 | 17 | 嘴 | 161 |
| 玉 | 186 | 地 | 330 | 年 | 16 | 老鼠 | 149 |

Table 4 shows the statistics of idioms that have typical forms of metaphor along with their frequencies in the idiom knowledge base. This information will help us know the distribution of tenors and vehicles used by idioms with metaphor.

**Table 4.** Distribution of tenors and vehicles used by idioms with metaphor

| 类型 | 本体 | 喻体 | 示例 | 总数 |
|---|---|---|---|---|
| 如A如B | 风景等 | 诗、画等 | 如诗如画 | 22 |
| 如A似B | 女子等 | 花、玉等 | 如花似玉 | 11 |
| A如B | 军队等 | 处子等 | 静如处子 | 601 |
| A似B | 感情等 | 水 | 柔情似水 | 46 |
| A若B | 人等 | 木鸡 | 呆若木鸡 | 211 |

It is shown in Table 5 that the most frequent nouns(mostly used for tenors), verbs(mostly used to describe actions in context) and adjectives(mostly used to describe attribute of the metaphors) used by *xiehouyus*.

**Table 5.** The most common nouns and verbs used by *xiehouyus*

| 名词 | 频率 | 动词 | 频率 | 形容词 | 频率 |
|---|---|---|---|---|---|
| 人 | 190 | 吃 | 600 | 好 | 238 |
| 瞎子 | 171 | 打 | 422 | 难 | 236 |
| 狗 | 166 | 做 | 332 | 大 | 217 |
| 老鼠 | 146 | 来 | 245 | 死 | 157 |
| 和尚 | 141 | 死 | 237 | 多 | 148 |
| 鸡 | 129 | 坐 | 180 | 硬 | 126 |
| 水 | 126 | 卖 | 179 | 高 | 114 |

# 5    Future Work

At present, in the MWE knowledge base of ICL/PKU, the idiom knowledge base and the *xiyu* knowledge base are quite complete in both entries and fields. In the future, emphasis will be laid on further correction of mistaken fields and research on possible applications.

Other than what we have introduced in this paper, the other knowledge bases are still under construction. Our goal is to collect more MWEs and attempt to apply more automatic methods to fill in the missing information by extracting them from available corpora. We also expect to do more work on the all-word sense tagging of MWEs in order for the MWE knowledge base to contribute more to semantic understanding and computing of texts.

We also hope the MWE knowledge base will be used on metaphor understanding and computing, which will definitely make great breakthrough in automatic text understanding.

**Acknowledgements.** Our work is supported by National Natural Science Foundation(Grant No. 61170163 and No. 61272221), Chiang Ching-kuo Foundation for International Scholarly Exchange(2009) and Open Project foundation of National Key Laboratory of Computational Linguistics(No. 201302), This work was partially supported by National High Technology Research and Development Program of China (863 Program) (No. 2012AA011101).

# References

Baldwin, T., Bannard, C., Tanaka, T., Widdows, D.: An Empirical Model of Multiword Expression Decomposability. In: Proceedings of the ACL 2003 Workshop on Multiword Expressions: Analysis, Acquisition and Treatment, Sapporo, Japan, pp. 89–96 (2003)

Fiedler, S.: English Phraseology: A Coursebook. Gunter Narr Verlag, Turbingen (2007)

Hu, Y.: Modern Chinese. Shanghai Education Press, Shanghai (1998)

Lv, S., Ding, S.: Modern Chinese Dictionary, 3rd edn. The Commercial Press, Beijing (1996)

Rchards,

http://books.google.com.hk/books?id=XSImdRh8gsgC&hl=zh-CN&source=gbs_similarbooks

Wang, L., Yu, S., Zhu, X., Li, Y.: Chinese Idiom Knowledge Base for Chinese Information Processing. In: Proceedings of the Chinese Language Semantics Workshop (2012), Wuhan, pp. 85–90 (2012)

Wu, Z.: A Handbook of Modern Chinese. Beijing Language University Press, Beijing (1986)

Yu, S., Zhu, X., Wang, H.: A Complete Specification of Grammatical Knowledge Base of Contemporary Chinese, 2nd edn. Tsinghua University Press, Beijing (1998)

Zhou, J.: On the Classicness of Shuyu. Research on Chinese (3) (1994)

Zhang, H., Yu, H., Xiong, D., Liu, Q.: HHMM-based Chinese Lexical Analyzer ICTCLAS. In: Proceedings of the Second SIGHAN Workshop on Chinese Language Processing, pp. 184–187 (2003)

# Construction of Multilingual Terminology Bank of Computational Linguistics[*]

Yanqiu Shao[1,2], Shiwen Yu[3], Chunxia Liang[1], and Ning Mao[1]

[1] Research Department, Beijing City University, Beijing, China
yqshao163@163.com, {nanyanglcx,maoning}@bcu.edu.cn
[2] Institute of Applied Linguistics, Beijing Language Culture University, Beijing, China
[3] Institute of Computational Linguistics, Peking University, Beijing, China
yusw@pku.edu.cn

**Abstract.** A multilingual computational linguistics dictionary involving English, Chinese, Japanese, German was built by Institute of Computational Linguistics of Peking University in the 1990s. The dictionary contains more than 5,400 terms of computational linguistics and it made great contributions to the development of NLP domain. In order to develop the prior achievements, more terms that occur in the past two decades are added into the expanded term bank (ETB) which includes about 13,000 English terms and the number of languages involved is also extended to seven. Now, the seven language core term bank is mostly done. The construction of ETB including the scale, source of terms and the design of the database management system is described in details in the paper. ETB will have a promoting effect on the development of computational linguistics.

**Keywords:** terminology bank, multilingual term, computational linguistics.

## 1 Introduction

With the development of computer and internet, a large number of academic literatures are emerging everyday, and many field terminologies are generated accordingly. The terminology refers to the general concept of specialized field[1]. In a sense, terminology embodies and loads the kernel knowledge of the field, and it always plays an important role in understanding and grasping the development of one field. Terminology is an important information resource and standard terminology is required in the academic communication. Terminology bank provides a convenient way to share the information resource and an important method to the management of terms.

Computational linguistics is an inter-discipline which involves many fields such as computer science, linguistics, psychology, mathematics, information theory, control theory, automatics and so on. Computational linguistics is becoming an important theoretical basis of many applied technology, such as machine translation, information retrieval, intelligent man-machine interface, etc. The multilingual terminology

---

[*] This work is supported by National Natural Science Foundation of China (No. 61170144).

P. Liu and Q. Su (Eds.): CLSW 2013, LNAI 8229, pp. 572–580, 2013.

bank of computational linguistics could help construct the relationship among different languages, and it is helpful for researchers to understand the concept of terminology and to ensure the consistence of the academic communication.

Professor Yu Shiwen of Institute of Computational Linguistics Peking University (ICL-PKU) developed a multilingual comparison lexicon of English, Japanese, Chinese and German which includes 5,415 terms of computational linguistics occurred before the early of 1990s. Based on this achievement, the Peking University Press published an English-Chinese Lexicon Computational Linguistics which is the first terminology dictionary of this field and one of the most important references of terminology translation. This term bank was incorporated into an information science and technology terminology base which includes about 100,000 terms developed by China National Institute of Standardization (CNIS) and ICL-PKU. The collection of these terms makes great contribution to the standardization of information technology terminology. In 2002, the China National Committee for Terms in Sciences and Technologies published the second edition of Chinese Terms in Computer Science and Technology which covered 23 branches[2]. Computational Linguistics is also one of these branches, and this branch includes 223 Chinese-English terms which are almost all selected from the ICL-PKU terminology bank.

Computational linguistics is one of the high-speed developing disciplines, and the field terminology is constantly changing and updating. In order to inherit and develop the existing research achievements, we collect some new terms which emerged in the last two decades. The scale and the language kind of the terminology bank are also expanded. A computational linguistics terminology bank with wide coverage, high quality, and multi-language is constructed. In 2007, ICL-PKU signed an agreement with NICT (National Institute of Information and Communications Technology) about the construction of computational linguistic terminology bank, so as to collaborate and promote the development of computational linguistics and natural language processing technology.

## 2    Terminology Sources and Languages Selection

### 2.1    Terminology Sources

As terminology is a kind of appellation of concepts, in most cases, terminology is noun. However, according to practical condition, some special verbs and adjectives could also be contained in term base, such as "parse", "anaphoric", and so on.

The expanded term bank (ETB) in this paper enlarges the original dictionary of "English-Chinese Lexicon of Computational Linguistics", and 5,415 terms in ETB come from the original dictionary[3]. Apart from the writer's collection, there were three main sources of these 5,415 terms in this original dictionary.

- Bibliography of natural language processing in the 1980s edited by Center for the Study of Language and Information of Stanford University. 1764 papers or tales of contents from 1980 to 1987 are included in this book.

- The appendix indexes of more than ten Japanese books about computational linguistics and natural language processing published in the mid or late 1980s.
- Terms compilation of language information processing. It was compiled by the Research Center of Information Development of the Ministry of Machine Building & Electronics Industry of People's Republic of China and Chinese Information Processing Society. Professor Yu Shiwen and Feng Zhiwei participated in the compilation of the first edition of the book.

In order to update the terms bank, many new terms in ETB are selected from the following sources.

- Three books written by Prof. Yu Shiwen and other researchers in ICL-PKU. 325 terms are from the book "The Introduction to Computational Linguistics"[4], 304 terms are from "Preview of Computational Linguistics"[5], and 782 terms from "The Grammatical Knowledge-Base of Contemporary Chinese-A complete Specification"[6]. All of these terms were checked repeatedly by the researchers who work on the frontier of the field and these terms have a very high reliability and authority.
- A math and computational linguistics terminology dictionary of English-French-Russian written by Y.VENEV in 1990[7].7697 shunting indexed items are listed in this dictionary. The real number of the items is much smaller. There are only about 3,900 terms in it. Each English term has one or several corresponding French and Russian terms. The indexes based on French and Russian are listed behind the book and each French and Russian term has the corresponding English term number.
- The book "Natural Language Understanding" written by James Allen. 602 terms come from the appendix of this book[8].
- Considering the important relation between natural language processing and information retrieval, some items of the field of information retrieval are collected in this paper to extend the terms bank. For example, the book "An Introduction to Information Retrieval" written by Christopher D. Manning is selected. 630 English terms of IR field are from it[9].
- Besides books, the key words from the papers of "Journal of Chinese Information Processing" are picked as the terms to the ETB. The publishing period of journal is shorter than book, so there are many new terms in journals. About 1,100 terms are chosen from these journals.
- About 1,300 terms come from the internet and the usual research work.

All of the terms mentioned above are got by many different methods such as automatic acquisition, manual input, machine scan, etc. All of the new terms are checked manually at last. Many repetitive and wrong terms are got from different sources, and they are deleted and corrected. In ETB, English term is taken as the primary key. There are about 13,000 English computational linguistics terms totally now. By using some dictionaries, some of the translation work from English to other languages is done. Besides, the terms from different sources are made intersection computation to form a core terms bank (CTB) which, to some extent, could represent those frequently-used and important concepts. These core terms will be defined in the bank and be looked as seed unions of domain terminology based on which the whole terminology definition could be completed gradually.

## 2.2    Languages Selection

Seven languages are selected in ETB which are English, Chinese, Japanese, German, Russian, French, and Korean. These languages belong to different language families. For example, Russian belongs to Slavonic family, English and German belong to Germanic family, French is the member of Latin family, Japanese and Korean are the ones of Altaic family, and Chinese is part of Sino-Tibetan. These seven languages are often used in research jobs. ICL-PKU maintains good communication and cooperation relations with many foreign institutes. Professor Yu Shiwen invited several experts and scholars from different countries to join the terminology translation work. Now, a seven-language computational linguistic terminology bank has initially been built.

# 3      The Characteristics of Multilingual Terminology Bank

The main file of ETB is one multilingual term comparison bank which includes seven languages. Each record uses English term as primary key. In the English term field, there is only one English term. However, apart from English term field, there may be several corresponding terms in other language term fields. In fact, the relationship is multi-to-multi among different language terms. In Table 1, it could be seen that one English term could correspond to several different Chinese, Russian and German terms, and conversely, one non-English term could also correspond to several different English terms. For example, the Chinese term "语法" has two corresponding English terms, "grammar" and "syntax". Although the relationship among different language terms is multi-to-multi, for the convenience of query and expression, the main file is represented as the form of one-to-multi relation, i.e., one English term corresponds to multi other language terms. Table1 gives several examples from multilingual ETB.

Although these languages vary from each other, there are some internal relations among them. For example, there are some Chinese characters in Japanese terms. Both the writing and the meaning of these Chinese characters are similar with the Japanese terms. But this does not always happen. Sometimes the same characters represent different concepts for Chinese and Japanese. For instance, the Japanese term "言語" corresponds to Chinese term "语言", and the meaning is "language". But the Chinese term "言语" generally means "speech" and the corresponding Japanese term is "音声, 発話". For English and German, they belong to the same language family. Many terms are represented in the same form of English and German, but there still exists some situations that the same representation corresponds to different meaning. For example, one meaning of German term "Ellipse" is "ellipsis" or "omission of a word or words", but English word "ellipse" only means "oval".

It might be seen that besides applying the multi-lingual term bank to machine translation and information retrieval application, this term bank is significant for correctly understanding the meaning of terminology, because referring to different language could help know the concept from different angles.

**Table 1.** Examples from multi-lingual terminology bank

| English | Chinese | Japanese | German | Russian | French | Korean |
|---|---|---|---|---|---|---|
| ambiguity | 歧义 | 曖昧性 | Ambiguität, Mehrdeutigkeit | двусмысленность | ambiguïté | 중의성 |
| grammar | 语法, 文法 | グラマー, 構文論, 文法 | Grammatik | грамматика | grammaire | 문법 |
| machine translation | 机器翻译, 机译 | 機械翻訳 | maschinelle Sprachübersetzung, maschinelle Übersetzung, Maschinenübersetzung | машинный перевод, автоматический перевод | traduction automatique | 기계번역 |
| syntax | 句法, 语法 | シンタックス, 構文, 統語論 | Syntax | синтаксис | syntaxe | 통사 |

# 4    Multilingual Terminology Bank System

## 4.1    Design of Base Table

- One Main File

The main file is a term comparison table of seven languages and it includes 9 fields, i.e., ID number, seven different language fields, and the sources which are listed in section 2.1. The table is arranged by English character order. Arabic number is listed at the front and the Greek letter at last. English term is the primary key, and for every record there is only one English term but may be several other language terms. It could be seen that according to English field, it is easy to find the corresponding other language terms. The structural form of the main file is expressed as Table 2.

**Table 2.** The structure of main file

| ID | English | Chinese | Japanese | German | Russian | French | Korean | Source |
|----|---------|---------|----------|--------|---------|--------|--------|--------|
| 1 | E1 | C11, C12... | J11, J12... | G11, G12... | R11, R12... | F11, F12... | K11, K12... | S11, S12... |
| 2 | E2 | C21, C22... | J21, J22... | G21, G22... | R21, R22... | F21, F22... | K21 ,K22... | S21, S22... |
| ... | ...... | ...... | ...... | ...... | ...... | ...... | ...... | ...... |

- Six Monolingual Term Index Tables

In order to find the terms of different languages conveniently and quickly, six index tables are built. Each table corresponds to one language. Because English terms could be found in main file, there is no English index table in the system. Table 3 gives the structure of the index table.

**Table 3.** The structure of monolingual index table

| Term | ID |
|------|-----|
| Term1 | ID11, ID12... |
| Term2 | ID21, ID22... |
| ...... | ...... |

In Table 3, the field "Term" means the monolingual term, and the field "ID" corresponds to the ID number in Table1.

Except for "Term" and "ID" fields, another field of "PinYin" (Chinese phonetic alphabet) is added to Chinese term index table, and the table is ordered by PinYin of the terms. Table 4 shows that the pinyin in pinyin field is also segmented according to the Chinese words. For example, the two tokens of the pinyin string "jisuan yuyanxue" respectively represents two Chinese phrases of "计算"(computational) and "语言学"(linguistics). In our system, the pinyin labeling is realized by a "Tool of Chinese term pinyin annotation".

For Japanese, terms are ordered by fifty sound-graphs, and the hiragana and katakana are mixed arranged. A transformation tool of Japanese hiragana and katakana is also developed in the system. For Korean, German, Russian, and French, the terms are all ordered by characters.

It should be noted that for each index table, there is only one terminology in term field, which means if there are more than one other language terms corresponding one English term, these terms should be put into the index table respectively. For example, in Table 4, Chinese terms "句法" and "文法" are represented by two records, but in Table 1 they are combined to one record, "grammar". The Chinese term "语法" has two corresponding English terms, "grammar" and "syntax", so it has two corresponding IDs.

**Table 4.** Examples from Chinese term index table

| Term | ID | PinYin |
|------|-----|--------|
| 计算语言学 | 2169 | jisuan yuyanxue |
| 句法 | 11571 | jufa |
| 语法 | 4769,11571 | yufa |
| …… | …… | …… |

- Seven Monolingual Basic Information Tables

It is incomplete for a term bank if it only contains the different language translation of the terms. The basic information tables are built for the researchers to find more information such as definition, pinyin, synonym, abbreviation, hyponym, hyponym and so on. Some information of the terms could be obtained by "The Grammatical Knowledge-Base of Contemporary Chinese" of ICL-PKU. As for those terms which are not in the dictionary, further work should be done. Because the number of the terms is large, it is difficult to construct the whole information tables. The terms in CTB will be considered first. Now, this information table is still under construction. Table 5 shows the structure of the basic information table of Chinese terms.

**Table 5.** The basic information table of Chinese terms

| Chinese Terms | Chinese PinYin | Synonymy | Hyponym | Hyponym | Definition of Terms |
|------|------|------|------|------|------|
| C1 | …… | ……… | ……… | ……… | ……… |
| C1 | …… | ……… | | ……… | ……… |
| …… | ……… | ……… | | ……… | …… |

Based on term information table, index table and the main file, it is convenient to automatically construct some dictionaries such as mono-linguistic information dictionary, bilingual information dictionary. In fact, the Chinese term information table is just one Chinese information dictionary. An English-Chinese term information dictionary could be constructed by using the main file, Chinese term index table, English term index table and Chinese term information table. Even the trilingual information dictionary could also be built.

## 4.2    The Function of ETB Management System

Based on the above basic tables, the management system of ETB has the following functions.

- Data maintenance. The records could be made the operation of adding, deleting and modifying which are the basic functions of database. Based on these functions, the database could be constantly updated and expanded.

- Data Inquiry. The records satisfied with the query condition could be found. The query condition is flexible, e.g., not only terms could be found, but the information such as "definition" could also be found.
- Duplicate checking. When the new records are added into the base, the system could find and delete the duplicate records, and by comparing, the record with rich information could be reserved.
- Re-order. When the records change after some operation, the system could reorder the whole bank. This is an ordinary function of database.
- Automatic indexing. The system could build the monolingual index table dynamically. For instance, the Chinese term index file is automatically built according to pinyin. Now, the key problem of pinyin index table is how to deal with the polyphonic. To find the polyphonic dictionary and using some rules is the main methods in this system.
- Dictionary Generation. The system could automatically build multi-lingual term dictionary such as mono-lingual term information dictionary, bilingual term information dictionary, and so on.

The management database system uses Visual Studio 2005 as development tool, and C# as the programming language. The platform of database is based on SQL Server 2005. The application of ADO.NET to the data access, and the objects such as SqlConnection, SqlCommand, SqlDataAdapter, DataSet etc. could help conveniently realize the function of adding, deleting, modifying and inquiring. Figure 1 shows the interface of the management system of ETB.

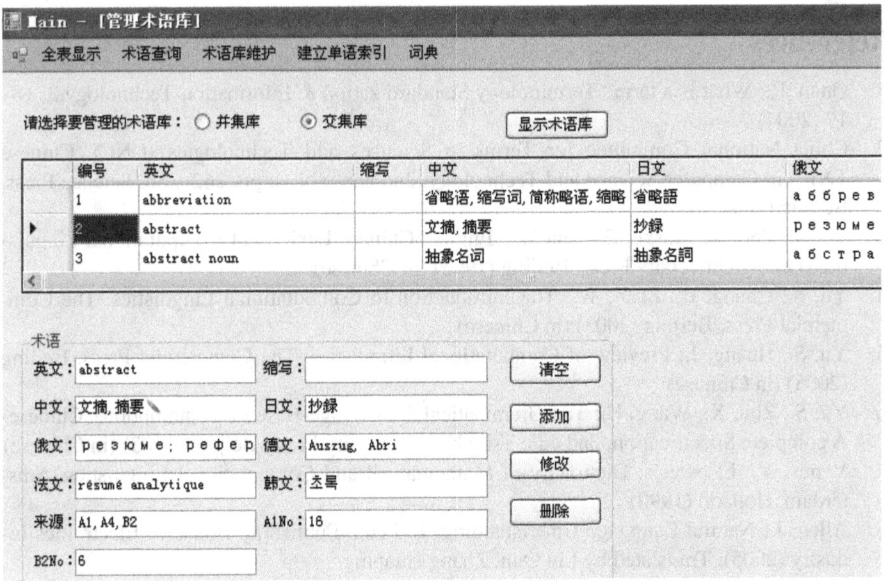

**Fig. 1.** The management system of ETB

# 5    Conclusion and Future Work

Based on the 5,415 terms from Computational Linguistic Lexicon which was built by ICL-PKU in the early 1990s, a new expanded computational linguistic terminology bank ETB is constructed. The number of languages is also expanded from the four to seven. CTB is built by intersection operation of different term banks and one database management system is also built. Currently, the expanding job and CTB construction have been finished, and the multi-linguistic translation of CTB is completed. The whole translation work of ETB is now in progress. The current ETB contains 13,016 English terms, 11,290 Chinese terms, 8,415 Japanese terms, 6,250 German terms, 5,747 Russian terms, 4,583 French terms, and 779 Korean terms.

To complete the whole translation is the key task in the future. Also, how to translate, define, arrange the terms by combining the manual and automatic methods, how to give the term information such as synonym and hyponym, and how to construct the term classification system are the further problems that should be dealt with.

**Acknowledgements.** ETB can hardly be constructed without the help from these experts, Prof. Yu Shiwen and Zhu Xuefeng from ICL-PKU, associate professor Elisabeth Kaske from Frankfurt University in German, Prof. Feng Zhiwei from Institute of Applied Linguistics Ministry of Education, Dr. Zhang Yujie from NICT of Japan, Dr. Jiang Binggui from University of Seoul, Li Liang (Лиля Холкина) from Russia, and Prof. Chen Min from Nanjing University. They are in charge of different language translation jobs. Thanks for the support and help from these experts and scholars very much.

This work is supported by National Natural Science Foundation of China (No. 61170144).

# References

1. Quan, R.: What is a term? Terminology Standardization & Information Technology 3, 18–19 (2004)
2. China National Committee for Terms in Sciences and Technologies (CNC). Chinese Terms in Computer Science and Technology, 2nd edn. vol. 4, pp. 262–268. Science Press, Beijing (2002)
3. Yu, S., Zhu, X., Kaske, E., Feng, Z.: English-Chinese Lexicon of Computational Linguistics. Peking University Press, Beijing (1996) (in Chinese)
4. Yu, S., Chang, B., Zhan, W.: The Introduction to Computational Linguistics. The Commercial Press, Beijing (2003) (in Chinese)
5. Yu, S., Huang, J.: Preview of Computational Linguistics. The Commercial Press, Beijing (2005) (in Chinese)
6. Yu, S., Zhu, X., Wang, H.: The Grammatical Knowledge-Base of Contemporary Chinese-A complete Specification, 2nd edn. Tsinghua University Press, Beijing (2003) (in Chinese)
7. Venev, Y.: Elsevier's: Dictionary of Mathematical and Computational Linguistics, Amsterdam, Holland (1990)
8. Allen, J.: Natural Language Understanding, 2nd edn. Publishing House of Electronics Industry (2005); Translated by Liu Qun, Zhang Huaping
9. Manning, C.D., Raghavan, P., Schützek, H.: An Introduction to Information Retrieval. Cambridge University Press, Cambridge (2008)

# On the Indicating Words of Idiom Annotation in CCD (6th ed.)

Hongyan Liu[1], Jiyan Li[2], and Huibin Zhuang[3]

[1] Hebei University, Baoding, China
[2] Yanshan University, Qinhuangdao, China
[3] Henan University, Kaifeng, China
{chlhy_youxiang,dayanlijiyan,zhuanghuibin}@163.com

**Abstract.** Seven years after the publication of the fifth edition, the sixth edition of Contemporary Chinese Dictionary (CCD) comes out. It is a systematic revision based on the former editions and allows the CCD to keep pace with time and advance to a new level. With the method of quantitative analysis, the paper examines the types and the amount of changes in the IWs of idioms in the 6th edition, aiming to analyze the possible causes, demonstrate its accomplishment and points out some remaining problems.

**Keywords:** IWs, changes, problems.

## 1 Introduction

In order to clarify the definition, when defining words, dictionary use certain expressions and symbol marks with special meaning [1] (p.51). Those words are known as IWs [2-4]. In the guide to Contemporary Chinese Dictionary (CCD) (sixth edition), it is clearly stated that one main aspect of the revision is to "make a unified revision on the indicating words (IW) in idiom annotation, such as 比喻 *biyu* 'metaphorize', 形容 *xingrong* 'describe', 借代 *jie dai* 'metonymize'." The change of IWs, is both due to the compilers' objective perception and ordinary people's view on the semantic development. The sixth edition of CCD is a systematically revised version on the basis of the fifth edition. The definition of idioms in the sixth edition inherits the main contents of the fifth edition and revises the IWs systematically. Through comparison, this paper pays close attention to the types and the amount of the revised IWs, analyzes the value of the revision, and ventures to put forward some understandings, with the hope for further discussion with the compilers of CCD and specialists in this area.

## 2 Changes of the Indicating Words

### 2.1 Types of IW Changes in Idiom Annotation

a. "比喻" *biyu* 'metaphorize' to "形容" *xingrong* 'describe' (100 entries in total). Examples are shown as follows:

P. Liu and Q. Su (Eds.): CLSW 2013, LNAI 8229, pp. 581–592, 2013.

壁垒森严 *bi lei sen yan* '(*fig*) closely guarded; strongly fortified or sharply divided'
比喻防守很严密或界限划得很分明。（5<sup>th</sup> ed.）
'To **metaphorize** close guard, strong fortification or sharp division.'
形容防守很严密或界限划得很分明。（6<sup>th</sup> ed.）
'To **describe** close guard, strong fortification or sharp division.'

如火如荼 *ru huo ru tu* '...to describe the mightiness of an army. Now used figuratively to indicate something prosperous, vigorous, or intense.'
原比喻军容之盛（语本《国语·吴语》），现用来形容旺盛、热烈或激烈。(5<sup>th</sup> ed.)
'...used to **metaphorize** the mightiness of an army. Now used figuratively to indicate something prosperous, vigorous, or intense.'
原形容军容之盛（语本《国语·吴语》），现用来形容旺盛、热烈或激烈。(6<sup>th</sup> ed.)
'...used to **describe** the mightiness of an army. Now used figuratively to indicate something prosperous, vigorous, or intense.'

举重若轻 *ju zhong ruo qing* 'Lifting something heavy is as easy as lifting something light. (*fig*) it seems easy to do something even though the assignment is actually complicated and hard to handle'
……比喻做繁难的事或处理棘手的问题轻松而不费力。（5<sup>th</sup> ed.）
'To **metaphorize** the easiness to do something even though the assignment is actually complicated and hard to handle.'
……形容做繁难的事或处理棘手的问题轻松而不费力。（6<sup>th</sup> ed.）
'To **describe** the easiness to do something even though the assignment is actually complicated and hard to handle.'

b. 比喻 *biyu* 'metaphorize' to 指 *zhi* 'refer to' (46 entries in total).
表里如一 *biao li ru yi* '(*fig*) think and act in one and the same way'
比喻思想和言行完全一致。（5<sup>th</sup> ed.）
'To **metaphorize** the state to think and act in one and the same way'
指思想和言行完全一致。（6<sup>th</sup> ed.）
'To **refer to** the state to think and act in one and the same way'

c. 比喻 *biyu* 'metaphorize' to 泛指 *fanzhi* 'generally refer to' (24 entries in total).
闭关自守 *bi guan zi shou* 'Close the country to the outside world by closing the pass; (*fig*) seclude oneself from the outside world'
闭塞关口，不跟别国往来。也比喻不跟外界交往。（5<sup>th</sup> ed.）
'Close the country to the outside world by closing the pass; **metaphorize** the seclusion of oneself from the outside world'
闭塞关口，不跟别国往来。也泛指不跟外界交往。（6<sup>th</sup> ed.）
'Close the country to the outside world by closing the pass; **generally describe** the seclusion of oneself from the outside world'

d. 比喻 *biyu* 'metaphorize' to 借指 *jiezhi* 'be used refer to' (17 entries in total).
黔驴技穷 *qian lü ji qiong* 'The Guizhou donkey has exhausted its tricks; (*fig*) be at one's wit's end; be at the end of one's resources.'

比喻仅有的一点伎俩也用完了。（5<sup>th</sup> ed.）

'To **metaphorize** the statement being at one's wit's end or at the end of one's resources.'

借指仅有的一点儿本领也用完了（多含贬义）。（6<sup>th</sup> ed.）

'To **refer to** the statement being at one's wit's end or at the end of one's resources.'

e. Deleting the IW 比喻 *biyu* 'metaphorize' (4 entries in total).

捷足先登 *jie zu xian deng* '(fig) the swift-footed arrive first; early bird catches the worm.'

比喻行动敏捷，先达到目的。（5<sup>th</sup> ed.）

'To **metaphorize** that the swift-footed arrive first; early bird catches the worm.'

行动敏捷，先达到目的。（6<sup>th</sup> ed.）

'The swift-footed arrive first; early bird catches the worm.'

风烛残年 *feng zhu can nian* 'candle guttering in the wind; (fig) (of a person or thing) may die or disappear at any moment.'

比喻随时可能死亡的晚年（风烛：风中之烛）。（5<sup>th</sup> ed.）

'To **metaphorize** the state (of a person or thing) may die or disappear at any moment (candle guttering in the wind).'

像风中的蜡烛那样随时可能死亡的晚年。（6<sup>th</sup> ed.）

'(of a person or thing) may die or disappear at any moment like a candle guttering in the wind.'

f. 形容*xingrong* 'describe' to 指 *zhi* 'refer to' (7 entries in total).

失之交臂 *shi zhi jiao bi* 'Miss somebody by a narrow chance; lose a good opportunity.'

形容当面错过，失掉好机会。（5<sup>th</sup> ed.）

'To **describe** the state missing somebody by a narrow chance or losing a good opportunity.'

指当面错过，失掉好机会。（6<sup>th</sup> ed.）

'To **refer to** the state missing somebody by a narrow chance or losing a good opportunity.'

g. 形容*xingrong* 'describe' to 比喻 *biyu* 'metaphorize' (3 entries in total).

绵里藏针 *mian li cang zhen* 'needle hidden in silk floss; an iron hand in a velvet glove.'

①形容柔中有刚（5<sup>th</sup> ed.）

'To **describe** needle hidden in silk floss or an iron hand in a velvet glove.'

①比喻柔中有刚（6<sup>th</sup> ed.）

'To **metaphorize** needle hidden in silk floss or an iron hand in a velvet glove.'

h. Deleting the IW 形容 *xingrong* 'describe' (8 entries in total).

不修边幅 *bu xiu bian fu* 'Not care about one's disappearance; be slovenly.'

形容不注意衣着、容貌的整洁。（5<sup>th</sup> ed.）

'To **describe** a person not caring about one's disappearance; be slovenly.'

不注意衣着、容貌的整洁。（6<sup>th</sup> ed.）

'Not caring about one's disappearance; be slovenly.'

i. 泛指 *fanzhi* 'generally refer to' to 比喻 *biyu* 'metaphorize' (3 entries in total)

超然物外 *chao ran wu wai* '(fig) be above worldly concerns; stay away from scenes of contention; stand aloof.'

②泛指置身事外。（5ᵗʰ ed.）

'To **describe** the state being above worldly concerns; staying away from scenes of contention or standing aloof.'

②比喻置身事外。（6ᵗʰ ed.）

'To **metaphorize** the state being above worldly concerns; staying away from scenes of contention or standing aloof.'

j. 泛指 *fanzhi* 'generally refer to' to 形容 *xingrong* 'describe' (2 entries in total).

赶尽杀绝 *gan jin sha jue* 'Kill all; ruthlessly exterminate; spare none.'

消灭净尽，**泛指**对人狠毒，不留余地。（5ᵗʰ ed.）

'To kill all; **generally refer to** the ruthlessnees to exterminate and spare none.'

消灭净尽，**形容**对人狠毒，不留余地。（6ᵗʰ ed.）

'To kill all; **describe** the ruthlessnees to exterminate and spare none.'

k. 泛指 *fanzhi* 'generally refer to' to 借指 *jiezhi* 'be used to refer to' (3 entries in total)

等因奉此 *deng yin feng ci* '…general reference to government documents; (fig) officialese.'

⋯⋯泛指文牍，比喻例行公事、官样文章。（5ᵗʰ ed.）

'…**generally refer to** government documents; (fig) officialese.'

⋯⋯借指例行公事的文牍或官样文章。（6ᵗʰ ed.）

'…It **is used to refer to** government documents or officialese.'

l. 指 *zhi* 'refer to' to 比喻 *biyu* 'metaphorize' (1 entry in total).

飞黄腾达 *fei huang teng da* 'Soar like the holy horse, leaving behind the toad.'

⋯⋯后来用"飞黄腾达"指官职、地位上升得很快。（5ᵗʰ ed.）

'Now *fei huang teng da* is used to **refer to** the situation of quick promotion.'

⋯⋯后来用"飞黄腾达"比喻官职、地位上升得很快。（6ᵗʰ ed.）

'Now *fei huang teng da* is used to **metaphorize** the situation of quick promotion.'

m. 指 *zhi* 'refer to' to 形容 *xingrong* 'describe' (7 entries in total)

颐指气使 *yi zhi qi shi* 'Order people about by gestures; be insufferably arrogant.'

⋯⋯指有权势的人随意支使人的傲慢神气。（5ᵗʰ ed.）

'**Refer to** the insufferably arrogance (of a person) when ordering people about.'

⋯⋯形容有权势的人随意支使人的傲慢神气。（6ᵗʰ ed.）

'**Describe** the insufferably arrogance (of a person) when ordering people about.'

n. 指 *zhi* 'refer to' to 借指 *jiezhi* 'be used to refer to' (1 entry in total).

围魏救赵 *wei wei jiu zhao* '…refer to similar strategies.'

⋯⋯指类似的作战方法。（5ᵗʰ ed.）

'…**refer to** similar fighting strategies.'

⋯⋯借指类似的作战方法。（6ᵗʰ ed.）

'…It **is used to refer to** similar fighting strategies.'

o. Deleting IW 指 *zhi* 'refer to' (2 entries in total)

兵临城下 *bing lin cheng xia* 'The enemy has reached the city gates; the city is under siege; the situation is dangerous.

指大军压境，城被围困。形容形势危急。（5th ed.）

'**To refer to** the situation where the enemy has reached the city gates; the city is under siege. It is used to describe the situation is dangerous.'

大军压境，城被围困。形容形势危急。（6th ed.）

'The enemy has reached the city gates; the city is under siege. This is used to describe the situation is dangerous.'

p. 借指 *jiezhi* 'be used to refer to' to 泛指 *fanzhi* 'generally refer to' (1 entry in total)

弱肉强食 *ruo rou qiang shi* 'The weak being at the mercy of the strong- the Law of the Jungle.'

指动物中弱者被强者吃掉，借指弱者被欺凌、吞并。（5th ed.）

'Weak animals are prey of strong animals. This **is used to refer to** the situation that the weak being at the mercy of the strong.'

指动物中弱者被强者吃掉，泛指弱者被欺凌、吞并。（6th ed.）

'Weak animals are prey of strong animals. **Generally** it **refers to** the situation that the weak being at the mercy of the strong.'

q. 表示 *biaoshi* 'indicate' to 指 *zhi* 'refer to' (2 entries in total)

万劫不复 *wan jie bu fu* 'Lost forever; beyond redemption.'

表示永远不能恢复。（5th ed.）

'To **indicate** the state being lost forever and beyond redemption.'

指永远不能恢复。（6th ed.）

'To **refer to** the state being lost forever and beyond redemption.'

r. 表示 *biaoshi* 'indicate' to 形容 *xingrong* 'describe' (1 entry in total)

连篇累牍 *lian pian lei du* 'lengthy and tedious; at great length'

表示用过多篇幅叙述。（5th ed.）

'To **indicate** that the statement being at great length.'

形容叙述的篇幅过多、过长。（6th ed.）

'To **describe** the statement that is lengthy and tedious.'

s. 转喻 *zhuanyu* 'metonymize' to 借指 *jiezhi* 'be used to refer to' (1 entry in total)

风花雪月 *feng hua xue yue* 'wind, flowers, snow and moon; originally they are the subjects in classical literature; now flowery, empty poetic prose.'

原指古典文学里描写自然景物的四种对象，后转喻堆砌辞藻而内容贫乏的诗文。（5th ed.）

'Originally they are the subjects in classical literature. Now it **meonymizes** flowery, empty poetic prose.'

原指古典文学里描写自然景物的四种对象，后借指堆砌辞藻而内容贫乏的诗文。（6th ed.）

'Originally they are the subjects in classical literature. Now it **is used to refer to** flowery, empty poetic prose.'

## 2.2    Analysis of the Changes

First, in the definitions of idioms, the literal surface meaning is directly stated usually, without IWs; the deep meaning is usually stated with IWs. In the fifth edition the IWs are 比喻 *biyu* 'metaphorize', 形容 *xingrong* 'describe', 泛指 *fanzhi* 'generally refer to', 指 *zhi* 'refer to', 借指 *jiezhi* 'be used to refer to', 表示 *biaoshi* 'indicate'; 转喻 *zhuanyu* 'metonymize'; while in the sixth edition, the IWs are 比喻 *biyu* 'metaphorize', 形容 *xingrong* 'describe', 泛指 *fanzhi* 'generally refer to', 指 *zhi* 'refer to', 借指 *jiezhi* 'be used to refer to', 表示 *biaoshi* 'indicate'.

Second, in items (a-e), the IW 比喻 *biyu* 'metaphorize' is revised, adding up to 191 entries, which is quite an extraordinary phenomenon in the sixth edition. The definition of 比喻 *biyu* is still the same in the two versions: *n. metaphor, analogy, figure of speech, a method of comparing one thing to another with which it shares some similarities with the aim of achieving a more vivid form of expression; draw an analogy.* The IW 比喻 *biyu* 'metaphorize' is used to explain the metaphorical or figurative meanings of the idioms whose integral figurative meaning is a must. The differences between figurative words and figurative meaning of words are extensively discussed among the experts [4-6], the related achievement of which is adopted in the compilation of the sixth edition. The sixth edition further distinguishes 'the idioms constructed in a figurative way' and 'the figurative meanings of the idioms' and revises the chaotic situation in the fifth edition that some idioms have the same structure but different IWs. For example, in the fifth edition, 如火如荼 *ru huo ru tu* uses the IW 比喻 *biyu* 'metaphorize', but 如胶似漆 *ru jiao si qi* which has the same structure uses the IW 形容 *xingrong* 'describe'. In the sixth edition, both of them use the IW 形容 *xingrong* 'describe'. All these reflect the compilers' deeper cognition and precise definition.

a. 形容 *xingrong* 'describe' in the two editions have the same definition: *to describe the image or nature of something.* The IW 形容 *xingrong* 'describe' is usually used to describe the image or nature of things. In the fifth edition, some idioms are pure description, but the IW 比喻 *biyu* 'metaphorize' is applied improperly, such as in 不刊之论 *bu kan zhi lun*. Some idioms contain parts with metaphorical meaning, but as a whole they are description instead of metaphors, such as 壁垒森严 *bi lei sen yan*. Some are constructed in a figurative way, but the whole meaning is a description rather than a metaphor. Some appear to contain metaphorical words, but they are not metaphor, but analogy, and the application of analogy is for description, such as 举重若轻 *ju zhong ruo qing*. These interpretations using the IW 比喻 *biyu* 'metaphorize' improperly in the fifth edition are revised with the IW 形容 *xingrong* 'describe' in the sixth edition.

b. Yu [7] proposes that 指 *zhi* 'refer to' is to show the semantic range clearly and is applied only to those with semantic range problems. However, in CCD, it is not in that way. The differences of 指 *zhi* in the two editions lie in that in fifth edition 指 is *to refer to something in meaning* while in sixth edition 指 *zhi* is *to target at something in meaning*. In the fifth edition, the IW 指 *zhi* is used to define the word itself. This kind of circular definition is absolutely unacceptable in the compilation of a dictionary. The author of this paper believes that it would be better to define 指 *zhi* as to point and the IW 指 should be applied to indicate the meaning of the words under the condition that the words have not only surface meanings but also deep meanings, and the deep meanings is non-figurative, non-overstated, non-transferred epithet. The definition of 表里如一 *biao li ru yi* has the non-surface literal meaning, but it does not have the overall figurative sense. Therefore, in its interpretation in the sixth edition, 比喻 *biyu* 'metaphorize' is revised as 指 *zhi* 'refer to'.

c. In the fifth edition, there are two items in the entry of 泛指 *fanzhi* 'generally refer to': *1. to generally refer to; 2. to use a particular subject to refer to a whole concept, as opposed to particularly refer to.* In the sixth edition, the entry of 泛指 *fanzhi* is deleted. The use of the IW 泛指 *fanzhi* 'generally refer to' in two editions shares one point, that is, the meanings of the idioms extend from a narrow scope to a broader one. Take 闭关自守 *bi guan zi shou* as an example. There is no overall figurative relationship between the surface meaning and deep meaning in this idiom. It is just that the meaning expands from the communication between countries to the communication with any other space beyond the community itself. Therefore, here the IW should not be 比喻 *biyu* 'metaphorize' but 泛指 *fanzhi* 'generally refer to' as has been revised in the sixth edition.

d. The definition of 借指 *jiezhi* 'be used to refer to' in the fifth edition is as follows: *to use something related to a particular thing to refer to this particular thing.* There is no entry of 借指 *jiezhi* 'be used to refer to' in the sixth edition. Generally speaking, the IW 借指 *jiezhi* 'be used to refer to' in both editions shows the situation that two related things generate new meaning because of their relevance. It differs from 比喻 *biyu* 'metaphorize' in the basis on which the two devices come into being. 比喻 *biyu* 'metaphorize' lays special emphasis on the similarity, while 借指 *jiezhi* 'be used to refer to' on the interrelationship. 黔驴技穷 *qian lü ji qiong* takes advantage of the typical image of the Guizhou donkey who when exhausting his tricks was at the end of his wits. The key element between the tenor and the vehicle is to borrow, instead of making a figurative speech. That is why the IWs of this kind of idioms in the sixth edition are revised.

e. The idioms don't have figurative sense, such as 捷足先登 *jie zu xian deng*, or both the tenor and the vehicle appear in the constitution of the idiom, but the vehicle is used only to illustrate the tenor inside the entry. That is to say, the figurative speech lies inside the idiom, and it can't produce figurative speech with components outside of the entry, such as 风烛残年 *feng zhu can nian*. Idioms like that don't have internal overall figurative sense. They can be explained directly from the literal meaning, and therefore do not match with the IW of 比喻 *biyu* 'metaphorize'. Thus, the revision in the sixth edition is very reasonable.

Third, the items (f-h) are about the revisions of IW 形容 *xingrong* 'describe', adding up to 18 entries. As an IW, 形容 *xingrong* 'describe' is generally used to describe the image and nature of things. However, in the fifth edition, some idioms do not describe the image and nature of things, but just deduce the deep meaning beyond the surface meaning, such as 失之交臂 *shi zhi jiao bi*. Some do not lay special emphasis on description, but carry overall figurative sense, such as 绵里藏针 *mian li cang zhen*. Some do not have deep meanings, and can be directly defined through the literal components. Hence, the IW 形容 *xingrong* 'describe' in the interpretation of these idioms are revised in the sixth edition.

Fourth, in items (q-r), the IW 表示 *biaoshi* 'indicate' is revised. In both editions of CCD, 表示 is defined as '(of sth.) indicate meaning through itself or through something else'. This definition shows that the IW 表示 has two meanings: *1. indicate meaning through itself; 2. indicate meaning through something else.* When following the first meaning, the IW 表示 *biaoshi* 'indicate' has basically the same meaning with 指 *zhi* 'refer to'. Considering the conciseness of the expression, in sixth edition, the IW 表示 *biaoshi* 'indicate' is revised as 指 *zhi* 'refer to' in such idioms as 万劫不复 *wan jie bu fu*. On contrary, the meaning of 连篇累牍 *lian pian lei du* should be 'putting particular stress on description', so the IW 表示 *biaoshi* 'indicate' is revised to the IW 形容 *xingrong* 'describe' in the sixth edition.

Fifth, the item (s) is about the revision of the IW 转喻 *zhuanyu* 'metonymize'. Now specialists on semantics, lexicography, grammar, rhetoric all use the word of 转喻 *zhuanyu* 'metonymize', but they mean differently. The entry of 转喻 *zhuanyu* 'metonymize' appears neither in the fifth nor the sixth edition. It can be regarded as a phrase which expresses its meaning through its two individual words. In the sixth edition, the definition of 转 *zhuan* is as follows: *(of orientation, position, situation, condition, etc.) turn; shift; change*; while the definition of 喻 *yu* is *analogy; figure of speech.* Thus 转喻 *zhuanyu* 'metonymize' can generally be defined as 'to make an analogy by turning (orientation, position, situation, condition, etc.)'. Since 借指 *jiezhi* 'be used to refer to' means 'to use something related to a particular thing to refer to this particular thing', it is clear that 转喻 *zhuanyu* 'metonymize' attaches more importance to the analogy and similarity while 借指 *jiezhi* 'be used to refer to' attaches more importance to the substitution and interrelation. For example, 风花雪月 *feng hua xue yue* originally means the four kinds of natural phenomena (wind, flowers, snow, and moon) and has by extension come to mean the flowery, empty poetic prose. But it does not change the objects to draw an analogy between the four kinds of natural phenomena and the poems and essays with fancy words and poor contents. Instead, it borrows the related things to refer to the flowery, empty poetic prose. Those poetic proses are correlated with wind, flowers, snow, and moon, the former being the manifestation of the latter and the latter being the contents of the former. Hence, the use of 转喻 *zhuanyu* 'metonymize' as the IWs in the fifth edition is improper.

The IW 转喻 *zhuanyu* 'metonymize' appears only once in the fifth edition, explaining the first meaning of 风花雪月 *feng hua xue yue*, but its connotation is not clear. This does not agree with the requirement of editing a dictionary that IWs should be scientific, rigorous and systematic. From this viewpoint, the revision in the sixth edition is correct.

Sixth, items (*i-p*) show the revision of the IWs 泛指 *fanzhi* 'generally refer to', 指 *zhi* 'refer to', and 借指 *jiezhi* 'be used to refer to'. The reason for the revision is largely the same as that for the revision of 比喻 *biyu* 'metaphorize', and 形容 *xingrong* 'describe', which demonstrates the clarification of the connotation of the IWs and the compilers' deeper understanding about the meanings of the idioms.

## 3    Remaining Problems in the Use of IWs in the Sixth Edition

It is remarkable progress to make a systematic revision of the IWs in the sixth edition, but there are still some problems.

First, the connotations of the IWs are not clear enough. As the metalanguage for definition, the IWs, in order to be of great help for standardized use, should be clear in connotation, scientific and rigorous. However, the fact is that the sixth edition does not list the entries of some IWs, such as 泛指 *fanzhi* 'generally refer to', 借指 *jiezhi* 'be used refer to' and that the definitions of some IWs are not exact or accurate, such as 指 *zhi* 'refer to'. These phenomena would contribute to the situation that the connotations of some IWs are vague and unclear. On the one hand, there is no unified concept in this area; on the other hand, the dictionary compilers do not have a unanimous understanding about these IWs. Thus, the casual use of IWs is unavoidable in the course of the dictionary compilation.

Second, the distinctive features of the IWs are not clear. The IWs 表示 *biaoshi* 'indicate' and 指 *zhi* 'refer to' have been analyzed in the previous parts. On some conditions, 表示 *biaoshi* 'indicate' and 指 *zhi* 'refer to' are basically the same, such as in the idiom 万劫不复 *wan jie bu fu*. In the latest edition, the IW 表示 *biaoshi* 'indicate' is revised in 3 idioms and is used in another 11 idioms, but there isn't much difference between the 11 unrevised idioms and those revised ones. For instance, 肝脑涂地 *gan nao tu di* is revised, but 大而化之 *da er hua zhi* which has the similar definition form is unrevised yet. The reason why some are revised but some are not can't be identified. The IWs are supposed to have distinctive features. If the distinctive features are not clear, or basically are synonyms, then they are unnecessary and should be deleted.

Third, some IWs are used improperly. Most of the revisions of the IWs in the sixth edition conform to the formation of the idiom meanings, yet some of them are unsuitable. Take 青红皂白 *qing hong zao bai* as an example. The IW of its definition in the fifth edition is 比喻 *biyu* 'metaphorize', while in the sixth edition, it changes into 借指 *jiezhi* 'be used to refer to'. However, the components of this idiom are four kinds of colors: green, red, black, and white, which have nothing to do with '是非 *shifei* 'right and wrong', 情由 *qingyou* 'hows and whys'. However, when used in negative context, i.e., 不分青红皂白 *bu fen qing hong zao bai*, the idiom has extended its meaning from 'not distinguishing between colors' to 'not distinguishing between right and wrong'. Between the two meanings there exists similarity but not relevance, an therefore the use of 比喻 *biyu* 'metaphorize' in the fifth edition is more suitable. Improper revisions in the sixth edition also happen with such idioms as 落花流水 *luo hua liu shui*, 粗枝大叶 *cu zhi da ye*, 弦外之意 *xian wai zhi yin*, etc.

The sixth edition continues to use some IWs improperly in the fifth edition. For instance, 逼良为娼 *bi liang wei chang* in both editions is defined as *'to force a young woman from a good family or a woman of virtue to engage in prostitution; (fig) force an honest person to do something dishonest'*. Both the surface meaning *'to force a young woman of a good family or a woman of virtue to engage in prostitution'* and the deep meaning *'to force an honest person to do something dishonest'* have one common point: to force a person to do something bad. There is no figurative sense; it's just that the semantic scope expands from a special area to a broader one. Hence, the IW should be 泛指 *fanzhi* 'generally refer to', rather than 比喻 *biyu* 'metaphorize'. In the sixth edition, idioms which follow the wrong IWs include 敝帚自珍 *bi zhou zi zhen*, 夫唱妇随 *fu chang fu sui*, 鞭长莫及 *bian chang mo ji*, 插科打诨 *cha ke da hun*, etc, whose IWs should be revised as 泛指 *fanzhi* 'generally refer to', 指 *zhi* 'refer to', 泛指 *fanzhi* 'generally refer to', and no IW.

Some idioms have the same structure but different IWs. In both editions, 背城一战 *bei cheng yi zhan* is defined as 背城借一 *bei cheng jie yi* whose definition is 'to wage a last-ditch fight with one's back against the city wall; generally refer to fight to the last ditch; put up a stubborn resistance; also known as 背城一战'. This means 背城一战 and 背城借一 are of different forms but the same meaning. In both editions, 背水一战 bei sh*ui yi zhan* is defined as 'to fight with one's back against the river or the wall; (fig) to fight to win to die; fight a last-ditch battle; conduct a desperate struggle to find a way out of a hopeless situation'. 背水一战 and 背城一战 are alike in the form and close in meaning, but their IWs are different. This definitely is a problem. Considering the relationship between the idiom and its meaning, the proper IW for 背水一战 should be revised as 泛指 *fanzhi* 'generally refer to'.

## 4    Conclusion

This paper compares the IWs of idioms in the 6th edition of CCD with those in the 5th edition, showing that it is a systematic revision based on the former editions and allows the CCD to keep pace with time and advance to a new level.

To sum up, the IWs in the sixth edition become more systematic, clearer in connotations, and more rigorous in use. Meanwhile, problems do exist. However, the small defects can't obscure the greatness.

We are looking forward to a more normative and scientific Contemporary Chinese Dictionary.

## References

1. Hu, M.: An Outline on Lexicography. People's Press of China, Beijing (1982) (in Chinese)
2. Su, X.: A quantitative study on the entries of Contemporary Chinese Dictionary. Chinese Teaching in the World 4, 39–47 (2001) (in Chinese)

3. Yu, G.: Interpretation and interpretative features of Chinese four-character idioms in Contemporary Chinese dictionary. Journal of Pingxiang College (2), 88–90 (2001) (in Chinese)
4. Long, Q.: The meaning type and dictionary paraphrase of metaphorical idiom. Journal of Yunmeng (2), 118–121 (2005)
5. Ying, Y.: Type and interpretation of the figurative phrases. Zhongguo Yuwen 4, 295–300 (1993) (in Chinese)
6. Zhou, J.: Metaphorical words and metaphorical meaning of words. Language Teaching and Linguistic Studies (4), 145–155 (1993) (in Chinese)
7. Yu, S.: On preposed indicating words in definitions. Lexicographical Studies 2, 17–21 (1996) (in Chinese)

# Appendix: A Table for the Changes in IWs

**a. "比喻"变为"形容"** (*biyu* 'metaphorize' to *xingrong* 'describe')（**100条**）

| | | | | | | | |
|---|---|---|---|---|---|---|---|
| 哀鸿遍野 | 唇齿相依 | 狼奔豕突 | 磬竹难书 | 深藏若虚 | 天昏地暗 | 行云流水 | 有血有肉 |
| 百孔千疮 | 粗枝大叶 | 狼心狗肺 | 热血沸腾 | 神出鬼没 | 投鞭断流 | 杳如黄鹤 | 源远流长 |
| 壁垒森严 | 大张旗鼓 | 雷霆万钧 | 如臂使指 | 十拿九稳 | 土崩瓦解 | 一波三折 | 云泥之别 |
| 冰清玉洁 | 翻江倒海 | 琳琅满目 | 如虎添翼 | 势如破竹 | 推心置腹 | 一触即发 | 运风成斤 |
| 波澜壮阔 | 非驴非马 | 落花流水 | 如火如荼 | 鼠目寸光 | 拖泥带水 | 一帆风顺 | 朝三暮四 |
| 不刊之论 | 浮光掠影 | 履险如夷 | 如梦初醒 | 束手无策 | 万紫千红 | 一气呵成 | 蒸蒸日上 |
| 不郎不秀 | 纲举目张 | 明察秋毫 | 如日中天 | 水乳交融 | 望尘莫及 | 一五一十 | 众口铄金 |
| 不蔓不枝 | 规行矩步 | 目迷五色 | 如汤沃雪 | 水深火热 | 无声无息 | 以汤沃雪 | 转弯抹角 |
| 不同凡响 | 火烧眉毛 | 盘根错节 | 如蚁附膻 | 丝丝入扣 | 五花八门 | 易如反掌 | 左右逢源 |
| 步步为营 | 间不容发 | 披肝沥胆 | 如影随形 | 四面楚歌 | 五体投地 | 莺歌燕舞 | |
| 沧海一粟 | 焦头烂额 | 迫在眉睫 | 如鱼得水 | 泰山压顶 | 息息相关 | 蝇营狗苟 | |
| 称王称霸 | 举重若轻 | 扑朔迷离 | 入木三分 | 天差地远 | 细针密缕 | 游刃有余 | |
| 吹灰之力 | 刻骨铭心 | 青云直上 | 若明若暗 | 天花乱坠 | 欣欣向荣 | 有口皆碑 | |

**b. "比喻"变为"指"** (*biyu* 'metaphorize' to *zhi* 'refer to')（**46条**）

| | | | | | | | |
|---|---|---|---|---|---|---|---|
| 宝刀不老 | 池鱼之殃 | 俯仰由人 | 狼子野心 | 前车之鉴 | 天诛地灭 | 弦外之音 | 异军突起 |
| 表里如一 | 重温旧梦 | 高山流水 | 两袖清风 | 倾箱倒箧 | 听天由命 | 偃旗息鼓 | 朝秦暮楚 |
| 不打自招 | 初露锋芒 | 高枕无忧 | 龙马精神 | 入主出奴 | 推襟送抱 | 夜郎自大 | 肘腋之患 |
| 不二法门 | 初露头角 | 光天化日 | 平分秋色 | 上下其手 | 望洋兴叹 | 一定之规 | 左右开弓 |
| 不落窠臼 | 独树一帜 | 狐朋狗友 | 旗帜鲜明 | 顺理成章 | 闻鸡起舞 | 一鼓作气 | |
| 称孤道寡 | 分庭抗礼 | 寄人篱下 | 企足而待 | 探骊得珠 | 稳操胜券 | 一席之地 | |

**c. "比喻"变为"泛指"** (*biyu* 'metaphorize' to *fanzhi* 'generally refer to')（**24条**）

| | | | | | | | |
|---|---|---|---|---|---|---|---|
| 闭关自守 | 沆瀣一气 | 开山祖师 | 身先士卒 | 寿终正寝 | 投桃报李 | 新陈代谢 | 欲擒故纵 |
| 趁火打劫 | 祸起萧墙 | 离经叛道 | 始作俑者 | 谈虎色变 | 退避三舍 | 摇旗呐喊 | 终南捷径 |
| 繁文缛节 | 江郎才尽 | 马首是瞻 | 嗜痂之癖 | 同病相怜 | 稳扎稳打 | 一笔勾消 | 自卖自夸 |

**d. "比喻"变为"借指"** (*biyu* 'metaphorize' to *jiezhi* 'be used to refer to')（**16条**）

| | | | | | | | |
|---|---|---|---|---|---|---|---|
| 暗度陈仓 | 独占鳌头 | 滥竽充数 | 毛遂自荐 | 黔驴技穷 | 嗜痂之癖 | 虾兵蟹将 | 愚公移山 |
| 等因奉此 | 鸡鸣狗盗 | 李代桃僵 | 杞人忧天 | 青红皂白 | 完璧归赵 | 渔人之利 | 终南捷径 |

**e. 删掉提示词"比喻"** (deleting indicating word *biyu* 'metaphorize') （4条）

风烛残年　　捷足先登　　金玉良言　　燃眉之急

**f. "形容"变为"指"** (*xingrong* 'describe' to *zhi* 'refer to') （7条）

鞍马劳顿　　拔刀相助　　别树一帜　　不知进退　　舍本逐末　　失之交臂　　食言而肥

**g. "形容"变为"比喻"** (*xingrong* 'describe' to *biyu* 'mmetaphorize') （3条）

白手起家　　绵里藏针　　舍近求远

**h. 删掉提示词"形容"** (deleting indicating word *xingrong* 'describe') （8条）

暴戾恣睢　　不修边幅　　风和日丽　　精明强干　　秋高气爽　　深藏若虚　　顺理成章　　死得其所

**i. "泛指"变为"比喻"** (*fanzhi* 'generally refer to' to *biyu* 'metaphorize') （3条）

超然物外　　数典忘祖　　先天不足

**j. "泛指"变为"形容"** (*fanzhi* 'generally refer' to *xingrong* 'describe') （2条）

赶尽杀绝　　犬牙交错

**k. "泛指"变为"借指"** (*fanzhi* 'generally refer to' to *jiezhi* 'be used to refer to') （3条）

等因奉此　　气冲斗牛　　清规戒律

**l. "指"变为"比喻"** (*zhi* 'refer to' to *biyu* 'metaphorize') （1条）

飞黄腾达

**m. "指"变为"形容"** (*zhi* 'refer to' to *xingrong* 'describe') （7条）

间不容发　　甚嚣尘上　　天荒地老　　听而不闻　　惜墨如金　　一尘不染　　颐指气使

**n. "指"变为"借指"** (*zhi* 'refer to' to *jiezhi* 'be used to refer to') （1条）

围魏救赵

**o. 删掉提示词"指"** (deleting indicating word *zhi* 'refer to') （2条）

兵临城下　　淡而无味

**p. "借指"变为"泛指"** (*jiezhi* 'be used to refer to' to *fanzhi* 'generally refer to') （1条）

弱肉强食

**q. "表示"变为"指"** (*biaoshi* 'indicate' to *zhi* 'refer to') （2条）

万劫不复　　肝脑涂地

**r. "表示"变为"形容"** (*biaoshi* 'indicate' to *xingrong* 'describe') （1条）

连篇累牍

**s. "转喻"变为"借指"** (*zhuanyu* 'metonymize' to *jiezhi* 'be used to refer to') （1条）

风花雪月

# Construction and Implementation of the Quantifier-Noun Collocation Knowledge Base for Proofreading Based on Multiple Knowledge Sources[*]

Lin Jiang, Yangsen Zhang, Jun Guan, and Zhenlei Du

Institute of Intelligence Information Processing,
Beijing Information Science and Technology University, Beijing 100192
my5261@126.com

**Abstract.** Due to specific semantic constraints between quantifiers and nouns and the frequent phenomena of quantifier-noun collocation error in real text, this paper proposes a new model of extracting quantifier-noun collocation and a new representation method of knowledge base. In this paper, by rules and statistical methods and the use of "The Grammatical Knowledge-base of Contemporary Chinese" and the "People's Daily" corpus resources, word-level quantifier-noun collocation knowledge base was established. On this basis, by analyzing the characteristics of the nouns and combining semantic class attributes in the "The Semantic Knowledge-base of Contemporary Chinese", semantic-level quantifier-noun collocation knowledge base was established. The experiment results show that the accuracy of checking quantifier-noun collocation errors reaches 77.38% by using quantifier-noun collocation knowledge base built by this method, and the scale of this knowledge base is expanded effectively.

**Keywords:** quantifier-noun collocation, semantic collocation, knowledge acquisition, quantifier-noun collocation knowledge base.

## 1  Introduction

Quantifier is a specific part-of-speech in Sino-Tibetan language as the representative of Chinese. According to relevant statistics, noun phrases containing at least a quantifier account for 20% of all noun phrases [1]. Thus, if we can dig up quantifier-noun collocations from a large number of texts, it will not only facilitate further study of linguistics, but also extend the research scope and refine the research subject. From another point of view, collocation knowledge base is the core of proofreading system knowledge base. Under current circumstance that the effect of syntactic parser for Chinese is not satisfied, it is necessary to first automatically identify quantifier-noun

---

[*] This paper is funded by the Natural Science Foundation of China (NSFC, Grant No.61070119), the Project of Construction of Innovation Teams and Teacher Career Development for Universities and Colleges Under Beijing Municipality(Grant No.IDHT20130519) and the Beijing Municipal Education Commission Special Fund (Grant No.PXM2012-014224-000020).

P. Liu and Q. Su (Eds.): CLSW 2013, LNAI 8229, pp. 593–602, 2013.

collocations from Chinese texts without collocation errors, and then establish quantifier-noun collocation knowledge base by using several types of resources. Finally, we can detect and correct collocation errors between quantifiers and nouns for any Chinese text.

Domestic researchers have studied collocation extraction between quantifiers and nouns for a period of time, the majority of them extracted word-level collocations from all kinds of dictionaries established by linguists or extracted from corpus by setting rules artificially. The former includes dictionaries such as the most representative of the "Mandarin Daily News Quantifier Dictionary" by Juren Huang and the "Quantifier Usage Dictionary of Contemporary Chinese"[2] by Xianzhen Guo, etc. The latter includes corpus like the "People's Daily" and Contemporary News & Novel Corpus, etc. There are also some researchers solving this problem from the perspective of class or semantics. For example, Meng Wang et al.[3] established a class knowledge base containing quantifier-noun collocations. It should be noted that the class is the core component of nouns. Fang Fang, Bin Li[4] proposed a back-off algorithm to extract quantifier-noun collocation based on $n$ words matching from the back forward. In essence, their idea is similar to that of [3]. Xuling Zheng et al.[5] summarized the usage of three kinds of quantifiers by making full use of the "Hownet". Hui Zhang[6] designed a noun-quantifier collocation dictionary with semantic information using data mining technology. However, the above methods have some drawbacks, for example, the range covered by the class sometimes is too large, or the study of quantifiers is not comprehensive, etc. Thus, further research is needed.

In this paper, we not only extracted quantifier-noun collocations by using dictionaries and corpus resources like previous researchers, but also for expanding the scale of the collocations, respectively generalized nouns modified by a specific quantifier to a certain semantic level while trying to maintain accuracy. This paper provides a new way for extracting quantifier-noun collocations.

# 2    The Construction of A Word-Level Quantifier-Noun Collocation Knowledge Base

## 2.1    Analysis of Noun Attributes in "The Grammatical Knowledge-Base of Contemporary Chinese" and the Construction of the Quantifier-Noun Collocation Knowledge Base

"The Grammatical Knowledge-base of Contemporary Chinese"[7] (abbreviated as GKB, hereinafter referred to as "The Grammatical Knowledge-base" ) categorizes words for information processing. It gives formal descriptions for each word correspondingly. There are various attribute fields related to quantifiers which probably collocate with each noun in its noun library. The differences between the values of each field are not hard to understand from the following Figure 1.

| 词语 | 个体量词 | 集体量词 | 容器量词 | 度量词 | 种类量词 | 成形量词 | 不定量词 | 动时量词 |
|---|---|---|---|---|---|---|---|---|
| 铜片 | 块 | 批 | 箱车袋 | 吨.公斤.千克... | 种 | 堆片块 | 些.点 | NULL |
| 立体电影 | 部.个 | 批 | NULL | NULL | 类种 | NULL | 些 | 场 |

**Fig. 1.** Each attribute field related to quantifiers in the noun knowledge base

The above figure shows that "The Grammatical Knowledge-base" carefully divides and lists various quantifiers that can modify the nouns. Therefore, we first gathered together each quantifier field for each record in the noun knowledge base, and then changed these data representation and established quantifier-noun collocation knowledge base. The knowledge base's format is "quantifier:noun (space) noun".

## 2.2 Using the Method of Combining Statistics and Rules to Extract Quantifier-Noun Collocations From Corpus Resources

After all, the number of extracted quantifier-noun collocations according to above step is restricted. Therefore, it is necessary to dig out collocations from a large number of real Chinese texts. On the one hand, doing so can compensate for the limitations of dictionary. On the other hand, that can extract quantifier-noun collocations with higher frequency of usage in modern language in order to optimize the knowledge base when checking errors. In this paper we selected the tagged "People's Daily" corpus with certain tagging specifications and accuracy as the source of corpus. Through analysis of the training corpus, quantifier-noun collocations will be extracted after rule templates are formulated. Finally, after further screening the candidate set by statistical strategies, the quantifier-noun collocation knowledge base will be established.

**Formulation of Collocation Rules**
Since the collocations between quantifiers and nouns are fairly complex, without simple regularity, so that it is difficult to cover all phenomena of quantifier-noun collocations with a few rules. In this paper we analyze the syntactic structures of more common quantifier-noun collocations. These examples of collocations are as follows:

1. 在/p 和平共处/l 五/m 项/q 原则/n 的/ud 基础/n 上/f (On the basis of the five principles of peaceful coexistence)
2. 成功/a 地/ui 召开/v 第十八/m 次/q 全国/n 代表大会/n (Successfully convened the Eighteenth National Congress)
3. 从/p 韩国/ns 进口/v 的/ud 五千/m 公斤/q 葵花仁/n (Five thousand kilograms sunflower kernels imported from South Korea)
4. 我/r 记得/v 第一/m 次/q 《/w 文学/n 概论/n 》/w 作业/n 。/w (I remember the "Introduction to Literature" homework that I did the first time.)
5. 胡/nr 富国/nr 悄悄/d 地/ui 来到/v 几/m 家/q 困难/a 企业/n 。/w (Fuguo Hu quietly came to several enterprises in difficulty.)
6. 一/m 本/q 由/p 少儿/n 出版社/n 发行/v 的/ud 图书/n (A book published by the Children's Press)
7. 淮河/ns 是/vl!B1 一/m 条/qe 怎样/ryw 的/ud 河流/n (What is the Huaihe River)

Through analyzing a large number of texts, the above examples show the sentence structure characteristics in the sentences obtaining quantifier-noun collocations. After summing up them, this paper has presented the corresponding rules templates:

**Rule 1:** If the right neighbor of the quantifier is a single noun(/n), then the noun will be taken as the collocation; If the right neighbors of the quantifier are several nouns that are linked together, then the last noun will be taken as the collocation. For example, when $q+n_1+n_2+...+n_i$, $q$-$n_i$ collocation will be extracted.

This corresponds to the above Example 1 and 2, the former, because the right neighbor of the quantifier "项"[xiang](a) is a single noun "原则"[yuanze](principle), the quantifier-noun collocation "项-原则"[xiang-yuanze](a-principle) was extracted. The latter, because the right neighbors of the quantifier "次"[ci](times) are several nouns, namely "全国"[quanguo](national)、"代表大会"[daibiaodahui](congress), the quantifier-noun collocation "次-代表大会"[ci-daibiaodahui](times-congress) was extracted.

**Rule 2:** If the right neighbor of the quantifier is a pause or conjunction(/wu or /c), then quantifier-noun collocation will not be judged.

After much analysis, we can find that such sentences like "产值[chanzhi](output)/n 超[chao](exceeded)/v 亿[yi](one hundred million)/m 元[yuan](yuan)/q" appear frequently, that is to say, the noun which collocates with the quantifier is at the front of that quantifier. As well as sentences like "女子 ５００米/q 和 ３０００米/q 接力/n" (the woman's 500m and 3000m relay) are also very common, in other words, there are other quantifiers after the conjunction or the noun collocating with the quantifier is omitted.

**Rule 3:** If the quantifier is one of "年[nian](year)/月[yue](mouth)/日[ri](day)/元 [yuan](yuan)/ 辈子 [beizi](lifetime)/ 斤 [jin](jin)/ 公斤 [gongjin](kilogram)/ 米 [mi](meter)" and the right neighbor of the quantifier is a noun, then the noun will be taken as the collocation; Otherwise, quantifier-noun collocation will no longer be judged.

This corresponds to the above Example 3. The reason why only the noun that is the right neighbor of a quantifier is extracted as the collocation, which leads to miss some effective collocations, is that like "以 １３３ 公斤/q的/u成绩/n"(by the results of 133 kg) such sentences abound in texts. We mustn't strive merely for quantity without taking into account quality, because doing so makes some wrong collocations taken as correct collocations, which seriously affects the accuracy of checking errors.

**Rule 4:** When traversing words on the right side of a quantifier, the " 《" or " （" is meet on condition that noun has not been detected, then start to judge after the "》" or "）"; If "/wky" is next to the quantifier directly on the right side of the quantifier, then we no longer continue to traverse backward.

This corresponds to the above Example 4, quantifier-noun collocation "次-作业"[ci-zuoye](time-homework) was extracted. If the quantifier is out of the range from " 《" to "》" or from " （" to "）", then the target word is not between the two pairs of marks. So, in order to avoid misjudgment, we set out this rule.

**Rule 5:** The word "的"[de] is not located behind the quantifier until the end of the current clauses: If the right neighbor of the quantifier is the word whose part-of-speech is "preposition/adverb/auxiliary word "地"[di]/verb/numeral" (/p/d/ui/v/m), then quantifier-noun collocation will no longer be judged; Otherwise, if it does not meet the [Rule 1], then the noun which is the nearest to the quantifier or the last noun in the sequence of nouns behind the quantifier will be extracted as the collocation.

This corresponds to the above Example 5. Because the word "的"[de] does not appear behind the quantifier "家"[jia](a) in the sentence and the right neighbor of the quantifier "家"[jia](a) is not the either word whose part-of-speech is mentioned above, then the quantifier-noun collocation "家-企业[jia-qiye](an-enterprise)" was extracted.

**Rule 6:** The word "的"[de] is located behind the quantifier until the end of the current clauses: If the right neighbor of the quantifier is the word whose part-of-speech is "adverb/verb/ preposition/conjunction/ numeral/adjective", then the noun which is the nearest to the word "的" or the last noun in the sequence of nouns behind the word "的" will be extracted as the collocation. Such as, when $q+$ $d/v/p/c/m/a$ $+...+/ud+(...)+/n$, then extract $q$-$n$; Otherwise, if it does not meet [Rule 1], then the noun which is the nearest to the quantifier or the last noun in the sequence of nouns behind the quantifier will be extracted as the collocation.

This corresponds to the above Example 6 and 7. Such sentences like Example 6 often appear in texts, in other words, the quantifier collocates with the central noun in the prepositional phrase and usually the noun is adjacent to the word "的". As shown in Example 6, quantifier-noun collocation "本-图书[ben-tushu](a-book)" was extracted. There are other cases, such as "一/m 座/q 有/v 三十/m 多/m 年/q 楼龄/n 的/u 大厦/n"(a building of 30 years old), then the quantifier-noun collocation "座-大厦[zuo-dasha](a-building)" was extracted. If there are no such sentence patterns like a prepositional phrase and etc., for example the Example 7, then the quantifier-noun collocation "条-河流[tiao-heliu](a-rivel)" was extracted.

**Statistical Filtering**

As mentioned above, the rules do not cover various flexible sentence patterns of the profound Chinese language, which leads to the extract some collocations that do not accord with the summarized general rules. Thus, filtering them using statistical strategies is also strongly needed. In this paper, the screening indicator is frequency and mutual information. 142987 sentences extracted from the "People's Daily" published in a half year are used as corpora. First, 23715 quantifier-noun collocations were extracted using collocation rules. And then through repeated test, filter conditions were ascertained at last, namely that the frequency should be greater than or equal to 2 and the mutual information should be greater than or equal to 4. According to them, 4497 pairs of collocations have been extracted as correct collocations.

## 2.3   Integration and Construction of Word-Level Quantifier-Noun Collocation Knowledge Base

At this point, firstly a union of the collocations extracted from "The Grammatical Knowledge-base" and the other part of collocations extracted from the "People's

Daily" was done, and then duplicates were removed, finally word-level quantifier-noun collocation knowledge base was established. The scale of the knowledge base is 44816 pairs of quantifier-noun collocations and its structure is shown in Figure 2.

安培:电流, 感生电流, 感应电流, 脉动电流
盎司:纯金, 黄金, 金块, 金子
把:白果, 白玉兰, 枹果, 耥子, 扳手, 板斧, 板栗, 包谷, 包米, 贝壳, 荸荠, 鼻涕, 匕首, 比例尺
瓣:蒜
帮:白领, 百万富翁, 败军, 半劳动力, 伴读, 绑匪, 包工头, 保镖, 鸨母, 报童, 兵痞, 病号, 伯爵

**Fig. 2.** Data representation of the word-level quantifier-noun collocation knowledge base

# 3    The Construction of Semantic Class Knowledge Base of Quantifier-Noun Collocation

The scale of word-level quantifier-noun collocation knowledge base established in Section 2 is restricted by the dictionary capacity, the type and size of the corpora, so it is necessary to level up the abstraction level of the collocations to some extent with the help of semantic class concepts. In this way, the knowledge base's storage space will not be so large that the efficiency of proofreading is declined. Moreover, the size of knowledge base will be increased so that more real and correct collocation pairs are contained. From another perspective, the word-level collocation knowledge base was established considering from syntax level. However, there are also semantic constraints between quantifiers and nouns, and syntax and semantics are always closely associated. Therefore, the combination of the both can mine out quantifier-noun collocations to the max.

We hope to analyze and summarize the nouns collocating with each quantifier respectively, and then extract the nouns which belong to the same category and have the same semantic features to form a noun semantics class respectively. The form of collocation is "quantifier:core component–semantic class (space) core component–semantic class". The construction algorithm of semantic class knowledge base of quantifier-noun collocation is shown in Algorithm 1.

**Algorithm 1.** The construction algorithm of semantic class knowledge base

---

**Step1 :  For each** quantifier $q_i$ **in** the word-level quantifier-noun collocation knowledge base

The quantifier $q_i$'s corresponding noun sets is $q_i=\{w_1, w_2, \ldots, w_i\}$
**For each** $w_i$ **in** $q_i$
Extract the $w_i$'s last single word，named as $c_j$, and establish or add to **hashtable[$c_j$]**

Sort the hashtable in reverse order according to **Values'** value, and then extract the core components according to **hashtable[$cj$]>4**, finally remove the items which do not accord with the condition;

**For each $w_i$ in $q_i$**
    **if(hashtable.contains**(the $w_i$'s last single word)) , then reserve the $w_i$;
    **else** delete the $w_i$;

**Step2：For each** quantifier $q_i$ **in** the word-level quantifier-noun collocation knowledge base

**For each $w_i$ in $q_i$**
    Search the $w_i$'s semantic class in "The Semantic Knowledge-base of Contemporary Chinese"(abbreviated as CSD, hereinafter referred to as "The Semantic Knowledge-base"), and then output the results combined with the $w_i$'s last single word to a set; the format is "class(namely the core component)-semantic class"
    Gather the same items together from the above set and count frequency respectively, and then extract the final semantic class nouns collocated with $q_i$ according to frequency>4.

**Step3** : The end.

---

In Chinese, the structure of nouns which express things of the same kind is always called Ding Zhong structure, and they usually have the same core component, for example, the core component of "包装费 [baozhuangfei](packaging fees), 学费 [xuefei](tuition),经费[jingfei](funding)" is all "费"[fei](fee). In essence, strong semantic constraints exist between the quantifier and the core component. Thus, in this paper, the core components of nouns with such characteristics will be extracted and the extraction method is shown in Step1. However, through experiments, part of such a phenomenon appears, that is to say that some nouns have the same last single word, but they have different semantic class in "The Semantic Knowledge-base". For example, "尺子"[chizi](ruler) and "榛子"[zhenzi](hazeinut) are nouns that collocate with the quantifier "把"[ba](a handful of), but they belong to different categories obviously, as shown in Figure3. So, it is sometimes inappropriate to extract the last single word only according to the practice of former researchers. Therefore, in this paper, semantic class attributes in "The Semantic Knowledge-base" will be introduced and combined with the core components to further explicate semantic information contained in nouns collocated with quantifiers. The method is shown in Step 2.

| 词语 | 词类 | 子类 | 拼音 | 义项 | 同形 | 释义 | 语义类 |
|---|---|---|---|---|---|---|---|
| 尺子 | n | NULL | chi3zi5 | 1 | NULL | NULL | 文具 |
| 榛子 | n | NULL | zhen1zi5 | 2 | 2 | 椿树的果实 | 食物 |

**Fig. 3.** The semantic class attributes of "尺子" and "榛子" in "The Semantic Knowledge-base"

So far, through experimental tests, 8241 pairs of collocations have been extracted from 44816 word-level collocations and then the semantic class knowledge base of quantifier-noun collocation has been established. Its data structure is shown in figure 4.

**Fig. 4.** Data representation of the semantic class knowledge base of quantifier-noun collocation

# 4    Error Checking Algorithm of Quantifier-Noun Collocation

If the word-level quantifier-noun collocation knowledge base and the semantic class knowledge base of quantifier-noun collocation are applied to the proofreading system for Chinese text, the system will automatically check quantifier-noun collocation errors in a given text. The error checking algorithm is shown in Algorithm 2.

**Algorithm 2.** The error checking algorithm of the quantifier-noun collocation

---

**Step 1:** Read the corpus and scan sentence by sentence, and then judge whether there are at least a quantifier in the current sentence or not. If it exists, then go to Step2, otherwise continue to scan the next sentence;

**Step 2:** According to the rules mentioned above, extract the noun collocating with the current quantifier, and then transform it to the corresponding semantic class (the format is "core component-semantic class"). Judge whether there exists the collocation in the semantic class knowledge base of quantifier-noun collocation. If it does not exist, then go to Step3, otherwise go to Step5;

**Step 3:** Search whether the current "quantifier-noun" collocation is contained in the word-level quantifier-noun collocation knowledge base. If it does not exist, then go to Step4, otherwise go to Step5;

**Step 4:** The current collocation is taken as a wrong collocation and related information will be recorded to the error list named "wrongList", and then go to Step5;

**Step 5:** Judge whether the current sentence is the last one in the corpus. If it is, then go to Step6, otherwise go to Step1 and continue to judge the next sentence;

**Step 6:** Sequentially read the wrong collocations recorded in the "wrongList" and change their font color to red in the current active interface, and then go to Step7;

**Step 7:** The end.

---

# 5    Experimental Results

## 5.1    Evaluation Criteria of Proofreading System

We use quantifier-noun collocation knowledge base established in this paper as one of the proofreading knowledge bases to assist the system in automatically judging whether the quantifier-noun collocations in sentences are correct or not. The criteria of evaluating system performance are precision, recall and F-Score.

$$precision = \frac{the\ NO.\ of\ correctly\ identified\ collocation\ errors}{the\ NO.\ of\ collocation\ errors\ identified\ by\ system} \times 100\% \quad (1)$$

$$recall = \frac{the\ NO.\ of\ corrently\ identified\ collocation\ errors}{the\ NO.\ of\ collocation\ errors\ contained\ in\ test\ texts} \times 100\% \quad (2)$$

$$F - Score = \frac{2 \times precision \times recall}{precision + recall} \quad (3)$$

### 5.2    Experimental Results and Analysis

In this paper, we selected the untagged "People's Daily" of December 2000 as the test corpus, and then extracted sentences containing a quantifier at least. By using wrong quantifier to replace the correct ones in every sentence artificially, finally the test corpus was formed.

To test the effect of applying the quantifier-noun collocation knowledge base to the proofreading system, namely the quality of the knowledge base, the following four parts were tested respectively. The experimental results are showed in Table 1.

**Table 1.** The experimental results of checking quantifier-noun collocation errors

|  | Precision | Recall | F-Score |
| --- | --- | --- | --- |
| Using the word-level quantifier-noun collocation knowledge base alone | 75.86% | 58.88% | 66.30% |
| Using semantic class knowledge base of quantifier-noun collocation alone | 73.26% | 61.68% | 66.97% |
| Combination of the both | 77.38% | 60.75% | 68.06% |
| The Black Horse proofreading system 2004 | 37.50% | 2.80% | 5.21% |

The experimental results show that the effect of using combination of the both to check quantifier-noun collocation errors is better than the effect of using the either of them alone. Furthermore, the test corpus was randomly selected. If such circumstance appears more frequent in test texts, namely that the noun collocating with the current quantifier does not exist in the word-level collocation knowledge base, but the nouns of its kind appeared in the training corpus and their quantity exceeded the threshold, then we can match the collocation in the semantic class knowledge base. Then misjudgment rate of error checking will decrease and the performance will be improved.

Because there is no uniform experimental data of error checking for quantifier-noun collocation and MS Word is still weak in checking syntax errors and semantic errors, so we conducted the contrast experiment with the highly practical Black Horse proofreading system 2004(the latest version we can download from the Internet). The experiment shows that overall the vast majority of collocation errors can be identified by the method in this paper. Thus, the research has certain practical significance.

## 6 Conclusion

In this paper, by the integrated use of dictionaries and corpora, we established the quantifier-noun collocation knowledge base from the perspective of syntax and semantic level. We also designed the error checking algorithm of quantifier-noun collocation, and then we applied it to the proofreading system. Finally we achieved satisfied results. However, there is still room for improvement. For example, in the case of quality assurance, we can further expand the scale of the knowledge base, or improve the storage mode of the knowledge base so as to reduce the load of the proofreading system. For the former, we can add and refine the rules of extracting collocations, or increase the size of the training corpus to expand the size of the semantic class knowledge base of quantifier-noun collocation. For the latter, we can build index, use method of multi-threaded parallel processing or change the storage structure.

## References

1. Zhou, Q., Sun, M., Huang, C.: Automatically Identify Chinese Maximal Noun Phrase. Technical Report 99001, State Key Lab
2. Guo, X.: Modern Chinese Quantifier Usage Dictionary. Chinese Press, Beijing (2002); (郭先珍.现代汉语量词用法词典. 北京:语文出版社)
3. Wang, M., Yu, S., Duan, H., et al.: Modern Chinese Quantifier-noun collocation research based on corpus statistics. In: Conference Proceedings of the Fourth National Student Conference on Computational Linguistics, Shanxi, pp. 42－48 (2008); (王萌,俞士汶,段慧明等. 基于语料统计的现代汉语量名搭配研究[A].第四届全国学生计算语言学研讨会会议论文集. 山西)
4. Fang, F., Li, B.: Numeral-quantifier-noun phrase Recognition Based on Corpus. In: Conference Proceedings of the Third Student Conference on Computational Linguistics, Shenyang, pp. 331－337 (2006); (方芳,李斌. 基于语料库的数量名短语识别. 第三届学生计算语言学研讨会论文集. 沈阳)
5. Zheng, X., Li, T., Chen, Y.: Restrictive Relationship between quantifier and related components in Chinese Phrase Disambiguation Application. Journal of Xiamen University 41(6), 715－719 (2002); (郑旭玲,李堂秋,陈毅东. 量词与相关成分的制约关系在汉语短语排歧中的应用. 厦门大学学报)
6. Zhang, H.: Construction of Noun-Quantifier Collocation Dictionary for Chinese Information Processing. Shanghai Jiao Tong University, Shanghai (2003); (张辉.构建面向中文信息处理的名量搭配词典. 上海:上海交通大学)
7. Yu, S., et al.: Detailed Explanation on the Grammatical Knowledge-base of Contemporary Chinese. Tsinghua University Press, Beijing (2003); (俞士汶等著. 现代汉语语法信息词典详解. 北京:清华大学出版社)

# A Genre Analysis of Chinese and English Abstracts of Academic Journal Articles: A Parallel-Corpus-Based Study

Guiling Niu

College of Foreign Languages, Zhengzhou University, Zhengzhou, Henan, China
mayerniu@163.com

**Abstract.** With the increasing prominence and importance of abstracts in international academic communication, research on abstract genre has become much more necessary. We aimed to make an overall and comprehensive study on journal abstracts at home and abroad from the perspective of genre analysis by building this large-scale Chinese-English Parallel Abstract Corpus (CEPAC) with advanced corpus and computer technology. Findings show that there is still a relatively significant difference in some aspects between Chinese and English abstracts. The present corpus will bridge the genre research of abstracts and its social functions, facilitate researchers' genre analysis, and benefit both Chinese and English abstract writing, translation teaching and dictionary compilation of academic terms.

**Keywords:** genre analysis, parallel corpus, RA abstracts.

## 1    Abstracts and Genre Analysis

### 1.1    Functions of Abstracts

What is an abstract? According to Cleveland [1], "an abstract summarises the essential contents of a particular knowledge record and is a true surrogate of the document". A similar definition is produced by Graetz [2]: "the abstract is a time-saving device that can be used to find particular parts of the article without reading it; … knowing the structure in advance will help the reader to get into the article; … if comprehensive enough, it might replace the article". An abstract should be concise and precise, indicating to the potential reader two things: (a) what was done, and (b) important results obtained.

In the past, most papers did not contain any abstracts; abstracts were only introduced into medical research articles first during the 1960s [3] and it took decades for it to be widely applied to other fields. Twenty years ago, it would seem that abstracts were an under- researched genre from a discourse-analytic perspective because of limited application. According to Montesi & Urdiciain's [4] survey in 2005, there were barely 28 studies with reference to research article (RA) abstracts then. In contrast, now, research world is facing "an information explosion", with several million research

P. Liu and Q. Su (Eds.): CLSW 2013, LNAI 8229, pp. 603–616, 2013.

papers being published each year, and there are also continual announcements of new journals being launched, either online or in hard copy or both. Many researchers have therefore to be highly selective in their reading, often focusing on skimming abstracts and key words, which has resulted in a noticeable upsurge in the amount of research devoted to abstracts, particularly RA abstracts in that abstracts "have become a tool of mastering and managing the ever increasing information flow in the scientific community" [5], and research perspectives involve grammatical, semantic, pragmatic and culture etc.

According to Huckin [6], RA abstracts bear four distinguishable functions, to which Swales & Feak [3] added a fifth: (1)They function as stand-alone mini-texts, giving readers a short summary of a study's topic, methodology and main findings; (2)They function as screening devices, helping readers decide whether they wish to read the whole article or not; (3)They function as previews for readers intending to read the whole article, giving them a road-map for their reading; (4)They provide indexing help for professional abstract writers and editors; (5)They provide reviewers with an immediate oversight of the paper they have been asked to review.

## 1.2    Genre Analysis

Genre was originally categorized as a literary term. Since the 1980s, Swales [7] combined the concept of genre with the communicative function of text and introduced it into ESP/EAP（English for Specific/Academic Purposes）teaching, research on Genre Analysis has been unfolding an ascendant trend and is attracting an increasing attention from world linguists and ESP/EAP teachers ever since.

Genre analysis falls into two main schools, one of which is called Swalesian School and represented by Swales and Bhatia, and the other school is named as Australian School while Martin is the representative. The former defines genre analysis as "type of discourse", believing that genre bears "consistency of communicative purposes" [8-9] They viewed genre analysis as the study of situated linguistic behaviour [10]. Australian school gives a definition as follows, "regularities of staged, goal oriented social processes" [11]. Qin [12] compares the two schools and finds that the two definitions conform to each other in nature, and the similarities lie in the following aspects: (1) communication objectives determine the existence of genre, forms its corresponding "Schematic Structure" of texts, and influences the choice of text content and style; (2) Conventionality of genre; (3) Differences among texts of the same genre.

Genre analysis involves both stylistic analysis and text analysis. It is the output of inter-disciplinary research, whose fundamental goal is to investigate communicative and applying strategy. Genre analysis is more than the simple description of textual linguistic feature in that it endeavors to interpret the motivation of textual structure, explores the socio-cultural and psycho-cognitive factors behind textual structure, and thus unfolds the special way to realize the communicative goal and the normalization of textual structure.

Genre is determined by the communicative purpose [7]· and therefore, with the increase of the importance and use of abstracts, they have developed into an increasingly important part-genre [13]·

The objective of this research is to generalize and illustrate the generic structural potential (GSP) of abstracts by using the advantage of big texts of corpus and analyzing the usage of   rhetorical MOVE in them, with genre analysis and schematic structure as the theoretical basis.

## 2     Methodology: Combination of Genre Analysis and Corpus Technology

Corpus-driven Approach has gained wide popularity among linguists and has been widely applied to language research.

In comparison with mono-lingual corpora, parallel corpora are more valuable and are mainly used for translation and language contrast, because they can be used to investigate the ways to express the same content with two different languages [14].

So far, there are limited studies on abstracts from genre analysis perspective and with empirical corpus method, not to mention the large-scale parallel corpora approach. Without adequate data support, conclusion based on traditional observation and small-scale survey only would be impractical, unpersuasive and conflicting.

## 3     Corpus Description

The corpus we built is computer-operable and is named as Chinese-English Parallel Abstract Corpus (CEPAC).

### 3.1     Representativeness and Time Effectiveness of Texts

CEPAC is characterized by its big sample and multi-discipline covering, which can well represent abstract genre texts and embody their universal features. The chosen journals are all influential top periodicals in the world or in China. The English journals are all indexed by SCI, EI, Elsevier, Springer or EBSCO, etc., while the Chinese journals are all included in the Core Journal list by Beijing University and indexed by CNKI.net, Wanfang Data or VIP INFORMATION.

In order to unfold the time effectiveness of texts and better reflect the genre features of recently-published RA abstracts, we only chose the articles published in 2008, 2009 and 2010.

### 3.2     Balance and Comparability of CC, CE and EE Abstracts

CEPAC parallel corpus is composed of three sub-corpora: Chinese Abstracts Corpus of Chinese journals (CC), English Abstracts Corpus of Chinese journals (CE), and English Abstracts Corpus of International journals (EE), in which all the CE abstracts are the translated versions of the CC ones and they are aligned for future annotation and inter-lingual comparison. Under each of the three sub-corpora, five disciplinary categories are respectively established: Health Sciences (H[1]), Social Sciences and Humanities (S), Physical Sciences and Engineering (P), Life Science and Biomedical Sciences (L), Language Sciences and Literature (Y) (divided from Social Sciences and Humanities due to our research purpose and interest). For each category under the three sub-corpora, 252 abstracts were chosen. The sub-disciplines chosen in the three sub-corpora basically also conform to each other, ensuring the balance of texts.

### 3.3    Corpus Size and Structure

CEPAC is aimed at representing the total of modern Chinese and Chinese RA abstracts. We collected 1260 Chinese and 1260 English abstracts respectively from Chinese journals, and 1260 English abstracts from international periodicals, 3780 texts altogether.

CEPAC covers 673246 Chinese and English words in all, including 209889 Chinese words (376972 characters) in CC, 221240 and 242117 English words in CE and EE respectively.

CEPAC is a dynamic parallel corpus and new texts can be added anytime, which is helpful for future dynamic observation of the ever-changing features of RA abstracts. Each of the three sub-corpora has an independent system that can be divided and combined freely to serve different research purposes. Concordance can be conducted inter-lingually (CC-CE or CC-EE) or just intra-lingually (CE-EE), as is shown in Fig.1, or it can be realized among different disciplines, and thus, comparison can be made at three levels: 1. inter-lingual comparison: CC abstracts versus CE abstracts; 2. intra-lingual comparison: CE abstracts versus EE abstracts; 3.interdisciplinary comparison.

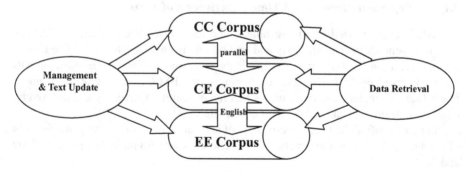

**Fig. 1.** Corpus Structure

---

[1] Each text is coded with a three-digit code following the sequence of "discipline (H, L, S, P, Y)+journal origin(C for Chinese journals, E for International journals)+language(C for Chinese, E for English)", eg. HCC001.

# 4    Genre Analysis of RA Abstracts

## 4.1    MOVEs and Steps

Researchers tend to start their text analysis with MOVEs and Steps when analyzing a text. The term MOVE means a text segment made up of a bundle of linguistic features (lexical meaning, propositional meanings, illocutionary forces, etc.), which give the segment a uniform orientation and signal the content of discourse in it [15]. It is a functional concept rather than a content one in that each move or step bears an independent and complete communicative function. As Lores [16] states, abstracts are an independent genre, share some common features with RA but are different from RA in some aspects, and one of the different points is the rhetorical MOVE structure.

Moves have different text lengths, which can be phrases or paragraphs. In genre analysis, each move begins with textual context and lingual context, and is identified and determined through the lingual clue of the text. Sentences conveying the communicative information of the same type are identified as the same MOVE.

## 4.2    Schematic Structure of Abstract Genre

Biber et al. [17] contended that analysing linguistic items regarding discourse moves and sections may provide more accurate interpretations of their functional work in the discourse. Adhering to this proposal, the texts used in this study were coded into rhetorical sections following the Introduction-Purpose- Methods-Results-Conclusion five-move pattern for abstracts. Swales & Feak [3] proved the scientificity and universality of this five-move pattern, stating, "Most researchers identify a potential total of five moves." Terminology varies somewhat, but the moves are in their typical order (Table 1).

**Table 1.** Macrostructure and Meaning of MOVE and Labels (from: Swales & Feak [13])

| MOVE | Typical Labels | Implied questions |
|---|---|---|
| MOVE 1 | Background/introduction/situation | 1. What do we know about the topic? 2. Why is the topic important? |
| MOVE 2 | Present research/purpose | What is this study about? |
| MOVE 3 | Methods/materials/subjects/procedures | How was it done? |
| MOVE 4 | Results/findings | What was discovered? |
| MOVE 5 | Discussion/conclusion/implications/recommendations | What do the findings mean? |

Based on the above analysis, we coded the texts with the five-move pattern, and the respective coding attributives are Introduction, Purpose, Method, Result and Conclusion.

### 4.3    Annotation Tool and Scheme

In the course of CEPAC construction, many tools were employed, such as EditPlus, ICTCLAS, Paraconc, AntConc, Smith Tools, etc.. The tool used to annotate texts was MMAX2[2] (Multi-modal Annotation in XML), a versatile, XML-based annotation tool which can be customized according to users' own needs and has already been used in a variety of annotation projects. This software also bears the merits that can serve multi-level annotation and support stand-alone storage of the annotated data at different levels without affecting each other.

CC Chinese texts and CE English texts were aligned prior to annotation for easy annotation work and inter-lingual comparison and EE English texts are processed independently. Well-designed schemes were used to define attributes, values and relations of the annotated items at different levels. Rigorous self-checking and cross-checking after annotation among annotators guaranteed the intra- and inter-agreement in annotation quality.

## 5    Data Analysis and Discussion

### 5.1    Distribution of Introduction and Conclusion

Not all sentences consist of independent moves. An abstract text is generally composed of several sentences, some of which are independent sentences (including both regular and irregular independent moves), while some others are compound ones (containing two moves or more in a single sentence). The MOVE distribution in the three sub-corpora will well illustrate this phenomenon (See Table 2).

As Hyland [18] finds, abstracts containing Introduction and Conclusion rose from 33% and 7% in 1980 to 47% and 22% in 1997. Data in Table 2 indicate that the percentage of abstracts containing Introduction and Conclusion moves has increased to 57.30% and 75.56% in EE sub-corpus, meaning a radical increase compared to the related data in Hyland's research result. This finding develops Hyland's research. However, Chinese RA abstracts still contain a lower percentage of Introduction and Conclusion, 37.54% and 44.44% for CC, 67.46% and 73.49% for CE. Difference is especially significant between CC and EE texts in this aspect. The percentage of other moves in EE is higher than that in CC and CE ones, and EE texts contain a lower percentage than CC and CE ones only in compound moves.

---

[2] For the software details, please refer to: http://www.eml-research.de/english/research/nlp/download/mmax.php

**Table 2.** Raw Frequency of MOVE Distribution in CC, CE and EE Sub-corpora（unit：text）

| Sub -corpora | Independent Moves | | | | | Compound Moves | Irregular Sequence Moves | Total No. of texts |
|---|---|---|---|---|---|---|---|---|
| | Introduc-tion | Purpose | Method | Result | Conclusion | | | |
| HCC | 30 | 218 | 225 | 232 | 232 | 23 | 3 | |
| LCC | 81 | 120 | 108 | 194 | 162 | 116 | 14 | |
| PCC | 84 | 97 | 163 | 136 | 136 | 135 | 8 | |
| SCC | 136 | 43 | 44 | 118 | 145 | 124 | 17 | |
| YCC | 142 | 72 | 23 | 62 | 175 | 127 | 18 | |
| sub-total | 473 | 550 | 563 | 742 | 850 | 525 | 60 | 1260 |
| percentage | 37.54% | 43.65% | 44.68% | 58.89% | 67.46% | 41.67% | 4.76% | |
| HCE | 40 | 222 | 234 | 238 | 236 | 9 | 7 | |
| LCE | 102 | 167 | 156 | 204 | 174 | 43 | 30 | |
| PCE | 108 | 120 | 197 | 161 | 165 | 82 | 12 | |
| SCE | 154 | 75 | 61 | 132 | 162 | 68 | 35 | |
| YCE | 156 | 106 | 47 | 66 | 189 | 72 | 23 | |
| sub-total | 560 | 690 | 695 | 801 | 926 | 274 | 107 | 1260 |
| percentage | 44.44% | 54.76% | 55.16% | 63.57% | 73.49% | 21.75% | 8.49% | |
| HEE | 161 | 174 | 168 | 217 | 204 | 15 | 23 | |
| LEE | 176 | 187 | 139 | 236 | 203 | 45 | 21 | |
| PEE | 130 | 205 | 124 | 161 | 175 | 54 | 31 | |
| SEE | 133 | 203 | 149 | 177 | 188 | 23 | 21 | |
| YEE | 122 | 183 | 165 | 172 | 182 | 29 | 17 | |
| sub-total | 722 | 952 | 745 | 963 | 952 | 168 | 113 | 1260 |
| percentage | 57.30% | 75.56% | 59.13% | 76.43% | 75.56% | 13.33% | 8.97% | |

## 5.2    Interdisciplinary Comparison

Fig. 2 presents a clear overview of the normalized frequency of move usage in five disciplines in the respective three corpora, while Table 2 provides a detailed move distribution concerned with raw frequency in them. The two sets of data basically agree to each other in reflecting the move distribution in the five disciplines of the three sub-corpora.

Data show that move distribution of the five moves in YEE, PEE and SEE texts is quite balanced while it is not so balanced in HEE and LEE in that they bear a higher frequency of Result than that of other Moves in HEE and LEE, which may be caused by the nature of the two disciplines, Health Sciences and Life and Biomedical Sciences, for most research concerning these two main disciplines is empirical and research results are supposed to be highlighted. Chinese and English abstracts of Chinese journals in the two disciplines (HCC, HCE, LCC and LCE) take on similar traits, with Result occupying a higher frequency. Besides, move distribution HCC, HCE, LCC and LCE is also relatively balanced like HEE and LEE, indicating Chinese journal abstracts and international ones in these two disciplines bear more similar features in move distribution and the distance between them have been shortened.

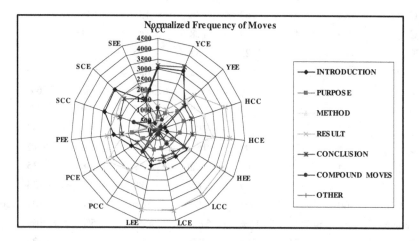

**Fig. 2.** Normalized Frequency of Moves (Every 10,000 running words)

However, there is an obvious difference between Chinese abstracts and international ones in the use of Introduction and Conclusion in Social Sciences and Humanities (S) and Language Sciences and Literature (Y) because frequencies of Introduction and Conclusion are abnormally high in SCE, and those of Introduction high and Conclusion low in YCE, in comparison with those in the corresponding international texts, SEE and YEE. Conversely, there is a great shortage of Purpose, Method and Result in YCC and YCE abstracts and a shortage of Purpose and Method in SCC and SCE texts, which indicates that the move distribution in these two disciplines is rather unbalanced and that the information in these tests is less informative. To see whether there is a significant difference in the use of the five moves in the two disciplines between Chinese journal English abstracts and International ones, Log-likelihood ratio and Chi-Square are calculated by using data in Table 2. Since the English abstracts of Chinese journals are the translated version of the Chinese texts and therefore they bear much similarity in move distribution, only the English abstract moves are selected to compare with the international ones.

Table 3. Chi-square & Likelihood Test for SCE & SEE

| MOVEs | SCE | SEE | Chi-Square Test | | Log-likelihood Ratio | | |
|---|---|---|---|---|---|---|---|
| | | | Chi-Square | Signific-ance(P) | Log-likeli hood | Sig. | |
| Introduc-tion | 154 | 133 | 1.7341 | 0.188 | 1.54 | 0.215 | + |
| Purpose | 75 | 203 | 66.2430 | 0.000*** | 61.22 | 0.000*** [3] | - |
| Method | 61 | 149 | 40.2286 | 0.000*** | 38.04 | 0.000*** | - |
| Result | 132 | 177 | 7.4693 | 0.006** | 6.58 | 0.010* | - |
| Conclu-sion | 162 | 188 | 2.2429 | 0.134 | 1.93 | 0.164 | - |

Table 4. Chi-square & Likelihood Test for YCE & YEE

| MOVEs | YCE | YEE | Chi-Squa re | Signi-ficance (P) | Log-likelih ood | Sig. | |
|---|---|---|---|---|---|---|---|
| | | | | | Log-likelihood Ratio | | |
| Intro-duction | 156 | 122 | 4.6739 | 0.031* | 4.17 | 0.041* | + |
| Purpose | 106 | 183 | 23.1731 | 0.000*** | 20.77 | 0.000*** | - |
| Method | 47 | 165 | 71.7122 | 0.000*** | 69.58 | 0.000*** | - |
| Result | 66 | 172 | 52.1338 | 0.000*** | 48.91 | 0.000*** | - |
| Conclu-sion | 189 | 182 | 0.1549 | 0.694 | 0.13 | 0.716 | + |

Judging from the data in Table 3 and Table 4, we may conclude that there is really a significant difference in the use of Purpose, Method and Result between Chinese journal abstracts and international ones, regardless of the difference level, both in Social Sciences and Humanities (S) and Language Sciences and Literature (Y) in which these three moves are all underused in Chinese journal abstracts. Still, Introduction is overused in YCE abstracts compared to their counterparts in YEE texts.

To add more Purpose, Method and Result content in Chinese journal RA abstracts and to leave out more Introduction content in YCE abstracts may partly solve this problem and make the move distribution more balanced and abstracts more informative.

## 5.3    Inter- and Intra-lingual Comparison

### 5.3.1    Explicitation in C-E Translation
Judging by the number change of moves in Table 2, there is an obvious rise in text length in the use of independent moves and irregular moves (reversed move order) in

---

[3] The asterisks (*) indicate significance level, and the "+" and "-" signs on the right column indicate "overuse" and "underuse".

CE texts, compared with CC texts (A fall only appears in the use of compound moves), showing the explicitation in translated English texts, the clarification of implied meaning by adding words or expressions. As Nida & Taber [19] argue, this feature is caused by the writers' intention of lowering the difficulty of translated version and results in the increase of redundancy. Explicitation is universal in other genres [20].

### 5.3.2    Comparison of MOVE Numbers

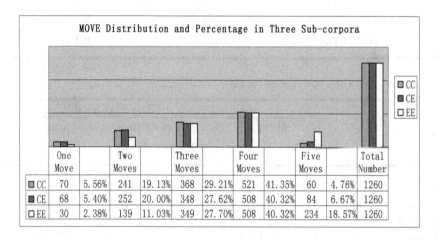

MOVE Distribution and Percentage in Three Sub-corpora

| | One Move | | Two Moves | | Three Moves | | Four Moves | | Five Moves | | Total Number |
|---|---|---|---|---|---|---|---|---|---|---|---|
| CC | 70 | 5. 56% | 241 | 19. 13% | 368 | 29. 21% | 521 | 41. 35% | 60 | 4. 76% | 1260 |
| CE | 68 | 5. 40% | 252 | 20. 00% | 348 | 27. 62% | 508 | 40. 32% | 84 | 6. 67% | 1260 |
| EE | 30 | 2. 38% | 139 | 11. 03% | 349 | 27. 70% | 508 | 40. 32% | 234 | 18. 57% | 1260 |

**Fig. 3.** MOVE Numbers and Percentage in Texts in Three Sub-corpora （unit : text）

As Swales & Feak [3] points out, it is important to stress that abstracts have the potential for all five moves, although in many cases, especially when there are tight word (or character) restrictions, not all five moves will be realized. It should be further noted that while the above order of the five moves is pretty regular, exceptions can be found when the sequence of the five moves is irregular, especially with regard to the Method move.

### 5.4    Coverage of Five Moves

As is shown in Fig.3, there are the most five-move-contained abstracts in EE sub-corpus, 234 texts, 18.57% of all 1260 abstracts, which is nearly 3 times and 2 times more than in CC and CE sub-corpora, 4.76% in CC and 6.67% in CE. Conversely, there is a lowest coverage of one-move-contained and two-move-contained abstracts in EE sub-corpus.

The data above, combined with the analysis in 5.1 and 5.2, reveal the generic structural potential in the CC, CE and EE abstracts: (1) There are the most abstracts covering all five moves in EE sub-corpus, in which the scheme is more complete and balanced, more valuable information is provided, and the texts are more worth indexing and readable. Conversely, there are many abstracts containing only one or two moves in CC and CE texts, providing less complete move distribution and less valuable information. (2) CC, CE and EE sub-corpora share a similar feature in coverage of four moves and coverage of three moves, esp. the four-move-contained abstracts which also cover the highest occurrences and percentage in all three sub-corpora, indicating Chinese journals have shortened the distance from international periodicals in this aspect, or maybe four-move pattern is the most preferable mode in most researchers' eyes, at home or abroad.

A sample EE abstract containing five moves is shown as follows:

**Sample** : [Sentence 1] Thousands of students in California learn English as a second language in schools that utilize exclusively monolingual — English Only — literacy programs. [Sentence 2] With such programs students do not have the opportunity to use the knowledge of their first language in order to acquire and master their second language. [Sentence 3] The project of cooperative bi-literacy described in this article was created to explicitly construct linguistic and cultural bridges between the language spoken at the community - in this case, Spanish — and the language of school, English. [Sentence 4] Through one school year, 2005-06, twenty- nine, fourth-grade students, their parents and two teachers read, deconstructed and analysed bilingual books to supplement the monolingual programs mandated by the school district. [Sentence 5] The outcomes of this project suggest that when teachers have the power to develop activities that analyse the connections between languages, students increase their academic performance and parents engage actively on the learning process of their children. [Sentence 6] Most importantly, the participants learn within a context that promotes cultural and linguistic coexistence.

There are 163 words altogether (including punctuations) in this example abstract, containing 6 sentences, of which Sentence 1 and Sentence 2 belong to Introduction, Sentence 3 Purpose, Sentence 4 Method, Sentence 5 Result, and Sentence 6 Conclusion. All the five moves are contained in the example text and all sentences are in the regular order.

## 5.5    Compound Moves

As is shown in Table 2, there are a large number of compound moves in all CC, CE and EE abstracts. A compound move = move1 move2 [movei]*, where * means a repetition between 0 and n, and i ranges from 3 to n + 2, n > 0. In brief words, a compound move means there are at least two moves in the same sentence, for example, "a purpose + a method". This kind of move is used to convey richer and ampler information with limited words.

The above data also reveals that CC, CE and EE abstracts share one feature in Method move, that is, many sentences containing Purpose are compound moves, combined with Purpose or Result. However, concerning the specific use of Method, as can be seen in Table 2, The number of independent Method moves is still much larger than that of compound moves, because the frequency of independent moves in all three CC, CE and EE corpora is nearly the same or larger than the frequency of compound moves composed of "Method + Purpose/Result/ Conclusion", while there are some other compound moves in not containing Method.

## 5.6      Irregular Moves

Moves of Abstracts are generally in such typical order as: IPMRC (Introduction-Purpose- Method-Result-Conclusion). Still, as Table 2 unfolds, the phenomenon of irregular sequence moves is also universal in abstracts. Swales & Feak[3] point out, "while the above order of the five moves is pretty regular, exceptions can be found, especially with regard to the Methods move."

### 5.6.1    Irregular Independent Moves

Data in Table 2 indicate that, the percentages of texts containing irregular moves in CC, CE, EE corpora are 4.76%, 8.49% and 8.97% of the respective corpora. This reversed phenomenon is most prominent in EE abstracts.

Another prominent phenomenon concerning irregular independent moves is the reversed sequence of Introduction, Purpose and Method, that is, Introduction is put behind Purpose or Method, and CC, CE, EE corpora respectively contain 16, 17 and 20 texts of this sort. In this case, the abstract writer puts forward research purpose or method first, and introduces research background later. This structure facilitates the author to draw readers' attention on present research, stating about the research itself straightforwardly, which makes statements more convincing. This kind of pattern is distributed relatively balancedly in three corpora, indicating that Chinese or foreign RA abstract writers have much in common in the use of this structure.

### 5.6.2    Irregular Compound Moves

In fact, there are also numerable irregular compound moves in the three sub-corpora, with Method-Purpose compound move occupying the highest frequency. According to statistics, the percentages of texts containing irregular compound moves in CC, CE and EE corpora are 14.21%, 7.14% and 3.57% of the respective total texts, of which there are fewest abstracts containing irregular compound moves in EE corpus, with CC occupying the highest frequency. This finding is just opposite to the statistical result of irregular independent moves.

The two series of data concerning irregular independent moves and irregular compound moves reflects the difference between CC abstracts and EE ones. In short, independent moves are more frequently used in the usage of irregular move in EE corpus to put the important move ahead, for example, Result or Conclusion ahead of Purpose or Method, while, compound moves are more often used in irregular moves in CC corpus to highlight key move, esp. in the description related to Method. In CC corpus, approximately one-seventh abstracts use "Method + Purpose" irregular compound move structure, by using "用...的方法/工具对...进行了研究/调查/分析" [yòng...defāngfǎ/gōngjùduì...jìnxíngleyánjiū/diàochá/ fēnxī] (performed/made a/an study/investigation/analysis on...by (doing)...) model. This structure is characterized by brevity and conciseness, and bears a highly generalized nature. The innate structural difference between Chinese and English may account for this phenomenon, or it may be related to Chinese and foreigners' different expressing ways. Chinese people tend to express more complicated content in a sentence, that's why there are more compound structures in Chinese. From another angle, Chinese are inclined to put "Method" prior to "Purpose", to highlight acts or behavior. Fore example, a Chinese says, "我是开车来的[wǒshìkāichēláide]。 ", in which "开车[kāichē](drive)" indicates the method, while "来[lái](come)" means the purpose, and Method is put prior to Purpose in this statement. While, expressed in English, it would be turned into: "I came here by driving." in which Purpose "came" is put ahead of Method "driving". Therefore the regular or reversed order of a compound move containing Method is closely related to the Chinese or English users' cultural background and language expressing customs. At this level, it is hard to judge which language is superior to the other.

# 6    Discussion

CEPAC is a comprehensive database. This corpus bridges the gap between abstract genre and its social function, and facilitates the international community of scholars and research students to make broad and all-around research on RA abstracts [3]. As for EAP teachers, genre analysis can provide the description of communicative activities and help students understand the implied meanings, so genre analysis can serve as important resources [3], and thus effectively enhance ESP/EAP and translation teaching. When it comes to researchers, abstracts are their passes to international top journals or conferences, and this corpus will facilitate them for their research achievements publicized and known to the world. Besides, research on academic genre will also benefit myriad journal editors and RA readers.

**Acknowledgement.** This work is supported by the Humanities and Social Sciences Research Project of the Education Department of China (No.10YJA740074) and the Open Projects Program of National Laboratory of Pattern Recognition.

# References

1. Cleveland, D.B.: Introduction to Indexing and Abstracting, p. 103. Libraries Unlimited Inc. (1983)
2. Graetz, N.: Teaching EFL students to extract structural information from abstracts. In: Ulijn, J.M., Pugh, A.K. (eds.) Reading for Professional Purposes. ACCO, Leuven (1985)
3. Swales, J.M., Feak, C.B.: From text to task: Petting research on abstracts to work. In: Ruiz-Garrido, M.F., Palmer-Silveira, J.C., Fortanet-Gómez, I. (eds.) English for Professional and Academic Purposes, pp. 167–180. Rodopi, Amsterdam (2010)
4. Montesi, M., Urdiciain, B.G.: Recent linguistics research into author abstracts. Knowledge Organizations 32, 64–78 (2005)
5. Ventola, E.: Abstracts as an object of linguistic study. In: Čmejrková, S., Daneš, F., Havlová, E. (eds.) Writing vs. Speaking: Language, Text, Discourse, Communication. Gunter Narr, Tübingen (1994)
6. Huckin, T.N.: Abstracting from abstracts. In: Hewings, M. (ed.) Academic Writing in Context. University of Birmingham Press, Birmingham (2001)
7. Swales, J.: Aspects of article introduction. The University of Aston, Language Studies Unit, Birmingham, UK (1981)

8. Swales, J.M.: Genre Analysis: English in Academic and Research Settings. Cambridge University Press, Cambridge (1990)
9. Bhatia, V.K.: Analyzing Genre: Language Use in Professional Settings. Longman, Essex (1993)
10. Bhatia, V.K.: A generic view of academic discourse. In: John Flowerdew. Academic Discourse. Longman, England (2002)
11. Martin, J.R., Rose, D.: Genre Relations Mapping Culture. Equinox Publishing LTD., London Oakville (2008)
12. Qin, X.: A Review of Genre-based Teaching Approaches. Foreign Language Teaching and Research 32(1), 42–46 (2000) ( in Chinese)
13. Swales, J.M., Feak, C.B.: Abstracts and the Writing of Abstracts. University of Michigan Press, Ann Arbor (2009)
14. Aijmer, K., Albtenberg, B. (eds.): English Corpus Linguistics. Longman, London (1991)
15. Nwogu, K.N.: The medical Research Paper: Structure and Functions. English for Specific Purposes 16(2), 119–138 (1997)
16. Lores, R.: On RA Abstracts: from Rhetorical Structure to Thematic Organization. English for Specific Purposes 23(3), 280–302 (2004)
17. Biber, D., et al.: Lexical bundles in university spoken and written registers. English for Specific Purposes 26, 263–286 (2007)
18. Hyland, K.: English for Academic Purposes. Routledge, Amsterdam (2006)
19. Nida, E.A., Taber, C.R.: The Theory and Practice of Translation. E.J. Brill, Leiden (1969)
20. Baker, M.: Corpus Linguistics and Translation Studies: Implications and Applications. In: Baker, M., Francis, G., Tognini-Bonelli, E. (eds.) Text and Technology: in Honour of John Sinclair. John Benjamins Publishing Company, Amsterdam (1993)

# A Corpus-Based Genre and Language Feature Analysis of Chinese and English Linguistics and Literature Article Abstracts

Chunxiang Fan

College of Foreign Languages, Zhengzhou University, Zhengzhou, Henan, China
fanchunxiang@zzu.edu.cn

**Abstract.** The development of computer technology has led the language research into a new age. In this research we take advantage of the corpus-driven approach to illustrate the differences and similarities in the generic structural potential (GSP) and the language features of Chinese and English article abstracts by building our own corpora of article abstracts and using AntConc. Results show that both the GSP and the language features have their own Chinese and English characteristics. This research will help Chinese writers know how to write an article abstract and lays a ground for those who will publish their works in the high-quality magazines and even in the foreign ones.

**Keywords:** Corpus-based, genre analysis, generic structural potential, article abstracts.

## 1 Introduction

With the development of computer science, approaching is the new era of the language research. It is no longer impossible to process the natural language. Teng Zhenru and Tan Wancheng [1] had analyses on the tense and voice differences and the cause to the differences in Chinese and English scientific article abstracts after giving an introduction of the previous research on the translated English version of Chinese scientific article abstracts. Lu Yuanwen [2] did research on the language features of English article abstracts. He Yuyin and Cao Zhenzhen [3] built a corpus of aerospace article abstracts including 50 Chinese and English respectively. Based on the corpus, they had a genre analysis on the abstracts and concluded the drawbacks in the translated English version of Chinese abstracts. Li Qingming and Zhang Min [4] made an analysis on the context of Chinese and English Academic Article Abstracts. What's more, Yan Meijuan [5] and Shi Wenxia[6] did research on the Medical and Scientific article abstracts respectively. Chen Ruina [7] and Ye Ning [8] made an analysis on English and Chinese article abstracts from the perspective of genre set while Li Yanfang [9] and Wang Zhou [10] did studies on hedges in Chinese and English RA abstracts.

We can not list all the studies on Chinese and English article abstracts here. But looking through the previous researches, we find there is little research on the linguistic and literature article abstracts. So in this research, based on the corpus-driven approach

P. Liu and Q. Su (Eds.): CLSW 2013, LNAI 8229, pp. 617–624, 2013.

[11], is pursued the regular usage pattern of the language in Chinese and English linguistic and literature article abstracts. The AntConc is used to retrieve and analyze the data in order to find the language traits.

To assure the objectivity and the reliability of the research, we establish a corpus by collecting the abstract of some essays on linguistics and literature. All the language material come from the authoritative linguistics and literature magazines of both English and Chinese language, such as Foreign Language, China Scientific Translation, Foreign Language Learning, Modern Foreign Language, Journal of Linguistics, Language Teaching Research, Language Learning, The Modern Language Journal. There are 252 Chinese and English abstracts respectively.

## 2     Analysis on the Generic Structural Potential (GSP) of Chinese and English Linguistic and Literature Article Abstracts

We did an analysis on 100 abstracts (50 Chinese and 50 English respectively) randomly drawn from the self-built corpus based on the move-step pattern produced by Swales [12] and the IPMRC (Introduction–Purpose–Method –Results-Conclusion) model to find the order of the five moves' appearance and their distribution frequency. Then the generic structural potential (GSP) of Chinese and English linguistic and literature article abstracts is suggested. The following is the table of the data from the analysis:

**Table 1.** The macrostructure of the material

| YCC (Chinese abstract) | | | | YEE (English abstract) | | | |
|---|---|---|---|---|---|---|---|
| Num. | structure of the material | Num. | structure of the material | Num. | structure of the material | Num. | structure of the material |
| No.1 | I- R-C-P | No.26 | I-P-M-C | No.1 | I-C | No.26 | P-M-R-C |
| No.2 | P-M-R-C | No.27 | C | No.2 | P-R-C | No.27 | I |
| No.3 | P-M-C | No.28 | P-M-C | No.3 | P-M-R-C-I | No.28 | P-M |
| No.4 | P-M-R-C | No.29 | P-C | No.4 | I-C | No.29 | I-P-M-C |
| No.5 | P-M-C | No.30 | P-C | No.5 | I-M-C | No.30 | I-P-M-C |
| No.6 | P-M-R-C | No.31 | C | No.6 | I-P-c | No.31 | P-M-R-C |
| No.7 | P-M-R-C | No.32 | I-C-P | No.7 | P-I-M-R-C | No.32 | I-M-C |
| No.8 | C | No.33 | I-M-P | No.8 | I-P-M-R-C | No.33 | P-M-R-C |
| No.9 | I-M-P-R-C | No.34 | M-P-C | No.9 | P-R-C | No.34 | P-M-R-C |
| No.10 | I-P-M-C | No.35 | C | No.10 | P-M-C | No.35 | I-P |
| No.11 | I-P-C | No.36 | I-M-P | No.11 | P-M-R-c | No.36 | P-M-R |

**Table 1.** (*continued*)

| No.12 | I-C | No.37 | I-M-R-C | No.12 | I-P-C | No.37 | P-M-R-C |
|---|---|---|---|---|---|---|---|
| No.13 | I-M-P-C | No.38 | P-C | No.13 | P-M-R-C | No.38 | P-M-R |
| No.14 | I-M-P-C | No.39 | I-P-C | No.14 | P-M-C | No.39 | I-M-C |
| No.15 | P-M-C-I | No.40 | I-P | No.15 | P-M-R | No.40 | P-M-R |
| No.16 | P-I-C | No.41 | I-P | No.16 | P-M-R-C | No.41 | P-M-R-C |
| No.17 | M-P-C | No.42 | P-C | No.17 | P-M-C | No.42 | P-M-R-C |
| No.18 | I | No.43 | I-C | No.18 | P-R | No.43 | P-M-R-C |
| No.19 | I-M-P-C | No.44 | I-R-C | No.19 | P-M-R-C | No.44 | P-C |
| No.20 | I-P-C-M | No.45 | I-C | No.20 | I-M-R-C | No.45 | P-M-R-C |
| No.21 | I-C | No.46 | I-C | No.21 | P-M-C | No.46 | P-M-R-C |
| No.22 | M-P-C | No.47 | I-C | No.22 | I-P-M-R-C | No.47 | I-P-R-C |
| No.23 | I-C-P | No.48 | I-M-P-C | No.23 | P-M-R-C | No.48 | P-M-R-C |
| No.24 | I-M-R-C | No.49 | I-M-P-R | No.24 | I-M-P-R-C | No.49 | P-M-R-C |
| No.25 | I-C | No.50 | M-P-R-C | No.25 | I-C | No.50 | P-M-R-C |

**Table 2.** Co-occurrences of moves and percentage

| Num. of | YCC | | YEE | |
|---|---|---|---|---|
| moves | Num. of abstracts with the moves | percentage | Num. of abstracts with the moves | percentage |
| 5 moves | 1 | 2% | 5 | 10% |
| 4 moves | 17 | 34% | 22 | 44% |
| 3 moves | 14 | 28% | 15 | 30% |
| 2 moves | 13 | 26% | 7 | 14% |
| 1 move | 5 | 10% | 1 | 2% |

**Table 3.** The frequency of the respective 5 moves

| Names of the moves | YCC | | YEE | |
|---|---|---|---|---|
| | Num. of abstracts | percentage | Num. of abstracts | percentage |
| Introduction | 31 | 62% | 19 | 38% |
| Purpose | 35 | 70% | 41 | 82% |
| Method | 25 | 50% | 41 | 82% |
| Result | 11 | 22% | 33 | 66% |
| Conclusion | 44 | 88% | 42 | 84% |

We can easily see the differences and the similarities between Chinese and English abstracts from the above tables. In both Chinese and English abstracts, despite the few differences on the order and the frequency, the number of abstracts with 4 moves is the highest, the second highest is those with 3 moves. It is indicated that most abstracts, whether Chinese or English, contain 3 or 4 moves. Among the 50 English abstracts, there are 5 which include all the 5 moves, while only one of the 50 Chinese abstracts contains 5 moves. Compared with English abstracts, Chinese abstracts show a relatively high irregularity, which is illustrated by the number of abstracts with one or two moves. The percentage of Chinese abstracts with one or two moves in the 50 ones is 36% while that of the English is only 16%. It is seen that English abstracts are relatively more complete than the Chinese ones. What's more, among the Chinese 50, the abstracts with only one move occupy 10%, which suggests that Chinese authors like to write descriptive abstract.

Table 3 indicates that whether Chinese or English, the frequency of the purpose move and the conclusion move is high, which shows that both Chinese authors and English authors will not omit these two moves and these two are likely to be the basic moves. There exists a large difference on the other three moves. The frequency of the method move and the result move in English abstracts is high (82% and 66% respectively), which suggests that these two are basic moves in English while in Chinese abstracts, the percentage of both the method and the result moves takes up 72%, less than that of the method move in English. However, the frequency of the introduction move in Chinese abstracts is quite higher than that in English, 62% vs. 38%. This is probably due to the fact that Chinese authors used to be criticized because of their ignorance of referring to the others' research and usually taking the others' research as the free resources and then trying to show their respect to the quoted materials. Hence Chinese authors put much emphasis on the introduction move [3].

To sum up, the generic structural potential (GSP) of Chinese and English linguistics and literature article abstracts tends to be different owing to the different Chinese and English cultures, and differences also exist in different abstracts in the same culture [4]. Although an absolute conclusion can not be drawn from the above data and analysis, which is due to the fact that among the 100 randomly chosen abstracts the frequency of no one move is 100%, we can obtain the relative generic structural potential (GSP) of Chinese and English linguistic and literature article abstracts by taking 70% as the standard frequency, with those more than or equal to 70% as the basic elements and those less than 70% as the optional ones:

A: the generic structural potential (GSP) of Chinese linguistic and literature article abstracts:

Of the 5 moves, IPMRC, the purpose and conclusion are the basic elements, and the introduction, method and result moves are optional. The frequency of the result move is the least and that of the introduction is relatively higher. However, the frequency of result move in YEE is 66%, which means most international English abstracts have the result move.

B: the generic structural potential (GSP) of English linguistic and literature article abstracts:

Of the 5 moves, IPMRC, the purpose, method and the conclusion are the basic elements, while the introduction and the result are optional. But the frequency of result move in English is 66%, which means most English abstracts have the result move.

# 3    Language Features of Chinese and English Article Abstracts

## 3.1    The Use of the First Person

By using the AntConc, we calculated the frequency of the first person words such as I, we, me, the author, the researcher etc. in the YCC, YCE (translated English version of the original Chinese abstracts) and the YEE, 252 respectively. At the same time, the number of word types and the number of word tokens of each sub-corpus are also counted to get the TTR (type/token ratio) per 3000 words. Then the standardized TTR [11] is got on the average 3000. The following is the statistical result.

**Table 4.** The Standardized TTR

|  | No. of word types | No. of word tokens | Standardized TTR |
|---|---|---|---|
| YCC | 4585 | 30895 | 33.8 |
| YCE | 6325 | 35699 | 34.75 |
| YEE | 6059 | 41824 | 35.93 |

**Table 5.** The No. of the first person words

|  | YCC | YCE | YEE |
|---|---|---|---|
| I | - | 1 | 61 |
| we | - | 47 | 140 |
| the author | - | 23 | 4 |
| the researcher | - | 1 | 0 |
| 我[wo]( I ) | 0 | - | - |
| 我们[women]( we ) | 0 | - | - |
| 作者[zuozhe]( author ) | 0 | - | - |
| 笔者[bizhe]( author ) | 0 | - | - |

We can see from Table 4 that in spite of the little difference of the standardized TTR in YCC, YCE and YEE, the TTR in YCE is, anyway, a little lower than that in YEE, which means Chinese authors' command of English vocabulary should be improved.

It can be seen from Table 5 that the first person words are not found in YCC. This may be due to the Chinese culture that holds modesty dear. We Chinese advocate being reserved, not aggressive. Also important is the Chinese article writing tradition that necessitates the objectivity in one's technical writing. Hence, the first person words, which are considered as the most subjective expressions by the Chinese, are surely avoided being used. To our gratification, the English translation of Chinese abstracts contains a lot of first person words, which suggests that Chinese translators are aware of the first person words using in the English world and can keep the pace with the international pattern. It is a new trend in English academic writing that there exist a lot of first person words since it is a tradition that in the academic writing the first person words should be avoided in order to hold the objectivity of the paper [2]. In today's academic world, the first person words are encouraged to be used to attach importance to the authors' responsibility and, at the same time, to remove the rigid appearance of the technical papers and make them more readable as well.

It can also be found that in the English translation of Chinese abstracts the word "author" is used many times as well as "we" while in English abstracts "author" is seldom found. It is probably also the result of the Chinese modesty. The word "author", on the one hand, has the same function as "we", on the other hand, is less aggressive than "we", which is typically Chinese.

We find another fact that even in English abstracts the frequency of "we" is quite higher than that of "I". We can interpret this as the following: There are more than one researcher; The plural form means more people's agreement and then leads more persuasive conclusion. Maybe there is the third reason, that is, no one is willing to shoulder, alone, the responsibility of the conclusion.

## 3.2     The Use of Passive Voice

The passive voice in Chinese is much more complicated than that in English. In addition to the marked passive voice, there are unmarked passive voice and implied passive voice. In this paper all the three kinds of passive voice are included.

We made a meta-information mark-up to the original texts and then randomly chose 50 texts from each sub-corpus (YCC, YCE, YEE) respectively. We annotated the passive voice feature and extracted the corresponding data as following:

**Table 6.** The No. of passive voice

|                             | YCC  | YCE | YEE |
|-----------------------------|------|-----|-----|
| Num. of passive voice       | 8    | 164 | 174 |
| Num. of sentences           | 250  | 330 | 335 |
| Percentage of passive voice | 0.3% | 50% | 52% |

As is shown in Table 6, the frequency of passive voice in Chinese abstracts is low, only 0.3% while in the English translation of Chinese abstracts and English abstracts it is similar, which means Chinese translators have no difference from English native speakers in the use of passive voice in the abstract writing. Although some researchers have noticed that English native speakers is now likely to use positive voice instead of passive voice in their abstract writing [1][3], what they have probed are all abstracts of the scientific articles. This paper is based on the data from the only linguistic and literature article abstracts. We can draw a conclusion that in the linguistic and literature article abstracts it is still popular to use passive voice. Meanwhile, the difference of the macrostructure between Chinese and English is proved, i.e. more positive voice in Chinese and more passive voice in English.

# 4    Conclusion

From the above analysis on the generic structural potential (GSP) of Chinese and English linguistic and literature article abstracts we can easily see the difference between the two languages, which will be a help to Chinese academic article writers. The writers know how to write a good abstract, both Chinese and English, and catch more publishing opportunities. After all, the authoritative magazines attach much more importance to the high quality abstracts. There are some writers who will publish their papers in the foreign magazines and a high quality English abstract is necessary.

The above analysis on the language features of Chinese and English article abstracts makes us know the difference of the first person and the passive voice between Chinese and English. It can help us make a good translation to Chinese abstracts and keep pace with the English ones.

However, we should not, at the same time, ignore the difference between the Chinese and the English culture. We'd better, in abstract writing, operate on the principle that we try our best to keep pace with the international pattern while not ignoring our own culture [1]. Therefore, we can exactly and timely convey our messages to the readers with a high quality abstract.

**Acknowledgement.** This work is supported by the Humanities and Social Sciences Research Project of the Education Department of China (10YJA740074)

# References

1. Teng, Z., Tan, W.: The Tense and Voice in English Abstracts. Chinese Science & Technology Translators Journal 17(1), 5–7 (2004) (in Chinese)
2. Lu, Y.: Linguistic Features of English Research Paper Abstracts: A Corpus-Driven Study. Journal of PLA University of Foreign Languages 35(6), 8–13 (2009) (in Chinese)
3. He, Y., Cao, Z.: Genre Analysis of Aerospace Article Abstracts. Journal of Beijing University of Aeronautics and Astronautics (Social Sciences Edition) 23(2), 97–100 (2010) (in Chinese)

4. Li, Q., Zhang, M.: An Analysis on the Context of Chinese and English Academic Article Abstracts. Journal of Changchun University of Science and Technology (Social Sciences Edition) 25(1), 66–68 (2012) ( in Chinese)
5. Yan, M.: Comparative Study on Abstract of Chinese and English Medical Research Articles. Journal of Liaoning Medical University (Social Science Edition) 9(4), 140–142 (2011) (in Chinese)
6. Shi, W.: An Economic Research on the English Abstracts of the Scientific Papers. Journal of Xi'an International Studies University 16(1), 25–27 (2008) (in Chinese)
7. Chen, R.: Analysis on the Abstracts and Introductions of English and Chi-nese Linguistic Journal Articles from the Perspective of Genre Set. Journal of Guizhou University (Social Science Edition) 29(4), 106–111 (2011) (in Chinese)
8. Ye, N.: Analysis and Compare on the Abstracts and Introductions of the Genre Set between English and Chinese. Journal of Jiangnan University (Humanities & Social Sciences) 7(4), 99–103 (2008) (in Chinese)
9. Li, Y.: Analysis on Hedges in English Abstracts. Journal of Hunan Medical University (Social Science Edition) 11(5), 215–217 (2009) (in Chinese)
10. Wang, Z.: A Corpus-based Contrastive Study on Hedges in Chinese and English RA Abstracts. Journal of Huazhong Science and Technology University (Social Science Edition) 22(6), 59–63 (2008) (in Chinese)
11. Liang, M., Li, W., Xu, J.: Using Corpora: A Practical Coursebook. Foreign Language Teaching and Research Press, Beijing (2010) (in Chinese)
12. Swales, J.M.: Genre Analysis: English in Academic and Research Settings. Shanghai Foreign Language Education Press, Shanghai (2000)

# Corpus Construction on Polarity Shifting
# in Sentiment Analysis

Shoushan Li[1,2], Sophia Yat Mei Lee[2], and Chu-Ren Huang[2]

[1] Natural Language Processing, Lab School of Computer Science and Technology,
Soochow University, China
[2] CBS, The Hong Kong Polytechnic University
lishoushan@suda.edu.cn, {sophiaym,churenhuang}@gmail.com

**Abstract.** Polarity shifting has been a challenge to automatic sentiment classification. In this paper, we create a corpus which consists of polarity-shifted sentences in the product reviews, where both the sentimental words and shifting trigger words are annotated. In particular, we group the polarity-shifted sentence structures into five main categories, i.e., negation, contrastive transition, modality, implication, and irrelevance Evaluation shows the statistics on the agreement of the annotation and the distribution of the five categories of polarity shifting is given.

## 1    Introduction

Sentiment classification is a special task of text classification whose objective is to categorize a text according to the sentimental polarity of opinions it contains (Pang et al., 2002). This task has received considerable interest and been widely studied in the community of computational linguistics.

One challenging problem in sentiment classification is the phenomenon of so-called polarity shifting (Li et al., 2010) which happens when the sentimental orientation of the whole text is different from its containing words or sentences. For example, in the sentence '*I do not like this book*', the polarity of the word '*like*' is different from the polarity of the whole sentence due to the polarity shifting caused by the trigger word '*not*'. It is one main reason why some bag-of-words based machine learning approaches fail under some circumstances.

Recently, polarity shifting has received more and more attention. Several studies have been conducted to detect the polarity shifting and apply the shifting knowledge to sentiment classification systems (Pang et al., 2002; Na et al., 2004; Kennedy and Inkpen, 2006; Ikeda et al., 2008; Li et al., 2010). However, some basic issues of this problem still remain unclear or unsolved. First, in linguistic studies, various linguistic structures or contextual clues could cause polarity shifting (Polanyi and Zaenen, 2004). The distributions of these structures, however, have never been carefully computed and analyzed. These distributions allow us to have a better understanding of the shifting phenomenon by indicating which parts of the structures are crucial and which parts are trivial. For example, considering negation alone has been reported to be negligible effect on improving the performance (Pang et al. 2002; Kennedy and

P. Liu and Q. Su (Eds.): CLSW 2013, LNAI 8229, pp. 625–634, 2013.

Inkpen, 2006). Even with a rather sophisticated classification approach with compositional inference (Choi and Cardie, 2008), the improvement is still very limited (about 1.5 percent). Intuitively, systems considering polarity shifting should have performed much better. One possible reason for the low improvement is that the proportion of negation to all the shifting structures is not as high as people have imagined.

Second, in computational studies, shifting detection is an essential component in a sentiment classification system in that the shifting knowledge is incorporated. Most existing shifting detection approaches are rule-based, which are highly restricted in terms of coverage. Although some machine-learning based approaches have recently been proposed (Ikeda et al., 2008; Li et al., 2010), the corpora used to train their machine learning models are automatically obtained and thus unavoidably contains considerable noises.

In this paper, we propose a categorization framework to specify different polarity-shifting structures in the document-level product reviews. Specifically, we first manually annotate the polarity-shifted sentences and categorize the shifting structures and cues into five main types: *negation, contrastive transition, modality, implication,* and *irrelevance*. We analyze each type of shifting structure and generalize its subcategories in detail. Then, a corpus is presented with the category information. Based on the corpus analysis, the distribution of these categories and subcategories are presented.

## 2   Related Work

Polanyi and Zaenen (2004) present an extensive analysis on polarity shifting structures in movie reviews. The trigger words of polarity shifting are categorized into two types: sentence-based shifters, e.g., *not* and *never*, and discourse-based shifters, e.g., *but*, and *however*. The analysis is thorough but the proposed taxonomy is not specifically designed for computational applications, such as automatic detection of polarity shifting structures. Furthermore, since the shifting information is not annotated in the corpus, the distribution of the different shifting structures cannot be computed and analyzed.

Negation shifting, a specific structure of polarity shifting caused by negation, has been widely studied, such as Pang et al. (2002), Na et al. (2004), and Kennedy and Inkpen (2006). They usually detect negation structures based on certain rules with trigger words. Their results show that considering negation could only slightly improve the performance of machine learning approaches on sentiment classification. When other kinds of structures, such as content-based negation and contrastive transition, are also considered along with general negation structure, the improved performance becomes more significant (Choi and Cardie, 2008; Ding et al., 2008; Wilson et al., 2009).

On top of the above studies, Ikeda et al. (2008) and Li et al. (2010) introduce other shifting structures at sentence-level and document-level sentiment classification respectively. They automatically generate a pseudo corpus containing polarity-shifted sentences and propose machine-learning approach to detect polarity-shifted sentences. However, both studies train the detection model with the automatically-generated training data, which makes the accuracy suffer.

Unlike all above studies, this paper is the first attempt to perform manual annotation for polarity shifting. This paper is an extension work of Zhang et al. (2011) and the categorization structure is modified and analyzed in more details.

# 3     Corpus Annotation

Polarity shifting is a kind of relationship between an expression (e.g., a phrase, a sentence or a document) and its components (e.g., a word, a phrase, or a sentence). If the polarity of the expression is different from the component, the component is regarded as polarity-shifted. In this study, the term polarity shifting is restricted to the relationship between a word and a document, in that the polarity of a word is different from the polarity expressed by the whole document. The sentences containing such polarity-shifted words are considered as polarity-shifted sentences.

## 3.1     Collection and Annotation of Sentimental Words

The sentimental words are collected from two resources. One is the domain-independent dictionary compiled by Wilson et al. (2005). The other is the word list (Blitzer et al., 2007) extracted from product reviews (Blitzer et al., 2007). Since this list of sentimental words is rather preliminary, we manually check the polarities of all the words and assign a general polarity to each word.

## 3.2     Annotation Process

The polarity-shifted structures are annotated in the product reviews of two domains: DVD and kitchen (Blitzer et al., 2007), where the polarity of each document is already given. The detailed annotation process is illustrated as follows.

First of all, the document is segmented into sentences with punctuations, e.g., '*?*' and '*.*', and some simple conjunctions, e.g., '*and*', '*but*', '*so*', '*although*', and so on. Second, the sentimental word is automatically marked (The symbol '*#*' is added after the sentimental word) when its general polarity is different from the polarity of the document. Third, the marked words are manually annotated to be polarity-shifted or polarity-unshifted.

The third step is to ensure the correct marking of polarity shifting between a word and a document. For example, '*like*' is a positive word in our dictionary and '*It looks like # a dog.*' is a sentence in a negative document. However, we cannot label the word '*like*' as polarity-shifted as it does not express any opinion at all.

## 3.3     Specific Label Format

Each polarity-shifted sentence in the corpus is annotated using a vector in the following format:

<*Category, Sentimental word, Shifting trigger word*>

The vector contains three main elements. The first element is the category information that will be presented in Section 4. The second element indicates the sentimental word and the third one indicates the trigger word causing polarity shifting. Examples are illustrated in Figure 1.

> (1) So i would not recommend # this film for families with young children, because of the nudity. [26] <NEGATION_functional, recommend, not>

**Fig. 1.** Some examples in our corpus

# 4    Analysis of Polarity Shifting Structures

We generalize five main categories of polarity shifting structures along with other subcategories, as illustrated in Figure 2. This section discusses each of these categories and its subcategories.

## 4.1    Negation

Negation is a very popular structure that causes polarity shifting. In this kind of structure, a clear trigger word, referred to as negator, is used to shift the polarity of the sentimental word in the same sentence. Generally, there are two types of negators: function-word negators and content-word negators (Choi and Cardie, 2008). Different from function-word negators (e.g., 'not' and 'never'), content-word negators themselves contain content meaning and can possibly be sentimental words (e.g., 'fail' and 'eliminated'). Accordingly, the negation can be further categorized into two subgroups: functional negation and contextual negation. For example, E1 belongs to functional negation while E2 belongs to contextual negation.

E1: I would **not** recommend # this electric kettle .
E2: **Lack** of dimensional stability # at 15 degrees f translates to poor heat conduction.

## 4.2    Contrastive Transition

Contrastive transition is one special type of transition for expressing contradiction or contrast when connecting one paragraph, sentence, clause or word with another. It is distinguished from other types of transitions by different connectives. Examples of contrastive transitions are connectives such as *however, but,* and *notwithstanding,* as compared to other transitions such as concluding transitions expressed by connectives such as *therefore, in a word, in summary,* and *in brief.*

A distinct difference between negation and contrastive transition is the shifting scope caused by trigger words. A negator could merely shift the polarity of the word in the same sentence while a connective in contrastive transition can shift not only the sentimental word from the same sentence but also the one from different sentence or even different paragraph.

According to the influenced scope of the trigger word, we group the structures of contrastive transition into three subcategories: *intra-sentence* (E3), *extra-sentence* (E4), and *extra-paragraph* (E5).

E3: I like # the idea of this product, ***but*** not the pre-filled one I received .

E4: When it works , this blender does a fine # job , and looks great # . ***However***, our first one quit turning the blades in less than a year .

E5: The heat distribution is excellent #, and unlike the copper bottom pan, the calphalon is light and easy # to use.

***But***, the good # stops here.

## 4.3    Modality

Modality is related to the attitude of the speaker towards her/his statements in terms of the degree of certainty, reliability, subjectivity, sources of information, and perspective (De Haan, 1995). This category is also a common structure that causes polarity shifting and yet underdeveloped in sentiment classification studies. Some subcategories are analyzed in detail as follows.

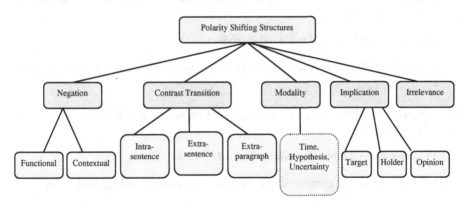

**Fig. 2.** The taxonomy of the structures causing polarity shifting

(1) **Time:** where the opinion does not exist at the present but in the past. For example:

E6: I ***thought*** it is a good # product.

The corresponding trigger words can be *should, would, thought* and so on.

(2) **Hypothesis:** where an assumption (Narayanan et al., 2009) or a hypothetical situation is described. For example:

E7: ***If*** they change the color, I will recommend # it.

The corresponding trigger words can be *wish, if, hope, would*, and so on.

(3) **Uncertainty:** where the statement of the sentence is uncertain. For example,

E8: It *probably* worked better # back in 96 '.

The corresponding trigger words can be *possible, possibly, perhaps, probably*, and so on.

We see in the corpus that these subcategories are frequently interrelated, i.e. often appear simultaneously (See E9). Therefore, we only assign the category label, i.e., modality, without subcategory information.

E9: I *thought* it *would* work great #.

## 4.4    Implication

This category is specifically proposed to detect the polarity of the opinion expressed by a holder on a specific target. Sometimes, the holder or the target in the sentence might not be the one concerned. Although the opinion in this case is from other holders or about other targets, it sometimes implies opinions on the target concerned. There are three subcategories.

(1) **Holder:** where the holder of sentimental expression is not the author, but may be other people. For example,

E10: *Other people* think it is a good # product.

The corresponding trigger words can be *other people, someone, another one*, and so on.

(2) **Target:** where the opinion is not expressed on the target object but on another thing. For example:

E11: I recommend # buy *something instead*.

The corresponding trigger words can be: *other, instead, something*, and so on.

(3) **Opinion:** where the opinion is expressed from the holder concerned or on the target concerned. But the expression implies a opposite opinion.

E12: *The only* small annoying # feature is every time the "talk " button is pressed.

The corresponding trigger word is *only*.

## 4.5    Irrelevance

The last category is called irrelevance. The sentences of irrelevance are not related to the topic concerned at all. For example,

E13: Every great # writer of every age and era, be it mark twain.

E13 is mainly concerned with the writer. It is irrelevant to the topic concerned, i.e., DVD or kitchen.   Different from all of the above categories, the polarity-shifted sentences in this category contain no explicit trigger word.

# 5    Experimentation

In our study, 1200 reviews with 600 positive and 600 negative ones are annotated. Every review has been annotated by two annotators. In this section, we first report the agreement analysis and important statistics regarding the proposed corpus. Then, a rule-based system for detecting polarity shifting is implemented and applied to sentiment classification with term-counting.

## 5.1    Empirical Study on the Proposed Corpus Annotation Agreement

As discussed in Section 3.1, we annotate the sentimental words from two resources: one is the dictionary (Wilson et al., 2009) and the other is word list generated from feature selection. The agreement of our annotation on the polarities of the words is given in Table 1. The disagreement often happens when the polarity of the word is hard to judge, for example, the words *'struggle'*, *'marvelous'*, *'surprise'*, and *'financial'*.

As far as the polarity-shifted sentences are concerned, two annotators very often give the same judgment on whether the sentence is polarity-shifted or polarity-unshifted according to our definition of polarity shifting.

**Table 1.** Annotation agreement on the sentimental words

| Source of the Sentimental Words | Markables | Agreement |
|---|---|---|
| Word list in product reviews | 1200 | 0.87 |
| Dictionary (Wilson et al., 2005) | 8200 | 0.90 |

**Table 2.** The proportion of the each category of polarity shifting

|  | DVD | Kitchen |
|---|---|---|
| Negation | 25.1% | 39.7% |
| Contrast Transition | 14.5% | 17.0% |
| Modality | 10.3% | 13.0% |
| Implication | 13.0% | 18.8% |
| Irrelevance | 42.6% | 17.5% |

## Category Statistics

As discussed in Section 4, we group the polarity shifting structures into five categories. Table 2 and Table 3 show the proportion of each category and the corresponding subcategories respectively.

From Table 2, we can see that there is a reasonable amount of each category of polarity shifting appears in the corpus. In particular, *negation* does not dominate over others in polarity shifting structures. This may explain why the improvements of considering negation alone is reported to be very limited (Pang et al., 2002; Kennedy and Inkpen, 2006). Table 4 shows that the percentage of contextual negation is about 9%, which confirms the finding of Choi and Cardie (2008) that contextual negation is very important for detecting the polarity of expressions.

**Table 3.** The distribution of all subcategories in each domain

| Domain | | Negation | |
|--------|--------|------------|------------|
| | | Functional | Contextual |
| DVD | neg | 14.2% | 5.8% |
| | pos | 3.5% | 1.7% |
| Kitchen | neg | 19.4% | 7.0% |
| | pos | 10.8% | 2.7% |

| Domain | | Contrastive Transition | | |
|--------|--------|----------------|----------------|-----------------|
| | | Intra-sentence | Extra-sentence | Extra-paragraph |
| DVD | neg | 7.5% | 3.1% | 0.4% |
| | pos | 2.4% | 1.0% | 0.1% |
| Kitchen | neg | 10.1% | 3.9% | 0.2% |
| | pos | 2.5% | 0.2% | 0.0% |

| Domain | | Implicit | | |
|--------|--------|--------|--------|---------|
| | | Target | Holder | Opinion |
| DVD | neg | 5.0% | 2.9% | 0.7% |
| | pos | 0.8% | 0.2% | 0.2% |
| Kitchen | neg | 10.2% | 7.9% | 1.2% |
| | pos | 2.8% | 1.5% | 1.5% |

Note that the percentage of *irrelevance* in DVD is extraordinarily high (42.6%). This is because there are many irrelevant discussions in a DVD reviews, especially the plot of a movie. The high percentage of *irrelevance* greatly hinders the polarity shifting detection due to the lack of explicit trigger words in such category. Therefore, some studies have shown that the improvements in domains like DVD are much less than the other domains like kitchen (Ikeda et al., 2008).

# 6    Conclusions and Future Work

In this paper, we classify the polarity shifting structures into five categories i.e. *negation, contrastive transition, modality, implication*, and *irrelevance*, to better understand the polarity shifting phenomenon in sentiment analysis. In particular, we propose a corpus containing the polarity-shifted sentences, together with the containing sentimental words, shifting trigger words, and the shifting category information. Empirical studies on the proposed corpus demonstrate that the polarity shifting phenomenon indeed appears very commonly in review texts. In addition, the category distribution is calculated and analyzed.

**Acknowledgments.** This work is supported by a General Research Fund (GRF) sponsored by the Research Grants Council, Hong Kong (Project No. 543810).

# References

1. Blitzer, J., Dredze, M., Pereira, F.: Biographies, Bollywood, Boom-boxes and Blenders: Domain Adaptation for Sentiment Classification. In: Proceedings of ACL 2007, pp. 440–447 (2007)
2. Choi, Y., Cardie, C.: Learning with Compositional Semantics as Structural Inference for Subsentential Sentiment Analysis. In: Proceedings of EMNLP, pp. 793–801 (2008)
3. De Haan, F.: The Interaction of Modality and Negation: A Typological Study. Garland Publishing, Inc., New York (1997)
4. Ding, X., Liu, B., Yu, P.: A Holistic Lexicon-based Approach to Opinion Mining. In: Proceedings of the International Conference on Web Search and Web Data Mining, WSDM 2008, pp. 64–71 (2008)
5. Ikeda, D., Takamura, H., Ratinov, L., Okumura, M.: Learning to Shift the Polarity of Words for Sentiment Classification. In: Proceedings of IJCNLP 2008, pp. 296–303 (2008)
6. Kennedy, A., Inkpen, D.: Sentiment Classification of Movie Reviews using Contextual Valence Shifters. Computational Intelligence 22(2), 110–125 (2006)
7. Li, S., Xia, R., Zong, C., Huang, C.: A Framework of Feature Selection Methods for Text Categorization. In: Proceedings of ACL-IJCNLP 2009, pp. 692–700 (2009)
8. Li, S., Lee, S., Chen, Y., Huang, C., Zhou, G.: Sentiment Classification and Polarity Shifting. In: Proceedings of COLING 2010, pp. 635–643 (2010)
9. Na, J., Sui, H., Khoo, C., Chan, S., Zhou, Y.: Effectiveness of Simple Linguistic Processing in Automatic Sentiment Classification of Product Reviews. In: Conference of the International Society for Knowledge Organization, ISKO 2004 (2004)
10. Narayanan, R., Liu, B.: Sentiment Analysis of Conditional Sentences. In: Proceeding of ACL-IJCNLP 2009, pp. 180–189 (2009)

11. Pang, B., Lee, L., Vaithyanathan, S.: Thumbs up? Sentiment Classification using Machine Learning Techniques. In: Proceedings of EMNLP 2002, pp. 79–86 (2002)
12. Pang, B., Lee, L.: A Sentimental Education: Sentiment Analysis Using Subjectivity Summarization Based on Minimum Cuts. In: Proceedings of ACL 2004, pp. 271–278 (2004)
13. Polanyi, L., Zaenen, A.: Contextual Valence Shifters. Computing attitude and affect in text: Theory and application. Springer (2006)
14. Turney, P.: Thumbs Up or Thumbs Down? Semantic Orientation Applied to Unsupervised Classification of Reviews. In: Proceedings of ACL 2002, pp. 79–86 (2002)
15. Wilson, T., Wiebe, J., Hoffmann, P.: Recognizing Contextual Polarity: An Exploration of Features for Phrase-Level Sentiment Analysis. Computational Linguistics 35(3), 399–433 (2009)
16. Yang, Y., Pedersen, J.O.: A Comparative Study on Feature Selection in Text Categorization. In: Proceedings of the 14th International Conference on Machine Learning, pp. 412–420 (1997)
17. Zhang, X., Li, S., Zhou, G., Zhao, H.: Polarity Shifting: Corpus Construction and Analysis. In: Proceeding of IALP 2011, pp. 272–275 (2011)

# An Event-Based Emotion Corpus

Sophia Yat Mei Lee[1], Huarui Zhang[2], and Chu-Ren Huang[1]

[1] CBS The Hong Kong Polytechnic University, Hong Kong
[2] Key Laboratory of Computational Linguistics, Peking University, Beijing
{ymlee,churen.huang}@polyu.edu.hk, hrzhang@pku.edu.cn

**Abstract.** As part of a larger project, this paper presents some of the work done regarding our proposal of an event-based analysis of emotion. We propose that an emotion is treated as a pivot event linking the events inducing (i.e. pre-events), and induced by (i.e. post-events), said emotion. Our study begins with the development of an emotion corpus annotated with pre-and post-events. We then provide a collocational pattern analysis as well as a linguistic analysis of the links between event structures and emotions in the text. The project goal is to develop a theory predicting the dependencies between emotions and events, based on linguistic cues in context.

## 1    Introduction

Emotions are universal human cognitive states elicited by actual or perceived external events. As such, emotions conceptualize and link cognitive experiences to potential consequences, and provide strong motivations for human behaviors. The emotion of anger, for instance, is elicited by unwanted or harmful circumstances which in turn motivates aggressive behaviors. Our project treats emotions as pivots linking reported events to potential actions by the experiencer. The three key issues we will address in the project are: 1) What are the event structures of emotions? 2) Is there any linguistically motivated empirical evidence for the event structures of emotions? 3) Is there any event-type selection and/or coercion between evoking events and emotion, and between emotion and caused events?

As part of the project, this paper aims to account for the linguistic correlations between evoking events (i.e. pre-events) and caused emotions, and the correlations between emotions and events induced (i.e. post-events). In doing so, we first construct an event-based annotated emotion corpus in Chinese. For each annotated emotion, we identify its pre-events and post-events. We then provide a collocational pattern analysis as well as a linguistic analysis of the links between event structures and emotions in the text. Such a study will offer rich structured data allowing the development of a theory of emotion as events.

P. Liu and Q. Su (Eds.): CLSW 2013, LNAI 8229, pp. 635–644, 2013.
© Springer-Verlag Berlin Heidelberg 2013

## 2     Related Work

The earliest scientific research on emotion has focused on the representation and processing of emotion in facial expressions and body language (Andrew, 1963; Ekman & Friesen, 1978; Gelder, 2009 for a review). More recently, there has been mounting research on the neurobiological basis of emotion (Olson et al., 2007; Craig, 2009; Hervé et al., 2012, among others) and how emotion is linked with other aspects of human cognition (Smith & Lazarus, 1993; Smith and Kirby, 2001; Bridge et al., 2010; Sweeny et al., in press, among others). Meanwhile, the object of research has been extended to cover emotion in verbal language (i.e. emotional language) as well. It has been shown that when humans encounter emotional language, the processing of language and the processing of emotion are highly intertwined (Hervé et al., 2012). The language-processing part of the brain is responsible for extracting linguistic cues for emotion, while the emotion-processing part makes inferences about the emotional content based on linguistic meanings. Thus it begs the question of which linguistic cues are used for encoding emotion and how they interact with each other.

In terms of applications, opinion mining and sentiment analysis have been hot topics in language technology for over ten years (Turney, 2002; Pang and Lee, 2008). Existing studies are dominated by polarity analyses focusing on positive and negative sentiment. The assignment of sentiment polarity to an object or a linguistic term tends to be domain-specific and perspective-specific; hence these applications face challenges in domain adaptation. Unlike polarity analysis, emotion is rather universal across all domains. Despite the difficulty in detecting and classifying emotions, there is a growing literature on emotion detection in computational linguistics (Tokuhisa et al., 2008; Lee et al., 2012).

## 3     Emotion as a Pivot Event

Various linguistic and psychological theories of emotions were proposed previously (e.g. Plutchik 1980, Fridja 1986, Weiss and Cropanozano 1996). However, there is no clear consensus among the theories on how to define or account for emotions with linguistic data. Most emotion theories agree that emotion is stimulated by an event. However, emotion state as a sub-type of event is rarely studied in linguistic study of event structure. This study aims to fill this gap and account for the emotions' interaction with pre-events (i.e. events that induce the emotions) and post-events (i.e. events that are induced by the emotions) for emotion processing in text. An example is given in Figure 1. Figure 1 shows the context of an emotion "生氣"[shengqi](*angry*) in which the pre-event "他說已約好牌搭子" (*She said [she] had made an appointment with her friends)* induced the emotion, which in turn led to the post-event "吵了 一架". Here we treat emotions as pivot event linking reported events to potential actions by the experiencer.

"由於下週我得到香港出差，雖然才五天，我總是覺得夫妻分離相思濃，有點捨不得，就在週末的前一天計劃我星期六下午的節目，誰知他說已約好牌搭子，我好**生氣**，吵了一架，背對背而眠。"

*(As I needed to go on a business trip to Hong Kong the next week, albeit just for five days, I felt that I would miss my wife dearly. So just before the week-end, I started to make plans for the two of us on Saturday afternoon. To my surprise, she said she had already made an appointment with her friends. I was very **angry**, and we had a quarrel. That night, we slept with our backs turned on each other.)*

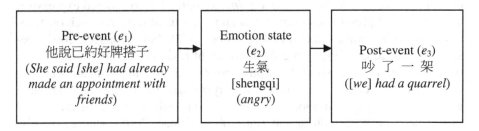

**Fig. 1.** Emotion-event interaction

A theory of event structure anchors this inter-disciplinary study of emotions. Although the study of event structure is well-established in philosophy and linguistics, it is a relatively new idea for computational linguists. The theoretical framework adopted in this study is the theory of Generative Lexicon (Pustejovsky 1995). The approach to represent event's internal structure goes back to Reichenback (1949) and Davidson (1967). Davidson reified events as individuals and tried to capture the appropriate entailment between propositions involving action and event expression. The thought provides a convincing tool for analyzing word meaning and arises out of the semantic research which attempts to model event into complex event structures - a causative outer event and a change of state inner event. Pustejovsky (1995) argued that finer-grained distinctions are necessary for event descriptions. He introduced a tree structure to represent the temporal ordering and dominance constraints on an event, with its inner events (subevents). Furthermore, Im and Pustejovsky (2009) constructed an Event Structure Lexicon which encodes Aktionsart and subevent structure frame. They defined event implicature as the lexical entailment or presupposition based on the event structure of event-denoting expression, consisting of pre-state, process, and result state of an event. The annotated corpus is thus used to make event implicature-based inference and recognize event structure-related entailments in text.

The observation that emotion is one of the most significant factors involving event comes naturally. Yet, little research focuses on the interactions of event with emotion, especially in linguists and computational linguists. From the perspective of social psychology, Ortony (1990) viewed emotion as paradigmatic psychological states of feeling that arise from attending to events which are appraised as being desirable or undesirable. Type specification (desirable/undesirable) of an event comprises the eliciting conditions for the emotion type (Joy/Distress emotion). Similar thoughts have also been presented by Roseman (1979), Scherer (1982), and Frijda (1987).

Emotion may be encoded in text. In general, emotion words are classified into two types, i.e., expressive and descriptive (Kövecses, 2000; Potts, 2007). For example, the sentence *"I was so angry that I left the party!"* is considered descriptive, while *"Damn it, what's going on here?"* is considered expressive. The study of expressive emotion has been the focus of most research on emotion in speech studies (Abelin and Allwood, 2000; Mozziconacci, 2002; Devillers et al., 2005). Despite a growing body of research on emotion, little has been done on the analysis of descriptive emotion as it is linguistically conventionalized and not as closely linked to physiological attributes as expressive emotion. Descriptive emotion, however, is frequently found to be embedded in textual context (Mihalcea and Liu, 2006; Ahmad, 2008). Hence, the discovery and interpretation of descriptive emotion is crucial for the application in knowledge representation as well as information technology. It also offers a better test for how emotion is represented in the complex linguistic system. This paper focuses on the analysis of descriptive emotions as illustrated in Figure 1.

## 4    The Event-Based Emotion Corpus

Based on our proposal that emotion is treated as a pivot event which connects the pre-events and post-events, we have constructed an event-based emotion corpus. As it is an ongoing project, we will present what has been done and what will be done in this section.

### 4.1    Data

Data are extracted from the Sinica Corpus using a pattern-based approach as described in Chen et al. (2009). Based on the list of 91 Chinese primary emotion keywords identified in Chen et al. (2009), we extracted 3,000 instances of sentences by keyword matching from the Sinica Corpus, which is a tagged balanced corpus of Mandarin Chinese containing ten million words. Each in-stance contains the focus sentence with the emotion keyword "<FocusSentence>," plus the sentence before "<PrefixSentence>" and after "<SuffixSentence>" it. A sample instance is given in Figure 2.

---

snc_11417 Y 0/生氣/Anger
<PrefixSentence> 過些時候，魯班的妻子懷孕了，肚子一天比一天大。
</PrefixSentence>

<FocusSentence>魯班的父親很<emo id=0>生氣</emo>，就她說：我兒子
在涼州做事，離家那麼遠，很久沒有回來過，你竟然懷孕了，真是可恥 ！
</FocusSentence>

<SuffixSentence>魯班的妻子受了冤枉，很不甘心，就把魯班每晚乘木鳶回
来的情形告訴他父親。</SuffixSentence>


snc_11417 Y 0/生氣/Anger
<PrefixSentence>After some time, Luban's wife became with child. Her pregnant belly grew with each day. </PrefixSentence>

<FocusSentence>Luban's father was <emo id=0>furious</emo>, scolding her: "My son works in faraway Liangzhou and has not come back for so long. Yet you have conceived. What a shameful act! " </FocusSentence>

<SuffixSentence>Luban's wife could not bear the wrongful accusation, and told her father-in-law of how Luban had returned home each night by riding a wooden kite to be with her. </SuffixSentence>

---

**Fig. 2.** A sample of an instance in the emotion corpus

## 4.2    Event Annotation and Linguistic Analysis

The event annotation scheme in this study is based on Pustejovsky's Generative Lexicon Theory. For each event-bearing verb, we identify the context-dependent event type and assign the appropriate event structure frame associated with the event type using Generative Lexicon Markup Language (GLML, Pustejovsky et al. 2009). We also collect paraphrases of the predicates associated with each subevent and assemble resulting information as a structured object for each verb. This part of research will benefit from Pustejovsky's previous work and has the potential of linking our data to event-annotated corpus in other languages for comparative studies.

---

snc_11417 Y 0/生氣/Anger
<PrefixSentence> 過些時候，[[魯班的妻子懷孕了]]，肚子一天比一天大。</PrefixSentence>

<FocusSentence>魯班的父親很<emo id=0>生氣</emo>，就{{她}}說：我兒子在涼州做事，離家那麼遠，很久沒有回來過，你竟然懷孕了，真是可恥 ！</FocusSentence>

<SuffixSentence>魯班的妻子受了冤枉，很不甘心，就把魯班每晚乘木鸢回来的情形告訴他父親。</SuffixSentence>


snc_11417 Y 0/生氣/Anger
<PrefixSentence>After some time, [[Luban's wife became with child]]. Her pregnant belly grew with each day. </PrefixSentence>

<FocusSentence>Luban's father was <emo id=0>furious</emo>, {{scolding her}}: "My son works in faraway Liangzhou and has not come back for so long. Yet you have conceived. What a shameful act! " </FocusSentence>

<SuffixSentence>Luban's wife could not bear the wrongful accusation, and told her father-in-law of how Luban had returned home each night by riding a wooden kite to be with her. </SuffixSentence>

---

**Fig. 3.** A sample of an event-annotated instance in the emotion corpus

For each annotated emotion, its pre-events and the post-events are manually annotated. Figure 3 shows an example of an event-annotated instance in which the pre-event is marked with "[[… ]]" and the post-event "{{…}}". Results show that, out of the 3,000 instances of emotion, 81% contain a pre-event and 19% contain a post-event in the context. We notice that pre-events tend to occur before the emotion keyword (67%) than after the emotion keyword (33%), while post-events mostly occur after the emotion keyword (85%). With the pre-events, they tend to be introduced by a list of linguistic cues, including prepositions such as 為[wei](*for*) and 對[dui](*for*), conjunctions such as因為[yinwei](*because*) and yushi[於是](*so*), epistemic markers such as kandao[看到](*to see*) and tingdao[聽到](*to hear*) and so on (Lee et al. 2012). As for post-events, it is observed that there is a close association between the emotion and the event type. For instance, the emotion of anger often triggers shouting events which are expressed as 罵 [ma](*to scold*),

大吼[dahuo](*to yell*), 咆哮[paoxiao](*to roar*), etc. More examples of emotion-event association are shown in Table 1. Since the annotation is still in progress, we expect that more data would show a clearer pattern of such an association.

**Table 1.** Emotion-Event Association

| Emotions | Event types |
|---|---|
| Happiness | 笑[xiao](*to laugh*)，起來[qilai](*to start to*)，擁抱[yongbao](*to hug*)，跑[pao](*to run*)，大叫[dajiao](*to shout*) |
| Sadness | 哭[ku](*to cry*)，死[si](*to die*)，離開[likai](*to leave*)，下定決心[xiadingjuetxin](*to determine*) |
| Fear | 不敢[bugan](*not dare*)，躲[duo](*to hide*)，身體[shenti](*body*) |
| Anger | 罵[ma](*to scold*)，大吼[dahuo](*to yell*)，咆哮[paoxiao](*to roar*)，破壞[pohuai](*to destroy*)，殺[sha](*to kill*) |

The next step of our project is to provide a deep linguistic analysis of the links between event structures and emotions in the text. We will provide a more comprehensive structural analysis as well as an analysis of collocational patterns and event's emotion attributes. Based on the MARVS event structure (Huang et al. 2000), which was proposed in representing verbal information and their semantic factors in our previous works, we will propose a unified emotion and event representation frame to decode the emotion as event types and semantic composition of event structures of emotions. We will also explore how the manual event-annotation and the linguistic analysis would help improve the automatic event-annotation by aligning the two sets of data.

### 4.3    Temporal Relation

With the annotated corpus, we will examine the temporal relation of the events involved in each emotion instance based on Allen's Interval Algebra. The 13 base relations presented in Figure 4 capture the possible relations between two intervals:

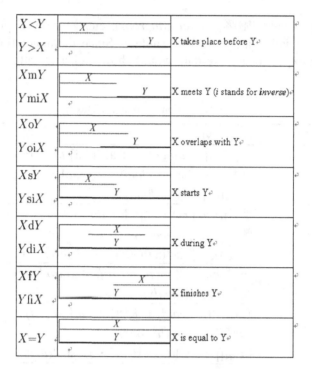

| $X<Y$<br>$Y>X$ | | X takes place before Y |
| $XmY$<br>$YmiX$ | | X meets Y (*i* stands for *inverse*) |
| $XoY$<br>$YoiX$ | | X overlaps with Y |
| $XsY$<br>$YsiX$ | | X starts Y |
| $XdY$<br>$YdiX$ | | X during Y |
| $XfY$<br>$YfiX$ | | X finishes Y |
| $X=Y$ | | X is equal to Y |

**Fig. 4.** Allen's Interval Algebra

For instance, the sentence

老鼠減少了許多，主人非常\<emo id=1\>高興\</emo\>，貓兒也很\<emo id=0\>得意\</emo\> 地繼續擔任守衛的工作。

(*As the number of rats decreased, the master was \<emo id=1\>pleased\</emo\>; as was the cat, which continued to perform its guardkeeping duties with \<emo id=0\>pride\</emo\>.*)

is formalized in Allen's Interval Algebra as follows:

[老鼠減少了許多] {<, m} [高興]
[高興] { d, s, f } [擔任守衛的工作]

[*the number of rats decreased*] {<, m}[*pleased*]
[*pleased*] { d, s, f }[*perform its guardkeeping duties*]

The annotation of temporal relation shows the temporal ordering and dominance constraints of the emotion and its pre-event and post-event. This would allow event implicature-based inference and event structure-related entailment in text.

# 5    Conclusion

In Emotions as pivots underlie our innovative approach towards a linguistic model for event and emotion classification. On the one hand, emotion-evoking events underpin our linguistic model of emotion classification. On the other hand, events causing emotion allow us to make better prediction of event coercion and contextual understanding of texts. Based on our event-annotated emotion corpus, we will propose accounts of the interaction between event type and elicited emotion, as well as between emotion type and caused events. By accounting for emotion states as events, we address a long-lasting gap in existing event structure theories. In particular, our event-annotated corpus and the linguistic account will lay the foundation of emotion analysis in language technology.

**Acknowledgments.** This work is supported by a General Research Fund (GRF) sponsored by the Research Grants Council, Hong Kong (Project No. 543810).

# References

1. Abelin, Å., Allwood, J.: Cross linguistic interpretation of emotional prosody. In: Proceedings of the ISCA ITRW on Speech and Emotion, pp. 110–113 (2000)
2. Ahmad, K. (ed.): Proceedings of the LREC Workshop on Sentiment Analysis: Emotion, Metaphor, Ontology and Terminology (2008)
3. Andrew, R.J.: Evolution of facial expressions. Science 142, 1034–1041 (1963)
4. Bridge, D.J., Chiao, J.Y., Paller, K.A.: Emotional context at learning systematically biases memory for facial information. Memory & Cognition 38, 125–133 (2010)
5. Chen, Y., Lee, S.Y.M., Huang, C.-R.: A Cognitive-based Annotation System for Emotion Computing. In: Proceedings of the Third Linguistic Annotation Workshop (The LAW III) (2009)
6. Craig, A.D.: How do you feel - now? The anterior insula and human awareness. Nat. Rev. Neurosci. 10(1), 59–70 (2009)
7. Davidson, D.: Causal Relations. Journal of Philosophy 64(21), 691–703 (1967)
8. Devillers, L., Vidrascu, L., Lamel, L.: Challenges in real-life emotion annotation and machine learning based detection. Neural Networks 18, 407–422 (2005)
9. Ekman, P., Friesen, W.V.: Facial Action Coding System. Consulting Psychology Press, California (1978)
10. Frijda, N.H.: Emotion, cognitive structure, and action tendency. Cognition and Emotion 1, 115–143 (1987)
11. de Gelder, B.: Why bodies? Twelve reasons for including bodily expressions in affective neuroscience. Philosophical Transactions of the Royal Society B: Biological Sciences 364(1535), 3475–3484 (2009)
12. Hervé, P.-Y., Razafimandimby, A., Vigneau, M., Mazoyer, B., Tzourio-Mazoyer, N.: Disentangling the brain networks supporting affective speech comprehension. NeuroImage 61(4), 1255–1267 (2012)

13. Huang, C.R., Ahrens, K., Chang, L.L., Chen, K.J., Liu, M.C., Tsai, M.C.: The Module-Attribute Representation of Verbal Semantics: From Semantics to Argument Structure. In: Biq, Y.O. (ed.) Special Issue on Chinese Verbal Semantics. Computational Linguistics and Chinese Language Processing, vol. 5(1), pp. 19–46 (2000)
14. Im, S., Pustejovsky, J.: Annotating Event Implicatures for Textual Inference Tasks. In: The 5th International Conference on Generative Approaches to the Lexicon, Pisa, Italy (2009)
15. Kövecses, Z.: Metaphor and Emotion: Language, Culture and Body in Human Feeling. Cambridge University Press, Cambridge (2000)
16. Lee, S.Y.M., Chen, Y., Huang, C.-R., Li, S.: Detecting Emotion Causes with a Linguistic Rule-based Approach. In: Computational Intelligence, Special Issues on Computational Approaches to Analysis of Emotion in Text, Wiley-Blackwell (2012)
17. Mihalcea, R., Liu, H.: A Corpus-based Approach to Finding Happiness. In: Proceedings of the AAAI Spring Symposium on Computational Approaches to Weblogs (2006)
18. Mozziconacci, S.: Prosody and Emotions. In: Proceedings of First International Conference on Speech Prosody (Speech Prosody 2002) (2002)
19. Olson, I.R., Plotzker, A., Ezzyat, Y.: The Enigmatic Temporal Poles: A Review of Findings on Social and Emotional Processing. Brain (2007)
20. Ortony, A., Clore, G.L., Collins, A.: The Cognitive Structure of Emotions. Cambridge University Press (1990)
21. Pang, B., Lee, L.: Opinion Mining and Sentiment Analysis. Foundations and Trends in Information Retrieval 2(1-2), 1–135 (2008)
22. Plutchik, R.: Emotions: A Psychoevolutionary Synthesis. Harper & Row, New York (1980)
23. Potts, C.: Expressive Dimension. Theoretical Linguistics 33(2), 165–198 (2007)
24. Pustejovsky, J.: The Generative Lexicon. The MIT Press, Cambridge (1995)
25. Reichenbach, H.: The Philosophical Significance of the Theory of Relativity. In: Schilpp, P.A. (ed.) Albert Einstein: Philosopher-Scientist, Tudor (1949)
26. Roseman, I.J.: Cognitive aspects of emotion and emotional behavior. Paper presented at the 87th Annual Convention. American Psychological Association, New York (1979)
27. Scherer, K.R.: The assessment of vocal expression in infants and children. In: Izard, C.E. (ed.) Measuring emotions in infants and children, pp. 127–163. Cambridge University Press, Cambridge (1982)
28. Smith, C.A., Kirby, L.D.: Toward delivering on the promise of appraisal theory. In: Scherer, K.R., Schoor, A., Johnstone, T. (eds.) Appraisal Processes in Emotion: Theory, Methods, Research. Oxford University Press, Oxford (2001)
29. Smith, C.A., Lazarus, R.S.: Appraisal components, core relational themes, and the emotions. Cognition and Emotion 7, 233–269 (1993)
30. Sweeny, T.D., Suzuki, S., Grabowecky, M., Paller, K.A.: Detecting and Discriminating Fleeting Emotions in Faces. Emotion (in press)
31. Tokuhisa, R., Inui, K., Matsumoto, Y.: Emotion Classification Using Massive Examples Extracted from the Web. In: Proceedings of International Conference on Computational Linguistics, COLING 2008 (2008)
32. Turney, P.: Thumbs up or thumbs down? Semantic orientation applied to unsupervised classification of reviews. In: Proceedings of the Association for Computational Linguistics, pp. 417–424 (2002)

# Number in Chinese: A Corpus-Based
# Computational Investigation

Lifeng Jin[1], Mao Ye[1,2,3], and Yunlan Fu[1]

[1] Peking University Founder Group Co. LTD
jinlf@founder.com.cn
[2] Institute of Computer Science and Technology, Peking University
[3] Postdoctoral Workstation of the Zhongguancun Haidian Science Park, China
{xjtuyemao,faith416elvin}@163.com

**Abstract.** This article explores the notion of number and plurality in Chinese based on word collocation analysis in a large corpus. It has been argued that although plurality may not be expressed systematically or completely in Chinese, the grammatical category of number may be evident through the collocations of the words which could be analyzed as singular or plural under different semantic circumstances with or without overt marks. Using word similarity measurement techniques, different local contexts of words were extracted from a large corpus and analyzed for their contextual similarities. It may be concluded that singular and plural forms of a word may have a clear distinction in their collocation behavior, and a mark-less noun, i.e. a noun without any numeral or classifier to express its number explicitly, could behave just like a plural noun.

**Keywords:** number, mark-less nouns, collocation differences, contextual similarity, plurality, Chinese language.

## 1   Introduction

Number in Chinese has been regarded by a number of experts as missing or incomplete (see Chen (2009)). The grammatical category of number in Chinese has been a controversial research topic and many ideas and theories have been proposed. Yet most of them may be regarded as analytic and descriptive. With corpus-based data analysis, word collocation analysis and text similarity measurements, the nature of number in Chinese may be investigated further with much more examples and details. In this research paper, the main focus would be to answer the fundamental question: "Are there any collocation differences between singular and plural words in terms of word collocation?" as well as the compelling question "Is a noun without any apparent number mark singular, plural or numberless in Chinese?"

Such an idea may be proposed that the notion of number in Chinese may have been expressed by the context in which the same noun with different kinds of number category could appear. Therefore one would surmise to see different contextual behaviors for nouns with different number categories.

P. Liu and Q. Su (Eds.): CLSW 2013, LNAI 8229, pp. 645–656, 2013.

## 2    Related Works

### 2.1    Number and Plurality

The controversy over number in Modern Chinese may have been a long and intriguing one. The earlier researchers such as Lü (1949) and T. Wu (1994) all argue that the category of number should be seen as absent in Chinese language.

In more recent studies, more researchers tend to agree that number is indeed present in Chinese grammar and pragmatics, and try to categorize a myriad of linguistic phenomena into several number categories. For example, Shi (2003) carefully examined the relationship of number and definiteness in Chinese, and came to the conclusion that "In Chinese, only the definite words have to be expressed with number marks." Chu (2000) examined the plural mark (i.e. "们"[men]) and argued that the plural mark is as grammatical mark as a pragmatic mark. Also, L. Zhang (2003) argued that the category of number in Chinese is more of a pragmatic problem than a grammatical problem.

**Table 1.** Expressions of Number in Chinese, Chen (2009)

| "Expression System of Number" | Expression Method of "Number" |
|---|---|
| {De-fined}{Objective}{Singular} | 1: "一 [yi](one)+ classifier+NP"<br>2: "这/那[zhe/na](this/that) + classifier + NP"<br>3: "proper noun"<br>4: "pronoun" |
| {De-fined}{Objective}{Plural} | 5: "defined numeral + classifier + NP"<br>6: "zhe/na + defined numeral + classifier + NP"<br>7: "words like '各位'[gewei](everyone) + NP"<br>8: "enumeration of proper noun" |
| {Unde-fined}{Subjective}{Singular} | 9: "normal noun"<br>10: "group noun" |
| {Unde-fined}{Objective}{Plural} | 11: "undefined numeral + classifier + NP"<br>12: "这/那[zhe/na](this/that) + undefined numeral +classifier + NP"<br>13: "一/这/那[yi/zhe/na] (one/this/that) + group classifier + NP"<br>14: "numeric adjective + NP"<br>15: "repetition of noun"<br>16: "repetition of classifier" |

The ways of express number in Chinese are also researched comprehensively. "们" [men] has been a traditional research topic where it has been interpreted in a number of different ways: a suffix (see Lü (1949)), a mark (see Shi (2003)), an auxiliary word (see B. Zhang (2002)) and so on. Regardless of what it may be, the function may be relatively undisputed: it expresses the notion of number for pronouns and certain nouns. In terms of the functional aspect of the word, there may be three ways to look at it: a plurality mark (see (Li & Shi, 2000)), a group/set mark (see Wen and Chen (2002)) and both under different circumstances (H. Zhang, 2010).

Chen (2009) had surveyed the topics related to the notion of number in Modern Chinese and also proposed a list of constructs for expressing number. He gave a table of the constructs for number expression (which are given ordinals to be used further down in the Experiment section):

Chen identified the nouns without any number reference ("normal noun" and "group noun" in the table) as singular, however there are also researchers who opine that this kind of nouns would be plural, such as H. Zhang (2010) and Wang and Mei (2004). However Lang (2008) suggests that they belong to the category of undetermined number, different from both singular and plural nouns.

## 2.2   Corpus-Based Word Similarity Analysis

Recent research around the topic of corpus-based word sense distinction may be mostly about distinguishing synonyms. A range of different differentiation tools and methods has been developed and applied to different sets of English as well as Chinese synonyms, such as collocation, mutual information: eg J.-d. Zhang and Liu (2005), Lin (2005), Wei (2007).

Hoey (2005) points out that it should be noticed in English that different grammatical forms of the word, or the lemma may be very different in terms of word collocations (Doyle (2003) and also Hoey (2005)), and these differences may be pervasive lexically, semantically and grammatically. He concluded that the collocation should be some kind of psychological association between words, not lemmas. Also he claims that "grammatical conditions have to be met before a semantic association can operate". This hypothesis would be the one that drives this research for new discoveries.

In this paper, it is proposed that the corpus-based synonym differentiation techniques could be utilized in search for collocation differences between words which share the same lemma, but are expressed in different grammatical forms. In Chinese, the so-called grammatical forms of number may be hardly seen, and Chinese language does not have plural marks as visible as English, therefore the proposed question would be also seen as "would an implicit category of human cognition show influence on word collocations in a language where such a language lacks grammatical category to express such notion?"

One noted experiment was conducted by J.-J. Zhang and Sun (2010). With psychological experiments conducted on the priming effect of implicit number tendency to following pronouns, they noticed that in Chinese, the effect of priming and number attraction show that number would be a universal concept and Chinese speakers do notice and try to convey it through various structures.

# 3    Experiment Procedures

In order to attempt to answer the questions raised in the previous sections of the paper, an experiment has been developed in the following steps:

1. Select the nouns.
2. Identify the number constructs
3. Extract the local context of the nouns
4. Form feature vectors for nouns and their numbers
5. Compute the similarity measure between the vectors
6. Analysis

These steps are explained below.

## 3.1    Select the Nouns

For choosing representative nouns as research objects, it is considered that nouns should be chosen from every major semantic field. Moreover, there are words in Chinese which lack plurality naturally, such as "天空"[*tiankong*](*sky*), so only words to which most of the constructs in Chen(2009)'s table could be applied get selected. Consequently, nine nouns are selected as the sample nouns for the research:

- Animal: 猫 [*mao*](*cat*);老虎 [*laohu*](*tiger*)
- Plant:树叶 [*shuye*](*leaf*);
- Object:桌子 [*zhuozi*](*desk*); 书 [*shu*](*book*)
- People: 学生 [*xuesheng*](*student*); 小贩 [*xiaofan*](*peddler*); 领导 [*lingdao*](*official*)
- Abstract:能力 [*nengli*](*ability*)

## 3.2    Identify the Number Constructs

To identify a noun in a sentence in Chinese singular or plural would be an interesting task. Taking references from Chen (2009), it is suggested that for the purpose of this research, three kinds of number categories need to be identified, i.e. singular (which corresponds to 1 and 2 in the table above), plural (which corresponds to 5, 6, 7, 8, 11, 12, 13, 14, 15, 16 in the table) and also undetermined (which corresponds to 9, 10). It would be very easy to see that singular constructs seem to be very few as well as undetermined ones, whereas plural constructs appear to be numerous and complicated. This phenomenon could be observed in the corpus data as explained in a following section.

## 3.3    Extract the Local Context of the Nouns

For the local contexts which have to be extracted from sentences, the corpus used for this task is the 2012 Sina News corpus[1] with every piece of news article from the

---

[1] www.sina.com.cn. All news articles are from the website and are processed into a corpus by the researchers of this paper.

website Sina for the entire year 2012. There is 226 million characters' linguistic material in the corpus. The corpus contains only raw materials. Basic word segmentation and p-o-s tagging are commenced using one of the open-source analyzers in Python: *Jieba* analyzer[2].

To extract the local context of the nouns, two steps have to be carried out. The first step would be to take out the nouns and its local context with it. According to Hoey (2005), the collocation expansion of a word would best be 4 at either side, therefore the local context $LC_{w,s} = \{w_{n-4}...w_{n+4}\}$ when the span parameter $s = 4$. The idea is also taken up, however to show the effect of the so-called feature selection mechanism on the result, 3 and 5 are also used as the span parameter. The second step would be to determine number of the noun based on the local context. With the grammatical number constructs from the 2nd step, it is possible to determine the number of a noun from the list according to its immediate neighbors. The number in the form of referential and common knowledge has been omitted in the process, leaving the grammatical/semantic number as the main focus.

The number determination process is inspired by the rule-based procedure in Lang (2008). Because the rules for singular and undetermined are much less than plural and the nouns to be processed are much fewer, it is possible for us to alter the original procedure and make it much simpler. The process is as follows:

```
Let K be singular rule, set K = [一 + classifier, 这/那
[zhe/na](this/that) + classifier]
Let Y be number rule, set Y = [classifier, numeral, 这
/那 [zhe/na](this/that)]
Let L be the list of words extracted from the corpus
to the left of the noun

Algorithm Compute()
input: K, Y, L
output: r
Begin
1 for each line l ∈ L do
2 {
3    r = undetermined;
4      if l ∈ Y do
5        {
6             r = singular;
7             if l ∉ K do
8             {
9                  r = plural;
10             }
11        }
12 }
End
```

---

[2] *Jieba* Analyzer: https://github.com/fxsjy/jieba

## 3.4    Form Feature Vectors for Nouns and Their Numbers

In order to compute the similarity score for different $LC$ with different number properties for different words, vectors need to be formed. The vector space would be all the words appeared around every noun in question. For every word, the undetermined, singular and plural vectors are labeled as 0, 1 and 2 vectors in the word-specific vector space. The value of the vectors consists of term frequency counts divided by the number of $LCs$ in the whole word-specific vector space.

## 3.5    Compute the Similarity Measure between the Vectors

With each number of the noun represented by a vector, the similarity of the vectors, or to be interpreted in linguistic terms, the similarity of the collocated words surrounding the noun would be calculated using the cosine similarity method.

$$\text{similarity} = \cos\theta = \frac{A \cdot B}{\|A\|\|B\|} = \frac{\sum_{i=1}^{n} A_i \times B_i}{\sqrt{\sum_{i=1}^{n}(A_i)^2} \times \sqrt{\sum_{i=1}^{n}(B_i)^2}} \tag{1}$$

As the term frequencies in the word vectors cannot be negative, therefore the result of the cosine similarity would be between 0 and 1, with 0 being orthogonal and 1 being the same. From the similarity results, collocation environments for different numbers could be observed and regularities would be investigable, be there any at all.

# 4    Results and Analysis

The results and analysis from the experiment are in three parts, the first of which would be the observed distribution of different number constructs in the corpus grouped by the chosen words. The second part would be the comparative results with the different span parameters, and the third part would be the similarity results when changing some of the parameters, e.g. when the $LC$ sample space for each number category gets restricted.

## 4.1    Observed Distribution of Number

**Table 2.** Observed distribution of different number categories of nouns ($s = 4$)

| Word | 0 | 1 | 2 | 0:1:2 Ratio |
|------|-----|-----|-----|-------------|
| 猫[*mao*] (cat) | 1874 | 183 | 639 | 10.2:1: 3.5 |
| 老虎[*laohu*] (tiger) | 1036 | 63 | 209 | 16.6:1: 3.3 |
| 树叶[*shuye*] (leaf) | 212 | 14 | 32 | 15.1:1: 2.3 |
| 书[*shu*] (book) | 4914 | 694 | 1519 | 7.1:1:2.2 |

**Table 2.** (*continued*)

| | | | | |
|---|---|---|---|---|
| 桌子<br>[*zhuozi*]<br>(*desk*) | 1360 | 219 | 262 | 6.2:1:1.2 |
| 学生<br>[*xuesheng*]<br>(*student*) | 37835 | 1121 | 13003 | 33.8:1:11.6 |
| 小贩<br>[*xiaofan*]<br>(*peddler*) | 738 | 44 | 147 | 15.7:1: 3.1 |
| 领导<br>[*lingdao*]<br>(*official*) | 25640 | 339 | 4372 | 75.6:1: 12.9 |
| 能力<br>[*nengli*]<br>(*ability*) | 29036 | 220 | 3058 | 132:1: 13.9 |

As aforementioned, because the rigid condition under which a singular construct may form, the number of singular constructs for every word is the least of the three. The number of undetermined number samples is the greatest, showing that it is evident that the mark-less category may be seen as dominating the language, and largely the nouns do not display any mark towards number. This finding actually may echo examples from Hoey (2005), where he found 1764 cases of 'consequence' and 3611 cases of 'consequences' in a corpus. Also from the table it may be obvious that the singular vs. plural ratio may reveal how individualized every word is. For example, the singular-plural ratio for 桌子[*zhuozi*] (*desk*) is the lowest, meaning that 桌子 [*zhuozi*] (*desk*) may be quite an individualized concept and it has a comparatively strong inclination to be singular. 能力[*nengli*] (*ability*) or 领导[*lingdao*] (*official*) however, has a comparatively strong tendency to be plural. Another reading from the table would be that it seems more frequently a word appear in text, more generalized and pluralized it would become. At the lower end, there may be comparatively individualized words such as 桌子[*zhuozi*] (*desk*) and 书 [*shu*] (*book*) which occur only thousands of times in the corpus, yet 学生[*xuesheng*] (*student*) or 领导[*lingdao*] (*official*) which occur tens of thousands of times would be comparatively pluralized.

## 4.2    Comparative Analysis of Number Similarity among Words

**Table 3.** Similarity scores for number pairs of each word (the pair is undirected, i.e. change 0 -1 to 1- 0 will not change the score)

| Word | Number Pair | Span = 3 | Span = 4 | Span = 5 |
|------|-------------|----------|----------|----------|
| 猫[*mao*] (*cat*) | 0 − 1 | 0.41 | 0.41 | 0.56 |
|  | 0 − 2 | 0.78 | 0.85 | 0.84 |
|  | 1 − 2 | 0.45 | 0.45 | 0.57 |
| 老虎[*laohu*] (*tiger*) | 0 − 1 | 0.42 | 0.51 | 0.54 |
|  | 0 − 2 | 0.76 | 0.74 | 0.80 |
|  | 1 − 2 | 0.41 | 0.40 | 0.52 |
| 树叶[*shuye*] (*leaf*) | 0 − 1 | 0.21 | 0.35 | 0.32 |
|  | 0 − 2 | 0.53 | 0.54 | 0.60 |
|  | 1 − 2 | 0.20 | 0.27 | 0.30 |
| 书[*shu*] (*book*) | 0 − 1 | 0.46 | 0.54 | 0.62 |
|  | 0 − 2 | 0.74 | 0.78 | 0.79 |
|  | 1 − 2 | 0.32 | 0.40 | 0.47 |
| 桌子[*zhuozi*] (*desk*) | 0 − 1 | 0.37 | 0.42 | 0.54 |
|  | 0 − 2 | 0.72 | 0.77 | 0.84 |
|  | 1 − 2 | 0.45 | 0.47 | 0.57 |
| 学生 [*xuesheng*] (*student*) | 0 − 1 | 0.47 | 0.61 | 0.68 |
|  | 0 − 2 | 0.83 | 0.88 | 0.91 |
|  | 1 − 2 | 0.56 | 0.67 | 0.72 |
| 小贩[*xiaofan*] (*peddler*) | 0 − 1 | 0.23 | 0.36 | 0.42 |
|  | 0 − 2 | 0.61 | 0.68 | 0.72 |
|  | 1 − 2 | 0.28 | 0.37 | 0.40 |
| 领导 [*lingdao*] (*official*) | 0 − 1 | 0.56 | 0.61 | 0.69 |
|  | 0 − 2 | 0.86 | 0.90 | 0.92 |
|  | 1 − 2 | 0.50 | 0.61 | 0.69 |
| 能力[*nengli*] (*ability*) | 0 − 1 | 0.43 | 0.52 | 0.63 |
|  | 0 − 2 | 0.88 | 0.88 | 0.92 |
|  | 1 − 2 | 0.41 | 0.51 | 0.62 |

From table 3, the most obvious reading one may infer would be the high similarity between 0 and 2, in other words between undetermined number category and the plural number category. Thus it may be safe to say that a noun without any obvious number mark around it may most possibly behave like a noun with plural marks around it, and or it could be said that mark-less nouns may be one grammatical variant of plural nouns. As Hoey (2005) suggested, the word association would have to be decided after the grammatical form of said word is decided, therefore there does seem to be a connection between the grammatical form of the mark-less noun and the association behavior of plural nouns. By the collocation behavior of the mark-less nouns, they could quite possibly be plural nouns.

Such observation may be further enhanced by the similarity between the 0 − 1 and 1 − 2 scores. In most cases, these two scores are very close which also proves that mark-less category and plural category indeed have a lot in common in terms of collocation words. There appears to be a conspicuous 0.3 similarity gap between mark-less to plural and mark-less to singular (or singular to plural) for almost every word and this gap appears to be somehow compensated by the increment of the number of spam parameters, yet even at 5, the gap would still be clearly discernible. This could demonstrate that although singular and plural forms of a word share words in their collocation patterns, there also appears to be very distinct behaviors for both forms so that they would be statistically obvious in a large corpus. This also echoes Hoey's findings (2005) in English.

Another noticeable phenomenon would be that the most frequently appeared words, such as 能力[*nengli*] (*ability*), also appear to be quite outstanding similar in terms of the mark-less variant of the word vs. plural form of the word. The low similarity scores for 0 – 2 category of less-frequent words may be caused by the underrepresentation of sufficient features.

## 4.3    Similarity Scores of Standardized Sample Space among Words

**Table 4.** Similarity scores of standardized sample space among words

| Word | Number Pair | Span = 4 |
| --- | --- | --- |
| 猫[*mao*] (*cat*) | 0 – 1 | 0.40 |
|  | 0 – 2 | 0.80 |
|  | 1 – 2 | 0.42 |
| 老虎[*laohu*] (*tiger*) | 0 – 1 | 0.33 |
|  | 0 – 2 | 0.57 |
|  | 1 – 2 | 0.34 |
| 树叶[*shuye*] (*leaf*) | 0 – 1 | 0.31 |
|  | 0 – 2 | 0.43 |
|  | 1 – 2 | 0.25 |
| 书[*shu*] (*book*) | 0 – 1 | 0.54 |
|  | 0 – 2 | 0.73 |
|  | 1 – 2 | 0.37 |
| 桌子[*zhuozi*] (*desk*) | 0 – 1 | 0.42 |
|  | 0 – 2 | 0.75 |
|  | 1 – 2 | 0.46 |
| 学生[*xuesheng*] (*student*) | 0 – 1 | 0.62 |
|  | 0 – 2 | 0.86 |
|  | 1 – 2 | 0.66 |
| 小贩[*xiaofan*] (*peddler*) | 0 – 1 | 0.30 |
|  | 0 – 2 | 0.55 |
|  | 1 – 2 | 0.38 |
| 领导[*lingdao*] (*official*) | 0 – 1 | 0.56 |
|  | 0 – 2 | 0.83 |
|  | 1 – 2 | 0.59 |
| 能力[*nengli*] (*ability*) | 0 – 1 | 0.49 |
|  | 0 – 2 | 0.83 |
|  | 1 – 2 | 0.49 |

Table 2 has demonstrated that different number category may possess different numbers of samples, therefore a further standardization has been carried out to examine to what extent the imbalance of sample numbers may affect the results.

The standardization restricts the number of samples in all categories to the number of the category where there is the smallest set of samples, which generally is the singular category. After the standardization, the vector space has shrunk dramatically yet the scores do not show large fluctuations. The tendency may be still apparent, and the 0.3 similarity gap is still present, although for some words, such as 树叶[*shuye*](*leaf*), the gap also shrinks to a little over 0.1. This may be because the sampling space is quite small so that the samples from categories where samples are abundant may be biased by the random selection process.

# 5     Discussions

With the observations, it may be clear that number in Chinese may be seen as two categories: singular and plural, and the mark-less noun would be in the category of plural. However, there are a few observations made during the analysis which may deserve further discussion. The first observation would be the "pluralization" of common nouns, and the second would be the mark-less noun as plural noun.

## 5.1     Pluralization of Common Nouns

From the comparative counts of number cases for the nouns, it is discussed that there seems to be a tendency of "pluralization" for the commonly-seen nouns, in other words the more often a word appears, the more likely the plural case dominates the number cases in which the word may appear.

Seen from a cognitive point of view, a word commonly-seen in a large corpus could be because that the signified appears more common in daily life or it is something the majority understand and usually talk about. The prevalence of the knowledge of such signified may require the speakers to drop the cognitive differences between individuals of such signified and use what is perceived as common features of the signified to start a conversation on it. Chen(2009) uses 'defined' and 'undefined' to denote the specificity of the signified. From the observation, it may be seen as special tactics for speakers to use when they try to objectify a concept or a notion in mind. The pluralization, especially when taken into account that the mark-less noun may also be a kind of plural noun, would be a piece of evidence that during the objectification process, the more one concept is subject to going through the process, the more likely the speakers try to avoid the process altogether and use pragmatic or nonverbal methods to deliver the information the receiver needs to duplicate the objectification process. Of course, this process would have to be executed to the nouns which may possibly appear in plural forms.

Zhang(2010) also briefly touches on the problem. The sentence " 客人来了"(*"The guest(s) is(are) coming"*) is given as an example to show that in such cases, the mark "们" may be omitted, because the understanding of the number of the noun would be common-sensical, and they tend to adapt a plural sense more often. The intuition here unravels itself in the data, and the common-sense of the understanding process as described in Zhang's paper could be just the state of the concept before and during the objectification process.

## 5.2     Mark-Less Noun as Plural

Chen(2009) categorizes the mark-less nouns as "Undefined Subjective Singular", which means that the number of such nouns (when there is no clear mark) may be seen in a deeper level, i.e. from the speaker's point of reference. By using such statements, it may be concluded that Chen believes that the nouns without any mark may reflect a more primitive or "deeper" state of them before the objectification process begins to work. By the collocation behavior, it is now known that such nouns would be plural instead of singular, which also reveals that the deeper state of a noun may well be plural instead of singular.

It is understood that meanings of words for individuals may be slightly different due to different life experiences, education and other social influences, yet people would be able to communicate because the concepts behind the words are highly abstract, resembling a series of prominent features of the categories the words represent or signify. It may be reasonable to speculate that during the process of abstraction, features of many objects which belong to the same concept category get extract from them, therefore the formed concept itself tend to exhibit high degrees of plurality. Therefore when the "deeper" state is expressed fully or partially through mark-less nouns, it displays more similarity towards the plural state which would be modified by the objectification process towards expressing a certain but plural variety of the concept.

In English, because the number of the noun may be seen as necessary to be expressed explicitly, the objectification process may also be seen as necessary to be complete. In Chinese however, the mark-less noun allows concepts to "leak out" without much interference from the objectification process, giving us a unique category of plural nouns and maybe a window to the raw concepts behind the language, at least in terms of number.

# 6     Conclusion and Future Work

This article utilizes a set of computational tools in order to explore the grammatical and semantic notion of number and plurality in Chinese. Although the notion of number may not be so clean-cut, the effect of it on word collocation may be obvious. With collocation analysis and similarity scores, it is discovered that in Chinese, mark-less nouns may behave very much like a plural noun. Also, the distinction between singular and plural forms of a noun may also be quite prominent with a clear similarity gap between the collocation words of the forms. The article approaches the questions of number and plurality in Chinese with a corpus-based and computational methodology and provides valuable insights and plausible answers to the questions.

There would be a lot more to be covered on number that this article does not go into, such as classification of nouns according to the similarity between singular and plural nouns, also more samples could be examined to see how widespread the phenomena are. The computational methods used in the article, such as word segmentation, cosine similarity and number detection could also be perfected in future research. The article mainly explores the domain of online news materials, so other domains such as popular culture, or maybe scientific texts may be examined.

**Acknowledgements.** The authors would like to thank the anonymous reviewers for their careful reading of this paper and for their helpful and constructive comments. This work was supported in part by the Beijing Postdoctoral Work Funding Program.

# References

1. Chen, J.: A Study on The Semantic Functions of "X+men" in Modern Chinese (PhD), Fudan University (2009)
2. Chu, Z.: Shuci yu Fushu Biaoji buneng Tongxian de Yuanyin. Minzu Yuwen (5), 7 (2000) (in Chinese)
3. Doyle, P.G.: Replicating corpus linguisitics: a corpus-driven investigation of lexical networks in text (Ph.D). University of Lancaster (2003)
4. Hoey, M.: Lexcal Priming: A new theory of words and language. Routledge, Oxen (2005)
5. Lang, J., et al.: Number Type Recognition of Chinese Personal Noun Phrase. Acta Automatica Sinica 34(8), 8 (2008)
6. Li, A.Y.H., Shi, Y.: The Story of Men. Modern Linguistics 2(1), 12 (2000)
7. Lin, C.: Jiyu Yuliaoku de Yingyu Jinyici Bianxi. Journal of China Three Gorges University (Humanities & Social Sciences) 27 (2005) (in Chinese)
8. Lü, S.: Shuo "Men". Guowen Yuekan (82) (1949) (in Chinese)
9. Shi, Y.: The Relationship Between the Two Grammartical Categories in Chinese: Number and Definiteness. Studies in Language and Linguistics 23(2), 11 (2003)
10. Wang, H.F., Mei, Z.: An empirical study on pronoun resolution in Chinese, Mexico City. Paper presented at the The 2nd International Conference on Computational Linguistics and Intelligent Text Processing, Mexico City (2004)
11. Wei, C.: Distinguishing Synonyms Verbs - A Corpus-based study on "develop, improve, advance, enhance and progress". Journal of Xinxiang Teachers College 21(4) (2007)
12. Wen, B.-L., Chen, Z.-L.: On the Syntactic Realization of the [Num] Feature in Chinese Nominal Phrases. Modern Foreign Languages 25(2), 9 (2002)
13. Wu, T.: Hanyu Meiyou Danfushu Yufa Fanchou dui Hanren Yishi Chansheng de Yingxiang. Journal of University of Heilongjiang (5) (1994) (in Chinese)
14. Zhang, B.: Xinbian Xiandai Hanyu. Fudan University Press, Shanghai (2002) (in Chinese)
15. Zhang, H.: The Expression and Mark of the Plural Form of Modern Chinese Nouns, MA, Nanchang University (2010)
16. Zhang, J.-D., Liu, P.: Corpus-based Approaches to the Differentiation of English Synonyms. Journal of PLA University of Foreign Languages 28(6) (2005)
17. Zhang, J.-J., Sun, P.-Z.: Implicit Number Tendency of Antecedent-Related Words Affects Choice of Pronoun in Chinese Sentence Production. Acta Psychologica Sinica 42(9), 11 (2010)
18. Zhang, L.: The Realization and Related Discussion of Number Category in Chinese Nouns. Chinese Language Learning(5) 5 (2003)

# The Scientific Literature Corpus for Chinese Negation and Uncertainty Identification

Zhancheng Chen[1,2], Bowei Zou[1,2], Qiaoming Zhu[1,2], and Peifeng Li[1,2]

[1] School of Computer Science and Technology, Soochow University, Jiangsu 215006, China
[2] Key Lab of Computer Information Processing Technology of Jiangsu Province,
Suzhou, Jiangsu, 215006, China
{whezex,zoubowei}@gmail.com,
{qmzhu,pfli}@suda.edu.cn

**Abstract.** Negative and uncertain expressions widely exist in natural language. Negation and uncertainty identification has become an important task in computational linguistics community. Lacking of corpus hinders the development of Chinese negation and uncertainty identification. This paper reports on a corpus annotation project for Chinese negation and uncertainty identification on scientific literature. We introduce several important aspects during our annotation, such as selection of raw text, framework of annotation, guidelines, data consistency and statistic data summarized from corpus. In this corpus, we annotate negation and uncertainty cues and their corresponding scopes. Statistic for corpus shows that there are a certain proportion of negative and uncertain expressions in Chinese scientific literature. Accordingly, this corpus is able to support the research of Chinese negation and uncertainty identification in the future.

**Keywords:** negation, uncertainty, Chinese corpus.

## 1 Introduction

Negation implies a proposition is false or something does not happen [1], while uncertainty reveals that a proposition is unreliable or speculative [2]. Negation and uncertainty identification task aims to identify the negative and uncertain fragments in natural language. Morante et al. [3] pointed that the negation and uncertainty identification task normally involved two subtasks: Cue Detection and Scope Detection. The former judges whether there exits negative or uncertain semantics in a sentence or not. If it exists, the task requires to find out the negation or uncertainty keyword (Cue). The later focuses on detecting the scope modified by negation or uncertainty cue. For example, see the following two sentences:

(a) Chinese: 这把椅子虽然坐上去[不舒服]scope1但价格很便宜。
Pinyin: *zhè bǎ yǐ zǐ sūi rán zuò shàng qù bù shū fū dàn jià gé hěn pián yí.*
English: *The chair is not comfortable but cheap.*
(b) Chinese: 女主人递给我一件礼物，[可能是一本书，或者一本照相簿]scope2。

P. Liu and Q. Su (Eds.): CLSW 2013, LNAI 8229, pp. 657–667, 2013.

Pinyin: *nǚ zhǔ rén dì gěi wǒ yí jiàn lǐ wù , kě néng shì yì běn shū , huò zhě yì běn zhào xiàng bù .*

English: *The hostess gives me a gift.I guess it may be a book or a photo album.*

In sentence (a), "不"[bù](not) indicates that the chair is not comfortable. The word is a negation cue to modify "舒服"[shū fú](comfortable), so the scope of "不"[bù](not)is "不舒服"[bù shū fú](not comfortable). In sentence (b), "可能"[kě néng](may) implies that the gift may be a book or some other things. It is not sure. The word is an uncertainty cue to modify "一本书，或者一本照相簿"[shì yì běn shū , huò zhě yì běn zhào xiàng bù](a book or a photo album).

Vincze et al. [4] claimed that it should be necessary to separate the negation and uncertainty information from the factual, especially in science literature. In science writing, authors always use uncertainty to express the hypothesis and to summarize experimental results. According to the statistic of Vincze [4], there are a significant portion of sentences on BioScope Abstract corpus (13.45% for negation and 17.69% for uncertainty). It shows that negation and uncertainty expressions extensively exist in scientific literature.

A suitable corpus is a vital necessity for natural language processing research [5]. At present, the public negation and uncertainty identification corpus are only the BioScope corpus [4] and the dataset for CoNLL'2010 share task [6]. The former provided not only the negation and uncertainty cues but also their corresponding scopes, while the latter only annotated the uncertainty cues. The BioScope corpus defined negative information as denying the existence of things or the truth of a proposition, and uncertain information as these attitudes or statements without facts to back up. During the annotation, a word or phrase is marked as cue depends on whether there exists negation or uncertainty in sentence. However, corpus for Chinese negation and uncertainty identification task is scarce.

This paper reports on a corpus annotation project that produces resources for Chinese negation and uncertainty identification task on *Chinese Journal of Computers*. There are three reasons for us to choose such corpus. First, identification of negative and uncertain information plays an important role in scientific writing. Negative and uncertain information such as unproved proposition is significant communicative resource for academics. This information can confirm the individual's professional persona, and remind author to clarify their attitudes or opinions cautiously [7]. Second, *Chinese Journal of Computers,* is an authoritative academic journal on computer science in China. On account of its rigorous expression, the annotation complexity could be reduced. Finally, the abundant texts make it easier to expand the corpus scale.

The rest of this paper is organized as follows. Section 2 introduces the annotation framework including preprocessing, annotation tool, and the storage of corpus. Section 3 reports on the annotation guidelines in detail. The statistical data are presented and discussed in Section 4. Finally, Section 5 concludes our work and predicts some possible future work.

## 2    Annotation

The annotation includes three steps. Firstly, we download full papers from the web-sites of *Chinese Journal of Computers[1]*. The redundant information, as charts, figures, math formulas, is filtered. Secondly, annotation work is carried out by two independent annotators and a chief linguist who is responsible for setting up the annotation guidelines. Thirdly, we transform the texts generated from the second step to XML format file.

### 2.1    Datasets and Pre-processing

The negation and uncertainty identification corpus consists of 19 full papers taken from the *Chinese Journal of Computers* in November 2012.The automatic segmentation to sentences of the documents was corrected manually. In order to facilitate the computer programs to process, we 1) transform Chinese punctuation to full-width; 2) delete the redundant space; 3) use *"[公式]"* to replace formulas or math expressions; and 4) filter the meaningless figures and charts.

### 2.2    Data Format

Both text documents and XML format files are commonly used to store corpus. The former is easy to use, but not suitable to store structure data. Many scopes are nested in negation and uncertainty identification corpus, so we adopt XML format file to store corpus. By this format, different scopes can be presented clearly. Fig. 1 shows two nested scopes of sentence (c).

---

*<sentence id="207">*首先从EED随机抽取规模M的数据集，再从中随机选取N个关键词作为规模N的词典，并*<scope id="s207.1"><cue ref="s207.1">*去除*</cue><cue ref="s207.2"><scope id="s207.2">*不*</scope></cue>*包含于词典中的数据关键词*</scope>*.  *</sentence>*

---

**Fig. 1.** XML format of sentence (c)

*(c)* Chinese: 首先从*EED*随机抽取规模*M*的数据集，再从中随机选取*N*个关键词作为规模*N*的词典，并⌐去除⌐不包含于词典中的数据关键词⌡$_{scope2}$⌡$_{scope1}$·

Pinyin: *shǒu xiān cóng EED suí jī chōu qǔ guī mó M de shù jù jí, zài cóng zhōng suí jī xuǎn qǔ N gè guān jiàn cí zuò wéi guī mó N de cí diǎn, bìng qù chú bù bāo hán yú cí diǎn zhōng de shù jù guān jiàn cí.*

English: *We extract data set size of M from EED randomly, and then select keywords set size N to make up dictionary size of N accompanying with removing part keywords including in dictionary.*

---

[1] http://cjc.ict.ac.cn/

## 2.3    Annotation Tool

In order to alleviate annotation burden and to improve the annotation efficiency, we develop an annotation tool shown in Fig 2. The annotators could choose cues and their corresponding scope in a given sentence. If there are several scopes, then they could click *"Add Instance"* button to add a frame tofill instance. After choosing, the annotators could click *"Generate"* button to generate annotation result.

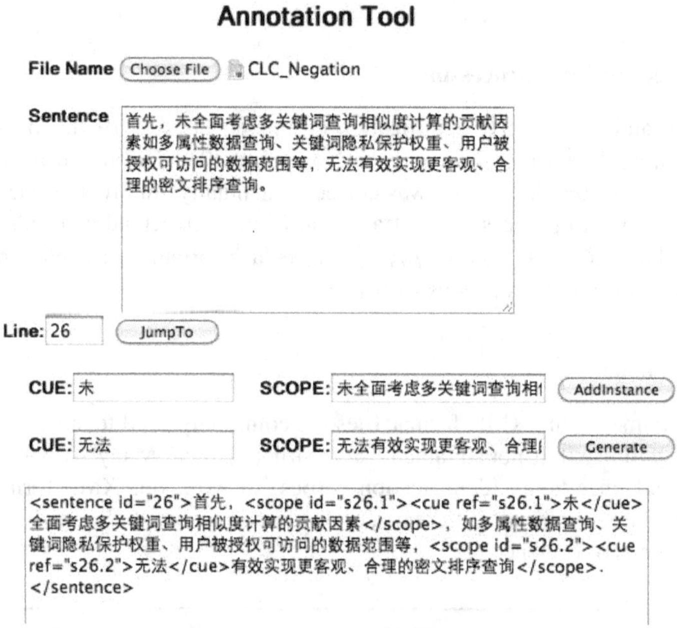

**Annotation Tool**

**File Name** ( Choose File )  CLC_Negation

**Sentence**  首先，未全面考虑多关键词查询相似度计算的贡献因
素如多属性数据查询、关键词隐私保护权重、用户被
授权可访问的数据范围等，无法有效实现更客观、合
理的密文排序查询。

**Line:** 26    ( JumpTo )

**CUE:** 未          **SCOPE:** 未全面考虑多关键词查询相{    ( AddInstance )

**CUE:** 无法        **SCOPE:** 无法有效实现更客观、合理{    ( Generate )

<sentence id="26">首先，<scope id="s26.1"><cue ref="s26.1">未</cue>
全面考虑多关键词查询相似度计算的贡献因素</scope>，如多属性数据查询、关
键词隐私保护权重、用户被授权可访问的数据范围等，<scope id="s26.2"><cue
ref="s26.2">无法</cue>有效实现更客观、合理的密文排序查询</scope>.
</sentence>

**Fig. 2.** Annotation Tool

# 3    General Guidelines

Negative and uncertain information are two common semantics in language, which are used to describe author's attitudes or opinions. We design suitable guidelines which describe the semantics of negation or uncertainty faithfully. This section describes how to annotate the negation and uncertainty cues and their corresponding scopes in detail.

## 3.1    Negation Annotation

1) The majority of negation cues are used as adverb to deny behaviors or properties. Such as *"不"[bù](not), "不能"[bù néng](can'not), "无"[wú](no), "无法"[wú fǎ](not), "不易"[bú yì](difficult), "难以"[nán yǐ](difficult)*. When these words become negation cues, the responding scopes are always the syntactic structures that modified by

cues. When adverb cue modifies a verb or a verb phrase, its scope is always the clause including the verb or the verbal phrase. When adverb cue modifies an adjective, its scope is always the clause including noun phrase that modified by the adjective. When adverb cue modifies another adverb, its scope is the part of which the latter modify. For example,

Chinese: *当存在多数据拥有者查询授权时，[用户查询过程**难以抵御**恶意数据拥有者与CSP的合谋攻击]*scope1*。*

Pinyin: *dāng cún zài duō shù jù yōng yǒu zhě chá xún shòu quán shí，yòng hù chá xún guò chéng nán yǐ dǐ yù è yì shù jù yōng yǒu zhě yǔ CSP de hé móu gōng jī。*

English: *when there is authorization of queries of multi-data owners, it is difficult for user queries to resists attacks from data owner and CSP.*

"*难以*"*[nán yǐ](difficult)* is an adverb cue to modify the predicate "*抵御*"*[dǐ yù](resists)*, and its scope extends to the clause labeled with *scope1* which consists of subject, negative adverb, predicate and object. In Chinese, there exists some ellipses (subject or object is always absent). In that case, scope consists of the clause lacking of component. For example,

Chinese: *如下所示：[公式].式（4）计算IDF的最大特点是去除[用户**无法**访问的无关数据]*scope1*对其查询排序的影响。*

Pinyin: *rú xià suǒ shì ：[gōng shì]. shì (4) jì suàn IDF de zuì dà tè diǎn shì qù chú yòng hù wú fǎ fǎng wèn de wú guān shù jù duì qí chá xún pái xù de yǐng xiǎng 。*

English: *Formula is shown as follow. The characteristic of computing IDF with formula is that it removes the effects of irrelevance data user can't access to rank.*

"*无法*"*[wúfǎ](can't)* is a negation cue modifying "*无关数据*"*[wú guān shù jù] (irrelevance data)* which is ahead word of a noun phrase. Here, the predicate "*去除*"*[qù chù](removes)* connects the subject "*最大特点*"*[zuì dà tè diǎn](the characteristic)* and the object "*用户无法访问的无关数据*"*[yòng hù wú fǎ fǎng wèn de wú guān shù jù](irrelevance data user can't access)*, but"*无法*"*[wú fǎ](can't)* and "*去除*"*[qù chù](removes)* is irrelevant in semantic level. Therefore, the scope of"*无法*"*[wúfǎ](can't)* extends to"*用户无法访问的无关数据*"*[yòng hù wú fǎ fǎng wèn de wú guān shù jù](irrelevance data user can't access)*.

2) Negation cue may be an adverb of degree, such as"*基本*"*[jī běn](mainly),*"*全面*"*[quán miàn](overall)* etc. For example,

Chinese: *因此，[目前解决TDSP问题的方法均**不能**解决本文面对的问题]*scope1*。*

Pinyin: *yīn cǐ，mù qián jiě jué TDSP wèn tí de fāng fǎ jūn bù néng jiě jué běn wén miàn duì de wèn tí 。*

English: *At present the method solving TDSP can't be used to solve the problem in this paper.*

"*不能*"*[bù néng](can't)*is an adverb cue to modify "*解决*"*[jiě jué](solve)* as predicate, and its scope is "*目前解决TDSP问题的方法均不能解决本文面对的问题*"*[mù qián jiě jué TDSP wèn tí de fāng fǎ jūn bù néng jiě jué běn wén miàn duì de wèn tí]*

*(At present the method solving TDSP can't be used to solve the problem in this paper)* which consists of subject, adverb of degree, negative adverb, predicate and object.

3) Negation cue sometimes is a verb, such as *"没"[méi](no)*, *"避免"[bì miǎn](avoid)*, *"排除"[pái chú](exclude)*, *"减少"[jiǎn shǎo](decrease)* etc. *"没"[méi](no)*, *"没有"[méi yǒu](no)* have common border with adverb and verb. Parts of these verbs are treated as negation cues. It depends on whether it implies negation semantics or not. When there exits subject ellipsis in sentence, the responding scope is the whole sentence lacking of subject. For example,

> Chinese: 基本算法BSL遍历出的图中所有q-clique均[缺乏良好的可伸缩性]scope1。
> Pinyin: *jī běn suàn fǎ BSL biàn lì chū de tú zhōng suǒ yǒu q-clique jūn quē fá liáng hǎo de kě shēn suō xìng。*
> English: *all q-clique, BSL algorithm finds out in graph, lack of enough scalability.*

*"缺乏"[quē fá](lack of)* is predicate to modify *"良好的可伸缩性"[liáng hǎo de kě shēn suō xìng](enough scalability)* which consists of nominal group.

Besides, there exist some negation adjectives, nouns and prepositions.

4) When negation cue is an adjective, such as *"非"[fēi](un-)*, *"不可行的"[bù kě xíng de](failure)*, *"不同"[bù tóng](different)* etc., there exist two cases. When the adjective negation cue is attributive, the responding scope is the noun phrase modified by the adjective. When the adjective negation cue is used as predicative, the scope is the sub-clause. For example,

> Chinese: 显然，[该结果是错误的]scope1。
> Pinyin: *xiǎn rán, gāi jié guǒ shì cuò wù de.*
> English: *Obviously, result is error.*

*"错误的"[cuò wù de](error)* is used as predicative to imply that result is not right, so scope is *"该结果是错误的"[gāi jié guǒ shì cuò wù de](result is error).*

5) Negation cue may be a preposition, such as *"除了"[chú le](except)*, *"不同于"[bù tóng yú](different to)* etc. In this case, the corresponding scope always is the adverbial modified by the preposition. For example,

> Chinese: [不同于传统的Trie树]scope1，RegionTrie中同一个前缀可能对应着多个结点。
> Pinyin: *bù tóng yú chuán tǒng de Trie shù, RegionTrie zhōng tóng yīgè qián zhuì kě néng duì yìng zhe duō gè jié diǎn.*
> English: *Different to traditional Trie Tree, the same prefix in regionTrie may be mapped to several node.*

*"不同于"[bù tóng yú](different to)* is used as preposition to imply the difference between *"传统的Trie树"[chuán tǒng de Trie shù](traditional Trie Tree)* and *"RegionTrie"*. Therefore, the corresponding scope extends to *scope1*.

### 3.2    Uncertainty Annotation

1) During annotation for uncertainty, adverb is used as cue to modify verb, adjective or noun phrase [8]. The scope of an adverb cue extends to the clause or sentence. For example,

Chinese: *使*[*查询时间***基本不受***M值的影响*]scope1*。*
Pinyin: *shǐ chá xún shí jiān jī běn bù shòu M zhí de yǐng xiǎng.*
English: *It makes query time mainly has nothing to do with M value.*

*"基本"[jī běn](mainly)* is used as an adverb cue to modify the predicate*"不受"[bù shòu](has nothing to do with)*. The scope of the adverb cue extends to clause labeled with *scope1.*

Besides, other adverbs such as*" 一般 "[yì bān](sometimes)*, *" 往往 "[wǎng wǎng](always)*, *"较大地"[jiào dà di](major)*, *"较大程度地"[jiào dà chéng dù di](mainly)*are used to imply uncertain information.

2) Verb cues sometimes imply the uncertainty semantics, such as *" 估计"[gu jì](suppose)*, *"试图"[shì tú](attempt),"假设"[jiǎ shè](suppose)* etc. The scope of a verb cue always extends tothe clause or the entire sentence. For example,

Chinese: [*文献***试图***通过扰乱排序实现查询隐私保护*]scope1*，但其内部用户完全可以根据自己所掌握的密钥与CSP合谋*[*推理出*其他用户的查询请求隐私]scope2*。*
Pinyin: *wén xiàn shì tú tōng guò rǎo luàn pái xù shí xiàn chá xún yǐn sī bǎo hù, dàn qí nèi bù yòng hù wán quán kě yǐ gēn jù zì jǐ suǒ zhǎng wò de mì yào yǔ CSP hé móu tuī lǐ chū qí tā yòng hù de chá xún qǐng qiú yǐn sī.*
English: *Literature attempts to protect privacy of query by disrupting the order, but internal users can estimate privacy of query of other users through master key they own and CSP.*

There are two uncertainty instances. First, *"试图"[shì tú](attempt)* is used as predicate to imply that *" 查询隐私保护"*will happen. Second, *" 推理出"[tuī lǐ chū](estimate)*indicates the fact that*"其它用户的查询请求隐私"[qí tā yòng hù de chá xún qǐng qiú yǐn sī](privacy of query of other users)* is not factual information.

3) Uncertainty cue may be a phrase(like *neither... nor* in English), such as *"成为......的问题"[chéng wéi......de wèn tí](question of)*, *"在......情况下"[zài......qíng kuàng xià] (suppose that)*, *" 当...... 时 "[dāng......shí](suppose that)."在...... 情况下 "[zài......qíngkuàng xià](suppose that)* implies that the proposition will occur with the condition that ellipsis occur.

4) Adjectives such as *"任意"[rèn yì](random)*, *"假定的"[jiǎ dìng de](hypothetical)* can be uncertainty cues. For example,

Chinese: *然而，*[*这些工作***假定的***时间模型是离散的* ]scope1*。*
Pinyin: *rán ér , zhè xiē gōng zuò jiǎ dìng de shí jiān mó xíng shì lí sàn de.*
English: *However, hypothetical time model we assign is discrete in this work.*

*"时间模型是离散的"[shí jiān mó xíng shì lí sàn de](time model is discrete)* is a hypothetical proposition which we cannot judge whether it happen or not.

5) Besides, conjunction sometimes implies the uncertainty semantics.

Chinese: *其中，[顶点代表道路的交叉口**或者**道路的端点]*<sub>scope1</sub>。

Pinyin: *qí zhōng, dǐng diǎn dài biǎo dào lù de jiāo chā kǒu huò zhě dào lù de duān diǎn.* For example,

English: *The vertex stand for intersection of the road or end of the road.*

*"或者"[huò zhě] (or)* is used as uncertainty cue to indicate what vertex stand for is uncertain. The scope extends to the whole clause. *"或"[huò](or)*, of the same mean to *"或者"[huò zhě](or)*, also can be seen as an uncertainty cue.

## 3.3    Special Cases

We have introduced the general guidelines above. However, there are some negative and uncertain words not implying negation and uncertainty semantics. In this section, we introduce these special annotation cases.

### Special Annotation Cases for Negation

1) *"不同"[bù tóng](different)* sometimes can't be seen as negation cue. For example,

Chinese: *时间子序列匹配，根据不同查询标准，可分为范围查询和k近邻查询两类。*

Pinyin: *shí jiān zǐ xù liè pǐ pèi, gēn jù bù tóng chá xún biāo zhǔn, kě fēn wéi fàn wéi chá xún hé k jìn lín chá xún liǎng lèi。*

English: *According to the different query criteria, we can divide the matching of time sequence into extent query and k-nearest query.*

*"不同"[bù tóng](different)* indicates the difference of *"查询标准"[chá xún biāo zhǔn](query criteria)*but notthe negation to *"查询标准"[chá xún biāo zhǔn](query criteria)*, so the word *"不同"[bù tóng](different)* cannot be seen as a negation cue.

2) When *"除了......之外"[chú le......zhi wài](except)* or*"除了"[chú le](except)* occurs in sentence, we annotate this word in according with context whether it implies negation. For example,

Chinese: *而隐私保护则要求除了保护数据隐私，还需确保密文索引和查询过程无隐私泄露。*

Pinyin: *ér yǐn sī bǎo hù zé yāo qiú chú le bǎo hù shù jù yǐn sī, hái xūquè bǎo mì wén suǒ yǐn hé chá xún guò chéng wú yǐn sī xiè lù.*

English: *Except protecting privacy of data, privacy protecting also ensure there are no privacy leaking out in process of index and query.*

*"除了"[chú le](except)*which represents the two sentences is climactic relation and does not imply negation. For example,

Chinese: [*除了*叶节点对所有序列保存所必须的开销*以外*]scope1，*索引所需要额外开销非常的小。*

Pinyin: *chú le yè jié diǎn duì suǒ yǒu xù liè bǎo cún suǒ bì xū de kāi xiāo yǐ wài,suǒ yǐn suǒ xū yào de é wài kāi xiāo fēi cháng de xiǎo.*

English: *Except necessary overhead leaf nodes stored for all sequence, other extra overhead index need is rare.*

"*除了......之外*"[*chú le......zhiwài*]*(except)* is used as a negation cue, because the meaning of the second clause is opposite to the first clause.

**Special Annotation Cases for Uncertainty**

1) Whether "*考虑*"[*kǎo lǜ*] *(consider)* can be seen as an uncertainty cue depends on the sense sentence imply. For example,

Chinese: *Zhu*等人对同时考虑结构信息和属性信息的近似图匹配问题进行了研究。

Pinyin: *Zhu    děng rén duì tóng shí kǎo lǜ jié gòu xìn xī hé shǔ xìng xìn xī de jìn sì tú pǐ pèi wèn tí jìn xíng le yán jiū。*

English: *Zhu et al. have done research about the matching of approximate graph which consider structure information and attribution information.*

"*考虑*"[*kǎo lǜ*]*(consider)* here has the same meaning with "*涉及*"[*shè jí*]*(refer to)*. It does not imply the uncertainty semantics.

2) When "*如何*"[*rú hé*] *(how)* is used as a noun to describe an event, it can't be seen as uncertainty cue. For example,

Chinese: 在本节中，我们介绍如何计算起点到终点的最小费用代价。

Pinyin: *zài běn jié zhōng ，wǒ mén jiè shào rú hé jì suàn qǐ diǎn dào zhōng diǎn de zuì xiǎo fèi yòng dài jià 。*

English: *In this section, we introduce how to calculate the minimum cost price from start to end.*

"*如何*"[*rú hé*]*(how)* modifies the event of "*计算起点到终点的最小费用代价*"[*jì suàn qǐ diǎn dào zhōng diǎn de zuì xiǎo fèi yòng dài jià*]*(calculate the minimum cost price)*.It does not imply the uncertainty semantics.

# 4    Corpus Statistics

The corpus consists of 19 full papers including 4842 sentences. Annotation is finished by two annotators respectively. Table 1 summarizes the chief characteristics on the corpus. The 2nd and 6th rows of table 1 show the number of cue set (42 and 59 for negation and uncertainty, respectively). The phenomenon that negation cue set is less than uncertainty cue set in Chinese is similar with that in English. The 3rd and 7th rows of the table show the ratio of sentences which contain negative or uncertain information (15.78% and 13.88%for negation and uncertainty, respectively).The 4th and 8th rows of the table show the average length of negation nor uncertainty scope (14.95 and 18.41 for negation and uncertainty, respectively). It is longer than that in English (8.81 [3] and 14.37 [9] respectively).

**Table 1.** Statistics of the corpus

| | | |
|---|---|---|
| Negation | Negation cues | 941 |
| | Negation cues set | 42 |
| | Negation sentences | 15.78% |
| | Average length of negation scope | 14.95 |
| Uncertainty | Uncertainty cues | 812 |
| | Uncertainty cues set | 59 |
| | Uncertainty sentences | 13.88% |
| | Average length of uncertainty scope | 18.41 |

We extract 1300 sentences randomly and adopt Cohen' kappa [10] to measure the agreement rate of annotating negative and uncertainty cues and their scopes. If both the cue and its scope labeled by one annotator are absolutely same to another, it is considered as coinciding annotations. The kappa values for negation and uncertainty are84.55% and 83.04%, respectively.

## 5    Conclusions and Future Work

This paper reports on the construction of negation and uncertainty identification corpus. During annotation, sentences in Chinese always lack of elements because of ellipse phenomenon, so scope identification by the machine cannot depend only on syntactic parsing. Besides, sentences in English contain one subject-verb structure, but there often exist several subject-verb structures in Chinese sentences. For this reason, we consider punctuation as the boundary of clause to identify scope. Our corpus statistics shows that uncertainty identification is more complicated than negation identification, because the formal kappa value is lower even for humans and the average length of uncertainty scope is longer. The corpus is available free of charge for research purposes and can be obtained for a modest price for business use. For more details, please contact us. In the future work, we will expand the scale of negation and uncertainty identification corpus. Besides, we will implement system to identify negation and uncertainty automatically.

**Acknowledgement.** The authors were supported by National Natural Science Foundation of China (No. 61070123, 61272260), the Natural Science Foundation of Jiangsu Province (No. BK2011282), the Major Project of College Natural Science Foundation of Jiangsu Province (No. 11KJA520003), the Graduates Project of Science and Innovation (No. CXZZ12_0818).

# References

1. Blanco, E., Moldovan, D.: Semantic Representation of Negation Using Focus Detection. In: Proceedings of the 49th Annual Meeting of the Association for Computational Linguistics, Portland, Oregon, pp. 581–589 (2011)
2. Medlock, B., Briscoe, T.: Weakly Supervised Learning for Hedge Classification in Scientific Literature. In: Proceedings of the 45th Annual Meeting of the Association of Computational Linguistics, Prague, Czech Republic, pp. 992–999 (2007)
3. Morante, R., Daelemans, W.: A meta-learning approach to processing the scope of negation. In: Proceedings of the Thirteenth Conference on Computational Natural Language Learning (CoNLL), Boulder, Colorado, pp. 21–29 (June 2009)
4. Vincze, V., Szarvas, G., Farkas, R., Móra, G., Csirik, J.: The BioScope corpus: biomedical texts annotated for uncertainty, negation and their scopes. In: BioNLP 2008: Current Trends in Biomedical Natural Language Processing, Columbus, Ohio, USA, pp. 38–45 (June 2008)
5. Sinclair, J.: Corpus Concordance Collocation. Oxford University Press, Oxford (1991)
6. Farkas, R., Vincze, V., Mora, G., Csirik, J., Szarvas, G.: The CoNLL-2010 Shared Task: Learning to Detect Hedges and their Scope in Natural Language Text. In: Proceedings of the Fourteenth Conference on Computational Natural Language Learning (CoNLL): Shared Task, pp. 1–12 (July 2010)
7. Hyland, K.: Writing Without Conviction? Hedging in Science Research Articles. Applied Linguistics 17(4), 433–454 (1996)
8. Xu, L.: Discuss negative sentence in Chinese (试论现代汉语否定句). Journal of Anqing Teachers College (Social Science Edition) (3), 108–118 (1986)
9. Morante, R., Daelemans, W.: Learning the scope of hedge cues in biomedical texts. In: Proceedings of the Workshop on BioNLP, Boulder, Colorado, pp. 28–36 (June 2009)
10. Cohen. A coefficient of agreement for nominal scales. Educational and Psychological Measurement, 37–46 (1960)

# Annotation Schema for Contemporary Chinese Based on JinXi Li's Grammar System

Jing He[1], Weiming Peng[2], Jihua Song[1], and Hongzhang Liu[1]

[1] College of Computer Science and Technology,
Beijing Normal University, Beijing 100875, China
[2] Institute of Computational Linguistics, Peking University, Beijing 100871, China
hejing8@mail.bnu.edu.cn, athing@tju.edu.cn,
{sjh13,laoliuya}@163.com

**Abstract.** The Sentence-based Grammar System which was created by linguist Jinxi Li, is one of the most representative Chinese grammar systems. After reviewing the outline of Li's Grammar Theory including some viewpoints on syntax, morphology and diagrammatic parsing method, the paper illustrated the formalization idea of the Sentence-based Grammar System from the perspective of Chinese Information Processing, and designed an annotation schema for contemporary Chinese sentence structure. Then a visual annotation tool was implemented, and a Treebank was built up by analyzing 11 thousand sentences from some Chinese text books. The fact that all these sentences can be analyzed and modeled within the annotation schema proves the correctness and completeness of Li's grammar system, and our work also provides the basic resources and theory for the study of Automatic Parsing and Machine Translation.

**Keywords:** Treebank, Annotation Schema, Jinxi Li's Grammar, Sentence-based, Sentence Pattern.

## 1   Introduction

With the rapid development of the Natural Language Processing (NLP), corpus that is considered to be the basic resource of the NLP becomes more and more important. The researchers never stop increasing the scale of the corpus, analyzing them in depth, and improving the annotation schema. Among the attempts, the Treebank construction is making an effort to create the high quality corpus by annotating the syntactic and semantic information. Now it is certain that Treebank construction will be the trend of corpus linguistics research [1].

The Treebank is a kind of text corpus in which every sentence has been parsed and annotated based on corresponding annotation schema. The grammar theories play a very important role in Treebank construction, so theoretical research always goes with the Treebank construction. For example, 973 Treebank built by Tsinghua University is based on Phrase Structure Grammar (PSG), while the HIT Chinese Treebank built by Harbin Institute of Technology is based on Dependency Grammar (DG) [2]. The advantage of the combination is obvious. The grammar research provides the

P. Liu and Q. Su (Eds.): CLSW 2013, LNAI 8229, pp. 668–681, 2013.

theoretical direction for the Treebank structure design, in the other hand, with the increasing of Treebank scale, we can summarize pattern from a more extensive linguistic phenomena, and improve the grammar theories. So the Treebank construction and grammar theoretical research complement and promote each other [3]. At present, a widely accepted grammar theory that can make efficient interactive between the lexical meaning and the syntactical structure is still in blank [4]. The developments of CIP urgently demand the grammatical rationale for further progress.

This paper will introduce the Sentence-based Grammar System, which is a representative Chinese grammar theory created by linguist Jinxi Li. The basic idea of Li's theory indicates as follow: grammatical analysis should take sentence as the observation point and basic point, and concentrate efforts on the syntagmatic layout of "sentence components" and their syntactic relations. [5]. Sentence is the smallest linguistic communicative unit for people to express their ideas. Sentence layout offers the macroscopic view of understanding, so it's the principle contradiction of the grammatical analysis while word-class (named parts of speech(POS) in CIP) as the secondary contradiction. In a word, word-class analysis follows syntax analysis and depends on it.

To illustrate the sentence structure and layout vividly, Li designed the Diagrammatic Parsing Method, which is the representation of the Sentence-based Grammar and also an essential tool to study this theory. The Diagrammatic Parsing Method contains finite diagrams to demonstrate the order of the words, the sentence components, the word-class and so on. In the diagram, the clauses' function in sentence, the phrases' function in clause and the word-class function in phrase are displayed clearly. Therefore, we implemented a visual annotation tool using Li's Diagrammatic Parsing Method as a prototype, and designed the corresponding storage format of the sentence structure. The annotation schema is a formal system composed of different diagrams and corresponding structure formats for all kinds of Chinese sentences. The following will briefly introduce the Sentence-based Grammar at first, and then illustrate the detailed design of the diagrammatic annotation system, as well as the overall progress of the Treebank construction.

## 2    The Overview of the Sentence-Based Grammar System

Generally, a grammar theory is considered to contain two aspects: the syntax, which controls the sentence structure, and the morphology, which classifies the word-class.

### 2.1    Syntax: Sentence Structure Layout and Sentence Component

The Sentence Structure Layout means a relative stable hierarchy and sequence of subject, predicate, object, attribute, adverbial, complement and other components in the sentence [6]. The Sentence Structure Layout of the Sentence-based Grammar can be represented by a Diagrammatic Formula which was created in Li's famous book *A New Chinese Grammar* [5].

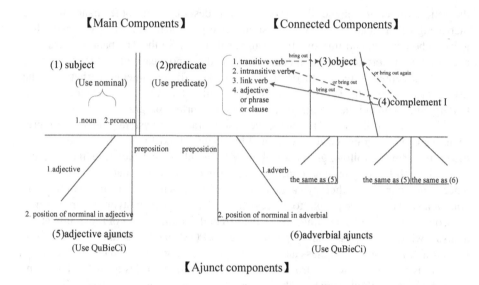

**Fig. 1.** Sentence Diagrammatic Formula[1]

As shown in Fig 1, the sentence is divided into two parts by a long horizontal line. Above the line lie the main and connected components which represent the truck of the sentence; while below the line lie the adjunct components which represent the branches. Just like branches adhere to trunk in a tree, the adjunct components adhere to the main and connected components. We can have a more intuitive understanding of the "Sentence Structure Layout" through this diagram. Different combinations of the widgets indicate different layouts of the sentence (hierarchy and order). The combination patterns of the trunk are finite, which reflect the sentence meaning roughly. Therefore, dividing the trucks and branches is the primary step in grammatical analysis. In short, the "Sentence Structure Layout" has laid the foundation for the analysis of the sentence meaning.

## The Six Components of the Sentence

Li's Grammar set up six "sentence components" in total, which can be divided into three layers as followings:

(1) Main components: 1. Subject; 2. Predicate
(2) Connected components: 3. Object; 4. Subject and Object Complement
(3) Adjunct components: 5. Adjective adjuncts; 6. Adverbial adjuncts

---

[1] In Li's work, there are two terminologies named "补足语"[buzhuyu] and "补语"[buyu] respectively. They are both translated as Complement in English. This paper refers to the former as Complement I, which means a complement of the subject or object located after predicate; and refers to the latter as Complement II, which means a modifier of the predicate but located below the predicate. See details in section 2.1.

Table 1shows some sentences that can help to understand the concrete connotation:

**Table 1.** example of the syntactic analysis

| example | (adjuncts) Subject | (adjuncts) Predicate | (adjuncts) Object | (adjuncts) Complement I |
|---------|--------------------|----------------------|-------------------|-------------------------|
| 1 | 日[ri] (the sun) | 出[chu]。 (rises) | | |
| 2 | 工人[gongren] (the workers) | 准备[zhunbei] (prepare) | 材料[cailiao]。 (materials) | |
| 3 | 工人[gongren] (the workers) | 是[shi] (are) | | 劳动者[laodongzhe]。 (laborers) |
| 4 | 工人[gongren] (the workers) | 推举[tuiju] (elect) | 张先生[zhangxiansheng] (Mr. Zhang) | 作代表[zuodaibiao]。 (as a delegate) |
| 5 | （勤劳的[qinglaode] ( industrious)) 工人[gongren] (the workers) | （在河岸[zaihean] (on the bank)) 准备[zhunbei] (prepare) | 材料[cailiao]。 (materials) | |
| 6 | 火车[huoche] (the train) | 开[kai] (drive) （得慢）[deman]。 (slowly) | | |

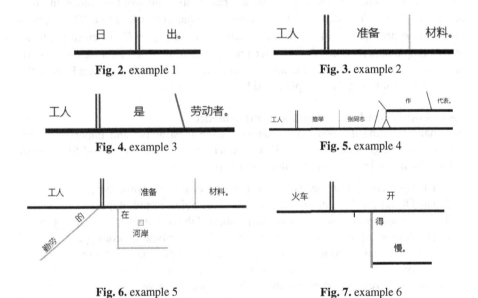

**Fig. 2.** example 1                    **Fig. 3.** example 2

**Fig. 4.** example 3                    **Fig. 5.** example 4

**Fig. 6.** example 5                    **Fig. 7.** example 6

Subject and predicate are the essential parts of the sentence. Fig. 1 depicts a simplest sentence with only two main components in diagram. According to the semantic of the predicate word, the predicate may lead different connected components, and result in different trunks as follows:

(1) When the predicate is an intransitive verb, the action of the subject will not influence other things, so it won't bring out connected component.(Fig. 2)

(2)    When the predicate is a transitive verb, the action (i.e. "准备") of the subject will influence other things (i.e."材料"), so it will bring out the object.(Fig. 3)

(3)    When the predicate is a link verb, the subject will bring out a complement I by which to describe the subject's situation, as we can see in the example 3: "是" complement "工人" with "劳动者".(Fig. 4)

(4)    The transitive verb as a predicate can lead a complement I for its object. These kinds of verbs, which mean command, engage or advice, will trigger the influenced object to change or to produce another action. e.g. "推举" makes its object "张先生" produce the action of "作代表".(Fig. 5)

Overall, there are only four combinations of the main components and connected components above the main line:

1. subject + predicate;
2. subject + predicate + object;
3. subject + predicate + complement I ;
4. subject + predicate + object + complement I .

The adjunct components extend from the main components and connected components. The attribute (i.e. "勤劳的") appears before its head word (nominal in common) (i.e. "工人"), and depicted as a leftwards oblique line or fold line. The adjuncts of predicate are divided into two types: adverbial (i.e. "在河岸") before predicate while complement II (i.e. "得慢") after predicate, and depicted as a rightward oblique line or fold line. Oblique line and fold line are used to distinguish the POS of the adjuncts, shown in Fig. 6. example 5 and Fig. 7. example 6.

**Seven Positions of Nominal and Variant Sentence**
Nominal (including the noun and pronoun) is the most active and important word-class in Chinese grammar system. Li's Grammar set up "Seven Positions" for nominal in the sentence's deep structure, named prototype, as follow:

1. The Subject-position means the position of the subject in prototype;
2. The Object-position means the position of the object in prototype;
3. The Complement-position means the position of the complement I in prototype;
4. The Attribute-position means the position of the attribute in prototype;
5. The Adverbial-position means the position of the adverbial in prototype;
6. The Appositive-position means the position of the appositive;
7. The Vocative-position means the position of the vocative.

The first five positions represent that a nominal can be used in the position of the five components above-mentioned. Appositive is placed with another nominal as an explanatory equivalent, both having the same syntactic relation to the other in the sentence. A vocative is used to represent the name of somebody or something being spoken to directly, and must be separated from the rest of the sentence.

Seven Positions set up a parallel terminology system, which plays a role when the surface structure and deep structure are inconsistent. For example, *A New Chinese Grammar* suggests the object of some verbs ( like "在[zai](*at*)", "往[wang](*to*)", "到

[dao](*arrive*)", "上[shang](*above*)", "下[xia](*below*)", "出[chu](*out*)", "入[ru](*enter*)", "进[jin](*enter*)", "过[guo](*pass*)", "回[hui](*back*)", "离[li](*away*)") to be called "adverbial object" (副性宾语[fu xing bin yu]) which means "the object form with the adverbial meaning". In analysis of the sentence "我在家。[wo zai jia](*I'm home*)", "家[jia](*home*)" is the object of "在[zai](*at*)" but still expresses a spatial semantic relation in the Adverbial- position [7].

Another utility of Seven Positions is in the analysis of variant sentence. Take the "把[ba]-construction" for example, the object being moved before the predicate by preposition "把" transforms to a prepositional-structure adverbial, but in the diagram it still occupies the prototypical Object-position. In the Diagrammatic Parsing, the Object-position should fold upward to represent this situation, as Fig. 8 shown:

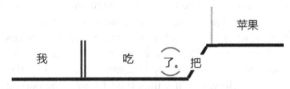

**Fig. 8.** "the object moves before the predicate"

There are 6 kinds of variants in Li's grammar system: "主退谓后[zhutuiweihou] (*the subject moves behind the predicate*)", "宾提动前[bintidongqian](*the object moves before the predicate*)", "宾置句首[binzhijushou] (*the object moves at the head of the sentence*)", "形附名后[xingfuminghou] (*the attribute moves behind the headword*)", "副冠句首[fuguanjushou] (*the adverbial moves at the head of the sentence*)", "副夺主位[fuduozhuwei] (*the adverbial takes over the position of the subject*)".

**Phrase and Clause**

There are some differences on the terminology "phrase" between Li's Grammar and prevailing grammar. Firstly, Li's Grammar considers subject-predicate structure as a Clause rather than a Phrase. Secondly, only if a verb-structure serves as one sentence component in whole, it could be called a Phrase in Li's Grammar. Otherwise, Li presumed that the verb as well as its adjuncts or connected components dissolved in the sentence layout, just like the chemical compound dissolved in water.

In the perspective of diagram, the component directly located at or adheres to the long horizontal line are in the same sentence layout. With the six sentence-components, there is no need to call the conjunction of any components "Phrase". If a verb-structure forms a "Phrase", it must have escaped from long horizontal line in Li's diagram, as shown in Fig. 9. In other words, Li's "Phrase" will break the natural hierarchy of the sentence layout.

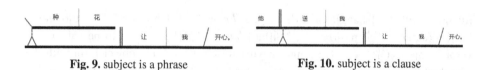

**Fig. 9.** subject is a phrase          **Fig. 10.** subject is a clause

Therefore, syntactic hierarchy in Li's Grammar contains two aspects: the grammar system itself determines the natural hierarchy of the sentence layout, while the phrase extension produces the other kind of hierarchy.

## 2.2     Morphology: The Viewpoint of "*For All Words, the Word-class Is Based on the Sentence*" and Word-Class Transformation

Li's word-class system contains nine categories which are noun, pronoun, verb, adjective, adverb, preposition, conjunction, auxiliary word and interjection. Li's Grammar proposed a famous viewpoint: "for all words, the word-class is based on the sentence". The Fig. 1 demonstrates POS and component have a relatively stable correspondence. Once the sentence is parsed by Diagrammatic Parsing, the word-class can be determined generally. However, it's important to note, the correspondence is not one-to-one relationship.

The viewpoint always leads to a problem called "words have no fixed class". In fact, it can only draw the conclusion that "tokens have no fixed class". Since lack of morphologic change in Chinese, the same token may stand for several word items. It is a very appropriate viewpoint suitable for Chinese word feature.

**Table 2.** the word-class of token "调查[diaocha](*investigate*)"

| 汉语[hanyu](*Chinese*) | 英语[yingyu](*English*) |
|---|---|
| 他已经调查过这件事了。<br>[ta yi jing diao cha guo zhe jian shi le] | He has **investigated** this event. |
| 调查很及时。<br>[diao cha hen ji shi] | The **investigation** is in time. |

As shown in the table, the two words share the same form: token "调查", but with different meanings. The first word is a verb which means "investigate" in English, while the second word is a noun which means "investigation". The latter has been nominalized already. Li's Grammar calls this phenomenon "Word-class Transformation".

To summary this section, Chinese morphology is controlled by the syntax. It makes sure that every word-class has their special functions, so the sentence structure layout becomes stable. That is convenient for the computer to analyze the Chinese sentence.

## 3     The Design of the Diagrammatic Annotation Schema

This paper utilizes a diagrammatic annotation tool to build a Treebank in XML format.

## 3.1    Data Structure Design

The following two tables illustrate the tag sets based on Li's Grammar, including the POS tag set and the syntax tag set.

**Table 3.** POS tag set

| POS | | tag | example |
|---|---|---|---|
| 实词[shici] (*notional word*) | 名词[mingci](*noun*) | m | 人民[renmin](*people*) |
| | 代名词[daiminci](*pronoun*) | i | 你[ni](*you*) |
| | 动词[dongci](*verb*) 附类：助动词（前附）[zhudongci qianfu] 助动词（后附）[zhudongci houfu] (*Auxiliary Verb*) | d d1 d2 | 建设[jianshe](*build*) 可以[keyi](*can*) 来[lai](*come*) |
| | 形容词[xingrongci](*adjective*) | x | 红[hong](*red*) |
| | 副词[fuci](*adverb*) | f | 已经[yijing](*already*) |
| 虚词[xuci] (*function word*) | 介词[jieci](*preposition*) 附类[fulei](*subclass*)： "的" [de] "地" [de] "得" [de] | j j1 | 在[zai](*at*) 的[de][2] 地[de] 得[de] |
| | 连词[lianci](*conjunction*) | l | 和[he](*and*) |
| | 语气词[yuqici](*modal particle*) | y | 吗[ma] |
| | 叹词[tanci](*interjection*) | t | 啊[a] |

**Table 4.** Syntax tag set

| category | term | tag |
|---|---|---|
| 成分[chengfen] (*component*) | 主语[zhuyu](*subject*) | zy |
| | 谓语[weiyu](*predicate*) | wy |
| | 宾语[binyu](*object*) | by |
| | 补足语[buzuyu](*complement I*) | bz |
| | 定语[dingyu](*attribute*) | di |
| | 状语[zhuangyu](*adverbial*) | zh |
| | 补语[buyu](*complement II*) | bu |
| | 同位语[tongweiyu](*appositive*) | tw |
| | 独立语[duliyu](*holophrastice*) | hw |
| 短语 (*phrase*) | 名词性短语[mingcixingduanyu](*nominal phrase*) | md |
| | 形容性短语[xingrongxingduanyu](*adjective phrase*) | xd |
| | 副词性短语[fucixingduanyu](*adverbial phrase*) | fd |
| 子句 (*clause*) | 名词性子句[mingcixingziju](*nominal clause*) | mz |
| | 形容性子句[xingrongxingziju](*adjective clause*) | xz |
| | 副词性子句[fucixingziju](*adverbial clause*) | fz |

As shown in Table 4, we have adjusted the terms in Li's grammar system:

---

[2] Some Chinese function words have no English equivalents, so you'll find some words haven't got the corresponding English word in this paper.

Divide "adverb adjuncts"(副词性附加语[fucixingfujiayu]) into two terms: "adverbial" and "complementⅡ";

Change "adjective adjuncts"( 形 容 性 附 加 语 [xingrongxingfujiayu]) to "adjective"(定语[dingyu]);

Add two components: "appositive" and "holophrastic" for Appositive-position and Vocative-position.

To summarize, there are nine sentence components in total. Besides, phrase and clause in Sentence-based Grammar can be divided into three types: noun, adjective and adverb.

We use the first letter of the pinyin to represent the POS tag. If there is a conflict, then take the second letter. The subclass of a POS is implemented by adding a number after the letter. Syntactic tag will be represented by the first letter of the pinyin of the two Chinese Characters. If conflicted, take the next letter of the first Chinese Character [6].

Take the following sentence for example, Fig. 11 shows the XML structure and we will explain the design principles.

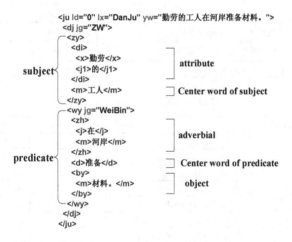

**Fig. 11.** XML data structure

The root node of the XML DOM tree is "ju" (means a sentence in Chinese pinyin, the same below), its attribute lx="DanJu" (means simple sentence) gives the information of the sentence type, and the attribute "yw" is used to record the original text. The child-node of the root is "dj" whose attribute jg="ZW" (means the trunk of the sentence is subject-predicate) represent the basic sentence structure, and if the sentence is a complex sentence, the count of the node "dj" is equal or greater than two. The node "zy" and "wy" which represent subject and predicate separately are the child-node of "dj". The DOM hierarchy further down follows the principle of "Head-word Analysis": the head-word of a sentence component must be the direct child of the component node, and the adjuncts as well as the connected components of the head-word locate in the same hierarchy as the head-word in DOM. Thus the attribute nodes "di" is the sibling node of noun node "m", while the adverbial node "zh" and the object node "by" are the sibling node of verb node "d". The attribute jg="WeiBin" (means predicate-object) illustrates the information of the truck-structure, so we can extract the head-words that can express the main idea of the sentence. This design pattern facilitates the information extraction of the syntactic structure.

Our design doesn't set a hard dichotomy rule on the structure of "adverbial-predicate-object", because it's a dilemma in most cases. Take the sentence in Fig. 11 for example, "在河岸准备材料[zai he an zhun bei cai liao] (*prepare some materials on the bank*)"  can actually be analyzed in two hierarchies ([[在河岸 准备] 材料] or [在河岸 [准备 材料]]). Chinese linguist Fuyi Xing regards this structure as "the interlock of two syntactic structure" (扣合[kouhe]) and considers that dichotomy is not essential in the analysis of some kinds of structures[8].

## 3.2    Variant Sentence

According to the design in the previous section, the sequence of the sentence layout is relatively stable. However, in some variant sentence the sequence goes against the normal sequence in the prototype layout. We use the attribute "bs" to store the information of variant.

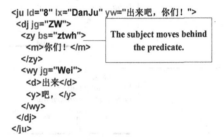

**Fig. 12.** the subject moves behind the predicate

Take the sentence "出来吧，你们！ [chu lai ba, ni men] (*come out, you!*) " as an example, the diagram still keeps the logical sequence "你们出来吧[ni men chu lai ba] (*means you come out*)". This can maintain the sentence pattern in a stable layout, and the sequence information stored by attribute bs="ztwh" (means the subject move behind the predicate) isn't lost.

There are six kinds of variants in Li's Grammar System in total.

## 3.3    The Complex Sentence

In the book *A New Chinese Grammar*, Li had classified the POS, and also analyzed several complex sentences and paragraphs. Based on those concepts, he divided *Chinese Grammar Teaching Material* into three parts, and the third part introduced the complex sentence and the paragraph structure in a systematic way. Here we will not evolve that.

# 4    The Practice of Building Treebank

The diagrammatic annotation tool and XML storage format follow the three principles:

First, make sure that the conversion between the diagram and XML storage format should be effective.

Second, make sure XML storage format is consistent to the sentence structure layout (with a relatively stable sequence and hierarchy).

Third, make sure the sentence with the variant can keep the original order of the sentence. Because any change of syntax may lead to the change of the semantics, pragmatics or rhetoric, so the "bs" attribute is essential [9].

*Chinese Grammar Teaching Material* has enumerated a lot of illustrative example sentences which are high-quality Chinese resources. We choose these sentences as the raw material of the Treebank. So far we have already built the Treebank including 11,044 sentences, 210,000 characters. The table below is the 16 sentence patterns for *Chinese Grammar Teaching Material* using sentence pattern code [10].

**Table 5.** Sixteen sentence patterns

| ID | Name | Example |
|---|---|---|
| 1 | subject-verb-object<br>动宾谓语句<br>[dongbinweiyuju] | 我调工作啦。<br>[wo diao gong zuo la]<br>(*I have changed my job*)<br> |
| 2 | subject-verb<br>单动谓语句<br>[dandongweiyuju] | 战争爆发了。<br>[zhan zheng bao fa le]<br>(*The war has broken out*)<br> |
| 3 | subject-adjective<br>单形谓语句<br>[danxingweiyuju] | 水流急。<br>[shui liu ji]<br>(*The water flow is very strong*)<br> |
| 4 | subject-noun<br>名词谓语句<br>[mingciweiyuju] | 老王南方人。<br>[lao wang nan fang ren]<br>(*Lao Wang comes from south China*)<br> |

**Table 5.** (*continued*)

| 5 | subject-link verb-complement I<br>判断句<br>[panduanju] | 这是闹市。<br>[zhe shi nao shi]<br>(*Here is a busy street*) |
| 6 | statements<br>说明句<br>[shuomingju] | 心情是愉快的。<br>[xin qing shi yu kuai de]<br>(*The feeling is pleasant*) |
| 7 | pivotal sentence<br>兼语句<br>[jianyuju] | 母亲叫闰土坐。<br>[mu qin jiao run tu zuo]<br>(*My mother asked Tu Run to sit down*) |
| 8 | subject-object-verb<br>提宾句<br>[tibinju] | 你把我们忘了。<br>[ni men ba wo men wang le]<br>(*You have forgotten us*) |
| 9 | inverted sentence<br>倒装句<br>[daozhuangju] | 怎么了，你？<br>[zen me le, ni]<br>(*What's wrong with you*) |
| 10 | holophrastic<br>独词句<br>[duciju] | 秋天。<br>[qiu tian]<br>(*The autumn*) |
| 11 | object-subject-verb<br>宾置句首句<br>[binzhujushouju] | 这我明白。<br>[zhe wo ming bai]<br>(*I can understand it*) |

**Table 5.** (*continued*)

| 12 | subject-(subject-predicate)<br>主谓谓语句<br>[zhuweiweiyuju] | 他头痛。<br>[ta tou tong]<br>(*He had a headache*) |
| 13 | subject-verb-object-object<br>双宾语句<br>[shuangbinyuju] | 指导员给他一本书。<br>[zhi dao yuan gei ta yi ben shu]<br>(*The instructor gave him a book*) |
| 14 | sentences with serial predicates<br>连动句<br>[liandongju] | 他站起来说话了。<br>[ta zhan qi lai shuo hua le]<br>(*He has stood up to speak*) |
| 15 | subject-auxiliary verb-predicate<br>助动句<br>[zhudongju] | 你得问他。<br>[ni de wen ta]<br>(*You'll have to ask him*) |
| 16 | existential sentence<br>存现句<br>[cunxianju] | 水上停着一渔船。<br>[shui shang ting zhe yi yu chuan]<br>(*There is a fishing boat in the river*) |

# 5    Conclusions

Building a Treebank using the Sentence-based Grammar is an attempt to apply traditional grammar to NLP. It requires a good understanding of the Sentence-based Grammar. The sentence layout has established the foundation of the further work that to abstract the main idea of the sentence. Since we are still in the early stages, there are so many things to do, such as concluding the basic sentence pattern, building the basic sense of sentence. We need to study more theories to make the Sentence-based Grammar become more complete.

# References

1. Zhiwei, F.: Empiricism-based Corpus Research. Terminology Standardization & Information Technology 1 (2007)
2. Jihua, S., Erhong, Y., Qiangjun, W.: Chinese Information Processing, p. 94. China Higher Education Press, Beijing (2011)
3. Qiang, Z.: Annotation Scheme for Chinese Treebank. Journal of Chinese Information Processing 18(4) (2004)
4. Guangjin, J., Li, F.: The construction of the Chinese Corpus-setting of the standard and inspection of the quality. In: The Third Application of Linguistics Workshop. Hong Kong Science and Technology Associated Press, Hong Kong (2004)
5. Jinxi, L.: A New Chinese Grammar. The Commercial Press, Beijing (2001)
6. Weiming, P.: Digital Platform Construction of Sentence-based Grammar and Its Application Study. Beijing Normal University, Beijing (2012)
7. Danqing, L.: Some Grammatical Terms Used by LI Jin-xi. Journal of Beijing Normal University (Social Sciences) (5) (2010)
8. Fuyi, X.: Chinese Grammar Theory. Journal of Northeast Normal University Press, Changchun (1998)
9. Hu, M.Y.: Basic Sentences and Transformations. Chinese Language Learning (1) (2000)
10. Weiming, P., Jing, H., Song, J.: The Design and Implement of Dia-grammatical Sentence-based Grammar Parsing System. In: The 4th International Conference of Digital Archives and Digital Humanities, Taiwan (November 30, 2012)

# Topicaliazation in the Model of Sentence Formation

Mengyue Yan[1,2]

[1] College of Chinese Language and Literature, Wuhan University, Wuhan, China
[2] College of arts, Chongqing Normal University, Chongqing, China
yanmengyue1979@aliyun.cn

**Abstract.** This paper explains Chinese topicalization phenomena from the perspective of the process of sentence formation. We propose a presupposed flow chart model to show the process by which the speaker arranges information materials into a sentence and explain many kinds of topic phenomena on it. We consider that topic itself is a complex component which exists in many layers in the sentence formation process, so we can get several different points of view on it. The so called "topicalization" is the process in which topic emerges from the information layer to the functional layer, the syntactic forms layer and the phonology layer one by one. This model not only explains the phenomena of topic but also can provides a theoretical basis for natural language processing.

**Keywords:** entence generation model, topicalization, layers, filters.

## 1 Some Problems of the Relevant Study

The previous researcher Yuan yulin (1996) used to define "topicalization" as such a process: under the certain pragmatic motivations, a NP at the end or the middle of a sentence be left dislocated to the initiation of it. During this syntactic operation, the NP becomes the topic or subtopic of the sentence. At the same time, the sentence be transferred from a basic sentence to a non-basic one. Furthermore, This process is relevant to some syntactic operation, such as pronominalization, identity deletion,imperativization. This definition can only adapt to a small part of topic phenomena. If we take a viewpoint of topic with broad sense, i.e. considering all the given entity information introduced to hearer is topic, then the definition can not adapt them adequately. For example, as in (1), the object "311 教室"[311jiaoshi](classroom 311) is a given information and the topic of the sentence, but we can't find a process of topicalization defined above in its formation.

(1) 谁打扫的<u>311教室</u>TOP。

    *Shui dasao de <u>311 jiaoshi</u> TOP.*

    *Who did he clean the classroom 311.*

    The topic in (1) is not moved and its formation is irrelevant to the grammatical process (pronominalization, identity deletion, imperativization) mentioned above. Given this situation, we set a new model of the formation of the sentences in Mandarin and try to use it to explain all kinds of topic sentences. Our aim is to find the universal

P. Liu and Q. Su (Eds.): CLSW 2013, LNAI 8229, pp. 682–691, 2013.

model of Chinese topic sentence formation. The model can be used to explain all sorts of Chinese topic sentence and is of value on the study of Chinese natural language processing. In our model, topicalization is viewed as a emerging process of a given entity information from the functional layer to the syntactic layer and phonological layer one by one.

## 2    The Flow Chart of the Model and Topic in It

In the practice of Chinese speech act, it has to go through four steps in the process of sentence formation from the time speaker has a communicative intention to the time it has been realized into vocal sentence. We describe it in a flow chart with layers and filters and embody it in figure1 below:

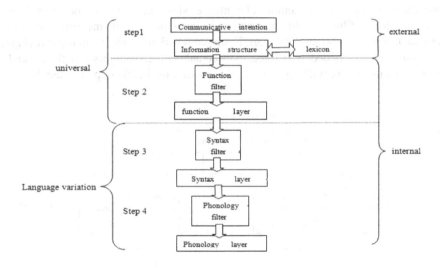

**Fig. 1.** flow chart of sentence formation

Step 1: From communicative intention to information structure.

The formation of Chinese sentence begins with the communicative intention layer. Having had a communicative intention, speaker will arrange the new and old information for the sentences and forms a information structure. It is the information structure layer. It is a process that speakers arrange new and old materials in their mind. The given information is old materials including but not limited to topic and the new information is new material including but not limited to focus. These two layers are the external layers in the formation of sentences. They universally exist and have no variations between different languages. Information structure has no word order and can be realized in any kind of word order only if it conforms to the grammar of this language. We called the topic in the information layer as "topic 1" and it is a universal component in human languages. There is a need for all the languages to arrange new and old information in a sentence but the ways they achieve it are different. For the reason that all the languages have these two layers, different languages can be translated or be code switched. We confine this paper to the sentence formation and put aside the discussion of lexicon and discourse. We number the topics in the different layers with "topic1" "topic2" "topic3" "topic4" and they exist in the information structure layer, function layer, syntax layer and phonology layer respectively. Topic1 is a component lies in information structure, it is an entity information that is given in direct or indirect context. Speakers consider that hearers have known it or can infer it indirectly. Topic1 is just the so called "topic referent", see in the discussion of Knud Lambrecht (1994).The fact that topic lies in information structure has been seen by some researchers, as in Nomi Erteschik-Shir (2007), he used to study the interaction of topic and focus in information structure.

Step 2: from information structure to function layer

In step2, the sentence information structure goes through the function filter and be output as the functional structure of it. Sentence functional structure is a theme-rheme construction, theme is the beginning of sentence while rheme is the core of it. The rule of functional filter is: old information is input into the theme part and new information is input into the rheme part. From the function of information conveying, theme part can be divided into three: conceptual theme, interpersonal theme and contextual theme, see in Halliday (1985). We can see flow in this step in figure 2:

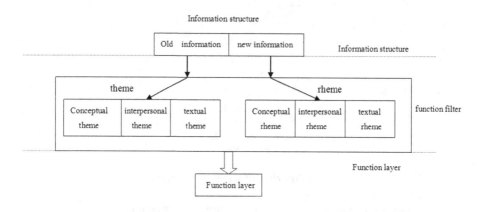

**Fig. 2.** Function filter in step2

Topic2 is the part of theme which convey given entity information, Zhang bojiang and Fang mei (1994) called it "topic theme" and consider it as the part which has conceptual function. We agree with them, but we consider that topic is the part which only conveys entity information and doesn't include concept of event, state, property etc. We see topic2 in (2).

(2) 饭前*TOP*要是不洗手，容易得病。

Fanqian-*TOP* yaoshi bu xishou, rongyi debing.

*If you don't wash your hands before eating, you are easy to be ill.*

The theme of sentence (2) is "饭前要是不洗手 [*Fanqian yaoshi bu xishou*]", "饭前 "[*fanqian*](*before dinner*) and "不洗手" [*bu xishou*] (*not wash hand* ) are conceptual theme, "要是[*yao shi*](*if*)" is textual theme, but only the theme"饭前" .[*fanqian*]which conveys entity conceptual information is the topic of the sentence. Topic2 in function layer still has no definite forms and the forms of it will be realized until it goes into syntax layer. Function layer is still a universal layer and locates in the grammar system with no language variations. The sentences of all the languages have this theme-rheme division in their function structure but the word orders they embody it are different. In our model, it is necessary to set a function layer between information structure and syntax layer. When the external components, such as the information components go into grammar system, they should go through an entry "function filter". This device differentiates the syntactic structure from the components outside language. Only if the materials go in this entry, speaker can realize communicative intention and information into the sentences in languages.

Step3: function layer to syntax layer

In this step, theme-rheme structures are input syntax filter and amended by the rule of it. The outcome of this process is sentence syntactic forms. We show the step in figure 3:

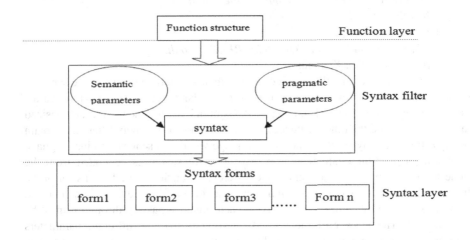

**Fig. 3.** Step3

As we all know, a grammatical sentence should not only conform to the rules of syntax but also be restricted by semantic and pragmatic factors. Theoretically, several sentence syntactic forms can be generated from the same set of functional components and each one of them has different semantic and pragmatic values respectively. They are showed in figure3 as "form1" "form2" "form3"and "form n" and have different meaning in particular context. Within the three factors (syntax, semantic and pragmatics) which restrict sentence forms, the rules of syntax are compulsory and the only way must be passed by sentence functional structure. Every functional structure must be filtered by syntactic rules then becomes grammatical sentence. The subscript "n" of form in figure 3 can be a very big number theoretically, but actually it can only span in a restricted interval value, eg: 1 to 6 or so. That is to say, for a determined function structure, the sentence forms we can get are determined and restricted. As in (3), for these three components: 小明(xiaomin, a boy's name), 打了(dale, break), 玻璃(boli, glasses), we can get at least six sentence forms of them.

(3) a. 小明打了玻璃。

   *Xiaomin   dale   boli.*
   *Xiaomin broke the window.*

   b.玻璃被小明打了。

   *Boli   bei-PASSIVE MARKER   xiaomin   dale.*
   *The window is broken by Xiaomin.*

   c.小明把玻璃打了。

   *Xiaomin   ba-MARKER of "ba" sentence   boli   dale.*
   *Xiaomin broke the window.*

   d. 玻璃小明打了。

   *Boli-main TOP   xiaomin-sub TOP   dale.*
   *The window is broken by Xiaomin.*

   e.是小明打了玻璃。

   *Shi-FOCUS MARKER   xiaomin   dale   boli.*
   *It is Xiaomin who broke the window.*

   f.小明打的是玻璃。

   *Xiaomin   dade   shi-FOCUS MARKER   boali.*
   *It is window that Xiaomin broke.*

These six sentences are all grammatical and their semantic meaning is the same, as in the translation. However, they each have particular pragmatic or semantic value. For example, (3) e focused the agent "Xiaomin" as the new and emphasized information. So are the other sentences in (3). This model of syntax filter can explain two questions: a. why a native speaker can judge whether a sentence in his language is grammatical or ungrammatical;   b. why a set of sentences generated from the same set of information components have different syntactic forms. The answer of the first question is that syntax is a compulsory part in the filter device; each sentence must unconditionally conform to syntax so each sentence passing through it must be grammatical. The answer of the second question is that the different parameters determined by semantic and pragmatic factors cause the sentences get different forms. However, these parameters are chosen optionally, so the different combinations of the parameters set different sentence forms. For the two reasons stated above, we find that it is the syntax filter that determines language variations.

From the perspective of our model, there is no essential distinction between the basic word order and non-basic word order for the same set of information components. The different word orders of a set of sentences are determined by the three factors above. The form with basic word order is the form which is most frequently used while the form with non-basic word order is relatively of a low frequency. The transformation between the basic word order and the non-basic word order can be seen as to take different forms for the purposes of different semantic and pragmatic values. Viewing the sentences generated from the same set of information components as integrity, the relations between them are complementary. From this syntax layer, languages' variations emerge.

As for topic2, it is filtered by syntax filter and be output as topic3 taking forms of subjects, objects, adverbials, modifiers and telescopicforms. See in (4)-(8).

(4) 他-*TOP*太小了，还不能去上学。(Subject)

*Ta-TOP  taixiao  le, hai  buneng  qu  shangxue.*

*He is too young to go to school.*

(5)_新中国成立那年-*TOP*，我才八岁。 (Adverbial)

*Xinzhongguo chengli nanian-TOP, wo  cai  basui.*

*In the year the Peoples republic of China founded, I was eight years old.*

(6) 厨房里-*TOP*的什么在响。(Modifier)

 *Chufangli-TOP  de  shenmo  zai  xiang.*

*What is sounding in the kitchen?*

(7) 我请小张-*TOP*负责业务工作。 (Telescopicform)

*Wo  qin  xiaozhang-TOP  fuze  yewu  gongzuo.*

*I ask Xiaozhang to be responsible for the professional work.*

The topics in (4)-(7) are topic3 in our model, we view all the given entity information in sentence as topic. We find topic3 is different from topic2 and topic1, the former we called it "topic expression" (see in Knud Lambrecht: 1994) contrasted to the latter as "topic referent". Topic3 has language variations in their forms. The typological distinctions between topic prominent language and subject prominent language are realized in topic3 but topic1 or topic2.

Step4: syntax layer to phonology layer

The syntactic form of a sentence is a mental symbol string with no vocal expressions. In this step, it is input into phonology filter and be output as a vocal symbol string. There are several phonetic spelling rules in the device and they can spell syntactic symbol strings to get termination product of this model: a vocal grammatical sentence in natural languages. For the reason of out paper's aim, we put aside the discussions of phonetic spelling rules. So in this step topic3 is transformed into topic4, a vocal form.

## 3    A Chinese Example for Model Explanation

To prove the validity of the model, we use a set of sentences to show the process of the sentence formation in our model, as in (8). (" | " designates the boundary of theme and rheme)

(8) a. 这个品种的栗子|不甜。

*Zhege pingzhong de-MODIFIER  lizi-TOP  | butian.*

*Chestnut of this variety is  not sweet.*

b. 不甜的|是这个品种的栗子。

*Butian de  | shi-FOC Marker  zhege pingzhong-Modifier de lizi-TOP.*

*It is this variety of chestnut which is not sweet.*

c. 栗子|这个品种的|不甜。

*Lizi-Main TOP    / zhege pingzhong de-SubTOP   / butian.*

*Chestnut of this variety is   not sweet.*

d. 栗子 |不甜的|是这个品种的。

*Lizi-TOP   / butian de  / shi-FOC Marker   zhege pingzhong de .*

*Chestnut of this variety is   not sweet.*

e. 这个栗子|是不甜的品种。

*Zhege lizi-TOP   / shi-VERB butian de pingzhong.*

*This chestnut is the variety which is not sweet.*

In step1, the five sentences in (8) a-b are formed with the same set of information components, so we put them together in our discussion.   Let us suppose, if the speaker tries to speak these five sentences, he should draw out these five information components ("inf" designates information components): inf1 (chestnut), inf2 (sweet), inf3 (not, negative), inf4 (this) and inf5 (variety). Information components itself have no forms and the speaker will replace them with the words in lexicon, as showed in step1 of figure1. An evident of the existing of the process is that different languages will have different outcomes of this replacement, i.e. words of different languages. Chinese will replace them with the five words: inf1-栗子[*lizi*](*chestnut*), inf2-甜 [*tian*](*sweet*), inf3-不[*bu*](*not*), inf4-这个[*zhege*](*this*), inf5-品种[*pingzhong*](*variety*) while  English will replace them with the word: inf1-chestnut, inf2-sweet, inf3-not, inf4-this, inf5-variety. Then in step2, the five information components are input function filter. According to the rules in figure2, the old information is input theme part while the new information is input rheme part. We can choose one or more members of the five components to be the given information or unknown information. Different choices determined different information structures. Theoretically, each of information has a chance to go into the theme part or the rheme part. How to arrange them in information structure is determined by expressive intention. Take (8) as an example, we can put inf1, inf4 and inf5 into the theme part and put inf2 and inf3 into the rheme part to get sentences a.b.c.d. And an alternative choice is to put inf1 and inf4 into the theme and put inf2, inf3 and inf5 into the rheme to get sentence e. From the different information structures we can get different functional structures, as in (8), we can get at least two functional structures as stated above. The functional structures only differentiate the sentences into the two parts (theme and rheme) from the perspective of information conveying and have no definite word order. The word order of sentences is to be decided until they go in step3. All in all, sentences are the permutation and combination of the different information components only if they conform to the grammar and expressive intention.

In step3 (as shown in figure 3), functional structures will be input syntax filter to be amended. In this step, the word order is determined, the assignment relations between NP and VP is determined, NP and VP will get the morphology. Even in the languages like Chinese which have little morphology, it will amend the sentences' forms in its own ways. First, sentence word order will be determined, as we all know, some languages put the theme before the rheme and some others maybe converse this word order. Even for the languages having "theme-rheme" word order sometimes will take the word order as "rheme-theme", so is Chinese. (8) a and (8)b have functional structure word order quite the reverse. In addition to this, speaker could choose some other functional structure for sentence. We called (8) c double-subject sentence traditionally, in fact its sentence functional structure is in two level. In the first level, inf1 is the theme; the other information components are the rheme. In the second level, in the functional structure formed with inf2 to inf5, inf4 and inf5 are the theme while inf2 and inf3 are the rheme. The difference between (8) a. b and (8) c is their level quantities are different, the former has only one level, the latter has two. Like (8) c, sentence (8)d also has a two level functional structure and they both take inf1 as their theme in the first level. The difference between them lies in the functional structure of second level, (8) d take inf2 inf3 as the theme and take inf4 inf5 as the rheme. The second syntactic amendment is adding marker, (8)a-d are the outcomes of the same set of information components, they can be divided into two groups by the using of focus marker "是1[shi-1](be)" . (8) a and (8)c have no focus marker and take the unmarked word order of theme-rheme structure. (8)b and (8)d have a focus marker "是1" to mark the word order conversed. The theme-rheme word order is set by the semantic parameters which need to     especially emphasize the rheme. Sentence (8)e also has a word "是[shi](be)", it is a verb designating   judgments but a focus marker. The third, the relations between NP and VP will be amended. Taking sentences (8) as example, because different NPs are assigned to the predicate "不甜 [bu tian](not sweet)" , we can get forms in (8)a.b.c.d.e. In (8)a, the predicate "不甜" dominates the NP formed by inf1 inf4 inf5. In this NP, inf4 and inf5 modify the head word inf1栗子[lizi](chestnut). In (8)c, "不甜" dominates inf5 but inf1, the modifier of inf5 is inf4. Then inf1 is dominated by the clause formed by inf2, inf3, inf4 and inf5. (8)b has the same argument structure as (8)a but its functional structure is reversed. (8)c and (8)d have the same argument structure only with reversed theme-rheme word order in inner functional structure.

For the reason we stated above, we put aside the discussions of the process of sentences (8) in step4.

## 4    A New Definition of Topicalization in Our Model

The research on topicalization has being centered on the topic sentences which are formed by the syntactic operations, such as "left-dislocation. This definition of topicalization can not explain the generating mechanism of all types of topic sentences. From the perspective of out model, we give a new definition on topicalization: topicalization is a process that speaker put the given entity information component into the function filter, syntax filter and phonology filters one by one and get a vocal sentence topic form. In this process, a given entity information is filtered by function filter and be out put as a topic-theme, then the topic theme goes in syntax filter and be output as several sorts of syntactic components: subject, object, adverbial, telescopicform. At last, it is put into phonology filter and be output as a topic with vocal form.

As for the definition of topicalization in the past research, we call it "topicalization in a narrow sense". It only discusses the process which topic is undergone in step3 in our model, i.e. how the topic theme is filtered by syntax filter and output as several syntactic components. From the perspective of our model, the formation of topic does not need an operation of left-dislocation. The typical topic-initial sentence is only one of the outcomes of this process.

# 5    The Features and Values of Our Model

This paper segregates topic into four kinds of existing form in the generation of sentence: topic1 (information topic), topic2 (topic-theme), topic3 (syntactic topic, registered as several kinds of syntactic components), topic4 (vocal topic). This model can explain the forming mechanism of all the topics in Chinese sentence and give topicalization a more reasonable definition. As we have known, many researchers have study Chinese topic sentence from the different perspective and get several kinds of conclusions on it. Some scholars view topic as a syntactic component (Xu liejiong & Liu danqing, 2005), some views it as a functional component (Zhang bojiang & Fang mei, 1994; Fang mei 1994; Cao fengfu 1995), some others view it as a information component (Nomi，Erteschik-Shir：2007). These views all have certain rationality, but their fundamental views of topic are different. The model can unite these views on Chinese topic sentence and explain why they got different conclusions on it. The answer of the question is topic itself is a component existing in the several layers in the model of sentence generation. On the other hand, there is some other researchers' study that can prove the rationality of this model. They consider that topic maybe is not a simple notion but can exist in the forms more than one. Lambrecht（1994）and Avery D. Andrews（1985）: "This common use of the term topic to denote a referent with a particular relation to a proposition should be sharply distinguished from the use of the term to refer to a LINGUISTIC EXPRESSION designating a topic referent in a sentence. To refer to such an expression, I will use terms like "TOPIC EXPRESSION…".

Except syntax and phonetic layers, the model in this paper sets information and function layers to explain the differences of opinions on the study of topic. We also hope that the model can be used to explain other language phenomena. For some of the controversial issues like double-subject sentence, postpositive topic sentence and the function of the focus marker "是"[shi](be), this model can give them explanation economically. If we restrict our discussions of these topics within the syntax, semantics and pragmatics, the conclusions we get usually are controversial. However, if we view them from the perspectives of information and function structure of sentences, some of the differences between the researches and exceptional case can be solved relatively easy. Human's language is a process that speaker uses the forms in languages to arrange the information materials in his mind. In this process, he should consider both expressive intention, context of a sentence and grammar including syntax and pragmatics. Therefore, such a model can be in accordance with language reality to a certain extent and be formalized on computer to imitate the process of sentence generation.

# References

1. Andrews, A.D.: The major functions of the noun phrase. In: Shopen, T. (ed.) Language Typology and Syntactic Description, vol. I: Clause Structure, pp. 62–154. Cambridge University Press, Cambridge (1985)
2. Halliday, M.A.K.: An Introduction to Functional Grammar. Edward Arnold, London (1985)
3. Li, C.N., Thompson, S.A.: Mandarin Chinese: A Functional Reference Grammar. University of California Press, Berkley and Los Angles (1981)
4. Lambrecht, K.: Information Structure and Sentence Form. Cambridge University Press, Cambridge (1994)
5. Nomi, E.-S.: Information Structure: The Syntax-Discourse Interface. Oxford University Press (2007)
6. Reinhart, T.: Pragmatics and Linguistics: an analysis of sentence topics. Distributed by Indiana University Linguistics Club, Bloomington (1982)
7. Yulin, Y.: Topicaization and the Relevant Grammatical Process. Chinese Journal of China (4) (1996)
8. Bojiang, Z., Mei, F.: The Theme-Structure of Spoken Chinese. Journal of Peking University (2) (1994)
9. Cao, F.: A functional study of topic in Chinese: the first step towards discourse analysis. The Chinese Press (1995)

# Chinese Verb Classification Based on 3 Dimensional Dynamic Concept Model*

Haoguo Feng, Na Ye, Qimeng Zhao, and Dongfeng Cai

Knowledge Engineering Research Center, Shenyang Aerospace University, Shenyang, China
fenghgnlp@163.com, yn.yena@gmail.com,
zhaomeng1123@126.com, caidf@vip.163.com

**Abstract.** This paper puts forward 3 Dimensional Dynamic Concept Model (3-DDCM) by combining philosophical analysis and thinking of materialist dialectics and inspiration of HowNet biaxial theory of events. According to the 3-DDCM, the paper proposes a method of verb classification through sentence semantic analysis. The method studies the correspondence between the verb classes and HowNet event taxonomy, verb classes in Verb Dictionary and related concepts in HNC on the whole. The paper is a preliminary exploration of integrated application of HowNet, Verb Dictionary and HNC.

**Keywords:** verb, verb classification, 3-DDCM.

## 1 Introduction

There exists deep semantic plane representing certain semantic structure in sentence. The deep semantic structure is mainly determined by the core verb of a sentence [1]. From the perspective of understanding and translating natural language by computer, the predicate verbs and adjectives act like the center of syntactic structure and semantic interpretation of a sentence [2]. If the semantic combinational relations between the predicate verb and nominal phrases are concretely and exhaustively described, we can greatly promote the performance of natural language understanding system and machine translation system. Chinese expresses a strong preference for semantic analysis and is characterized by analytic and parataxis. Therefore, it is very important to make intensive research on Chinese verbs and relative concepts in semantic or even deeper layer.

The verbs in *Verb Dictionary* are classified into two categories, i.e. *relation verbs*, *action verbs*. *Relation verbs*, moreover, only include *possessive* relation and *isa* relation. In contrast with HowNet relation events which include nine categories, it is not that rich in the classification of *relation verbs*. Besides *relation events*, *states* and *actions* are also incorporated into HowNet events. Furthermore, the *actions* are classified into two categories, i.e. *ActGeneral* and *ActSpecific*. *ActApecific* events are classified into more than 800 categories and the classification of *ActSpecific* of HowNet is

---

* This paper was supported by the National Key Science & Technology Pillar Program during the 12th Five-Year Plan of China under Grant No. 2012BAH14F00.

P. Liu and Q. Su (Eds.): CLSW 2013, LNAI 8229, pp. 692–701, 2013.

extremely elaborate. By contrast, *action verbs* in Verb Dictionary only include four categories. Certainly, *Verb Dictionary*'s bidirectional research on verbs is a great progress.

The verbs in linguistics are not only related to HowNet events, but also related to the primitive concepts and basic logic concepts in HNC. Owing to a large number of classes of events, it's very hard to manually tag corpus by HowNet event taxonomy. The proposal of the *Generalized Function-effect Chain* in HNC has made a great progress on NLU. The presentation of relation and state in HNC, however, is not as subtle as the presentation of *relation* and *AlterRelation*, *state* and *AlterState* in HowNet. The semantic resources, such as *Verb Dictionary*, HowNet and HNC, have different characteristics respectively. Whereas, lack of compatibility and mapping between each other in these semantic relative resources or theory has made them form isolated islands and resulted in the difficulty for integrated application and comprehensive exploitation.

This paper puts forward 3 Dimensional Dynamic Concept Model (3-DDCM) by combining with philosophical analysis and thinking of materialist dialectics and inspiration of HowNet *biaxial theory* of events. The paper, using the 3-DDCM and according to the verb frequency of corpus and daily examples, puts forward a method of verb classification through sentence semantic analysis. This method studies the correspondence between the verb classes and HowNet event taxonomy, verb classes in *Verb Dictionary* and related concepts of HNC on the whole. The paper is a preliminary exploration for the integrated application of HowNet, *Verb Dictionary* and HNC, which contributes to reducing the cost of building knowledge bases concerned. Furthermore, it would be helpful for precise logic reasoning of triples extracted by Open Information Extraction which views the core verbs as relation of entities.

# 2    Related Work

*Verb Dictionary* is an excellent achievement that has deepened case relation research on verbs of contemporary Chinese language. The dictionary put previous researchers' achievements and their practical experiences together, and looked backward at the object and forward at the subject, and investigated verbs in a bidirectional way. According to the semantic relation between subject and object that is a correlative of state or action indicated by verbs, verbs are classified into four action subordinate categories and two relation subordinate categories.

HowNet is a powerful semantic system, it makes calculability of Chinese concepts and relations come true. Event is something that happens in a given time and space, and linguistically in most situations are denoted by verbs [3]. It discovered a perfect correspondence between the concepts of *static events* and the concepts of *dynamic events (actions)*. Its *biaxial theory* of events unveils an intrinsic biaxial scheme of events [3]. Horizontal axis is the correspondence between *dynamic events* and *static events*. Vertical axis is the development of things. What we called progress indicates a process that shows the development of the birth, existence and death of things. For example, one from birth to growing, robust (fine state), then goes into decline state, such as one can't be cured and death follows, at last, vanishes (cremation). Spirit product may also experience a process involves birth, development and death. For example, angry, at first a little, then very, at last calm down. The correspondence between "give birth to", "bring up", "kill" and "alive", "growth", "death" is the correspondence of dynamic and static. Biaxial theory of HowNet, especially its discovery of correspondence between *static events* and *dynamic events*, has given new significant meaning to inference.

HowNet(Version 2006) defines 812 classes of events. Event concepts can be classified into two groups: *dynamic events* and *static events*. *Static events* are subclassified into two sub-groups: *the event of relation* and *the event of state*. The event *of relation* includes *isa, possession, comparison, suit, inclusive, connective, causeResult, timeOrSpace, arithmetic*, etc. *The event of state* includes *statePhysical* and *stateMental*. *statePhysical* includes existence, begin, normal, good, recovered, change, end, disappear, etc. And *stateMental* includes feeling, attitude, volition, cognition state, etc. *dynamic events* is sub-classified into two sub-groups: *actGeneral*(general actions) and *actSpecific*(specific actions), *actGeneral* is classified into five subgroups: start, do, DoNot, cease, wait, etc., and *actSpecific* is classified into two subgroups: *aterGeneral* and *aterSpecific* which includes *alterRelation* and *alterState*. Furthermore, *alterRelation* includes *alterPossession, alterIsa, alterComparison, alterFitness, alterInclusion, alterConnection, alterCauseResult, alterLocation, alterTimePosition, alterQuantity*, etc. And *alterState* includes *alterPhysical, makeAct, alterMental*, etc.

Using Fillmore's Frame Semantics as theory foundation, referring to English FrameNet and according to Chinese corpus facts [7], a Chinese word semantic database called CFN has been built. Frame is a structured scope system, which is in accordance with some motivating contexts, and is a graphical circumstance stored in human recognition experiences [8]. The lemma that motivate frame includes verb, adjective and event noun, etc., and verb is the main lemma among these lemmas. The principal relations include inheritance relation (superior frame and subordinate frame), whole-part relation (whole frame and part frame), whole domain and part domain, subsequent process, consequence process, referring, etc.

Chinese Concept Dictionary (CCD), compatible with WordNet, is a Chinese semantic dictionary developed by the Computational Linguistics Research Institution of Peking University. 15 initial concepts of verbs in CCD are verbs' semantic scopes [9]. There are four kinds of inclusive relation between verb concepts. CCD defines association relation between noun and verb concepts and Closed Semantic Constraint of verb concepts. The main relations, i.e. inheritance relationship between concepts, in other words, hypernym-hyponym relation, and some additional relations make CCD form a concept network [9].

HNC is abbreviation of *Hierarchical Network of Concepts* and a theory about natural language understanding and processing by computer. HNC overlooks natural language space by standing in concepts space and proposes four propositions, i.e. infinite concepts but finite *Concept Primitives*, infinite sentences but finite *Sentence Categorries*, infinite *Sentence Groups* but finite *Sentence Group Unites*, etc. HNC *Generalized Function-effect Chain* penetrates into concepts, chunks and *sentence categories*, not only used for characterizing feature chunks, but for classifying semantic categories of a sentence. Among all of HNC's concepts, primitive concepts and basic logical concepts are relative to verbs, and primitive concepts include main primitive concepts, two kinds of labour and three kinds of spiritual life. Basic logical concepts mainly correspond to western language's copula and modal verb [10].

**Table 1.** The contrast among verb-related concepts of five semantic theories or resources

| | Verb Dictionary | CCD | CFN | HowNet | HNC |
|---|---|---|---|---|---|
| theory foundation | Case Grammar | Compatible with WordNet | Frame Semantics | HowNet | HNC |
| corresponding concepts | verb | verb concept | lexical unit | event | Primitive Concept |
| Relations between corresponding concepts and verbs | No | hypenymy, hyponymy, entailment, etc. | frame-frame relations | Biaxial theory | Generalized Function-effect Chain |
| sequences of chunks or the characteristics of sentence | Basic sentence pattern, extended sentence pattern | Sentence Frame, Closed Semantic Constraint | frame | Semantic parsing | Sentence Category parsing |

# 3    Dimensional Dynamic Concept Model (3-DDCM)

## 3.1    Act Axis, Static Axis, Evolution Axis and Chaos Origin

*Dynamic concept*, used for describing move, motion, alteration, change, evolution, etc., correspond to roughly to the HowNet events, *Generalized Function-effect Chain*, and verbs. Motion is the mode of existence of matter. All equilibrium is only relative and only has meaning in relation to one or other definite form of motion. Therefore, as is shown in figure 1, 3 Dimensional Dynamic Concept Model (3-DDCM) has been studying the cause of motion named *act* and relative equilibrium named *static*. *Static axis* puts emphasis on relative equilibrium, however *act axis* puts emphasis on absolute motion, i.e. the cause of motion. *Evolution* is a general process everywhere apparent in Nature and Society. Therefore, *evolution axis* puts emphasis on the description of different stages of development or evolution. *Chaos origin*, the point of intersection of *act axis*, *static axis* and *evolution axis*, is an original state of complete confusion and disorder.

As is shown in figure 1, *static* includes *relation* and *state*, and describes the relative equilibrium. The *state* is external and describe the trend of changes, i.e. the physical, mental or emotional condition that a person or thing is in. The *relation* is internal, i.e. the relevance or way in which two or more things that is systematic and its active elements behave towards each other or deal with each other. The *state* includes *stateMaterial* and *stateConscious*. *stateMaterial* includes *statePhysical* and *stateMental*. The *stateConscious* means temporary situation of human conscious. The *relation* includes *classicRelation* and *otherRelation*, and the *classicRelation* is the positive result of absorbing and reforming the event taxonomy of HowNet and classification of *Verb Dictionary*. The *classicRelation* includes *allosomePossession* , *autologous-Possession, metaphorIsa, attributeIsa, inclusive, comparison, suit, connective, cause-Result, timeOrSpace, arithmetic*. The *otherRelation* is the development of *relation*, i.e. follow, accompany, lead, guide, carry, bring ,cooperate , etc. *3-DDCM* reflects the unity of state and relation and deepens the realization of *static* by the process of *chaos, state* to *relation*.

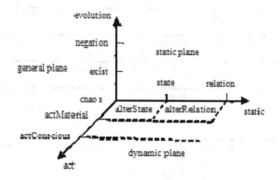

**Fig. 1.** 3 Dimensional Dynamic Concept Model (3-DDCM)

*Act* is the agent which results in some alterations about *static* and the interaction among systematic things and its inner active elements. The world united in the material, and the consciousness is a product of a certain stage of development of the material world. Therefore, *act* includes *actMaterial* and *actConscious*. Meanwhile, the thought that Matter is primary and Consciousness derivative is given in visual image in figure 1. The *actMaterial* is only defined as the motion of material and didn't specify what altered and acted. The consciousness, the function of human brain, reflects and reacts against objective. The *actConscious* is only defined as the motion of consciousness and didn't specify what altered and acted. Therefore, *actMaterial* and *actConscious* are classified as generalized *dynamic concept* shortened to *general*. 3-DDCM reflects unity of material and consciousness and promotes the realization of *act* by the process of from *chaos, actMaterial* to *actConscious*.

Never anywhere has there been matter without motion and evolution. There are both development and change of from small to large, from simple to complex, from lower to higher and occasional setback, such as ShiKai Yuan restoration of the monarchy, atavism, etc. *Evolution axis* reflects the stages of development or evolution and the law of metabolism. Things are in common in terms of their basic process of from living to death, from appearance to disappearance. They undergo the same basic process of development, that is, a process of development of coming into being, then growing up and maturing, gradually becoming old and weak, finally passing from physical life.

*Chaos origin*, the point of intersection of *act axis*, *static axis* and *evolution axis*, is an original state of complete confusion and disorder. In the application of NLP, *chaos origin* can be marked with language, i.e. Chinese, English, etc. It means the research on a certain language verbs.

## 3.2     Dynamic Plane, General Plane and Static Plane

As is shown in *dynamic plane* of figure 1, any relation or state is caused or changed by its corresponding action, any action is caused to happen by its corresponding relation or state. If the behavior of the *dynamic concept* of a specific action indicated a relation altered, the *dynamic concept* belongs to *alterRelation*, as is shown in the intersection formed by two dashes drawn from act axis *actMaterial* and *static axis* relation. For example, *dynamic concept* denoting the relation of possession such as "own" or "not have" are a correlative of the *dynamic concept* denoting the change of the possession relation such as "buy" or "sell". If the behavior of the *dynamic concept* of a specific action indicated a state altered, the *dynamic concept* belong to *alterSate*, as is shown in the intersection formed by two dashes drawn from *act axis actMaterial* and *static axis state*. *Dynamic concept* denoting the state of *statePhysical* such as "hungry" or "full" are a correlative of the *dynamic concept* denoting the change of the physical state such as "eat" or "excrete". As is shown in *general plane* of figure 1, "alter" or "act" itself didn't specify what altered and acted and it is classified as "general" which includes *actMaterial* and *actConscious*, i.e. begin ,wait ,lazy ,etc. The *static plane*, formed by *static axis* and *evolution axis* , is used for describing those relations and states in different stages of evolution or development.

The direction of *act axis* and the sequence of *actMaterial* and *actConscious* reflect that material is primary and consciousness derivative. Pondering over particularity and active reaction of consciousness, the dotted lines drawn from *actConscious* of *act axis* and *relation* and *state* of *static axis*, however, did not intersect. According to whether Mind continued and essence of consciousness, *dynamic concept* in this area (including corresponding part of act-axis) are classified into three categories, i.e. *thinking, judge, logic*, etc. The *thinking* concepts mean *dynamic concept* describing continued consciousness, i.e. ponder, consider, think over, etc. The *judge* concepts mean *dynamic concept* making decision, i.e. decide, judge, diagnose, etc. The *logic* concepts mean *dynamic concept* describing the thought about logic and ideology, i.e. deduce, induce, inference, abstract, summarize, etc.

## 4     Chinese Verb Classification Based on 3-DDCM

Based on the 3 Dimensional Dynamic Concept Model (3-DDCM) and according to the verb frequency of corpus and daily examples, this paper puts forward a method of verb classification through sentence semantic analysis. Verbs are classified into three types: *general, static* and *dynamic*. The *general* verbs include *actConscious* verbs and *actMaterial* verbs. The *static* verbs include *state* verbs and *relation* verbs. The *dynamic* verbs include *alterRelation* verbs, *alterState* verbs, *thinking* verbs, *judge* verbs, *logic* verbs.

### 4.1     General Verbs

Based on the 3-DDCM, the *general* verbs are only defined as the motion of material and didn't specify what altered and acted, i.e. prepare, beginning, wait, etc.

*General* verbs include *actMaterial* verbs describing material movement and *actConscious* verbs describing conscious movement.

## 4.2   Static Verbs

Based on the 3-DDCM, *state* and *relation* are the description from the shallower to the deeper to the *static*. Therefore, in this paper, *static* verbs are classified into two categories: *state* verbs and *relation* verbs.

### State Verbs

Any *relation* or *state* is caused or changed by its corresponding action, any action is caused to happen by its corresponding *relation* or *state*. As a consequence, the *state* includes *stateMaterial* which results from the behavior action that material verbs point and *stateConscious* which results from the behavior action that conscious verbs point. The *state* verbs include *stateMaterial* verbs and *stateConscious* verbs. The *stateMaterial* verbs include *statePhysical* verbs and *stateMental* verbs.

### Relation Verbs

The *relation* verbs are classified into two categories: *classicRelation* verbs and *otherRelation* verbs. Analyze *classicRelation* verbs first.

   *allosomePossession*

   (1) Zhang San has a car.

   *autologousPossession*

   (2) That equipment has tablets with head ……

   (3) The dragonfly has two rightnesses of wings. [2]

   From the perspective of Verb Dictionary, The verb "has" in these examples is classified as Possession verb. In the example (1), the subject "Zhang San" and the object "a car" don't belong to the same individual. In the example (2), however, the subject "that equipment" and objective "tablets" belong to the same individual. In the example (3), the subject "dragonfly" and object "wing" belong to the same individual too, and the subject "dragonfly" as whole and object "wings"as part of whole. As a result, Possession verbs, such as have, own, has, etc., are classified into two categories: *allosomePossession* verbs and *autologousPossession* verbs. The verb "has" in the example (1) is classified as *allosomePossession*, but the verb "has" in the example (2), (3) is classified as *autologousPossession* . Then analyze the *isa* verbs.

   *metaphorIsa* (can also be called allosomeIsa)

   (4) I am a very small rock.

   (5) These words mean nothing. [2]

   (6) Because the shape of the outer shell seems the lamp bulb well known……

   *attributeIsa*(can also be called autologousIsa)

   (7) I am a teacher.

   (8) His surname is Zhang.

   (9) So, drive unit 6 is small……

From the view of Verb Dictionary, the verbs am, is, seem, mean, etc. belong to *isa* verbs. The subject "I" and the object "a very small rock" in (4) is a kind of relation of rhetorical, which is subjective. And in fact the subject "I" and the object "a very small rock" have no relation. "Mean" "seem" in (5) and (6) are also the case. However, the subject "I" and the object "a teacher" in (7) describe the same object. "A teacher" is the attribute of "I", so the verb "am" is classified as *attributeIsa*. The verb "is" in (8) and (9) are also classified as *attributeIsa*. Therefore, *isa* verbs are classified into two categories: *metaphorIsa* verbs and *attributeIsa* verbs.

In addition to the above four types of relation verbs: *allosomePossession, autologousPossession, metaphorIsa* and *attributeIsa*, absorbing and reforming the seven types of relation verbs such as *inclusive, comparison, suit, connective, causeResult, timeOrSpace* and *arithmetic* of HowNet event taxonomy. The seven types of relation verbs are illustrated with example respectively: *inclusive* relation, usually relate to whole and parts of roles, such as include, belong to, etc.; *Comparison* relation, such as smaller, bigger, compare, lower, more, etc.; *Suit* relation, such as suit, be suitable for, appropriate, adaption, etc.; *Connective* relation, such as relevance, connective, interconnection, associate, etc.; *CauseResult* relation, such as result in, lead to, cause, depend on, etc.; *TimeOrSpace* relation, such as be located, toward, etc.; *Arithmetic* relation, such as add, subtract, multiply, divide and add up to, etc. These 11 relation verbs mentioned above are classified as *classicRelation* verbs. Considering the following examples, this paper, then, puts forward *otherRelation* verbs.

(10)You accompany this expert and enter. [2]

One of the definition of the HowNet event "accompany" is DEF={follow|跟随}, the sememe "follow|跟随" is classified as *AlterLocation*|变空间位置. The verb "enter" changes the space of "you" and "this expert". Therefore, it is more appropriate that "Accompany" is regarded as a relation between "you" and "this expert". "Accompany" "follow behind" and "follow" are also the case.

(11)Carrying a dagger，he entered the dormitory. [2]

One of the definition of the HowNet event "carry" is DEF={bring|携带}, the sememe "bring|携带" is classified as *AlterLocation*|变空间位置. As far as example (11) is concerned, the verb "enter" changes the space of "dagger" and "he". Therefore, it is more appropriate that "carry" is regarded as a relation between "he" and "a dagger". "Bring" and "lead" are also the case.

## 4.3   Dynamic Verbs

According to the dynamic plane of 3-DDCM, dynamic verbs are classified into five categories: *alterState* verbs, *alterRelation* verbs, *thinking* verbs, *judge* verbs and *logic* verbs.

**Table 2.** The relations between verb classes in this paper and HowNet event taxonomy, verb classes in *Verb Dictionary*, related concepts in HNC on the whole

| Verb classes in this paper | | | Event Taxonomy in HowNet | | Verb classes in Verb Dictionary | Related concepts in HNC |
|---|---|---|---|---|---|---|
| static | state | stateMaterial | static | state | action | Generalized Function-effect Chain related concepts |
| | | stateConscious | | | | |
| | relation | classicRelation | | relation | relation | |
| | | otherRelation | | | | |
| act | actMaterial | | act | actGeneral actSpecific | action | |
| | actConscious | | | | | |
| dynamic | alterState , alterRelation | | | | | |
| | Thinking , judge , logic | | | | | |

## 5    Conclusion

This paper proposes the 3-DDCM. Using the 3-DDCM and according to the verb frequency of corpus and daily examples, this paper puts forward a method of verb classification through sentence semantic analysis. This method studies the correspondence between the verb classes and HowNet events, verb classes in Verb Dictionary and related concepts in HNC on the whole. The paper is a preliminary exploration for the integrated application of HowNet, *Verb Dictionary* and HNC, which contributes to reducing the cost of building knowledge bases concerned. Furthermore, it would be helpful for precise logic reasoning of triples extracted by Open Information Extraction which views the core verbs as relation of entities.

Many more tasks will be considered in future work, such as verifying the approach's feasibility and perfecting the proposed classification of verbs through tagging and relative experiments, and drawing up semantic tagging standard and trying to map the verb classes onto HowNet event taxonomy, and studying the space structure of 3-DDCM.

Many thanks for Zhengdong Dong's patient help with HowNet.

## References

1. Zhu, X.: Studies on Semantic Structure Patterns of Sentences in Modern Chinese (现代汉语句模研究). Peking University Press, Beijing (2001)
2. Lin, X., Lu, C., Wang, L.: Verb Dictionary (动词大词典). China Material Press, China (1994)
3. Dong, Z., Dong, Q.: HowNet and the Computation of Meaning. World Scientific Publishing Co. Pte. Ltd., Singapore (2006)
4. Dong, Z., Dong, Q.: HowNet, http://www.keenage.com
5. Ruppenhofer, J., Ellsworth, M., Petruck, M.R.L., Johnson, C.R., Scheffczyk, J.: FrameNet II : Extended Theory and Practice (printed September 14, 2010)

6. Bos, J.: A Survey of Computational Semantics: Representation, Inference and Knowledge in Wide-Coverage Text Understanding. Language and Linguistics Compass 5(6), 336–366 (2011), 10.1111/j.1749-818x.2011.00284.x
7. Liu, K.: Research on Chinese FrameNet Construction and Application Technologies. Journal of Chinese Information Processing (汉语框架语义网构建及其应用技术研究) 25(6) (2011)
8. Hao, X., Liu, W., Li, R., Liu, K.: Description Systems of the Chinese FrameNet Database and Software Tools (汉语框架语义知识库及软件描述体系). Journal of Chinese Information Processing 21(5) (2007)
9. Yu, J., Yu, S.: The Structure of Chinese Concept Dictionary (中文概念词典的结构). Journal of Chinese Information Processing 16(4) (2002)
10. Huang, Z.: HNC (Hierarchical Network of Concepts) Theory (HNC (概念层次网络) 理论). Tsinghua University Press, Beijing (1998)
11. The HNC Theory, http://www.hncnlp.com
12. Jia, Y.: Chinese Semantics (汉语语义学). Peking University Press, Beijing (1999)
13. Zhou, L.: A Frame-Semantic Approach to the Motion of Chinese FrameNet (汉语移动域框架语义分析). Social Sciences Academic Press, China (2012)
14. Ma, Q.: The Chinese Verb and Verbal Constructions (汉语动词和动词性结构·一编). Peking University Press, Beijing (2004)
15. Wang, Z., Qiu, Q., Feng, P., Xie, S.: Information Extraction Method of Technical Solution from Mechanical Product Patent (机械产品专利技术方案信息抽取方法). Journal of Mechanical Engineering 45(10) (October 2009)
16. Chen, P.: Reach on status verbs' Semantics construction and Sentence transformation (状态动词的语义结构及句式投射——以静态存在动词为例). In: Proceedings of 12th Chinese Lexical Semantics Workshop (2011)
17. You, L., Fan, K., Liu, K.: Comment on Models in Chinese Semantic Representation (汉语语义分析模型研究述评). Journal of Chinese Information Processing 19(6) (2005)

# Research on Semantic Metadata Online Auxiliary Construction Platform and Key Technologies

Jie Li[1], Ruijia Wang[2], and Yao Liu[2]

[1] He Ze University
hzxylijie@163.com
[2] Institute of Scientific and Technical Information of China

**Abstract.** The semantization of library resources is the general trend in a networked environment, therefore, we propose methods using natural language processing technology and machine learning to promote library resources semantization process. We develop semantic metadata online auxiliary construction platform of Chinese information resources to do semantic label of related literature, and generate initial semantic metadata by utilize traditional organizational resources (such as thesaurus) with machine learning method based on the relatively semantization of a large amount of content, and realize simultaneously implementation of semantic metadata system construction and organizational resources semantization. The system proposed in this paper can help to construct the semantic metadata of scientific and technical information based on the Web, and utilize up-to-date semantic technologies to realize domain thesaurus and effectively integrate various kinds of metadata, it can also realize the edit, development and maintenance of a certain semantic metadata project by automatic or auxiliary construct the semantic metadata system using the semi-structured text. The realization and implement of this method can provide technical support and theory reference for accelerate the progress of Chinese resource semantic annotation.

## 1 Overview

A great deal of literature resource is stored in the library, therefore, how to help users to find knowledge in the literature comprehensively, quickly and accurately, to showcase the knowledge from different knowledge dimensions and find the relevance between the knowledge, in order to help users to create knowledge innovation more effectively have become key problems of achieving leap development of next generation literature services in library and reaching the stage of knowledge service based on literature information retrieval services. So the semantization of library resources is the general trend in a networked environment. Semantization means choose suitable semantic label to change the resource into the format that computer can recognize with the semantic features reflected from label content in the resource, and make the computer understand and master the resource content to some extent.

In this paper we consider that semantization of library resources can be regarded as shallow labeling of library resource, and is the interactive implementation of content

P. Liu and Q. Su (Eds.): CLSW 2013, LNAI 8229, pp. 702–716, 2013.

semantization and form semantization. Therefore, based on NLP theories and methods, we propose this method to utilize the traditional library resource organization mode, construct semantic metadata system, and construct integrated platform of auxiliary construction and annotation. Two key problems of this research are semantic metadata generation and semantic annotation.

## 2     Research Status at Home and Abroad

Semantic metadata[1] (also called Tag Ontologies) can provide semantic information of data, and is the important tool in library resource organization semantization, it has an important role in changing the information that can be read by people into the information that can be processed by computer. So semantic metadata generation, which can provide semantic information of data, has got more and more attention of researchers.

Semantic metadata generation technology and domain knowledge base (also called domain ontologies) construction technology are basically the same in the perspective of technical implantation, the methods and ideas of the technologies are relatively mature, and our research group has got good results on this research from hard study and exploration (see the references) [2-5].

Semantic annotation is the other key problem. At the present stage, a lot of work focus on designing automatic semantic metadata generation model and methods, in order to realize thoroughly automatic annotation. For example, Huang et al have proposed a Web based automatic thematic metadata generation system[6]. Yang and Lee proposed an approach for automatic metadata generation for Web pages[7]. A. Dingli et al proposed a framework named Armadillo[8]. H. Graubitz et al proposed DI-AsDEM framework[9]. LI J showed a machime learning method to generate semantic annotation for domain specific sentences, and change them to RDF format based on syntax[10]. DILL et al described a project for automated largescale semantic annotation—semTag[11]. Specia, Motta and Hak Lae Kim proposed methods to integrate folksonomies and ontologies, in order to improve the semantic expression of labels. The advantage of folksonomies is that it can integrate all the interested and labeled information, and can help to organize the network information, but it is too casual for library resource organization. Therefore, our research group proposed NLP based theory and method, utilize traditional library resource organization methods and domain ontology construction technologies to construct semantic metadata system, and construct integrated platform of auxiliary construction and annotation, in order to find the theory and method to synchronized realize system construction and resource organization semantization.

## 3     Ideas and Methods

In this paper we use NLP technologies and machine learning methods to develop the semantic metadata online auxiliary construction platform of Chinese information resources, semantically label the related literature, and generate initial semantic metadata by utilize traditional organizational resources (such as thesaurus) with machine learning method based on the relatively semantization of a large amount of content, and realize simultaneously implementation of semantic metadata system construction and organizational resources semantization. The process and structure are shown in figure 1.

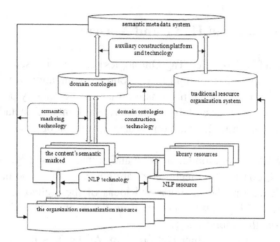

**Fig. 1.** Process and structure

## 4     Key Technologies

### 4.1     Research on Part-of-Speech Segmentation and Labeling Technologies of Professional Corpus

In this paper we segment selected literatures according to part-of-speech and label them, and utilize field semantic dictionary to realize professional knowledge annotation of literature resource. On one hand, we do the words sense labeling according to semantic dictionary. On the other hand, we modify, enlarge and adjust related information of semantic dictionary according to the real appearing of words in corpus, in order to implement a virtuous circling integration of semantic dictionary construction and words sense labeling corpus construction, and finally synchronous achieve optimal semantic dictionary and words sense labeling corpus.

### 4.2     Research on Knowledge-Intensive Text Segments Oriented Natural Language Processing Technology

In this paper we utilize comprehensive language knowledge-base and statistical techniques to design and implement knowledge-intensive text segments oriented natural language processing technology. We combine syntax rules and semantic information to analyze syntax, and get semantic restrictive information at the same time. We get shallow case frame by semantic role labeling on predicate head and the main valence components, in order to analyze and understand the natural language part of knowledge-intensive text segments[15].

### 4.3   Style Characteristics Expression, Obtain and Application of Knowledge-Intensive Text Segments

We learn the language expression patterns which represent the relations between domain concepts by conduct term recognition and shallow analysis on major textbook, monograph and encyclopedia. Then gather these language expression patterns to get style characteristics of knowledge-intensive text. After that, based on these characteristics of knowledge-intensive text and the structure tag set of traditional library literature resource organization methods, we choose knowledge-intensive text segments as the source of domain new knowledge from extensive text resources, and construct the training corpus[16].

### 4.4   Research on Semantic Annotation Technology

In this paper we use semantic indexing to store the results of semantic annotation based on tag data description depth collaboration research. The main idea of semantic indexing is that we do not index according to documents, but separately index text segments of different grades, and add domain to indicate grades and semantic information in the indexing.

## 5   Development and Implementation of Auxiliary Construction Platform

Integrated platform system of semantic metadata auxiliary construction and annotation can support multiuser online to auxiliary construct and edit semantic metadata. This system can realize joint edit, development and maintenance of a semantic metadata project by letting multiuser expediently visit, create and maintain semantic metadata based on BS technology, and managing users in Web page way. The main features include users' authorization management, semantic metadata projects management, semantic metadata online edit, semantic metadata projects comparison, conversion processing of semantic metadata in different formats, semantic metadata project format management and import and export of semantic metadata.

### 5.1   Import of Domain Thesaurus

Firstly upload the domain thesaurus with neat format and clear hierarchy to this system through the Web, then the system would convert it to semantic metadata base model and show it as tree form in the Web.

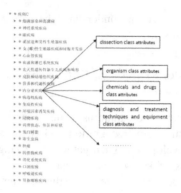

**Fig. 2.** Structure chart of domain thesaurus

## 5.2    Import of Metadata

Import the structured metadata or semi-structured text (data file or network) into base semantic metadata model generated by thesaurus, in order to enrich the contents of domain semantic metadata.

5.2.1. NLP automatic analysis and processing functions. NLP automatic analysis and processing functions include structured vocabulary processing function (as shown in figure3), it mainly process resources with structured information, such as traditional Chinese medicine thesaurus, thesaurus, classification vocabulary, classification thesaurus, and so on; textbooks and other text processing function (as shown in figure4), it mainly process relatively standard electronic text, such as textbooks; professional dictionary processing function, it mainly import and process professional dictionary.

**Fig. 3.** Professional dictionary automatic processing interface

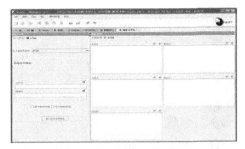

**Fig. 4.** Textbooks and other text automatic processing interface

5.2.2. Internet content extraction and mining (the interface is shown in figure5). Internet content extraction and mining functions include batched internet content extraction function (off-line), with this function we can input batched medical website address, regularly and actively download all the webpages and build indexes, and input concept categories to accomplish automatic extraction and batch fill of medical knowledge; concept related batch internet content extraction function, with this function we can input a kind of disease, provide batched medical website address related to this disease, and accomplish automatic extraction and batch fill of medical knowledge.

**Fig. 5.** Network data automatic processing interface

### 5.3    Conversion Processing between Different Formats of Semantic Metadata

The other function of this system is the conversion between different knowledge storage ways. That is to say, it can resolve each class in the semantic metadata project into text file that could be recognized, and import it into the data base for users to edit and update its content, and then reflect the updated content in the semantic metadata project files.

Open the synchronous web data option, we can see the interface as the following figure:

**Fig. 6.** WEB data synchronization function

Click the option "synchronize Web data" to start synchronizing Wiki data into semantic metadata project, as shown in the following figure:

**Fig. 7.** Synchronize Web data

After successfully synchronizing Web data, there will be a successful prompt, and the data is successfully synchronized into semantic metadata project. The semantic metadata project can be opened by ontology generation tool, as shown in the following figure:

**Fig. 8.** The data is successfully synchronized into ontology generation tool

The data is successfully synchronized into semantic metadata project.

### 5.4    Semantic Metadata Edit

Semantic metadata can be browsed and modified by this system, such as editing the class and its attributes. The edit of semantic metadata include the open, edit and save of semantic metadata project; the add, delete and modify of basic concepts defined by semantic metadata knowledge expression model; the tree form expression of semantic metadata project in the Web page; the data management of different users, users with expert authorization can audit the semantic metadata edited by different users, and submit the data which passed audits.

a. Open the edit semantic metadata project, we will see the interface shown as follow:

**Fig. 9.** Open the edit semantic metadata project

b. Click the "demographic characteristics" option, we can see the interface as follows:

**Fig. 10.** Demographic characteristics

c. Edit the "English name" option, we will see the interface as follows:

**Fig. 11.** English name

d. After modification, the save interface is shown as follows:

**Fig. 12.** After modification

## 5.5    Export of Semantic Metadata (OWL, RDF Format)

Export the semantic metadata in OWL, RDF and other common general storage format, so that we can use it in other application systems. The construction platform provide "import" and "export" functions, including rdf, owl export function, log record function and so on. This system export the semantic metadata project as rdf files for users to download, and export the semantic metadata project as owl files for users to download, and write the log in the log directory.

5.5.1. Import owl files.

**Fig. 13.** Import owl files

5.5.2. Import RDF files. Users can see the interface as follows by enter into "import RDF files":

**Fig. 14.** Import RDF files

## 5.6    Semantic Metadata Backup and Recovery

The semantic metadata is constantly modified, therefore, users can selectively backup and recover the ontologies, in order to manage the historical data.

The other main function of this system is that it can recover the semantic metadata into previous version.

**Fig. 15.** Backup and recovery

## 5.7    Realize Develop Authorization Management of Semantic Metadata

This system has strict authorization control. Users can creat semantic metadata initial system, users can also add users or groups, and designate read and write authority for the users and groups. Users can take action to the content within their extent of authorization.

5.7.1. User management module. User authorization is used to control different semantic metadata visit authorization of different users, it can be divided into three classes.

Normal users. Normal users can open and edit the semantic metadata project within their domains.

Expert users. Except the authorization of normal users, the expert users can also audit the semantic metadata modified and edited by normal users.

System administrator users. Except the authorization of normal users and expert users, the system administrator users can also create users with different authorizations.

5.7.2. User login module. Users can login from the following page:

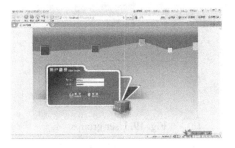

**Fig. 16.** User login module

Ⅰ. Non-system members can use the user name "Guest", and the password "guest" to login and browse semantic metadata project.

Ⅱ. System members can use their own user name and password to login in.

5.7.3. User authorization management module. User administrators can see the interface as follows after login in:

**Fig. 17.** User authorization management module

"User management" module can be used to check and modify user name, password, description information and user groups.

**Fig. 18.** User management

Administrators can edit users' information through the edit button in the figure above, as shown in the following figure.

**Fig. 19.** User groups

Administrators can choose groups they want to add by selecting new pages popping up. Group is associated with user visit authorization, it can control visit by the settings of project management. The following figure shows the interface after clicking add user groups:

**Fig. 20.** User groups

5.7.4. Project management module. User administrators can control the user visit authorization through "project management". As shown in the following figure, semantic metadata project column shows all the information of semantic metadata project. In the right side of semantic metadata project column, detailed information of semantic metadata project is given, such as the project path, the owner, readable user groups and the writable user groups.

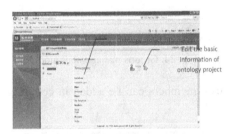

**Fig. 21.** Project management module

Edit the basic information of semantic metadata project: edit the description information, the path and the name of semantic metadata project, as shown in the following figure.

**Fig. 22.** Edit button

Add or delete reader and writer groups of semantic metadata project, and owner information of semantic metadata project. Moreover, the semantic metadata project can also be added or deleted through the following button.

**Fig. 23.** Add or delete project

5.7.5. Groups management module. Administrators can set user visit authorization through "groups management".

**Fig. 24.** Groups management module

In the edit mode, user members can be added in certain group. As shown in the following figure:

**Fig. 25.** Add or delete users

# 6    Conclusions

In this paper we propose methods using natural language processing technology and machine learning to promote library resources semantization process. We develop semantic metadata online auxiliary construction platform of Chinese information resources to do semantic label of related literature, and generate initial semantic metadata by utilize traditional organizational resources (such as thesaurus) with machine learning method based on the relatively semantization of a large amount of content, and realize simultaneously implementation of semantic metadata system construction and organizational resources semantization. With the methods proposed in this paper, even the natural language processing technology is not yet fully mature, we can also greatly improve the automaticity of resource semantic annotation, and provides reference for quickly implement organization semantization. Resource processing way determines its service providing way, therefore, realization and implementation of the methods proposed in this paper can effectively promote the process of library resources semantization, and make the semantic annotation processing and knowledge service possible.

The system proposed in this paper can help to construct the semantic metadata of scientific and technical information based on the Web, and utilize up-to-date semantic technologies to realize domain thesaurus and effectively integrate various kinds of metadata, it can also realize the edit, development and maintenance of a certain semantic metadata project by automatic or auxiliary construct the semantic metadata system using the semi-structured text. The realization and implement of this method can provide technical support and theory reference for accelerate the progress of Chinese resource semantic annotation.

**Acknowledgment.** This work is partially supported by National Social Science Fund No. 12BTQ006, National Key Project of Scientific and Technical Supporting Programs No. 2011BAH10B04, The authors also gratefully acknowledge the helpful comments and suggestions of the reviewers, which have improved the presentation.

# References

1. Han, X.-P., Zhao, J.: Semantic Metadata Generation: A Method Based on Wikipedia. Journal of Chinese Information Processing 23(2), 108–114 (2009)
2. Yao, L., Zhifang, S.: Research on Construction Method of Ontology Description in Domain Ontology. Journal of Academic Libraries (5), 28–33 (2006)
3. Liu, Y., Sui, Z.-F., Hu, Y.-W.: Automatic Construction on of Domain Ontology. Journal of Beijing University of Posts and Telecommunications (Z1), 65–69 (2006)
4. Liu, Y., Sui, Z.: On method and automatic construction theory of domain ontology based on depended text. In: International Conference on Innovative Computing, Information and Control, pp. 63–66 (2006)
5. Liu, Y., Chen, X., Sui, Z.: Study on evolution of domain ontology. In: Second International Conference on Innovative Computing, Information and Control, pp. 1–4 (2007)
6. Huang, C.C., et al.: Using a Web based categorization approach to generate thematic metadata from texts. ACM Transactions on Asian Language Information Processing 3(3), 190–212 (2004)
7. Yang, H.-C., Lee, C.-H.: Automatic metadata generation for Web pages using a text mining approach. In: International Workshop on Challenges in Web Information Retrieval and Integration, pp. 186–194 (2005)

8. Dingli, A., et al.: Automatic semantic annotation using unsupervised information extract on and integration. In: Gennari, J., et al. (eds.) Proceedings K-CAP (2003)
9. Graubitz, H., et al.: Semantic tagging of domain-specific text documents with diasdem. In: Saake, G., et al. (eds.) Proceedings of DBFusion 2001, pp. 61–72. ACM, USA (2001)
10. Li, J., et al.: Learning to generate semantic annotation for domain specific sentences. In: Gil, Y., et al. (eds.) Proceedings of K-CAP, pp. 44–57 (2001)
11. Dill, S., et al.: A case for automated largescale semantic annotation. Web Semantics: Science, Services and Agents on the World Wide Web 1(1), 115–132 (2003)
12. Specia, L., Motta, E.: Integrating folksonomies with the semantic Web. In: Franconi, E., Kifer, M., May, W. (eds.) ESWC 2007. LNCS, vol. 4519, pp. 624–639. Springer, Heidelberg (2007)
13. Kim, H.L., et al.: The state of the art in tag ontologies: a semantic model for tagging and folksonomies. In: International Conference on Dublin Core and Metadata Applications (2008)
14. Liu, Y., Duan, H.-M., et al.: Research on Corpus Creation and Development of Chinese Traditional Medicine. Journal of Chinese Information Processing (4), 24–30 (2008)
15. Sui, Z., Liu, Y., Hu, Y.: Extracting hyponymy relation between Chinese terms based on term types' commonality. ICIC Express Letters 3(4), 1233–1238 (2009)
16. Yao, L., Zhifang, S., et al.: Research on Automatic Construction of Chinese Traditional Medicine Ontology Concept's Description Architecture. New Technology of Library and Information Service (5), 21–26 (2008)

# Author Index